Contemporary
Literary Criticism

Guide to Gale Literary Criticism Series

When you need to review criticism of literary works, these are the Gale series to use:

If the author's death date is: **You should turn to:**

After Dec. 31, 1959
(or author is still living)

CONTEMPORARY LITERARY CRITICISM

for example: Jorge Luis Borges, Anthony Burgess,
William Faulkner, Mary Gordon,
Ernest Hemingway, Iris Murdoch

1900 through 1959

TWENTIETH-CENTURY LITERARY CRITICISM

for example: Willa Cather, F. Scott Fitzgerald,
Henry James, Mark Twain, Virginia Woolf

1800 through 1899

NINETEENTH-CENTURY LITERATURE CRITICISM

for example: Fedor Dostoevski, Nathaniel Hawthorne,
George Sand, William Wordsworth

1400 through 1799

LITERATURE CRITICISM FROM 1400 TO 1800
(excluding Shakespeare)

for example: Anne Bradstreet, Daniel Defoe,
Alexander Pope, François Rabelais,
Jonathan Swift, Phillis Wheatley

SHAKESPEAREAN CRITICISM

Shakespeare's plays and poetry

Antiquity through 1399

CLASSICAL AND MEDIEVAL LITERATURE CRITICISM

for example: Dante, Homer, Plato, Sophocles, Vergil,
the Beowulf Poet

Gale also publishes related criticism series:

CHILDREN'S LITERATURE REVIEW

This series covers authors of all eras who write for the preschool
through high school audience.

SHORT STORY CRITICISM

This series covers the major short fiction writers of all nationalities
and periods of literary history.

ISSN 0091-3421

Volume 52

Contemporary Literary Criticism

Excerpts from Criticism of the
Works of Today's Novelists, Poets,
Playwrights, Short Story Writers, Scriptwriters,
and Other Creative Writers

Daniel G. Marowski
Roger Matuz
EDITORS

Sean R. Pollock
Thomas J. Votteler
Robyn V. Young
ASSOCIATE EDITORS

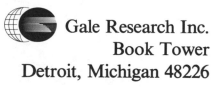 Gale Research Inc.
Book Tower
Detroit, Michigan 48226

STAFF

Daniel G. Marowski, Roger Matuz, *Editors*

Sean R. Pollock, Thomas J. Votteler, Robyn V. Young, *Associate Editors*

David Segal, Anne Sharp, Jane C. Thacker, *Senior Assistant Editors*

Cathy Beranek, Bridget Travers, *Assistant Editors*

Melissa Reiff Hug, Debra A. Wells, *Contributing Editors*

Jeanne A. Gough, *Production & Permissions Manager*
Lizbeth A. Purdy, *Production Supervisor*
Christine A. Galbraith, David G. Oblender, Suzanne Powers, Linda M. Ross,
Lee Ann Welsh, *Editorial Assistants*
Linda M. Pugliese, *Manuscript Coordinator*
Maureen A. Puhl, *Senior Manuscript Assistant*
Donna Craft, Jennifer E. Gale, *Manuscript Assistants*

Victoria B. Cariappa, *Research Supervisor*
Maureen R. Richards, *Research Coordinator*
Mary D. Wise, *Senior Research Assistant*
Joyce E. Doyle, Rogene M. Fisher, Kevin B. Hillstrom, Karen D. Kaus,
Eric Priehs, Filomena Sgambati, *Research Assistants*

Janice M. Mach, *Text Permissions Supervisor*
Kathy Grell, Mabel E. Gurney, *Permissions Coordinators*
Josephine M. Keene, *Senior Permissions Assistant*
H. Diane Cooper, Anita Lorraine Ransom,
Kimberly F. Smilay, *Permissions Assistants*
Melissa A. Brantley, Denise M. Singleton, Sharon D. Valentine,
Lisa M. Wimmer, *Permissions Clerks*

Patricia A. Seefelt, *Picture Permissions Supervisor*
Margaret A. Chamberlain, *Picture Permissions Coordinator*
Pamela A. Hayes, Lillian Tyus, *Permissions Clerks*

Mary Beth Trimper, *Production Manager*
Anthony J. Scolaro, *Production Assistant*

Arthur Chartow, *Art Director*
Linda A. Davis, *Production Assistant*

Laura Bryant, *Production Supervisor*
Louise Gagné, *Internal Production Associate*

Contents

Preface   vii

Authors Forthcoming in *CLC*   xi

Acknowledgments   439

Literary Criticism Series Cumulative Author Index   451

CLC Cumulative Nationality Index   513

CLC-52 Title Index   523

Preface

Literary criticism is, by definition, "the art of evaluating or analyzing with knowledge and propriety works of literature." The complexity and variety of the themes and forms of contemporary literature make the function of the critic especially important to today's reader. It is the critic who assists the reader in identifying significant new writers, recognizing trends in critical methods, mastering new terminology, and monitoring scholarly and popular sources of critical opinion.

Until the publication of the first volume of *Contemporary Literary Criticism (CLC)* in 1973, there existed no ongoing digest of current literary opinion. *CLC,* therefore, has fulfilled an essential need.

Scope of the Work

CLC presents significant passages from published criticism of works by today's creative writers. Each volume of *CLC* includes excerpted criticism on about thirty-five authors who are now living or who died after December 31, 1959. Nearly 2,000 authors have been included since the series began publication. The majority of authors covered by *CLC* are living writers who continue to publish; therefore, criticism on an author frequently appears in more than one volume. There is, of course, no duplication of reprinted criticism.

Authors are selected for inclusion for a variety of reasons, among them the publication of a critically acclaimed new work, the reception of a major literary award, or the dramatization of a literary work as a film or television screenplay. For example, the present volume includes Najīb Mahfūz, who was awarded the 1988 Nobel Prize in literature; William Faulkner, whose widely studied novel *Absalom, Absalom!* is the focus of the current entry; and Woody Allen, whose popular and acclaimed films are complemented by such collections of short stories and essays as *Getting Even, Without Feathers,* and *Side Effects.* Perhaps most importantly, authors who appear frequently on the syllabuses of high school and college literature classes are heavily represented in *CLC;* Joyce Carol Oates and Jean-Paul Sartre are examples of writers of this stature in the present volume. Attention is also given to several other groups of writers—authors of considerable public interest—about whose work criticism is often difficult to locate. These are the contributors to the well-loved but nonscholarly genres of mystery and science fiction, as well as literary and social critics whose insights are considered valuable and informative. Foreign writers and authors who represent particular ethnic groups in the United States are also featured in each volume.

Format of the Book

Altogether there are about 600 individual excerpts in each volume—with approximately seventeen excerpts per author—taken from hundreds of literary reviews, general magazines, scholarly journals, and monographs. Contemporary criticism is loosely defined as that which is relevant to the evaluation of the author under discussion; this includes criticism written at the beginning of an author's career as well as current commentary. Emphasis has been placed on expanding the sources for criticism by including an increasing number of scholarly and specialized periodicals. Students, teachers, librarians, and researchers frequently find that the generous excerpts and supplementary material provided by the editors supply them with vital information needed to write a term paper, analyze a poem, or lead a book discussion group. However, complete bibliographical citations facilitate the location of the original source and provide all of the information necessary for a term paper footnote or bibliography.

A *CLC* author entry consists of the following elements:

- The **author heading** cites the author's full name, followed by birth date, and death date when applicable. The portion of the name outside parentheses denotes the form under which the author has most commonly published. If an author has written consistently under a pseudonym, the pseudonym will be listed in the author heading and the real name given on the first line of the biographical and critical introduction. Also located at the beginning of the introduction to the author entry are any important name variations under which an author has written. Uncertainty as to a birth or death date is indicated by question marks.

- A **portrait** of the author is included when available.

• A brief **biographical and critical introduction** to the author and his or her work precedes the excerpted criticism. However, *CLC* is not intended to be a definitive biographical source. Therefore, *cross-references* have been included to direct the reader to these useful sources published by Gale Research: *Contemporary Authors,* which includes detailed biographical and bibliographical sketches on more than 90,000 authors; *Children's Literature Review,* which presents excerpted criticism on the works of authors of children's books; *Something about the Author,* which contains heavily illustrated biographical sketches of writers and illustrators who create books for children and young adults; *Dictionary of Literary Biography,* which provides original evaluations and detailed biographies of authors important to literary history; *Contemporary Authors Autobiography Series,* which offers autobiographical essays by prominent writers; and *Something about the Author Autobiography Series,* which presents autobiographical essays by authors of interest to young readers. Previous volumes of *CLC* in which the author has been featured are also listed in the introduction.

• The **excerpted criticism** represents various kinds of critical writing—a particular essay may be descriptive, interpretive, textual, appreciative, comparative, or generic. It may range in form from the brief review to the scholarly monograph. Essays are selected by the editors to reflect the spectrum of opinion about a specific work or about an author's literary career in general. The excerpts are presented chronologically, adding a useful perspective to the entry. All titles by the author featured in the entry are printed in boldface type, which enables the reader to easily identify the works being discussed. Publication information (such as publisher names and book prices) and parenthetical numerical references (such as footnotes or page and line references to specific editions of a work) have been deleted at the editor's discretion to provide smoother reading of the text.

• A complete **bibliographical citation** designed to help the user find the original essay or book follows each excerpt.

Other Features

• A list of **Authors Forthcoming in *CLC*** previews the authors to be researched for future volumes.

• An **Acknowledgments** section lists the copyright holders who have granted permission to reprint material in this volume of *CLC*. It does not, however, list every book or periodical reprinted or consulted during the preparation of the volume.

• A **Cumulative Author Index** lists all the authors who have appeared in *CLC, Twentieth-Century Literary Criticism, Nineteenth-Century Literature Criticism, Literature Criticism from 1400 to 1800,* and *Classical and Medieval Literature Criticism,* with cross-references to these Gale series: *Short Story Criticism, Children's Literature Review, Authors in the News, Contemporary Authors, Contemporary Authors Autobiography Series, Contemporary Authors Bibliographical Series, Dictionary of Literary Biography, Something about the Author, Something about the Author Autobiography Series,* and *Yesterday's Authors of Books for Children.* Readers will welcome this cumulated author index as a useful tool for locating an author within the various series. The index, which lists birth and death dates when available, will be particularly valuable for those authors who are identified with a certain period but whose death date causes them to be placed in another, or for those authors whose careers span two periods. For example, Ernest Hemingway is found in *CLC,* yet a writer often associated with him, F. Scott Fitzgerald, is found in *Twentieth-Century Literary Criticism.*

• A **Cumulative Nationality Index** alphabetically lists all authors featured in *CLC* by nationality, followed by numbers corresponding to the volumes in which they appear.

• A **Title Index** alphabetically lists all titles reviewed in the current volume of *CLC*. Titles are followed by the corresponding page numbers where they may be located in the series. In cases where the same title is used by different authors, the authors' surnames are given in parentheses after the title, e.g., *Collected Poems* (Berryman), *Collected Poems* (Eliot). For foreign titles, a cross-reference is given to the translated English title. Titles of novels, novellas, dramas, films, record albums, and poetry, short story, and essay collections are printed in italics, while all individual poems, short stories, essays, and songs are printed in roman type within quotation marks; when published separately (e.g., T.S. Eliot's poem *The Waste Land*), the title will also be printed in italics.

• In response to numerous suggestions from librarians, Gale has also produced a **special paperbound edition** of the *CLC* title index. This annual cumulation, which alphabetically lists all titles reviewed in the series, is available to all customers and will be published with the first volume of *CLC* issued in each calendar year. Additional copies of the index are available upon request. Librarians and patrons will welcome this separate index: it saves shelf space, is easily disposable upon receipt of the following year's cumulation, and is more portable and thus easier to use than was previously possible.

Acknowledgments

No work of this scope can be accomplished without the cooperation of many people. The editors especially wish to thank the copyright holders of the excerpted essays included in this volume, the permissions managers of many book and magazine publishing companies for assisting us in securing reprint rights, and the photographers and other individuals who provided portraits of the authors. We are grateful to the staffs of the Detroit Public Library, the Library of Congress, the University of Detroit Library, the University of Michigan Library, and the Wayne State University Library for making their resources available to us. We also wish to thank Anthony Bogucki for his assistance with copyright research.

Suggestions Are Welcome

The editors welcome the comments and suggestions of readers to expand the coverage and enhance the usefulness of the series.

Authors Forthcoming in *CLC*

To Be Included in Volume 53

Edward Albee (American dramatist and script-writer)—Acclaimed for such plays as *The Zoo Story, The American Dream,* and *Who's Afraid of Virginia Woolf?,* Albee was considered one of the most prominent avant-garde American dramatists of the 1960s. In his recent work, *Marriage Play,* Albee examines the complex motivations underlying a middle-aged couple's determination to endure their marriage despite dissatisfaction and conflict.

Paul Celan (Rumanian-born Austrian poet, translator, and essayist)—Recognized as among the most important poets to emerge in Europe after World War II, Celan frequently drew upon his experiences as an inmate of Nazi labor camps to create lyrical poetry rich in dreamlike imagery.

William Demby (American novelist)—Best known for his novels *Beetlecreek* and *The Catacombs,* Demby is praised for universalizing black concerns by focusing on characters who examine their ethnic heritage in relation to such issues as love, personal growth, and artistic freedom.

Nuruddin Farah (Somalian novelist and dramatist)—In such novels as *From a Crooked Rib, Sweet and Sour Milk,* and *Maps,* Farah explores the effects of colonization, independence, and civil war upon twentieth-century Somalian society.

Robert Harling (American dramatist)—Harling's first play, *Steel Magnolias,* which is being adapted into a major motion picture, is a dark comedy that examines everyday life in a small Southern town.

William Kennedy (American novelist, script-writer, short story writer, and critic)—Kennedy is best known for his novel *Ironweed,* for which he received a National Book Critics Circle Award as well as the Pulitzer Prize in fiction. In his recent novel, *Quinn's Book,* Kennedy extends his series of works set in Albany, New York, combining history and magic realism to depict a young man's quest for freedom and love during the nineteenth century.

Louis MacNeice (Irish-born English poet, critic, translator, dramatist, scriptwriter, and novelist)—A member of the "Oxford Group" of poets of the 1930s that included W. H. Auden, C. Day Lewis, and Stephen Spender, MacNeice is known for verse in which he examined social concerns and the vagaries of the human condition.

Bharati Mukherjee (Indian-born novelist, short story writer, and nonfiction writer)—Mukherjee's writings largely reflect her personal experiences as an exile and immigrant while investigating clashes between native Indian culture and Western society. Works to be covered in Mukherjee's entry include the novels *The Tiger's Daughter* and *Wife* and the short fiction collections *Darkness* and *The Middle Man and Other Stories.*

Pierre Reverdy (French poet, novelist, critic, and editor)—An important figure in the development of literary cubism and surrealism, Reverdy founded the influential magazine *Nord-Sud,* which provided a forum for such innovative writers as Guillaume Apollinaire, Louis Aragon, André Breton, and Max Jacob. In his own verse, Reverdy employed sharp visual imagery and fragmentary language, blended philosophical and mystical elements, and endeavored to reveal what he termed "the sublime simplicity of true reality."

Anatoli Rybakov (Russian novelist)—Rybakov attracted a wide readership in the Soviet Union with his novel *Heavy Sand,* an epic portrait of two Russian-Jewish families before and during World War II. His recent novel, *Children of the Arabat,* examines events leading to the purges initiated by Communist leader Joseph Stalin in the late 1940s and 1950s and their effect upon the collective Soviet conscience.

Gina Berriault (American short story writer and novelist)—An author who first attracted critical attention during the 1950s for stories of alienation and frustration, Berriault employs a compact, unsentimental prose style to examine the often disturbing reactions of characters to psychological or moral crises.

André Breton (French poet, novelist, nonfiction writer, and critic)—One of the major figures of the Dada and Surrealist movements, Breton is perhaps best known for his *Surrealist Manifesto,* which espouses artistic tenets that are still held in high regard. Criticism in Breton's entry will focus upon his poetry and such prose works as *Nadja* and *Mad Love.*

Luis Cernuda (Spanish poet and critic)—Among the most controversial members of the "Generation of 1927," a group of Spanish artists that included such acclaimed authors as Federico García Lorca and Jorge Guillén, Cernuda was best known for surrealist poetry in which he often explored the individual's alienation from society.

Don DeLillo (American novelist, dramatist, and short story writer)—Regarded as an important satirist of modern American culture, DeLillo is acclaimed for his novel *White Noise,* which won the American Book Award for fiction. Commentary in this entry will center on *Libra,* DeLillo's acclaimed recent novel about the assassination of President John F. Kennedy.

Ralph Ellison (American novelist, essayist, short story writer, and editor)—A prolific nonfiction writer, Ellison is best known for his only novel, *Invisible Man.* Regarded as a formidable contribution to American postwar fiction, this portrait of black repression and the search for identity will serve as the focus of Ellison's entry.

Gert Hofmann (German dramatist, novelist, short story writer, and essayist)—Recipient of Germany's prestigious Alfred Döblin Prize for his novel *The Spectacle at the Tower,* Hofmann is respected for his fabulistic fiction that has been compared to the works of Franz Kafka and Günter Grass.

Tadeusz Konwicki (Polish novelist, short story writer, filmmaker, and journalist)—In such novels as *A Dreambook for Our Time* and *The Polish Complex,* Konwicki reflects upon the grim realities of modern Polish life, including the devastating effects and memories of World War II and the subsequent Communist domination of his homeland. Criticism in Konwicki's entry will examine such recent works as *Moonrise, Moonset* and *A Minor Apocalypse.*

Antonine Maillet (Canadian novelist, dramatist, and short story writer)—Regarded as the foremost contemporary chronicler of the Acadians, a French-speaking Canadian ethnic group, Maillet is renowned for her drama *La sagouine* and her novel *Pélagie-la-charrette,* which was the first French-Canadian work to be awarded the Prix Goncourt.

William Saroyan (American dramatist, short story writer, and novelist)—A prolific author of works in diverse genres, Saroyan was praised for his romantic and nostalgic celebrations of American innocence and idealism. Critical commentary in Saroyan's entry will focus upon his Pulitzer Prize-winning drama, *The Time of Your Life.*

Léopold Sédar Senghor (Senegalese poet, essayist, and editor)—President of Senegal from 1960 to 1980, Senghor is largely responsible for establishing the concept of négritude, a literary aesthetic adopted by French-speaking African authors who uphold tribal traditions and values in their work.

Peter Ackroyd

1949-

English novelist, biographer, critic, nonfiction writer, poet, and editor.

In his fiction, Ackroyd focuses upon the interaction between artifice and reality and emphasizes the ways in which contemporary art and life are profoundly influenced by events and creations of the past. Often described as pastiches, Ackroyd's novels blend historical and invented material, parody, multiple narratives, and self-reflexive techniques to explore the lives and writings of such noted personages as Oscar Wilde, Nicholas Hawksmoor, and Thomas Chatterton. By frequently depicting characters who lead dual lives, Ackroyd examines such topics as deception and disguise, forgery, imitation, and plagiarism. Ackroyd's use of Gothic elements contributes to the aura of mystery and decadence that he establishes in his works. Karl Miller commented: "[Ackroyd] can be seen to contribute to the tradition of romantic fabulation which began with the Gothic novel—a tradition in which darkness is privileged, in which a paranoid distrust is evident, in which can be read the evergreen message that the deprived may turn out to be depraved, and in which there can be two of someone."

In his first novel, *The Great Fire of London* (1982), Ackroyd depicts a contemporary filmmaker who wants to produce a documentary on Marshalsea Prison, a vividly evoked setting in Charles Dickens's 1857 novel *Little Dorrit*. Like Dickens's fiction, *The Great Fire of London* details relationships between odd, grotesque, and innocent characters, including a young woman who becomes possessed by the spirit of Dickens's heroine, Amy Dorrit. *The Last Testament of Oscar Wilde* (1983) takes the form of a journal in which Wilde comments on events during the last few months of his life. Ackroyd blends actual statements by Wilde, witty observations rendered in the Wildean manner, and factual and invented incidents to depict the various problems that confronted the famous playwright following his imprisonment and exile from Great Britain for homosexual activities. In particular, Ackroyd concentrates on the personas that Wilde cultivated in his life and work. Andrew Hislop noted: "[*The Last Testament of Oscar Wilde*] rewrites Wilde—employs, mutates, promotes, even mutilates his writings, sayings and actions. Ackroyd has adopted the mask of a man who wrote that 'it is only when you give the poet a mask that he can tell you the truth.'"

In his next novel, *Hawksmoor* (1985), Ackroyd employs alternating narratives, one of which is set during the Augustan era in England, the other in contemporary London. The earlier story line centers on a character named Nicholas Dyer, who is based on Nicholas Hawksmoor, a baroque architect of the Augustan Age best known for having designed several elaborate churches. Dyer promotes the sublime by constructing churches with labyrinthine structures and intimidating forms that emphasize shadow and gloom, and he consecrates each of his creations with a human sacrifice. The modern narrative focuses on a present-day detective named Nicholas Hawksmoor, who is investigating a series of murders committed at the same churches. The two stories, which are connected through a series of recurring images and events, eventually converge with a mystical encounter between Hawksmoor and Dyer in

one of the churches. Alan Hollinghurst commented: "Parallels between the two periods, and between the words and experiences of Dyer and Hawksmoor, are plentifully established: the art of shadows has them both in its grip, and Dyer shadows and foreshadows Hawksmoor in a hundred details." Critics were particularly impressed with Ackroyd's use of Augustan vernacular in the Dyer sections and his probing of conflicts between reason and emotion, logical deduction and intuition. *Hawksmoor* won the Whitbread Award in Great Britain and the Goncourt Prize in France.

Ackroyd also makes use of a multinarrative structure in *Chatterton* (1987). One story line concerns Thomas Chatterton, a poet who committed suicide in 1770 at age seventeen after gaining attention for writing antiquated verse that he claimed was the work of a medieval monk. A second plot depicts events surrounding the completion of Henry Wallis's famous painting "The Death of Chatterton," for which poet George Meredith posed as Chatterton during the 1850s. This section also details Wallis's seduction of Meredith's wife. A third narrative is set in contemporary London and concerns a sickly, obscure young poet who discovers lost manuscripts supposedly written by Chatterton which imply that he staged his death and continued writing into the nineteenth century. Through these premises, Ackroyd examines the ambiguities of truth and illusion and such issues as plagiarism, forgery, and imitation. Several critics noted that *Chatterton,* like all of his fiction, contains a wealth of allusions and references to other literary figures and texts, reflecting Ackroyd's belief that writers develop their craft by imitating other authors. This theme is also explored in Ackroyd's biographies, *Ezra Pound and His World* (1980) and *T. S. Eliot: A Life* (1984), and critics have detected numerous parallels in *Hawksmoor* and *Chatterton* to Eliot's life and work.

In addition to his novels and biographies, Ackroyd has published *Notes for a New Culture: An Essay on Modernism* (1976), *Dressing Up: Transvestism and Drag, the History of an Obsession* (1979), and several volumes of poetry, including *London Lickpenny* (1973), *Country Life* (1978), and *The Diversions of Purley and Other Poems* (1987). He has also served as an editor and critic for the *Spectator* magazine.

(See also *CLC,* Vol. 34 and *Contemporary Authors,* Vol. 123.)

THE TIMES LITERARY SUPPLEMENT

[In *London Lickpenny*] Peter Ackroyd makes not only an odd poetry, but a poetry out of the oddness of the world, which is much more difficult and a good deal more entertaining. Mr Ackroyd is a delicate and insistent stylist, based very firmly on American models. The familiar routines of floating syntax, collages of disparate image and idiom, found poetry, fragmentation and, for the most part, total incomprehensibility on a rational level—features which normally produce poems of truly brutal boredom—here yield many rather beautiful effects as well as some agreeably comic ones.

> *"Cold Comfort," in* The Times Literary Supplement, *No. 3765, May 3, 1973, p. 471.*

PETER PORTER

Peter Ackroyd's poems [in *London Lickpenny*] are neither parodies nor collages but make use of both techniques. They have a prevailing tone of friendliness and good humour. Bits of our literature, ordinary sayings, clichés and remarkable propositions glitter in his nests of words like a magpie's garnerings. But I can no longer conceal that I do not understand most of the poems, and I am inclined to fall back on what little I know of him biographically. Certainly, Cambridge language-analysis seems to have left its mark on his work. . . . *London Lickpenny* is perhaps too cool, but it is dapper and engaging.

> *Peter Porter, "Hearts and Sleeves," in* The Observer, *January 27, 1974, p. 30.*

GALEN STRAWSON

The Great Fire of London starts inauspiciously with two errors of fictional fact. Its opening paragraph, "The story so far", summarizes the plot of the first half of Dickens's *Little Dorrit*. But, first, it is not Arthur Clennam who, "with the help of Pancks, an agent" discovers that William Dorrit is in fact heir to a fortune. Pancks makes the discovery on his own, verifies in with the help of "RUGG, GENERAL AGENT, ACCOUNTANT, DEBTS RECOVERED", and astonishes Clennam with it. Secondly, it is not Little Dorrit's simple protégé Maggy, but Little Dorrit herself, who is "Little Mother"; it is Maggy who calls her "Little Mother". This second error recurs, harm-

lessly, throughout *The Great Fire of London*—harmlessly, because most fiction is made from altered fact, and can be made from altered fiction too.

Peter Ackroyd's novel is a tissue of allusion: to past and present, real and fictive. . . .

"This is not a true story, but certain things follow from other things", Ackroyd writes in the closing paragraph. A great deal of the novel follows from Dickens's witty, delicate masterpiece *Little Dorrit*—it is, after all, "the story so far". Ackroyd is clearly intrigued by the idea of past fiction working great changes in present (fictional) reality, and he misses few chances to make further connections and to elaborate the network of coincidences. Dickens's fiction is at work not only within the plot of the book but also in its composition. . . .

Moving over the surface of things in a distracted but attractive manner, this book lacks a strong design. It is often curiously perfunctory in its details, and the ending is most unsatisfactory—an easy way out, a rapid tying up of unimportant strands in accordance with some imperfectly worked out formal scheme whereby "certain things follow from other things" and everything connects. At the same time, however, it contains some very precise rendering of the rags and patches and scattered movement of unfocused thought; . . . Ackroyd is acute about his characters' small bad-faithed embarrassments, indelicacies, disappointments, cruelties, demeaning accommodations and failures of sympathetic imagination. He is continually alive, too, to that hidden presence in many people's lives which he calls "the vast sphere of unremembered wishes", and to the effects it has on their conscious thoughts and actions. There are some very poignant sketches of people together (some couples, some not) simply failing to think properly about each other, failing to take each other seriously, their thoughts veering sideways at difficult moments. It is these things one remembers as one forgets the scrappy plot. They are simply pictured, not analysed or ruminated, and, despite its structural self-consciousness, this is an oddly artless novel—even the acuity is simple. This is its virtue.

> *Galen Strawson, "Failing to Connect," in* The Times Literary Supplement, *No. 4113, January 29, 1982, p. 105.*

FRANCIS KING

If a novel-reviewer is as incisive and abrasive as Peter Ackroyd, then it is an act of courage for him to publish a first novel himself. There will, of course, be those who will be disappointed if he fails; but there will also be those who will be disappointed if he succeeds. For the people in the second category, still resentful of Mr Ackroyd's louring or mocking presence over the cradle of their literary hopes, the news is bad: no miscarriage has taken place [in *The Great Fire of London*] and, despite one or two blemishes, the infant is lusty.

The point of departure for this tidily succinct novel is an untidily sprawling one, *Little Dorrit*. Spenser Spender (what name could be more poetic than that?) is a minor director who persuades the 'Film Finance Board' to back the movie that he proposes to make of the first part, dealing with the Marshalsea Prison, of Dickens's work. His locations will be the disused wing of a present-day South London prison and the area around it. Spenser, whose egotism makes it difficult for him to make more than intermittent contact with others, is married to Laetitia—whom he calls 'Lettuce' (*sic*—but surely this should be

'Lettice'?) or 'Letty', when not using some such nauseating endearment as 'Shrimpy'. 'Their relationship was close, based as it was upon a mutual inability to understand each other,' is Mr Ackroyd's characteristically epigrammatic summing-up. . . .

Both these characters are wholly convincing. So, too, is the strand of the novel that deals with the relationship between a homosexual Canadian writer and Cambridge don, Rowan Philips, commissioned by Spenser to produce a script for the film, and a working-class youth, Tim. . . .

Tim has a girl-friend, Audrey, who works in a telephone-exchange. While at a seance with Tim and a female friend, Audrey is 'taken over' by Little Dorrit, with whom she then increasingly identifies herself, producing, apropos of nothing, such scraps of Dickens dialogue, understandably bewildering to her uncultured auditors, as 'Bless you, my love, my dearest love' and 'Poor, poor creature.' The inane chatter of Audrey and the other girls at the telephone-exchange is a lovely piece of virtuoso writing, with their remarks to their callers jumbled up in surrealistic confusion with their remarks to each other. ('He needs his head examining he does. The number you want, madam, is 106. Sex, sex, sex, that's all he thinks about . . .'). But Audrey's growing schizophrenia and the spectacular way in which she sets about putting a stop to the film are less convincing.

Nor was I wholly convinced by the dwarf child-murderer Arthur, an inmate of the prison, who, like Audrey, becomes a dark and demented angel of catastrophe. In the case of both these characters, the novel, for all the vivacity and vividness of its writing, suffers from a mysterious failure of realisation. This ability to 'realise'—to create a world, however gimcrack and cockeyed, that the reader instantly accepts as a paradigm of the real one—is one which many unintelligent writers command with ease and many intelligent ones with difficulty; and Mr Ackroyd, most intelligent of writers, sometimes finds it slipping from him.

The best chapters, impressive in their descriptive economy, are the last two. In the first of these, Audrey sets fire to the empty, dilapidated riverside warehouses used as a location by Spenser and so to a whole area of South London; and in the second, the dwarf, having clambered from his inhabited section of the prison to the empty wing, short-circuits the electricity cables that he finds there and thus deprives the authorities of their power (in both senses of the word) and enables his fellow prisoners to make a get-away. Although the symbolism of these events remains cloudy, with a number of different interpretations suggesting themselves, they certainly bring the book to an appropriately wild and lurid close.

As when he finds a pair of ancient corduroy trousers 'oddly out of place with the patina of modern life' (a patina is the result of age and long use), Mr Ackroyd sometimes makes surprising miscalculations in coming up with his images; but the majority of them—like 'an expression in which a smile curled like a stale piece of bread'—are arresting in their bizarre appropriateness. Nocturnal London itself—neatly summed up by Mr Ackroyd's 'In other cities the night is full of movement and possibility; in London it is like a cloth placed over the cage of a bird'—is evoked with a haunting, if rancid, poetry.

Francis King, "Lusty Début," in The Spectator, *Vol. 248, No. 8012, January 30, 1982, p. 20.*

MELVYN BRAGG

Peter Ackroyd has lit a squib on the great bonfire of Dickens and although it does not go off BANG! there are sparkles all the way. The idea of *The Great Fire of London* is ingenious. In short, Little Dorrit walks again. Ackroyd takes this great tower of Dickens's London and through various media—film, a seance, scholarship, documentary and copy characters—draws it into our own day. It's full of fun. . . .

[There is] a bold attempt to conscript a cohort of contemporary Dickensian characters. I enjoyed his ambition. I like the way Ackroyd casts his fiction on the waters and ways of London and eschews the "Arty"—inbitten fictions of some of the younger novelists.

It fails though in its lack of energy, its lack of length and its lack of the determination to make us feel. Again and again Ackroyd sets up a scene and lets it go in a sketch or even a quip when it needed pages of care and slow—yes, Dickensian building with all the cliches and sentimental exploration, the necessary packings and full explanations which would have fed this kindling into a fire worthy of our greatest novelist.

Yet, and yet . . . *The Great Fire of London* is a dashing debut. Its faults are more the common faults of early novels—uncertainty, haste, anxiety—rather than any central fault in an author who has proved his worth in other areas. I enjoyed the book a lot and look forward to the next with pleasure.

Melvyn Bragg, "The Hulk's Gal," in Punch, *Vol. 282, February 3, 1982, p. 201.*

JOHN SUTHERLAND

The Great Fire of London's preface is a scenario based on *Little Dorrit* but falsified by an inauthentic sentimental climax. Dickens's novel, and his fiction generally, echo disconcertingly through Ackroyd's. (p. 19)

Ackroyd is a versatile writer (though this is his first novel). One of his earlier productions was *Notes for a New Culture*. This novel recalls Eliot and his maxim about the impossibility of gumming leaves back on trees: the culture of the past, that is to say, cannot easily be brought into line with that of the present. *The Great Fire of London* plays with this idea of cultural irrecoverability. The Cambridge expert (whom Spender hires as a scriptwriter) cannot bring back the Dickens world. Nor can Audrey, a lunatic telephonist who claims to have séance contact with Little Dorrit and thinks herself possessed by the Victorian heroine. Least successful of all is Spender's film reconstruction, for all its authenticity of set and location. In elaborating this pattern, Ackroyd may have had in mind that Dickens himself was describing Marshalsea not as it stood, but consciously inventing it. . . . Spender is thus engaged in reconstructing, not Dickens's London, but Dickens's imagination of London. *The Great Fire of London* is cleverly resonant and sharply observed as to scene and character. Ackroyd is especially good on Cambridge high tables and low London gay bars. But he seems reluctant to surmount his favourite level of bitchy caricature and offhand smartness. In the flood or fire manner of the great Hollywood novels, the narrative ends apocalyptically: but the event is given with all the drama of a *Keesing's Archive* entry: 'it inflicted disaster and destruction on the city,' we are told. (pp. 19-20)

John Sutherland, "Generations," in London Review of Books, *Vol. 4, No. 4, March 4 to March 17, 1982, pp. 19-20.*

ANDREW HISLOP

In [*The Great Fire of London*], Peter Ackroyd rewrote *Little Dorrit*. In *The Last Testament of Oscar Wilde* he turns his talents to one of the most renowned purveyors and purloiners of words. Superficially, he has written what Wilde did not write—a journal of the last months of his life—but this "historical fiction" tells little of what "happened" during this time. Its main concern is to explain what went before. To do so it rewrites Wilde—employs, mutates, promotes, even mutilates his writings, sayings and actions. Ackroyd has adopted the mask of a man who wrote that "it is only when you give the poet a mask that he can tell you the truth". The result is inevitably two-faced and the truth of *The Last Testament,* though redolent with fact, is a fiction. But this is not inappropriate for a man who was in many of his aspects (and certainly not always in a pejorative sense) two-faced. Wilde, who could show a feminine as well as a masculine countenance, thought "A man's face is his autobiography. A woman's face is her work of fiction." By adopting the mask of biographical fiction Ackroyd gives us Wilde both ways.

The relationship between an author and his works, between the cultivation through conversation of a "personality" and the art of writing, was a subject which Wilde delighted in and was tormented by. . . . His trials gave further poignancy to this relationship (Wilde, though able to defend his works when they were speaking for themselves and to transcend them when they appeared to be speaking against himself, condemned himself on occasion by being unable to control his brilliant conversational retorts). And he probably would not object to Ackroyd's making him continue his exploration of the relationship beyond the grave. ("One's real life is so often the life that one does not lead.") When alive he was always tolerant to the point of generosity of colourful and even pale imitations of his personality. . . .

Wilde's writings are well suited to modern literary games of intertextuality, toying with tropes, fabricating faction, for his masterly manipulation of the fictions of life did not prevent him getting up to a literary trick or two. His most formal and "proper" use of the writings of others was not a modest reworking of Shakespeare . . . but the adaptation in *Salome* of the Bible. . . . But with less lofty subjects he was no respecter of linguistic and literary property: "I appropriate what is already mine for once a thing is published it becomes public property".

Ackroyd, not surprisingly, makes great play with both the imitators of Wilde—he makes much imaginative use of the occasion when Howson, who played a Wildean figure in *Patience,* pretended to be Wilde when they journeyed together in America—and Wilde's appropriative and manipulative literary practices. He continually uses Wilde to justify his use of Wilde, though often it is not exactly Wilde but pseudo-Wilde or just plain Ackroyd who, though clever and witty, at times very witty in a Wildean way, never matches the rhetoric of the original at his most majestic. Numerous references are made by him and the Wildes to such themes as literary property, imitation changing not the impersonator but the impersonated, the meaning of Wilde's life existing in the mind of others, an artist's life being determined by what he forgets not what he remembers, borrowing other voices, mastering masks, art and life finding their highest expression in parody, etc. We are shown Wilde dipping into Landor's *Imaginary Conversations of Literary Men and Statesmen* and with reference to his own exercise in speculative biography, *The Portrait of Mr WH* (which argued that Shakespeare's sonnets were addressed to a boy actor), he boldly declares "It was of no concern to me if the facts were accurate or inaccurate: I discerned a truth which was larger than that of biography and history." He even records in his journal his friends remarking on the inaccuracy of his journal.

The Last Testament of Oscar Wilde is, without doubt, a remarkable achievement. What is less certain is what it has achieved. Ackroyd has played a clever but precarious game. The reader is required to have a certain knowledge to know that the game is being played (and that Ackroyd's suggestion, for instance, that Wilde's mother told him during his trials that he was illegitimate is a truth larger than history). Too much knowledge, however, threatens the artifice of the novel's authority. The Wildean scholar who knows every source, and marks every diversion from the "accepted" truth will see exactly where Ackroyd lurks behind the mask. And because Ackroyd has chosen a medium in which it is difficult to find him, the discovery of his presence destroys his subject—much more so than if he were an actor obviously playing Wilde. The audience accept an actor as a subject, they mask him because it is obvious that he is another. Ackroyd's success of interesting his readers will drive them to other writings which will unmask him and make his efforts redundant. Perhaps in his next novel he will use his many talents to show more of himself. But then if Wilde's opinion that "Most people are other people. Their thoughts are someone else's opinions, their lives a mimicry, their passions a quotation" is correct, he might well wish to rewrite himself.

Andrew Hislop, "An Imitation Game," in The Times Literary Supplement, *No. 4176, April 15, 1983, p. 375.*

KAY DICK

To write Oscar Wilde's autobiography would seem to be an impossible task, with the danger of pastiche overshadowing, but in *The Last Testament of Oscar Wilde* Peter Ackroyd achieves a triumph of imaginative construction. Clever and spritely-minded Mr Ackroyd has a sureness of touch, wit that strikes the right pitch, and a perceptive selective chronology for events and issues which haunted Wilde's last days. That his research has been all-embracing and subtle is clear: the Wilde bibliography is a positive labyrinth of confusion. The proposition that Wilde may have kept a journal during the last year of his life is an acceptable thesis, since we have his apologia, *De Profundis,* that searingly agonising, self-pitying and often spiteful letter to Lord Alfred Douglas, written in Reading Gaol, to remind us that Wilde's art was to explain himself.

In his point of departure Mr Ackroyd is shrewd. He gives us Wilde in 1900, the year of his death, finally down on his luck, living frugally, if not wholly uncomfortably, in one room at the Hôtel d'Alsace in Paris. A Wilde then beaten to a very great extent by his circumstances, in spite of the fact that he was not exactly penniless nor friendless. . . . Wishing to protect him from himself, his friends conspired to keep him from his love, but Wilde wrote to Douglas that "my only hope of again doing beautiful work in Art is being with you," and with him again, in Naples and Capri, the final fire of that ruinous passion was burnt out. There was little then left for Wilde to save or survive on.

It is this last desolation which Mr Ackroyd so brilliantly conveys, with mood changes from despair to whistling-in-the-dark bravery which turn Wilde to thoughts of past triumphs. So we have this Wilde, stumbling yet still prideful, towards death, aware of final disintegration.... Reasonable that for consolation—in Mr Ackroyd's imagination—Wilde should have turned to his past in journal form.

So Mr Ackroyd takes us through the landmarks and influences of that life, and gives us a man who, in spite of horrific years, retains a sparkle and an elegance of spirit. He has him telling us how his mother confessed to his illegitimacy—new to me, taken I'm told from Terence de Vere White's book. His guilt about his wife Constance. Of Douglas: "I was lost as soon as I loved him." His pride—so needed by him then—about his conversational art and his ability to turn it into perfect theatre. There is a superb dialogue between Wilde and Ada Leverson, the famed and beloved Sphinx who harboured him at the time of the trial.... Mr Ackroyd has Wilde writing lyrically about Socratic love—difficult since this was the peak of Wilde's defence at his trial—telling how Ross introduced him to his own nature. These passages about London's male brothels of the time powerfully annotate Wilde's recklessness and his strange conviction that his fame would protect him from censure. Credible also that Wilde should assess his own work, and Mr Ackroyd sums it up for him: "I constructed fine, light work, as sensuous as Maeterlinck, as witty as Sheridan." All the horrors of the trial and three years in prison are recalled with just the right mixture of self-explanation, self-deception and self-pity.

"You should see the things I shall write now," Mr Ackroyd makes him say to Ross at the end, and it rings true, because Wilde at no time denied his genius. Mr Ackroyd adds, "Then I broke down and wept"—a moving finale to this tragic story. (pp. 77-8)

Kay Dick, "Oscar Ceremony," in Punch, Vol. 284, No. 7431, April 27, 1983, pp. 77-8.

ROGER LEWIS

Peter Ackroyd is a master of disguise. But it is not he who dresses up: His talent is to divine the masquerades of other people. He has already essayed Ezra Pound [*Ezra Pound and His World*], an author whose endless *Cantos* form a ventriloquial epic. (p. 39)

Ackroyd has also written a book called *Dressing Up.* Ostensibly about transvestism, it charted the couturial aids which help blur sexual distinctions. But looked at with a critical eye, free from moral and social distaste, the concept of a man trying to turn himself into a woman enacts something important. With the looks of a lady and the appendages of the male, the transvestite is a creature closest to androgyne (*andros* male, *gunē* woman, in Greek). If our commentators about myth are to be believed, androgyne is the primal, undivided whole from which the rest of us have sprung.

This combination of masculine and feminine traits is the basis of comic confusion in much of Shakespeare (where girls turn into boys) and is the major convention in British pantomime (where the Ugly Sisters are vamps played by comedians and the handsome prince is in fact a strutting girl). Superannuated, androgyne appears as Tiresias in T. S. Eliot's *The Waste Land* ("throbbing between two lives / Old man with wrinkled female breasts") and in an elliptical way underpins Ackroyd's latest book, *The Last Testament of Oscar Wilde.* "Although I possess the wonder of Miranda, I have also the faintness of Prospero who forswears his art as soon as life has quite matched his

expectations." In feature a Boer farmer, in manner a vestal virgin, as Wilde says of Walter Pater.

Wilde it is who throbs between two lives. On the one hand he was a famous author, aphorist of the Café Royale with a respectable wife and family; on the other he was a frequenter of male brothels, a wallower in his own sins. Ackroyd's novel pretends to be a journal of the writer's last few weeks when these two halves of his nature clashed together like fatal cymbals. His dandyism and fame were ruined and mocked by the discovery of his secret proclivities. "I have lied to so many people—but I have committed the unforgivable sin, I have lied to myself. Now I must try to break the habit of a lifetime."

Wilde has been on trial, imprisoned, and now exiled to the continent. He wanders Paris, bearing his past like a curse. What makes *Last Testament* so breathtaking is that this invented diary is dangerously plausible. It is as though Ackroyd had been chosen as the amanuensis for Wilde's spectral jottings. He is sometimes more Wildean than Wilde. (pp. 39-40)

Wilde's lifelong quest, as Ackroyd perceives, was to turn conversation into an art and his personality into a symbol. What in fact happened was that his personality became entangled in a drama which not even his conversation could outface. "Instead of mastering life, I allowed it to master me; instead of being the extraordinary dramatist which I was, I became an actor merely, mouthing the lines of others and those which fear and cowardice murmured to me." How do we know when an actor is acting? Wilde certainly could not have put an unevasive answer to this kind of discrimination.

His trials saw him pilloried: The version of himself which performed deeds shocking to Victorian England stripped the finery from the peacock he had striven to become. "When I entered the courtroom of the Old Bailey it was as if I were going upon a stage." The tragedy was that Wilde was neither the stage manager of his own performance nor placed within the safety of a script known to the actor in advance. "I have always worshipped at the altar of imagination, but I never believed that I would become a sacrifice upon it." (p. 40)

The genius of *The Last Testament* is that the squalor which was the reality of Wilde's last days is transfigured into art. We see Wilde convert his degradation into a symbol of the theological Fall. He also views himself as a martyr, a stumbled messiah. He even affects a disinterested inquisitiveness about his own fate....

Wilde hid himself in words. He highlighted the disguise with real costumes for "dress is the most complete representation of modern civilization." Decorousness betrays the sham within. The idea is an old one. Oswald in *King Lear* is sneered at because "a tailor made thee" and Parolles in *All's Well that Ends Well* is dismissed for "the soul of this man is his clothes." But Wilde's dressing up—both linguistic and sartorial—reflected the brilliance of his vital intellect. He hid himself in words for in sentences his personality could unfurl as in a sanctuary. He used language as Pope used a couplet: a machine to hide in which was simultaneously a weapon to wield. Ackroyd's Wilde is as fluent as the genuine article and in addition achieves wisdom from his humiliations. (p. 41)

Roger Lewis, in a review of "The Last Testament of Oscar Wilde," in The American Spectator, Vol. 17, No. 3, March, 1984, pp. 39-41.

JONATHAN KEATES

Of all [England's] better-known Baroque architects, it is Nicholas Hawksmoor who most insistently tugs at the imagination. Wren, for all his unchallenged primacy, is still too much the virtuoso, the mathematician and astronomer indulging his curiosity in stone, while Vanbrugh plays the wit and the dabbler to perfection. The genuine one-off among them was their assistant, the backroom boy at Blenheim and St Paul's, whose language of sinister monumental massiveness and starkly incised gloom embodies a proto-romanticism matched in the morbidity of contemporary poems like Pope's ''Eloisa to Abelard'' and Parnell's ''A Night-piece on Death.''

The maggots and conundrums, the quirkish allusions to pagan antiquity, the sense of a haunted fancy at work on St Mary Woolnoth, Christ Church Spitafields and St Anne Limehouse have proved irresistible to Peter Ackroyd, whose evocation of their creator lays an icily compelling touch upon us. *Hawksmoor* is hardly, as its publishers claim, 'a novel . . . of total originality' and is much the better for not being so. The long-cherished fable of the artist who acquires wisdom at the price of damnation is given a lurid new gloss, and the appeal is to an authentically English tradition of the macabre, something out of Sheridan Le Fanu or M. R. James, to a desired accompaniment of gooseflesh, nervous backward glances, creaking floorboards upstairs and something ominously indistinct outside the window.

Ackroyd's unflaggingly precise pastiche registers the rhythms and colours of Augustan vernacular so truly that even the spellings—'alwaies,' 'Cloaths,' 'rowling'—are infallibly hit off. He has steeped himself in the antiquarians, the anatomists, the prophets, mountebanks and dreamers of the age, and their crinkum-crankum scatters its phosphorescent brilliance across both narrative and plot.

As a chronicle of the balefully obsessive transmuted into the screaming bananas, the work hurls us towards its unforeseen resolution in the luminous calm of recollected childhood, a visionary gleam from Vaughan or Traherne. Inspector Hawksmoor, alter ego of an eighteenth-century architect named Dyer (who is—well, you guessed it), never finds his infanticide quarry, pursued among the East End graveyards and doss houses, and Dyer himself never ultimately arrives at the demoniac theophany which his temples are designed to celebrate. The pair achieve their destined synthesis via the children's singing games which run through the novel in a mingled stream of menace and beatitude.

What flaws there are derive mainly from Ackroydian exuberance laying too many false trails and from a certain flimsiness in the handling of the contemporary episodes, but such things pale beside the overwhelming accomplishment with which Dyer's private empire of unreason is given its ghastly reality, and with which the primal voids and shadows of London are disclosed in all their ancient, dank, crepuscular horror.

> Jonathan Keates, ''Creaking Floorboards,'' in The Observer, *September 22, 1985, p. 27.*

ALAN HOLLINGHURST

Peter Ackroyd is much possessed by possession. In his first novel, *The Great Fire of London,* he aimed to trace the map of the Dickensian metropolis under its present form, and allowed one of his characters to be taken over by the spirit of Little Dorrit. In *Hawksmoor,* which includes the Great Fire of London in its narrative, he again shows the twentieth-century city malignly haunted by its fictional past—though this time it is not by a pre-existing fiction, but by one created in the novel itself. Ackroyd has reinvented early eighteenth-century London, and with it one of its greatest geniuses, Nicholas Hawksmoor. In his fictional form Hawksmoor becomes Nicholas Dyer: Nicholas Hawksmoor is the name of the present-day police officer who is possessed by his spirit.

Ackroyd himself, like some theatrical spirit-medium, has raised to an art the act of being possessed. He do the baroque architect—as he did Oscar Wilde in his previous novel—in different voices. *The Last Testament of Oscar Wilde* was consummate ventriloquism, so Wildean that it was easy to forget it was make-believe and the result of research, hard work and a brilliant ear. Alternate chapters of *Hawksmoor* are written as if by Dyer, and for these Ackroyd has forged a vigorous, eccentric pastiche style, of the late seventeenth as much as of the eighteenth century, which in its personal and irregular cadences is a finer achievement than his mimicry of Wilde's monotonous periods. It is a livelier and more literary style than Hawksmoor's own (although it does adopt and adapt a number of passages from his letters to his assistants and patrons); it is at once dramatic and confessional, and this gives these chapters something of the aural and claustrophobic quality of an epistolary novel. Such period voices, funny spelling and all, have a certain chic these days; none the less, Ackroyd has agglomerated a medium perfect for his purpose: the self-portrait of a fanatical and secretive schemer, alert, violent and solipsistic.

This is not quite the picture we have of Hawksmoor, but Ackroyd has taken his cue from the eccentricities of his buildings, which so disturbingly combine the barbaric grandeur of the antique with a kind of atavistic feeling for Gothic forms. His was a vocabulary that, more than any other in the brief epoch of the English baroque, seemed even in its own time a kind of Babylonish dialect in stone, and that was soon discredited by the fashionable correctness of Palladianism. Ackroyd's trick is to fix on this bizarrerie, and in turning Hawksmoor into Dyer to exaggerate it, subvert it and reinterpret it. In the process he aggravates Hawksmoor's differences from Wren, and from the empirical and scientific ethos of the Royal Society in general. The detail in which this is done is ingenious, with a kind of covert ingenuity like Dyer's own, and will be invisible to most readers. Few will recognize, for example, that Dyer's chance exclamation, ''Curved lines are more beautiful than Straight'', is an inversion of a dictum in one of Wren's *Tracts,* that ''Strait Lines are more beautiful than curved''. . . .

The alternating chapters recount a series of inexplicable strangulations which occur in the environs of the six ''real'' Dyer churches, and the understandable failure of Detective Chief Superintendent Hawksmoor to find the murderer. The victims, like those of Dyer, are all ''virgin boys'' or else vagrants who have ''become as a child''. Parallels between the two periods, and between the words and experiences of Dyer and Hawksmoor, are plentifully established: the art of shadows has them both in its grip, and Dyer shadows and foreshadows Hawksmoor in a hundred details.

But all this is easily done. Dyer's pagan mysteries of the Renaissance have a compulsion, even an authority, in the idiom of their time, but as Ackroyd sets up facile parallelisms the trickery of the technique is somehow revealed, and the mechanics of possession appear trumpery after all. The eighteenth-century passages have the force of a revelation, even if a bogus one; the present-day chapters show it all to be a kind of hokum.

It must be said, too, that when he is not in his possessed mode, Ackroyd does not write nearly so well. The cumbrous physical immediacy of the Dyer chapters is lost in the Hawksmoor ones, which try to generate mystery through portentous vagueness. Many of the echoes, such as children's street-games and songs (a rich treasury of superstition, of course), stick out clumsily in the modern passages, and the dialogue is obstinately implausible. As in *The Great Fire of London,* sketchy characters stagger as much from their symbolic burden as from their own hardships.

The end of the novel is hard to understand. In the penultimate chapter we leave Dyer in an exultant state in Little St Hugh, Black Step Lane. He may even be dying: his name has marked him as both an artist and a mortal, but his death would raise tricky, even tricksy, problems about the epistemological status of his text. The last chapter brings Hawksmoor in his (black) steps, and to a mystical confrontation with "his own Image". There is a visionary dance, or greeting of spirits, which might be a dream or might not. Hawksmoor becomes "a child again"— and so perhaps himself at last a sacrificial victim, entering the occult labyrinth of the church. There is an Eliotic mood to it— the church at smokefall, the dancers of *East Coker*—and Eliot, whom Ackroyd has most recently possessed [in his biography, *T. S. Eliot: A Life*], plays his part in the novel's concern with the City churches, its vision of purgatorial London, and its reflections on time. Dyer even has a servant called Eliot and there are a number of echoes from the poetry. What Ackroyd may be saying is that time present and time past are both present in time future, and that the essence of Dyer's possession of Hawksmoor is the simultaneity of experiences centuries apart, to which Dyer's churches are perversely capable of granting access—as all great art may be thought to transcend time. But *Hawksmoor* does not, alas, sustain that conviction; for all its sporadic brilliance and intricacy it has a lowering effect. It is a dark, cold novel, almost wholly untouched by altruism or responsibility.

Alan Hollinghurst, "In Hieroglyph and Shadow," in The Times Literary Supplement, *No. 4304, September 27, 1985, p. 1049.*

FRANCIS KING

The epithet 'clever' has tended to become a pejorative among reviewers themselves obtuse. But however great my obtuseness about Peter Ackroyd's new novel in particular or about fiction in general, I intend it to be in no way pejorative when I describe his *Hawksmoor* as diabolically clever.

'Diabolically' is here as much the right adverb as 'clever' is the right adjective, since the central character of the novel, to whom the author ascribes most of the major architectural achievements of Nicholas Hawksmoor.... but a far shorter life span (1654-c.1715 instead of 1661-1736) and a different name, is a secret adherent of the old pre-Christian religion of Britain and therefore, in essence, a Manichean.

The name that Mr Ackroyd gives to this weird character is Nicholas Dyer. St Nicholas is, of course, the patron saint not merely of sailors, pawnbrokers and Aberdeen but also of small boys. However, so far from protecting small boys—though the last of his churches, Little St Hugh, bears the name of a boy martyr—this character offers them up as human sacrifices whenever he embarks on the raising of one of those edifices....

As could at once be perceived from his *The Last Testament of Oscar Wilde,* Mr Ackroyd is the most adroit of pasticheurs. In consequence, much of the pleasure of this new novel derives from his extraordinary ability to speak through the thin lips of his Nicholas Dyer with total conviction. Inevitably, the pedantic will find occasional words and phrases either not in use in the early 18th century or else in use with meanings subtly different; but the sense that this unloving, unloveable, half-demented man of genius is truly speaking to one across a gap of some 350 years is uncanny. (p. 29)

In general, Mr Ackroyd is more successful with the obviously difficult than with the apparently easy—with Dyer more than with Hawksmoor, with the London of Wren and Vanbrugh more than with the London of Spence and Seifert. In the Dyer sections one finds oneself constantly gasping with admiration at the way in which there emerges, as out of a swirling fog, a recreation of early 18th-century London in all its squalor, poverty and danger on the one hand and all its elegance, rationality and intellectual vigour on the other. Here is a fitting battle-ground for a contest between past and future, superstition and scepticism, darkness and light. The sections set in a present-day London of gloomy lodging-houses, rancid doss-houses and playgrounds raucous with children possessed of the age-old wisdom of the slums, are less vivid in their observation, less arresting in their tone. Like a spiritualist medium, Mr Ackroyd seems best able to grip the attention when he is the instrument for a voice not his own.

Precisely what links Dyer the architect and Hawksmoor the detective to each other so ineluctably and so what knits together the alternating sections of the novel is something that, for the moment at least, remains obscure to me. In building his churches, Dyer's self-confessed aim has been to create a mystical 'Figure', an 'everlasting Order', with the seven noble edifices representing the seven planets, the seven circles of heaven, the seven stars in Ursa Major and in the Pleiades, the seven marks of the martyrdom of Little St Hugh, and, above all, the seven demons. This aim has been apprehended by the detective Hawksmoor through no process of logic but through a revelation that flashes on him because of a mysterious affinity between him and the revenant from the past.

At the close of the book, detective and mass-murderer find themselves seated side by side in 'the great square room' that is the Church of Little St Hugh (the one church that, significantly, has no existence in reality). Even though their eyes do not meet, each becomes the mirror-image of the other, each 'a child again, begging on the threshold of eternity'.

The scene, like so many others in the novel, is hauntingly written. Yet, somehow, it does not quite come off, leaving the reader like a child begging for elucidation on the threshold of comprehension. There is no doubt, as I have already said, that the book is a diabolically clever one; but it poses the question whether the obfuscation from which one struggles to emerge at the end is the fault of oneself or of an author who seems, essentially, to have conceived his book as a series of brilliant scenes rather than as an organic whole. (pp. 29-30)

Francis King, "A Voice from the Past," in The Spectator, *Vol. 255, No. 8203, September 28, 1985, pp. 29-30.*

PAT ROGERS

It takes no time to see that Peter Ackroyd's *Hawksmoor* is a book wrought with extreme cunning. A slower discovery arrives, that this virtuosity on the surface goes with imaginative density and profundity of inquiry. Inquiry into many related topics: the vagrancy of youth, the corruption of obsession, the permanence of evil. Allusive throughout, the text (though it contains a character named Eliot) does not utter the passage from *The Waste Land* which seems to underlie its themes, the one on the 'unreal city' at dawn:

> I had not thought death had undone so many.
> Sighs, short and infrequent, were exhaled,
> And each man fixed his eyes before his feet,
> Flowed up the hill and down King William Street,
> To where Saint Mary Woolnoth kept the hour
> With a dead sound on the final stroke of nine.

The novel at a crucial point reaches the same mood as well as the identical locale; and Stetson's corpses 'planted last year in your garden' are likewise mimicked in the plot.

Ackroyd's double-track narrative switches between London in the period of the Queen Anne churches (say 1714 to 1715, though the building process is telescoped) and the city of today. Across the divide of idiom and landscape, there is a parallelism of event: murders committed in identical places—around the site of Hawksmoor churches, in fact. But history, as one might suppose, has suffered an alteration, and the architect of these Baroque edifices turns out to be one Nicholas Dyer—with a career as Wren's protégé but a life-history significantly different from the real Hawksmoor's. Here Superintendent Hawksmoor turns out to be a senior detective based on (new) New Scotland Yard, where his predecessor had worked from the Board of Works in Old Scotland Yard. For that matter, the two men each inhabit an obscure lodging round about Seven Dials: topographic coincidences mortice together a staggeringly well-made plot. Hawksmoor, assigned to the modern murders, stumbles on the dark events of an equally neurotic and frightening past. . . .

The older world is rendered with total conviction and an unflagging sense of period. Ackroyd is able to do as much because he achieves what is emphatically one of the best reproductions of 18th-century language that any modern writer has essayed. Not only does he catch the cadence and syntax, which parodists generally miss: he is brilliantly exact in trapping the stage of semantic decay which had set in among words, and he hardly puts a foot wrong in his displacement of idiom. The text is replete with proverbs, saws, stock formulas, all chosen with remarkable taste. There are also numerous snatches of riddles, children's rhymes, catches and ballads—the detective is always overhearing potent but unconnected phrases, as though he has eavesdropped on the inner griefs and shames of a dissociated community. Such things are not unexpected in a book which often focuses on boyhood, but they are enlisted here with consistent point—the language and lore of schoolchildren seem not to be drawn from a season with the Opies but from a deep Augustan street-wisdom.

So, curiously, the author is able to impart a fresh and first-hand quality to a book bristling with antiquarian detail. We are given entry to Execution Dock and Rag Fair, the glass-houses of Ratcliff Highway, and the foredoomed 'fields' where the churches are set, like markers on a battle-plan, as the urban tide flows irresistibly out to the east. The tramps and waifs in the earlier period might have stepped from *Colonel Jack*, though their inner life is more richly apprehended by Ackroyd. The modern derelicts are cast out by institutions, and grow strange in their isolation: 'He was a collector, and at weekends he would search paths or fields for old coins and artefacts; the objects he discovered were not valuable, but he was drawn to their status as forgotten and discarded things.' In general, the modern narrative is comparably effective, except when it turns into a police-procedural near the end as the detective thrashes about to find a line on the murders, or a plot to connect the grisly churchyard profanations. Sometimes the symmetry becomes a perfect mirror-image in the story, as when a 1980s character reverses the journey which Dyer makes from London to Stonehenge. A sign of the times, by the way, that both Ackroyd and John Fowles, in his latest novel, should send their Georgian creations crawling about Stonehenge, which not long ago would have seemed one of the purest un-Augustan activities.

Ackroyd has taken Hawksmoor's known interest in pre-Gothic architectural theory and made Dyer into a kind of rebel against the Enlightenment. He encounters Christopher Wren in the role of a devotee of Gresham's College empiricism, and then takes part in a dialogue (appropriately, in a Restoration comedy mode) with John Vanbrugh, cast as inquisitive modern in contrast with Dyer's suspicious loyalties to the ancient. He believes with the most credulous antiquarians in the reality of a Temple of Diana beneath St Paul's. And the modern Hawksmoor in turn is forced to look for truth in the flickering signs of an electronic age, in the desperate semiology of urbanism. Ackroyd makes an intense and memorable logic of such phantasmagoria, in a novel remarkable for power, ingenuity and subtlety alike. (p. 18)

> *Pat Rogers, "Street Wise," in* London Review of Books, *Vol. 7, No. 17, October 3, 1985, pp. 18-19.*

JOYCE CAROL OATES

Hawksmoor is a witty and macabre work of the imagination, intricately plotted, obsessive in its much-reiterated concerns with mankind's fallen nature. It is less a novel in the conventional sense of the word (in which, for instance, human relationships and their development are of central importance) than a highly idiosyncratic treatise, or testament, on the subject of evil. "I like to make Merry among the Fallen and there is pleasure to be had in the Observation of the Deformity of Things," Dyer tells the reader. And, elsewhere:

> This mundus tenebrosus, this shaddowy world of Mankind, is sunk into Night; there is not a Field without its Spirits, nor a City without its Daemons, and the Lunaticks speak Prophesies while the Wise men fall into the Pitte. We are all in the Dark, one with another.

(Half the novel—its most energetic half—is related by Dyer himself in the years 1711-1715. The other half belongs to Detective Hawksmoor, whose voice, like his imagination, is far less inspired.) By the end of the novel the reader is likely to concur with Dyer's conviction that there is "no Light without Darknesse and no Substance without Shaddowe," if simply because Dyer's voice is so skillfully done.

Mr. Ackroyd's sense of drama is fiercest when it involves ideas rather than people. Indeed, *Hawksmoor* is primarily a novel of ideas, a spirited debate between those who believe (like Dyer and his fellow mystics) that "the highest Passion is Terrour" and those who believe (like Dyer's superior in Her Majesty's Office of Works, Christopher Wren) that the new science of rationalism and experimental method will eventually eradicate superstition. While Dyer argues that man cannot avoid the rage of evil spirits except by participating in evil, Wren and his fellow members of the Royal Society argue that man's reason will one day vanquish "those Wilde inhabitants of False worlds." Dyer's is the voice of the most despairing (and exulting) anti-intellectualism, a throwback to medieval notions of the necessary primacy of the irrational; Wren's is the civilized voice in which we should like to believe. As for the luckless Detective Hawksmoor, whose voice is perhaps meant to be our own—he not only fails to solve his case but appears, on the novel's final page, to have fallen victim to the malevolent Dyer himself.

At first glance this singular work of fiction would seem to have little in common with Peter Ackroyd's excellent biography, *T. S. Eliot,* published in 1984. But Dyer's obsession with physical corruption—in particular his disgust with sex—echoes the dysphoria of Eliot's most characteristic poems; his evocation of London as the "Capital City of the World of Affliction" and his scorn for the optimism of the Enlightenment strike an unmistakably Eliotic tone. Women are sluts and prostitutes. There is even a passing reference to "hollow men." Clearly Mr. Ackroyd shares Eliot's high regard for the language of the Renaissance and for Elizabethan and Jacobean drama. Dyer's voice is often Shakespearean (echoing Iago, Edmund, Thersites, Lear) in its rhetorical brilliance, as well as in the extremity of its disgust, and one of Dyer and Wren's debates is a dramatic set piece that skillfully echoes the characteristic tone (mordant, funny, terse) of Elizabethan-Jacobean drama. Mr. Ackroyd is a virtuoso writer whose prose is a continual pleasure to read. . . .

If *Hawksmoor* is less than perfect as a mystery-suspense novel it is primarily because Detective Hawksmoor is no match for his mad 18th-century counterpart: he lacks Dyer's passion as well as his uncanny sensibility. It is not surprising that he fails to catch his man, or even to grasp the pattern underlying the series of seemingly motiveless crimes. . . .

But in all, *Hawksmoor* is an unfailingly intelligent work of the imagination, a worthy counterpart in fiction to Mr. Ackroyd's much-acclaimed biography of Eliot. It will be interesting to see what this gifted and ambitious English writer will embark upon next.

> *Joyce Carol Oates, " 'The Highest Passion Is Terrour'," in* The New York Times Book Review, *January 19, 1986, p. 3.*

ALAN JENKINS

Peter Ackroyd's *The Diversions of Purley* contains poems from three earlier collections, and some new pieces. The most diverting thing about it is the title: the poems themselves trot out a repertoire of post-symbolist and surrealist and post-modernist devices and manners and tricks, parading a highly developed literary 'wit', a facility for parody and a kind of melting wistfulness.

Elliptical narratives fade and blur, directionless, drift goes on drifting, associations free themselves, all on cue; anything goes, in Purley, except the verbal imagination regularly praised in Ackroyd's fiction. He seems, in this dreamy suburb of the mind, a gifted mimic, a rather winsome prankster—and the first of those attributes, at least, has since found more effective expression. Get out at East Croydon, or go on to Hayward's Heath.

> *Alan Jenkins, "Suburban Lines," in* The Observer, *March 22, 1987, p. 27.*

KARL MILLER

[*Hawksmoor* and *Chatterton*] are books which do much to explain one another. Both books mingle old times and new times, and both give expression to fantasies of replication, with *Hawksmoor* a hard act to follow.

Its old times are brilliantly rendered, and its appeal is in part generic. The biographer of T. S. Eliot, who was himself to speak of the 'dark' experience, of the 'rude unknown psychic material', incorporated in his poem *The Waste Land,* can be seen to contribute to the tradition of romantic fabulation which began with the Gothic novel—a tradition in which darkness is privileged, in which a paranoid distrust is evident, in which can be read the evergreen message that the deprived may turn out to be depraved, and in which there can be two of someone.

Hawksmoor speaks the words of romantic duality, and is in a number of ways a double book. It consists of two alternating narratives, one of which is set in the 18th century and the other in the present, with the earlier delivered in the first person. Each of the two principal actors [Dyer, an 18th-century architect, and Hawksmoor, a present-day detective] glimpses his double in passing, as a reflection in a glass, and each stands to the other in the same relation—a relation which presupposes, as in many other Gothic texts, some sort of metempsychosis or rebirth. (p. 17)

Peter Ackroyd is all of the formidable pasticheur that he is praised for being, and Dyer's tale, which affects to be that of someone who lived in the 18th century, and in which the element of imitation, present in writing of every kind, is more obtrusive than it is in the other tale, is the livelier of the two. Pastiche is a dualistic activity, and it is an activity which can lend itself to the expression of paranoid feelings and unacted desires. A writer is copied by 'someone other' than himself, and that 'someone other' can in a manner of speaking become the writer he copies: the biter bit. The expression I am quoting is uttered by Dyer, and it is an expression which Ackroyd is given to using in his books. In pretending here to be someone other than himself who keeps murdering people, he does a tremendous job: this is a convincing argot for the age in question. The suffering and self-conscious first-person singular manifested in Dyer could be considered a creation of the Gothic novel that came after him, and Dyer can also bring to mind the magus of a time before. But there is no nagging sense of anachronism. How could there be? the novel seems to be saying. There is no such thing as anachronism. All ages are one.

The later stranglings look like a copy of what happened, at the hands of a sorcerer, in the loamy past, and Peter Ackroyd is very interested in copies. The present one is not exact, as indeed is usual in such cases. Dyer's doings are the same as but also different from those investigated by the fretful man he resembles, just as Hawksmoor's investigative Scotland Yard is the same as but also different from the architects' department of that name attended by Dyer. Ackroyd has given some readers the impression that the modern narrative, the paler of the two, is paler on purpose—in obedience, presumably, to the doctrine of time, of its runnings-down and recurrences, which figures in the novel.

The pale Hawksmoor is an inhabitant of the present day who reminds one not only of Dyer but of P. D. James's recurrent character Inspector Dalgliesh—one of her novels, *A Taste for Death,* published the following year, has a church murder in London, draped in the poses of this sensitive, cultivated policeman, and it also has, like *Hawksmoor,* a suspected tramp.

Both inspectors are presented as more interesting than the colleagues and suspects they move among. With the James, we are told who did it; in the Ackroyd, the matted fellow who is the chief suspect is never very securely identified as the author of the crimes—it is almost as if the inspector could have done it: so that Ackroyd's is an authorially uncertain work in which the authorship of its crimes is uncertain too. Meanwhile the interesting Hawksmoor is less interesting than Dyer, and may be meant to be. 'Time will tell, sir,' a colleague remarks, and Hawksmoor replies: '"Time will not tell. Time never tells." Once more he raised his arm involuntarily, as if in greeting.' It is hard to think that the novelist *intended* the reader to find this even more gnomic and exasperating than the colleague seems to find it. But there may indeed be some such aim.

Can the author be detected in this novel—come upon in his dark corner? The attitude to time might tell us what he thinks, but it is the most inscrutable aspect of the novel. *Hora e sempre*—this motto is inscribed on the front of Hawksmoor's, the real Hawksmoor's, Classical house at Easton Neston in Northamptonshire: the reputed original of Mansfield park, a house imagined by an opponent of the Gothic novel. The motto refers to a dynastic permanence: but it could be stolen for this novel, where a 'now and always' is on show. We may be meant to think that time is simultaneous, in a way that may owe something to the simultaneity propounded, 'perhaps', in Eliot's *Four Quartets;* or that it is cyclical, a turning wheel, with human depravity paling into insignificance as the wheel turns into modern times.

Interpretation is allowed to copy what it finds, and to distort it, and it may be that the novel can be interpreted as an entertainment which conveys that doctrines of science and improvement can't encompass what happens in a frightening world, where motive is dark and ill will ubiquitous. The Gothic novel was shaped to take account of such a world, and to do so, very often, in the guise of entertainment. Since its arrival in the 18th century, this is a literary mode which has recurrently been pronounced dead but which has been capable of renewal, and now Ackroyd has given a further turn to the wheel. Once again, a sufferer is seen to be mad, and his fearful sense of what he is up to can be seen to dominate the book in which it is in the end defeated or controverted. Such a book has to be divided—between hope and fear, improvement and depravity. It will be the work both of one hand and of the other. And one of these hands may wield the instrument of pastiche.

Hawksmoor was preceded by the Eliot biography of 1984 [*T. S. Eliot: A Life*], which was preceded by *The Last Testament of Oscar Wilde* of the year before, and now these annual events have been pressed upon by the new novel, *Chatterton*. All four books reveal a steady concern with imitation and interpretation, and to read them together is to be clearer about what it is that the writer intends us to think that he thinks about things. He would appear to believe in an invented truth, an invented reality—a Rortyan reality, one might be inclined to call it at times. He believes that a writer will often find himself through exposure to some other writer. And it is apparent that Ackroyd has found himself in this manner—through exposure to Wilde, Eliot, and now Chatterton. This brings with it the corollary that it is not always apparent whether the beliefs he expresses are Ackroyd's or those of the writer to whom he is exposed, or both. Interpreters must therefore beware.

All four books speak of a 'someone other'. In *Hawksmoor* Ned the tramp encounters a 'someone other' in his double, and in *Chatterton* Charles Wychwood's double is another 'someone

other'. Eliot was able to 'recognise himself through someone other'—a changeable other, but at one point it was the Frenchman Laforgue. 'The first law of the imagination,' states Ackroyd's Wilde, is that 'in his work the artist is someone other than himself.' Greek love is virtuous, Wilde is also represented as saying, because 'men can live in perfect equality, each finding in the other the image of his own soul.'

It is plain that there are many ways of being and of imagining a someone other. Art may imagine one, and Greek love may. Paranoia imagines one, and so does pastiche. And Ackroyd comes to vivid life as a pasticheur. 'The truest Plagiarism is the truest Poetry,' claims Thomas Chatterton, warming to Ackroyd's theme, and perhaps overdoing it, along with Ackroyd's Wilde, who had been able to believe that 'almost all the methods and conventions of art and life found their highest expression in parody.' Still, such claims do seem to have force when fitted to the case of the writer who is making or mediating them: Ackroyd's truest prose occurs when he applies himself to the imitation of ancient writers. This is, of course, what Chatterton, Wordsworth's 'marvellous boy', did in the plagiaristic 18th century. Like Chatterton, Ackroyd is a 'great Parodist', a 'great Plagiarist'.

It is deemed to follow from such claims that human history is 'a succession of interpretations', a piling-up of imitations, an accumulation of metaphor which will be perceived as reality. And literature will amount to the same thing: all writers are copycats. Those who prefer to believe in an indivisible single self capable of originality will be sceptical of the Ackroyd scepticism. They will make less than he does of that part of Eliot which was a 'good ventriloquist'. And they will undoubtedly object to the more unbridled formulations that enter the three fictions (the biography of Eliot maintains a comparative, and suitable, reserve on the subject). They won't accept with Charles Wychwood that 'everything is copied,' and won't accept his opinion of Chatterton:

> Thomas Chatterton believed that he could explain the entire material and spiritual world in terms of imitation and forgery, and so sure was he of his own genius that he allowed it to flourish under other names.

The second half of this, however, happens to coincide with the opinion of Chatterton which is expressed by Ackroyd's Wilde: 'a strange, slight boy who was so prodigal of his genius that he attached the names of others to it'. Peter Ackroyd has here performed the rare feat of plagiarising himself—while leaving the reader in doubt as to whether the writer shares this implausible estimate of Chatterton's marvellous buoyancy. (pp. 17-18)

In the literature of duality it is the outcast or victim who has dealings with a double, and in the new novel Charles Wychwood is an outcast whose condition copies that of Thomas Chatterton, who committed suicide in 1770 at the age of 17, having invented a medieval monk, Rowley, and written poems for him. Romantic poets were keen to vindicate Chatterton, and to cherish his untimely death as that of a sacrificial victim: here was a spilling of young blood that might have watered the purlieus of a church. Charles belongs, moreover, to a cast of outcasts, monsters, hustlers and impostors which composes a literary London reminiscent of the early novels of Muriel Spark, and far from brutally inauthentic. The queen is Harriet Scrope, novelist, plot-stealer and ferocious egotist, whose war against the world she inhabits extends to her best friend and her cat. As a comic portrait of the artist, Harriet scores high. She is estranged and she is hostile. She is a bit like Dyer.

'Tho' I was young Thomas Chatterton to those I met, I was a very Proteus to those who read my Works': Chatterton's story is mostly told by himself, and with a felicity of cadence and of reference which can be caught in the sentence I have just quoted. His story is interwoven with, and is replicated by, a modern tale, in which Charles Wychwood's comet-like career is featured. He, too, dies the early death of romance—*en poète,* as the poet Burns put it with reference to his own fate—and his end is enveloped in the consequences of his supposing that he has lit upon some Chatterton manuscripts. Charles is touchingly done—a frail unpublished poet kept going by his wife and son (the wife is called Vivien, presumably by design, though she is no copy of the first Mrs Eliot), their household a breath of fresh air in the conniving, phrase-making milieu to which Charles clings. Then there is a third story. Chatterton is as much as anything the famous painting of his death in a Holborn attic done in the 1850s by Henry Wallis—with the poet lying across the bed in a kind of frozen entrechat. It looks like an enlargement of the postcard which, in an age of mechanical reproduction, it was to become, commemorating the tourist attraction which it was also to become. The third narrative tells how George Meredith modelled for the corpse in the painting and how his wife then ran away with the painter (see also the sonnets in *Modern Love*). The three tales are deftly assembled and get on very well together.

Chatterton is represented in the novel as an accidental suicide—slain by a cocktail of arsenic and laudanum swallowed for a venereal infection. Poor Charles brings him to life again, however, for some further plagiarisms: a nest of antique-dealers, of antic disposition, in Chatterton's native Bristol, have passed to Charles a cache of papers which, together with the discovery of what seems to be the portrait of an adult Chatterton, persuades him that the poet lived on. The portraits of Chatterton have something of the importance to the novel that the living and ageing likeness has in *The Picture of Dorian Gray.*

Like **Hawksmoor** and **The Last Testament of Oscar Wilde**, this novel is a *tour de force.* And it could be said that not only is it about imitation—it is also, as are other *tours de force,* itself an imitation of something. Like other *tours de force,* it is done in a spirit of play and of emulation. It is a contender. It observes one of Wilde's principles of literature in responding to the importance of not being 'serious'. It shows what the writer can do rather than tells what he thinks. In order to find out more of what this writer thinks about imitation, we can consult a work where a treatise on the subject is developed at intervals and where he writes *in propria persona.* In [*T. S. Eliot: A Life*] we read about a major poet who was a good ventriloquist; a man of multiple personality who swore by a principle of impersonality in art, and whose art bears the indelible signature of that distinctive protean character of his; a man who led a miserable and tormented life. The book says Eliot's truest poetry was a form of plagiarism, in the benign sense that 'it was only in response to other poetry that Eliot could express his own deepest feelings.' A little earlier, a view of Eliot's has been paraphrased: that 'there is no "truth" to be found' in the world, 'only a number of styles and interpretations—one laid upon the other in an endless and apparently meaningless process'. Ackroyd notices that the Eliot who had once called poetry a 'mug's game' was eventually, in his play *The Elder Statesman,* to use the same expression for forgery. Ackroyd warns us not to jump to a conflation here, but he is intrigued by the coincidence, and it might almost serve as an emblem of his concern throughout the biography with the connection between poetry and feigning, and with the potency of parody.

The biography suggests that Eliot was never to lose the divided sense of his youth that human life is futile and meaningless—that man is 'a finite piece of reasonable misery', in the words of William Drummond of Hawthornden, a good poet who was also a great plagiarist, and a great seeker of shelter in books—but that an absolute order might be felt for, or invented. That order was eventually discovered in the teachings of Christianity. When he turned to God it was to someone other: he was surrendering to 'something outside oneself'.

The book depicts Eliot as a parodist, a plagiarist, a responder to other people's poems, and as a seeker of shelter. And yet in its closing passages we learn that as a poet he had 'no real predecessors'. He was his own man, after all. The book is cursory in its treatment of Eliot's literary background: there is no mention, for instance, of Wallace Stevens, Ivy Compton-Burnett, of Empson or Leavis, and no adequate picture of what Eliot meant to later generations of intellectuals in Britain. In other respects, however, this is a cogent and sensible account (which was constrained by a barbarous embargo on quotation). I don't think that its readers can have had much trouble in finding in the life and work the responsiveness Ackroyd finds in them. But perhaps it is the paradox conveyed by that closing glimpse of a parodic but unprecedented Eliot which carries the sharpest conviction of any feature of the book.

Eliot comes across as the sad man who sees double, as a living embodiment of the proposition that the double has to do with pain and with relief from pain, with the search, in such circumstances, for someone other. From the ordeal of his first marriage to the late happiness of the second, the book locks, at one level, into a recital of misfortunes and a medical record. Influenza after influenza. Constant debilitating 'work', in publishing and public life, and a constant invocation of the claims of such work. Lecture after lecture, accompanied by complaints about the futility of lectures and his reluctance to give them. The book makes one conscious of Eliot in the sarcophagus of his upper-class eminence; of a sad face of clerical cut—once the face of a delightful shy child—bleakly sprouting from a sartorial apparatus that resembles the mourning clothes of a cabinet minister; of a masterly poseur, an honoured invalid and recluse, of someone snobbish and sometimes unkind, who sought relief in literature and in imitation, and who also embodied the opposite of these qualities.

It is almost as if we are confronted here by a replication of the poor Tom described in Ackroyd's novel by another poor Tom of later times. And perhaps we might imagine that they are the same but different. Eliot was to tell the poet F. T. Prince: 'Not everything you write is very *interesting.*' This could be said with some emphasis of Chatterton, but not of Eliot himself, who moreover survived, who grew to be famous, who did not kill himself, though he was to wonder how one might set about dying. As the tradition might have it, as romance might have it, Chatterton died the early death of the divided, the invaded man, while Eliot did not.

It isn't that Ackroyd asks us to compare these two poor Toms, in pursuit of a theory alleging the importance of imitation. But they are brought together, in successive books, by the force of this preoccupation, and the reader has to make what he can of the resemblance between two figures quite remote from one another in any coarser understanding of the matter, to do this while adjusting his sight to a vista of copycats, impostors and successive interpretations—a vista which is not, however, unfamiliar now and can be glimpsed, for instance, in the productions and reproductions of contemporary literary theory.

Imposture is shown in Ackroyd's new novel, in this burlesque of the literary life, to be an interesting business, and the result may be that Chatterton's reputation will climb back towards what it was in the retrospects of the Romantic period. He was worshipped then for his talent and untimely death—perhaps a little as Eliot was to be worshipped, in the 1940s and 50s, for his saintly abstention from the world. Keats placed him among the stars, where Keats himself, for similar reasons, was to be placed by Shelley. Chatterton became a topos, and the numbers lisped: 'O Chatterton, how very sad thy fate,' 'Flow gently, sweet Chatterton,' 'Good for you, Chatterton.' Readers can be expected to spot which of these quotations are forgeries, and they must also have doubted in their time whether this writer was as good as the early tributes made out.

Chatterton needn't have had prodigious talent for the talent expended in the novel to take effect. It is a novel which communicates the notion that the talented and untalented meet in that country of the mind where everyone copies and steals from everyone else, where everything is reproductive or reminiscent of everything else, where one thing leads to another and this person passes into that. It plays with such ideas, to a Shavian pitch of exaggeration: but it is not a novel of ideas, any more than it is a heartless game. It has people in it, with lives to live. It has Charles in it, whose plight is more touching than anything in the 19th-century retrospects of Chatterton. It has its predecessors in the romantic tradition—a tradition which includes the self-important single self nevertheless prone to dispersal and division, invasion and impersonation, which includes the victim and his alter ego. At the same time, both here and in *Hawksmoor*, Ackroyd, too, is his own man. For all his standard procedures, I don't think he is actually imitating anybody. (p. 18)

Karl Miller, "Poor Toms," in London Review of
Books, *Vol. 9, No. 15, September 3, 1987, pp. 17-18.*

RUPERT CHRISTIANSEN

Thomas Chatterton, the 'marvellous boy' who died in 1770 at the age of 17, after a brief career as a forger of medieval poetry and an even briefer attempt to storm Grub Street, has already made two sorts of appearance in Peter Ackroyd's fiction. In *The Last Testament of Oscar Wilde,* he is judged by Ackroyd's Wilde to be 'the great tragedy of the 18th century . . . a strange, slight boy so prodigal of his genius that he attached the names of others to it'; while in *Hawksmoor,* he is unmistakably prefigured by the isolated and antagonised young apprentice Nick Dyer, ambitious to make his way out of the gutter and into the profession of architecture.

Now, in [*Chatterton*], he is presented full-face and central, although needless to say the result is far from a conventional fictional reconstruction of a historical figure: Ackroyd is up to his old tricks, and some new ones too. At one level, the game is an indisputable success, ceaselessly entertaining, dazzlingly clever and written in a prose of colour, fluidity, and panache. Whether it rises to any other level—as a significant work of novelistic art or as a rich statement of its purported themes—is less easy to determine.

Like *Hawksmoor, Chatterton* moves between different historical periods and shows the not-quite buried past wreaking its revenge on the innocent present. The contemporary layer of the novel follows a failed or failing young poet, Charles Wychwood, who happens upon an apparently authentic portrait of Thomas Chatterton in middle age, dated 1802; the subsequent

discovery of a hoard of manuscripts leads him to the conclusion that Chatterton merely staged his teenage death in order to continue his poetic forging unhindered, churning out verse in the manners of other famous 18th-century poets. Parallel to this runs a pastiche narration of Chatterton's few sad months living and dying in London, and a novelettish version of the events surrounding the painting of *The Death of Chatterton* . . . by the Victorian painter Henry Wallis, for which the model was the young George Meredith. Between these three areas of plot is a whole complex of echoes and interconnections, manipulated with Ackroyd's characteristic virtuosity, as well as a number of *voltes-faces* which no tactful reviewer could conscientiously reveal.

But these are the old tricks: what distinguishes **Chatterton**, the advance it makes in terms of Ackroyd's *oeuvre*, is the emergence of the influence of Dickens, whose biography Ackroyd is currently writing. In *Hawksmoor,* Nick Dyer proposes to the neo-classicist Vanbrugh the virtues of a 'huge, lushious style . . . of outlandish Phrases and fantasticall terms': here the baroque flamboyance is not so much linguistic as psychological, bodied forth in a gallery of grotesques and eccentrics. . . .

Yet there is an emotional scope in Dickens that Ackroyd cannot yet match, and I would guess that it is from another Dickens disciple, Angus Wilson, that he has acquired both the high-pitched camp repartee in which most of the minor characters relentlessly indulge and the fascination with the unsavoury habits and morals of the elderly. More specifically, one could point to the model of Wilson's *Anglo-Saxon Attitudes,* another novel about the consequences of forgery, which contains various possible sources for the personality traits of **Chatterton**'s most memorable figure—the lady novelist Harriet Scrope, whose sheer nastiness and unscrupulous attempts to exploit Wychwood's discoveries provide some of the most uninhibitedly and inventively funny passages I have encountered in any novel published in the last 15 years.

To suggest the existence of such links is only to follow Ackroyd's own insistence that 'there is no real *origin* for anything': the illusoriness of the divisions between the authentic and the plagiarised, between reality and imitations of it is **Chatterton**'s theme—and it is here that Ackroyd falls short, in as much as the idea is not so much developed as led through a hall of mirrors: virtually every page contains some instance of the fact that we are all, inevitably and continually, borrowing from each other.

And there lies the ultimate disappointment of this otherwise enormously enjoyable novel: it doesn't settle the doubt that arose over *Hawksmoor* as to whether Ackroyd is simply a brilliant pasticheur, who, in the phrase of his previous biographical subject T. S. Eliot, can 'do the police in different voices'; or whether he is in pursuit of something genuinely distinctive, a new form of Gothic fiction perhaps. **Chatterton**'s retaliation is to defend the creativity involved in pastiching; and yet at the end of the novel a writer friend of Wychwood's announces that he is planning a novel about the events to which he has been witness: 'I might discover that I had a style of my own, after all' he remarks. Is this Ackroyd's last little joke against himself? **Chatterton** certainly doesn't provide the answer, but it constitutes a fascinating evasion of the whole question.

Rupert Christiansen, "Borrowers Amok," in The
Listener, *Vol. 118, No. 3028, September 10, 1987,
p. 22.*

MARTIN DODSWORTH

"Peter Ackroyd's *Chatterton* is about death. It is about plagiarism. It is about the nature of poetry." And, one might add to the publisher's dust-jacket description, it does not sound much fun. Yet, like its predecessor, *Hawksmoor,* it is best thought of as a game played between the author and his reader—"Art is just another game", says George Meredith in this latest fiction—or, to come a little closer to the point, as a game played by words themselves in the field of meaning. . . .

In the new novel a character describes his own failure as a novelist to capture the *given* quality of the world in which "everything just exists in order to exist", and no significant pattern can be found. Whenever he tried to write he found himself imitating other people, and this wouldn't do because "none of them seemed to feel how *odd* it is that life is just the way it is and no other." *Chatterton* is a novel that does affirm that oddity, and does so by means entirely paradoxical. Its unpatterned world is presented in a frame as elaborately patterned as the novelist can make it. . . .

The question is, in what spirit these patterns are offered the reader. It is not unlike the question proposed by Ackroyd's previous novel, *Hawksmoor,* in which a patently fictitious diabolist, more than two hundred years dead, apparently secures death after death in present-day London. Reviewers compared that book with M. R. James, but James had the sense to write short stories. If *Hawksmoor* were simply meant to make the flesh crawl, the reader could have been spared much verbiage. Others represented the book as an account of "modern evil", but here again something seemed wrong; the modern parts of the novel were by far the weaker and the underlying *donnée* of the criminal and his partner seeking each other out too banal to demand such seriousness.

There is none of this banality in *Chatterton,* at least at the level of plot. Something is always happening; the novel accumulates in brief episodes and the reader is kept guessing what will happen next. On the other hand, characters are continually flitting into conversations about what is real and what is unreal, what is a fake and what is not, and these conversations lack bite. . . .

It is easy to become impatient with this novel. Ackroyd at times seems intent on goading the reader to the point when the book must definitively be given up, and then sweetly relaxing, offering an unexpected morsel of plot, a new twist to the tale. Charles, for example, gets his portrait of Chatterton from an incongruously Dickensian antique-dealer, Mr Leno, who advertises his shop by a sign: "Leno Antiques. Don't Linger. Make Us Very Happy. Walk Up, Do." This amuses Charles, who likes to address his small son of indeterminate age as "Edward the Impossible", "Edward the Unprepared" or "Edward the Unexpected" as the mood takes him. The reader is under no compulsion to find amusing either Mr Leno's Dickensian manners or Charles's roguish name-calling; if he does not, Ackroyd may lose a reader even before he has had time to present the Firbankian Harriet Scrope or Vivien's employer Cumberland, who always refers to his partner as "someone", or Charles's friend Flint, who speaks his own rum lingo: "This is the inner sanctum," he said apologetically. "Can I tempt you?"—"Excuse Me?"—"Nunc est bibendum?"—"What?"—"A drinkie?"

If this is Ackroyd's idea of being amusing, just what is his game? Something fearfully semiotic by the look of some of the many jokes in which characters find themselves caught up:

Charles entering Harriet's house thinks she has been reading *Andromaque* or *Bérénice* because he has misread RACING on the cover of her form-book. This is a bad start to a scene in which he replies to Harriet's explanation, "the reason I telephoned . . . is, that I am not myself", by asking "Who are you?" Such misunderstandings do not only foreshadow the impending crisis produced by Charles's brain-tumour, but exemplify that slippage of meaning which is Derrida's subject-matter; Charles's friend Philip has a vision of the Derridean universe in the basement of the library where he works "a world where there was no beginning and no end, no story, no meaning", the very world which, as a novelist, he wants to celebrate.

Ackroyd, too, wants to celebrate it, and in order to do so he must somehow forego the element of story which suggests that there are beginnings and endings. In *Hawksmoor* the very banality of the plot was to make it dispensable; in *Chatterton* the object is to make it clear that whatever the plot does it cannot represent events in a real world. The camp stylization of much of the dialogue, the clash of styles within the book, both undermine the status of the plot as an ordered, Aristotelian representation of reality. It is not possible to reconcile all the patterned elements of the novel with each other, or all the details which in a conventional book would confirm the imagined reality of the world presented. The red-haired boy who watches Philip in the library, for example, has the air of being Chatterton manifesting himself once more, but the novel will not confirm such an identification. In his death Chatterton links hands with Meredith and Charles, according to the novel's penultimate paragraph, but not with Philip.

Perhaps that is because Philip's artistry only exists within the novel in the future tense: he thinks that he is about to become a "real" writer, thanks to Charles's example (though what this is remains appropriately mysterious), but we do not see him become one. Indeed, there is reason to think that he will not do so, since, he thinks, "I might discover a style of my own, after all", a thought which the book with its insistence on the way in which books are made out of books and on the artistry of the faker seems to deny. On the other hand, perhaps it does not, since there is no gainsaying that *Chatterton* is distinctively the creation of its author and "in the style" of both *Hawksmoor* and *Notes for a New Culture.*

Peter Ackroyd's new novel is, then, ingenious and extraordinarily self-sustaining, not to say self-conscious. It presents itself in such a way that it is difficult to pass judgment on it. In a secular world, where everything exists merely in order to exist, existence itself escapes judgment—that is to say, any judgment that may rightly claim a general validity. Nevertheless, only the most committed of Ackroyd's readers will be willing to eschew all judgment on his book. *Chatterton* sustains itself perfectly as an idea; but if art is about feeling as well as ideas, and a reading of other authors, among them Chatterton and Meredith, suggests that it is, then *Chatterton* is vulnerable to criticism. Its stylistic strategy, so brutal in its treatment of the reader, while it may be justified as an idea may not prove tolerable in practice. Its refusal of representation may, if the reader neglects or even rejects the novel's idea, look suspiciously like the alibi for a failure to represent what in a slipshod way could be called reality. The material circumstances of Charles and his wife, like their place in the perpetual exchange of social relations, are utterly unconvincing, and all the more so for Ackroyd's evident success in the "representation", within his fiction, of the imagined past, whether Chatterton's or Meredith's.

This does not cancel out the inventive power of this new book. But it does diminish the extent to which that power weighs with the reader. All about the fiction there lie hints of an uncertainty not kept fully at bay, and never more so than in the last pages. Chatterton's death is imagined with physical details that rebuke the idealized image of Wallis's painting, but the physical death gives way to a vision that represents Chatterton's idea of immortality, an idea which seems to be the book's also. This immortality is the *perpetuum mobile* of meaning that constitutes a literature, and in Chatterton's case it brings him into the company of the artists with whom he will be associated after death: Meredith and Charles Wychwood:

> They stand silently beside him. I will live for ever, he tells them. They link hands and bow towards the sun.
>
> And, when he is found the next morning, Chatterton is smiling.

At the end of the game, this note of solemnity sounds false. However much Ackroyd's own view of literary immortality differs from that which the book offers, solemnity fits badly with the outrageous taunting of the reader earlier in the novel. It gestures too easily to a conventionality that for most of the way has been repudiated. But then, to take Chatterton as the type of the artist at all has its conventional quality too. Convention entangles even the wariest of the avant-garde. Peter Ackroyd must console himself with the thought that he is, at least, *quite* wary.

> Martin Dodsworth, "Existing in Order to Exist," in The Times Literary Supplement, *No. 4406, September 11-17, 1987, p. 976.*

DENIS DONOGHUE

[Like Oscar Wilde and Thomas Chatterton, Peter Ackroyd] is preoccupied with the double or multiple life. In 1979 he published *Dressing Up: Transvestism and Drag, the History of an Obsession.* The fifth chapter deals with "Transvestism as Performance," and the whole book is an attempt to understand the desires, compulsions and gratifications involved in impersonation. Why do some men dress up as women? Is it necessary that the pretense of being another self be incompletely realized; that is, that it remain recognizable as a pretense? In literature, when Wilde, Yeats and T. S. Eliot take upon themselves a mask, or several masks, is it necessary that the self-effacement be complete?

Given these interests, Mr. Ackroyd cannot be content to write historical novels, even though many of the events he narrates have indeed happened. He is not interested in discovering "how it was," or even in provoking a sense of historical periods and scenes. In this respect he differs from the Irish novelist John Banville, whose novels *Kepler* and *Doctor Copernicus* give the impression that if we knew more about Kepler and Copernicus, our knowledge would coincide with Banville's imagining. Mr. Ackroyd's novels are historical romances, because they refuse to discriminate between the life a character apparently lived and the other lives he or she performed. Mr. Ackroyd seems to reject the implication, in the historical novel, that people coincide with themselves and settle for the one life which the decorum of historical narration gives them.

In all his books, the people who interest Mr. Ackroyd are those who do not consent to coincide with their official lineaments.

In *The Last Testament of Oscar Wilde* he gives more privilege to the experiences which Wilde imagined and proclaimed than to those he merely happened upon and suffered. In *T. S. Eliot: A Life* he makes much of Eliot the impersonator, the ventriloquist, the poet who preserved his voice by pretending that he didn't have one, who kept himself concealed behind the masks of Prufrock and Gerontion. In *Chatterton* the hero is allowed to strut through many roles. . . . (pp. 1, 40)

Mr. Ackroyd's procedures differ from those of the dramatic monologue or the historical novel because he links events, real or imagined, by likeness and not by chronology. He sets aside the official privilege of sequence, cause and effect, and produces a simultaneous concatenation of likenesses and differences, regardless of temporal impediments. Wilde is allowed to quote Eliot, without acknowledgement, of course. Simile and metaphor exert their authority over and-then-and-then-and-then. The passive form of similitude is coincidence, gratefully received or imagined; the active form is impersonation, by which a different life is appropriated to one's own.

But we are not accosted with mere ingenuities. Mr. Ackroyd is not interested in conceits. His new novel has itself a multiple life or, to be more precise, four lives at the cost of one. In different ways, it is easy to care about them all. Perhaps one of them, the story of Charles Wychwood—I hear an allusion to Wishwood, the scene of Eliot's play *The Family Reunion,* another tale of double lives—needs our care most urgently. The modern hero of Mr. Ackroyd's novel is a failed, doomed poet, engrossed in a portrait which may be of Chatterton: dated 1802 and signed George Stead, it may or may not be genuine. If it is genuine, it raises the possibility that Chatterton may not have died in 1770 after all. Wychwood bears some resemblance to Eliot in the early years of vulnerability and bad nerves, but the resemblance goes no further. He has a precocious son and a splendid wife named, like Eliot's first wife, Vivien, but unlike that woman in virtually every respect. The second life is Harriet Scrope's: she is an aging popular novelist, an amiably caustic fake, a plagiarist, trying to write her memoirs. Her friend Sarah Tilt is an art historian trying to write a study of death paintings. These two have dealings with a mysterious painting which may or may not be genuine.

The third tale is true. In 1856 Henry Wallis completed his "Death of Chatterton," now one of the most perused paintings in the Tate. His model for the painting was the poet George Meredith, with whose wife Wallis was soon to be illicitly engaged. Mrs. Meredith ran off with Wallis, who abandoned her when she became pregnant. In *Chatterton* Meredith is to be found miming death in a Holborn garret some time before he writes "Modern Love," a sequence of sonnets on his destroyed marriage.

And finally there is Chatterton, present by way of an autobiographical document which has come into Charles Wychwood's hand; he is present, too, as an unnamed young man who appears to Charles, in a moment of the latter's collapse, and restores him to health.

These four tales are elaborately interlinked. Ingenuity is exerted in ways that leave us free, while the reading lasts, to be unaware of it. Plausibility is not an issue: by disconnecting the orthodoxy of sequence and causation, Mr. Ackroyd makes it seem natural that any event should summon its kin. . . .

Chatterton is a wonderfully vivid book, continuously at home to its many lives. Mr. Ackroyd has relaxed a little from the constantly directed pressure of *Hawksmoor,* but there is no loss of vitality. The several styles of the book are most persuasively managed, and even if the memorable bits of dialogue are neo-Wildean flourishes, they are lively enough to live in Wilde's vicinity. An art dealer says to Stew Merk, a forger of his master's paintings: "We will buy your paintings. We will go on with your story, but only on condition that nothing happens next." I balked only once: when Mr. Ackroyd has the same art dealer quote Ackroyd. Examining a fake picture, he remarks: "And the hair is quite wrong. Men's hair was the greatest tragedy of the eighteenth century, with the possible exception of George Stubbs's animal paintings." It was better the first time, in *The Last Testament of Oscar Wilde.* A few sentences are a bit arch, I suppose: "Crocodile tears and crocodile shoes are matching accessories." Elsewhere: "A wig can cover a multitude of gins." But I'm not quarreling. The book is superb. (p. 40)

> Denis Donoghue, "One Life Was Not Enough," in The New York Times Book Review, *January 17, 1988, pp. 1, 40.*

DAVID LODGE

It is not surprising that Thomas Chatterton should have attracted the attention of the versatile and prolific young British writer Peter Ackroyd as a subject for fiction. His first novel, *The Great Fire of London* (1982), was a Dickensian novel about Charles Dickens; his second, *The Last Testament of Oscar Wilde* (1983), was an astonishingly convincing attempt to imagine the journal Wilde might have written in the last months of his life. *Hawksmoor* (1985) was based on another tour de force of literary pastiche, crosscutting between the first-person narrative of a seventeenth-century architect, whose churches in the City of London were the products of Satanism as well as geometry, and the story of a twentieth-century detective investigating a series of macabre murders in those same churches. In short, Mr. Ackroyd's fiction has always been characterized by the writer's effort to think himself back into the past by a dazzling feat of stylistic imitation—which would be a charitable way of describing the forgeries perpetrated by the young Chatterton. "The truest Plagiarism is the truest Poetry," declares [the title character of *Chatterton*], and on one level the novel can be read as an exploration of that paradox and an implicit defense of Ackroyd's own self-consciously intertextual methods.

As Louise J. Kaplan observes, in a psychoanalytical biography of Chatterton [*The Family Romance of the Imposter-Poet Thomas Chatterton*] which by a happy coincidence appears at almost the same time as Ackroyd's novel, Chatterton was not a plagiarist in the normal sense of the word—one who seeks to purloin the credit due to other men's words; but rather the inverse—one who passed off his own brilliant inventions as the work of someone else (the fictitious Rowley). To be sure, Chatterton's pseudomedieval verse is full of echoes of his precocious reading in Chaucer and in Percy's *Reliques,* but such borrowing occurs in all poetry, indeed all art. . . . The most obvious example is Eliot's *The Waste Land,* a poem stuffed with echoes of and allusions to precursor texts, especially in the original draft, from which Ezra Pound persuaded Eliot to prune many lines of pastiche and parody. A critic quoted by Kaplan has said of these omitted passages that "they are not simply imitations but rather creative borrowings of another style and syntax which releases [*sic*] a plethora of voices and perceptions." That critic was Peter Ackroyd, in his prize-winning biography, *T. S. Eliot* (1984).

The example of Eliot has contributed to the structure as well as the texture of Ackroyd's *Chatterton:* just as Eliot switches between several "narratives" (the Grail legend, the New Testament, the sordid and neurotic lives of various twentieth-century social types, etc.), setting up resonances and resemblances between them, so Ackroyd cuts abruptly backward and forward between the story of Chatterton, the story of Wallis and the Merediths, and the story of fictitious characters in modern London in whose lives the two historical narratives suggestively echo and intertwine. But since it is a novel and not a poem, there is more narrative logic in *Chatterton* than in *The Waste Land.* As in *Hawksmoor,* a causality of occult coincidence knits the three stories together.

The greater part of the text is devoted to the modern story, which is not altogether good news for Ackroyd's readers, since his touch is surer in recreating the past than in representing the present. The modern characters in *Chatterton* fall into two sharply differentiated groups: good guys and bad guys. The good guys are mostly rather poor and unworldly, and somewhat colorless; the bad guys are outrageous grotesques who might have been invented by a collaboration between Dickens and Firbank. Their behavior is extravagantly eccentric and their speech is highly mannered, peppered with bad puns and facetious quips. They are occasionally amusing but their chatter quickly becomes tiresome, grating on the nerves like squeaky chalk on a blackboard. Fortunately, Ackroyd never lingers with any single set of characters for very long.

The chief good guy is a youngish unpublished and unemployed poet, Charles Wychwood, with a wife, Vivien (the name of Eliot's neurotic first wife, though there the resemblance ends—Vivien Wychwood is a simple soul, with an uncomplicated devotion to her husband), and a young son, Edward. Charles's sometimes odd behavior (he is, for instance, fond of tearing strips out of his favorite books and eating them) turns out to be a symptom of the brain tumor that eventually kills him. The story starts with his attempt to raise some money by selling an eighteenth-century book on flute-playing to a couple of Dickensian grotesques called Mr. and Mrs. Leno. In their antique shop, Charles is much struck by an early nineteenth-century portrait of a middle-aged literary man, and accepts the painting in exchange for his book. Various clues suggest that it is a portrait of Thomas Chatterton, and when Charles, accompanied by his faithful librarian friend, Philip, goes down to Bristol to investigate the provenance of the painting, he discovers some old manuscripts apparently written by Chatterton which suggest that, faced with the imminent exposure of his Rowley forgeries, he conspired with a bookseller to fake his suicide so that he could go on with his career as a literary forger. The excited Charles speculates that "half the poetry of the eighteenth century is probably written by him" and hopes to make his own fortune by publishing the discovery.

Charles refuses to admit that he is ill, but as his symptoms grow worse he more and more identifies himself with the spirit of Chatterton. When he suffers a fatal collapse in the course of a party at an Indian restaurant he sees the ghostly figure of the eighteenth-century poet hovering behind his chair. The apparition is seen at the same moment by an elderly novelist called Harriet Scrope, a foul-mouthed, witchlike figure. . . . She has got wind of Charles's discovery and schemes to relieve Charles's widow of the Chatterton papers and portrait.

Harriet Scrope herself has been guilty of plagiarism in her early work, as Philip discovers when he stumbles upon an obscure Victorian novelist called Harrison Bentley, whose plots Harriet

Scrope evidently borrowed and adapted for her own purposes. . . . When Harriet Scrope takes the putative portrait of
Chatterton to be verified by the art dealers Cumberland and
Maitland (for whom Vivien works as a secretary) she is told
that it is "a fake. . . That is, if it's meant to be what you think
it is," because some of the details are incorrect for the alleged
date of the painting. Scrope, being privy to an artistic forgery
at which the art dealers have connived (they are selling paintings by a recently deceased artist called Seymour knowing that
they were executed by his assistant Stewart Merk during the
painter's last illness), blackmails them into employing Merk
to make the necessary adjustments to the Chatterton portrait;
but when Merk starts cleaning the painting the picture of a
younger man (a genuine portrait of the young Chatterton?)
becomes visible before both layers of pigment dissolve and
melt in a fashion heavily reminiscent of the climax of *The
Picture of Dorian Gray.*

Thus does Peter Ackroyd duplicate and deconstruct the op-
positions of truth/falsehood, authenticity/forgery, originality/
plagiarism. It is a brilliantly ingenious, consciously artificial,
and mercifully unpedantic performance. The reader feels as if
he is groping his way through a mirrored labyrinth; whatever
threads are furnished to guide him lead not to an exit into
"reality" but only to more texts—and more often than not,
texts by Peter Ackroyd. The title of one of Harrison Bentley's
novels is *The Last Testament,* the same as Ackroyd's imitation
of and homage to Oscar Wilde. The title of the other is *Stage
Fire.* This recalls a cryptic remark of Harriet Scrope's to a
blind man, earlier in the novel: "All you need, old man . . .
is a circle of stage fire." Ruskin said famously of Charles
Dickens, "Let us not lose the use of Dickens's wit and insight,
because he chooses to speak in a circle of stage fire." Dickens,
the inspiration of Ackroyd's first novel, **The Great Fire of
London,** and the subject of his current biography in progress,
first came to fame through writing copy to accompany the
sporting prints of an artist called Seymour, who, jealous of his
collaborator's success with *The Pickwick Papers,* committed
suicide. The chain of allusions recedes into infinity.

There is some ambivalence in the novel, and perhaps in the
author's mind, whether the artist's vocation as represented by
Chatterton is a blessing or a curse. Charles's obsession with
the painting he discovers in the antique shop is associated with
his fatal illness, and is instinctively disliked by his wife and
son. It starts a trail that leads back to a repellent old homosexual
in Bristol whose ancestor, it turns out, faked the portrait and
forged the manuscripts in order to blacken the character of
Thomas Chatterton, in revenge for being denied the opportunity
to publish Chatterton's poems in his lifetime. This painting
seems to represent the evil that is generated by, or parasitic
upon, the artistic life. The Wallis painting, on the other hand,
just as much a fake in its own way, and associated with much
human anguish in the person of George Meredith, is seen as
benign. . . . Philip comes across a story to the effect that George

Meredith, in despair at his wife's desertion, was saved from
committing suicide by the apparition of the young Thomas
Chatterton. I do not know whether this story is true, apocry-
phal, or invented by Ackroyd for the occasion. In a sense it
doesn't matter. The impossibility of establishing the plain truth
of any human history is the underlying theme of **Chatterton.**

Perhaps, therefore, it was unwise of Ackroyd to use his authority as a storyteller to decide the historically undecidable
mystery of Chatterton's death. He shows us Chatterton waking
on the fateful day in good spirits, slightly dashed by the discovery that he has symptoms of gonorrhea, presumably con-
tracted from his amorous landlady. He recalls a remedy recommended by a friend, a mixture of opium and arsenic, and
purchases these ingredients from an apothecary who warns him
of the deadly properties of arsenic. At the end of the day,
returning to bed in his cups, he drinks the potion with agonizing
and fatal consequences.

Louise Kaplan carefully considers this theory of how Chatterton
died, and presents the evidence to support it. . . . The theory
is plausible—but no more so than several others, and less so
than some, all of which are scrupulously investigated and weighed
by Dr. Kaplan. She herself inclines to the traditional view that
Chatterton committed suicide, but acknowledges that it will
never be possible to establish this with any certainty. (pp. 15-16)

If Chatterton died of a quack remedy for the clap, the Romantic
cult of the marvelous boy who perished in his pride seems
rather foolish, as unfounded as Charles Wychwood's belief
that Chatterton lived on to middle age. But, as if reluctant to
accept the cynical implications of his own narrative, Ackroyd
adds a coda in which Charles's friend Philip vows to keep the
fantasy (and thus in a sense Charles himself) alive, by writing
it up in his own way. The novel ends with Chatterton smiling
in death, united beyond time and space with the spirits of the
other two poets who lived and died after him.

If Mr. Ackroyd ingeniously teases us with a multiplicity of
meanings, Dr. Kaplan (whose elegantly designed book is not
without its elements of literary pastiche in the form of mock-
eighteenth-century chapter headings) pursues a single line of
argument, observing but not being distracted by the plethora
of myths, rumors, and downright lies that accumulated around
Chatterton after his death. Both books are excellent of their
kind, and they complement each other beautifully. They are,
as it happens, identical in size, and unsurprisingly both bear
on their dustjackets full color reproductions of Wallis's famous
painting. To hold them, one in each hand, looking from one
to another, is like glancing between two mirrors in which the
same image is endlessly replicated—an apt emblem for the
insoluble enigma of Chatterton's death. (p. 16)

David Lodge, "The Marvelous Boy," in The New
York Review of Books, *Vol. XXXV, No. 6, April 14,
1988, pp. 15-16.*

Conrad (Potter) Aiken

1889-1973

(Also wrote under pseudonym of Samuel Jeake, Jr.) American poet, novelist, short story writer, autobiographer, critic, editor, author of children's books, dramatist, memoirist, essayist, and journalist.

Aiken is considered by many critics to have significantly influenced the development of modern poetry. Although a contemporary and associate of such writers as Ezra Pound and T. S. Eliot, Aiken eschewed literary groups and movements, instead focusing on his personal sensibility and the delineation of self—what he termed "that passionate sense of identity which has always been the most preciously guarded possession of the poet." Deeply affected by the theories of Sigmund Freud and George Santayana, Aiken blended spiritual, philosophical, and psychological elements in his works to explore facets of modern existence and the evolution of human consciousness. He also employed numerous devices and styles and is particularly noted for adapting musical structures to literature. By combining physical detail and psychological drama, Aiken synthesized his preoccupations with conscious and unconscious reality while creating complex works that reveal significance on several levels. Commenting in 1953 on the autobiographical aspect of Aiken's work, R. P. Blackmur stated: "What he writes shines with the expanded light—perhaps the idiopathic light, perhaps the light of self-healing or idio-therapy—of what he has seen and been; and the hope is that, with the aid of the traditions and forms of poetry, it may be light for others also."

Born in Savannah, Georgia, to parents of Scottish descent, Aiken moved to Massachusetts at the age of eleven to live with relatives after his father, a Harvard-educated physician and surgeon, shot his wife to death and then committed suicide. Profoundly affected by this experience, Aiken later wrote that in discovering his parents' bodies he "found himself possessed of them forever." In 1907, Aiken entered Harvard University, where he studied literature and wrote for the Harvard *Advocate*. Among several notable classmates was T. S. Eliot, with whom Aiken maintained a lasting personal and professional relationship. After missing classes to complete a translation of a work by nineteenth-century poet Théophile Gautier during his senior year, Aiken was placed on probation for absenteeism. His ensuing withdrawal from the university divested him of duties as class poet, and he spent the next year in Europe, visiting Eliot in Paris. Aiken returned to Harvard in the autumn of 1911 to complete his degree and subsequently pursued a career as a freelance writer. Aiken's early verse, much of which was composed during the years following his graduation in 1912, is generally considered to emulate the works of such poets as John Masefield and Edgar Lee Masters while evidencing his initial experiments in adapting musical forms to poetry and his use of common individuals as central characters. In these poems, collected in *Earth Triumphant and Other Tales in Verse* (1914), *Turns and Movies and Other Tales in Verse* (1916), *Nocturne of Remembered Spring and Other Poems* (1917), and the belatedly published *The Clerk's Journal: Being the Diary of a Queer Man* (1971), Aiken utilizes narrative and dramatic verse forms to explore such themes as disillusionment, guilt, nostalgia, and anxiety.

While living in Cambridge, Massachusetts, between 1915 and 1920, Aiken composed a unified sequence of poems that is regarded as the major work of his early career. These six long pieces, which he called "symphonies," strive to achieve the contrapuntal effects of music by juxtaposing patterns of narrative repetition and variation. Aiken traced the origins of his symphonies to a "passing passion for Richard Strauss," yet he abandoned Strauss's smooth, chronological structures in favor of a more modern symphonic tradition, featuring abrupt transitions and elements of cacophony similar to the works of composers Anton Bruckner, Arnold Schoenberg, and Igor Stravinsky. Concerned with themes of personal identity, these poems specifically center upon what R. P. Blackmur defined as "the struggle of the mind which has become permanently aware of itself to rediscover and unite itself with the world in which it is lodged." *The Charnel Rose*, Aiken's earliest symphonic composition, was written in 1915 and first published in *The Charnel Rose, Senlin: A Biography, and Other Poems* (1918). Focusing on the theme of nympholepsy, which Aiken defined as a desire for the unattainable, this piece features dreamlike visions of lamias and death and examines the elusiveness of love. *The Jig of Forslin: A Symphony* (1916) presents the fantasies of an ordinary man haunted by prostitutes, vampires, and demons. Compared by some critics to Berlioz's *Symphonie Fantastique*, with allusions to the hallucinations of characters in the works of Rimbaud, Baudelaire, and Flaubert, this poem portrays the modern world as alienating and hostile. *The House of Dust: A Symphony* (1920), composed in 1917, is considered a marked improvement in thematic development and technique over Aiken's previous symphonies. Lengthy and complex, this work explores analogies between the city and the human body, focusing on the narrator's quest for identity while exploring dimensions of awareness in societies and individuals. In Aiken's 1918 composition *Senlin: A Biography,* which is generally regarded as his most successful symphony, the title character represents an all-encompassing consciousness that seeks individual form. Even as he assumes the physical appearances of his world in manifestations as a forest, a desert, a city, and a house, Senlin simultaneously exists independently of them. *The Pilgrimage of Festus* (1923) returns to a more concrete conception of personality and consciousness in which Festus, searching for truth and knowledge, dreams of encounters with Buddha, Confucius, Jesus Christ, and Mephistopheles. Aiken's concluding symphonic work, *The Changing Mind,* was composed during 1924 and 1925 and later added to the sequence when it was reorganized and published as *The Divine Pilgrim* (1949). This poem directly confronts problems of identity by focusing on both external and internal reality.

During 1917 and 1918, Aiken completed the narrative poem *Punch: The Immortal Liar, Documents in His History* (1921), which was described by Amy Lowell as "one of the most significant books of the poetry renaissance." Based on the figure from the Punch and Judy puppet shows, Aiken's protagonist is presented from several points of view which alternately depict life as mysterious, ironic, and deterministic. In 1921, Aiken moved his family to England, living initially in London and eventually in Rye, Sussex, and began to contribute reviews and commentaries on contemporary poetry to such periodicals as the London *Athenaeum* and the London *Mercury.* Between 1922 and 1925, in addition to these pieces, Aiken published prose fiction and continued writing poetry. In *Priapus and the Pool* (1922; published in an enlarged edition in 1925 as *Priapus and the Pool and Other Poems*), Aiken introduces experiments with serial form, a musical structure that is based on a series of tones arranged in an arbitrary but fixed pattern in which themes are explored by increment and variation. This volume focuses on the myriad aspects of love as symbolized by the mythical figures of Priapus and Narcissus. *John Deth: A Metaphysical Legend and Other Poems* (1930) is a symbolic treatment of death that incorporates Freudian notions of ritual and routine, portrayals of grotesque dream landscapes, and sexual themes.

In the late 1920s and early 1930s, Aiken experienced a period of intense personal suffering which resulted in a divorce from his first wife in 1929, remarriage in 1930, and a suicide attempt in 1932. These years also initiated an extraordinarily productive literary phase during which Aiken produced much of his most enduring and significant work. His next four volumes of verse, *The Coming Forth by Day of Osiris Jones* (1931), *Preludes for Memnon; or, Preludes to Attitude* (1931), *Time in the Rock: Preludes to Definition* (1936), and *Landscape West of Eden* (1934), which was intended as an epilogue to the entire series although published earlier than *Time in the Rock,* form a related cycle of poems, known as "preludes," that Aiken described as an "all-out effort at a probing of the self-in-relation-to-the-world." *The Coming Forth by Day of Osiris Jones* is a funerary book of parables, myths, letters, and other documents that borrows from the Egyptian *Book of the Dead.* Assimilating several voices in colloquy, choral response, and dialogue, this

piece utilizes fragmentary and prosaic language and serves as a prologue to the two volumes of preludes that follow. *Preludes for Memnon* furthers Aiken's experiments with serial form begun in *Priapus and the Pool* and addresses problems encountered in the narrator's search for self-knowledge. *Time in the Rock* explores such themes as the transience of innocence, the nature of love and betrayal, and the attainment of understanding and transcendence. Highly philosophical and lyrical, these poems are also concerned with the ability of poetry to extend consciousness and awareness. *Landscape West of Eden,* which has been viewed as one of Aiken's most difficult poems, is an allegorical narrative in which a spiritually developing God leads Adam out of Eden in search of knowledge.

From 1934 to 1936, Aiken served as London correspondent to the *New Yorker* under the pseudonym of Samuel Jeake, Jr. In 1939, following a divorce from his second wife and his subsequent remarriage, Aiken returned to the United States, and his poetry during the next decade chiefly reflects his experiences in New England. Collected in the volumes *And in the Human Heart* (1940), *Brownstone Eclogues and Other Poems* (1942), *The Soldier* (1944), *The Kid* (1947), and *Skylight One: Fifteen Poems* (1949), these pieces feature various stanzaic, rhythmic, and rhyme patterns and concentrate on Aiken's interest in cultural and ancestral heritage. Aiken's poetry of the 1950s and 1960s is collected in four volumes: *A Letter from Li Po and Other Poems* (1955), *Sheepfold Hill: Fifteen Poems* (1958), *The Morning Song of Lord Zero: Poems Old and New* (1963), and *Thee* (1967). These works emphasize themes relating to language and art while displaying a renewed affirmation of life. Aiken's poetry has been compiled in several volumes, including *Selected Poems* (1929), for which he was awarded a Pulitzer Prize, *Collected Poems* (1953; published in an expanded edition in 1970 as *Collected Poems, 1916-1970),* which received a National Book Award, *Selected Poems* (1961), and *Preludes: Preludes for Memnon/Time in the Rock* (1966).

Aiken's fiction, which blends symbolic, philosophic, and psychological elements and demonstrates a predilection for the surreal and the macabre within an often lyrical prose style, is closely related to his poetry. Several of his short stories, which are collected in the volumes *Bring! Bring! and Other Stories* (1925), *Costumes by Eros* (1928), *Gehenna* (1930), and *Among the Lost People* (1934), have been widely anthologized. "Mr. Arcularis," a well-known piece in which an elderly man close to death during an operation imagines himself recuperating on a sea voyage, was later adapted by Aiken for the stage. In his novels, Aiken frequently employs the voyage motif as an analogy of the quest for knowledge and self-discovery. *Blue Voyage* (1927), Aiken's semiautobiographical first novel, and *Great Circle* (1933), which Sigmund Freud is reputed to have considered a masterpiece, are related in stream-of-consciousness narratives that fuse musical structure and principles of psychoanalysis. *King Coffin* (1935) is a psychological horror novel focusing on the plotting of an unmotivated murder. In *A Heart for the Gods of Mexico* (1939), a woman travels from New England to Mexico to obtain a divorce so that she can remarry before a heart ailment claims her life. *Conversation; or, Pilgrims' Progress* (1940) is set in Cape Cod and deals with a man's conflicting roles as husband, father, and artist. Aiken's fiction, like his poetry, has been collected in numerous volumes, including *The Short Stories of Conrad Aiken* (1950), *The Collected Short Stories of Conrad Aiken* (1960), *The Collected Novels of Conrad Aiken* (1964), and *Three Novels: Blue Voyage/Great Circle/King Coffin* (1965).

In addition to his accomplishments in poetry and fiction, Aiken is recognized as a formidable literary critic. His essays and reviews have been assembled in *Scepticisms: Notes on Contemporary Poetry* (1919) and *A Reviewer's ABC: Collected Criticism of Conrad Aiken from 1916 to the Present* (1958; reprinted in 1968 as *Collected Criticism*). Aiken's other publications include the children's books *Cats and Bats and Things with Wings* (1965), *Tom, Sue, and the Clock* (1966), and *A Little Who's Zoo of Mild Animals* (1977); his celebrated experimental autobiography, *Ushant: An Essay* (1952); *A Seizure of Limericks* (1964); and the posthumously published *Selected Letters of Conrad Aiken* (1978).

(See also *CLC,* Vols. 1, 3, 5, 10; *Contemporary Authors,* Vols. 5-8, rev. ed., Vols. 45-48 [obituary]; *Contemporary Authors New Revision Series,* Vol. 4; *Something about the Author,* Vols. 3, 30; and *Dictionary of Literary Biography,* Vols. 9, 45.)

R. P. BLACKMUR

Some poets concentrate, compound, and construct their experience into words. Others, like Aiken, expand and extend and exhaust their experience. Their unity is in all their work, not in single efforts, where indeed the unity may evaporate. This is because such poets, and especially Aiken, work in a continuous relation to the chaos of their sensibilities (Houston Peterson called his book about Aiken *The Melody of Chaos*), and each separate poem issues with a kind of random spontaneity: the least possible ordering of experience, what is possible within the devices of prosody (such as the couplet, the quatrain, the sonnet, and so on), never the maximum possible ordering under what Coleridge called the coadunative powers of the mind. There is no generalizing power of the mind. Yet all the poems together make a generalization.

Perhaps we cannot say what that generalization is, though we may feel it. Who can say what the sphinx generalizes?—or a change in weather?—or Jacob wrestling in the stream? Yet we know very well, and try our best to say. So with Aiken. We must see if the shifts and alternations in his weather do not make a climate which generalizes them. Luckily Aiken himself supports this effort. If he did not exactly choose he somehow found it necessary to write in the mode of imagination here described.

In his autobiographical narrative called *Ushant,* Aiken gives an account of a prophecy of his life made to him by an eccentric "Unitarian-minister-and-clairvoyant" one morning in a Bloomsbury boardinghouse. "You have the vision, the primary requisite," said this gentleman.

> You will be a true seer: it is, I fear, in the communication that you will fail. You will always tend to rush at things somewhat prematurely: you will see beyond your years, ahead of your maturity, so that continually, and unfortunately the immaturity of your expression, a certain glibness and triteness, will tend to spoil your excellent ideas, leaving them to be adopted and better expressed—better organized because better understood—by others.

And he went on:

> You will touch [life] at almost every possible point; and, if you do die spiritually bankrupt, you will have

known at least nearly everything—known and seen it, even if ultimately without the requisite power, or love, or understanding, or belief, to harmonize it into a whole, or set it into a frame. . . . You will want to taste your own spiritual death.

To this, and the rest of it, Aiken gives full assent: "How devastatingly true!" We all have such an uncle in the cupboard who says such words in our ears, if we listen: it is under such words that we see the divisive nature of our politics, our culture, and our individual selves. Aiken has written one version of the poetry of that condition, just as Eliot has written another version, which Aiken will not quite understand, thinking Eliot's version a betrayal of his. "That [Eliot's] achievement was unique and astounding, and attended, too, by rainbows of creative splendor, there could be no doubt. Indeed, it was in the nature of a miracle, a transformation. But was it not to have been, also, a surrender, and perhaps the saddest known to D. in his life?"

D. is Aiken objectively observed, spun out, developed, and coiled round himself as endlessly as possible within a single volume. And that volume, *Ushant,* is the best key we have to what Aiken the man was up to in creating Aiken the poet. From *Ushant,* then, it is easy to clarify and support what Aiken (or D.) undertook to believe the prophetic Unitarian from California meant in the Bloomsbury room. At one place Aiken says D. had a bias for form as form, "that inventions of form must keep a basis in order and tradition" and must be related to "a conscious and articulated *Weltanschauung,* a consistent view." On the next page he remarks that through Freud "at last the road was being opened for the only religion that was any longer tenable or viable, a poetic comprehension of man's position in the universe, and of his potentialities as a poetic shaper of his own destiny, through self-knowledge and love." The combination (of the philosopher and the maker) was expressed in the two volumes of 'Preludes" which he here [in *Collected Poems*] calls "serial essays towards attitude and definition."

But there are three other sets of remarks which would seem to clarify the way in which Aiken actually approached his double problem. One is where he refers to himself as the priest of consciousness in flight. A second is where he develops the notion that the true theory of art is, necessarily, the unwritten book; that the true aesthetic is of the impossible, where the act of initiation is taken as an end in itself. The third set of remarks summarizes his underlying philosophy:

> One must live, first, by seeing and being: after that could come the translation of it into something else. This constant state of his 'falling in love,' falling in love with all of life, this radiant narcissism, with its passionate need to emphasize and identify, this all-embracingness, must find something to do with itself. Subject and object must be brought together, and brought together in an apocalypse, an ecstasy, a marriage of heaven and hell.

It might be supposed that everyone has a little more life—a little more seeing and being—than he can quite manage; but there is no need to quarrel with Aiken about that. What is interesting here is the "radiant narcissism" which is the radical quality of all his acts of apprehension, or at any rate of those which get into his poems and other fictions. His autobiography is itself an act of radiant narcissism. What he writes shines with the expanded light—perhaps the idiopathic light, perhaps the light of self-healing or idio-therapy—of what he has seen and been; and the hope is that, with the aid of the traditions and forms of poetry, it may be light for others also.

Aiken's life is a self-feast mediated in poetry, and what is so attractive about his poetry is that each of us, by letting his own egoism shine a little, may eat of himself there. This is also why he can speak of his world as a "rimless sensorium," and why the Unitarian prophet was right in telling the young Aiken that he would never set life into a frame.

But not everybody needs to make frames. If Aldous Huxley complained in 1920 that Aiken would have to find "some new intellectual formula into which to concentrate the shapelessness of his vague emotions," he was not reminding us of Aiken's obligation so much as he suggested our own. So long as this Narcissus remains radiant it will be our business to find a frame or frames for the radiance. The Narcissus is only ourselves at a desirable remove: the heightened remove of poetry in which even our worst selves seem authentic and our best impossible of attainment. For it is poetry like this which teaches us we could never put up with our best selves.

What then does Aiken do—what is his radiance—between the double blows of life and theory? What is his music and how does he sing it? He sings on two trains of thought or themes and he sings like the legendary bard, improvising old tunes as if they were his own by discovery or inheritance, or both. To expand into clarity and towards judgment these phrases will be the remaining task of this essay. What are the themes and how does a bard sing?

One theme is the long, engorged pilgrimage of the self coming on the self: the self creating the self as near objectively as possible. The second theme has to do with the dramatization—in theatrical terms, so far as a poem can be a theater—of the selves of others. *The Jig of Forslin* edges towards a fusion of both themes: where the self comes on a dramatization of the self, full-fledged and self-creative. *Turns and Movies,* his next set of poems, represents the second theme; *Senlin,* a few years later, represents the first. If there is a single theme in Aiken's work, it is the struggle of the mind which has become permanently aware of itself to rediscover and unite itself with the world in which it is lodged.

When the soul feels so greatly its own flux—the flow of itself recalling and eddying upon itself—it becomes very difficult to reassess the world other people inhabit. Very difficult and of absolute necessity. Bertrand Russell wrote his most lucid book, *Introduction to Mathematical Philosophy,* while in prison during the First World War as a conscientious objector to that world. In Aiken it is the self that is such a prison; one bursts out of it without ever leaving it, and one bursts into it without ever having been there. It is the contest of our private lives with the public world.

No theme could be closer to us; almost every mode of the modern mind tends to make the private life more intolerable and the public life more impossible. Only what used to be called ejaculations of the spirit suggests the blending of the tolerable with the possible. Arnold thought poetry could do the job of religion, but Arnold had never heard of psychology (psychiatry, psychoanalysis, and psychosomatics). Aiken could not help having Arnold for an uncle, but he had "psychology" for his other self, the hopeful and destructive brother of his heart.

In his poems there is always the cry: "Am I my brother's keeper?" But it is both brothers who cry, not one: sometimes they cry alternately, sometimes together. The attractive force of Aiken's poetry lies in these joined cries; they make the radiance of this Narcissus. Narcissus is only the personal, anecdotal, and legendary form for that frame of mind known as solipsism: the extreme subjective idealism that believes the mind creates the world when it opens its eyes. It lies in the background of the whole movement in modern art called expressionism (the feeling that what one says commands its own meaning) and is related to make the artist or outsider, as such, the characteristic hero of modern literature. Solipsism is the creative egoism, not of the primitive savage who believes in nothing he does not see, but of the civilized and excruciated consciousness which claims credence for everything it does see and, by the warrant of sincerity of feeling, everything it might see.

This is why we speak of so many levels of consciousness, all of them our own, and for that reason all valid; but none of them dependable for others, none of them showing to others any surety of motive. Dostoevsky invented buffoons who acted out of caprice. Gide invented criminals who made *actes gratuites.* Kafka invented his hero "K" who could not act at all. Aiken's work belongs in this train of thought with his deliberate egoism, his structure by series and repetitions and involutions, his preludes to attitude and definition, the emphasis on the incomplete or aborted act of the incomplete or aborted ego. Your solipsist, because for him no action can ever be completed, is bound to be violent in expression.

Readers of Aiken's novels will easily understand the application of these remarks to all his work. Indeed the long poems will come immediately to seem themselves novels in a philosophico-lyric mode. The chaos under the skin of perception has become both part of the body, its bloodstream, and united with the mind, its creative matrix. For the mass of Aiken's work is deliberately pre-morphous; it is prevented from reaching more than minimal form. He attempts to preserve the chaos he sees and he attempts to woo the chaos he does not see. The limit of form which attracts him is the form just adequate to keep the record with grace: the anecdote, the analysis, and the prelude. He has the sense that as things are finally their own meaning (as he is himself), so they will take up immediately their own form.

This is true with the poems, and increasingly so from the earlier to the later volumes. *Turns and Movies* is a series of dramatic monologues, hard, rapid, and anecdotal, rather like *Satires of Circumstance* or *Time's Laughing-stocks* by Thomas Hardy, full of murder, open and hidden hatred, wrong marriages, and burning infidelities: an effort to grasp the outside world by its violent sore thumbs. *Punch, the Immortal Liar,* the next volume, is Aiken's first conscious effort to fuse the two halves of his theme, and we get the violence of the inner man seizing that of the outside world. *Senlin,* four years later, is philosophical, meditative, musical, and repetitive, the free onward solipsism of the pilgrim trying to come on himself.

Something like one of these sets of attitudes can be applied to any of the original volumes. *Festus* is part of the pilgrimage. *The Charnel Rose* is a kind of theatrical or *Turns and Movies* version of romantic love. In *John Deth* we have the solipsist working towards annihilation, as in *Osiris Jones* we have him working towards epiphany. *Priapus and the Pool* is free erotic expressionism moving into philosophy. *The Kid* is an historical version of *Turns and Movies,* a frontier version of the civilized soul, remarking tradition as he goes. *And in the Human Heart* is an effort to make the inner violence transform the outer through love. *The Preludes of Attitude and Definition* exhibit in infinite variety both the tension and the distension of the two violences, what keeps the soul together in every moment but the last in its lifelong series of fallings apart.

The attitude breeds the vital chaos of definition. (Which may remind some readers of Aristotle's remark that there is an optimum definition for any point at issue, and one should never define more than necessary. In Aiken's preludes the right amount is reached when the vitality of the chaos is reached.) Lastly, though not last in chronology, the *Brownstone Eclogues* most clearly fuse, join, and crystallize the two violences of Aiken's theme. . . . (pp. 77-8, 80)

So for his theme. How does the bard sing? In the easiest language and the easiest external forms of any modern poet of stature. He sings by nature and training out of the general body of poetry in English. He writes from the cumulus of cliché in the language, always, for him, freshly felt, as if the existing language were the only reality outside himself there were. There is hardly ever in his work the stinging twist of new idiom, and the sometimes high polish of his phrasing comes only from the pressure and friction of his mind upon his metres.

It is hard to make clear, in a period where so many poets play upon their words and so many readers think the play is all there is, that this superficially "easy" procedure with language has long since and will again produce poetry—even the difficult poetry of the soul wrestling with itself. But it is so with Aiken, and it is worth while to end these remarks by trying to make this matter clear. Aiken depends on the force of his own mind and the force of metrical form to refresh his language. The cumulus upon which he really works is the cumulus of repetition, modulation by arrangement, pattern, and overtone. He writes as if the words were spoken to let the mind under the words sing. He writes as if it were the song of the mind that puts meaning into the words.

Thus, as in popular songs, the words themselves do not matter much, yet matter everything *and* nothing to those who sing them and those who hear them. This is to say Aiken takes for granted that his words are real; he never *makes* his words real except by the agency of the music of their sequence. No method works all the time, and when Aiken's method fails, you get the sense of deliquescence in his language, as if any words would do because none would work. To understand the successes of the method takes time and familiarity. In his language, but not in his conceptions, he depends more on convention than most poets do in our time, almost as much as Dryden or Pope. The point is, if you look into his conventions you will find them right, just, genuine, and alive. What more do you want? You have brought with you what was required.

Finally—for poetry is an affair of skill at words—Aiken demands of you, at a serious level, the same skill that newspaper poets demand at no level at all. Your newspaper poet merely wants to say something to go with what he feels. Aiken is looking hard to find, and make real, the emotion that drives, and inhabits him. Aiken, as Croce might say, has a vast amount of the same talent the newspaper poet has so little of. The amount of talent makes all the difference. The existence of poets like Aiken make poetry possible. (p. 82)

> R. P. Blackmur, "Conrad Aiken: The Poet," in *The Atlantic Monthly, Vol. 192, No. 6, December, 1953, pp. 77-8, 80, 82.*

RUFUS A. BLANSHARD

Of our very few major poets over the past forty years, Conrad Aiken is probably, at the moment, the least known. It is time for a full critical treatment, which should be at once a survey of the evolution of his modes and themes and a definition of his abiding value. For such a protracted engagement, this paper does not pretend to do more than suggest a stance.

The point that eludes a short view is the evolution. Considered together, Aiken's twenty-odd books of poetry give the lie to two notions that have had some currency (despite their incompatibility): that he is always the same, and that he has no identity. The first can be traced to the early reviewers' comments on his "ready-made technique" and his "single idea." The second goes back to—and does not go beyond—a young poet's diverse "influences," his experiments in more than a single manner: the manners of Keats and Masefield, then of Masters and Gibson, then of Eliot and the Symbolists; and having so far sacrificed his integrity, the chameleon could only continue in his modesty, taking next the color of Freud and Joyce, then of Shakespeare and nineteenth-century Shakespeare, and finally of Eliot again and Stevens (with a daub of Whitman). Both notions are entertaining substitutes for the critical reading of more than a few pages of Aiken's poetry. What the reading does is to yield a superior entertainment: the prospect of an organic progress and the sound of an authentic voice.

To show the evolution, one begins before the published beginnings and listens for the crack in the adolescent voice. Aiken was not precocious as poets go, either in thought or in technique, but from the start he saw things at least partly with his own eyes and rendered them fluently. At Harvard in 1911 he wrote a long narrative poem called *The Clerk's Journal: Being the Diary of a Queer Man.* In it, the little clerk's drab urban routine—before Prufrock or Mr. Zero—is transfigured by his cheap love for a waitress in "a justly far-famed eating joint." Here are the gaucheries of diction and taste one might expect, and the sentimentality of subject insufficiently disguised by irony. But already Aiken was experimenting in the direction of the later symphonies and the serial poems, already mixing the quotidian and the "poetic," already charting a mind's successive moods with repetition and contrast of "emotion-masses" (as he later called them), already preoccupied by the correspondences between outer and inner weather and the "music" those chords make. . . . (pp. 135-36)

Aiken's first three published books (not counting *Forslin,* one of his "symphonies") are both auspicious and disappointing. *Turns and Movies,* the title poem of the second book, was more boldly realistic than we may now see it to be, unused as we are to the poetic gentilities it flouted. For this reason Aiken has rightly included it in his *Collected Poems.* From the other two volumes, he tells us, perhaps too self-critically, "it was difficult to find anything worth keeping." They contain some of those obstacles to acceptance that modern criticism, with a pained expression, calls "romantic": vagueness, sentimentality, prolixity, facility, and euphony—in a word, softness. Instead of making a synthesis of a group of incidents and attitudes and gestures, he too often made a mélange, including elements that dissipate rather than focus attention. He was not sure himself what, in an experience, was important and what not, and he sometimes conveyed little more, as an aesthetic impression, than the moony malaise which this uncertainty had produced in him. The texture of his verse reflected this slackness. . . . Aiken sensed his failures of "softness" as well as any of his critics; he even supplied them with ammunition in his early pieces on himself, as he continued to do in subsequent critical and autobiographical writings. What he also sensed was the partial virtue, for the development of his talent, in that very softness. The theme of disillusioned nostalgia, for example, . . . the dominant theme in *Nocturne of Remembered Spring,* is a romantic one. But Aiken knew that for all its dangers it was a good theme, and a good one for him. Nostalgia is one of the sad tricks of the mind: we cannot banish it, nor would we want to, by banishing it from poetry. What Aiken was trying to do was to *use* it: to arrange into a ''musical'' flow of sounds the emotional ''resonances'' of things, so that the reader's heart might be struck to a ''bitter-chorded music'' (as he put it in **''White Nocturne''**) of its *own,* like the strings of one violin set to humming by those of another. The musical analogy is basic; it does not excuse the failures, but it relates them to the successes.

The five ''symphonies'' that make up what Aiken later called *The Divine Pilgrim,* all written before 1920, are a prodigious achievement. That they are entirely successful no champion of Aiken would wish to argue. That they carry him forward, that they *contain* successes resulting from earlier gropings, is abundantly demonstrable. The subject alone—''the consciousness of modern man''—is original enough to have made Aiken important. The over-all treatment—the musical form—is nearly equal to the subject. And both subject and form evolved from within, from the crude beginnings evident in *The Clerk's Journal,* even from the ''objective'' sketches in *Turns and Movies* which now seem, in a sense, sequential metaphors for the fragmentary components of a single consciousness. The way subject and form work together in the symphonies is exemplified by the part which repetition plays in them.

Repetition in the symphonies is Aiken's poetic equivalent of musical restatement. Sometimes a whole section reappears as a reprise: the closing sections of *The House of Dust* and *Festus,* for example, exactly repeat the openings. More often it is a selective repetition, a variation. The first section of the final part of *Senlin* begins with a nearly exact repetition of the first five lines of the poem, ''placing'' Senlin before us, then dissolves into a new series of metamorphoses, which however become more and more echoic of the original ones. And the very last section of the poem is a pastiche of lines, slightly and significantly changed, from various earlier parts. . . . This works like so-called incremental repetition in ballads, only with great spaces between for a delayed effect. (In the shorter poems, and most movingly in the latter ones, it works rhythmically, like breakers on a shore.)

Another sort of repetition is the glimpse of something seen earlier, which has quite literally on the reader the effect of *déjà vu.* This is one of the usual ways of symbolic imagery, but in Aiken it works in harmony with a dominant theme, which is the poignant elusiveness of experience in the memory. *Déjà vu* is a haunting flicker, not a clear identifiable light. (What was said earlier about vagueness and nostalgia has its bearing here.) Thus a single image like the peach tree in *Senlin* comes back upon the reader to tease his memory. The peach tree in II, 7, which ''dreams in the sun'' but suddenly ''braces itself'' against an unseen ferocious power that threatens it, has a special force because of its ''overtones.'' What is threatening the tree, and men with it, is death; that much is obvious from this section and the one immediately preceding it. What is not obvious, what the reader is not expected quite to remember in its details, is how the peach tree figured many pages earlier, in I, 5, as

the image of man in ''his dark origins'' and his shining achievements. . . . (pp. 136-39)

The effect of the echo of this in the later passage is to enrich unaccountably the latter—unaccountably for the reader who *as he reads* does not place the echo. He ''feels'' the outer threat of the later passage as also an inner one, the dark underground self of tree and man containing the vital and destructive forces to which the bright conscious life is oblivious. The symphonies are vast interweavings of such cumulative motifs, consciously designed to have the effect of not being consciously designed.

Between the symphonies and the *Preludes for Memnon,* Aiken's thought and technique became more maturely focused. The revisions for the 1925 edition of *Senlin* make it tighter and surer poetry without a loss in suggestiveness. In the same year appeared the enlarged edition of *Priapus and the Pool,* a major event in Aiken's development. From that volume of extraordinary successes it must suffice to single out **''The Room,''** for its characteristically parabolic statement of a central theme, its use again of the tree symbol to carry the full meaning, and its nightmarish power. Through a window from outside, the poet sees in a room ''the struggle / Of darkness against darkness.'' From this chaos of pain, of darkness killing itself, is born a single leaf: ''For the leaf came, / Alone and shining in the empty room.'' Twig, bough, and trunk then appear, in a fantastic but credible reversal of normal sequence:

> and last the one black root.
> The black root cracked the walls. Boughs burst the window:
> The great tree took possession.
> Tree of trees!
> Remember (when time comes) how chaos died
> To shape the shining leaf. Then turn, have courage,
> Wrap arms and roots together, be convulsed
> With grief, and bring back chaos out of shape.
> I will be watching then as I watch now.
> I will praise darkness now, but then the leaf.

This is ''bare'' poetry, virtually untranslatable: It means just what it says, and it means a whole world. What Aiken was doing at this time was forging for himself a set of symbols in which he could convey his personal vision of consciousness and the unconscious, life and death, creation and destruction, and their endless inversions and interrelations, with the immediate elemental force which that vision had for him. The symphonies have many inklings of the process, such as the tree figure in *Senlin,* but they dissipate the shock, as it were, by adhering to their elaborate form. Besides, the semblance of a realistic narrative with a central ''character''—even if the narrative ended where it began and the character was supposed to be Everyman—demanded a more literal (if ''Freudian'') treatment of experience than a wholly allegorical frame. *Punch* and *John Deth,* although they use many of the symphonic devices, are really allegories; and what seems in them to be merely a gain over the symphonies in realism—the rendering of outward events, the characterizations—is in fact a departure in symbolism for these ''legends'' have their own laws. In **''The Room''** and the other *Priapus* poems, and in the shorter poems of the *John Deth* volume, the allegorical mode is concentrated and intensified, so that each is a sort of translation of a single vivid moment of awareness, each a result of what Aiken calls ''the difficult and . . . painful process of cryptoiesis.'' And in this process a few dominant symbols—tree and forest, sea and mirror, star and clock—figure more and more powerfully: symbols of the ambiguous and unfathomable nature of man, love, time, and the universe.

All this was on the way to the *Preludes,* in which the "philosophy" and the form it took came alike to full ripeness. The two volumes of *Preludes* (1931 and 1936) must be the central exhibit in the demonstration that Aiken is a major poet. "Major" poetry (like "minor") is more easily illustrated than defined, but part of a poet's claim to majority consists in his concern with immensities, with the meaning of things: he must be in some sense a "philosophical" poet. If we forget for a moment what we all by now know, that the nineteenth century hopelessly mixed sense and sensibility, we can see how a mind like Aiken's (or one like Hardy's), nourished on its modes, could aspire to ask—and what is more, to answer—some of the great impossible questions. Pope told Spence that light verse was hardest to do, since it took more work to make people think it was worth reading. Aiken, who was capable of writing the kind of "charming" lyric that gets into all the anthologies, thought Pope artificial and small. For him, at least as far back as the Harvard seminar in which Santayana was formulating his notions for *Three Philosophical Poets,* poetry has been the more or less successful embodiment of "major" attitudes. In his own case, as he progressed, the embodiment became more successful, and part of the reason for this was his growing conviction, during the twenties, that he *had,* if he could bring it to focus, a "consistent view." This view, as he puts it in *Ushant,* "had shaped itself slowly and intermittently out of the incredibly rich pour of new discoveries, new ideas, the miraculously rapid expansion of man's knowledge, inward and outward, whether into the ever farther-reaching astrophysics of the heavens, or of man's mind." Put that way, of course, it sounds like a neo-Victorian version of the best of all possible worlds. But this was only what helped to shape the view, not the view itself, for by the time it had thoroughly crystallized it was a vision *through* man's knowledge, in both directions, outward and inward of chaos. (pp. 139-41)

The Elizabethans saw the macrocosm in the microcosm, the universe in man, and vice versa, and saw it all divinely ordered. Aiken also sees the correspondence of outer and inner worlds, but ordered by a sort of sublime aimlessness. Human consciousness is, like the cosmos, a stage across which passes, in series, an infinite variety of vaudeville acts (the similarity to Hume's image of a stage has been noted, though Aiken did not read Hume), of which the "pattern," if there is one, is only another act, neither more nor less meaningful than, on that larger stage, "the whisper / Of time to space." Man and the universe are, alike, "dark fluxions, all unfixable by thought"—a line of Coleridge's which made a lasting impression on Aiken, who extended its application to both worlds. It is a correspondence at once exciting and unconsoling, the dark self in a dark void: "a vast everything," as he puts it in one of the preludes, "whose sum is nothing."

It must be granted that such a view, if not rigorously worked out "philosophy," is the sort of attitude toward the nature of things which has sufficient intellectual viability, along with its sweep and magnitude, to form a basis for major poetry. Still, the expression must suit the vision. Aiken talks, again in *Ushant,* of having in his earlier poetry "walked round this 'consistent view,'" of having only touched on it by "intermittent and musical reference, by counterpoint and implication," used it for "thematic material, something on which to play variations. . . . Not for another decade . . . was the consistent view . . . to receive his consistent attention, and to find at last its own expression in the two volumes of *parerga,* the serial essays towards attitude and definition." The *Preludes,* then, ask for judgment on the very highest plane of poetry.

Preludes for Memnon, the first of the two volumes, is one of the most original and powerful books in our literature, and *Time in the Rock,* the other, is even better. On this high plane, the first is not without some characteristic faults, which fall under the generic head of "rhetoric." Certain old-fashioned locutions, amounting to clichés, are overused ("Such precious nonsense as no god foresaw," "such reasons / As have no reason"), and the scornful or peremptory vocatives ("Poor fool," "Woman") are overinsistent. Sometimes, too, the incantatory repetition and inversion and transposition of phrases seems to be a tic, with the effect, as one critic has put it, of making a poem say more than it means. But the devices of rhetoric are not faults when they work, and they often do work here. To take the example of the opening lines of Prelude L: "The world is intricate, and we are nothing. / The world is nothing: we are intricate." One reader threw up his hands and declared, "After a page or two, one finds oneself supplying the subsequent line before it arrives." This is nonsense, of course; one doubts that he *has* read the page or two; but it shows most of all a failure to see the way the inversion in that very poem is set up only to be knocked down:

> Alas, how simple to invert the world
> Inverting phrases! And, alas, how simple
> To fool the foolish heart to his topmost bent
> With flattery of the moment.

On the whole question of rhetoric Aiken himself has the last, ambiguous word in Prelude LVI, *Rimbaud and Verlaine,* where, at the end, we are to "take godhead by the neck— / And strangle it, and with it, rhetoric"—the *form* of the poem, however, with its diminishing stanza and final couplets, being an ironic comment on the proposal. ("Rhetoric and eloquence—?" Aiken once wrote of Dylan Thomas. "Of course, and why not? And all the rest of the poet's bag of tricks.")

Like rhetoric that after all works, the over-all form of the *Preludes* is likely to be regarded as an artistic flaw until it proves itself. The best defense of any form is that it could have been no other. Aiken's idea of "series" as the only intelligible order of experience, an idea at the core of the *Preludes,* is as it were imitated formally by the "serial essays" that make them up. It is far short of a first-hand reaction to this marriage of form and content, a marriage which any poet proposes, to see in it, as some have seemed to do, nothing but "the fallacy of imitative form." The main aesthetic objection to the *Preludes* as a whole is that they are "formless"; which is to say that they have an indeterminate structure too nearly like the structure of experience; which is to say that the objection is a too narrow one, *even aesthetically.* R. P. Blackmur ought to have given pause enough to the a priori formalists when he called the *Preludes* "not rigid and right, but amorphous and honest," with "the inconclusiveness of a perfect balance, the indecision of a bewilderment perfectly resolved." And if one only looks for a rhythm in them less mechanical than one expects in a sequence of poems, one finds it in alternations like those of the mind itself. One prelude (XVI) is a love poem, the poet ecstatic with the mystery of the touch of a woman's fingernail on his; the next is a vision which a smirking Narcissus has, in his usually flattering hand glass, of "dumb, tumultuous, all-including horror"; the next is another love poem, but with what poignance after the other two—for what the poet asks his lady to be is "brightness, music, God, my self" (thus echoing the first), and yet the "self" is what Narcissus was (in the second). So the preludes are juxtaposed, and such is the rationale of their "form."

As for the individual poems, aside from the way they fit with others, it is precisely in the *shape* they give to Aiken's perceptions that they are remarkable. The articulation on this primary level, where "form" in a narrow sense is of the first importance, is both elaborate and controlled, and the images flow one into another naturally, extending the thought without running away with it. (pp. 141-43)

Time in the Rock is an even more impressive single volume than *Preludes for Memnon*. One reason is Aiken's growing concern with language as a theme in itself, a theme more inclusive than previously of the other preoccupations: language as the extender of consciousness (as consciousness is of language), poetry as the medium of awareness, the *word* as the net to catch reality in—though never for long, and never quite. Aiken had been tending in this direction; now (in XII, XIX, XLII, XLVIII, and many others) he went ahead more surely. There is a striving for simplicity in complexity: "The flower's simplicity" (XCVI) became a sort of poetic model. There is also an increased conviction, amounting to religious persuasion, that God is the *ding an sich* which poetry suggests, "such a margin as thus lies between / the poem and the page's edge" (LXXVII). If man's consciousness is the only godhead, consciousness is now seen, more than ever, to reside in poetry: Poetry is therefore a religious act. To say, as some have done, that Aiken is more "reverent" in his later poetry is to make him sound too orthodox, too much like Wordsworth in his decline; but he is more devout, in the sense in which Wallace Stevens was devout, in his dedication to poetry, in his laborious care over language. As early as *Senlin,* where the final "secret" is that language is a poor groping for reality, but the nearest approximation to it that we have, the theme was important. But he was more interested then in finding ways to represent the composite and discordant self than in examining the verbal counters with which alone he or any poet can do so. He did not lose interest in the one pursuit—the *Preludes* are the fulfillment, in this, of what the symphonies promise—but he gained interest in the other; so that, as he now says looking back, the *Preludes* seem to be as much "about" language as about anything else. *Time in the Rock* develops the theme, and, twenty years later, *A Letter from Li Po* fuses it with all the other interests early and late. *Time in the Rock* (LXXVIII), which is about God, love, and poetry, is a preview of much of Aiken's latest work. (pp. 145-46)

"Poetry without music is at bottom a contradiction in terms." So Aiken said in 1917, when free verse was still a controversial subject. His own poetry then and since . . . not only exploits all the analogies between the two arts, and makes music like poetry a symbol of the highest consciousness, but also in its very texture presses the one into the service of the other. His early rhythms and "sound effects," though too obvious, were his best technical equipment. As his thought and imagination matured in power and subtlety, his "ear" developed a more and more fitting harmony for them, so that what was at first sometimes a factitious euphony became a necessary and inevitable one. It would be profitable to devote pages to that harmony alone, to show the mastery in the long paragraph and the short stanza, the tight and the loose blank verse, the easy and sure rhymes, the chiming of syllabic patterns. But here may be noted only one of the signs of that mastery, perhaps the most striking sign of its *development:* Aiken's sense of what can be done in a single line to vary the rhythm. A comparatively late poem, **"Voyage to Spring,"** has a predominantly five-beat line which usually scans but runs into extra syllables: it is very loose blank verse. The first variation that one notices

is the heavy mixture of six- and four-beat lines with the pentameter:

> and the small mouth, *bocca tremante,* trembling and timid,
> that asks but says no, denies but says yes—
> with what pathos, with tremulous empathy,
> prefiguring all, foretasting all,
> it offers to be shaped, or to shape itself, to yours.

The third line alone is unquestionably of five beats, the fifth may be; the first is of six, the second and fourth of four. Then within those lines (and Aiken scarcely ever "runs over" completely, so that his lines *are* lines) the variations in placement of accent and distribution of unaccented syllables are the work of an audioprestidigitator. Two other consecutive lines show the full range. Each has five accents; the first has seven syllables, the second nineteen:

> False, false, false, all of it false,
> the necessary inevitable illusion, chromatic deception.

Aiken's latest long poem, **"The Crystal,"** is mainly in triple-time pentameter, like the last two sections of the early **"Te-télestai"** and the Epilogue of *Punch,* and within this loose line he subtilizes sound in such a way as to justify for good his lifelong devotion to "music."

These notes for a survey must conclude with less attention to the late poetry than it deserves. Although it maintains and refines the qualities that have already been noted in the two books of *Preludes,* it also strikes new notes of its own which prove that Aiken never rests on what he has done. One of these is the personal-historical note. From *The Kid,* which is Aiken's rediscovery of America, through **"Mayflower"** and **"Crepe Myrtle"** to *A Letter from Li Po* and **"The Crystal,"** which show his search for roots and associations in the shifting soil of the spirit, Aiken has worked the theme of the double frontier, outer and inner, which constitutes for him the essence of American individualism and the key to his own past. Like *Ushant,* this poetry spirals out from intensely personal, and at the same time serenely objectified, experience. (pp. 146-47)

The title of this paper was meant to imply, in addition to what has been sketched, what Delmore Schwartz called Aiken's "long progress and pilgrimage." It is the pilgrimage of a modern spirit in the modern world, one who like Festus has continually struggled in the net of himself and perceived in a mirror his own vacuity, and has had the self-knowledge and the irony ("Is it divine?" he asks in one of the preludes, "or maudlin?") to call what he is and sees "The Divine Pilgrim." His poetry is a monument to the difficulty and the integrity of a multiple pilgrimage. (p. 148)

> *Rufus A. Blanshard, "Pilgrim's Progress: Conrad Aiken's Poetry," in* The Texas Quarterly, *Vol. I, No. 4, Winter, 1958, pp. 135-48.*

CALVIN S. BROWN

Conrad Aiken's death in Savannah, Georgia, last August closed the remarkably symmetrical pattern of his eighty-four years of life. As a boy he had been brought up in a house only a couple of doors down the street from the one in which he died. I believe that he was born there, it is certain that it was in that house that his world had fallen apart when he was eleven years old and (in his own words, fifty years later) "after the desultory early-morning quarrel, came the half-stifled scream, and then the sound of his father's voice counting three; and the two loud pistol-shots; and he had tiptoed into the dark room, where the two bodies lay motionless, and apart, and, finding them dead, found himself possessed of them forever." The young orphan was sent to relatives in New England who saw to his education (without his ever being adopted or quite belonging anywhere) up to and almost through Harvard. (p. 477)

His death not only closed the circle of Aiken's own life: it ended a cycle in American poetry as well. Edwin Arlington Robinson, Robert Frost, Edgar Lee Masters, Carl Sandburg, and Amy Lowell were considerably older than Aiken, but their significant work, or, in some cases, their recognition, was in general so late that they can be counted as belonging to Aiken's generation in literary history. . . . These older poets combined with Aiken's own generation—Ezra Pound, T. S. Eliot, Robinson Jeffers, e. e. cummings, "H. D.," and John Gould Fletcher—to produce the revolution in American poetry about the time of the First World War which is still a dominant force in our literature. Aiken was the last survivor of this distinguished group.

It is only in the chronological sense that Aiken can be called a member of this—or of any—group, for he never had the group-mentality or any taste for group-politics. He was a sociable man, but never a joiner—a fact which probably helped his poetry and certainly hindered his recognition. (p. 478)

The variety of Aiken's work is astonishing. We usually think of him as a poet because poetry was his principal and abiding interest throughout the whole of his long career, and his poetry is itself a body of diverse work using a great variety of forms and approaches. But he also wrote five novels, three collections of distinguished short stories, one play, a remarkable autobiography, and a considerable body of sensitive and penetrating literary criticism. There was also a fair amount of journalistic hack-work which he recognized for exactly that, and which need not concern us here.

For a general overview of Aiken's work, perhaps the best starting point is his *Ushant: An Essay,* published in 1952. It is a sort of autobiography, but a very different sort from the usual factual, chronological, and complacent chronicle. Aiken's version of his life is both a literary and a psychological experiment. The whole thing is placed in the hero's mind on shipboard as he passes the Ile d'Ouessant (Ushant / You shan't), off the tip of Brittany, and approaches England once again. The word *hero* is not really accurate, since Aiken often appears in his own eyes as anything but a heroic figure. But we cannot properly call this person Aiken, since the author calls him D (for Demarest, in his autobiographical novel *Blue Voyage*), and puts the whole account in the third person. D's thoughts on his past proceed by free association, so that the whole life is present at all times, and there are frequent references to things which have not yet been presented. Thus there are many allusions to the domestic tragedy of D's childhood, but it is five sixths of the way through the book before a short passage (which I have already quoted) tells what actually happened. Through all the memories weave the dominating themes of ships and bells—and woman, always woman, "that wingèd body of delightful chaos," as Aiken once called her. His three wives appear as Loreleis One, Two, and Three, with an attendant court of less important "Loreliebchens." The search for a certain degree of objectivity by the avoidance of actual names leads to amusing and transparent encipherments. Aiken's first novel was *Blue Voyage,* but D's was entitled *Purple Passage.* Ezra Pound is Rabbi Ben Ezra. T. S. Eliot's initials are reduplicated so that he becomes the Tsetse, with a fine

ambivalence that suggests both a gadfly and a carrier of sleeping sickness.

Ushant is certainly an "experimental" literary production, but not for the sake of being original or different. Aiken's own introspective tendencies were intensified by the early and abiding influence of Freudian psychology. What he is attempting is to see himself and his life as clearly as possible, and as honestly. The changed names and the use of the third person are an aid to objectivity. The chronological chaos is due to the fact that the book is not supposed to be the *story* of a life, but an attempt to answer the question "Who—or what—am I?" And all his past is, of course, present, both as memory and as a shaping force, in his consciousness during the brief period of introspection that *Ushant* represents.

This introspection is as honest as is humanly possible. Biographical dictionaries tell us that Aiken left Harvard in protest over some penalties for cutting classes, because that is what he said at the time. But in *Ushant* he tells us that he was ducking out of the ordeal of a public appearance as class poet, because that is what he finally came to realize. He tells how his attempted suicide was thwarted when he left the gas-filled kitchen to destroy an illicit love-letter that he suddenly remembered—but he wonders whether that letter was really a reason, or only a pretext. He regrets the dishonest prettying up of some biographical facts in his autobiographical novels. But along with all the soul-searching there is wit, comedy, merriment, and always a keen appreciation of the sensuous natural beauty of the world and the contrived beauties of the arts.

Since *Ushant* gives us a long, hard look into Aiken's character and interests, it also provides a key to all the rest of his work, where the same character and interests appear in a remarkable variety of forms and disguises. This is true even of his literary criticism. In *Ushant* he devotes a long discussion to his short novel *A Heart for the Gods of Mexico* (there called *A Heart for the Barranca*)—"for, of all D's many failures, this had been the most lamentable." He even admits that one section of it "was worse than anything in Thomas Wolfe—which was saying a great deal." He finds, characteristically, that the failure can be attributed to a closely interrelated set of literary and psychological causes. He had tried to do an easy pot-boiler, and it had not come off. The literary devices had often been merely a bag of tricks instead of serious artistic techniques. He had tried to substitute empty "fine writing" for perception and accuracy of expression. He had tried to adapt personal experience into literature instead of absorbing and transmuting it.

Here we have the essentials of his literary criticism. It is as objective as possible. It never dawdles on the surface, but goes right to the heart of the matter. It sets high standards, both artistically and ethically, for the art of literature, and is merciless towards any betrayal of these standards. No wonder he could not participate in the mutual puffery of literary cliques! And, by the same token, it is no wonder that his book-reviews often turned out to be real literary criticism of permanent value, and that he was able to understand and evaluate difficult writers like Eliot and Faulkner at a time when most reviewers were floundering in bewilderment or dismissing them with snide witticisms.

Aiken's prose fiction, consisting of five shortish novels and some forty short stories, is all of a piece and can be considered as a single unit. The short stories are probably better than the novels, though Graham Greene once called Aiken "perhaps the most exciting, the most finally satisfying of all novelists." Practically all the fiction is psychological in that, no matter how interesting the events of the plot or the actions of the characters may be, the essential drama is played out in their minds. We could even classify some of the works in technical jargon by saying, for example, that the much-anthologized short story **"Silent Snow, Secret Snow"** is a study of the onset of schizophrenia and that the novel *King Coffin* is a case history of paranoia. But such a statement would be misrepresentation. The point of view is all-important. Studies and case-histories aim at objectivity, which means seeing things from the outside. These stories are told from the point of view of the "subjects" (as a psychologist would call them), with the result that what is conveyed to the reader is not information, but experience. A case-history tries to tell how the schizophrenic looks to the normal world, but **"Silent Snow, Secret Snow"** tells how the normal world looks to the schizophrenic, or, in other words, what it is like to be one.

The short story **"Mr. Arcularis"** (which is the basis for the play of the same name, Aiken's only venture into the field of drama) begins with a man recuperating from a desperate operation and takes him from the hospital briefly to his home and on to a sea-voyage which is fraught with continued weakness, horror, premonitions of death, and a general nightmarish quality. At the end the patient dies on the operating table and we realize that the whole story took place in the unconscious mind of the anesthetized dying man.

Not all the fiction is as directly psychological as these examples, but it is true that in all of it the internal drama predominates and the external events are primarily a setting for it. The effect, however, is far from abstract or analytical. In his settings Aiken is a naturalist who exploits the concrete details of everyday life for a maximum sense of the real and even the trivial. We are constantly told how things looked, and who ordered what drinks, and what the waitress said, and what the band or the juke-box was playing. We are frequently given tantalizing fragments of conversation overheard from the next table or from people passing on the street or in the subway. Much of the effect of Aiken's fiction springs from the tension between the two worlds—outer and inner—in which his characters live. Since all of us live in this same tension, this method is actually far closer to reality than the so-called realism that confines itself to the external world, or than the opposite pole, the stream of consciousness, which represents only the inner one. From this point of view, Aiken's fiction can be said to be a synthesis of the two dominant fictional schools during the period from 1920 to 1940, when practically all of it was written. (pp. 479-83)

Poetry was, of course, Aiken's lifelong love and his primary activity. He had always wanted to be a poet, and after various childish efforts he began seriously working at it as a student at Harvard. It was his cutting of all classes to work full-time on a poem which precipitated the crisis that led to his departure from the university. (He returned quietly and finished his degree the following year.) His volumes of verse appeared over a span of well over half a century. There was the inevitable short period of apprenticeship at the beginning, and towards the end there was a slackening of effort—a shift to playing with verse rather than working at it—but during most of his long life Aiken was busy writing first-rate poetry.

This poetry exhibits an astonishing variety of forms and types. Beginning with narrative verse, he soon reduced the narrative element to a mere scaffolding—often perilously flimsy—to support an investigation of the minds and inner lives of his characters. In this vein he produced a series of "symphonies," as he called them, large poems subdivided into a few main sections, with further subdivisions on several levels, so that in a poem of fifty pages there might be no section longer than a page and a half. Individual sections are in blank verse, free verse, and rhymed verse, sometimes in fixed stanzas, sometimes irregular. These poems do not attempt to reproduce the sonata-form of the symphony, but they deliberately borrow many of the techniques and effects of music. Six of these poems, written between 1915 and 1925, are conceived all together as a single work, and were finally so published (with extensive revisions) in 1949, under the title *The Divine Pilgrim.* This is a difficult work with an easy surface of sharply observed sights, sounds, and events, forming endless chains of interrelated allusions and implications. It is perhaps best described in the terms that Aiken later used to characterize a recurring symbolical dream: "It was a continuum of shimmer, one meaning dissolving beautifully and naturally into the next, no one of them central, but all of them primary."

After these "symphonies," Aiken went into a period of more overtly philosophical poetry, with *John Deth: A Metaphysical Legend* (actually written during the period of the symphonies) and *Preludes for Memnon.* In 1931 he published *The Coming Forth by Day of Osiris Jones,* a strange but sometimes powerful work based on the ancient Egyptian *Book of the Dead* (whose title is actually *Chapters of Coming Forth by Day*). It represents the trial of the soul of the deceased—the common man—by the testimony of the people, places, and things that knew him, and ranges all the way from conventional romantic stanzaic lyrics to scattered, disjointed phrases in the most "modern" manner. During the rest of the thirties and the forties, Aiken published a number of volumes of good poetry in various veins— *Landscape West of Eden, Time in the Rock, And in the Human Heart* (a sonnet sequence), *Brownstone Eclogues, The Soldier. The Kid* (1947) is a striking, though uneven, performance. Aiken's preoccupation with his parents had led to the pursuit of his New England ancestors and a concern with the American past generally. The Kid is a sort of incarnation of the American spirit, distilled from (and with specific allusions to) characters as various as William Blackstone, Anne Bradstreet, "Johnny Appleseed," Kit Carson, Billy the Kid, Audubon, Melville, Whitman, and Emily Dickinson. . . . While *The Kid* is not the best of Aiken's poetry, it is a striking work and possibly the one most immediately accessible to that mythical beast, the general reader.

Skylight One (1949) and the poems in the volumes that followed in the fifties and early sixties—*A Letter from Li Po, Sheepfold Hill,* and *The Morning Song of Lord Zero*—took a new direction. In many of these poems Aiken returned to the subdivided, intricately suggestive and interwoven type of poetry that marked the early "symphonies," but with a difference. The symphonies were long poems, about thirty to seventy-five pages long with, in spite of their virtues, a tendency to be diffuse. These new poems use similar techniques and structures, but they are three to five pages long, are much more tightly built, and are under a firmer and surer artistic control. Their subjects range all the way from the atomic bomb (**"Skylight One"**) to specific concern with the poet's ancestors (**"Hallowe'en"**) and intricate philosophical and aesthetic concerns (**"The Crystal"**).

Finally, Aiken took a well-earned rest from work, and began to play, producing *A Seizure of Limericks* (1964) and a set of children's verses on animals written to go with a set of drawings by Milton Glaser, *Cats and Bats and Things with Wings* (1965). This last work is uneven, but has some fine playing with language.... After this, bad health began to close in, and Aiken wrote little more.

In spite of the great variety of his poetry, it is possible to see a set of basic themes and ideas that run through it all. One of these is the common man. Aiken's novels are full of artists because they are basically autobiographical, but he has none of the narcissism that makes many poets incapable of writing about anything else. He is as fond of the music hall as he is of the string quartet. His second volume *Turns and Movies and Other Tales in Verse* (1916), is devoted to performers on the vaudeville circuit, and he returned to this theme in a section entitled **"The Tinsel Circuit"** in his last collection of serious poetry. The principal character of *The Jig of Forslin* (probably the best of the "symphonies") is a juggler. **"Tetélestai"** is a fine poem in specific praise of the common man as such. The title is the New Testament Greek for Christ's last utterance (John: 19:30), translated in the King James version as "It is finished." The gist of the poem can be seen from its beginning and ending:

How shall we praise the magnificence of the dead,
The great man humbled, the haughty brought to dust?
Is there a horn we should not blow as proudly
For the meanest of us all, who creeps his days,
Guarding his heart from blows, to die obscurely?

　　　　　　　•　•　•

　　This, then, is the humble, the nameless,—
The lover, the husband and father, the struggler with shadows,
The one who went down under shoutings of chaos, the
　　weakling
Who cried his "forsaken" like Christ on the darkening
　　hilltop! ...
This, then, is the one who implores, as he dwindles to silence,
A fanfare of glory.... And which of us dares to deny him?

In Egyptian ritual the soul of the dead was identified with and called by the name of the god Osiris. Thus *The Coming Forth by Day of Osiris Jones* indicates that the poem represents the final balancing of the books on the common man. Osiris Jones had a mother (who was to him little more than a lovingly remembered face), and he had a cat that he once kicked (for the common man is not canonized), as well as various love-affairs. But he has no profession or career or birthplace, no local habitation or name, because he is man in general rather than any particular man. And even when all his faults and pettiness are honestly faced, he comes off pretty well.

Another permanent characteristic is Aiken's sharp eye for the external world, and delight in it. His early work was related to that of the Imagists, and the fondness for the sharp, detailed image remained with him. Because of his many clear observations of such things as wet leaves, rain, the robin in the chinaberry tree, wild flowers (the fruit of boyhood ramblings with a botanizing uncle), and the varied effects of sunlight and moonlight, it is hard not to think of him as a poet of nature. But he is equally fascinated by the modern metropolis, even in its most sordid manifestations.... He observes street-walkers as lovingly as sunsets, and as accurately.

But Aiken is very far from being a mere pictorial or descriptive poet. Always he is concerned with the aspect of the world specifically explored in **"The Crystal"**—the miracle of interconnectedness. All the rich sights and sounds of the phenomenal world are a part of our consciousness—but who and what are we, and what and why is consciousness? How do the dewdrops on the garden stones stand with respect to Aiken's char-

acter Senlin and the universe? How can we know, and what is the nature of knowledge? The trivial world of everyday actions, the local scene, and the infinities of the universe are to be simultaneously perceived and interrelated—not kept in separate compartments of the mind, as is usualy done.... (pp. 483-88)

Aiken's love of the physical world and fascination with the mysteries of the conceptual world combine to form what might be called a religion of acceptance:

　　Mysticism, but let us have no words,
　　angels, but let us have no fantasies,
　　churches, but let us have no creeds,
　　no dead gods hung on crosses in a shop,
　　nor beads nor prayers nor faith nor sin nor penance;
　　and yet, let us believe, let us believe.

This passage from *Time in the Rock* states the theme of his last poem (so far as I know), **"THEE,"** dedicated to his wife and published in 1967.

Though no tidy formula can ever express the whole truth about an artist, we can say that Aiken combines the sensuous eye of an imagist with the mind of a philosopher. It is a striking combination, and the merits of the best poetry it produced have not yet been fully recognized. (p. 488)

Calvin S. Brown, "The Achievement of Conrad Aiken," in The Georgia Review, *Vol. XXVII, No. 4, Winter, 1973, pp. 477-88.*

DOUGLAS ROBILLARD

Writing a study of some American poets not long ago, Denis Donoghue called them, after a phrase of Wallace Stevens, "connoisseurs of chaos." Although the poets he chose to discuss, including Melville, Stevens, Eliot, Robinson, and Frost, were surely apt for his theme, he might well have added Aiken to their number, for Aiken is an authority on the subject of chaos, perhaps more authoritative than any connoisseur could possibly be. His poetry has always shown an extraordinarily keen insight into the impermanent and desperate condition of man in the world; poem after poem describes the situation vividly, and everywhere the poems strive to lift man, all impermanence and desperation clinging to him, out of the despair that the conditions of his existence have brought him to. (p. 5)

Aiken seems bent upon something more than finding the design [within chaos]; his effort is no less than finding a mode of living with the terrors of what is apparently a meaningless existence. Commenting upon his work, the late Frederick Hoffman summed up the position he assumes by saying "he sees himself as a part of the chaos he is observing," and reminding us that this is an inversion of the transcendental idea; he must, concludes Hoffman, "*accept* the paradoxical isolation that is his lot." In the magnitude of his effort, Aiken often seems to see man in terms similar to those used by Albert Camus, though Aiken's own poetic conception was put forth long before the philosophical stance assumed by Camus. Defining the "absurd man" in *The Myth of Sisyphus*, Camus asserted that he must live without appeal and know the limits of his mortality. Both the poet and the philosopher are well aware that what man very nearly cannot do at all is to live without appeal and with full consciousness of his limits; it is virtually impossible for him to recognize and accept his end.

Although Aiken's preludes, published originally in 1931 and 1936, state and comment upon man's disastrous knowledge, they are not the earliest of the poet's ventures to the edge of chaos. Several of the poetic symphonies touch on various aspects of the theme, as do a number of later poems. The supreme difficulty of man in his striving in the world comes from his lack of self-knowledge, the gaps in his consciousness. He is capable of evolving in his consciousness, "ever widening and deepening and subtilizing his awareness," and as he does this he approaches a state of being in which he has all he will need of a sort of religion; "he can, if he only will, become divine," says Aiken, taking for a moment the thought of the nineteenth-century American transcendentalists. Obviously, there is much to be said in favor of such a prospect for man; but he is almost unable to achieve such a happy station and, instead, remains frighteningly human, although he does possess the lineaments of godhead. . . . (pp. 5-6)

In the symphonies that Aiken wrote between 1915 and 1920, the protagonists were seekers and victims. The anonymous searcher in *The Charnel Rose,* afflicted with nympholepsy, the desire for what is unattainable, nevertheless moves, inexhaustibly, "from one dream or ideal to another . . . creating for adoration, some new and subtler fiction." The hero of *The Jig of Forslin,* who is either a romantic or a weakling, depending upon how you view him, realizes that, for the most part, he can do little to change the movement of his life and so depends upon wish fulfillment and fantasy to give him the balance he needs in an otherwise unbearable world. Senlin, the little man, has a sharper awareness of his problems than his predecessors in the series of poetic symphonies; he wants to know who he is and why he is who he is, and, by implication, what he can do about it. He learns that he is not simply Senlin and that being is not simple in any case. And further, he learns that nothing can be done about it and that he is unable to communicate the fact that he is really a whole world of people. Senlin has attempted to reach beyond the world that we know day by day; but generally, as Aiken admonishes us in another of the symphonies, *The House of Dust,* "we live for small horizons," and see only "The small bright circle of our consciousness, / Beyond which lies the dark." Senlin and Forslin do move within the small circle and their attempts to widen it are hardly successful, because they have bound themselves to seek only within its limits. But in *The Pilgrimage of Festus,* we have a conqueror whose desire is for knowledge, and the poem is his quest for the varieties of power and knowledge. Obviously, temporal power, with all its attractions, offers no useful kinds of knowledge. Even in his search for the spiritual, he is disappointed to find that Buddha, Christ, and Mephistopheles cannot bring him deeper into the darkness of self and help illuminate it. Festus has to conclude that he can find no point at which he can say he has reached the goal he was attempting to reach. Only the appeal of the search itself is left to him; he has, in fact, reached that point where, in the later preludes, the whole question of purpose is examined. Unlike the protagonist of the preludes, Festus does not really find a theme in seeking a theme and does not find something to love; but he does find something to think and say, and he does have the joy of plunging "into the world of himself." It is his kind of reckless and exuberant action, of going forward restlessly, of looking for significance when faced with chaos and meaninglessness, that makes him, and man, into a very human but heroic figure. The artist of *Changing Mind* (1925), the last of Aiken's symphonies, is more complex, for he not only seeks enlightenment but must articulate what he learns.

Before leaving the symphonies, we might well remind ourselves that in one of them, *The House of Dust,* though it has no central human figure upon which it focuses, Aiken catalogues his progress as poet, and, by implication, the progress of man, who proceeds from a kind of romanticism, "eager for color, for beauty," through a "bickering into metaphysics" and "strange aesthetics," till finally he reaches a central chamber of thought and feeling, brought there by the increasing subtlety, through labyrinths of ideas. And, having reached this central place, he finds it to be

> the last, and cunningest, resort
> Of one who has found this world of dust and flesh,—
> This world of lamentations, death, injustice,
> Sickness, humiliation, slow defeat,
> Bareness, and ugliness, and iteration,—
> Too meaningless; or if it has a meaning,
> Too tiresomely insistent on one meaning:
> Futility. . . .

It is hardly surprising to find the argument continued and advanced in the whole brilliant group of poems composed between the symphonies and the preludes, that is, during the decade of the twenties. These are the poems that Aiken was to call parables, considering them symbolic narratives that "might lend force to one's ideas which in a more strictly reflective manner would be lacking." They include the meditation upon **"King Borborigmi,"** whose name, like the stomach growling it signifies, is the image of the persistently earthbound character of man, and who sees a vision of the universe that can only move him to helpless laughter: "The infinite octopus / With eyes of chaos and long arms of stars, / And belly of void and darkness." Likewise, the narrator of **"Dead Leaf in May"** sees the skeleton of a leaf lodged among blossoms and finds in it a metaphor for the shaky position of humanity, "ripeness at top" and "rottenness beneath." What we find, as always in Aiken, is the cautionary statement, the advice to accept the world on its chaotic, impermanent, death-giving, and terrifying terms: "Thirst in the There, that you may drink the Here."

In symbolic terms, chaos is large, all-encompassing; it is a galaxy, as in **"King Borborigmi,"** or it is all that exists outside the tiny, torchlit area of the consciousness. In contrast, the order that somehow must come from the encircling chaos is often the simple form, very often as simple as the single leaf or flower. The struggle to shape out of the huge shapelessness a semblance of a coherent pattern is the result of terrific pressures and concentration, for it is essentially an act of creation. . . . The terrific act of creation can be an act of nature, or it can be an act of the human mind and spirit. When it releases itself through the human agency, the mind must traverse all the powers of chaos, all the terrors of mortality, and all human fears and suffering before it discovers self in creation and consciousness. This is the theme of the preludes. (pp. 7-9)

To call the preludes a cycle seems appropriate, for they should be read as though they constitute one very large work. Read out of context, the sonnets that compose Rossetti's *The House of Life* or the lyrics that make up Tennyson's *In Memoriam* are often impressive performances, but they take their main meaning from their relationship to the other poems in these larger works. And so it is with Aiken's preludes; they constitute a cycle, in that there is a movement of thought and feeling, of plot, perhaps, if they are considered sequentially.

The preludes present us once again with the man whom we so often see in Aiken's poetry, the frail, despairing, all too mortal creature whose only possible bulwark and weapon is consciousness, for in consciousness, as Jay Martin says of the poems, "lies the salvation of life; for the consciousness of them transcends them.'' Since the essence of cyclic treatment of a theme is repetition, the poems treat the few subjects in a variety of ways. In some schematic form, they include: mortality, death and the fear of death; man as demonic angel, sometimes as god; the meaning of this apparently senseless and cruel cycle of life and death; the mystery of nature, the constant urge and glory of life; the mystery and power of love; the immortality of the word, and the problem of communication. Half of the paradox of man is that he bears the lineaments and perhaps some of the powers of his creator, and certainly some of His imagination; the other half is that he is mortal and fears death. The first poem in *Preludes for Memnon* presents the first half of this vision: ''Tears form and fall from your magnificent eyes, / The brow is noble and the mouth is God's.'' But the second prelude immediately puts the other half before us: ''What winding sheet for us, what boards and bricks, / What mummeries, candles, prayers, and pious frauds.''

The wavering, uncertain image of man persists through the early preludes; he is nothing and he is godlike. In XI he is magnificent, even though his incomprehension weighs him down, for ''a fool, a pool of water, speaks the star.'' But in XII he is set back again as ''Poor fool, deluded toy, brief anthropomorph,'' who thinks of himself as the center of the universe. He is thinking centrifugally, like the spider at the center of the web. But if he learns to think centripetally, he will have to conclude, quite rightly, that ''You dream the world? Alas, the world dreamed you.'' Quickly then we are thrown back to the other side of the debate, and in XIV see a little drama enacted, in which the consciousness penetrates to the inmost mystery of life and learns of its complexity and irreducibility. . . . A trip like this, to the verge of the world or the verge of being can produce the answers that one seeks; and, miraculously, in his seeking, he does not find disaster, but only a truth that he must learn plainly:

> It is to self you come,—
> And that is God. It is the seed of seeds:
> Seeds for disastrous and immortal worlds.

Such is the method of the preludes. Since they are, as Aiken hinted, preludes to attitudes that we must learn and consider, they never do pose definite answers. Instead, they range over the whole area of possibility, offering the entire bewildering multiplicity of choice. No side is given an extra advantage in the debate because all are fairly and fully presented.

And always we find that there is too much complexity of thought to allow of any simple formula. In the thirteenth prelude, we are told that there is no beginning, no ending, no convenient point at which we might begin our considerations. Later, when chaos begins to envelop the poem, there is praise for art as an organizing principle. When, like Narcissus, one begins to see order only within himself, and, like the spider, begins to think centrifugally, he is immediately faced by a truthful mirror image in which he sees the ''mad order, the inhuman god.'' So he must conclude that in the beginning and the end are nothing, silence, chaos; but in between there are brightness, music, God, self, love, glory, and bewilderment. (pp. 10-11)

The method of the preludes requires that the arguments, probings, and attempts of the poet take him around the subject without, apparently, getting to the heart of it. In essence, the heart of it is too simple to be easily grasped. We go on living because we must, for all our futile intelligence and feeling, just as the unintelligent and unfeeling live: ''There is no doubt that we shall do, as always, / Just what the crocus does.''

In the twenty-eighth prelude, we encounter Memnon, the mythic figure that the preludes are ''for.'' Memnon is the Ethiopian warrior who was the son of Eos and Tithonus. As an ally of Troy, he killed Antilochus in battle and was himself slain by Achilles. The mythical elements that surround the interment and subsequent worship of Memnon are relevant to the poem and to all the preludes. Night, in sympathy with the grief of Eos, the Dawn, covers the heavens with clouds, and all nature mourns the death of the hero. Zeus turns the sparks of the funeral pyre into birds that fight and are consumed by the flames. On the Nile, a colossal statue is supposedly raised to the memory of Memnon; and, as the first rays of the rising sun strike the wonderful statue, it resounds with a sound like that of a harp string. In the poem, the poet will have us learn from the tale of Memnon, after we have engaged in self-deception and suffered from lack of love: ''if you have the strength to curse the darkness, / And praise a world of light, remember Memnon.'' Here we are put in possession of an ''attitude,'' a stance to assume, one which receives the poet's approbation. If we are planted, like Memnon, in the dark, or in the desert of life, then like Memnon we must sing the daybreak before it comes. Knowledge may not break for us, but day will, and so we must sing.

It has to be in the various unreasoning ways that man must seek what comfort he can get from his situation. He can die ''for such reasons / As have no reasons,'' for whatever structure of argument he builds is all too easily turned over: ''Alas, how simple to invert the world / Inverting phrases.'' All the resources of reason and the forms of discourse they can take are brought together in the fifty-sixth prelude, one of the poems most often reprinted. Rimbaud and Verlaine appear in a little dramatic scene, playing chess and discussing poetry and rhetoric. Verlaine's famous conclusion about rhetoric is invoked— ''Prends l'eloquence et tords-lui son cou.'' But Aiken wants to do more than wring the neck of eloquence. However pleasing the situation, the two geniuses discussing rhetoric, Sophocles, and ''fate as Plato loved it,'' there intrudes always the vision of death and chaos. . . . The stanzaic pattern of the poem parallels its meaning. Starting with an eight-line stanza, Aiken makes each succeeding stanza one line shorter, so that the poem moves toward briefer and plainer statement, from couplet, to single line, to silence. As Aiken remarks, the form becomes an ''ironic comment on the accompanying dismissal of 'rhetoric.''' But, as a dismissal of godhead as well, the poem is central to the meaning of the whole poetic cycle. We are nearing the end of the preludes to attitude, and the attitude they present at this point brings the feelings of the poem to a low ebb. Resignation in the sixty-second prelude, no ''message of assuagement'' in the next, and we have reached the conclusion of the first part of the cycle; the preludes to ''definition'' will have to be put forward to attempt a resolution of the problem.

In the forty-fifth of the *Preludes for Memnon,* the poet provides the title for the second set of preludes: ''I have read / Time in the rock and in the human heart''. If he has achieved a semblance of attitude in the first half of the cycle, it is in the longer second part that he begins to organize a methodology of definition. The first poem sounds again the theme of man as god. . . . The very look of this new set of preludes seems to indicate a new poetic power. The earlier set followed the conventional pattern of capitalization for the first word of each line and for standard punctuation; here, both punctuation and capitalization are minimal, as though the speaker has impatiently decided that they hinder definition. Some of the poems have different shapes from those we have become accustomed to seeing in the first part; two carry epigraphs and one of them, the fourteenth, is a set of variations upon the quotation from Anne Bradstreet that prefaces it.

In the whole series of poems in *Time in the Rock,* angels and the angelic order of feeling and knowledge appear again and again as symbols of what man can reach. In a world from which the poet has dismissed godhead, or else strangled it, along with rhetoric, he must deal with a world where consciousness takes the place of the dismissed godhead. As the great instrument of consciousness, poetry then assumes the responsibility for taking this place. The result, as Rufus Blanshard puts it, is that "poetry is therefore a religious act" [see excerpt above]. . . . (pp. 12-14)

Aiken does not see poetry as a translation of experience, but rather as a "direct emotional experience, which happens to be in terms of language rhythmically arranged." It is assuredly part of the angelic nature of man that he is capable of using this supremely effective instrument; it raises him, somehow, above the creature who is seen, satirically, as "the one with teeth and tongue, insatiable belly," or, in a sadder moment as "we who walk only because we walk / we who think only because we think / feel for no reason."

And thus the whole poem moves forward, suiting its parts to the discourse of the poet who takes, in a leisurely and meditative way, theme after theme, to examine, comment upon, and put away for a moment while he goes on to another side of his multifaceted subject. He accepts bewilderment as a natural condition of living and admits, as Whitman does, that "all goes on, as always." As usual, the problem is one of belief, without the necessary bases for belief. The crickets who conduct a ridiculous and repetitive dialogue say over and over the words which should be meaningful—love, hate, act, give, speak, take—but they conclude, finally, "what is the use of speech." It is possible, we are told, that the universe is a chaos, controlled by a gypsy god. It takes the angelic quality in man to respond properly to the complexity and fearfulness of the world, rather than just hiding himself from it: "Seeing, to know the terror of seeing: being, / to know the terror of being: knowing, to know / the dreadfulness of knowledge."

The process of definition is to destroy the custom-made answers and evasions and to put in their place the honest recognition that however plain and disastrous the truth may be, once it is accepted it releases the angelic and nobler quality of man from the bindings of his terror and his consequent attempts and failures at either avoiding or somehow covering his fears. A turning point in the cycle is reached when the poet asserts, in the seventy-first poem that "disaster is no disaster on a starlit night." If the world has movement and intent, it is impossible to deny that man, too, must have a destiny of some splendor. And, from this point, it is only a step to assure man that he is capable of making his own destiny, that his destiny is "love without end," that once he has overcome his fear and opened his vision to the delight of the living world, his calculations "fall in with those of god," lies become truths, and one looks, loves, and believes. Assurance, support for this new vision, comes from everywhere, often from the things which are seemingly least significant, the casuals of daily life. (pp. 14-16)

Finally, poetry is made to assume its place in the scheme of things. In the eighty-second prelude, a child makes a poem on the tiny scale of childlike play, of the things that he plays with on the sand before the sea. He triumphs over the absolute, the sea, by leaving it out of his poetic conception. The next poem

compares music to verse and emphasizes its superiority as an expressive medium, subtle and flexible; but the poem is itself subtle and flexible in its use of rhyme and quick rhythms. There is the mystery that we are nothing and yet we can still speak, "And thus in speaking come / to something, which is yourselves." In a subsequent poem, the second of the three that make up the eighty-ninth prelude, the poet invokes the presence of Confucius, Virgil, Dante, and Joyce; and the ninety-second prelude is about the symbolic language of poetry, the revocation of the familiar symbols that will no longer serve and the search for a new phrase. Perhaps it is not in the fashioning of a new phrase that the poet will succeed in composing an ode to death. After all, the things about him, the things of nature, seem to be capable of expressing without words all that he means, and he has to conclude that the "ode to death is not in a phrase, / nor in a hymn to darkness, nor in a knowlege / of timelessness." It is all rather simpler than the use of words will allow to the expression of it. The poet is able to conclude with a double vision of man, for in this doubling "is the profound duplicity, the ambiguity / which appeared your easy theme." By this duplicity, as it were, man may at the same time assume and maintain his identity and idiosyncratic individuality and be the other "who said yes, but with a separate meaning, / who said no with an air of profound acceptance."

The form that the poet has chosen to employ in his cycle of poems allows him at once the assurance of structure and limitation and the flexibility of the musical form implied in the title. . . . Constant work with musical form in poetry, from the early sonatas, nocturnes, improvisations, and the like, to the large structures of the poetic symphonies had given Aiken a sense of what it was possible to do with musical form and poetic content. The preludes are not as bound to a program as the earlier symphonies seemed to be; there is no need for narrative, no requirement that movements be conceived and filled, no limitation as to lengths and shape.

We must come at last to the realization that the brief and intense is not the only characteristic poetic utterance of the twentieth century. The poets themselves have understood the need for the larger forms, and, each proceeding in the ways best suited to his talents, they have constantly made large poems of the materials and forms that are not available to the creator of lyrics. As a result, our experience of contemporary poetry will be incomplete till we come to grips with the longer poetic works of Pound, Stevens, Aiken, and others among our most notable poets. It is to Aiken's credit that he has worked unceasingly to extend the borders of expression in the long poem. In moving from narrative and drama to the avenues opened by experimentation with forms that approximate the form of music, he has given us new ways of considering the long poem; and in the preludes, he has put forth a poem which by its seriousness of theme and excellence of form ranks high among the poems of our time. (pp. 16-17)

Douglas Robillard, "Conrad Aiken's Preludes and the Modern Consciousness," in Essays in Arts and Sciences, *Vol. III, May, 1974, pp. 5-18.*

HARRY MARTEN

[The *Selected Letters of Conrad Aiken*], ranging over a 75-year period (1898-1973), crackle with energy from beginning to end. By turns hopeful, angry, playful, gossipy—sometimes nasty, bitter, occasionally despairing and even suicidal, almost always passionate, they reveal a man of immense intelligence, integrity and generosity, and astonishing humor in the face of poverty and public neglect. One feels after all that Aiken was in love with words, and that despite the sour notes of what he identified as "the theme-song" of his career—"each new book is panned, but in the background is the implication that all the previous ones were good"—his life was a series of constant creative renewals.

[The editor's] selection of letters makes clear that Aiken drew a lifetime of revitalizing intellectual sustenance from the works of Henry and William James, Richard Strauss and George Santayana (his teacher at Harvard). And even readers already familiar with Aiken's interest in Freud (the poet H. D. reported in 1934 that she found Aiken's psychoanalytic novel **Great Circle** in "the Master's waiting room") will be surprised by the continually developing exploration of psychoanalysis and creativity in the correspondences with his close friends Henry A. Murray, a psychologist, and George B. Wilbur, a psychiatrist.

Aiken's intense response to people and to physical places, however, seems to have energized him most. Each of his three wives, of course, shared and helped to shape his creative life during the years of their marriage—Jessie, 1912-29; Clarissa, 1930-36, and Mary, 1937 until his death. And his lifelong friendships with publisher Robert Linscott (recipient of many of his best and fullest letters), Maurice Firuski, a book dealer, and Edward Burra, a painter, gave him sympathetic but intelligently critical audiences whose conversations and letters both stimulated and tested his ideas.

The letters suggest again and again that Aiken's sense of physical locale was an elemental force in his work. Like many other Americans, he was drawn to the England of his ancestors, with its "finished forms and ritual of a fixed and conscious society" (*Ushant*), and yet he identified his lot, too, with "magically beautiful" Savannah (*Ushant*) and with the intellectual and emotional spareness of New England. For much of his life he alternated residences between Rye, England, and Cape Cod and Cambridge. In later years—as in his earliest—Georgia was part of the domestic framework. Out of the tension of double, then triple location—longing for one place while living in and responding to another—came explosion after explosion of creative activity, visible in the novels and poems, and now everywhere in the letters, where the half-perceiving half-creating eye works its moving and beautiful landscape magic.

Speaking of the great writers of our literature, Melville, Hawthorne and company, Aiken once write: "We isolate, we exile our great men, whether by ignoring them or praising them stupidly. And perhaps this isolation we offer them is our greatest gift." If this is so, Conrad Aiken was more gifted than most. [This] edition of Aiken's letters, however, offers a greater gift, in its careful, affectionate attention to the work of a master craftsman, a shaper and shape-shifter of language and emotion, who believed from first to last that "there is NOTHING so completely and exclusively fascinating as the *control of form*. And the simultaneous intertwining with it of the Eye—the 'I'—the inner voice, that comes up from undersea." In his letters, as always throughout his long career, Aiken was able to "give the effect of LIFE, the pour-in-stillness of LIFE."

Harry Marten, "Energetic Messages," in The New
York Times Book Review, May 14, 1978, p. 28.

CALVIN S. BROWN

[The editor of **Selected Letters of Conrad Aiken**] has done a skillful job of editing some seven percent of the approximately 3,500 letters of Conrad Aiken available to him. With such a strict limitation on what to include, he decided to unify the selection by choosing letters to reflect "the continuous arc—or 'great circle' of Aiken's life." For this purpose he divides the letters into periods and supplies for each period a headnote briefly outlining the biographical facts, often buttressed by quotation from Aiken's own experimental autobiography, *Ushant*. Footnotes are provided when really necessary, as well as three useful indexes: a "Cast of Correspondents" giving thumbnail sketches of the recipients of the letters, an index of Aiken's works mentioned in the letters, and a general index of names.

Aiken did distinguished work in a bewildering variety of styles and genres. He was poet, critic, short-story writer, novelist, autobiographer, even dramatist, as well as a dedicated punster and limerickist. We can now add another accomplishment to the list: he was one of the great letter-writers. The letters not only trace the arc of his life; they also give us a much more complete picture of the man than could be drawn from his varied works, including the stylized and fictionalized autobiography.

The secret lies in two facts which are immediately apparent. First, these are genuine letters, written for the recipients only, not the rigged productions of a man of letters (to make an Aikenian pun) written with an eye to subsequent publication. Second, Aiken quite obviously enjoyed writing them, even when they were expressions of misery and frustration. He put himself into them completely, with all his wit, charm, bawdiness, love of art and nature and liquor and life (whether high or low), artistic integrity, and lifelong struggle to attain complete honesty. (p. 673)

This stubborn integrity was one of Aiken's lifelong handicaps. It is probably the principal reason for the fact that, in spite of high praises by intelligent and influential critics, his work has never received anything like the general recognition it deserves. Several letters show his awareness of the jungle of literary politics and the viciousness of its denizens. "'Literary people are shits,' gravely observed [T. S.] Eliot to me at lunch this winter; he said a mouthful. I recognized myself instantly." That was in 1922. The next year Aiken himself commented, "Poets are fools and criminal and don't know what truth or honesty is." And twenty-eight years later he still holds the same opinion, adding the mob-spirit of literary cliques: "I more and more think poets are to be avoided whenever possible, they really stink. Especially in large numbers, when herding. They are such incorrigible eager beavers." Aiken consistently refused to join a herd, and said that the complications and shifts of factions are too intricate and ephemeral to be followed closely, "but fun, just the same." The well-oiled mutual-promotion machine of the Fugitives and New Critics "is becoming a menace, and with widening rings, and ought to be dealt with, but they're tough babies." (p. 674)

It is greatly to Aiken's credit that he refused to play the game, but he really couldn't have done it even if he had wanted to. The game depends largely on specialization, on developing and touting some little fiefdom like imagism or metaphysical wit; but Aiken's work was too varied and his tastes too catholic for this sort of narrowness. He loved movies, vaudeville, and comic strips, as well as all sorts of literature. "I don't see why D. Richardson should prevent one's enjoying V. Woolf. Any more than Chekhov spoils Mansfield." A man with this sort of breadth and lack of highbrow pretensions was inevitably, as he put it, "always outside the main 'thing'." But if he did not meet the literary establishment's standards, it was because his own were considerably higher. As he wrote to the editors of the *Nation,* apropos of Randall Jarrell's snide review of *The Kid,* "It is the prevalence of this sort of smart-alec and pretentious parti-pris reviewing that still prevents our having a single good critical paper in the country, one that can be relied on in advance for criticism that is informed without being bigoted or personally biased, which combines an ordered sense of the past with a knowing gusto for the contemporary, and is based on trained perceptions and disciplined taste." That is still as true as when Aiken wrote it, thirty years ago.

But fine as this comment is, it is not typical, for Aiken is seldom so solemn. He could find the literary jungle appalling, but fun. He could recognize himself in Eliot's forthright characterization of poets, and could be wittily honest about himself. . . . What will remain with a reader of Aiken's letters, after the names, dates, opinions, and literary infighting are forgotten, is the impression of an engaging, witty, and wise man (not merely a mind, but a man) living his life up to the hilt and enjoying every bit of it, including his real and frequent miseries. (pp. 674-75)

> *Calvin S. Brown, in a review of "Selected Letters of Conrad Aiken," in* The Georgia Review, *Vol. XXXII, No. 3, Fall, 1978, pp. 673-75.*

HAROLD L. WEATHERBY

A volume so varied in subject, setting, mood, and tone as [the] recent edition of Conrad Aiken's correspondence [*Selected Letters of Conrad Aiken*] defies any single reaction or logically coherent assessment. To which Aiken are we to respond? The mocking, adolescent, faddishly cynical Aiken of a great many of the letters from the beginning until almost (but not quite) the end of his career? The very nearly tragic Aiken, confounded objectively by poverty and subjectively by a near psychotic depression who somehow survives the dark thirties in Sussex? The Aiken who twice falls in love with "another woman" and does not hesitate in either instance to abandon the previous wife? The Aiken who writes enormously (and convincingly) affectionate letters to his children and who is domestically entrenched, whether in Rye, Sussex, Brewster, Massachusetts, or Savannah, with cats, flowers, and vegetables? The Aiken who contemplates suicide and finally attempts it? Aiken the man of letters in witty correspondence with or about Amy Lowell, Henry James, T. S. Eliot, W. H. Auden, Robert Frost, John Crowe Ransom, Allen Tate, John Gould Fletcher, Ezra Pound, and William Faulkner? Aiken the critic (and some of these letters contain remarkably penetrating interpretations and assessments of the work of his contemporaries)? Or Aiken as guide to his own not inconsiderable literary achievement? There is a sense in which one has his choice, and the mutually exclusive characters of these various Aikens virtually demands a choice. I have never read a body of correspondence from which a less consistent impression of personality and character emerged. The result is a volume which is at once remarkably engaging, fresh on every page, and at the same time undeniably frustrating.

This multiplicity is in part the fruit of the editor's stated intention, for he tells us in a prefatory note that his aim "has been to include letters that reflect Aiken in the variety of his interests and styles," and that the volume's unity "lies in the continuous arc—or 'great circle'—of Aiken's life. . . ." Be-

yond editorial policy, however, one suspects that self-contradiction, lack of personal coherence, is an inescapable characteristic both of Aiken and his circumstances. In fact the letters offer some reason to believe that incoherence was Aiken's deliberate choice as well as his editor's, and it is in reflecting that choice that [the editor] . . . may have done his most perceptive work—in showing Aiken in the only way in which he could honestly be shown. In any event the scattering effect gives the book its peculiar character and a great deal of its charm.

It is that same effect, moreover, which is responsible for the work's significance as a twentieth-century document, as a kind of minority report on the major literature of our times. Because Aiken registers experience as it comes, making no effort to interpret it in light of a consistent pattern of thought and feeling, he provides us with a much more vivid impression of the social and spiritual conditions of our literature than emerges from the more philosophically coherent comments of his contemporaries. Unlike most of those contemporaries, he never embraced a theology or a philosophical system of any kind. Eliot became an Anglo-Catholic, the Fugitives became Agrarians, and Frost (ideologically) a New Englander, but Aiken remained uncommitted to any shaping principle. All of these writers, in order to write, had to come to terms with the chaos of a dissolving civilization, and whereas most of them embraced a traditional (theological or social) alternative to the dissolution, Aiken may be said to have fed on the disorder itself, to have remained (helplessly but also deliberately) open to the chaos. (pp. 212-14)

[During the 1960s], and in far better physical and psychological circumstances, Aiken is prepared to make a kind of affirmation, but it amounts to little more than an endorsement of his earlier position. In a letter (1965) to the President's Council on Aging he proclaims an "animal faith, [a] primal love of earth and sky and water and air," and he urges us "to renew every day our astonishment at being permitted to be present with these, and conscious of them." His tone in the sixties may be more hopeful than in the twenties, but an "animal faith" or a "primal love of earth," though appealing in themselves, scarcely constitute an ordering metaphysical principle. I think it fair to say that he remained consistent in his nihilism, and that consistency, however appalling its spiritual cost, is, as I have suggested, what makes this correspondence so interesting and ultimately so valuable. Eliot and Aiken's other philosophically committed contemporaries produced (I believe unarguably) much greater literature than he; and I suspect that whether one is fortunate enough to inherit a system of thought and belief, as Medieval and Renaissance writers did, or whether he must adopt one deliberately by an act of will, as twentieth-century writers were constrained to do, some such system is requisite for literature of the first magnitude. On the other hand an "open" sensibility can provide what Aiken recognized himself to be—a not wholly attractive but an honest and engrossing index of an age. "You may not like him," he remarks of himself, "but he is at least a little history of his time, and if he offers you no moral or social beliefs, and not even much belief in personality or character . . . , he seems anyway to imply that there might be a kind of tragic virtue in this, and is for the most part consistent in his self-unwinding. . . ."

We are indebted to [the editor's] . . . excellent editorial work for making us privy to that unwinding and for giving us, through Aiken, a firsthand encounter with the spiritual preconditions of our century's major literature. We are also indebted to him simply for presenting Aiken in all his self-contradiction and chaos; for, however repelled we may be at moments in this correspondence, we finally do "like him." That is partly because he can say of his "unwinding," "And I think it all stinks, myself!" and because he can poke such delicious fun at "tomeliot" and his solemnity. But beyond those charms lie traits more deeply and lastingly likable, which are never far from the surface of the letters—honesty, compassion, true friendship, and, to a remarkable degree, humility. (p. 214)

Harold L. Weatherby, "A Little History of His Time,"
in Modern Age, *Vol. 23, No. 2, Spring, 1979, pp.*
213-14.

Woody Allen

1935-

(Born Allen Stewart Konigsberg; name legally changed to Heywood Allen) American director, scriptwriter, dramatist, essayist, short story writer, and actor.

Respected for his contributions in several genres to the development of twentieth-century comedy, Allen is recognized as one of the foremost filmmakers to emerge during the 1960s. Essentially a humorist in all of his writings, Allen uses satire and parody to exploit contemporary stereotypes and neuroses. In his early films, the typical Allen protagonist is a *schlemiel,* or Jewish bungler, at odds with machines and nature, insecure with women, and overwhelmed by society. Allen's later motion pictures are more introspective, exploring such topics as love, God, death, artistic integrity, the consequences of fame, and personal relationships. Nancy Pogel observed: "[Allen's] finest work exposes a culture that simultaneously promises and frustrates the fulfillment of our desires, while his comic spirit reminds us of our humanity and of our stubborn resistance to all life-denying, closed systems."

Born in Brooklyn, New York, and raised in a middle-class Jewish environment, Allen was a shy, morose child and a poor student who spent most of his time writing gag lines. While still in high school, he began sending jokes to New York newspaper columnists Earl Wilson and Walter Winchell, who in turn published them or passed them on to celebrities. As a result of these prestigious references, an advertising agency hired Allen as a jokewriter. This capacity led to others in which he wrote for such television stars as Sid Caesar, Art Carney, and Jack Paar during the 1950s. Allen soon began to perform his own material at nightclubs and universities across the United States, and his popular and critical success as a stand-up comedian enabled him to secure the position of scriptwriter for the film *What's New Pussycat?* (1965). Looking for greater artistic control, Allen acquired a Japanese spy movie, reedited it, and added his own incongruous dialogue. The resulting film, *What's Up, Tiger Lily?* (1966), received widespread acknowledgment for Allen's animated comic genius.

In *Take the Money and Run* (1969), the first film for which he was credited as both actor and director, Allen burlesques cinema verité and biographical documentaries, employing blackouts and interviews to depict the life of an ineffectual thief. Sacrificing structure for humor, this movie relies on rapid-fire verbal and visual gags which subvert the conventions of gangster films. Similarly, in *Bananas* (1971), Allen emphasizes madcap, absurd humor at the expense of continuity in a story about a meek individual who unexpectedly becomes the leader of a Latin American country while trying to impress a female political activist. *Play It Again, Sam* (1972) details a neurotic film critic's hapless attempts to regain confidence in relationships with women after his divorce. The protagonist tries to emulate the invulnerable, romantic ideal represented by Humphrey Bogart but ultimately realizes that it is best to retain one's individuality. *Sleeper* (1973), the last of Allen's motion pictures to accentuate physical and visual humor, spoofs futuristic science fiction films to ridicule follies of contemporary society.

With *Love and Death* (1975), Allen began to develop greater thematic and technical sophistication. Set in czarist Russia, *Love and Death* satirizes Russian literary and cinematic classics in its examination of such topics as despair, mortality, and concepts of God. *Annie Hall* (1977), for which Allen won Academy Awards for best picture, director, and screenplay, is generally regarded as his masterpiece. A semiautobiographical romantic comedy, *Annie Hall* examines the troubled relationship between Alvy Singer, a Jewish comedy writer, and Annie Hall, his gentile lover. Originally drawn to each other by their similar neuroses, they drift apart when Annie begins to exhibit self-confidence and intellectual independence, while Alvy becomes jealous and remains unable to enjoy life. *Interiors* (1978) marks a departure for Allen into serious drama. An austere film reminiscent of Ingmar Bergman's work, *Interiors* treats human frailty in much the same manner as *Annie Hall* but without relying on Allen's usual backdrop of visual and verbal humor. In *Manhattan* (1979), Allen blends comedy and pathos while exploring the consequences of professional compromises and the vagaries of love among neurotic intellectuals in New York City. This film centers on middle-aged television writer Isaac Davis, whose wife has left him for another woman. Isaac begins an affair with seventeen-year-old Tracy but remains noncommittal and finally loses her. Ironically, despite her youth, Tracy displays more maturity and wisdom than the other characters.

Stardust Memories (1980), another of Allen's semiautobiographical films, focuses on director Sandy Bates's disillusionment with fame and his own creations. Set at a convention honoring his achievements, this work examines relationships between reality and film, the artist and his work, and the artist and his public. Thematically and stylistically similar to Federico Fellini's *8½*, *Stardust Memories* was faulted for self-indulgence and a self-pitying tone. *Zelig* (1983) also offers a scathing portrait of the nature of celebrity in the form of a mock-documentary about Leonard Zelig, a fictitious historical figure who desperately desires friendship and adulation. Allen weaves interviews, newsreel footage, and scenes of psychiatric sessions to show how assiduously Zelig yearns to be accepted by society. In *The Purple Rose of Cairo* (1985), Allen again investigates relationships between fantasy and reality through the device of a film actor leaving the screen and entering the "real" life of a downtrodden woman in the audience. Allen's recent films, including *Hannah and Her Sisters* (1986) and *Radio Days* (1987), explore many of his usual thematic concerns.

Most of Allen's essays and short stories were published in the *New Yorker* and are composed in the tradition of such humorists for that publication as S. J. Perelman and Robert Benchley. In his collections *Getting Even* (1971), *Without Feathers* (1975), and *Side Effects* (1980), Allen often parodies literary genres, including the memoir, the philosophical treatise, and the hard-boiled detective story, deriving humor from puns, non sequiturs, inverted clichés, surreal situations, literary and cinematic allusions, and juxtapositions of lofty, abstract ideas with practical, mundane matters. In his review of *Side Effects,* Sanford Pinsker remarked: "Allen's imagination works best in that special realm where the High Brow idea and the urban (read: Jewish) detail are forced to share space, often on opposing sides of a semi-colon."

Allen achieved success on Broadway with his first two plays. *Don't Drink the Water* (1966) revolves around an American family's frustrations while visiting an Eastern European country, while *Play It Again, Sam* (1969) served as the basis for Allen's 1972 film. *The Floating Light Bulb* (1981), a realistic autobiographical play reminiscent of Tennessee Williams's *The Glass Menagerie,* focuses on a reclusive teenager who performs magic tricks in his bedroom while his family dwells on its unrealized dreams. In the comedies *Death* (1975) and *God* (1975), Allen addresses such themes as faith versus doubt, art versus life, and the nature of artistic creation. Both plays feature surreal juxtapositions of classical drama with elements borrowed from the Theater of the Absurd.

(See also *CLC*, Vol. 16; *Contemporary Authors,* Vols. 33-36, rev. ed.; and *Dictionary of Literary Biography,* Vol. 44.)

ROBERT LASSON

Getting Even, a collection of seventeen humorous pieces from various sources, proves that [Woody Allen] is truly a Renaissance schlemiel.

His prose is a minefield laid down by an inspired loon sired by Groucho Marx out of Lizzie Borden. Words bend. Logic withers. The synapses miss connections. . . .

Allen shoots at—and hits—a diversity of targets. In "**Mr. Big,**" a metaphysical Whodunit, a great-looking chick calls on a private eye. His assignment: find God. "My first lead was Rabbi Itzhak Wiseman, a local cleric who owed me a favor for finding out who was rubbing pork on his hat."

In "**Spring Bulletin,**" Introduction to Psychology includes such courses as Introduction to Hostility, Intermediate Hostility, Advanced Hatred, and Theoretical Foundations of Loathing. Another course at Allen U. is in elementary philosophy: "Aesthetics: Is art a mirror of life, or what?"

In "**My Philosophy,**" Allen ponders, "Can we actually 'know' the universe? My God, it's hard enough finding your way around in Chinatown." . . .

As funny as these excerpts are, it must be noted that Allen doesn't hit every time. Some of the pieces are little undeveloped buds. Others depend too much on technique rather than content and the result is more pyrotechnic wheel-spinning.

But what sour ingrate would argue with a collection that contains five or six pieces of contemporary humor which are bound to last forever? (Here let's invoke Mark Twain, who defined "forever" in this context as thirty years.)

Why is Woody Allen funny? Please. Let's not throw our maiden author to the graduate students just yet. He's too young to dry. But Allen's best pieces—"**My Philosophy,**" "**Conversations with Helmholtz,**" "**Mr. Big,**" "**Hasidic Tales,**" and others— are those which attempt to explain one basic absurdity—with a superimposed absurdity. You look into a funhouse mirror but for a hundredth of a second, you see *through* it. This is not the task that humor ordinarily sets for itself. But then, Woody Allen is an extraordinary humorist.

> Robert Lasson, "*By Groucho Out of Lizzie Borden,*" in Book World—Chicago Tribune, *October 17, 1971, p. 4.*

ISA KAPP

[Starting with the title, *Without Feathers*], lifted pessimistically from Emily Dickinson's line "Hope is the thing with feathers," this second collection of [Allen's] writings has high intellectual pretensions. Taken mainly from his contributions to the *New Yorker* (as was the earlier *Getting Even*), it is meant for those who have read Mary McCarthy, seen Tom Stoppard's *Jumpers,* and are no strangers to veal cordon bleu.

For the benefit of the cognoscenti Allen volunteers "**A Guide to Some of the Lesser Ballets,**" covering only scenes (dear to choreographers) that accentuate the moribund. In "**The Spell,**" a woman who is half swan enchants Sigmund; though he "is careful not to make any poultry jokes," the affair ends disastrously. "**The Predators**" is about two insects who dance slowly to French horns and fall in love. They plan a nuptial flight, but "the female changes her mind and devours him, preferring to move in with a roommate." "**A Day in the Life of a Doe**" is a model of poignant brevity: "Unbearably lovely music is heard as the curtain rises . . . a faun dances and nibbles at some leaves. . . . Soon he starts coughing and drops dead."

Closer to the neurotic kink of Allen's mind is "**The Irish Genius,**" a satire on annotation to a poem that struggles to evoke Yeats' "Sailing to Byzantium," Sean O'Shawn's "Beyond Ichor." The notes, by a Columbia professor named Hyman "Bojangles" Lefkowitz, clear up esoteric references like: "*The Beamish brothers.* Two half-wit brothers who tried to get from Belfast to Scotland by mailing each other,'' or "*Homer was blind*. Homer was a symbol for T. S. Eliot . . . a poet of immense scope but very little breadth.'' Always finely disattuned to the academic mind, Allen is fervently preoccupied with notes and critical introductions to literature—no doubt the main blocks he stumbled over in dropping out of City College and New York University. He lingers with allergic intensity over classic phrases out of the critical vocabulary—"this obdurate and sparkling book,'' or "clearly the most fully realized woman in Lovborg's plays''—the baggage of trivia and excess that travels with a modern education.

Nevertheless, it must be admitted that in his new collection he has lost some of his patience and more of his coherence. He took more time for the objects of his scorn in *Getting Even*. (p. 9)

Humor has to set up its own logic, and then perpetrate the switch that undermines us. Laurel and Hardy are masters of this discipline within madness when they try to move a grand piano across a narrow suspension bridge slung over a chasm between two Alps. Midway they meet a gorilla! In [*Without Feathers*], Woody Allen often lacks that strong center, that vital takeoff point, and his febrile imagination runs amok.

He envisions neurotic and erotic attitudes toward food (cheese fondling or immersing an arm in custard); he conjures up parrots who become Secretaries of Agriculture, woodchucks who try to claim his prize at a raffle, or beavers who take over Carnegie Hall and perform *Wozzeck*. There is, in fact, a procession of birds, fish and small animals through *Without Feathers*, and frequently dark hints are dropped about improper relations with them. Zaniness certainly has a place in humor, yet Allen's latest fancies are so weird that we laugh shakily, reluctant to establish ourselves too definitively on his haphazard wavelength.

The play *God* . . . presupposes at least the approximation of a context for his jokes. It encompasses a vast panorama of inaction, giving us a capsule history of "new theater" from Pirandello to Beckett and Stoppard. The playwright creates a writer who invents an audience that stays to quarrel about the outcome of the play. Incorporating certain hollow pauses out of *Waiting for Godot*, the drama asks ultimate questions destined never to be answered, and one-ups the appearance of the nude girl on a swing in Stoppard's *Jumpers* by lowering Zeus onto the stage in a very suitable contraption, a *deus ex machina* (not unexpectedly, the god, on arrival, is dead). Going on the assumption that life is disorganized and irrational, the pay holds a distorting mirror up to it and gets completely out of hand.

What really confounds us about *God* is why, with perfectly plausible material for ridicule and a theoretically sound comic strategy, it is not in the least funny. Perhaps first-class humorists like Mark Twain, Robert Benchley, Peter de Vries and, on a lower rung, Nichols and May and Mort Sahl, have all had a greater capacity than Woody Allen to be serious. Their starting points have been exact perceptions of reality, of something intrinsically laughable not about man's creations but about man himself. Allen, pondering dance, drama, literary criticism, educational curricula, pursuing art rather than life, is often awkwardly suspended between the devils of comedy and the deep unnavigable sea of culture.

Still, Woody continues to be sharp, active and ingenious, a few paradoxes ahead of the audience that groans over his jokes. After all, culture comedy, like caricature, must be based on a formidably precise understanding of attributes. Most of us can-

not, like David Levine, differentiate the fine lines that constitute hypocrisy or complacency; the best we can manage is a slippery grasp of their elusive general contours. Similarly, when we see an Ibsen play, we don't, like Woody Allen in "**Lovborg's Women**," isolate out of the craft and astute characterizations the purely ludicrous aspects: the devastating disclosures, the gratuitous exhortations to courage, the sudden swerves from exaltation to gloom. Allen has caught, through a trick of selective concentration, only the cadences, the exasperating high-mindedness, the peasoup of morality and moroseness. If you could shut out the sense of his words, you would be sure you were actually reading Ibsen.

The funniest story in the book is "**The Whore of Mensa**," in which a private eye tries to crack a callgirl racket for men who want a quickie intellectual experience. The shamus walks through the Hunter College bookstore where, behind a secret panel,

> "Pale nervous girls with black-rimmed glasses and blunt cut hair lolled around on sofas, riffling Penguin Classics provocatively. . . . For fifty bucks, I learned, you could 'relate without getting close.' For a hundred, a girl would lend you her Bartok records, have dinner, and then let you watch while she had an anxiety attack. For three bills you got the works. A thin Jewish brunette would pretend to pick you up at the Museum of Modern Art, let you read her master's, get you involved in a screaming quarrel at Elaine's over Freud's conception of women, and then fake a suicide of your choosing. . . . Nice racket. Great town, New York."

In an age of brazen culture-vulturism, only a cowering man of sensibility, a secret sharer, could have written that. (pp. 9-10)

Isa Kapp, "A Cowering Man of Sensibility," in The New Leader, *Vol. LVIII, No. 11, May 26, 1975, pp. 8-10.*

ARTHUR COOPER

Except for two or three pieces that flirt dangerously with self-parody his new collection, *Without Feathers*, is the funniest book since *Getting Even*, which also had Allen's name on it. Of course Woody wrote neither. Both were stitched together by a Ukrainian dwarf from the unpublished nightmares of Fyodor Dostoevski, Ingmar Bergman, Franz Kafka and Xaviera Hollander.

Anything carrying the Woody Allen trademark appeals to the shnook residing in every contemporary urban male—that hapless, feckless creature befuddled by gadgets, perplexed by a lack of faith, lusting for sexual encounters but scared to death of any emotional involvement. This loopy universe is captured in a surreal, throwaway style in which philosophical profundity is given a hotfoot by the ridiculously mundane. . . .

Allen's forte is the inverted one-liner, the Big Non Sequitur. But his best pieces—"**The Whore of Mensa**" and "**No Kaddish for Weinstein**"—reveal just how well he can sustain his wit. . . .

"**No Kaddish for Weinstein**" is a parody of the Saul Bellow-Bernard Malamud antihero, whose brain is the mortal enemy of his body. Weinstein

> "had been a precocious child. An intellectual. At twelve, he had translated the poems of T. S. Eliot into English, after some vandals had broken into the library and translated them into French . . . He was impotent with any woman who finished college with higher than a B-minus average. He felt most at home

with graduates of typing school, although if the woman did over 60 words a minute he panicked and could not perform."

(p. 87)

Allen embodies the contradiction found in most comic artists: he's an intelligent, serious man who derives his funniest material from his darkest obsessions—God, sex and, particularly, death, which nags his consciousness like a carping wife. "As Tolstoy said," notes Allen, "'Any man over 35 for whom death is not the main consideration is a fool'." That's a heavy thought for the funniest 39-year-old in America to carry around. But Allen can even punch Tolstoy's line until it laughs. "It's not that I'm afraid to die," he allows. "I just don't want to be there when it happens." (p. 87A)

> *Arthur Cooper, "Allen the Author," in* Newsweek, *Vol. LXXXV, No. 25, June 23, 1975, pp. 87-87A.*

RICHARD R. LINGEMAN

There are gags [in *Without Feathers*], of course, and slapstick, as in a piece on precognition that has a man dreaming his grandfather's death scenario only to learn that the actual demise was a result of the old man's slipping on a chicken salad sandwich and falling off the Chrysler Building. Similarly, in **"No Kaddish for Weinstein,"** a very funny parody of Bellow and Malamud, among others, Weinstein's relationship with his wife employs George Burns-Gracie Allen: "How are the kids, Harriet?" "We never had any kids, Ike." Weinstein and his ex-wife are a couple with a private joke neither of them understands.

Mr. Allen is also a master of the juxtaposition of the banal with the cosmic, as in transubstantiation's being "not a bad way to travel, although there is usually a half-hour wait for luggage." And he can take a brilliant premise and run with it as in **"The Whore of Mensa,"** in which Kaiser Lupowitz, private eye, uncovers a ring of intellectual call girls who satiate men's lust for intelligent conversation. . . .

Some of the pieces strike me as primarily finger exercises in nonsense, and the parody **"If the Impressionists Were Dentists"** makes me wish that anyone committing dental humor be sentenced to compulsory fluoridation. Two plays, *God* and *Death,* show Mr. Allen's debt to Pirandello, Beckett and Kafka, not necessarily in that order. Still, give Woody Allen credit for dealing with the great themes of sex, death and God; the entire universe is his banana peel. Even if he received absolute assurance of an afterlife, he would ask, "Is it rent-controlled?"

> *Richard R. Lingeman, "God, Death and Woody Allen," in* The New York Times, *July 9, 1975, p. 35.*

MICHAEL WOOD

There is a characteristic cadence in many of Woody Allen's jokes. A broad, old-fashioned gesture meets a narrow, uncooperative bit of contemporary reality. Allen waves casually to make a point and the record he is holding slips out of its sleeve and hurtles across the room. Smiling sardonically at himself in a mirror, Allen gets ready for a night on the town. When he turns on his hair-dryer, it blows him about as if it were a hurricane. He tries to make Beef Stroganoff in a pressure cooker, and someone asks him how it tasted. "I don't know," Allen says. "It's still on the wall."

More often these mishaps are set up in language, clashes of perfectly unsympathetic contexts. "Still obsessed by thoughts of death, I brood constantly. I keep wondering if there is an afterlife, and if there is will they be able to break a twenty?" "There is no question that there is an unseen world. The problem is, how far is it from midtown and how late is it open?" "If only God would show me a miracle. Like a burning bush, or the parting of the Red Sea, or Uncle Sasha picking up a check."

Similarly the whole strength of Allen's film *Love and Death* (1975) comes from a constant contrast between a carefully pastiched Russia, taken from Tolstoy and Dostoevsky, played out in predictable costumes and thick accents, and an unmistakable America, present in all kinds of gags and in every move and sound of Allen and his co-star Diane Keaton. "What do you mean, man is made in God's image?" Allen asks indignantly in his own rather thin voice, American accent entirely unmodified. "You mean God looks like me? God wears glasses?" Keaton looks at him thoughtfully, tilts her head slightly. "Maybe not with those frames."

These are very good jokes, but they are also quite traditional ones: incongruities, pratfalls, versions of the banana peel. Allen is right to insist that he is not an intellectual. "I'm a one-liner comic like Bob Hope and Henny Youngman," he told Eric Lax. "I do the wife jokes. I make faces. I'm a comedian in the classic style." There is a little more to Allen than that. He reads a lot, he is very intelligent, and he is not only a stand-up comic: he is also an actor, a playwright, a screenwriter, and a movie director. He used to work up gags for Garry Moore and Sid Caesar, and he has become a *New Yorker* humorist in the tradition of Robert Benchley. But he is after laughs rather than meaning, and we don't need hefty theories about the Insecurity of Our Times to account for his success. Allen is very funny, his gags have familiar structures, and these are *our* banana peels he is stepping on. A whole modern world can be constructed out of the things Allen runs into: dentists, analysts, rent-control, rabbis, racing at Aqueduct, high culture, old movies, college, brand names . . . , air travel. . . . (p. 14)

Even Allen's most allusion-packed material belongs here. "By the fifth grade," he says, "I would be doing references to Freud and sex, too, without knowing who he and what it really was but sensing how to use them correctly." He is still doing this, and his frequently esoteric-looking jokes almost always depend on our sensing the *sort* of reference that is being made rather than our knowing anything much about the actual source. Here, for example, is Kaiser Lupowitz, a private eye on a tough case, trying to find God ("So that's how it was. The Jews were into God for a lot. It was the old protection racket. Take care of them in return for a price"), and discovering that He is dead. The phone rings:

> The voice on the other end was Sergeant Reed of Homicide.
>
> "You still looking for God?"
>
> "Yeah."
>
> "An all-powerful Being? Great Oneness, Creator of the Universe? First Cause of All Things?"
>
> "That's right."
>
> "Somebody with that description just showed up at the morgue. You better get down here right away."

And here is Kaiser, in another story, investigating a racket in which pretty girls will talk over intellectual matters with any man who has the right kind of money. Kaiser poses as a client and says he wants to discuss Melville (*"Moby Dick* or the shorter novels?" "What's the difference?" "The price. That's all. Symbolism's extra") but is distressed by the cynicism of his partner ("She was barely nineteen years old, but already she had developed the hardened facility of the pseudo-intellectual"), and decides to turn her in:

> "I'm fuzz, sugar, and discussing Melville for money is an 802. You can do time."
>
> "You louse!"
>
> "Better come clean, baby. Unless you want to tell your story down at Alfred Kazin's office. . . ."

The madame in charge of the whole affair is called Flossie, and she turns out to be a man in a mask. A sad story:

> "I devised a complicated scheme to take over *The New York Review of Books* [Flossie confesses], but it meant I had to pass for Lionel Trilling. I went to Mexico for an operation. There's a doctor in Juarez who gives people Trilling's features—for a price. Something went wrong. I came out looking like Auden, with Mary McCarthy's voice. . . ."

Now I suppose none of this would be very funny if you had not heard the rumors of God's death or didn't know who any of these people were, or what *The New York Review* was. But it was a fairly safe bet to assume that readers of *The New Yorker,* where the second of these stories first appeared, would know such things, and the joke, in any case, requires no reading of Trilling, or Auden, or anyone else, for its comprehension. It requires only that we know the names, and "how to use them correctly." Allen's central perception is that culture, high, low, and middling, is very often a matter of moving tokens about, literally dropping names; that we live largely in a magical universe, clustering in often belligerent groups because of passwords spoken and banners waved. And Allen's great gift is for muddling the tokens, for an equivalent of that terrible operation in Juarez: Nietzsche and Matthew Arnold come out sounding like Mickey Spillane, passwords become gibberish, banners droop, and with any luck we can begin to think for ourselves again. Allen is out for laughs, as I said, and he gets them. But it won't do us any harm to reflect on our laughter. What if we are a nation of half-educated people, and have got the wrong half?

These are rather complicated bananas, and I should try quickly to give an impression of Allen's range as a comedian. He can echo the escalating tones of Groucho Marx . . . and the treacherous seriousness of S. J. Perelman. (pp. 14-15)

He also has a line in inspired nonsense of his own . . . and he is particularly adept at seeking out and sending up a whole variety of official voices, from those of reviewers ("this obdurate and sparkling book") to those of college catalogues ("Students interested in these aspects of psychology are advised to take one of these Winter Term courses: Introduction to Hostility; Intermediate Hostility; Advanced Hatred; Theoretical Foundations of Loathing") and historians ("the vibrant, cruel Darwinian force of nature, which was to blow through Europe for the next fifty years and find its deepest expression in the songs of Maurice Chevalier").

There are also moments when a genuine helplessness seems to peep through the jokes, and this of course is the personality Allen projects as an actor: distraught, ineffective, underconfident, given to whining. It *is* a projection; but it clearly reflects Allen's difficulties and preoccupations. The painful diffidence

of his public character is a disguise of some sort; it is not likely to be an outright fiction. . . .

Allen told Jack Kroll that he thought his anxieties might shorten the range of his appeal, and said W. C. Fields, for example, had "a certain neurotic quality, whereas Chaplin had a greater feeling for the human condition." But if Fields was neurotic Allen is in hiding, and the charm and the limitation of his work are in its display of sheer incapacity. Allen has none of the grace of Chaplin and Buster Keaton, none of Fields' seedy elegance, none of Groucho's threatening energy. All he has are his mistakes and a wonderful air of passive, hopeless innocence. (p. 15)

> Michael Wood, *"Allen's Alley,"* in The New York Review of Books, *Vol. XXV, No. 11, June 29, 1978, pp. 14-16.*

DAVID M. FRIEND

Though Allen is developing as a serious dramatist . . . it is through his comedy that we can focus most clearly on the wandering Jew shrugging in the shadows of Woody Allen's art. Very little of Allen's humor is directly concerned with Jewish themes. He is a comedian of modern alienation and *anhedonia* before he is a Jewish comedian. . . .

Woody Allen's father once remarked that his son "put on black-face and did an imitation of Al Jolson" at his bar mitzvah. In the context of such irreverence the chore here is to examine Allen's changing use of "things Jewish" in his evolving comedy and to decipher how this irreverent genius became, to borrow one critic's praise, "the funniest neurotic of our time." (p. 59)

During his career, the Jewish edge of his comedy has altered much in the same way that the assimilated American Jewish mythos has changed during the past two generations: unconscious love of Judaism to rebellion against same to a distilled cultural Judaism, one stripped, finally, of almost everything but its preoccupation with broader feelings of alienation and marginality. . . .

In early Allen everyone is Jewish whether they live in Brooklyn or Peking. (p. 60)

And often Allen turns the tables, using Jews in non-Jewish settings strictly for absurdity's sake. . . .

Total absurdity that *happens* to have Jewish components: that is the final criterion in these early bits. The joke's the thing. . . . [Early] on in his career the pure laugh takes priority over everything: Jewishness, politics, philosophy. Allen, pre-***Annie Hall,*** is, according to Michael Wood in the *New York Review of Books,* "after laughs rather than meaning" [see excerpt above]. (p. 61)

[The] Jew in Woody Allen plays it tame in his early comedy. When Judaism slides a banana peel under his feet, it is a Jewish American aura, writ lovingly, in broad strokes of *shlimazel,* self-pity, and intellectual Kuni-Lemmel that are eons away from harsh criticism of his upbringing.

It is not until Allen's middle and later films that he seems to feel Judaism is often smashing a pie in his face and, of course, he returns the disfavor: (pp. 61-2)

The film ***Everything You Always Wanted To Know About Sex*** presents a rabbi tied up on a game show being whipped by a woman in leather while his wife eats pork at his feet. ***Sleeper*** shows a party guest arriving at the door wearing a swastika-emblazoned shirt with a *talis* draped nonchalantly around his neck like a scarf. Jewish women, so *Love and Death* cautions, don't believe in sex after marriage. . . .

These gags are not violently anti-Jewish. Allen's no religious rebel. They *are* disturbing to most people with a strict Jewish sensibility. However you slice it, he has made unkosher many of our sacred cows. But what this irreverence expresses—and I balk at over-interpretation—is a certain backlash accompanying Allen's growing lack of concern for Judaism in his art (as Judaism and as a comic outlet).

Preoccupation with things Jewish is not a threat or hindrance to Allen at this point. At its very worst, Judaism seems to sidetrack his comedy to one vicinity when it desires, ideally, to inhabit other arenas of humor. Judaism, it seems, merely becomes less important to him as his comedy and characters mature (as Allen himself matures). Allen the private philosopher has designed some strange breed of self-taught existentialism, and it finally surfaces at the gut of his interviews, writings, and motion pictures at this stage in his career. He undergoes the trials of all good 20th century absurdist/neurotics, Jew or Gentile. Religion is a sour spot on the *punim* of a Godless world. Though this is never a conscious realization, the fact remains that Judaism, for whatever other reasons, cannot be even incidentally valid since God, to Allen, does not exist.

Like director Ingmar Bergman, Allen's acknowledged idol, he becomes obsessed in his plays and in *Love and Death* and *Sleeper* with mortality and the silence of God, nursing these themes with fetishistic abandon. . . .

Is this comedy? Certainly Allen has pushed black comedy to an absurd precipice. What Camus calls the anxious "climate of absurdity" Allen makes comically bearable in his own way. He diverts us from despair by the cushions and canopies of some crazy comic irony. God's joking. Or, in the absence of God, we might as well laugh at the nothingness. It spares us pain.

If not black comedy, the comedy of . . . *Love and Death* is "grey matter" comedy, the artfully delivered gibberish of a cerebral jester at the door of purgatory, defying God and most of humanity, reveling in the queer laughter that, as Francine du Plessix Gray points out, accompanies Allen's deep "anxiety toward the nameless persecuting enemy essential to Jewish humor."

Jewish or not, his comedy can be sore stuff if taken in excess. It rests on the Freudian doctrine of a man eternally possessed by the fears of sex and death, love and death. (p. 62)

It is curious that at this juncture in Allen's comedy the main characters in his works, for the most part, shed their *shlemiel*-ness and graduate to the level of the urban cynic spouting Freud, Kafka, and Dostoevski. For contrast consider Virgil Starkwell of Allen's film *Take the Money and Run*. . . . Virgil cannot carry out a hold-up because he misspells the note he gives to the bank teller. He is almost late to another heist because he can't decide what color shirt to wear. "Call the other guys," his wife advises. "See what they're wearing."

But no longer is he the bungling tramp. . . . Here in his . . . middle films is the brooding, self-involved alien, the stranger; by turns, a self-assured picaroon and an ill-at-ease social drop-out. . . .

Who, then, is the archetypal Woody Allen character, let alone Jewish character? (Hint: there is no archetype.) The Allen Felix role in *Play It Again, Sam,* written just prior to *Sex* and *Sleeper,* though, seems to best compress the flow of characters in Allen's career. Surely, Jewish references abound. At the grocery store Felix mistakes *Yahrtzeit* candles for mood candles. . . . He is not the *shlemiel* but the New York Jewish angstnik—though to call that type necessarily Jewish is, errantly, to call a rose a Rosen. Allen Felix turns from *nebbish* to frustrated sexual athlete to a finally self-confident neurotic (each a more palatable echelon of hopelessness).

But if Felix is the most complete fossil of all Woody Allen characters, *Annie Hall* is the film in which Felix's primitive imprint finds maturity and through which Allen finally settles the thoroughly unconscious question: How do I utilize my Judaism in my comedy? In fact, he resolves it so well in this film that he practically abandons it later. . . .

Having exhausted, for the time being, the themes of death and Godlessness in *Love and Death* and his late plays, Allen steps back in *Annie Hall* to present a more human comedy. Its Jewish facets have little resemblance to the loving Yiddishisms of Mel Brooks's or even Allen's early films. Allen, like Bergman, has braved the furnaces of existential philosophy. His comic anguish could never incorporate a "return to love" of things Jewish as, say, Saul Bellow's or Philip Roth's have. Nor does religion seem important enough for him to turn *against* it. So Judaism becomes for Allen, as it has for many modern Jews, a benign facet of his artistic personality. It is only of import in questions of dislocation or persecution. . . .

Alvy Singer [in *Annie Hall*] seems to cure the aches of estrangements by criticizing everyone else in one form or another—placing himself on a safe self-made island. But even from that island he has a persecution complex the size of Manhattan. He uses his Judaism as a scapegoat, an "out" for the rest of his personality. They are after him, he reduces it easily, because he is Jewish. . . . (p. 63)

A paranoid kibbitzer, Alvy uses Judaism as an excuse for all his daily alienations. His happens-to-be Jewish aspect speeds up a process. It propels the fact that he is on the "outs" with the outside world.

Love relationships translate into similar equations of distance and anxiety. However comic or tragic, you can't fuse two egos. Alvy's attraction to Annie . . . shows the religious differences, though not serious drawbacks, don't *help* matters any. . . .

Love inevitably fades, Allen tells us in *Annie Hall.* But Alvy and Annie start out on the wrong side of the waterbed. Annie's grandmother gives her Christmas presents. Alvy's never gave him anything since "she was too busy being raped by Cossacks." . . .

[The] life of the modern materialist, the urbanite, the intellectual has repressed a large share of our consciousness of Jewish history and replaces it with a less urgent self-consciousness where Judaism is used only conveniently as it fits the persecution or shtick-at-hand. . . .

Annie Hall has significantly more to do with the strange comedic chemistry of paranoia, of love-lost, and of modern social discomfort in general than it has to do with Jewish alienation in specific. *Manhattan* takes this point a step further.

Of the six Jewish-oriented jokes in *Manhattan,* two are about Nazis, and one is about his mother, the Castrating Zionist.

This is strictly armor humor, just as *Annie Hall*'s humor often revolves around the notion that a Jew's strength—and, surely, much of the strength of humor itself—is derived, in part, from fighting back at his persecutors. But, more crucially, the Jewish persona post-*Annie Hall,* virtually absent in *Interiors,* is *buried* in *Manhattan.* It is no longer a point of reference as in the early films, or a point to lampoon as in his middle works. . . .

Allen has reached a stage where he has refined Judaism *per se* out of his art. It plays a minor, not a major chord. (p. 64)

For the mature Allen, Jews have no monopoly on persecution, on knowledge of the bleakness of existence, or on humor's armor as a mechanism for coping with persecution and bleakness. . . . Allen's art has taught us that the time has come to stop laughing, begin confronting, revolt, shrug hopelessly, and commence laughing again. (pp. 64-5)

At the bottom line, the punch line, Woody Allen's humor is not Jewish humor, if there *is* such an animal. He is, instead, one of the best Jewish humorists, black comedians, culture critics, absurdists, et. al. His use of the Jewish condition in his humor is a convenience but not a contrivance. Like any good writer, he is best (he is funniest) when operating in a context he knows with a certain intimacy. It just happens to be part of his character which he doesn't seem to take seriously. He traces the path of muddled assimilation taken by many modern Jews.

But whether he admits it or not, he *appeals* to what is often termed (for reasons of shading and lack of precise definition) "the assimilated American Jewish sensibility": preoccupation with persecution, a history of urban estrangement, resilient self-confidence, Freudian frustrations, Yiddish cynicism albeit ability to smile or smirk at doom. Each of these may be central to any urban agnostic intellectual Puerto Rican. . . . But they are particularly "Jewish" concerns inasmuch as they are largely a product of part of a culture that claims these strengths and ills as its own. (p. 65)

> *David M. Friend, "Woody Allen's Jewish American Gothic," in* Midstream, *Vol. XXV, No. 6, June-July, 1979, pp. 59-65.*

JOHN LEONARD

As in his previous collections, *Getting Even* and *Without Feathers, Side Effects* is full of what might be called intellectual brand names. Igor Stravinsky and Hannah Arendt are the favorites, but references are also made to Proust, Chekhov, Socrates, Tolstoy, Flaubert, Wordsworth, Goethe, Novalis, Einstein, Saul Bellow, Joseph Heller, Jacques Monod, Lao-tse, T. S. Eliot, Bach, Vivaldi, Matisse, Robert Rauschenberg, Yasser Arafat and the Egyptian *Book of the Dead.*

Indeed, Kafka, Bernard Malamud, Philip Roth and, if I am not mistaken, Jean-Paul Sartre and André Malraux are all parodied. It is as if *The New York Review of Books* were the only magazine to which S. J. Perelman subscribed.

These big boys, however, get pushed around by the little guys—the Marx Brothers, Johnny Cash, Spike Mulligan, Helmut Berger, O. J. Simpson, Ralph Lauren, Rupert Murdoch and the Flying Wallendas. Everybody in the book has a problem, and the problem is usually sexual, and the sex as usual is unthreatening. Mr. Allen gets away with so much, in his stories, in his movies, in his monologues, because he is perceived as not being dangerous. Schizophrenia is made cute. . . .

Nothing in *Side Effects* is quite so good as **"The Whore of Mensa"** in *Without Feathers,* which was to his fiction what *Manhattan* is to his movies—that is, perfect of its sort. In his fiction, unfortunately, there isn't any Diane Keaton. The women in his fiction either listen to Stravinsky and think like Hannah Arendt, or they listen to Johnny Cash and think like the Flying Wallendas, except for Madame Bovary, who has an affair with Sidney Kugelmass, a professor of humanities at City College. With Madame Bovary, Mr. Allen had some help.

But every story is funny; Mr. Allen can't help being funny. And one story, **"Retribution,"** which is more or less about incest, might have been more than funny; it is acquainted with nuance as well as brand names. Mr. Allen, however, backs off. Whether he is writing for *The New Yorker, The New Republic* or *The Kenyon Review,* he seldom bothers to finish a story; he simply stops making jokes.

Of course, it may be unfair to ask of Mr. Allen more than he wants to give us, when what he gives us is more than what we deserve. Civilized wit is not to be taken for granted; to parody Kafka, and to parody Philip Roth parodying Kafka, in a country largely ignorant of both Kafka and Philip Roth is, if not perhaps heroic, at least better than Rupert Murdoch and prettier than Ernest Borgnine. We must also remember that when Mr. Allen does get serious, a movie like *Interiors* is likely to be the result.

And yet, said the review. The odd effect of reading these stories in a single sitting is to feel that not only have anxiety and schizophrenia been made cute, but so also have Kafka and high culture. There is no threat; literature and philosophy aren't dangerous. We finish one story after another, smile and go untroubled to our waterbed.

> *John Leonard, in a review of "Side Effects," in* The New York Times, *September 19, 1980, p. C23.*

S. SCHOENBAUM

Besides stories [in *Side Effects*] there is a one-act play about an incident in Abraham Lincoln's life; a restaurant review of Fabrizio's Villa Nova, with follow-up correspondence, in "one of the more thought-provoking journals" ("The green noodle does not amuse us. . . . The linguine, on the other hand, is quite delicious and not at all didactic"); even a graduation address happily not deficient in the mind-boggling pseudo-profundities expected, and, alas, usually forthcoming, on such occasions: "More than any other time in history, mankind faces a crossroads. One path leads to despair and utter hopelessness. The other, to total extinction. Let us pray we have the wisdom to choose correctly."

Allen's literary endeavors are rather more than, as his title would have it, side effects. . . . In some of the present pieces Allen comes across as a stand-up comic working sitting down.

"Keep it light," Lenny Mendel muses in **"The Shallowest Man"** while visiting a dying friend, "keep the one-liners coming." The American comedic genius flourishes on them. Our most successful entertainers, Bob Hope, Henny Youngman, Ronald Reagan, and the rest, not to mention Neil Simon on Broadway, all keep the one-liners coming. I found a lot of them in *Side Effects* quite funny. In **"Remembering Needleman,"** Sandor Needleman, obsessed with death, confides, "I much prefer cremation to burial in the earth, and both to a weekend with Mrs. Needleman." He is in the end cremated with a hat on: "A first, I believe," the narrator notes. (pp. 1-2)

Other gags fall flat. ''He has two sons by Margaret Figg—one normal, the other simpleminded, though it is hard to tell the difference unless someone hands them each a yo-yo.'' Any attempt to get a laugh out of a yo-yo carries some air of desperation. The hallucinating hero of **''Nefarious Times We Live In''** recalls ''seeing Frankenstein stroll through Covent Gardens with a hamburger on skis.'' Frankenstein references are fairly desperate too, and Allen surely knows enough to distinguish between the Doctor and his Monster. At such moments the subliminal laugh track becomes intrusive, although this fan was never tempted to switch channels.

Between covers, as on film, the Big Apple defines Allen's favored perimeters. We are in the Manhattan of *Manhattan:* I think of the prologue, stunning despite, or maybe in part because of, the black and white; all Gershwin and fireworks. It is the New York of subscribers to *The New Yorker* and *The New York Review of Books*, of concert goers taking in Brahms at Lincoln Center, art lovers enjoying a Matisse exhibition at the Museum of Modern Art, apartment dwellers knocking back Valpolicella and finger foods in their Manhattan towers on Central Park West. Genteelly educated, middle-class Jewish.

We hear of shrinks and high holidays; Aunt Rose waxes hysterical over the prospect of her young nephew marrying a 55-year-old *shiksa*. The references may at times puzzle WASPs in the sticks. (pp. 2, 14)

Mostly, though, the name-dropping and other references are not calculated to stir cultural anxieties. The reverse rather; they reassure Allen's audience that they too have indeed paid their dues to the intelligentsia. Existentialism, ontology, hermeneutics. Malraux, Kafka, Wittgenstein, Max Planck, Hannah Arendt, and Willie Maugham. Murals by Orozco, Emil Jannings in *The Blue Angel,* the figure in Edvard Munch's ''The Scream.'' For *New York Review* regulars, Robert Craft on Stravinsky. Invoking T. S. Eliot, listening to Vivaldi. Uplift without strain. You don't have to have visited the Huntington Library art gallery in San Marino to realize that, when Moses Goldworm in **''A Giant Step for Mankind''** turns ''a shade of blue invariably associated with Thomas Gainsborough,'' you are expected to think of ''The Blue Boy'' everybody associates with that master. And you don't have to be able to tell contemporary ontology from Heinz baked beans to enjoy **''Remembering Needleman.''**

But the greatest treat of *Side Effects* is **''The Kugelmass Episode,''** which is alone worth the not exorbitant admission tab. A professor of humanities at City College and miserably married, Kugelmass yearns for romance. One night a magician phones to bring a little exotica into Kugelmass' life. For a double sawbuck The Great Persky tosses his client and a paperback *Madame Bovary* into his magic cabinet, and three taps later Kugelmass is transported to Emma Bovary's bedroom in Yonville. She speaks in the fine accents of the paperback English translation. They stroll in the French countryside, and Kugelmass, from City College, rescues the bored matron from her crass rural existence.

Students in lit classes across the country begin to ask, ''Who is this character on page 100? A bald Jew is kissing Madame Bovary.'' Months pass; a passionate liaison develops. Kugelmass transports Emma to a suite at the Plaza. '''I cannot get my mind around this,' a Stanford professor said. 'First a strange character named Kugelmass, and now she's gone from the book. Well, I guess the mark of a classic is that you can reread it a thousand times and always find something new.''' Retri-

bution inevitably follows. In Allen's moral world the joys of proscribed sex exact their Talmudic penalties. The last story is, indeed, appropriately entitled **''Retribution,''** and its last word are ''Oy vey,'' best translated as—well—''Oy vey.'' (p. 14)

> *S. Schoenbaum, ''What Woody Wrote,'' in* Book World—The Washington Post, *September 21, 1980, pp. 1-2, 14.*

JOHN LAHR

As schlepper triumphant, Woody Allen is living refutation of every Jewish mother's nightmare: a 60-pound weakling who has parlayed his inheritance of fear, self-hate and love of finger foods into a fortune big enough to buy up all the chopped liver on the Upper West Side. Even when he lays an egg—and in *Side Effects* he lays a cake (10 eggs)—you can't be too stern with a man who asks, ''How is it possible to find meaning in a finite world given my waist and shirt size?''

Two of these 16 short pieces—**''The Kugelmass Episode''** and **''Fabrizio's: Criticism and Response''**—are brilliant flights of fantasy whose comic detail and inspired silliness are at once dramatic and controlled. In **''The Kugelmass Episode,''** an aging professor from C.C.N.Y., tired and terrified of his second wife, dreams out loud to his psychiatrist of being reborn by a passionate relationship. He wants sex with no strings; and he ends up going to a magician who puts him in a time machine with his favorite work of fiction, *Madame Bovary*. Kugelmass can hardly believe his luck. ''My God, I'm doing it with Madame Bovary! . . . Me, who failed freshman English.'' But ingeniously, Kugelmass not only walks into the book but into everybody else's copy of *Madame Bovary;* nobody can understand where he's come from. Kugelmass brings Emma to New York, sets her up at the Plaza, and she soon becomes as much a virago as his wife. ''Get me back into that novel or marry me,'' Emma says to him. ''Meanwhile I want to get a job or go to class, because watching TV all day is the pits.'' Finally, with Emma back in the novel, Kugelmass tries to go on another trip. But, by mistake, a remedial Spanish textbook is thrown into the machine; and Mr. Allen gives his story one final superb surrealist filip with Kugelmass ''running for his life over a barren, rocky terrain as the word *tener* ('to have')— a large and hairy irregular verb—raced after him on its spindly legs.''

In **''Fabrizio's: Criticism and Response,''** Mr. Allen uses as his premise an intellectual debate about an Italian restaurant to send up the uses and abuses of learning, and the letters column of the *New York Review of Books*. He is never in higher spirits or in more terrific form than when Fabian Plotnick is describing the social implications of the chef's antipasto: ''Was Spinelli trying to say that all life was represented here in his antipasto, with the black olives an unbearable reminder of mortality? If so, where was the celery?'' Plotnick has a hilarious line of lit-crit name-dropping. ''As Hannah Arendt told me once,'' he concludes, the restaurant's prices are ''reasonable without being historically inevitable.'' There ensues a correspondence about the article, with Plotnick being reminded of his own essay ''Eliot, Reincarnation and Zuppa di Clams'' and taken to task for his ''revisionist history'' by a writer who calls the restaurant a Stalinist hotbed. . . .

Many of Mr. Allen's stories indulge in broad burlesque imagery that might work on the screen but lies like latkes on the page— a man suffocated by a rolltop desk (**''Remembering Needle-**

man''), a murderer's gun stuck in his victim's ear ("**The Condemned**"), a toupee shooting through the roof ("**The UFO Menace**"). Mr. Allen is better when he gets closer to the anger and panic in his heart. In "**Nefarious Times We Live In**," Mr. Allen's paranoia has a field day as he explains the events leading up to Willard Pogrebin taking a shot at Gerald Ford. Pogrebin is kidnapped by a religious sect and made to witness ''a black mass in which hooded adolescent acolytes chanted the words, 'oh wow,' in Latin.'' He becomes a follower of the Reverend Chow Bok Ding, ''a moon-faced charismatic, who combined the teachings of Lao-Tze with the wisdom of Robert Vesco.'' He is almost tortured to death by two men ''who sang country and western music to me until I agreed to do anything they wanted.'' Wit is a great pesticide; and here Mr. Allen uses the wisecrack to swat away many of the harassing stupidities of American life. (p. 3)

In "**Nefarious Times We Live In**" and "**Fabrizio's**", Mr. Allen's trivializing wit finds its target. But too often in *Side Effects* Mr. Allen's potshots are wide of the mark. In "**My Speech to the Graduates**" he writes: ''The Government is unresponsive to the needs of the little man. Under five-seven, it is impossible to get your Congressman on the phone.'' It's easy to imagine Mr. Allen giggling over the typewriter at the line, but his silliness often gets the best of him. In "**By Destiny Denied**," a parody treatment of a best seller, Mr. Allen goes in for sub-Perelman baroque: ''Years ago, Blanche would have been considered pretty, though not later than the Pleistocene epoch.'' And in "**Reminiscences: Places and People**," Mr. Allen's appetite for the outrageous image gets him nowhere: ''Six months later, I awake in a Mexican hospital completely bald and clutching a Yale pennant. It has been a fearful experience, and I am told that when I was delirious with fever and close to death's door I ordered two suits from Hong Kong.'' The broadness of the joke defeats Mr. Allen's surreal intention and shows his sloppiness. The words sound funny, but the situation doesn't support them, and so they sink. (pp. 3, 55)

The attenuation of Mr. Allen's talent is nowhere more apparent than in his tired one-act President Lincoln play, "**The Query**." At one point Lincoln admits to his wife: ''I was too preoccupied with getting the quick laugh. I allowed a complex issue to elude me just so I could get a few chuckles from my cabinet.'' Mr. Allen is a smart man; he knows when he's vamping even when the public doesn't.

The reader picks through this beggar's banquet, looking for good bits. Mr. Allen's meditations on philosophy provide the choicest laughs, showing off his keen intelligence and his persona as cosmic kvetcher. He parodies Sartre, Kafka, Socrates. . . .

In a throwaway culture, Mr. Allen presents himself as wisecracking detritus, an empty shell with a big mouth. An entrepreneur of impotence, his persona is perfect for the society's sense of retreat. (p. 55)

> *John Lahr, "A Shrug in Place of a Pratfall," in* The New York Times Book Review, *October 26, 1980, pp. 3, 55.*

SANFORD PINSKER

[*Side Effects*] is preoccupied with the fate of modern man, that endangered species Allen defines as ''any person born after Nietzsche's edict that 'God is dead,' but before the hit recording 'I Wanna Hold Your Hand'.'' The sixteen sketches . . . rake over the usual Allen coals of love and death, angst and despair, bagels and lox. . . . (p. 634)

Granted, much of the humor in *Side Effects* has a familiar ring. Allen's imagination works best in that special realm where the High Brow idea and the urban (read: Jewish) detail are forced to share space, often on opposing sides of a semi-colon. In "**Remembering Needleman**," for example, we are told that Sandor Needleman ''differentiated between existence and Existence, and knew that one was preferable, but could never remember which . . . 'God is silent,' he was fond of saying, 'now if we can only get Man to shut up.''' Or in "**The Lunatic's Tale**," we are encouraged to shower ''an appropriate hostility toward all deserving targets: politicians, television, facelifts, the architecture of housing projects, men in leisure suits, film courses, and people who begin sentences with 'basically'.''

That much said, however, let me now suggest that Woody Allen's comic writing differs from his previous work as a stand-up comedian and from his ongoing career as a filmmaker, however much the same preoccupations persist. The discipline comic writing requires makes one literary, bookish, part of a Tradition that includes the likes of Robert Benchley, George Ade, James Thurber, E. B. White and S. J. Perelman. It is no coincidence that most of these comic giants are associated with *The New Yorker* magazine, nor is it surprising that Allen would want to count himself in their number. What looks for all the world like a stream-of-very-funny-consciousness is, in fact, the product of hard work and a half-dozen drafts. But to twist a phrase made famous by Harold Ross, *The New Yorker*'s founder: Woody Allen does not write for the pimply teenager from Dubuque. His congenial turf is not restricted to what passes for our popular culture and this, more than anything else, separates his humor from the trendy, and shallower, high-jinks of ''Saturday Night Live'' or stand-up comics like Steve Martin and David Brenner.

Put another way: one of the more pleasant ''side effects'' of modernist culture is Woody Allen's humor. His sketches are a way of gauging what happens when the solemn manifestoes of Kierkegaard or Heidegger or Kafka become the stuff of college courses. . . . The dilemma, of course, is that modernist ideas have been debased and contemporary ''ideas'' are vacuous. Choose the former and you runt the risk of sounding pretentious; opt for the latter and you are reduced to saying ''you know'' far more than is good for any of us. The result is a neurotic stand-off, one that, for Woody Allen, is likely to produce more collections of humor and more films than it is solutions.

Meanwhile, Allen adds his comic asides to our century's stockpile of images for ontological frustration. Consider the following from "**By Destiny Denied**":

> Pinchuck is a nervous man who fishes in his spare time but has not caught anything since 1923. ''I guess it's not in the cards,'' he chortles. But when an acquaintance pointed out that he was casting his line into a jar of sweet cream he grew uneasy.

Granted, there are lesser moments in *Side Effects;* not every non sequitur manages to avoid the sophomore slump. For example, in a parody of the Socratic dialogues one character can't quite resist pointing out that Isosceles ''has a great idea for a new triangle.'' One wishes that he would have, because discretion is at least as much a part of humor as it is of valor. But small reservations aside, the general level of *Side Effects* makes it painfully clear that Woody Allen has no serious competition as our generation's most sophisticated, most significant humorist. (pp. 635-36)

Sanford Pinsker, "Angst & Despair, Bagels & Lox," in Commonweal, Vol. CVII, No. 20, November 7, 1980, pp. 634-36.

FELICIA HARDISON LONDRÉ

Sex, Death, and *God* are three one-act plays by Woody Allen on the three subjects that preoccupy him most. Sex, death, and God are also important in the work of British dramatist Tom Stoppard.... Both Allen and Stoppard instinctively resort to comedy in handling philosophical concerns about human existence. Sex has always been spoofed in the theatre, and death has had its share of humorous treatments, but a jocular approach to questions about the nature of God is less commonplace. Therefore, in comparing Allen's and Stoppard's use of comic devices to make serious points, I shall concentrate on two plays that feature philosophical discussion of the existence of God: Woody Allen's *God* (1975) and Tom Stoppard's *Jumpers* (1972). (p. 346)

The Woody Allen character is not the protagonist of *God,* although Allen does have a role in the play. In *God,* the hero is called simply The Actor, and the action occurs on a stage. At the beginning and at the end of *God,* the Actor complains to a character named The Writer that the play lacks a satisfactory ending. This circular construction reinforces the metaphor of man as actor in repetitive cycles of human existence on the stage of life. Both the Actor and the Writer are aware that they are characters in a play created by Woody Allen. They telephone Woody Allen in the course of the action to check with him about the apparent departure from the script when a girl named Doris Levine comes out of the audience to interact with them on stage. Thus, on one level, Woody Allen, who is heard but not seen, functions as God. (p. 347)

Within Woody Allen's *God* is an ancient Greek drama called "The Slave" by the Writer, who plays Hepatitis in his own play. The Actor—Diabetes—plays the title role, and Doris Levine participates in the action as the slave's girlfriend. Since Hepatitis does rewrites on the script and authorizes the rental of a God machine to improve the ending of his play, he too is a creator at a certain level. Another contender for god-status is Lorenzo Miller, a writer who claims to have created the audience that is present in the theatre. His claim seems legitimate when certain audience members behave exactly as he predicted they would. Finally, there is Zeus in the God machine, who declaims: "I am Zeus, God of Gods! Worker of miracles! Creator of the universe! I bring salvation to all!" The multiplicity of possible gods in *God* recalls a theme that runs through much of Allen's work: the difficulty of distinguishing between the real and the ersatz.

At every level of *God* the characters pose the question: "Is there a god?" In Hepatitis's play, the slave carries the one-word message "yes," but even that assertion proves ambiguous. The content of Woody Allen's play tends to deny the existence of God, but its form suggests otherwise. For one thing, it progresses backward from a modern, godless dramatic construct to the classical Greek idiom, in which religious ceremony and theatre were synonymous. Despite the chaos of a dramatic action that includes Groucho Marx chasing Blanche DuBois across the stage, and a man in the audience ripping the blouse off an usherette and chasing her up the aisle, we know that there is an ultimate authority for what occurs in the theatrical production. This is pointed out by Woody Allen's telephoned intervention in the play-within-the-play, as well as in the frame story. Even if the script—like human existence—*seems* uncontrolled to those who are caught up in it, there is still a script and there is a creator behind it. (pp. 347-48)

That modern man is confused and helpless without God is a basic premise of both *Jumpers* and *God.* Both plays dramatize this quandary by setting it in contrast to a survival from a more stable order when truths could be taken "on trust."... In *God,* stability is sought within the ritual framework of classical Greek drama; this refuge deteriorates when Diabetes, the Actor, rebels against the Writer's script and tries to change it to make himself a hero. Hepatitis, the Writer, cries: "This is a very serious play with a message! If it falls apart, they'll never get the message." With a mere actor taking things into his own hands, the work does indeed fall apart—a snowballing build-up of nonsensical actions that sweep the Actor and the Writer back to zero again.

The technique of building to some kind of climactic statement and then undercutting, deflating, or trivializing it is used by both Allen and Stoppard. Allen's handling is always concise, as in this line spoken by Doris Levine: "But without God, the universe is meaningless. Life is meaningless. We're meaningless. *(Deadly pause.)* I have a sudden and overpowering urge to get laid." (pp. 349-50)

Another frequently used comic device is the reversal of expectations.... In *God,* having learned that a messenger bearing bad news is customarily put to death, Diabetes hesitates to deliver his one-word message, "yes," to the king until he can be sure that the question is not something like "does the queen have the clap?" The king reveals his "question of questions: is there a god?" and Diabetes confidently responds, "yes." Our expectations are reversed when, instead of giving Diabetes a reward for good news, the king tells him: "If there is a god, then man is not responsible and I will surely be judged for my sins.... Judged for my sins, my crimes. Very horrible crimes, I am doomed. This message you bring me dooms me for eternity."

Other sources of comedy in both plays are incongruity and the deflation of pretentiousness. Allen's *God* abounds with anachronisms, as when the Greek chorus forgets what show it is in and sings, "Poor Professor Higgins—." Comic mix-ups of props, a standard farcical device, occur in both plays. Twice, in *God,* the wrong message is read. Diabetes at first produces, instead of the message for the king, one that reads, "For Best Supporting Actor, the winner is—(the name of the actor playing Hepatitis)." Later, a Western Union Delivery Boy arrives with a telegram from the author to the audience; he starts to sing "Happy Birthday," then realizes his mistake and switches to "God is dead. You're on your own." (pp. 350-51)

Verbal comedy is the mainstay of both *Jumpers* and *God,* and it ranges from the lowly pun to in-jokes for literati. In *God,* the actor who is to descend in the God machine is told to get into his "Zeus suit."... *Jumpers* contains a number of *double entendres,* but only Woody Allen manages to integrate sexual meaning with a reference to God or philosophy. In *God,* Blanche DuBois explains her unmotivated entrance: "I've got to get into another play, a play where God exists ... somewhere where I can rest at last. That's why you must put me in your play and allow Zeus, young and handsome Zeus to triumph with his thunderbolt." The joke is richer with meaning if one recalls the scene in *A Streetcar Named Desire* in which Blanche attempts to seduce a young newspaper boy, and, in another scene, Blanche's line when Mitch finally proposes to her: ''Sometimes—there's God—so quickly!''

Such jokes based on literary or philosophical allusions are probably the most frequently recurring comic device in both *Jumpers* and *God.* Both plays contain variations on Descartes's dictum *Cogito, ergo sum.* Doris Levine in *God* says: ''I think, therefore I am. Or better yet, I *feel.*''... In *God,* most of Allen's intellectual jokes depend upon a knowledge of classical Greek dramatic literature, as in this exchange: ''King Oedipus?'' ''Yes.'' ''I hear he lives with his mother.'' (pp. 351-52)

Although Allen and Stoppard are best known for their verbal humor, *God* and *Jumpers* contain liberal doses of visual humor, including slapstick and sight gags.... In *God,* Diabetes recalls reading about a woman who was stabbed to death in the subway while sixteen people looked on and didn't help. ''If one person had the guts to help her,'' he says, ''maybe she'd be here today.'' Immediately, a woman enters with a knife in her chest and announces, ''I am here.'' Finally, there are such spectacular visual effects as the pyramid of philosopher-gymnasts in *Jumpers,* and in *God,* the deus ex machina. Zeus, in a trial demonstration, descends ''hurling thunderbolts majestically'' to the accompaniment of ''thunder and fabulous lightning.''

In both plays the comedy lurches to a momentary, sickening halt just before the end.... In *God,* the actor playing Zeus is strangled on the wires of the God machine. Somebody pulled the wrong lever, and his neck is broken; this God is indeed dead.

In neither play does the shocking moment of truth actually resolve the question of God's existence. As thoughtful writers, neither Stoppard nor Allen is inclined to offer a simple or intuitive answer to a problem that defies their considerable analytical skills. Stoppard has said: ''My plays are a lot to do with the fact that *I just don't know.*'' The frequency with which the ultimate question crops up in Woody Allen's short prose pieces and in his films (most notably *Love and Death*) suggests that Allen does not know either. What is most to the point, however, is not that the two dramatists are manifestly unable to supply answers, but that they are willing to grapple, in the commercial theatre, with ponderous and abstract issues. Today's theatre abounds both with thought-provoking serious plays and with mindless comedies, but Tom Stoppard and Woody Allen stand apart because they are able to marry ideas with fun. (pp. 352-53)

The comic devices that both playwrights use—deflation of a climactic build-up, reversal of expectations, incongruity, mix-up of props, and spectacular effects that fizzle—vitalize the same basic premise: that man's uncertainty about God is a cause of extreme confusion in modern life. From *God* one may infer that society is all too ready to embrace an array of phony creators or false gods. *Jumpers* depicts a society that can reason the one God out of existence but which, without the mystery of that God, cannot apply any sort of logic to its own social structure. The uncertainty that still exists at the end of both plays corroborates Woody Allen's observation that ''when comedy approaches a problem, it kids it but it doesn't resolve it.''

Tom Stoppard and Woody Allen use comic devices not so much to provide an answer to the ultimate question as to examine it and to wonder at its continuing importance in the mind of modern man. The plot and the philosophical argument in *Jump-*

ers and in *God* are propelled forward on waves of laughter, but the maddening inconclusiveness that finally stalls them is a purposeful reminder that comedy is serious business. The laughter provoked by these plays is intended to serve as a stimulus to thought. (p. 353)

Felicia Hardison Londré, ''Using Comic Devices to Answer the Ultimate Question: Tom Stoppard's 'Jumpers' and Woody Allen's 'God','' in Comparative Drama, *Vol. 14, No. 4, Winter, 1980-81, pp. 346-54.*

JACK KROLL

We tend to use up our favorite artists—chew them up and spit them out. A certain amount of pre-spitting mastication is going on now with Woody Allen. Some people think his recent movies have shown signs of arrogance and conceit. Maybe that's why Allen's new play, ***The Floating Light Bulb***, is such a modest work. Allen is a self-taught artist in every way—we've been watching his education in films now for fifteen years. ***The Floating Light Bulb*** is his third play and his first since ***Play It Again, Sam***, twelve years ago. So there's a kind of time warp in his theater education; this play is redolent of Clifford Odets, Tennessee Williams, Arthur Miller, the main line of American theater. Well, it makes sense that Allen doesn't come on after twelve years as some post-Beckett, neo-absurdist playwright with sprinkles of Grotowski, Peter Brook and East African tribal rites. Give him time, he'll get there. But seriously, folks, Allen has given us a small but sweet, shrewd, funny and loving comedy of heartbreak.

All of Allen's work is about heartbreak—he can hear the seismic crackling in his own heart without a stethoscope. In ***Light Bulb,*** 16-year-old Paul Pollack lives in a Brooklyn tenement, like the young Woody. His down-at-the-heels family is a platoon of balked dreamers. Paul is a homely, shy, stammering boy who plays hooky and keeps to his bedroom practicing mail-order magic tricks like the floating light bulb. Enid, his mother, always wanted to be a Broadway dancer and devises pathetic at-home business enterprises that lose money. Max, her husband, is a struggling waiter who plays the numbers, is deep in debt to loan sharks and is about to take off with his girlfriend Betty. The family realist is Paul's younger brother, Steve, the wise-cracking mini-jester of this seedy dynasty of fantasts. In the pivotal scene, Enid pries Paul loose from his bedroom to audition for Jerry Wexler, a theatrical manager who turns out to be just another tacky dreamer.

This scene, which finally focuses the play's somewhat scrappy structure, is an Allen classic. Not only do everyone's dreams collide and collapse like slapstick comics, but one final dream is born and dies right before your eyes. That's Wexler's instant infatuation with Enid, which is no more practical than his hope of stardom for his talking-dog act. You'll never see anything more heartbreakingly hilarious than chubby [Jerry Wexler], perspiring with passion that he instantly sublimates as he holds out his hand to Enid and, with a smile of suicidal sincerity, says ''Shake.''

Jack Kroll, ''The Heartbreak Kid,'' in Newsweek, *Vol. XCVII, No. 19, May 11, 1981, p. 93.*

ROBERT BRUSTEIN

Woody Allen is a newcomer to realism, which seems to be another stage in his development as a literary impersonator.

Hitherto we have seen Woody Allen trapped inside a novel by Tolstoy, Woody Allen sequestered within a movie by Bergman; now we have Woody Allen entombed in a play by Tennessee Williams. The Jewish talent for impersonation may be linked to Jewish survival (imitation being the pathway to assimilation). But whereas Norman Mailer seriously believes himself to be Ernest Hemingway and Arthur Miller confuses himself with Henrik Ibsen, Woody Allen has usually maintained a satiric distance between himself and the objects of his mimetic gifts, deflating himself along with the works he was parodying. As his fame increased, however, and he began to take himself more seriously as an artist, the distance between Woody Allen and his models began to narrow until he is in danger of becoming something of a satiric object himself.

This shrinking distance can be seen in the way his work has become increasingly autobiographical in recent years, reflecting his increasing sense of self-importance. His new play [*The Floating Light Bulb*], may not be exactly true to Allen's childhood history, but it is close enough to what we know about the author to raise suspicions about his continuing self-absorption. And the central figure has been cast with an actor bearing such a close physical resemblance to his creator, including a prominent Woody Allen schnozz, that it is difficult not to conclude that we are witnessing personal secrets. If so, the play catches Woody in a moment of profound self-pity. It seems to be the intention of the writing (not to mention the playing) to create a climate of understanding for the young hero in his relations with his family—one of the elements usually associated with a playwright's first play. Another symptom of juvenilia is the close relationship of the work to a literary model—in this case, Williams's *The Glass Menagerie*. As critics have already noted, Allen has cast his young surrogate in the role of Williams's Laura, substituting the boy's collection of magical tricks for Laura's collection of glass animals. In place of Williams's decaying southern belle with delusions of grandeur, Allen has created a hearty Jewish mama from Canarsie, but one with the same inflated expectations of her children. And he has replaced the Gentleman Caller with a visiting theatrical manager named Jerry Wexler, for whom, like Laura, the young boy is expected to perform. (As expected, the audition is a flop when the boy gets sick.)

The visit is a flop for the mother, too, whose husband is preparing to desert her. Allen contrives a long and rather irrelevant romantic scene between the mother and the manager in the second act which is concluded when he reveals that he is going off to Arizona with his sick mother. The play ends with the family trapped in its misery. I half-expected to see a Williams legend descend from the flies: "Things have a way of turning out so badly." The only variant from the Williams borrowings comes when Allen steals a device from Albee's *Virginia Woolf;* the mother starts to hit her husband with a cane, only to have it turn into a bouquet of flowers—one of her son's discarded magical tricks. (pp. 26, 28)

I hope this brief affair with American realism, unhappy though it must be, will have some salutary effect on his future work, if only to convince Woody Allen that he creates his best art out of his observation of others, and his most convincing reality out of the distance he maintains between himself and the objects of his satire. (p. 28)

> *Robert Brustein, "The Limits of Realism," in* The New Republic, *Vol. 184, No. 21, May 23, 1981, pp. 25-6, 28.*

MARK SHECHNER

Although American Jews are no longer bilingual and the striking antinomies of ghetto life are nowhere to be found in the smooth-as-velour continuities of the American middle-class, habits of mind that were fostered in the Old Country stubbornly persist as deep structures of consciousness. The habit of self-irony remains long after certain ironies native to the ghetto have been eradicated, gaining reinforcement from new discrepancies that are uniquely American, discrepancies that attend upward mobility and cultural assimilation. The contradictions of the ancient Semite, who, in the words of the British Arabist C. M. Doughty, "sits in a cloaca up to his neck, but his brow touches the heavens," has been replaced in some measure by the ironies of cultural change and generational succession. The modern Jew sits in Brooklyn up to his neck, but he works in Manhattan. . . . The scale of irony is infinitely reduced and the distance is now spanned by the IRT instead of prayer and ceremony, but the form is familiar. As Woody Allen has advanced its techniques, such irony produces the comedy of the modern Jew versus his ancestors, or Beverly Hills in light of Warsaw, or, so foreshortened is the scope of our history, Beverly Hills in light of New York. In purely diagrammatic form it is the comedy of Allen's **"Hasidic Tales"** (in *Getting Even*), in which Rabbi Baumel of Vitebsk embarks on a fast "to protest the unfair law prohibiting Russian Jews from wearing loafers outside the ghetto" or Rabbi Yitzchok Ben Levi, the great Jewish mystic, applies cabalistic numerology to horse racing and hits the daily double at Aqueduct fifty-two days running. Now, such inventions are sheer formula: place the ancient and the modern side by side and you've got a joke. And it is precisely in such cases where the humor is nothing more than the routine application of technique, and not very funny, that its machinery is most clearly visible.

Yet when Allen lets the habits of self-irony and cultural aggression float free and create their own fiendish combinations, fantastic scenarios begin to emerge, such as Fielding Mellish's dream, in *Bananas,* in which two monks bearing enormous crosses come to blows over a parking place on Wall Street, or the routine in *Everything You Always Wanted to Know About Sex But Were Afraid to Ask* in which Gene Wilder takes an Armenian sheep to a hotel for a night of lovemaking, or the wonderful lobster-chasing scene in *Annie Hall,* where the gourmet in Alvy Singer suddenly yields to the nervous boy from Brooklyn who isn't quite ready to handle the aggressive, snapping *traif* (unkosher food) that his dreams of *savoir faire* have conjured up.

That the Yiddish element in Allen's comedy merges so easily with the American tells us something about the current state of American comedy and culture. Allen's humor almost never puts the Jewish side of him against the American; it customarily levels both barrels side by side against Europe and *Kultur:* Ibsen and Strindberg, Tolstoy and Dostoevsky, Ingmar Bergman, Kierkegaard and Freud. Bogart and baseball, gin rummy and the protracted sexual adolescence stand for much the same thing, Brooklyn, which is as distant from Manhattan as it is from Europe culturally, making it a convenient base of operations for strikes on both. What Americanness and *Yiddishkeit* have in common is a sense of cultural inferiority before the high culture of *Mitteleuropa,* making their assaults upon that culture exercises in *ressentiment.*

The dialectic at the heart of Allen's comedy recalls in rough outline Van Wyck Brooks's conception of American culture as a realm divided between the spiritual and the practical, the incorporeal and the commercial, the highbrow and the low-brow. But where Brooks, in *America's Coming of Age,* was describing the broader antinomies at work in American life, the Jewish version of the dialectic appears to be at work within the individual Jew, who is highbrow and lowbrow unto himself. A substantial line of humor that runs through comedians as different as Jack Benny, Henny Youngman, Morey Amsterdam, Harpo Marx, and Allen himself is built upon the standoff between *Kunst* and candy store. (pp. 234-36)

As we now know from watching Woody Allen's career, the logic of cultural subversion is reversible, and comedy can be unmasked to reveal *its* latent content, which may be depression or despair or terror. It is abundantly clear by now that Allen, in bringing his comedy to bear on the great masters of gloom like Kafka, Kierkegaard, and Bergman was not just dropping banana peels in the path of Western thought but mulling over concerns that had been dredged up by his own distraught imagination; setting up troublesome preoccupations of his own and then pulling out the rug.

Allen has been something of a closet tragedian all along, and the air of cosmic befuddlement that now colors his thought was there from the start. He has taken to telling interviewers, "My real obsessions are religious," and, "Death is the big obsession behind all I've done," and "The metaphor for life is a concentration camp. I do believe that." This last, he told *Time* magazine after *Manhattan* was released, was a line he had cut from that film but intended to use in his next. And despite efforts on Allen's part to keep *Manhattan* from drowning, as *Interiors* did, in too metaphysical a view of the modern condition, the void sneaks inexorably in. So, when Isaac Davis and Mary take refuge from a storm in Hayden Planetarium and conduct a flirtatious tête-à-tête amid lunar and nebular skyscapes, Allen, as director, is not just having fun with his sets; he's also reminding us that "we're lost out here in the stars."

Since depression, as everyone knows, is the special malaise of intellectuals, the comedian who admits to being even mildly depressed is bound to be taken for an intellectual comedian, as Allen often is, despite his frequent pleas that he is nothing more than a funnyman out in pursuit of the next laugh. It is true that his exploitation of ideas can scarcely conceal his ambivalence toward them, even now that he has taken to brooding in public over God, death, and *l'univers concentrationnaire.* He has the autodidact's contempt for formal schooling, and his comedy employs general ideas in much the same way that a hamburger employs meat. (pp. 236-37)

Allen's world of late has been of singles in distress, who are predominantly urban, affluent (or, at any rate, not pressed for money), educated, divorced, schooled in breakup and breakdown, for whom the analysis is a substitute for the marriage and the analyst a surrogate for the family. It is, then, a social enclave that best exemplifies what Christopher Lasch calls "the culture of narcissism." As such, it is not a place at all (New York) but a way of life that has taken hold wherever the middle class has graduated from sufficiency to surplus and found the end of the rainbow to be also the end of the rope. It is here that success breeds despair, leisure yields to boredom, and the cost of modern life is more visible for being so much higher than that of the goods that are conspicuously consumed. ("I ran into my ex wife the other day, and I hardly recognized her with her wrists closed.") In a faltering monologue at the beginning of *Manhattan,* Allen's Isaac Davis speaks portentously of Manhattan as "a metaphor for the decay of contemporary culture," as though to prepare us for a tour through the city

of dreadful night. Scarcely. There isn't an act of terror in the film and not even a subway joke, let alone a subway mugging. Culture decomposes at the highest tax brackets, among tea rooms and sculpture galleries, to the strains of Gershwin. And Central Park is still for lovers. What distresses Allen is not what is happening to society but what is happening to that social class whose dreams were once scored by Gershwin, and which, having ascended to the skyline, has nothing left to look forward to save sexual adventurism. What do you give the man who has everything? A divorce.

We might well ask what is so Jewish about any of this, since Allen plays this as a Jewish drama. At first glance, little is. Jews have no patent on success and despair, and a footloose Jewish bachelor like Allen's Isaac Davis is scarcely going to reflect on the Torah or the tragic history of his people while cruising the Dalton School for a pickup. In fact, what is most Jewish about *Annie Hall, Manhattan,* and *Stardust Memories* is what is most American about them. The Jews, having found a home in the heart of the American middle-class, have inherited its conflicts: ambition vs. ethical probity, commerce vs. spirit, family vs. career, and it makes some sense to see Allen's recent films as footnotes to the history of immigrant success and therefore as reflections of the life that began on the Lower East Side and eventually arrived uptown by way of Brooklyn. It might well be said that Allen's ambiguous celebrations of uptown Manhattan are predicated upon a boyhood spent in Brooklyn, from which the Brooklyn Bridge must have seemed like a stairway to paradise. In a sense, Allen is following the lead of Abraham Cahan's *The Rise of David Levinsky* and, more recently, Saul Bellow's *Humboldt's Gift,* both examinations of the ironies of Jewish success. If his talents permitted, Allen might become the tragic historian of Jewish achievement.

I scarcely think, however, that Allen is conscious of so bold an intention, unless he is more socially conscious than he lets on. In *Manhattan,* a film basically about class and taste, he appears to take up social themes whose full ironies elude his grasp. But social history isn't always recorded best by those who have reflected on it most. The migration from Brooklyn to Manhattan may put a man in touch with the social drama of a culture without granting him any conceptual understanding of it. Allen plays catch-as-catch-can with his social themes, attacking them with whatever weapons come to hand: the one-liner, the cameo, the throwaway, the fragments of overheard conversation. But largely he approaches society through the bedroom door, as though the sexual habits of a culture could stand for its entire life, which, in some measure, they can. After all, the history of psychoanalysis is also the history of a particular phase of Western civilization, and psychoanalysis itself has been instrumental in forming the values of the modern world. Whether it is true or not that, as John Murray Cuddihy argues in his book, *The Ordeal of Civility,* Freud's sexual interpretation of culture is a special manifestation of Jewish alienation and rage, it does seem the case that both psychoanalysis and Jewish comedy share in common a genius for debunking social pieties by calling attention to their hidden motives. But whether Allen's brand of bedroom analysis is equal to the job of social analysis is another question. Consider *Manhattan.* It opens to find Isaac Davis twice-divorced, unemployed, about to have his private habits exposed in print by his second wife (now a lesbian who left him for another woman), and taking refuge in the arms of a seventeen-year-old senior at the Dalton School named Tracy, whom he is, in embarrassment, trying to dump. Enter Mary, a dippy, neurotic critic (of everything, it would seem) who is involved with Isaac's married friend, Yale, and romance slowly kindles between them, presided over by the lush strains of Gershwin's "Embraceable You," "Lady Be Good," and "Someone to Watch over Me." It culminates in a brief affair that lasts only until Yale can summon up the courage to leave his wife, claim Mary, and leave a heartbroken Isaac alone, full of regrets, and feeling very much the fool. The conclusion finds him at Tracy's door, begging for a reconciliation as she is preparing to depart for London and drama school. This sort of bed-swapping, home-breaking, breakup, makeup, 'cause I love you brand of living is Allen's version of the "decay of contemporary culture," and it does seem fairly bleak. Allen tries to play it as a romance, but there aren't enough moonbeams to go around. Post-Freudian culture, we're meant to understand, frees us for pleasure at the cost of loneliness and guilt; and modern guilt, unlike its Victorian antecedent, is not over the impulses we've repressed but over those we've acted out. This is a film about freedom and its discontents, and Allen never once has to invoke the death of God in explanation. Sex and boredom explain everything.

There is material here for a substantial criticism of the culture of narcissism, but Allen turns out to be doing something different, writing a romance (albeit a depressive one) and a comedy of manners in which the narcissism of taste that is under attack finally wins out because, it seems, Allen wants it to. Allen appears to be uncertain whether he wants to denounce middle-class ennui or exalt it, and so he does both, as though George Gershwin could be assimilated to, say, Herbert Marcuse without anyone's noticing the difference. Let us accept for the moment the film's romantic premise—that Isaac, at forty-two, has been foolish to give up his seventeen-year-old Tracy for the neurotic Mary, who was bound to drop him just as soon as Yale could get up the gumption to leave his wife. What are the appeals of Tracy that prompt Isaac to tell her at one point that she is "God's answer to Job?" Of course there is her low threshold of arousal, which makes her want to do most of her homework in Isaac's bed. She does respond passionately, much to the relief of Isaac, whose last wife has charged him with having changed her from a bisexual into a lesbian. But you needn't be seventeen to be embraceable. It is not for nothing that Allen's sex goddess is a kid, because the film's deepest idea, which is quite apart from any of that stuff about the decline of values, demands it. The underlying myth of *Manhattan* is that in a world of corrupt adults, redemption may come through the love of a child, or, since the redemption is sexual, the love of a teenager. *Manhattan* is a fairy tale for an age of sexual freedom, in which the hero is released into innocence *and* orgasm, providing a new twist to an old moral: *And they came together happily ever after.* Only thinking stands in the way of this; it is known as "intellectualizing," and it blocks the avenues to self-realization and erotic fulfillment. (pp. 238-41)

Allen has often been compared to Philip Roth, though it might be more pertinent just now to compare him to J. D. Salinger, a *New Yorker* writer of another generation in whose books a similar irony lends cover to an overwhelming sentimentality. For Salinger, too, sex is a threat, intelligence invariably a pretentious show of bogus erudition, and innocence a cherished and elusive virtue. Of course, Allen can admit sex while Salinger can only deny it frantically. But when Allen celebrates the adolescent love goddess in *Manhattan* he gives us an unwitting parody of *The Catcher in the Rye*, in which Phoebe Caulfield, by her innocence, proves to be her brother's only refuge. The fact that Allen's heroes, unlike Salinger's Seymour Glass in the story "A Perfect Day for Bananafish," use the bedroom for love and not death, doesn't mitigate their fear of women; it only promotes their terror a few grades, from junior high to high school level. The innocence Allen yearns for is that of the eternal sexual high school, while Salinger's is that of the threshold years, where all is yet a vast and terrifying portent. The latter trades on the kind of sexual mystification that points the way to the monastery or the ashram, while Allen's sexual mythos takes him to the playground. In *Manhattan*, Tracy is seventeen because Isaac Davis is scarcely older than that himself. Perpetual adolescence is Allen's great secret and his weapon. His film persona is nothing without it. He is the eternal kid.

Great comedy can be launched from that position, because the kid is granted special insights into the follies of the adult world, and because he has a dispensation from that world to be as sentimental or as belligerent as he pleases. Boys will be boys. Thus armed and vulnerable, he gives free rein to his imagination. Now, the kid's-eye view of the adult world won't always give you a persuasive criticism of society, since its powers of analysis are likely to be primitive, but it does permit explosive combinations of outrage and wit. Yet Allen has chosen to repudiate the imaginative advantages of playing the kid overtly, as he did in his earlier comedies, for more sober points of view. The kid is still very much there steaming with envy and resentment, but he is now cunningly disguised as a social critic. . . . In an effort to lend his work more contemporary significance, Allen has managed, in *Interiors* and *Manhattan,* to go off the shallow end. Taking leave of comedy, he has taken leave of his imagination as well. (pp. 241-42)

It is the sign of Allen's midlife maturation that where id once was now only ego is visible, and we can only lament the passing of a rare and gifted childhood. (p. 242)

> *Mark Shechner, "Woody Allen: The Failure of the Therapeutic," in* From Hester Street to Hollywood: The Jewish-American Stage and Screen, *edited by Sarah Blacher Cohen, Indiana University Press, 1983, pp. 231-44.*

JOHN LAHR

As America has become more educated and self-conscious, its humor has become more verbal and less physical. Allen is the bellwether of this change. The great American clowns of the early twentieth century were kinetic. Their antics epitomized both the panic and purposefulness of the industrial boom. . . . The new rhythm brought a new kind of laughter, which admitted the agitation and the credulity of a people that had always been restless in the midst of abundance. . . . The old clowns fed a young generation's will to run wild. The clown's pratfall was the emblem of the society's resilient hopefulness.

Where the old-timers reflected myths of hope, Allen reflects a myth of defeat. A sense of elegant dread has replaced hilarious excess. ("It's impossible to experience one's own death, and still carry a tune," Allen writes in *Getting Even*.) His humor is about emotional paralysis. It was the right subject for uneasy times when Allen first came on the scene in the mid-sixties. A conventional society wanted the titillation of the unconventional. Lenny Bruce found vulgarity; Mort Sahl found politics; and Allen—best exemplifying his narcissistic era—found himself. Allen's losing battles with his psyche substitute the shrug for the pratfall. . . . Allen is a veteran of more than two decades of psychoanalysis, his introspection reflects a society that now looks on behavior not as a mystery but as a system of motives and explanations. The old-timers were not in the habit of analysis: they concentrated on mayhem and left the meanings to others. "I never realized that I was doing anything but trying to make people laugh when I threw my custard pies and took my pratfalls," said Buster Keaton. The old-guard clowns promoted their fear as playfulness; Allen promotes it as exposition. Both are obsessed, the old-timers with their product and Allen with the added burden of his problems. The difference reflects a change in the society that made the clown and the audience that applauds him. The charm of action has been replaced by the charm of agony. (pp. 89-90)

Allen's conservative self-absorption is typical of his times. Whereas the early clowns took the dead world around them—the classroom, the courtroom, the boring job, the abusive authority figure—and gave it life, Allen's specialty is taking life and giving it a sense of death. . . . Allen's jokes turn death into a commercial proposition. The gags about evading terror are themselves evasions. They raise serious issues but refuse any serious conclusions:

> —The key here, I think, is to not think of death as an end but to think of it more as a very effective way to cut down on your expenses.
>
> —I don't believe in an afterlife although I'm bringing a change of underwear.
>
> —I don't want to achieve immortality through my work, I want to achieve it through not dying.

These funny lines have the shape of ideas, but are without insight. What they achieve is a mood of decline.

For the old guard, parody was just part of their comic arsenal; for Allen, it's his statement about life. Parody is skepticism acted out. When Groucho sent up the soliloquies in Eugene O'Neill's *Strange Interlude* or Bert Lahr's "Song of the Woodsman" skewered the vibrato of Chaliapin, they were mocking pretension. But Allen uses parody to show off his mastery of styles while trivializing the content. . . . (pp. 92-3)

Allen's compulsion to parody is the reflection of an imagination submerged more in art than in life. It signals an absence of curiosity and of will. The range of Allen's vicariousness is best dramatized in *Manhattan* (1979), in which his spokesman Ike Davis lists his reasons for staying alive: "I would say . . . Groucho Marx . . . Willie Mays. . . . the second movement of the Jupiter Symphony . . . Louis Armstrong's recording of 'Potatohead Blues' . . . Swedish movies, naturally . . . *Sentimental Education* by Flaubert. . . ." Unlike the proletarian funny men of the first half century, who read little and late . . . , Allen is the archetypal middle-class culture vulture for whom art is a false god. (p. 93)

Allen has filled his solitude with reading and movies; his mind percolates with references and borrowed images. In his brilliant story **"The Kugelmass Episode,"** the beleaguered Professor Kugelmass seeks emotional rebirth in some passionate relationship with no strings and finally goes to a magician, who puts him in a time machine with his favorite work of fiction. ("My God, I'm doing it with Madame Bovary," Kugelmass exclaims, hardly believing his luck. "Me who failed freshman English!") Kugelmass not only walks into the book but into everybody else's copy. When they see Madame Bovary, they see him. In his plays and movies, Allen has been doing the same thing: living in his favorite fictions.

This promiscuity with art forms is an affair from which Allen seems fated never to escape. "When I get an idea for a play," he told a biographer, "I think to myself 'What play does this most closely resemble that was successful?'" **Don't Drink the Water** (1966) is built on the premise of George S. Kaufman's *You Can't Take It With You* and the structure of John Patrick's *Teahouse of the August Moon,* **Play It Again Sam** (1972) amalgamates Bogart pastiche from *Casablanca* structured in imitation of George Axelrod's *The Seven Year Itch* in a story about a writer (as the stage direction reads) *"who daydreams of someday doing something important in either literature or film."* **God** (1975) is Allen's *Waiting for Godot,* except that God appears, strangled, toward the finale. Allen parodies great films in his attempt to be a significant filmmaker; as a result, his films end up being as much about film as life. **A Midsummer Night's Sex Comedy** (1982) is his vain attempt to marry Bergman's *Smiles of a Summer Night* with the farce in Renoir's *Rules of the Game;* **Stardust Memories** attempts Fellini's self-probing in *8½;* **Interiors** (1978) is Allen being Bergman via Chekhov's *The Three Sisters;* **Love and Death,** his parody of Russian literature, combines Bergman's *The Seventh Seal* with pastiches of Eisenstein and Chaplin. In all these films, Allen uses the camera as Kugelmass uses the time machine—to get himself into the classics. **Zelig** (1983) is the acme of this ambition, a cinematic conjuring trick that allows Allen to put himself among the fantasy figures of his past and present. Zelig's protean personality is parody incarnate. He can't help becoming like the people he's around. (pp. 93-4)

The problem with parody is that it takes its energy from other sources. This works fine for Allen in his early films, where he wants a plot on which to hang his jokes. But in his "serious" films, parody shows up his deficiencies. Allen doesn't have within himself the emotional resources to re-create in his own terms the narrative ideas and styles he admires. . . . Allen's inability to write from the inside of other people's predicaments reaches its apex in **Interiors,** which would have been more aptly titled *Exteriors.* This deadpan chronicle of a wife's vain attempt to win back her husband, and the impact of her anguish on her three daughters, attempts the profounder ironies of a philosophical overview. But mistaking gravity for seriousness, Allen weighs his stick-figure characters down with meanings. (p. 95)

In his prose, Allen thankfully is not worried about wisdom; he gives up the pose of rabbi and adopts the role of trickster. In the story **"Fabrizio's: Criticism and Response,"** Allen shows up the uses and abuses of education and dramatizes in three pages what *Manhattan* in an hour and a half never quite clinches, that education doesn't lead to understanding or wisdom. Using as a premise a debate about an Italian restaurant carried out in the style of the letters column of the *New York Review of Books,* Allen's cunning wit has a field day, with no abstractions and no apologies for his high spirits. (pp. 96-7)

Allen cannot rest on his substantial achievements as a comic writer. As he tries to force his comedy to carry more weight than it can hold, his real concerns become postures. The pose of the characters in his art films is that they are searching for meaning in a godless, decadent world. In **Love and Death,** Allen dances with Death. In **Annie Hall,** the very first speech announces: "Well, that's how I feel about life. Full of loneliness and misery and suffering and unhappiness and it's all over too quickly." Alvy Singer gives two books to Annie as clues to his character: *Death and Western Thought* and *Denial of Death.* Angst can be boned up; and Allen, like his characters, has learned it well. "Maturity has borne out my childhood," he says. "I'd always thought death was the sole driving force: I mean that our effort to avoid it is the only thing that gives impetus to our existence." Wonder has been replaced by worry; and instead of letting laughter renew life, Allen is in danger of scaring his comedy to death. In *Stardust Memories,* Sandy Bates revels in disintegration. "Hey," he asks his entourage of lawyer, press agent, and doctor, "did-did anybody read on the front page of the *Times* that matter is decaying? Am I the only one that saw that? The universe is gradually breaking down. There's not gonna be anything left . . . I'm not talking about my stupid little films here. I'm—Uh, eventually there's not gonna be any, any Beethoven or Shakespeare." Bates, who worries that his career is nothing more than a lifelong affair with his own image, flatters himself that such insights show his connection to the world.

Such confessions are a form of hiding, a means of exempting Allen and his characters from action. "Should I change my-my movie? Should I change my life?" whines Sandy Bates. But change requires sacrifice; and none of Allen's egotists is willing to risk that. "He saw reality too clearly," says Bates's analyst in a fantasy sequence of his film retrospective. "Faulty denial mechanism." In fact, Bates sees no reality at all: he merely chews the cud of his own emptiness. Bates, like Allen and all his comic spokesmen, suborns himself and others to his self-absorption. Far from wanting to shed despair, Allen and his comic surrogates relish it, savor it, wrap themselves in it, because the lacerations rationalize their sensational self-ishness. Inevitably, they *must* find no meaning. They have given up everything that imparts meaning, unwilling to commit themselves to relationships, to children, to life outside their immediate work, to a community larger than their own charmed circle. Isolated variously by work, fame, money, and self-consciousness, Allen's comic spokesmen see people more as a threat than as a promise of salvation. *"The mass of people looks slightly off-kilter, almost carnivorous in their need to see and touch Sandy,"* reads a stage direction for *Stardust Memories.* The implication of this attitude as dramatized in *Stardust Memories* and epitomized in Allen's self-absorption is that other people are not worth caring about. His showy vulnerability hides the pride of his despair. He pretends to be concerned about the world; but he is temperamentally unwilling to do anything about it. (pp. 97-8)

As a social reporter and cosmic kvetcher ("If God is testing us, why doesn't He give us a written?"), Allen is terrific. He can juggle adroitly with the academic jargon of the day (the philosopher-monster Sandor Needleman in "**Remembering Needleman**" is the author of *Styles of Modes* and *Non-Existence: What To Do When It Suddenly Strikes You*). But when he gives up the wisecrack for the role of wise man, Allen runs into trouble. His art films dramatize his separation from life and make this alienation seem like maturity. Allen is an entrepreneur of his alienation; his success at exploiting his wound makes it impossible for him to heal it. Suffering itself becomes a posture. (pp. 98-9)

> *John Lahr, "Woody Allen," in his* Automatic Vaude-
> ville: Essays on Star Turns, *Alfred A. Knopf, 1984,*
> *pp. 89-99.*

PEARL K. BELL

What is it about Woody Allen's style and our culture that has made him such a phenomenon? What is so strikingly different about his approach to the art of film? There may be three innovations that account for his success; and they are impressive.

One is the cunning skill with which he has adapted a modernist literary device for the cinema. Most movies still tell a story in the straightforward manner of the 19th-century novel. A linear narrative unfolds; and we sit in the dark, watching fictitious characters enact an invented story. But Woody Allen turns the conventional way of telling a story on its head. He invites us into his own life, and intrudes on the action with his own voice, commenting like a Greek chorus, or a *kibbitzer,* on the images he has devised. He doesn't stay behind the scenes, like most directors, but talks right into the camera, sharing with the audience his thoughts and his uncertainties about the right way to get the film moving. (p. 72)

The second: as we sit through such films as *Annie Hall, Manhattan,* and *Stardust Memories,* we don't feel we're looking at actors impersonating made-up characters. We seem to be looking at real people: the crowds waiting to get inside the cinema; the celebrities and groupies at Elaine's; above all, a man named Woody Allen, a neurotic Jewish intellectual who looks like a wimp but is really a very smart cookie. (pp. 72-3)

The third: Woody Allen has created a new kind of Jewish comedian who is not only smart and sassy but erudite as well. His wisecracks are festooned with names and titles covering a vast range of intellectual reference, from Socrates to Kafka, like the college reading-list for Humanities 101. For the millions in the audience who consider themselves part of the *culturati,* Allen's gags, crackling with literary know-how, dispense the balm of self-esteem. And the jokes are no mere laughing matter, but profound reflections on the foibles and hang-ups of our time. This comic must be a *khukhem,* the wise man of old. (p. 73)

Though Woody Allen thinks of himself as a highbrow, he is decidely uncertain about the way to play this role. Despite all the cultural baggage he unloads in his movies, he can't stop taking pot-shots at the brainy types who think he's nothing but a clown. He wants to be acclaimed as a serious artist, but doesn't have much use for those who do. . . .

He wants to have it both ways: to make art films that mock art films, to be intellectual and anti-intellectual at the same time, to show that Woody Allen knows the score and can't be aced by anyone. When Alvy Singer is driven nuts in *Annie Hall* by the trendy jargon of the Columbia professor (of "TV Media & Culture") standing behind him in the cinema queue, Allen brings Marshall McLuhan on camera (as if we're all waiting together) to puncture the fatuous "McLuhanesque" posturing. But if we've listened, the prof's terms *were* McLuhanesque, so who's kidding whom? He who laughs last may not know why he's laughing. (p. 74)

Woody Allen does have an identity problem, and it isn't funny. It is rooted most disturbingly, not in his dilettantism or in the irreconcilable demands of the jester and the *auteur,* but in his sense of himself as a Jew. Seen from one angle, Woody Allen the comedian seems to be a younger, more sophisticated, better-educated descendant of the older American Jewish entertainers . . . who became prominent in the first half of the century. Particularly in the early decades, many of those comedians, born to Yiddish-speaking immigrant families, mangled the *mamalushen* into Yinglish, mocked the accents of the "mockies", and had no inhibitions about being boisterously, manically crude. But no matter how broad the routine, they were aggressively asserting themselves *as* Jews, flaunting their Jewishness as a way of jeering at the genteel sensibility of the gentiles. For that dynasty of comedians, as Irving Howe has observed, "Jewishness was cause neither for self-denying shame nor ethical nail-biting". What sets Woody Allen apart, far apart, from the older generation is the vagrant self-contempt that seeps into his movies.

Much of his wit springs from the prickly Jewish talent for ironic self-deprecation, and his aspirations as an intellectual have been shaped by the style and manner of Jewish novelists like Saul Bellow and Philip Roth, Jewish humorists like S. J. Perelman, and the Jewish critical intelligence associated in the past with *Partisan Review*. But what he can't come to terms with, can't accept and certainly doesn't like, is the Jewish world that made him. For Allen the lower-middle-class Brooklyn family is not remembered with any of the affection some New York intellectuals summon up, but with the embarrassed distaste it evokes in many others. In his films he depicts the Jewish family as irredeemably loud, vulgar, and ugly; and though he's come a long way from Flatbush, he can't quell the clawing anxiety—for all his worldly success, and the interminable years of psychoanalysis—that he has been irrevocably tainted by that petty-bourgeois world. The Jewish self-loathing imprinted by his Brooklyn beginnings remains as unalterable as a fingerprint.

His compulsion to ridicule the vulgarity of the lower-middle-class Jewish family would seem to place Woody Allen in the same camp with the young Philip Roth, who was a merciless satirist in the stories of *Goodbye, Columbus,* and in *Portnoy's Complaint.* But Roth, in *The Ghost Writer* (1979)—and his new novel, *The Counterlife* (1987)—has grown more thoughtful about his Jewishness, and has shown himself capable of shedding the spite that fuelled his earlier fiction; for he has the mind, the voice, and the ear that can endow experience and feeling with unquestionable authenticity. Woody Allen can't get beyond the malice of farcical crudity. Since he can't resolve the contradiction between wanting to be a Jewish intellectual and scorning his Jewish origins, and won't ask himself what

it means to be a Jew, he remains stuck on the treadmill of burlesque.

When he was more of a writer than a movie-maker, he could portray the *schlemiel* and the Jewish mother with a modicum of affection. But in his films the innocent fun turns to vinegar. (pp. 74-5)

Why has Woody Allen's rebarbative travesty of Jewish life, his contempt for himself as a Jew, been so little remarked, and raised so few hackles among the critics and the public? Even the magazine *Hadassah,* of all places, in an article on Jewish humour, kindly informs us that "Woody Allen, having donned the *schlemiel* persona, gives us permission to laugh and recognise our weaknesses and gain acceptance, as did Sholem Aleichem." Aside from Pauline Kael and John Simmon, no film critic, as far as I know, has noticed, much less been bothered by, the way he portrays the Jews. Why was Philip Roth pilloried for his caricatures while Woody Allen's larger-than-life images give no offence? Are words in fact more wounding than images on a screen, which are readily defanged with "Look, fellas, it's only a movie"?

The critics now deconstruct Allen's films as fast as he can make them, and these days he churns them out at the dizzying pace of one a year. He has become the darling of the semi-skilled intelligentsia that is flattered by jokes with a literary flavour, like the post-coital wisecrack in *Annie Hall:* "As Balzac said, 'There goes another novel'. . . ." His movies suit the cultural mood of the moment to perfection: with their quick and easy allusions, they are all surface, self-aggrandisement and self-indulgence. He thumbs his nose at high culture while proving, with his collection of intellectual bric-a-brac, that he can play the game. What Woody Allen, the cultural phenomenon, most trenchantly demonstrates is a simple truth: If you can make people laugh, they won't question anything you do. But why are they laughing? and at whom? (p. 75)

Pearl K. Bell, "Woody Allen, Cultural Phenomenon: The 'Schlemiel' as Intellectual," in Encounter, *Vol. LXXI, No. 1, June, 1988, pp. 72-5.*

Clive Barker

1952-

English short story writer, novelist, dramatist, and scriptwriter.

Barker is considered one of the most promising horror writers to have emerged in the mid-1980s. His fiction often focuses upon ordinary characters forced to confront senseless brutality, sudden decadent obsessions, or supernatural terrors. Critics praise Barker as a witty stylist whose shocking and unsettling stories are enhanced by well-crafted plots and vivid descriptions.

Barker first gained attention among aficionados of horror literature with the short story collection *Clive Barker's Books of Blood, Vols. I-III* (1984). Each volume of this set contains pieces that elaborately detail exotic forms of mayhem. "Rawhead Rex," for example, is a story about a monster that devours human infants, while "Son of Celluloid" concerns an infectious cancerous growth which begets murderous ghouls that resemble famous film stars. Barker's short fiction proved so popular that he rapidly produced *Clive Barker's Books of Blood, Vols. IV-VI* (1985), which was published in the United States under the individual titles *The Inhuman Condition* (1986), *In the Flesh* (1987), and *The Life of Death* (1987). Critics noted that these later volumes evidence maturation in Barker's work, with less reliance on grisly detail and more of the wit and exuberant narrative techniques that characterize his best writings. Among the most highly praised stories in the latter *Books of Blood* are "The Age of Desire," about an aphrodisiac that turns a normal man into a sexual psychopath, and "The Body Politic," in which rebellious hands sever themselves from their bodies in order to wage a war of liberation.

Barker's first novel, *The Damnation Game* (1985), is a nightmarish thriller relating a wealthy businessman's forty-year struggle to regain his soul, which he lost in a card game to a human-like being with supernatural powers. His next novel, *Weaveworld* (1987), places greater emphasis on fantasy than horror. In this work, a young man and woman living in Liverpool, England, become involved with a race of seers who have magically retreated to another world that is represented in the elaborate designs of a carpet. John Calvin Batchelor noted: "Reaching into [contemporary England's] degraded and strangely fertile streets, [Barker] creates a fantastic romance of magic and promise that is at once popular fiction and utopian conjuring."

In addition to his fiction, Barker has adapted some of his stories to film and has composed several plays. *The Secret Life of Cartoons* (1986), his best-known drama, is a farce about an animator whose animal cartoon characters come to life and interfere with his marriage.

(See also *Contemporary Authors,* Vol. 121.)

MICHAEL A. MORRISON

The publication of this massive collection of well-crafted, original, disturbing stories [*Clive Barker's Books of Blood, Vols.*

1-3] heralds the arrival of an important new voice in horror fiction. The reader new to Barker's fiction is struck immediately by the gleeful carnage, graphic violence, and explicit sex that abound in these tales. . . . All this carnality and mayhem is lovingly described in Barker's vivid, sensory cinematic style.

Yet *Books of Blood* cannot be dismissed as mere splatter fiction; the philosophical and thematic content of these visceral stories elevates them from this category. Indeed, *Books of Blood* bristles with ideas: feminism (**"Jacqueline Ess: Her Will and Testament"**), the interplay of fiction and reality (**"New Murders in the Rue Morgue"**), man's attitude towards violence (**"Dread"** and **"Midnight Meat Train"**), and a host of others.

With a single exception—the hysterically funny **"The Yattering and Jack"**—Barker's fiction reflects a bleak, nihilistic world view. His characters drift through grey, hopeless lives that are interrupted only by random encounters with the appallingly powerful evil that rules his cosmos.

The bleakness of this vision is alleviated solely by the strong current of manic wit that surges through most of these stories. . . .

Barker sometimes loses control of his material, the excessive blood and gore overwhelming story ideas. Also, many of his characters are so unsympathetic that we are hard pressed to care about or empathize with them. Perhaps because of these faults, Barker's stories are rarely *terrifying*. . . .

Although similar thematically to the stories of Ramsey Campbell . . . Barker's horrors are closest to the no-less-extreme films of David Cronenberg. Like Cronenberg, Barker forces us—by his craftsmanship and intelligence—to confront our deepest anxieties about the nature of man and life in the late 20th century. And, like Cronenberg's films, Barker's radical stories are sure to provoke controversy, even among aficionados.

> *Michael A. Morrison, "Blood without End," in* Fantasy Review, *Vol. 9, No. 6, June, 1985, p. 15.*

CHRIS MORGAN

While Clive Barker is undoubtedly an immensely talented writer, his previously published work—the novelettes in six volumes of *Books of Blood*—has been full of promise but flawed. That promise is amply fulfilled here in his first novel [*The Damnation Game*], a tour-de-force of gruesome supernatural horror. The most startling features of his work are the fact that he allows no depth of nastiness, cruelty or perversion to go unplumbed, and the beautifully figurative and allusive nature of his prose style. . . . The combined effect of these two features is that not only is *The Damnation Game* attractively written, it is also very hard hitting—very graphic. . . .

In this novel Barker overcomes most of the flaws of his novelettes by having a plausible plot that is only partly dependent upon the supernatural, and by giving himself enough space to develop his characters as real people. While it is easy for the reader to laugh at supernatural horror, the impact of gruesome physical or psychological horror inflicted upon characters one has come to know over a couple of hundred pages is much more shocking—and it is this shock value that Barker exploits.

Briefly, the plot revolves around supernatural revenge meted out to millionaire Joseph Whitehead and his daughter. The main viewpoint character is Marty Strauss, a young hoodlum on parole from prison who is taken on as Whitehead's bodyguard. While Marty is an unpleasant type, Barker tries to portray him as a noble savage, more loyal and trustworthy than the rich, against whom the novel is strongly biased.

Although the novel is, on the whole, brilliantly executed, Barker's writing does show signs of immaturity in places. He uses a fully floating viewpoint, showing us the thoughts of so many characters (including, at one point, a dead dog) that one is occasionally unsure of whose head one is intruding into. . . .

Potentially, Barker is a better writer than Stephen King or Peter Straub; he is more usefully compared with that other startlingly able young British horror writer, Iain Banks (author of *The Wasp Factor*). *The Damnation Game* is an important novel, helping to establish links between graphic horror and high quality literature.

> *Chris Morgan, "Brilliant First Novel," in* Fantasy Review, *Vol. 8, No. 9, September, 1985, p. 16.*

COLIN GREENLAND

The Damnation Game, [Clive Barker's] first novel, bears out the extraordinary reputation he has already made. The protagonist is a gambler, Marty Strauss, who has ruined his life by a single desperate and disastrous crime. He is offered a con-

ditional reprieve from his Wandsworth Prison sentence to become the bodyguard of Joseph Whitehead, a pharmaceutical magnate. A grim encounter with an intruder who shrugs off guard dogs and an electric fence convinces Strauss that the attacker his employer fears is not altogether human.

Barker is generous with the gore and grue currently fashionable in horror novels, but he is also a highly literate fantasist, and makes powerful use of the subtleties and ambiguities inherent in the situation. Though the agents of evil are identified and intriguingly depicted, the reader, like Strauss himself, remains uncertain of the nature of the Damnation Game and the size of the stakes until quite late in the book. By then Barker has firmly engaged our interest and sympathy with quite a number of uncommonly complex and vital characters. . . .

The author's experience with short stories, and also with stage and film plays, shows strongly in his organization of the action by tableaux. At times he is apt to load more emotional or symbolic weight onto a scene than its position in the plot will easily bear, but he never loses his grip on the reader's nerve-ends.

> *Colin Greenland, in a review of "The Damnation Game," in* British Book News, *December, 1985, p. 742.*

KIM NEWMAN

On first acquaintance, this second batch of *contes cruels* [*Clive Barker's Books of Blood, Vols. IV-VI*] does seem less directly offensive than the fistful of shockers in the first three volumes. With the attention-grabbing debut tales out of the way, Barker can afford to experiment with a more literary style. Semicolons have crept in, paragraphs have grown and the stories are more elaborately plotted. But the nastiness hasn't gone; there are still repulsive demons, flesh-twisting monstrosities, crawling severed hands, disgustingly purposeful diseases and obscene elder Gods in the Lovecraft tradition. Barker has never been content simply to scare his readers; in these books, the fright quotient is almost completely irrelevant to the effects he is after.

Having burrowed his way into the genre with his first books, Barker is now eating away at it, *transforming* it from within. There are filler stories, semi-comic misfires and a few repetitions in volumes IV-VI, but they are outweighed two to one by unhealthy triumphs—**"The Age of Desire"**, **"Madonna"**, **"In the Flesh"**—which either tread new ground or seed the old with spores that germinate into mutant blossoms. With Ramsey Campbell increasingly proving himself Britain's leading horror novelist, Barker has single-handedly demonstrated the potency and marketability of the horror story collection as an art form. (p. 29)

> *Kim Newman, "Living Hell," in* New Statesman, *Vol. 112, No. 2886, July 18, 1986, pp. 29-30.*

DOUGLAS E. WINTER

There is little mystery about Clive Barker's sudden success. [*Clive Barker's Books of Blood, Vols. I-III*] offer a strikingly bold vision, and some of the most provocative tales of terror ever published. . . .

The *Books of Blood* are patterned after Ray Bradbury's *The Illustrated Man*, each story said to be etched into the skin of an unfortunate charlatan whose psychic shenanigans have offended the dead. Any resemblance to Bradbury's gentle fantasies (or, indeed, those of Stephen King) ends, however, with the series' first story, **"Midnight Meat Train,"** a harrowing sojourn that depicts the New York subway as a rolling abattoir. It is what the reader will come to recognize as quintessential Barker: graphic, grotesque, and yet compellingly readable. He is the literary equivalent of those special-effects geniuses who unleash convincing and blood-splattered monstrosities on the motion picture screen.

Never has horror fiction been as consistently explicit in its sex or violence or indeed, in its linking of the two. Barker's creations include **"Rawhead Rex,"** a babyeating monster of pure sexual appetite, and **"Son of Celluloid,"** a moviehouse cancer that spawns bloodthirsty replicas of classic film actors. On the face of it, the *Books of Blood* might seem just the thing to set the hearts of the Meese Commission [on pornography] aflutter. But Barker never panders; indeed, he seems intent on forging something that might well be called the antihorror story.

Conventional horror fiction progresses from the archetype of Pandora's Box: the tense conflict between pleasure and fear that is latent when we face the forbidden and the unknown. The *Books of Blood* are founded on the proposition that there are no taboos, no mysteries. Barker's eye is unblinking; he drags our terrors from the shadows and forces us to look upon them and despair or laugh with relief.

Conventional horror, particularly in film, has also always been rich with Puritan subtext: if there is a single certainty, it is that teenagers who have sex in cars or in the woods will die. Most horror stories offer a message as conservative as their morality: Conform. Their boogeymen are the hitmen of homogeneity. Don't do it, they tell us, or you will pay an awful price. Don't talk to strangers. Don't dare to be different. And the monsters (who, by definition, *are* different) are typically destroyed by proper behavior, whether symbolized by virginity, silver crucifixes, or, indeed, conformity.

For Barker, conformity is the ultimate horror; many of his characters are dimensionless by design. Only through the intrusion of horror, he tells us, may we see our world clearly, know both its dangers and its possibilities. . . .

The Inhuman Condition begins a second cycle of "Books of Blood.". . . These stories reflect a decided maturation of style and find Barker relying more often on craft than sheer explicitness of image to convey his horrors.

But the extremity of Barker's aesthetics has not flagged. In the collection's title story, a knotted string, symbolic of life's mysteries, brings violent death to its possessors as it is unraveled. **"The Body Politic"** imagines human hands tearing themselves from the wrists of their masters and crawling spiderlike to a bloody revolution. In **"The Age of Desire,"** a powerful aphrodisiac unleashes ghastly sexual urgings whose fulfillment can be found only in mating with death.

"There is no delight the equal of dread," writes Barker, and it is precisely this enthusiasm for invoking terror that propels his fiction. His prose, particularly in the first three *Books of Blood,* is rough-edged (he has, among other things, a lamentable propensity for anarchic shifts of point of view), but its energy is unstoppable. Like Stephen King, with whom he must inevitably be compared, he is unashamed to confront the terrors of our daily lives, and to do so in a genre that is too often relegated to the ranks of tawdry-looking paperbacks. But while

King, the avuncular storyteller, holds our hands as we face a darkening world, Barker thrusts us forward into the night. . . .

Douglas E. Winter, "Clive Barker: Britain's New Master of Horror," in Book World—The Washington Post, *August 24, 1986, p. 6.*

KEN TUCKER

[Clive Barker] avoids the breathless tone that makes most modern horror tales seem foolish, instead setting scenes in a measured voice with meticulous details that accumulate to create an atmosphere of dread and foreboding. This sets you up properly for the scary parts—in this, Mr. Barker is mindful of such predecessors as H.P. Lovecraft and Arthur Machen. What he adds to this tradition is a wicked willingness to use vivid images of violence to provide a jolt of R-rated realism to his fiction. Try to imagine *The Texas Chainsaw Massacre* with a screenplay by V. S. Pritchett and you have some idea of Clive Barker at his most effective in these five tales [*The Inhuman Condition*]. . . . **"The Age of Desire"** is sort of an erotic parody of *Frankenstein,* as a group of doctors develop "an aphrodisiac that actually works"—all too well, turning an ordinary man into an uncontrollable psychotic, as Mr. Barker's prose moves from the Gothic to the graphic in a sleek, subtle shift. The most powerful story here is **"The Body Politic,"** whose premise sounds like a joke—a pair of hands literally sever themselves from a man's body and scramble off, dragging a hatchet, in the hope of persuading other hands to "liberate themselves" from *their* bodies. It's a measure of Mr. Barker's cool control that he makes this bad dream seem not only creepily disturbing but plausible.

Ken Tucker, in a review of "The Inhuman Condition," in The New York Times Book Review, *September 21, 1986, p. 26.*

MICHAEL A. MORRISON

The Inhuman Condition is aptly named. These five "tales of terror" from the first volume of Barker's second *Books of Blood* trilogy, tell of humans transformed into something more than human. It is their obsessions—sexual, religious, or intellectual—that drive Barker's protagonists to transformation, fulfillment, and doom. Although some of the characters are superficially drawn, their reactions are rarely stereotypical.

Take, for example, Jerome Tregold, the hapless test subject of an experiment in drug design that goes awry; suddenly inflamed with sexual cravings, he is compelled to a variety of vividly rendered excesses ("sex without end") that presage the dawning of "The Age of Desire." Like most of the transformed humans that people Barker's tales, Tregold reacts to his new state of being not with panic or revulsion but with exuberance and relief. . . .

There is also the slight fable **"Down, Satan!"** in which a rich businessman and lapsed Catholic seeks to restore his faith by luring Satan himself to a newly constructed "hell on earth . . . a modern inferno so monstrous that the Tempter would be tempted"; this is one of Barker's wittiest tales. However, none of these stories are the equal of the best in the first trilogy; none, for example, have the powerful imagery of **"In the Hills, the Cities"** or the morbid fascination of **"Dread."** Still, Barker remains daring, imaginative, and self-assured, and there is much to savor in this collection: Sadie's *joie de morte* in **"Revelations"**; the inspired metaphor for evolution underlying the knotty problem posed in the title story; a macabre romp of liberated limbs in the wacky **"The Body Politic."** Seekers after the off-trail who have not experienced Barker's bizarre fiction are in for a treat; the rest of us can only await whatever else he has in store.

Michael A. Morrison, "Visions of the Joyous Apocalypse," in Fantasy Review, *Vol. 9, No. 9, October,*
1986, p. 19.

MICHAEL BILLINGTON

The idea of the creator devoured by his own invention goes back at least as far as Mary Shelley's *Frankenstein*. It resurfaced, in the form of the ventriloquist devoured by his dummy, in films like *Dead Of Night* and *Magic*. But this notion, rooted in Gothic horror, is transmuted by Clive Barker in *The Secret Life Of Cartoons* into crude, frantic, anything-for-a-laugh farce and the result is not pleasant to watch.

The basic concept has a surreal potential. The hero, who has spent 22 years in animation, finds that his life and libido have been poured into the creation of Rosco, a lewd, pacifist, transvestite cartoon rabbit. So we watch Rosco, his furry biped of an ultra ego, cutting loose and seducing his wife while hotly pursued by a cartoon rabbit hunter and a camp duck.

Lest we miss Barker's point about the ominivorous nature of fantasy, we also see the hero himself randily traced by a pneumatic cartoon cat until a studio boss rodent in black Homburg arrives to reclaim his creatures and permit the animator to return to marital normality.

Mr Barker's problem is that his verbal invention is out of sync with his imagination and that his ideas about farce might have been garnered from a lifetime exclusively spent at the end of seaside piers. I never thought to hear again exchanges like "I appeal to you"—"No you don't," and I hope never to hear again puns like"I'm a quack shot" or "Sit down and have a mouseful."

Under the puerile dialogue Mr Barker seems to be saying not merely that animators are dominated by their creations, but also that we expect cartoons to be based on violence rather than sex. But his plea for adult sexuality in animation is not helped by his own creation of a lisping, limp-webbed duck who does old Ginger Rogers numbers in a blue frock and who makes the queen in *Privates on Parade* look like Rambo.

This, in short, an evening of uniquely hideous vulgarity. . . .

Michael Billington, in a review of "The Secret Life
of Cartoons," in The Guardian, *October 17, 1986.*

NICK ST. GEORGE

[In *The Secret Life of Cartoons*] make-believe becomes uncomfortably (and often hilariously) real as an animator's comic creations leave the safety of celluloid and come home to roost (in one particular case in the cartoonist's bed with his wife). A number of illustrious critics have been somewhat unkind about Mr. Barker's play. It is not great art, but it is great fun. That's not to say it isn't also heavily flawed, but the problems are as much (if not more so) a fault of the production as the text. . . . [Dick] has put his heart and soul (and sex drive) into his star turn: Rosco—a 6′4″ rabbit with the liveliest libido this side of Watership Down. In doing so he neglects his wife . . . , who is instantly seduced by the Rabbit when he turns up one

day in their apartment; and why not? Rosco . . . has all the attractive attributes her husband used to have. For so long, when Rosco was just pencil and ink, he came between husband and wife, now he's fur and blood he does it for real.

This initial act of cartoon anarchy is then followed by further mayhem, as the entire cast of Dick's cartoons come in search of the Rabbit . . . reality and illusion become well and truly blurred.

Barker takes far too long to set up the initial chaos, but after that the lunacy is virtually non-stop—a mixture of bedroom farce, deliberately bad jokes and animation techniques that may be frequently groanworthy and dramatically uneven, but are just as frequently justified and very, very funny. . . .

The Secret Life of Cartoons is full of holes, yet it has at its heart such a marvellous basic idea, bucketfuls of imagination and a healthily daft sense of humour that it really is extremely difficult to dislike.

Nick St. George, in a review of "The Secret Life of
Cartoons," in a radio broadcast on BBC Radio—
London, October 25, 1986. Reprinted in London
Theatre Record, *Vol. VI, No. 21, October 8-21, 1986,*
p. 1136.

RICHARD GEHR

For all I know, Clive Barker could be the Antichrist. He sure makes me feel uncomfortable in this mortal coil. The bloody Englishman turns the reader into a sadistic voyeur, an indictable conspirator in the grisly little game of horror writing, gleefully lapping up each nasty bit of Barker business. That in itself is pretty darn frightening. Stephen King, in comparison, comes off a humanitarian. When a writer flips out in one of his books, you know that King identifies with that writer. Barker, on the other hand, is nowhere to be found in his own fiction, which at least partially explains why many find his violence a tad extreme.

Like the way he tends to go for the eyes. In **"Son of Celluloid,"** from volume 3 of his *Books of Blood,* a fugitive with cancer crawls into a run-down rep house and dies, but his tumor lives on, filling the theater with ghosts of movies past. The subject is the cinematic spectacle, and eyeballing in general. These specters want it all: "His eyes had been scooped out of his head. Not neatly: no surgeon's job. They'd been wrenched out, leaving a trail of mechanics down his cheek." (The orbs end up between the legs of Marilyn Monroe.) Barker's slickest bit of deoculation takes place in **"The Body Politic,"** from [*The Inhuman Condition,* the fourth volume of the *Books of Blood*]: "Her nails, her pride and joy, found her eyes. In moments the miracle of sight was muck on her cheek."

If Barker is hard on eyes, he's no easier on the rest of the anatomy, forcing every body to tell its story. "Every body is a book of blood; wherever we're opened, we're red," he says in the epigraph to the collection. A master of detail, Barker believes in proper introductions. Short yet intimate relationships set the stage for hideous catastrophes. He describes the everyday agonies of the human corpus before putting his characters through whatever fictive grinders he has in mind. . . .

If David Cronenberg wants us to "watch the unwatchable," Barker tempts us to read the unreadable. His visuals are no less inventive and tumultuous than Cronenberg's. In **"Confessions of a (Pornographer's) Shroud,"** the spirit-possessed sheet clambers down a murderer's throat, gathers up his innards, and turns him inside out. In **"Scape-Goats,"** Barker spends two sad and elegant pages describing the drowning and subsequent decomposition of a decent young woman among a sea of dead men. Barker writes without limits. Even though his characters are hip, now, and kind of wow, bad things inevitably happen to good people in his stories, and frequent glib asides distance both him and his readers from the gore. (pp. 63-4)

Whether he becomes a name brand or not, he writes strong stuff. Something discomfiting lies between the gags and the Grand Guignol—something that makes me feel a little queasier about myself the morning after. (p. 64)

> *Richard Gehr, "Barker's Bite," in* The Village Voice,
> *Vol. XXXI, No. 48, December 2, 1986, pp. 63-4.*

ELIZABETH GLEICK

[In *In the Flesh*] Clive Barker plays upon our unconscious terrors—a man transmutes into a woman after a strange sexual encounter, leaderless world governments are on the verge of running amok, a man realizes he has the potential to commit murder—and also on our innate fascination with the lurid. The author has not selected his victims arbitrarily; they are naturally adventurous and compassionate, and like the avid reader, they search out the horrible, compelled against their better judgment to discover the very worst. The title piece shows Mr. Barker at his most adept. In it, Cleve, a petty criminal who is in jail for the third time, spends his days reading theories about how sin came into the world (being in jail, he's pretty skeptical about the subject). When his new cellmate, Billy Tait, calls forth the ghost—no, something infinitely more horrendous and complex—of his grandfather, a murderer who is buried on the prison grounds, Cleve follows Billy in his dreams to an acropolis where he discovers firsthand the birth of evil. Mr. Barker's intelligence and humor creep out of these tales from the unlikeliest places—what a breath of fresh, if chilling, air.

> *Elizabeth Gleick, in a review of "In the Flesh," in*
> The New York Times Book Review, *February 15,*
> *1987, p. 20.*

STEFAN R. DZIEMIANOWICZ

Those who liked *The Inhuman Condition* will have no reason not to like *In the Flesh*. The book displays the same strengths, weaknesses, and—eerily enough—format: the title story, about a tug of war between the dead and the living over the fate of a boy, roughly corresponds to the parallel worlds of the dead and undead seen previously in **"Revelations"**; the overt political commentary of **"Babel's Children"** mirrors the overt allegory of **"The Body Politic"**; the terror of uncontrollable sexuality is a theme of both **"The Madonna"** and the earlier **"Age of Desire"**; and if the plot of **"The Forbidden"** doesn't exactly match that of **"The Inhuman Condition,"** urban squalor and the sensibilities it produces are significant to the development of both. Fortunately, Barker exercises enough imagination that these stories never read like rehashed formulae.

The most commendable thing about Barker's approach to horror is that he always tells a story before he tries to scare you. You're as interested in finding out how his very real characters are affected by their experiences as in seeing how they walk into (and, very rarely, out of) the traps he has laid. This strength helps the reader over his endings, which often over- or understate the case he has been building throughout the story. If **"The Madonna"** has no coherent plotline, you can at least

relish how two different men respond to the mutual incoherence of their situations. There is no need for Barker to have the malignant force in **"The Forbidden"** explain itself, nor explicitly to answer in the closing sentence the question raised throughout **"In the Flesh,"** nor to bring on cartoon representations of the authorities he lampoons in **"Babel's Children."** But you'll read each of these stories through to the end. And you'll buy *Book of Blood VI*, whatever its new title, for more of the same.

> *Stefan R. Dziemianowicz, "Sure Thing," in* Fantasy
> Review, *Vol. 10, No. 3, April, 1987, p. 32.*

ALAN CARUBA

The Liverpudlian writer Clive Barker, who has established a reputation as a writer of short horror fiction, has now written his first novel [*The Damnation Game*] set on a vast estate outside London. In fairness, those who like this genre will, no doubt, enjoy the book for its unremitting devotion to the most sickening imagery. For others, however, it will be more like struggling to awaken from a nightmare. Near the end, a major character says, "Sense? There's no sense to be made." In fact, the absence of any meaning in all this is the flaw that runs through what might have been an allegory of evil, an extended commentary on the various addictions that entrap people. The characters are little more than pathetically obvious metaphors. . . . [All] we get is a forced march through the dank, fetid quicksand of a story whose every page drips with images of horrible wounds, blood and other human effluents and effluvium.

> *Alan Caruba, in a review of "The Damnation Game," in* The New York Times Book Review, *June 21, 1987, p. 22.*

LAURENCE COVEN

In his first novel, *The Damnation Game* . . . , Clive Barker plunges straight to hell with a remarkably powerful portrait of post-war Warsaw. The nightmare is not of mere destruction, for Barker also evokes the much more horrible imagery of a teeming and utter decadence that seems to ooze from the rubble of the city.

Here the Thief and the Cardplayer meet, two fable-like characters who begin their hideous game that lasts for 40 years.

Abruptly Barker pulls us into present-day London, the Thief is now Whitehead, the elderly head of a multi-million dollar empire. He has betrayed the Cardplayer, Mamoulian, and now fears his vengeance. And well he should, for Mamoulian has survived for more than 200 years, and his powers include reanimating the dead who serve as his bond slaves. . . .

Time after time Barker makes us shudder in revulsion. In pure descriptive power there is no one writing horror fiction now who can match him. And to his credit, Barker does not write in a social vacuum. His terrors arise, at least in part, from a profound sadness and misery he perceives in the human condition.

However, there are only so many unspeakable acts one can speak about. No matter how brilliant the language, many readers will eventually be numbed by Barker's excess. His overkill deprives us of a sense of anticipation, and without anticipation there is no suspense.

Both here and in his six volumes of stories, *The Books of Blood,* Barker has proven that he is a master of horror who has yet to write his masterpiece.

Laurence Coven, "Unspeakable Acts," in Book World—The Washington Post, *June 28, 1987, p. 10.*

KIRKUS REVIEWS

Britisher Barker, horror's *Wunderkind,* has dazzled in several short-story collections (*The Inhuman Condition, In the Flesh,* etc.), but disappointed in his one previous novel, the unwieldy *The Damnation Game* (1985). Never mind: his new dark fantasy [*Weaveworld*], an epic tale of a magic carpet and the wondrous world within its weave, towers above his earlier work—and, despite some serious flaws, manages via its powerful and giddy torrent of invention to grasp the golden ring as the most ambitious and visionary horror novel of the decade.

Barker attempts nothing less here than the resurrection of the imagination as the prime force in human destiny. To do so, he posits a race of magicians—the Seerkind—as always having cast spells of delight alongside humankind. But at the dawn of this century, modernity's onslaught forced the Seerkind to retreat within a magical fortress—a carpet. As the story begins, young Cal Mooney, an office grind with a fanciful heart, chances upon the rug and is transported into the enchanted fields and towns of "The Fugue"—the marvelous land woven within the rug. Cal faints from this vision; when he awakes, the rug is gone—and in its place are Immacolata (a demonic/erotic spirit) and Shadwell the Salesman (a human embodiment of the Seven Deadly Sins), veteran seekers for the rug who, believing that Cal knows its location, pursue him with all the hounds of hell. After ferocious battles with evil entities, Cal links up with Suzanna—descendant of the carpet's dead caretaker—who soon learns that Seerkind blood courses in her veins. . . .

Like Barker's earlier fiction, this complex work erupts with explicit sex and violence—but now the shocks punctuate a raging flood of image and situation so rich as to overflow Barker's abilities to formalize it. Nearly every page teems with original ideas; what's missing, however, is an emotional vigor to backbone all this activity; Cal and Suzanna remain distant creations. Here Barker has unleashed literary genius without taming it—though cemented his position as *the* major horror rival to King.

A review of "Weaveworld," in Kirkus Reviews, *Vol. LV, No. 15, August 1, 1987, p. 1085.*

PHIL NORMAND

Before television became the children's home companion, I would often wake early and stare long at the ceiling. In the random, stuccoed patterns or in the loose spatter design of the 1940s linoleum floor, I knew where the goblins lived. When I got older and was drawn into the regimented life of school and a few other responsibilities, I tried to keep one foot in the land of Camelot, Sherwood Forest, or the odd countries of Oz. Later still, it was Barsoom, Opar, Hyperborea, or Zothique. Deep within me, these worlds are sewn together into a patchwork nation of images where my dreams have bodies and act out their dark or bright lives. That world is at once exciting and serene; it is the home of the spirit. Some call it wonderland; Clive Barker [in *Weaveworld*] calls it the Fugue.

Calhoun Mooney's grandfather was a poet, a lunatic Irishman, and, though most talk of him was banished, Cal can't escape the mixed blessing of Mad Mooney's blood. He didn't know he had the poet's curse, didn't know he had the longing for the "fields beyond." Cal Mooney didn't know he'd ever stand in wonderland until he stumbled upon the Weave.

The Weave is a carpet woven with strange and jumbled designs. It was kept by old Mimi Laschenski for all the years she had lived alone. Her granddaughter, Suzanna Parrish, though grown now, has feared the old woman since childhood, sensing they share a secret bond. When Mimi falls ill and her apartment furnishings are sold to cover debts, Suzanna is finally confronted with her destined charge. She becomes the wielder of the menstruum, a powerful female energy, and she inherits the guardianship of the Weave.

Cal and Suzanna are thrown together by different fates. Cal, having once seen the Weave and a bit of wonderland, knows he can never be content with the everyday life of Liverpool and a mundane marriage. Suzanna, who has been brought up to honor the rational, finds, through the confrontation of old fears, a place within her more alive than she had ever dreamed. Together they are renewed in the salvation of the Fugue from evils both human and magical.

Near the end of the last century the Scourge had begun to cleanse the world of the last vestiges of the fantastic and magical. These "mistakes" of creation were hounded from the habitations of men and ruthlessly destroyed. Those few places where the Families of the Seerkind still held sway banded together, not without tension, to weave a spell of sleep and protection that resulted in the Fugue, the Weaveworld, a simple carpet to the eyes of men. (p. 21)

Clive Barker's chilling *Books of Blood* are filled with the sweating terror and unique visions of the bizarre—a sentient cancer and fastidious subway slaughterer, a troupe of long dead actors who continue to tour Shakespeare, and the monstrous giant of Popolac alive with thousands of people for cells. Barker continues to parade wonders before the eye and ear with the showmanship of his carnival namesake and the fluid language of a poet. *Weaveworld* contains novel delights . . . and horrors. . . .

Nothing is clearcut in Weaveworld. The Seerkind are not all sweetness and light. Lust and vanity are present in that congregation along with loyalty and love. Cal and Suzanna are often rejected by the Families who look upon them as Cuckoos, powerless, greedy beings that, for some reason, the earth tends to favor. . . .

The cast of secondary characters is ample. Inspector Hobart is obsessed with keeping the law, certain that the strange manifestations he witnessed are the work of terrorists and murderers. Apolline, Nimrod, and Jerichau St. Louis, Seerkind on the edges of the Weave, are outcasts who hope to take their pleasure from the ignorant Cuckoos. Lemuel Lo and his orchard of Giddy Fruit hold perpetual poetry readings in the sacred grove of the Fugue. Each character, human or magical, moves the story onward and helps or hinders as no one else can. Most are seed or echo of archetypal forces, which continue beyond the tale.

Many fantasy and horror novels in recent years have been overlong exercises that lose direction after a few shocking episodes. We have the feeling we are wandering through pages waiting for the terror to strike. When it finally does, it is accompanied by a slight feeling of guilt, of voyeuristic pleasure; we know we're only turning pages to find out when the blood will spurt, who the next monstrously violated victim will be. Clive Barker is skillful enough to create that kind of blood feast. But he also does much more.

Barker's *Weaveworld* lives up to its title; it is a tapestry of themes and characters. Beyond the chase-and-capture plot, we are called to rejoice in the strength of dream. This is a book of fantasy *about* fantasy, the struggle for man's dominion over the ungovernable casts of the imagination. It is about regaining the heart's true desire, about finding a place as close as breath where all things have a special purpose and meaning, where each man and woman is valued for his or her uniqueness, a place where each finds love. (p. 25)

> *Phil Normand, in a review of "Weaveworld," in* The Bloomsbury Review, *Vol. 7, No. 5, September-October, 1987, pp. 21, 25.*

JOHN CALVIN BATCHELOR

[In *Weaveworld*] Clive Barker reveals his prodigious talent for erecting make-believe worlds in the midst of Mrs. Thatcher's tumbledown kingdom of Windsorian privilege and secretly policed ghettos. Reaching into its degraded and strangely fertile streets, he creates a fantastic romance of magic and promise that is at once popular fiction and uptopian conjuring. The result here is post-post-post Malory. Cal Mooney, a poetic clerk living by the train tracks in modern-day Liverpool, stumbles upon a magic carpet that contains within its weave an antediluvian world of smarmy folk who might be the kindred of the wizard Merlin.... [Chaos] appears in the form of a winningly loathsome traveling salesman named Shadwell and his beloved witch friend Immacolata, who want either to sell or destroy the carpet. There is great wit in the struggle that ensues, and keen attention to the facts of poverty and exile, as well as the matter of what it is like to dream of a better world while scrabbling by the Mersey.

> *John Calvin Batchelor, in a review of "Weaveworld," in* The New York Times Book Review, *November 22, 1987, p. 32.*

JOHN CLUTE

After a long first novel [*The Damnation Game*], six volumes of *Books of Blood,* and with a budding career as a film director, Clive Barker has also had time to produce *Weaveworld,* an immense second novel. This intense, intriguingly busy fantasy is what one might call a tale of portals. Within the warp and woof of the carpet of the title, the land of Faerie reposes until threats posed by its internal enemies and by the secular world outside have passed. But the carpet is soon unwoven—catastrophes loom while Suzanna Parrish and Cal Mooney fight off the machinations of fallen fairies, of a corrupt and fallen police officer from Liverpool and of a dire, deluded fallen angel. After 700 pages, too many portals have opened and shut too often but excess is the essence of Mr. Barker's craft. And the rollercoaster he has constructed bears its rug with bravura ease.

> *John Clute, "The SF Silly Season," in* The Observer, *December 27, 1987, p. 17.*

COLIN GREENLAND

[*Weaveworld*] is almost classically a romance, a heraldic adventure in which figures possessed by principles, of love or greed or despair, pursue one another headlong with spells or pistols through a vague locality full of numinous things that begin with capital letters: the Fugue, the Firmament, the Gyre, and so forth. The secret land inside the carpet is threatened by a rough association of villains, all of them, on first introduction, the most promising elements in the book. They are Shadwell, the salesman, inside whose magic jacket is stowed every heart's desire; Hobart, the brutal, crusading police inspector; a loathsome trinity of weird sisters; and a mad djinn that thinks it is the angel Uriel.

On further acquaintance all these characters prove less interesting. In fairyland, Shadwell, for example, becomes a mere demagogue and tyrant. The fairies themselves are rather disappointing, their magic no match for machine-guns, and their much-prized innocence no more than routine mob gullibility. Helped and hindered by them, our heroine and hero (both human) strive, suffer and surmount. Titanic events continually sweep them apart, then together again. The plot reeks with the pathos of loss and reunion, forgetting and remembering. Barker lays on the sentiment with a palette knife, and rounds each chapter with a plangent phrase ("'Ah, the ladies', said Shadwell; and Death flew in at the door"). All this, as he knows well, will endear him to the consumers of novels that are thick; but in substance it is thin, compared to the robustness of Ramsey Campbell, let alone the richness of John Crowley's *Little, Big* or Robert Holdstock's *Mythago Wood,* two rediscoveries of fairyland much more thorough and disconcerting.

> *Colin Greenland, "The Figures in the Carpet," in* The Times Literary Supplement, *No. 4428, February 12-18, 1988, p. 172.*

Gregory (Albert) Benford

1941-

American novelist, short story writer, and editor.

An astrophysicist who is also considered among the most prominent authors of science fiction to emerge in the early 1970s, Benford is praised for his extensive knowledge of scientific phenomena and his literate style and characterizations. Although he attempts to evoke the sense of wonder and adventure commonly associated with literature of science fiction's "Golden Age," Benford avoids the often simplistic ideas of this period in favor of the literary and psychological emphases of the genre's "New Wave" movement of the 1960s. Many of Benford's works examine the processes of scientific discovery through contact with alien cultures, and his protagonists often include scientists whose dissatisfaction with their own societies leads them to identify more closely with otherworldly beings than with humans. Benford maintains that his major concerns include "the vast landscape of science, and the philosophical implications of that landscape on mortal, sensual human beings. What genuinely interests me is the strange, the undiscovered. But in the end it is how people see this that matters most."

As a teenager, Benford coedited the science fiction fan magazine *Void* together with several of the genre's established authors. After receiving his doctorate in theoretical physics from the University of California, San Diego, in 1967 and becoming a professor of physics at the University of California, Irvine, Benford contributed short stories to science fiction magazines, later expanding many of these pieces into full-length works. His earliest books conceived in this manner include *Deeper than the Darkness* (1970; revised as *The Stars in Shroud*), a conventional science fiction adventure story, and *Jupiter Project* (1975), a tale of space exploration intended for young adults. While these works attracted little attention, Benford garnered substantial acclaim for his next novel, *If the Stars Are Gods* (1977), which he coauthored with science fiction writer Gordon Eklund. The book's title section, based on the authors' novella of the same title for which they received a Nebula Award, concerns an astronaut who defies orders to destroy an unidentified alien ship that is considered a threat to earth's armed forces. Judging the military's reaction to be xenophobic, the astronaut attempts to communicate with the inhabitants of the alien vessel and attains insight into the true nature of the universe.

Like the protagonist of *If the Stars Are Gods,* the hero of Benford's next novel, *In the Ocean of Night* (1977), disobeys military orders to destroy an asteroid that is discovered to encompass an alien ship. As the only British astronaut to serve in the American space program, Nigel Walmsley is prompted by feelings of alienation from his comrades to establish contact with the spacecraft, which contains a form of mechanical intelligence. His experience later enables him to approach another conceivably hostile civilization of intelligent machines. In the novel's sequel, *Across the Sea of Suns* (1984), Walmsley and his crew become marooned on a distant planet after investigating an alien broadcast of mysterious English messages. Meanwhile, human existence is threatened when a malignant machine civilization places an intelligent but destructive organic life form in the earth's oceans.

In 1980, Benford collaborated on two novels: *Find the Changeling,* authored with William Rotsler, about the pursuit of a highly adaptable extraterrestrial being intent on initiating anarchy on Earth, and *Shiva Descending*, written with Gordon Eklund, in which various nations must overcome their rivalries to avert Earth's imminent collision with an asteroid. Benford's next novel, *Timescape* (1980), earned him both a John W. Campbell Award and a Nebula Award. In this work, a group of British researchers from the year 1998 use tachyons—atomic particles that travel faster than light and can, theoretically, be used to journey backward in time—to warn a California physicist in 1962 of a forthcoming ecological disaster. David N. Samuelson called *Timescape* "a full-fledged novel about people who live, who make love, who fight for their identity and survival, in the context of doing for a living an intellectually obsessing activity known as science, with all of the attendant politics of the scientific community, past and future."

Several critics compared Benford's subsequent novel, *Against Infinity* (1983), to Ernest Hemingway's novella *The Old Man and the Sea* and William Faulkner's short story "The Bear" for its exploration of conflicts between humanity and nature and its focus on a young man's coming-of-age. This work revolves around the annual hunt of a mysterious alien artifact known as the Aleph, which wanders the recently settled Jovian moon of Ganymede. Although Manuel Lopez attains manhood by terminating the Aleph, the artifact is revealed to contain the universe, and its destruction carries serious repercussions. *Artifact* (1985) blends science fiction, adventure, and intrigue in depicting an international struggle to reveal the mysteries surrounding an ancient artifact discovered in a Mycenaean tomb. Critics generally praised Benford's characterizations in this work and his ability to dramatize the excitement of scientific endeavors. In *Heart of the Comet* (1986), which Benford co-wrote with science fiction author David Brin, a scientific colony attempting to establish an outpost at the nucleus of Halley's comet in the year 2061 faces biological obstacles as well as a rivalry between the expedition's ordinary humans and genetically improved people, known as Percells. Although this novel received mixed reviews, Gary K. Wolfe maintained that *Heart of the Comet* ''works just fine as a sweeping adventure-cum-problem story in the classic mold,'' and Keith Soltys called it ''one of the best [science fiction] novels of the last few years.''

Benford's first volume of short fiction, *In Alien Flesh* (1986), examines such characteristic topics as alien contact and the possibility of mechanical or artificial intelligence. Pascal J. Thomas commented that ''the best stories in the collection are suffused with the sense of wonder arising from the divergent potentialities of the human mind.'' In his recent novel, *Great Sky River* (1987), Benford makes use of allusions to Homer's *Odyssey* to examine the struggles of a human colony that is controlled by a superior machine culture. Just as Homer's hero Odysseus invokes the ghosts of dead heroes to help return him to Ithaca, the protagonists of this novel obtain access to the memories and personalities of their dead ancestors through silicon chips implanted in their nervous systems. John G. Cramer called *Great Sky River* ''an ambitious work that sets new standards for hard science fiction.''

(See also *Contemporary Authors*, Vols. 69-72; *Contemporary Authors New Revision Series*, Vols. 12, 24; and *Dictionary of Literary Biography Yearbook: 1982*.)

GERALD JONAS

One of the more endearing traits of modern science fiction is the tendency, in novels and short stories, to wrap things up with a bang rather than a whimper. The crudest planet-hopping adventure tale . . . will suddenly blossom into apocalypse in the last few sentences—in which the earth is destroyed, or the hero achieves godlike powers or the secret of the universe . . . is revealed. What makes these cosmic punchlines endearing, rather than off-putting, is their deadpan manner of delivery. In most cases, the reader is obviously not expected to give any more credence to the final paragraph than the reader of fairy tales gives to the words ''And they lived happily ever after.''

In [*If the Stars Are Gods*], co-authors Gregory Benford and Gordon Eklund make the mistake of trying to sustain the apocalyptic mood throughout. The novel is actually three parable-like stories, tied together by an improbably ubiquitous character named Bradley Reynolds. Reynolds is on hand when the first expedition to Mars discovers life on the surface of the Red Planet; and as the expedition's sole survivor, he is in a position to tell a white lie about the nature of the discovery, so as to ensure mankind's continued interest in space travel.

Reynolds is also present a few years later when an enormous alien spaceship enters the solar system on what turns out to be a religious pilgrimage: The aliens have come to worship our sun, which they insist is a super-sentient being. Reynolds communes with the aliens and, through them, with the sun itself. . . . [Reynolds is finally] called back to space to command a team of scientists who are trying to decipher a mysterious message from a distant stellar civilization. (The star-worshipers have long since moved on.) The success of this mission leads to a final encounter with alien life-forms, in the course of which Reynolds attains a kind of immortality and meets a lot of old friends.

Two things must be said about this ambitious and deadly serious book. First, there is no satisfactory plural of ''apocalypse,'' and the attempt to provide one every 50 pages or so is self-defeating. Second, a truly apocalyptic vision (as opposed to a cosmic punchline) demands expression in language that rises above locutions like: ''This is one of the most significant events in the history of the human race. If anyone ought to know that, it's you. Christ.''

> Gerald Jonas, in a review of ''If the Stars Are Gods,'' in The New York Times Book Review, *March 27, 1977, p. 42.*

[RICHARD E. GEIS]

The dustjacket of [*If the Stars Are Gods*] proclaims it a major philosophical science fiction novel.

That's almost enough to prejudice anyone, even me, against it.

But I started reading, and found it to be a very well-written episodic story . . . Not a story, a narrative of the space career of Bradley Reynolds. . . .

I was impressed with Reynolds, with his wisdom, his character, his understandings of people. HE is the book. The philosophy is overlooked, and forgettable, strictly speaking. And the final revelation, on the last page . . . is something that I may have read in *Astonishing Stories* in 1939 or so.

Even so, the book is recommended, because there is a strength and grace in the style, in the narrative, in Bradley Reynolds, that makes the reading a pleasure. This is mature writing, adult science fiction.

> [Richard E. Geis], in a review of ''If the Stars Are Gods,'' in Science Fiction Review, *Vol. 6, No. 2, May, 1977, p. 53.*

LESTER DEL REY

[*In the Ocean of Night*] is the second novel in the Quantum Science Fiction Program. . . . I don't know what that program is trying to achieve, but I can't find myself very impressed as yet with the results.

Benford knows science fiction and he also knows science, since he's a professor of physics. In his shorter works, he has proved himself one of the more interesting younger writers in the field. But so far, I haven't found his novels very satisfactory. There is a great deal of good material in this one, but the totality somehow isn't convincing.

There are three steps in the development of the novel, each dealing with an alien ship, and all related through the hero of the book, Nigel. In the first, which I consider the best of these steps, Nigel is an astronaut who is sent to the asteroid Icarus during one of its close approaches to Earth. Seems Icarus has been spouting out gas like a comet and that jet of gas is changing the orbit, threatening to send the little world into collision with Earth. Nigel is supposed to blow it up with a bomb. But he discovers an alien ship buried inside the rocky worldlet. And he determines to save some evidence of that ship despite orders from Earth. It's a good section of the novel, well handled and convincing.

But then we skip fifteen years. Now working in the space agency, Nigel discovers that another alien ship is entering the Solar System. Here the story of Nigel's discovering the nature of the ship and his experiences with it are fascinating—but they're surrounded with too obvious "with it" sex for three, a new religion, and even a mysterious return from death that may be cleverly developed but somehow doesn't amount to anything in the long run.

And the final events begin when another ship is found buried on the Moon. (pp. 172-73)

Don't ask how long the ship was buried in Icarus, nor how that happened—but it had to be a long, long time. And the ship on the Moon must have lain there for over half a million years. Yet both of those suddenly develop activity that leads to their detection in a twenty-year period during which the second alien ship comes calling. There's a kind of common reason for the ships—but having three pop up so conveniently in such a limited part of the time of their existence is a bit too much to accept. . . .

A lot of [*In the Ocean of Night*] was published as short fiction in the magazines from 1972 on. That probably explains some of the trouble with the novel, since tying such material, written over several years, into a coherent whole is difficult. But for whatever reason, I found the novel hardly worth the effort of reading it. (p. 173)

> *Lester del Rey, in a review of "In the Ocean of Night," in* Analog Science Fiction/Science Fact, *Vol. XCVIII, No. 1, January, 1978, pp. 172-73.*

SPIDER ROBINSON

Lester del Rey has already reviewed *In The Ocean Of Night* in these pages [see excerpt above], freeing me from the necessity of dwelling on its flaws and obliging me to rebut.

Because, while some of Lester's criticisms were quite well-founded, I liked the book one hell of a lot, and expect to nominate it for a Hugo when the time comes. It has some of the finest characterization I have ever seen in a science fiction novel, the more astonishing when you consider that it is one of those books that was originally written over a period of 5 or 6 years as a series of novelettes. Atypically, it has been substantially rewritten so that no seams show; its parts are combined rather than simply welded together. The advantage is that you get genuine and profound character growth over a period of many years, both of his life and the author's. The result is a protagonist so real that I feel I've known him all my life. Furthermore, I *like* him.

All the characterization is first-rate; the dialogue is excellent; the writing itself is economical, vivid and quite literate. But what I think I liked most was that *Ocean* is one of the most successful attempts to infuse a work of sf with genuine spiri-

tuality. This is something rarely attempted and even more rarely achieved; I beat my palms bloody in applauding it and Benford.

The book is almost *too much* like real life; perhaps that's a fair statement of Lester's objection to it. It's one of those books that leaves some major questions unanswered—just like life does. This may or may not make you uncomfortable with it as a work of fiction. I can only say that it impresses the hell out of me. . . . Benford mailed me a galley out of the blue, saying, "If you're going to review *one* of my books, let this be the one," and I'm very glad he did. He has a right to be proud.

> *Spider Robinson, in a review of "In the Ocean of Night," in* Analog Science Fiction/Science Fact, *Vol. XCVIII, No. 6, June, 1978, p. 173.*

PUBLISHERS WEEKLY

[*The Stars in Shroud* is a] fine and superbly written science fiction novel. . . . The tale is based on an earlier [novella] (*Deeper Than the Darkness*) and is here developed into a full-length novel of adventure in space. Earth, after atomic wars, is taken over by the survivors, Orientals, who have built a space empire. Ling, a space captain and the book's hero, is sent to look into a disease fostered by the Quarn civilization. Ling himself contracts the disease, yet still is drawn into a plan for Quarn to take over Earth. Benford's imaginary worlds and imaginary people are fascinating as they carry on their lives in a, to us, surrealistic universe where empires crash and marriages crumble and human life goes on in much altered ways. Benford can write. SF fans will find their sights lifted with this pro at work.

> *A review of "The Stars in Shroud," in* Publishers Weekly, *Vol. 213, No. 26, June 26, 1978, p. 106.*

ALGIS BUDRYS

Greg Benford has been coming along, coming along as a professional SF writer after years of high status in the SF fan community. Working alone and with Gordon Eklund, Benford has been contributing important stories to the field. . . . Now he has produced *In the Ocean of Night,* a novel made by welding some of these parts into a unified structure, and it is a major novel.

Something very good is happening in SF. A new generation has arrived in the ranks of writers, and is establishing a clear voice of its own, taking the best of what it can assimilate from the past and creating a characteristic new sound by melding that with its own contemporary view of the world. (p. 54)

I think Gregory Benford, George R. R. Martin, and John Varley, have joined Joe Haldeman and become the nucleus of a group which probably also includes James Tiptree, Jr. (Sheldon), as well as many other writers who ought to be doing novels. . . .

The central identifying characteristic of this new school is that it takes science fiction seriously. This represents a sharp reversal of a fifteen-year-old tendency toward satire and allegory which made mere "science fiction" a totally inadequate label and necessitated the use of "SF" as a covering term.

Collaterally, this means the reappearance of the effective hero. Male or female, the protagonists of these stories are not the helpless victims of massive irreversible forces. They are people whose energies and intelligence have been directed to the acquisition of skills which make changes in the situation. Not great changes, some of them. But changes which rise from an understanding that the universe is real, with real rules, and a feeling that even though one may not grasp their full extent, nevertheless it is possible to use the known rules in dealing with problems. (p. 56)

What we have now from Benford, *et al*, is unique because while it turns from the view of the decade which ended in the early 1970s, it does not embrace wholeheartedly the seeming simplicism of the 1940s. (p. 57)

The hero of *In the Ocean of Night* is Nigel Walmsley, a British astronaut attached to NASA in the later years of this century. A skillfully drawn character—especially for a writer who is a California physicist—Walmsley thus enjoys that slight aura of alienation which represents a recurrent theme in "modern" science fiction. But he lives in a triadic marriage very reminiscent of the social arrangements of antiscience SF. As an active participant in technology, he is sent on a mission to divert or destroy Icarus, the eccentric asteroid, which suddenly begins a plunge toward Earth. As a self-directed personality, he disregards Ground Control upon discovering that Icarus is actually a long-abandoned alien interstellar vessel, lands, and explores. . . . As a man skilled in the verbal knife-fights of bureaucracy, he manages to capitalize on his actions, and to preserve his status so that he can continue to participate in the events which follow.

As you will recall if you have read, here, Benford's "**A Snark in The Night**," Walmsley next must cope with the problem of an alien drone entering the Solar System, while simultaneously attempting to resolve his emotional problems as one of his wives, suffering from a disease born of technological pollution, gradually succumbs. But Benford is too much a Post-Allegorist not to intertwine these two seemingly discrete developments. He makes each dramatically stronger in the process, and then merges them into one unifed development which to some extent transforms [Walmsley], changes both Earth and, to an appropriate extent, the universe, and leads on to further story developments. Those developments steadily increase the physical scope of the story, involving greater and greater perspectives, until at the end his novel evokes a truly majestic feeling for the vast distances and time-scales upon which the universe operates. But he never loses focus on Walmsley, who continues to be a distinct human being.

This is work on the award-winning level. More important even than that, I think, is that it presents a coherent view of people who, though seemingly born and dead in a twinkling, and far too feeble to affect the falling of a star, nevertheless can not only dream greatly but can, on occasion, do that which endures. I came away from this piece of work with a sense that though the heavens are wide, yet the human spirit can fare well upon them. . . . Welcome, Dr. Benford, *et al*; you are making something else of us all. (pp. 57-8)

*Algis Budrys, in a review of "In the Ocean of Night,"
in* The Magazine of Fantasy and Science Fiction, *Vol.
55, No. 1, July, 1978, pp. 54-8.*

DAVID N. SAMUELSON

Can anything new be said about alien contact, after countless variations on the themes defined by Wells? Eighty years later, we know the moon as a familiar desert, Venus as a cauldron and Mars as a fabulous landscape without any recognizable life forms. . . . We know as much as Wells did, and no more, i.e. nothing.

But we continue to spin tales about contact with aliens which can be little more than projections of human aspirations and despair. Those who believe they will come in peace, and soon, can take heart from the positive if pallid counterpoint to the mindless hostility of Fifties films offered by Stephen Spielberg's movie, *Close Encounters of the Third Kind*. Nonbelievers may still find refuge behind the words of J.B.S. Haldane, which may serve as a continuing goad to generations of science fiction writers: "The universe is not only queerer than we imagine; it is queerer than we can imagine."

As both a scientist and an artist, Gregory Benford is more at home with this agnostic position. Recognizing the statistical probability that there are intelligent aliens, and the improbability that we and they have actually met, he is also aware of the irrelevance of statistics to the actuality of possible contact, past or future, and to the desire for contact in the human imagination. He is also concerned with the theme of the alien for its artistic potential, not only for word-pictures, but also as an index to human sensibilities. (p. 5)

Benford generally takes great care with verisimilitude, especially including the scientific factors. But he finds representing the alien more than a trick, more than putting human beings into funny costumes. Confronting the alien is in large part his rationale for writing, even for reading, science fiction.

Benford published two novels in 1977, *If the Stars are Gods* (co-authored with Gordon Eklund) and *In the Ocean of Night,* which were the product of years of speculation on and contemplation of the alien mystique. A temporary culmination of his development with both theme and handling, they represent an extension of and a reaction to the use of aliens in other science fiction. A close examination of these books . . . may tell us something not just about Benford, but also about the resonance of the alien theme, which meshes here with human problems central to his thought, to the popularity of science fiction, perhaps to civilization in the latter half of the twentieth century. (pp. 5-6)

Although *In the Ocean of Night* was begun earlier, it was completed later [than *If the Stars are Gods*], and the collaboration with Gordon Eklund on *If the Stars are Gods* seems to have been instrumental in Benford's achievement in the other novel as well. When Benford proposed the novelette version, Eklund was already a full-time writer whose name and experience he hoped to gain from. Given the parallels with Benford's other work, it is apparent who was the dominant partner in the collaboration, but the best parts of the book resulted from the most balanced sharing of the work.

The protagonist of *If the Stars are Gods* is an alien-seeker, Bradley Reynolds, whose progress the book chronicles through several variations on the theme of alien contact. Though naturalistic speculation is predominant, in the title story the mythological roots of alien-hunting obviously are intertwined, in a way that points toward the transcendence sought at the novel's end. Dissatisfaction with the here-and-now is also evident in the protagonist, reflecting less the aspirations of the entire race than the ambiguous quest of an isolated individual.

Part One shows how Reynolds became the sole survivor of an ill-fated expedition which found life on Mars, but couldn't be sure whether it was indigenous or brought there by an unsterilized Soviet space capsule. Published separately (**"Hellas is Florida"**), this was written mainly by Eklund. Not an ineffective story in its own right, it serves mainly to introduce the hero and the uncertainty factor involved in dealing with the alien. Whether it was necessary for the book is contestable, since it is concisely summed up and overshadowed by Part Two. Rich in conception, characterization and handling, this story, which gave the title to the book, won the Nebula award for best novelette of 1974. From its frequent revision before publication, it acquired a complexity and polish from the collaboration which neither partner might have accomplished on his own.

Twenty-five years later, in the year 2017, Reynolds is now 58, a man who is doubly "alienated". Ill at ease with other people, dissatisfied with the state of society and of his own life, he has more or less devoted it to the quest for the impossible. By occupation, he is now an astronomer, no longer an astronaut-explorer; by fate he has been chosen to establish communication between humanity—(that is, the United States) and the giraffe-like beings who have apparently come to "worship" our sun.

Communication is imperfect at best, but Reynolds, predisposed to distrust his own kind, comes to believe he has established fairly firm rapport with the aliens. Sorting out what he thinks are truth and lies, he delivers to his nominal superiors various pieces of information about the aliens and their world. Of their goals, one is immediately comprehensible in human terms: their apparent need to resettle on a congenial world, their own being threatened by changes in its climate that may induce racial psychosis. The other goal makes no sense to people trained in Western science, but Reynolds accepts that they believe in divine stars; he even shares, subjectively, their communion with our sun. At this climactic point, the alien Vergnan sings a "hymn" to the sun and Reynolds, joining in, feels guided to a contact that is mind-jarring, not only in its apparent revelation of the sun's living intelligence (reminiscent of Stapledon's *Star Maker*), but also in the sun's message for him. At the core, Reynolds senses cold, valueless nothingness, which parallels the aliens' judgment that our sun is not as benevolent as they had hoped. But it is also consistent with Reynolds's own doubts and with the alternative explanations—hypnosis, hysteria, drugs—he later offers for his experience.

Whether he actually makes more than superficial contact with the aliens is never clearly resolved, even in his own mind. Certainly parts of the story he relays to his colleagues seem inconsistent, whether because of misunderstandings or misrepresentations. A race of giraffe-like beings . . . , the aliens are represented as technophobic nomads whose Rube Goldberg-like starship is a gift from a manlike race from "the true center of the universe". Despite their distrust of machines and their limited manipulative ability, they can pilot the ship, and have done so for over a century's trip. They have encountered other intelligent races, none of which pose any danger to them or to man, and they have exhibited a considerable amount of diplomacy along with a remarkable facility for languages. How much of this is true, the reader can not know, having Reynolds as a filter, nor can we necessarily judge what is relevant. . . . More important to the reader's uncertainty is the very alienness of the creatures, of which Reynolds continually has to remind the others, *and himself.*

Reynolds's objectivity is in doubt because more and more he comes to identify with what he thinks is the alien viewpoint, which progressively alienates him further from his fellow humans. At first he looks down at their technophobia, their re-

jection of his books and tape recorder, their treatment of the ship as a stable. . . . Finally, he takes a little perverse joy in ordering other humans accompanying him on his last trip inside the starship not to wear spacesuits, deprecating their xenophobia. Their questions, too, he sees as faintly ridiculous, representing the attitude he once had of getting *facts*—physical sizes, shapes, distances and dangers—without looking for meaning. Crazy as the aliens seem, they believe in something, though their spokesman, Johnathon, says that he—that everyone—has doubts, and Reynolds comes to share at least a portion of their belief. By the end of the story, meaning transcends for him the material quests of ordinary human beings.

There are echoes here of Gulliver among the Houyhnhnms . . . , but nothing is quite as clearcut as in Swift's masterpiece. Aliens and Americans are as different in their own way as Oriental and Occidental or scientific and "prescientific" man. Though we are warned against oversimplifying such distinctions, the human characters draw parallels between the aliens' beliefs and those of such "discarded" human faiths as sun-worship, astrology and nomadic Judaism. Like adherents of these faiths, the aliens may be looking at the same phenomena, but they do not see the same things that we do, and human theories as to what they actually see must be largely guesswork. (pp. 9-11)

Though he frequently feels confident and buoyant in his role of interpreter, Reynolds gradually comes to distrust that feeling as vanity, after several jolts indicate he has seriously misjudged the aliens. . . . His quest for transcendent meaning has led him into alien pathways, but not necessarily those of the aliens; ultimately, this quest must take him inside himself, to inner as well as outer space.

Technophobia and transcendence are related to the theme of achieving maturity, which has directed many a science fiction hero. . . . [Reynolds] has lived through much, much of it boring. He has cultivated a studied independence from both military spit-and-polish and administrative caution. He warily studies his reactions and weighs his words. Acquainted with fame and thoroughly tired of other people, he is tired enough to request that the aliens take him with them, wherever they go next. Though this may seem a rash, impulsive act, the foundation of it is credibly laid beforehand.

In this mental sea-change, there is a respect for age and apparent wisdom, and a repugnance for childish arrogance which reflect Reynolds's feeling of neglect by his own society. This attitude is made more explicit in Part Five of the novel, with its epigraph from Yeats's "Sailing to Byzantium": "An aged man is but a paltry thing / A tattered coat upon a stick, unless / Soul clap its hands and sing, and louder sing. . . ." Implicit here, however, is the sense from the same poem that "That is no country for old men", because "Caught in that sensual music all neglect / Monuments of unaging intellect", as well as the desire of Yeats's persona that the "sages" of Byzantium become "the singing masters of [his] soul".

Where Yeats asks the sages to "consume my heart away", Reynolds's revelation begins with an entrance into a rather different part of the anatomy. Entering the starship, he takes part in "the act of being swallowed", and finds himself in "tight passages" all but gagging at the smell of "vintage manure". . . . [This] alien ship combines digestive, excretory and copulatory associations, with overtones of the womb from which rebirth may follow. Furthermore, the pastel colouration of the walls is reminiscent of a nursery, and the aliens recall childhood memories of zoos and animated cartoons. The first alien's voice "reminded him of a child", the second's voice was identical, and the fluttering eyes of one and the acts of "obeisance" of the other, splaying all four legs to belly down to the floor, have something quaint and ludicrous about them to our eyes.

Reynolds, however, though at first he sees them as childish, gradually comes to the realization that he, though old among active spacemen, is as a child to the aliens, who apparently live for centuries, and whose wisdom must be ancient. His approach to solar communion, which clinches his elevation of their wisdom, is undertaken in the spirit of a disillusioned Westerner prostrating himself at the feet of a guru, whose promise of Eastern wisdom is commonly seen by the West as ancient, regardless of whether we accept it or not.... After this, the posturing of humans and their mere factual questioning and bickering come to seem childish indeed. Reynolds's own actions become not exactly a matter of indifference to him, but the plane of objective reality becomes something to which he is more or less resigned. It comes as no surprise to find in Part Three that he spends some thirty-five years in monastic meditation before the call of the alien tempts him once more from retirement.

The world from which he retires, and from which he longs to escape, is that of our near future, of which we are given only tantalizing hints.... We may assume, I think, as in other Benford fiction, that a crash of some sort is imminent, perhaps always implicit in his conception of technological society, and the alien theme represents in part a desire to escape that crash.

Whether the aliens are really old or wise, or even technophobic, is as uncertain as the answer to the implied question in the title. The concept of gods introduced here is man-made, however, and it does not necessarily fit the aliens, the stars or the Earth itself. What is evident is that we can not know, that the alien is precisely that, a concept Benford shares with Lem, most notably in *Solaris*. All of the meanings we deal with are man-made categories, as suggested by the novelette's epigraph from Wittgenstein: "A dog cannot be a hypocrite, but neither can he be sincere". Though the apothegm seems aimed at the aliens, whose sincerity is in doubt, it is also appropriate to Reynolds, who is both explicitly and implicitly likened to a dog. Wittgenstein, with his concern for how little we can positively know, and his love of paradox, might well approve.

Recognizing perhaps the dog in himself and seeking to find the alien in himself, Reynolds goes into seclusion, in transitional Part Three, only to be seduced from his meditation by the siren call of an alien message received from deep space. This interlude brings us to Part Four, which broadens still further the concepts of alien and alienation. Published independently ("**The Anvil of Jove**"), this is a collaborative effort, but mainly Benford's, with much less give-and-take between the partners in its production. The result is primarily a "hard" science fiction "puzzle-story" in which some of the puzzles are human. Because the alien message (it is actually called "the Puzzle") seems to suggest that its senders might inhabit a world like Jupiter, the research project has been set up there. Beyond the solving of "the Puzzle", the story also leads to the discovery of Jovian life-forms, spherical, floating, and intelligent, though the actions are largely independent of each other. What connects them is that both problems were solved by "alien" human beings, envied and detested by the "normal" human beings of the project.

Called "Nippies" because they are results of genetic manipulation, Mara and Corey are alien from each other as well as from everyone else, and theirs is the human involvement that makes the story go round. Mara is a beautiful young woman of eccentric habits, whose superior intelligence is demonstrable, whose "paranoia" is justified by verbal and physical attacks on her, and whose talents finally become useful to the project only when Corey's life is doomed and hers is in danger. The soft spot in her unemotional armor is her affection for her "brother", Corey, a cyborg, literally a box, whose gender is in doubt until the end. Responsible for attempts on Mara's life, he finally atones for his acts and ends his own suffering by volunteering for hazardous duty in the Jovian atmosphere, from which he reports back his discovery of native life forms, and triggers Mara's solution of the Puzzle. (pp. 11-13)

Part Five (based on a discarded ending for the 1975 version of *Jupiter Project*) takes [Reynolds] to Titan, which Benford, virtually unassisted, naturalistically brings to life.... Though the motivations of the other characters are somewhat in doubt, Reynolds is there for one purpose alone, a logical extension of his previous contacts with the alien. The alien artifact on Titan is hard to recognize by human categories, but Reynolds finds it and merges with it, the configurations of his mind being preserved by these crystal lattices after his death. (p. 14)

In an epilogue, Benford explains—not clearly enough for some reviewers—that "the lattice was a transmitter" from which Reynolds's "intense experience" was broadcast to the home planet of a "stasis life" form, "trying to fix what [it] knew as an impermanent form, *fluxlife* (emphasis his)". Increasing jumps of time and space distance the reader, in structural counterpart to the shifts in viewpoint in Part One which finally ended up with Reynolds, but this is still an awkward way to end a book. The episodic structure mars the continuity, as in Clarke's *2001* and *Childhood's End,* and the failure is perhaps inevitable in the conception. Melodrama and sentimentality weaken Parts Four and Five; One and Three and Six are almost tacked on to suggest the intellectual and emotional continuity of Reynolds's quixotic existence. And the very richness and complexity of Two and Four make them top-heavy for the chronicle form implied by the overall shape of the novel. Still, invention and characterization almost carry it off, if the reader can take the assemblage simply as variations on a theme.

More ambitious, and more successful, is *In the Ocean of Night,* although it is also assembled from separately conceived and published parts. Nurtured, perhaps, by the ongoing collaboration with Eklund, they grew into a more organic form, in which the parts complement, rather than simply follow each other. Almost twice as long as the collaboration, and as complicated as the centerpieces of the other work, this novel will inevitably be shortchanged by a brief critical analysis. Thematically, however, it can be tied in to the complex of alienness and alienation, without leaving too much out.

The focus is again on an astronaut, Nigel Walmsley, who is in the prime of life and thus may be easier for the reader to accept. He is alienated from the start, as the sole Englishman in the American space programme, and intelligent enough to look critically at both NASA and the United States. A man without a country in several senses of the term, he is most at home in confrontations with the alien, which he sees as the *raison d'etre* of any space programme. The enemy, if there is one, is not so much the alien.... Rather it is the rigid, paranoiac bureaucracy of the American government, which is understandably concerned about the security and territorial integrity of the Earth. It is also threatened by economic rivals from abroad and increasingly under pressure from irrational religious elements more in tune with the inward, subjective movement of its own people.

The reduced economic situation of the United States and the general social setting of the story are more in evidence than in other Benford fiction. Characterization is richer than ever before, especially of the protagonist, but also for some of the secondary characters. Sexual activity is again a measure of vitality, and East-West relationships once more counterpoint the human-alien dichotomy. But male-female, astronaut-groundling, scientist-worshipper antitheses are also important, and fully established through characters in action.

This time the alien is a representative of a machine-civilization, to which we are one of those relatively rare and transitory organic life forms that sometimes threaten the stability of things, before they either give way to machines or wink out of existence. The "Snark" as Nigel calls it, emphasizing its unknowable qualities via the allusion to Lewis Carroll's poem, interacts with human beings in several ways, most of which involve Nigel. First, to identify it as an alien he circumvents NASA intentions by working out a communications system linking it directly to himself. Through his unwitting agency, the Snark takes over a human body, that of Nigel's lover, Alexandria, at the moment of her death. Later, it uses Nigel's own senses as tool for further explorations of the terrestrial environment. Nigel's friend, Mr. Ichino, helps programme messages to the Snark, chief among which are artifacts of our culture that help it better to understand us, and serve to enrich the loneliness of its journey. Finally, the Snark confronts Nigel in space, in a NASA "interceptor" inadequate to its job, and educates him in the realities of the Universe, "the ocean of night".

That confrontation might have been the end of a lesser novel. Here it is only the second of Nigel's three connections with alien vessels. The first, based on the novelette "Icarus Descending," is a hulk, misidentified for years as an asteroid. Nigel is one of two astronauts sent to prevent its probable collision with the Earth, by blowing it up if necessary. Names and details have been changed since first publication, but the central thrust remains: discovering the ship's true nature, Nigel delays its destruction in order to explore its interior, risking the wrath of a panicky planet. His conviction that we have much to learn from the aliens is hardly vindicated at that time, fifteen years before the main sections of the novel, but his motivation and his first experience of the alien are convincingly represented.

The rupturing of this ship, resulting in an escape of atmosphere which propels it toward Earth, is coincident with the sending of a distress signal summoning the Snark, away from its intended course. That Nigel is still in position, with Pasadena's Jet Propulsion Laboratory, to interact with the second alien vessel is due to his tenacity for bureaucratic infighting and his stature as a "public figure" earned from press conferences, talk shows, etc. Having maintained his astronaut's rating, he is a logical if resisted choice, not only for interceptor pilot, but also for the lunar project of the last third of the novel, in which Earth scientists pry information from still a third alien ship, activated by the Snark in passing.

In this section, the fragmented Nigel of the earlier narratives comes closer to wholeness in his human affairs, as well as in his grasp of human-alien similarities and differences. His *ménage à trois* with Alexandria and Shirley, another Occidental woman, was wrecked by Alexandria's acquiring lupus, then by the defection of both women to a charismatic religious cult, the New Sons of God. Alexandria's death and her transfiguration by the Snark wins fame for the faith and plunges Nigel into a "dark night of the soul" from which he emerges better able to love in a more unselfish way. This is indicated by his sexual liaison with Nikka, an Oriental girl he meets in his lunar research, but also by his asexual relationship with Mr. Ichino, an older, more ascetic version of what Nigel could become. In this second triangle, Nigel is involved in a merging of East and West, of course, but also in a bipolar connection with male and female, young and old, in love relationships which are also held together by shared interests and outlooks.

The work of all three is less dramatic than Nigel's earlier confrontation, but it is intellectually exciting nonetheless. Nigel and Nikka extract secrets from the alien hulk, interact with each other in analyzing them, and manage to make much of their information public, despite attempts by the bureaucracy, infiltrated by New Sons, to block transmission of material that might upset mankind's mythological self-portrait.... Neither Nikka nor Ichino understands the alien as well as Nigel, who absorbs a charge of alien information on the moon which builds on his previous contacts, and radically reorganizes his world view. (pp. 14-16)

Nigel's last series of revelations parallel the concluding statements of potential Clarke and Heinlein gave the protagonists of *2001* and *Stranger in a Strange Land,* without the mysticism and metaphysics they felt compelled to use. Nigel's situation is always explicable in naturalistic terms; the beauty of his vision of a Universe alien to man is in its existential reality. It is not evident how Nigel will use his new-found perceptions, but his insights are accessible to others, in the book, and in the reader. (p. 16)

Resemblances to *2001* and *Rendezvous with Rama* are inevitable, as also to countless other stories of first contact and rebels rewarded, not to mention dystopian or at least deteriorating futures. Where **In the Ocean of Night** advances on them, while still adhering to formulas, is partly in artistry, in the fusing of themes, in the embedding of a minimal metaphysic in the solid ground of naturalistic description and psychologically convincing characterization, in structural and stylistic effects that are perhaps better dealt with in other contexts than this one. Suffice it to say that this is a remarkable step in the direction of the science fiction novel, rather than the simpler romance.

And the major reason may be the development of the astronaut-hero, the alien-seeker silhouetted . . . against the background of an Earth society declining in resources and the will to risk them on off-planet adventures. Benford recognizes the seductiveness of self-sufficiency as well as the lure of the unknown; though he sees in the latter the potential for renewal, not just of the individual but also of the race, he does not succumb to the temptation to make his hero a knight in shining armour. Nigel has a touch of the adventurer about him, a bit of the child, and more than his share of irritability and impatience with those around him who can not see as far as he can. But for all that he is a rebel against constraints, he recognizes the reality of those constraints. The environment of space is unforgiving; he cannot disregard its limits and survive. But neither can he take for granted his own superiority to social controls and bureaucratic enforcement of them, simply because he knows his cause is just. He has had to learn the rules and how to circumvent them, how to use publicity and bureaucratic hierarchies as tools, and how to play the game better than his rivals and opponents. And finally, he has had to come to recognize the limits of himself, not just of his body but also of his mind, of the shape it has been given by his society and its myths.

Nigel's longing for space and its potential, his victories over the forces of darkness are appropriate to the formula demands of the Western, adapted to the space frontier. His dependence on technology, on society, even on family, however, contrast starkly with the rejection of all three by the lone gunslinger riding into town out of the desert. . . . Though his mind may be an "outlaw", yearning for the impossible, he knows he can never merge with the "other". But as a scientist, he must try, he must learn what he can, he must approximate in his terms what he senses that is beyond him. As a child progressively internalizes the world outside, Nigel encompasses the alien, formulating a paradigm which unites even organic and machine civilization against the awesome backdrop of the emptiness between civilizations.

This paradigm is implicit in Benford's equation of the alien with the future, in his arguments, proffered in lecture, that alien contact and artificial intelligence are the prospective last nails in the coffin of man's anthropocentric world view. As a creative physicist, he is aware of the role of science in familiarizing the unknown, at the cost of knowing its reality. As a human being, he is also aware of the fears of the unknown which we try to allay by means of religion, art and science, in progressively less—or less obviously—anthropocentric terms. The mythological component of religion traditionally looks backward, analogizing with past images of the unknown, such as the god and devil figures of *Childhood's End* and Promethean archetypes from *Frankenstein* to *Dune,* and beyond. Science ostensibly looks forward, carrying us into physical and mental arenas for which most of us are singularly poorly equipped.

Art, theoretically, can mediate between religion and science, using both new and traditional images and patterns, juxtaposing differing world-views. Science fiction, as a "lay mythology", performs this function for increasingly large numbers of people. Although most science fiction may do this badly, pandering more to the desire to return to a simpler existence, where magic works or Mother can make it all better, some science fiction is up to the task, not of exorcizing the alien, but rather of assimilating it. . . . If responding to [this challenge] is possible (pace Toynbee), to preserve what is worth preserving of our civilization, imagining that response is a must, not in the puerile terms of *Close Encounters of the Third Kind* or *Star Wars,* but in a hard-nosed manner which recognizes the adamancy of the physical and psychical materials with which we have to work. (pp. 16-18)

[Although] *In the Ocean of Night* is a culmination of Benford's work with the theme up to now, it is only a temporary resting-place. In preparation are three more volumes dealing with aspects of the alien, broadly conceived. . . . Whether or not these variations on the theme measure up to . . . *In the Ocean of Night* artistically, they're certain to add more depth and resonance to the alien theme in Benford's work, and in science fiction, and just possibly in the world outside. (p. 18)

> David N. Samuelson, "From Aliens to Alienation: Gregory Benford's Variations on a Theme," in Foundation, *No. 14, September, 1978, pp. 5-19.*

DAN MILLER

A superbly written novel of the far distant future, [*The Stars in Shroud*] tells of the moral and physical degeneration of

Earth's space empire in the face of persistent and sinister attacks from the mysterious Quarn. . . . [The Quarn's] biggest conquest comes in duping starship captain Ling Sanjen in their drive toward the empire's heart, Earth. Benford neatly weaves in an examination of the nature of religious experience with fast-paced action, all set against the well-conceived background of a pathetic Earth culture.

> Dan Miller, in a review of *"The Stars in Shroud,"* in Booklist, *Vol. 75, No. 3, October 1, 1978, p. 275.*

DAVID N. SAMUELSON

Is it really appropriate for science fiction to be about science? Ever since Hugo Gernsback, someone's been arguing over whether the first word in "science fiction" is anything but an honorific, or . . . a curse. Gregory Benford has been known to straddle that line himself, declaring himself a "hard science fiction" writer, a member of a class of which there are no members, since fantasy is essential, requiring fancy footwork to cover over the questions science cannot (yet) answer.

But being a practicing physicist and a conscientious artist, concerned with the knowledge won from experience, Benford has tried at times to make science central to his fiction, almost to the point of excluding the fantasy altogether. (p. 24)

At moments, a character might stop and reflect, taking time out from other adventures to actually do some science, observing, hypothesizing, testing, before he had a result worth announcing. For some readers, this slowed up the action, as in, for example, *In the Ocean of Night.* But in *Timescape* this *is* the action, in so far as it departs from living in the real world with all of its demands and distractions.

The science fiction of *Timescape* is, loosely speaking, time travel, complete with paradoxes, both potential and actual. Technically, it's time *communication,* by means of a technique that's dramatically plausible but theoretically impossible. Scientists in Cambridge, England (1998) try to bombard indium antinomide in La Jolla, California (1963), with tachyons, theoretical particles that can only travel faster than light, hence backwards in time, directed in space to where Earth was at the target time. Success is urgent, since life, or at least civilization, is threatened by a biochemical reaction that might be reversible before it gets started, i.e. "if only we knew then what we know now".

Doesn't sound promising? Sounds like an interminable lecture? Like one of a dozen past novels of ecotastrophe? Or a story in which a nameless technician discovers a strange message, precipitating a successful rescue by some equivalent of the U.S. Cavalry coming over the rise? It's nothing of the kind, any of those kinds.

What Benford has done to spotlight this action is to write a full-fledged novel about people who live, who make love, who fight for their identity and survival, in the context of doing for a living an intellectually obsessing activity known as science, with all of the attendant politics of the scientific community, past and future.

The people of 1998 are, understandably, on the edge of desperation. Cambridge is beset by shortages—of food, electricity, raw materials, law and order—but the academic middle class is surviving, in a civilized, barely flappable way. . . .

The most serious threat, a new cloud-borne life form resulting from ocean pollution, is officially known to very few beyond the Emergency Council, whose efforts to fight on all fronts at once both the causes and effects of the past's profligacy seem doomed. But that Renfrew's tachyon experiment is worth supporting is agreed by Council member Ian Peterson and visiting American physicist Gregory Markham, who seek help from British, American and Continental sources. . . .

The situation in La Jolla, thirty-six years earlier, seems contrasting in the extreme. America has just entered the Sixties (the book's action starts in 1962, making 1980 a midpoint between its two presents), ebulliently optimistic. Nowhere is it more so than at the La Jolla campus of the University of California (now UC San Diego), madly recruiting science faculty, with Nobel prizewinners seemingly around every corner.

Heady with this atmosphere, Gordon Bernstein is an Assistant Professor of Physics, dependent on the good graces of senior faculty not only for tenure and promotion, but also for research grant support and approval. . . .

Bernstein is the reluctant recipient of Renfrew's inexplicable and garbled message, for which he must fight for acceptance and interpretation, against the weight of the scientific establishment and the publicized wrong guesses of well-meaning colleagues and competitors. . . . Gordon risks his future for the sake of a puzzle that won't go away, and that turns out to involve the risk of everybody's future.

All of this is treated with loving, sensuous detail, much of it taken from life. . . . Benford is familiar with both Cambridge, where he has taught and studied, and La Jolla, where he was a graduate student at the time of the novel. Numerous real-life scientists make cameo appearances, including Benford and his brother (under another name) and a headline-hunting send-up of Carl Sagan.

The imaginary details are also in place, however, from Bernstein's confrontations with his mother and family over living with a *shiksa*, to Peterson's fulfilling long-laid plans to survive the catastrophe on his family's country estate. But central to the book is the recurrent experience of *doing science,* in the laboratory, in the classroom, in the colloquium, in the board room and especially in the mind.

Science is not a swashbuckling adventure, but an intellectual activity, and one in which a single flash of revelation may lead to endless philosophical repercussions and even mystical overtones, but seldom before a thousand obstacles, rebuffs, distractions, wrong turnings and after-the-fact reservations. For all of its vaunted teamwork, science is also an essentially solitary activity, like life: in *Timescape* the "community of scholars" continually threatens to turn into a school of sharks, just as the traditionally sought-after "love of a good woman" can be transformed into a model of miscommunication.

The result is a thoroughly engrossing novel, about interesting and real-seeming people, in an intellectually and emotionally charged setting, or pair of settings. At the least, it's the best science fiction novel since *A Canticle for Leibowitz,* but there really is no precedent for *Timescape* in science fiction. The closest competition outside science fiction, the novels of C.P. Snow, are no match for Benford in vision or style. If Simon and Schuster and Gollancz are at all successful in marketing it as general fiction, it should be the next big book about which people will say "This can't be science fiction . . . it's good!" (p. 25)

> *David N. Samuelson, in a review of "Timescape,"
> in* Science Fiction Review, *Vol. 9, No. 3, August,
> 1980, pp. 24-5.*

TOM EASTON

[A] great many current SF novels are set in a future of scarcity that might have been avoided or at least put off by more rational consumption patterns. Greg Benford's *Timescape* (there's a pun in there) is an example. The context includes resource shortages. It also includes overpopulation and ecodisaster. By 1998, the chemicals we have put on the land—pesticides, herbicides, fertilizers, etc.—have washed into the sea, there to begin a self-sustaining process that promises to end human life. The world is run by a World Council which, among other things, controls the trickle of funding for scientific research. In England's Cavendish Laboratory, a young researcher, John Renfrew, is working with tachyons. He has the idea that they can be used to communicate back across the years, to send a message that will prevent disaster. To do so, he has to focus a tachyon beam on suitable experiments, involving super-cooled indium antimonide, in which the beam can influence the noise level. Fortunately, such experiments were being done in the early 1960s by a California physicist, Gordon Bernstein.

When Renfrew tries his message sending, Bernstein notices the Morse code in the noise. He deciphers it, experiences suitable amazement, and then tries to convince others. No way. He is clearly seeing things in his data. However, he eventually prevails, and steps are taken to prevent disaster. . . .

There are vast stretches of physics, intended to display the difference between past and future, the doing of physics and the nature of physicists, and to show off Benford's familiarity with the recent past of his own discipline, but also to analyze the problem of time-travel paradoxes (as convincingly as any other SF writer) and demonstrate that time must branch into alternate histories.

One does care about Benford's characters, about their problems and fates. *Timescape* is a disaster novel, after all, and it shares a certain grippingness with the rest of the genre. It is well enough written, too. But for all that it fails to hold the attention as well as it might. I believe this is because Benford has spent so much time on his characters, on developing the lives and thoughts and feelings affected by his plot that the plot itself loses momentum. The story would have more impact if it were trimmed by a quarter or a third, and Benford's people would still be alive enough. But don't let my grumblings stop you from reading the book. When you consider that well-developed characters often leave readers wishing a story didn't end so soon, Benford may well please more people than not. If so— well, I still think he overdid it. I praise him more for his idea of the history-message time loop, and I wonder if such a thing could possibly help us out of our resource-shortage bind.

> *Tom Easton, in a review of "Timescape," in* Analog
> Science Fiction/Science Fact, *Vol. C, No. 10, October, 1980, p. 164.*

TOM EASTON

[The title of *Shiva Descending* refers to] an asteroid over two kilometers in diameter, aimed dead at Earth and offering the likely end of all surface life on our planet. The only possible solution is to blow it off course with a 400-megaton Russian hell-bomb and a couple of dozen 20-megaton jobs. The world has less than a year to get its act together, and that act depends on an egomaniac astronaut.

The novel details the deterioration of the human psyche faced with total disaster. . . . As meteors turn cities into craters and rubble, fatalism becomes the philosophy of the day.

You know the ending. Too few authors dare to live up to the dire threats they utter. But the story is not just the tale of victory. It is also a tale of ongoing disaster, and it seems tailored for the same folks who love gruesome headlines. It's a pot-boiling disaster novel, and not worth a dime as literature. But it'll probably make a bundle, so—more power to the authors. Both Lit and Non-lit have their places in the world, and though we may wish the one could appeal like the other and the other were written like the one, it just ain't in the cards, and even writers have to live. I only wish I could live so well.

> *Tom Easton, in a review of "Shiva Descending," in* Analog Science Fiction/Science Fact, *Vol. C, No. 11, November, 1980, p. 171.*

RICHARD E. GEIS

[A] Changeling can alter his body to mimick any living form he wishes, and he firmly believes the nature of the universe is chaos and unpredictability. He is a dedicated, religious anarchist and he and his species—few, growing fewer—are hunted and killed by humans, by the Earth Consortium, as they individually slip into a society and sow disorganization, riot, ruin.

[In *Find the Changeling*], Fain—the veteran Changeling killer, and Skallon, an idealistic anthropologist sent with him—arrive on the plague-infested colony planet Alvea in hot pursuit of a clever, ruthless Changeling. (pp. 24-5)

The Changeling plays games with them, kills, adroitly seeds the fragile society with destruction . . . and in the end attempts the ultimate emotional destruction of its hated enemy—Fain.

Here's everything you want in a sf novel—action, sex, violence, pace, depth of characterization, an intriguing, terrible alien, a strange human society . . . and a thought-provoking philosophical problem to consider.

A superior science fiction novel. (p. 25)

> *Richard E. Geis, in a review of "Find the Changeling," in* Science Fiction Review, *Vol. 9, No. 4, November, 1980, pp. 24-5.*

JOHN CLUTE

[*Shiva Descending*] is probably not the worst novel about a huge meteor on a collision course with our planet, but then who's keeping score. Will Shiva total Terra? Will the President go bonkers from too much strain and too much sex with his secretary? . . . These questions, and many many more, receive answers. It all takes 400 pages. . . . Shiva is eventually diverted, shifted into orbit, and slated to become a space station: ending all these woes. Of main interest, at least to readers of Benford's other books, may be the way in which the bureaucratic corruption of NASA and of government in general can be read pretty explicitly as a description of the entropic loss of vigor of Western civilization itself as the century passes on beyond the Moon landing. Though ostensibly a tale of human valor and technological triumph against almost insuperable odds, beneath all the acres of blockbuster filibustering there is a fin-de-siecle melancholy to the book, telling us that not all is well,

and even suggesting a few reasons for our sense of unease. It's some compensation for all the nonsense on top.

> *John Clute, in a review of "Shiva Descending," in* The Magazine of Fantasy and Science Fiction, *Vol. 59, No. 6, December, 1980, p. 42.*

JOHN CLUTE

Few science fiction novels are about science. . . .

Gregory Benford's *Timescape,* which is by far the best novel yet from this working physicist and successful writer, is an exception. Its protagonists are physicists deeply and obsessively involved in the entangled arduous pursuit of (relatively) pure knowledge; its plot involves them in what might be called imaginary science in a real garden. The world of 1998 is close to terminal ecocatastrophe. . . .

Of the recourses available to the world's failing governments, one of the more remote seems to be a project—lovingly described—to induce morse-coded tachyon transmission through time and space to the earth of 1963, warning of the disaster to come. . . . Most of the novel, set in an expansive dawn-like America circa 1962-63, before the Kennedy assassination, deals with the efforts of a rising young physicist at the University of California (La Jolla branch) to make sense of an experiment involving indium antimonide, a substance whose atomic structure, sensitive to tachyon bombardment, is registering interference effects in morse code.

Gordon Bernstein, the physicist in question, is a well-realized character; his ultimately triumphant obsession with his problem, his New York Jewish enthralment with a California *shiksa* convincingly deep into surfing, sex and Goldwater, his befuddled immersement in university politics and rivalries, all bring the reader to an elated sense that the haecceity of scientific cognition is being laid bare for him, and that to be a working physicist is to be in the world, where we all are.

> *John Clute, "Faster than Light," in* The Times Literary Supplement, *No. 4053, December 5, 1980, p. 1378.*

THOMAS M. DISCH

Of a book as good as Gregory Benford's *Timescape,* a reviewer can say very little except, Take my word, this is superlative, read it. Not only does *Timescape* accomplish the specific task of science fiction (what that task is may be assumed, in these pages, to be self-evident), but it also clears the hurdles of the mainstream novel with strength, grace, and intellectual distinction. Its prose is lucid, flexible, and eloquent without straining after 'poetic' effects. Its characterizations have a precision and amplitude of observation rare in even the best sf, since it is difficult to be precise or observant about hypothetical social structures. Contemporary realism necessarily has the edge in that regard, but Benford is able to possess himself of that advantage by setting half his novel in 1962. His scrupulous treatment of the recent past becomes his touchstone for that part of the book set in 1998, a date equidistant (from 1980) in the near future. (p. 46)

The plot concerns the efforts of a group of Cambridge physicists in 1998 to get a message back to the scientific establishment of the year 1962 warning them of the world's impending doom. . . . It will give away few turns of the plot to note that the tachyons get through to 1962, since the story's suspense depends rather on how the message is interpreted and whether it is to be believed, a drama that allows full scope to Benford's ability to portray scientists in the round—as politicians, as professional intellectuals, as members of a common culture. As a group portrait of the scientific community *Timescape* compares favorably with the novels of C. P. Snow or even with a non-fiction work like Watson's *The Double Helix.*

As a work of the imagination, comparison becomes more difficult, since sf writers so seldom attempt anything of this magnitude and seriousness. (Seriousness is usually a term I cringe at, since it implies a kind of moral superiority in a work of art. Nevertheless, I would call this 'serious fiction' in the sense that it eschews playfullness and works with the simplest materials on the largest possible scale to create a moral paradigm of great hortatory force.) Beside it even such admirable recent works as *The Dispossessed* or *The Fountains of Paradise* (to cite works that share Benford's 'seriousness' and his determination to express the imaginative core of scientific thought) seem thin and schematic.

While I can't pretend to judge the physics of the book as a physicist, I'm willing to defer in such conjectures to the authority of Dr. Benford, who . . . is accounted *the* expert on tachyons. I'll take his word on tachyons. However, when the characters began to speculate about standard time-travel paradoxes, such as "Was that my grandfather I murdered last night and should I *warn* him about me?" I feel no such compunction. The only answers to such eternal quandries are those that art provides, the sense of closure that comes when an engrossing story finds the tellingly right cadences for its finale. (pp. 46-7)

Timescape is a superlative novel, i.e., beyond comparison. Read it and proselytize for it. This is one of those rare works of sf, like *A Canticle for Leibowitz,* that can speak to the unconverted. (p. 47)

Thomas M. Disch, in a review of ''Timescape,'' in The Magazine of Fantasy and Science Fiction, *Vol. 60, No. 2, February, 1981, pp. 46-7.*

GEORGE R. R. MARTIN

Benford, fresh from the overwhelming triumph of *Timescape,* turns away from that novel's portrait of working scientists to a concern that informed much of his earlier work: the confrontation of human and alien. In *Against Infinity,* the human is Manuel Lopez, a 13-year-old boy living in one of the human settlements that are busily terraforming Ganymede, and the alien is the Aleph, a strange artifact left behind by some ancient nonhuman race which spends eternity moving up and down and through the mountains . . . until Manuel "kills" it during one of the settlement's jolly Aleph-hunts. When the Aleph ceases to move, there are dire consequences for Manuel, his friends, his father, and ultimately for everyone on Ganymede.

It would be nice to report that Benford has done it again, that he has captured a truly *alien* alien as successfully as he captured the workings of science in *Timescape.* Unfortunately, it's not so. Benford's writing is never less than fine, and *Against Infinity* is a perfectly good coming-of-age novel, and the bioengineered animals used in the terraforming are a splendid stroke of invention. But the Aleph, alas, is not a creation to stand with Lem's Solaris or Lovecraft's color out of space. Instead of seeming alien and unknowable, it comes across as arbitrary and badly-described, always a danger in this kind of

story. And the ending, with its heavy mystical overtones, seems glaringly inappropriate to the cold, gritty texture of the book. The great sf alien novel remains to be written.

George R. R. Martin, in a review of ''Against Infinity,'' in Book World—The Washington Post, *May 29, 1983, p. 10.*

ALGIS BUDRYS

[*Against Infinity*] is likely to be considered one of the best SF novels of 1983. It certainly deserves to. Set on a colonized Ganymede in the earliest days of that Jovian satellite's terraforming, the book proceeds in a straight line of powerful narrative, telling the story of Manuel Lopez, whose life is tied inextricably with that of old Matt Bohles and of Aleph, the totally self-possessed alien artifact that has been wandering the moon for billions of years.

It begins when Manuel is thirteen, taken for the first time out into the wastelands beyond Sidon Settlement. He is a member of a hunting party of men. Ostensibly out just to cull the synthetic life-forms that have been set loose to graze on the Ganymedan ecology and thus transform it, he then becomes aware of Aleph as a presence.

That presence looms over the men, coloring every thought and deed. Alien artifacts have been found all over the moons of Jupiter, all ancient, all enigmatic. But only Aleph moves, pursuing its mysterious courses through the deeps . . . , occasionally brushing aside the works of mankind, and men, and their cyborg hunting animals, never responding in the slightest to any human attempt at contact or study, surfacing at its own need, sounding down into the depths again at its own mercy, inviolate.

Manuel's father, Colonel Lopez, is a commanding figure, stern and lawgiving, marshalling the resources of his men in the face of Ganymede's implacable environment. Sidon Settlement lives constantly on the thin edge of insufficiency. Life is not cruel: it is doomed unless meticulously cared for. So what fondness there may be between the Colonel and Manuel is far less accessible to the boy than is the tutelage offered by Old Matt, who assumes the role of a grandfather. . . . Old Matt knows what the fatal mistakes are. More important, over the years as Aleph looms larger and larger in their lives, he and Manuel—and a ravening maniac named Eagle, reconstructed from the partial brain of a human and given a killer body—gradually work out a way to stop Aleph.

The thing of it is, of course, that since Aleph is the men's obsession, it's thus part of Manuel's manhood as he accesses toward it. (pp. 31-2)

[Whenever] Aleph appears, it immediately becomes the focus of a barrage of weaponry, even though everyone knows full well that no weapon has ever had the slightest effect on it. The scenes in which the men and animals plunge into tumultuous, shouting pursuit of the uncaring artifact contain some of the most effective and evocative writing in a powerfully evocative book. Not since Ahab thrust his lance at the lightning and swore the white whale's doom have I read anything much like it.

And that brings me to my other point, which is that I don't know how much this is a good book in its own right and how much it reminds me of a good book. This is a very important point.

I say I don't know. I suspect. I suspect this is a very good book in its own right. Benford, who has just been getting better and better, has here evolved into a prose stylist who creates his effects in the way the really good writers do. He does it not with words, per se, but with patterns of words. . . . Benford, a physicist by trade, has not only emerged as the latest in a long but slim line of scientist-poets but also as one who promises to be one of the best ever. If I were trapped into some fresh episode of the timeworn debate about whether SF and the "Mainstream" will ever merge, I would bring forward ex-Fan Benford and rest my case.

But I know what a hostile critic could say. He could say that Benford is too conscious of precursors to be *sui generis;* that his book is reminiscent of Hemingway's *The Old Man and The Sea,* and Faulkner's "The Bear," and of course *Moby Dick* (and even more so of Robert Ruark's *The Old Man and the Boy*), and thus is good by virtue of its models, but only by virtue of its models.

The question comes down to this: given a long, honorable literary tradition of rite-of-passage stories built around the metaphor of the hunt, is an SF story made any the less by being aware of that tradition? If Hemingway is allowed to model on Melville, why isn't Benford? (pp. 32-3)

> *Algis Budrys, in a review of "Against Infinity," in* The Magazine of Fantasy and Science Fiction, *Vol. 65, No. 1, July, 1983, pp. 31-3.*

GENE DeWEESE

Against Infinity is Benford's first novel since *Timescape,* and there's little doubt that it's good. I'm not sure, however, whether or not I like it.

The basic story, though simple, is not all that predictable. A few hundred years from now, while Earth itself has turned to a rigid form of socialism, Ganymede, one of Jupiter's moons, is being terraformed by a colony of pioneering settlers. The massive amounts of ice they are melting, however, threaten the stability of the moon's crust, and the herds of animals they have genetically engineered to eat the existing ammonia compounds, convert them into usable oxygen compounds and defecate, the results are mutating at an alarming rate. The mutations, unfortunately, don't always eat and defecate what they should, so they have to be destroyed, either by hunting parties of settlers or by other animals created specifically to prey on the mutants. Those, of course, mutate too, and the problem goes on. (p. 39)

The picture of Ganymede itself and the terraforming procedures is not only detailed but vivid and thoroughly convincing, and the settlers are similarly believable. Still, for me at least, *Against Infinity* was not nearly as enjoyable as *Timescape* or other Benford novels, and I'm not altogether sure why. Perhaps it was the characters. It's not that they were mostly unlikeable. Good villains, after all, are always interesting. The problem is that I got the feeling that I was supposed to like these people, which I just couldn't manage to do.

Then there was the fact that no matter what trouble they got into, they had mostly themselves to blame. And unlike *Timescape,* where the entire Earth and billions of innocent bystanders could be wiped out as a result of the foulups of others, if these settlers destroyed themselves, it wouldn't seem to be that much of a loss. Or maybe my mindset is so anti-hunting and pro-science that treating a billion-year-old artifact like a rogue elephant instead of as a vital and intriguing mystery turned me off from the start. For that matter, Benford may even have been purposely presenting a warning that whether humans stay on Earth or go exploring, they're going to foul things up unless something can be done to change "human nature."

In any event, *Against Infinity* is an impressive if ambiguous book, and everyone should try it and then make up his or her own mind whether or not to like it. (pp. 39-40)

> *Gene DeWeese, in a review of "Against Infinity," in* Science Fiction Review, *Vol. 12, No. 3, August, 1983, pp. 39-40.*

TOM EASTON

[In *Against Infinity*] we are hard put to find a story worthy of the word. Message, on the other hand—well, it's gotta be there. You can tell. The thing's lit'ry as all get out in tone, so there's got to be one. In fact, the message is clearly more important than the story.

So what's the message? Damfino! But enough mock philistinism. There *is* story, and the message isn't that hard to pin down. The moons of Jupiter have long been settled by colonists from socialist Earth, and they're being terraformed, even unto wrapping Io in a plastic baggy. Too, the moons are studded with artifacts: mysterious, incomprehensible, abandoned billions of years ago. . . .

The story opens when Manuel Lopez, on his first culling, meets the Aleph. Thereafter, their destinies are linked. He assumes a hunter's mission, uses cyborg dogs on his hunts, and finally prevails. The Aleph, the mystery of the frontier, is dead, and the air is thick with futility.

It's a tale of growth, maturation, fate, and destiny. It's Hemingway SF. Perhaps it's a rewrite of Faulkner's "The Bear." Certainly it does *not* really deserve the hyperbole with which I began this review, for hyperbole my remarks were. There's story here, and story of a sort we're more accustomed to seeing in "higher" forms of literature. There is theme, too, and theme as valid as anything we might ask for.

Perhaps I don't appreciate lit'ry doings well enough. If I did, I suspect I'd like *Infinity* a lot more. After all, it does at least one thing I love to see—the technical "furniture" of Benford's future are practically invisible, almost as taken for granted by the characters as they might be in life. Here is the stamp of thorough imagination, and of a fictional world that feels real.

My ambivalence is clear, isn't it? *Against Infinity* is good, but it's not quite my cup of tea. Is it yours? Maybe. Try it and see.

> *Tom Easton, in a review of "Against Infinity," in* Analog Science Fiction/Science Fact, *Vol. CIII, No. 9, September, 1983, p. 163.*

RUDY RUCKER

[*Across the Sea of Suns*] is so good it hurts. . . . Benford puts it all together in this one—adult characters, rich writing, innovative science, a grand philosophical theme—it's all here.

The novel interleaves two narratives: one about an alien invasion of Earth, the other about the voyage of the fusion-drive starship *Lancer*. The main character on the *Lancer* is Nigel

Walmsley, an aging scientist who some readers will remember from Benford's 1977 book, *In the Ocean of Night.*

The first planet the *Lancer* visits is inhabited by some remarkable beings who see, and communicate, by emitting bursts of electromagnetic radiation in the form of radio waves. Acting as a kind of cosmic Mormon Tabernacle Choir, these "EM" creatures have been beaming signals Earthward in their spare time.

What is the signal they are sending? A playback of a 1956 Arthur Godfrey radio show which they picked up from Earth! Ludicrous, yes, but it makes scientific sense, and by the time one of the humans lands on the EMs' windy, barren planet to boom out, "It's Arrr-thur God-frey time," it's not funny, it's genuinely scary and out-of-this-world. . . .

Meanwhile, some mysterious aliens are invading Earth—creatures called Swarmers, who infest our oceans, and pull down any ship that dares to venture into the open sea. We see the Swarmers bring down a storm-tossed ship; and after the shipwreck, we follow the adventures of a sailor called Warren, who has escaped on a crude raft. He finds a way to kill the Swarmers that attack the raft, eating their flesh and drinking their fluids to survive. These chapters are wonderfully taut and clear—one suspects that Benford has recently reread *The Old Man And the Sea.*

Warren soon realizes that the Swarmers are only the larval stage of an intelligent life-form, the Skimmers. He learns to talk with the Skimmers, and they reveal a shocking fact: a vast, malignant civilization of machines—robots gone mad—has deliberately seeded our seas with the Swarmers in order to destroy our biosphere. Meanwhile on the *Lancer,* Nigel Walmsley is finding mounting evidence that this same evil race of super-machines is out to destroy organic life everywhere in the galaxy.

At the book's end, the machines seem to have the upper hand; yet in a lovely, Faulknerian closing passage, Benford celebrates the power of life. . . .

One is left with a final vision of life as an on-going process, already diffused throughout the universe—life as an overarching whole greater than each of us isolated parts. Perhaps no person now living will make it to the distant stars, but no matter. We are here in any case.

> *Rudy Rucker, in a review of "Across the Sea of Suns," in* Book World—The Washington Post, *February 26, 1984, p. 8.*

JERRY L. PARSONS

A sequel to *In the Ocean of Night* (1976), this powerful novel [*Across the Sea of Suns*] continues the account of man's discoveries of sentient alien life forms and civilizations. Nigel Walmsley, the protagonist in the earlier novel, is again the primary character. An old man whose savoring of humanistic pursuits contrasts vividly with the many mechanistic, insensitive specialists and politicos on the starship *Lancer,* Nigel is a pariah to the many group-think types. *Lancer* has been sent to investigate the source of radio signals from Isis, a one-face world that, it is discovered, once supported a thriving, sophisticated civilization. Sentient beings still exist, but are primitive except for their radio communications. In addition, Isis is guarded by computerized weapons satellites similar to others stationed near planets which could support organic life. Nigel,

cued by his earlier contacts with alien artifacts in *Ocean,* deduces that the satellites are "watchers," left by a machine culture to ensure that sophisticated organic civilizations do not evolve. . . .

After botched attempts to contact the beings on Isis and to board one of Isis's "watchers" end in mayhem and death for many *Lancer* crew members, the ship travels to other planets which formerly supported civilizations, and finally to Pocks, another body from which signals have been monitored. There, the *Lancer's* drive is destroyed in a battle with that system's "watcher." Nigel discovers sentient beings related to those on Isis living under the ice and water surface of Pocks. The book ends there, with the surviving crew stranded on Pocks, having no hope of returning to Earth. Can they collaborate with the resident sentients in building a civilization? Can they defeat the "watcher?" The unnamed third novel in this series may provide answers. (p. 25)

[*Across the Sea of Suns*] is well written and thought provoking, but not optimistic. Character development is minimal, even in primary characters such as Nigel. *Across the Sea of Suns'* greatest strength is its theme which is at once cosmic, exciting, depressing and tantalizing. (p. 26)

> *Jerry L. Parsons, "Cosmic, Exciting, Depressing, Tantalizing," in* SF & Fantasy Review, *Vol. 7, No. 2, March, 1984, pp. 25-6.*

TOM EASTON

Greg Benford's *Across the Sea of Suns* is the sequel to *In the Ocean of Night,* in which Nigel Walmsley found an ancient spacecraft. Now, thirty years later, he is aboard the starship *Lancer,* off to seek the origins of mysterious signals, fragmentary messages in English. He is older than most of his shipmates, and hence his competence is suspect, but though he continues to age, failing and unregarded, he insists on taking part. He insinuates himself among the explorers of the source world to see the strange beings who play back fragments of old radio shows with built-in transmitters. He is there when a strange satellite turns out to be a mechanical ravener, and he is the first to realize that the galaxy is occupied by mechanical intelligences that brook no organic competition.

Meanwhile, back on Earth, alien Swarmers and Skimmers drive humanity from the seas and threaten civilization itself. . . .

Benford shows an impressive breadth of vision, an awesome compassion, and a striking skill with his characters—his treatment of Nigel and his two paramours is deft and sympathetic. At the same time, his skills as a writer are impressive, and when he tries to capture the sense of multipletrack conversation in multitrack prose, he succeeds admirably. I heartily recommend the book and the Benford name.

> *Tom Easton, in a review of "Across the Sea of Suns," in* Analog Science Fiction/Science Fact, *Vol. CIV, No. 9, September, 1984, p. 171.*

GARY K. WOLFE

Even science fiction's most ardent defenders have long complained that the genre (if it is a genre) has yet to produce its Hemingway or its Faulkner. Next to "sense of wonder" and "literature of ideas," this complaint may in fact be our longest standing critical cliche. (p. 9)

My own candidate [for such a position] is Gregory Benford, for two reasons. One is that with such novels as *Timescape, In The Ocean of Night,* and *Across a Sea of Suns,* he has established for himself the clear, authoritative, and passionate voice of a writer equally comfortable with the environment of physics and the vagaries of the human heart. On his own terms, he may be as fine a writer as science fiction has.

The Second reason is that Benford may have ended the debate about a science-fictional Faulkner once and for all. ''Why wait for science fiction to produce its own Faulkner?'' Benford seems to be saying in his most recent works. Why not have Faulkner *himself*?

Let me explain. The two specific works I have in mind are *Against Infinity* . . . and **''To The Storming Gulf.''** . . . The former novel is a version of Faulkner's novella ''The Bear,'' and the latter novella a version of Faulkner's novel *As I Lay Dying.*

But the parallels go deeper than mere pastiche or *hommage.* Near the beginning of *Against Infinity,* for example, we have the following passage:

> The boy was thirteen. He watched it all with wide eyes. For five years now he had waited and listened to the talk of the ice ridges and ammonia rivers. . . . What he knew most deeply was the bigness of the wilderness they now crawled into, bigger than any of the puny human Settlements, vast and powerful and with a reason and logic to itself.

That's the second paragraph of the novel. The second paragraph of ''The Bear'' begins:

> He was sixteen. For six years now he had been a man's hunter. For six years now he had heard the best of all talking. It was of the wilderness, the big woods, bigger and older than any recorded document. . . .

Close, but perhaps a reasonable tribute to a powerful style. There are parallels of plot, too—Benford's hunt for the alien artifact known as ''The Aleph'' recurs over roughly the same time-frame as Faulkner's hunt for the legendary bear, Old Ben. There is in each story a sequence laid some years after the hunt is ended in which the young protagonist comes to question his inheritance.

And there are parallels of character, especially Faulkner's young Ike McCaslin, the old hunter Sam Fathers, and the dog, Lion. Benford gives us the young Manuel Lopez, the old pioneer Matt Bohles, and the spirited half-machine, Eagle. A few reviewers commented on these parallels, and by and large they seem to work. Ganymede makes a fine Mississippi wilderness, and *Against Infinity* gradually builds its own power, turning into a kind of *tour de force* of literary adaptation and, in its final chapters, using this momentum to develop ideas that go well beyond what could reasonably be presented in a non-science fiction narrative.

''To The Storming Gulf,'' I think, is another matter, and one that raises some interesting questions regarding the proper boundaries of literary borrowing, the relationship of science fiction to ''literature,'' and which techniques might be appropriate to improve that relationship. The story is additionally interesting in that it is one of the first works by a major science fiction writer to address the ''nuclear winter'' issue, and it may gain somewhat wider attention for that reason alone.

Concerning the cross-country pilgrimage of a group of people who have survived a limited nuclear war by hiding (cleverly) in a nuclear power plant, it uses exactly the same narrative technique as Faulkner's 1930 novel *As I Lay Dying:* multiple viewpoints presented in short sections titled with the name of the narrator for each section. . . . The family name in the Faulkner novel is Bundren; in Benford it is Bunren. One of Faulkner's characters, a rather mechanical, logical type, chooses to number the paragraphs in his section. So does a similar character in Benford. A major crisis in each story is the crossing of a flooded river with a coffin (in Faulkner) or a coffin-like life-support unit (in Benford). In each case, a floating log strikes the wagon (Faulkner) or the truck (Benford). But there is more. Here is a passage from Benford: . . .

> The tidal flats were achurn, murmuring ceaseless and sullen like some big animal, the yellow surface dimpled with lunging splotches. . . . Like there was something huge and alive, and it waked for a moment and stuck itself out to see what the world of air was like.

Faulkner:

> Before us the thick dark current runs. It talks up to us in a murmur become ceaseless and myriad, the yellow surface dimpled monstrously into fading swirls . . . as though just beneath the surface something huge and alive waked for a moment of lazy alertness out of and into light slumber again.
>
> (pp. 9-10)

Benford has borrowed not only a general plot and a narrative technique and a vivid style from Faulkner, he has actually borrowed specific images and phrases. ''The yellow surface dimpled,'' ''something huge and alive,'' . . . and the like are striking, powerful phrases, and to the reader unfamiliar with Faulkner, they are Benford's. To the reader familiar with Faulkner they are a bit disturbing. But I don't think they quite constitute plagiarism, and I don't believe there is anything venal or deliberately dishonest going on.

The one time that I met Benford, I came strongly to believe in his integrity, and this integrity shows in his other fiction as well. I doubt that it is in him to engage in undergraduate-style plagiarism. More tellingly, he is a talented enough and successful enough writer on his own terms that he simply doesn't need to do such a thing.

The obvious question then becomes, why? Is Benford enjoying a little joke at the expense of science fiction readers, who if they have read Faulkner at all may only have done so years ago? Does he have some moralistic idea that SF can become a kind of ''classic comics'' for literary masterworks that people ought to read but won't? Has he become ambitious to experiment with new styles and narrative techniques, but is unsure how to go about it? Or is this, after all, part of the old grand scheme to turn SF into ''literature'' by bizarrely turning ''literature'' into SF?

For that matter, did he start with an SF idea and find in Faulkner a congenial framework for that idea, or did he start with *As I Lay Dying* and find an SF plot to superimpose upon it? Most of **''To The Storming Gulf,''** it must be said, does not echo Faulkner as closely as the passages I have quoted, but some parts read as though Benford had his Faulkner in one hand and his keyboard in the other.

I don't know the answers, but I fear that Benford just wants to be ''literary.'' I've noticed echoes of Wallace Stevens and

T. S. Eliot in his other work, and *Timescape* may owe something to C. P. Snow. . . . Other science fiction writers have borrowed often from literary sources; we can see Joyce in Blish and Aldiss, and Justin Leiber's *Beyond Rejection* starts with a nice pastiche of *Finnegan's Wake*. . . .

But there is a difference between assimilating a style, or deliberately writing a pastiche, and simply sifting another author for words and characters and narrative techniques. It is one thing when Benford writes, as he does in *In The Ocean of Night*, ''Do not go softly into this good sky''; the allusion to Dylan Thomas is familiar enough to be clear and open. Borrowing less recognizable phrases from a novel-length work such as Faulkner's is not this kind of allusion.

If Benford wants to be more ''literary,'' I think this is an ill-advised way to do it. SF arguably needs masterpieces, but shouldn't they be masterpieces which derive from the material of the genre, and not simply recastings of material from the 1920s or 1930s? I doubt, in fact, that any mainstream writer could get away with **''To The Storming Gulf.''** It is literary regress, not progress. It will only lead to verse plays and epistolary romances. Huck Finn belongs on a raft, not a ramjet, and the dangers of transplanting Conrad's Kurtz should be apparent to anyone who has seen *Apocalypse Now*.

Benford's best bet for becoming more ''literary,'' it seems to me, lies in continuing to develop the unique voice he has displayed in his Nigel Walmsley novels and elsewhere. That science fiction and science fiction writers deserve more respect I do not argue. But first they perhaps need a little more self-confidence. And like respect, this they must gain on their own terms, with their own words and images and structures. Huck may not belong on a ramjet, but some fictional hero perhaps does, and I as a reader—even a ''literary'' reader—have come to depend on talents like Gregory Benford's to find out who that person is, to introduce me to him or her, and to make me care. (p. 12)

> *Gary K. Wolfe, ''Gregory Benford's Introductory Survey of American Literature,'' in* Fantasy Review, *Vol. 8, No. 4, April, 1985, pp. 9-10, 12.*

GREGORY BENFORD

When a friend read Gary Wolfe's essay [see excerpt above], he was certain I would be angry. To my surprise, I felt no anger at all, but rather a familiar sadness. To write science fiction is to be misunderstood, as always—but from a critic who has said many intelligent things in the past, obtuseness is doubly vexing.

Wolfe's work on sf iconography . . . led me to believe that he looks deeply into texts. Yet **''To the Storming Gulf''** brings forth only textual comparisons and his question, *why?*—followed by a series of progressively more absurd conjectures, ending with the fear that I ''just want to be literary.''

Since the story has been in print less than a month, and he has been fretting over Faulknerian influences ever since *Against Infinity,* one would think he might've just asked. But critics reflexively fire broadsides rather than inquire; so be it.

Still, I am disarmed by such a remorselessly reductionist reading. In both works I tried to find a way to comment on both the future and the past, on cultures imaginary and real. But to see that demands comparison at a structural level, and that's what Wolfe resolutely avoids.

I do hope that anyone interested in this will read the novella first, *then* the discussion here. Otherwise, it'll be ruined for them.

A clue comes from the fact that in fact the vast body of **''To the Storming Gulf''** doesn't follow Faulkner at all. Only the general opening situation is similar; plot, character, stress, even regional accents are different. . . . (p. 9)

The second half has no parallel other than those called up by the implied rereading of *As I Lay Dying* which I'd hoped to signal in the first half, and particularly by the river scene.

Whereas *As I Lay Dying* concerns a family moving a corpse, and the relations between them all, in **''To the Storming Gulf''** the stored body recalls civilization itself, which the characters (not a family) are struggling to hold onto. In the second half, they encounter evidence of what the Third World War was truly like, how the presence of anti-ICBM defenses altered events, and similar ideas which have no parallel in Faulkner. Even more, the story then jumps forward decades, to reflect back on the generation that is once more devoted to high tech and the future, and has forgotten the sacrifice of the old folks.

All this is bridged by the crucial scene at the river, where in both stories natural forces nearly overwhelm the people. That's where I displayed the explicit similarity to *As I Lay Dying*. Why? Lots of reasons, some of which I can't state in flat terms. It's the fulcrum of the story.

I was trying to contrast the old South with the spirit infusing **''To the Storming Gulf,''** among other things. My people never submit to Nuclear Winter, never consider setting up some post-holocaust utopia, never allow their involuted selves to halt their progress.

Why Faulkner? I find it a bit hard to believe the salute Wolfe gives me at the opening of his essay, mostly because he's said nothing about my work in the past, and because he seems to have missed totally the fact that I'm from the rural South. (pp. 9-10)

Faulknerian methods are just plain storytelling to me. The voice, the story lines—these are common Southern folklore. Most critics have never understood that about Faulkner. I went hunting long before I even heard of ''The Bear.'' We had to carry my Uncle Roy out of a backwoods still after a heart attack, across hills and fair-sized creeks, when I was twelve. He died before we got him out to the road—decades before I read *As I Lay Dying*.

Indeed, when I got to the passages where I wanted to echo Faulkner, I could remember the way Faulkner had done things (though I didn't actually look up the text; I have a magpie memory for phrases) and I used that, too, to underline the parallels.

I'm not good at explaining my own work, and had hoped that the whole method I was using in *Against Infinity* and **''To the Storming Gulf''** would emerge with time. I expected a reader who knew Faulkner to extract another reading, without imposing anything on an uninformed reader. I'm trying to convey how humans change and yet recall the past, too. In *Against Infinity* the theme of the Aleph drawing humans out, where they can display their age old patterns of hunting and bonding, is basic to the novel. Only by couching it in terms we already knew from literature could I make this clear—and even then a lot of critics missed it. But there are a lot of other matters, too, that I tried to bring forth by writing specifically and unmistakably out of a Southern tradition: that sf is dominated by the Heinleinian mold of always being about the winners, never the downtrodden or ordinary; that in American experience that role has fallen to the South; that in sf the wilderness (the South) has gotten confused with the frontier (the West)—a common confusion in all literature; that attitudes don't change rapidly, and sf has never acknowledged that enough, never used its relation to the past and past literature to grow wiser; and that persisting in its narrow Northern ethnocentrism, sf hobbles itself.

All this Wolfe has reduced to the quoting of text and fretting over plagiarism. Okay, I confess—I tried in these two works to say something differently, something that's best done by indirection, I think.

And I failed. If as bright a critic as Wolfe is doesn't get it, I'm doing something wrong. I wanted *NOT* to continue "to develop the unique voice he has displayed in his Nigel Walmsley novels and elsewhere," but to do something new.

Bob Silverberg has been telling me for years that putting such effort into sf was a waste, and in the last year I have begun to conclude that he is right. There is only so much freight the field will bear, and one easily overloads it. Trying to satisfy both literary and scientific constraints in sf compresses and heightens problems, and adding more dimensions to the discourse worsens them.

I say this without bitterness toward Wolfe or indeed toward anyone. But it is something we all need to admit, and something that will help me in my slow steady retreat from the genre. (pp. 10, 12)

> *Gregory Benford, "Some Comments from the Minority Culture," in* Fantasy Review, *Vol. 8, No. 4, April, 1985, pp. 9-10, 12.*

GARY K. WOLFE

At first glance, *Artifact* appears to be Gregory Benford's *hommage* to the bestseller lists. . . . At the same time, there are the familiar Benford elements—a very believable and at times satirical portrayal of academic politics, a fully-realized near-future world which is kept discreetly in the background . . . , and a lot of real physics, carefully worked out and meticulously confined to a few plausible speculations. The novel is, if one can imagine it, a cross between *Timescape* and *Raiders of the Lost Ark*.

Since the whole mix makes for great fun, and is compulsively readable, not all readers will care to speculate on what it all means. After all, many SF writers in recent years have turned from what might be termed "high science fiction" to more accessible popular forms, and I don't believe anyone can prove the genre is the worse for it. But I don't think that what Benford does here is as simple as that. He is one of the most sophisticated writers we have. . . . For critics (and for many authors), "expanding the boundaries" usually means producing works which retain some science fiction content while otherwise coming more and more to resemble the mainstream classics we were all trained to admire. While there is some of this in *Artifact,* there is also a strong (and somewhat playful) element of deliberately mixing popular forms, of seeing if SF and the international thriller have anything to offer one another, and if the conventions of both can be sustained without resorting to purely formulaic characters and incidents.

In this latter sense, I think *Artifact* yields mixed results. Its central conceit—that singularities may exist at random within the earth, that one may have been "captured" by an ancient Mycenaean king and unearthed by modern archaeologists—is worked out with such scientific rigor that the science may delight SF readers while absolutely terrorizing the thriller crowd, many of whom only want a macguffin to get the action going. The central characters, a young archaeologist and a physicist who become lovers, are as interesting and fully-rounded as any in *Timescape*—but the villain, a Greek colonel who is also an archaeologist, is almost a pulp stereotype. There is a whole gallery of believable scientists, and it is interesting that even when Benford tends toward stereotypes, they are not really the stereotypes of science fiction. While many SF "bestsellers" seem intent on introducing the Heinleinian superhero to the world, no such figure appears in Benford's thriller. The style is that of a cliffhanger, and the special effects are indeed worthy of Spielberg, but the passages dealing with academe and working scientists are fully developed on their own terms, and equally successful for sympathetic readers.

I suspect that *Artifact* is about as successful as an experiment like this can get. The novel doesn't compromise its intellectual content for the sake of its outward form, and yet it doesn't grossly violate the conventions of that form. It represents one of the few honest attempts I know to transplant the substance of science fiction into another narrative mode, and as such it offers an alternative direction for the genre. *Artifact* isn't deadly serious "mainstream" SF, nor is it a pop novel which takes the iconography of SF into bestsellerdom with the intellectual baggage. Instead, it suggests that there are still resources within the realm of popular fiction that SF can exploit, and that can be enriched in turn by SF's own resources. (pp. 17-18)

> *Gary K. Wolfe, "Benford's Latest Cast in 'Thriller' Format," in* Fantasy Review, *Vol. 8, No. 9, September, 1985, pp. 17-18.*

DON D'AMMASSA

Despite the extreme length of [*Artifact*], I read it through in a single sitting. Archaeologists in Greece discover an artifact that seems totally out of place in an ancient burial vault. . . . Political problems force the team to leave the country, but they are able to smuggle the artifact back to the United States, where it ends up in the physics department instead of archaeology. The military government of Greece wants it back, even though there is evidence it may be a danger to the entire world. There is a fast moving, well constructed plot, excellent characterization, an interesting scientific puzzle, and a satisfying solution. Benford goes right on getting better with each book.

> *Don D'Ammassa, in a review of "Artifact," in* Science Fiction Chronicle, *Vol. 7, No. 1, October, 1985, p. 42.*

GREGORY FEELEY

Modern science fiction, which was launched in this country under the banner of dramatizing the scientific wonders of the world to come, has always had trouble reconciling its twin ideals of scientific plausibility and artistic ambition. The commercial magazines which shaped sf for most of its history subordinated both ideals to the gospel of telling a good story. . . . The '60s, a cauldron of controversy in sf as elsewhere, saw the polarization of these camps, and for some years afterward serious sf was marked by a relative reluctance to engage its seminal themes of scientific breakthrough or the strangeness of the universe.

Gregory Benford comes closer than any other writer to healing this rift, as his much-admired *Timescape* has shown. For Benford and many younger sf writers of a high-tech, post-Space Race generation, the science/art dichotomy was always a spurious one, and the hard details of a future world, its subatomic and interstellar particulars, are valid not simply as metaphors with respectably literary purposes but for having their own textures and poetry....

Artifact, Gregory Benford's latest and longest novel, deals once more with scientific research, although the field has shifted, at first glance anyway, from the particle physics that informed *Timescape* to the more mundane world of archeology. Claire Anderson is overseeing a Greek dig into a Mycenaean tomb when the eponymous artifact is discovered, a cubic meter of black rock that appeared to hold unusual signficance to the Mycenaeans and soon exhibits unusual behavior to scientists....

Deteriorating political conditions in Greece lead to the artifact's surreptitious removal to Boston, whereupon the novel shifts gears from exoticism and political intrigue to the world of scientific research. As before, Benford effectively dramatizes the excitement and procedures of discovery, and his evocation of academic research, its protocols and rivalries, is impeccable. Less assured are his descriptions of Boston, which have a worked-up, guidebook quality to them, as though Benford knew the locale less well than he does Mycenae. When Greek operatives steal back the cube, which destroys their boat and sinks in Boston harbor, the tone shifts again, to international thriller, as U.S. security forces, alerted by now to the artifact's destructive potential (and aware that a kindred phenomenon was left behind in Greece) take charge of things. Benford handles the location and recovery of the cube with the authoritative élan of one who loves the intricacies of procedures, but the novel's climax, an extravagant shoot-out on the Greek coast, seemed a final, forced shift into highest gear, and held less excitement for this reader than did the moments of discovery in the Boston labs.

Benford, unusually for a modern writer, acknowledges a division in his writing between serious novels and what Graham Greene calls "entertainments," and it is instructive to remember that Benford published two other novels the same year as *Timescape,* each essentially an adventure novel. *Artifact,* despite its wealth of detail and the careful speculation that Benford has put into the nature of his artifact, has more in common with these efforts than with *Timescape,* and is at its weakest when it imitates the conventions of the international thriller. Benford remains unsurpassed in describing the artistry of a theoretical insight, but his occasional desires to fold these into the yeastings of the popular novel (*Shiva Descending,* a near-disaster novel written with William Rotsler, had similar ambitions) can hobble his best efforts.

> Gregory Feeley, "High-Tech Goes Haywire," in Book World—The Washington Post, *October 27, 1985, p. 6.*

GENE DeWEESE

The setting [of *Artifact*] is a near future world that will require very little—say the theft of a Greek archeological artifact by an American—to spark a war. The characters, in addition to [American archeologist Claire] Anderson, are a well-done collection of scientists, an overly macho Greek colonel, and bureaucrats sharing varying degrees of short-sightedness and self interest. The plot, aside from the unravelling of the mystery of the artifact, is a mixture of international intrigue and disaster.

The main difference between this and other similarly constructed books is that the author, besides being an excellent writer, knows both science and scientists inside and out, and he has created a new and scientifically plausible, if unlikely, menace in the form of a super-massive (one ton) elementary subatomic particle. For those who want more information or need more convincing, there is even a "Technical Afterword" explaining the science involved.

The only major fault I can find is that, at 500 + pages, *Artifact* is itself a bit too massive. Still, it's probably Benford's best and most readable novel since 1980's award-winning *Timescape.*

> Gene DeWeese, in a review of "Artifact," in Science Fiction Review, *Vol. 14, No. 4, November, 1985, p. 22.*

GARY K. WOLFE

[In *Heart of the Comet,* a] scientific colony exploring Halley's comet in 2061 is threatened by mysterious plagues and attacked by giant purple man-eating space worms.... A brilliant scientist, in the nick of time, invents a ray gun to battle the worms and a cure for the worst of the space plagues. "He stared at the horrible things closing in on him from all sides, and knew what loathing was." Mutineers steal the spaceship, leaving the colony abandoned on the comet.

What is going on here? Gregory Benford and David Brin, two of the most respected scientist-authors in all of science fiction, have collaborated on what promises to be the year's big comet novel (there had to be one, didn't there?), and a third of the way into it we might as well be in a 1936 issue of *Astounding.* With plot lines drawn from authors as diverse as Verne, Van Vogt, Asimov, and Heinlein, dramatic scenes of battles on the icy comet surface, and characters who are frankly heroic in the grand tradition, the authors seem bent on paying homage to the whole of Golden Age science fiction. And, to a great extent, they succeed on that level: *Heart of the Comet* works just fine as a sweeping adventure-cum-problem story in the classic mold.

But, as we might expect from these authors, that's not as far as it goes. In the first place, the various menaces and their solutions are thought out much more ingeniously than in pulp science fiction, and each new solution involves provocative ideas that place the novel firmly in the newer tradition of "literate" hard SF that Brin and Benford have helped define. In the second place, after verging on parody in some of the early chapters, the novel takes an unsuspected turn and becomes almost a critique of Campbellian science fiction. The brilliant solutions don't work quite as neatly as planned, and factionalism and despair, together with the still virulent diseases, threaten the colony's survival. Earth, the traditional image of home and hope in earlier space operas, becomes the enemy, and the alien life forms in the comet itself become almost allies. Much of this depressing middle third of the novel borrows from the "Universe" tradition of the long space voyage, but cast in a much darker hue.

Finally, after setting up a scenario worthy of Van Vogt and then systematically dismantling it, the novel arrives at what may be its real subject—the redemption of the old heroic SF tradition in light of later revisionism. (pp. 17-18)

Benford and Brin seem to be writing for two audiences—mainstream readers who may be vaguely interested in something about Halley, and their own readers. Sometimes the balancing act shows; there are a few too many *dei ex machina* for most hard SF readers to be comfortable with, and much is made of the Jewishness of the brilliant doctor who saves the day. Nor is the idea of a group of exiles learning to live together and create a new society especially original, even though it provides the narrative with a surprisingly rich social texture. But the overall strategy works, echoing classic SF themes in ways that may introduce these to new readers while reinvigorating them for veterans. I doubt that *Heart of the Comet* will disappoint either audience. (p. 18)

> Gary K. Wolfe, "Off on a Comet," in Fantasy Review, *Vol. 9, No. 2, February, 1986, pp. 17-18.*

GREGORY FEELEY

[*Heart of the Comet*] must have seemed a publisher's dream. Both [Benford and co-author David Brin] are practicing scientists, and an impressive amount of research went into the study of cometary phenomena and Halley's Comet in particular. The story of an international expedition to Halley's Comet in the next century seems to have everything: a large cast, a span of 80 years and billions of miles, love, conflict, and a succession of perils to face.

Yet while Benford and Brin are both experienced if unequally accomplished novelists, Benford-Brin writes like an amateur, and the result is something of a disaster. Quite possibly the novel was rushed in order to reach us soon after Halley itself did; a reference in the acknowledgements to "laboring under 'astronomical' deadlines" suggests that opportunism may have informed inspiration. Benford at least is a demonstrably punctilious writer whose novels often reach their final form only after successive stages of published expansion and revision. *Heart of the Comet* seems to have enjoyed no such consideration in composition, and the result shows.

In the mid-21st century the world's nations have begun to recover from decades of ecological disaster but are riven by a new controversy: a strain of genetically "improved" humans have been bred, called Percells after their creator. . . . [The] crew colonizing Halley contains both Percell and "Ortho" humans. When it is discovered that Halley contains life, which is "awakened" by the heat of the explorers' tunnels and begins to threaten the survival of the expedition, tension between Percell and Ortho spills over into mutiny and civil war.

This is material for a gripping story, but the execution is awkward and forced. Much of the first hundred pages is given over to exposition and long political arguments that are too plainly staged for the reader's benefit. A militant group of Percells, led by a Soviet crewmember, vows war against the reactionary Orthos, who in turn engage in a campaign of extermination. The novel's four main characters (American or American-educated Israeli) are left to hold things together with the foreigners acting to irresponsibly, and save the mission more or less singlehandedly. They also contribute a running romantic subplot that proves depressingly schematic: Lani loves Carl, Carl loves Virginia, Virginia loves Saul.

In the end the Halley life forms are tamed and become symbiotic beneficiaries of mankind. Saul, who helped create the Percells decades earlier and thus bridges the Ortho-Percell conflict, reacts especially well and is rendered immortal. As he is also the greatest mind on the mission and has by the novel's end filled the comet with his equally brilliant clones, he ultimately takes on the godlike attributes of a late Heinlein hero. Benford's protagonists have been showing this disconcerting tendency for a few years now. This, plus the concomitant trend in Benford's last few novels for his antagonists to be killed off in increasingly spectacular ways, prompts deep foreboding about the direction in which Benford and his fiction are going. *Heart of the Comet* ends on a note of visionary affirmation, but its triumphs seem unearned, its victories fixed.

A much more accomplished book is Gregory Benford's collection *In Alien Flesh*. . . . All of the stories here stand on their own, and show aspects of Benford's talent that do not really appear in his books. Several, such as the novelettes **"In Alien Flesh"** and **"Relativistic Effects,"** possess that breadth of detail that suggests the germinal novel, but it is the short stories, such as **"Nooncoming"** and the madcap **"Doing Lennon,"** that are especially welcome here, showing as they do Benford working as jeweler rather than muralist. Interestingly, the longest story, **"To the Storming Gulf,"** seems the least finished, and Benford perhaps tellingly remarks that it may someday form part of a longer work.

> Gregory Feeley, "Scientists at Work," in Book World—The Washington Post, *March 23, 1986, p. 8.*

ELTON T. ELLIOTT

[*In Alien Flesh*] shows Benford at his most erudite in the introductions and at his dazzling, innovative best in the thoughtful stories. **"Doing Lennon"** (1975), the last story in the volume, is the most typical and atypical of the stories here. It is about a person from the future who meets Lennon—it is eerily predictive of Lennon's death—or the obsession that caused it.

The rest are excellent gems including the magnificent title story [**"In Alien Flesh"**] which is one of the best attempts—and most successful—to portray aliens.

> Elton T. Elliott, in a review of "In Alien Flesh," in Science Fiction Review, *Vol. 15, No. 2, May, 1986, p. 53.*

KEITH SOLTYS

When I first heard that Greg Benford and David Brin were collaborating on a novel called *Heart of the Comet,* my first thought was "cashing in on Halley's Comet, eh." Well, I hereby apologize to the authors. *Heart of the Comet* is one of the best SF novels of the last few years.

The story is set around a mission to establish a base on the nucleus of Halley's comet, during its next return in 2062. . . . The colonists must not only battle against the strange environment they have chosen to make their home but against the divisions that they bring with them from Earth, divisions that are more threatening than anything the comet can muster.

Benford and Brin haven't neglected the human element in their story. The central love triangle between Carl Osborn, an American astronaut and percell, Virginia Kaninamanu Herbert, a Hawaiian computer programmer and Saul Lintz, an Israeli biologist, is one of the most moving in recent science fiction. There's a deeper level at work here too. Heinlein's Competent Man, the Wandering Jew and Koestler's Ghost in the Machine all come to mind as archetypes that add another level of depth to the characterization.

Heart of the Comet is science fiction at it's best, a powerful story that both stretches the mind with its ideas and examines the limits of the human spirit. If Benford and Brin continue to collaborate, and if they improve, they will likely be regarded as the best collaborative team in the history of the genre. (pp. 58-9)

> *Keith Soltys, in a review of "Heart of the Comet,"*
> *in* Science Fiction Review, *Vol. 15, No. 2, May,*
> *1986, pp. 58-9.*

TOM EASTON

[Benford and Brin] want their massive novel, *Heart of the Comet,* to be a heart-stopper, a show-stopper, a best-seller, and they need a little excitement. And they find it. The Earth of 2060 is a world of factions. There are the "Percells," people whose genes have been engineered to eliminate genetic diseases and to confer advantages the "norms" distrust. There are the members of the Arc of the Rising Sun, equatorial ecofreaks who distrust the attitudes that spoiled so much of Earth's environment during the "Hell Century." And more.

Each faction has its representatives on the mission, but they are unified by a single vision—until Halley springs its big surprise. Just as Hoyle once guessed, it bears life. Slime grows in the halls. Worms break the vacuum seals. Plague attacks the crew. And under stress, the factions separate, hostilities ripen, and unity disintegrates.

Fortunately, the crew includes a number of highly competent people. There is Virginia, a computer whiz who cultivates an artificial intelligence in a semi-organic machine. . . . There is Carl, who yearns for Virginia but cannot have her; his talents go to coordinating the crew's efforts to survive after the commander must be slotted for the duration. There is Saul, genetic engineer who once worked with Simon Percell himself and now strives to find a way for humans to weather the attacks of Halley's indigenous life; Virginia loves him, and in time he reciprocates. Together, Carl, Saul, and Virginia solve their technical problems and struggle as best they can with the human ones.

Yet some problems are beyond their reach. Earth knows of the plague, and it is not at all willing to let its pioneers come home. When mutineers capture the expedition's sole ship and try to reach Earth, they are blasted from the sky. And even the comet itself is not safe.

All the excitements, on technical, personal, and political levels, work together very well to make *Heart of the Comet* a crackerjack yarn. It will bore no reader. Yet the part I liked best (as a biologist) was the puzzle part of the tale. Benford and Brin did a marvelous job of portraying the possibilities of cometary life, the reasons why it might mesh enough with our chemistry to be dangerous, and the possible mechanisms of coexistence. I won't say their scenario is likely, but it does strike me as intriguingly possible, and that is enough for science fiction. (pp. 179-80)

> *Tom Easton, in a review of "Heart of the Comet,"*
> *in* Analog Science Fiction/Science Fact, *Vol. CVI,*
> *No. 7, July, 1986, pp. 179-80.*

PASCAL J. THOMAS

Considering his distinguished career as a novelist, it is rather surprising that we have had to wait so long for [*In Alien Flesh*], a collection of Benford's short fiction: perhaps it is because of the market defiance towards collections, perhaps because Benford used to mine his stories for novel material, (as in *In the Ocean of Night* and *Timescape*). Gathered here, what stories have survived the winnowing of time become more impressive in their diversity.

The theme of artificial intelligence—robots and computers—occurs several times, running he gamut from the wise to the smartass. But artificial intelligence here seems devoted to the exploration of what makes minds work. . . . The study of simple, machine-like models of thinking can turn into a dry intellectual game (as in "**Time's Rub**"), but the best stories in the collection are suffused with the sense of wonder arising from the divergent potentialities of the human mind. Benford's dual life, it seems, provides a good example of how varied these can be; and on those grounds he can be forgiven for shamelessly cannibalizing his own experiences in stories like "**Exposures**" and "**Of Space/Time and the River.**"

Though ideas rule in this kind of SF, characters do not take a backseat. ["**In Alien Flesh**"] deals with the psychological after-effects of an intellectual experience bordering on the transcendental—the experience, in raw form, of the mathematics of an alien species. If the human mind is a rich field, it only makes sense that the fireworks of this collection come when the cognitive and aesthetic fantasies of alien minds are tackled. In that sense, "**Space/Time and the River**" is the best, wildest story of the lot.

Time is the ultimate adversary for the human mind—man may try to bridge it ("**Relativistic Effects**"), but his efforts will likely end up pitiful ("**Time Shards**"). When survival is the theme, the intellectual game loses ground, and I tend to be less interested ("**To the Storming Gulf**"). . . . Only artificial intelligences can hope to survive time—as in "**Time's Rub**," or "**Doing Lennon**,"—and they come to look suspiciously like us, to the point of sharing our artistic emotions.

Less diverse stylistically than it is intellectually, the book in that area is not without experiments or without merits; but what sticks in my mind are brilliant notes on the aesthetics of science from a very clever writer.

> *Pascal J. Thomas, "In Human Minds," in* Fantasy
> Review, *Vol. 9, No. 7, July-August, 1986, p. 20.*

DON D'AMMASSA

[In *Great Sky River,* the] remnants of a human colony on a far world live as nomadic fugitives amongst the robotic "mech" culture, a star travelling society of mechanical creatures whose origins are shrouded in mystery. But the enemies of the humans are evolving after a fashion, developing new weapons and new ways of dealing with the surviving human population. The story follows one family group as it attempts to find a place in the world, or a way to escape it. *Great Sky River* is not typical of Benford's work; it uses a clipped, idiosyncratic form of dialogue, and different type faces as the characters interact with Aspects, elements of the surviving personalities of dead humans. It displays a different side of Benford's writing, one that will attract an entirely new group of readers to his work. (pp. 52-3)

Don D'Ammassa, in a review of "Great Sky River," in Science Fiction Chronicle, *Vol. 9, No. 2, November, 1987, pp. 52-3.*

JOHN G. CRAMER

Great Sky River is an important new work of hard science fiction. The novel is set several thousand years in the future of Benford's previous novels, *In the Ocean of Night* and *Across the Sea of Suns,* two books of a projected trilogy. *Great Sky River* does not complete that trilogy, but leaps beyond it to a time when the ragtag human remnants of a once thriving civilization are being hounded to extinction by a technologically superior culture of intelligent machines. The machines have, over the past thousand years, wrested Snowglade, a rich world near the center of our galaxy, away from its human colonists. The war between men and machines has destroyed the humans' proud citadels, leaving them to exist like vermin on the machine-dominated planet, now transformed from a green fertile world rich in organic life to a cold, dead, arid brown planet better suited to the needs of the machines.

The Mantis, a machine intelligence that tirelessly pursues and herds the survivors is faster, smarter, and better equipped than the human fugitives who now wander the devastated planet in search of a safe haven. This novel is hard S-F, but the survivors' problems cannot be resolved with the usual techno-fix. The machines hold all the technological aces. . . .

In *Great Sky River* Benford turns for inspiration to Homer's Odyssey for a wealth of literary allusions and resonances. Benford's protagonists have nervous systems augmented by Aspects and Faces, which are downloads into the immortality of silicon chips of the knowledge and personalities of their dead ancestors. These desiccated personas of the dead lurk at the borders of consciousness of the living, striving for the sensory stimulation of real-time, waiting eagerly until they are summoned by their carriers to provide canned knowledge and technical skills and to experience a brief re-exposure to life.

This motif creates an atmosphere in *Great Sky River* which is an eerie synthesis of the high-tech neuro-circuitry of cyberpunk mixed with the Hades scene from Book XI of the Odyssey, in which Odysseus . . . summons up the ghosts of dead heroes to tell him how he may return home to Ithaca. Benford's protagonists summon up similar ghosts to aid them in coping with alien technology. . . .

Benford drives home the point that it is a serious mistake to cast alien intelligence in human terms. "Thing about aliens is, they're *alien*," is wisdom that the male protagonist has learned from his father. And this is the key to the salvation of the humans. The machine civilization's essential alienness finally allows a remnant of humanity to triumph and indeed to outwit, perhaps even destroy, the hyper-intelligent Mantis.

Great Sky River is an ambitious work that sets new standards for hard science fiction. Benford's previous contributions to the S-F field include the highly acclaimed *Timescape,* the innovative *Against Infinity,* the splendid, underappreciated *Across the Sea of Suns,* and a very successful collaboration with David Brin to produce *Heart of the Comet.* With the publication of *Great Sky River* this impressive body of work must place Benford firmly among the new generation of masters of the S-F genre, along with Gene Wolfe, Ursula LeGuin, and perhaps a few others. *Great Sky River* is a challenging, pace-setting work of hard science fiction that should not be missed.

John G. Cramer, "If Homer Were to Write Science Fiction," in Los Angeles Times Book Review, *December 27, 1987, p. 11.*

TOM EASTON

It is a pleasure to see another book from Gregory Benford. *Great Sky River* continues his future history of a galaxy dominated by machine intelligences who leave little place for fleshly life (see *Across the Sea of Suns* and *In the Ocean of Night*). Here we have a far-distant time on a world, Snowglade, once settled by humans, then found by the machines, or mechs. Over millennia, the mechs have changed the planet's climate and forced humans into a fringe existence of no relevance in the mechs' larger schemes.

Do you sense that humans occupy the place of contemporary Earthly wildlife? The parallel does seem deliberate, especially when we find, after following the flight of the remnant Family Bishop across the desolate face of Snowglade, hunted by the bizarrely unkillable Mantis, a mech with an eye for aesthetically motivated conservation. But that parallel, though it adds a nice level of resonance to the story, is only a subtheme. Benford skillfully and convincingly portrays a fallen humanity, vermin in a world they neither made nor wanted, stripped to the basics of survival. But those basics are high-tech basics—power-assisted suits hand built from mech parts, wired-in communications and sense-extenders. . . . (p. 180)

In this context, we watch Killeen, his son Toby, and the rest of Family Bishop, running, hunted, taking refuge where they can, fighting back when they get the chance, adapting, and running again. The Mantis strikes, they are overwhelmed by a sense of helplessness, and their flight brings them to another Family, one that is building a settlement with the aid of a renegade mech. It dreams of reestablishing humanity's dominance. But Killeen soon discovers the shaming truth, and then an out for those bold enough to take it: An ancient human robot, enslaved (or co-opted, really) by the mechs, reveals that its human masters long ago provided for an escape when humanity might wish to flee the mechs. That escape waits. . . . Those who follow Killeen have a destiny awaiting, and Benford has more books to write.

Don't miss this one. It's a masterful job, and it promises to be essential to Benford's future history. (pp. 180-81)

Tom Easton, in a review of "Great Sky River," in Analog Science Fiction/Science Fact, *Vol. CVIII, No. 3, March, 1988, pp. 180-81.*

Maryse Condé

1937-

Guadeloupean novelist, dramatist, short story writer, and critic.

A French-language author who is not widely known outside of France and her native Guadeloupe, Condé writes novels that are rich in historical detail and political discussion. Emphasizing the effects of transition upon ordinary individuals, Condé places her protagonists in situations where they must choose between the existing West African social order and cultural changes prompted by Western influence. Condé is praised for her authentic rendering of such diverse locales as the Caribbean, Africa, and Europe as well as for the lyrical qualities of her prose.

Condé's first novel, *Hérémakhonon: On doit attendre le bonheur* (1976; *Heremakhonon*), is set in an unidentified West African country and details the adventures of a Paris-educated Guadeloupean woman who, some critics suggest, bears a strong resemblance to Condé. The protagonist unwittingly becomes involved in the nation's political turmoil through her relationships with a bureaucrat and a radical schoolmaster. In her second novel, *Une saison à Rihata* (1981), Condé again focuses upon an African nation beset by internal problems to relate the story of a prominent family threatened by corruption and antigovernment sentiments. Charlotte and David Bruner observed: "[Here], as in *Hérémakhonon*, Condé draws upon . . . her knowledge of Guadeloupe, West Africa, and Paris to create credible people in a credible social environment. It is not herself she writes about—except, of course, in that limited sense that Flaubert recognized Emma Bovary with his 'C'est moi.'"

In her next two novels, *Ségou: Les murailles de terre* (1984; *Segu*) and *Ségou: La terre en miettes* (1986), Condé combines historical fact with fabulation to recreate events in the West African kingdom of Segou, which is now Mali, between 1797 and 1860. These works chronicle the experiences of members of a royal family whose lives are destroyed by such developments as European colonization, the slave trade, and the introduction of Islam and Christianity into Segou's largely animistic culture. Most critics praised Condé for her authentic and anthropologically informative portrait of pre-colonial African society. Charles R. Larson commented: "[Condé's] knowledge of African history is prodigious, and she is equally versed in the continent's folklore. The unseen world haunts her characters and vibrates with the spirits of the dead." Condé's fifth novel, *Moi, Tituba, sorcière, noire de Salem* (1986), is a fictionalized biography of Tituba, a Barbadian slave who was executed for practicing witchcraft in colonial Massachusetts. Condé presents the title character as a mystic and healer whose gifts were misunderstood and feared by her Puritan masters. Ann Armstrong Scarboro stated: "Condé weaves the threads of the novel so tightly that we are not fully aware of its social implications until we have stopped reading."

In addition to her novels, Condé has written two dramas, *Dieu nous l'a donné* (1973) and *Mort d'Oluwémi d'Ajumako* (1975), and a collection of short stories, *Un gout de miel* (1984). She has also published several volumes devoted to an examination of Francophone literature.

(See also *Contemporary Authors,* Vol. 110.)

DAVID K. BRUNER

It is to be expected that many of the dramas and works of prose fiction now being produced by Caribbean and African writers would deal with scenes of political struggle. The difficulties of a newly independent nation, or of a nation struggling for integrity and viability, are certain to occupy the mind and the spirit of creative artists, as well as of the rest of us. Current efforts of various leaders or leadership groups to make one or another political philosophy succeed are sure to catch the attention of the writer—who may, in his daily life, be a committed activist himself.

An obvious question arises: can drama and prose fiction of compelling interest and artistic value arise in such a situation? Or will literary efforts result merely in reiterations of stereotype plots and characters and political advocacy? The proper answer is, of course, that many plays and novels are merely vehicles for preaching a theory of social structure, but they need not be so limited. So long as a writer faces his creative task honestly, puts aside all temptation towards political propaganda, and believes in his characters as individuals, he may possibly achieve a work of artistic merit. We, as readers, may of course recognize patterns of belief and a world outlook which we take to belong to the writer. Our inferences, however, are made after the fact—and in part according to our own complex belief and value systems.

With respect to the double role of person and writer, Maryse Condé of Guadeloupe gives an excellent account of herself. Anyone who talks seriously with her for as long as a quarter of an hour is sure to discover that she cares about social, political, and ethical questions and is more than willing to make and defend her case openly. Anyone who has read her skillfully expressed rebuttal of what many négritude enthusiasts have claimed knows that her views are neither timid nor casual. Her essay, **"Pourquoi la négritude? négritude ou révolution?"** delivered in January 1973 at a colloquium organized by Le Centre d'Études Littéraires francophones de l'Université Paris-Nord. . . , leaves little doubt that her opposition to the social and political orders of colonialism, neo-colonialism, and race-based nationalism are vehement and individualistic. Her onslaught upon the idea that race, rather than poverty and weakness, is the base upon which the exploitation of Africans and exiled Africans was brought into being leads her into head-on rejection of some often-cited words of Sartre, Césaire, and Damas— among others—and she scorns to see a testament to the virtue of négritude in the political realities of her world, and ours.

She argues that in the struggles against the outsider who invades, colonizes, and exploits a people, race is not a causative factor—not even when it is later used as a "justification" by the conqueror for what his past actions have been. . . . Ms. Condé's point is that it was not black people who happened to be weak who were enslaved; it was weak people who happened to be black. Therefore, she argues, it is the weakness which needs to be dealt with, not the blackness. (pp. 168-70)

As a writer of creative fiction and drama, Ms. Condé is interested in people who are caught up in social and political struggle: what they do, what they believe, and how they are motivated. But, as an artist, she recognizes that, though there may be some rather commonly held beliefs and some rather commonly developed situations in all "revolutions," each revolution *is* an individual event and each person in a revolution is an individual person. Although she believes that a single person does not "make" a revolution . . . she finds "leaders" to be of compelling interest and good pivots for dramatic action. The leader may become the focus of drama; the reader or the viewer may live with and through him. But he must be convincing as a person. He, and his associates, must succeed or fail in various ways, not because of ideological reasons alone, or even principally, but because of all that they are and all that their environment is. Often, indeed, the dramatic catastrophe is hastened because of some motivation of the leader's having nothing at all to do with political or social matters.

In *Dieu nous l'a donné*, Ms. Condé's first published play, there are two "leaders," two quite different persons. One, a young, European-educated doctor, has come to Grand Anse because he believes it to be about as miserable a place as there is in the world; he has come to help the people to rebel against the corrupt government. . . . But the young doctor is clearly too naïve to be a success. He is, also, somewhat less than honest in his willingness to "use people for their own good." But he is attractive to two women in the play, and he does elicit the help of an old native-tyrant, a sort of doctor-magician, to help him in his effort to form a rebel group. But he fails, fully and even ridiculously. Though his failure might be in part due to poor planning and naïveté, it is more directly the result of the jealousy and injured pride of the two women, who betray him,

and of the jealous rage of the tyrant-doctor, who stabs him. The bizarre tragedy, in other words, is not really one of a failed revolution; it is one of a naïve (and a bit crude) egoist caught up in a web of human greed, jealousy, and vanity. Still, the play does take place in a social milieu where the viewer might well be praying for a revolution.

The second "leader" in the play, the native doctor, reveals a dark past of violent crime, based upon jealousy and including incestuous lust, which haunts him in terrifying dreams. His terror, however, is not sufficient to bring repentance and a change of behavior. Both "leaders" are flawed, inadequate in different ways to lead a revolution—for which the people are not ready anyhow!

Ms. Condé's next play again deals with power and a ruler of people. Here, in *Mort d'Oluwémi d'Ajumako,* the leader is an old native ruler in flight from his people. He has ruled by reason of traditional inheritance and by support of "the government" (external) which has used and protected him. But an old traditional ritual requires the king's self-slaughter after a period of twenty years of absolute rule. Oluwémi has almost successfully deceived his people into believing that he has followed the tradition honorably; he has substituted his slave in the slaughter ritual and has made the first part of his own physical escape. But the fraud has been discovered; greed has prompted a grave-robbery and revealed the slave's corpse. The people now will pursue and kill him if they can. The dramatic action of the play turns upon the ultimate decision of Oluwémi to sacrifice himself, and thus expiate his crime. But he can hardly be honored for "rising" to the deed; the old king is callous of his past of cruelty, luxury, lechery, and deceit. . . . In his movement to the ultimate decision, he is interesting— and even awesome—but not exemplary. The play is not a prescription for magistrates, nor a commentary upon traditional or colonial rule; nor is it a treatise upon the corrupting force of power any more than *King Lear* is a treatise upon the governance of daughters or the effect of storms upon the reason.

Ms. Condé's two plays are good ones, I think; they would go well upon the stage. The characters are sharp and individualized and the interaction of characters is a continuing source of plot. One has the feeling of conviction. (pp. 170-72)

Ms. Condé's third publication is a novel, *Hérémakhonon,* in many ways more complex and stronger than the plays, but concerned with people placed in much the same situation: in or near the seat of political power and affected by the applications of that power. . . . The narrator, Veronica, is the eyes of the reader, but she turns those eyes inward as well as outward. Sometimes she talks directly to the reader, revealing bits of her earlier life in the Caribbean island from which she moved to Paris as a student; sometimes she places the reader in Paris as she remembers herself there; sometimes she takes him into the novel's foreground, an unidentified West African country where she is finding herself in the middle of events involving her friends, her lover, and herself in some sort of political activity. As a free narrator, she can and does jump from time period to time period and locus to locus as the artistic unfolding of the story requires; she can theorize, speculate, or simply make verbatim report of an event. . . . But the *drama* of the whole book is encompassed in a battle between her lover, Ibrahim Sory, and her Institute associate and revolutionary, Saliou—a battle waged in and against the name of the titular ruler, Mwalimwana. Veronica does not early recognize the fact of the battle, and she never fully understands it. For the most part Saliou and Sory impinge upon her non-politically—as do other characters caught in the struggle. . . . The political issues force themselves upon her, and upon us, the readers, and it is for political reasons that her stay in Hérémakhonon is terminated. The reader speculates—and often he feels that he knows more than Veronica does about the power struggle, yet he always remains dependent upon her for confirmation or refutation of his judgments.

In *Hérémakhonon,* as in the two plays, there are "leaders" of considerable strength and fascination. In *Hérémakhonon,* the political situation is that of a nominally freed and independent, democratic nation, but actually one ruled by the force of old, inherited power. In this nation, a second revolution is in embryo and has as one of its centers the Institute where Veronica teaches and where ardent students—as well as students not ardent, but allied with their ardent peers—are involved in an act of futile resistance. The revolution fails, but not as ridiculously as the one in *Dieu nous l'a donné.* Indeed, the two *milieux* are different; the leaders are different. Each fiction is an artistic entity; neither is intended as "typical" or "illustrative." (pp. 172-73)

Obviously, Ms. Condé sees politics as very much a part of life. Commendably, however, she does not confuse drama and fiction with analysis and history. Whatever her literary objective—she strives for integrity, so much so that in anticipation of adverse criticism she has remarked, "I do not believe writing is meant to please people. . ."

From such convictions in a person of talent, energy, and intelligence, one has every reason to look for works of artistic merit and value. (p. 173)

> David K. Bruner, "Maryse Condé: Creative Writer in a Political World," in L'Esprit Créateur, Vol. XVII, No. 2, Summer, 1977, pp. 168-73.

DAVID K. BRUNER

Like Armah's title, *The Beautyful Ones Are Not Yet Born,* Condé's *Hérémakhonon* (*on doit attendre le bonheur*) implies that though the good may arrive, it has not arrived as yet. *Hérémakhonon* is based upon the conviction that a single leader does not make a revolution; revolution can come only when a whole people moves. Leaders may be influential, of course, but they may also be tragic, futile, demagogic, tyrannical or absurd. *Hérémakhonon* does not deal with this large theme in a heavy-handed way, however. It tells a story by means of a rather simple device and draws its reader into its central character, Veronica, to see and to speculate upon events unfolding in a country unidentified but obviously in French West Africa of the Senegal-Mali-Upper Volta region. . . . But the reader also reflects upon Veronica's past in the Antilles and in Paris, where she went to school. An internal dialogue intermingles the three time periods throughout the novel, as Veronica attempts a journey into her self to find whether a métisse has roots and ancestors in Africa.

The novel is not a treatise, however. Although it clearly shows Condé's impatient rejection of all clichéd thinking on the subjects of negritude, Maoism, democracy, et al., and although it clearly shows her hatred of exploitation, hypocrisy and cant of all sorts and her sympathy with people, it does so by means of involving the reader in a dominantly personal story. Veronica is quickly attracted to Ibrahima Sory and takes him as her lover. Sory, whom she thinks of half-facetiously as *un Oronoko,* is a strong man in the new order under the figurehead

leader Mwalimwana. Veronica also becomes the affectionate and beloved friend of Saliou, the revolutionary school director who sees Sory and Mwalimwana as tyrant-traitors to the new nation. . . . To her dismay, she is unable to stay out of the political struggle, and yet she is aware that she does not know enough to understand what is happening.

The novel ends, properly, with Veronica's return to the West— *her* world insofar as she has one. It provides no illuminating answers to the serious questions which abound in the Third World. . . . But it does reveal a great deal, honestly and often harshly in personal conflicts, about a dozen characters. It introduces types of people and situations which are clear and recognizable as part of political life generally, and at the same time it denounces the practice of thinking in types and reifying one's general concepts. . . .

[*Hérémakhonon*] is fascinating and fast-moving. It is also embellished with wit and wry allusions which delight the reader. When the school children, in public, take the oath of allegiance to Mwalimwana and are restored to good standing, "aprés chaque serment, l'assistance répond gravement. *Amin!*" One is tempted to reply to Condé: "An *i* for an *e*, that is to say?"

> David K. Bruner, in a review of "Hérémakhonon," in World Literature Today, Vol. 51, No. 3, Summer, 1977, p. 494.

CAROLE BOVOSO

Caught between sexism and racism, we black women find our identities divided, our loyalties strained. In addition, we must seek temporal security in a society centuries and continents away from our racial origins. The memory of our long-ago culture can be burden or benefit; often it calls up confusion and loneliness that we mask with a show of indifference. Alienation can become a self-inflicted disease.

Such is the case with Veronica, heroine of Maryse Condé's *Heremakhonon.* Although she resembles a typical Parisian tourist on her way to exotic Africa, Veronica is in fact a young, self-exiled Guadeloupan who soon reveals herself to be "a tourist, but one of a new breed, searching out herself, not landscapes." . . .

This land of flame trees, identical to those of her homeland, seems the perfect place to seek a cure for her sickness—that sense of alienation dating from the time the first slave ships departed Africa, dispersing ancestors she has been unable to trace.

"I want to escape from the black bourgeoisie that made me, with its talk of glorifying the race and its terrified conviction of its inferiority," Veronica confides as she lies defiantly beside her African lover, the country's minister of defense. The minister's villa is called Heremakhonon ("Welcome House" in Mandingo); Veronica is drawn there, and spends much of the novel being chauffeured past poverty to the minister's bed.

Amid conflict and danger, Veronica remains uncommitted. Incapable of choosing sides, she seeks a past that no longer exists; the present seems as anachronistic to her as the tank that rolls ominously past the mud huts of the strife-torn village. . . .

Condé's insinuating prose has a surreal, airless quality as she assembles a complex mosaic of African and Antillean imagery. There were times I longed to rush in and break the spell, to shout at this black woman and shake her. But no one can rescue

Veronica, least of all herself; Condé conveys the seriousness of her plight by means of a tone of relentless irony and reproach. As she awaits the DC-10 which will take her away from chaos and murder that have left her untouched, it is clear that Veronica is yet another victim of the diaspora. Indifference has become her true homeland; for her there is no cure.

Carole Bovoso, in a review of "Heremakhonon," in VLS, *No. 12, November, 1982, p. 3.*

HAL WYLIE

Born in Guadeloupe in 1937, Condé has gone far. She has been teacher, scholar, critic, journalist, radio and TV personality, dramatist and novelist.... It seems that her travels and extensive publications indicate a rather privileged person, much like the protagonist of *Heremakhonon,* Veronica. Although Condé stated in an interview that she created Veronica as an "anti-moi" to make her more credible and to avoid producing a "slogan-novel," Three Continents Press claims on the back cover that *Heremakhonon* is both a "tract" and a "self-analysis." Veronica and her author indeed have much in common. (p. 157)

[Veronica] is cynical, tough, blasé; a modern anti-feminine, anti-childbirth, anti-family "feminist"; overeducated and footloose. Her conception of independence seems to be related to her vision of herself as an outsider who identifies with outcasts and renegades. Her psychology is the main flaw in the novel. Veronica chooses the reactionary chief of police, a torturer with a feudal mentality, as her lover, even though warned by her colleagues. This facilitates Condé's work in sketching a newly independent African nation, since Veronica has friends in both the parasitical establishment and the revolutionary opposition. (pp. 157-58)

The connections between the sociology of the nation and the psychology of commitment are handled well. Only the protagonist's character rings false. Can a philosophy teacher really be this dumb? How can she fail to see that her lover is a murderer? If she was intended as neurotic, she comes across as psychotic. Her keen insights into the dialectics of race, class, sex and power and her analyses of identity and commitment all clash with a certain basic lack of awareness.

The novel is quite readable and revealing. But might not the time have come to dispense with the psychotic protagonist? (p. 158)

Hal Wylie, in a review of "Heremakhonon," in World Literature Today, *Vol. 57, No. 1, Winter, 1983, pp. 157-58.*

CHARLOTTE BRUNER AND DAVID BRUNER

One of the assertions often made about contemporary women writers, particularly those of the Third World, or more precisely those whose cultures have not afforded them any opportunity to write or be heard until recently, is that they of course have an interesting personal and domestic story to tell. They do; so does everyone. The trouble with this assertion is its implied limitation to the allegedly simple narrative of one's domestic experience, and the attribution of this limitation to women's writing or to women writers. An additional implication is that such subject matter is, after all, trivial. Such implications are of course insupportable, as the works of Buchi Emecheta and Maryse Condé amply demonstrate....

With respect to Maryse Condé's writing, the case for scope and depth is perhaps much easier to make, not necessarily because her perceptions are more profound, but because they have been apparent over a longer period of time and in most of her dramas, stories, articles, and novels. Although Condé, like Emecheta, deals with characters in domestic situations and employs fictitious narratives as a means of elaborating large-scale activities, she has also produced critical analyses based on scholarly research....

Condé's dramas *Dieu nous l'a donné* (1972) and *Mort d'Oluwémi d'Ajumako* (1973) also are concerned with the manipulation of social mores and myths by individuals seeking political power and influence. Her three novels *Hérémakhonon* (1976), *Une saison à Rihata* (1981), and [*Ségou: les murailles de terre*] (1984) attempt to make credible on an increasingly larger scale the personal human complexities involved in holy wars, national rivalries, and migrations of peoples. (p. 9)

Condé, as a critic, has explored the literary contribution of African and Caribbean women writers. She finds many of them confused, undirected, unfocused. In her own fiction she may invent female narrators or lead characters, but her concerns are for all human beings, their rights as individuals to self-fulfillment in a world of political corruption and unrest....

Condé, in her fiction as well as in her criticism, reflects her concern for the art of writing. Though her characters are not self-portraits, their remarks appear often to echo her experience and her critical opinions....

Condé has also stated that Véronica of *Hérémakhonon* is not a self-portrait and is perhaps even an *anti-moi*. Nonetheless, Véronica's black bourgeois family in Guadeloupe somewhat resembles Condé's, cherishing blackness and white cultural values all at once. Véronica is also like Condé in that French, not the local Creole, is her first language. A product of a classical education, Véronica sprinkles her speech with epigrams ("Life is a bitch with a bum leg"), with puns, and with allusions to Pascal and Marivaux as well as to Césaire, Fanon, and Simone de Beauvoir. Condé's erudition and wit, and her fascination with history and the Middle Passage, are reflected in Véronica's assertion:

> After all, where would we be if Christopher Columbus hadn't crossed the Atlantic with his ship's hold full of sugarcane plants taken from the Moslems in Cyprus? We ought to make it our emblem, our standard. If man is a (thinking) reed [Pascal's *roseau*], the West Indian is a stalk [*roseau*] of sugarcane.

"I have the unfortunate habit of seeing symbols everywhere," Véronica wryly remarks. (p. 10)

It is not that there has been a change in Maryse Condé's basic understanding, nor even in her narrative skills, that one is impelled to view *Ségou,* her latest novel, as a truly remarkable book, a work to be considered according to the same criteria one applies to *God's Bits of Wood, The Grapes of Wrath,* or *War and Peace.* Indeed, the ability to make the truth of fiction compatible with the data of historical events is discernible in all her writing. In her early plays, like *Dieu nous l'a donné* or *Mort d'Oluwémi d'Ajumako,* as well as in her novels *Hérémakhonon, Une saison à Rihata,* and *Ségou,* her management of fact and fiction would satisfy most Aristotelians. She is unwilling to accept a popular belief or to reject it just because it is popular, she is willing to refrain from drawing inferences and theorizing on the basis of inadequate or confusing evidence, and she has a persistent curiosity which sharpens her powers of observation. This same analytical intelligence and critical integrity are evident also in her many essays and scholarly critiques; they have often put her into bold relief against a popular attitude, as did her article **"Pourquoi la négritude? Négritude ou révolution?"**. . . In that essay she refuted as ill-founded Léon Damas's enthusiastic perception of a healthy, triumphing *négritude,* citing Haiti as a prime counterexample, among others. Here, however, our discussion of Maryse Condé will limit itself to a consideration of the three novels, each of which deals fictionally with sociopolitical material.

Hérémakhonon invents a political conflict in an unspecified but obviously West African nation into which Véronica, a *métisse* from the Antilles by way of Paris, enters, searching to see whether she will find any African roots. (pp. 11-12)

The telling of the narrative is most effective; the reader believes in the characters and tends to see them as rather ordinary people occupying positions of extraordinary power and having somewhat distorted perceptions of themselves. Justly or not, one gains a comprehension of what a revolution is like, what new African nations are like, yet one is aware that this comprehension is nothing more than a feeling. The wise reader will go home as Véronica does—to continue more calmly to reflect, and to observe.

Une saison à Rihata, like *Hérémakhonon,* presents a revolution in progress toward failure in a West African nation. It involves a fairly large family of characters whose ethnic and social foci are Africa, Paris, and the Antilles. There is a difference in the telling of the story, however, which is noteworthy. The main character is not a visitor-woman, but an indigenous man whose birth and position have thrust social obligations upon him which he, however, has not accepted. Much of what the reader sees is seen through this man's eyes, but not all. The reader is permitted into the thoughts and feelings of other characters also, and the narrative becomes more a family chronicle than a spectator piece. The major actors in the chronicle are two sisters, two brothers, various children, a powerful father in the background, and a number of political activists. As the family drama of conflicts, loves, hates, and betrayals unfolds, the social implications in the abortive attempt at political overthrow move into the foreground. Here . . . , as in *Hérémakhonon,* Condé draws upon her real-life experience: she makes use of her knowledge of Guadeloupe, West Africa, and Paris to create credible people in a credible social environment. It is not herself she writes about—except, of course, in that limited sense that Flaubert recognized Emma Bovary with his "C'est moi." (p. 12)

Upon reading *Ségou,* at least one difference from the two previous novels is immediately clear: its magnitude. The magnitude is not wholly one of the number of pages (nearly five hundred), but also the years covered (sixty to eighty), of the localities involved (perhaps a dozen different nations or kingdoms), of the number of major historical and fictional characters extensively developed (over a dozen), of the major historical events integrally involved (the march of Islam over north central Africa, the later years of the slave trade, the "repatriation" in West Africa of Brazilian slaves, et cetera).

With such an overwhelming mass of data and with so extensive a literary objective, the risks of writing a *roman à thèse* (a genre not favored by Condé) or of producing a heavy, didactic treatise are, of course, great. The main reason that Condé has done neither is, perhaps, because she has written here essentially as she did in her two earlier novels: she has followed the lives of the fictional characters as individuals dominated by interests and concerns which are very personal and often selfish and petty, even when those characters are perceived by other characters as powerful leaders in significant national or religious movements. In *Ségou,* for example, one bit of factual data involves the conquest of most of North Africa by Islam and specifically of the struggle of Islam with the Bambara religion, a sort of animism. In the narrative fiction, one of the sons of Dousika Traoré, Tiékoro, becomes a convert to Islam, even against his family's wishes and its feeling of security. The family loyalties are strong, and Tiékoro is permitted to pursue his own course. He becomes fanatically determined to convert all Bambara; the family stresses are great, and hate-love-betrayal-envy feelings arise by turns in many of its members. Tiékoro, almost by chance, is slain as an enemy of the people and then is seen as a martyr and revered as a hero-saint by the people. Ironically, however, the reader knows that Tiékoro was often skeptical about his own motivations, often felt himself a sinner and a sham; the reader cannot share the family's awe for a legendary hero. Condé does not generalize from the fiction of Tiékoro's life; she does not draw inferences to explain why Islam was in fact successful in its holy war. The reader, however, who has seen Tiékoro from the inside, may be tempted to wonder how many really ordinary human beings like Tiékoro are the actual bases of great national and religious movements, just how substantial a part mere chance and erratic behavior have in such movements. It is not Condé's purpose to give voice to such questions, much to her credit as a writer of fiction.

The great historical matters like the slave trade, the governance of women, and the conflicts of nations and religions, which are in the background of the story of the Traoré family in Segou, are similarly dealt with. Condé avoids the intrusion of her own voice, directly or indirectly. In such areas of judgment, she feels that the reader should be permitted to act *tout seul.* To the present date, very little of Condé's writing has been translated into English; much more should be. (pp. 12-13)

Condé some time ago spoke of writing directly about her early life in Guadeloupe. It will be good for us if she does so; the Caribbean is only recently entering the general literate consciousness. We know it is not one entity, but many entities. To know one of these entities (Guadeloupe) better, as well as to know Maryse Condé even better, would be a good thing. (p. 13)

Charlotte Bruner and David Bruner, "Buchi Eme-cheta and Maryse Condé: Contemporary Writing from Africa and the Caribbean," in World Literature Today, *Vol. 59, No. 1, Winter, 1985, pp. 9-13.*

JURIS SILENIEKS

With [*Ségou: les murailles de terre*], Maryse Condé, a Guadeloupean writer with several critical and creative works to her credit, embarks upon an ambitious venture, situating her novel at the interstices of fiction and history. The genre, of course, has always tempted many and seems to be of some currency today among Francophone Caribbean writers (Glissant, Maximin, Placoly, et alia), who are well aware of the fictional import to the interpretation of history as exemplified by the great Latin American novelists.

Ségou is set in the late eighteenth and early nineteenth centuries, and the central narrative locale is the Bambara kingdom of Segu. The saga follows more or less three generations of the Dousika family, whose members, after the disgrace of the family head, are dispersed throughout West Africa, some of them even reaching the New World and England. Incessant internecine wars, consolidation and dissolution of political alliances, the expansion of Islam into territories that still cling to forms of animism or fetishism and occasion violent religious contentions, the last decades of the slave trade, the growing presence of the Europeans as traders, colonizers, and missionaries—all these constitute a colorful backdrop, richly embroidered with graphic vignettes of intrigue, suicide, murder, rape.

The narrative, while tracing the life paths of the four sons of the Dousika family, gives a panoramic overview of African societies within this rapidly changing world. . . . Throughout the novel, however, the narrative focus frequently dwells on the lot of African women, who, slaves or legitimate wives, are bartered and swapped, humiliated and exploited, with no pangs of conscience or reflection on the part of the male.

The reading of the saga is engaging. The historical/anthropological accuracy cannot be faulted, and the author has mercifully provided the reader with geographic and historical maps, glossaries, and genealogical tables. Still, the saga does not rise much above the level of an inspired soap opera, failing to stop and to reflect, to distill a deeper meaning from the chaos and absurdities that crowd the narrative. Carlos Fuentes argued that every novel, while anchored in history, must at the same time transcend it to bring truth to the lies of history. *Ségou,* unfortunately, does not illustrate Fuentes's contention. (pp. 309-10)

> *Juris Silenieks, in a review of ''Ségou: Les murailles de terre,'' in* World Literature Today, *Vol. 59, No. 2, Spring, 1985, pp. 309-10.*

DAVID K. BRUNER

With the appearance of [*Ségou: La terre en miettes*], Maryse Condé has strengthened her position as a writer of historical fiction of the highest order. Together with volume 1, *Les murailles de terre*, it tells a convincing story of two generations of a Bambara family, the Traorés, in the midst of at least three international movements: the slave trade, the sweep of Islam across North Africa, and the colonization (mainly French) of central North Africa.

In *Les murailles de terre,* the sites of action include central and western North Africa, Brazil, and England; in *La terre en miettes* the sites are central and western North Africa and Jamaica. The stories told of individual members of Dousika Traoré's extended family are fascinating and convincing as they bring the reader into intimate contact with each separate and distinctly individual character. . . . Though Condé never speaks in her own name as apologist, advocate, or critic, the reader recognizes that her ability to produce a compelling fiction must necessarily rest upon a profound and judicious observation of people and what Bertrand Russell called "the springs of human action."

That myths are built upon incomplete and false evidence only to become worshiped and "factualized" by posterity is easily inferred. In volume 1 the execution of Tiékoro as a traitor and his subsequent elevation as a revered "founding father" of Islam among the Bambaras are, the reader knows, incongruous with the persistent internal doubts and contradictions which were the facts of his life. So also in volume 2 the elevation of Omar to the status of *madhi* whose doctrine of "Nous sommes un. Un" is accepted and incorporated into Bambara life after having been scorned and rejected while he lived is incongruous

with the facts of *his* internal life of doubts and contradictions. Even though Omar's wife is aware of the incongruity, she knows the created myth is now an "irrefutable" cultural fact.

The three or four main streams of action in both volumes are complex but nevertheless are well integrated into the objective facts of history, which Condé has researched in great depth. As strongly impressive historical fiction. [*Ségou: La terre en miettes*] makes one think of the kind of opus Jean-Paul Sartre produced concerning the French prelude, life and postlude of World War II in *Chemins de la liberté*. A nondoctrinaire novel—no thesis novel—*Ségou* is a major addition to the world's literary treasure.

> *David K. Bruner, in a review of ''Ségou: La Terre en Miettes,'' in* World Literature Today, *Vol. 60, No. 3, Summer, 1986, p. 509.*

PUBLISHERS WEEKLY

Lively, interesting and unusual, this family saga [*Segu*] is set in the warlike kingdom of Segu (roughly present-day Mali) in the late 19th century. Furthermore, Condé is a born storyteller. The cummulative effect is marred, however, by such a bewildering array of characters and such a density of cultural detail that the storyline becomes both sluggish and hard to follow. . . . Taken piecemeal, it's a vivid tale that provides what appears to be a scrupulously authentic picture of an African nation turned into a crucible of conflict by the thrust of militant Islam from the East and the thrust of slavery from the West, with Christian missionaries adding to the cultural confusion. It's a pity Condé, herself a descendant of the Bambara, did not fashion her material into several novels.

> *A review of ''Segu,'' in* Publishers Weekly, *Vol. 231, No. 5, February 6, 1987, p. 84.*

ANNABELLE M. REA

Maryse Condé's *Pays mêlé,* the first of the two short pieces in [*Pays mêlé*], is an important historical text, important for non-Antilleans and also for West Indians who traditionally have known more of European history than their own. It is not, however, a historical text in the usual sense but a history of "unimportant" people, a history that begins with the death of "un jeune comme les autres," in the violent events of 1984.

The narrator, a French-trained doctor, representative of the elite whose tastes lean toward European art and other aspects of foreign culture, feels a need to search out the story of the young revolutionary, Antoine Suréna, and that of his mother, Berthe, whose death follows as a consequence of her son's. *Pays mêlé* is also the story of the unnamed doctor's emerging identity as an Antillean; he begins and ends with confusion between "mon histoire" and "leur histoire." As a bachelor, he represents the end of a family line while the "insignificant" people whose story he tells will continue, even though two of their representatives have died. (pp. 905-06)

The text surveys the evolution of popular mentalities, mentioning along the way specific events of Guadeloupe's history, with proper names changed, however. The sweep through history shows the difficult relationship of mothers and daughters, the transience of the fathers, and the male frustrations and angers which lead only to fights among themselves instead of toward revolt against the system. Although the physical geography is a composite fiction, the "social geography," with its jealousies and its narrowness, remains very true to life. In both of the short texts we see the distinctions of skin color, the alienation of many who don't fit society's mould, and the attraction of Protestant sects.

The second narrative, *Nanna-ya,* set in the English-speaking Caribbean, also focuses on a historical writing project. In his search for revenge against the humiliations caused both by society and his wife, George Pereira decides to tell the story of the eighteenth-century Jamaican slave revolt leader, Tacky, because he resents his wife's pride in her descent from the legendary Maroon heroine, Nanny. George's text, however, must be shaped by a female, the mulatto Joyce, before it can become readable. Joyce's theft of his manuscript leads to her social advancement and George's reconciliation with his wife. Only through collaboration between male and female, through a re-examination of the relationship so distorted by slavery and colonization can Antillean society progress.

The *Pays mêlé* volume represents a "return to the native land" for Guadeloupean writer Maryse Condé. These tales, after the vast panorama of African history celebrated in *Ségou,* spotlight contemporary Caribbean culture approached through an understanding of the past. (p. 906)

> *Annabelle M. Rea, in a review of "Pays mêlé," in The French Review, Vol. LX, No. 6, May, 1987, pp. 905-06.*

CHARLES R. LARSON

In *Segu,* Maryse Condé has written a wondrous novel about a period of African history few other writers have addressed. Some have dwelt on the late 19th century, when Christianity swept the continent and gave rise to an iconography that played off the contrast of black and white. But Ms. Condé has chosen for her subject an equally chaotic stage, when the animism (which she calls fetishism) native to the region began to yield to Islam. The result is the most significant historical novel about black Africa published in many a year.

Ms. Condé's work is epic in scope, in part because the author weaves together the stories of four sons of a Bambara patriarch, Dousika Traore. The book covers the years from 1797 to 1860, when Segu (a city located between Bamako and Timbuktu in present-day Mali) underwent continued ravages as a result of religious confrontations. . . . The differences among the four brothers—and among the fascinating women who become part of their lives—are both startling and comfortably familiar.

Much of the novel's radiance comes from the lush descriptions of a traditional life that is both exotic and violent. Noblemen surround themselves with wives and concubines, often supporting their hedonism through the active slave trade. Though the author is particularly sympathetic to her female characters, she neither condemns nor condones these activities, but presents them as realities of the time. She also makes it clear that bodily pleasure, especially sexuality, was one of the major points of conflict between fetishism and Islam. . . .

Besides depicting rural life in both West Africa and Brazil, the narrative evokes half a dozen major African cities during the early 19th century: Timbuktu, Cape Coast, Lagos, Fez, Ouidah, Freetown. There is even a madcap sequence set in London—one of the highlights of the novel, in fact—describing one of Dousika's grandsons trapped in the heart of darkness:

> The dirt and overcrowding horrified Eucaristus, and caused a stench never swept away by cleansing breezes

such as those of Freetown. A few yards from the Strand and its rows of luxury stores you came upon lanes and alleys strewn with filth and human excrement, and these led to hovels filled with human wrecks sleeping and copulating on heaps of straw or rags crawling with vermin.

Although the story brings us back repeatedly to Segu, in a broader sense Ms. Condé's story is about the inability of different cultures to combine. Along with important Moslem characters (based on historical figures), there are cameo appearances by the British explorer Mungo Park; the first African Bishop of Nigeria, Samuel Adjai Crowther; as well as other harbingers and byproducts of Western penetration. Ms. Condé is a Guadeloupan by birth, but she clearly identifies with her Bambara forebears. Her knowledge of African history is prodigious, and she is equally versed in the continent's folklore. The unseen world haunts her characters and vibrates with the spirits of the dead.

As the author of several novels (both *Segu* and its sequel [*Ségou: La terre en miettes*] were best sellers in France), she knows how to keep the narrative engrossing. . . . Still—in spite of its richness—the story at times almost totally engulfs the reader. The novel cries out for an annotated list giving the linkages among the 50 or so important characters, several of whom Ms. Condé simply drops as if she had grown weary of them.

> *Charles R. Larson, "Converts and Concubines," in The New York Times Book Review, May 31, 1987, p. 47.*

ANN ARMSTRONG SCARBORO

Moi, Tituba, sorcière, Noire de Salem (I, Tituba, sorceress, Black woman of Salem), by Maryse Condé, . . . is a striking example of recent fiction from the Caribbean. The literature from this area is coming of age—we have moved from works that portray political and social injustice exclusively to writing that uses these issues but focuses on the individual's dilemma, that of choosing a personal moral path. Tituba decides that she will not work evil even when she is in the heartland of the evildoers. She is constantly tempted to use her gift of magic to harm her enemies, and yet she resists, growing in stature because she resists. She invites us instead into a spiritual and ethical world that permits her—and the rest of us—to rise above the pain caused by slavery and religious discrimination even as we learn from Condé more about the horrors of these worlds.

Although much of the action takes place in America, Barbados is always present in Tituba's imagination. . . . The whole Caribbean configuration of ancestral spirits, native folklore, and Vodoun wisdom is essential to the working out of Tituba's interior journey. She communicates frequently with the spirits of her deceased mother and grandmother, Abena and Man Yaya. Instructed by Man Yaya, she uses herbs, roots, and animal sacrifices to heal black and white alike. Tituba's positive concept of sorcery is the life-giving, healing version of that dark Satanic power the Puritans ascribed to their notion of witchcraft. . . .

The Caribbean configuration provides a dramatic contrast to the Puritan world of guilt and closure, making the latter seem unimaginative and lonely as well as repressive. These elements are never more clearly or more repugnantly depicted than in Condé's portrait of the minister, Samuel Parris: "However fanatic and somber were the parishioners who shared his faith, they were less so than Parris, he with his enormous, angry silhouette, his mouth shouting reprimands and exhortations, frightening everyone to the very core.'' The novel is a triple indictment of slavery, of religious intolerance, and of a world in which men dominate women. Condé is lyrical yet brutally direct in her presentation of these indictments. When we think about Watts, the resurgence of the Ku Klux Klan, and Khomeini, the novel is uncannily pertinent.

Moi, Tituba, sorcière, Noire de Salem is a fictionalized biography of Tituba, the slave from Barbados who was tried for witchcraft along with Sarah Good and Sarah Osborne in Salem, Massachusetts, in 1692. Tituba is a documented historical figure who appeared in Arthur Miller's scathing condemnation of the Salem witch trials, *The Crucible,* and in Ann Petry's novel for young readers, *Tituba of Salem Village.* Condé uses numerous historical facts, telling us how Tituba is born aboard a slave ship bound for Barbados, marries the slave John Indian, is sold along with him to the Puritan minister Samuel Parris, and goes with the Parris family to America and eventually to Salem. Intense irony emerges from small details like the names of the slave ships—Tituba was conceived when her mother was raped by a sailor on *Christ the King,* she is transported to America on *Blessing,* and she goes home to Barbados on *Bless the Lord.*

Tituba violates her personal code of ethics when, on trial for witchcraft, she implicates two women who have been most hateful to her, to avoid being hanged. She condemns herself for lying even though she knows she is the victim of a system based on falsehoods. Condé explicitly links discrimination against Jews to discrimination against blacks when she introduces Ben-

jamin Cohen as Tituba's new owner. We are reminded of Hitler's Germany when Benjamin's children are killed in a pogrom. We admire the depth of Benjamin's generosity when he sets Tituba free because he knows that her deepest desire is to return home to Barbados. We think of Toussaint L'Ouverture in St. Domingue (later Haiti), and countless other renegades, when Tituba joins a band of runaway slaves who are planning a rebellion, the same kind of rebellion that occurred frequently during the 1800s in the Caribbean. . . .

When Tituba discovers she is pregnant, she vows to keep the child and decides to fight with the rebels, still, however, not using her sorcerer's art as a weapon. The rebels are betrayed and the English colonists hang Tituba for witchcraft.

This novel represents an evolution in Condé's writing. In her first two novels, *Hérémakhonon (Happy Homecoming)* and *Une Saison à Rihata (A Season in Rihata),* external political reality is at least as much a focus as is the heroine's choice of a personal moral path. In the two-volume best seller in France, *Ségou: les murailles de terre* and *Ségou: la terre en miettes,* a series of eloquent but brief interior journeys portrays a detailed saga of religious and social history in Africa and the Caribbean. . . . In *Moi, Tituba, sorcière, Noire de Salem,* it is the moral experience combined with an exploration of love and sorcery that binds the work together. Condé weaves the threads of the novel so tightly that we are not fully aware of its social implications until we have stopped reading.

Ann Armstrong Scarboro, ''Womb of Shadow,'' in The American Book Review, *Vol. 9, No. 6, January-February, 1988, p. 8.*

Elizabeth Daly

1878-1967

American novelist.

Daly earned an enthusiastic readership during the 1940s and early 1950s for her mystery novels written in the tradition of the classic English detective story as practiced by such authors as Sir Arthur Conan Doyle and Agatha Christie. Usually focusing upon affluent East Coast American communities, Daly's works feature protagonist Henry Gamadge, an author and rare books appraiser whose bibliophilic skills draw him into investigations of crime and murder. Daly was acknowledged by Barbara C. M. Dudley for having "charmed and intrigued [mystery readers] over and over with humor, careful plotting, a delicate handling of surprise, and telling sketches."

Daly's first novel, *Unexpected Night* (1940), chronicles Henry Gamadge's efforts to locate the murderer of an heir to a family fortune. In *Deadly Nightshade* (1940), Gamadge investigates the poisoning of three children on the coast of Maine. *Murders in Volume 2* (1941) concerns the cryptic relationship between a missing volume of Lord Byron's poems and the reappearance of an English governess who was assumed to be dead. In *Evidence of Things Seen* (1943), Daly employs elements of Gothic fiction to relate a mystery in which Gamadge's wife sojourns to a remote Connecticut summer house and views a specter wandering the grounds prior to a murder. In *The Book of the Dead* (1944), mysterious markings in a copy of William Shakespeare's play *The Tempest* lead Gamadge to the solution of a murder. *Any Shape or Form* (1945) sends him to an East Coast estate where a contemptuous millionairess has been fatally shot during a tea party. In *Night Walk* (1947), Gamadge becomes involved in the investigations of two brutal murders while vacationing in an isolated rural village. *And Dangerous to Know* (1949) details his search for an elderly woman of means, and *Death and Letters* (1950) involves a young woman who uses crossword puzzles to communicate information to Gamadge about her imprisonment by relatives. Other Daly mysteries featuring Henry Gamadge include *The House without the Door* (1942), *Nothing Can Rescue Me* (1943), *Arrow Pointing Nowhere* (1944; reprinted as *Murder Listens In*), *Somewhere in the House* (1946), *The Wrong Way Down* (1946; reprinted as *Shroud for a Lady*), *The Book of the Lion* (1948), and *The Book of the Crime* (1950). Daly also authored *The Street Has Changed* (1941), a novel of manners in which she documents the history of four New York families involved in the theater.

(See also *Contemporary Authors*, Vols. 23-24, Vols. 25-28, rev. ed [obituary] and *Contemporary Authors Permanent Series*, Vol. 2.)

KAY IRVIN

The title [of *Unexpected Night*]—so happily portentous and delightfully grim—is from Thomas Lovell Beddoes: "Eventful unexpected night, which finishes a row of plotting days." And the story fulfills all that phrase's implications. The author is a writer of light verse who has not hitherto essayed this type of light fiction. But . . . with her skill and wit and suavity we hope she is in this field to stay.

A rich lad in an impoverished family, Amberley Cowden, will be sole master of his fortune when he reaches the age of 21. On his twenty-first birthday he dies of the heart disease which has kept him a lifelong invalid; and since he hasn't had time to sign the will he has just made, his young sister Alma gets all the money. But why is his body found at the foot of a cliff on the Maine coast? What is Alma Cowden afraid of? Are his conventional cousins, the Barclays, trying to conceal something? And in the Summer theatre in an all-but-inaccessible cove what is his extremely unconventional actor-cousin up to?

To the basic essential of an ingenious plot Miss Daly adds consistent characterization, a light and easy style, and realistic atmosphere.

> *Kay Irvin, in a review of "Unexpected Night," in* The New York Times Book Review, *March 10, 1940, p. 26.*

RALPH PARTRIDGE

[In *Unexpected Night*, a] young man with a weak heart is heir to a million dollars if he lives to be twenty-one; he is found dead at the foot of a cliff on the morning of his twenty-first birthday. This should make a nice plot, and Miss Daly has marshalled a wide group of predatory relatives round her victim for us to pick a murderer; but in the novice's anxiety to keep the cat in the bag she goes to great—intolerably great—lengths. Driving golf balls at people a hundred yards off is not a recognised way even to simulate murder. The style is very readable, but why must one of the characters constantly be called a "leprechaun"? The solution is deductively sound, but not notable for anything but extravagance. (p. 680)

> Ralph Partridge, "The Progress of Simenon," in The New Statesman & Nation, Vol. XIX, No. 483, May 25, 1940, pp. 678, 680.

THE TIMES LITERARY SUPPLEMENT

Miss Elizabeth Daly is an American novelist who, we believe, is a newcomer to the British public. She has written [*Unexpected Night*], a pleasant murder story, if murder stories may be reckoned pleasant, which concerns a rich family and a group of poor actors on a Maine sea-coast resort. The amateur detective named Gamadge sets himself to solve a series of murders which follow that of a wealthy young man who dies either just before or just after the hour at which he was due to inherit. The characters are as distinct as detective story characters can be. Possibly readers of *Unexpected Night* who have read Mr. Sinclair Lewis's latest novel [*Bethel Merriday*] may be a trifle disappointed with the description of a "summer theatre" which could have been written more interestingly, but that is a stern comparison and Mr. Gollancz [the publisher of the book in Great Britain] may be wholeheartedly congratulated on his discovery.

> "Kidnappers and Killers," in The Times Literary Supplement, No. 2000, June 1, 1940, p. 269.

WILL CUPPY

Why worry if you can't believe every word of this tangled tale [*Deadly Nightshade*]? Puzzling is the main show, and Miss Daly has her jigsaw pieces arranged for a prime guessing game. Some kiddies up in Ford Center, Me., got hold of some deadly nightshade berries, and right away there's one child dead, another missing, an enigmatic little boy at the gypsy camp and panic abroad in the countryside. Maybe the death of Trooper Trainor in a motorcycle spill is significant, too. Enter Henry Gamadge, whose skill with ink and old documents endeared him to fans in *Unexpected Night*. He also knows about chess, astronomy, kittens, painting and atropine and has a gift for handling all sorts of suspects, several of them touched in the head. . . . The plot thickens amazingly toward the end, with a flurry of romantic gambits, and Miss Daly proves herself as deft at juggling hints as the armchair sleuth could wish. A pleasing yarn, tall in spots.

> Will Cuppy, in a review of "Deadly Nightshade," in New York Herald Tribune Books, September 29, 1940, p. 23.

KAY IRVIN

Elizabeth Daly rose like a star on the mystery fans' horizon with *Unexpected Night*. . . . [*Deadly Nightshade*] is another, also original and highly civilized, also excellent, and also with its scene laid on the Maine coast and its chief sleuth in the

person of Henry Gamadge, who runs down forgeries in old (or not so old) manuscripts by profession and untangles crime puzzles for fun. This new puzzle is not only intricate. It was the sort of thing the investigators simply couldn't get a grip on. Three children had eaten deadly nightshade berries, and one had died. Another child, a gypsy, was ill, too. When Detective Mitchell asked Gamadge's help, there was nothing to connect the mishaps, no way to tell whether they were crimes or accidents, no motive, no sense. . . .

The plot is complicated but the action is brisk; and both people and scene are alive. Miss Daly has done it again; and started in, we hope, as a regular.

> Kay Irvin, in a review of "Deadly Nightshade," in The New York Times Book Review, September 29, 1940, p. 20.

WILL CUPPY

Miss Daly, whose admirable work you may have sampled in *Unexpected Night* and *Deadly Nightshade,* has turned in a four-star job this time, no fooling. . . . *Murders in Volume 2,* herewith highly recommended on all counts, is one of those fortunate combinations of plot, people and writing that should stand the puzzlers on their heads, excepting maybe the more determined and desperate roughnecks. . . . Henry Gamadge, that expert thinker and authority on old books, is present with a glittering line of logic, . . . one of the main characters is suspected of having disappeared into the fourth dimension and come out again, and that the second volume of a set of Lord Byron's poems is Exhibit A. Murder strikes in the midst of the aristocratic Vauregards, riddles of the past pop up for modern solving, and Henry Gamadge gives you the answer in a burst of powerful reasoning.

> Will Cuppy, in a review of "Murders in Volume 2," in New York Herald Tribune Books, March 9, 1941, p. 17.

KAY IRVIN

That young expert in old books, Henry Gamadge, may now be counted a regular member of the choice company of the best fiction sleuths. In the latest Gamadge chronicle [*Murders in Volume 2*] he is called in as book expert to solve a puzzle of attempted fraud with which a volume of Byron's poems is strangely connected. And although no murder takes place for some time, our interest in the singular designs on Imbrie Vauregard's fortune burns high from the start. Lydia Wagoneur, a charming young lady, disappeared from the Vauregard garden in May, 1840; a century later to a day her impressive presentment steps, it seems, out of the fourth dimension; and the 80-year-old master of the Vauregard millions is completely taken in.

It is old Imbrie's likable middle-aged niece who calls in Mr. Gamadge. But that astute thinker is not slow in guessing that the impoverished Vauregard relations themselves may not be able to present a full roll of innocence. . . .

[The plot is] complex. But the book is delightfully original and suavely written, with lively characters and a vivid scene. This is Elizabeth Daly's third mystery novel. They are all excellent.

> Kay Irvin, in a review of "Murders in Volume 2," in The New York Times Book Review, March 9, 1941, p. 20.

CHARLOTTE DEAN

[In *The Street Has Changed,* Elizabeth Daly's] theme is the theatre and what it did, and by inference always will do, to the people caught in its coils. . . .

The story follows the fortunes of four families living in handsome brownstone houses just off Fifth Avenue for more than forty years. Each family finally has at least one representative in the theatre in some capacity. As their fortunes rise and fall and rise again, the fine houses are occupied by these fashionable families, turned into small apartments later on, and still later torn down to make way for grand apartment buildings or otherwise altered beyond recognition. . . .

For all its leaps through time, the story is not jerky. It has a firm unity and continuity, and is told with subtlety, wit and sometimes clever indirection. Yet it is always perfectly clear. Like Sardou's well-made play, to which it refers, it is deftly planned and neatly finished, and people who have read Miss Daly's mystery stories will be pleased to see her again applying her skill to fastening each loose end. In its research into the past, its solid plot, its bright, illuminating dialogue it is a book for adult entertainment.

> Charlotte Dean, "The Theatre," in The New York Times Book Review, October 5, 1941, p. 34.

FRANCES SMYTH

[In *The Street Has Changed,* Daly] has abandoned the mystery field for a study of four New York families whose lives are inextricably tied together by a passion for the theatre. . . . It begins with Miss Fay Beacham, rebelling against her life as a *jeune fille bien élèvée,* and bullying George Dominick, the famous manager, into taking her to London with his company. It ends, fifty years later, in 1941, with Fay emerging as the anonymous "angel" who is putting up twenty-five thousand dollars to back the first production of George Dominick's grandson. In the interval, the street has changed: brownstones have given way to small flats that have in turn yielded to great apartment houses, but, Miss Daly intends to suggest, the hold the theatre exerts has not changed at all; its strength, in fact, increases yearly.

Miss Daly's thesis may very well be true. However, neatly contrived and fitted as her novel is, she remarkably fails to communicate to the reader any of the glow and glamor to which her characters are evidently in thrall. Consequently, it is difficult for the reader, himself so untouched by the reported magic, to accept its announced dominion over the lives of the people in the book. This fact tends to thwart any very lively interest in Miss Daly's novel.

> Frances Smyth, "Daly. . .," in The Saturday Review of Literature, Vol. XXIV, No. 26, October 18, 1941, p. 33.

ISAAC ANDERSON

The case with which [*The House without the Door*] deals is a peculiar one. Mrs. Vina Gregson, who has once been tried for murder and acquitted, reports to [Henry Gamadge] that she has received anonymous letters of a threatening nature and that several attempts have been made upon her life. To call in the police would mean a recurrence of the unpleasant notoriety which was her lot during her trial and after. Gamadge, on the other hand, can carry on a secret investigation and, so Mrs.

Gregson hopes, eventually prove that the person who is persecuting her is the one who actually committed the murder of which she was accused.

Gamadge feels that he must work fast if he is to accomplish anything at all, but he is not able to work fast enough to prevent another murder. That brings the police into the case, and Gamadge has to resort to unorthodox tactics to keep them from pinning the crime upon the wrong person. He is aided by several assistants, including his wife, but none of them knows whom he suspects or just what he is doing. The plot is an unusual one, and it is developed with all the skill that Elizabeth Daly has made manifest in her other books.

> Isaac Anderson, in a review of "The House without the Door," in The New York Times Book Review, July 26, 1942, p. 15.

ISAAC ANDERSON

[In *Nothing Can Rescue Me*], Florence Hutter Mason is trying to write a novel, and some unknown person is adding cryptic and vaguely menacing quotations to the manuscript. It may be a practical joke, but Mrs. Mason thinks not. She is so worried that her nephew, Sylvanus Hutter, begs Henry Gamadge to come to Underhill, the ancestral home of the Hutters, to find out who is responsible. When Gamadge has heard the story at first hand he is convinced that some deadly purpose is behind the interpolations in the manuscript. And Gamadge is right, although it is a bit difficult to see the connection between the preceding events and the two murders that follow soon after Gamadge's arrival at Underhill. It is quite clear that the murders must have been done either by some one in the Underhill household or by some one who has easy access to the house and is familiar with it and with the habits of those who live there. There are too many such persons to make the going easy for Gamadge, but he comes through with the right solution at the right moment. It is all a bit involved, but what mystery isn't?

> Isaac Anderson, in a review of "Nothing Can Rescue Me," in The New York Times Book Review, January 24, 1943, p. 20.

ISAAC ANDERSON

The figure of a woman in a faded purple dress and sunbonnet plays an important part in [*Evidence of Things Seen*]. Clara Gamadge sees it several times—the last time just before a murder is committed. There are those who believe that Clara has seen a ghost, and there are others who consider her the victim of a hallucination. Still others think that she has concocted her story to cover up her own guilt. When Henry Gamadge arrives on the scene a day later he knows that it is up to him to learn the truth if his wife is to be cleared of suspicion. And learn the truth he does, although it takes some doing. So ingenious is the plot of this story that we feel safe in predicting that most readers will be completely fooled and will then wonder how they ever happened to muff the solution.

> Isaac Anderson, in a review of "Evidence of Things Seen," in The New York Times Book Review, June 27, 1943, p. 8.

WILL CUPPY

If you want to wake up screaming, [*Evidence of Things Seen* is] a story that should serve your purpose and give you a dandy jigsaw workout besides. It's one of Elizabeth Daly's finest, with Henry Gamadge detecting like a house afire and his young wife, Clara, in dire peril from several directions. Clara took an isolated Connecticut cottage for the summer, expecting some friends to join her and not counting at all on the sinister old woman in a sunbonnet who always appeared at sunset, not to speak of the attic door that opened every time she came and other matters better not mentioned. It's fair to say that something awful happened to Miss Alvira Radnor, the egg woman who used to live in the cottage with her sister, now deceased. Main exhibit is that twilight figure, as scary a number as you're likely to meet in 1943 fiction. Could it be a ghost bent on vengeance, or don't you believe in spooks in sunbonnets? Gil Craye, a rich neighbor, knows something and won't tell. Where did Alvira hide the $106,000 (less taxes) that she inherited from Mrs. Hickson? And so forth to a climax and untying that may leave you limp if you read it at one sitting, as you probably will. No fooling, it's the kind of mystery you can't lay down until you find out whodunit and why.

Henry Gamadge may be said to surpass all his previous performances this time. Returning on leave from war service to find Clara suspected of murder, his efforts to forestall a trial and possible verdict of guilty but insane are nothing short of terrific. Superhuman is the word as he takes over the puzzle and unreels it with masterly skill. Miss Daly hands you a jolt when she's ready to unveil the killer, after leading you up several garden paths. Murderers' motives and general psychology being what they are, this person might very well have done the deed, though it sort of bowled us over at the time. The Gamadges and their friends are a little tonier than we would choose as playmates and we couldn't make up our mind about Clara's "half a minute of semioblivion" at the scene of the murder; which are no faults at all. . . . *Evidence of Things Seen* is a top-notcher of the polite school, unreservedly recommended to those who wander around in Mystery Land.

> *Will Cuppy, in a review of "Evidence of Things Seen," in* New York Herald Tribune Weekly Book Review, *July 4, 1943, p. 9.*

WILL CUPPY

Elizabeth Daly is one popular baffler who could probably write a creditable non-mystery novel if she chose. Not that we want her to do so, since she serves a useful and comforting purpose where she is: she's a lifesaver to fans who demand the civilized point of view, characters who resemble human beings as we know them and writing to match. She is right there, too, with puzzle interest, without which a whodunit would be neither here nor there. [*Arrow Pointing Nowhere*], indeed, may puzzle you too much in the first few pages, but it carries on nobly once Miss Daly has got into her stride with Henry Gamadge, private detective, authority on old documents and good fellow in general. He is after the lowdown about the rich but not haughty Fenways, and you may be sure he gets it, after a smooth series of investigations involving rare books, family secrets and violent deaths. . . .

For mystery joy of the better sort, with all the excitement you need and positively no tripe, grab *Arrow Pointing Nowhere*.

> *Will Cuppy, in a review of "Arrow Pointing Nowhere," in* New York Herald Tribune Weekly Book Review, *January 9, 1944, p. 6.*

ISAAC ANDERSON

Henry Gamadge is an amateur detective in the true sense of that term; he loves mysteries and solves them without hope of reward. In the case with which [*Arrow Pointing Nowhere*] deals he does not, in the beginning, know what he is expected to investigate nor by whom he is employed. All he knows is that he has received a cryptic summons to the home of Blake Fenway—and thither he goes and talks to the various members of the household. He learns that a page has been torn out of a book which Blake Fenway prizes highly, but he is sure that the problem he has been called upon to solve lies much deeper. Three violent deaths intervene before he is able to probe the mystery to the bottom. All this and more is told with all the skill that Miss Daly has at her command, and she has plenty.

> *Isaac Anderson, "More Murders, Plain and Fancy," in* The New York Times Book Review, *January 9, 1944, p. 22.*

BEATRICE SHERMAN

[*The Book of the Dead*] begins in a thin way and quickly builds up to keen interest and excitement. Gamadge, who's a dilettante at studying old documents, has a young woman visitor at his New York town house. A drab person, she has a fixed idea that Mr. Crenshaw, a casual summer acquaintance with no friends and relatives, is the victim of queer happenings. She suspects Crenshaw feared his man Pike. Her only clue is a volume of Shakespeare he lent her with some cryptic underlinings and notations. There doesn't seem any reason for mystery about a man dying in his bed of leukemia with all his funeral expenses paid in advance. But plenty of hocus-pocus develops. A second death, a violent one, occurs before Crenshaw is buried. The plot is compactly and fairly worked out. Dangerous doings are told in a smooth Park Avenue manner that makes them seem grimmer. The book is an absorbing yarn that holds up to the end.

> *Beatrice Sherman, in a review of "The Book of the Dead," in* The New York Times Book Review, *July 16, 1944, p. 16.*

THE NEW REPUBLIC

[In *Any Shape or Form,* an] elaborate Connecticut estate furnishes the scene for some pretty weird antics on the part of a group of assorted snobs, plus one sun-worshiper, wealthy old Josephine Malcolm. In fact, Henry Gamadge, the criminologist, is the only bearable person at the tea party which is the prelude to Mrs. Malcolm's murder. Since the victim was within a few paces of him when she was shot, Gamadge feels obliged to ferret out the killer, but his heart doesn't seem to be in the job. Neither was this reader's. A terrific letdown from the A-1 work Miss Daly had been giving us lately.

> *E. H., in a review of "Any Shape or Form," in* The New Republic, *Vol. 112, No. 23, June 4, 1945, p. 798.*

ISAAC ANDERSON

[*Somewhere in the House* depicts] a sealed room in the old Clayborn mansion, and in it is one of the secrets of the Clayborn family. So much is known when Henry Gamadge is asked to be present when the room is opened after twenty years. What else is in the room is known to only one person, although it may be suspected by one other. Who it is that knows is revealed when Gamadge succeeds in solving the mystery of three murders. Gamadge, as you may remember, is a bibliophile. That is how he happens to know what a solander is and to what uses it may be put. He knows also what is meant by the "Sacrifice of Sugar" and the "Consecration of the Pickaxe," and his knowledge of these things helps him to trap the murderer. Enough is explained about them to enable you to appreciate this expertly plotted story, written with the skill for which Elizabeth Daly is so well known.

> *Isaac Anderson, in a review of "Somewhere in the House," in* The New York Times Book Review, *March 10, 1946, p. 30.*

WILL CUPPY

[*The Wrong Way Down* is] a good one and no mistake by an author who is fast becoming America's mystery darling. Henry Gamadge, now a "thinnish, tallish, green-eyed man of forty," is faced at first by the disappearance of a Bartolozzi engraving of a Holbein portrait, right up his antiquarian alley, then by murder foul and puzzling. . . .

Miss Daly scores her mystery points quietly and impressively, wins you completely with her polite moods and finally springs one of those knockout surprises, the kind you can believe.

> *Will Cuppy, in a review of "The Wrong Way Down," in* New York Herald Tribune Weekly Book Review, *October 13, 1946, p. 23.*

ISAAC ANDERSON

[In *The Wrong Way Down,* a] framed engraving hanging on the wall of the house where [Miss Paxton] is acting as caretaker has suddenly sprouted a printed title where no title had been a day earlier. Henry Gamadge, who knows about such things, discovers that a comparatively worthless picture has been substituted for a more valuable one. It does not appear to be a serius matter until Miss Paxton is found dead, apparently as the result of a fall from what was the front door before the high stoop was sheared away. Gamadge is sure that she has been murdered, and the police are inclined to agree with him when another woman is shot dead at Gamadge's front door. The case proves to be a real puzzler, and much patient sleuthing has to be done before Gamadge comes up with the correct solution. The story has far more thrills than the comparatively mild beginning would lead one to suspect.

> *Isaac Anderson, in a review of "The Wrong Way Down," in* The New York Times Book Review, *October 27, 1946, p. 36.*

ISAAC ANDERSON

[In *Night Walk,* a] prowler by night alarms some of the residents of the hitherto peaceful village of Frazer's Mills. That there has been good reason for alarm is demonstrated when it is found that Mr. George Carrington, a semi-invalid, has been bludgeoned to death in his bed. The general opinion is that it is the work of a maniac, but Henry Gamadge, who has been persuaded to make an investigation, reserves judgment. Ostensibly Gamadge has come to Frazer's Mills for a rest at what might be called a home for convalescents run by Miss Studley. After the second murder, however, there is no longer need for concealment. Frazer's Mills is such an oddly self-contained and self-centered community, almost feudal in character, that it is difficult for any of its residents to believe that any other of them could possibly be a murderer. Gamadge, as an outsider, sees people as they are, not as they are thought to be by their neighbors. Because of this and also because of the knowledge acquired in his real profession, that of an examiner of disputed documents, he is able to solve the case of two apparently motiveless murders. It is a good story, beautifully told.

> *Isaac Anderson, in a review of "'Night Walk,'" in* The New York Times Book Review, *September 14, 1947, p. 32.*

WILL CUPPY

Good thing Henry Gamadge stopped off at Frazer's Mills, where somebody had smashed the head of Mr. Garrington, the town's rich man. Some thought the fiend must be the same person who had been prowling around Miss Studley's rest home. . . . After a session at the library and other brain waves of the first order, Gamadge completes his theory—and it's correct. [*Night Walk* is another] top-drawer Daly item with human characters. Grade A detection and a garnishing of young love. Two killings.

> *Will Cuppy, in a review of "Night Walk," in* New York Herald Tribune Weekly Book Review, *September 21, 1947, p. 17.*

WILL CUPPY

We often wonder if Henry Gamadge, Miss Daly's adored bibliophile-sleuth, isn't a little too good for this workaday world. Here he is again [in *The Book of the Lion*] in all his cold perfection, both as sleuth and fellow creature, if we may venture to speak of him thus, tossing off a difficult solution having to do with several murders and an engaging rigmarole about a fifteenth century copy of one of Chaucer's lost works, said to have been sold to Eigenstern for a cool $100,000. True or false? Chief corpse is Paul Bradlock, pifflicated avant garde poet slain in Central Park maybe by one of his Left Bank cronies—a very sad affair. With his knowledge of the book field, Gamadge is just the man to go chasing literary clews as casualties mount and tension tightens.

A shrewd judge of pace, Miss Daly opens up on the home stretch, where you'll be full of problems about Paul's widow, her intimates, and their various documents—young love, too. Gamadge lets you in on a big surprise without bothering much about the cops and justice. He functions without anything so crude as a fee, apparently from pure love of snooping. Well, he's fine at that. Why carp if he is smarter than the rest of us?

> *Will Cuppy, in a review of "The Book of the Lion," in* New York Herald Tribune Weekly Book Review, *May 30, 1948, p. 9.*

ELIZABETH DALY

[In the essay excerpted below, Daly's general remarks about detective fiction also serve as commentary on the nature of her own work.]

No kind of fiction requires good writing more than detective fiction does; a puzzle unadorned makes dull reading. I know but one detective novelist of the first rank who ever said that apart from the research involved this form of writing was easy. Goaded by the bitterest envy, I can only think that he was suffering from forgetfulness or even from self-deception. Did he really toss them off? Was good writing ever easy? And in the case of detective fiction the writing has to clothe material closely reasoned, carefully arranged, which demands originality of treatment and the most delicate handling of incident.

But the problem is the thing; and I do not think that the problem ought to deal directly, as direct propaganda, with issues which lift it out of the field of entertainment. The detective story is by its own nature too impartial to function on any party line. Politics and religion enter the field on legitimate service—to explain motive; there will be plenty of implications as to the author's point of view, because (as it has been pointed out by its friends) the detective novel has its own ethics—without them it could not exist. It stands for the broad principles of law against chaos, justice for the individual, a fair trial for all; and if its principles were not generally known it would not, unpretentious form of amusement though it is, have been banned under totalitarian governments. . . .

Detective fiction does not gain many converts. It is a special taste, and seldom an acquired one. I know of no drearier sight than that of an intellectual—the kind of intellectual who doesn't like detective stories—sitting down and grimly trying to appraise them. He is lost. His standards fail him—there are no signposts and no landmarks for him in this corner of the country. He cannot criticize, he can only scold.

Here are a great many people, he complains, who would otherwise be reading something good, wasting themselves on stuff that has no message for humanity, no more significance than a Chinese puzzle. It does not (he should hope!) reflect life. It has conventions as absurd as opera, as rigid as the sonnet. If it seems now and then to have been slipped into literature by Poe and the author of *Edwin Drood,* by other distinguished but misguided persons, that is illusion. The stories would have been better without it.

It is a special taste. I yield to none in my affection for a good crime story, suspense story, adventure story; but I do not think they can ever take the place of the straight detective story while there remains a new problem to be solved, or a writer to present it in an original way. (p. 187)

> *Elizabeth Daly, "Are You Sure They Are All Horrid?" in* The Writer, *Vol. 61, No. 6, June, 1948, pp. 186-87.*

THE NEW YORKER

[In *And Dangerous to Know,* Henry Gamadge] is consulted by the attorney for the Dunbar family about the disappearance of one of the daughters of that conservative New York clan. In the course of pondering problems . . . , Gamadge runs into two corpses and several other tokens of skulduggery. Although his final interpretation is sound enough, his method of trapping the scoundrel may seem, even to his admirers, to be on the shaky side. Agreeably written and moderately wry.

> *A review of "And Dangerous to Know," in* The New Yorker, *Vol. XXV, No. 30, September 17, 1949, p. 116.*

WILL CUPPY

Henry Gamadge, bibliophile-detective, seems more fun to read about [in *And Dangerous to Know*], maybe because he's taking a vacation from musty old manuscripts. Anyway, he's all over the place with the light touch but no lack of solid brainwork as he flies at the case of Miss Alice Dunbar, who left home one day and disappeared into space. . . . Miss Daly concludes a remarkably easy-to-read riddle with a quick surprise trick by the invaluable Gamadge.

> *Will Cuppy, in a review of "And Dangerous to Know," in* New York Herald Tribune Weekly Book Review, *September 18, 1949, p. 15.*

ANTHONY BOUCHER

"Gentility" is a word rarely used seriously in these days, but nothing else quite so well describes the atmosphere of Elizabeth Daly's novels. Henry Gamadge, her charming and sympathetic bibliophile-detective, is a man so well-bred as to make Lord Peter Wimsey seem a trifle coarse.

A few restive readers find all this a trifle tenuous and thin. The rest of us have reveled in a series of novels that at once portray a vanishing era of New York society and chill the blood with exquisitely refined accounts of the most genteel evil.

The central character of [*And Dangerous to Know*] is a spinster who seeks to break away from her sterile background and vanishes from the earth. The quest for her leads Gamadge into more nearly straight detection than is his wont, free from antiquarian arcana, but still delightfully subtle and indirect—and far harder on the nerves than the blatant hypertension of standard "suspense."

> *Anthony Boucher, "Modish Mayhem," in* The New York Times Book Review, *September 18, 1949, p. 29.*

THE NEW YORKER

In the course of [*Death and Letters,* in which he investigates] the incarceration of a lovely young widow by her formidable in-laws (she is not allowed to telephone or to write letters, but deviously manages to communicate by means of some crossword puzzles in the London *Times*), Henry Gamadge proves that her husband was the victim of murder, not a suicide, and characteristically turns up a literary motive for the crime. This time it is the secret sale of love letters written by an eminent Victorian poet to the proud family's skittish grandmother. Using his special knowledge and lively imagination, Mr. Gamadge uncovers a shrewd and unlikely murderer in this literate and superior work. (pp. 123-24)

> *A review of "Death and Letters," in* The New Yorker, *Vol. XXVI, No. 13, May 20, 1950, pp. 123-24.*

HILLIS MILLS

The world of Elizabeth Daly's famous bibliophile-detective, Henry Gamadge, has much in common with the crime-fiction world of English country houses. In polite surroundings, among soft-spoken gentle folk, murder and other such sordid goings-on take on an extra edge of horror.

Because Gamadge is a remarkably clever fellow with highly specialized knowledge, he is able [in *Death and Letters*] to read a half-finished crossword puzzle as a cry for help from a lady in distress. Also, he is able to solve one murder and thwart a second one by properly interpreting some musty old love letters written by a Victorian poet. Gamadge richly deserves his popularity with readers. His creator has no need to insist on the kind of man he is. Every move he makes and every sentence he speaks prove him to be a likable, intelligent gentleman of wide book learning.

> Hillis Mills, *"Edge of Horror," in* The New York Times Book Review, *June 4, 1950, p. 20.*

NEW YORK HERALD TRIBUNE

Miss Daly's Henry Gamadge is one of the more captivating sleuths in detective fiction. His elliptical wit, his erudition, his friendship for the underdog, and his relationship with his steadily growing family, all add up to a great deal of charm. You can always pick up a Henry Gamadge book with a sense of pleasurable anticipation, and you're seldom disappointed. In [*The Book of the Crime*] he espouses the cause of Serena Austen, who left her young war-hero husband because she was afraid of him. Although they had been married only a year, she had long realized that they didn't love each other. And finally when he saw her with the slim copies of two old books in her hands and came toward her with murder in his eyes, she fled the house. Unfortunately, she hadn't noticed what the books were. That's why she went to Henry Gamadge for help. And that's why Henry had to go back to the narrow, dark old Austen house, and probe into the pasts of Grey Austen and his brother and sister before he could find the answer to her question. There's murder, too, which is also solved in the riddle of the two books.

> *A review of "The Book of the Crime," in* New York Herald Tribune, *March 4, 1951, p. 18.*

HILLIS MILLS

[In *The Book of the Crime*], a pretty, 19-year-old bride innocently picks a book off a shelf and looks up to see murder in her husband's eyes. When an unidentified body is found in a near-by alley Gamadge suspects that it has some connection with the case of the terrified bride.

Miss Daly's plots carry undercurrents of suspense and terror, but even the villains, until Gamadge finally turns them over to the law, speak in well-bred accents and try to mind their company manners.

> Hillis Mills, *"Terrified Bride," in* The New York Times Book Review, *March 11, 1951, p. 20.*

Stephen Dixon

1936-

American short story writer, novelist, and editor.

A prolific experimental writer, Dixon combines disjointed prose and extended passages of dialogue to examine the lives of individuals who are overwhelmed by the frantic pace of modern civilization. By focusing on sensitive young male characters involved in problematic romances, Dixon explores such themes as the difficulties of friendship and communication, the clash between mundane and aberrant elements of human existence, and the significance of consequence, coincidence, and chance in life and art. Commenting on the antiheroic nature of Dixon's protagonists, Peter Bricklebank stated: "This repetition of error, failure to learn from experience, [makes for] much humor and humanity in Dixon's characters. Compounded with the tragedy that it inevitably brings, it screws the lens through which we look at the world into a disquieting blur, giving disproportion a clarity all its own."

Dixon's short stories, many of which were originally published in such periodicals as *Harper's, Playboy,* the *Paris Review,* and the *Atlantic,* are often set in urban surroundings and feature fast-paced narratives, satire, wordplay, and lengthy portions of dialogue. In his initial collection, *No Relief* (1976), Dixon uses first-person narration to probe disparate facets of failed love and the role of fate in daily life. *Quite Contrary: The Mary and Newt Story* (1979), a volume comprising eleven interrelated short pieces, focuses on the three-year courtship of a young couple whose frequent breakups become their primary bond. Dixon's use of self-reflexive techniques and fragmented structures prompted Jerome Klinkowitz to describe this work as "a perfectly natural reinforcement of form and content." Dixon's third volume, *14 Stories* (1980), collects short fiction from throughout his career, including the often discussed title piece, which documents a series of events that results from a man's suicide, and "Love Has Its Own Action," in which the narrator seeks his ideal woman through a rapid succession of affairs and marriages. In the stories contained in *Movies* (1983), Dixon implements realistic dialogue, elaborate digressions, and surreal effects to explore the realms of fantasy and reality. Peter Bricklebank remarked: "Not only does [*Movies*] repay attention with humor, insight and originality, but it shows us just how hectically absurd our world really is." In *Time to Go* (1984), which includes a section of stories focusing on the private and professional experiences of Will Taub, a mild-mannered teacher and writer, Dixon examines various dimensions of death and loss.

In his first novel, *Work* (1977), Dixon depicts a man's efforts to find and maintain employment and also presents lengthy digressions on aspects of low-wage occupations. Noting this book's apparent lack of form, Thomas A. Stumpf observed: "There is an attractive aimlessness about [*Work*], and it reflects the sort of structure that we all experience from day to day: actions that are dropped or begin again at unlikely times, digressions that are never wholly irrelevant, events that are never quite to the point, characters that appear and disappear.... All this could be made more intense, but the lack of intensity is part of Dixon's truth. Life is neither grand opera nor the babbling idiot's tale." *Too Late* (1978) concerns Art A. Ali-

man's paranoid imaginings of his girlfriend's fate when she disappears following her early departure from a film which they attended together. Indulging his worst fears, Aliman engages in a frantic search that causes him to lose his job, alienate his friends and relatives, and commit violent acts. In *Fall and Rise* (1985), Dixon focuses on the personal anxieties and social incompetence of a man who pursues an alluring woman he had briefly encountered at a party. Reflecting on Dixon's use of language in this novel, Roy Kasten asserted: "By disturbing grammar, narrative voice takes on an immediate, nervous, neurotic quality. The text becomes a kind of neurotic performance, moving with frenetic, stream of conscious speed."

(See also *Contemporary Authors,* Vols. 89-92 and *Contemporary Authors New Revision Series,* Vol. 17.)

FREDERICK H. GUIDRY

The five stories in [*No Relief*] show a fine talent for getting at the sound of a particular voice—that of a sensitive young man with a romantic problem. (Maybe these protagonists are not all that young; but their thought and speech patterns have the ring of early adulthood—never mind the age.)

The settings are all New York, but the particulars of streets and neighborhoods do not get in the way of a reader's recognizing them as everyday urban. The truly universalizing element, however, is the sense of helpless grappling with boy-girl relationships, of friendships crumbling despite frantic efforts to keep things going, of communication taking place but failing to do the job it was hoped to do.

There is wry humor in all of these tales, which counteracts the potentially tiresome viewing of life always from the single standpoint of a goodwilled, aggressive-diffident narrator. To be sure, this discerning and fairminded person faithfully records conversations involving him, and even surmises the judgments others make concerning him. But the voice stays the same.

If you happen to recognize the voice as remarkably like your own, this book will warm your heart. Even if you have outgrown the viewpoint but have an affectionate regard for the post-adolescent stage of life, it will still have a certain nostalgic appeal.

"**Mac in Love**" typifies the collection, with its account of an absolutely irrepressible young suitor, who genially ignores the firmest farewells of his ex-girl friend. Shut out of her apartment, he attempts conversation from the street, and when that fails, he tries to involve neighbors with shouted entreaties. He is annoying and likable; his plight, the author seems to be saying, is just one of those things.

Indeed, the stories as a group stick to a formula, fashioning a pleasant, questing hero and generating sympathy for his hesitant approach to life, while populating his world with individuals on deliberately different wavelengths, for the reliable, mild pathos this creates. And the modest undertaking succeeds.

> Frederick H. Guidry, "Catching the Sound of a Suitor," in The Christian Science Monitor, *January 10, 1977, p. 22.*

JULIA O'FAOLAIN

Stephen Dixon's publishers describe him as "one of the decade's most widely published fictioneers," and Webster defines fictioneer as "a prolific writer of mediocre fiction.". . . His lead story [in *No Relief*], "**Mac in Love**," might be a parable about unloved wordmen. Mac, repulsed by Jane, keeps yelling wistful nonsense at her balcony until she calls the police. He promises to stop. They let him go. He yells again. They come back, and so on *da capo*. All the stories in the book—Dixon's first—are about matings and mismatings.

Bad taste is probably so deliberate it is naive of me to mention it. It is most blatant in "**Last May**," a story in which Bud and Marlene keep vigil in hospital, he by the bedside of his dying dad, she of her dying mother. Need I say that as life ebbs from the progenitors the young engage in the life-making activity? The dying die and so does passion. Bud ditches Marlene. To quote another Dixon story: "It was probably better in the end for us both and other rationales and I left, walked, took a bus, went to a movie, couldn't stay, cafeteria, couple of bars, got home." If you read this fast, it has the pulse of life. If you keep reading, it may affect your syntax.

> Julia O'Faolain, "Small Goods in Small Packages," in The New York Times Book Review, *July 31, 1977, p. 15.*

THOMAS A. STUMPF

[Form] within formlessness characterizes Stephen Dixon's novel *Work* and, to a lesser extent, his collection of short stories, *No Relief*. One could say that Dixon has no sense of form at all, or one could say that he deliberately avoids structure in an attempt to express the anarchy of the world, or perhaps just the random character of life in the city. Happily, neither of these statements would be true. The careful and programmatic cultivation of chaos seems to appeal to theoretical critics and French publicists more than to practicing writers, who know that the arrangement of words on a page is a serious matter requiring intelligence as well as luck. And besides, those carefully contrived pieces of anarchy are much easier to talk about than to read, and Dixon keeps his reader turning the pages in a very old fashioned way, from beginning to end. In fact, both *Work* and "**Last May**," in my opinion Dixon's best short story, have primitive but vigorous plot lines: man gets job; man loses job—man gets woman; man gives her up. They are not intricate plots to be sure, but they are fundamental and functional.

The charge that he has no sense of form at all is tantamount to a charge that he is a bad writer or a madman. This charge is a little harder, though by no means impossible, to refute. What gives it some substance is Dixon's occasionally maddening sense of pace. *Work* is 189 pages long. The main action is that the hero, an unemployed actor named Claude Martez, gets a job as a bartender and then, for various interesting reasons, loses it. But it is not until page 62 that the hero applies for his job at "BurgBrew Drew's." Before that, we get an account of some other jobs he's had, some tedious telephone conversations with his girl friend, Oona, and descriptions of attempts to find work writing captions or collecting blood. Much of this is, if not irrelevant, uneconomical. The novel is full of issues and characters that are raised and dropped. With the obvious exception of Claude himself, not one of the characters, Oona included, to whom we are introduced at such length in the first part of the novel, is mentioned again after page 62. The fact that Claude is an actor is also, finally, of no significance. Dixon simply lets his character wander about at random for sixty pages or so until he catches the thread of an action, at which point the irrelevant narrative bric-a-brac is tidied away and we begin to concentrate exclusively upon the matter at hand.

Even after Claude gets work as a bartender, however, our interest tends to wander off into odd corners. How does a fast food chain hire its employees, transfer them, check up on them? What is a bartender's *modus operandi*? How do his responsibilities relate to those of cooks, waiters, dishwashers? These things prove to be interesting in themselves, and Dixon obligingly, even lovingly, leads us through all the details of a bartender's daily routine. The relevance to Claude's character and to the narrative line, while never wholly forgotten, is charmingly incidental.

There is an attractive aimlessness about all this, and it reflects the sort of structure that we all experience from day to day: actions that are dropped or begin again at unlikely times, digressions that are never wholly irrelevant, events that are never quite to the point, characters that appear and disappear. Once we give up on the hope that everything will be drawn together in a giant, symmetrical web, we are pleased by occasional glimpses of pattern: the bartender's rituals, the constant return of regular customers, the consistently shiftless, consistently shifted, managers, the inevitable, and inevitably unmerited, loss of the job, which closes the circle. All this could be made more intense, but the lack of intensity is part of Dixon's truth. Life is neither grand opera nor the babbling idiot's tale. Its rhythms and the rhythms of art are at variance.

The short stories in *No Relief* are more tightly constructed, but there is the same sense of episodes proceeding in an almost random fashion. The best of the stories, **"Last May,"** describes the love felt by a young man whose father is dying for a young girl whose mother is dying. They meet in a sickroom and make love there, but the love survives only until the last funeral is over. Then, for no obvious reason, the young man breaks off this affair, whose soil was death. The apparent motivelessness of the characters in this story is a feature of all the other stories, all of which are about love. Love begins and ends mysteriously. It has its own, unknown, cycle and laws, and the characters are as puzzled by it as the readers. No one in the stories falls in or out of love willingly. It happens, as death happens, and they adjust to it as best they can. It is the characters more than the author who refuse, or are unable, to provide a structure.

They are not, to be sure, apathetic. They are self-willed, stubborn, and deeply passionate—romantic characters, really—but they are not in the habit of criticizing their desires. They know what they want but not why they want it. All of the works are informed by the suspicion that any analysis of human behavior is bound to be false and laughably pointless. This is reflected to some degree in technique and style. Dixon has no use for omniscient narrators, whose very existence suggests a serene perspective from which the pitiful flounderings of a character can be made to make sense. He does not let us view things from the distance which might allow them to fall into place. Everything is written from the first-person point of view, but this too is handled in a characteristic way. The narrators do not engage in much interior discourse; they do not analyze their own actions. Instead we are given a high proportion of dialogue, sometimes witty and gamy, more often a parody of critical analysis in which dialogue becomes formless monologue.

> Rose, the best thing for you right now is to be outside on your own having your own experiences and testing yourself out on the unknown or something, I'm convinced of that, because I'll tell you, no matter what we say or do here tonight I see the same things happening with us and you over and over again till you do have a lot better idea what you want or don't want, I know that for sure now or almost . . . and I'll also tell you, I'm tired of people feeling I'm a burden on them because they know I care deeply for them and especially when I thought that deep feeling was being returned or because they know I mostly like what I've done and am now doing with my life and because they didn't do what they wanted to before they met me or aren't doing now what they think they can or must do and for some reason think it's because of me or even not because of me but just whatever, all of which might sound senseless or too muddled or high-toned or pedantic or something.

A passage like this, from the story **"Rose,"** is not ridiculous, though there is a whiff of ridiculousness about it. We feel, however, something hurried and *pro forma* in the speech. An explanation is required, though author, characters, and reader know that no explanation, no critical analysis, will ever get to the heart of anything. The dialogue, the speeches—and this is true throughout both books—cover everything with a thin lacquer of logic with which we must be content, though we know how much more there is that we cannot know.

I don't want to sound more enthusiastic about these books than I really am. Dixon's characters talk like a curious amalgam of Damon Runyon and James Joyce, and though you get used to this after a while, it's never really a strength. His fastidious avoidance of conventional punctuation is a fashionable tic which requires a speedy cure. Finally there is, despite the realistic details of *Work,* despite the avoidance of self-analysis in the stories, something curiously narcissistic about all of Dixon's characters. They begin alone and they end alone. Loves and jobs are put on and shucked off like the incidental accoutrements they are. These is a fine, old-fashioned, existentialist gloom in all of this; but a little of it goes a long way. Three hundred pages of this wintry, stoical, urban landscape is enough to drive one, giggling to a Maypole.

Nevertheless, Dixon has his claims upon the truth, upon nature perhaps more than upon art, though he is by no means artless. His feckless, occasionally dismal world with its small momentary triumphs and large, permanent sorrows is real enough; and if we are troubled by the absence of great and satisfying patterns in his work, why then we are meant to be. **"Last May"** and **"Rose"** are painful but unforgettable stories, and *Work,* despite its many flaws, has its roots in life itself, not in some morbid secretion of the imagination. The dissatisfaction we feel when we close Dixon's books is finally not unlike the dissatisfaction that most of us feel at the close of each of the days of our lives. (pp. 129-31)

> *Thomas A. Stumpf, in a review of "No Relief" and "Work," in* The South Carolina Review, *Vol. 11, No. 4, November, 1978, pp. 129-31.*

ALLEN WIER

Most of the stories in Stephen Dixon's collection [*14 Stories*] are shaggy-dog stories. There are few resolutions. The book presents a Rube Goldberg fiction in which elaborate diagrams become the ends rather than the means. Sometimes there is great pleasure in watching Dixon invent, juxtapose, make connections; sometimes I wish there were more beneath the surface.

There are 13 stories in the book. The title story [**"14 Stories"**] refers to the 14th story of a hotel in which a man named Eugene Randall commits suicide, and the title suggests the many other stories we glimpse because of this one story, the many lives touched: the hotel maid who hears the shot, the lovers who find a suicide note that blew out of the window, the boy on the roof of a nearby building where the spent slug falls, the boy's neighbor who calls the police, the boy's mother who meets the neighbor who asks her out, the hotel operator who relays calls about the suicide, etc. The point of this and other stories in *14 Stories* seems to be the odd cause and effect relationships connecting so many things in the universe—simultaneity, coincidence, chance.

Dixon is aware of the possibilities of language; his prose is flat, clean, wry. At times he overdoes jokes, at times he extends word play until it becomes predictable, as it is in **"Milk is Very Good for You"** and **"Names."** A good deal that could have been comic in *14 Stories* strikes me as too obvious, too heavy-handed. The stories that do work, especially **"Love Has Its Own Action,"** **"Cut,"** and **"The Security Guard,"** do so because their deeper implications are subtler and resonate longer.

> *Allen Wier, "Glimpses into the Heart," in* Book World—The Washington Post, *February 22, 1981, p. 10.*

JEROME KLINKOWITZ

"**14 Stories**" would be a good title for a volume's collection, and it is (*14 Stories*, 1980), but for Stephen Dixon the notion is adequate to describe just one short piece, the book's title story (twelve others follow). "Eugene Randall held the gun in front of his mouth and fired," Dixon begins, where others might conclude. "The bullet smashed his upper front teeth, left his head through the back of his jaw, pierced an ear lobe and broke a window that overlooked much of the midtown area." Already we know more about the shell's trajectory than we do about poor Eugene, but who's to say the little signs and symbols of his worldly life were more important than the path of that utterly realistic bullet?

As a lesson in phenomenology à la Alain Robbe-Grillet, "**14 Stories**" might stop right there. But for Steve Dixon there's always more to say. Even his rigors of surface description take us elsewhere: the gun's sound has penetrated several floors of the hotel, one of his suicide notes has drifted out the broken window, and the bullet itself lands a block away on a brownstone roof, startling a boy and beginning a complicated episode, the effects of which reach far into the future. A maid must clean up the gory mess (suicides are so thoughtless!), a young couple argue over what to do with the recovered note, and on and on through a series of consequences no less real because they don't touch Eugene Randall's fading life in the cozily humanistic way conventional realists have taught readers to expect.

"Novels are cluttered with all kinds of signals," experimentalist Gilbert Sorrentino has complained, "flashing and gesturing so that the author may direct our attention to a particular configuration of character or plot in order that his work, such as it is, may be made simpler for him, and for us." Hence all the bits and pieces from real life which fill up conventionally realistic novels: makes of autos, tastes in music, styles and quality of clothes. . . . Fiction becomes less art and more news from the world; by pantomiming with signs, the writer has been able "to slip out from under problems that only confrontation with his materials can solve."

Dixon's talent is to stick it out with his materials, *to write fiction with them*, and so he never lets his signifiers rush off into the world in search of the things they represent. Eugene Randall's suicide in a shabby hotel room could easily start a movie running in our heads, but then Steve Dixon's story would be out of control, happening somewhere off the page. Thus we're given no more than one line of it before the chambermaid downstairs starts worrying about the sound, and no more than a single line of that before an equally interesting narrative begins about the kid up the block who's nearly nicked by the shot. Conventional realism may be in part a moral statement about the world, but Steve Dixon is more the experimentalist. Realism, he shows, is a lot more than lazy readers have thought it is, and from sentence to sentence there's a great deal of writing to be done before anyone can sit back and say they know it all.

Unlike the conventional realists who pretend the world is an easy place to have and hold, Dixon knows that things go on. At least six distinct actions take place in ["**14 Stories**"], more if every new involvement is counted. Moreover, within each little tale there's an endless regression of fact. . . .

So many simultaneous interests might be a strategy prompted by the short attention spans and precipitous boredom of contemporary audiences, but this habit of stretching things to their full extent runs through all five of Dixon's books and serves a deeper purpose. In "**Mac in Love,**" the opening story of his first collection *No Relief* (1976), the narrator's girlfriend is breaking off their affair (a perennial Dixon theme), and under these conditions nothing is simple. A nice day? Sure, blue sky, but there's pollution which can't be seen by the naked eye "because of something to do with particles and refraction," and on and on while the relationship, tenuous even in its best days, is sustained now only by language. Even on his way out the door there are conversations to be stretched to infinity. . . . (p. 54)

In Dixon's work a five-hundred word sentence is not unusual. What begins as an attempt to capture it all, as in the sketch of a narrator's comatose father dying in a hospital, ends as a virtual recreation of the old man's helpless state. Simple instructions for communication—blink once if you hear me, twice if you don't—soon extend themselves to the ridiculous even as they try harder and harder, through qualification after qualification, to be effective. The hallmark of this behavior, and of this style, is persistence. Both Dixon's sentences and his narrators' go on and on, until credibility turns incredible and then back into believability again. Mac keeps saying goodbye until the police warn him, and then again as they carry him off. Another narrator bugs a woman in a cafeteria through all sorts of brushoffs, rejections, threats, physical violence, and mayhem. In Steve Dixon's work there is no simple end to anything.

Dixon's novels are built on similar situations, and their plots show that his way of writing sentences and setting scenes works for full length plots as well. *Work* (1977) is a testimony both to the dogged persistence it takes to find employment and, even more comically, the ridiculous length one must go to to hold a job. Hunting one down take his narrator one-third of the novel, and that's the easy part. Once employed as a bartender in a restaurant chain he has to cope with a self-contained universe of rules and relationships: how to mix drinks, charge for specials, move traffic, scan papers for bar-talk news, spot company spies, handle rush hour jams, deal with the company union, foil stick-ups, soothe tempers, counsel neurotics, and keep the whole wacky symphony of waiters, dishwashers, assistant managers, cashiers, and customers in tune. And this is just three or four pages into the story. *Work* is a natural for Steve Dixon. If job hassles did not exist, he would have to invent them.

Dixon's second novel, *Too Late* (1978), takes his two favorite topics—breaking off relationships and suffering complications which run on *ad infinitum*—and rushes them through a breathless experience in the urban jungle, during which four days pass like four minutes of excitement or four centuries of maniacal torture. The narrator's girlfriend leaves him in a movie, the violence of which has sickened her. But she never makes it home. Where is she, and why? The police want to treat it as a brushoff, but the narrator resists this (as always) and is seduced by the universe of other possibilities: abduction, rape, murder, or worse. The very worst that a frightened person can imagine is just what transpires. Kooks and crazies who feed on news sensationalism rush into the narrator's life, and he himself goes through a Jekyll-and-Hyde transformation of losing his job, annoying friends, hassling neighbors, tearing up his apartment, forging a ransom note (to motivate the police), and running off helter-skelter after the shadiest of clues to his lover's whereabouts. *Too Late* is a tangled web of disruptions and distractions, the very stuff of Steve Dixon's fiction which is here shown to be an ever-present possibility of city life.

The question which stands at the center of Dixon's work—the fragile stability of human relationships or the danger reality has of running off into infinite digressions and qualifications—is answered by the work which synthesizes his talents as a story writer and novelist: the integrated collection, *Quite Contrary: The Mary and Newt Story* (1979). These eleven fictions treat the three-year off-and-on affair of a couple the likes of whom run through nearly all of Dixon's work. Such involvements, he says, include endless complications; love begets much more than love in return. . . . Dixon's couples are a fated mismatch: he is "too demanding," she has just departed one marriage and doesn't want to be tied down again too soon. Their tendency to break up is in fact the cement of their relationship. If Newt tries to tell a friend that he and Mary are "this time really through," he faces the reply that "Nah, you two are never really through. You're a pair: Tom and Jerry, Biff and Bang. You just tell yourselves you're through to make your sex better and your lives more mythic and poetic and to repeatedly renew those first two beatific weeks you went through."

Like the parting scene in **"Mac in Love,"** these peculiar qualities of the Mary and Newt story lend themselves to articulation—endless articulation—and what otherwise in a relationship might not even be noticed is here endlessly explained. Conversely, a less self-conscious affair might be over and done with before much fiction could be made of it, but Mary and Newt's experience is sustained by language and therefore kept before our imaginative attention.

The story-collection form of *Quite Contrary* lets Dixon use form as well as content to tell his story, and here we see how his views of human relationships and the quality of reality are one. Mary and Newt's rocky affair provides materials for narrative, but also hints for different ways to structure their tale. Indeed, the telling is the story. **"Man of Letters"** prints sixteen drafts of a single break-up letter which concludes with the decision not to split up at all—a choice encouraged by the textuality of the narrator's own writing. **"The Meeting"** tries to explain the odd circumstances of a relationship which began with a sustained parting. Under the gun of explaining such odd behavior the narrator finds he can't tell a straight story and so pleads "Let me start again, though keeping my confusion in. I don't know why, but right now that seems important to me"; this self-questioning continues throughout the story and makes its own point (which the puzzling content alone might have obscured). **"Em"** and **"Mary's Piece"** are the two narrators' attempts to make sense of one another, and *making sense* is defined as a writing problem (they even discuss submitting these stories to magazines). **"The Franklin Stove"** begins with the narrator off at a writers' colony, composing a Mary and Newt break-up story; it ends back in his apartment with Mary herself seducing him away from his typewriter (and away from his apparent intention to leave). When the affair does reach its finish (as finally as possible, for the book itself is coming to a close, only ten pages are left) the writer presents an aptly named **"Prolog"** in which his grief is so massive and disruptive that it can no longer be screamed, spoken, or even typed, "so I type goodnight."

14 Stories collects several years' worth of Steve Dixon's best. He's published over 125 in all, more than Fitzgerald or Hemingway and at a better rate than John O'Hara's hundred per decade—this in an age which prints very few short stories at all. Without the thematic integration of either *No Relief* or *Quite Contrary, 14 Stories* shows how the true synthesis for any good writer is finally on the level of form. An old man dying in a hospital (**"Cut"**) is the focus of a dozen different actions, including that of relatives, visitors, doctors, nurses, orderlies, and so on, not to mention his own interests. Shifting point of view from paragraph to paragraph thus tells the same story and many different stories all at once; the most common of realistic techniques is here used experimentally, showing how many different realities compete around this pitifully wasted man. Speech and dialogue, two more simple parts of realism, yield marvelously transformative effects simply by juggling consonants ("We were in red, Jane heated on top of me, my sock deep in her funt and linger up her masspole . . ."). A simple event, such as a whirlwind romance and just-as-sudden breakup, is told again and again with the winds of love and disaffection whirling faster each time (**"Love Has Its Own Action"**); writing this way soon changes reality into utterly absurd improbability, though each step has been small enough that one never knows just where common sense turns crazy.

Life is problematic, Dixon shows, in both its experience and depiction. The type of honesty each demands creates a realism one can never take for granted. Knowing the world—and all that can happen in it—is an epistemological adventure, and it is Steve Dixon's achievement that familiar conventions can be used for such a unique process of reading. There are no *conventions* in his story, for everything is happening quite literally for the very first time. (pp. 54-6)

Jerome Klinkowitz, "Stephen Dixon: Experimental Realism," in The North American Review, *Vol. 266, No. 1, March, 1981, pp. 54-6.*

LEE ABBOTT

In *Work,* his first novel, and *No Relief,* an early collection of stories, Dixon proved himself a comic but careful chronicler of mania in megalopolis, bringing us cabbie and cop, bozo and bureaucrat in prose quick and fine enough to be the best of works, art. His strengths, like city-living itself were many and apparent: energy, variety, and invention. His weaknesses, equally apparent to the country mouse in any critic, were few: surface mistaken for substance, eccentricity for character, and material for matter. The good news now is that Mr. Dixon remains the ever-watchful writer-baron of the asphalt jungle; the bad news is that, well, life in the city can be boring.

Too Late, a 1978 novel, is a dash, dizzying of pace, provoking of yawn—a dash through the mean streets attended by those good 20th-century villains Nightmare, Paranoia and Malaise. At the movies one evening, Art A. Aliman learns from his girlfriend Donna that the film is too violent. She's going home, alone. She'll meet him later. She doesn't, of course, and what follows is a horror-show of high-jinks, Chaplin-like slapstick and heavy-duty cruelty as our hero-narrator-victim takes to the streets and the phone to find a woman who, even at book's end, remains beyond the beck of kith and ken; she's vanished into a Pandemonium of murder and mayhem, of wist and woe. At his best, Dixon uses his plot to fix Art's place among and relationship to, as Mr. Rogers says, "the people in the neighborhood"—from junky to jerk to street-corner Jesus. At his worst, Dixon wastes his considerable skills and eye for detail showing us what we've seen before: *Mondo Cane* cavalcade of lunacy and loss. For all its verve and comedy, *Too Late* is more atlas than novel, a sore misreading of Mr. James's notion that "landscape is character."

Quite Contrary, a 1979 collection of connected stories, on the other hand, is tuneful testimony to Dixon's ability to exploit

Gotham's hugger-mugger to the lasting advantage of his people. Caught on what's billed as "the cutting edge of NYC," Mary LeBroom and Newt Leeb suffer each other as only lovers dare—through break-up and reconciliation, through abortion and infidelity, through want and wealth—in a chronicle, told from end to beginning (a sweet way of having your ache and eating it too!), that works from the glory and gut of a character. In this 11-story volume, Mr. Dixon, with the care and patience that seriousness brings, thrusts us into a relationship run at full tilt, a relationship fueled by need and hope and dread—the right stuff that's real *and* realized.

More recent is *14 Stories* (actually 13, but that's a story itself), part of the Johns Hopkins series of poetry and fiction. His clunkers aside, of which there are a handful, Dixon's finer efforts (**"The Security Guard,"** **"The Intruder"** and the title story [**"14 Stories"**]) recall the virtues of Michaels (Leonard), Barthelme (Donald), and Marx (Groucho)—namely, passion, daring and elan. Especially noteworthy is **"Love Has Its Own Action,"** in which love, the peril and promise of it, hustles the narrator at break-neck speed through a series of affairs and marriages, searching for a woman who had "intelligence, understanding, and a good nature and sense of humor and was thoroughly feminine, seemingly talented and self-sufficient and she very much appealed to my groin." High-order Action, indeed. In this collection, Dixon has turned his interest from city to citizen, his stories swift with the sense of folks, modern and therefore crazed, busy with the business of living and, uh, loving—in the Village, in the Streets, and in hotels without a 13th storey.

Lastly, what remains notable about even Dixon's less accomplished work is style: pure Nighttown, a Broadway-Bowery of zip, pop and snap-crackly. When he presses, when he's setting you up, when his reach exceeds his etcetera, he's cute, self-indulgent, lazy: "Maybe me because so far it's so far from what's what I believe." When he's right, he's as true as fine science: "Donna has very small breasts, way below average. She was either ultra-high newspaper and magazine fashion, shampoo or bubbly soap on tv or gloves or stockings or shoes with the top of her body removed." Ah, such is meet and choice, writing to remember and to celebrate—even outside the city limits. (pp. 133-34)

> *Lee Abbott, in a review of "Too Late," "Quite Contrary: The Mary and Newt Story," and "14 Stories," in* The South Carolina Review, *Vol. 13, No. 1, Fall, 1981, pp. 133-34.*

PETER BRICKLEBANK

Movies contains all that is characteristic Stephen Dixon.... Not only is he again holding his slightly distorted mirror up to life, but his tape recorder is running apace. The dialogue is uncannily accurate but yet constantly surprising. Shuffling through contradiction and digression, hesitation and inversion, each step of a character and twist of a tale is gloriously funny—and often a wrong step, and often a tragic twist. But in addition to previous collections such as *14 Stories* and *Quite Contrary,* these pieces seem less convoluted and more straightforward in narrative line. In **"The Frame,"** a customer wishes to hang a photocopy and returns to a store he's not visited for many years. There he is struck by the likeness of the assistant to his dead sister; and past is 'framed' in present. This more obviously 'literary' quality provides counterpoint to Dixon's lusher linguistic jungles.

I was reminded in these stories of T. S. Eliot's magic lantern which threw "nerves in patterns on a screen." In the title piece [**"Movies"**], a couple's polarized reactions to a new rave flick casts their relationship into the grotesque. The movie is incomprehensibly surreal—giant lips amidst a nauseating array of cinematography—and the man retreats to a peep show and television. These are at least understandable escapes, if ineffectual ones. But as often in Dixon, mis- and multi-interpretation is always possible, always a problem. Variations on telling a story—**"The Barbecue"**—or telling the truth—**"Small Bear"**—are open ended yet limited. What is the man to do when the surreal slips from screen into real life and his wife announces that she wishes to separate? Deal with it, perhaps; it's an everyday occurrence. But when she adds she'll move in with the woman who took the seat next to her when he left? And this because of one movie? In a marvellous speech as off-the-wall as that movie, the wife attempts to put everything in focus. The movie showed, she explains (and summarizes this collection), "'. . . the sometime absurdity of living together as couples and the possibility of undiscovered courage . . . the voices we hear. . . .'" There is a direct link then between the fantasy world of the cinema screen and the man in the street. Finding and understanding the borderline of the irrational that separates the two leads to much questioning throughout these 17 tales. . . . But there is no escape from the inevitably useless answer, or the super-realism associated with the screen but more accurately of the sidewalk.

Even with this heightened 'realism,' it is not much of a comparison, as has been made, to see Dixon's work as "Kafkaesque." There are no unusual events here, no symbols or secondary levels of meaning. These are stories of cops and robbers, lovers, the un-streetwise, all that is first slapstick and then tragic. Characters are rarely described in any detail. Unless, like the misunderstood 'hero' of **"Cy,"** they are hit by grenade, car and bicycle beyond redemption of that ultimate of make-up artists, the plastic surgeon. They are extras in their own B-movie horror; superfluous to their employers, hardly the heart-throbs of their lovers. If they come remotely close to becoming pin-ups, it's only because they're Wanted—or have socially skewered themselves—perhaps on the boom mike—and are still trying to talk their way out of it.

These are ordinary people surprised by the fickleness of mundanity: sometimes life unprovokedly bites. As those rendered goofy by "Candid Camera" or voluble by a news lens, they perform accordingly. They stare or say the wrong thing. They get what they think is a joke when there isn't one. They cherish their mother (who's awaiting them with an axe). They arrive blithely on the scene of a construed crime oblivious that they are stepping into the spotlight of interrogation as prime suspect.

Often their predicaments are self generated by the most humane of errors and motives. They mistakenly give a pocket watch instead of a coin to a panhandler on the spur of the moment (**"The Watch"**), or they are embroiled in their conscience and debate over borrowing a wheelchair to visit their sick baby (**"Not Charles"**). Often they fight back at a world too grossly unfair with a kind of celluloid courage spliced with true concern, but they are harshly treated. After great emotional and financial loss, they find themselves howling "You bum, you bum" after the panhandler or find, having finally secured the wheelchair, they're too late, their baby is dead, their hopes and journey in vain. There is a hopelessness about many of the characters' predicaments. In the 1982 O'Henry Prize story, **"Layaways,"** the all too familiar events of a store robbery occurs. When one young man tries to fight back, he manages to get his mother killed, only to repeat his mistake later with his best friend. He proves only that screen heroism has no place in our murky urban badlands. This repetition of error, failure to learn from experience, is one that makes for so much humor and humanity in Dixon's characters. Compounded with the tragedy that it inevitably brings, it screws the lens through which we look at the world into a disquieting blur, giving disproportion a clarity all its own.

The tattered social fabric through which these individuals rush pell mell is uncomfortably recognizable. Throughout **"The Hole"** bombings occur in civic places with spiralling frequency and death tolls, in the same heartlessly casual way as those in the news of recent months. But these are the background to the (in)human story of a teacher who refuses to let his trapped class escape until all, including himself, can be saved. When his son is beaten to death, so too is the possibility of any happy endings, leaving a disquiet verging on paranoia that suffuses not only these tales, but very possibly the street or bookstore (remember the bag check?) where you bought this review. (pp. 85-7)

Dixon's narratives run and jump through hoops of possibilities, taking on, as always, lives of their own. Ringing true of the rhythms of life—the spoken word, the unspoken thought— these tales are 'documentaries.' They are also farce; Dixon makes us laugh, cry, and feel the world of the little man or woman, inescapably the one we're in. It is only by seeing the minutiae of life, its hassles, its waiting in lines *outside* cinemas, that we can come to terms with that inside. The small people here wonder whether it will be worth it as they wait in line. They check that they have the increased price of admission and yearn alternatives. Of these—as many characters here— reading is one. Certainly *Movies* would be a fine investment. Not only does it repay attention with humor, insight and originality, but it shows us just how hectically absurd our world really is. (p. 87)

> *Peter Bricklebank, in a review of "Movies," in* Carolina Quarterly, *Vol. XXXVI, No 3, Spring, 1984, pp. 85-7.*

TOM LeCLAIR

Stephen Dixon's *Time to Go* . . . suffers from sameness: all the stories are about loss—taking leave of parents, children, lovers, friends, students, places—and are composed in a militantly banal style, as if Samuel Beckett were recording the telephone conversations of middle-class Baltimoreans. Several are wonderful, arresting in their simplicity: **"The Bench,"** about a handyman who tries to learn from gossip and speculation where a loving father and infant daughter he used to watch have gone, and the title story [**"Time to Go"**], in which a grown son can't get rid of his father's voice, advising, cajoling, criticizing, loving. But too many are either sterile completions of Dixon's "going" pattern or lack any imaginative lift, a quality of perception or style that raises a trivial subject to attention. Particularly weak are the stories about the writer Will, whose problem is lack of subjects. (p. 9)

> *Tom LeClair, "Overheard Stories," in* Book World— The Washington Post, *August 5, 1984, pp. 8-9.*

PATRICIA BLAKE

Among his seven books, published mainly by small presses, [Dixon's] latest, *Time to Go,* emphatically establishes him as one of the short story's most accomplished if quirky practitioners.

Almost obsessively, Dixon has doomed the protagonist of most of his stories to repeated and often farcical failures in love. Whether named Mac, Jules or Will, he is conspicuously a loser. Speaking with a strikingly distinctive voice, this hapless character is alternately self-pitying and self-mocking, weepily sentimental and stonily sharp-witted. He unceasingly endures abuse, rejection, infidelity and most of the other mortifications that can befall a man in the throes of passion.

"End of Magna" catches the antihero talking himself out of the love of his life. "She's too good for me. She's too beautiful, too intelligent, too perceptive, too creative, too everything," begins an interior monologue that could be a manual of masochism. In that story the woman walks out kindly. Not so the 20-year-old in **"For a Man Your Age,"** whose explanation of why her lover is too old for her is cruel beyond the call of love or duty. She knows all a man's vulnerabilities and has deadly aim. . . .

Much of the satiric power of Dixon's stories springs from his reversals of sexual stereotypes. His women tend to be aggressive, and his standard male character is at best foolishly romantic. Yet the final cycle of stories in this collection suggests that a wimp can turn into a mensch. For the first time in the Dixon canon his male character gets the girl. In the title story [**"Time to Go"**] he actually marries her, in spite of an imagined, ironic commentary on his courtship by his late father. The story **"Wheels"** lovingly tells of the baby that is born of the marriage. In one affecting and indeed surprisingly beautiful scene, the man, in diapering his child, is reminded of a time when he nursed his dying, incontinent father. Evidently the resolution of the hero's romantic miseries has brought to Dixon's work not only joy, but insight into the keener shadings of grief.

> *Patricia Blake, "Wimps in Love," in* Time, *New York, Vol. 124, No. 7, August 13, 1984, p. B4.*

MIKE MOYLE

Unfortunately, and as is often the case in the work of writers who are prolific, Dixon's short fiction . . . has been a bit uneven, some of his more than two hundred published stories if technically proficient, downright bad; on occasion he wastes his time, and he shouldn't always trust his belief: I'll even go as far as to say that Dixon has written *too* much, that he seems unable at times to pass over what's better left alone. *14 Stories,* generally an impressive 1980 collection . . . , offers a few examples. **"The Sub,"** for the most part an interior monologue about a substitute teacher's fantasies and their relationship to reality, is skillfully sustained but, I'm afraid, dull; and **"Signatures,"** the story of a man who for a living collects the John Hancocks of the famous, the near-famous, and the potentially-famous and who has an unmemorable encounter with a playwright, is mercifully brief but insipid. . . . When we read Dixon, we sometimes feel that production is all he's interested in.

Though in the end they shine quite brightly, *Movies* and *Time to Go,* Dixon's newest collections and the ones under consideration here, provide more of the same. In the former, **"Stop"** contains vintage Dixon material—a man is being chased by the police through the streets and across the rooftops of a New York waterfront neighborhood—but is curiously lifeless; and "Joke," despite Dixon's limiting himself to three incredibly fast-paced pages, is tedious in its recounting of what could be but isn't a prank played on the narrator by a woman with whom he's sexually involved. In *Time to Go,* "**Self-Portrait,**" a monologue from a writer-teacher who goes on ad nauseam about how he'd like to draw himself, rather than get down to his real business for the day, is well written but self-indulgent: the story ostensibly concerns one Will Taub (as do all the stories in this second section of the book), but we feel as if we're reading a Dixon warm-up exercise. "**The Beginning of Something,**" which *is* in part about Taub's limbering up for a few hours' bout with his typewriter, made me plain angry—it is a lamentable piece of metafiction that caused me momentarily to forget how good Dixon can be. Finally, in "**Magna Takes the Calls,**" during the course of which Taub receives the news of the passing of his uncle and the murder of a friend's wife, Dixon takes what Yeats considered one of the two great subjects, death, and makes us yawn.

Fortunately, these kinds of clunkers clearly constitute a rarity, not a rule. By and large the two volumes contain stories that range from the recommendable to the just-can't-be-missed. At his absolute best, and he's there surprisingly often, Dixon is both gut-wrenching and funny. For instance, the *Movies* tale "**Darling**" touches us with its depiction of the plight of the ne'er-do-well narrator, whose wife has kicked him out of their home and who has found a job a thousand miles away taking care of a bedridden invalid, at the same time that it makes us giggle over some of the torments the narrator inflicts upon his charge because he can't take the pathos and frustrations of their combined situations any longer and wants her to fire him—doing everything except what she asks of him and intentionally spilling water on her. Similarly, *Time to Go*'s "**Goodbye to Goodbye,**" an account of another narrator-loser's efforts to come to grips with his wife's abandoning him, stabs our emotions as it teases our brains: trying to bid adieu to bidding adieu, the man gives us five versions of his predicament, four uproariously outrageous (and each in its turn acknowledged as a lie), one presumably—and sadly—true. In addition, the title story ["**Time to Go**"] and "**Don**" work on us in similar ways. The latter is brilliant, a seemingly random outpouring of paragraphs that jump around in time and tense to form a full portrait of the titular character, a portrait that many lesser writers would have stretched into a novel. . . . (pp. 113-14)

Only a little less pleasing is Dixon's ability to be purely serious, or nearly so, in a fashion that makes us feel the practically unutterable pain of some of his characters while it assiduously avoids sentimentality. In "**The Frame,**" the final story in *Movies,* for example, the male narrator goes into a small shop to buy a picture frame and is aided by a deformed woman; she poignantly reminds him of his dead sister, who hobbled through a significant portion of her twenty-five-year life with a similar ailment. "**The Package Store,**" the last piece in the first section of *Time to Go,* presents the quiet tragedy of a small-business owner and his wife trying to eke out a living in a Baltimore neighborhood consisting of more robbers, it nearly seems, than customers. And "**Cy,**" a standout among even the best stories in *Movies,* is reminiscent of *The Elephant Man,* though perhaps more heart-rending; here's the terribly disfigured, purblind, but in his own way savvy title character-narrator telling us of his reunion with his mother, who's been under the impression that he's dead, after he has been virtually chased by unbelievably cruel neighbors out of the apartment he has called refuge:

"I don't dare kiss her cheek yet. I kiss the air instead. I've forgotten what it's like to hold another human being. The feeling can't be physically or mentally reproduced. How often I've hugged my pillow. Myself, if only to embrace some person's flesh . . . Not even a dog have I kissed the nose of or hugged in ten years." Moving stuff, that.

Last are the stories, slightly less satisfactory because ultimately more ephemeral than those which are humorously tragic or simply devastating, that I can classify only as knee-slappers and wild fun. In *Movies* we have "**The Hole,**" hilarious mania about a rash of bombings in the "City" and the off-duty policeman who gets involved in the rib-tickling rescue of some of the victims, one unreasonably reasonable schoolteacher in particular. And in *Time to Go* there's "**Eating the Placenta,**" a romp about Will Taub's frantic attempt to escape the verbal clutches of a pestering student and run home to his pregnant, almost let's-get-to-the-hospital-I-think-it's-time wife—only to be harried by the persistent undergraduate over the phone when he reaches his destination, though Taub's final triumph is sweeter than aspartame.

I would enjoy going on at greater length showering praise on gems like "**Layaways**" and "**Not Charles**" in *Movies* and "**Wheels**" and "**Reversal**" in *Time to Go,* but the limitation of allotted space prohibits me. So since I've written rather specifically of Stephen Dixon, purposely treating him as someone with whom you're likely familiar if you're a regular reader of these pages, let me end more generally. These two books aren't as unified as their publishers make them out to be, and once in a while Dixon doesn't dazzle. But as an unidentified reviewer says on the dust jacket of *Movies,* Dixon is "always professional," and his most pedestrian efforts usually bristle and pulse with life. (pp. 114-15)

> *Mike Moyle, in a review of "Movies: Seventeen Stories" and "Time to Go," in* The South Carolina Review, *Vol. 17, No. 1, Fall, 1984, pp. 113-15.*

JOHN DOMINI

Mr. Dixon's imagination [in *Time to Go*] sticks close to home. His principal subject is the clash of the mundane and the aberrant, those unsettling run-ins with wackos or former lovers all too familiar to anyone who's ever lived in a city. Here that city is nearly always New York, where Mr. Dixon has spent most of his life, and most of the time the protagonist is an unmarried male writer in early middle age. On top of that, more than half the stories are about the same writer, Will Taub, who teaches in a university very much like Johns Hopkins University, where Mr. Dixon teaches.

Time to Go does have touches of exotica. The title story ["**Time to Go**"] features a running conversation between Taub and his dead father (the ghost proves one of the liveliest talkers in the book), while other stories disrupt chronology or, Barth-like, reflect on the story in process. But only one story genuinely breaks away from the metropolitan settings and writerly circumstances. And that one, the surreal "**Come on a Coming,**" is grounded in such obvious symbolism and is so patly predictable as to suggest Mr. Dixon is better off with his more down-to-earth urban encounters.

In these stories, everyone arrives eventually at the same conclusion—that the day-to-day is preferable to the outlandish—and their logic provides the best moments. Mr. Dixon allows every character his or her moment of enjoyably lunatic self-defense. There is a prolonged analysis, for instance, of how best to catch the eye of a woman you once lived with. Such bits are entirely familiar but rich with cranky charm nonetheless.

Outside of such moments, however, *Time to Go* is awfully underdone. The opening story, **"The Bench,"** concerns some subdued and pointless gossip about an unnamed father and his baby girl, and the last story, **"Reversal,"** offers nothing more than the depressing thoughts of a character diapering his child.

When some excitement does occur—even the robbery of a wedding ring—it too is handled with a stick-figure soullessness. . . .

All Mr. Dixon's encounters lack any but the most general physicality. And the quieter moments, which a writer interested in day-to-dayness would be expected to savor, are handled with the same abstraction. The changing of diapers in **"Reversal"** is presented as it might be in a how-to manual:

> He raises her bottom by holding her feet up in one hand, slips the double diapers out from under her, sets her down, keeps one hand on her chest so she won't roll off the changing board to the floor, drops the wet diapers into the diaper pail and closes it.

The repression of rhetoric and an emphasis on the trivial are hallmarks of many contemporary short stories. But Mr. Dixon is so unrelenting in both regards that he ends up compounding a lack of imagination with a near absence of passion. His characters' theorizing all starts to sound the same after a while, and his endings, deprived of even the least bubble of poetic effect, suffocate. Despite its sensitivity to its characters' bad moments and its pleasing attention to structure, *Time to Go* amounts to less than Mr. Dixon's *14 Stories*. Its failures point up the dangers in the fashion for the understated.

John Domini, "Day-to-Dayness," in The New York Times Book Review, *October 14, 1984, p. 34.*

JOHN HOUSE

Like an old Woody Allen routine, Stephen Dixon's third novel [*Fall & Rise*] is full of personal anxieties and social pratfalls. For, like the Woody Allen of old, Daniel Krin is a chump—a failed shoeshine boy, a draft and family dodger, a translator of execrable Japanese verse. In a single night, Krin—in his fantasies at first and then in reality—pursues "her," a literature teacher named Helene Winiker. But *Fall & Rise* is hardly a love story; it's a home movie about metropolitan life, a foot-dragging wade through Manhattan at ebb tide. Krin's gradual progress uptown and Helene's evening at a wedding reception are a series of urban trials. He's left bloodied and coatless when he tries to stop a newsstand holdup; she ends up angered and alone after the former lover she's gone home with announces he has herpes. Krin's largest obstacles to winning Helene, however, are verbal. Language is like a pot of mucilage, and each time he dips into it, his thoughts come out a little stickier. "No," he imagines saying to her, "that's confusing and tumescent, just as that phrase was when I could have more accurately and less clumsily said 'affected and bombastic,' though I'm still being vocally showy, and even still with that last adverbial phrase." Played against Helene's insistent need for clarification, Krin's loopy delivery becomes a comic exercise in thwarted intercourse. Mr. Dixon is a fluent and articulate writer, and he might have brought this novel off had Krin's confusion remained just a part of the story. Using

him as a narrator, though, hampered as he is by a crippling awareness of what words can't do, is asking for trouble. Ultimately language undoes *Fall & Rise* as surely as it undoes Daniel Krin.

John House, in a review of "Fall & Rise," in The New York Times Book Review, *July 7, 1985, p. 16.*

JEROME KLINKOWITZ

Stephen Dixon's work continues to grow. Unlike the entropic fiction, from Pynchon to Beattie, which has found such favor with academic critics, his novels and short stories expand thematic possibilities rather than constrict them, at the same time showing how within the range of familiar narrative techniques there remains a world of fresh discovery. . . .

Since their first appearance in book form ten years ago, his story collections and novels have spoken for expansion, both in the lives they describe and the forms with which they do it. The pieces in *No Relief* (1976) enlarge situations which would be otherwise constrictive: breaking off with a lover, saying goodbye to a dying father, and having to tell people how large such vacancies loom. *Work* (1977) is a novel which shows how complete and complex a supposedly menial job can be, a virtual intertext of increasing considerations. Dixon's next work, *Too Late* (1978), confirms this method for his full-length fiction: how the simplest occasion, such as a girlfriend leaving a movie early, can lead to hundreds of pages of consequences, a style of casuistry which delights philosophers and drives neurotics mad, but which in the hands of a good novelist shows how rich the world of narrative can get. *Quite Contrary: The Mary and Newt Story* (1979) follows this belief in interconnectedness to its logical generic conclusion: that the story of a man and woman's relationship may fragment itself into an infinity of action, yet will still cohere by virtue of its mutually attractive subjects—a perfectly natural reinforcement of form and content. (p. 90)

His new novel, *Fall & Rise,* is notable not just because it's his first longer work in nearly a decade, but because it confirms the writerly tendencies developed in the three short story collections with which Dixon began the Eighties, *14 Stories* (1980), *Movies,* (1983), and *Time to Go* (1984). His finest stories are found in these volumes, where the tendency to interconnect is kept within each text's bounds, with the result that those boundaries of the text generate the possibilities of narrative. A suicide's bullet crashing through the window and initiating other stories all around town, a couple's parrying relationship as they attend a movie, the memory of a father physically haunting a son's and his fiancée's trip to the jeweler for wedding rings—these stories show how Dixon views limits not as inhibitions but rather as invitations to write, and write, and write. Like the human heart beat, his stories go on, vitalistic and never boring. It's the oldest narrative principle that stories impel themselves toward their conclusion, that their endings are implicit in their first words. It is human nature to resist these inevitable endings, and just as in the urge to draw another breath Dixon's writing finds ways within the material itself to draw another breath and live on.

Fall & Rise breathes a universe of life into the smallest of narrative situations: a man meets an alluring woman at a party, and from the briefest of encounters sustains an imaginative involvement as he spends the evening and early morning wandering the streets with thoughts of her and finally calling her near daybreak for shelter. "I meet her at a party," Dixon's narrator begins, and from the ongoing present tense evolves a seemingly endless story. Such a life of syntax recalls the limits of fiction, from Valéry's inability to write "The Marquis went out at five o'clock" to Tolstoy's success at generating a novelistic universe from the unlikely resource of "Happy marriages are all alike." Dixon's approach is destined to succeed because he aligns his narrative situation with the conditions of storytelling themselves: as his narrator, Daniel Krin, tries to take imaginative hold of his subject, Helene Winiker, he must literally write himself into her life. The novel's action, spoken in his voice, is to incorporate her character, all from the slightest of provocations. The novel's present tense, which includes lots of dialogue registered in the same tone, speaks to the reader as another character. It is the influential sense of *presence*, then, that dominates the writing, and that sense stays with the reader long after the smaller details of plot, action, and character are forgotten.

Not that the narrative situations are inconsequential—although of small substance, such as choosing what to wear and whether to eat before going to the party, they are occasions which produce language (as opposed to language having to generate situations, a ploy of less successful fiction). Daniel Krin quite literally has his story grow around him, as his subway ride over (through a world of narrative graffiti), early moments at the party (a kaleidoscope of dropped conversations and abandonments for more attractive guests), and snatch of stairway conversation with Helene (to whom he is never formally introduced) all conspire to create a situation he must take over and write himself to have any success. Even then, his story becomes one of missed intentions:

> Go over, say hello or if she's still with the man then stay close to say hello when he momentarily looks away or talks to someone else and maybe even leaves her. I head for the bar, turn to the food table, I wouldn't know what to say. "Hello, how's by you, the family?" Might be original enough to tickle her but I doubt it. A funnyman she might think, one who isn't afraid to make a fool of himself, but I doubt it. Earnest approach then. "I wanted to meet you, plain as that, what can I say?" She looks earnest but the approach might what? Put her ill at ease or touch her in some not too positive way and then she could silently blame me for her sudden awkwardness or whatever it might come to when before she was feeling so good. Just go over. Say and do nothing. Or say nothing but do something. Pretend to want more wine. Just want more wine, since when do you have to pretend, and while there look at her and if she's not looking at you continue to look at her and if she then looks at you, maybe then you can make one of a number of moves. But finish your wine first. Or go over with it. She'll know the real reason you're coming over, but if she's interested, and for an intermittent minute she seems to be, she won't care what's the excuse.

Daniel never gets to her in time for any of these ploys—their contact at the party will be limited to a few words on the stairs as she leaves and Daniel's postscript shouted from the window—but Dixon has shown how the situation is so rich in linguistic possibilities that it takes over 300 words to cover logical options even when they don't eventually happen. Each sentence is generated by the syntactical arrangement which precedes it, and a subliminal order to the mental events makes the narrative cohere. (pp. 91-2)

The novel's visible events are keyed to its seven chapters, as from The Party Daniel moves to The Park across the street, then into The Bar and out again into The Street, where he joins in the analytical aftermath of an accident involving The Car. Then the action shifts to Helene for her own chapter, which she narrates, filling in the evening's action after she's left the party but before she returns home to The Apartment, where Daniel calls and asks for the shelter which concludes *Fall & Rise*. At each stage there are entire stories, from panhandlings to tavern squabbles to a robbery and mugging. Pick up the phone and there's another story—a Mother's loneliness and lack of heat—and any contact on the street invites a new branch to the narrative. But organizing it all is Daniel's attempt to get to Helene—past panhandlers and muggers, through her answering service and many other obstacles, until he's bedded down on her livingroom floor for what remains of the night. The novel ends with Daniel still "writing"—this time the adventures of a dream—which is halted only by Helene's sunrise invitation to have breakfast and depart. Her stopping of the narrative is the only way Daniel's story can end.

Like the act of breathing in and breathing out, *Fall & Rise* impels its story onward, the effect of one action leading obversely yet completely to the next. Only a blank page can end it, but even that blankness implies that there is a world of language to be heard if the storyteller is given just one more word. Six words have begun it, and led to another 120,000. Yet every one has been spoken within the bounds of a coherent situation, filling the hours from 9 PM to daybreak with a world of possibilities. Rarely has a novelist's sense of life, and how it operates, been so complete. (p. 92)

Jerome Klinkowitz, in a review of "Fall & Rise," in The South Carolina Review, *Vol. 19, No. 1, Fall, 1986, pp. 90-2.*

ROY KASTEN

Daniel Krin, the protagonist of Stephen Dixon's third novel *Fall and Rise*, is a translator of modern Japanese poetry. His pursuit of Helene, a beautiful redhead he meets at a party, and the numerous delays to his pursuit form the novel's structure. Krin moves through a frenetic, sometimes chaotic, sometimes mundane urban labyrinth in search of Helene. But while Krin is continually defined as a translator, the novel suggests little of the translation of his experience, of the meaning underlying the detours, encounters, embraces, and risks of Krin's quest. The text is something like the unedited videotape recording of a day in the life of the New York literati, focused mainly through Krin, though making an unexpected and pleasurable shift to Helene for a long chapter. The reader is allowed to enter the thoughts of the two principle characters; indeed, the world perceived and the language revealing that perception are ordered by their thoughts. The last chapter, "The Apartment," shifts from a first person narration to third person ordered and shaped by Krin and Helene. Although Dixon plays with language throughout the novel, often fragmenting and shattering, occasionally freeing language from conventional prose, the language of *Fall and Rise* continually obeys the convention of a mind, of a vehicle of perception that plays with language in precisely plausible and often comical forms. (pp. 175-76)

The bulk of Dixon's novel relies, unsurprisingly, on dialogue. But his dialogue is not so much *realistic* as it is always plausible and logically sensible. The form of dialogue is alone a disruption and breakage of the text (Dixon seems to sense this, juxtaposing single paragraphs that unravel like streamers for 10 pages with pages of pure dialogue). But ultimately in *Fall and Rise,* dialogue is characterized by a trivial and *uninterested* "party chit-chat" quality. Dialogue is not concerned with tension or driving wedges into meaning. Dialogue is always translatable.

There are moments in this novel that lead me to believe that its reading must take the seeming vacuity and flaccidity of much of the dialogue as well as the narration as a kind of guide. That this novel is about a quest through a wasteland of chit-chat for those few moments of resonant language. And those moments, though few, do happen:

> I want to hold her face in my hands and lean over the two or three inches I think it'd take if what I'm remembering now is right about her height and if she doesn't raise herself on her toes to kiss. I want to. Yes. Very much. To open my eyes and find hers closed. Then open them again and find them open. Hers. Her to smile when I find her eyes open when I open mine. Her to take my face in her hands and bring it down to hers and kiss my lips. Want to. I lie my head on a pillow beside hers on a pillow or both ours on the same pillow and our lips almost touching but not speaking and then touching and our eyes closing, though I don't know why not speaking.

In this gentle, complex moment, language resonates because all the nervous, neurotic, sexual, dislocated language that strays absentmindedly throughout this novel joins together in a tender rhythm. Dixon is not merely celebrating a beautiful moment, but creating the beautiful, as William Gass might say.

But these moments remain too rare, like bluejays flashing over an endless landfill. They are squelched in a monotonous urban drone. Even in the above passage, Dixon's language retains the same explicative tone of the bulk of the novel. His prose is never metaphorical, rarely imagistic or suggestive (the number of analogies in the novel can be counted on one hand) and by denying metaphor, Dixon denies a fundamental need—a need almost totally unexplored in the thought processes and perceptions of Krin or Helene. Instead, the music of this novel plays out in the severing of the name or pronoun as subject from sentences. . . . (pp. 176-77)

By disturbing grammar, narrative voice takes on an immediate, nervous, neurotic quality. The text becomes a kind of neurotic performance, moving with frenetic, stream of conscious speed—but lacking texture. And Dixon's prose is not the "dreck" of language that Barthelme explores, but grinding, pulverized language. This is a dense and rambling novel: reading it is like driving 90 mph over an endless gravel road full of potholes. (p. 177)

Roy Kasten, in a review of "Fall and Rise," in Quarterly West, *No. 23, 1986, pp. 175-77.*

William (Cuthbert) Faulkner

1897-1962

American novelist, short story writer, and scriptwriter.

The following entry presents criticism on Faulkner's novel *Absalom, Absalom!* (1936). For discussions of Faulkner's complete career, see *CLC*, Vols. 1, 3, 6, 8, 9, 11, 14, 18, 28.

Regarded by many critics as the culminating achievement of Faulkner's series of works set in Yoknapatawpha County, a fictitious region of his native Mississippi, *Absalom, Absalom!* is a complex and controversial novel of guilt, expiation, and revenge that asserts the overwhelming necessity for responsibility in human affairs. This novel chronicles the efforts of Thomas Sutpen to establish a family dynasty near the imaginary town of Jefferson, Mississippi, prior to and following the American Civil War. A commercial failure at the time of its publication, *Absalom, Absalom!* initially received negative reviews but later challenged *The Sound and the Fury* (1929) for supremacy in Faulkner's canon. Although some early critics favorably compared the density and symbolism of *Absalom, Absalom!* to the style of lyric poetry, most were confused by Faulkner's use of nonchronological narration and multiple points of view, which later commentators contended he had deliberately employed to provide fragmentary, overlapping, or contradictory perspectives of Sutpen's story. Originally interpreted as an obfuscated Gothic romance, *Absalom, Absalom!* received minimal scholarly attention until the publication of *The Portable Faulkner* (1946), a collection of previously published fiction edited by Malcolm Cowley that revived interest in Faulkner's work. Although many early reviewers regarded the novel as an allegory of the fall of the aristocratic order of the old South, most contemporary critics maintain that *Absalom, Absalom!* is an intricate examination of evil and irrationality, echoing the opinion of Robert E. Scholes that its depiction of Southern society serves less as criticism than "as a condition of a particular human drama."

Most early reviewers of *Absalom, Absalom!* treated Thomas Sutpen as the novel's central character. An impoverished mountain youth who experiences no contact with blacks or the South's caste system prior to moving with his family to Virginia, Sutpen conceives of the ambition he later refers to as his "design" when, sent on an errand by his father to a neighboring plantation, he is instructed to use the back door because of his inferior social status. Humiliated, Sutpen determines to gain revenge by becoming a respected member of the Southern aristocracy and establishing a family dynasty. Critics frequently compare Sutpen to Captain Ahab of Herman Melville's novel *Moby Dick*, as well as to the title character of F. Scott Fitzgerald's novel *The Great Gatsby*, in his ruthless but naive pursuit of power over his destiny. Traveling to the West Indies to work as a plantation overseer, Sutpen marries Eulalia Bon, the daughter of a plantation owner, whom he acquires as a reward for suppressing a slave rebellion. Sutpen deems his wife and newborn son nonconducive to his design, however, when he discovers them to possess a trace of black ancestry. After arranging financially for his family, Sutpen deserts them and moves to Jefferson, where he acquires one hundred square miles of land and uses twenty black West Indian slaves and a

captive French architect to construct his mansion, Sutpen's Hundred.

Critics also liken Sutpen to the biblical David, whose moral blindness is described in Books I and II of Samuel in the Old Testament. Promised a specific daughter by King Saul for killing the giant Goliath, David feels morally justified in leaving Israel when Saul delivers a different daughter. After David becomes King of Israel, the prophet Nathan promises that God will wreak retribution upon his house because of his adulterous procurement of Bathsheba. A similarly inescapable fate awaits Sutpen, who marries the daughter of the respectable Coldfield family and raises two children, Henry and Judith, as well as Clytie, his illegitimate daughter by a mulatto slave, prior to becoming the wealthiest landowner in Jefferson. When his son Henry invites his college friend, Charles Bon, to Sutpen's Hundred, Sutpen recognizes the young man as the child he abandoned but refuses to acknowledge him as his son because he fears such recognition could entitle Bon to declare himself Sutpen's firstborn heir and endanger his design. When Bon announces his intention to wed Judith, Sutpen forbids the marriage and informs Henry that Bon is his half-brother. Henry refuses to accept this fact, and he later fights alongside Bon as a Confederate soldier in the Civil War. Upon their return to Sutpen's Hundred, however, Henry inexplicably shoots and kills his half-brother and flees from the authorities. His second wife dead, his legitimate heir a fugitive from justice, his lands seized for debt, Sutpen finds his design ironically defeated by the same means he conceived to protect it.

Like Agamemnon in the Hellenic myth described in the *Oresteia* of Aeschylus, Sutpen sacrifices a child for what he regards as honorable reasons but finds his sins tragically inherited by his children. The irony of Sutpen's situation is further compounded by his inability to grieve for Bon. The title of *Absalom, Absalom!* refers to David's lament for his son Absalom, who was slain by David's servants for killing his half-brother Amnon in revenge for Amnon's rape of Absalom's sister Tamar. Although critics disagree as to which of Sutpen's sons functions as the figure of Absalom, most concur on the crucial point of the biblical allusion: whereas David recognizes the curse upon his house and, in grieving for Absalom, laments the immutability of fate, Sutpen remains unable to comprehend what he refers to as the "flaw" in his design. Sutpen attempts to father another male heir by Milly, the granddaughter of a poor white retainer, but provokes her grandfather to kill him when he callously rejects Milly after she delivers a baby girl. When Henry returns to die at the Sutpen mansion years later, his aunt, Rosa Coldfield, sends an ambulance for him out of family responsibility. In an ironic parallel to the story of Clytemnestra, the wife of Agamemnon, who set fire to the house of Atreus in response to her husband's sacrifice of their daughter Iphigenia, Clytie ignites Sutpen's Hundred rather than submit to the police that she believes have come for Henry. The only survivor of Sutpen's dynasty is Jim Bond, the illegitimate grandson of Charles Bon, whose inheritance is "to lurk around those ashes and howl."

During the late 1940s and early 1950s, scholars began to examine how Faulkner's intricate imagery, style, and narrative structure inform the subject matter and theme of *Absalom, Absalom!* Although critics have reached no definitive consensus regarding the cumulative effect of these elements, most agree that Faulkner's use of delayed revelation, vague pronoun references, and long, convoluted sentences reflect his attempt to convey a sense of oral history, to negate distinctions between legend and fact, and to invest melodramatic subject matter with dramatic intensity and ambiguity. *Absalom, Absalom!* is largely recounted by Quentin Compson, Henry's cousin, who commits suicide in Faulkner's novel *The Sound and the Fury* due to his guilt over harboring incestuous feelings for his sister Caddy. Sutpen's story is related from several viewpoints. The first is that of Rosa Coldfield, Quentin's repressive spinster aunt, whom Sutpen proposed to marry following Bon's death and Henry's disappearance if she could produce a male heir prior to wedlock. Rosa characterizes Sutpen as a "demon" for forbidding the marriage of Judith and Bon, but her neurotic disdain is soon revealed to derive from her ignorance of Bon's relationship to Sutpen. That Bon is Sutpen's son is revealed by Quentin's father, who learned this from Quentin's grandfather and Sutpen's closest friend, General Compson. Details become further obscured when Quentin travels to Sutpen's Hundred with Rosa and ostensibly discovers the circumstances of Bon's mixed racial heritage from Henry Sutpen, who has returned home to die. In the final section of *Absalom, Absalom!*, Quentin engages in discourse in his Harvard University dormitory with his roommate, Shreve McCannon, offering a variety of conceivable motives for Henry's murder of Bon. Among other complex observations, Quentin and Shreve conclude that the incident must have arisen from the threat of miscegenation rather than incest, reasoning that Henry knew much earlier of

his blood relationship to Bon, and that Bon probably had no actual interest in marrying Henry's sister, Judith, since some evidence suggests that he used her to force Sutpen to recognize him as his son.

Many contemporary critics view *Absalom, Absalom!* as Quentin's story, since he emerges as the novel's ordering factor and since Sutpen's saga of miscegenation and racism seems to determine his own fate in *The Sound and the Fury*. Because Quentin's examination is self-reflexive, some commentators link *Absalom, Absalom!* with the metafictional works of such authors as Vladimir Nabokov and Alain Robbe-Grillet, while others, citing retrospective narration and dual plots, discern similarities in structure to the classic detective novel. Interpreted in this manner, Quentin functions as the book's investigator, while Shreve McCannon exists to qualify inconsistencies and overcome reader objections, much like Doctor Watson in the Sherlock Holmes mysteries of Sir Arthur Conan Doyle.

Two major points of controversy surrounding *Absalom, Absalom!* relate to questions of racism and sexism. Although some critics consider Sutpen a racist because he determines to revenge himself by adopting the dehumanizing social codes of his tormentors, many view his behavior as motivated by the need to conform to prevailing rules of conduct rather than as an expression of personal belief. Like the proud Byronic hero, Sutpen emerges as a man incapable of recognizing his own flaw, which is rooted in his refusal to acknowledge the emotional needs of others. Although most contemporary critics agree that Sutpen's downfall results from his inability to temper ambition with compassion, many early reviewers contended that his major sin relates to his cohabitation with blacks, since his design is largely ruined by Eulalia Bon, her son, Charles, and Clytie, Sutpen's mulatto daughter. Some commentators asserted that Faulkner was decrying the demise of the chivalric old South and equating the emancipation of blacks with the problems of the new South, yet most modern scholars agree that the puritanical Henry Sutpen and Rosa Coldfield function as the book's only genuine Southern racists, echoing John V. Hagopian's assessment that the "novel as a whole clearly repudiates Southern racism" in its portrayal of the destruction that arises from relations based on racial designations. Several explicators have also attributed sexist ideology to *Absalom, Absalom!*, identifying Thomas Sutpen as a godlike figure and the novel's women, in the words of Thomas M. Lorch, as symbols of "the passive but sustaining and indomitable life forces of nature" that provide strong men with the ability to shape and elevate their existence. Critics seeking to confirm Faulkner's sexism have pointed to his negative portrayals of Clytie and Eulalia Bon, who function as figures of retribution. More recent interpreters, however, applaud the character of Judith—who invites Bon's octoroon mistress to visit his grave following his death and attempts to raise his illegitimate son as her own to atone for her father's transgressions—as one of Faulkner's most sensitive affirmations of female compassion.

Despite critical disagreement, *Absalom, Absalom!* is often considered one of Faulkner's most fully realized works. Although many commentators acknowledge that Sutpen does not attain tragic stature because he fails to comprehend his flaw and neither suffers nor atones for his sins, others contend that his children become tragic figures—Judith in her self-sacrifice, and Henry in his ambivalent confrontation with Bon, who forces him to choose between fratricide and the racial acceptance that his Southern upbringing could not allow. Scholars generally concur that by focusing upon the perversion of human interaction, *Absalom, Absalom!* emerges as one of Faulkner's most powerful rejections of racism and the pre-Civil War South.

(See also *Short Story Criticism,* Vol. 1; *Contemporary Authors,* Vols. 81-84; *Dictionary of Literary Biography,* Vols. 9, 11, 44; *Dictionary of Literary Biography Yearbook: 1986;* and *Dictionary of Literary Biography Documentary Series,* Vol. 2.)

CLIFTON FADIMAN

At one point in *Absalom, Absalom!* William Faulkner makes Quentin Compson, who is telling the story, say to his auditor, "You can't understand it. You would have to be born there." This seems to me not merely one (or two) of the few comprehensible sentences in the entire novel, but also beyond a doubt the truest. At any rate, it is my particular Out. Not hailing from Mississippi . . . , I figure I'm not required to understand Mr. Faulkner's novels. I should like to state, therefore, in all humility, that I do not comprehend why *Absalom, Absalom!* was written, what the non-Mississippian is supposed to get out of it, or, indeed, what it is all about. Nor do I understand why Mr. Faulkner writes the way he does. And, having gone so far, I may as well break down and state my conviction that Mr. Faulkner's latest work is the most consistently boring novel by a reputable writer to come my way during the last decade. Duty also bids me report the opinion of the publishers, who see it as a major work, "his most important and ambitious contribution to American literature."

One may sum up both substance and style by saying that every person in *Absalom, Absalom!* comes to no good end, and they all take a hell of a time coming even that far. The story runs from 1807 to 1910, with the major action concentrated between 1833, when Thomas Sutpen appears in Jefferson, Mississippi, and 1869, when he is rather regretfully murdered by an old family retainer. Thomas Sutpen is a monomaniac, known familiarly to the other characters as The Demon. It is never quite clear what makes him so villainous, except that he has a habit of engaging in gouge-as-gouge-can fights with Negroes, and has the odd power of scaring ladies first into marrying him and then into conniption fits. However, he's the fellow you're supposed to shudder at, and if you understand Mr. Faulkner, you'll shudder. If you don't, I guess you just won't. The Demon's second wife, Ellen Coldfield, gives birth to two children, Henry and Judith, goes dotty, and dies after a while. Her younger sister, Rosa, is insulted by The Demon and also goes dotty, though it takes her much longer to die. The father of Rosa and Ellen goes nuts when the Civil War arrives, nails himself up in a garret, and perseveringly starves himself to death. Now, young Henry, upon finding out that his best friend, Charles Bon, engaged to be married to his sister Judith, is (a) his half-brother and (b) part Negro, also goes dotty in a complicated way, and finally shoots Charles dead. By the end of the story Henry has been reduced to straight, simple idiocy and is kept shut up in the attic. Judith, after some years passed in a vacant-eyed trance, passes out as a result of smallpox, a death so natural as to strike a rather jarring note. There is also Clytemnestra Sutpen, daughter of Thomas Sutpen (that's dat Ole Demon Sutpen) and a Negro slave. Clytie sets fire to herself and the idiot boy Henry, and so finishes her career in a fine blaze of pyromaniacal lunacy.

Then there are the Joneses. Wash Jones is a daft hanger-on of Ole Demon Sutpen. He has a granddaughter, Milly. Milly gives birth to a child (it's the Ole Demon's handiwork), Ole Demon insults her, Wash gets sore, [kills Milly and] the child, cuts Old Demon in two with a scythe, and then commits suicide. The Joneses furnish the nearest thing to comic relief in the book. Now, if you'll think back a few lunatics or so, you will remember Charles Bon, preserved from incest and miscegenation by Henry Sutpen's fraternal bullet. Charles had an octoroon mistress, name and mental condition unrecorded, by whom he engendered the boy Charles Etienne. Charles Etienne, realizing that he is a few thirty-seconds Negro, promptly runs amuck. He dies rather dully, of smallpox, but not before he has begotten, with the assistance of a full-blooded Negress, a son Jim. Jim is the real McCoy, a legitimate idiot. (I mean one specifically so called by Mr. Faulkner.) At the end of the book, he is the only living descendant of the accursed Sutpens, which shows you what can happen to a family once they have committed themselves to Mr. Faulkner's tender care.

I think I've got them all in. There's a stray lunatic aunt here and there, but I'm no stickler for details. Come to think of it, there's the young man named Quentin Compson, whose grandfather had befriended Ole Demon Sutpen, and who tells the Sutpen saga to his college chum many years after all these murders, near-incests, fires, suicides, etc., occurred down on the Sutpen farm in Old Mississipp'. Neither Quentin nor his roommate carries on what you would call normal conversations, but as there is no evidence of either of them having married his grandmother, or roasted his grandfather over a slow fire . . . , I think they should be accepted as Mr. Faulkner's concession to the gray, tawdry, non-Mississippian universe in which the rest of us poor folks live, if Mr. Faulkner can bring himself to call it living.

This cheerful little fable is filtered through the medium of a style peculiar to Mr. Faulkner. It seems peculiar to me, too. First, we have the Non-Stop or Life Sentence. The first two and a half pages of *Absalom, Absalom!* consist of seven sentences. . . . To penetrate Mr. Faulkner's sentences is like hacking your way through a jungle. The path closes up at once behind you, and in no time at all you find yourself entangled in a luxuriant mass of modifiers, qualifications, relative clauses, parenthetical phrases, interjected matter, recapitulations, and other indications of a Great Style. All of Mr. Faulkner's shuddery inventions pale in horrendousness before the mere notion of parsing him.

After the Life Sentence comes the Far Fetch, or Hypertrope. Very few things in the book remain themselves. Each one reminds Mr. Faulkner of something else. "Her legs hung . . . clear of the floor with that air of impotent and static rage like children's feet." See it? No? Join me at the foot of the class, where you belong.

Then we have what may be called Anti-Narrative, a set of complex devices used to keep the story from being told. Mr. Faulkner is very clever at this. He gets quite an interesting effect, for example, by tearing the Sutpen chronicle into pieces, as if a mad child were to go to work on it with a pair of shears, and then having each of the jagged divisions narrated by a different personage: the author, Rosa, Quentin, Quentin's father, Quentin's grandfather. All these people do a neat job of mixing up the time sequences, delaying climaxes, confusing the reader, and otherwise enabling Mr. Faulkner to demonstrate that as a technician he has Joyce and Proust punch-drunk. I should add that everybody talks the same language, a kind of

Dixie Gongorism, very formal, allusive, cryptic. . . . On the other hand, it is only fair to say that there are a score of pages (Rosa Coldfield's section of the narrative) full of remarkable prose poetry, beautiful in itself, if magnificently irrelevant.

Seriously, I do not know what to say of this book except that it seems to point to the final blowup of what was once a remarkable, if minor, talent. I imagine that many of my respected colleagues will see in it a tragic masterpiece, a great lament for the old dead South, a Sophoclean study of a doomed family. Perhaps they are right. For me, this is a penny dreadful tricked up in fancy language and given a specious depth by the expert manipulation of a series of eccentric technical tricks. The characters have no magnitude and no meaning because they have no more reality than a mince-pie nightmare. If we are to have tales of violence and sadism, let the violence and sadism be drawn from the behavior of grownups, let them be more than the melodramatic gestures of childish maniacs. A study of defeat can have great tragic weight, but only if the defeated are akin to us, which these mumbling, muttering, frozen-faced Sutpens surely are not. I fail to see why we must go into a spasm of ecstatic shivering just because Mr. Faulkner is a clever hand at fitting up a literary asylum for the feeble-minded. It takes more than these fake sepulchral voices, these synthetic incests, these Monk Lewis allusions, to scare ordinary sober citizens. Ole Demon Sutpen is a mechanical bogeyman, and the rest of his gang are no better. . . . I have the horrid suspicion that if enough people were to say boo the entire structure of *Absalom, Absalom!* would disappear in smoke. Does anyone care to say boo? (pp. 62-4)

> Clifton Fadiman, "Faulkner, Extra-Special, Double-Distilled," in *The New Yorker, Vol. XII, No. 37*, October 31, 1936, pp. 62-4.

BERNARD DeVOTO

It is now possible to say confidently that the greatest suffering of which American fiction has any record occurred in the summer of 1909 and was inflicted on Quentin Compson. You will remember, if you succeeded in distinguishing Quentin from his niece in *The Sound and the Fury*, that late in that summer he made harrowing discoveries about his sister Candace. Not only was she pregnant outside the law but also, what seared Quentin's purity much worse, she had lost her virginity. In the agony of his betrayed reverence for her, he undertook to kill both himself and her but ended by merely telling their father that he had committed incest with her. This blend of wish-fulfilment and Southern chivalry did not impress Mr. Jason Richmond Compson, who advised his son to take a vacation, adding, in one of the best lines Mr. Faulkner ever wrote, "watching pennies has healed more scars than Jesus." Quentin went on to Harvard, where, however, the yeasts of guilt, expiation, and revenge that are Mr. Faulkner's usual themes so worked in him that he eventually killed himself, somewhere in the vicinity of the Brighton abattoir. But at the end of *The Sound and the Fury* not all the returns were in. It now appears that only a little while after he was pressing a knife to Candace's throat—I make it about a month—Quentin had to watch the last act of doom's pitiless engulfing of the Sutpens, another family handicapped by a curse.

Mr. Faulkner's new fantasia [*Absalom, Absalom!*] is familiar to us in everything but style. Although the story is told in approximations which display a magnificent technical dexterity—more expert than Mr. Dos Passos's, and therefore the most

expert in contemporary American fiction—and although the various segments are shredded and displaced, it is not a difficult story to follow. It is not, for instance, so darkly refracted through distorting lenses as *The Sound and the Fury*. Though plenty of devices are employed to postpone the ultimate clarification, none are introduced for the sole purpose of misleading the reader. . . .

Thomas Sutpen, the demon of this novel, has a childhood racked by the monstrous cruelties to which all Faulkner children are subjected. He has immeasurable will—like evil, will is always immeasurable in Faulkner. He forms a "design": to found a fortune and a family. In pursuit of it he marries the daughter of a Haitian planter, has a son by her, discovers that she has Negro blood, abandons her, and rouses in her a purpose of immeasurable revenge. He takes some Haitian slaves to Mississippi, clears a plantation, becomes rich, marries a gentlewoman, and begets Henry and Judith. At the University Henry meets his mulatto half-brother, Charles Bon, who has been sent there by his vengeful mother. . . . Henry worships Charles at sight and helps to effect his engagement to Judith. Thomas Sutpen inconceivably does nothing to prevent the engagement till, just before the Civil War, he tells Henry the secret of Bon's birth, though not (and here again the motive is what Mr. Faulkner would call unmotive) that of his Negro blood. Through four years of war Henry remains jubilant about the contemplated incest, but when his father at last reveals the secret he cannot accept incestuous miscegenation, and so shoots Bon when he goes to claim his bride. Henry then disappears and Thomas Sutpen, still demonic, comes back to rehabilitate both his estate and his posterity. . . . Sutpen begets a child on the fifteen-year old granddaughter of a poor-white retainer. The child is a daughter and so Sutpen's design is ruined forever. The grandfather kills him with a scythe, kills the granddaughter and the child with a butcher's knife, and rushes happily into the arms of the lynchers. The relicts then send for Charles Bon's son and raise him, a mulatto, with further tortures. He rebels, marries a coal-black wench, and begets a semi-idiot, the last of the Sutpens who gives a tragic twist to the title of the novel. The horror which Quentin Compson has to undergo occurs many years later, when Henry Sutpen has crept back to die in the ruined mansion. . . . (p. 3)

Mr. Faulkner, in fact, has done much of this before. This off-stage hammering on a coffin—Charles Bon's coffin this time—was used to make us liquefy with pity in *As I Lay Dying* where it was Addie Bundren's coffin. And when Addie's coffin, with the corpse inside, slid off the wagon into the flooded river, the effect then gained discounted the scene in *Absalom, Absalom!* where the mules bolt and throw Thomas Sutpen's corpse and coffin into the ditch. . . . When Charles Bon forces Henry Sutpen to shoot him, moved by some inscrutable inertia of pride and contempt and abnegation (or moved by unmotive)—he is repeating whatever immolation was in Popeye's mind when he refused to defend himself against the murder charge of which he was innocent, near the end of *Sanctuary*. These are incidental repetitions, but many fundamental parts of *Absalom, Absalom!* seem to come straight out of *Light in August*. It is not only that Etienne Bon undergoes in childhood cruelties as unceasing as those that made Joe Christmas the most persecuted child since Dickens, . . . and not only that the same gigantic injustices are bludgeoned on the same immeasurable stubbornness and stupidity in the same inexplicable succession. It is deeper than that and comes down to an identity of theme. That theme is hardly reducible to words, and certainly has not been reduced to words by Mr. Faulkner. It is beyond the boundary of explanation: some undimensional identity of fear and lust in which a man is both black and white, yet neither, loathing both, rushing to embrace both with some super-Tolstoian ecstasy of abasement, fulfillment, and expiation.

The drama of *Absalom, Absalom!* is clearly diabolism, a "miasmal distillant" of horror. . . . And it is embodied in the familiar hypochondria of Mr. Faulkner's prose, a supersaturated solution of pity and despair. In book after book now he has dropped tears like the famed Arabian tree, in a rapture of sensibility amounting to continuous orgasm. The medium in which his novels exist is lachrymal, and in *Absalom, Absalom!* that disconsolate fog reaches its greatest concentration to date. And its most tortured prose. Mr. Faulkner has always had many styles at his command, has been able to write expertly in many manners, but he has always been best at the phrase, and it is as a phrase-maker only that he writes well here. Many times he says the incidental thing perfectly, as "that quiet aptitude of a child for accepting the inexplicable." But, beyond the phrase, he now—deliberately—mires himself in such a quicksand of invertebrate sentences as has not been seen since *Euphues*. There have been contentions between Mr. Faulkner and Mr. Hemingway before this; it may be that he is matching himself against the Gertrude-Steinish explosions of syntax that spattered *Green Hills of Africa* with bad prose. If so, he comes home under wraps: the longest Hemingway sentence ran only forty-three lines, whereas the longest Faulkner sentence runs eighty lines and there are more than anyone will bother to count which exceed the thirty-three line measure of his page. They have the steady purpose of expressing the inexpressible that accounts for so much of Mr. Faulkner, but they show a style in process of disintegration. When a narrative sentence has to have as many as three parentheses identifying the reference of pronouns, it signifies mere bad writing and can be justified by no psychological or esthetic principle whatever.

It is time, however, to inquire just what Mr. Faulkner means by this novel, and by the whole physiography of the countryside which he locates on the map of Mississippi in the vicinity of a town called Jefferson. This community is said to be in the geographical and historical South, and the Sutpens, together with the Compsons and the Sartorises and the Benbows and the Poor Whites and the Negroes, are presented to us as human beings. Yet even the brief summary I have made above shows that if we are forced to judge them as human beings we can accept them only as farce. Just why did not Thomas Sutpen, recognizing Charles Bon as his mulatto son, order him off the plantation, or bribe or kill him, or tell Judith either half of the truth, or tell Henry all of it? In a single sentence toward the end of the book, Mr. Faulkner gives us an explanation, but it is as inadequate to explain the tornadoes that depend on it as if he had tried to explain the Civil War by the annual rainfall at New Granada. Not even that effort at explanation is made for most of the behavior in the book. Eulalia Bon's monotone of revenge is quite inconceivable, and her demonic lawyer is just one more of those figures of pure bale that began with Januarius Jones in *Soldiers' Pay* and have drifted through all the novels since exhaling evil and imitating the facial mannerisms of the basilisk. Miss Rosa (another Emily, without rose) is comprehensible neither as a woman nor as a maniac. Why do the children suffer so? Why did Emily's father treat her that way? Why did Sutpen treat Henry and Judith that way? Why did Judith and Clytie treat Etienne that way?. . . Just what momentary and sacrificial nobility moved Wash Jones to kill three people? Just what emotion, compulsion, obsession, or immediate clairvoyant pattern of impotence plus regeneration

plus pure evil may by invoked to explain the behavior of Charles Bon, for which neither experience nor the psychology of the unconscious nor any logic of the heart or mind can supply an explanation?

Well, it might answer everything to say that they are all crazy. As mere symptomatology, their behavior does vividly suggest schizophrenia, paranoia, and dementia precox. But that is too easy a verdict, it would have to be extended to all the population of Jefferson, the countryside, New Granada, and New Orleans, and besides the whole force of Mr. Faulkner's titanic effort is expended in assuring us that this is not insanity.

A scholarly examination might get us a little farther. This fiction of families destroyed by a mysterious curse . . . , of ruined castles in romantic landscapes, of Giaours and dark "unwill," may be only a continuation of the literature of excessive heartbreak. The Poe of "Ligeia" and kindred tales, Charles Brockden Brown, Horace Walpole, and Mrs. Radcliffe suggest a clue to a state of mind which, after accepting the theorem that sensation is desirable for itself alone, has moved on to the further theorem that the more violent sensation is the more admirable, noble, and appropriate to fiction. Surely this reek of hell and the passage to and fro of demons has intimate linkages with Eblis; . . . and yet that tells us very little.

Much more central is the thesis advanced in these columns a couple of years ago, that Mr. Faulkner is exploring the primitive violence of the unconscious mind. Nothing else can explain the continuity of rape, mutilation, castration, incest, patricide, lynching, and necrophilia in his novels, the blind drive of terror, the obsessional preoccupation with corpses and decay and generation and especially with the threat to generation. It is for the most part a deliberate exploration, Mr. Faulkner is at pains to give us Freudian clues, and he has mapped in detail the unconscious mind's domain of horrors. . . . (pp. 3-4, 14)

Haunted by the fear of impotence and mutilation and dismemberment, hell-ridden by compulsions to destroy the mind's own self and to perpetrate a primal, revengeful murder on the old, cataleptic in the helplessness of the terrified young, bringing the world to an end in a final fantasy of ritual murder and the burning house—the inhabitants of the prodigy-land of the unconscious are also fascinated by those other primal lusts and dreads, incest and miscegenation. In Joe Christmas and Etienne Bon, neither white nor black, repudiating both races, . . . we face a central preoccupation of Mr. Faulkner, a central theme of his fiction, and, I think, an obligation to go beyond the psycho-analytical study of his purposes. In spite of his enormous labor to elucidate these two mulattoes and their feelings and their symbolism in society, they are never elucidated. What is it that bubbles through those minds, what is it that drives them, what are they feeling, what are they trying to do, what do they mean? You cannot tell, for you do not know. A fair conclusion is that you do not know because Mr. Faulkner does not know. I suggest that on that fact hinges the explanation of his fiction.

It is a fact in religion. For the energy derived from primitive sources in the mind projects a structure of thought intended to be explanatory of the world, and this is religious, though religious in the familiar reversal that constitutes demonology and witchcraft. William James has told us how it comes about. The simple truth is that Mr. Faulkner is a mystic. He is trying to communicate to us an immediate experience of the ineffable. He cannot tell us because he does not know—because what he perceives cannot be known, cannot therefore be told, can never be put into words but can only be suggested in symbols, whose content and import must forever be in great part missed and in greater part misunderstood. This is a mysticism, furthermore, of what James called the lower path. There are, James said, two mystical paths, the one proceeding out of some beatitude of spiritual health which we may faintly glimpse in the visions of the saints. It is from the lower path, the decay of the vision, that witchcraft always proceeds. And witchcraft, like all magic, is a spurious substitute for fundamental knowledge.

The crux of the process by which witchcraft came to substitute for the ordinary concerns of fiction in Mr. Faulkner's work may be observed in *Sartoris*. . . . [With *Sartoris*], he became a serious novelist in the best sense of that adjective. He undertook to deal fairly with experience, to articulate his characters with a social organism, and to interpret the web of life in terms of human personality. Wherever he was factual and objective . . . , he imposed a conformable and convincing world of his own on a recognizable American experience, in symbols communicative to us all. But he failed in the principal effort of the novel. What he tried to do, with the Sartorises themselves, was to deliver up to us the heart of a mystery—to explain the damnation, the curse, of a brilliant, decayed, and vainglorious family doomed to failure and death. And he did not do it. They were a void. We did not know them and he could not tell us about them. They were without necessity, without causation. When he faced the simple but primary necessity of the novelist, to inform us about his characters, he backed away.

He has been backing away ever since. All the prestidigitation of his later technique rests on a tacit promise that this tortuous narrative method, this obsession with pathology, this parade of Grand Guignol tricks and sensations, will, if persevered with, bring us in the end to a deeper and a fuller truth about his people than we could get otherwise. And it never does. Those people remain wraiths blown at random through fog by winds of myth. The revelation remains just a series of horror stories that are essentially false—false because they happen to grotesques who have no psychology, no necessary motivation as what they have become out of what they were. They are also the targets of a fiercely rhetorical bombast diffused through the brilliant technique that promises us everything and gives us nothing, leaving them just wraiths. Meanwhile the talent for serious fiction shown in *Sartoris* and the rich comic intelligence grudgingly displayed from time to time, especially in *Sanctuary*, have been allowed to atrophy from disuse and have been covered deep by a tide of sensibility. (p. 14)

Bernard DeVoto, "Witchcraft in Mississippi," in The Saturday Review of Literature, *Vol. XV, No. 1, October 31, 1936, pp. 3-4, 14.*

HAROLD STRAUSS

Out of the tenebrous mind of William Faulkner there comes another strange tale of the people of Jefferson, that remote corner of Mississippi out of which Faulkner has carved his literary empire and which has produced such novels as *Sanctuary* and *Light in August*. *Absalom, Absalom!* is not strange, however, for its shocking theme, as was *Sanctuary*. Indeed, the underlying fable is no more than the tragic story of a man from nowhere who tried to establish himself as a Southern gentleman and plantation lord in the years before the Civil War, with but a touch of incest and miscegenation, modestly

and inoffensively added, to remind us of Faulkner's old preoccupation with the psychopathology of sex.

Nor is it strange for its time-stopping intensity and for its detailed and hypersensitive examination of the flow of mental images during moments of violent physical action—matters in which Faulkner is a recognized master. No, it is strange chiefly because of the amazing indirectness with which Faulkner has managed to tell a basically simple story. In fact, he does not tell the story of Thomas Sutpen—of his descent upon Jefferson in 1833 with his twenty wild Negroes and his eventual fate—at all; rather, he gets inside the mind of a young man by the name of Quentin Compson, who went to Harvard in 1910 and who by accident was impelled slowly to piece the old story together and who was permitted to witness its epilogue.

First one ancient of Jefferson who knew Thomas Sutpen and then another muse over particular aspects of the old and puzzling story in Quentin's presence. Not one of them knows the whole story. . . . It remains for Quentin, after he has witnessed the conflagration of the great manor house at Sutpen's Hundred in which Henry and Clytemnestra Sutpen died, to piece the story together with the help of his Harvard roommate, Shreve, and to examine the moral impulses behind the actions of the Sutpens. It is their shuttling back and forth over the motives, their toying with hypotheses and alternatives, that chiefly dooms the book to obscurity.

That, and the style. Faulkner has always written in an involved style, but his earlier writing shines with the clear light of eloquence against the obscurity of the intricate page-long sentences in *Absalom, Absalom!*—sentences that occasionally deal simultaneously with the doings of young Quentin in 1910 and of the Sutpens in 1860. The truth seems to be that Faulkner fears banality. Now that . . . he has abandoned his more shocking themes, he is compelled to distinguish himself from the generality of authors by employing one of the most complex, unreadable and uncommunicative prose styles ever to find its way into print. It represents an entirely new departure into complexity for Faulkner. He has been complex before, but never uncommunicative.

Occasionally there are passages of great power and beauty in this book, passages which remind us that Faulkner is still a writer with a unique gift of illuminating dark corners of the human soul. There are other passages which, while hardly communicative, drop into a pure blank verse and are estimable for their sheer verbal music. For the rest, *Absalom, Absalom!* must be left to those hardy souls who care for puzzles.

Harold Strauss, "Mr. Faulkner Is Ambushed in Words," in The New York Times Book Review, *November 1, 1936, p. 7.*

MALCOLM COWLEY

Among all the empty and witless tags attached to living American authors, perhaps the most misleading is that of Southern Realist as applied to William Faulkner. He writes about one section of the South—that much is true—and he writes in what often seems to be a mood of utter distaste. But critics have no excuse for confusing realism with revulsion, or rather with the mixture of violent love and violent hatred that Faulkner bears toward his native state. No, there is only one possible justification for classing him with the novelists who try to copy the South without distortion. It lies in the fact that he can and does write realistically when his daemon consents. He can and does give us the exact tone of Mississippi voices, the feel of a Mississippi landscape, the look of an old plantation house rotting among sedge-grown fields. On occasion he even gives us Mississippi humor . . . that is as broad and native as anything preserved from the days of the steamboat gamblers. But Faulkner's daemon does not often permit him to be broadly humorous or to echo the mild confusions of daily life. The daemon forces him to be always intense, to write in a wild lyrical style, to omit almost every detail that does not contribute to a single effect of somber violence and horror.

And this gives us a clue to Faulkner's real kinship. He belongs with the other writers who try to produce this single and somber effect—that is, with the "satanic" poets from Byron to Baudelaire, and with the "black" or "terrifying" novelists from Monk Lewis and the Hoffman of the *Tales* to Edgar Allan Poe. The daemon that haunts him is the ghost of the haunted castle—though it is also Poe's raven and Manfred's evil spirit. And the daemon is especially prominent in his new novel. Not only is *Absalom, Absalom!* in many ways the strongest, the most unified and characteristic of his twelve books, but it is also the most romantic, in the strict historical sense of the word.

Thomas Sutpen, in 1833, comes riding into a little Mississippi town with twenty coal-black Negroes straight from the jungle. He despises his new neighbors who in turn regard him as Satan in the flesh. He is the lonely Byronic hero with his mind coldly fixed on the achievement of one design. And the plantation house built with the help of his naked slaves—the great mansion literally hewn from the swamps—is the haunted castle that was described so often in early nineteenth-century romances. Like other haunted castles, Sutpen's Hundred is brooded over by a curse. Years ago in the West Indies, Thomas Sutpen had deserted his wife and his infant son after discovering that they had Negro blood. He now marries again; he has two children and a hundred square miles of virgin land; but in the midst of his triumph the curse begins to operate: the deserted son reappears and tries to marry his own half-sister. Here the note of incest suggests Byron, but elsewhere it is Poe whose spirit seems closest to the story—especially at the end, where Sutpen's Hundred collapses like the House of Usher. And indeed one might say that Faulkner is Poe in Mississippi—Poe modernized with technical and psychological devices imported from Joyce's Dublin and Freud's Vienna.

But this is a great deal different from saying with Granville Hicks that Faulkner is "in danger of becoming a Sax Rohmer for the sophisticated." It is different from saying that "he is not primarily interested in representative men and women; certainly he is not interested in the forces that have shaped them." Hicks's judgment seems to be based on the false theory that romantic authors are always trying to evade the life of their own times. The truth is that they know and can write about nothing else. The men and women they present in romantic disguises are their own selves, with their friends, mistresses and enemies. The issues they deal with are derived from their own lives and are frequently social as well as personal or pathological. And the general result is that romantic novels are likely to be written on two planes, with one subject below, in the foreground, and above it another subject that is half-revealed by conscious or unconscious symbolism.

In Faulkner's new book, the second or hidden subject is the decline of the South after the Civil War. Sutpen's Hundred, the mansion that rotted and finally burned, is obviously a symbol of Southern culture. Thomas Sutpen himself seems to represent the Southern ruling caste, though here the symbolism is

confused by the fact that he also represents the proud Byronic hero hated by his fellow men. But it is clear enough that Sutpen's curse is a result of his relations with Negroes, and that he is finally murdered by a poor white. . . .

Faulkner is not presenting this picture as the reasoned conclusion of an essay on the South. . . . He is not arguing anything whatever. He is giving us perceptions rather than ideas, and their value is not statistical but emotional. To the critic their importance lies in the fact that they explain a great deal not only about *Absalom, Absalom!* but also about Faulkner's earlier novels. His violence here and elsewhere is not a means of arousing pointless horror: it is an expression of a whole society which the author sincerely loves and hates and which he perceives to be in a state of catastrophic decay.

But Faulkner's new book falls considerably short of the powerful mood that it might have achieved. Possibly this is because he has failed to find a satisfactory relationship between the horror story in the foreground and the vaster theme that it conceals: the two subjects interfere with each other. But the partial failure of *Absalom, Absalom!* is chiefly explained by the style in which his daemon forced him to write it—a strained, involved, ecstatic style in which colloquialisms and deliberate grammatical errors are mingled with words too pretentious even for Henry James. Too often it seems that Faulkner, in the process of evoking an emotion in himself, has ignored the equally important task of evoking it in the reader.

Malcolm Cowley, "Poe in Mississippi," in The New Republic, *Vol. LXXXIX, No. 1144, November 4, 1936, p. 22.*

MARY M. COLUM

What makes for the marked superiority of the southern novel? For there is no doubt in my mind but that the young southern novelists are superior to the young northern novelists; that their best novels have a poetic quality, a depth of communication with life that we find all too rarely in the northern work. Before me is a novel, *A World I Never Made*, by a highly praised northern writer, James T. Farrell, and two southern novels, *The Tallons*, by William March, and *Absalom, Absalom!* by William Faulkner; and the quality of the southern novels is so far above *A World I Never Made* that they make it seem ordinary and commonplace. (p. 33)

How does the second southern novel, *Absalom, Absalom!* compare with *The Tallons*? Certain single passages have a dramatic beauty and tension beyond anything that March accomplishes in single passages. William Faulkner can do things with language, with the sound of words that March cannot do. He is making a struggle with form and with language; but his form in this novel seems to me to be too incoherent, and his long, trailing sentences are often difficult, if not exasperating, reading. He is too dazzled by wondrously involved sentences and wondrously involved sounds. Yet there are powerful scenes in the book, all done in the narrative manner in which there is no action and hardly any dialogue, all related by different people.

The cry of King David gives title to the novel. The David is Thomas Sutpen, who builds the house called Sutpen's Hundred. His son, Charles, by a part-negro Haitian wife, is killed by Henry, the son born to him by his second wife. Here there enters the ancient theme of the girl who wants to marry her own father's son. Thomas Sutpen's daughter, Judith, wants to marry his negroid Charles, and it is for this that Charles is killed by Henry, who had loved him as Jonathan was loved.

Thomas Sutpen is an enigmatic character, and before he comes to the town of Jefferson he has been a robber and a fighter like King David. (pp. 35-6)

We see grouped around him his band of wild niggers, like beasts half tamed to walk upright like men, in attitudes wild and reposed, and manacled among them the architect who was to build the vast house:

> Immobile, bearded and hand palm-uplifted the horseman sat; behind him the wild blacks and the captive architect huddled quietly, carrying in bloodless paradox the shovels and picks and axes of peaceful conquest.

This sort of writing is the precise opposite of Farrell's, though the word *exaggeration* might be applied to both. Farrell's exaggeration is always toward farcical comedy and toward making what is individual generalized, while Faulkner's exaggeration is toward a mystical and mysterious tragedy and toward making what is individual unique to the point of being demoniacal. Farrell's revolutionary novels are really very soothing, because they give us the sense that men and women are tamed creatures who can eventually be made satisfied with bread and circuses and with easy sensual gratifications. Faulkner's novels are very disturbing, because they give us the sense that human beings will never be satisfied with anything that society can give them, that they are so tortuous, so mutually destructive, and so self-destructive that there is no possibility of any social change making very much difference in human existence.

Yet, while this book of Faulkner's show a powerful talent, it is an unsuccessful novel. We regret that this should be the net result of all that power for creating situation and atmosphere and producing sentences of deep import and beauty. His people all have the same kind of tension; they all feel the same terror; all the narrators in the story relate their tales in the same manner, with the same kind of words. Yet it is giving great praise to **Absalom, Absalom!** to say that it actually brings *Wuthering Heights* to our minds.

William Faulkner is struggling with a difficult technique, and one cannot help believing that, if he had the opportunity (as writers in other countries naturally have) of threshing out his technical ideas around a café table, his accomplishment would not be so incoherent as it is. Obviously he has studied Joyce and Proust, as well as *Wuthering Heights* and *The Fall of the House of Usher;* but Joyce knew George Moore, and George Moore knew Dujardin—who invented the interior monologue—and he knew Zola and Turgenev; and, as for the artists Proust talked with and studied, the list is too long to write down.

Could we sum up in a few lines what is in these southern writers that is absent from the bulk of the northern novels? There is a complexity of interior life; there is a sense of tragedy; there is a sense of the relation of life to the soil, to the earth and the people around. The authors have an inherited culture, a culture and emotions that come out of leisure, as a Mexican or Italian peasant has a culture that comes out of leisure and as the busy president of a great university might not have. The fire in their emotions does not all come from the body or the brain but from the spirit and the spirit's longing for some meaning to life. They have not the simple illusions of the northern industrial city novelists, that all life's frustrations can

be settled the minute capitalism is liquidated and the "bourgeois ideology" banished from life and that the incompleteness of human destiny can be made complete by some economic arrangements. (p. 36)

> *Mary M. Colum, "Life and Literature: Fiction and Fact," in* Forum and Century, *Vol. XCVII, No. 1, January, 1937, pp. 33-8.*

THE TIMES LITERARY SUPPLEMENT

It would not be fair to assess Mr. Faulkner's new novel [**Absalom, Absalom!**] by the standards of what may be termed library fiction. Every book, and the novel more than some kinds, represents a compromise between author and reader. Unoriginality hides itself in lifeless conventionalisms, overoriginality in impenetrable esotericisms; balanced originality walks the middle of the road, speaking to both present and future.

Mr. Faulkner makes almost no concessions. He presents his work in his own way, and those who do not like it must—and will—leave it. It is undeniably something very odd and very special he desires to communicate—a sense of life as frustration, as decay, as evil, the sins of the fathers forever compelling the children to new transgressions—and to that end he devises, as in earlier works, not only a story of unusual brutality and horror but a narrative-method as involved and allusive as anyone this side of surrealism has proposed. He does in fact less narrate than adumbrate his tale, depicting events invariably not direct but as refracted through two or three or even more minds, and in an extraordinary labyrinthine prose, cadenced, involved, its often page-long sentences demanding to be taken at their own slow, drugging pace. . . . The dream-quality is persistent. Shapes and shadows and actions are evoked, thrust tantalizingly forward, drawn back, fogged over with mists of restless, surging, indeterminate words before they can be grasped, and then again produced, niggled at, clarified inch by inch, till something like the full truth is, if scarcely stated, able to be guessed at.

To give the bare outline of the story is, in these circumstances, possibly to misrepresent the book; but for those who would wish to know . . . it may be stated as embodying the history of the Sutpen family, and centrally of Thomas Sutpen, who came in 1828 to that tragic township of Jefferson, Mississippi, an appended sketch-map of which formally declares Mr. Faulkner its "sole owner and proprietor." Sutpen is, at his first appearance in Jefferson, already a sombre, bitter, demonic figure of vaulting ambition, and it soon becomes apparent that his actions have had (for all is told in very remote retrospect) the most dreadful results, but not for many pages does one learn of the origin in his earlier youth of his inexorable impulsion, and of the innocent error thereafter dogging him and all the heirs of his body over nearly a century to their doom. The details of that doom are too involved to suggest even in outline, and it is more important to ask who Sutpen is, what he stands for in his creator's mind, that he should warrant this elaborate and essentially aggrandizing presentation. Is he, the last pages force one to question, the very figure of the Old South itself, seeking to establish and bequeath a noble civilization, but from the first bearing in itself, and especially in its involved relation to the negro slave, the seed of its inevitable downfall; passed now for ever, and rightly passed, yet centering still the love and hate of its children upon those yesterdays, upon "a kind of vacuum filled with wraithlike and indomitable anger and pride and glory at and in happenings that occurred and ceased fifty years ago''?

The book has almost everything against it—a tiring prose, an exasperating method, a distasteful subject-matter dubiously attaining the dignity of the tragedy it hints at. Yet the author's very passion, that conflicting love and hate finding no rest or resting-place, gives to its pages indubitable vitality; it lives as unquestionably, and if too often as awkwardly then sometimes also as beautifully, as others of Nature's more eccentric creations.

> *"Doom in Mississippi," in* The Times Literary Supplement, *No. 1829, February 20, 1937, p. 128.*

GRAHAM GREENE

Mr. Faulkner's reputation has suffered lately from the exaggerated claims his admirers made for him on the strength of the rather obvious technical experiments in his early novels, **Soldiers' Pay** and **The Sound and the Fury.** He isn't another Joyce, any more than he is another Stein, that bogey of the Sunday reviewer. Indeed in his historical novels he is rapidly matriculating into the Book Society. Horsemen riding at night, the clank of holsters, niggers shrieking in the dark, Southern gentlewomen and the scent of wistaria, family Honour and family Doom: his historical novels are full of quite charming, traditional, bogus romance.... (p. 517)

Let the devil's advocate have his way for awhile, explain how Mr. Faulkner's new novel [**Absalom, Absalom!**] belongs to the worst, the **Sartoris,** side of his achievement: the deep South and the picturesque Civil War costumes, the doom-ridden hero, "this Faustus, this demon, this Beelzebub," riding in..., hiring a French architect, working naked on the house with his niggers, marrying the most respectable girl in the town, overtaken by his Fate, his son murdering his daughter's betrothed to save her from incest and the taint of black blood, all culminating years later, in 1910, in a huge conflagration and the last survivor's death in the flames. That advocate will point out that the method of the novel, the story related by various people years later, the events falling into their order in the mind only on the last pages, has been far more skilfully managed by Mr. Ford who knows how to give intrinsic value and character to the narrators—all Mr. Faulkner's narrators speak the same bastard poetic prose. And as for this prose the advocate will remark how often it falls into blank verse rhythms, how fond the author is of resounding abstractions.... (In the first paragraphs of the novel—a devil's advocate is always a bit of a pedant—there are forty-one adjectives in twenty-seven lines qualifying only fifteen nouns.) And the advocate will wind up his speech with the claim that Mr. Faulkner has not created a single character of recognizable humanity and that the intellectual content of his novel is almost nil. Strip away the fake poetry, and you have the plot of a "blood," while Mr. Faulkner disguises the complete absence of a theme with pseudo-tragic talk of doom and fate and the furies.

Alas! it is all true. Mr. Faulkner's is a talent quite easy to condemn, but there does remain over—Something: at the least a gift of vivid phrase heard too seldom through the Otranto thunder ("the ghost mused with shadowy docility as if it were the voice which he haunted where a more fortunate one would have had a house")...; at its best—not to be found here or in **Sartoris**—an individual blend of the romantic and the realistic which makes the gangster Pop-Eye in **Sanctuary** so memorable a figure, a sense of spiritual evil which away from the contemporary scene becomes unconvincing and stagey. And finally we should consider whether, if the romantic costume subject is to be treated at all (if Southern gentlefolk, horsemen at night and wistaria blossom, which do speak in certain moods like common songs to the imagination, deserve an occasional appearance), it can be treated in any other way. It can't be treated plainly, like Pop-Eye's rape on the cornhusks of the college girl, or the crazy antique planes in **Pylon:** the artificial subject has to be carried by an artificial manner, and even at its vaguest and most resounding Mr. Faulkner's style is welcome when we consider the alternatives: Anthony Adverse and Gone With the Wind. (pp. 517-18)

> Graham Greene, "The Furies in Mississippi," in The London Mercury, Vol. XXXV, No. 209, March, 1937, pp. 517-18.

OSCAR CARGILL

In **Absalom, Absalom!** (1936) Faulkner gives a Southern recipe for avoiding incest, which is to set one of your sons to shoot his half-brother when the latter becomes engaged to his sister. For the man who has read all of Faulkner, or who reads this book in connection with **The Sound and the Fury, Absalom, Absalom!** has a dramatic import that is no part of the story itself, for the events of the narrative are strained through the consciousness of Quentin Compson, a Harvard student in 1910, who, shortly after this, is to commit suicide because he, too, has been involved in incest with his sister. Quentin receives the story through Rosa Coldfield, one of the actors, picks up details from his father and grandfather, witnesses one final episode, and pieces together the rest in a five-hour discussion with his roommate. His own connection with the story at so critical a juncture in his life is highly improbable and has the effect of weakening both novels. That is, the suicide of Quentin in **The Sound and the Fury** was explicable enough; but now with this added commentary seems extraordinarily dubious. Possessor of this staggering tale and of the guilty knowledge of his own crime, Quentin more probably would have laughed both off as a man who has taken an overdose throws off poison. Some lack of artistic sensibility has permitted Faulkner to attach the monstrous cancerous growth of **Absalom, Absalom!** on to his most artistic novel. The relation of the two novels is better forgotten.

Absalom, Absalom! by itself is the story of Thomas Sutpen, poor mountain white, who conceives the idea of founding a family. He unfortunately forms a union with the daughter of a Haitian sugar grower, whose tainted blood is kept a secret from him. When he buys her off and starts again in Mississippi in 1833, she follows, watches, plans revenge. The engagement of her son to Sutpen's daughter by his second wife precipitates an involved series of tragedies, rehearsed and re-rehearsed from every possible angle. The tedium of the telling in this tale is the greatest in all of Faulkner's books. Further, there is no relief of any sort from the snarled twine of his sentences—no humor, no pathos, no dialogue; the knots of Quentin's "ratiocinations" (Faulkner's word) simply have to be picked one after another. It is a dull book, dull, dull, dull. The one moment in it is in the last paragraph when honest Shreve asks Quentin (as one might ask Faulkner), "Why do you hate the South?" and he reiterates, "I don't. I don't! I don't hate it. I don't hate it!" (pp. 380-81)

> Oscar Cargill, "The Primitivists," in his Intellectual America: Ideas on the March, The Macmillan Company, 1941, pp. 311-98.

MAXWELL GEISMAR

[In his review of *Absalom, Absalom!* (see excerpt above)] Mr. Fadiman has understood both the plot and technic of the novel, which is no simple feat. The publishers of *Absalom* themselves, after confessing their belief that it is Faulkner's major work—'his most important and ambitious contribution to American literature'—talk, on the jacket of the novel, about 'demonic Stephen Sutpen' when they obviously mean Thomas Sutpen. The Faulknerian genealogy of *Absalom* is complex enough without the publishers adding their own characters. And in one sense *Absalom* deserves Mr. Fadiman's rebuke. It is certainly the most pretentious of Faulkner's works, which all have their degree of pretense. It is the most self-conscious, technically the most elaborate product of this rather self-conscious technical virtuoso. There seems to be a Henry Jamesian influence at work here too in the polished writing, the involved patterns of behavior which circle around an enigmatic horror story. *Absalom* is in this respect a kind of Mississippian *Turn of the Screw*, and like the later Henry James, sometimes its effect of mystery seems a little strained; it pants intricately with suspense; it becomes a gothic novel of the emotions. Yet once *Absalom* has been subjected to this deflationary process, and the air let out of it, the novel does get the 'interesting effect' which Mr. Fadiman allows it, and its remarkable prose is not always so irrelevant. Once we have worked through the pretensions of *Absalom* the story holds us, at times moves us, and certainly provides the last missing pieces in the pattern of Faulknerian discontent. *Absalom* is indeed a mystery story we must solve, and the mystery is that of the author as well as his work. (pp. 171-72)

[In *Absalom, Absalom!*, it] is the Negro who is the fundamental source of Thomas Sutpen's destruction, and with Sutpen his southern dynasty, and with this the whole framework, for which it stands in the novel, of Southern culture before the Civil War. It is, in fact, the 'monkey nigger,' barring the door of the great southern estate, who starts the poverty-stricken and ignorant young Sutpen off on his monomaniacal vision of himself building such an estate and founding a dynasty to inherit it—the vision to which all else was sacrificed during Sutpen's life, but which as it was induced by the negro was thwarted by him: the monkey nigger barring the door at the end of Sutpen's mad and indomitable life, as at the start. For the woman whom Sutpen marries in Haiti, Eulalia Bon, proves to have negro blood in her. In a curious pattern, partly accidental, part design, seeking his revenge on the father who has disowned him, but also the father's recognition and love, Eulalia's son, Charles Bon, meets young Henry Sutpen in college. Through his own volition Bon corrupts Henry; against his volition he becomes Henry's close friend, almost lover; meets Henry's sister Judith; and the tragedy opens which will destroy the Sutpen line. So here Faulkner has joined his twin Furies. It is Eulalia Bon, both the female and the negro, who is at the root of the disaster, the original cause of that 'dread and fear of females which you must have drawn in with the primary mammalian milk.' In many passages of *Absalom* Faulkner makes quite implicit the evil which proceeds from the 'female principle which existed, queenly and complete, in the hot equatorial groin of the world long before that white one of ours came down from trees and lost its hair and bleached out. . . .' But if the Faulknerian complex of the Female and the Negro has been fused in *Absalom*, is the prime movement of the novel, there is here a sort of elevation to the action, in contrast to the pollution which marks *Light in August*. Charles Bon himself, the active instrument of the drama, if he is biologically akin to [the character of Joe Christmas in *Light In August*], both of them apparently white with the hidden negro blood, is temperamentally very different. Where Christmas is the brutish and criminal negro principle, Bon is complex, civilized, and tragic. And as we read *Absalom* we realize that not only Bon, but all the central figures in the novel have a human stature which has been missing in Faulkner's work since *The Sound and the Fury*. This comparison arrests us in *Absalom*, puzzles us—until we realize also that these figures are closely related to those of *The Sound and the Fury*. The Quentin who tells the story here is the same Quentin Compson, the Sutpens are part of the same lineage as the Compsons and the Sartoris family, and, in short, Faulkner is once again dealing with the aristocratic South of the Civil War. And returning to the old South, endowing *Absalom* with the mark of genuine tragedy which has been lacking in his writing for seven years, Faulkner has dropped off the bitterness, the stale perversions which characterize his portraits of the new South. He has once again caught, on this odd sabbath, the sense of human grandeur, where for a long and harsh aesthetic tilling he has been able only to feel that of human bondage.

It is worth noticing how closely the pattern fits. If the negro Charles Bon of *Absalom* is the curse again of the white Sutpen dynasty, Bon is nevertheless the product of the old South, as compared to Joe Christmas, the 'emancipated' new negro, who must be punished with all the devices of Faulkner's hatred. And now we see also the cause for all the indignities which Faulkner heaps upon the Miss Burden of *Light in August*, this respectable, decent, well-meaning abolitionist spinster. Miss Burden is respectable. She is decent and well-meaning. But she is also the abolitionist spinster who is attempting to raise the freed negro, the pair seeming to symbolize for Faulkner all the evils which have befallen his land. And what better expression of his scorn can the southern writer produce than to have the sterile female accept the emancipated negro as her sexual partner, to have her humiliated by the negro, and to have her murdered by the negro. We see now, if Faulkner is the misogynist (we shall come to the root of this a little later), it is the modern woman, and particularly the 'northern' woman who is the special object of his venom. Thus the Miss Coldfield of *Absalom* differs radically in her fate, though it is not either a very pleasant one, from Miss Burden—both spinsters, equally frigid and neurotic, and equally deserving, one should think, of Faulkner's sympathy or aversion. But the southern lady in her historical setting retains at least her dignity, while the northern woman retains nothing, not even her life. Judith Sutpen in *Absalom*, if she is hardly very compelling as a person, being much more the vehicle through whom the affection of Henry and Charles Bon is being consummated, nevertheless has a 'serene, tranquil repose' befitting the southern belle. Judith reminds us of the Narcissa of *Sartoris* who had equal poise, if as little charm, so long as Faulkner described her within the aristocratic tradition. But transposing Narcissa to the new South of *Sanctuary*, he turns this musing madonna (Faulkner's single type of 'good' woman, and usually a madonna of somewhat imperfect mentality) into the malignant shrew. We recall now the significance of *Sanctuary* itself beyond its commercialism. Presenting us with the first flow of Faulkner's modern discontent, the new stage of Memphis society on which strut only pimps and prostitutes, it also portrays the losing struggle of the aristocratic Horace Benbow, the old-fashioned liberal statesman, against the new southern corrupt politicians. We see more clearly now why, holding as it does all the elements of tragedy, *As I Lay Dying* was not after all tragic, since the poor-white Bundrens were not capable of receiving tragedy. The pattern fits, so perfectly, so mechanically, so rather inartistically for a major artist dealing with the complexities and not the simplifications of life, that we may feel it to be an almost unconscious expression of Faulkner's feelings—as if the writer were in the power of these deep prejudices rather than their master.

And the Thomas Sutpen of *Absalom,* ragged, ignorant, poor boy whom Faulkner paints, is he not very comparable in his origins to these same Bundrens? Or his rise to state not without equivalents to the modern Snopeses whom Faulkner castigates [in *The Hamlet*]? Violent, rapacious, marked by the same lust for power, Thomas builds his Sutpen's Hundred out of the virgin forest by tricking his friends and intimidating his enemies, Sutpen who is after all the type of Robber Baron of the old South, as Snopes is of the new. But against the lecherous idiocy of the new southern mercantile rulers, what dignity does Faulkner invest his Sutpen with! What iron will (lost to the modern epoch) working out its tragic rôle, and thwarted, gaining the grandeur of a defeat which for Faulkner seems attributable only to the past, belonging only to that bygone 'high (and impossible) destiny of the United States.' A destiny high only to these Sutpens, Sartorises, and Compsons of Faulkner's ancient mythology; impossible for their heirs. For indeed they have no heirs. Closing, the chronicle of *Absalom* holds this message also. We see the new age implicit in the country store which Thomas Sutpen now runs, returned home, broken by the 'bloody aberration' of the Civil War; we see this 'ancient varicose and despairing Faustus' fling his final main now—

> . . . with the Creditor's hand already on his shoulder, running his little country store now for his bread and meat, haggling tediously over nickels and dimes with rapacious and poverty-stricken whites and negroes . . . , using out of his meagre stock the cheap ribbons and beads and the stale violently-colored candy with which even an old man can seduce a fifteen-year-old country girl. . . .

With this country store, of course, we are back in the land of the Bundrens, a country girl, a human life, worth only cheap ribbons and beads. How Faulkner's imagery itself conveys his moral, the despairing Faustus and the stale candy! But this last desperate effort of Sutpen's to gain a son and carry on his line is blocked also. [Milly Jones, the] woman of the post-Civil War South, bears Sutpen no male. And the aristocrat himself is killed by the girl's grandfather, Wash Jones, gangling, malaria-stricken, imbecilic poor-white Jones who is now to inherit the southern earth. (pp. 172-76)

[In his recent novel *The Hamlet*], Faulkner seems now to accept the antics of his provincial morons, to enjoy the chronicle of their low-grade behavior; he submerges himself in their clownish degradation. And in one sense why should he not? If the Snopeses are all the writer can discover in the modern world, the descendants of the gangling and giggling Wash Jones, if they now tread omnipotently the southern acres where Sutpen had his vision of dynasty, they are after all the victims and not the victors, they are the blind vessels of the final wrath. For in the Faulknerian mythology, the Wash Jones of *Absalom, Absalom!* will himself be superseded by another sort of Sutpen, the illegitimate Sutpen from the colored branch, the Jim Bond of the novel, the final type of brutish negro idiot:

> I think that in time the Jim Bonds are going to conquer the western hemisphere. Of course it won't quite be in our time and of course as they spread toward the poles they will bleach out again like the rabbits and the birds do, so they won't show up so sharp against the snow. But it will still be Jim Bond; and so in a

few thousand years, I who regard you will also have sprung from the loins of African kings.

(pp. 178-79)

So we see, just as Faulkner was punishing the northern woman in *Light in August,* now he threatens the entire western hemisphere with the rape of the Negro. And what better images, after all, could the artist have found to express his discontent—this great hatred of the entire complex of modern northern industrial society—than the Negro and the Female? The emancipated negro who to the southern writer is the cause of the destruction of all he held dear. And now showing this negro as Joe Christmas, as Jim Bond, as the inhuman criminal, the degenerate who will dominate the civilization which freed him, Faulkner proclaims at once his anger and his revenge upon those who have destroyed his home. What more appropriate symbol than the woman, who to the southern writer is the particular treasured image of the bygone, cavalier society he is lamenting and lost in: the southern Lady, elevated and sacrosanct, the central figure of the southern age of chivalry. . . . How shall the artist better show the universal debasement of modern times than to turn the pure Lady into the contemporary Female, now wanton, graceless, and degraded? . . . How shall the artist more aptly convey his total protest than to portray the Female source of life as itself inherently vicious? And as the last step in his sequence of discontent, Faulkner mates the Female with the Negro, the savage as Faulkner feels for whom the southern Lady was sacrificed, and spawns out of his modern union the colored degenerate who is to reign supreme, the moronic emperor of the future.(pp. 179-80)

What a strange inversion it is to take the Female and the Negro, who are if anything the tragic consequence, and to exhibit them, indeed to believe them as the evil cause! This turning of the logical coin is psychological prestidigitation which ends with the head becoming the tail, and all respectable sense lost! The using of the one object that is certainly not responsible for our woes as being the single creator of them (so the Fascists use the Jew)—this is an inversion all too familiar to us today in other areas, another symptom of the confused emotions of our time. What genuine ills can be ignored by this again infantile preoccupation with scapegoats (so the child blames its mother), the infatuation with chimeras, what terrible ills can be created by it. . . . I have [elsewhere] used the title of Maurice Samuel's penetrating study of the Fascist superstitions, *The Great Hatred,* to best describe Faulkner's work as a whole. For it is in the larger tradition of reversionism, neo-pagan, and neurotic discontent (from which Fascism stems) that much of Faulkner's writing must be placed—the anti-civilizational revolt which has caught so many modern mystics, the revolt rising out of modern social evils, nourished by ignorance of their true nature, and which succumbs to malice as their solution. It is not accidental that in Faulkner's novels we have watched the retrogression from the affecting era of infancy to that of infantile corruption; and that returning in *Absalom, Absalom!* to the only society he can believe in, Faulkner's affection is nevertheless thinner, and the pretension of his novel greater. Hatred, as we know, feeds upon itself, while living in the past is apt to be an attenuating process.

Yet these are dangers dormant in parts of the Faulknerian reversion rather than immediate. It would be a tragedy if the major talent of Faulkner were to yield to any such gross chicanery, or to any other smaller trickeries. But it would be unjust to claim that on the whole, really, it has. . . . If we notice the dangerous possibilities of Faulkner's position, moreover, we must remember it is still the southern world of the nineteen-twenties that the novelist rejects. It is the earlier impact of the American industrial ethics he denies. . . . In the repudiation of our society from 1860 to 1929, Faulkner thus presents another aspect of the total cultural rejection of the American artist over this epoch. Alone among the major writers of the twenties Faulkner has remained without change, our unreconstructed rebel, like the Hightower of *Light in August* still bemused in the vision of a nobler southern past where his life began and ended. Yet to Faulkner . . . , viewing the modern scene, what may have seemed like perpetuity was after all only an American adolescence. The new age, as it reached the Michigan woods of Hemingway and the metropolis of Dos Passos, may yet rout the phantoms and ghouls of Faulkner's Jefferson. . . . A developing American maturity, this maturity that Faulkner despairs of, must at last penetrate even to Jefferson, even to the Snopeses; and may awaken in our artist that magnificent compassion which he has vouchsafed only to the children of a disintegrating aristocracy. (pp. 181-83)

> *Maxwell Geismar, "William Faulkner: The Negro and the Female," in his* Writers in Crisis: The American Novel Between Two Wars, *Houghton Mifflin Company, 1942, pp. 141-83.*

MALCOLM COWLEY

William Faulkner is one of the writers who reward and even in a sense demand a second reading. When you return to one of his books years after its publication, the passages that had puzzled you are easier to understand and each of them takes its proper place in the picture. Moreover, you lose very little by knowing the plot in advance. Faulkner's stories are not the sort that unwind in celluloid ribbons until the last inch of them has been reflected on a flat screen, with nothing to imagine and nothing more to see except the newsreel, the animated cartoon and the Coming Repulsions; instead his books are sculptural, as if you could walk round them for different views of the same solid object. But it is not merely a statue that he presents: rather it is a whole monument or, let us say, a city buried in the jungle, to which the author wishes to guide us, but not at once or by following a single path. . . . Reading the same book a second time is like soaring over the jungle in a plane, with every section of the landscape falling into its proper perspective.

And there is another respect in which our judgment of the author changes when we return to not one but several of his novels in succession. On a first reading what had chiefly impressed us may have been their violence, which sometimes seemed to have no justification in art or nature. . . . After a second reading, most of these nightmares retain their power to shock, but at the same time they merge a little into the background, as if they were the almost natural product of the long unbearable Mississippi summers; as if they were thunder showers brewed in the windless heat. We pay less attention to the horrors as such, and more to the old situation out of which they developed and the new disasters it seems to foreshadow.

The situation itself, and not the violence to which it leads, is Faulkner's real subject. It is, moreover, the same situation in all his books—or, let us say, in all the novels and stories belonging to his Yoknapatawpha County series. Briefly it is the destruction of the old Southern order, by war and military occupation and still more by finance capitalism that tempts and destroys it from within. "Tell about the South," says Quentin Compson's roommate at Harvard [in *Absalom, Absalom!*], who

comes from Edmonton, Alberta, and is curious about the unknown region beyond the Ohio. . . . And Quentin, whose background is a little like that of the author and who often seems to speak for him—Quentin answers, "You can't understand it. You would have to be born there." Nevertheless, he tells a long and violent story that he regards as the essence of the Deep South, which is not so much a region as it is, in Quentin's mind, an incomplete and frustrated nation trying to recover its own identity, trying to relive its legendary past.

There was a boy, Quentin says—I am giving the plot of *Absalom, Absalom!*—a mountain boy named Thomas Sutpen whose family drifted into the Virginia Tidewater. There his father found odd jobs on a plantation. One day the father sent him with a message to the big house, but he was turned away at the door by a black man in livery. The mountain boy, puzzled and humiliated, was seized upon by the ambition to which he would afterwards refer as "the design." (pp. 343-45)

A dozen years later, Sutpen appeared in the frontier town of Jefferson, Mississippi, and, by some transaction the nature of which is never explained—though it certainly wasn't by honest purchase—he obtained a hundred square miles of land from the Chickasaws. He disappeared again, and this time he returned with twenty wild Negroes from the jungle and a French architect. On the day of his reappearance, he set about building the largest house in northern Mississippi, with timbers from the forest and bricks that his Negroes molded and baked on the spot; it was as if his mansion, Sutpen's Hundred, had been literally torn from the soil. Only one man in Jefferson—he was Quentin's grandfather, General Compson—ever learned how and where Sutpen had acquired his slaves. He had shipped to Haiti from Virginia, worked as an overseer on a sugar plantation and married the rich planter's daughter, who had borne him a son. Then finding that his wife had Negro blood, he had simply put her away, with her child and her fortune, while keeping the twenty slaves as a sort of indemnity. He explained to General Compson in the stilted speech he had taught himself that she could not be "adjunctive to the forwarding of the design." (p. 345)

Sutpen married again, Quentin continues. This time his wife belonged to a pious family of the neighborhood, and she bore him two children, Henry and Judith. He became the biggest landowner and cotton planter in the county, and it seemed that his "design" had already been fulfilled. At this moment, however—it was Christmas in 1859—Henry came home from the University of Mississippi with an older and worldlier new friend, Charles Bon, who was in reality Sutpen's son by his first marriage. Charles became engaged to Judith. Sutpen learned his identity and, without making a sign of recognition, ordered him to leave the house. Henry, who refused to believe that Charles was his half-brother, renounced his birthright and followed him to New Orleans. In 1861 all the male Sutpens went off to war, and all of them survived four years of fighting. Then, in the spring of 1865, Charles suddenly decided to marry Judith, even though he was certain by now that she was his half-sister. Henry rode beside him all the way back to Sutpen's Hundred, but tried to stop him at the gate, killed him when he insisted on going ahead with his plan, told Judith what he had done, and disappeared. (p. 346)

But Quentin's story of the Deep South does not end with the war. Colonel Sutpen came home, he says, to find his wife dead, his son a fugitive, his slaves dispersed (they had run away even before they were freed by the Union army) and most of his land about to be seized for debt. But still determined to carry out "the design," he did not even pause for breath before undertaking to restore his house and plantation as nearly as possible to what they had been. The effort failed; he lost most of his land and was reduced to keeping a crossroads store. Now in his sixties, he tried again to beget a son; but his wife's younger sister, Miss Rosa Coldfield, was outraged by his proposal ("Let's try it," he said, "and if it's a boy we'll get married."); and later poor Milly Jones, with whom he had an affair, gave birth to a baby girl. At that Sutpen abandoned hope and provoked Milly's grandfather into killing him. Judith survived her father for a time, as did the half-caste son of Charles Bon by a New Orleans octoroon. After the death of these two by yellow fever, the great house was haunted rather than inhabited by an ancient mulatto woman, Sutpen's daughter by one of his slaves. The fugitive Henry Sutpen came home to die; the townspeople heard of his illness and sent an ambulance after him; but old Clytie thought they were arresting him for murder and set fire to Sutpen's Hundred. The only survivor of the conflagration was Jim Bond, a half-witted, saddle-colored creature who was Charles Bon's grandson. (pp. 346-47)

The reader cannot help wondering why this sombre and, at moments, plainly incredible story had so seized upon Quentin's mind that he trembled with excitement when telling it and felt that it revealed the essence of the Deep South. It seems to belong in the realm of Gothic romances, with Sutpen's Hundred taking the place of the haunted castle on the Rhine, with Colonel Sutpen as Faust and Charles Bon as Manfred. Then slowly it dawns on you that most of the characters and incidents have a double meaning; that besides their place in the story, they also serve as symbols or metaphors with a general application. Sutpen's great design, the land he stole from the Indians, the French architect who built his house with the help of wild Negroes from the jungle, the woman of mixed blood whom he married and disowned, the unacknowledged son who ruined him, the poor white whom he wronged and who killed him in anger, the final destruction of the mansion like the downfall of a social order: all these might belong to a tragic fable of Southern history. With a little cleverness, the whole novel might be explained as a connected and logical allegory, but this, I think, would be going beyond the author's intention. First of all he was writing a story, and one that affected him deeply, but he was also brooding over a social situation. More or less unconsciously, the incidents in the story came to represent the forces and elements in the social situation, since the mind naturally works in terms of symbols and parallels. In Faulkner's case, this form of parallelism is not confined to *Absalom, Absalom!* It can be found in the whole fictional framework that he has been elaborating in novel after novel, until his work has become a myth or legend of the South.

I call it a legend because it is obviously no more intended as a historical account of the country south of the Ohio than *The Scarlet Letter* is intended as a history of Massachusetts or *Paradise Lost* as a factual description of the Fall. Briefly stated, the legend might run something like this: The Deep South was settled partly by aristocrats like the Sartoris clan and partly by new men like Colonel Sutpen. Both types of planters were determined to establish a lasting social order on the land they had seized from the Indians (that is, to leave sons behind them). They had the virtue of living single-mindedly by a fixed code; but there was also an inherent guilt in their "design," their way of life, that put a curse on the land and brought about the Civil War. After the War was lost, partly as a result of their own mad heroism . . . , they tried to restore "the design" by other methods. But they no longer had the strength to achieve

more than a partial success, even after they had freed their land from the carpetbaggers who followed the Northern armies. As time passed, moreover, the men of the old order found that they had Southern enemies too: they had to fight against a new exploiting class descended from the landless whites of slavery days. In this struggle between the clan of Sartoris and the unscrupulous tribe of Snopes, the Sartorises were defeated in advance by a traditional code that prevented them from using the weapons of the enemy. But the Snopeses as price of their victory had to serve the mechanized civilization of the North, which was morally impotent in itself, but which, with the aid of its Southern retainers, ended by corrupting the Southern nation. In our own day, the problems of the South are still unsolved, the racial conflict is becoming more acute; and Faulkner's characters in their despairing moments foresee or forebode some catastrophe of which Jim Bond and his like will be the only survivors. (pp. 348-49)

Faulkner presents the virtues of the old order as being moral rather than material. There is no baronial pomp in his novels; no profusion of silk and silver, mahogany and moonlight and champagne. . . . All the planters lived comfortably, with plenty of servants, but Faulkner never lets us forget that they were living on what had recently been the frontier. What he admires about them is not their wealth or their manners or their fine houses, but rather their unquestioning acceptance of a moral code that taught them "courage and honor and pride, and pity and love of justice and of liberty." (pp. 349-50)

The old order was a moral order: briefly that was its strength and the secret lost by its heirs. I don't wish to give the impression that Faulkner is the only Southern writer to advance this principle. . . . The fact is that most of the ideas embodied in Faulkner's legend are held in common by many Southern writers of the new generation; what Faulkner has done is to express them in a whole series of novels written with his own emotional intensity and technical resourcefulness. But his version of the legend also has features that set it apart: most notably its emphasis on the idea that the Southern nation (like most of his own fictional heroes) was defeated from within.

In Faulkner's reading, the old order not only had its virtues of dignity and courage and love of justice; it also bore the moral burden of a guilt so great that the War and even Reconstruction were in some sense a merited punishment. (pp. 350-51)

Colonel Sutpen himself has a feeling, not exactly of guilt, since he has never questioned the rightness of his design, but rather of amazement that so many misfortunes have fallen on him. Sitting in General Compson's office, he goes back over his career, trying to see where he had made his "mistake," for that is what he calls it. Sometimes the author seems to be implying that the sin for which Sutpen and his class are being punished is simply the act of cohabiting with Negroes. But before the end of *Absalom, Absalom!* we learn that miscegenation is only part of it. When Charles Bon's curious actions are explained, we find that he was taking revenge on his father for having refused to recognize him by so much as a single glance. Thus, heartlessness was the "mistake" that had ruined Sutpen, not the taking of a partly Negro wife and Negro concubines. (pp. 351-52)

In Faulkner's novels, the Negroes are an element of stability and endurance, just as the octoroons (like Charles Bon and Joe Christmas) are an element of tragic instability. His favorite characters are the Negro cooks and matriarchs who hold a white family together: Elnora and Dilsey and Clytie and Aunt Mollie Beauchamp. (p. 354)

Always in his mind [Faulkner] has an ideal picture of how the [South] and the people should be—a picture of painted, many-windowed houses, fenced fields, overflowing barns, eyes lighting up with recognition; and always, being honest, he measures that picture against the land and people he has seen. And both pictures are not only physical but moral; for always in the background of his novels is a sense of moral standards and a feeling of outrage at their being violated or simply pushed aside. Seeing little hope in the future, he turns to the past, where he hopes to discover a legendary and recurrent pattern that will illuminate and lend dignity to the world about him. (pp. 360-61)

> *Malcolm Cowley, "William Faulkner's Legend of the South," in* The Sewanee Review, *Vol. LIII, No. 3, Summer, 1945, pp. 343-61.*

CHARLES I. GLICKSBERG

Practically all of Faulkner's novels are bathed in an atmosphere of, and culminate in, implacable tragedy. Though there are occasional touches of tenderness, there is no intrusion of irony, no attempt at metaphysical or religious consolation and certainly none at justifying the actions of the characters, nearly all of whom are at the mercy of their biological impulses or caught in a web of circumstance from which they cannot possibly escape. (p. 46)

Absalom, Absalom! has the quality of a continuous nightmare. There is no relief from the slow but relentless unwinding of the spool of evil, the sense of impending tragedy. And the method of narration, retrospective, crablike, presenting the central events of the plot bit by bit as seen by different characters and from different points of vantage and perspectives of time, adds cumulatively to the mounting horror. In this novel interest is centered not so much on the action itself as on the tangled skein of motives that led up to the tragic culmination. Which means that concern with the dynamics of character transcends the importance of the logic of plot. Not that Faulkner fails to skirt the edge of melodrama with his detailed account of shooting, fighting, sinister crimes, seductions, violated codes of honor, but he avoids it by seeking to probe, in each instance, beneath the passion and violence to the psychological forces that made these men and women behave in this eccentric, abnormal manner. Since the background of the story is Mississippi, this means that attention is concentrated on the environment, the soil and place, the mores of the plantation, the influence of slavery, the disturbing presence of the Negro.

The style of narration is adapted to the needs of the plot, which spins itself endlessly, uncoiling, winding up again and then unrolling with a new insight, a new revelation. What lends a touch of the nightmarish, of Laocoönic violence, to these scenes and incidents is that they deal with a proud, gracious, picturesque past. Beneath its pomp and circumstance, however, beneath the traditional façade of elegance and chivalric dignity, we can see the working out of tameless, abysmal passions, frustrations that are rooted in the cells of the blood, in the germ plasm. Through the eyes of his characters Faulkner draws a composite picture of life in the South, a picture lighted from multiple angles. The sentences pour out copiously, in a stream that overflows its banks, in a language of the night, a curiously involved language of reminiscence, introspection, and retrospection, the past taking on sinister hues of foreboding and

disaster, until the town of Jefferson, the people, the landscape are bathed in a lowering, crepuscular atmosphere, as scenes of the past, emerging in no strictly ordered succession, confused, repetitious, but tied together at the end to form a unified tale, enact their doom-decreed destiny. This is a Greek drama, but without the intercession of the gods, of evil and retribution in a Southern environment.

In *Absalom, Absalom!* the style is mannered, baroque, turgid, even pretentious, but it must be considered effective as a whole in light of the special atmosphere and mood it seeks to produce. Joyce, in *Ulysses* and *Finnegans Wake,* was a pioneer in the field of composing "night language." One recalls in particular his masterly use of nocturnal dream-monologue in the last section of *Ulysses.* . . . [But] Faulkner is bent on suggesting the increment of horror, the ghostliness and ghastliness, connected with the romantic shell of a past that is the South. Therefore, it is not so much dream-sequences that he relates but remembrances of things past, recollections filtered through the memory of lingering ghosts who have long brooded on the wrongs of the past, the passions, the murder, the revenge, recognizing at last the continuity of life, the fatality of events, the working out of the law of Karma.

As in his other novels, only gradually does the full force of the creative design strike us: the complexity of the plot, the repetitive cyclical pattern, something new revealed with each forward and backward movement of the story—the motives for which we have been searching at last brought forth into the light of day, though even then obscured and tangled, as all motives are bound to be in the human soul. Piece by piece the jigsaw puzzle falls into place and a clear-cut pattern finally emerges, but the suggestion of horror and doom is maintained throughout. The secret that is finally disclosed, the secret on which the resolution of the plot hinges, is the discovery that Charles Bon has part Negro blood in his veins; he is the illegitimate son of Colonel Sutpen, but the boy's mother, when she finds herself rejected by the Colonel, devotes herself with paranoiac energy to the pursuit of revenge, with her son as the chosen instrument to wreak ruin on the man who has cast her aside. The father refuses to acknowledge this product of miscegenation. When the knowledge of this dreadful secret is finally brought home to the legitimate son, Henry, he kills Charles Bon rather than allow him to marry his sister, who is thus condemned to spinsterhood.

It is the mark of Faulkner's genius that he has seized upon this theme—the race problem and all that it involves—as the central problem of his novel and the dominant problem of the South, and handled it with scrupulous honesty and objectivity. If Faulkner is the Dostoyevski of the South, [then] this land and its people, haunted by ghosts of the past, tormented by a crushing sense of guilt, burdened with an antiquated and iniquitous caste system, present a handicap and a complication. There is Charles Bon, with his dreadful "secret," pleading with Henry the justification for incest. There is also the realization that our illusions are as integral a part of us as our flesh and bone. But it is the miscegenation, not the incest, which is the insuperable barrier. (pp. 53-5)

No Faulkner novel is complete without its compounded plot of horror, its ingredients of rape, seduction, prostitution, illegitimate children, incest, perversion, miscegenation. . . . Overriding all these elements of plot, of course, is the theme of the Negro: "black" blood as an abomination, a source of defilement, an inexpiable curse. It is an obsession that is present not only in the horror-haunted mind of Faulkner but also in the collective psyche of the South.

But horror, cumulative and intense, is only part of the picture. Though these scenes of tragic violence take place against the peaceful, somnolent background, the fields shimmering gold beneath the hot sun, the crickets sounding musically at night, Faulkner's object is to make it clear that these seemingly self-contained, God-fearing men and women of Mississippi are subject to gusts of murderous passion, bestial lusts, destructive impulses. . . . Now in all these tales of miscegenation, rape, seduction, degeneration, and crime, there is no implication, no hint even, that life can fulfill its appointed rounds graciously, "normally," without morbid complications and inevitably tragic outcomes. If Faulkner is the Dostoyevski of the South, he is without the Russian's universality of vision, his saving grace of compassion. What Faulkner is doing is to impose a romantic psychopathological point of view on starkly realistic material, with the result that what he produces is a Freudian nightmare. There is sin without any hope of redemption, struggle without the possibility of victory, suffering without meaning or purpose, sex without love, life without fulfillment. It is all a tale told by an idiot and, as in parts of *The Sound and the Fury,* in the idiot's own words and impressions. Faulkner does not succeed—he does not attempt to do so—in holding steadily before our gaze the knowledge that other patterns of life exist, that other perspectives are possible.

The critic is perhaps not justified in demanding of an author that which he is not prepared to give. Faulkner is not understandable if we seek to impose a sociological or metaphysical gloss on his work, least of all if we judge him by Marxist standards. He is neither a philosopher nor a socialist but a writer of fiction. If he dwells on the slow stages of decadence in the South, he is not concerned about pointing a moral but in presenting the process dramatically and objectively in terms of human suffering. The stream-of-consciousness method he employs is more profound and subtle and varied, certainly more passionate, than its counterpart in the novels of Virginia Woolf. This stream is colored and turbulent, responsive to the complex emotions—the memories and lusts, the desires and guilt and remorse—that agitate the minds of various characters. Through it all Faulkner remains practically invisible, a medium of communication but never a participant in the course of the action, venturing no commentary of praise or blame. The people in his fiction are stricken with fatal desires, moved by impulses they cannot control, driven to compulsive actions of guilt and fantastic rituals of expiation and flight. The mind, as Faulkner sees it, cannot cease its gyrations, memory will not die. In the end, these victims must go under and meet defeat. Having no philosophy of life to offer except one of absolute nihilism, Faulkner creates characters who reflect his baffled uncertainty, the torment of his unknowing.

William Faulkner has been criticized severely for a number of reasons, but for none more sharply than for his morbidity and nihilism. What is reprehensible, it seems, is that his work is overshadowed by a sense of utter futility. When this is combined with the theme of decadence, developed brilliantly with a plethora of naturalistic details, the humanistic critic has had more than he can stomach. He cannot be led to believe that the decadence of the South after the Civil War was as vicious and depraved as it is made out to be in the lurid pages of Faulkner. Such objections on moralistic grounds will not, however, carry weight. Faulkner is primarily concerned to tell the truth as objectively and effectively as he can within the limits of fiction, without compromising his integrity of vision. If he finds cruelty and obscenity, incest and perversion and horror in the South, characters that are abnormal, spiritually lost and doomed, it is because such things exist; he has seen them happen, and his conscience as a writer forbids him to gloss them over. (pp. 56-8)

Charles I. Glicksberg, "The World of William Faulkner," in Arizona Quarterly, *Vol. 5, No. 1, Spring, 1949, pp. 46-58.*

RICHARD POIRIER

[The essay from which this excerpt is taken was originally published in William Faulkner: Two Decades of Criticism, *edited by Frederick J. Hoffman and Olga W. Vickery, 1951.]*

Almost without exception, existing criticism of Faulkner has ignored *Absalom, Absalom!* or has examined it either as a naturalistic novel full of Gothic horror and romantic attitudinizing or as little more than a curious source book, significant only for what it can tell us about the problems of Quentin Compson in *The Sound and the Fury.* The only notable exception of which I am aware in Malcolm Cowley's essay "William Faulkner's Legend of the South" [see excerpt above]. But the commentary on *Absalom, Absalom!* which is included in that essay is not meant by Mr. Cowley to be extensive, and it only partially succeeds, it seems to me, in suggesting the true character of the novel.

An understanding of the environment which we see conditioning Quentin in *The Sound and the Fury* is of course helpful. We can perhaps better appreciate his response to experience in *Absalom, Absalom!* if we have learned from the earlier book that Quentin's disillusionment, the vacuity of purpose which plagues him, cannot be divorced from the spiritual dead end which his mother represents and which his father pathetically articulates. The latter, summing up his view of life, tells Quentin that "Time is your misfortune." . . . The father has slowly undermined for Quentin the myth of any spiritual transcendence of what seems to be the mechanism of historical fact. This is in great part the problem faced by Quentin in *Absalom, Absalom!* as well. It is a problem which makes Quentin, as an organizer of Thomas Sutpen's story, the dramatic center of this novel. Indeed, in *Absalom, Absalom!* Quentin is nearly allowed to appropriate the position of the author.

But this is not to say, as many have, that Quentin or some other character is Faulkner's spokesman. Faulkner is extremely careful to prevent his novels from ever being controlled by the "efficient confessionals" which Kenneth Burke claims to find in them. The form in both *The Sound and the Fury* and *Absalom, Absalom!* prevents any one of the narrators from seducing the reader to a restricted, wholly individual point of view. It is quite clear that the author sympathizes in the earlier book with Benjy and Quentin. But if we are looking for Faulkner to express himself, we shall find that he does so impersonally in the structure of the work itself. Benjy, Quentin, and Jason tend, in different degrees, to neutralize one another. It is the structure of *The Sound and the Fury* which emphasizes the wholeness of Dilsey's point of view and which affirms the presence, if only as a choral effect, of a traditional and moral context in which we can place the whole novel.

The adaptation of this method to a new set of circumstances constitutes the most significant connection between *The Sound and the Fury* and *Absalom, Absalom!* In the formal arrangement of this later novel, for example, we see Faulkner's sense of history played off against the social irresponsibility of Rosa Coldfield, the most consciously incantatory of all his narrators. We see Thomas Sutpen try to make history begin in his own image and, when the damage is done, Quentin Compson attempt to discover the meaning of his historical background with Sutpen as the central figure. The attempt to create history is both the story of Sutpen and, with a difference, the conscious effort of Quentin as a narrator of that story. Faulkner has joined the two themes so that the persisting disruptions caused by Sutpen almost fatally effect Quentin's attempt to discover the meaning of his heritage.

Because Quentin, if he is to define himself, must confront these persisting disruptions, it is little wonder that Faulkner is so obviously fond of him. The preoccupations and the difficulties of the two are not dissimilar. Within the chaotic nature of Sutpen's history and Rosa's "demonizing," Quentin tries to find some human value adhering to what is apparently a representative anecdote of his homeland. In doing so, he must somehow overcome a problem such as confronts the contemporary writer. As T. S. Eliot defines it, it is the problem of overcoming "the damage of a lifetime and of having been born into an unsettled society." (pp. 12-14)

In Quentin's mind, the career of Thomas Sutpen is the most persistently disturbing element in the history of his native region, and one in which all of his family have been involved. . . . But it is well to remember that Quentin's interest in Sutpen's story transcends any reference he finds in it for . . . personal problems, which, after all, we are acquainted with only from observing his activity outside the context of *Absalom, Absalom!* Had Quentin assumed the luxury of treating the Sutpen story merely as an objectification of some personal obsession, the total effect of the novel would have partaken of the overindulgent and romantic self-dramatization of Rosa's soliloquy.

Quentin tries to place Sutpen in a social and historical context. By doing so he can perhaps discover his own tradition and the reasons for its collapse. . . . Perhaps Malcolm Cowley is right and the Sutpen story represents for Quentin the essence of the Deep South. But *Absalom, Absalom!* is not primarily about the South or about a doomed family as a symbol of the South. It is a novel about the meaning of history for Quentin Compson. The story of Sutpen simply represents that part of the past which Quentin must understand if he is to understand himself. In this respect, Quentin's dilemma is very similar to that of Stephen Dedalus in *Ulysses.* (pp. 14-15)

Like the violence of Joe Christmas in *Light in August,* Sutpen's "design" is directed as much against a terrifying sense of his own insufficiency as against a society which apparently standardizes that insufficiency by caste or class systems. When his family moves from the primitively communal society of their mountain home to settle in the Tidewater, young Sutpen finds everything in the new environment phenomenal. . . . He is naturally humiliated and confused when, carrying a message to the plantation owner, he is ordered away from the front door by a Negro in livery. Because he has been brought up in a society outside the one in which he now lives, he cannot fit the action of the "monkey nigger" into any acknowledged social pattern. It can be seen by young Sutpen only as a wholly personal affront. At the door, he finds himself "looking out from within the balloon face" of the Negro, and at himself. Having no past, no background of his own by which he could appreciate the social complexity of the incident, he prejudicially assumes the position of his insulter, or the agent of his

insulter, and both pities and degrades himself. . . . [He] finally decides that the best thing he can do is to become as rich and powerful as the man from whose door he has been turned. This ambition develops into what he later calls his "design."

When Sutpen tells Quentin's grandfather about this incident, he claims that he felt then that "he would have to do something about it in order to live with himself for the rest of his life." . . . [The] rest of his life is dedicated to a vindication of that little boy at the door, what he himself calls "the boy symbol."

The "boy symbol" motif persists throughout the novel and becomes connected with Sutpen's desire for a son. Indeed, the whole "design" is a calculated bid for a kind of immortality. His son and the rest of his descendants shall have all Sutpen lacked: wealth, power, untainted respectability. To that end, he first goes to Haiti to make a fortune only to abandon it and to repudiate his first wife and son, Charles Bon, when he discovers that she has a trace of Negro blood. The hundred-square-mile plantation called Sutpen's Hundred which he later builds in Mississippi is really a second and, it seems, unassailable foundation of the power and wealth that his heir, Henry Sutpen, shall perpetuate. . . . It is characteristic of Sutpen that in selecting his wife he chooses, in place of the aristocratic connection he wishes to make, a marriage into a family which is merely priggishly proud. Without any sense or knowledge of the past, Sutpen, through his son, would belong only to the future. . . . As a reflection of the vindicated boy symbol, Henry becomes for his father a means of disowning the past. (pp. 15-17)

According to Quentin, "Sutpen's trouble was "innocence." . . . Part of that "innocence" is, of course, the belief that any woman will accept money as a final recompense for desertion. Bon's sudden and ironically unintentional appearance with Henry at Sutpen's Hundred makes that expression of Sutpen's "innocence" seem purblind indeed. Sutpen, who at least gave Bon the name he bears, is the only one in the family who is aware of the guest's real identity. But all he can do for the present is to remain silent. To acknowledge that Charles Bon is his son would be to infuse humanity into the "ingredients" of his "design." He is simply incapable of doing it. He fails to realize that Bon is demanding only the same sort of recognition denied him as a boy at the plantation door. And he can forget human need so completely that he cannot understand how or why his plans could be so affected by what he calls "a maelstrom of unpredictable and unreasoning human beings."

Sutpen's story might well be about his opportunities for becoming human. There are countless opportunities, like the appearance of Bon, which he has ignored. . . . Sutpen, as we have seen, comes totally to express the very inhumanity and injustice which he would have us believe compelled the "design" in the first place. When Judith's life is ruined as a consequence of the complications which lead to the murder of Bon, she complains to Quentin's grandmother that the fulfillment of her life was frustrated by forces over which she had no control. . . . Actually, it is her father's "innocence" of anything but his own compulsion which disorders her life. . . . Quentin, only with much pain, finally discovers in the career of Thomas Sutpen not the essence of his past so much as a force which disrupts all that was possibly coherent, orderly, and humane in the past. (pp. 17-18)

The structure of *Absalom, Absalom!* is a reflection of both the nature and the method of Quentin's search, in a confusion of historical fact, for value. Consideration of that structure might begin simply by dividing the novel into two parts of four chapters each, leaving Rosa's monologue, which separates them by exclusively occupying all of Chapter V, for special consideration. The first four chapters, in which the whole of Sutpen's story is continually repeated with changing emphases, are really a dramatization of Quentin's activity at the sources of his information. In the last four chapters, during which he is at Harvard College, Quentin, with the help of his roommate, Shreve, pieces together all of the facts and opinions about the story held by Rosa, his father, and his grandfather, along with a good deal of information which is apparently a part of his heritage. (pp. 19-20)

The events of the Sutpen narrative are neither so contemporary nor, except for Rosa, so personally consequential to the speakers [in *Absalom, Absalom!*] as are those in *The Sound and the Fury.* Yet neither Rosa nor Mr. Compson, both of whom first tell the story to Quentin in the early chapters, are wholly trustworthy narrators. . . .

[Rosa's] description of Sutpen's first years in Jefferson is wild and incredible. Sutpen becomes *"an ogre, some beast out of tales to frighten children with."* But the distortions resulting from her nightmarish sensibility are continually being revealed to the reader by the contradictory nature of Rosa's own testimony. At other times, her version of an incident may remain consistent throughout her conversation, only to be invalidated by some other narrator who is either more informed or at least less prejudiced. (p. 20)

The detailing of incidents by Quentin's father, in Chapters II, III, and IV, if not as distorted as Rosa's, is no less riddled with faulty information. On the basis of what he knows, Mr. Compson, believes, for example, that Sutpen forbade Judith's marriage merely because her fiancé, Charles Bon, kept an octoroon mistress in New Orleans. . . . But Quentin, after his trip to Sutpen's Hundred with Rosa, comes into possession of more information. In the process of retelling the story in Chapter VII, he corrects his father's error in Chapter II. We learn what only Sutpen knew at the time: the real identity of Charles Bon. Judith's betrothal to him was forbidden by Sutpen because it would have resulted not only in incest, but in miscegenation. This new information not only partially invalidates Mr. Compson's analysis, but also reflects adversely on the already questionable account of the story given by Rosa. In the first chapter she tells Quentin that she "saw Judith's marriage forbidden without rhyme or reason or shadow of excuse." It is this belief, based on ignorance of the facts, which partly explains the peculiar quality of her hatred of Sutpen. Rosa's bitterness and frustration at being the last child of cold and unloving parents finds total expression in the collapse of the romantic life she had lived vicariously in that of her niece, Judith.

In the light of the new facts uncovered by Quentin, the reader must now re-evaluate Rosa's emotional state which has its reference in the incredibility for her of Sutpen's prohibition of the marriage. By doing so the reader sees that the attitude of Rosa, or it might be of any other narrator, is understandable not in terms of what actually has happened but because of either her lack of information or her inability to change her mind when new information is made available. . . . Quentin's version of the Judith-Bon affair causes a reorientation of the whole Sutpen story. Sutpen's attitude toward the marriage becomes a coherent element in his "design" and Bon's insistence on returning to marry his half-sister becomes a dramatically powerful gesture activated by his need for paternal recognition. (p. 21)

Before dealing with Rosa Coldfield in greater detail, I want to suggest once again that the emphasis here is primarily upon Quentin, that neither Rosa nor Sutpen can serve as the dramatic center of this novel. Quentin's acts of remembrance actually determine the form of the novel. . . . Before he and Shreve begin the job of historical recreation, Quentin can see in Rosa's approach to the Sutpen story the great difficulty which will beset him in his effort to discover the human content of his heritage. From her involvement in the "design," Rosa seems to conclude that history fulfills itself not through the efforts or aspirations of human beings, but wholly in an impersonal, antagonistic universe, through abstract "designs" or by the action of Fate. If that is the case, Quentin's tradition is devoid of human value. Eventually, his attempt to discover a meaningful tradition depends for its success upon his discovery of a participant in the conflict with Sutpen with whom he can share an active sense of association. Whoever that individual is, he must be able, as Rosa is not, to acknowledge the world outside himself; he must surrender some of his individuality in order actively to participate in society. Rosa simply compounds for Quentin the already frightening phenomena of Sutpen. She is no more aware than her "demon" of any necessary relationship between her aspirations and the moral codes and social disciplines of the community. (p. 22)

Although she has never seen him, Rosa has fallen deeply in love with her vision of the man who she never learns is Sutpen's unrecognized son. She has heard him discussed by Ellen, whose plans for an engagement between him and Judith, also made in ignorance of Bon's identity, come to objectify Rosa's own romantic longings. Her dream of Bon is a dream of a future, a "living fairy tale." Like Sutpen's dream of the future, it is a "fairy tale" which is foolishly isolated from the world of other human beings in which it must, if at all, exist. Rosa's dream was concocted in the [womblike] hallways of her darkened house. (pp. 22-3)

When Wash Jones shouts beneath her window that Henry has "kilt" Charles Bon "dead as a beef," she leaves this "hallway" and rushes out to Sutpen's Hundred. She does not go, as she claims, to rescue Judith from the curse which seems to be on the house. Rather, she is trying desperately to save some of the enchantment of Judith's proposed wedding, her own "vicarious bridal." But when she rushes into the hall calling for Judith, her *"shadow-realm of make-believe"* comes into direct conflict with Sutpen's *"factual scheme."* This is embodied for Rosa in Clytie, Sutpen's daughter by a Negro slave. . . . Clytie has blocked Rosa's path, which leads to Judith's room, to Bon's body, which has been placed there. The moment of conflict has finally been achieved. . . .

At this point the narrative stops. Attention is focused by Rosa upon the significance of Clytie's grip on her arm. She cries out, not at Clytie but at what she calls the *"cumulative overreach of despair itself."* In attempting to define its elements, Rosa expands this single moment, which is in a sense out of time, into her whole experience of life. Her immediate response becomes enlarged into the total response of an individual who has encountered the disabling grip of a damaging past as she tries to realize her dream of the future. . . . Only when she is released by Clytie are her illusions completely shattered. She finds that though Bon is dead, she still is denied by Judith the chance to look at him, that Judith, left nearly a widow, refuses to grieve for him. Rosa at last faces what Sutpen optimistically refused to face: *"that sickness somewhere at the prime foundation of this factual scheme."* That "sickness," one might say, is primarily an ignorance of context. The pattern of events which Rosa had chosen to recognize was only a dream. (p. 23)

The poverty of Sutpen's imagination and the neurotic richness of Rosa's place the two figures at poles. Yet in their different ways, both express a wholly nonsocial, dangerously individualistic point of view, [and both pursue illusive goals]. . . . It is sufficient to say that Sutpen represents all that [Rosa] would but cannot be. In her soliloquy he is given alternately the face of an ogre and the "*shape of a hero.*" She recalls that her life "*was at last worth something*" when she helped care for him after the war. His proposal is accepted simply because he is a man and, she thinks then, a heroic one. . . . The breaking of the engagement occurs only when he intimates that she is merely the means to provide him with another son to carry on the "design." In a rage, she returns to her "womb-like corridor" to live on the charity of the town and to continue her "demonizing" of Sutpen, a role which her aunt "seems to have invested her with at birth along with the swaddling clothes."

But the very attitudes implicated in her final revulsion and hatred of Sutpen further the ironic similarities already suggested as existing between Sutpen and Rosa Coldfield. Both of them try desperately to disown the past. Rosa has had her own design, one by which she was obsessed with a future even more impossible of achievement than Sutpen's. Sutpen's scapegoat is the "monkey nigger"; Rosa's is Sutpen. She uses him, as Sutpen used his experience at the plantation door, to objectify an exclusively egocentric and romantic view of life which has been wrenched apart by forces and events for which she holds this remarkably childish man too exclusively responsible. She never sees in the very nature of her illusions—nor does he in his—the source of their destruction.

Faulkner's own literary position is powerfully suggested by the dramatic function in the novel of Rosa's self-negating soliloquy [in Chapter V]. . . . In Rosa Coldfield's soliloquy, Faulkner has dramatically fused literary with social disorders. These very disorders are in large part what T. S. Eliot is concerned with in *After Strange Gods*. Both Rosa's point of view and the career of Thomas Sutpen, which concerns her, are illustrative of the heretical sensibility on the loose, of the danger, which Eliot defines for us, of overindulgent individualism: "when morals cease to be a matter of tradition and orthodoxy . . . and when each man is to elaborate his own, then *personality* becomes a thing of alarming importance."

This sort of "elaboration" is clearly dramatized by Rosa's obliviousness to anything but her own needs and compulsions. But its literary applications are made most evident by the stylistic quality of her version of the Sutpen story. Through the style of Rosa's soliloquy, we are made aware that Sutpen is not alone in his pursuit of "strange Gods." A rather peculiar Eros intrudes upon Agape despite Rosa's incantations to an avenging God. Perhaps because of this, her soliloquy is reminiscent of the Gerty McDowell sequence in Joyce's *Ulysses*. . . . Such tortuous, verbalized relieving of emotion . . . is a consequence of Rosa's neurotic self-absorption. She is bringing herself to life through emotional paroxysms. Eliot observes much the same thing happening, but not with Faulkner's ironic purpose, in the novels of Hardy. Indeed, Eliot's definition of the kind of "heresy" Hardy is supposed to have committed in his novels applies exactly to those qualities of Rosa's soliloquy which I am anxious to point out. Eliot observes

> . . . an interesting example of a powerful personality uncurbed . . . by submission to any objective beliefs; unhampered by any ideas, or even by what sometimes

acts as a partial restraint . . . the desire to please a large public. [Hardy] . . . seems to me to have written as nearly for the sake of self-expression as man well can. . . .

The point I should like to make is that Eliot's remarks can apply to Rosa but cannot in any sense be applied to Faulkner. This is precisely the mistake made by those critics who have accused Faulkner of being irresponsibly romantic. Mr. Alfred Kazin, for example, asserts that Faulkner represents "a tormented individualism in the contemporary novel, a self-centered romanticism." If this were true, we might use Rosa Coldfield's soliloquy to direct irony against the author himself. Obviously, the novel does not allow us to do this. The context in which Faulkner places her soliloquy prevents it from having any persuasively incantatory effect upon the reader. Rosa's romantic verbalization is consistent with her avocation as a poet but reflects only in a most negative way Faulkner's sense of his own vocation. . . . [The] reader will be disappointed who tries to discover in Rosa's soliloquy the moral basis for her hatred of Sutpen. All that she can reveal to Quentin is the "undefeat" not of moral rigor but of an essentially unregenerate personality.

When Rosa is finished, Sutpen remains where Quentin found him, bewilderingly inexplicable. The explanation for this is part of the logic of Faulkner's method which is really the method of historical research and re-creation. But the historical method has to this point proved, so far as Quentin is concerned, tragically unsuccessful. . . . Both Rosa and Sutpen are really ignorant of what is going on about them. Knowledge is the basis of historical perspective and knowledge is essentially an act of remembrance, an awareness of tradition.

The form of *The Sound and the Fury,* of *Absalom, Absalom!,* and of most of Faulkner's major works is determined by this conception. The reader is witness to a conscious stockpiling of information by the characters as the story is repeated over and over again with a different focus upon the material, a persistent encirclement of alien facts and enigmatic personalities by all the accumulated knowledge of an individual, a family, or an entire community. (pp. 24-7)

Quentin's persistent acts of remembrance in the last four chapters finally are successful in placing Sutpen in a comprehensible human context. Quentin and his roommate, Shreve McCannon, bring both a fairly complete knowledge of the facts and an inventive curiosity to the job of historical re-creation. Sutpen himself ceases to be a phenomenon in Quentin's past.

In their final ordering of the story, Quentin and Shreve are primarily concerned with the activity of Charles Bon and Henry Sutpen. (p. 27)

The account of the Bon story which finally emerges from the conversations of Quentin and Shreve may be viewed as an attempted rejection by Quentin of both his father's and Rosa's points of view. The effect, in terms of the novel, is a rejection of naturalism. The activity of Bon and Henry, as it is seen by Quentin, simply does not sustain a conception of history either as an impersonal mechanism or in which "blind Fate" slowly and solemnly triumphs. Faulkner quite admirably makes his own job extremely difficult. He endows Bon's career with all the material which should by its very nature keep Rosa's "current of retribution and fatality" moving on unaffected by Bon's own feelings and desires. Bon's childhood, according the Shreve, was almost a ritual in which his mother prepared him as an agent of her revenge on her husband. . . .

Actually, however, Bon gives Sutpen numerous opportunities to correct his "mistake.". . . . [If] he had once perceived Bon's human motive, then [Bon] would, he claims, have sacrificed the love of Henry and whatever claim he might have to the love of Judith. . . .

But he at last falls victim, as Sutpen himself is a victim, to the ravages of this abstract "design." Incest with Judith or death at the hands of his brother become the only ways in which Bon can identify himself as Sutpen's son. Henry, after four years of painful indecision, kills his friend and brother at the gates of Sutpen's Hundred. For Bon, this was the ultimate recognition of his sonship. For Henry, it was a terribly difficult moral act. It had to be carried out in a world which his father, like Quentin's mother in *The Sound and the Fury*, has almost wholly corrupted. Henry acts not in obedience to his father, but to an inherent sense of a moral code which is stronger than his love for Bon. The act, though Sutpen insisted upon it, is really a transcendence by Henry of the dehumanized quality of his father's "design." (pp. 28-9)

But the conversations of Quentin and Shreve do not end with the killing of Bon, with a personal action carried out in painful recognition of a moral code. As they continue with the Sutpen story, its natural sequence is significantly disrupted. Chronologically, though all of the details are made available to us in earlier chapters, the death of Bon should be followed by Wash Jones's murder of Thomas Sutpen and by the violent escapades of Bon's son, Velery Bon, who has been brought by Clytie and Judith to Sutpen's Hundred. Structurally, however, the next incident with which Quentin and Shreve concern themselves is the final catastrophe of the Sutpen family, a catastrophe which seems to affirm the workings of a grotesquely deterministic universe. Such a focus on the material as a chronological ordering of the Wash Jones and Velery Bon stories would have allowed might have permitted Quentin a more substantial mitigation of the meaning which Shreve desperately assigns in the end to the idiot who alone survives at Sutpen's Hundred.

The actions of Wash Jones and of Velery Bon suggest as clearly as the final actions of Bon and Henry a distorted but eloquent sense of moral revulsion at the corruption and inhumanity of Sutpen's "design." When there seems no hope of reinstituting that "design," Sutpen perhaps consciously provokes Wash into killing him. In Wash's hearing, he crudely repudiates Milly, Wash's granddaughter, when she fails to bear him a son. But we can as easily view the murder less as a credit to Sutpen's scheming than as an assertion by Wash of human pride. In order to reaffirm his manhood and his dignity, he must destroy the man who has been his hero. (pp. 29-30)

[Like] Wash, Velery Bon discovers that he, too, is a part of the rejected residue of his grandfather's career. His subsequent conduct is a comment upon the consequences of Sutpen's invalidation of the habits and customs of the community which, taken together, constitute a kind of moral or social discipline. Having no family of his own, his real identity hidden from the town, Velery Bon seeks literally to make a name for himself by violent and extraordinary action. Though he could pass for a white man, he marries a woman who is an extremely dark Negress, and insists on being recognized as a Negro himself. Considering the social consequences, this is really a conscious form of self-degradation similar in its motivation to that of Joe Christmas in *Light in August*. . . . In Sutpen's world, all Velery Bon can do is to assert negatively his potential dignity as a man.

But the structure of the final episodes dramatically excludes from the immediate attention of Quentin and Shreve the moral affirmations, however deformed, of Wash and Velery Bon. Instead, we have in the sharpest possible juxtaposition, the circumstances of Bon's death and the almost theatrical horror of the burning of Sutpen's Hundred. Velery Bon's son [Jim Bond], the heir to the estate and a Negro idiot, is left to "lurk around those ashes and howl."

The Negro idiot seems powerfully to reintroduce the apparently inhuman and mechanistic nature of Sutpen's history and of Quentin's heritage. Shreve is moved almost as much as Quentin by the ambiguous quality of the story they have finally pieced together. . . . But he rather pathetically disguises his feelings and doubts. He grasps what is for him the easiest solution, what is for Quentin an emotionally impossible solution—the cliché of the idiot as symbol of predestined doom. This final catastrophe, he tells Quentin, "clears the whole ledger, you can tear all the pages out and burn them, except for one thing." That one thing, Shreve facetiously concludes, is the [reproductive] mechanism itself by which "the Jim Bonds are going to conquer the western hemisphere." . . . (pp. 30-1)

Annoying to Quentin as Shreve's easy and terrible solution might seem, the possibility exists for him even at the end of the novel that man and his history are mutually hostile and alien; that he is merely the reflex of some impersonal and abstract historical process. But it is a possibility to which he refuses wholly to succumb. Inherent in the tragically suggestive ambiguity of the conclusion is the justification for the structure of *Absalom, Absalom!* The form of the novel itself insists that the act of placing Sutpen in the understandable context of human society and history is a continually necessary act, a never-ending responsibility and an act of humanistic faith. (p. 31)

Richard Poirier, "'Strange Gods' in Jefferson, Mississippi: Analysis of 'Absalom, Absalom!'" in Twentieth Century Interpretations of Absalom, Absalom! A Collection of Critical Essays, *edited by Arnold Goldman, Prentice-Hall, Inc., 1971, pp. 12-31.*

CLEANTH BROOKS

[*The essay from which this excerpt is taken was originally published in Brooks's study* William Faulkner *in 1954.*]

Absalom, Absalom!, in my opinion the greatest of Faulkner's novels, is probably the least well understood of all his books. The property of a great work, as T. S. Eliot remarked long ago, is to communicate before it is understood; and *Absalom, Absalom!* passes this test triumphantly. It has meant something very powerful and important to all sorts of people, and who is to say that, under the circumstances, this something was not the thing to be said to that particular reader? To the young Frenchman who had served in the *maquis,* to the young writer in New York interested in problems of technique, a little weary from having given his days and nights to the prose of Henry James, to the Shrevlin McCannons all over Canada and the United States with their myths of the South compounded out of *Uncle Tom's Cabin* and *Strange Fruit*—to all these *Absalom, Absalom!* had something to give. That is important, and I do not mean to disparage it. Yet the book has its own rights, as it were, and in proportion as we admire it, we shall want to see not merely what we can make of it but what it makes of itself. In any case, the book is more than a bottle of Gothic sauce to be used to spice up our own preconceptions about the history of American society.

Harvey Breit's sympathetic introduction to the Modern Library edition provides a useful—because it is not an extreme—instance of the typical misreading that I have in mind. Mr. Breit writes:

> It is a terrible Gothic sequence of events, a brooding tragic fable.... Was it the "design" that had devoured Sutpen and prevented him from avowing the very thing that would have saved the design? Was it something in the South itself, in its social, political, moral, economic origins that was responsible for Sutpen and for all the subsequent tragedy? Quentin can make no judgment: Sutpen himself had possessed courage and innocence, and the same land had nourished men and women who had delicacy of feeling and capacity for love and gifts for life.

These are questions which the typical reader asks. Shreve, the outsider, implies them. But it is significant that Quentin does not ask them. The questions are begged by the very way in which they are asked, for, put in this way, the questions undercut the problem of tragedy (which is the problem that obsesses Quentin). They imply that there is a social "solution." And they misread Sutpen's character in relation to his society and in relation to himself.

It is the quality of Sutpen's innocence that we must understand if we are to understand the meaning of his tragedy, and if we confuse it with innocence as we ordinarily use the term or with even the typical American "innocence" possessed by, say, one of Henry James' young heiresses as she goes to confront the corruption of Europe, we shall remain in the dark. Sutpen will be for us, as he was for Miss Rosa, simply the "demon"— or since we lack the justification of Miss Rosa's experience of personal horror, we shall simply appropriate the term from her as Shreve, in his half-awed, half-amused fashion, does.

Faulkner has been very careful to define Sutpen's innocence for us. "Sutpen's trouble," as Quentin's grandfather observed, "was innocence." ... It is this innocence about the nature of reality that persists, for [according to Quentin's grandfather], Sutpen "believed that the ingredients of morality were like the ingredients of pie or cake and once you had measured them and balanced them and mixed them and put them into the oven it was all finished and nothing but pie or cake could come out." That is why Sutpen can ask Quentin's grandfather, in his innocence, not "Where did I do wrong" but "Where did I make the mistake ... what did I do or misdo ... whom or what injure by it to the extent which this would indicate? I had a design. To accomplish it I should require money, a house, a plantation, slaves, a family—incidentally of course, a wife. I set out to acquire these, asking no favor of any man."

This is an "innocence" with which most of us today ought to be acquainted. It is par excellence the innocence of modern man, though it has not, to be sure, been confined to modern times.... But innocence of this sort can properly be claimed as a special characteristic of modern man, and one can claim further that it flourishes particularly in a secularized society.

The society into which Sutpen rides in 1833 is not a secularized society. That is not to say that the people are necessarily "good." They have their selfishness and cruelty and their snobbery, as men have always had them. Once Sutpen has acquired enough wealth and displayed enough force, the people of the community are willing to accept him. But they do not live by his code, nor do they share his innocent disregard of accepted values. (pp. 295-97)

That Sutpen does remain outside the community comes out in all sorts of little ways. Mr. Compson describes his "florid, swaggering gesture" with the parenthetical remark: "yes, he was underbred. It showed like this always, your grandfather said, in all his formal contacts with people." And Mr. Compson goes on to say that it was as if John L. Sullivan "having taught himself painfully and tediously to do the schottische, having drilled himself and drilled himself in secret ... now believed it no longer necessary to count the music's beat, say." (pp. 297-98)

Mr. Compson is not overrating the possession of mere manners. More is involved that Miss Rosa's opinion that Sutpen was no gentleman. For Sutpen's manners indicate his abstract approach to the whole matter of living. Sutpen would seize upon "the traditional" as a pure abstraction—which, of course, is to deny its very meaning. For him the tradition is not a way of life "handed down" or "transmitted" from the community, past and present, to the individual nurtured by it. It is an assortment of things to be possessed, not a manner of living that embodies certain values and determines men's conduct. The fetish objects are to be gained by sheer ruthless efficiency.... [One] is tempted to say that Sutpen's unwillingness to acknowledge Charles Bon as his son does not spring from any particular racial feeling. Indeed, Sutpen's whole attitude toward the Negro has to be reinspected if we are to understand his relation to the Southern community into which he comes.

It would seem that the prevailing relation between the races in Jefferson is simply one more of the culture traits which Sutpen takes from the plantation community into which he has come as a boy out of the mountains of western Virginia. Sutpen takes over the color bar almost without personal feeling. His attitude toward the Negro is further clarified by his attitude toward his other part-Negro child, Clytie. Mr. Compson once casually lets fall the remark that Sutpen's other children "Henry and Judith had grown up with a negro half sister of their own." The context of Mr. Compson's remarks makes it perfectly plain that Henry and Judith were well aware that Clytie was indeed their half-sister, and that Clytie was allowed to grow up in the house with them. This fact in itself suggests a lack of the usual Southern feeling about Negroes. Miss Rosa is much more typically Southern when she tells Quentin, with evident distaste, that Clytie and Judith sometimes slept in the same bed.

After Sutpen has returned from the war, Clytie sits in the same room with Judith and Rosa and Sutpen and listens each evening to the sound of Sutpen's voice. When Sutpen proposes to Rosa, he begins, "'Judith, you and Clytie—' and ceased, still entering, then said, 'No, never mind. Rosa will not mind if you both hear it too, since we are short for time'." Clytie is accepted naturally as part of the "we." She can be so accepted because acceptance on this level does not imperil Sutpen's "design." But acceptance of Charles Bon, in Sutpen's opinion, would. For Sutpen the matter is really as simple as that. He does not hate his first wife or feel repugnance for her child. He does not hate just as he does not love. His passion is totally committed to the design. Not even his own flesh and blood are allowed to distract him from that.

As for slavery, Sutpen does not confine himself to black chattel slavery. He ruthlessly bends anyone that he can to his will. The white French architect whom he bring into Yoknapatawpha County to build his house is as much a slave as any of his black servants: Sutpen hunts him down with dogs when he tries to escape. (pp. 298-99)

Sutpen is not without morality or a certain code of honor. He is, according to his own lights, a just man. As he told Quentin's grandfather with reference to his rejection of his first wife: "suffice that I . . . accepted [my wife] in good faith, with no reservations about myself, and I expected as much from [her parents]. I did not [demand credentials]. . . . [Yet] they deliberately withheld from me one fact which I have reason to know they were aware would have caused me to decline the entire matter." But Sutpen, as he tells General Compson, "made no attempt to keep . . . that [property] which I might consider myself to have earned at the risk of my life . . . but on the contrary I declined and resigned all right and claim to this in order that I might repair whatever injustice I might be considered to have done [in abandoning my wife and child] by so providing for" them.

Moreover, Sutpen is careful to say nothing in disparagement of his first wife. Quentin's grandfather comments upon "that morality which would not permit him to malign or traduce the memory of his first wife, or at least the memory of the marriage even though he felt that he had been tricked by it." It is Sutpen's innocence to think that justice is enough—that there is no claim that cannot be satisfied by sufficient money payment. (p. 300)

Sutpen thinks of himself as strictly just and he submits all of his faculties almost selflessly to the achievement of his design. His attitude toward his second wife conforms perfectly to this. Why does he choose her? For choose he does: he is not chosen—that is, involved with her through passion. The choice is calculated quite coldbloodedly (if, to our minds, naïvely and innocently). Ellen Coldfield is not the daughter of a planter. She does not possess great social prestige or beauty and she does not inherit wealth. But as the daughter of a steward in the Methodist church, she possesses in high degree the thing that Sutpen most obviously lacks—respectability. . . . For Sutpen, respectability is an abstraction like morality: you measure out so many cups of concentrated respectability to sweeten so many measures of disrespectability—"like the ingredients of pie or cake."

The choice of a father-in-law is in fact just as symbolically right: the two men resemble each other, for all the appearance of antithetical differences. Mr. Coldfield is as definitely set off from the community as is Sutpen. With the coming of the Civil War, this rift widens to an absolute break. Mr. Coldfield denounces secession, closes his store, and finally nails himself up in the attic of his house, where he spends the last three years of his life. No more than Sutpen is he a coward: like Sutpen, too, his scheme of human conduct is abstract and mechanical. . . . (p. 301)

Mr. Coldfield is glad when he sees the country that he hates obviously drifting into a fatal war, for he regards the inevitable defeat of the South as the price it will pay for having erected its economic edifice "not on the rock of stern morality but on the shifting sands of opportunism and moral brigandage."

Some critics have been so unwary as to assume that this view of the Civil War is one that the author would enjoin upon the reader, but William Faulkner is neither so much of a Puritan nor so much of a materialist as is Mr. Coldfield. The truth of the matter is that Mr. Coldfield's morality is simply Sutpen's turned inside out. (p. 302)

Sutpen is further defined by his son, Charles Bon. Bon is a mirror image, a reversed shadow of his father. Like his father, he suddenly appears out of nowhere as a man of mystery. . . .

Like his father, Bon has an octoroon "wife," whom he is prepared to repudiate along with his child by her. Like his father, he stands beyond good and evil. But Bon is Byronic, rather than the go-getter; spent, rather than full of pushing vitality; sophisticated, rather than confidently naïve.

Sutpen is the secularized Puritan; Bon is the lapsed Roman Catholic. . . . The one has gone beyond the distinction between good and evil; the other has scarcely arrived at that distinction. The father and the son define the extremes of the human world: one aberration corresponds to—and eventually destroys—the other. The reader is inclined to view Bon with sympathy as a person gravely wronged, and he probably agrees with Quentin's interpretation of Bon's character: that Bon finally put aside all ideas of revenge and asked for nothing more than a single hint of recognition of his sonship. Faulkner has certainly treated Bon with full dramatic sympathy, as he has Sutpen, for that matter. But our sympathy ought not to obscure for us Bon's resemblances to his father, or the complexity of his character. Unless we care to go beyond Quentin and Shreve in speculation, Charles Bon displays toward his octoroon mistress and their son something of the cool aloofness that his father displays toward him. If he is the instrument by which Sutpen's design is wrecked, his own irresponsibility (or at the least, his lack of concern for his own child) wrecks his child's life. We shall have to look to Judith to find responsible action and a real counter to Sutpen's ruthlessness.

These other children of Sutpen—Judith and Henry—reflect further light upon the character of Sutpen—upon his virtues and upon his prime defect. They represent a mixture of the qualities of Sutpen and Coldfield. Judith, it is made plain, has more of the confidence and boldness of her father; Henry, more of the conventionality and the scruples of his maternal grandfather. It is the boy Henry who vomits at the sight of his father, stripped to the waist in the ring with the black slave. Judith watches calmly. And it is Judith who urges the coachman to race the coach on the way to church.

Henry is, of the two, the more vulnerable. After Sutpen has forbidden marriage between Bon and Judith and during the long period in which Henry remains self-exiled with his friend Bon, he is the one tested to the limit by his father's puzzling silence and by his friend's fatalistic passivity. But he has some of his father's courage, and he has what his father does not have: love. At the last moment he kills, though he kills what he loves and apparently for love. It is the truly tragic dilemma. Faulkner has not chosen to put Henry's story in the forefront of the novel, but he has not needed to do so. For the sensitive reader the various baffles through which that act of decision reaches us do not muffle but, through their resonance, magnify the decisive act.

Henry's later course is, again, only implied. We know that in the end—his last four years—he reverted to the course of action of his grandfather Coldfield, and shut himself up in the house. But there is a difference. This is no act of abstract defiance and hate. Henry has assumed responsibility, has acted, has been willing to abide the consequences of that action, and now, forty years later, has come home to die.

If it is too much to call Henry's course of action renunciation and expiation, there is full justification for calling Judith's action just that. Judith has much of her father in her, but she is a woman and she also has love. . . . It is Judith who invites Charles Bon's octoroon mistress to visit Bon's grave. It is Judith who, on his mother's death, sends to New Orleans for

Bon's son and tries to rear him. . . . [We also] know that Judith did take him into the house when he was stricken with yellow fever, and that she died nursing him. The acknowledgement of blood kinship is made; Sutpen's design is repudiated; the boy, even though he has the "taint" of Negro blood, is not turned away from the door.

Both Henry's action, the violent turning away from the door with a bullet, and Judith's, the holding open the door not merely to Bon, her fiancé, but literally to his part-Negro son, are human actions, as Sutpen's actions are not. Both involve renunciation, and both are motivated by love. The suffering of Henry and Judith is not meaningless, and their very capacity for suffering marks them as having transcended their father's radical and disabling defect. (pp. 302-05)

One must not alter the focus of the novel by making wisdom won through suffering the issue. But the consequences entailed upon Judith and Henry have to be mentioned if only to discourage a glib Gothicizing of the novel or forcing its meaning into an over-shallow sociological interpretation.

Miss Rosa feels the Coldfields are all cursed; and certainly the impact of Sutpen upon her personally is damning: she remains rigid with horror and hate for forty-three years. But it is Miss Rosa only who is damned. Judith is not damned; nor am I sure that Henry is. Judith and Henry are not caught in an uncomprehending stasis. There is development: they grow and learn at however terrible a price. (p. 305)

Sutpen, as has been pointed out, never learns anything; he remains innocent to the end. As Quentin sees the character: when Charles Bon first comes to his door, Sutpen does not call it "retribution, no sins of the father come home to roost; not even calling it bad luck, but just a mistake . . . just an old mistake in fact which a man of courage and shrewdness . . . could still combat if he could only find out what the mistake had been." I have remarked that Sutpen's innocence is peculiarly the innocence of modern man. For like modern man, Sutpen does not believe in Jehovah. He does not believe in the goddess Tyche. He is not the victim of bad luck. He has simply made a "mistake." (p. 306)

Sutpen resembles the modern American, whose character, as Arthur M. Schlesinger has put it, "is bottomed on the profound conviction that nothing in the world is beyond [his] power to accomplish." Sutpen is a "planner" who works by blueprint and on a schedule. He is rationalistic and scientific, not traditional, not religious, not even superstitious.

We must be prepared to take such traits into account if we attempt to read the story of Sutpen's fall as a myth of the fall of the Old South. Unless we are content with some rather rough and ready analogies, the story of the fall of the house of Sutpen may prove less than parallel. The fall of the house of Compson as depicted in *The Sound and the Fury* is also sometimes regarded as a kind of exemplum of the fall of the old aristocratic order in the South, and perhaps in some sense it is. But the breakup of these two families comes from very different causes, and if we wish to use them to point a moral or illustrate a bit of social history, surely they point to different morals and illustrate different histories. Mr. Compson, whose father, General Compson, regarded Sutpen as a "little underbred," has failed through a kind of overrefinement. He has lost his grip on himself; he has ceased finally to believe in the values of the inherited tradition. He is a fatalist and something of an easy cynic. His vices are diametrically opposed to those of Thomas Sutpen, and so are his virtues. (pp. 306-07)

Up to this point we have been concerned with the character of Thomas Sutpen, especially in his relation to the claims of the family and the community. We have treated him as if he were a historical figure, but of course he is not. More than most characters in literature, Thomas Sutpen is an imaginative construct, a set of inferences—an hypothesis put forward to account for several peculiar events. For the novel *Absalom, Absalom!* does not merely tell the story of Thomas Sutpen, but dramatizes the process by which two young men of the twentieth century construct the character Thomas Sutpen. Fascinated by the few known events of his life and death, they try, through inference and conjecture and guesswork, to ascertain what manner of man he was. The novel then has to do not merely with the meaning of Sutpen's career but with the nature of historical truth and with the problem of how we can "know" the past. The importance of this latter theme determines the very special way in which the story of Sutpen is mediated to us through a series of partial disclosures, informed guesses, and constantly revised deductions and hypotheses.

Young Quentin Compson, just on the eve of leaving Mississippi for his first year at Harvard, is summoned by Miss Rosa Coldfield and made to listen to the story of her wicked brother-in-law, Thomas Sutpen. Sutpen had been a friend of Quentin's grandfather, General Compson, and as Quentin waits to drive Miss Rosa out to Sutpen's Hundred after dark, as she has requested, Quentin's father tells him what he knows about the Sutpen story.

Nobody had really understood the strange events that had occurred at Sutpen's Hundred—the quarrel between Thomas Sutpen and Henry, the disappearance of Henry with his friend Charles Bon, the forbidding of the marriage between Judith and Bon, and later, and most sensational of all, Henry's shooting of his friend Charles Bon at the very gates of Sutpen's Hundred in 1865. Mr. Compson makes a valiant effort to account for what happened. What evidently sticks in his mind is the fact that Charles Bon had an octoroon mistress in New Orleans. Presumably Judith had told General Compson or his wife about finding the octoroon's picture on Charles Bon's dead body. But in any case the visit, at Judith's invitation, of the [octoroon] woman to Charles Bon's grave would have impressed the whole relationship upon his son, Mr. Compson. Mr. Compson thinks that it was the fact of the mistress that made Thomas Sutpen oppose Bon's marriage to his daughter, but that Henry was so deeply committed to his friend that he refused to believe what his father told him about Bon's mistress, chose to go away with Charles, and only at the very end, when Charles Bon was actually standing before his father's house, used the gun to prevent the match.

It is not a very plausible theory. For though it could account for Sutpen's opposition to Bon, it hardly explains Henry's violent action, taken so late in the day. (pp. 308-10)

Quentin's other informant about the Sutpens is Miss Rosa Coldfield, Sutpen's sister-in-law. Miss Rosa clearly does not understand what happened. She exclaims that "Judith's marriage [was] forbidden without rhyme or reason," and her only theory for accounting for the murder is that Sutpen was a demon, and as a demon, dowered his children with a curse which made them destroy themselves. (p. 310)

By the time we have reached the end of section 5—that is, half way through the book—we have been given most of the basic facts of the Sutpen story but no satisfactory interpretation of it. We know the story of Sutpen's life in the Mississippi community pretty much as the community itself knew it, but the events do not make sense. The second half of the book may be called an attempt at interpretation. When section 6 opens, we are in Quentin's room at Harvard. . . . Quentin and Shreve discuss the story of Sutpen and make their own conjectures as to what actually happened. In this second half of the book there are, to be sure, further disclosures about Sutpen, especially with reference to his early life before he came to Mississippi. Sutpen, it turns out, had once told the story of his early life to General Compson, and his information had been passed on to Quentin through Mr. Compson. As Shreve and Quentin talk, Quentin feeds into the conversation from time to time more material from his father's and grandfather's memory of events. . . . But as the last four sections of the book make plain, we are dealing with an intricate imaginative reconstruction of events leading up to the murder of Charles Bon—a plausible account of what may have happened, not what necessarily did happen.

If the reader reminds himself how little hard fact there is to go on—how much of the most important information about the motivation of the central characters comes late and is, at best, vague and ambiguous—he will appreciate how much of the story of Sutpen and especially of Sutpen's children has been spun out of the imaginations of Quentin and Shreve.

Absalom, Absalom! is indeed from one point of view a wonderful detective story—by far the best of Faulkner's several flirtations with this particular genre. It may also be considered to yield a nice instance of how the novelist works, for Shreve and Quentin both show a good deal of the insights of the novelist and his imaginative capacity for constructing plausible motivations around a few given facts. This theme would obviously be one dear to Faulkner's heart. Most important of all, however, *Absalom, Absalom!* is a persuasive commentary upon the thesis that much of "history" is really a kind of imaginative construction. The past always remains at some level a mystery, but if we are to hope to understand it in any wise, we must enter into it and project ourselves imaginatively into the attitudes and emotions of the historical figures. Both of the boys make this sort of projection, though one would expect it to be easy for Quentin and difficult for Shreve. Actually, it does not work out in this way, for Shreve enters into the reconstruction of the past with ardor. He finds it, in his lack of any serious emotional commitment, a fascinating game—in fact, he consistently treats it as a game, saying "Let me play now.". . . Quentin, on the other hand, is too much involved—too fully committed to the problems and the issue—actually to enjoy the reconstruction. He feels a compulsion to do so, of course, the same compulsion that had caused him, against his better judgment, to go up into the bedroom at Sutpen's Hundred and look upon the wasted face of Henry Sutpen.

To note that the account of the Sutpens which Shreve and Quentin concoct is largely an imaginative construct is not to maintain that it is necessarily untrue. Their version of events is plausible, and the author himself—for whatever that may be worth—suggests that some of the scenes which they palpably invented were probably true. . . . But it is worth remarking that we do not "know," apart from the Quentin-Shreve semifictional process, many events which a casual reader assumes actually happened. (pp. 310-12)

One of the most important devices used in the novel is the placing of Shreve in it as a kind of sounding board and mouthpiece. By doing so, Faulkner has in effect acknowledged the attitude of the modern "liberal," twentieth-century reader, who is basically rational, skeptical, without any special concern for history, and pretty well emancipated from the ties of family, race, or section. In fact, Shreve sounds very much like certain literary critics who have written on Faulkner. It was a stroke of genius on Faulkner's part to put such a mentality squarely inside the novel, for this is a way of facing criticism from that quarter and putting it into its proper perspective. (p. 313)

It is curious that Shreve, all of whose facts have been given him by or through Quentin, is allowed in the latter chapters to do most of the imaginative work—far more, I should say, than is allowed to Quentin. . . . Perhaps the fact that Quentin is so involved makes it difficult or distasteful for him to talk. At any rate, it is the "outsider" who does most of the imaginative reconstruction. Quentin's role at times becomes merely that of a check or brake upon Shreve's fertile imagination. (pp. 313-14)

In remarking on how little of hard fact one has to go on, we should bear in mind particularly the question of Bon's Negro blood and of his kinship to Henry. Quentin says flatly that "nobody ever did know if Bon ever knew Sutpen was his father or not." Did anyone ever know whether Bon knew that he was part Negro? In their reconstruction of the story, Shreve and Quentin assume that Bon was aware that he was Henry's part-Negro half-brother (though [later] Quentin and Shreve assume that Bon did not know that he had Negro blood). If in fact Bon did have Negro blood, how did Shreve and Quentin come by that knowledge? As we have seen, neither Judith nor Miss Rosa had any inkling of it. Nor did Mr. Compson. Early in the novel he refers to Bon's "sixteenth part negro son." (pp. 314-15)

The conjectures made by Shreve and Quentin—even if taken merely as conjectures—render the story of Sutpen plausible. They make much more convincing sense of the story than Mr. Compson's notions were able to make. And that very fact suggests their probable truth. But are they more than plausible theories? Is there any real evidence to support the view that Bon was Sutpen's son by a part-Negro wife? There is, and the way in which this evidence is discovered constitutes another, and the most decisive, justification for regarding *Absalom, Absalom!* as a magnificent detective story. (p. 315)

[When] Quentin tells Shreve of Sutpen's long conversation with General Compson about his "design" and about the "mistake" that Sutpen had made in trying to carry it out, Shreve asks Quentin whether General Compson had then really known what Sutpen was talking about. Quentin answers that General Compson had not known; and Shreve, pressing the point, makes Quentin admit that he himself "wouldn't have known what anybody was talking about" if he "hadn't been out there and seen Clytie." The secret of Bon's birth, then, was revealed to Quentin on that particular visit. Shreve's way of phrasing it implies that it was from Clytie that Quentin had got his information, but, as we shall see, it is unlikely that Clytie was Quentin's informant. In any case, when Shreve puts his question about seeing Clytie, he did not know that another person besides Clytie and her nephew was living at Sutpen's Hundred.

Miss Rosa has sensed that "something"—she does not say *someone*—was "living hidden in that house." When she and Quentin visit Sutpen's Hundred, her intuition is confirmed. The hidden something turns out to be Henry Sutpen, now come home to die. Presumably, it was from Henry Sutpen that Quentin learned the crucial facts. Or did he? Here again Faulkner may seem to the reader either teasingly reticent or, upon reflection, brilliantly skillful. (pp. 315-16)

At all events, the whole logic of *Absalom, Absalom!* argues that *only* through the presence of Henry in the house was it possible for Quentin—and through Quentin his father and Shreve and those of us who read the book—to be made privy to the dark secret that underlay the Sutpen tragedy.

At the end of the novel Shreve is able to shrug off the tragic implications and resume the tone of easy banter. . . . Though the spell of the story has been powerful enough to fire his imagination and involve all his sympathies, he is not personally committed, and we can see him drawing back from the tragic problem and becoming again the cheery, cynical, common-sense man of the present day. . . .

From his stance of detachment, Shreve suddenly, and apropos of nothing, puts to Quentin the question "Why do you hate the South?" And Quentin's passionate denial that he hates it tells its own story of personal involvement and distress. The more naïve reader may insist on having an answer: "Well, does he hate it?" And the response would have to be, I suppose, another question: "Does Stephen Dedalus hate Dublin?" (p. 317)

At this point, however, it may be more profitable to put a different question. What did the story of Sutpen mean to Quentin? Did it mean to him what it has apparently meant to most of the critics who have written on this novel—the story of the curse of slavery and how it involved Sutpen and his children in ruin? Surely this is to fit the story to a neat and oversimple formula. Slavery was an evil. But other slaveholders avoided Sutpen's kind of defeat and were exempt from his special kind of moral blindness. (pp. 317-18)

The story embodied the problem of evil and of the irrational: Henry was beset by conflicting claims; he was forced to make intolerably hard choices—between opposed goods or between conflicting evils. Had Henry cared much less for Bon, or else much less for Judith, he might have promoted the happiness of one without feeling that he was sacrificing that of the other. . . . Had Henry been not necessarily wiser but simply more cynical or more gross or more selfish, there would have been no tragedy.

To say that Quentin was peculiarly susceptible to this meaning of Henry's story is not to make of Shreve a monster of inhumanly cool irrationality. But Shreve is measurably closer to the skepticism and detachment that allow modern man to dismiss the irrational claims from which Quentin cannot free himself and which he honors to his own cost.

The reader of *Absalom, Absalom!* might well follow Quentin's example. If he must find in the story of the House of Sutpen something that has special pertinence to the tragic dilemmas of the South, the aspect of the story to stress is not the downfall of Thomas Sutpen, a man who is finally optimistic, rationalistic, and afflicted with elephantiasis of the will. Instead, he ought to attend to the story of Sutpen's children.

The story of Judith, though muted and played down in terms of the whole novel, is one of the most moving that Faulkner has ever written. She has in her the best of her father's traits. . . . She endures the horror of her fiancé's murder and buries his body. She refuses to commit suicide; she keeps the place going for her father's return. Years later it is Judith who sees to it that Bon's mistress has an opportunity to visit his grave, who brings Bon's child to live with her after his mother's death and, at least in Quentin's reconstruction of events, tries to get the little boy to recognize her as his aunt and to set him free, pushing him on past the barriers of color. When she fails to

do so, she still tries to protect him. . . . She is one of Faulkner's finest characters of endurance—and not merely through numb, bleak Stoicism but also through compassion and love. Judith is doomed by misfortunes not of her making, but she is not warped and twisted by them. Her humanity survives them.

Because Henry knew what presumably Judith did not know, the secret of Bon's birth, his struggle—granted the circumstances of his breeding, education, and environment—was more difficult than Judith's. He had not merely to endure but to act, and yet any action that he could take would be cruelly painful. He was compelled to an agonizing decision. (pp. 318-19)

Absalom, Absalom! is the most memorable of Faulkner's novels—and memorable in a very special way. Though even the intelligent reader may feel at times some frustration with the powerful but darkly involved story, with its patches of murkiness and its almost willful complications of plot, he will find himself haunted by individual scenes and episodes, rendered with almost compulsive force. (p. 320)

Absalom, Absalom! is in many respects the most brilliantly written of all Faulkner's novels, whether one considers its writing line by line and paragraph by paragraph, or its structure, in which we are moved up from one suspended note to a higher suspended note and on up further still to an almost intolerable climax. The intensity of the book is a function of the structure. The deferred and suspended resolutions are necessary if the great scenes are to have their full vigor and significance. Admittedly, the novel is a difficult one, but the difficulty is not forced and factitious. It is the price that has to be paid by the reader for the novel's power and significance. There are actually few instances in modern fiction of a more perfect adaptation of form to matter and of an intricacy that justifies itself at every point through the significance and intensity which it makes possible. (pp. 323-24)

> *Cleanth Brooks, "History and the Sense of the Tragic ('Absalom, Absalom!')," in his* William Faulkner: The Yoknapatawpha Country, *Yale University Press, 1963, pp. 295-324.*

HYATT H. WAGGONER

Absalom, Absalom! has no close precedent, even in Faulkner's own works. Hindsight suggests now that much in modern fiction, and in modern opinion, should have prepared us for it, but it is not really surprising that most of the early reviewers were bewildered. Like *The Waste Land, Absalom* has many voices but no official, sanctioned Voice. The voices in it speak from many points of view, none of them removed from the criticism of irony. *Absalom* demonstrated once more Faulkner's artistic courage. (p. 148)

[In *Absalom, Absalom!,* Faulkner often uses the voice of] Quentin, who speaks with no special authority, mostly in the words of others, and who does not act at all; and [that of his college roommate] Shreve, who speaks as one amazed, even outraged, by a tale hard to credit and almost impossible to understand, and who, when he is not repeating what Quentin has told him, invents a version based on no uniquely privileged knowledge of the facts. Quentin and Shreve together finally imagine a version of Sutpen's story that has both plausibility and meaning, but the plausibility rests upon our willingness to accept as correct certain speculations of theirs for which they can offer no solid proof, and the meaning is left implicit. . . . (p. 149)

As Quentin tells his college roommate what he has been told and what he discovered for himself the night a few months before when he went to the ruined house with Miss Rosa, the two of them imaginatively recreate and relive Sutpen's story. The novel that emerges from their cooperative retelling has seemed to many readers best defined as a lyric evocation of the Southern past: the novel as poem. Quentin and Shreve retell the facts about Sutpen and his children in order to discover the feelings that can make the facts credible, rehearsing the deeds to discover the motives. The result is a kind of poem on time and death and the presentness of the past which seems so remote when we know only the "facts," a poem on the failure of the old order in the South, created by an evocation of the "ghosts" that have haunted Quentin's life. Quentin and Shreve are young, imaginative, easily moved to sympathetic identification. The joint product of their efforts, as they work with memory and imagination, evokes, in a style of sustained intensity of pitch, a feeling of the mystery and a sense of the pain and defeat of human life. It conveys its impressions through some of the most sharply realized images in modern writing in a rhetoric strained almost to the breaking point by an agony of identification with the suffering of the characters.

But *Absalom* cannot be completely understood in terms of this analogy with a lyric poem. The insight is useful in its pointing to pure evocation achieved through a strategy of indirection, but it leaves the central fact of the form of *Absalom*—its multiple retellings of what is in one sense already known and in another sense eludes knowing—unrelated to the feelings evoked and the meanings created by the form. Much of Faulkner's fiction may be called lyrical, and criticism today forces on us a recognition of the fact that all successful novels are in some sense like poems. The uniqueness of *Absalom* is not to be found here, so much as in the fact that it takes its form from its search for the truth about human life as that truth may be discovered by understanding the past, in which actions are complete, whole, so that we may put motive, deed, and consequence all into one picture. (pp. 149-50)

The whole effort of Quentin and Shreve, who end by becoming twin narrators, is to comprehend what is "not quite comprehensible." (p. 151)

The story they finally put together is a product of their imagination working as best it can toward truth with the overabundant, conflicting, and enigmatic material at hand. As bias is balanced against bias and distorted views give way to views with different distortions, fragmented and overlapping pictures of people and actions emerge from the multiple mirrors and screens of the telling. Then the fragments begin to fall into place for us and at last they cohere in a story possessing an immediacy, a distinctness of outline, and an evocativeness almost unparalleled in modern fiction. The dim ghosts evoked by Miss Rosa out of the distant past take on flesh and their actions finally take on meaning as we move from Miss Rosa's memories to Shreve's and Quentin's imaginings. A story is told, and a meaning expressed, despite a technique seemingly designed to delay the telling and withhold meaning. (p. 152)

Shreve and Quentin supplement and correct each other; and Shreve, Quentin, and the reader join with Miss Rosa and Quentin's father and grandfather in a joint effort to understand Sutpen and search out what is hidden. Sutpen cannot be questioned, and Quentin's experience in the house has to be understood in relation to matters that cannot be known with certainty; and then it becomes hardly distinguishable from what has been posited, imagined. The tale that finally takes shape in the mind of the reader of *Absalom* is in several senses a cooperative construct—not a figment or a fantasy but something creatively discovered.

As it may be said of the naturalistic novel that it attempted to probe behind conventional interpretations and values to get at "fact," so it may be said of *Absalom* that it tries to get behind not only received interpretations but the public facts themselves to get at what Faulkner has called in the introduction to **"Monk"** in *Knight's Gambit*, "credibility and verisimilitude." One of the meanings of *Absalom* is that the central effort of the naturalistic novel, to transfer a "slice of life" onto the printed page without any shaping act of imagination, interpretation, and judgment, is impossible. It is impossible not because the sacrifice of art to truth is too great a price to pay but because without the kind of imaginative effort and creation we find always at the center of art, there is not only no art but no truth.

The complications of the telling can be clarified somewhat if we think of the basic story—Sutpen, from his early youth through the death of his remaining son and half-Negro daughter—as having not one but several narrative frames. The telling of the story by Quentin to Shreve—and partly later by Shreve to Quentin—makes the frame which encloses all the others. But this telling and retelling is based on versions of the same story, or of parts of it, given to Quentin by Miss Rosa and father; and father's version is based in large part on a version given him by his father, who got it in part from Sutpen himself. Since in Quentin's version each of these people speaks in his own voice, often at great length and circumstantially, with unintended revelation of himself in the process, what we have in effect is a series of frames, one within the other, like the picture of a picture containing a picture, and so on. (pp. 152-54)

As the frames are shifted and the implicit distortions discovered, we see the motive for the continual retelling. Each new version is a part of the search in which Quentin and Shreve involve the reader, the search for a truth beyond and behind distortion. (p. 155)

The motive for the retellings, the reinterpretations, each of which adds new facts as well as a new perspective and makes necessary a reinterpretation of the facts already known, is constant, and it supplies the organizing principle of the novel.

Shreve's role as interpretive listener and finally as partial narrator is crucial. By the time we discover his presence we are more than halfway through the book and we realize now that both Miss Rosa's telling and father's retelling are part of the past which Shreve and Quentin have rehearsed. Now a new frame, more distant from Sutpen, comes in focus. As father had been less intimately involved in the Sutpen story than Miss Rosa, so Shreve the Canadian is less involved than father. The movement is one of progressive disengagement, a moving outward from the center. Yet the parts of the story that Shreve retells are among the most vivid and circumstantial in the whole book. Shreve's imagination moves freely. His presence in the story makes possible the widest of the circling movements through which the subject is approached. (pp. 155-56)

[Shreve puts Sutpen's story in] perspective when he says, toward the end, "'So he just wanted a grandson . . . That was all he was after. Jesus, the South is fine, isn't it. It's better than the theater, isn't it. It's better than Ben Hur, isn't it.'" *Absalom* has been called Gothic and obsessive, but true Gothic cannot survive irony, and obsession does not admit criticism. Here the irony and the criticism are central. (p. 156)

[What] emerges is substantially different from what would have emerged had there been no Shreve for Quentin to talk and listen to. . . . [We] are ready now, prepared by the interchange between Quentin and Shreve, to speculate with them, to invent probable characters and fill in details to make the story, the given incomprehensible facts, plausible. This is one of the most extreme examples of the conjectural method of the whole search that Quentin and Shreve are engaged in; and it is made to seem natural, right, because Shreve, who cannot be accused of excessive closeness to the material, offers the speculation. (p. 157)

[It is also] Shreve who at the end offers the prediction that "the Jim Bonds are going to conquer the western hemisphere" and asks Quentin why he hates the South. Shreve adds distance, controlling irony, to a story that otherwise might be obsessive or too shrill. If his final question to Quentin is, perhaps, somewhat unprepared for, so that we may find the ironic effect a little forced at this point, nevertheless he discharges his crucial function in the story with wonderful economy. His point of view is not the final one because there is no final one explicitly stated anywhere in the book. (pp. 157-58)

In the absence of chronologically related plot as the controlling factor, the relations of points of view govern the order of the chapters. Chapter One is Miss Rosa's. Miss Rosa lives in the past, in the cherishing of her hatred and her frustration. . . . Her view of the past is simple, moralistic, and, to Quentin, quite incredible. For her Sutpen was an evil man, satanic, with no redeeming qualities.

The next three chapters are Quentin's father's. His point of view is that of the interested but emotionally uninvolved rational observer. Unlike Miss Rosa, father is impressed by the mystery of human action and frequently confesses himself baffled in his search for understanding. If he is biased in any way it is slightly in Sutpen's favor, partly because the town condemned Sutpen and father is an iconoclast who has little respect for conventional opinion, partly because much of his information he got from his father, who was Sutpen's one friend in the community, the only one willing to defend him against outraged public opinion.

Chapter Five is Miss Rosa's again. We are now prepared for a verbatim report of a part of what she said to Quentin that afternoon. Miss Rosa, it is clearer now, not only hates Sutpen but judges him from a point of view not wholly distinct from his own. . . . She shares, it begins to appear, both his racial and his class prejudices, and she hates him chiefly because he destroyed for her that social eminence, respectability, and security which it was the aim of his design to secure for himself and his posterity. Yet though we recognize and allow for her obsessive hatred, we learn much from her account that we should not otherwise know, and we cannot entirely discount her judgment.

Chapter Six is Shreve's retelling of what Quentin has told him of what Quentin's father has told Quentin. . . . The snow on Shreve's overcoat sleeve suggests the distance from which he views this tale which began for us in the "long still hot weary" afternoon when Quentin sat with Miss Rosa. And Shreve himself, with his ruddy vitality, contrasts sharply with the other narrators—with the passive Quentin and with Miss Rosa herself. . . . (pp. 158-59)

Parts of Sutpen's story have been told and retold now from points of view both hostile and friendly or neutral, by narrators within his own culture, and again from a point of view entirely external. . . . Chapter Seven gives us Sutpen's story, the first part of it largely in a paraphrase of his own statements and some of it in his own words, as he told it to Quentin's grandfather—and as grandfather told it to father and father told it to Quentin and Quentin told it to Shreve: there is no certainty even in *ipsissima verba,* no possibility of getting back to "the thing in itself" of Sutpen's consciousness.

Sutpen saw himself alternately in the role of innocence betrayed and the role of a man who had made some mistake in adding a row of figures. Grandfather does not question his self-evaluation, simply passes it on. We are given almost no reason and very little opportunity, within the early part of this chapter, to question Sutpen or to step outside his frame of reference. The poor child who had been turned away from the door of the rich man's house conceived a design for his life calculated to put him in a position where he could never again be humiliated by anyone. Since he could see that the rewards in life went to the "courageous and shrewd" and since, though he felt sure he had courage, he had failed in his design, he must have made a mistake, a miscalculation somewhere. What could it be? (pp. 159-60)

Most of the material of this chapter comes ultimately from [Quentin's] grandfather, who was not only Sutpen's "advocate" but the only one in Jefferson who knew about the past which had shaped him to be what he was. Since this report of Sutpen's history has the additional advantage, if "inside knowledge" is an advantage, of resting on Sutpen's own self-awareness, it constitutes an effective foil to the "demonizing" of Miss Rosa, through whom we first met Sutpen.

Chapter Eight is Bon's chapter, his story (and Henry's, but chiefly his) as interpreted sympathetically by Shreve and Quentin. Shreve is no longer amused, ironic. He has been drawn into the tale now: this is a part he can feel, thinks he can understand. And for the first time he and Quentin are in complete agreement in their interpretive reconstructions. It no longer matters who is speaking: each is capable of taking up where the other left off, completing the other's thought. This is the most direct and circumstantial segment of the whole tale. It might be called interpretation by immersion, or by empathy. It penetrates Bon's consciousness to discover his point of view, reporting his experiences in detail, complete with imaginary conversations for which there is no warrant in the literally known facts. In place of Miss Rosa's bald summaries of Sutpen's whole career, mingled with moral judgments, we have here a detailed "realistic" rendering of the qualitative aspects of a few of Bon's experiences. There is no certainty, of course, that Shreve and Quentin are right in the details of their reconstruction. . . . Yet the reader is led by the circumstantial solidity of this chapter to feel more certain that this sympathetic account of Bon is correct than he is of any other interpretation he has encountered so far in the book.

Chapter Nine presents what might be called a general perspective on the whole tale. We are beyond the uniquely biased views of those who were closest to Sutpen. Two things happen at this point. First, Quentin and Shreve come into the foreground of the picture explicitly as narrators. No longer merely voices speaking to us in the words of the past, chiefly through direct and indirect quotation, they now appear as preservers of a past which must in some degree be created in order to be preserved. (pp. 160-62)

The second thing that happens is that as the appearance of objectivity evaporates the "facts" come back into focus and we move out again from subjective to objective. We learn for the first time in this last chapter what Quentin experienced that night when he went with Miss Rosa to Sutpen's decaying mansion. Everything before this has been hearsay, rumor, conjecture, hypothesis, or, at best, biased accounts of matters of fact. Here we are in the presence of something that we know ''really happened,'' the terrible culmination of the Sutpen story. We are in a position to understand and to respond emotionally and imaginatively. Quentin does not need to theorize, or even create an atmosphere. The bare, elliptical, subjective record, the fragmentary memory, of what happened that night is enough. Without what has preceded the record would be meaningless. (p. 162)

Though Quentin's meeting with Henry is the one thing in the novel which may conceivably justify a charge of pointless mystification—why are we not told what Quentin learns from Henry?—yet I think the bareness of this climactic episode suggests its own justification. This meeting was a confrontation with a flesh-and-blood ghost. Here is proof that the past is ''real'' (though not yet, for Quentin at the time, explicable). This is the shock that motivates the search for understanding. In giving us the incident only in the barest outline, Faulkner is following the Jamesian formula of making the reader imagine. By the time we come to the episode in the book we have plenty of material for the imagination to work with. We discover, better than if we were told, that the past is still alive, still with us, demanding to be understood.

We end, in this last chapter, sharing Quentin's and Shreve's certainty about just two other matters of the first importance: that Sutpen brought his destruction upon himself, and that Bon asked only for recognition. But the first of these certainties rests upon the second, and the second is itself ''certain'' only if we either decide to trust Quentin and Shreve to be right or if we have so far shared their imaginative adventure as to arrive with them at the same conclusion. It is, at any rate, beyond proof. The whole meaning of Sutpen's history hangs on this leap of the imagination.

But *Absalom, Absalom!* is not an exercise in perspectivist history, it is a novel; it tells a story. Each chapter contributes something to our knowledge of the action. It is true that we know something of the end of the story before we know the beginning, but what we know of the end is tantalizingly incomplete until we get to the end of the book; and what we know of the beginning of Sutpen's story, by the end of the book, could not have been understood earlier. If tricks are being played with time here, if the form is less conspicuously temporal than spatial or conceptual, it is not in the interest of obscuring the story but of making possible an existential understanding of it.

The versions of the Southern past that Quentin has grown up with he recognizes as inadequate, but he is not interested in adding to them one more subjective version, his own. What he is interested in is ''the truth.''. . . [Because] Quentin is interested in truth he must reject too simple a view of it. The ''spatial'' form of the novel *is,* from one point of view, *symbolizes,* from another, Quentin's probing beyond and behind appearances to get at reality. *Absalom* is conspicuously an orderly book, but the order in it springs from within, from the human need and effort to understand, not from anything external to itself. It substitutes an aesthetic and human order for temporal order. The result is a story inseparable from its meanings.

But the screens, the baffles that keep us from getting directly at the facts, are not only thematically expressive, they serve a more elementary, but indispensable, need of fiction. They do not lessen but increase the suspense. We learn in the first chapter, for instance, that Sutpen must have said or done something outrageously shocking to Miss Rosa to precipitate her departure from his house. We do not learn what it was until much later, but meanwhile we have never been allowed entirely to forget it. Again, we hear of Wash Jones early as an ill-mannered ''poor white'' who brought Miss Rosa the news of Bon's death. We learn later that he was responsible for Sutpen's death, but not how. We find out later still something of the manner of the death, hearing of the rusty scythe. But only toward the end do we witness the death itself, one of the great scenes in literature. Meanwhile our conception of Jones has been growing so that by the time we see him kill Sutpen we are prepared to see the action of this grim and silent avenger as both psychologically motivated and far-reaching in its symbolic implications. Our knowing ahead of time something of what would happen—as though we had a premonition at once certain and indistinct—has not lessened but actually increased the impact of the scene.

The characters of *Absalom* grow, emerge and develop, as we catch glimpses of them from different angles. When we finally confront Judith directly, after we already know the outline of her life, we are prepared to feel her few words and actions reverberating in areas that would have been closed to us without the preparation. She has become a figure of tragic proportions. The fluid and subjective quality of *Absalom*'s sifting of memory implies no diminution or beclouding of the world of significant action.

If Shreve and Quentin are right in their sympathetic estimate of Bon, then the immediate cause of the tragic events that resulted in the failure of Sutpen's design was his refusal to recognize his part-Negro son. Bon, Shreve and Quentin both believe, would have given up Judith and gone away if he had had any sign at all from his father, even the most private and minimal acknowledgement of their relationship. Shreve and Quentin cannot be sure that they are right. If they are wrong and Bon was a conscienceless extortioner, then the failure of Sutpen's design was caused, not by moral failure but as he himself thought, by ignorance, by the simple fact of his not knowing when he married her that Bon's mother was part Negro.

The title of the book, with its Biblical allusion, supports the hypothesis of Shreve and Quentin. Sutpen would not say ''My son'' to Bon as David said it to Absalom even after Absalom's rebellion. And different as he was from his father, Henry acted in the end on the same racist principle, killing Bon finally to prevent not incest but miscegenation. One meaning of *Absalom* then is that when the Old South was faced with a choice it could not avoid, it chose to destroy itself rather than admit brotherhood across racial lines.

But the theme is broader and deeper than the race problem which serves as its vehicle and embodiment. Sutpen was a cold and ruthless man motivated by a driving ambition to be his own god. His intelligence and courage won him a measure of success, but his pride destroyed him. . . . Sutpen was the new man, the post-Machiavellian man consciously living by power-knowledge alone, refusing to acknowledge the validity of principles that he cannot or will not live by and granting reality to nothing that cannot be known with abstract rational clarity. He lives by a calculated expediency. (pp. 162-66)

When he came to [Quentin's] grandfather to review his life, [Sutpen] was concerned to discover not which of his actions had been morally right and which wrong but where he had made the mistake which kept them from being, as modern scienteers would say, "effective." "Whether it was a good or a bad design is beside the point.". . . [Sutpen] could calculate no advantage to be gained by recognizing Bon as his son, and he was not one to be moved by the incalculable. There is point as well as humor in Shreve's characterization of him as Faustus. He is also related to Ahab and Ethan Brand.

The total form of the novel implies the ultimate reason for the failure of Sutpen's design. Considered as an integral symbol the form of *Absalom* says that reality is unknowable in Sutpen's way, by weighing, measuring, and calculating. It says that without an "unscientific" act of imagination and even of faith— like Shreve's and Quentin's faith in Bon—we cannot know the things which are most worth knowing. Naturally Sutpen failed in his design, and naturally he could not imagine where his error had been. His error had been ultimately, of course, in the moral sense, that he had always treated people as things. Even Bon falls into the same error when he tries to use Judith as a lever to move Sutpen, to get recognition.

Absalom also has implications about the nature and role of history that are worthy of further thought. Quentin's effort to understand Sutpen is an attempt to interpret all history, man's history. Quentin encounters two conflicting modes of interpretation, is satisfied by neither, and creates, with Shreve, a third that has some of the features of both. (pp. 166-67)

[Quentin and Shreve finally] find room for moral judgment: Sutpen's *hubris*, his narrow rationalism, his lack of love, all these are descriptions that imply the relevance of moral judgment. But Quentin and Shreve do not categorize Sutpen as simply a "bad" man: they know that to do so is to substitute judgment for explanation. . . . The view in terms of which they operate is that of classical-Christian tragedy, at once Greek and Biblical: history contains both God's judgment and man's decision, both necessity and freedom, and it has sufficient intelligibility for our human purposes. But its meaning is neither given nor entirely withheld. It must be achieved, created by imagination and faith. Historical meaning is a construct.

Such a view of history contrasts sharply with Marxist and "scientific" theories of history, but it has much in common with the best historiography of the thirties and of our own time. . . . As a novel built from the clash of conflicting views of history, *Absalom* seems to me as relevant now as when it was written.

No doubt *Absalom* gets its chief effect as a novel from our sense that we are participating in its search for the truth. *Absalom* draws us in, makes us share its creative discovery, as few novels do. The lack of an authoritative voice puts a greater burden on us as readers than we may want to bear. Faulkner ran this risk when he wrote it. He has had to wait long for a just appreciation of its greatness. Few readers were ready for it in the thirties. But if we can and will bear our proper burden as readers we shall find the rewards correspondingly great.

Absalom is the novel not denying its status as fiction but positively enlarging and capitalizing upon it. It appropriately closes Faulkner's period of most rapid and successful productivity with a full-scale thematic exploration of what had been implied in all the major works so far: that fiction is neither lie nor document but a kind of knowledge which has no substitute and to which there is no unimaginative shortcut. Adding to this the implication that fiction is not unique in its dependence upon imagination and the necessary deviousness of its strategy, it

suggests a view of life that Faulkner was to make increasingly explicit in later works. (pp. 167-69)

Hyatt H. Waggoner, "Past as Present: Absalom, Absalom!" in his William Faulkner: From Jefferson to the World, *University of Kentucky Press, 1959, 279 p.*

ROBERT E. SCHOLES

Literary critics often discuss something called "The Modern American Novel" as if a homogenous body of literature appropriately designated by that title really existed. Actually, there is no such thing. In those many assumptions about manners and morals which may be called the "premises" of fiction the novelists of the North and those of the South have been in fundamental opposition for many years. This division is closely related to the grave political division which has separated these two sections of the country and stems from the same source. The North and the South represent two distinct cultures, though they speak the same language.

The effects of this cultural division on literary works may be observed if novels representative of these societies are closely compared. For this purpose I have selected several novels dealing with related themes. In Faulkner's *Absalom, Absalom!* and Fitzgerald's *The Great Gatsby* we may examine two studies of the so-called "innocent" young man from the provinces attempting to rise in a more complex society. (p. 193)

At first, William Faulkner's *Absalom, Absalom!* appears to have a good deal in common with *The Bostonians, The Rise of Silas Lapham, Sister Carrie, The Great Gatsby* and the other Northern novels in the near-genre of stories about innocent young persons from the provinces. This view of *Absalom* has resulted in considerable misunderstanding and misinterpretation. In reality *Absalom, Absalom!* is a very different kind of book from those Northern novels, because Thomas Sutpen is presented by Faulkner in a way which differs radically from the way in which Scott Fitzgerald, for example, saw Jay Gatsby. To read Faulkner's novel as an indictment of Southern society (as Richard Rovere does in his introduction to the Modern Library edition) is to misread it grossly.

"Sutpen's trouble was innocence." With these words Quentin Compson begins to explain the actions of Thomas Sutpen to the outsider, Shreve McCannon, the Canadian who is curious about this alien Southern culture. Since many of us are in a position similar to Shreve's, since we approach *Absalom, Absalom!* as curious, sympathetic, and sometimes defensively facetious outsiders, Quentin's explanation may be for us also the best course toward comprehension of this novel. . . . (pp. 193-94)

It was Quentin's Grandfather who diagnosed Sutpen's trouble as innocence when he heard from Sutpen himself the history of his early days, and who repeated the story, along with the diagnosis, to Quentin. . . . Sutpen discovered both his ignorance and his innocence when he was turned away from the front door of a plantation house by a "monkey nigger" in "broadcloth and linen and silk stockings," and he lost his ignorance but not his innocence, "which he had never lost, because after it finally told him what to do that night he forgot about it and didn't know that he still had it." What Sutpen's innocence told him to do was to "combat them." (p. 194)

Sutpen's combat took the form of what he called his "design," which was the plan dictated by his innocence to revenge himself on "them." His design was a work of heroic simplicity. "To accomplish it," he told Quentin's Grandfather, "I should require money, a house, a plantation, slaves, a family—incidentally of course, a wife." In his simplicity Sutpen does not distinguish between the material and the intangible; he does not realize the difference between progeny and a family. His plan does not recognize the existence of love and other emotional intangibles which ultimately prevent the achievement of his design. And this is because the design is based on Sutpen's innocence. . . . (pp. 194-95)

[To attain] his design, Sutpen brought himself a virgin to his first marriage, because "that too was a part of the design which I had in my mind.". . . And when he found that his wife, and hence his son, had Negro blood, he simply began his recipe again with new ingredients, or, in his own words, "I merely explained how this new fact rendered it impossible that this woman and this child be incorporated in my design." So he "put aside" the woman and child who could not be incorporated into his design, after making an equitable financial settlement which he called and believed to be "justice," not knowing, in his innocence, that what had once been a part of his life, of his design, would always be a part of it. (p. 195)

For it is this woman, of course, and her child, Charles Bon, who are the principal instruments of the destruction of Sutpen's design, and they are able to act as such agents because of the blood relationships which Sutpen denied and because of the intangible, love, which unites Sutpen's children of two marriages in a terrible bond. . . .

Sutpen, like Adam and Eve in paradise, simply has no conception of sin or of evil. But Sutpen is not living in paradise. (p. 196)

Sutpen's actions repeatedly alienate him from the society of Jefferson, and, ultimately, from the whole human community. His penchant for engaging in hand-to-hand combat with his "wild niggers" is just one of those characteristics which, together with his suspicious past and rapid acquisition of wealth, set him off from Jefferson society. His record in the war seems to give him a chance to be assumed into the society around him, but he manages to alienate the Sartorises by displacing John Sartoris as Colonel of the local regiment, and finally to lose whatever good-will and acceptance he may have gained despite the Sartorises, by refusing to join the night-riders who were organizing against the carpet-baggers after the war. The incident is important, and Faulkner gives us two versions of it with interesting differences: one is narrated by Miss Rosa Coldfield in *Absalom, Absalom!;* the other, by Bayard Sartoris in **"An Odor of Verbena."** The different sympathies of the narrators naturally color their versions, but consistent in both stories is the attitude of Sutpen that the South can "save itself" only through individuals working on their own land, and the attitude of John Sartoris that collective action is needed, that the sum of all the individual Southern selfishnesses is not enough. The innocent Sutpen still thinks that every man can work out his own design alone and unaided, while John Sartoris speaks for those who place their faith in society.

But Sutpen is not only alienated from Jefferson society. He is cut off from the whole race of men. His innocently conceived design caused him to put aside the wife and child who did not fit in it; and throughout the novel his failure to distinguish between what is human and what is not is manifest. He purchases his second wife as methodically as he abandoned his first; he proposes to Miss Rosa that they breed like dogs and

see what they get; and finally he tells Wash Jones's granddaughter, who has just borne him a daughter for whom there is no place in the design, "Well Milly; too bad you're not a mare too. Then I could give you a decent stall in the stable," and this is his last evidence of inhuman blindness; for that grotesque parody of the grim reaper who unites all men in death, the absurd, shambling Wash Jones, waits outside with his rusty scythe to restore Thomas Sutpen to the human condition.

Sutpen's innocence serves primarily to make him inhuman, to deprive him, as Adam and Eve in their pre-human state were deprived, of the knowledge of good and evil and of sin and death; to make him what Rosa Coldfield and Shreve McCannon perpetually call him: a demon. Yet Thomas Sutpen is a man also, though his dream, his design, cloak his humanity in a ruthless, demonic exterior. The last time Sutpen appears in the novel is in the tent in Carolina where he has his final interview with his son Henry; and here, as Shreve and Quentin recreate the scene, Sutpen's humanity is more evident than anywhere else in the novel, when he embraces Henry, kisses him, and repeats the phrase with which King David mourned his lost son Absalom, "My Son." For the moment Sutpen seems redeemed into the human race—but did the situation really occur as Shreve and Quentin see it? Or do they do Sutpen more than justice through their intense sympathy? We do not know, any more than we know whether Jay Gatsby was actually graced by the moment of insight which Nick Carraway believes he may have had as he lay in the warm sunlight on "the pneumatic mattress that had amused his guests during the summer" and felt—or did not feel—that he had "paid a high price for living too long with a single dream."

The comparison between Gatsby and Sutpen is instructive, for they are both innocents in much the same way: men with a dream, who do not know good and evil as most men do, who believe in the future and are haunted by the past, yet who are presented in very different ways. The ruthlessness which Gatsby must have possessed to establish himself financially is only suggested by the Wolfsheim "gonnection," never displayed. As an innocent, Gatsby is more sinned against than sinning. His death is not a retribution but a mistake. While Sutpen's innocence serves to set him off, apart from society and humanity, Gatsby's tends to make him quintessentially human. The figure which appears at a distance as the Great Gatsby, on closer examination is revealed as "the poor son of a bitch." Gatsby's dream is the product of "a heightened sensitivity to the promises of life." Sutpen's design is conceived and executed in "abysmal and purblind innocence." For Fitzgerald the innocent is a seer; for Faulkner he is a blind man.

Fitzgerald's criticism in *The Great Gatsby* is not of his deluded hero but of the "foul dust [that] floated in the wake of his dreams," of the society which was not "commensurate to his capacity for wonder." The society of Jefferson and by extension the whole structure of Southern society is not taken by Faulkner as an object for criticism in *Absalom, Absalom!,* but as a condition of a particular human drama. Sutpen is, as Bayard Sartoris observed, "underbred." His opportunism is carefully distinguished from that of John Sartoris, who preserves always some notion of the community while pursuing his own ambitious course. The Sartorises and the Compsons represent a kind of aristocracy which a man well might wish to associate himself with; clearly they are more appealing as an ideal, however imperfect, than the Buchanans of *The Great Gatsby*. It is significant that Sutpen does not wish to join this society but to "combat" it. He sees his goal in terms of the acquisition of things which will help him "to combat them."

Sutpen sins, and compounds his sin by calling it a mistake. Sin is a word—like honor—which would echo strangely in the world of *Gatsby,* but which is of overmastering importance in the novels of William Faulkner. . . . The Calvinistic sense of sin which ebbed out of the Northern novel after Hawthorne is still strongly alive in the fiction of the South. (pp. 197-99)

It is at this point that the portentous question of the possibility of tragedy in modern literature might well arise. For, clearly, Faulkner's emphasis on the ability of man to sin and suffer and on the value of such suffering tends to place him in the company of the great tragic writers of the past. But the direction of this study is not esthetic but cultural. The question asked here is not whether this is indeed True Tragedy, but rather, why does this tendency toward tragedy exist at all in the writings of a Southern novelist like Faulkner and not in his Northern counterparts? In his study of tragic modes of fiction (*Anatomy of Criticism*) Northrop Frye has shrewdly observed that

> Tragedy belongs chiefly to the two indigenous developments of tragic drama in fifth-century Athens and seventeenth-century Europe from Shakespeare to Racine. Both belong to a period of social history in which an aristocracy is fast losing its effective power but still retains a good deal of ideological prestige.

In the Southern part of the United States since the Civil War a close approximation of this situation has existed. The social conditions have been of the sort which produce tragedy. The South has looked back regretfully toward its vanishing aristocratic ideal, while the North, preoccupied with the "orgastic future," has looked ahead to the culmination of its ideal of progress and prosperity. It is an ideal which has failed in *The Great Gatsby.* It is a man who fails to measure up to an ideal in *Absalom, Absalom!* (pp. 203-04)

> *Robert E. Scholes, "The Modern American Novel and the Mason-Dixon Line," in* The Georgia Review, *Vol. XIV, No. 2, Summer, 1960, pp. 193-204.*

IRVING HOWE

[*The essay from which this excerpt is taken was originally published in 1952 and revised in 1962.*]

From its place at the center of the Yoknapatawpha chronicle, *Absalom, Absalom!* gains an unsuspected stature; what might in isolation seem a stylized frenzy becomes a tone essentially right, even if all but unbearable. How else, one must concede, could Faulkner manage this lacerating return to the past? how else invest his one great story—the story of the fall of the homeland—with that foaming intensity which might warrant still another recapitulation?

Because the material of *Absalom, Absalom!* was so oppressively close to him, Faulkner had to find a device by which to hold it, so to speak, in suspension; and that device, perhaps the only possible one, was Gothic. To see the purpose and shape of the novel one must understand why Faulkner draped it in Gothic remnants; that much done . . . , the book can be judged as a solitary work of art and its three main elements examined: the character of Sutpen, the formal arrangement of its parts, and its uses of language.

In several of Faulkner's books a character is quickly placed beyond the perimeter of the ordinary; he stands apart from and

towers over the smaller creatures of his world. But no other Faulkner character rules a book so completely as does Sutpen in *Absalom, Absalom!* To be sure, there are several striking figures in the novel: old Mr. Coldfield starving himself in protest against the War; Wash Jones cackling the news of Charles Bon's death and years later cutting off Sutpen's head; Velery Bon marrying a lamp-black Negro woman so as to flaunt his own ambiguous status before anyone, whatever his color. But these figures are not meant to be more than full-scale. Present even when not seen and dominating whether seen or present, Sutpen fills the novel with his smoldering resolution. . . . This single-mindedness is less fanaticism than a grandiose solipsism. He is ready to exalt this purposes above the wisdom and convenience of society not because he despises it but because it does not exist for him; and he has the terrifying gift for hurrying to his fate without an interval of self-doubt.

Given his energy, his commitment to a mythic role, his impersonality in behalf of personal vindication—given all this, what could the mirror of his mind reflect but a rigid duplicate of his behavior? Faulkner's neglect of his inner consciousness is, therefore, no failure at all; for this hero need not be analyzed, he need only be stared at from a distance as he lives out his destiny.

Few things in Faulkner astonish more than Sutpen's power to make himself continuously felt. . . . Everything in the novel, from Charles Bon's doglike yearning for acceptance by his father to Wash Jones's ultimate rearing-up to manhood, is a function of Sutpen's will. (pp. 221-23)

Throughout the book Sutpen is finely controlled, his doom an inevitable culmination of his first clash with the world. In a curious sense Sutpen is innocent: he cannot fully reckon the consequences of what he does, the hunger that impels his "design" remains obscure to him. He harms no one out of malice or sadism, and he is not without sense, particularly in the hysterical years after the War. These very qualities serve only to intensify his destructiveness, for Faulkner realizes that a premeditated and impersonal act of evil can be more dangerous than a quick impulse to hurt.

Sutpen's life is a gesture of *hubris;* what prevents him from rising to the greatness of the tragic hero is a failure in self-recognition. . . . Sutpen is not struck by a weight of knowledge; he neither searches the source of his fall nor assumes responsibility for its consequences. Because he is incapable of that rending of the self and tearing out of pride which forms the tragic element, Sutpen dies as he lived, a satanic hero subject only to his own willfulness and the check of fate. He is one of the few heroes in twentieth-century literature who rejects the passive role, but his creator is sufficiently a writer of the century to withhold from him the cleansing ritual of tragedy.

Sutpen cannot be grasped through a single apprehension; he must be reached through ambush and obstacle, confusion and delay. Only gradually do we accustom ourselves to a man who is large and grand in his evil, and from this complexity in his character follows the technique of the novel. Suspensions of incident, apparent mystifications, calculated affronts to continuity—all are used in behalf of Faulkner's executive purpose. Not that every patch of rhetoric or device of structure springs from ineffable necessity; Faulkner is a craftsman all too ready to indulge his excesses. But the remark of one critic that Faulkner's complex structures derive "from an obscure and profligate confusion, a manifest absence of purpose rather than from an elaborate and coherent aim'' is, at least with regard to *Absalom, Absalom!,* wrong.

Of all Faulkner's novels *Absalom, Absalom!* most nearly approaches structural perfection. By presenting the effect of an action on spectator or narrator long before the action itself, the novel creates sudden eddies of confusion but also arouses large and exciting expectations; the emotional response of the characters, instead of stemming from the action, prepares for it. As long as action is adequate to expectation there need be no complaint, and for the most part it is—though one occasionally feels, as in reading Conrad's *Heart of Darkness,* that nothing could possibly satisfy all the hungers the author has stirred.

The scrambling of narrative cause and emotional response, like the circling back and forth in time, is warranted by the material itself. Faulkner is probing the under-tissues of the past, fearful that he will locate some secret evil—and that is hardly to be done with brisk directness. Were he merely trying to render the past in pictorial breadth and immediacy, *Absalom, Absalom!* would surely contain many more dramatic scenes than it does but since Faulkner and his central narrator Quentin Compson refuse to surrender to the past even as they cannot tear themselves away from it, the story is told rather than shown. And since the past is to be seen as a ''dead time,'' an almost incredible passage of nightmare, it must be presented in a ghostly flatness. The sense of time established by the novel is thus extraordinarily complex and ingenious. Through a delicate interaction of past times, the novel creates an illusion of timelessness within a strongly felt present. Time stops; the past is not recaptured in flow—that would be too dangerous—but broken, as it were, into a series of stills. And is this not one reason for Faulkner's use of Gothic—to stare at the ''old ghost times'' from a preserving distance?

For the details of this scheme there can be only praise: for the flares of inventiveness . . . ; for the moments of scenic vividness . . . ; for the balanced relation between chapters, each carrying its fraction of the story and together forming a comprehensive pattern; and for the skill with which Faulkner deploys shocks of climax. . . . (pp. 223-25)

While several characters are employed as narrators, they are not sharply distinguished, their voices blending in a drone of eloquence. Mr. Warren Beck has claimed that Faulkner ''does make some differences among these voices: Miss Rosa rambles and ejaculates with spinsterish emotion, Mr. Compson is elaborately and sometimes parenthetically ironic, Quentin is most sensitively imaginative and melancholy, Shreve most detached and humorous.'' These differences are indeed present, though not drawn quite so sharply as Mr. Beck formulates them. It does not very much matter, since Faulkner is trying not to identify the narrators as individuals but to arrange them as parts in a chorus. They seem, in the structure of the book, echoes of a master ventriloquist rather than individual voices attuned to Jamesian distinctions.

The style of *Absalom, Absalom!* is a style of oratory. . . . [The] oratory of *Absalom, Absalom!* evokes an image of a man rasping from the heart, perhaps to no one but himself. . . . The convolutions of Faulkner's prose mirror the reactions of his narrators to the events they uncover. And Faulkner's reactions too; the voice of the ventriloquist laments in romantic cadence and lifts to appalled shriek. *Absalom, Absalom!* is packed with the incongruities and complexities of consciousness, each sentence approaching, remembering, analyzing and modifying the material that has preceded it. ''To this end,'' remarks Warren

Beck, ''the sentence as a rhetorical unit (however strained) is made to hold diverse yet related elements in a sort of saturated solution. . . .'' And sometimes, one might add, supersaturated.

The uses to which Faulkner puts this prose are surprisingly varied, though *Absalom, Absalom!* is not a book likely to shine in isolated quotation. But for all its dragging periods, its lifeless Latinisms, its shrillness of pitch, the writing is often capable of fine modulations of tone and a wide range of effects. (pp. 225-27)

For its major fault in style—the absence of change of pace—only the book itself can serve as illustration. It lacks, and badly needs, those intervals of quiet and warmth provided in other Faulkner novels by such characters as Lena Grove and Dilsey. But a second characteristic weakness, a forcing of imagery, can be shown by quotation. The child Rosa Coldfield is facing Sutpen:

> The face, the smallest face in the company, watching him across the table with still and curious and profound intensity as though she had actually had some intimation gained from that rapport with the fluid cradle of events (time) which she had acquired or cultivated by listening behind closed doors not to what she heard there, but by becoming supine and receptive, incapable of either discrimination or opinion or incredulity, listening to the prefever's temperature of disaster, which makes soothsayers and sometimes makes them right, and of the future catastrophe in which the ogre-face of her childhood would apparently vanish so completely that she would agree to marry the late owner of it.

Faulkner himself seems uncertain about the communicative value of this sentence: how else explain the parenthesis? ''Rapport with the fluid cradle,'' ''temperature of a prefever,'' ''the unfortunate soothsayers''—all are signs of language being driven to do the work of imagination. Sometimes the writing breaks down in an excess of abstraction, as in sentences which cannot be read but must be deciphered. . . . (p. 230)

But the distinctive vice in the writing of *Absalom, Absalom!* is that the prose is whipped into a fury so habitual as to become mechanical and dull, a mere surrender to the monstrous. (p. 231)

[Despite the range of style in *Absalom, Absalom!*], it must be remembered that the book is an integral work of art in which success and failure can be distinguished but not separated. An artist deserves to be accepted, ultimately, in his completeness—his clarity and obscurity. Faulkner's greatest risk, *Absalom, Absalom!* is never likely to be read widely; it is for *aficionados* willing to satisfy the large and sometimes excessive demands it makes upon attention. Wild, twisted and occasionally absurd, the novel has, nonetheless, the fearful impressiveness which comes when a writer has driven his vision to an extreme. (pp. 231-32)

> *Irving Howe, in his* William Faulkner: A Critical Study, *third edition, The University of Chicago Press, 1975, 308 p.*

LAWRANCE THOMPSON

The average reader is likely to find that *Absalom, Absalom!* presents so many difficulties in style and plot and structure that the first discouraging effect may be one of apparent confusion and chaos, similar to the first effect of starting to read *The Sound and the Fury.* Yet Faulkner's ways of ordering and controlling his materials and his meanings in *Absalom, Absa-*

lom! are very strikingly different from the ways employed in *The Sound and the Fury.* Each of his best novels, and this is certainly one of them, has its own distinct and original pattern, which would seem to be determined by what Faulkner wants to make a particular story emphasize in regard to underlying meanings. If we proceed once again, then, with the assumption that our understanding and enjoyment of the parts and of the whole may be increased by a retrospective consideration of a few important technical principles of ordering, a convenient starting place may be found by noticing that four plots in *Absalom, Absalom!* are interwoven to make a unified whole. One kind of confusion disappears as soon as a reader begins to notice which of those plots is made to dominate the other three.

Of those four plots, a pivotal and yet minor one has a short-story shape and may be summarized as follows. . . . [One evening in 1909, Rosa Coldfield] asked Quentin if he would get his father's horse and carriage . . . and drive her to the splendid but decaying Sutpen mansion on the outskirts of Jefferson. She wanted to make that drive in order to learn whether a particular son of the late Thomas Sutpen might be hiding there as a fugitive from justice. . . . [As] soon as Miss Rosa found the fugitive from justice, as expected, and found him an invalid, she returned quietly to Jefferson with Quentin. . . . [She later] arranged to have an ambulance drive out to the Sutpen mansion for the purpose of rescuing the invalid from death. But as the ambulance approached, the inmates set the house on fire and two descendants of Thomas Sutpen, including the invalid, willingly perished in the flames. (pp. 53-54)

Thus summarized, that pivotal plot is very nearly meaningless. But a second plot, more important, may be pieced together from the fragments of information about Thomas Sutpen which Quentin Compson gathered during his talks about Sutpen, at first with Miss Rosa Coldfield and then with his father. That second plot may be summarized briefly, and in a way which also makes it relatively meaningless, as follows. Thomas Sutpen was born a poor white in western Virginia. While still a very young man he conceived an idealistic plan to build a fine mansion on a fine plantation somewhere in the South. Part of his plan was to marry well and to establish a noble line of descent. . . . [But he later discovered] that one event had caused the collapse of his plan to establish a noble line of descent. He never did learn or understand what mistake in his planning might have caused that unforeseen event. (p. 54)

That second plot obviously has the makings of a novel in itself; but Faulkner did not choose to handle that plot separately. In fact he interwove it with the third and fourth plots which in turn he interwove with the first and second. The third plot might be described as the story of what happened to Miss Coldfield, in early days, to make her so much interested in the latter days of the Sutpen mansion and the Sutpen descendants. It might be summarized, also somewhat meaninglessly, as follows. Miss Rosa Coldfield had been a child when her older sister Ellen was courted by and married to Thomas Sutpen. . . . After the death of her sister Ellen, and after the War, Miss Rosa was courted by Thomas Sutpen. But the courtship was conducted so crudely that his proposal was rejected as an insult, and Miss Rosa never could forgive Sutpen. Yet she could pity Sutpen's children and could worry over them, because they were also the children of her dead sister Ellen. Hence her attempt to rescue one of them from the Sutpen mansion, years later, even though she knew he was a murderer and a fugitive from justice.

Although it might seem that Faulkner could have interwoven those three plots adequately, without any addition, he chose instead to add what might be called a fourth plot, in such a way as to make it determine the entire significance of the other three plots. Instead of merely asserting what that fourth plot is, and of asserting that it achieves a dominant quality of importance, a more convincing way to marshal evidence may be to turn briefly from these considerations of plot to some brief considerations of structure and setting.

There are nine structural units or chapters in *Absalom, Absalom!* and they are built around three meaningful tableaux in three different settings. The first tableau occurs at the beginning of chapter one, where Quentin Compson is sitting in Miss Rosa Coldfield's parlor. . . . The second tableau (which is preserved throughout chapters two, three, and four) represents Quentin Compson, again sitting and listening; but this time the setting is the front gallery of his own home, and he is listening to his father's version of the Sutpen story, together with his father's comments on what Miss Rosa had told Quentin. Chapter five is a flashback, and the italics imply a stream-of-consciousness remembering, on Quentin's part, of certain details about the Sutpen story told him by Miss Rosa that afternoon—details which have become more meaningful to him (and to the reader) now that an improved perspective has been provided by new details given in Mr. Compson's version of the story. The third tableau, established at the beginning of chapter eight, represents Quentin Compson sitting and talking with his Harvard roommate Shrevlin McCannon in their Harvard dormitory room—talking across a letter from Mr. Compson announcing the death of Miss Rosa Coldfield. (pp. 54-5)

Those controlling aspects of structure and setting, plus those three tableaux, require the reader to realize that Quentin Compson is represented by Faulkner as being more than a center of consciousness through whom the reader ''sees'' or learns all the details of the other three plots. In a very important sense, Faulkner arranges the focus of the entire narrative to make the reader primarily concerned with what happened to Quentin Compson and what Quentin Compson happened to make out of the other three plots, in terms of *meaning, meaning, meaning.* From start to finish, Quentin is dramatically shown as trying to get at the underlying truth of Miss Coldfield's story and of the Sutpen story; trying to piece the fragments of evidence together; and finally trying to imagine or create fictions which have the quality of truth, in this larger fiction. (pp. 55-6)

So far, then, some clear advantages should have been gained from noticing the Faulknerian techniques of ordering and controlling his meanings through ingenious and original arrangements of tableaux and structure and setting and plots. Noticing those factors, the reader can be guided and directed by them, until the total story may be seen in a sharper focus. But Faulkner uses these same techniques in ways which further control the reader's attention. Because Quentin is the center of consciousness, through whose restricted vision the reader's own vision is also restricted, a curious effect is achieved. In a sense, the reader is thus forced to dramatize, or to act out, a very important aspect of theme which has to do with the processes by which human beings search for truth through insufficient evidence— the processes by which human beings employ their imaginations creatively to reinterpret knowledge, and thus to endow relatively meaningless facts with significant and useful meanings.

Now we may return to our first observations, and extend them. It would seem that Faulkner had artistic and thematic reasons for confronting the reader, initially, with difficulties in style and plot and structure—with apparent confusion and chaos. As we look more closely at the total structure, and recall the way in which Faulkner made Quentin (and with him the reader) circle back and back over so many of the same details concerning the Sutpen story, it becomes clear that an effect was achieved which was more than mere circling. Each return brought with it some new information, and therefore some improvement in perspective, so that the motion was one of a spiraling ascent. But as we have noticed, all those improvements in perspective bring Quentin (and with him the reader) to the ultimate vantage point only when Quentin and Shreve collaboratively perform their own creative process of imagining fictions within the fiction.

If these insights concerning the relationship between matter and meaning, or techniques and themes, may be extended to include another technical factor of ordering, even the confusing difficulties of style acquire new significance. Much of the narrative is provided through Quentin's stream-of-consciousness rememberings, which dramatize his puzzling search for meanings on the basis of insufficient evidence. The initial motion of Quentin's effort depends on what he is able to make out of Miss Rosa's obscure swirl of rhetoric, warped as it is by the narrowness of her own prejudices. The second motion of Quentin's effort depends on the antithetical, yet still obscure, swirl of Mr. Compson's rhetoric, also warped by the narrowness of his prejudices. Quentin's task is to perform a dialectical process of synthesis by combining Miss Rosa's thesis with Mr. Compson's antithesis. But the reader can go beyond Quentin, in this regard, by noticing that Faulkner arranged to let the rhetoric of each provide a pertinent aspect of characterization for each. For example, Miss Rosa's rhetoric employs a vocabulary which bristles with the terminology of Calvinistic Methodist dogma when she tells Quentin how this demon, this devil named Thomas Sutpen, first saw and courted Miss Rosa's sister Ellen. . . . (pp. 56-7)

In the counterpoint or antithesis provided by the rhetoric of Mr. Compson, correctives are offered from his very pessimistic and agnostic viewpoint, buttressed with what he understands (or rather misunderstands) of Greek tragedy. Mr. Compson views the long-dead Thomas Sutpen as a modern Agamemnon, doomed by circumstances beyond his control—doomed by a meaningless fate. (p. 57)

Even as Quentin makes use of and yet resists the interpretations of Sutpen offered by Miss Rosa and Mr. Compson, so the reader resists. For example, Mr. Compson keeps referring to Sutpen as a modern Agamemnon and guesses that Sutpen mistakenly gave the name of Clytemnestra to one of his daughters by a Negro slave; that he had "intended to name Clytie, Cassandra, prompted by some pure dramatic economy not only to beget but to designate the presiding augur of his own disaster." The reader should use and resist those analogies in ways which have bearing on theme. As yet, however, other factors need to be considered before such bearing becomes sufficiently meaningful. (p. 58)

As Quentin explained to his Harvard roommate, after Sutpen had built his mansion near Jefferson and after he had married Miss Ellen Coldfield and after he had raised a son named Henry and a daughter named Judith, Henry had brought home from college, as his closest friend, Sutpen's disowned son named Charles Bon. According to Quentin, that must have been the moment when Sutpen felt his plan put to the test. (p. 59)

Sutpen had told Quentin's grandfather that his first marriage had been annulled, but he had not told him why. . . . Before Quentin returned from that visit to the Sutpen mansion, his own father had not known about Charles Bon's background. But even after Quentin knew, even after he had told his father, the crux of the mystery in the Sutpen story was a murder. After Sutpen had forbidden the marriage of Judith and Charles Bon, Henry Sutpen had turned against his father and had sided with his half brother without knowing of their blood-relationship. . . . [At the gate of the Sutpen plantation], Henry had shot and killed Charles Bon.

Of course, by the time Quentin tried to explain all this to Shreve, at Harvard, they could understand enough to wish to reconstruct the details of that love story, which had involved Henry and Charles and Judith. As Quentin and Shreve try to imagine crucial conversations during crucial moments, Faulkner makes two important editorial intrusions for purposes of commenting on their creative process. (pp. 59-60)

Those two passages concerning these two creators of fictions within a fiction help to correlate and extend ideas which have been recurrent and questions hinted earlier concerning not only the limitations of human knowledge but also the ways in which limited knowledge searches for truth. The art of fiction, not unlike the art of historiography, is an imaginative process of creating possibilities which make the past, thus interpreted, more meaningful and useful to the present. But both arts require the collaboration of readers who are willing to arrange a "happy marriage of speaking and hearing," a joint effort of collaboration "wherein each before the demand, the requirement, forgave condoned and forgot the faulting of the other."

A more central aspect of a favorite Faulknerian theme is hinted and foreshadowed when Shreve and Quentin "overpass to love" in their imaginative creations and interpretations. Part of their imagining is that Charles Bon, informed by his mother that he has been disinherited by his father, re-enacts the familiar ritual of the orphan seeking his own identity—the son in search of the father. Quentin should be particularly interested in this aspect of theme; he himself was already represented as involved in it, throughout *The Sound and the Fury*. . . .

They imagine that Charles does finally arrange to make Henry do precisely what Charles wants him to do. But before they reach that stage in their creative process they imagine that when Charles Bon first knew he was to be taken home as a guest at Christmas time, by Henry, Bon must have hoped for some kind of recognition-scene between his father and himself. . . . (p. 61)

Quentin and Shreve imagine that perhaps Henry's deep love for Charles, after he learned of their half-brother relationship, was so powerful that during the War he gradually overcame his repugnance to the unavoidably incestuous element in the possible marriage of Bon to Judith; they imagine that only after the War, when Sutpen still refused to show Bon any indication of their kinship, and yet privately revealed to Henry that Bon had the very slightest "taint" of Negro blood, then and only then Henry may have found himself faced with what Henry might consider to be a tragic choice. Or perhaps Bon had precipitated the final crisis from motives of revenge and retaliation, bitterly and desperately planned, not against Henry but against the father who had refused to be a father. Maybe, Quentin and Shreve agree, Bon had decided to deprive Sutpen of two sons by making the gesture of insisting that he would marry Judith unless Henry stopped him. (p. 62)

[Bon's decision, together with Henry's fear of miscegenation], suggests the ironic possibility that the two sons of Thomas Sutpen, each finding his own way to force the crisis into a tragic conclusion, thus brought the Sutpen saga full circle by figuratively re-enacting precisely the same kind of self-centered and ruthless logic which their father had employed when he unconsciously established the matrix for this tragedy. That possibility is strengthened by a refrain which Quentin establishes and repeats, while considering the love stories of the Sutpens: "But it's not love," Quentin said. "That's still not love."

Throughout the narrative, Faulkner has arranged to concentrate more and more attention on those two sides of his thematic coin, love and not-love; but once again he has arranged to define the positive largely in terms of the negative. Because love was not one of the "old virtues" possessed by Thomas Sutpen, all the other virtues came to naught. And the last two love stories involving Thomas Sutpen put the clinching evidence on that thematic point. . . . The cold logic of his need was so clear that he proposed to Miss Rosa Coldfield that "they breed together for test and sample and if it was a boy they would marry." That was the end of that love story. The final love story brought the end of Sutpen. . . . [When] the desperate Sutpen transferred his biological attentions from the disgusted Miss Rosa to the passive and submissive granddaughter of Wash Jones, no complaint was possible. . . . For Wash Jones, the terrible moment of disillusionment came only when he stood outside his own shack on the morning Milly gave birth to a girl, and heard Sutpen say to her as he stood beside the bed holding mother and child, "Well, Milly; too bad you're not a mare too. Then I could give you a decent stall in the stable." Having uttered those casual not-love words, Sutpen left the shack to find Wash Jones waiting for him with the nearest weapon handy. It happened to be a rusty old scythe. Like Father Time, or like Fate, the furious man effectively used that symbolic weapon and mowed old Sutpen down. As one character in *The Unvanquished* phrased it, "Sutpen's dream was only Sutpen."

By way of conclusion, we are now in a position to notice how Faulkner has arranged to reinforce and corroborate his thematic meanings, throughout, by manipulating mythic analogies. One of these is Hellenic in its source and the other Hebraic: the Oresteia trilogy of Aeschylus, in which the violation of sacred family ties brings retribution and tragedy, and the old Testament story of David and Absalom, again involving the violation of sacred family ties and again bringing retribution and tragedy. Quite obviously, Faulkner gives his first hint of the primary mythic analogy by drawing his title for this novel from David's celebrated lament. But he reinforces that first hint by invoking and implying repeated analogies. Also quite obviously, Faulkner permits Mr. Compson's comparisons of Sutpen with Agamemnon to hint at the secondary mythic analogy. (pp. 62-4)

Any correlation which is made between what might be called the Sutpen myth and the pertinent Hellenic myth must be held loosely and must be taken poetically. But remember that in the Oresteia trilogy the curse on the house of Atreus was heightened by that violation of sacred family ties which occurred when Agamemnon sacrificed one of his children, for reasons he considered idealistic and noble. As a result, he brought on himself the vengeful fury and retribution of Clytemnestra, and the sins of the parents were at least figuratively "inherited" by the children, in a succession of tragic consequences. That may press the analogies far enough. But it should be clear that when

Faulkner arranges to endow the Sutpen story with elements of a Greek tragedy he did not accept Mr. Compson's reading of Greek tragedy. . . . Faulkner variously revealed his awareness that in Greece the concept of tragedy evolved through various stages; that originally the fall of a man of high degree, through a meaningless and inexplicable act of Fate, was considered an adequate concept of tragedy; and that Aeschylus modified that concept in his plays and also in one celebrated remark: "I hold my own mind and think apart from other men. Not prosperity but human faults and failures bring misery." But Faulkner's fondness for dialectical procedures may have made him enjoy the reconciliation of those two opposed concepts. As we have noticed, he was willing to admit that human beings were indeed victimized, at times, by inexplicable and meaningless forces beyond their control. He was also willing to admit that human faults and failures bring tragedy. But in novel after novel he demonstrated his preference for that concept of tragedy which represented an inextricable relationship between determinism and freely willed actions. So here, is the tragedy of Thomas Sutpen; a tragedy without a self-recognition scene.

Perhaps the mythic analogy drawn from the Old Testament has less to do with illuminating the Faulknerian concept of tragedy and more to do with corroborating the reader's awareness of what was lacking in Thomas Sutpen. But first notice how many analogies between the story of David and the story of Thomas Sutpen are arranged by Faulkner, before any of those analogies pay off significantly, in terms of Faulknerian themes. It will be remembered that Sutpen, like David, was sent by his father on an errand which changed the entire course of his life. David was told that whoever should kill the giant Goliath would receive as wife the daughter of the king. But after David had killed Goliath he was tricked by Saul, who promised him one daughter and gave him another. As a result, David felt morally justified in leaving that wife and in fleeing from that country. Much later, after he had established himself as a king, David used questionable means to obtain another wife, Bathsheba, even as Sutpen used questionable means in obtaining Ellen Coldfield. For that theft of Bathsheba, David was reprimanded by the prophet Nathan: "Thus saith the Lord, Behold, I will raise up evil against thee out of thine own house . . . the child also that is born unto thee shall surely die." That prophecy fits Thomas Sutpen's predicament. But consider further analogies. David had his own family problems involving incest. There came a time when David's son Amnon forced incestuous relations with his half sister Tamar, and was killed by his brother Absalom, who rebelled against his father and thus ruined the house of David. Even so, when David received the news of the death of Absalom, he uttered his grief-stricken lament:

> O my son Absalom, my son, my son Absalom! would God I had died for thee O Absalom, my son, my son!

Thus David took on himself or at least shared part of the responsibilities for the estrangements between father and son which caused the ultimate death of two sons. More than that, David achieved the tragic height of anguished dignity and nobility, through self-reproach and repentance. How do the analogies operate here? Did Thomas Sutpen make any such lament? He did not. It is thus at the very point where the mythic analogy breaks down, or becomes inverted, that the most important values of all those analogizings illuminate the crucial point in the Sutpen story. The ultimate tragedy here is that Sutpen's dream was indeed only Sutpen. (pp. 64-5)

Lawrance Thompson, in his William Faulkner: An Introduction and Interpretation, *Barnes & Noble, Inc. 1963, 184 p.*

MICHAEL MILLGATE

Absalom, Absalom! is Faulkner's most impressive achievement, a work of technical virtuosity and moral anguish on a scale not seen in American literature since Henry James's *The Wings of the Dove*. Some critics have considered the structural complexity of *Absalom, Absalom!* to be a mere act of perversity on Faulkner's part. It is in fact fundamental to the whole meaning of the book, but there is no doubt that it often dismays readers coming to *Absalom, Absalom!* for the first time. The language of the opening chapters is the most difficult of any in the novel: grandiose, intricate, convoluted, often unsyntactical, almost Elizabethan in its complexity and its splendour. The atmosphere is dark, violent, melodramatic. The action seems confused, full of obscure hints of future catastrophes and enigmatic glimpses into a mysterious past, and it is only gradually that a firm pattern begins to emerge. Once the pattern has emerged, however, it is never lost sight of—though always shifting, always appearing in new lights, always being modified—and it grows steadily richer in its implications, more compelling in its power over our imaginations, more compelling in its power over our imaginations. This is true above all of the last pages when the fall of the house of Sutpen is revealed; for it is here that the organisation of the novel brings to bear the whole weight of the tragedy upon Quentin Compson, . . . the chief medium through whom the story of *Absalom, Absalom!* is told.

Quentin is the novel's "medium" in a very special sense, for it is through him that we hear the voices of men and women absent and dead, and it is in his imagination, and in the precisely-attuned imagination of his Harvard room-mate Shreve, that the final poetic reconstruction of the story takes place. The reconstruction is "poetic" because we are never presented, in this extraordinary book, with the "truth" about Thomas Sutpen. (pp. 52-3)

We are given in the novel three different interpretations of . . . the whole Sutpen story; that of Rosa Coldfield, Ellen's much younger sister, to whom the ageing Sutpen, returned after the four heroic years of the Civil War to a plantation and a family in ruins, once proposed a marriage that would be conditional on her ability to produce the son and heir he needed; that of Mr Compson, father of Quentin, son of the General Compson who had been Sutpen's only friend; and, finally, that of Quentin himself as he sits with the Canadian Shreve McCannon in their icy room at Harvard a few months before committing the act of suicide we have already learned of from *The Sound and the Fury*. Rosa's story, which occupies most of Ch. I and the whole of Ch. V, is a tale of Gothic horror, an essay in demonology, with Sutpen himself cast in the role of Beelzebub. Mr Compson's version, occupying Chs. II-IV, is more objective than Rosa's, and much saner, but we come to realise that it goes too far in the opposite direction; it is too balanced, too self-consciously rational, to take the full measure of Sutpen's obsession, and Mr Compson himself realises that his account of Charles Bon's death seems to leave something unexplained

The final chapters of the novel (VI-IX) are taken up with the attempt of Quentin and Shreve to assemble all the extraordinary events and characters of the Sutpen story and make sense out of them. Quentin, in particular, is like a detective of genius, collecting all the available evidence, and then, with the aid of his more matter-of-fact assistant, imaginatively reconstructing what "must" have been the course of events and the pattern of motivation. Because of the imaginative sympathy, amounting in Ch. VIII to a sense of actual identification, which Quentin and Shreve feel for the dead Henry and Charles, their version achieves a "poetic truth" of a wholly convincing kind. It is not, however, to be taken as a factually accurate account—despite the fact that it is based on fuller information than the two earlier ones and is obviously much nearer the "truth"—for to do so would be to miss an important aspect of the book's richness.

The three accounts do not simply fill out the story and clothe it with meaning, they brilliantly illuminate the personalities of the respective story-tellers. Thus Rosa's account concentrates on Sutpen's relations with his womankind, Mr Compson's on Sutpen's relationship to the society of Jefferson and of the South generally, Quentin-Shreve's on the relationships between Sutpen, Charles, Henry, and Judith; and what emerges so vividly from these different versions is Rosa's frustrated bitterness, Mr Compson's ineffectual cynicism, and the eager romantic idealism of the two young men, qualified on Quentin's part by his personal involvement with the South and with that theme of incest which is of such importance in *The Sound and the Fury* and in the Biblical story of Absalom in II Sam. XIII-XIX.

At one level, then, *Absalom, Absalom!* is a study of the characters of Rosa, Mr Compson, and Quentin, as revealed by their different reactions to the same set of events; and, to this extent, it is in the same experimental line as *The Sound and the Fury* and *As I Lay Dying. Absalom, Absalom!* differs from these earlier books, however, in several important ways. The different reflexions or interpretations of the central story, instead of being separated out into distinct sections, are intimately interwoven within an extremely complex and carefully-articulated novel structure. The different versions constantly overlap, contradict, confirm, and revalue each other, and it is by this means that Faulkner achieves those audacious ambiguities, juxtapositions, and effects of delayed revelation which give the novel its extraordinary qualities of moral complexity and narrative suspense.

The structural complexity of *Absalom, Absalom!,* far from being an arbitrary imposition, thus embodies the very meaning of the work. Not only does the "story" exist solely in terms of its various reflexions, the whole novel is "about" the inextricable confusion of fact and fiction, of observation and interpretation, involved in any account of human experience. Or we might say that it is a demonstration of the difficulties of writing history, of the impossibility of defining "Truth," of the evolution of a myth, or even of the way in which a simple idea may grow in the hands of an artist into a thing of beauty and grandeur—as perhaps the short story **"Wash"** of 1934, which contains the germ of *Absalom, Absalom!,* evolved gradually in Faulkner's mind into the major novel of 1936.

It is useful, up to a point, to think of *Absalom, Absalom!* as a demonstration of this kind, but there is certainly nothing about it of a coldly-undertaken literary exercise. It bears, on the contrary, all the marks of having been written out of an intense inner compulsion. (pp. 54-7)

For Quentin, as for Faulkner, the story of Sutpen is in some sense an image of that South of which he is himself inescapably a part. In historical terms, Sutpen is a late-comer to the ranks of Southern gentlemen, but his achievement of that rank in a single generation is only a violent condensation of a process which in most families went over several generations, and by the magnificence of his house and his outstanding bravery in the Civil War Sutpen proves himself a worthy representative of his new class. For Wash Jones, in the story **"Wash,"** Sutpen is the supreme embodiment of all that is best in the South, but what Wash comes to realise is that the South at its best cannot bring itself to recognise even the simplest human need of its inferiors, the need to be recognised as human.

The point of view in the story is that of Wash rather than of Sutpen, and the point about Sutpen's lack of human feeling is quickly and economically made, but in the novel we are at first stunned by the sheer audacity and splendour of Sutpen's design and it is only gradually that we become aware of its fatal flaw.... Sutpen's "mistake," of course, is inherent in the design itself, in the monstrosity of its attempt to make human flesh and blood conform to the rigid contours of an abstract idea. His failure as a man lies in his refusal to regard even his own family as other than the instruments of his design. His failure as a Southerner lies in his refusal to regard the Negro as a human being.

The distinction is not wholly valid, of course, for the two themes in the novel are closely intertwined. Thus the tragic event at the heart of the novel, that shooting of Charles by Henry to which Quentin's tortured imagination again and again returns, is the direct outcome of Sutpen's refusal to acknowledge Charles as his son; and this refusal is due entirely, or so we gather, to the same taint of Negro blood as had caused him to repudiate Charles's mother. Since Charles repeatedly makes it clear that he would be satisfied with the least sign of recognition, the barest acknowledgment of his human identity, Sutpen's refusal becomes an apt image of the South's tragic failure to acknowledge and accommodate the minimal human needs of the Negro. (pp. 57-8)

Looked at in yet another way, Sutpen's story is an extended example of that theme of rigidity which Faulkner earlier explored, particularly in terms of religious belief, in *Light in August,* and the fate of Joe Christmas in that novel is recalled here by the story of Valery Bon, son of Charles and the octoroon, who violently flaunts his Negro blood in a similar attempt to gain recognition for himself as a human being. Like Christmas, however, he fails in his attempt: even to Judith and Clytie, who love him after their fashion, he is not Valery Bon but "Negro," as the sleeping arrangements made for him clearly show. All that Valery Bon does do is produce a son, the idiot Jim Bond, who is left at the end of the novel to haunt Quentin with his howls and to represent, like Benjy in *The Sound and the Fury,* the final degradation of his line. (p. 59)

> *Michael Millgate, in his* William Faulkner, *revised edition, 1966. Reprint by Capricorn Books, 1971, 120 p.*

THOMAS M. LORCH

In reconstructing Henry Sutpen's journey to New Orleans, Mr. Compson describes his introduction to "a female principle which existed, queenly and complete, in the hot equatorial groin of the world," and which "reigns, wise supine and all-powerful." What role does the female principle, to adopt Mr. Compson's term, play in *Absalom, Absalom!*? The novel contains no earth mother comparable to Lena Grove of *Light in August* or Eula Varner in *The Hamlet,* nor any compulsive bitch whose perverted sexuality wreaks destruction as does

Temple Drake in *Sanctuary.* Nevertheless, the female principle emerges as a significant force in *Absalom, Absalom!* Many of the reasons for Thomas Sutpen's failure to fulfill his design have been amply considered: for example, his lack of moral sense, his inability to recognize and treat others as human beings, his refusal to accept Charles Bon as a boy at the door like himself, and his blind acceptance of the Southern social codes of caste and color. I intend to show that Sutpen also comes in conflict with the forces of the female principle throughout the novel, and that these forces help to cause his downfall.

What are the characteristics of the female principle? Fundamentally, it is the passive but sustaining and indomitable life forces of nature. Faulkner's generic Woman, especially his pregnant women, Karl E. Zink points out in his excellent study of this subject, "are akin to the 'fecund' earth, like the earth itself potential sources for renewal and development, for physical continuity within the continuous process of Nature." But there is another side to this coin. Faulkner's women, as Cleanth Brooks observes in his chapter on Faulkner in *The Hidden God,* stand aside from good and evil, and from the abstract codes and standards men seek to establish. Their ability to sustain life amidst destruction and disintegration enables them to achieve what Rosa Coldfield defines as "*that doom which we call female victory which is: endure and then endure, without rhyme or reason or hope of reward—and then endure*"; but this indomitable female endurance approaches perilously close to the minimal maintenance and reproduction of physical life.

Faulkner's men, according to Brooks, "cannot be content merely with being natural." They must work out their fates in terms of good and evil, and of virtues, ideals, and goals they set up for themselves. As a result, Faulkner's men come in conflict with the female principle. His women come to represent the material which his men seek to shape and elevate, resembling in this conflict what Faulkner describes in *Intruder in the Dust* as "the massy intolerable inertia of the earth itself," the "land's irrevocably immitigable negation." The danger is that what Jody Varner calls his sister Eula's "rich mind- and will-sapping fluid softness" will absorb and stifle man's efforts.... The female principle is capable of absorbing man's aspirations and ideals just as the woman physically absorbs him and his seed.

Absalom, Absalom! presents male aspiration and will and the passive, enduring, absorbent Female in more closely balanced conflict than we find in Faulkner's other novels. Thomas Sutpen is Faulkner's most powerful male figure. In terms of Sutpen's conflict with the female principle, the novel is divided into two parts: the first ending with Rosa's monologue, and the second consisting of Shreve and Quentin's reconstruction at Harvard. The first part depicts Sutpen's male achievements in a predominantly masculine world. In the hands of Rosa and Mr. Compson Sutpen emerges as a god-like creator-spirit, a greater than life-size heroic figure.... The swamp from which Sutpen drags his plantation represents the primordial slime which was the source of all life, and Sutpen is portrayed as the creator who alone can give birth to life. (pp. 38-40)

In the first half of the novel, women and the land combine to provide the materials out of which Sutpen shapes his design. He possesses the creative force which enables him to dominate these materials and to impose himself, his aspirations, and his ideals upon them. His finest quality is his indomitable will. In the instant his design is conceived at fourteen, it becomes a mission; and for almost fifty years he pursues it with unflagging determination. . . . He possesses "*some spark, some crumb to leaven and redeem that articulated flesh,*" the male force capable of raising human life above the female level of existence. Sutpen's triumph in the first part of the novel is the triumph of the male principle. His creation of a plantation out of the inarticulated mud, and of a dynasty from the appropriately named "Coldfields," is perhaps the outstanding male achievement in Faulkner's works.

However, Sutpen remains successful only so long as he lives in a predominantly male world. He passes through Jefferson with his wild Negroes and builds his plantation out of sight of any women. For five years he opens his home only to men; he hunts, drinks, gambles, and fights with his slaves. Even after his marriage his way of life remains relatively unchanged; he continues to fight and live among men until the Civil War ends. But after the war, everything is changed. The South's defeat coincides with the death and destruction of Sutpen's heirs; the social and familial or personal disaster correspond. After these events, Sutpen moves in a female world.

The war's end and Henry's killing of Charles Bon also correspond to the transition from the first to the second part of the novel. . . . Whereas the first part centers upon Sutpen himself, the second emphasizes the vessels into which he pours his creative energies. In respect to the conflict between male and female, Sutpen is presented in the first part as a mysterious, isolated heroic figure. . . . Only in the second part do we learn about Sutpen's past and discover the motives behind his design and the reasons for his choice of means. We find that Sutpen felt forced to channel his efforts within the structure of Southern society and to found a dynasty by begetting male heirs.

The vessels Sutpen chooses, the society and the women, finally absorb and stifle his creative spark. Instead of harnessing his immense creative energy for constructive purposes, Southern society perverts it and renders it self-destructive. The South's artificial codes, particularly the color line, lead him to repudiate his first wife and son, and later cause his heirs to turn against each other and destroy themselves. Mr. Coldfield's oft-quoted condemnation—that "the South . . . was now paying the price for having erected its economic edifice not on the rock of stern morality but on the shifting sands of opportunism and moral brigandage"—contains the quicksand image of absorption which also relates Southern society to the female principle.

In the second part of the novel, the women who have fought him constantly gain the upper hand. When Sutpen returns to his house, he finds it dominated by three women, Judith, Clytie, and Rosa, who had learned that they "*did not need him, had not the need for any man.*" From the first, Rosa wars against him and "the entire male principle," and she ultimately outlasts him and all that he created. Judith, whom Brooks calls "one of Faulkner's finest characters of endurance," . . . also outlasts him in a similar manner. And Clytie represents a fusion of factors which have thwarted him: the fatal Negro blood, the surviving daughter instead of the son, and the enduring female; it is she who presides over the final holocaust which eradicates his efforts forever. Also in the second part, Shreve and Quentin conclude that Sutpen's first wife Eulalia Bon ultimately brings down his grand designs, and she too is at war with "the old infernal immortal male principle." And lastly, Milly Jones betrays his final hope; although she conceives for him, she bears him a daughter, . . . but, significantly, not [a] son. "You cant beat women anyhow," Shreve concludes. "The old imbecile stability of the articulated mud," Mr. Compson asserts

in another connection, ". . . outlasts the victories and the defeats both."

Nevertheless, both in *Absalom* and elsewhere, Faulkner's presentation of this theme is far from wholly pessimistic. He recognizes female nature as necessary and good, because it provides the living material for the male to shape and elevate. And if his demand that his men rise above this matrix in pursuit of higher ideals dooms his heroes to failure, it also opens up to them the possibility of moments of transcendence. The interaction between man's aspirations and the female principle in *Absalom, Absalom!* is analogous to certain philosophical or theological conceptions of the relationship between spirit and matter, or body and soul. Spirit can express itself only through matter or the body; but once the spirit enters into this matrix, it is transformed, burdened with matter's inertia, and subject to time, change and death. Throughout Faulkner's works, the weight of female nature resists man and pulls him down. But at least for a time, the creative spirit, the "spark" within men such as Thomas Sutpen, makes it possible for them to impose themselves and their wills on the female matrix, to infuse it with form and order, and to make transcendent flights toward the ideal. These moments of glory enable Faulkner's men to give meaning to the constantly flowing life, the female principle which both sustains and destroys them. (pp. 40-2)

Thomas M. Lorch, "Thomas Sutpen and the Female Principle," in The Mississippi Quarterly, *Vol. XX, No. 1, Winter, 1966-67, pp. 38-42.*

ELIZABETH SABISTON

Absalom, Absalom! has always been one of William Faulkner's most controversial or problematical works. Cleanth Brooks calls it "the greatest of Faulkner's novels," and Michael Millgate sees it as "Faulkner's most impressive achievement, a work of technical virtuosity and moral anguish on a scale not seen in American literature since Henry James's *The Wings of the Dove*" [see excerpts above]. It is the quintessential Faulkner work, a compendium of all his major themes and concerns. It covers a far greater time span than any of the other novels, and it demands the total participation of the reader, much of it through the "outsider" within the work, Shreve McCannon the Canadian. Above all, it is Faulkner's rationale for the writing of fiction; he implies that through the creative process he, together with the reader, may attain a higher truth than the history which provides his raw material. Faulkner himself has said that *Absalom, Absalom!* is one of his two hardest novels— both to write and to read, one infers. The other is, of course, *The Sound and the Fury* (1928), closest to his heart and his "most magnificent failure." *Absalom, Absalom!* (1936) is in a sense its sequel, completion and culmination, as in a different sense it is also, though written eight years later, its forerunner, inasmuch as the fall of the Sutpen dynasty historically precedes the fall of the Compsons and interlocks with it. Its virtue resides in its openness and reverberations.

The theme of the creative process has evidently become obsessive with Faulkner, who simply cannot let go of Quentin Compson. Quentin, who has been likened to Joyce's Stephen Dedalus, is here seen clearly to function as an artist figure, piecing together his sparse clues and transforming them through the power of his imagination. (p. 15)

The subject of the novel is the creative process shared by Quentin, Shreve, Thomas Sutpen, Faulkner, and the reader. As Harry Levin rightly points out, the most provincial novel can also often be the most universal in theme. Faulkner himself has said about using the South as his microcosm: "I simply was using the quickest tool to hand. I was using what I knew best." If the South is Faulkner's raw material, it is also Sutpen's, but in the latter an idealistic vision precludes any cognition of reality. Sutpen, in fact, resembles the romantic egoist Jay Gatsby far more than he does the fatalistic, defeatist Compsons. Like Gatsby, he is uncultivated, and like Gatsby he takes ruthlessly what he wants. He eventually uses his trump card to prevent Bon's marriage to Judith for, it is implied, he tells Henry that Bon is not only his half-brother, but that he is partly Negro, and it is the threat of miscegenation, not that of incest, which impels Henry to kill Bon. (p. 17)

The concatenated themes of creativity and heredity constitute the novel's center of gravity, but those who hold the key to these themes are the sometimes silent, sometimes volubly misguided sufferers in the work, the women and the Negroes, whose plights mutually reinforce and complement each other.

At the beginning of the novel Rosa compares Sutpen to the God of Creation, "creating the Sutpen's Hundred, the *Be Sutpen's Hundred* like the oldentime *Be Light*." Rosa at this point speaks more wisely than she knows, for Sutpen has confused a godlike creativity with a merely biological or agricultural creativity. Again, it is Rosa who describes the founding of the plantation as a caesarean birth, for Sutpen "tore violently a plantation." It is important to remember that Rosa's own birth was caesarean: she was torn from living flesh, thereby rendering her mother a "hollow woman."

Sutpen is neither a racist nor a sexist in any simple terms, but rather a monomaniac, like Melville's Ahab, whose mania is his "grand design." His perceptions of women and blacks are equally distorted because he sees them as only instrumental or contingent to his design, and therefore he dehumanizes them. As he puts it, he needs a wife only "incidentally" after establishing his claim to property, and his vision of the Negro never transcends that of the "monkey nigger," the balloon on a stick, the necessary appendage to the plantation who had turned the child from the door. Thus the Negro, like the woman, becomes a symbol for him, "no actual nigger, living creature, living flesh to feel pain and writhe and cry out." In fact, Sutpen never comprehends the essence of women or Negroes *or* of his own children, and Faulkner stresses the interconnections of these three by indicating that the black blood is introduced through the female line. Sutpen's children, we are told, are "just illusions that he begot." His progeny have the "fecundity of dragons' teeth," or of Abraham's sons, and Faulkner describes his tragedy as that of a man who has attempted to found a dynasty by begetting *too many* sons. "Sutpen's Hundred" refers literally to the plantation, but obliquely to the "fecundity of dragons' teeth," his children. Sutpen has been grafted onto the Southern tradition without really comprehending its *idées-forces;* he is always in a sense alienated or estranged from it. If Gatsby hangs his dream onto a dying past, Sutpen ties his to a dying or passing present. All he perceives of the Southern tradition are its appearances: a great plantation tilled by Negro slaves, a mansion serviced by Negro slaves, a dynasty rooted in a respectably white marriage producing respectably white children, supported if need be by a half-Negro progeny to serve as house rather than field slaves. (pp. 17-18)

[Sutpen's] misappropriation and misapplication of the Southern myth lay bare some ugly truths underlying the myth itself. Sutpen's understanding of surfaces emphasizes the fragility of the twin pillars on which the Southern tradition stands. For there is a sense in which Sutpen is right, that the whole glorious rainbow has, at one end of the spectrum, slavery, and at the other, the exploitation of the legitimate white wife for the sole purpose of procreation, lust and pleasure being restricted to the master's activities with the more comely of the female slaves.... Quentin's own half-formulated perception of this sickness at the root of Southern society triggers Quentin's fierce denial at the end that he hates it: "*I dont hate it* he thought, panting in the cold air, the iron New England dark; I dont. I dont! I dont hate it! I dont hate it!" He seems to be trying to refute what Conrad's Kurtz calls "the horror! the horror!"— in this case the corrupting power of the South, not as reality, but as myth. Sutpen is a well-intentioned forger of myths who builds a dream on outgrown materials with a soft center of corruption he fails to detect, much less articulate.

Faulkner has always shown himself to be perceptive, if somewhat bewildered, about women. He has remarked, "I think that women are much stronger, much more determined than men." This attitude represents a major undercurrent in *The Sound and the Fury.* Faulkner suggested that the central image around which the entire novel was structured was that of Caddy, the little girl in muddy drawers climbing a tree.... Caddy represents the feminine principle in the novel in open revolt against a class-ridden, sterile, and incestuously exclusive tradition built on dynasties, property, and a supposedly aristocratically pure blood line. (p. 18)

This "female principle" is even more subtly shaded and nuanced in *Absalom, Absalom!* In terms of the implied link between Faulkner's women and the novel's center of gravity, the twin themes of creativity and heredity, it is no mere desire for obfuscation and mystery that impels Faulkner to begin the novel with the narrative of Rosa Coldfield.... Rosa's is the most disjointed narration of all, and even her role in the novel is defined as peripheral. This is, indeed, the very source of her rage—that she is only at the circumference of truth.

Rosa, however, for all her nightmarish distortions, does introduce all of the major themes of the novel. She brings Sutpen on in a sort of mythic apotheosis, and the rest of the novel reveals how Sutpen's legend grew. Moreover, Rosa serves as a foil to Sutpen in terms of the theme of creativity. Like him, she is a mythologizer, and her obviously mad attempts to force a dimly perceived reality into a pattern serve as an ironically dubious commentary on Sutpen's own avowedly rational "grand design," which is also transmuted into an heroic legend. Like Sutpen, Rosa's ambition is supposedly to help others, but only those others who can be viewed as narcissistic projections of herself. Thus, we are told that she would like to play God for plain girls—a female god—in much the same manner as Sutpen sees himself as a godlike creator of a plantation and a dynasty.

Rosa compensates for a redundant, thwarted, and stultified existence by becoming "the county's poetess laureate." She sends to the local paper "poems, ode, eulogy and epitaph, out of some bitter and implacable reserve of undefeat." Like Mark Twain's Emmeline Grangeford, she cultivates her own graveyard school of poetry. While her father is evading the Confederate soldiers, she is writing heroic poetry "about the very men from whom her father was hiding and who would have shot him or hung him without trial if they had found him." Her unequivocal revulsion at the pharisaically self-righteous masculine principle represented by her father—a principle that she considers killed her mother—helps to explain her ambivalent attraction-repulsion for the heroically apocalyptic masculine principle represented by the man on a horse, Thomas Sutpen.

However Rosa consciously repudiates and condemns Sutpen, she also consistently supports his characteristic metaphors and patterns of imagery, as well as those associated with him by others: the stallion, with its clearly sexual overtones . . . , war, the fallow field. (p. 19)

Sutpen does see life as a war, but the tragic irony resides in the fact that he chooses to combat the system with its own weapons, not in order to destroy it, but in order to join it. It never occurs to him to question its moral, ethical, or metaphysical assumptions or validity, so he ends by extending it rather than levelling it in favor of a new order. Granted this failure to ask ultimate questions, his dehumanization of women and Negroes into mere instruments of his will, tools for the acquisition and perpetuation of property, is inevitable. Sex becomes only another battle in Sutpen's private war. . . . Sutpen impregnates Milly Jones when he realizes that he "had at best but one more son in his loins, as the old cannon might know when it has just one more shot in its corporeality." Rosa Coldfield herself never reaches a plane where she can coolly dissect and analyze the sickness underlying the heroic, gallant, chivalric Walter Scott-like pretensions of the Confederacy. . . .

Rosa also resembles Sutpen in seeing herself as a suppliant child. As Mr. Compson tells Quentin his grandfather remarked, "'Suffer little children to come unto Me': and what did He mean by that? how, if He meant that little children should need to *be* suffered to approach Him, what sort of earth had He created; that if they had to *suffer* in order to approach Him, what sort of Heaven did He have?" Thus the fate of all Faulkner's characters in the novel hinges on a pun between the Biblical sense of "suffer," *to allow,* and the contemporary usage of "suffer," *to agonize.* The final suppliant, or suffering, child within Sutpen's life span is Bon, who comes to Sutpen's door as Sutpen years before came out of the hills to another plantation door. . . . The Prodigal Son is to be welcomed with a feast and rejoicing; but how about a son who is living evidence of a Prodigal Father?

Rosa speaks for all the women in the novel, including her sister Ellen. The women are seen as the ghosts of the old South, and Rosa is Faulkner's "Representative Woman"—a voluble and angry ghost. As Mr. Compson says of Rosa, "Years ago we in the South made our women into ladies. Then the war came and made the ladies into ghosts. So what else can we do, being gentlemen, but listen to them being ghosts?" But, it should be noted, it is the men who have elevated their women into ladies, thereby burying some kind of strong "female principle" which nevertheless survives, if often in inverted form, in the female ghosts. (p. 20)

Finally, Rosa is associated with what I take to be the central metaphor of the novel: she is a rose in a cold field. With her projected engagement to Thomas Sutpen, she is seen as "suddenly sprouting and flowering like a seed lain fallow in a vacuum." But the engagement is aborted (almost in the literal sense), and Rosa's virginity is left intact. Rosa can be linked with so many of Faulkner's spinsters for whom he exhibits a profound understanding and sympathy: Joanna Burden of *Light in August*; the neurotic Minnie Cooper of **"Dry September"** who accuses a Negro of rape; Miss Emily Grierson of the Gothic **"A Rose for Emily"** who goes to bed with her lover's skeleton for forty years. Because Rosa begins life by hating her father, she detests "the entire male principle (that principle

which had left the aunt a virgin at thirty-five)." She is seen as "Cassandralike"—Cassandra, the prophetess of doom in the saga of the House of Atreus, taken as a concubine by Agamemnon as part of the spoils of war. (p. 21)

The field image has resonances beyond Rosa's name and situation and the literal tearing of a plantation out of the wilderness. It is importantly associated also with Judith, Rosa's niece, who is actually older than Rosa herself, and through whom Rosa hopes to celebrate a "vicarious bridal" with Bon. As Henry describes his sister to Bon during their days at the University of Mississippi, Bon thinks, "I am not hearing about a young girl, a virgin; I am hearing about a narrow delicate fenced virgin field already furrowed and bedded so that all I shall need to do is drop the seeds in, caress it smooth again." Bon himself uses the same image of seduction for Henry as for Judith, that of planting seeds, of "preparing Henry's puritan mind as he would have prepared a cramped and rocky field." Although Henry is the legitimate Sutpen heir, he is actually the only "Coldfield" member of the family, with the puritanical morality of his Aunt Rosa.

In his use of the field metaphor, Bon is the "obverse reflection" of his father, as the Negro is of the white in *The Sound and the Fury.* It is almost as though the two brothers mutually seduce each other, as well as their sister. Mr. Compson says, in fact, that "it was Henry who seduced Judith: not Bon." This incestuous wish is the logical outcome and reflection of Sutpen's own self-love which pervades his entire biological and dynastic creativity. Judith and Henry themselves have no separate identities: they are "that single personality with two bodies both of which had been seduced almost simultaneously by a man whom at the time Judith had never seen." . . . The sexual symbolism associated with the field-property image becomes explicit as we witness Bon's son ploughing what should have been his father's fields, linked with his mule "by the savage steel-and-wood male symbol, ripping from the prone rich female earth corn to feed them both."

In a climactic scene in the novel, Thomas Sutpen is cut down by Wash Jones wielding Sutpen's own rusty scythe—"that scythe, symbolic laurel of a caesar's triumph—that rusty scythe loaned by the demon himself to Jones more than two years ago to cut the weeds away from the shanty doorway to smooth the path for rutting." Although critics have generally viewed the scythe as the traditional symbol for Death, the Grim Reaper, Father Time, or Fate, it seems to me that Faulkner is also punning on his central metaphor of the ploughed field. The manner of Sutpen's death reflects not just a Gothic horror, a mortality that visits us all, but also a poetic justice. I would suggest that Faulker is punning on the Biblical injunction, "As ye sow, so shall ye reap." The reference to preparing the path for "rutting" links the death scene with the planting of the virgin field, and Wash Jones exacts retribution from his adored master, Sutpen, because the latter has cruelly and even jokingly rejected Milly Jones for having produced a *female* child from his very last seed. He is, in fact, cut down for failing to acknowledge the basic needs and humanity of *all* his offspring, the female and mixed blood as well as the white "legitimate" heir.

Thomas Lorch assumes that Sutpen's point of view about women is essentially Faulkner's own [see excerpt above], and that "women and the land combine to provide the materials out of which Sutpen shapes his design." Women are, according to this theory, purely natural entities like the open fields, and Lorch quotes Cleanth Brooks to the effect that Faulkner's men ''cannot be content merely with being natural.'' For this reason the male principle comes into conflict with the female. As a final sop to the female sex, Lorch concludes that the novel is not wholly pessimistic since the female principle is ''necessary and good because it provides the living material for the male to shape and elevate.'' On the other hand, according to Lorch, female resistance and passive absorption invariably drag men down from their highest ideals.

An assumption of the virtue and rightness of Sutpen's creative vision subtends such an interpretation. Lorch fails to perceive that the field metaphor is Sutpen's own and shadows forth his constant failure to distinguish ''the otherness of the other'' or, in fact, to locate a metaphor which is equal to his vision. It is crucial to realize that the various narrators' failings are not necessarily Faulkner's, and that he may in fact be using them to signal the mythopoeic Thomas Sutpen's proclivity for abstracting generalities from living, breathing human flesh.

Sutpen fathers, on various wives and mistresses, four off-spring who are central actors in the novel, two male, two female, one of whom in each sexual pairing is black and the other white. This sexual and racial symmetry brings us close to the core of the novel. Sutpen has exercised an imaginative as well as biological creativity in that he has named them all. The legitimate white Henry's name may suggest the scion of a princely line. . . . The irony is that Henry, the heir in whom all Sutpen's hopes are vested, is the least like Sutpen of all his children.

On the other hand, the fact that Charles Bon uses Sutpen's obsessive field metaphor to describe his relationships with both Henry and Judith suggests that he is his father's son in more ways than Sutpen ever realizes. Like Sutpen's, his arrival in Jefferson is mysterious, almost apocalyptic. Like his father, he comes close to playing God with the octoroon, a member of an hereditary class of mistresses. Still assuming himself to be white, he says that such women are not whores because ''We—the thousand, the white men—made them, created and produced them.'' Although he cannot save them all, he adds, ''we save that one. God may mark every sparrow, but we do not pretend to be God, you see.'' But he does pretend, at least in a small way. (pp. 21-3)

[Bon's treatment of Judith] reveals the same single-mindedness as his father's egoism even though it is directed to other ends. He never demonstrates any understanding of Judith's separate identity and needs, but treats her as a pawn in a struggle for the recognition of his father. Once that recognition can be forced through Judith, he has every intention of abandoning and sacrificing her. One could generalize, in fact, that Bon is to Judith as the father is to Bon. Judith seeks from Bon, as Bon seeks from his father, some *human* recognition that one is finally more than a woman, a Negro, a commodity or an instrument, but a complete and integral personality.

On the level of his relationship with his father, Bon is in a sense crucified. He is Charles Bon, Charles the Good. . . . He first arrives in Jefferson on a Christmas day, and he dies at the age of thirty-three, buried by three ''Marys''—Rosa, Judith, Clytie. Shreve and Quentin guess that he has asked for and chosen his own fate by taunting Henry with the possibility of miscegenation, and references to the loaves and fishes and the thorny crown are his in his one letter to Judith. In his relationship with Judith, on the other hand, he is not the victim but the manipulator.

Images of the Crucifixion are associated with Rosa as well as with Bon, and Rosa identifies very strongly with Judith. Of the two legitimate white Sutpens, it is the girl, Judith, who is most clearly her father's daughter. . . . Her spirited character gives the lie to any attempt to reduce her to the metaphor of a passive virgin field. As a child, it is she who causes the team of horses to bolt for the sheer deviltry and excitement of it, and it is the two female Sutpen offspring, she and Clytie, who watch their father wrestling with his savage slaves while the boy Henry get sick. She, Rosa, and Clytie form a ruling triumvirate while the men are away in battle, and far from being associated with fertility, they are seen as three nuns in a convent.

Judith's allegiance is always less divided than her brother Henry's. Faulkner would probably agree with the Quentin-Shreve interpretation that ''women will show pride and honor about almost anything but love.'' I do not think, however, that this is said critically, but rather with admiration and awe. Whatever Bon asks, she will do, for ''Judith, being a female and so wiser than that [Henry], would not even consider dishonor.'' Thus she takes charge of Bon's child by the octoroon and, even if she treats him as black, does tell him to call her Aunt Judith. She dies from love, nursing Bon's son, and Faulkner seems to confer tacit approval on Mr. Compson's statement that women lead ''beautiful lives'' of courage and fortitude. She wages a peculiarly feminine version of her father's never-ending battle against time, though not by founding a dynasty. In the Melvillean sense, she wants something to last in the loom of fate, so she gives Bon's letter to Grandmother Compson. . . . She is apparently named for the Biblical Judith, who is a fighter for her people.

The black daughter Clytemnestra, or Clytie, cannot, unlike Bon, pose a threat to Sutpen's dynastic dream. Nevertheless, Clytie and Bon are the two dangerous variables or volatile elements in Sutpen's equation, whom he cannot understand viscerally although they are flesh of his flesh. Although Cytie is also, like Rosa, called a Cassandra, a presiding genius over the events, she is appropriately named for Clytemnestra, the murderess who precipitates the fall of the house of Atreus: in the end it is Clytie who literally burns to the ground the house of Sutpen. (pp. 23-4)

In **Absalom, Absalom!** it is Sutpen's mythopoeic drive which blinds him to the individuality of Negroes, women, and of his own children. I would agree with Lawrance Thompson's view [see excerpt above] that the affirmation of the novel is in the passage which tells us that we must ''overpass to love, where there might be paradox and inconsistency but nothing fault nor false.'' As far as we can tell, within the novel only Judith, and perhaps Clytie, attain this transcendence. (p. 24)

At the end of the novel the sole survivor of the holocaust is Jim Bond, and Shreve's prophecy is only half-facetious:

> I think that in time the Jim Bonds are going to conquer the western hemisphere: Of course it won't quite be in our time and of course as they spread toward the poles they will bleach out again like the rabbits and the birds do, so they won't show up so sharp against the snow. But it will still be Jim Bond; and so in a few thousand years, I who regard you will also have sprung from the loins of African kings.

The comment about bleaching could be taken as a white supremacist statement, but it seems to me that this would be to misread the intention of the entire novel as well as the unmistakably serious, majestic tone of Shreve's last sentence. Faulkner is concerned throughout to explode the myth of miscegenation and of hereditary inferiority. Both Mr. Compson and Bon attack racial definitions and the myth of "purity." Rather, racial adaptability becomes a mere question of climate and protective coloration, related to Faulkner's major themes of survival and endurance, the great virtues of the Negro, even when "the Good" has become the "Bond slave."

Jim Bond's idiocy is also in no way to be construed as a racial slur on his black blood. Bon and Clytie, after all, are "anything but mindless," and the white Benjy Compson, one of the last survivors of *his* dynasty, is also an idiot who sees "truth in madness." Rather, Jim Bond will inherit the earth because the meek will inherit the earth, when the Negro ceases to be an obverse reflection of the white man. A future Sutpen will finally be able to recognize his son and for once subsume his own ego in the suffering of another. Only then can he exclaim, as did King David: "Would God I had died for thee, Absalom, my son, my son!"

Whether the Absalom figure is Henry or Bon remains ambiguous, but the point is that it does not matter as Quentin and Shreve, and ultimately the reader, identify with them both in turn. All of Sutpen's sons—and his daughters—are crucified, but we are dormant in their "living blood and seed." As with Melville's monkey-rope in *Moby Dick*, we are tied together by the same umbilical cord.... If we recognize our own suffering in these other sons of Man, if we avoid Sutpen's mistake and "overpass to love," there is an important sense in which Sutpen produced us all. Perhaps, in fact, in the imaginative if not genealogical sense, Sutpen has had his dynasty after all. (pp. 24-5)

Elizabeth Sabiston, "Women, Blacks, and Thomas Sutpen's Mythopoeic Drive in 'Absalom, Absalom!'," in Modernist Studies: Literature & Culture 1920-1940, *Vol. 1, No. 3, 1974-75, pp. 15-26.*

LYALL H. POWERS

In *Absalom, Absalom!* (1936) Faulkner returns to the character who perhaps most nearly embodied his own anguished view of the South's decline, Quentin Compson.... Relying on the reports of Miss Rosa Coldfield and of his father, on his own brief encounter at the ruins of Sutpen's Hundred, and on his creative imagination as it is prodded and challenged by Shreve McCannon, Quentin pieces together Sutpen's life. Whether or not his recreation is truly accurate, or factually verifiable, is beside the point. It is sufficiently true and convincing for Quentin—and that is what matters finally. It is, in the full sense of the phrase, Quentin's story, terrifically meaningful for him and for us, since, through Quentin's recreation of Thomas Sutpen's career, we gain Faulkner's most searing penetration into the evil at the heart of the antebellum South's social organization, his most revealing exposure of the rot at the base of the Southern edifice.

The narrative strategy of disturbing regular chronology in the rehearsal of Sutpen's career contributes significantly to the novel's verisimilitude, as it reflects the way in which one might actually learn someone's life story—as does Ford Madox Ford's similar technique in *The Good Soldier.* But much more important is the way in which the narrative arrangement carefully manipulates our responses. Sutpen emerges for us and for Quentin as a somewhat ambiguous and equivocal creature—part hero, part demon.... (pp. 106-07)

Our introduction to Thomas Sutpen comes from the amazed and still outraged Miss Rosa, who, while she does some justice to Sutpen by admitting to certain of his virtues, nevertheless paints a portrait of him as a rather horrific demon. He seems to be a frantic version of the American ideal of the self-made man fiercely obsessed with the design of founding an endless future. He has vigor, creative energy, and undeviating determination as he both leads and drives the creatures he has brought suddenly into Mississippi—from no one knows where—to establish his estate. But he is, if not malevolent, then certainly maleficent as he rigorously uses (or abuses) anyone who can serve his ends—the band of unrecognizable Negroes, the evidently kidnapped French architect, the Coldfields, et al. (p. 107)

[Halfway] through the novel, a chronological shift affords us Mr. Compson's account of Sutpen's childhood and early life, modifying rather considerably Miss Rosa's depiction of her demon, and raising in us some feelings of guilt for having judged Sutpen prematurely and perhaps too harshly. For Sutpen's trouble, Quentin explains to Shreve, was innocence.... The rude shock of his initial encounter with the antebellum Southern way of life, administered to him by the black servant who sent him from the front door of the big house, awakened the young Sutpen to the hard "facts" of life in the real world: slavery, caste, prejudice, and the power of ownership. In that prolonged moment of shaken innocence, during which he ponders and contemplates this novel phenomenon of actuality, Sutpen comes to recognize what was necessary and required if one were to succeed in that world—much like the innocent James Gatz (not yet become Jay Gatsby) climbing aboard Dan Cody's yacht to discover the rules of the world's game. Hence came Sutpen's design.

If he is reminiscent of Jay Gatsby, he is also very similar to Joe Christmas of *Light in August.* Like Joe, Sutpen was not born bad nor was he, in the usual sense of the term, simply corrupted. Like Joe, he was educated by the "best" teachers, educated in the "proper" ways of the Southern system. Both characters are exactly the product of the society in which they must function. The evil they subsequently do, we cannot help but feel, results from their training, and hence their careers will seem to be pathetic and even to have a distinctly tragic cast.

The rest of Sutpen's early life, then, follows naturally from his epiphany, his discovery of the way of the world. He goes like any romantic adventurer to Haiti to make his fortune. He works on a rich plantation, puts down a rebellion there, and consequently takes the boss's daughter to wife.... But here reality intrudes into Sutpen's life . . . , and Sutpen discovers the taint of blackness in Eulalia's blood—a distinct disqualifier.... Eulalia and their son, Charles, just would not do. Having corrected that misstep, Sutpen removed to Mississippi, there to begin again the founding of his dynasty, the realization of his design, according to the Southern system as he had learned it.

In time, however, Sutpen the product would almost indistinguishable from the producers. Sutpen himself lived into the role which the South had presented for his admiration and emulation. And as he participated in its life, he necessarily assumed (even if unwittingly and unintentionally) responsibility for its fate. Early and late in the novel Sutpen is included in the group of Southern leaders responsible for the fiasco of the Civil War. (pp. 108-09)

Of course the parallels between Sutpen's career specifically and the history of the South generally are obvious; his career is a microcosmic emblem of the Southern macrocosm. Understanding of Sutpen yields understanding of the South, for Quentin and for us. Sutpen's Hundred was established upon two evils that taint the actions of most of Faulkner's Southern pseudoaristocrats—piratical land procurement . . . and inhuman use of human beings, especially of the enslaved Negroes. Sutpen's casting aside Eulalia and Charles, fathering Clytie, and driving his band of wild Negroes are all culpable features of his preparation to establish his estate and found his dynasty. His use of people as pawns is not restricted to blacks, as he used Coldfield to procure a wife and Ellen, in turn, to provide the necessary male heir, but it is the novel's central concern.

The chickens come home to roost; the nemesis appears with the return of the son he has denied, Charles Bon. And of course he must be denied again—and finally. In the midst of the Civil War, the great American fratricidal holocaust, Sutpen obliges Henry to murder Charles. Now the bitter irony is that with that fratricide Sutpen loses both his sons, for the darker brother is dead and the "legitimate" heir has disappeared, is in fact as good as dead. (And the typical Faulknerian equation of fratricide with suicide is again patently evident.) Furthermore, Sutpen's inhumanity has turned most vengefully against himself: the impelled fratricide has broken his dynasty. There is, too, the additional irony that Sutpen's seed has been more fertile than he thought or could have desired, as Charles's progeny continues in a line stretching toward the furthest horizon—"grandsons and great-grandsons springing as far as eye could reach."

The postbellum attempt to recoup and reconstruct proves too much for the old man. His desperate attempt to refound his dynasty drives him to behavior as inhumane and vicious as ever. He proposes to Miss Rosa a trial at procreation, and then imposes that trial on Milly Jones. Her failure to produce a male heir (whom he presumably would have legitimized) [causes him to reject her] . . . and causes Wash Jones to rise like the Grim Reaper and slay him. The sense of fit retribution is inescapable. Sutpen's heartlessness, however it was instilled, seems to merit the fate that has descended on him. And insofar as the novel has made him the South's representative, we feel that the South too has earned the wrath of the gods. (pp. 110-11)

The two principal allusions Faulkner has employed in this novel augment that sense of merited vengeance, of deserved divine punishment. The first, obvious and frequently commented upon, is the allusion to the biblical story of King David carried by the very title of the novel. That allusion has properly enough encouraged identification of Thomas Sutpen with David, Charles Bon with Amnon, Judith with Tamar, and Henry with Absalom. The title, echoing the words of David's lament over the death of his son ("O my son Absalom, my son, my son, Absalom! would God I had died for thee, O Absalom, my son, my son!" . . . , tends to restrict the allusion to that part of David's story which immediately precedes and accounts for Absalom's death. But the significance of that allusion is enhanced and its application more sharply focussed and defined by the appearance within the novel of a most important reiterated allusion to classical myth.

The allusion is established by Quentin's father and then reiterated by Quentin himself. Mr. Compson comments on Sutpen's naming his progeny: "Yes. He named Clytie as he named them all, . . . with that same robust and sardonic temerity, naming with his own mouth his own ironic fecundity of dragon's teeth." Quentin recalls this much later in the novel as he tells Shreve (with fuller knowledge now) that Sutpen "named them all—the Charles Goods and the Clytemnestras and Henry

and Judith and all of them—that entire fecundity of dragons' [*sic*] teeth as father called it." (p. 112)

Now the allusion to the myth of Cadmus (sower of dragon's teeth) is important because of its parallels to the story of David and Absalom. The two stories share several features, and their presence together focusses the relevance and controls the application of each to Sutpen's career. (1) Both stories involve the founding of kingdoms or dynasties—David his house and control of Jerusalem, Cadmus the city of Thebes. (2) Both tell of fratricide, of internal strife within the respective families, and also of enmity between fathers and sons. (3) In both, the fratricidal strife results from the principals' incurring divine wrath; it descends upon David and Cadmus as a punishment earned. David has sent Uriah to certain death in battle in order to take Bathsheba unto himself. In chapter 12 of the second Book of Samuel we read the prophecy that follows God's displeasure with David, "Now therefore the sword shall never depart from thy house," and "Behold, I will raise up evil against thee out of thine own house." Absalom kills Amnon, turns against David, and is himself finally killed. Cadmus slays the dragon that has killed his men when they violated its sacred wood and spring; bereft, he is told to sow the dragon's teeth to produce new offspring. Since the dragon was sacred to Mars, however, Cadmus' crop is a mixed blessing: the armed sons who sprout from the soil fall upon each other in lethal civil war and warn Cadmus not to interfere. (4) In both stories we have the case of "ironic fecundity," as both David and Cadmus have, in a sense, more sons than they can manage (which is also the case with Thomas Sutpen). (5) Both stories, finally, include a character who might be called the abused sister. Amnon's incestuous rape of Tamar, a crucial item in Absalom's career, has its counterpart in the threatened relationship of Charles Bon and Judith Sutpen. While there is no exact counterpart to this in the Cadmus myth, a kind of displaced equivalent may be seen in the fate of Cadmus's sister, Europa, seized and carried off by Jupiter disguised as a bull; and Cadmus's peregrinations have as their original motive the recovery of Europa. In spite of the inexact similarity, one sees that in both stories as in Faulkner's novel, the themes of unjust war and improper love play a prominent part.

These two important allusions—to Absalom and to the dragon's teeth—lend breadth of significance to the story of Thomas Sutpen and serve to give it the dimensions of myth. Furthermore, those features of the two which receive particular emphasis serve, in turn, to cast a searching light upon the crucial features of Sutpen's career as it is recreated for and by Quentin Compson: the earning of divine displeasure and the consequent internal, fratricidal strife. Now this is not to equate Sutpen fully with King David or with Cadmus; his career certainly does not promise the calm and happy outcome of either of those figures. And whether his career even has the distinctly tragic cast that has often been claimed for it seems rather dubious. It seems to me that the tragic possibilities are to some extent undercut, both by the controlled relevance of the two allusions just discussed—i.e., controlled to emphasize the punitive suicidal fratricide—and also by Faulkner's strategy here of situational repetition, in a word, by what I . . . [call] the theme of the Second Chance.

The crisis in Thomas Sutpen's career occurs when Henry brings Charles Bon home from college with him at Christmastime (appropriately) in 1859. The meeting is critical as a repetition of the past—the father facing again that son who he earlier decided could not form any part of his grand design, and obliged once again to decide whether or not to recognize him. The Second Chance is offered, the opportunity to make the correct moral choice which would justly compensate for the earlier moral failure. Of course Sutpen must fail again, lacking the wherewithal—the moral imagination, the simple humanity, the "pity or honor"—to do otherwise.... There is in Sutpen's attitude to this reappearance something almost equivalent to the *anagnorisis* of classical drama—a little like Macbeth's recognition of Macduff. He sees, thus, that he has no right option open to him, that whatever response he makes will lead to the destruction of his design, i.e., to "the same result." And as always, of course, Faulkner manages to make Sutpen's specific dilemma representative of the Southern dilemma in general, drawing an explicit parallel between the appearance of Charles at the door of the big house of Sutpen's Hundred and the much earlier appearance of the boy Thomas Sutpen at the door of the big house on another Southern plantation.... The South has once again affirmed its principles of caste, of exclusiveness and discrimination and segregation, as Sutpen fulfills his representative role.

He rejects Charles the second time in two steps, first through refusal of him as potential fiancé on the grounds of threatened incest, and second—the "trump card"—through refusal on the grounds of threatened miscegenation.... [He] is obliged to make sure by taking that second step which will get rid of Charles once and for all through death. The pathetic irony is provided by Charles's convincing explanation to Henry, now armed with the knowledge Sutpen trusts will lead to Charles's death, that he would have made no exorbitant demand whatsoever.... (pp. 113-15)

But Sutpen could not run the risk. His trouble, Quentin insists (quoting his grandfather), was innocence. Sutpen's reported actions and comments argue persuasively, however, that his trouble was much rather overweening pride, first rudely awakened by the initial rebuff that started his vengeful design to take shape. His trouble was hubris. Sutpen's design reflected his learned desire to transcend the normal human condition, to aspire to godhead and so overcome the human facts of mutability and mortality. (pp. 115-16)

The more healthy and humane Judith expresses the folly of that attitude by a modest counterstatement of the theme.... [Her] words constitute an emphatic statement of the human necessity of recognizing mutability and mortality as twin facts of life. Failure to do so ... means failure to be truly alive and human oneself and leads to inhuman regard and treatment of actually living things. It is Sutpen's failure ... and thus responsible for his baleful view of those who come into contact with him.... (pp. 116-17)

Mr. Compson characterizes [Henry] early as "the provincial ... who may have been conscious that his fierce provincial's pride in his sister's virginity was a false quantity which must incorporate in itself an inability to endure in order to be precious, to exist, and so much depend upon its loss, absence, to have existed at all ... the brother realizing that the sister's virginity must be destroyed in order to have existed at all." ... [Henry's] difficulty in facing the real possibility of Judith's losing her virginity is compounded by the fact that her fiancé is Charles Bon and that part of Sutpen's means of rejecting Charles a second time is to discover to Henry that he is half brother to him and Judith—the discovery of threatened incest. The second part of course is Sutpen's "trump card," the disclosure that Charles is Negro. That knowledge involves Henry in the pattern of the Second Chance: he, like his father thirty

years earlier, must choose to accept or reject this relative with "tainted" blood, and he has the chance to do right where his father had chosen to do wrong. Henry, alas, proves tragically to be his father's son, the full inheritor of commitment to the rules governing Southern social organization that his father had learned.

[Henry has] much difficulty (according to Shreve's conception) accepting the incestuous union of Charles and Judith.... Henry's recollection that kings and dukes "have done it"—especially the Lorraine duke named John something, excommunicated by the Pope—seems to have made the union of Charles and Judith finally acceptable to him. (pp. 118-19)

The basis on which Charles is to be rejected is either the threatened incest or the threatened miscegenation. We know Henry has managed to come to terms with the former, and we face the bitter recognition that he cannot come to terms with the latter. Charles puts it to him: *"So it's the miscegenation, not the incest, which you cant bear."* And he continues to press him, threatening now to go through with his pursuit of Judith, and pointing out to Henry the only way to stop him. He gives Henry the pistol and urges him on—*"Then do it now, he says."* At this moment of crisis Henry's response is the simple and tragically laconic *"You are my brother."* Charles is, however, relentless and drives Henry to the act he must commit—the fratricide which is always tantamount to suicide.

So Henry—and, by the usual extension, the South generally—has faced the Second Chance and rejected it in rejecting his brother. He is his father's son, and with his father shares a representative role. He has proven to be as exclusive, segregationist, and destructive as Thomas Sutpen—the South's demon. And the reports of Shreve and Mr. Compson prompt us to conclude, from his attitude to his sister, that he is in his way as unwilling to face the actual world of mutability, and thus as anxious to fix or to escape it.... Henry's motivation in rejecting Charles is a refusal to recognize him as a fellow human being—in spite of the spontaneous and tragic claim of brotherhood.

This shared hubristic attitude is, then, the tragic flaw in these quasi-tragic figures, Henry and Thomas Sutpen. They are not, however, truly tragic. Their shared flaw is not simply a blemish on an otherwise admirable character; it is the very heart of their being. And as they are the South's representatives, one may say that the "flaw" is the very base of the whole Southern structure.... [The "flaw"] is the fundamental and pervasive evil that has led to the frustrating of all of Thomas Sutpen's ambitions, of all of Henry's expectations, and hence to the collapse of the South in the Civil War. It was the disease which only that feverish holocaust could arrest.... (pp. 120-22)

While the story of Thomas Sutpen does not, I believe, carry for us or even for Quentin, the full impact of tragedy, its final impression is no more pessimistic, no less morally instructive than true tragedy. We have seen and understood, not simply that Sutpen and his South were bitterly frustrated and defeated, but also for what reasons—why God let them lose the War.... The mistake, the flaw (as Quentin may well want to see it), has been clearly identified, described, defined, and dramatized; and we recognize it as the evil which proves self-destructive. One looks vainly perhaps for hopeful signs of the Saving Remnant—unless it be in that ironically unrecognized progeny of Sutpen's, the product of his ironic fecundity springing (as it "bleaches out") as far as [the] eye can reach: the descendants of Charles Bon.

This is what Quentin has seen and what he has enabled us to see and contemplate. His vision of it all, however, we must call "tragic" in the more colloquial sense of the term, since for him it can only be depressing. Particularly in that he can so readily identify with Henry Sutpen, and especially with that facet of Henry that attracts him cerebrally to his sister—a principal symptom of the Southern "disease." In his own attitude to Caddy, as we found it in *The Sound and the Fury,* he imitates the fond Henry and shares with him that tendency to impotence, to self-defeat, ultimately to suicide. (pp. 122-23)

We recall [from *The Sound and the Fury*] that it was not actual incest ("i was afraid to i was afraid she might and then it wouldnt have done any good") but the idea of it that Quentin wanted; and that too strengthens his identification with Henry. The cerebral or vicarious incest only would do for both young men. And the final element in the parallel encouraging identification is exactly this conception of incest as a means of escape to hell. Quentin imagines Henry thinking about his incestuous Lorraine duke:

he could say now, "It isn't yours nor his nor the Pope's hell that we are all going to: it's my mother's and her mother's and father's and their mother's and father's hell, and it isn't you who are going there, but we, the three—no: four of us. . . . And we will all be together in torment and so we will not need to remember love and fornication." . . .

Quentin's early twentieth-century world we saw in *The Sound and the Fury* lacks even the pretension of glamorous chivalry that decorated the antebellum South. . . . It is not Quentin's world. His is the world of Thomas and Henry Sutpen as he has recreated it in *Absalom, Absalom!* in most terrifically believable detail. . . . *Absalom, Absalom!* is indeed Quentin's story. It is about him and his, and about who made him so: Thomas Sutpen and beyond him the whole South. What other final words, then, could Quentin utter than *I dont. I dont! I dont hate it! I dont hate it!* (p. 124)

Lyall H. Powers, in his Faulkner's Yoknapatawpha Comedy, *The University of Michigan Press, 1980, 285 p.*

Thomas (James Bonner) Flanagan

1923-

American novelist, essayist, short story writer, and critic.

Flanagan received considerable recognition following the publication of *The Year of the French* (1979), a historical novel in which he reconstructs events of the unsuccessful French-supported rebellion of Irish peasants against the British in 1798. An episodic work featuring narrative perspectives from various segments of late eighteenth-century Irish society, this novel interweaves excerpts from journals, memoirs, song lyrics, and speeches to portray occurrences and characters while illuminating history's ironies, myths, and misrepresentations. Described by Julie Moynahan as "a permanent contribution to the new, demythologized history of Ireland," *The Year of the French* illustrates conflicts of class, religion, and politics in its examination of the relationship between ideology and reality, the significance of myth in preserving the past, and the nature of historical inquiry.

In his second novel, *The Tenants of Time* (1988), Flanagan focuses on the lives of several veterans of the Battle of Clonbrony Wood, the final skirmish in the failed Irish nationalist uprising of 1867, and depicts the efforts of a young Irish intellectual to compile information and write a book about this rebellion. Implementing various techniques from *The Year of the French*, including numerous narrators, rapid shifts in time frame and point of view, and a fusion of historical fact, mythology, and imagination, Flanagan represents the significance of individual action while evoking the physical, sociological, and intellectual milieus of nineteenth-century Ireland. R. Z. Sheppard observed: "For all its size and sweep, *The Tenants of Time* is an intimate book, a narrative that constantly adds personal tones and shadings to 'take a moment of history, a week, a month, and know it fully.'"

In addition to his works of fiction, Flanagan has published *The Irish Novelists, 1800-1850* (1959), in which he compares the artistic achievements, social background, and political viewpoints of five Irish authors from the early nineteenth century. The combination of historical fact and literary scholarship in this volume prompted Vivian Mercier to comment: "The more one knows about Mr. Flanagan's subject matter, the more exciting his book seems and the better one appreciates his originality. He is never afraid to discard the accepted view in either history or literary criticism; and where, as so often in Irish matters, there is no accepted view, he carves out an intelligent position for himself. *The Irish Novelists* is a remarkable pioneering survey."

(See also *CLC*, Vol. 25; *Contemporary Authors*, Vol. 108; and *Dictionary of Literary Biography Yearbook: 1980*.)

BENEDICT KIELY

[In *The Year of the French*], Thomas Flanagan has George Moore of Moore Hall in the County Mayo writing a letter in the year of 1798 to the Rt. Hon. Edward Barrett, member of parliament at Westminster. This is not, as the date might indicate, George Moore, the novelist, but his grandfather: a man in his youth noted for duelling and gallantries in the great world of London. But being also of a philosophical cast of mind, he returned to his native Mayo and devoted his time to writing the history of the Girondins: a work never to be published.

Flanagan's management of the character of George Moore displays at its highest the expertise with which he brings people out of the past and sets them living beside us and relevant to our present: thus transforming his amazing book from what we might call, pejoratively, an historical novel into a profound comment on our time, or on any time that we know of since our modern western civilization took shape. His management of Moore's character is also a prime example of the many subtleties that delight and instruct in *The Year of the French*. (p. 3)

Moore is writing to London on behalf of his brother John, who, following on the landing of General Humbert and his handful of French at Killala, has got himself involved in rebellion against the British crown to the absurd extent of allowing himself to be appointed the first president of the republic of Connacht. Very conscious that he is writing from the wilds of Mayo to what was then the world's most powerful city, or one of the four of them, Moore allows himself a little meditation on the history of his benighted and misgoverned country:

How many dramas of modern history have chosen for setting this God-forsaken bog, and always without any recompense for my unfortunate countrymen save further misery. What were the rebellions of Desmond and Tyrone but chapters in the struggle between Elizabeth and Spain and thus of Reformation and Counterreformation? What were the wars of Cromwell here but a sideshow to the English Civil War, in which the divine right of kings was challenged and overthrown? When James and William, the two kings, faced each other at the Boyne, the game was Europe, and Ireland but a board upon which the wagers were placed.

The history of Ireland, as written by any of our local savants, reminds me of a learned and bespectacled ant climbing laboriously across a graven tablet and discovering there deep valleys, towering mountains, broad avenues, which to a grown man contemplating the scene are but the incised names of England, Spain, France. Now the name of France appears a second time upon the tablet.

An elegant, if cynical, point-of-view, yet from what we know of George Moore, the historian, it seems certain that he would have thought and written exactly like that: and his is only one of the many points-of-view that Flanagan uses in a novel elaborately and brilliantly constructed. Nor do his people speak to us out of a history book and about a dead past. They are contemporaries telling us about matters common to us all: and I find that reading this novel I am afflicted with an odd feeling of two things happening at the same time. It is so close to what we know of the history that it seems the author must have come on a hundred old books, not known to anyone else, in which it is all written down exactly as he has it. It is also so close to life as we know it now that he must have taken the liberties with history that could only be taken by a reckless recording angel.

He calls to his aid five narrators who, along with about fifty characters, make up a considerable cast: a large crowd to handle as the Russian high command might have said at the battle of Stalingrad: and there are also the French, the Irish rebels, and the army of Cornwallis. Yet nowhere—and I have searched the book carefully—can I find any fault in logic or coherence. The simplest reader need nowhere be confused. The professional writer will be (and one might as well confess it) more than a little ill with envy.

The books opens quietly, casually. Four men are in a tavern by Kilcummin Strand, there in all its innocence waiting for the French. They talk of rumors of thousands of rebel men out on the roads of Wexford, of the prophesied army of the Gael marching at last, of English yeomanry and hireling militia beaten and redcoats dead on thick-grassed fields: and of the French upon the sea and sailing to save the Poor Old Woman, Mother Ireland: and of Cooper, a small landlord whose people had come over with Cromwell: and of the Big Lord himself, owner and master of all the land as far as you can see. But the man himself is as far away in London as the Lord Almighty in the high heavens. They talk of and belong to the Whiteboys, nightriders of the long warfare of the peasants against those who owned the land that they slaved on. Sometimes on nocturnal exploits they wore long white shirts: a fashion that crossed the ocean as did the fiery cross of the Scottish Highlanders. But not nightriders exactly. For want of the means and the steeds they went on foot.

The men are Connacht peasants sunk as low into serfdom as a depressed rural class could be. Among them a wandering Gaelic poet from the province of Munster: Flanagan could easily have been thinking of Eoin Rua O Suilleabhain, the 18th Century poet. His fictional Munsterman is conscious of the plight of the people he talks with: and of his own plight. He will, in a mood of contempt and cynicism, write for these pitiful people their Whiteboy proclamations: they themselves are unable to do so. He will go, almost like a sleepwalker, with the rabble of peasantry, canon-fodder, in the tail of the French, to the fatal battle of Ballinamuck, and be dragged back to Mayo to the gallows. His head filled with poetry, he is very conscious that in Mayo he is Ovid: "banished to wild Tomi."

A wandering Gaelic poet might seem an obvious choice for a character in a novel about the period: but Flanagan makes of him a gigantic tragic figure and places him in a telling relationship with the throng of people he moves through. With the Protestant clergyman, Arthur Vincent Broome, M.A., (Oxon), he has a most ironic conversation about the exact meaning of the Irish verse that tells of Troy and Rome and Caesar and Alexander and their passing, and prophetically holds out the hope that the power of England might go the way they went: and Tara, once the halls of the High Kings of Ireland, itself is grass. Broome is conscious of the irony and, writing about it afterwards in a self-mocking effort to be the Edward Gibbon of the events that happened at Killala, he says: "How little we will ever know these people, locked as we are in our separate rooms . . . He (the poet) dwelt deep within the world of his people, and theirs is an unpredictable and violent world."

Yet when Broome looks at the bare white walls and slender windows of his own church, at the two battleflags brought home from the wars of Marlborough, at the memorial plaques to those who fell serving the king of the fields of France and Flanders, he fears that he is less a minister to Christ's people than "a priest to a military cult, as Mithra was honoured by the legions of Rome." An instinct bred in the bone, nourished by childhoods of Sundays spent staring at the battleflags, compelled the Protestant gentry of Ireland to send their young men into the British army or the army of the East India Company.

Yet (he thinks) it is also true that the arts and benefits of civilization, an orderly existence, security of person and property, education, just laws, true religion and a hopeful view of man's lot on earth, follow the British flag and sword. Many then, and before and since, would dispute the matter with him who would have less quarrel with his final conclusion: "Only here have we failed, in the very first land we entered, for reasons which were in part our fault, and in part the fault of the natives. But I think it pernicious to rummage over the past, sorting out wrongs and apportioning guilts."

It is possible that the novelist's greatest achievement in blending the broodings of his imagination and historical truth so as to create a living reality is in the character, and statements, of this same Arthur Vincent Broome. At the time of the landing of the French a Protestant Bishop Stock was in residence in Killala. He kept a journal. Some professional historians of my acquaintance have asked petulantly why Flanagan dropped Bishop Stock. Walter Scott could have told them that Flanagan was wise to do so, and to substitute Mr. Broome: for, shall we say, greater mobility, mental and physical. Bishops can be cumbersome.

Mary Renault has said very well of this novel that in it the ironies of time and the disasters of war are seen with contemporary eyes and to great effect, and that it should not be missed by anyone prepared to learn from history. But Hegel said that we learn from history that men never learn anything from history: and that ironic reflection allows Flanagan to allow Broome some of the profoundest paragraphs in the book. For Broome had once asked a learned and sagacious friend if man learned anything from history and was told that he did not, but that it was possible to learn from historians. To this matter, while reading the capacious works of Hume and Gibbon, he had given much thought. Then follows a meditation on history in relation to Edward Gibbon, as striking as anything I have ever read on the matter. It is a long passage either to quote or summarise, but since it is, from a certain point-of-view, the core of the book, it is worth much consideration: and brutally and totally to summarise would pay little respect to the style.

Flanagan-Broome or Broome-Flanagan writes:

> Gibbon gives to us the breadth of the classical world, from the Hellespont to the pillars of Hercules, a vast temple with colonnades and recesses, glowing white marble beneath a blazing Mediterranean sun, and displays to us then its hideous and shameful destruction. How firm a sense do we derive of all its constituent parts, of their intricate relationships. How certain is its destruction, with alien creeds subverting its powers and alien races wearing away its far-flung frontiers. Each cause and reason is locked securely into place. And over all the mighty drama presides the awesome authority of Gibbon's splendid language, his unimpassioned rationality. Here, we think, is the chief civil drama of human history, in which tens and hundreds of thousands played their parts, but a drama compelled by the human mind to yield up its uttermost secrets. Great was Rome and catastrophic was its fall, but great too is the energy of the historian's mind, the cool deliberation of his judgment.

But then afterthoughts come to the Rev. Mr. Broome, the Gibbon of Killala. Perhaps it had not been at all as Edward Gibbon had described it, perhaps everything had been chaos, chance, ill-luck, or simply the judgment of God—as had, in more pious ages, been believed. Perhaps everything that he had read had been only Gibbon's imagination: "And the past remains therefore unknowable, shrouded in shadow, an appalling sprawl of buildings, dead men, battles, unconnected, mute, half-recorded. Perhaps we learn nothing from history, and the historian teaches us only that we are ignorant."

Broome sees himself as vain and affected in his own poor narrative: and here Flanagan is being at his most subtly ironic. Broome sees himself, his poor self as he puts it, for he is a genuinely humble man, as a confused clergyman with an indifferent education, a lover of comfort and civility and buttered toast: and so he is made to seem to the reader. But also (and he is not allowed to know it himself) he is a man of gentleness, sensitivity and humanity. In electing to play Gibbon to the events that happened around him he finds that he has written only about a squabble in a remote province, a ragbag army of peasants, files of yeomen and militia, ploughboys hanged from crossroads gallows.

André Gide telling us that the novel about the novel might be more interesting than the novel itself could not be more astute than Flanagan is on that page.

The hopeless war goes east to the County Longford to end in defeat and slaughter at Ballinamuck or the Place of the Pig: in Irish *Baile na Mhuiche*. The dire events that are, at some time in the future, to take place in the Valley of the Black Pig are imbedded in ancient Irish legend. But neither myself nor the Shell Guide to Ireland know where that valley is: and the fatal field of Ballinamuck in 1798 may merely have justified and fortified a folktale.

Out of the whole tragic story this moment remains most vividly in the memory of Arthur Vincent Broome. While the Rebels held Killala, and the French and their ragged allies marched eastward, Broome had made a friendship with Ferdy O'Donnell, who kept the Rebels in the town in order. One late evening they sit together in Broome's kitchen: " . . . the light is thin, the far corners of the room are in shadow. Neither of us speaks. Men are shouting in the street outside. At last he raises his hand, then drops it again to the table. I have a vivid recollection of the scene, and yet it lacks significance, a random memory. But what if the mysterious truth is locked within such moments? Memory urges them upon us, implores us to ponder them, a hopeless message."

Albert Camus living uncomfortably and in ill-health in occupied France planned an introduction to an anthology on Insignificance. Because it would "practically describe not only the most considerable part of life, that of small gestures, small thoughts and small moods," and also our common future: and even great thoughts and actions end up by becoming insignificant.

The doomed, drunken poet, the dryasdust clergyman who would be an historian are only two in Flanagan's crowded field of folk. Apart from Broome there are four other narrators plus Flanagan himself to help out, and, as I've said, fifty other characters and a host of bystanders who are yet not content to stand idly by: as somebody said somewhere. His people range from Humbert in the bogs to Boney in the desert; from Tone and Teeling in Paris and on the sea with the French to a half-crazed prophecy-man hanged for shouting out about the Place of the Pig, or just for existing; from Cornwallis in the field to the Big Lord in London concerned about the condition of chimney-sweeps and the abolition of negro-slavery, but with his scrawny withers unwrung by the woes of his tenants on his lands in Mayo.

For some of the throng Flanagan had copious historical material to work on, for others less, and some had birth only in his brain. All are alive and memorable. (pp. 3-8)

This vast book moves slowly, but with a majesty that the more compels the further you advance. The attempt to write about it afflicts me with a sense of inadequacy. That a book of such quality should join the bestsellers is most unusual, but must not be held against the author who approached with great style a high and universal theme: and has singularly triumphed.

Do not mistake me here. There is not a writer in the world (myself included) who would not like for various reasons, money being one of them, to sell good, better or best. But that best-selling should by some people be accepted as a commendatory critical adjective is indeed odd. Herman Melville had stern views on these matters and said bluntly that, looking around him, he would not wish to write the sort of books that were popular. But Herman Melville was stronger-minded than most of us and had, in his own time, his wish.

Thomas Flanagan has written a book that, by a quirk of whatever gods now manage these matters, is selling and will sell so well that many copies of it may still be around, after the great catastrophe, for a new and hopefully chastened world to meditate on. (p. 8)

Benedict Kiely, ''Thomas Flanagan: The Lessons of History,'' in The Hollins Critic, *Vol. XVIII, No. 3, October, 1981, pp. 1-8.*

GERARD REEDY

On Aug. 22, 1798, a French force of about 1,000 men landed at Kilcummin Strand, a few miles from Killala, a village in northern Mayo, in the Irish province of Connaught. The French invasion responded to a call from the Society of United Irishmen, a few of whose members lived in Paris and encouraged the French Directory to action. The society sought to overthrow English rule of Ireland not from sectarian motives, but in the name of the rights of man. The French force, joined by thousands of native Irish, took a few central towns in Mayo, then made a dash to the Irish midlands to bolster an uprising there. That uprising failed, the French expedition marched, perhaps willingly, into the trap set for it by Lord Cornwallis, Viceroy of Ireland, and on Sept. 8, at Ballinamuck in County Longford, the combined French and Irish force was defeated by the English. English troops cleared the last pocket of resistance from Killala on Sept. 23. The sorry, month-long affair involves, as its one, great distinguishing feature, the last foreign invasion of Ireland.

There are a few, but not many books and monographs devoted to the events of August and September 1798 in Connaught. Many historical surveys bracket these events between the risings in Leinster and Ulster earlier in the year and the Act of Union in 1801. This act abolished the Protestant Irish Parliament sitting in Dublin and incorporated Ireland further into the United Kingdom. The Connaught rising proved to the English what they thought they already knew: that Ireland was incapable of self-government. The larger events of the last years of the Irish 18th century have distracted historians from attention to the events of the northwest and of the rising in County Mayo.

Five years ago this scholarly neglect was remedied in an extraordinary manner by Thomas Flanagan in his historical fiction, *The Year of the French*. First of all, this large fiction brings its readers to a day by day witness of the month-long rising. *The Year of the French* also attempts history greater than fidelity to fact. Valerian Gribayedoff's *French Invasion of Ireland* (1890) and Richard Hayes's *Last Invasion of Ireland: When Connacht Rose* (1939), two standard works, hint toward a fuller, scholarly history of the French invasion. Flanagan's research shows that he honors their contribution. His fiction shows his unwillingness to write only at the level of reconstruction of historical fact. *The Year of the French* is history and more than history. It causes us to reflect not only on Irish history, but on the very possibility of ordered and true historical narrative.

Flanagan's primary intuition as he approaches his historical material concerns the fragmentary nature of Ireland at the end of the 18th century. This Ireland is divided not only between Roman Catholics and Protestants, Irish and English. Protestants rebel while Catholic landowners remain loyal; the teaching of civilized Dublin corrupts the idealism of wild Mayo.

Given this complex diversity, it would have been difficult to have created one narrative voice sufficiently universal to sympathize with the disparate elements it must encounter. Flanagan solves this problem by allotting much of the narration to several principal characters: Owen MacCarthy, a wandering schoolmaster and poet caught up in the rising; Malcolm Elliott, a Protestant landowner and member of the United Irishmen; Sean MacKenna, a Mayo shopkeeper and a prudent nonbelligerent; Harold Wyndham, an aide to Cornwallis; and the Rev. Arthur Vincent Broome, Protestant Rector at Killala. Through these varied voices the narrative successfully encloses the fragmentariness of the rising and of Ireland itself in 1798. The divided narrative allows us to sympathize with the points of view of the several narrators and, at the same time, to understand their shortcomings.

Flanagan's division of narrators is especially interesting for at least two reasons. First, while these principal narrators come from opposing sides of the armed conflict of 1798, no one narrator is a rabid exponent of his cause. Each of the narrators tempers his commitment with an ironical glance at the inevitability of his own point of view.

Second, it is interesting that the standard historical works on the French invasion do not verify any of these narrators as historical persons, although many other historical persons move through their narratives. (pp. 185-86)

It is here that one sees the power of Flanagan's controlling intelligence, which prefers imaginative truth to the limits of facticity. It is unlikely that any varied group of historical persons could have served the purposes he has in mind. To have portrayed a company of embittered narrators, such as we find in some of the historical records, at war with one another to the death, would have sufficed for melodrama. But to create narrators who are trying to understand, and who at the same time maintain war with one another—this strategy reaches out toward establishing a much more complex and satisfying fiction.

The Year of the French is a long book, though not as long as it may seem to readers who come to it in search of briskly historical melodrama. Especially in the march from Mayo to the midlands, Flanagan conducts a detailed exploration of conflicting points of view. Thus on Sept. 4, in Tobercurry, County Sligo, the reader encounters Dick Manning, an Irish Protestant landowner, who climbs the Norman keep on his farm to watch and hope that the French and Irish force will pass him by. . . .

In Manning, Broome and Elliott, *The Year of the French* explores the Protestant reaction. The fiction also involves, as it must, Roman Catholic points of view. (p. 186)

When the French marched on Killala in August 1798, many Roman Catholic clergymen responded to the call. In two fictional figures, Flanagan images the Roman Catholic clergy of Mayo with economy. Mr. Hussey, the pastor in Killala, interprets the rising as a violation of the authority of God handed down to princes and preaches against involvement; Mr. Murphy, his curate, joins the invaders and becomes a chaplain to the army as it moves into the midlands. Malcolm Elliott gives an account of his preaching: "He saw our army, that improbable combination of bogtrotters and French conscripts, as God's hammer, forged to batter down foreigners and heretics." It is curious that in a fiction so generous to conflicting points of view we learn of Father Murphy's theology through the eyes of a Protestant landowner. No Roman Catholic clergyman—no Father Cooley, Gannon, Monnelly or Prendergast, historical figures in the rising—achieves the status of narrator.

The ambitions of *The Year of the French* do not cease with its imaginative involvement in probable points of view in the Connaught rising of 1798. The fiction also reflects on the kinds of sources and ordering that feed any re-creation of history. How, it asks, is history made? Does historical writing, with its need for order and consistency of motive and narrative, adequately respond to such complexity? The fiction calls our attention to several ideas or models of history. Some of these are:

History as the past entering the present: In *The Year of the French* the narrators and many other characters see their own actions as continuations of past events, often in the distant past.

In 1798 the past puts pressure on the present in the form of remembrance of the Elizabethan campaign of the 1590's, the invasion of Cromwell and his generals in the 1650's, that of William III in the 1690's, and, more recently, the defeated risings in Ulster and Leinster earlier in the year. Moreover, the past drearily recites the inevitability of defeat for any native rising. For John Moore, "1641 and 1691 were as young as yesterday shaping conduct and governing passions. It was history without triumphal arches or squares named after victories. It clung to the dour, treeless bogs and the low, abrupt hills, a history of defeats and dispossessions, of smoke rising from gutted houses." Moore hopes that the United Irishmen will provide a new departure: "For the first time in the history of this country," he claims, "Protestant and Catholic have united in a common purpose." Flanagan positions his readers at a point of expectation, where we think that a few at least of these participants will escape from the tyranny of the past.

The complex narrative also gives voice to an Irish Protestant sense of the past. Irish Protestants "have their hagiography," writes Arthur Broome, "above all Cromwell wrathful and implacable in a suit of black armour clanking across the countryside, crushing out rebellion and Popery with each tread of his metal boots." Broome is embarrassed that in the enlightened year of 1798 such historical bogeymen exist. Cornwallis, too, is shocked at "a religious war, at this time in the world's history" and tries to reduce the conflict to one involving a "war against property," an idea allowed by his enlightenment, Lockean categories.

In this fiction, the advanced thinkers are wrong; the narrated facts do not allow us to rest in a vision of progress. Sectarian visions of the past rule the present conflict. Mr. Murphy's idea of the rising as a hammer against heretics conquers John Moore's dream of the rights of man; the moderation of Broome and Cornwallis means little to the pragmatism of lesser officers, who presume that Catholic means enemy, and that victory must involve slaughter of the peasants. *The Year of the French* offers no escape from the prison of the past. The future belongs to the likes of Dennis Browne, High Sheriff of Connaught as the book ends. Browne covers his historical bias with the veneer of opportunism: Catholic landlords are to be cultivated; Catholic peasants will meet with fire and sword. For most of the Irish in Mayo, the '98 has made no difference.

History as the record of great events: "My own parish in poor, barbarous Mayo," writes Broome, "had been seized by the scruff of the neck and flung into history." Others ponder the improbability that distant Mayo, so divorced from the centers of power, should equal Yorktown and Paris in the geography of history.

The Year of the French excels at investing events of the '98 with spectacular interest. Cornwallis's magisterial dismissal of General Lake, who had lost his cannon to the French and Irish at Castlebar, the bravado of Bartholomew Teeling, a United Irishman, before the English guns, the private apprehension of her selfhood by Ellen Treacy, John Moore's fiancée, as the men of Mayo elsewhere fight their sad battles, and the breath-taking, drunken ride of George Moore across Ireland after the '98 is lost—these are powerful and memorable creations, rivaling those of other writers, like Thackeray and Tolstoy, showing the fate of the individual caught up in great events. These are Flanagan's own creations, and they are extraordinary.

The Year of the French repeatedly calls our attention to those who, without the language of self-definition and history, participate in the great event. The peasants, George Moore tells us, "lived below history, and there they died." We glimpse them by indirection: in Owen MacCarthy's visits to the cottages and Malcolm Elliott's confession that he cannot understand the very rising his enlightened ideas have caused. *The Year of the French* insists on the presence of the masses for whom the rising is the one great event and who suffer most for it.

History as order and disorder: The Year of the French narrates many self-conscious acts of writing. A frequent theme involves the provisional nature of the words, images and political categories that we use to order history. George Moore knows that the words in which he encloses his history of the Girondins give him a pleasurable distance from the facts; he also suspects that no one has yet discovered a proper language and point of view to narrate properly the Irish history of his time. In one way or other, several narrators are conscious of the divorce between the order of historical writing and the disorder of history.

For many of the participants in the '98 there is no writing at all. For the peasants, architecture and song embody the past. The hovels in which they live and the grand houses of the landowners provide the symbols of powerlessness and oppression that shape their history. Glenthorne Castle, the house but not the home of a prominent English landlord, "was an image by which their imaginations grasped historical and political reality." Soon after the French landing, peasants sack the castle; the French general forbids further destruction. The peasants must leave standing the symbols of their oppression.

Songs and ballads provide alternate peasant meanings for the past and present. Several literary narrators complain that the evolving ballad tradition of the '98 distorts fact: Local figures are unrecognizable in the heroic forms in which the ballads cast them. Yet, bereft of literary history, the peasants need the ballads to provide simple motives for fighting and, in the future, the heroic memories that make the oppression of history bearable.

A few of the literary forms the narrative offers have no irony about their own truthfulness, especially the periodic sentences and rationalized images of the United Irishmen. "The Rights of Man," reads a circular letter received by Elliott, "may be likened to a powerful sun, beneath which ancient bigotry will melt like wax." "I believe that every man," writes poor John Moore to his fiancée, "is a locked casket of virtue, of which freedom is the key." The preciosity and smug liberalism of these aphorisms may, depending on one's tastes, amuse or annoy. "The formulations of the Society," writes Owen MacCarthy, "although I gave and give them my full assent, are but abstract things less real than a blade of grass or a drop of blood."

The Year of the French, while exploiting limited narratives, is not an experimental fiction. We must depend on the various narrators for an approximation of the facts of the rising. Thus Elliott and Broome exercise intermittent irony: They tell us what aspects of their apprehensions of things we ought to doubt.

Elliott asks about the peasants: "What have we ever known of these people? . . . How could we have supposed a connection to exist between our ideas, city bred, and the passions of peasants?" He also feels that political language has divorced him from the complexity of himself. At his trial he wants to make a "simple and honest declaration" of his principles—but knows at the same time that such a declaration will falsify, in its simplicity, the complex fact of being an Irish Protestant in the '98. "May not political passion," he asks, "be a net which holds the heart distant from all that has nourished it?"

Broome repeatedly tells us of the difficulty of knowing what is going on in Ireland. For him, Ireland gloats over its own "incomprehensibility." There "is no way of knowing the roots of the present conflict. The first link in the chain of human passions is often undiscoverable." Broome also enters more deeply into problems of point of view for a historian. He suggests the possibility that no narration of history, however hungry for order, will ever digest the "chain of human passions" and the disparate worlds such narration strives to rationalize for its readers.

In a powerful epilogue, Broome goes to London late in 1798 to visit Lord Glenthorne, the absentee landlord of north Mayo. An ascetic evangelical, Glenthorne campaigns against the servitude of chimneysweeps, not a pressing problem in that area of Mayo in his stewardship. He wishes also to reform the management of his estates. Broome tries to tell him that land reform will put hundreds of peasants on the road. Glenthorne objects that he does not control the laws of "supply and demand, of property, of the marketplace, laws of commodities." The peasants of Mayo will be sacrificed to an economic model and an idea of history that, among other faults, has no sense of irony about itself.

It is risky business for a historical fiction like *The Year of the French* to criticize acts of writing and points of view because they fail to capture reality. Prodded by these criticisms, the reader focuses on the total fiction itself. How does the whole become reliable when its parts confess unreliability? Flanagan addresses this question by means of two implicit contracts with his readers. First, we learn that this fiction encompasses not only the facts of the Connaught rising but also varied consciousness apprehending those facts. We read that these probable narrators doubt their own omniscience. Because of the diffidence of the narrators, we contract, as we would in life, to trust the controlling intelligence of the book; its candor in admitting error leads us to give it greater credence.

Second, readers enter into a contract of compassion with the fiction. Narrators consistently avow that it is precisely the condition of the peasants that resists their understanding. Beyond speech and ordering, peasant hope and desperation make up the compassionate heart of *The Year of the French*. Because imperfect narrators admit that they cannot represent the peasant masses to us, a sense of the reality of those masses, too real to be worded, grows strong. We contract to sympathize with the unimagined misery of the landless Irish of Mayo because our humanity, which must at least equal the narrators', will not allow us to do otherwise. This is not, strictly speaking, a literary response; our own personal and ethnic histories get involved. On the other hand, for all its balancing of fictions, *The Year of the French* and the sorrow it encompasses intentionally challenge anemic readers to enlarge their categories of fiction and history.

Very near the end, a brilliant allegory captures the fragility of constructed worlds and the method of *The Year of the French*.

Broome remembers that he and his brother, as children, were given a glass globe that enclosed a village. When shaken, the globe filled with white flecks of snow. When the globe cleared, the village reappeared, "always the same but always looking slightly different, because we had not the wits to keep every part of it firm in our memories." One day the brothers fought over the globe; it fell to the floor and shattered.

It is tempting to read this as a political allegory, with the fight of the two brothers signifying the destructive forces of sectarianism. But I do not think that a political reading will suffice. The allegory seems to be a surrogate of the entire fiction itself, encompassing both imaginative invention and historical research. The brothers represent history and fiction; like so much storytelling in *The Year of the French,* the allegory reflects on the method of the book in which it appears. The snows of prejudice and time make it difficult to keep the wits to see Ireland clearly. But history and fiction childishly war with one another; working together in compromise, they provide rich insight. (pp. 186-89)

> *Gerard Reedy, "More than History: Flanagan's 'Year of the French'," in* America, *Vol. 150, No. 10, March 17, 1984, pp. 185-89.*

GEORGE GARRETT

What we have in *The Tenants of Time* is a powerful story—set in 19th-century Ireland—made up of many stories, of stories within stories, all told by many voices, appropriate for that land of great storytellers. Some of it is wildly funny, much is beautiful and more is brutal. All of it adds up to a tragedy, a tragic tale of love and death arriving at last at an ineffable sadness made all the more moving by Thomas Flanagan's choice to end his story with the terrible future of Ireland and the rest of the world just out of sight and beyond the imagination of everyone except the reader.

In a serious sense, *The Tenants of Time* is about the making of history, the confusion and complexity of motives and events (and Irish history is breathlessly complicated), the selectivity and fallibility of memory, the constantly changing nature of all past time. The novel is beautifully structured, a rush of almost cinematic narrative and transition, to make its points. But it (and thus history) becomes more than its points. In a variety of styles, depending on who is doing the perceiving and feeling, Mr. Flanagan evokes a country, its countryside, its weathers and seasons, its earth and old stones, and the long, dark shadows of its history. And the writing is so clear and clean; every sentence seems to shine. Moving in this created landscape we have memorable people. They eat and drink (Lord, they do drink!) and they sing and fight and murder and make love. They suffer and rejoice. And in this vivid world we find ourselves suffering and rejoicing with them. It is not often that we find ourselves wincing with the wounds of the dead, but we do so here.

All this is a special pleasure since *The Tenants of Time* is a novel of history, a historical novel, then, like it or not. And even though it is still a widely practiced (and sometimes widely read) literary form, the novel of history has some real problems these days. (pp. 1, 26)

Any novelist who turns to history to make fiction . . . inevitably embraces great difficulties. Information, even in the form of simple exposition, becomes a seriously demanding problem, especially since most Americans seem to know less actual history than ever before. Information must be there and yet must always be (somehow) adroitly introduced. Places and times must be known enough to be imagined and recreated in such ways that the reader is able to imagine them fully. Texture of time and place must be as real and complex as the edges and hunks, corners and curves of the here and now. Characters must rise up from two-dimensional graves to reappear as rounded and as mysterious as if they were living and breathing with us, not as friends and neighbors really, but alien, though human beings. And above all, from whatever sources and examples are at hand, the writer must invent a new language, not pedantically of the period, yet not of ours either, a tongue invented for the characters to speak and for the telling of their stories.

Thomas Flanagan proved demonstrably that he could do all these things (and more) with his brilliant first novel, *The Year of the French* (1979), a rich and complex narrative dealing with the attempt of the Irish, in conjunction with the French, to defeat and drive out the English in 1798, and seeking, successfully, in the words of one review, "to recreate, from barroom to manor hall, the entire intellectual and emotional climate of the time." *The Year of the French* was admirably successful, recognized commercially by being chosen as a main selection of the Book-of-the-Month Club and critically by receiving the National Book Critics Circle Award. The rare negative reviews complained about the difficulty of keeping up with Mr. Flanagan's multiple narrators. These things have some importance because Mr. Flanagan has elected this time to expand and develop and deepen some of the techniques he exploited in *The Year of the French.*

There are, again, multiple narrators and likewise sharp, sometimes rapid shifts in point of view, first person to third and back again, in scenes presented and remembered, sometimes speculative, other times purely and simply imagined. In the hands of a less skilled writer, or of a writer more interested in virtuosity than substance, it could be too tricky and difficult for words. It is not. It is gracefully controlled and easy for the attentive reader to follow. Every trick or turn serves to advance the story and to support its themes. What we have, then, is a solidly constructed historical novel, faithful to the requirements of its form, yet using the technical freedom we associate with the most advanced contemporary fiction. (pp. 26-7)

Mr. Flanagan has created *The Tenants of Time* with a sure and certain authority, the confidence gained not only from the extraordinary achievement of *The Year of the French,* but also from the bountifully bestowed recognition which that work received. . . .

The story of the novel covers, from many angles and with subtle connections, fore and aft, spoken and implied, that time in Irish history between the Fenian Rising of 1867 through the death of Charles Stewart Parnell in 1891 and on into the summer of 1908. Although the world is the stage and we have scenes in Dublin, London, New York, Chicago, Venice and elsewhere, the primary setting is the town of Kilpeder in Munster, and the action is centered on the efforts of a young historian, Patrick Prentiss, to make something out of his belief "that what happened in Kilpeder between the rising of 1867 and the fall of Parnell had a shape, a design, a theme which worked itself out in the variations of a dozen lives." He is helped and guided in this research by the retired schoolmaster Hugh MacMahon, a wise man and something of a historian himself, especially of the dying Gaelic culture, and by Lionel Forrester, cousin to Thomas Forrester, Earl of Ardmor and "owner" of Kilpeder. Lionel (called Lee) is a writer of historical romances

and of elegant travel books. Both he and MacMahon tell a lot of the story and tell Prentiss a great deal (though not quite everything) of what they know and remember.

The story they share with Prentiss involves themselves and others in and around Kilpeder. Hugh MacMahon was close friends with fellow Fenians Robert Delaney, Vincent Tully and the American Capt. Edward (Ned) Nolan. All were involved—and variously punished for their involvement—in the failed attempt to capture the police barracks in 1867, which ended ignominiously in Clonbrony Wood, but nevertheless became the subject of a popular ballad that inspired many who came after, embarrassed, in its false heroism, many who were there, and enraged some of the best of them.

Ballads are always a part of it, and there are ballads and the texts of letters and journals and notebooks and pamphlets and political speeches, sermons, and debates in the House of Commons. All these things are at least shadowed by an elegant and functional use of apt literary allusions—for everybody in the story is a reader of one thing or another.

Parallel with, and in many places overlapping the life stories of the four young Fenians of '67 and how they grew and changed for better and worse, grew in wisdom and stature and took on a weight of sorrow with the years, is the story of the gentry, of Lionel and of Tom Forrester, Earl of Ardmor, a gifted painter, "the real thing" in the eyes of James Whistler (who makes a few brief appearances), and his Countess, the beautiful Sylvia. Sylvia is a marvelous and surprising character as, in truth, are all the women characters, wives and lovers, kith and kin, in this novel, as deeply and complexly rendered as any women I have encountered in recent fiction created by writers of either gender and any sexual preference. The women emerge as entirely convincing, and I believe some readers may have their comfortable and stereotypical notions concerning Victorian women shaken to the core.

I mentioned earlier the authority of Thomas Flanagan. By the end it is overwhelming. Even as we wholeheartedly agree with his characters that the true history of the times cannot be written, we are aware that he has just done it, in a work of fiction, this work of fiction. It takes some time and space to work these wonders. *The Tenants of Time* is a fast-moving story, but it runs to 824 pages. Mr. Flanagan must have been tempted, however briefly, to cut it down to a more fashionable, mildly minimal size. I am grateful that he ignored that temptation. I would not have it one word less. (p. 27)

George Garrett, "Young Fenians in Love and History," in The New York Times Book Review, *January 3, 1988, pp. 1, 26-7.*

R. Z. SHEPPARD

The very first page of [*The Tenants of Time*] . . . contains a reference to an unspecified night in June 1904, when "Patrick Prentiss came for the first time to Kilpeder and booked a room at the Arms." The time may be of little consequence to most readers, but some will not be able to ignore that, by coincidence or design, the author begins his plunge into Irish history with a suggestion of the most famous date in modern literature. That would be Bloomsday (June 16, 1904), the day of James Joyce's *Ulysses.*

The tweedy Prentiss does not make as splashy an entrance as Joyce's stately, plump Buck Mulligan in his yellow dressing gown, "bearing a bowl of lather on which a mirror and a razor lay crossed." Yet there is a strained relationship. Buck begins Joyce's stream of subversive epiphanies with a mockery of religious ritual, and Pat launches Thomas Flanagan's *The Tenants of Time* with a polite spoof on the rituals of orthodox history. Prentiss is a young Irish pedant, fresh out of New College, Oxford, and itching to write a book about a failed nationalist uprising in 1867. The final skirmish, known as the Battle of Clonbrony Wood, has become exaggerated in story and barroom ditty: "Let all true Irishmen be good, / And fight for what they hold. / Like all those heroes brave and bold, / Who held Clonbrony Wood."

Blarney Clonbrony was a fiasco that began when a band of poorly organized and inadequately armed Fenian nationalists tried to take the local police barracks, and ended with the attackers scattered into the trees and hunted down one by one. Blood was drawn but no honor satisfied. The participants became public heroes and martyrs, but privately their failure bred resentment, which thrived on blame, which in turn sought enemies within. They were not in short supply, given the tangle of feudal alliances and tribal betrayals that confounded the ideals of nationhood. The wounds of Clonbrony festered and spread violence and discord for decades.

Prentiss's book never gets written, not because he lacks vision ("If . . . one could take a moment of history, a week, a month, and know it fully, perfectly, turn it in one's fingers until all the lights had played upon its surfaces . . .") but because the facts and mysteries he encounters exceed his intentions. Or so he claims. When a friend suggests that history is a form of narrative fiction, Prentiss replies a little too glibly that "a taste for fiction has always seemed to me the unfailing mark of an imaginative deficiency."

The hook in this remark is that the speaker happens to be an innovative character in a historical novel of a high imaginative order. . . . [Flanagan] first demonstrated his gift for evoking the past in the constant shimmer of good fiction eight years ago, when he published *The Year of the French*. The work received broad acclaim and was the National Book Critics Circle's choice as the best novel of 1979. It is a rich and complex telling of a rebellion on the west coast of Ireland, where in 1798 an army of the French Revolution landed and briefly allied itself with the restless peasantry against their English and Anglo-Irish masters. As one of many preludes to Clonbrony, the episode ended badly when Lord Cornwallis arrived with a superior force. The French were treated as prisoners of war and eventually sent home. The surviving Irish were denounced as traitors to the British crown; many were hanged.

A century later, and the noose is still tight around *The Tenants of Time*. Absentee landholders and bankers squeeze the squires, who drain the tenant farmers. Eviction, the workhouse and starvation are common fates. The women cling to the church and the men to the bottle, but a growing number, like Edward Nolan, take to the gun. Nolan was a Fenian leader at the time of Clonbrony; later he is hardened in Portland prison and becomes experienced in conspiracy and vengeful murder on both sides of the Atlantic.

Ned Nolan is the remorseless spirit whose actions unify much of the book's cause and effect. He spans the quarter-century of Flanagan's story, from Clonbrony to the decline and fall of the Irish republican hero Charles Stewart Parnell, who is quoted as saying "A passion for history—an Irish failing." Real figures from the past interact with fictional characters, making

107 in all, alphabetically listed and identified at the end of the book.

The principals—Terrorist Nolan, Schoolteacher Hugh MacMahon and Politician Robert Delaney—are all veterans of Clonbrony who pursue different paths to freedom from British rule. Flanagan follows the twists and turns from Kilpeder and Dublin to London and New York City. His settings, from Ardmor Castle to the local pub, are natural and unforced; the language of his characters hints at hidden poetry without breaking into showy lyricism or stage Irish. . . . (p. 75)

For all its size and sweep, *The Tenants of Time* is an intimate book, a narrative that constantly adds personal tones and shadings to "take a moment of history, a week, a month, and know it fully." Patrick Prentiss would envy this grand illusion, the best historical novel to be published in the U.S. since Thomas Flanagan's *The Year of the French*. (p. 76)

R. Z. Sheppard, "Connoisseurs of Lost Causes," in *Time, New York, Vol. 131, No. 2, January 11, 1988*, pp. 75-6.

RHODA KOENIG

Thomas Flanagan's *The Tenants of Time*, the new novel by the author of *The Year of the French*, fragments the last third of the nineteenth century, the years of bloody rebellion, into a kaleidoscopic view; minor characters play showier parts than established stars, and events are glimpsed from oblique angles.

To the West Cork market town of Kilpeder—"property," as the legend on an old print has it, "of the Earl of Ardmor"—comes Patrick Prentiss, historian, to seek the true story of the rising of 1867, more than 30 years before. The local schoolmaster, Hugh MacMahon, took part in the attack on the police barracks, earning him six months in prison, along with Robert Delaney, later to become the town solicitor and a member of Parliament, and Vincent Tully, spendthrift son of the moneylender, the gombeen-man. Prentiss wants to go beyond the "electroplated fact" and "accurate lies" of convention, beyond the colored lithographs and clubfooted ballads that have enshrined the three as "bold Fenian men." Along with our discoveries of the motives and acts of the rebellious three, we learn about their anticlimactic decades. MacMahon returns to happy domesticity and the schoolroom, Tully plays out a perpetual bachelorhood among the whores of Paris and the maidens of Cork, and Delaney breaches the laws of morality and property by having an affair with the mistress of the falcon-guarded castle, the Countess of Ardmor.

None of these characters, however, engages Flanagan as much as his embroidery work, building up a picture of the time from the flash of a cigar case or a glass of Chartreuse, from swathes of color like the description of an assassin in London who,

> no warrant sworn against him, saunters through fashionable quarters, intricate fanlights, the wood freshly-painted yearly, the glass polished by platoons of lads and skivvies. . . . But now he lay alone, frightened, wide awake at two in the morning, seeing the great centreless web of black and grey, save for a sudden dab, a dab of red blood in Chelsea.

This rather self-infatuated writing, all foreground and background, suffocates the characters before they can spring to life; they are forever congealing into tableaux, compared with paintings and engravings and posters.

Tenants is a very talky novel, with much musing and jawing, much Irish summoning up of the dear, dead days over a bit of the creature, but little of this stream of talk sticks in the mind. A hundred pages and more can go by, and concern themselves with the pouring of tea, the iniquities of the system, and a swirl of color and movement in the street. When the schoolmaster MacMahon, who narrates much of the novel, has the floor, the talk is often about history. "What history can ever be written truly," he wonders, "whether of the Fenians of Kilpeder or of the empire of the Assyrians?" and muses on the victims of the historical moment or the failings of history texts. Another character says, "History is the curse of this country. . . . When we take the train back to Dublin, I shudder—history closing in upon me, like these hedges to our either side here." One could have done with more forceful and dramatic illustrations of this rather simple (and fashionable) theme, and fewer periodic announcements of it, like a conductor's reminder to the drowsy of an approaching station. *The Tenants of Time* may have been intended as a novel of mysterious, shifting perspectives, but it comes across, instead, as a listless book-club historical encumbered by a thesis. (p. 86)

Rhoda Koenig, "Irish Bull," in New York Maga-
zine, Vol. 21, No. 3, January 18, 1988, pp. 86-7.

Alice Fulton

1952-

American poet and critic.

Fulton celebrates the nuances of contemporary life in poems that abound with wordplay, puns, and irreverent wit. Employing both free verse and traditional structures, Fulton explores such topics as art, music, love and death, and the importance of familial bonds and romantic relationships. While her linguistic dexterity has occasionally been faulted for overshadowing her subjects, Fulton is admired for her energy and originality. Matthew Gilbert commented: "Reading [Fulton's] poems is something like listening to a set of the most spirited and peculiar jazz: you cannot always make rational sense of what you hear. Instead you must sharpen your spirit in order to be moved by what is uncanny and rare."

Fulton's first major volume of verse, *Dance Script with Electric Ballerina* (1983), elicited critical attention for the playfulness with which she addresses her primary themes. Reviewers especially noted her evocation of dance and song motifs in the title piece, in which Fulton recalls personal experiences, and praised her use of musical cadences in "You Can't Rhumboogie in a Ball and Chain," a sestina about the late rock singer Janis Joplin. In *Palladium* (1986), Fulton continues to examine life and art in colorful, decorative language. The poems in this volume are divided into six sections, each revolving around a different definition of the word "palladium." Mark Jarman noted: "For [Fulton] all the fun's in how you name a thing. . . . Like [Marianne] Moore's poems, which she called her 'things,' Fulton's poems are also things, rather amazing ones."

(See also *Contemporary Authors,* Vol. 116.)

In the title poem of [*Dance Script with Electric Ballerina*] she describes her own poetry—as also her life—in dance terms and a dancer's "getup":

> feet bright and precise as eggbeaters,
> fingers quick as switch-
> blades and a miner's lamp for my tiara.
> You've seen kids on Independence Day, waving
> sparklers to sketch their initials on the night?
> Just so, I'd like to leave a residue
> of slash and glide, a trace-
> form on the riled air.

Her life seems to have been a succession of dances, dancers, performers, costume. . . . As alter ego she chooses a different sort of performer, Janis Joplin, who wants "No Chiclet-toothed Baptist boyfriend"—and shows it in her "brass-assed language, slingbacks with jeweled heel," her voice like she'd "guzzled fiberglass," and, above all, the costume we see her in, sell her on: "It's your shade, this blood dress. . . ." "It's you."

How many of the poems are concerned with dress—the costume of dancers, which is so often the costume of lovers. For unwanted lovers we see her (or her poems' speakers) going to bed bundled into macintoshes, galoshes, oiled wool sweaters, "everything but skin." (pp. xi-xii)

W. D. SNODGRASS

In *How to Read,* Pound identifies three ways the language of poetry is charged or energized: *melopoeia, phanopoeia,* and *logopoeia.* He describes the last of these as "the dance of intellect among words." He deems it untranslatable and "the latest come, and perhaps most tricky and undependable mode." I would add that it is conspicuously lacking from recent American poetry—as from recent American criticism, thought, politics, American life generally. Just when American dance itself is enjoying such an illustrious resurgence, the American intellect has to show itself creaky, overweight, and downright lubberly. *Logorrhoea?*—it's an epidemic; *Logopoeia?*—where? Yet, just when many of us had written off the American intellect as extinct, probably mythical, here steps into our dark and cheerless vale Alice Fulton, scattering "brio and ballon" on every side, the veritable Lady of Logopoeia.

Yet even when dance/song/performance is not the immediate
subject of Alice Fulton's poems, we are always engaged by
her dance of intellect, the sense of linguistic virtuosity Old Ez
described. There is a constant delight and dazzle in language
textures, the ever-shifting shock and jolt of an electric surface.
This makes me want to quote longer sections, lest by excerpt-
ing, I make her imagery, her diction, seem more predictable,
more readily graspable than it actually is. Let me turn, however, to a few passages where she treats the sky, the passing
day, the seasons:

> the new moon's just a luminous
> zilch. Under it, dawn's
> first nude streak startles
> like a bikini line.

When a man (a lover?) sends her a tape of his singing, her
heart "flap[s] like a screen door in a tempest." Intoxicated,
she notices

> night just sliding by
> gentle and majestic as a battleship
> with cut engines.

> (p. xiii)

It may be that at times the fancy footwork obscures the overall
shape of the dance—which is to say, I suppose, that she has
not quite decided whether she is a poet of style, like cummings
or Berryman, or a poet of subject, like Hardy or Frost. If this
is a fault, I must say it's a loveable one, the kind most young
poets could brag about. How many have the hope, much less
the choice, of being either? On every side manuscripts appear,
with high praise, exactly like seven other volumes one has read
that year; if you accidentally dropped and scrambled all eight
manuscripts, not even their authors could tell. In place of real
talent, energy, passion, one sees poem after poem written to
fit the fashion, the political or literary movement of the week,
the needs of 1,000 half-dead graduate students, the obsession
and power-hungry theories of critic A or B. Alice Fulton once
remarked that, victory or defeat, she hoped at least to be counted
among the lively ones. If my vote counts for anything, she is
a shoo-in. (p. xiv)

Returning to Pound, we remember that he said of his persona,
Hugh Selwyn Mauberley, that "His true Penelope was Flaubert." I shall think myself little poorer in my predilections in
claiming that my true Pavlova shall be henceforward Fulton.
(p. xv)

> *W. D. Snodgrass, in an introduction to* Dance Script
> with Electric Ballerina *by Alice Fulton, University
> of Pennsylvania Press, 1983, pp. xi-xv.*

MATTHEW GILBERT

In his lecture "The Music of Poetry," T. S. Eliot distinguished
between "poems in which we are moved by the music and
take the sense for granted," and "poems in which we attend
to the sense and are moved by the music without noticing it."
Our newer poets tend to write for the non-musical ear. The
meaning in their poems is presented in plain language with just
a hint of accent and other traces of standardized form. But in
her outstanding first book of poems, [*Dance Script With Electric
Ballerina*], Alice Fulton steers away from the "sense" school,
and heads along the less traveled road of verbal music. Each
poem in *Dance Script With Electric Ballerina* is so filled with
sound effects, is such an aural curiosity, that even if at times
the ideas seem incidental and accessory, the language itself
always thrills us.

Fulton's poems are filled with striking words like "carbon-
ado," "wrasse," "bobbled," "baubles," and "brio." She
gives odd, fetching titles like **"How To Swing Those Obbli-
gatos Around," "Agonist Of The Acceleration Lane," "Reeling Back The Saffron"**—phrases difficult to make sense of,
but marvelous to hear.... In **"Toward Clairvoyance,"** an
eloquent characterization of dust, Fulton's acoustic flair matches
that of James Merrill:

> You hold all our home truths,
>   nil-colored one.
> Silk lingerie and high-rag notebooks
>   are pilfered
> sooner or later to your dumb
>   dimension.

Not only are such passages alive with piquant sound repetitions,
but the diction is so eccentric that, as in Merrill's poems, you
never know just what word might show up next. This unpredictability is perhaps the key to Fulton's music: it lends an
improvised, irregular beat to the movement of her poems.

Of course verbal music alone does not first-rate poetry make.
In Pope's words, "The sound must seem an echo to the sense."
Certainly Fulton's sense is not quite as dazzling as her sound:
she writes about wanted lovers, unwanted lovers, the value of
imagination ("kicking like a worm in a jumping bean") in a
numbing world—nothing astoundingly innovative or sagacious. And her sound effects are often undirected and do not
provide particular, pointed emphases within the poem. Still,
Fulton's poems never *lack* sense. Amid the busy, stylish score,
she also delivers an engaging and skillful intellectual performance.

For example, witness her dexterous treatment of clairvoyance,
a recurrent subject in the collection. Clairvoyance is the "painful grace" of acute intuition, of being—

> sensitized to the least cheep and twinge
> of other beings and especially to my
> own twinges.

We are often unable to—

>   . . . see the gulf
> between gestures as a chance
> to find clairvoyance—
> a gift that thrives on fissures
> between then and now and when. . .

Fulton elucidates this rather indistinct notion with distinction
and ease. She is similarly fluent when, in her sestina for Janis
Joplin titled **"You Can't Rhumboogie In A Ball and Chain,"**
she describes the "Little Girl Blue" of rock 'n' roll as having
a voice "rasping like [she'd] guzzled fiberglass."

What lifts these poems above gimmickry, though, is their unusual mixture of passion and estrangement. The voice of this
collection is desirous of, yet somehow a fugitive from earthly
satisfaction....

[*Dance Script With Electric Ballerina*] won the 1982 Associated
Writing Programs Award, an honor Fulton well deserves. She
has the most unusual and entertaining voice I've heard in recent
years. Reading her poems is something like listening to a set
of the most spirited and peculiar jazz: you cannot always make
rational sense of what you hear. Instead you must sharpen your
spirit in order to be moved by what is uncanny and rare.

> *Matthew Gilbert, in a review of "Dance Script with
> Electric Ballerina," in* Boston Review, *Vol. IX, No.
> 1, February, 1984, p. 31.*

WILLIAM LOGAN

[In *Dance Script with Electric Ballerina* Fulton] reaches into a grab-bag of simile and pulls out whatever's handy. Fulton works from a wildness of association reminiscent of Jorie Graham's wayward charm, the abstractions tossed carelessly in, the metaphors whipped into pure froth. The lines hurtle on, and we can tell they're poetry because they're so violently enjambed. Significant enjambement is often a pleasure, but much of Fulton's is so obviously dramatic that it hurts (as in, "I didn't create this pain-/ ful grace").

For Fulton, imagery is intended to distract, so its meanings or implications can never cohere, but must scintillate from a center like subatomic particles after collision. However inventive or ingenious, her images have little precision, and rely completely on our trust in a fancy that reaches the equivocal far more easily than the complex. This conception of the trope as merely the shimmering ornamentation of a poem may corrupt the poem itself. A rape is attended to more as an opportunity for fanciful images ("He is a squeezed tube / spurting words that knife / and twine like eels / under ice") than as a chance to render this violation of the flesh imaginable or horrible, or horrible because imaginable. In her scene there is no feeling at all, only chattering metaphors.

Such amiable, light-hearted, and even light-headed verse could be over-criticized. Fulton at least has the courage of the experimenter. She doesn't *seem* to care what she writes about—any old thing will do; yet her subjects are often personal (her father's death, the machinations of various lovers), and to some extent they alleviate the glamour and transient frissons of the high-wire act she is so intent on performing. A sestina for Janis Joplin ["**You Can't Rhumboogie in a Ball and Chain**"], of all people, shows how easily a high-spirited imagination can master form by being mastered by it. Fulton's occasional leaps of invention (the "calm quantum" of dust) and her ravenous vocabulary ("mingy," "ballon," "melisma," "corm," "dalmatics," "taphephobia," "nyctophobia" [Fulton suffers from phobophilia]) suggest that underneath the glittering surfaces a mind operates:

> All winter the trees tossed in their coma.
> Beneath them fields unrolled
> like a pallet. Snow came,
> the universal donor, the connective
> in all the ready metaphors. . . .

There are still only glimpses of that mind. "It's true," she says, "I've dispensed with some conventions." This book doesn't so much dispense with conventions as prove itself ignorant of their purpose. (pp. 102-03)

> *William Logan, in a review of "Dance Script with Electric Ballerina," in* Poetry, *Vol. CXLV, No. 2, November, 1984, pp. 102-03.*

MARK JARMAN

Alice Fulton's energetic, inventive language in *Dance Script with Electric Ballerina* is justly praised by W. D. Snodgrass in his introduction to the book [see excerpt above]. However, I find inaccurate his claim that intellect is somehow dancing through Fulton's work. I would not call Fulton a particularly intelligent poet, but she does bring a lot of verve to her mostly occasional poems. To call a poem about jogging "**Agonist of the Acceleration Lane**" and speak of herself "alive in the stretch/& the resting of sinews" is clever. But intellect, if it

were really on its toes, would make for some restraint and restraint is rarely present in her poems. The problems of "**You Can't Rhumboogie in a Ball and Chain**," a sestina for Janis Joplin, begin in the title and do not cease until the poem's envoy. The last three lines do seem fitting:

> Like clerks we face your image in the glass,
> suggest lovers, as accessories, heels.
> "It's your shade, this blood dress," we say. "It's you."

But this is preceded by all sorts of pseudo-bluesy rock-talk:

> You called the blues' loose black belly lover
> and in Port Arthur they called you pig-face.
> The way you chugged booze straight, without a glass,
> your brass-assed language, slingbacks with jeweled heel. . .

Et cetera. The reference to Joplin's childhood in Texas is genuinely painful ("pig-face"), but the rest is forced, mannered.

It may be, like the title of the above sestina, that Fulton's own presiding metaphor, dancing, is what leads to excess. The poem in this book where possibility flickers most strongly, where success is near, is "**The Perpetual Light.**" It recounts a visit with her mother to her father's grave. The poem is good step by step, but her mother's reminiscences raise it to another level altogether, apparently by a will of their own. . . . What we have here . . . is a writer who is weakest when her verve, her *logopoeia* as Snodgrass calls it, takes over, singing "Gotta dance!" The mother's voice ends and the poet responds, noting the different ways people suffer today, "Oh, Ma/ how the world has changed us!". . . . Alice Fulton's gift is certain; what she must decide is when to sit one out. (pp. 83-5)

> *Mark Jarman, "Acts of Will," in* The Missouri Review, *Vol. VII, No. 3, 1984, pp. 83-94.*

STEPHEN C. BEHRENDT

Like so much of contemporary poetry, [*Dance Script With Electric Ballerina*] is a collection about interiors and exteriors, about self-discovery and self-definition in a world whose value and significance is continually shifting. Indeed, the title poem, "**Dance Script With Electric Ballerina,**" derives at least obliquely from the question Yeats posed at the end of "Among School Children": "How can we know the dancer from the dance?" Fulton's answer, as revealed in her poems, tends to be that the question is ultimately irrelevant, that dancer and dance (poet and poem) are mutually defining, mutually reflective, that poet and poem alike are both the embodiment and the record of human response to the experience of life. But in a thoroughly Romantic impulse, the poet goes beyond merely recording, moving on to reshaping and restructuring what is observed, what is experienced, to produce an alternative, heightened reality that is perpetually stimulating (to poet and reader alike), whether it be satisfying or frustrating. . . . These are poems in and about art and life, poems that weave the techniques of music—indeed of the several arts—into a lively and compelling fabric of experience. They are delightful, energetic poems, alive with the exhilaration of creation.

The single unsettling—indeed downright annoying—aspect of *Dance Script With Electric Ballerina* is the awkward and intrusive introduction (by no less a poet than W. D. Snodgrass) the publishers felt called upon to include [see excerpt above]. We are seeing more and more of this sort of thing; not only university presses like Pennsylvania but regional ones like Ahsahta Press are inserting such prefatory puffs in their editions. One wonders why. It is curious that publishers seem oblivious to the detrimental effects of such essays, which are inevitably contrived and condescending. Don't they trust the reader to read and appreciate with intelligence and sophistication? Apparently not, for over-written introductions of this sort invariably lecture readers about not only what to look for but also what to *appreciate*.... Were the poetry less interesting, less inspired, less original than Fulton's is, for instance, such a procedure might conceivably have some merit, though if poetry needs either an *apology* or a prefatory critical essay (or advertisement) for the reader's "benefit," then perhaps it ought not to be published at all. Alice Fulton's poetry needs no such treatment, no such crutch: indeed, the quality of the poetry makes all the more striking the obtrusiveness of the lecture to the reader. (pp. 121-22)

Stephen C. Behrendt, in a review of "Dance Script with Electric Ballerina," in Prairie Schooner, *Vol. 60, No. 2, Summer, 1985, pp. 121-22.*

J. D. McCLATCHY

Quite a number of people, I'll bet, have had their eye on Alice Fulton. I have. Her first book, *Dance Script with Electric Ballerina* (1983), made readers sit up and take notice. In his introduction to that book [see excerpt above], W. D. Snodgrass called her the Lady of Logopoeia and celebrated her razzy exuberance.... And he rightly noted that she is a poet of style, like Berryman, rather than a poet of subject, like Frost. The same can be said for *Palladium.* It's not that she lacks subjects; it's clear she could write about anything—Mme. Curie's middle name or why male ballet dancers don't wear moustaches. But her subjects are sometimes lost in the dazzle of her performance. Her poems are "like the convention / of majorettes to lead the Labor / Day parade, zipped in vinyl thigh / boots, suits molten as new pennies / above predictable kicks, batons / that soar, catch the light and twirl / before they're caught." I imagine that poems in this style go over very well when they are read to an audience; they're flashy—a pinball machine, an evangelist's tent, a casino floorshow. Page after page, however, can be wearing.... Each poem is crammed with idioms and metaphors that race by. She makes most other poets seem diffident to a fault. Fulton's hopped-up, with a hard metallic tone and a cranky line. She prefers equivalents to definitions, but in this is only following Wallace Stevens's adage that things seen are things *as* seen.

A style like this needs certain subjects to feed it—the eccentric, the debased, the high-flying.... She is variously a nun, a stripper, and an oil rigger in this book, and she can manipulate her own voice and circumstances to hilarious, satirical effect. When she writes of her family, as she does in a fine series of six poems, she quiets down. She remarks on her mother's "affinity with the fabulous," and indeed her whole tribe is an endearingly weird one. Fulton writes of them with love and respect. When she has hold of a worthy subject, her muscled style has more edge—as when she writes of Lord Pain's "bad oboes, / calliopes fueling the Silver Flash, / the Whip, the Tilt-A-Whirl, that is the bed / with its chipped grab bars." Or **"603 West Liberty Street"** with its take on faith.... There are other poems as deft and controlled—**"Terrestrial Magnetism," "Traveling Light," "Fugitive."** This poet's like a natural force that can run amok but when harnessed is a source of energy. I hope it powers many more books. (pp. 43-5)

J. D. McClatchy, "Mortal Listeners," in Poetry, *Vol. CXLIX, No. 1, October, 1986, pp. 31-47.*

SVEN BIRKERTS

Alice Fulton's first book, *Dance Script with Electric Ballerina,* careered around the poetry corner like a cartoon fire-engine, with two wheels in the air and an extension ladder cantilevering perilously over the street. Well, that might be an exaggeration; it was certainly a distinctive—and much remarked—debut. Fulton's quick, jaggy lines caught the music of growing up tough ("This boy liked me once: / / / two cries and a clutch"), and her gift for transforming commonplace objects and actions into lit-up signals was singular....

All first books are, in a sense, written to the world; second books tend to have a smaller target—mainly, the readers of the first. Improvement or departure are obligatory. As Fulton had achieved a kind of perfection within her chosen mode in *Dance Script,* the latter choice was natural. In *Palladium,* therefore, we see the artist installed in front of a larger canvas, equipped with more brushes and paints. The poems are longer, the subjects and stances have greater variety—the results are mixed.

Fulton's ambition is evident straight-off in the organization of the book. There are six sections, each prefaced by a different definition, or legend, of the word "palladium": a platinum-like element, a safeguard, a music hall, a photographic printing process, a legless effigy or cult object, and a magic-working totem which dropped from the heavens into the city of Troy, only to be stolen by the besieging Greeks. Though Fulton does work out certain thematic connections between the section headings and the poems—the music hall section, for instance, presents lively character studies of relatives—the unifying strategy is finally unconvincing. Why palladium? The reader feels either that some larger significance eludes him, or else that arbitrariness has donned the mask of order.

In her irrepressible inventiveness, as well as in her aesthetic of profusion, Fulton recalls Amy Clampitt. Both poets are capable of stunning virtuoso turns, but both are also capable of switching on the image-making machine while they rest from their exertions. When her heart is in it, Fulton can come across with a Gould-playing-Goldberg effervescence....

At other times, though, an equally persuasive rhythm can get undermined by the surface clutter of similes and metaphors:

> up North where windows ignite early,
> hanging the dark
> with inner lives like tiny drive-in screens
> showing underrated grade B stars,
> and bingo-playing ladies
> hover, intent as air controllers
> above their cards in social halls.
> At tables long as football fields, they acquire
> a taste for the metallic:
> coins, flat Coke; and Bic lighters
> puff like the souls of exclamation
> points as winners collect
> their macrame plant cradles.

(from **"Aviation"**)

In thirteen lines we have inner lives likened to grade B drive-in scenarios, bingo ladies to air controllers, tables to football fields, and Bic lighters to exclamation points. Passages like this convince me that Fulton's pen holds a bottomless reservoir of images, that she has only to move the point across the page for a poem to start shaping up.

This is my central complaint about this prodigiously gifted poet: I cannot always feel the pressure of inevitability, the sense that here is a poem that *had* to be written. I find this most often with her longer, more discursive meditations. . . . My cavils notwithstanding, *Palladium* is a collection to own and explore; like its namesake metal, it will not tarnish at ordinary temperatures.

Sven Birkerts, in a review of "Palladium," in Boston Review, *Vol. XI, No. 6, December, 1986, p. 29.*

PETER STITT

Palladium, Alice Fulton's second volume, was chosen by Mark Strand for inclusion in the National Poetry Series for 1985; her first book, *Dance Script with Electric Ballerina,* won the 1982 Associated Writing Programs Award in poetry. The new collection is divided into six sections according to the areas of meaning possessed by the word *palladium:* 1) it is a metallic element related to platinum, used in alloys and as a catalyst; 2) it is something that provides protection, a safeguard; 3) it is a name given to music halls that featured variety bills; 4) it is a process in photography so subject to variables that its prints "may be considered . . . one-of-a-kind images"; 5) it is a talismanic doll, rock, or other object; and 6) it is a felled asteroid and therefore heavenly; a monolith.

Fulton gives the impression of having structured her book according to these meanings. Even after having read through the volume several times, however. . ., I am unable to see much correlation between the definitions for a given section and the poems that follow. The method does, however, indicate Alice Fulton's interest in words, her commitment to language, to linguistic structures, as an element capable of giving shape and meaning to the reality contained within a poem.

This preoccupation with language shows up in both the subject matter and the style of the poems. **"Babies,"** for example, begins with a striking series of images and an event that demonstrates the power of verbal communication. . . . Within the content of the lines, it is the languagelike sounds made by the mother that define the world as perceived by the baby.

As baby grows up in this swiftly moving poem, language continues to be the agency through which reality's lessons are taught and understood. . . . Once a pair of these babies has reached physical maturity—that is, when, "Like a child's first school pencils / in their formal brilliance / and sharp new smells, / they lie / / as lovers"—the plot begins to thicken. The word *lie,* of course, is intentionally ambiguous, as language continues to drive life: "Maybe one cries / the wrong name . . ." Apologies in this scenario do not avail, for ". . . the beloved may stay bitter as an ear / the tongue pressed / into, unwanted." Eventually, ". . . the word *end:* spiney, finally-formed, / indents them and is / understood."

The poem comes to its own end in lines that reemphasize the importance, the solidity of communication. . . . It is not just subject matter that insists here that language gives substantial meaning to reality. Fulton's style has so much texture, thanks to her images and to her use of words, and that texture places a palpable surface on the abstract construct of the poem.

In terms only of subject matter, one other organizing principle plays an important role, albeit a negative one, in these poems. Along with such poets as David Bottoms, Alice Fulton shares an interest in the structure of ritual, myth, and belief offered by organized religion. Fulton's maternal relatives are, or were, Roman Catholic; in this regard we hear mostly about her mother, Mary Callahan Fulton, and grandmother, Catherine ("Katey")

Callahan. The dramatic monologue **"Sister Madeleine Pleads for Our Mary"** is spoken by the grandmother's sister-in-law and concerns the family's desire that Mary, then a schoolgirl, be chosen to portray the Holy Mother in a forthcoming pageant. The poem is addressed to "Sister Immaculata," who has it in her power to make this choice.

Sister Madeleine is a wonderfully salty character; she speaks of God as "that Chiseler / / of Souls for Paradise" and praises the Virgin for her rich contributions to the feminist cause. . . . As for the younger Mary, namesake to the Blessed Virgin— although saucy enough to ask questions about the Sisterly Vocation ("how we open doors / without a squeak of hinge, walk / with grounded eyes and never run / some innocent wayfarer down, keep / our spines 'straight as stickpins'"), she still is not irreligious: "High-spirited, yes, a chatterbox, / perhaps, but unholy never; never / / truly bold is Mary."

The same cannot be said for the speaker of most of these poems, whose belief is only "in the quantum world's array of random / / without chaos, its multiplicity." What she thinks of religious faith is expressed in lines about those who move "through austere ranges.". . . To the eyes of Alice Fulton, faith provides no help for understanding the world's incessant multiplicity. Perhaps it is because language is itself multiple, slippery, difficult to pin down, that it provides so much more satisfactory a vision. (pp. 801-04)

Peter Stitt, "To Enlighten, to Embody," in The Georgia Review, *Vol. XLI, No. 4, Winter, 1987, pp. 800-13.*

MARK JARMAN

[*Palladium*] is divided into six sections, each headed with a different definition of "palladium.". . . The definition is the form her poems most often take; as if in acknowledgement that a single thing or word can have many meanings, she attempts to give as many as she can think up. For her all the fun's in how you name a thing. In this, her guiding genius is Marianne Moore. Although Fulton's exuberance is not as strictly controlled as Moore's, it could be argued that the great Modernist's elaborate syllabic forms were disguises for a chaos of associations. Like Moore's poems, which she called her "things," Fulton's poems are also things, rather amazing ones, too.

They can include fanciful guidebooks to the lifestyles of hell (**"Orientation Day in Hades"**) and phantasmagoric trips through contemporary underworlds as in **"The Body Opulent."** She is savvy about female and male forms of identity, in **"Fictions of the Feminine"** and **"Men's Studies: *Roman de la Rose."*** I like her poems best for the way they say a thing, as in these lines from **"Everyone Knows the World is Ending."**

> Everyone knows the world is ending.
> Everyone always thought so, yet
> Here's the world.

Or the pun that closes **"Days Through Starch and Bluing"** ("Tomorrow's pressing."). (p. 349)

Reviewing her first book I complained that the poems were often overwritten [see excerpt above]. They still are, but to say so is also to object puritanically to their abundance. This long book covers quite a bit of ground, some of the best of it focused on Fulton's own family, mother and aunts, her father, and Troy, New York, her hometown, which she mythifies with a gossamer touch ("We loved a ruin"). As good company as these poems are, they are best when we can, to paraphrase Marianne Moore, admire what we understand.

> Oh, you will never know me. I wave and you go
> on playing in the clouds
> boys clap from erasers. I am the pebble
> you tossed on the chalked space and war-
> danced toward, one-leg two-leg, arms treading air.
>
> **"Fierce Girl Playing Hopscotch"**
> (p. 350)

Mark Jarman, "A Scale of Engagement, from Self to Form Itself," in The Hudson Review, *Vol. XL, No. 2, Summer, 1987, pp. 343-51.*

CALVIN BEDIENT

[In *Palladium,* Alice Fulton] is about equally energetic and novel and is a lot more limber—she does a sort of kicking dance as a poet, rapid, athletic, and with a wicked intelligence takes on a wider range of material. She too feeds on detail, only with gusto, and garrulously. She revels in her own youthful energy for life; her temptation is to do a verbal star turn, to entertain. Witness, beginning with the title, **"My Second Marriage to My First Husband"**:

> we lollygagged down the aisle, vowed
> to forsake dallying, shilly-shallying, and cleave
> only onto one another, to forever romp
> in the swampy rumpus
> room of our eccentricities: that sanctum
> sanctorum where I sport
> bedsocks and never rise
> till noon. . .

High-spirited, but a bit egoistic and noisy. . . . Fulton invites you to have a good time along with her, and if we judge from the blurbs, critics respond as if starved for just such an invitation. But Fulton is capable of piercing and disinterested contemplation (you get a glimpse of it in the arresting conclusion to the marriage poem—"Our eyes burn / stoplights in the Instamatic squares"), and I look forward to her years of middle-age sag, when her energy will be easier to bear. (pp. 142-43)

Calvin Bedient, "The Wild Braid of Creation," in The Sewanee Review, *Vol. XCVI, No. 1, Winter, 1988, pp. 137-49.*

Isaac Goldemberg

1945-

Peruvian novelist and poet.

In his fiction, Goldemberg examines the psychological consequences of the Jewish diaspora in his native country. He investigates the spiritual rootlessness and loss of personal identity of his frustrated protagonists in a subdued prose while often incorporating comedy and irony into a disjointed narrative style. Ellen Lesser observed: "Goldemberg fuses the best of two potent traditions: the Latin Americans' labyrinthine inventiveness and the irony and black humor of Jewish literature, all mixed up with some magic of his own." Although some critics claim that Goldemberg's style is excessively sentimental, most praise his ability to distance himself from his highly personal work.

The son of a Peruvian Indian and a Russian Jew, Goldemberg experienced during his adolescence the alienation and exile illuminated in his fiction. After emigrating to New York City in 1964, he produced several poetry collections written in Spanish but initially elicited critical attention with the publication of his first novel composed in English, *The Fragmented Life of Don Jacobo Lerner* (1976). The story of a dying Russian Jew struggling to come to terms with his disappointing life, this work dramatizes Jacobo Lerner's ungratifying existence through the viewpoints of his friends and enemies and his insane illegitimate son. Having left Russia because of Jewish persecution, Lerner settles in Peru, hoping to establish a new, affluent life. Although he fails to achieve his goal, Lerner's dream of becoming the patriarch of a large Jewish family is ironically and humorously realized in his ownership of a prosperous Lima brothel. Goldemberg juxtaposes Lerner's story with historical details and newspaper clippings which reveal escalating anti-Semitic tensions in Peru and the frustration and despondency felt by the Jewish community. Frank MacShane stated: "Just as Flaubert revealed for the first time the quality of bourgeois life in 19th-century France, so Goldemberg has created the whole world of provincial Peru—and by extension, of South America as a whole." Goldemberg's second novel, *Tiempo al Tiempo* (1985; *Play by Play*), involves the fatal search for identity of Marcos Karushansky Avila, an alienated Peruvian youth who moves in with his Orthodox Jewish father after living for years with his Gentile mother. Goldemberg presents his protagonist's story in the form of a surrealistic soccer match during which a manic broadcaster transmits a play-by-play account of Marcos's life and suicide. J. J. Hassett wrote: "Goldemberg heightens our appreciation of his character's estrangement by never allowing us to draw too close to him. He remains an enigmatic figure to the end, but the depth of his tragedy lingers with us long after we close the book."

Goldemberg has also written *Hombre de pase/Just Passing Through* (1981), a bilingual collection of verse which shares many of the concerns of his novels. Julio Marzán remarked: "Effectively rendered in English, these poems translate an uncommon Peruvian-Jewish background into a common language. They evoke Goldemberg's past as an enormous composite *before,* which imbues his present and preordains his future." *Tiempo de silencio* (1969) is a compilation of Gol-

demberg's early verse. In addition, Goldemberg composed the poetry collection *De Chepen a la Habana* (1973) in collaboration with Cuban-born author José Kozer.

(See also *Contemporary Authors,* Vols. 69-72 and *Contemporary Authors New Revision Series,* Vol. 11.)

MARGO JEFFERSON

When this haunting novel [*The Fragmented Life of Don Jacobo Lerner*] begins, Jacobo Lerner, a prosperous brothel owner from Russia, is lying on his deathbed in Lima, Peru, considering the "mild catastrophes" that will be incurred by his passing. The hypocritical brother who swindled him years before will now go bankrupt; his loyal mistress will be mocked "because she had not known how to squeeze money out of him in payment for her love"; his illegitimate 10-year-old son will struggle to piece together a picture of the absent father, and his son's mother, a Catholic woman of Indian and Spanish descent, will endure the insults of her father "for not having married the Jew while it was still possible."

In this first novel, Isaac Goldemberg, a young Peruvian Jewish writer, chronicles the "fragmented life" of Jacobo Lerner in a compelling range of tones and devices. Straightforward narrative alternates with monologues and historical and journalistic documents to illuminate the elements of his mosaic: the Russian and the Latin American cultures; Judaism and Catholicism; the public world of commerce and community; the private one of dybbuks and exorcism. . . .

All of this forms the rich backdrop for the painful saga of Goldemberg's Wandering Jew. Jacobo Lerner arrived in Lima in 1921 determined to make money, marry a Jewish woman and have many children, like "one of the patriarchs in Genesis." By 1931 he is a community disgrace. He socializes only in his brothel, with other men "deformed by solitude.". . . Eventually, the guilt-ridden Jacobo comes to feel that he is possessed by a dybbuk—the wandering soul of a dead childhood friend who was obsessed with visions of pogroms, war and holocaust. When the dybbuk is finally exorcised, Jacobo has nothing left to believe in but "the fact of his own imminent death."

Goldemberg shows with great perception how history, belief and myth can burden people with more contradictions than they can bear. This insight, joined to well-observed details . . . makes this novel a wonderfully promising debut for a gifted writer.

> *Margo Jefferson, "Wandering Jew," in* Newsweek, *Vol. LXXXIX, No. 19, May 9, 1977, p. 103.*

FRANK MacSHANE

We like to think of the United States as the principal haven for the "wretched refuse" of Europe's "teeming shore" (as the inscription on the Statue of Liberty puts it), but South America has also offered asylum to those trying to escape civil wars, poverty and racial bigotry. The New World has provided shelter, but the burden of exile is heavy. Spiritual rootlessness cannot be quickly overcome. In the recent surge of fiction from South America, this theme has nowhere been more fully treated than in [*The Fragmented Life of Don Jacobo Lerner*] by the Peruvian writer, Isaac Goldemberg.

The novel opens with Don Jacobo Lerner on his deathbed in Lima, looking back over his years as a Jewish immigrant who left Russia in the 1920's and began his life in Peru as an itinerant peddler. (p. 15)

Jacobo finds himself isolated in a small provincial town that is governed by the bourgeoisie whose sense of class structure and Roman Catholic morality set the tone. He tries to make a life for himself in this alien society, but he either does too much or too little. . . .

The drama of Don Jacobo's isolation is played out against the background of Peru in the 1930's, where his paranoia is shared by other Jews fearful of the Nazis and of pogroms such as Europe had already experienced. Some of the Jews seek protective coloration by becoming Peruvian citizens, hoping that their backgrounds will not be noticed; at the same time, they feel at home only within the Jewish community. Goldemberg reveals these opposed tensions most effectively by quoting articles, advertisements, letters to the editor in the *Jewish Soul*, a journal based on an actual Peruvian newspaper. The journal also publishes historical documents about the Inquisition to remind its readers of the long history of anti-Semitism among Spanish-speaking peoples.

Yet this is not a Jewish book in a narrow sense. Coping with the opposed impulses of solitude and companionship is a universal task, almost the touchstone of 20th-century experience. But there is more to this book than that. Just as Flaubert revealed for the first time the quality of bourgeois life in 19th-century France, so Goldemberg has created the whole world of provincial Peru—and by extension, of South America as a whole. Only Manuel Puig before him has given us a sense of the terrible solitude of small town life, the cultural poverty that exists everywhere except in the capital cities.

This first novel by Isaac Goldemberg gives us something quite different from what we have received from Gabriel García Márquez, Mario Vargas Llosa and Carlos Fuentes. It is a nightmare world of frustrated hopes, of narrowness and claustrophobia where no one can afford to be generous and where people become insane and destructive. Goldemberg allows his characters to tell their own stories and interrupts these private narratives with notices, documents and newspaper headlines to give a sense of the public dimension of the life of these exiles. This technique also insures that the novel, ably translated into idiomatic English, remains refreshingly free of the exotic trimmings that are often associated with Latin American fiction: it is a moving exploration of the human condition. (p. 33)

> *Frank MacShane, "American Indians, Peruvian Jews," in* The New York Times Book Review, *June 12, 1977, pp. 15, 33.*

MICHAEL IRWIN

[*The Fragmented Life of Don Jacobo Lerner*] reconstructs, through hints and snatches, the unsatisfactory life that is about to end. . . . There is no clear chronological sequence. The shifts and discontinuities reflect the disjointedness of Lerner's career. . . . He has seduced one woman, loved another, proposed to a third and kept a fourth. His son, whom he has never seen, is being brought up a Catholic, and has in any case gone mad. . . .

Only nominally is this the story of one man's life. Lerner scarcely has a personality, or even an identity. In one context he is a liar and betrayer, in another a victim, in another a benefactor. His "fragmented life" stands for the fragmented lives of all the Jews in the Peruvian community—characters who are glimpsed in the interstices of the narrative, struggling to come to terms with an alien land and a hostile religion. *The Fragmented Life of Don Jacobo Lerner* is an anatomy of Jewish immigrant experience.

The economy and restraint of Isaac Goldemberg's style can tend towards colourlessness. If the place-names were changed the novel might be set in another country, or even another continent. The author's self-denial is to be regretted, because where he does describe he describes delicately.

In technique and often in substance this novel is strongly reminiscent of Faulkner's *As I Lay Dying;* and it poses rather similar problems. To grasp, and sort, and cross-relate the component fragments the reader must be constantly alert and responsive. There are a dozen or more major characters, and as many minor ones, to be extricated and identified. . . . *The Fragmented Life of Don Jacobo Lerner* is a difficult novel to get into, since all the labour of exposition has been assigned to the reader. And what incentive has he, given that the prose is low-keyed and the narrative obscurely dispersed? Only an implicit suggestion of authorial control which seems to promise that these scattered fragments will eventually fall into a pattern.

Perhaps this is enough, but I doubt it. The kind of attentiveness this novel demands seems more appropriate to a mystery story or a memory test. . . . The narrative complexity does not adequately justify itself. But it must be said that the story for which these fragments are a substitute could have been a massive and original work. This is a first novel of unusual poise, flavour and promise.

Michael Irwin, *"As He Lay Dying,"* in The Times Literary Supplement, *No. 3963, March 10, 1978, p. 274.*

JULIO MARZÁN

[Isaac Goldemberg's *Hombre de Paso/Just Passing Through*] reminds us that hemispheric borders and national labels obscure a shared American experience. Effectively rendered in English, these poems translate an uncommon Peruvian-Jewish background into a common language. They evoke Goldemberg's past as an enormous composite *before*, which imbues his present and preordains his future.

Swept by time's flow, everything lived remains real for a short span, then becomes surreal; to recall the bygone present, Goldemberg acts like the man in **"One Day,"** who "touches his childhood / floats toward his memories." This couplet, which summarizes the principal activity of these poems, also conveys a sense of how, throughout the book, the poet travels to recurrent memories of ceremonies, traditions, events, and places surrounding the ghostly characters in the story of his life. Even those poems that realistically touch his childhood have the dreamlike quality of his other poems stripped of nonessential particulars: "1945 / is witness / to a mother who was never there / and a grey-haired father / who came into and left / my world at the same time."

No mere graphic detail, the "grey-haired" image reiterates this book's sustained theme of overpowering time. Goldemberg's aged father imparted both a sense of fleetingness and the long chronology of Jewish history; his mother contributed the indestructibility of the Incas. From an improbable union, Goldemberg inherited a sense of distance—between ancient, incompatible myths, present hardships and glorified histories, Incan-Christian Peru and its Jewish minority, his mother and father. . . .

This distance also helped Goldemberg convert the inevitable identity crisis into a drive to see through deceptive surface signs; "who cared if Wiracocha was born in a Bethlehem manger / or if Jesus was Lake Titicaca's son / we didn't need sperm tests / but tests of conscience." Distance also rescues his ethnic poems, like **"Bar Mitzvah,"** from remaining plainly sociological. . . . But it is the least explicitly personal poems which surprise with unexpected music and some of Goldemberg's finer images—as in **"A Peddler's Memories"** of a beautiful woman who daily, indifferently, passes by his corner: "and what if I were to see her pass this peddler's corner / slowly draining and embezzling the rest of my days."

Julio Marzán, *in a review of "Hombre de Paso/Just Passing Through,"* in VLS, *No. 7, May, 1982, p. 4.*

JONATHAN TITTLER

Titles are to books as proper names are to people. They identify the thing to which they allude, and in so doing distinguish it from the other discrete entities of its species. Predicated upon the uniqueness and stability of the object denominated, names facilitate reference by circumventing the (infinitely) long description necessary to capture adequately the essence of a particular phenomenon. The title of Isaac Goldemberg's recently published novel, **The Fragmented Life of Don Jacobo Lerner,** is thus tantamount to its name, even as it contains within it another proper name, that of its pathetic protagonist. Between the name of the character and that of the book there appears to be a simple rapport: the latter promises an account of the existence of the former. The simplicity soon proves to be illusory, however, owing to the qualifier "Fragmented," a loose translation of the Spanish *a plazos* (installment plan). "Fragmented," it turns out, indicates that the life in question is temporally extended, discontinuous, and, most important, not entirely one's own. If we follow the implication that one whose life is not quite one's own is not quite oneself, it is apparent that a name may serve as a sort of mask. It covers the deep-seated alterity, the movement and change of the world, with a veneer of constancy. Goldemberg's novel's title, then, as it performs its onomastic, idenfitying function, puts into question the self-sameness of the character Jacobo Lerner and in the same gesture problematizes the principle of naming that depends on that self-identical property.

In the novel, the difficulty inherent in nomination begins with the name Jacobo Lerner, which discloses immediately a circumstance of estrangement. It is the unlikely Hispanic version of a plainly Jewish appellation. Jacobo's namesake—*Ya'akov* of the Old Testament—is the son of *Yitzchak* (Isaac in both Spanish and English) and the sire of twelve sons who become the patriarchs of the twelve tribes of Israel. As well as a prodigious progenitor, he is a dreamer who envisages himself climbing a ladder to heaven and wrestling with an angel of God. Though his dreams are toubled, they are bounded by an implicit faith in a holy, plenipotentiary diety.

Ya'akov is derived from a word which means "supplanter" or "replacer," a sense which is consistent with Jacobo's ambitious visions. The present Jacobo's surname—Lerner—means in Yiddish "student" or "apprentice," a tag which, if it denotes subalternity, at least admits the possibility of future mastery. Within the novel's *unheimlich* Peruvian setting, however, all these labels suffer a perceptible distortion. To the extent that Jacobo learns anything, it is knowledge in its most negative sense. That is, he becomes undeceived, totally and cynically disillusioned from a lesson learned the hard way and too late. Rather than a supplanter, he is a transplantee, a displaced personage, an exile both within and without. His dreams, moreover, incoherent icons of dismal descent, have closer affiliations with the infernal than the celestial. And in stark contrast to the profuse genealogy engendered by his biblical archetype, Jacobo Lerner has but one illegitimate offspring, Efraín, who is both infirm and insane, and on whom his father never so much as sets eyes. Jacobo is thus not one with his name, which, like his life, seems also not to be entirely his own.

The fissures between the character and his proper name, suggested in the title and opened in the textual corpus, obey a single principle that manifests itself throughout the text: disjunction. Rupture and partition dominate the heterogeneous narrative on levels that range from the individual word to the most abstract textual movement. This tendency perhaps comes to the reader's attention first via the novel's many images of decimation. Efraín is obsessed with visions of his own physical decomposition, for example, as in the following hallucinatory passages: "They chop my head off and Father Chirinos throws me in the river so the crabs will eat me"; and "One day they're going to eat me alive. All that will be left of me is skin and little white bones spread throughout the house." On a historical plane (within the fiction), Sara, Jacobo's brother's wife, recalls the suicide shooting of her brother-in-law, "Daniel with his face blown off." And, in certain interpretive moves, Jacobo's "chaotic life" is characterized as "a past that was quickly breaking into small fragments." These are but a few samples of represented fragmentation that are "local" in scope. (pp. 173-75)

The principle of disjunction applies on a broader scale as well. In that separations of various kinds in the plot are far more numerous than reunions, the tendency is thematized and thus available to the reader as schemata in retrospect. His family devastated, Jacobo leaves his Russian *shtetl* of Staraya Ushitza for Poland and eventually for Peru. When the potentially happy coincidence occurs that his old friend Léon Mitrani has also emigrated to Chepén, a northern Peruvian village, Jacobo must again depart for Lima in order to avoid his paternal responsibilities. He enters a shoe business in partnership with his brother Moisés (another character with an ill-fitting name), but the tandem venture dissolves in the wake of Moisés' swindling his incredulous next of kin. Formerly a devout member of the Jewish community, a jaded Jacobo makes of himself a pariah by becoming proprietor of a brothel. Late in his life, when, for all his tainted wealth, he is despairingly ill and alone, Jacobo is assessed as "a man completely unattached, cut off from his traditions, and with absolutely no sense of direction."

Although Jacobo is central, his is only one of the numerous cases of disenfranchisement in the novel. His Gentile lover, Juana Paredes, receives from him no confirmation of their relationship other than a periodic allowance. She is thus subjected to a limbolike, installment-plan life of her own. More cut off still is his former lover, Virginia (Bertila in the English translation), with whom he engenders Efraín. Not only does she receive no financial consideration for her trouble, but she is additionally severed in the sense of losing her mind. . . . Indeed, insanity—an extreme form of divorce from communal norms—enjoys a disproportionately high incidence among those who figure in Jacobo's life story. In addition to Virginia there is her demented son, Efraín, of whom [Wolfgang A.] Luchting has said, "He disintegrates, almost literally, for not knowing who he is or who his father is." Jacobo's lifelong friend León Mitrani and his wife are also so stricken ("If it was true that the wife was not sound and sane, it was also true that León was not far behind"). Mitrani, in turn, after his death, contributes to Jacobo's mental derangement. Mitrani's body is lost en route to its interment and thus, according to lore, his spirit is condemned to roam the earth as an *ánima en pena*. In the last year of his life, Jacobo feels himself possessed by Mitrani's dibbuk, a condition which is alleviated only by an exorcism. The ostensible conjunction with "reality" implicit in Jacobo's return to his right mind, then, is attenuated by the disintegration of souls realized in the cure. There is thus ample evidence of inter- and intra-subjective breakage throughout the referential dimension of the text.

The antidote for the ubiquitous estrangement I have been describing, of course, should be the Jewish community, the organ of cultural and religious continuity and commonality. The ex-

iles form a synagogue, organize social gatherings, and keep in touch via the periodical *Jewish Soul,* many of whose pages are reproduced sporadically in the novel. . . . The solace one could hope to find among such a collectivity is . . . always already subverted, undermined by the initial loss (Lima can never be Jerusalem) that precipitates its attempt at recuperating unity.

In a way very typical of the Diaspora, the feeling of Jewry is further diluted by a tension between at times irreconcilable loyalties, for each member is split between the region into which he is born and the nation in which he has gained asylum. This division between two continuities (one implied in assimilation and another implied in cultural retention) is dramatized through Edelman, who tempers his solitude by marrying a Christian woman, and Jacobo, who does not. In addition to these and other examples of severing and dispersal in the novel, we should recognize the extent to which Judaism is primordially fragmented; that is, loss of wholeness constitutes a hallmark of its myths and ceremonies. . . . The lack of development and unity in Don Jacobo's life is not to be remedied by attending dances, bazaars, or theatrical performances. The sense of ubiquitous insufficiency in him, a transcendental "not-quiteness," is a structure that has informed the Jewish psyche for millennia. The mythical underpinnings of Goldemberg's novel are thus already riddled with rupture long before Don Jacobo begins his own truncated journey.

There is still room for differences of degree, however, and Jacobo's case certainly appears to be bleak in the extreme. His piecemeal existence, in fact, . . . leads him to the realization that "neither the affection he feels for his sister-in-law, nor his relationship with Doña Juana, nor the satisfactory economic situation in which he finds himself have been enough to give meaning to his life." But it is not the ambition of Goldemberg's novel merely to *describe* the senselessness of a particularly solitary existence. If such were the case, one could point to a few thematically comprehensive passages and dispense with the rest of the textual minutiae. To say that the work is "about" fragmentation per se is to say that in addition to the pervasiveness of that motif in the characters' lives, the novel is composed in such a manner as to *reproduce* for the reader the acute inconsequentiality that Jacobo judges his life to embody. Such a sensation clearly cannot be reduced to a single line, no matter how pithy. (pp. 175-79)

In addition to the images already described, the experience of scattering occurs at the level of language, where the fragmenting impulse is quite vigorous. Goldemberg's admirably controlled prose is sprinkled liberally with Yiddish and Hebrew. . . . Beyond the heterogeneous lexicon required for the mimetic portrayal of a Jewish-in-exile thematics, there are also select passages that create a heterogeneity of syntax. Some of Samuel Edelman's locutions, for example, such as: "Thank God tomorrow I leave Chepén and no more return, since I got here everything like a dream, reliving the past again, why have to remember things give pain in heart?", provide an insight into the rhythms and ellipses of an alien tongue spoken through a Yiddish grid. Similarly, journalistic prose, advertisements, and official documents are interspersed among narrative passages to give rise to, among other things, a disparity of graphic textures. Some of these narrative sections are of striking lyricism. (p. 179)

Along what might be called an axis of decorum, one finds discontinuity in the incongruous, sporadic juxtaposition of humorous material with more solemn writing. In addition to the illness, suicide, and madness already mentioned, other misfortunes are visited upon the protagonist. . . . (p. 180)

Nevertheless, passages of a clearly comic nature lighten the novel and skirt maudlin pathos. Jacobo's aspiring in-laws, for example, are drawn in caricaturesque proportions when they gullibly take him for ''a kind of Count of Monte Cristo, owner of vast shining treasures buried deep in the earth, lord of enchanted palaces in distant kingdoms, consummate swordsman, and tireless traveler destined for prodigious adventures.''. . . And Efraín, in an innocent and demented state that allows for outrageous candor, provides numerous instances of (mostly scatological) comic relief. At one point his mind wanders to a quarrel in which his grandmother scolds his grandfather as a ''shitty old man. Where the hell was he when they were fucking his daughter?'' Later he reports that ''Uncle Pedro died in the toilet. He farted, and then he died.'' As if uniform tragedy would lend too much importance to a series of events whose significance gestures toward an ultimate meaninglessness, inconsistency in mood (and narrative mode) plays a major role in buttressing the novel's fragmenting enterprise.

The overall narrative configuration further contributes to a kaleidoscopic, mystifying effect. The mystery is actually a sort of puzzle whose key resides in Samuel Edelman's talmudic dictum: ''But when man thinks he is finished then everything begins anew.'' It is Jacobo's sense of impending death in December of 1935 (he thinks he is finished) that generates the narration of his episodic existence (everything begins anew). (pp. 180-81)

The Fragmented Life of Don Jacobo Lerner should be recognized as a novel whose poetics is at the service of its politics. Worthy of recognition, too, is its place among the leading ironic works of contemporary Spanish-American fiction, for it accomplishes its aim of persuasion with admirable restraint. . . . (pp. 184-85)

> Jonathan Tittler, '' 'The Fragmented Life of Don Jacobo Lerner': The Esthetics of Fragmentation,'' in his Narrative Irony in the Contemporary Spanish-American Novel, *Cornell University Press, 1984, pp. 172-85.*

KIRKUS REVIEWS

Goldemberg's *The Fragmented Life of Don Jacobo Lerner* was nearly *sui generis*: a look into 30s Peruvian Jewish life, that particular outpost of the Diaspora. [In *Play by Play*] a culture that finds itself speaking Spanish, Yiddish, *and* Quechua (on occasion) is the focus again, now embodied in a young boy, Marquitos Karushansky, during the 50s. Marquitos' own abridged history of the Jews begins when he leaves his Gentile mother's house to live with his Jewish father in Lima. At 12 (with no time to waste) he's circumcised (the book's most striking scene, comic and grisly and symbolic); at 13, bar-mitzvahed. Schooled first at a Jewish academy, he then moves to a military school where his exceptionalness reoccurs mightily.

As Marquitos' father lies across him during the circumcision (to keep him from moving), ''he felt the pressure of his father's dead weight on him as a reproach, the embodiment of all the insults he had ever had to take.'' And as he recovers, stream-of-consciousness takes over in the form of a play-by-play of a soccer game that features Marquitos trying at once to uphold the honor of Peru/Israel/Judaism and his own questionable identity. ''Didi takes the foul: He serves it to Rabbi Goldstein: But he loses the ball to Marquitos: who enters the eighteen-yard-line of his hometown: His mother comes out trying to get the ball . . .'' A hundred and more pages of this is a little wearying, though. . . .

[*Play by Play* is less] accomplished, formally, than its predecessor—but with the same inherent fascination of its context.

> A review of ''Play by Play,'' in Kirkus Reviews, *Vol. LIII, No. 11, June 1, 1985, p. 490.*

ARIEL DORFMAN

Troubled adolescents have been a staple of fiction at least since Goethe's time—and because so much of their trouble has come from identity crises, some of the more interesting adolescents have been Jewish, their sorrows and apprenticeships complicated by uncertainty about national or cultural loyalties. One thinks of characters in the work of Proust, Philip Roth and Elias Canetti. Marcos Karushansky Avila, the protagonist of the Peruvian writer Isaac Goldemberg's brilliant second novel, *Play by Play,* is a fascinating addition to that group.

Marcos is the product of a Russian Jewish father and a Peruvian Catholic mother. As he undergoes the rites of initiation that will lead him to adulthood, he is pressured to choose a single culture, one model for his life. . . .

Marcos incarnates that perennial Jewish figure, the outsider, the wanderer who can find no final home. And he must define his relationship with a country that is a hybrid, born from a coupling of the native and the foreign (the rape of the Indians by the Spanish), and that has struggled ever since to understand its origins and its successive, borrowed masks. So the novel illuminates the condition not only of the Jew but of the Latin American as well.

Though it is tempting to call Mr. Goldemberg a Latin American Bellow or Malamud, as some have done, it is also misleading. North American Jews do not seem to have the same ferocious need to experiment in language that drives so many Latin American writers, including those who happen to be Jews. The source of Mr. Goldemberg's blend of fantasy and reality could be Isaac Bashevis Singer, but Mr. Goldemberg can more plausibly be compared to his Latin American contemporaries— Mario Vargas Llosa and Manuel Puig or equally talented writers who are not as well known in the United States, like Antonio Skarmeta and Osvaldo Soriano. . . .

Like these younger writers, Mr. Goldemberg employs the myths and language of the mass media to explore an elusive reality. . . . In *Play by Play,* the adolescent's struggle not to be expelled from either of the cultures he belongs to and his sexual advances and defeats are narrated by a television broadcaster as if they were a soccer game in Lima's National Stadium.

In Spanish, this merging of the individual life and a collective sports spectacle works splendidly, because Latin Americans are so used to sports announcers' poetic, chaotic kitsch that Mr. Goldemberg's surreal shifts in reality (Marcos's mother suddenly appears as a goalie), his mixing of Quechua and Yiddish, his metaphors and interruptions seem quite normal. In spite of the fine translation . . . , readers in the United States may lose much of the tender, bitter humor that derives from such familiar associations and that makes the book so subtly rewarding. They will gain by playing this game to the end, though. In his writing Mr. Goldemberg is able to bring together the conflicting elements of the two cultures that Marcos Karushansky Avila cannot reconcile in his fractured life.

Ariel Dorfman, ''Mother Is the Goalie,'' in The New York Times Book Review, *August 4, 1985, p. 12.*

ELLEN LESSER

[Isaac Goldemberg] writes about alienation and assimilation, exile and self-definition; his own story, like his characters', would seem a case study in multiple identity crisis. Yet Goldemberg presents a picture of balance amid contradiction. . . .

Like the boy in his first novel, **The Fragmented Life of Don Jacobo Lerner,** Goldemberg was born in the provincial Peruvian town of Chepén—child of a Russian Jewish immigrant father and a native mother, part Catholic, part Indian. Like Marcos in his most recent book, **Play by Play,** he left his mother and the village behind at age eight to live with his father in Lima's small Jewish community. For Goldemberg's fictional half-breeds, the inability to fuse the two sides of their heritage is crippling and finally tragic. . . .

Goldemberg is best known for his prose, but he also writes poetry. In his bilingual collection, **Hombre De Paso/Just Passing Through,** he speaks from a place where two ancient cultures might come together. ''Thousands of years of exile'' flutter around the eyes of a woman named Esther dying in Lima; the ''twisted silence'' of a father's Yiddish words meets the echo of his son's words in Quechua. Rooted as they are in the reality of modern Peru, Goldemberg's novels also exist in a realm where myth and history get entangled with daily life; his fathers and sons are fated to walk a ''road that neither began / nor ended in Jerusalem or Cuzco.'' In chronicling their misadventures along the way, Goldemberg fuses the best of two potent traditions: the Latin Americans' labyrinthine inventiveness and the irony and black humor of Jewish literature, all mixed up with some magic of his own. (p. 51)

For Jews like Jacobo—unloosed from the past, unconnected to a meaningful present—Peru [is] ''a big hourglass, full of sand, in which time breaks into little pieces.'' Following Jacobo's story, the reader puts those pieces together. The novel hopscotches between the early 1920s and 1935; segments of the tale are presented by a third-person narrator, but first-person accounts from a variety of characters fill in key parts of the puzzle. There's Samuel Edelman, a Jewish salesman taking the route Jacobo rejected, wedding a Peruvian woman and raising a family; Sara Lerner, Jacobo's sister-in-law and lover, leading lady of Lima's Jewish community; Sara's sister, Miriam, whose husband shamed the community by shooting himself; Juana Paredes, Jacobo's mistress, who loved the ''infidel'' and would gladly have made him a home. And most important, there's the bastard son, Efraín—unwanted and cruelly neglected in anti-Semitic Chepén—whose chapters trace a terrifying and moving descent into madness. (pp. 51-2)

In direct but lyrical prose, Goldemberg captures the lives moving between Chepén and the capital. At the same time, he uses a scrapbook technique to place his characters in the larger worlds of community, country, and history. Shuffled into **The Fragmented Life** are historical ''Chronicles'' and fictitious columns from the Lima newspaper **Jewish Soul,** with reports on subjects from the latest Hebrew Union ball to the murder of Jews in Bucharest, from digestive ailments to autos-da-fé. The Jews hoped to leave Europe's persecution behind, but they find themselves in a Peru at war with Colombia, on a continent whose Spanish colonies carried the Inquisition into the 18th century. The **Jewish Soul** excerpts become a vehicle for a pointed satire of Lima Jews—their desperate preoccupation

with the ceremonies of social life, their patriotic fervor for the Peruvian ''homeland.'' Without detracting from the tragic cast of his story, Goldemberg invites us to laugh at how seriously they take themselves and the institutions they've built in a shaky New World. . . .

Jacobo Lerner's permanent exile seems a waste of a life, but Efraín's fate is also tragic. At the novel's conclusion, he's crouched in a corner addressing a spider: ''That's why I am going to cut your little legs off, and I squeeze your head with my fingers, and I tear it off, slowly, and I crunch your body so that you can't feel anything when I chew you . . .''

In **Play by Play,** Goldemberg takes this metaphorical suicide of the son one step further; Marcos Karushansky Avila, born like Efraín of an immigrant Jew and native Peruvian, ''blows his brains out.'' We learn of Marcos's suicide—as we did of Jacobo's imminent death—early on, and the rest of this novel represents an attempt to piece together the life. Once again, Goldemberg builds a swirling, competing chorus of voices around his protagonist. But the humor, somewhat submerged in **Jacobo Lerner,** breaks out in **Play by Play,** turning what might have been a doleful tale into a wild, wise-cracking satire.

Say Efraín's early boyhood in Chepén had been happier, Jacobo more respectable and responsible; say the boy turned eight and his father fetched him to bring him up as a Jew. **Play by Play** opens with the son's violent initiation—trial by Hebrew lessons, circumcision, bar mitzvah: ''FIVETHOUSANDSEVENHUNDRED and thirteen years of Judaism hit Marquitos Karushansky like a ton of bricks.''. . .

Two italicized passages from Marcos's point of view describe the boy's conversion and symbolic sacrifice at the hands of his father. The picture gets filled in by the voices of his Jewish schoolmates, who nickname him ''Cholo''—Half-Indian—and his fellow cadets at the military academy where he's later sent, who call him ''the Jew.'' But the bulk of this technically daring narrative is delivered by a TV broadcaster, giving the play-by-play of a surreal soccer contest that's not a game at all, but Marcos's existence.

While Peru battles Brazil for a Latin American championship, Lima's National Stadium changes into the crumbling small town church that haunts Marcos's dreams, the synagogue of his bar mitzvah; the goal becomes his favorite prostitute's mouth or the anus of a young cadet in the academy barracks. Goldemberg's broadcaster plays fast and loose with reality and also with language; the idiom of this soccer game is rife with double-entendres—sexual, political, religious, historical. . . . As the prose rushes headlong through this manic melee . . . the broadcaster breaks for station identification, turns the microphone over to special commentators, plugs soda and beer. ''And don't say beer: say CRISTAL: THE CHAMPION OF BEERS. Don't say ADONAI: say WIRACOCHA.''

Can Marcos love Yiddish without losing his ear for the music of Quechua? Can Abraham and Manco Kapac, the first Inca king, play on the same winning team? Will the boy come to terms with his dual identity? These are the questions that propel the soccer game, but the broadcast isn't live; we already know the score. When Marcos is expelled from the Leoncio Prado Academy for his sexual practices, old man Karushansky ships him off to Israel, where he will not—as the community myth would prefer it—die a hero in the Six-Day War, but where he'll kill himself. The sins of the father are visited on the son: one can't help concluding that if Karushansky hadn't been so intent on erasing the boy's other half, Marcos might have made it as a whole person.

The crazy momentum of Goldemberg's broadcast technique pulls the reader breathlessly through *Play by Play*'s 172 pages, but when the clock runs out, Marcos remains almost as slippery as Pele's shots. The TV announcer circles again and again around certain crucial events, but he never stays in one place long enough to get all the way inside Marcos's experience. To meet the twin challenge of fitting in while not disappearing, Marcos went through both the Jewish School and the academy lying, evading, and making like a chameleon, so the evidence provided by his so-called friends is at best circumstantial. The pieces of Goldemberg's fragmented narratives don't necessarily add up to a complete image; both novels leave troublesome questions hanging in the air. But even if Marcos and Jacobo remain elusive, they allow Goldemberg to reveal the worlds around them—the Peruvian worlds of both Jews and non-Jews—with exceptional clarity.

"There is a distance you get when you belong and yet don't belong to a place." When Goldemberg describes his particular slant, he alludes to both the half-breed's paradoxical insider/outsider status and the perspective of exile. This complicated, equivocal stance has conditioned not only his work but its reception; Goldemberg has received a critical response in his native land that mixes recognition with disavowal. Reviewers found in *Jacobo Lerner* a kind of humor foreign to Peruvian literature. . . . Some of Lima's Jews didn't think the book was so funny. When *Jacobo Lerner* appeared in Peru, a self-appointed Jewish community spokesman attacked Goldemberg as an anti-Semite. On the other side, non-Jewish Peruvian critics tended to address themselves to the novel's Jewish aspect alone, "as if it were about Peruvian Jews only and not about Peru itself. One critic, whose name I wish to forget, said, 'What does Goldemberg have to do with Peru? Just look at his name. He doesn't represent any of our traditions.' ". . .

Play by Play, published this summer in Peru as *Tiempo al Tiempo*, has provoked some discomfort. Goldemberg says he's "noticed a tone in the reviews—even when they are positive—of not understanding what's going on.". . . Peruvian critics also seem confused about Goldemberg's use of the soccer game. "When it comes to soccer, Peruvians and the rest of Latin America are really fanatics, but they don't view the game as a symbol, they don't see the language of soccer as a language that has to do with anything else." Yet growing up a player and fan in Peru, Goldemberg felt that "the games and the way they were described were a sort of metaphor that you could use to explain other things happening in the country.". . .

While the distance of exile has helped shape Goldemberg's work so far, he's now convinced that going back home will stimulate his writing, that he needs to close the circle and reconnect with his source.

> When I was there, I spent hours and hours with my family, listening to stories. They're all storytellers, especially the women. You know how it is when you're a writer: you're listening on a very personal level, but at the same time, you're looking at the possibilities of using that material in order to write. Not only the content, but the way they tell it, the language. I didn't write anything down, but it's all up there. I would leave one house, and 30 blocks later I would end up in the house of another relative, and I knew exactly why—for the stories. These are people who never read anything, but they do realize that I am a writer. And I think unconsciously they knew that I needed to be fed.
>
> (p. 52)

Ellen Lesser, "Home Is Where the Head Is," in The Village Voice, *Vol. XXXI, No. 4, January 28, 1986, pp. 51-2.*

Trevor Griffiths

1935-

(Has also written under pseudonym of Ben Rae) English dramatist, scriptwriter, and author of children's books.

A leading British political playwright, Griffiths explores problems and dilemmas faced by proponents of social change, particularly emphasizing differences between socialist and capitalist ideals. While focusing on conflicts between individuals with opposing political ideologies as well as on weaknesses of various social orders, Griffiths presents characters with diverse personalities to emphasize the multitudinous emotional commitments that human beings must confront and accept. Oleg Kerensky commented: "[The success of Griffiths's plays] is due mainly to the skill with which [he] balances political, practical and emotional problems and presents his characters in depth. His presumptions are that reform or revolution are worth striving for, and that this is hard, perhaps impossible, to attain." Griffiths established his reputation during the early 1970s with three plays: *Occupations,* which examines conflicting forms of political commitment; *The Party,* which involves characters who reflect various factions of socialism in contemporary England; and *Comedians,* which addresses the social and political functions of art and humor. Reflecting his desire to reach a mass audience, Griffiths has also written several works for television.

Griffiths is frequently associated with a group of English playwrights that includes David Hare, Howard Brenton, Howard Barker, and Stephen Poliakoff, all of whom rose to prominence during the 1970s by composing dramas informed with socialist views. These writers are often categorized as members of the "Fringe" Theater because many of their plays, on which they often collaborated, were originally produced in small theaters or makeshift venues. The Fringe playwrights also contributed to the success of London's National Theatre in the mid-1970s, prompting Michael Billington to declare: "We've got three generations of [contemporary British dramatists] all functioning—the Osborne-Pinter one, the middle generation of Tom Stoppard and David Storey, and the new one of Griffiths, Howard Brenton and Stephen Poliakoff."

Occupations (1970; revised, 1980), Griffith's first drama to receive significant attention, is based upon a revolt that took place among workers at an automobile manufacturing plant in Turin, Italy, in 1920. This play focuses on two men, one of whom is genuinely concerned with social reform and the plight of the working class, while the other, a Russian spy, wants to provoke confrontations between workers and factory owners as part of an international communist revolution. Critics admired Griffiths's blending of the intellectual and emotional concerns of his characters. *The Party* (1973) was roundly scorned by reviewers, many of whom remarked that this play depended too heavily on ideological discussions and that the characters were not as well developed as those in *Occupations. The Party* revolves around a gathering of British socialist representatives and explores the reasons for their ineffective attempts to bring about political change. *Comedians* (1975), which enjoyed critical acclaim in London and on Broadway, is generally considered Griffiths's best play. This work centers upon a group of aspiring comedians whose coach believes that humor can serve

as a means for exposing truth. The teacher's view is contrasted by that of an agent before whom the students will perform in hopes of gaining a contract, who argues that comedy serves mainly as escapist entertainment. A third view of the function of comedy is manifested by a student who uses dark humor to vent his personal frustrations. *Real Dreams* (1986), Griffiths's next major theatrical play following a decade largely spent writing for television, is set in the United States in the late 1960s and concerns a group of young radicals who become embroiled in violent activities.

Griffiths's television dramas explore a variety of social and political issues. *All Good Men* (1974) centers on a member of the British Labour Party who becomes the subject of a favorable television documentary following his retirement, despite his exposure as a weak and ineffective administrator. *Absolute Beginners* (1974) addresses personal and political issues confronted by leaders of the Russian Bolshevik revolution. In *Through the Night* (1975), which is based on an incident in the life of Griffiths's late wife, a woman enters a hospital for a routine examination and, without being informed, undergoes a mastectomy to remove a cancerous growth. This work focuses on the failure of medical professionals to treat patients individually and personally. *Country* (1981) examines how the British upper class maintained power and status despite political defeats during the mid 1940s. Griffiths has also written the eleven-part television series "Bill Brand" (1976), which emphasizes the frequent compromises and sacrifices made by an idealistic young member of the British Parliament, and has collaborated with Warren Beatty on the script for *Reds* (1981), a film version of the life of John Reed, an influential proponent of communism in the United States early in the twentieth century.

(See also *CLC*, Vol. 13; *Contemporary Authors*, Vols. 97-100; and *Dictionary of Literary Biography*, Vol. 13.)

BENEDICT NIGHTINGALE

[*Occupations* is] a naturalistic piece about industrial unrest in Turin in 1920. It is rather awkwardly set in the hotel bedroom of a visiting Bolshevik, one Kabak; but some of the confrontations therein are vividly theatrical and, by British standards, distinctly unusual. How many writers can sustain a credible, intelligent action on a political as well as human level, and without sentimentalizing or unnecessarily simplifying the issues involved? How many take politics seriously at all? Too few—though, in Griffiths's case, the compliment seems somewhat double-edged. There is also a harrowed, furrowed, sameness of tone about his play that makes one long, if not for a joke or two, at least for a little irony, a little more detachment. . . .

His workers occupy their factories—can revolution be engineered? Their mentor, Gramsci, . . . believes the danger to them too great; . . . puts ends before means. The word 'love' hovers between them. Extract fellow-feeling, and the revolution lacks motive and justification; add it, and there may be no revolution. It is a dilemma well pointed—and worth consideration today, too. (p. 598)

> Benedict Nightingale, "Moonlit Master," in New Statesman, *Vol. 82, No. 2119, October 29, 1971, pp. 597-98.*

ADRIAN RENDLE

It is not all that often that a really political play emerges. Politics have a habit of becoming slogans and attitudes rather than characters and true situations. This often seems true of the East European scene where the game of politics is fashioned out of subversive activities and a continual fear of the police. It is as though we have been conditioned by the oversimplification of 'goodies' and 'baddies' on an international scale. Such a play as *Occupations* by Trevor Griffiths is therefore refreshing in its political shape since the action depends more on the personality of the characters than on the simple opposition of communism versus capitalism. *Occupations* deals with a period of industrial unrest in Italy during the 1920s and allows us to share the problems of Kabak, a Bulgarian/Soviet agent arriving in Turin to investigate secretly the strength of the communist party there and to stiffen its resolve. Kabak has an ailing aristocratic mistress with him who symbolically bleeds from her womb, and he carries out his interviews while she remains drugged by cocaine on the bed. This relationship of sick, dying woman and strong, passionately determined political agent provides a thread of humanity with enough weaknesses on both sides to make the political struggle with fascist-orientated Italy mean something more than a parade of

systems and methods of control. In the final analysis Kabak is discovered and let down by a simple political double-crossing. He finds himself ordered to leave at once and the dying mistress is left to end the play with a speech that recalls all her aristocratic wastage and hope for life after she herself has dismissed her servant Polya and overdosed herself with enough cocaine to make death a certainty. These scenes and those dealing with the real-life hunchback left-wing leader Gramsci, in fact the play's most important figure, are powerfully and truthfully written. . . .

> Adrian Rendle, in a review of "Occupations and The Big House," in Drama, *London, No. 108, Spring, 1973, p. 82.*

BENEDICT NIGHTINGALE

[The characters in *The Party* include] Joe, a working-class boy turned TV meteor, brilliant in his career, drab in everything else. We meet him in the buff, notably failing to impress his wife with his virility, and leave him aimlessly chatting to her about her latest lover; and, in between, he throws the 'party' of the ambiguous title, an inconclusive chinwag involving assorted radicals, chief among them an LSE sociologist [named Ford] and a Scots [Trotskyite named Tagg]. This pair presents us with the nub of the play, and a pretty solid nub it is, as nubs go: two 15-minute monologues, each a sort of party political broadcast for a different revolutionary stance. First, [Ford] finds hope in national liberation movements in the Third World, then [Tagg] urges everyone to put their faith in the British urban proletariat, and then the curtain falls for the interval. The party is over—though *The Party* drags on, since Griffiths, a conscientious host, still has some dramatic leftovers to tidy away.

True, there's a black on hand to cry 'right on', an unsmiling feminist from the *Guardian*, a couple of earnest girls from the International Socialists ('what are we doing here, for Christ's sake?'), a trendy literary agent, and someone called Grease, who works in street theatre and, faced with political theory, says 'it's just books, what's the point I mean?'. But none of these adds anything either to the debate or to the reality of the situation; and, indeed, the only remaining character of the least substance is a drunken, self-pitying TV playwright, whose function is to stumble through the throng, looking like Thersites and puncturing the others' pretension with remarks like 'excuse me, is this where they're going to have the revolution?' or (less facetiously) 'what do you lot *know*, eh? It doesn't *hurt*, does it?' I should add that it is May 1968, and that Cohn-Bendit and the Paris cops appear intermittently, both in the conversation and in projections at the back of the stage.

As you've guessed, [the TV playwright] is as near to a moral touchstone as we're offered, and his view of the coming revolution may reasonably be taken as the author's own. Briefly, it is that ordinary people's willingness to swallow placebos and adjust to capitalism is limited, and that one day they'll simply 'do it', ignoring the ideologues. Certainly, Griffiths would appear to condemn [Ford's] thesis as too bland . . . and [Tagg's] as too rigid and dogmatic. . . . [Tagg] and his author are at their most effective in cool denunciation. True radicalism, they declare,

> means deliberately severing yourself from the prior claims on your time and moral commitment of personal relationships, career advancement, reputation and prestige. And from my limited acquaintance with

the intellectual stratum in Britain I'd say that was the greatest hurdle of all to cross. Imagine a life without the approval of your peers. Imagine a life without success. The intellectual's problem is not vision, it's commitment. You enjoy biting the hand that feeds you, but you'll never bite it off.

And the accusation, if not the preceding analysis, reverberates long afterwards, giving the evening such point and force as it has.

Faced with this Jesuitical singlemindedness, [Joe] turns helplessly to Revelations, injecting a sort of shudder into 'because thou art lukewarm, and neither hot nor cold, I will spew thee out of my mouth'. I myself was less apocalyptically reminded of Matthew 19: isn't the play best seen as a modern secular translation of the story of the rich young ruler, a warning to all 'progressives' who think they can keep their conscience and comfort equally intact, be they readers of the *New Statesman,* theatre critics, or members of the National Theatre audience? This is the sort of wisdom we'd despaired of hearing in such surroundings, and Mr Griffiths does well to confront us with it. But it would surely have strengthened the sermon, not weakened it, if he'd managed to make his literary agent, his *Guardian* amazon and the other left-wing layabouts a little more credible: how else are we to feel accused by their existence?

Again, I could wish he'd resisted the temptation to associate sexual with political impotence. This sort of Reichian equation is becoming something of a cliché nowadays, and I don't think Griffiths satisfactorily reclaims it for reality. Almost everything [Joe] does seems painfully 'significant', whether he's miming masturbation, or remaining tongue-tied throughout his own party, or belying his anti-capitalist conscience by setting up his brother as a master-tailor: we're always more aware of his function in the dramatic scheme than of a personality with whom we might uncomfortably identify ourselves or our friends. It's the theatre's special strength to be able to belabour its adversaries with lessons, not only drawn from, but palpably consisting of, life itself; but *The Party* comes to us from the study via the lectern and pulpit, leaving us scarcely more scathed than an average congregation at an average matins in an average Anglican church.

Could Griffiths have resuscitated the play by confronting his characters with some immediate, challenging situation, such as the strike in his earlier (and better) *Occupations?* Perhaps. But it is, of course, his point that we British have become the world's political voyeurs, musing over our gins in our moulded armchairs while others fight and die in Angola or Harlem or, as here, Paris. We peer at international reality from our cosy island corner: we even manage, most of the time, to ignore the bumps under our own back-stairs, in Belfast. On the other hand, was it really necessary to reiterate this lamentable truth with quite such deadly literalness? I think not, and would invoke in my support the plays of David Mercer and (more particularly) David Caute's *The Demonstration*, which brought a supple and elaborate sense of irony to a markedly similar theme. It is no good dismissing such a play as 'mandarin' or 'elitist', as I daresay Griffiths would, if you're already writing for a mandarin and elitist theatre, as he is. It is no good at all if all you have to offer instead is two-and-a-half hours of illustrated lecture. Lantern slides, unless very expertly managed, tend to bore and alienate mandarins. In fact, they bore and alienate everyone.

My suspicion is that Griffiths felt conscientiously unable to contribute to the National Theatre unless he ruthlessly excluded 'entertainment' and 'art', and smacked his ideas straight at us, between the eyes: the paradox is that this has doomed him to be less effective than, with his proven talent, he certainly could be. There's a self-indulgence in his attack on our self-indulgence. It is a sad waste of rare opportunity.

Benedict Nightingale, "Socialist Sunday School," in New Statesman, *Vol. 87, No. 2233, January 4, 1974, p. 25.*

KENNETH HURREN

Griffiths is the kind of writer, seething with a rough and independent talent that the commercial theatre inevitably finds intimidating, whom the National Theatre is almost committed to encourage. His chosen subject matter [in *The Party*]—the dilemmas of the political left—cannot have seemed unpromising either, at a time of failed gods and vanishing illusions, and there is, anyway, always room for a decent dialectical play tangling with the knottier issues of the day. Unhappily the piece that turned up from Griffiths was not exactly the bold and challenging dramatic statement that might have been anticipated, full of flexing intellectual muscle. *The Party,* I'm sorry to say, is not much more than a restatement of conflicting left-wing attitudes, which might seem enormously stimulating at a Communist Party seminar, but which is likely to strike a less dedicated audience as a touch humdrum, especially as it flouts the humblest demands of the theatrical form (I am not thinking of anything as sophisticated as a plot) in a manner that might easily be confused with impertinence.

Obviously this was a manuscript which, commission or no commission, should have been regarded with the gravest suspicion, and somebody tactful delegated to explain to Griffiths that yes, well, hmm, it was, of course, wonderfully sincere and terribly literate, but that even National Theatre audiences don't altogether take for granted the urgent desirability of socialist revolution and may not be quite able to share his glumness over the indifferent prospects of its happening. . . .

Anyway, . . . [the] production does everything possible for it, including tarting it up with a sexy prologue that I suspect was an afterthought to the main proceedings. "You have this pinko telly producer," I can imagine them telling Griffiths when he rolled up to the Old Vic from Salford or wherever, "and the big thing about him is his political ineffectualness, isn't it? So why not make him sexually ineffectual too? A sort of symbol, see? Especially as you've made him so damn successful in television, you've got to have him failing at *something* besides politics. And we've got this girl . . .—remember she stripped off in *Equus?*—to play his wife. We'll open with them having a bedroom grapple, but *he* can't make it—okay? Those Marxist slogans you wanted to open with? Don't *worry*, Trev, old mate, you can still have them—we'll flash them on screens at either side of the bed."

This is indeed what happens . . . and more or less concludes the active part of the entertainment, to use the courtesy term. Thereafter the screens are used mostly to show moving and still film of the students' revolt in Paris in May, 1968—the time at which *The Party* takes place—framing the stage discussion group, which takes the form of a meeting of members of the Revolutionary Socialist Party in the South Kensington flat of the television producer. Less than a dozen people are present, and since this may well be the entire membership of the party and since there is nothing to suggest that they enjoy enthusiastic support in the outside world, it seems a little bleak to criticise them by implication for merely talking while Cohn-Bendit's lot are actually *doing* something about the revolution.

The RSP's trouble, it emerges from the chat about Marx and Engels and Trotsky and Marcuse, is that they can't get together on revolutionary principles and priorities; but the choices before them are not sensationally seductive. The main speakers of the evening are a smooth lecturer [Ford] . . . who summarises, not too succinctly, the revisionist position, and a veteran Trotskyite from the Clydeside shipyards [Tagg] who listens to this bland theorist with gloomy tolerance before erupting into a blistering affirmation of faith in a world proletarian revolution that has only so far been thwarted by the unsympathetic leadership of men like Stalin and, he hints darkly, by the likes of the present company: "You bite the hand that feeds you," he accuses them aggrievedly, "but you will never bite it off.". . .

The rest of the assembled RSP members have nothing much to do, except for a drunken television playwright, made miserable—but also engagingly sardonic—by his success within a system he would destroy if he could lay off the sauce for ten minutes. . . . The host is also depressed by his subservience to the reactionary demands of the medium that feeds him; he doesn't visibly brood over his sexual performance (which encouraged my notion that this was a sprightly afterthought), but is awfully worried over whether he should lend his brother £300 to help him set up his own business and thus become a capitalist—eventually he does, and the hell with his misgivings. If I'd cared more about the question Griffiths was posing, I suppose I might have cared more that his answer was to throw up his hands in despair; but this is all merely the peripheral trivia of society, rather—to borrow a genial phrase from my colleague, Clive Gammon—like the sound of mice farting behind a distant skirting board.

> Kenneth Hurren, "Kenneth Hurren on the National Socialist Party," in The Spectator, Vol. 232, No. 7593, January 5, 1974, p. 17.

DENNIS POTTER

People are more than, or other than their opinions, so any play which deliberately confines itself to lengthy exchanges of familiar ideas, however well-phrased and passionate, is in perpetual danger of collapsing into itself. Trevor Griffiths's *All Good Men* . . . was only about what it was about, so to speak—a heavily loaded debate on the achievements or, rather, non-achievements and therefore betrayals of Labourism. I prefer to see plays in which the 'ideas' are not exposed on the surface like basking sharks (or, in some cases, stranded cod) but arise with the insistence of discovery out of the fumbling yearnings, uncertain liaisons and perilous stratagems we usually make out of life. ('Life, in short, is more than . . .' yessir). People even react to those things in each other which are beyond the reach of 'reason'. But *All Good Men* almost overcame its self-imposed schema. Griffiths clothed the debate with some of the sharpest, most telling and intelligent speeches ever heard on television.

> Dennis Potter, "Prickly Pair," in New Statesman, Vol. 87, No. 2238, February 8, 1974, p. 198.

BRIAN WINSTON

Doctors, as a breed, have conducted the most successful and effective image-making exercise in recorded history. Helped by a lot of science, they have transformed themselves from bloodstained hacks into citizens above reproach. As such, they are very jealous of their prerogatives. One dissenting medic can hold up the airing of a public health issue on television far more easily than, say, any one politician similarly placed on another topic. Thus, medicine becomes a prime example of the phenomenon, noted by Anthony Smith, that it is now easier to examine many social issues on television under the guise of drama than as current affairs.

Trevor Griffiths's play, *Through the Night,* offered a compelling corrective to the public face of the doctors as it has been presented all year long by the news media—the sort of corrective that current affairs almost never manages to make. As if in acknowledgement of this, the play was immediately subjected, in the ["Tonight" discussion show] that followed it, to a veracity test. Two doctors did not deny the essential, observational truth of the piece. Griffiths's thesis about the essentially dehumanising processes of modern medicine, as practised for the mass of the population, stands. It is unlikely, said the medics, that all the things that happened to his heroine would happen to any one patient. Unlikely, but not impossible.

Yet a number of problems are raised by this fashionable strand of super-realistic drama. People, surprisingly, . . . find it difficult to draw the simple distinction between art and life in such works. Prominent critics have recently been complaining that such works have given up on plot. . . . [In *Through the Night*] obvious dramatic structures were not only apparent, but were the basis of my problems with the play. Griffiths resorted to some pretty creaky, non-naturalistic plotting, made all the worse by the dominant supernaturalistic, quasi-documentary style of the piece.

The crux of *Through the Night* was that nobody told the patient what was wrong with her, or, indeed, what had been done to her, until the dénouement. The result was that the dénouement was, in contradistinction to the rest of the piece, totally artificial and two other scenes, where such information could have been given, were equally artificially handled to prevent us getting it. . . . [The patient] in post-operative shock, not realizing that her biopsy had turned into a full-scale mastectomy, was only comforted by the nurse. Nothing was said. Her husband subsequently spoke to the ward sister—a scene played in long shot. We heard nothing. These two scenes seemed to be obeying a dramatic rather than a documentary-style necessity. And, even so, the dénouement required the radical doctor . . . to get drunk and utilize a different acting style for the contrivance of the small-hours chat in his room, wherein the patient was finally told the truth about her condition. That is the problem. Utilizing the supernaturalism made possible by film and television, legitimising it by referencing documentary, creates perhaps unavoidable conflicts with what we understand to be dramatic.

Nevertheless, *Through the Night* illuminated an area of our social life as no other television form could have done.

> Brian Winston, "Public and Private Medicine," in The Listener, Vol. 94, No. 2436, December 11, 1975, p. 798.

PETER PRINCE

I have no idea how well Trevor Griffiths managed to convey the feelings of a woman threatened by a mastectomy in *Through the Night*. It looked as if he had done a good job, but then who are we to say? Best to move straight on to the play's other main theme, its indictment of the casual, almost hostile fashion in which hospital patients are so often treated by the medical profession, that everyday situation in which a human being is reduced, as one character notes, to merely 'the sum of his symptoms'.

Here there was much to admire. I liked especially the constant sharp depiction of the hospital hierarchy—janitorial staff being hurried from their necessary duties and out of the ward to avoid offending the consultant's eye, a junior doctor reduced to making his intelligent and pertinent observations in the form of cheeky asides to salve the egos of his seniors. And there was a wonderful little scene which had the surgical team gathered round the patient's bed, discussing her post-operational condition. One couldn't hear a word the doctors said—that was the point. But what a rogue's gallery of nudges, sighs, frowns and secret smiles—utterly terrifying to the poor patient, of course, but presumably satisfying the professionals' desire to be seen as sole possessors of the Mystery. . . .

My only real reservation about **Through the Night** was that at times its message seemed to come across in a strangely muted fashion. For a play of protest it was a very *sensible* item. There were no out-and-out scoundrels. The worst that could be said of anyone, it appeared—even about the wretched surgeon who took off the woman's breast with only the most cursory of by-your-leaves and then refused to talk to her afterwards—was that he was 'one of the old school'. There was never a hint at any time that anything absolutely unforgivable was going to happen or be said, nor really anything particularly unexpected. Which is odd coming from the author of **Comedians** who, if anyone, ought to be relied on to put the boot in with smashing style. One can see good reasons for holding back on this particular subject. It would be tragic if any woman was deterred from going for a check-up by a TV play that presented her prospects in too harrowing a light. Of course she would be better off in hospital under any circumstances. But I wish some other way had been found of conveying that message to the public. It should not, for art's sake, have been built into the texture of the play. Intelligent, sensitive, responsible, **Through the Night** lacked in the last resort a vein of brilliant unfairness that might have made it memorable. (p. 766)

Peter Prince, "Soft Centre," in New Statesman, *Vol. 90, No. 2334, December 12, 1975, pp. 766-67.*

PETER ANSORGE

Although his 1973 play **The Party** . . . was given a disappointing reception by the majority of critics, Griffiths has deserved his reputation as our most capable explorer of the dilemmas which confront the radical imagination. **Occupations** is, possibly, the most successful political *play* (as opposed to polemic) written in the period [spanning 1968 to 1973].

Griffiths' work frequently includes discussions of complex political ideologies as part of an overall dramatic effect. In **Occupations,** for instance, there are two long speeches addressed by Gramsci, the founder of the Italian Communist Party, to the workers who are occupying the Fiat factories of Turin. The play depicts Gramsci's gradual disillusionment with the revolutionary powers that be—both as represented by the Italian union leaders of 1920 and the figure of Kabak, a secret spy sent by Moscow with instructions to survey the potential Italian revolutionary moment. . . . Griffiths is a strong political writer because he is able to reveal the pressures against which political idealism can crumble. Obviously, the play is written from the perspectives of the present—but that the Fiat bosses under-

mined the socialist movement in Italy with a welfare programme for its workers is an established fact of post-World War Two life. Kabak's agreement with Fiat also hints at a secret *détente* between East and West based upon mutual profit. Writers like David Edgar tend to 'underestimate' their enemies—a mistake which Griffiths never makes.

Kabak is in fact the central figure of the play, an 'occupational' revolutionary whose idealism has long burned out. Love, he tells Gramsci during an earlier discussion, has nothing to do with the revolution. Gramsci delivers a moving rebuke:

> '. . . how can a man bind himself to the masses, if he has never loved anyone himself, not even his mother or his father . . . how can a man love a collectivity, when he has not profoundly loved single human creatures. And it was then I began to see masses as people and it was only then that I began to love them, in their particular, detailed, local, individual individual characters. . .'

The professional revolutionary, like Kabak, who cannot love the people he is meant to represent is clearly a figure which fascinates Griffiths (one of the failings of the would-be revolutionary who gathers his radical friends together in **The Party** is that he *cannot* love either himself or his guests. The Trotskyite John Tagg, who emerges as the most powerful figure in **The Party,** admits at one crushing point that he has never married and no-one is likely to mourn his death). Yet ironically, Kabak does love a 'single human creature' in **Occupations.** It marks his only weakness. Kabak's mistress, Angelica is a white Russian, an aristocrat with whom he fell in love during 1917. She is with Kabak in the Turin hotel, dying of cancer, neither understanding nor believing in his 'occupation'. The play ends with her death—a powerful speech addressed to the audience about the way the revolution destroyed her life:

> '. . . All things will bend to Lenin's iron will. They will. They will. Nicholas. Her. The Friend. Grand Dukes, bankers, ballerinas. They've all had their last winter. Everywhere. They will. Will. Will. Will. What will stop them? Will anything stop them?'

We then see film slides of Mussolini, the March on Rome, Hitler, Stalin, the signing of the Russian-Nazi non-aggression pact. Clearly we are shown what halted the march of socialism—the fascist backlash throughout Europe and in Russia itself—through the figure of the totalitarian Stalin. Angelica's love for Kabak must count as a positive factor in the play—yet it contains the emotional seeds of political reaction. Do revolutionary politics depend on love or power? The suppression or encouragement of private emotion? These themes are worked subtly into the texture of the play. (pp. 64-5)

Peter Ansorge, "Plugged into Politics: John Mc-Grath, Trevor Griffiths and David Edgar," in his Disrupting the Spectacle: Five Years of Experimental and Fringe Theatre in Britain, *Pitman Publishing, 1975, pp. 56-67.*

CHRISTOPHER PRICE

If we are not going to televise Parliament just yet, I suppose [**"Bill Brand"**] is the next best thing. I am becoming a bit of an addict.

I have always watched it in the [Members of Parliament] TV room at the top of the House of Commons, to the accompaniment of a ribald and witty chorus of interjections, as we sit there waiting to do our duty in the lobbies at 10 pm sharp. The ambience is not that of the average living-room, so I cannot quite judge how it comes over to the ordinary viewer. . . .

By normal . . . standards, it is preposterous that innocent viewers should be inflicted with the strangled soul of a haggard, young, left-wing politician every Monday for weeks on end. But even some of my apolitical friends seem to enjoy it. . . .

The idea, of course, is not a new one. . . . But although I liked Arthur Hopcraft's *The Nearly Man*, and although I can and do niggle at detail after detail in the Brand saga, in the end I suspect Trevor Griffiths has done a fuller, rounder job. At least, there is some development in Brand. . . . Griffiths has tried to portray a political odyssey.

He has, however, created a pretty excruciating Odysseus. If I have difficulty with Brand's credibility, it is that I do not think it very likely that any Labour Party selection committee could pick as their candidate anyone with such a unique combination of tortured humourlessness and dumb naivety. Unlikely, but I suppose just possible. But, then, there are the totally impossible bits. Like voting in the wrong lobby because he just had not realised the Journal Group (i.e., *Tribune* Group—geddit?) had changed their minds, and were not going to vote against the government after all. The peculiar intimacy of the House of Commons 'sheep-dip' voting system, under which MPs are herded into a corridor and let out one at a time, ensures that it is quite impossible to vote the wrong way *by accident*. . . . Then there is that chief whip, who, I am told, occasionally used to bully MPs the way Griffiths makes him bully Brand, 20 or 30 years ago; but such is the collapse of authority and deference in Parliament, as well as society at large, that they just would not dare talk like that any more. Not in the Labour Party, anyway.

And one could go on and on, and complain that it is all an absurd collage of different parliamentary eras and none at all, pasted together just to knock the system and sate the paranoid fantasies of the loony left.

I, however, am happy to forgive the clangers for two reasons. First, because when Griffiths gets it right, he gets it beautifully right—the brittle tea-room conversation, the seedy Blackpool hotel bedroom, the haggling over composite resolutions before the Labour Party conference, the Home Secretary . . . at a Ruskin summer school, and, above all, . . . Brand's long-suffering agent. . . .

Secondly, Brand's dilemmas are real ones, the stuff of what politics ought to be but usually isn't. . . . The Brand crisis and the real thing are just too uncannily parallel.

In many ways, we are back in 1931 and 1966, with a sizeable bunch of Labour MPs (among whom I count myself one) who believe that changes can be wrought in our nation by a combination of imagination, vision and radical policy; and the government we support is forced by external pressures more and more on to orthodox, predictable tramlines, and protestations that imagination, vision and radical policy must await more prosperous days. This argument of the left, about pace and direction of policy, the purposes of political power and the use to which it is put, is a real one. The advantage of the naive, neo-Marxist school of political expectation, which emerged from our universities during the 1960s and of which Griffiths and his *alter ego,* Brand, are products, is that, like an awkward gadfly, it forces the parliamentary left to ask itself fundamental questions about what it is in business to do.

It is because Bill Brand persistently addresses himself to these questions . . . that I think the series is a worthwhile piece of dramatic political education. (p. 85)

Christopher Price, ''Haggard Odysseus,'' in The Listener, *Vol. 96, No. 2467, July 22, 1976, pp. 85-6.*

MARTIN GOTTFRIED

[*Comedians*] is a wonderful subject for a play and Trevor Griffiths, an Englishman, has written an irresistible serious comedy on it. His play is also very good on the whole and it is as funny and painful as a play about comedians should be, though it does have its weaknesses and is more than slightly influenced by David Storey.

It is about a provincial English night class for comedians, run by an ex-comic who might have been a star had it not been for the purity of his standards and the uncertainty of his drive, a not uncommon coupling. The students are young men, hardly tested, and the author has given them believably natural senses of humor.

His generally amusing first act is set in the classroom, where the teacher gives the final instructions in preparation for performances the student comics are going to give in the second act. These performances are to take place at a local workingman's club and they will be judged by a professional agent.

The play makes it clear, too clear, that there is a difference between the teacher's taste in comedians and the agent's. The teacher believes that the comedian draws pictures of the world. It's not his jokes that matter, it's the attitudes behind them. He sees the truth about people.

I hadn't meant to start pointing up problems so early on, but there you are, the play is preachy. For the agent, black villain, is a philistine who does not appreciate real comic art: ''We're not missionaries . . . philosophers . . . we're suppliers of laughter.''

I'm afraid the author is overly critical of that attitude and so appears to denigrate, or at least minimize, the comic side of being a comedian. That is, sheer funnyness. This is a common problem among analysts of comedy.

The second act, at the workingman's club, is wonderful. Griffiths sets up the students' routines with a magnificent introduction by the master of ceremonies: ''This'll last a half hour at the most. Then we'll get straight back to the Bingo.''

The author's idea is to fold the monologues back on themselves. At first purpose they are supposed to be five variations on comic routines. But they are also to represent corruption or resistance to it. For these young men have just become aware that the agent does not agree with their teacher and he's the one with jobs to offer. . . .

This subtext does not work as cuttingly as the author designed. The actors have a difficult time showing that they are corrupting their monologues. Often as not, it just seems as if they are being amateurish comedians. Also, one of the purists—the Irish comic doing the Catholic routines—is too funny for any agent to not like while one of the vulgarizers is funny enough for the teacher. The main problem is that the creative purists aren't as funny as the joke-tellers.

As for the purest purist, Griffiths makes him so artistic—a mime, no less—that he is aggressively unfunny. There is a daring idea in his routine: strip away the facade of entertaining and present the naked, raging hostilities, of the comic. (A generalization I happen to disagree with). But when this is done without black laughs, there is no way to feel that the best comedians are being lost to us. A comic just has to be funny.

The third act takes place in the classroom after the performance. The agent returns to present his criticisms. He offers contracts to the least talented in the group. Trash is on its way to the public. Each of the students is given an exit bequeathing the stage to the teacher and his best student—the mime. . .—for a reprise of the author's philosophy of comedy. . . .

As for the Storey influence, it is pervasive—in the assembly of intentionally characterless working class men with the group having the leading part; in the use of an inherently theatrical, everyday setting in the muted stylization of the naturalistic dialogue; in the plotless structure.

Still, Griffiths has a voice of his own. His idea is ingenious and theatrical. He has warmth, he has vigor, he has an affirming attitude. In this play he is affirming quality above shoddiness, high standards not just in stand-up comedy but of course in all of art and finally in all of life. He uses the music hall as the symbol for that natural high quality he feels lost by England. This is not revolutionary advice but it never hurts to be warned of cheap success at the expense of standards, nor does it hurt to be given a fresh kind of serious entertainment.

> *Martin Gottfried, '' 'Comedians'—An Affirming Attitude,'' in* New York Post, *November 29, 1976.*

CLIVE BARNES

[*Comedians* is] one of the funniest, and almost certainly the dirtiest, of comedies to be seen on Broadway in some seasons. It is comedy with an esthetic, moral and, above all, political purpose.

You can, if you like, just go along and have a few belly laughs. . . . Yet there is much more to *Comedians* than this superficial glance, and, surprisingly, also a little less.

Comedians does not always deliver the depth charge of its messages. . . . For this is drama with a double standard, and Mr. Griffiths is brilliant at writing the play he was less interested in writing—the play about life, rather than the play, running concurrently, about comedy and politics. Mr. Griffiths, by the way, is a Socialist, one presumes with a sense of humor.

Ostensibly *Comedians* is about comedians. It is set in a night school in Manchester, and in a workingmen's club just down the road. The class at the night school teaches comedy—how to be a stand-up comic in a few painful lessons. The teacher is a retired comic himself. Once very successful, he never had the killer instinct to continue on to fame. You are not told this by the playwright, but I imagine he just did not have the will to make the transition from radio to television. Many North Country and Cockney comics fell by the wayside there. But note, I am already taking a character outside his time in the proscenium arch. This is because Mr. Griffiths makes us believe in his people. They wander on in a striking semblance of reality.

Part of the reason for this is the play's shape. It starts at class. This is a kind of graduation—a graduation by fire. The six aspirant comics have run the course, and tonight, watched by a London talent scout, they are going to do their routines in front of a live audience at a club. You see them at class, you watch them in performance and you hear the summing up by the agent/scout. Mr. Griffiths has found himself a perfect form— or, at least a perfect form to discuss the weighty matter of comedy. Its function, purpose and reward.

He introduces us to his comedians carefully, even tantalizingly. They filter on one by one, baring their characters as competing wrestlers might bare their chests. Their teacher arrives and they play games—a warm-up for this first, possibly crucial, test before a live audience. The teacher is now a coach, testing his team. The agent arrives—he happens to be the teacher's worst friend—and it is clear that he has a quite different view of comedy.

The agent thinks comedy is a narcotic. The teacher thinks comedy is a stimulant. The agent believes comedy confirms. The teacher believes comedy questions. And by now Mr. Griffiths has got his play into conflict. A decent, worthy conflict.

The performance. For the second act the playwright quite shamelessly gives us five nightclub acts. Nothing less, but a great deal more, for each act, while funny in itself, offers a view not so much of comedy as of humanity. For some of the comedians have adapted their act, hurriedly, nervously, to what they imagine the agent will want. Others have remained true to their teacher's concept of comedy with its social purpose. Then there is a last, the maverick, Gethin Price, who calmly makes an outrageous, even disgusting, attack on society— which is caustically brilliant but not funny.

The agent's summing up is predictable. The guys who get the contract are the guys who bought it, and intractability brings its own blank reward. But it is Gethin's act that is important. This is a scene based on the classic clown Grock, who died in the 50's. He was a savage clown, a dark clown, a Brighella of a clown. He was not Chaplin, whose anger was transmogrified by the exigencies of commerce, into pathos. Grock was different.

This part of the play is quite unpleasant, and shines like a dark diamond in an elegant toad's forehead. And this represents the political roots of the play. At the end of the act . . . Gethin evokes "The Red Flag" and Socialism. Mr. Griffiths is apparently suggesting to world Socialists something less compromising or smug than social democracy. If you choose to disregard the politics you can just laugh at the jokes, savor the characters, and contemplate the difference between a comedian and a comic, a Harry Langdon and a Bob Hope.

The evening is full of laughter. This is not entirely because of Mr. Griffiths's script, although I am sure that if he ever needs to work at Las Vegas or Gomorrah—I say nothing of Sodom— he will find gorgeous employment. He can twist old jokes into life, which is the test of survival. (p. 34)

> *Clive Barnes, "The Weighty Matter of Comedy Gets Wry Treatment in 'Comedians'," in* The New York Times, *November 29, 1976, p. 34.*

JACK KROLL

When I saw Trevor Griffiths's [*Comedians*] in London last winter, I thought it was the best new play I had seen in years. Now it is on Broadway, and it's still the best new play I've seen in years—but it is not quite the same play. . . .

Griffiths had the idea of using the stand-up comic as a metaphor of the knocked-down society. The play is a rite of passage for six young workingmen in Manchester who are taking classes in comedy from Eddie Waters, a legendary comic. For them, becoming a comedian is a chance to blast off from a grinding life, and they're about to perform at a workers' club for a talent agent. Waters is more than a teacher, he's a Socrates of comedy. When Gethin Price, his favorite student, invents a limerick about a woman masturbating, Waters is repelled. "We work *through* laughter, not *for* it," he says. "Most comics feed prejudice and fear, but the best ones, the comedians, illuminate them, make them clearer to see . . . We've got to make people laugh till they cry. Till they find their pain and their beauty." But the agent, Challenor, declares, "I'm not looking for philosophers. I'm looking for comics," and cites Bob Hope as a shining example.

In the second act, the auditions are a gruesomely funny updating of the ancient Greek *agon*—a struggle between the comics and also a struggle between the moral forces represented by Waters and Challenor who sit flanking the tawdry little stage. Some of the comics, stampeded by Challenor, have desperately vulgarized their carefully planned routines. The Jew Sammy Samuels and the Irishman George McBrain unleash a torrent of gags about Jews, Irish, blacks, women. . . .

The play detonates with the appearance of Gethin Price, shorn, whitened and booted. He has built his savage routine out of a mixture of the great clown Grock and a British "bovver boy"— a skin-headed street terrorist. With deadly precision, Price . . . converses with two dummies of a posh couple, rising to an insanely logical pitch of anger as they ignore him. With evil gallantry he pins a marigold on the girl's dress, drawing a dizzying fall of blood that becomes a fearsome flag of class hatred as he stalks off the stage. It's the soliloquy of a bomb.

It's in the confrontation between Price and Waters in the third act that the production falters. Waters hates Price's brilliant but pitiless routine. Price accuses Waters of copping out on a social truth he expressed as a young comic. In the original play Waters makes a long, powerful speech about touring Germany after the war. At Buchenwald he found to his horror that the ambience of omnipotent destruction gave him a surge of sexual excitement. The grave dignity and terrible self-knowledge of Waters is vastly more moving than the skimpy abstractions that remain in the new version. Why was it changed? My guess is that somebody didn't trust the Broadway audience to absorb the dark but truthful humanity of Waters's confession.

This is too bad, because the production is a brave and largely successful graft of an English plant onto American soil. (pp. 97-8)

> *Jack Kroll, "Send in the Clowns," in* Newsweek, *Vol. LXXXVIII, No. 24, December 13, 1976, pp. 97-8.*

RONALD HAYMAN

[In *Comedians*] Griffiths, who seems genuinely worried about the relationship between artistry and aggression, is telling a story which brings the problem into focus. The central conflict involves three attitudes. Eddie Waters, who is running a class for would-be comedians, represents the value of liberal humanism. 'Hate your audience,' he tells his students, 'and you'll end up hating yourself.' The talent-spotter Challenor, who can help them into their first professional jobs, feels nothing but contempt for audiences. According to him, the art of the comedian is escapist art. 'I'm not looking for philosophers,' he says. Nothing matters except success, which can be achieved by giving the public what it wants. 'We can't all be Max By-

graves, but we can try.' The antagonism between Waters and Challenor is initially defined in terms of the class war. Waters tells his students that he never joined Challenor's Comedy Artists' and Managers' Federation because he'd been a union man all his life and believed that 'No comedian worth his salt could ever "federate" with a manager.'

Later the antagonism is developed in terms of conflicting attitudes to the function of the comedian, and here it becomes obvious that Griffiths is simultaneously writing about the function of the playwright and the function of art. (p. 98)

This is partly a camouflaged apologia for didactic art, but it is grooved into the plot. Performing in a bingo hall to audition for Challenor in front of an audience, some of the budding comedians will make last-minute changes to the acts they have prepared, steering away from Waters's principles towards Challenor's.

The third attitude is represented by Gethin Price, the most talented pupil in Waters's class. After arriving in a mood of prickly restiveness, he stays aloof from the easy camaraderie of the others, and when it is his turn to speak the tongue-twister 'The traitor distrusts the truth', he is accurate but puzzlingly vehement. That he is no longer willing to accept his teacher's principles is revealed when he recites an obscene limerick. . . . And when Waters is out of the room, Gethin cruelly mimics him in front of the class. In the climactic audition sequence, Gethin's deviation from the act he has been working on with Waters is not impelled by any wish to please Challenor. Dressed and made up to look like a football hooligan with a clown-white face, he spreads a filthy handkerchief on his shoulder to perform a routine with a tiny violin, which he finally smashes by stamping on it. After performing a series of Kung Fu exercises, he ends the act with a venomous monologue addressed to two beautiful dummies in evening clothes. They both have 'a faint unself-conscious arrogance in their carriage'. As if they could have responded, and as if he had the right to feel insulted by being ignored, he alternates between exaggerated chumminess and self-righteous resentment, gradually becoming more aggressive. He then starts telling them dirty jokes: 'You can laugh, you know, I don't mind you laughing. I'm *talking* to you. . . There's people'd call this *envy*, you know, it's not, it's hate.' When he produces a flower from his pocket and pins it between the girl's breasts, a dark red stain starts to spread over her white dress. Finally he picks up another tiny violin to play four bars of "The Red Flag."

Griffiths's intention is to make Gethin's performance approximate to the style of the Soviet clown Grock. 'Thing I liked was his hardness,' says Gethin, who has read about him in a book. Waters pronounces the act 'brilliant', and for the play to succeed fully, it is necessary for the audience to endorse this verdict, and to agree when Gethin tells Waters that without hatred there is no truth:

> Nobody hit harder than Eddie Waters, that's what they say. Because you were still in touch with what made you . . . hunger, diphtheria, filth, unemployment, penny clubs, means tests, bed bugs, head lice. . . Was all *that* truth beautiful?. . . Nothing's changed, Mr. Waters, is what I'm saying. When I stand upright—like tonight at that club—I bang my head on the ceiling. Just like you fifty years ago. We're still caged, exploited, prodded and pulled at, milked, fattened, slaughtered, cut up, fed out. We still don't belong to ourselves.

This explanation may seem suspiciously emotive, but the speech that follows is still more rhetorical. Accused of having gone soft, Waters defends himself by describing a visit to Buchenwald: 'It was a world like any other. It was the logic of our world . . . extended. . . .' But he did not find it merely repulsive: something inside him loved it so much that he had an erection. . . . Nazism is being invoked to prove that hatred is necessary and admirable.

It is not very plausible that a man like Waters, who objects so strongly to jokes that depend on prejudice against coloured people, the Jews, the Irish, or women, would be so impressed by a performance centered on prejudice against the upper middle class. Gethin is confusing class hatred with truth, and Griffiths is unaware of his mistake. Another fallacy built into the scheme of the play is that the only alternative to being an escapist comedian is to be a didactic comedian. In so far as vaudeville is serving as an analogy for art, the schema is misleading. But the main flaw in the play is not a flaw in its argument: it is the flaw that results from structuring the action on an argument. With Challenor as spokesman for escapism and Waters as spokesman for the view which is intended to seem antithetical, Gethin's view is meant to emerge as more acceptable than either. But because he cannot trust the audience to be as impressed as Waters is by Gethin's performance, which forms the play's natural climax, coming at the end of the second act, Griffiths adds a third, which culminates in the discussion between Gethin and Waters. All this is disappointingly static by comparison with the second act.

At the same time, Griffiths has missed a good opportunity to dig more deeply into his central ambivalence about love and hatred. In his 1970 play *Occupations,* Kabak, the Soviet agent, tries to reprove Gramsci for loving the working classes. 'You can't love an army, comrade,' he says. 'An army is a machine. This one makes revolutions. If it breaks down, you get another one. Love has nothing to do with it.' Gramsci argues that nothing is more relevant than love. . . . (pp. 99-101)

But in *Comedians* Griffiths adopts an anti-love position. (p. 102)

> Ronald Hayman, *"The Politics of Hatred,"* in his British Theatre Since 1955: A Reassessment, *Oxford University Press, Oxford, 1979, pp. 80-128.*

STEVE GRANT

[Griffiths] regards himself primarily as a TV writer, largely because as a Marxist he wishes to reach mass audiences. Nevertheless he is in many ways the most traditional playwright of his kind, a working-class Mancunian keenly concerned with the topic of revolutionary change, its necessity, its problems, its relationship with the often unfulfilled lives of individuals. Griffiths is, above all, a moral writer who believes, in the words of one of his political mentors, Antonio Gramsci, that "It is a revolutionary duty to tell the truth".

Though several of Griffiths' plays have been autobiographically based, the three that stand out in his career to date are the least personalized—*Occupations* (1970), *The Party* (1973) and *Comedians* (1975). The first two are explicitly concerned with the eternal Catch-22 of revolution: how do you create a new order without irredeemably damaging yourself and others, both morally and physically, in the process. . . . [*Occupations*] is set during the 1920 Turin Fiat motor strike. It opposes two different kinds of revolutionary ideology: the Stalinism of Kabak, a tough, pragmatic Bulgarian agitator who regards the masses as a machine for making revolutions, and Gramsci's commitment to total liberation, based on his intense love of the people "in their particular, detailed, local, individual character". Griffiths spreads the play generously, filling out this basic contrast with other quasi-symbolic personages, such as Kabak's mistress, an aristocrat stricken with cancer, whom he cheats on and finally abandons in a terribly cruel manner, and Valletta, a Fiat executive who illustrates capitalism's ability to adapt to situations which seem to threaten its stability.

The Party . . . carries on the same theme in a more complex if often excessively naturalistic fashion. . . . Set in the plush Kensington flat of a trendy TV producer during the Paris riots of 1968, it is concerned with the inability of the British Left to organize itself into a revolutionary weapon. As in *Occupations* the language has an uncompromising didactic tone which is all the more impressive for being direct and uncloyed by theatrical artifice. There are two long accounts of Marxian theory—a revised account by Ford, an LSE lecturer who preaches support for third-world revolutionary groups, and by Tagg, an ageing Glasgow Trotskyist whose analysis is uncompromisingly Bolshevist and contemptuous of the "moral exhaustion" of left-wing intelligentsia. Set cleverly against such theorizing is the living experience of each of the central protagonists: Tagg is stricken with cancer; Shawcross, the producer, by both professional and personal impotence (sexuality is an important factor in the motivation and make-up of Griffiths' characters); while Sloman, an alcoholic writer, is reduced to drunken cynicism, chauvinist snides, and a peculiarly British arid class hatred and Ford, the LSE Marcusian, is revealed as something of a lady-killing smoothie. *The Party* is certainly a fascinating play despite its formal shortcomings. Though himself a committed Socialist, Griffiths never falls for easy sermonizing or pat solutions. His numbed producer, Shawcross, ends by giving his younger brother the money he needs to set up in business. An act stemming from Shawcross' obvious distaste for the cold self-sacrifice of Tagg's Revolutionary Socialist Party (obviously modelled on the then Socialist Labour League) it is typically rooted within the complex and often contradictory loyalties of the British working class and its successful disenchanted sons and daughters. Though inspired by and set during the days of May, 1968, *The Party* continues to be topical and pertinent and certainly has a polemical strength far greater than most contemporary plays of political ideas. (pp. 132-33)

Like so many genuinely original theatre works, *Comedians* uses form both to embody and reinforce its content. On one level *Comedians* is a play about laughter and about what makes us laugh—comedy as a barometer for the measurement of our joy, of other people's pain, of racial intolerance in which (in the words of its central character, Eddie Waters) "Every joke was a little pellet, a final solution", and even a revolutionary instrument for saying the unsayable and liberating the will. (pp. 133-34)

For Waters, comedy is ultimately a didactic art: "We work through the laughter, not for it." For Challenor, the agent, it is a means of escape for the audience: "We can't all be Max Bygraves but we can try." But the play's great strength lies in the dialectical process by which Griffiths structures his own internal debate. Waters' best pupil is the sullen, aggressive Gethin whose suddenly changed act is a terrifying explosion of finely tuned hatred, part mime's ferocious integrity, part revenging Jacobean malcontent, part raging, disenfranchised yobbo. And yet Gethin's violent vision of 'ice and fire' is presented in direct contrast to Waters' more humanistic view of progress: "We've gotta get deeper than hate, Gethin. Hate's no help."

Comedians is not without faults. In the third-act confrontation between Waters and Gethin, Waters gives an account of a visit to Buchenwald during a post-war ENSA tour. He tries to explain his disillusionment with 'jokes' and the description ends with the revelation that the place gave him an erection. This latest attempt to relate sexual desire to our basic, darker urges fails not only in terms of character but also dramatically as it seems to be almost immediately swallowed up within the general argument despite its obvious intended shock value. More interestingly because the play contains a second act composed largely of live comedy, Griffiths' intended points fall foul of audiences who may not always oblige by laughing in the right places! For example, Mick's act, the kind of detailed, sympathetic comedy of which Waters approves, actually goes down better with live theatre audiences than it is obviously meant to.

Nevertheless *Comedians* is a remarkable play, a beautifully written, open-ended yet powerful piece of heightened naturalism. (p. 134)

> Steve Grant, "Voicing the Protest: The New Writers," in Dreams and Deconstructions: Alternative Theatre in Britain, *edited by Sandy Craig, Amber Lane Press, 1980, pp. 116-44.*

MIKE POOLE

Cross-scheduling is normally my pet hate. Yet ITV's running of the second episode of *Brideshead Revisited* against Trevor Griffiths's *Country* could not have been more apt or more fascinating. Here were two major pieces of television drama dealing with the same upper-class milieu, at the same time, but in diametrically opposed fashion. [*Brideshead Revisited* offers] a sumptuous and intoxicating recreation of aristocratic style;. . . [*Country* takes] that style apart and [interrogates] it for its class meanings and historical repercussions.

Watching *Brideshead* to the first commercial break and then channel-hopping to *Country* induced a striking sense of being confronted by two totally differing versions of the past. *Brideshead* presented us with a politically quiescent understanding of history in nostalgic period format. *Country,* on the other hand, worked to subvert the received assumptions about history that go with such a format. It delved into the past not to escape from the present, but to explain it.

And what it specifically sought to explain was, of course, the worm in the bud of the Welfare State: the process whereby ruling interests survived the election of a Labour government in 1945 virtually intact and were therefore able to dictate the terms of the post war reconstruction. As Philip—the central character and heir to the Carlion brewing empire—observes of workers celebrating news of the Labour victory: 'They think they are at a funeral. They haven't realised yet that the grave is empty.'

Ironically, Waugh too seems to have had no inkling that the grave was empty. *Brideshead* was written in 1945 very much as a valediction to a dying class; democracy was presumed to have taken its toll and the sense of loss that pervades the novel is in large measure historically determined. But, as we now know, Waugh's class was merely re-forming to reappear as a different kind of élite. (p. 33)

Country attempted to focus this class re-grouping by examining how one family with large business interests received the Labour landslide, gauged its likely consequences and then prepared to ride them out. The dream-like opening sequence—of Eton schoolboys on fire-drill bailing out of upper-floor windows into safety blankets—suggested that this instinct for survival was something passed on from generation to generation and inculcated at a very early age.

Griffiths was greatly influenced here by a group of recent plays—*Brassneck* by David Hare and Howard Brenton, *Licking Hitler* by Hare for TV, *Touched* by Stephen Lowe and Ian McEwan's *The Imitation Game,* also for TV—which set out to re-think the popular understanding of the Second World War. Drawing on historian Angus Calder's seminal *The People's War,* they questioned the myth of a united, classless Britain and explored the repressed links between the conduct of the war, the nature of the post-war reconstruction and the subsequent evolution of a Welfare State which still worked to enshrine privilege and inequality. What *Country* did was to present the covert manoeuvrings of capital which made this process possible and which constitute its real history.

The Carlion brewing dynasty and its associated 'families' was originally to have been the basis for a series of six plays. Griffiths intended a sort of English version of *The Godfather*—Carlion is after all only one syllable away from Corleone—with the Mafia element being replaced by political wheeling and dealing at government level. . . . Changes in the brewing industry—first keg, then lager, then multinational mergers—were to have served as a metaphor for the re-structuring of British capital. But beer was also chosen because of its importance within working-class culture, the area where consumerism, the multinationals and, eventually, monetarism were to wreak the profoundest changes of all.

We got a hint of how the series might have worked towards the end of *Country* when workers drinking to the new Labour government are shown to be consuming Carlion beer. Their future appeared already to be in somebody else's hands as chants of 'Roll Out the Barrel' ominously modulated to an Eton choristers' version of the song and the closing titles went up.

This highly stylised ending was typical of a play in which Griffiths had broken with the kind of dialectical structure that normally characterises his work. . . . In *Brideshead*, aristocratic *hauteur* had retained a beguiling kind of Nineties appeal, but [in *Country*] it signalled a world devoid of human feeling. The reek of corruption and decay was everywhere—madness, senility, disease, deviant sexuality, drugs—and the overall effect was close to the kind of mood generated by Bertolucci's epic study of political decadence, *1900*. (pp. 33-4)

Staggeringly, this major piece of television drama slipped through the schedules virtually unnoticed. Recession had made the cosy nostalgia of *Brideshead*—a production which, for all its virtues, takes no risks and in the end merely confirms Waugh's none-too-wholesome prejudices—much more appealing, and *Country* didn't even make it into *The Times* Pick of the Day. Bill Grundy used his column in the London *Standard* to mount an attack on Trevor Griffiths ('People like Mr Griffiths make me think I am reading a Labour Party Manifesto'). If I were Griffiths I wouldn't be too bothered though—when Mr Grundy crawls out of the woodwork to be counted it is a sure sign that somebody has hit the nail on the head. And *Country* certainly did that. (p. 34)

Mike Poole, "Another Country?" in New States-man, *Vol. 102, No. 2641, October 30, 1981, pp. 33-4.*

KENNETH O. MORGAN

Trevor Griffiths's television play, *Country,* is set against the background of the Labour election landslide in 1945. The Communist Phil Piratin's return for Mile End is faithfully included. Political upheaval is projected against the internal turmoil of a brewing dynasty of suitably distasteful character, and the desperate efforts of Sir Frederick Carlion to secure the succession, as managing director and chairman, for his white-suited black sheep of a son, the homosexual, non-soldiering anti-hero, Philip. There is a measured stillness about the family exchanges deliberately contrasted with an outside world convulsed by social conflict. "The people have declared war on us", one Carlion declares, as revolting Kentish peasants occupy, and then burn down, the family stables and let loose the horses all over the grounds. Even the police are on the side of the common people, up to a point. In the end, predictably enough, Philip triumphs over the man-eating malice of sister-in-law Alice, the scepticism of his mother, and the sullen hostility of fellow directors. The Carlions brace themselves to survive, to refloat the "sinking ship" of capitalism, weighed down with rats and plunder. On July 27, 1945, one day after the deluge, the fight back has begun.

It is easy to see why this superbly-paced production won such instant acclaim from television critics. The interaction of characters is quite gripping. . . . [The] wispy steeliness [of] Philip [is] countered by both the death-bed brutality of his father, the disenchanted dottiness of his mother and the carnivorous qualities of his sister-in-law. . . . Only Virginia . . . , a kind of up-dated Medusa exiled in France and of Communist inclinations, proclaiming the imminent and bloody end of capitalism with "the people banging on the door", does not quite ring true. . . .

Whether any of this bears much relation to the Labour victory in 1945 is quite another matter. Trevor Griffiths seems to take his cue from Evelyn Waugh—"it feels as if we are under enemy occupation". The reality was different, and the Carlions know it already. The inclusion in the play of Labour's election manifesto (with such bloodthirsty proposals as the nationalizing of the Bank of England, which even Churchill supported), the reproduction of Attlee's family-solicitor tones on victory night, telling jubilant Labour voters of the need for discipline and self-sacrifice, show how the Labour triumph was some way short of an apocalypse.

The Carlions, in their country-house cocoon, seem to have been propelled in from another planet, so total is their insulation. The war of 1939-45 apparently never happened for them, apart from a few tired remarks about injuries at the hands of "Jerry" and incoherent mutterings about India. The social changes of wartime, with their taxes, rationing, Beveridge scheme and evacuees, somehow affected forty million other people, but not them. The fictional background of a popular *jacquerie,* symbolized by besotted, dirty hop-pickers rising up against the beerage, would have been appropriate for 1789 but hardly for the realistic, dogged mood of 1945. But like other historically-based television ventures, this work simply isn't historical.

Nor can it really be claimed to be, in any serious way, social comment or analysis. Mr Griffiths has prefaced his play with radical utterances in the newspapers about the coming social revolution, somewhat loosely defined. "I'm sick of broad churches", he has declared. In fact, his play is largely innocent of Marxism or almost any other variant of socialism. It has nothing to say about class relationships or the economic system. As a Welsh Mancunian, Griffiths hates large country houses and idle, parasitical horsey gentry, public schools and vicars, adulterous army officers and adulterated beer. So do many of us. On the other hand, as with other purported critics, it is the rich who fascinate him, with their confident ritual and hermetic impregnability, the rich who are always with us. Like many another muckraker, his tract for the times is inadvertently written in praise of the robber barons. The Marxist playwright, like the New Left dramatist of the "glittering coffin" of the 1960s, is now in some danger of becoming the licensed rebel of the establishment. Instead of the gravedigger of the bourgeoisie, he is the darling of the halls. No more enchanting vision of our late-capitalist society has been presented than by this socialist propagandist. But, then, no more passionate celebration of the virtues of capitalism was ever written than that in *Das Kapital* by the old master himself.

Kenneth O. Morgan, "Loving Your Class Enemies," in The Times Literary Supplement, *No. 4100, October 30, 1981, p. 1266.*

MICK MARTIN

[If] a social activist play is to fall short of complete success, then to err on the side of entertainment is by far the happier alternative. *Occupations* was first performed in 1970, and first published in 1973, the recent new version [in 1980] being the fruit, the author states in an introductory note, of 'a decade's intermittent but intensive effort to arrive at a definitive text of the play'. Sadly, however, it is difficult to see that the effort has been directed towards the central problems of the play, which is set at the time of the ultimately unsuccessful attempt by workers in Northern Italy in 1920 to win control of production, and which focuses on two different political approaches to revolution, expressed through the two main characters Kabak and Gramsci. The former, a representative sent by the Third International to Turin to hasten the conversion of unrest into full-scale revolution, matches his belief in political opportunism against Gramsci's equally fervent belief in love, a love of the masses he speaks for, which prevents him risking their sacrifice in the total confrontation that Kabak advocates.

The argument is of far wider import and interest than is perhaps immediately apparent, and the historical context in which Griffiths sets it is not without dramatic possibilities. It is curious then that the author repeatedly sidesteps those possibilities, and in so doing jeopardises proper consideration of the views his play debates. For there is desperately little here for a director to exploit in seeking to win the attention of the spectator, desperately little for the spectator to fasten on to in seeking to come to terms with the issues that confront him. The setting of the play is limited (with the exception of two scenes in which Gramsci makes speeches) to Kabak's hotel room where those issues are debated, its action is limited to the comings and goings of those who partake in the debate. The climax of the argument is also, or rather stands in place of, the climax of the play, while the effective defeat of the workers' movement occurs during the interval. The two main protagonists are merely spokesmen of different points of view, and any consideration of their characters (in Gramsci's case particularly the play cries out for some exploitation of the dramatic potential suggested by the nature of his beliefs) is carefully eschewed in favour of a painstaking delineation of the positions taken up by Kabak as he changes from provocateur to counter-revolutionary in line with the modification of Soviet policy occasioned by the failure of the uprising in Italy. The one concession that Griffiths does appear to make in this context by the inclusion of Kabak's mistress Angelica turns out to be a crudely utilitarian image; the relationship dates from 1918 when Angelica's husband fled as the family estate at Kiev was occupied: now she lies dying of cancer in Kabak's hotel room, a last reminder of a bygone age. In the final analysis, indeed, important and interesting though the ideas debated in *Occupations* are, they remain, like Angelica herself, very much in a world of their own, an impenetrable world that makes little or no concession to its audience, and which fails in particular to provide the spectator with the means whereby he may relate what he sees back to the terms of his own experience. (pp. 51-2)

> Mick Martin, "The Search for a Form: Recently Published Plays," in Critical Quarterly, Vol. 23, No. 4, Winter, 1981, pp. 49-57.

EDWARD BRAUN

No television dramatist today is more articulate than Trevor Griffiths in his appreciation of the multiple hazards confronting anyone wishing to exploit the medium as a means of raising the audience's political consciousness. Yet equally, no other writer has expressed such confidence in the possibility of this aim. . . .

This belief in the vitality and political awareness of the British working class is a major theme that runs through practically all Griffiths' plays. (p. 56)

In *All Good Men* the action centers on the preparations for an 'in-depth' interview of Edward Waite, retiring Labour MP, ex-miners' leader and cabinet minister, and soon to be elevated to the peerage. On the eve of the interview, Lord Waite celebrates his seventy-first birthday with his daughter Maria, an art teacher in a comprehensive school, his son William, a research graduate in politics at Manchester University, and Richard Massingham, the ex-public-school television interviewer. Ostensibly to rehearse the forthcoming interview, William challenges his father to justify the record of the Labour Party in office over the past fifty years. This Waite does in a flow of impatient rhetoric, a shade too familiar in tone to be wholly convincing and subtly undercut by inflections and mannerisms that allude to George Brown, Lord Robens and, particularly with the cunningly deployed pipe (never smoked, as we later learn), Harold Wilson. Yet it remains a powerful and sincere display, and seemingly, enough to crush William particularly, as he says, 'Look. You're old. And you're ill. And you're my father. There's no way I can win. I asked my question, you answered it.' For Griffiths has taken care to invest the situation with a more urgent excitement: first, we have seen Waite a few days earlier suffer a mild heart attack, so we know that now he may be in danger of collapse; secondly, William is not just any chance left-wing adversary, but his own son, and a reflection of the young working-class idealist that he himself may once have been. Much of William's resentment towards his father springs ironically from the fact that he has been given the chances Waite never had; early in his life the family had moved from a dingy two-up, two-down in his Beswick constituency to 'Didsbury, four bedrooms, attics, cellars, gardens, playschools, parks. . .'—and on to this sequestered property in Surrey, where the worst problem is the squirrels

attacking the yew-trees. William is objecting both to his own and to his father's deracination, and by analogy to the Labour Party leadership's loss of touch with true working-class origins and aspirations.

Goaded by his father's patronising scorn, William resumes the attack and gives his version of Labour's achievements: not a social revolution, but 'a minimal social adjustment'. The debate reaches a climax of acrimony when son challenges father on his conduct during the General Strike, and thus we arrive at the true motive behind William's original challenge: in the course of his research he has gained access to confidential Miners' Union files, which have revealed that Waite opposed the strike in Union District Executive voting from start to finish, and then acted as vice-chairman of the committee to agree pay reductions and redundancies—a fact that Waite has been careful to exclude from his autobiography. There is no defence, and Waite can only align himself with Beatrice Webb's view of the General Strike as 'a proletarian distemper that had to run its course'. For good measure, he reveals his acceptance of a peerage to William, and retires to bed, apparently discredited. Yet an uneasiness persists: as Waite has already remarked, William has set up the exposure of his father in Massingham's honour, and he now reveals that he has had photocopies made of the incriminating minutes for use in the forthcoming interview. For his part, Massingham is probably planning a hatchet job on Lord Waite in any case, so they emerge as an unappealing alliance, and William is not much redeemed by his contempt for Massingham's phoney objectivity, his claim to be 'simply the film camera, the tape recorder, the lighting man'. His collusion with the derided 'media man' is not unlike Kabak's deal with Fiat in *Occupations*.

The closing scene shows the first take of the interview in the conservatory, with Massingham immediately broaching the question of Waite's view of the General Strike. As Waite starts to reply, his lips move soundlessly and the image is bright, washed out, like a pallid waxwork. The camera pulls back and cranes up to show him alone in a deserted space, draped in his baronet's robes. The credits roll, to the strains of "There'll Always Be an England", as though sounding a requiem for a whole era of Labour government.

Yet even if the play has persuaded one to question the shabby pragmatism of Labour in office, the alternative represented by William of high-minded social revolution has a certain dogmatic certitude about it that is no closer to working-class humanity. Whether the audience can find any alternative between these two extremes is doubtful: whereas Waite's daughter, Maria, is shrewd, warm, uncompromised and equally a product of the same family background, she remains in terms of political alternatives a peripheral figure, merely suggesting qualities that her father and brother have lost sight of. But if Griffiths does not present a solution, it is perhaps because in the early 1970s he could see none within the spectrum of British socialism, only qualities that endure and might yet be translated into action: the working-class faith is there, but in fragmented form.

Briefly reviewing *All Good Men* in *New Statesman* [see excerpt above], Dennis Potter acknowledged 'some of the sharpest, most telling and intelligent speeches ever heard on television'. . . . Yet, at the same time, he complained that the play 'was only about what it was about . . . People are more than, or other than their opinions, so any play which deliberately confines itself to lengthy exchanges of familiar ideas, however well-phrased and passionate, is in perpetual danger of collapsing into itself.'

This criticism seems to me to misread Griffiths' dramatic purpose entirely: the central point of **All Good Men** is that Waite is very much other than his opinions, and this we discover as his beliefs and actions are revealed. Whereas it may be common enough knowledge that Labour ministers are, for the most part, something other than 'men of the people' (a fact that has become a good deal more apparent in the aftermath of the Wilson resignation), yet television is still deployed constantly to reassure us that they remain precisely that. The very fact of locating Waite in a setting of Home Counties ease is enough to set him at an ironic distance from his Manchester back-to-back origins. Not only that: William and Maria are the children of his first, presumably working-class, marriage; but he has a second, estranged wife from higher up the social scale. Early in the play (Scene 3), when he suffers his heart attack over a solitary dinner, we hear in voice-over his recollection of the mocking, contemptuous words of the second wife as he engages in some guilty sexual activity with her. The words follow directly on snatches from past events: Chamberlain's 'peace with honour', Attlee in 1945, Bevin's 'naked into the conference chamber', Gaitskell's 'we will fight, fight and fight again'. The whole passage becomes associated with a sense of inner guilt, which seems to precipitate the heart attack. Given the taunts of his wife, the idea conveyed is that of inadequacy, in sex as well as in government, born of a sense of class inferiority. This is confirmed later when William berates Labour leaders for their need to be thought of as 'responsible' men.

Possibly the first indication of Waite's subconscious guilt is too fleeting to lodge in the viewer's mind, the voices-over too confusing; but there is no doubt that Griffiths is trying in **All Good Men** to reach far deeper into the Labour Party's collective psyche than Dennis Potter was able to grasp. It was an exploration that was to reach far deeper two years later with the greater scope afforded by the eleven-part series **"Bill Brand,"** where fundamentally the concerns were the same as those of **All Good Men.** (pp. 60-3)

[In] terms of political complexity and density of argument, **Absolute Beginners** [Griffiths' next play] makes no concessions whatsoever to what is derisively termed 'popular taste'. After a brief introductory scene at Tsar Nicholas's Summer Palace, in which Minister of the Interior Von Plehve briefs the Tsar on the measures required to quell revolutionary agitation, the action moves to the Bloomsbury flat of Lenin and Krupskaya. By rapid stages the conflict is established between Martov and Zasulich, the advocates of a revolution based on the ideals of human brotherhood, and Lenin, ruthlessly set on forging a dedicated vanguard leadership. In between stand Krupskaya, torn between loyalty to Lenin and respect for the ideas and feelings of their old friends and comrades, and the young Trotsky, flamboyant, opportunistic and prepared to back the winning side. In the distance is Plekhanov, the father of Russian Marxism, living in serene émigré retreat in Geneva, but ready to back Lenin.

As he had done in earlier plays, Griffiths establishes the personal-political dichotomy, using an authentic incident at an *Iskra* editorial board meeting when Lenin refuses the demands of Martov and Zasulich to accept proof of gross immoral conduct by the agent Bauman as reason for his expulsion from the party. According to Lenin's rigid revolutionary code, Bauman's value as an agent overrides all personal misdemeanours. . . . Importantly, the conflict is seen to be not merely one of view-points, but personal and emotional. By this stage, the close affection between Lenin and Martov is well established.

Dramatic tension arises from the fact that Lenin will sacrifice this intimacy if need be, but Martov only with the deepest pain, and this has its profound political as well as personal meaning.

When Griffiths wrote **Occupations** he could allow himself a certain freedom to compress historical events and even to invent a major character such as Kabak, the Soviet agent, together with his countess mistress, in order to give life to the antithesis to Gramsci's political beliefs. In **Absolute Beginners,** whilst seeking to explore similar issues, he was much more tightly bound by history, and there is nothing of significance in the script that cannot be traced back to an authentic source. The problem for Griffiths was that, apart from Lunacharsky's *Revolutionary Silhouettes* and Krupskaya's memoirs of Lenin (written under the constricting circumstances of the Soviet period), there is little information about the major revolutionary figures as *people,* since historians tend to portray them in terms of absolutes to correspond to their own particular version of events. . . . So what he did was to take what anecdotal detail there was and transform it into images and incidents which are significant yet realistic in terms of human behaviour.

Lenin's refusal to entertain the complaint against Bauman is one example; another is his delirious resistance to the agony of shingles, which suggests his determination to surmount all human frailty. Similarly, our first sight of him in the play is as he completes fifty press-ups before breakfast. Conversely, when first we see Martov, he is in impassioned debate with anarchists in a pub by the British Museum, and he is 'thin, smallish, bearded, untidy; papers and pamphlets bulge from his person'. Lenin, by contrast, is seen at this point against the background of the British Museum; 'He carries a roll of galleys under his left arm; stares sombrely at the entrance of the pub across the way.' In other words, Martov, for all his likeness to Lenin, is an émigré, 'Dilettante, intellectual. Unreliable'. He epitomises the weaknesses that Lenin seeks to purge from the party organisation. Similarly Georges Plekhanov is first encountered in his home in Geneva; his study is 'Large, expensive, tastefully and expensively got out. Double doors join to the next room. A view of the mountains from the window. The room is full of books and "objects".' It is evident that he belongs to the theoretical past of Russian Marxism, but not to its revolutionary activist future. The key contrasting image of Lenin is at the London Congress: at the crucial stage of the debate he is seen backed by an impressive semicircle of 'hard men'.

Yet the character is far from monolithic: . . . there are the moments of intimacy with Krupskaya, when she feeds him bread and milk on his sickbed, shyly offers herself at night, quietly defies him to console Zasulich. Then there is the final ironic impression after the awkward farewells have been exchanged by the conference delegates over Karl Marx's grave in Highgate: Lenin and Krupskaya 'Turn, walk off towards the gate, two simple bourgeois on a Sunday morning stroll'—cutting abruptly to Tsar Nicholas shooting crows in the park at Tsarskoe Selo to the ominous opening bars of Shostakovich's Fourth Symphony. What comes across is perhaps more predetermined than Griffiths intends, partly because one cannot help superimposing on the action what one knows of subsequent historical events, but also because the play as transmitted ran fifty minutes compared with the eighty plus of Griffiths' original text. In consequence, some depth is lost, specifically from the relationship between Krupskaya and Zasulich, from the portrayal of Bauman (and the justification of Lenin's retention of him), and above all from the depiction of Tsarist absolutism in the opening scene, designed to motivate Lenin's ruthless aim of 'a party built like a fist, like a brain balled'.

Deprived of this early view of the barbarism and total lack of scruple in Nicholas's police state, the viewer is in danger of concluding that the London Congress was where Russian Communism lost its soul and set itself on the course that led to the thirties terror. Nothing could be further from Griffiths' intentions: what he was seeking to pose was the classic dilemma of ends and means in terms of human, as well as political, behaviour.

Nor did he consent to compromise with the conventional demands of a popular series: there is no simplification of the interfactional debate within the ranks of the Social Democrats, and indeed the viewer is as hard put as Martov himself to keep pace with Lenin's manoeuvres in the final stages. However, the broad lines of conflict are clear enough, and the personal tragedy of the brave Vera Zasulich deeply moving at the end. (pp. 64-7)

Originally, *Through the Night* arose out of a commission . . . for a play based on an experimental prison in Sheffield. Griffiths' interest in this subject was overtaken by his reaction to a diary that his wife, a social worker, had kept when she was admitted to hospital for a biopsy operation on a lump in her breast and came round to discover that the breast had been removed. Out of this recorded experience and Griffiths' own reaction to it there emerged a rapidly written script, called originally *Maiming of Parts*. . . . (p. 68)

The experience of Christine Potts, a working-class mother in the play, follows closely that of Jan Griffiths. Diagnosed initially as a non-urgent, low-cancer risk, she is admitted for a biopsy after a three-week delay, signs an open consent-form when drowsy with anaesthetic in case the operation reveals 'anything, well, nasty', as the house surgeon puts it. The operation follows, and a malignant tumour is discovered. . . . (pp. 68-9)

Christine recovers to find her breast amputated, but is given no explanation beyond what her diffident husband, Joe, is granted by the Ward Sister: 'Well, she said when they opened you up it were nasty tissue and there were some sort of infection, so the specialist decided you'd be better off without'—plus a vague and frightening reference to 'more tests and that'.

When Stourton, the surgeon, makes his ward round, we share Christine's point of view of the muttered conference at the bottom of the bed and her confusion at the barely audible exchanges. Of the surgeon, she gets no more than a sight in half-profile 'as though [he were] shy or embarrassed'. Later, Chatterjee, the Indian nurse who attends to her dressing, can only admire the 'excellent wound' and marvel at Stourton's skill. Finally, in depression Christine seeks night-time sanctuary in a lavatory cubicle and is persuaded to emerge only by the intervention of the friendly and unkempt houseman, Dr Pearce. Over cocoa in his room she finally extracts an explanation by a great effort of will; she learns that a malignant tumour has been removed and finds the courage to put the question 'What are the chances?' The chances, it seems, are good, but await confirmation from the tests she is to undergo. 'But from now on [says Pearce] you live every day for keeps. The rest of us may continue to cherish the illusion that we're immortal. You know you're not.' Christine now has the strength to face her scar, even to joke about it to the scandalised Chatterjee: 'What did he do it with, a bottle?' The play ends with her joining in an anarchic drink-up in the ward organised by

Mrs Scully, a regular visitor to the operating theatre, to which the scant remains of her stomach testify.

Whereas in *All Good Men* Griffiths interpolated a critique of the celebrity interview and the sham of the 'objective' presenter, and conceived *Absolute Beginners* partly as a terse corrective to the fond nostalgia of the *Fall of Eagles* series [which focused on modern autocratic dynasties], *Through the Night* was calculated to cut across expectations born of the more predictable examples of the television hospital genre. . . . The extreme of impersonality is conveyed by the pathologist, Mount, who falls with voracity on his fifty grammes of infected tissue. Griffiths wished to go much further by including the horrific image of the amputated breast dumped casually into a waste-bin, but this was resisted in production. The point he is making, I think, is that the medical profession allows the necessary scientific detachment of its treatment of the patient's *parts* to extend to its care of the *whole* individual, leaving him or her adrift in ignorance and fear. . . . Thus the play's broader political implications are indicated, and the continuity with Griffiths' other work emerges: as Gramsci had said, the army not only can, but *must* be loved.

In the course of production, the script was extensively revised, particularly in response to solicited medical opinion. As Griffiths said to me, Scene 36 between Christine and Pearce 'bears all the torsions of organised BBC advice'. Specifically, he was confronted with the moral obligation to ensure that the play did not deter women from referring lumps in their breasts to their doctors, advice he could hardly ignore, but not relevant to the main argument about the way patients are treated when they are in hospital.

Immediately following the screening on BBC-1 on 2 December 1975, watched by an estimated audience of over eleven million people, the Corporation's duty officer logged close to a hundred phone calls, the producer's office and the *Radio Times* received many letters, and Griffiths personally some 180. Marjorie Proops in the *Sunday Mirror* opened her columns to readers with experience of mastectomy treatment and received over 1,800 letters in ten days. Thus the play loosened the taboo on the most feared of diseases. . . . (pp. 69-71)

Whereas, in terms of public response at least, *Through the Night* has been Trevor Griffiths' most successful play, **"Bill Brand"** (1976) remains an unequalled example of television drama as a form of extended political dialogue, surpassing even the controversial *Days of Hope*, broadcast by the BBC a year earlier. (p. 72)

Brand is introduced in the opening episode, the bye-election in 'Leighley', a Manchester suburb, at which he is elected to parliament. Ex-International Socialist and liberal studies teacher at the local tech, he describes his political stance in an interview for local radio:

> I am a socialist of the sort that Bernard Levin and his trail-blazing claque would describe as reactionary. I actually believe in public ownership and exchange. I actually believe in workers' control over work, community control over the environment. I actually believe that the real wealth of any society is its people—all of them, not just the well-off, the educated and the crafty, which I suppose makes me a democrat too.
>
> (Episode 1, Act 2)

Brand's struggle to maintain these principles in the face of parliamentary and constituency pressures during his first year at Westminster at the same time as he copes with the conflicting demands of his private life, furnishes the basis for the series. The crises Brand gets involved in all closely resemble events of recent history, or, at times, of history yet to be made: massive redundancies in the textile industry followed by non-union work-ins; the struggle for party leadership when a Wilsonian prime minister resigns mid-term; a 'Further Prevention of Terrorism Bill', designed to extend the police's power of detention; secret deals with union leaders leading to the cancellation of nationalisation plans and the curbing of wage demands.

Through all this Brand becomes inevitably involved in skirmishes with the whips' office, Tribune Group (here 'Journal Group') debates, censure motions by his constituency party, the compositing of conference resolutions, the procedural wrangles and frivolous badinage of select committee meetings. It is here that the series was at its most revelatory. . . . (pp. 73-4)

Brand has to learn to accept the compromises of everyday politics: the case of a woman denied an abortion cannot be publicly pursued in a constituency with 23,000 Catholics, most of them Labour voters; a Trades Council engagement must be cancelled for the sake of a fund-raising wine-and-cheese party organised by the 'Heaton Moor crowd', the right wing of the party, whose support and votes Brand still needs; faced with a possible snap election in the autumn, 'the wild man of Leighley' must restore confidence by opening fêtes, judging beauty contests and joining in Wolf Cub sponsored runs. But there is no compromising of principles amongst the hard core of constituency party workers, only a rigid sense of reality. As Albert Stead, the veteran Party and Union Regional Secretary, advises Bill, 'You've got to stay in touch. You can't run all the time.' And, quoting Gorky, he puts the question 'Is this the rabble on which we are to build a revolution?', to which the answer is 'Yes, comrade, it is: they're all you've got'.

It was at constituency level that Griffiths could draw on his personal experience of Labour Party membership, and it furnishes one of the key relationships of the series, that of Bill and his agent, Alf Jowett. Brand is answerable to Jowett for his voting at Westminster, his public utterances, his image in the press, his conduct in the constituency, even the irregularities of his private life: anything that might affect his chances of remaining an MP. Jowett is pragmatic, abrasively critical, but immovably socialist. When, in the final episode, Bill is contemplating voting against the Venables government in a vote of confidence, Alf supports him. . . . (pp. 77-8)

Thus, with Albert Stead and others, Jowett embodies the continuity of struggle and belief within the Labour movement, a continuity emphasised when Bill's unemployed brother, Eddie, shakes off his earlier apathy, joins the Fight for Work movement, and marches alongside Albert Stead.

Standing to the other side of Bill, and in virtual opposition to Alf Jowett, is Bill's mistress, Alex Ferguson. It is not only that she threatens to undermine the image Bill presents to the electorate, but, more important, she embodies the world of alternative politics that he has left behind, but which still conditions his responses. Moreover, her independent, feminist view of sexual politics implies a radical critique of the power structures that Bill, in becoming an MP, appears to endorse, and which now threaten their relationship. Add to this Bill's tendency to revert to the male-dominant role of his Northern, working-class conditioning, and one has a nexus of ideas so complex as to be incapable of proper development within this

series. In fact, as Trevor Griffiths concedes, the Bill-Alex relationship is properly a series in itself. A further problem was the impossibility of depicting their sexual relationship with the explicitness that Griffiths required to convey their powerful mutual attraction. The one scene of their lovemaking that was shown was by normal televison standards highly explicit, but, in Griffiths' judgement, merely risible. Even though the relationship had greatly deepened by the time it ended in Episode 8, it remained problematic, and the correlation between sexuality and politics never became sufficiently clear—a criticism I have already made of *All Good Men*.

One would not expect the final episode of **"Bill Brand"** to offer conclusions; as Griffiths said in an interview in *The Times Educational Supplement*, 'I'll probably never complete a play in the formal sense. It has to be open at the end: people have to make choices, because if you're not making choices, you're not actually living.' Hence, it is acceptable that we see Brand at the end still skirmishing with the whips' office and stubbornly invoking the ringing phrases of the party manifesto which others have conveniently forgotten. Any resolution of his ambivalent position at Westminster would be a falsification of the real-life truth. But one argument is affirmed without qualification, an argument that has run through the entire series and, for that matter, through every play that Griffiths has written before it: if socialism comes, it will come from nowhere but the working class. In the final episode (entitled 'It Is the People Who Create'), Bill houses an agitprop theatre group for the weekend, whilst they give a performance at the Leighley Labour Club. Discussing their ludicrous débâcle there, one of the actors says, 'If you're going to make connections, raise consciousness, you've got to start where people are actually at, not from some notional point in the middle of your own middle-class guilt-ridden hang-ups'. Bill Brand readily acknowledges the point—and so does Trevor Griffiths, never losing sight of it in his plays. That is the reason why, more than any of his contemporaries in television, he can be described as a socialist realist—socialist realist, that is, in the broad tradition of Gorky, O'Casey, Sholokhov, Steinbeck and Brecht, aiming, as Lukács says, 'to describe the forces working towards socialism *from the inside . . .* to locate those human qualities which make for the creation of a new social order.' (pp. 78-9)

Edward Braun, "Trevor Griffiths," in British Television Drama, *edited by George W. Brandt, Cambridge University Press, 1981, pp. 56-81.*

DIANA DEVLIN

[In *Oi for England,* six] characters convey the different attitudes towards the crushing social pressures on young working-class people in England today. Griffiths risks much by focusing so closely on skinheads, a group who already arouse fear and insecurity in other sections of society. . . . Griffiths shows us young men who loot and play urgent and disruptive music. Reading the script, protected by the safety of the page, I was better able to deal with the harshness of their conditions, understand how limited their moral choices are and differentiate between their loyalties, than when I was confronted with it through the frightening realism of television production.

Diana Devlin, in a review of "Oi for England," in Drama, *London, No. 147, Spring, 1983, p. 53.*

BENEDICT NIGHTINGALE

We haven't heard much from Trevor Griffiths of late, and that's a pity, since no dramatist on the Left better combines incisiveness and heart, none has written about the urgency of political change with greater sophistication of mind or generosity of spirit. Those qualities mark his *Real Dreams,* too, though it's not always easy to discern them. How could it be otherwise when the play's protagonists range from the muddled and naive to the floundering and foolish, and regard lucid argument and clear analysis with mistrust, preferring the shambling idiom of the right-on generation to the language of a supposedly corrupt establishment?

The time is 1969, the setting a commune in the Cleveland grot. The inhabitants, five male and four female, belong to an organisation which Students for a Democratic Society would no doubt reject as excessively radical, but the Weathermen maybe find not hard enough. They want to reach the local working class, they want to contact fellow-revolutionaries. They're less articulate than him, with their 'aw shit, man', 'I can dig on that', and so on; but they'd seem ideologically akin to the character in Griffiths's *Party* who sees hope for the future, less in marshalling disciplined battalions, more in identifying with the struggles of the Blacks, the urban poor, the Third World dispossessed and other oppressed groups.

So what should they do when a strutting Puerto Rican in vaguely military garb instructs them instantly to prove their solidarity by burning down that symbol of economic imperialism, the neighborhood A and P store? Understandably, they demur, complaining that the proposed action is unplanned. But what when Ramon, as he's called, flies into an almighty tantrum, deriding their revolutionary credentials? This time, they give in and drive with their molotov cocktails to what turns out to be a comically abortive raid, with Ramon himself drunkenly making obscene gestures at a motorist who has spotted the would-be saboteurs. Nor are the demands on them finished. What should they do when the Puerto Ricans insist on 'interrogating' one of their number as a suspected spy, and threaten to massacre the entire commune if this request is denied? Suddenly, the radicals find themselves ranged with guns against the very people they're hoping to liberate: 'This is fucking waggon-trail—we're protecting our goddam womenfolk from the savages, when what we're supposed to be doing is joining the savages.'

Somehow Griffiths resists the temptation to mock as thoroughly as he resists that to romanticise. He doesn't disguise the callow attitudinising, the macho bravado, or the contradictions and hypocrisies to be found in the commune. He doesn't pretend there isn't something absurd in talking violently about smashing the pig-state from the Louis Seize sofa your mother has given you, or begging to help burn down a supermarket because 'I've got to get into the heavy shit sometime—I'm 27, and I've never even been busted yet'. . . . Yet the feeling is never allowed to evaporate that these are sincere if confused young people, making principled sacrifices in conscientious hopes of changing a world which genuinely afflicts them with pain, disgust and guilt. They're dreamers, as western history in the last 20 years has proved; but they are, in the careful phrasing of the title, *real* dreamers, dreaming substantial dreams, dreams which 'will not go away'. (p. 30)

> *Benedict Nightingale, "The Way We Were," in* New Statesman, *Vol. 111, No. 2878, May 23, 1986, pp. 30-1.*

TONY DUNN

This kind of play gives the Sixties a bad name. [*Real Dreams*] tries to recreate on stage the American counter-culture of hippies, communes, obscenity, Vietnam and the Weathermen. But that's archival now, a moment which created its own, unique theatricality. Important social challenges were made but in a form and a language which is now comically dated. Griffiths seems to live in a time-warp. His college communards, trying to establish contact with a local Puerto Rican group called SPIC (sic), wander around their living room drinking wine, eating wholefood and actually saying 'The meeting was outta sight'. Someone sings, very badly, a Bob Dylan song and someone else quotes Wittgenstein. They're driven into bombing a supermarket by the locals, it's a fiasco; they're accused of betraying the operation to 'the pigs' and they wait, guns at the ready, for a revenge-attack by the Puerto Ricans. A glance at the cast list and the Pit's dimensions will tell you that the shoot-out will never come. So, as always in this kind of meandering closet-drama, tension is created by periodic telephone-rings. The last scene is a beautifully choreographed sequence of Tai Chi movements by the whole cast. It has nothing to do with the rest of the play but has the great merit of being wordless. . . .

This was supposed to be the work in which Griffiths moved from didactic to imagistic writing, but the long monologues of *Occupations* and *The Party* are infinitely superior to this nostalgic rant. Halfway through one of the women says 'This is really awful' and a little later one of the men says 'Maybe the whole evening has been a test' and that just about sums up this play.

> *Tony Dunn, in a review of "Real Dreams," in* Plays & Players, *No. 394, July, 1986, p. 27.*

PENNY KILEY

Trevor Griffiths' new, female version of *Comedians* has not turned into a feminist play, or at least not directly. The play does have a strong social thrust beneath its jokes—as it tells you a joke must have—but the messages are not simple, and the audience are made to draw their own conclusions.

However, the play does seem at first to be a little schematic. It's structured carefully with two acts in the classroom on each side of the central club showcase of Act 2. There are characters who seem to fit the comic stereo-types under discussion: Jews, Irish, Pakistanis, and women. And teacher Ella Waters and agent Bert Challoner have two directly opposing theories about the nature of comedy. But the twist in the end transcends everything that has been said before.

Perpetrator of the shock is Glenys Price, cool, tough, and alone. . . .

[She] stands out from her classmates: three years unemployed, the most passionate about the comic art, unconforming in looks as in everything else. The rest are older, typical working-class women with peripheral or part-time jobs, families to worry about, and dreams of escape. They are introduced as the play opens on an atmosphere of pre-test nerves and bravado, while they prepare for the culmination of three months of evening classes: the chance to win a career in comedy. . . .

The problem is that the characters are sketched in so lightly that they fail to engage sympathy. Around the auditorium are blown-up black and white photographs of the class in their outside occupations—cabbie, make-up saleswoman, bar-maid, cleaner, lollipop lady—but we are told little else about them. All that is revealed by the end of Act 1 is an indication of the relationships between the women and, after the appearance of the agent, of which side each is on.

Act 2 makes that clear, with a stage converted into a typically tacky Northern club, the theatre audience converted into clubgoers, and each 'turn' doing their bit. The laughs, of very different kinds, come fast, and the audience soon know which performer has lived up to Challoner's conventional commercial demands, which has stayed true to Ella Waters' ideals, and which they really shouldn't have laughed at. (p. 29)

It's all forgotten with the last. It's Glenys, turning class hate into art in a bizarre, cold, angry, inventive tour de force that would not last 30 seconds in clubland. No-one understands it. After that everything else must be an anti-climax. . . . [In] the end the play says no more—or less—about women than the 1975 version. (pp. 29-30)

Penny Kiley, in a review of "Comedians," in Plays & Players, *No. 404, May, 1987, pp. 29-30.*

Lillian (Florence) Hellman

1905?-1984

American dramatist, scriptwriter, memoirist, short story writer, director, critic, and editor.

Hellman was one of the most acclaimed American dramatists of the first half of the twentieth century. Her plays explore the human capacity for malice, the allure of power and money, and the dichotomy between individual interests and social consciousness. Ellen Moers observed: "[Hellman's characters] are not pleasant, and don't want to be, but most of the harm they do is to one another, and none of it seems meant to kill." In an era that largely featured lighthearted romantic plays and drawing-room comedies, Hellman's preference for confronting more complex issues of modern society earned her the reputation as an innovative contributor to the American theater and the foremost female playwright in the United States. Hellman also authored several acclaimed and controversial memoirs that span such historical events as the Spanish Civil War, the Moscow Purge Trials, World War II, and the McCarthy era.

Born in New Orleans, Hellman was the only child of a southern Jewish shoe manufacturer and a Manhattan socialite whose family had moved from Alabama. She attended New York University and Columbia University, leaving Columbia after her junior year in 1925 to work as a manuscript reader at the publishing firm of Boni and Liveright. After Hellman resigned her position the following year, she married publicist Arthur Kober and began contributing book reviews to the *New York Herald Tribune*. In late 1925, Hellman and Kober left New York for Paris, where her husband assumed the editorship of a new literary journal, the *Paris Comet;* during this period, Hellman published short stories and traveled extensively throughout Europe. The couple returned to New York in 1929, and Hellman served as a reader for several Broadway producers before moving with her husband to Hollywood in 1930. While working in a similar position at Metro-Goldwyn-Mayer studios, Hellman met detective novelist Dashiell Hammett, and their friendship evolved into a thirty-one-year personal and professional partnership during which Hammett guided Hellman in her initial attempts at playwriting and supplied her with material that she incorporated into several of her best-known dramas. Hellman subsequently divorced her husband and returned to New York City with Hammett.

Hellman's first play, *The Children's Hour* (1934), is based on an actual British court case cited in William Roughead's *Bad Companions* in which two headmistresses of a Scottish girls' academy were falsely accused by a student of homosexual behavior. Set at a private boarding school, *The Children's Hour* concerns a manipulative girl who accuses two of her teachers of engaging in a lesbian affair after she is suspected by her classmates of stealing from another student. The girl convinces her grandmother of this relationship, and the woman in turn influences parents to withdraw their children from the school. One of the teachers commits suicide before the student's lies are exposed at the play's end. *The Children's Hour* was a resounding critical and commercial success and was nominated for a Pulitzer Prize. The play was not awarded the honor, however, and it was later revealed that one of the Pulitzer judges had not seen the play because he found its subject matter

morally offensive. To counteract what they considered artistic censorship, the leading New York City drama reviewers subsequently formed the New York Drama Critics Circle Award committee for the purpose of establishing its own annual prize for theatrical works. *The Children's Hour* garnered notoriety in other cities besides New York; the play was banned in Boston and Chicago and was clandestinely staged at a private theater club in London to avoid government censorship during an international tour. Hellman's second play, *Days to Come* (1936), revolves around the lives of several people involved in a labor strike at a small Ohio factory. Much less successful among critics and audiences than *The Children's Hour, Days to Come* closed after seven performances.

The Little Foxes (1939) is the first of four dramas in which Hellman explores the conflict between self-interest and moral responsibility. Set in a small Southern town in 1900, *The Little Foxes* depicts greed and sibling rivalry among members of the affluent Hubbard family, who are offered the opportunity to become wealthier by investing in a local cotton mill. The business venture turns into a catastrophic conflict between Ben Hubbard, his brother Oscar, and their sister Regina, as their quest for power and money results in double-dealings, theft, blackmail, and death. Hellman also renders the South in cultural transition, as the aristocratic gentry succumbs to the entrepreneurs largely responsible for the emergence of the industrial New South. *The Little Foxes* received widespread acclaim for its strong characterizations, tightly woven plot, and spirited dialogue. Hellman's next play, *Watch on the Rhine* (1941), for which she won her first New York Drama Critics Circle Award, centers upon a family involved in the anti-Nazi movement. This work takes place in Washington, D.C., where Sara Müller, her husband, Kurt, and their children have returned to visit her parents after living abroad for over twenty years. Kurt is a German anti-fascist leader whose mission to gain American financial support is discovered by another houseguest, Teck de Brancovis, who in turn demands ten thousand dollars from Kurt in exchange for concealing his activities from the German embassy. During a struggle, Kurt knocks de Brancovis unconscious and leaves him for dead in an abandoned car, and the drama concludes with Kurt's departure for Germany alone. Commenting on the play's 1980 revival, Brendan Gill stated: "[*Watch on the Rhine*] is still charged with meaning; the moral and political questions with which it deals continue to torment us."

The Searching Wind (1944) also addresses anti-fascist sentiments in its examination of well-meaning, affluent Americans who fail to use their money and influence to stop the threats of Benito Mussolini and Adolf Hitler. Many critics contended that this play's multiple scenes and numerous major characters divert audiences from Hellman's thematic intentions. In *Another Part of the Forest* (1946), Hellman returns to the milieu of the Hubbard family twenty years prior to the action of *The Little Foxes* to trace the origins of the villainy and greed that destroyed their lives. This play centers on Marcus Hubbard, the family patriarch, who made his fortune as a storekeeper during the Civil War. Hellman constructs an intense parent-child relationship between the elder Hubbard and his youngest son, Ben, who discovers his father's indirect involvement in the deaths of twenty-seven Confederate soldiers and eventually blackmails Marcus into naming him the heir of the family business. *Another Part of the Forest* garnered mixed reviews, and Wolcott Gibbs summed up critical opinion by stating that the drama was "merely an untidy sequel to an infinitely superior play."

In the years following the composition of *Another Part of the Forest*, Hellman's involvement in various political movements prompted significant controversy. During the 1930s, she had raised money for the Spanish loyalists fighting the dictatorship of Generalissimo Francisco Franco and had lent her name to various radical causes. In addition, Hellman had visited Russia and other Communist countries and had continued to support Soviet premier Joseph Stalin after most American intellectuals and political writers had repudiated his regime. In 1947, Hellman wrote a scathing editorial published in the Screen Writers' Guild magazine in response to the Congressional House Un-American Activities Committee hearings held in Hollywood, during which several writers and film directors were cited for contempt of Congress for refusing to identify their peers as members of the Communist party. Although Hellman was never formally accused of being a Communist, she discovered in 1948 that she had been included on the Committee's blacklist. In 1952, Hellman was served with a subpoena to appear before the HUAC and responded by writing a letter to the Committee indicating that she would only answer questions related to her political activities. She stated: "I cannot and will not cut my conscience to fit this year's fashions, even though I long ago came to the conclusion that I was not a political person and could have no comfortable place in any political group." Dur-

ing this time, Hellman wrote and directed *Montserrat* (1949), the first of several adaptations on which she worked. Taken from a play by Emmanuel Roblès, *Montserrat* was followed by *The Lark* (1955), a reworking of Jean Anouilh's drama *L'alouette*, and *Candide* (1956), adapted from Voltaire's classic novel.

Hellman's last two original dramas, *The Autumn Garden* (1951) and *Toys in the Attic* (1960), examine personal relationships. *The Autumn Garden* concerns a group of middle-aged individuals vacationing on the Gulf of Mexico. Considered an unusually introspective work in Hellman's canon, this play garnered positive reviews and drew comparisons to the works of Anton Chekhov for its emphasis on characterization and dialogue. Richard Moody observed: "[Hellman] has captured the universal human experience of the middle years: the last desperate grasp at the dreams of what might have been, the sad and inexorable discovery that time and habit have fixed a mold that cannot be broken." The plot of *Toys in the Attic* was conceived by Dashiell Hammett, who suggested that Hellman write a play about a man who deliberately squanders his fortune when he discovers his family's resentment to his newfound wealth. Hellman incorporated Hammett's ideas into a Southern Gothic piece revolving around the obsessive and destructive relationship between spinster sisters Carrie and Anna Berniers and their younger brother Julian, whose sudden wealth and marriage threaten their domination of him. After being accused by his sisters of adultery and questioned about his reasons for marrying his wife, Julian loses his money in a robbery. Regarded by many critics as Hellman's finest work, *Toys in the Attic* won the New York Drama Critics Circle Award for best play.

Following the 1963 production of *My Mother, My Father, and Me*, an adaptation of Burt Blechman's novel *How Much?*, Hellman retired from the theater and renewed her political involvement as a staunch opponent of the Vietnam War. In 1969, Hellman published *An Unfinished Woman: A Memoir*, a respected autobiographical work that introduced her to a larger, mainstream audience. This book contains sketches of such literary figures as Ernest Hemingway and Dorothy Parker as well as a poignant tribute to Hammett, who died in 1961. In *Pentimento: A Book of Portraits* (1973), Hellman provides anecdotes of people and events from various periods of her life. Perhaps her best-known sketch is "Julia," which recounts Hellman's enduring relationship with a childhood friend whose involvement with the European Resistance led to her murder by Nazi collaborators. In this extended piece, Hellman recalls an incident in which Julia enlists her aid to smuggle fifty thousand dollars for the underground to help pay for the safe emigration of German Jews threatened by Hitler's regime. Hellman eventually attempts to locate her friend's illegitimate child but is rebuffed by Julia's estranged family. "Julia" was adapted into a critically acclaimed film.

Hellman's next memoir, *Scoundrel Time* (1976), chronicles her political involvement and provides a detailed account of the events which led to her appearance before the HUAC. This volume provoked much controversy for Hellman's unflattering portraits of such liberal intellectuals and writers as Lionel and Diana Trilling, Clifford Odets, and Elia Kazan, all of whom, she believed, had compromised their political beliefs for fear of retribution from Congress. *Scoundrel Time* also initiated reassessment of her previous autobiographical works, and many critics subsequently accused Hellman of deliberately distorting historical facts for her own self-interests. Perhaps the most serious threat to Hellman's integrity occurred in 1980, when novelist and critic Mary McCarthy called her "a bad writer and dishonest writer" on national television. This incident fueled further debate concerning the accuracy of Hellman's nonfiction works, particularly "Julia," and several writers published detailed essays discrediting the portrait of her friend and her brief participation in the Resistance movement. Hellman responded to these charges by filing a defamation suit against McCarthy that was dismissed following Hellman's death in 1984. Anita Susan Grossman observed: "It remains to be seen whether Hellman left behind further autobiographical fragments for eventual publication which will cause us to reevaluate her collection of memoirs. . . . [It] seems likely that the issue of truth in autobiography raised by her work will continue to arouse debate among her readers for years to come."

In addition to her work for the theater and her memoirs, Hellman wrote screenplays for the films *Dark Angel* (1935), with Mordaunt Shairp, *Dead End* (1937), adapted from Sidney Kingsley's play of the same title, *The North Star* (1943), and *The Chase* (1966). She also adapted several of her dramas for the cinema, among them *The Children's Hour* (filmed as *These Three*, 1936), *The Little Foxes* (1941), and *The Searching Wind* (1946).

(See also *CLC*, Vols. 2, 4, 8, 14, 18, 34, 44; *Contemporary Authors*, Vols. 13-16, rev. ed., Vol. 112 [obituary]; *Dictionary of Literary Biography*, Vol. 7; and *Dictionary of Literary Biography Yearbook: 1984*.)

BERNARD F. DICK

All we know about Julia is what Hellman has told us. Julia was her childhood friend, whose name she will not reveal. Her father was a Detroit millionaire, her uncle, a governor. Julia was raised by her grandparents, who were more interested in her fortune than in her. She had a fabled childhood: summers in the Adirondacks, trips to Rome and Cairo. Her life was short; she must have been in her early thirties when she was killed by Nazis.

The rest is conjecture. She and Hellman may have attended Waldleigh High School together in New York, from which Hellman was graduated in 1922. Perhaps Julia was the friend with whom she went spy-hunting along Riverside Drive in 1917, looking for German agents and mistaking a Hunter College classics professor for one. If so, it was a rehearsal for Hellman's exposure to espionage twenty years later.

Some of Hellman's detractors have denied that there ever was a Julia. The charge is never made so blatantly, but the implications are unmistakable. When Mary McCarthy appeared on the Dick Cavett Show in January 1980, she charged Hellman with being a "dishonest writer," whose every word is "a lie, including 'and' and 'the.'" McCarthy's animosity toward Hellman is part of a much broader antagonism that views her plays as melodramatic, her politics as intractably left-wing, her memoirs as unreliable, and her editorial dependence on Hammett as proof that he was her collaborator on the plays.

With any backlash, the stripes overlap. Thus, if one regards Hellman's plays as examples of "oily virtuosity," as Mary McCarthy does, one may be inclined to think similarly of the memoirs; and if one finds Hellman's politics offensively left-wing, one will call *The Little Foxes* a work of "Socialist re-

alism," as Elizabeth Hardwick did in her review of the 1967 revival, while a more temperate critic would have used the term "social realism." It is doubtful that Anatoli Lunacharsky, who originated the term "Socialist realism," would have found *The Little Foxes* revolutionary.

Hardwick was at least specific about what she disliked in Hellman; McCarthy, on the other hand, was bluntly general: "I've never liked what she writes." But the reason she gave had nothing to do with literature. It seemed that, in 1948, McCarthy overheard Hellman telling some students at Sarah Lawrence College that John Dos Passos had betrayed the Spanish Loyalists. . . . Presumably Hellman told them that Dos Passos was supposed to collaborate with Hemingway and Joris Ivens on *The Spanish Earth* until he came disillusioned by the conduct of the Communist Loyalists. Whether she told the students the reason for his disillusionment is another matter. When Dos Passos arrived in Valencia, he heard that his friend, José Robles Pazos, had been arrested for treason; in Madrid, he discovered that Robles had been executed, apparently by the Communists.

It is not surprising that the Spanish Civil War played such an important factor in McCarthy's dislike of Hellman, for it was a war that had the same polarizing effect on intellectuals as Vietnam had three decades later. Hellman's position was unequivocal: an anti-fascist supports the Loyalists. It was not an uncommon view. Anyone in doubt could look to Auden, who, in *Spain* (1937), resolved the Loyalist-Nationalist dilemma: "I am your choice, your decision; yes, I am Spain." McCarthy made her own decision; she would not unilaterally support the Loyalists because of the Stalinist faction within the Loyalist ranks.

Stalinism was another source of contention between the two women. After the Moscow purge trials, McCarthy became an anti-Stalinist, while Hellman did not, although she was in Moscow at the time and later chided herself for being so oblivious to the trials. In *Scoundrel Time,* she also admitted her blindness to the "sins" of Stalinism, which "for a long time [she] mistakenly denied." If, by a Stalinist, one means someone who signed a statement supporting the purge trials, as Hellman did in *The Daily Worker* (28 April 1938)—along with Hammett, Nelson Algren, Malcolm Cowley, Richard Wright, Langston Hughes, and others—then, naturally, she was. But such an endorsement should be viewed as the act of a hard-line Popular Fronter who steadfastly avoided criticizing the Soviet Union because it was the declared enemy of fascist aggression. . . . Even Sidney Hook, her fiercest critic, agrees she is no longer a Stalinist, although he seems to want a formal recantation of the sort the Inquisition demanded of heretics.

Had Hellman never written *Scoundrel Time,* one doubts that her critics would have raked up the coals of the past, searching for embers. Rarely has such a slender book occasioned such controversy. The prose was unadorned, although not as colorless as it was in *An Unfinished Woman*. The pacing suggested that Hellman had not lost her dramaturgical gifts. Yet unless one equates reminiscence with hagiography, *Scoundrel Time* is not "the record of a virtually unique personal heroism" that Diana Trilling claims it is. To call it such is to detract from the true hero, Joseph Rauh, Hellman's attorney, but for whom she would never have written her famous letter to the House Committee on Un-American Activities and quoters would have lost one of Bartlett's best. (pp. 153-55)

The Hellman who emerges from *Scoundrel Time* is a woman subject to fear and anger as well as a woman in need of reassurance, which she certainly did not get from Hammett, who thought she might be going to jail and spent the evenings telling her about the rats that scamper about the cells. Regardless, Hellman stood by her letter and refused to name names; it was an action that should never be minimized, not because it was heroic but because it was human. Integrity is not heroism; it is clearly within a mortal's capabilities. Yet a third of the mortals who appeared before the House Committee lost their integrity.

Integrity is also not the prerogative of martyrs and saints, although no one would know it from Garry Wills's introduction. . . . The introduction did not help Hellman, nor did the action taken by her publishers, Little, Brown, who regarded *Scoundrel Time* as such a sacred text that they demanded that Diana Trilling delete four unfavorable references to Hellman from *We Must March My Darlings* before they would publish it. When Mrs. Trilling refused, Little, Brown terminated her contract. (pp. 155-56)

Actually, Mrs. Trilling revealed nothing about Hellman that was not known. Even her discussion of Hellman's politics, while lucidly written, tells us more about the author as an anti-Communist liberal than it does about Hellman, who took another of her unequivocal stands during the McCarthy era—a stand that reflected a Popular Front mentality with McCarthyism replacing fascism. To Hellman, opposing McCarthyism meant opposing anti-Communism, which, in effect, meant being anti-anti-Communist. But to the right, a double negative was still a positive. The anti-Communist liberals did not have that problem. One could be anti-Communist and anti-McCarthy without the risk of being branded a Red.

Finally, to call *Scoundrel Time* an "unreliable history of the McCarthy era," as Mrs. Trilling does, is to misunderstand what the book really is: one individual's account of an event in which she participated. *Scoundrel Time* is to the history of McCarthyism what Edith Hamilton's *The Greek Way* is to the study of Hellenism: a primer, an introduction. What the memoir succeeded in portraying, and quite vividly, was an America under a kind of moral quarantine, where the illness was not severe enough to be an epidemic but only bothersome and nasty, like a prolonged case of flu that weakens the spirit and leaves the body smelling of flannel.

Yet the charge of unreliability is one that continues to haunt Hellman. Unlike the plays, which were often meticulously researched, the memoirs took an impressionistic view of history that would understandably infuriate anyone who wants a memoir to resemble a ship's log, with a strict correlation of date and event. One can appreciate Martha Gellhorn's exasperation at Hellman's seemingly cavalier attitude toward dates, especially since Gellhorn was a former war correspondent and journalist. Naturally one can respect Gellhorn's insistence on factual accuracy. But Hellman was not aiming for factual accuracy in her memoirs; she was seeking the essence of the event. To her, chronology was not the essence of the past, only one of its accidents. While it might seem laudable of Gellhorn to emend Hellman's chronology, she was not acting entirely in the interest of historical truth. (pp. 156-57)

Sometimes Hellman is vague because she does not remember; sometimes her vagueness is deliberate. The visit to Spain and the trip to Berlin took place within the same time period. Since Hellman has gone to great lengths to conceal Julia's identity, she may be using an inconsistent chronology to confound the curious. In *An Unfinished Woman,* she gave the name of Alice

to the friend who became Julia in *Pentimento,* stating that she died in 1934, which became 1938 in the second memoir.

Nor is it an earth-shattering revelation to discover that Hellman's dating is sometimes off by a year. In *Scoundrel Time,* she gave the date of her divorce from Arthur Kober as 1931, although it was a year later. A Freudian might argue that it was because Hellman was born a year later than the records indicate—in 1906, not 1905. Even Garry Wills seems to have picked up the habit, citing 1944 as the release date of *Song of Russia* when it was the previous year.

Therefore, Hellman's statement that Hemingway brought a print of *The Spanish Earth* to Hollywood in 1938 is not the whopper that Gellhorn imagines it is. Obviously it was 1937, since the film was released in August of that year. Yet to say, as Gellhorn does, that Hellman could not have been present at "Hemingway's only showing of the film in Hollywood" is incorrect. Hellman claims she saw the film at the home of Fredric and Florence March, and there is no reason to doubt her word: "In the summer of 1937, Hemingway and Ivens brought *The Spanish Earth* to Hollywood. . . . The screenings—at Fredric March's home, at Salka Viertel's house, at the Ambassador Hotel, and in the Philharmonic Auditorium—brought in more than $35,000 for the cause.

"But memory for us all is so nuts," Hellman observed rather prosaically in *Maybe.* . . . However, she anticipates any criticism of her chronology by invoking her memory that sometimes "won't supply what I need to know," as she admits candidly in *Maybe.*

If the intent of Gellhorn's argument was to show that Hellman had no talent for reportage, one would agree. Yet as well researched as Gellhorn's piece is, it seems to be another chapter in the humbling of Hellman. Interspersed among the documentation are references to Hellman the "important lady" whose *An Unfinished Woman* reads like a novel and whose *Pentimento* reads like short stories. Twice, she quotes a sentence from "**Julia,**" once italicizing it in disbelief: "But I trust absolutely what I remember about Julia."

Gellhorn ends her corrigenda by admitting she has many more questions about Hellman's accuracy, and even about "**Julia.**" There is much one would like to know about Julia, but demanding personal and historical vindication will not lead to an understanding of the woman who was the model for many of Hellman's characters. And regarding Hellman as a Stalinist will make one even more skeptical that such a person ever existed. (pp. 157-59)

It is one thing to say, as the *Times Literary Supplement* reviewer did in the context of a favorable notice, that "**Julia**" resembles a film scenario; it is something else to say, as James did, that it reads "like a spy-sketch by Nichols and May." For the moment, let us take a tabula rasa approach to Hellman, putting aside the image of Hellman the imperious doyenne whose face with its bisecting lines looks like the map of some uncharted land.

The land can be charted, and one might start with James's spy-sketch comparison. Certainly "**Julia**" has the ingredients of a spy thriller, and the role Lilly is required to play conjures up incidents in Eric Ambler, Graham Greene, and Helen MacInnes. Anyone who knows the thriller only from television or the movies would even sense something familiar about "**Julia.**" By reducing the entire experience to a *pentimento* or an outline, Hellman has universalized it. If Lilly and Julia seem familiar, it is because one has seen them before in other incarnations. Lilly is the innocent drawn into a circle of intrigue; the lady on a train making a perilous journey. Julia is the radical who rejects the affluence from which she came; the saint from the privileged class who elects to serve the poor without desire for recognition. Unwilling to be styled a heroine, Julia will not allow others to playact at being heroic. In her second note to Lilly, Julia dashes any hope of recognition Lilly may have: "There is no thanks for what you will do for them. . . . But there is the love I have for you." Julia has achieved total freedom from the nothingness of being-for-itself. Therefore, she evokes similarly committed women like Joan of Arc, Edith Cavell, Edith Stein, and Odette Churchill.

But Julia also evokes classical rebels like Prometheus and Antigone, and it is this archetypal link that makes her seem mythic. By spinning a narrative around Julia, Hellman has enclosed her within a myth—a truth that has been imaginatively universalized. However, as Suzanne K. Langer observed in *Philosophy in a New Key* (1948), myths are contradictory, as opposed to fairy tales, which remain simplistic. In one version of the Atreus myth, for example, Iphigenia is sacrificed by her father, Agamemnon; in another a stag is substituted for her, and Iphigenia goes off to Tauris. Hence, one should not be surprised to find inconsistencies in Julia.

In *An Unfinished Woman,* Hellman recalls a childhood friend called Alice, a millionairess who turned to Socialism and died in 1934 during the violence that erupted in February of that year when Engelbert Dollfuss, the right-wing chancellor of the Austrian Republic, closed Parliament and put down the protest strikes of the Viennese Socialists. Hellman would have been in Europe at that time, staying in Paris at the Hotel Jacob, where she was trying to complete *The Children's Hour.* In an incident common to both the memoir and the film, Hellman learned that her friend was hospitalized in Vienna. When Hellman arrived at the hospital, she found her friend speechless and almost completely wrapped in bandages.

Clearly Alice and Julia are the same person, whose identity Hellman simply will not divulge. It is also possible that in 1969, when Hellman published *An Unfinished Woman,* she had no plans of continuing her friend's story or of using it as the basis of a memory piece. A few years later, when she was ready to publish her second memoir, she decided otherwise; and so the friend who died as Alice in 1934 is given four more years of life.

Thus far we have been speaking of the mythico-historical Julia of the memoir; but there is also the Julia figure of the plays. Hellman was fascinated by the name of Julia. It was her mother's name, yet Hellman favored her father's side of the family. Hellman's mother was a Newhouse, and the Newhouses, as Hellman conceded, were the model for the predatory Hubbards of *The Little Foxes* and *Another Part of the Forest.* But the Hellmans were different. It was from her father that Hellman learned what it meant to be a liberal and to believe in racial equality. . . . The Newhouses, on the other hand, merely thought blacks had a distinctive odor. Julia Newhouse was the exception: "She was the only middle class woman I have ever known who has not rejected the middle class," Hellman wrote of her mother in *An Unfinished Woman.* Julia Newhouse found God everywhere and in everyone; in synagogues and cathedrals, in blacks and whites. Spiritually, she was a Julia—one of several.

In her very first play, *The Children's Hour,* Hellman transferred the homoerotic feelings she had for Julia, "the sexual yearning

of one girl for another" as she phrased it in the memoir, to Martha, with Karen and Martha becoming the tragic counterparts of Lilly and Julia. Other details in *The Children's Hour* corroborate what Hellman has written in her memoir. In the play, a child accuses her teachers of lesbianism; in "**Julia,**" Sammy Travers makes a similar allegation about Lilly and Julia. Hellman was in Vienna early in 1934 when Julia was hospitalized; in *The Children's Hour,* which premiered in November 1934, Joe Cardin offered to take Karen and Martha to Vienna, where he studied medicine. In *These Three,* [Hellman's screen adaptation of *The Children's Hour,* she] supplied a happy ending for Julia's story. Learning that Joe is in Vienna, Karen goes there and is reunited with him. If life imitated the movies, Lilly and Julia would have enjoyed a similar reunion in Vienna.

In her second play, *Days to Come,* Julie Rodman, the wife of an industrialist, has an affair with a labor organizer. Julie embodies some of the more superficial features of the Julia figure: she is widely traveled, well bred, and wealthy. But intrinsically, Julie Rodman is more like Hellman. Like the young Hellman, whom Julia thought of as a student rather than a teacher, Julie Rodman was always searching for "something I could be" and for "somebody to show me the way." In *An Unfinished Woman,* Hellman confessed a similar desire: "I needed a teacher, a cool teacher. . . ." (pp. 159-61)

In *The Little Foxes* screenplay, Hellman added a character called Julia. In a scene written especially for the film, Alexandra (Zan) finds the elegant Julia dining with David Hewitt and becomes jealous because she is interested in him herself. Zan is a composite of Julia and Hellman. Like Julia, she rebelled against her family's avarice; like Hellman, who once charged her family with being immoral when she was going through her righteous phase, Zan accused the Hubbards of "eating the earth."

Watch on the Rhine was a blueprint for "**Julia.**" In the play, Kurt Müller carried $23,000 in a briefcase, not unlike Lilly, who carried $50,000 in a hat and a candy box. Both Kurt and Julia bear the scars of commitment. Kurt's face is bullet-marked, and the bones in his hands have been broken; during the Vienna riots, Julia, in addition to being badly beaten, lost a leg.

In [another screenplay], *The North Star,* the Nazis tortured Sophia by breaking her arm and leg. At the end of *The Searching Wind,* Sam Hazen was about to lose a leg because of injuries sustained during World War II.

The Julia figure is transmogrified in *Toys in the Attic* along with Hellman's father and aunts. The entire play is a kind of dream displacement, as if the Hellmans had merged with the Newhouses and assumed their worst features. Julia's virtues (sharing of wealth, commitment to a cause) undergo a bizarre inversion as they are acquired by characters who turn them into vices. Instead of using money constructively as Julia did, Julian squanders it on pretentious gifts that alienate Carrie and make her his enemy. The victim of Julian's folly is Charlotte Warkins, also a Julia parody. Charlotte's face is slashed not because she is fighting fascism but because she has deceived her husband. And the cause of her disfigurement is the destructive naiveté of Julian's wife, an anti-Lilly in a play that is an "anti-Julia."

If Hellman has her way, we will never know Julia's identity. And would it really matter? Julia was a higher version of Lillian Hellman; she was everything to which the "aimless rebel," the "uncommitted" and "unfinished" woman aspired but never became. Julia was also Hellman's tribute to Dashiell Hammett, who lived by his principles as Julia lived by hers, expecting no recognition for doing what was right and deflating the egos of those who wanted it—he once told Howard Fast, who boasted that he was going to jail, that he would get more out of prison if he took off his crown of thorns. Most people find their models in books or movies. Hellman was fortunate; she found hers in life. (pp. 162-63)

> *Bernard F. Dick, in his* Hellman in Hollywood, *Fairleigh Dickinson University Press, 1982, 183 p.*

LINDA W. WAGNER

If autobiography is at once a personal and a fictional mode, as William Spengemann has recently suggested, then Lillian Hellman's last four books provide apt illustration of the conflict inherent in that description. *An Unfinished Woman* (1969), *Pentimento* (1973), *Scoundrel Time* (1976), and *Maybe, A Story* (1980) tell and retell the story of parts of Hellman's life, but one telling may differ from the account told elsewhere. Clearly, Hellman is using the process of autobiography both to explore her memories and to challenge the notion that recollection is a means to truth. . . . (p. 275)

The progression from her first memoir, *An Unfinished Woman*, through *Pentimento* and *Scoundrel Time* to the "story" of *Maybe*, helps the reader chart Hellman's search for personal truth, and for a means of recording it. *An Unfinished Woman* seems to be conventional autobiography, at least the first two-thirds of it. Hellman appears at its center; she is on stage throughout, and she also interprets happenings so that "truth" and "meaning" are in some episodes translated for the reader. *An Unfinished Woman* begins appropriately enough with a lengthy description of Hellman's birth to a prominent New Orleans family, that of the Newhouses, and of her fascination for her father's comparatively poor German family. She makes her fig-tree hideaway come alive, and shows the insecurity of herself as hesitant only child in several scenes. That she takes only twenty-seven pages to bring her persona to her first job— at age nineteen with Liveright Publishers—shows the economy and selectivity of her account. (pp. 275-76)

Once the chronology of the memoir becomes fragmented (Hellman's memories of the 1930s and 1940s coalesce around her relationship with Dashiell Hammett, about which she seldom speaks directly, and her stays in both Spain and Russia), the style begins to fit the experience in a way different from that of the opening section. The accounts of Spain and Russia are given as journal entries, scene leading to scene, and the presumption seems to be that the reader knows the contexts of the trips. The texture and tone of the experience is the valuable focus, not mere facts and dates. . . . Hellman by the very mode of telling her story emphasizes the insignificance of factual information. Poem-like, the whole of *An Unfinished Woman* asks the reader to believe that the juxtapositions, the breaks in narrative, the sense of timelessness (scene fused with scene, Hellman's personality recognizable as fragile, dependent yet rebellious, regardless of time) are all calculated to bring the life of Lillian Hellman into comprehension, even if partial. Throughout these books, Hellman ducks the role of author as oracle. In her narrative method of setting scene beside scene, she more nearly assumes the role of observer: here it is; remember the image; appreciate it. And perhaps later, on your own, experience these fragments as a whole. The "knowl-edge" of Lillian Hellman, both subject and observer, is—and must be—limited. (pp. 276-77)

The ending of *An Unfinished Woman* conveys this sense of failure at achieving the full memory. Chapters fourteen through sixteen are devoted to separate people, Dorothy Parker, Hellman's maid Helen, and Hammett. There is no attempt to tie these chapters to the body of the memoir. Each a try piece in a different sense, they foreshadow the method of *Pentimento*, as if Hellman had by the ending of her first book of autobiography realized the futility of plot and chronology. (pp. 277-78)

Pentimento is a book made of named "chapters," most of them about individual characters. Continuing on from the closing pages of *An Unfinished Woman*, Hellman perfects her method in **"Bethe," "Julia," "Arthur,"** and others. Again, she tells *her* story by refraction: we are forced to look at Hellman differently in every episode. With Bethe, good German cousin become Mafia girlfriend, Hellman is a fascinated child, strangely drawn by her conviction that passion is a necessity. With Julia, Hellman is unpredictably brave, risking her own life to carry funds for political causes not her own. With Arthur, Hellman is nearly pathetic, looking for affection as she gives it within an unconventional set of circumstances.

Her narrative method is not only effective in that it holds our interest; it more importantly enables her to present multiple facets of her personality. This is near-biography set in an autobiographical frame. It achieves coherence because of the patterns Hellman creates within the separate chapters. (p. 278)

Each episode allows her a climactic learning experience; central to the entire memoir is Hellman's understanding of Bethe as a woman who loves passionately, beyond reason or safety or moral code. (pp. 278-79)

Bethe's life itself is important but what is more telling, eventually, to Hellman who suffers all her life from her southern girlhood is the way her aunts Jenny and Hannah have responded to it. For all their outrage about Bethe's living in sin and her involvement with the Mafia—through Arneggio, who is brutally murdered—they never desert Bethe. Secretly, they visit her, give her gifts and money, and spirit her away after her lover's murder. When Hellman takes Hammett back to New Orleans with her to visit Hannah after Jenny's death, Hannah also accepts and befriends him. (p. 279)

Much less directly than Virginia Woolf, Edith Wharton, or Ellen Glasgow, Hellman faces the problems of being aggressive enough to be a successful woman writer while simultaneously being passive in a male-dominated culture, through her focus on other kinds of experience. Indeed, except for the **"Theatre"** chapter, *Pentimento* might very well be about any woman, not necessarily a woman writer. Metaphoric as Hellman often is, that tactic here may be germane for treatment of this theme. It may be too that she saw the conflicts she as writer experienced to be no greater than those Bethe, Hannah, Jenny, and Julia had known.

The primary relationship in Hellman's life—that with Hammett—gave her many opportunities to explore strengths and weaknesses, aggression and passivity. She often presents scenes with Hammett through metaphor. An early scene between them shows Hammett angry about her interest in other men, using a metaphor to give his command to her:

> One day, a few months after we met, he said, "Can you stop juggling oranges?"
>
> I said I didn't know what he meant.

He said, "Yes, you do. So stop it or I won't be around to watch."

A week later, I said, "You mean I haven't made up my mind about you and have been juggling you and other people. I'm sorry. Maybe it will take time for me to cure myself, but I'll try."

Similarly, Hellman chooses an episode in which she and Hammett kill a snapping turtle to try to image their relationship. Hammett's study of turtles has been mentioned throughout both *An Unfinished Woman* and *Pentimento,* so when the "three-foot round shell" appears (in **"Turtle"**) we expect Hammett to be in charge of ridding the farm of it. The conflict between Hellman and Hammett in the process of killing the turtle reveals character as well as interaction: Hellman sees herself as judgmental, happiest when putting people in moral categories she has designed. Hammett is singly-moral, living his life without making judgments. In this instance, however, Hammett is intent on killing the turtle. Even a gun wound behind the eyes and decapitation by ax ("severing the head to the skin") will not do the trick, and in the night the headless turtle moves from the kitchen out to the garden. Once found, the turtle becomes the point of controversy, Hellman insisting that "it has earned its life" and Hammett convinced it is long dead. Hellman finally buries it, against Hammett's wishes; and in the argument that continues, their own individual wills show clearly. Hammett comes to respect her feelings that the turtle's struggle to live, as she interpreted what was a biological post-death heartbeat, was worth commemoration, and when some animal digs up the buried turtle and eats it, he re-buries it for her. (pp. 279-81)

The tone of this book differs a great deal from that of *An Unfinished Woman.* Just as the method there was ostensibly direct and reasonably factual, the technique in *Pentimento* forces the reader to find the rationale for the choice of images, metaphors, juxtapositions. Hellman herself writes in the 1979 commentaries to the three memoirs, published as *Three* in that year, that "*Pentimento* was written by what psychoanalysis calls . . . 'free association.' I did not know from one portrait to another what I would do next, with the exception of 'Julia' where, without much hope, I wanted to try once more. I had not, for example, consciously thought of Bethe for perhaps thirty years. . . . I knew I was waiting each time not for what had been most important to me, but what had some root that I had never traced before." (pp. 281-82)

If *Pentimento* is the process of "repenting," seeing the earlier lines and shapes under the present paint on a canvas, a way of "seeing and then seeing again," *Scoundrel Time,* the third of her memoirs, is almost a scenario for a single episode. Focus is direct: Hellman is to appear before the House Un-American Activities Committee. . . . *Scoundrel Time* is almost entirely plot-oriented; it is a record of what happened from March of 1952 through May of that year, especially May 21, the day of the hearing. To be truly moving, the book needs to be read in sequence, following the other two memoirs, because in this one, Hellman says so little about herself or Hammett, or her professional life. (pp. 282-83)

The toll of Hellman's anxiety about the hearing took on her is clear in her several-day bout of vomiting after the session was over, and in her comment in *Scoundrel Time* that "for almost a year after my hearing before the Committee and after the sale of the farm, I have very little memory and only occasional diary notes." And, later, "I have only in part recovered from the shock that came . . . from an unexamined belief that sprang from my own nature, time, and place"—that people would not betray others, that the intellectuals and artists involved in many of the hearings would not succumb to pressures about their own futures and finances. *Scoundrel Time* is a record of those betrayals, and as such was much maligned in reviews soon after its 1976 publication. Hellman, characteristically, named names; and many of those named resented her forthright charges. (p. 284)

Three was published in 1979; *Maybe, A Story* followed in 1980. If one views *Scoundrel Time* as Hellman's character metaphor much in the same vein as the chapters in *Pentimento,* then the entire book of *Maybe* can be viewed as the Sarah Cameron character in suspended image and metaphor. . . . Parts of Sarah Cameron's life are recounted, always tentatively, always through the eye of some observer other than Hellman, but the explicit meaning of Sarah's story is left for the reader to deduce. As Hellman takes the risk of writing a "story" that is neither biography nor autobiography, that crosses the line between fact and fiction without recognition of that line, one recalls her *Paris Review* (*Writers at Work, III*) comment in the mid-1960s: "You write as you write, in your time, as you see your world. One form is as good as another. There are a thousand ways to write, and each is as good as the other if it fits you, if you are any good. If you can break into a new pattern along the way, and it opens things up, and allows you more freedom, that's something. . . ."

The necessity to break with conventional form, evident throughout these later writings, seems to reflect Hellman's increasing cognizance of the fragility of what had been her earlier convictions. . . . If she has reached a position closer to that of Hammett, she has not done so easily; and the fragmented sentence patterns and the casual building of paragraphs suggest the groping of the author-persona. (pp. 285-86)

Perhaps Hellman will later write a "commentary" about *Maybe, A Story,* but until she does, let me make this conjecture: Sarah Cameron's life crossed Hellman's in several important ways, important for Hellman's sense of herself as woman. The first was the sharing of Hellman's first lover, the malicious Alex, who suggested in leaving her that she had an unusual body odor. This comment caused a near-obsession with cleanliness (three baths daily) that lasted long into her life; the first third of *Maybe* deals with this obsession in one way or another; it is a connection to several memories of Hammett, to the Pleasantville Farm, and to other women friends. Sarah became Alex's lover soon after Hellman and, indeed, was said to have taken Alex from her.

Toward the close of *Maybe,* Carter Cameron, Sarah's former husband, became a lover of Hellman's for an extended period, in a pleasant and non-demanding relationship that was marred (and ended) only when Hellman questioned him about his feelings for Sarah. Both her early and late life as sensual woman was shaped in part by men close to Sarah.

Sarah Cameron herself was a creature of the imagination, a phoenix who might more closely resemble the writer and artist than does Hellman herself. Sheer fantasy wrapped Sarah's life: was the woman seen on the terrace with her dead a decade before? Was Sarah the mistress of a gangster and involved in a murder? Was she a member of the international jet set? Sarah was unpredictable; she was also unforgettable. And in Hellman's mind, she was also a symbol of death. (pp. 286-87)

The reader moves past the author-persona at the abrupt close of *Maybe:* is it Carter, then, who has the connections with the underworld? Has it been Carter's erratic behavior that has so conditioned Sarah to madness that she must experience it herself? Is Sarah's identity much more intimately bound up with the men in her life than even Hellman's? Trained as we are in what kinds of information to expect from writers, having Hellman leave us with such fragments can be upsetting, until we remind ourselves that Hellman's choices are intentional. The point of *Maybe* is that happenings exist both in themselves and as images which change according to the viewer. For most of her life, Hellman tried to impose order on those happenings (particularly in her plays, but also in the experiences she recounts in the earlier memoirs). By the time of *Maybe,* she has relaxed the need for control and is willing to offer the "story" as the mosaic she remembers. An informative paragraph occurs midway in the text: "Maybe the strange mixture is why I don't remember very much. Or, as time and much of life has passed, my memory—which for the purpose of this tale has kept me awake sorting out what I am certain of, what maybe I added to what, because I didn't see or know the people—won't supply what I need to know."

Hellman's willingness to try to tell the Sarah Cameron story, and another part of hers in that process, is proof again of the belief the writer has in the process of coming to words. The text of the story may be vague; she may even call attention to that elusiveness by titling the work *Maybe;* but the process of writing is more valuable than tentative. If Hellman continues to create more characters who figured prominently—whether imaginatively or directly—in her life, she may achieve what few women writers have in literary history: some credible account of the life, anxiety, conflict, love, and death of an important female writer. (pp. 287-88)

Linda W. Wagner, "Lillian Hellman: Autobiography and Truth," in The Southern Review *(Louisiana State University), Vol. 19, No. 2, Spring, 1983, pp. 275-88.*

SAMUEL McCRACKEN

In February 1980, Lillian Hellman brought a libel action against Mary McCarthy. Miss McCarthy, appearing on the "Dick Cavett Show," had called Miss Hellman a bad and dishonest writer, and had then repeated on television a judgment she had made earlier in an interview: "Every word she writes is a lie including 'and' and 'the.'"

Whether this statement constitutes a libel is properly a concern for the courts. But quite apart from the libel action, which may anyway never come to trial, the incident raises a more general question, the question of the credibility of a very well-known and highly esteemed author. Lillian Hellman's memoirs have received adulatory notices and are taken as authoritative sources on the life not only of their author but of such prominent literary figures as Dorothy Parker, Ernest Hemingway, and the man with whom Miss Hellman lived, Dashiell Hammett. Moreover, Miss Hellman is widely credited with having set a heroic example when she appeared before the House Committee on Un-American Activities during the McCarthy period and announced, before taking the Fifth Amendment and refusing to answer a question, that she would not "cut [her] conscience to fit this year's fashion." It is, therefore, a question of some consequence whether Mary McCarthy is right about Miss Hellman's honesty.

The answer to this question is to be found in Miss Hellman's series of memoirs: *An Unfinished Woman* (1969), *Pentimento* (1973), *Scoundrel Time* (1976), *Three* (an annotated compendium of the earlier memoirs, 1979), and *Maybe* (1980).

The best known of these is undoubtedly *Pentimento,* which contains a portrait, "**Julia,**" about a childhood friend. The heroine of this piece, a rich young American, attends Oxford and then the University of Vienna medical school; undergoes analysis at the hands of Sigmund Freud; becomes involved in anti-fascist underground work during the 30's; and at one point enlists Miss Hellman's aid in delivering money to the underground in Germany. According to Miss Hellman, Julia had a daughter by one of her fellow students; also, as a result of her work, she had lost a leg. In 1938, fatally wounded by Nazis in Frankfurt, she is smuggled, dying, to London. After her death Miss Hellman receives a telegram from London asking her to advise a funeral home there as to the disposition of the body. In the event, Miss Hellman herself goes to London where she takes charge of the body, brings it back to America, and has it cremated after Julia's family refuses to accept it.

Miss Hellman fleshes out this outline with her customary taut prose, pungent detail, and barbed expressions of contempt for those actors in the story who fail to meet her moral standards. . . . In 1978, "**Julia**" was made into a film starring Jane Fonda as Lillian Hellman, Vanessa Redgrave as Julia, and Jason Robards, Jr. as Dashiell Hammett. All three were nominated for, and Miss Redgrave and Mr. Robards received, the Academy Award.

In 1981, Martha Gellhorn, the well-known reporter who was the second wife of Ernest Hemingway, published an article in the *Paris Review* severely critical of Miss Hellman's veracity. Although she dealt largely not with *Pentimento* but with *An Unfinished Woman* (in which Miss Gellhorn and Hemingway figure prominently), and thus did not confront "**Julia**" directly, she raised *en passant* grave doubts about the internal consistency of Miss Hellman's account of the travels which included the delivery of money to Julia. (p. 35)

Then, in 1983, the psychoanalyst Muriel Gardiner published a memoir, *Code Name: "MARY,"* which disclosed startling similarities to the life story of Miss Hellman's Julia. Dr. Gardiner, like Julia, was born to wealth, enrolled at Oxford, and then traveled to Vienna in the 1920's where she attended the University of Vienna medical school and underwent analysis; like Julia, too, she became involved in anti-fascist underground work during the 1930's. The main differences between Dr. Gardiner and Miss Hellman's Julia are that Dr. Gardiner failed to persuade Freud to undertake her analysis, did not lose a leg, and survived to tell the tale. (pp. 35-6)

To accept the striking parallels between Muriel Gardiner and Julia as mere coincidence would require something like an act of faith. We must believe that all during the 1930's, one of Muriel Gardiner's fellow students in Vienna was, quite unknown to her, also at the center of the anti-Nazi resistance. Moreover, we must believe that this other freedom fighter escaped the notice of the documentation archives of the Austrian resistance—for Dr. Gardiner tells us that the director of those archives knows nothing of her presumed *Doppelgänger*. Indeed, he has taken pains to ask many survivors of the resistance whether they knew a second American woman, and the answer has always been "No. Only 'Mary.'"

But did Miss Hellman have access to information about Dr. Gardiner? Nothing about Dr. Gardiner's career was published until 1973, when her husband, the historian Joseph Buttinger, contributed a brief memoir to a professional journal. But as it happens, Wolf Schwabacher, a close friend of Dr. Gardiner and her husband, was for some years also Miss Hellman's attorney. Dr. Gardiner recounts that Schwabacher frequently told stories about Miss Hellman, and that he had been much interested in Dr. Gardiner's own work in the Austrian underground. Miss Hellman, for her part, denies that Schwabacher ever told her about Dr. Gardiner. Since he died in 1951, the issue cannot be finally resolved. . . . (p. 36)

Miss Hellman's own account of Julia presents difficulties to an investigator. To begin with, she tells us she has changed "most" of the names. Her reason for changing Julia's name in particular is that Julia's mother is still alive. But Miss Hellman never mentions Julia's *last* name, so presumably what she means is not that she has changed it but that she has suppressed it. It is not clear why, however, since her contempt for Julia's family—"bastards all"—is close to uncompromised. We may in any event presume that Julia is a real name since we are told that Julia described Donne's poem "To Julia" as a "tribute" to her.

Another suppressed name is that of a heavy woman with whom Miss Hellman rode on a train from Paris to Berlin. Miss Hellman is protective of her because she thinks the woman still lives in Cologne, and she is not sure whether even now the Germans like their premature anti-Nazis. This is rather an odd remark for two reasons: nothing in the account suggests that Miss Hellman ever had contact with this woman after leaving her in the train station in Berlin; and one would have thought, from the career of Willy Brandt alone, that the Germans are reasonably tolerant of their premature anti-Nazis.

Other names in *Pentimento* are equally elusive. Miss Hellman designates a "Moore's funeral home in Whitechapel Road," but the London telephone book for 1938 does not show a listing for such an establishment. . . . Likewise for the non-existence of a "Dr. Chester Lowe," said by Miss Hellman to have been in custody of Julia's body at 30 Downshire Hill; or for any named person in **"Julia"** other than those who, like Miss Hellman and Dashiell Hammett, are elsewhere attested.

But verification of Miss Hellman's account does not hang on names and streets. Much can be achieved by a close analysis of the text of **"Julia"** against the background in which it is set. Here the spadework has been done by Martha Gellhorn, who has demonstrated that there are very serious problems with the chronology of Miss Hellman's comings and goings in the fall of 1937. The discussion that follows is deeply indebted to Miss Gellhorn.

The *Normandie,* carrying Miss Hellman, Dorothy Parker and her husband Alan Campbell, as well as Miss Gellhorn, reached France on August 27, 1937. Miss Hellman tells us in one memoir that she spent three weeks, in another a month, in Paris before going to Moscow, where she was to attend a world theater festival. This means that her trip to Moscow cannot have begun earlier than the last week of September. The date is further nailed down by Miss Hellman's noting that she subsequently told Julia's grandmother that she had seen Julia in Berlin "in October," when she was on her way to Moscow. She tells us further that her trunk arrived in Moscow "two weeks" after leaving Berlin. October 1 is therefore a *terminus a quo* for Berlin, and she must have been in Moscow at least until October 15. She spent "several" weeks in Prague before returning to Paris. She was thus not back in Paris before the first of November; she spent "a few" days in Paris before proceeding to Spain.

One problem with all this is that in *An Unfinished Woman* Miss Hellman gives a detailed chronology for her activities in Spain, starting with October 13, a date on which she was presumably still in Moscow. It does not seem likely that her memory is playing her false about the date of her arrival in Spain, since it is given in what is apparently a *verbatim* extract from her diary. Besides, Miss Gellhorn reports seeing Miss Hellman in Madrid on October 15.

There is a further difficulty with Miss Hellman's chronology. The world theater festival in Moscow, as Martha Gellhorn notes, ran from September 1 to September 10, 1937. It is a little hard to understand how Miss Hellman could have attended this event if she did not get under way for Moscow before October 1. Even if her memory of having seen Julia "in October" is a slip for "in September," she would not have been able to spend three weeks or a month in Paris and still have made the festival.

Moreover, Miss Hellman reports that the only play at the festival that impressed her was a production of *Hamlet;* according to Miss Gellhorn, there is no record of a production of this play in Moscow during 1937.

Miss Hellman could not, therefore, have carried out the entire program she describes in her memoirs in the time she said she had for it. Some of these events, if they happened at all, must have happened at times and in ways other than she says they did. (pp. 36-7)

While in Paris, Miss Hellman talks on the telephone with Julia, and tells her that she will make a detour on the way to Moscow to see her in Vienna. Julia proposes instead a rendezvous in Berlin, the purpose of which will be explained by an emissary she will send in a few days. In due time, a man who calls himself Johann approaches Miss Hellman at her Paris hotel and tells her that Julia wants her to smuggle $50,000 for the underground as she passes through Berlin on the way to Moscow. Johann is to meet Miss Hellman at the train station the next morning, and if she is willing to undertake the task she will say "hello" to him.

The next morning Miss Hellman arrives at the station in the unwanted company of Dorothy Parker and her husband, and after a *contretemps* in which Johann is nearly driven off, she conveys her willingness to carry the money. Once on the train, she meets a young man who says he is Johann's nephew. He presents her with a hatbox and a box of candy, saying that they are from "Miss Julia." There is a note from Julia attached to the hatbox, advising her that at the border crossing she should leave the candy box on the seat and wear the hat when she leaves the train to go through immigration control. Once the train is on its way, Miss Hellman realizes that she has no idea whether the border will come in a few minutes or a few hours.

In her compartment, Miss Hellman has found two German women, one thin and one heavy. At lunch time, the heavy woman invites her to go to the restaurant car for lunch, and Miss Hellman demurs, saying that she doesn't know when they will be crossing the border. Assured that they will not reach the border until late afternoon, she goes off to lunch, where she learns that the heavy woman is a graduate student returning to her home in Cologne. When the border crossing is reached, the thin woman insists that Miss Hellman wear the hat. Once Miss Hellman has returned to the car, during which time there is a customs examination, the thin woman, over her protests, opens the box of candy, removes a piece, and eats it.

At the station in Berlin, where all three women leave the train, Miss Hellman is met by a man and woman; the woman greets her effusively, regretting that she cannot stay longer, but consoling herself that they will have a visit of a few hours. The woman then disappears and the man tells Miss Hellman to get a restaurant recommendation from the official at the gate, to go to the recommended restaurant but, should it not be Albert's, to proceed from the recommended restaurant to Albert's. At Albert's, Miss Hellman encounters Julia on crutches, minus a leg. She transfers the hat to Julia. After appropriate thanks, they talk, and Julia tells Miss Hellman—whose visa will not allow her to stay in Berlin overnight—to get her train at Bahnhof 200 (presumably a typographical error for Bahnhof Zoo). She will be shadowed by the underground to the station and then on the train to Warsaw; her unseen escort will be in the car to her left.

Miss Hellman boards the train, and in the morning, as the train pulls into Warsaw, she sees a figure gesturing at her from the platform; she recognizes the young man who had sat with her at dinner the night before. Shortly thereafter a voice—presumably that of the young man—speaking English from the corridor informs her that all is well but that the Germans have taken her trunk off the train; she should wait a few hours before inquiring about it, advice which Miss Hellman follows.

This narrative is shot through with improbabilities. The first of these is the mission itself. As Muriel Gardiner's memoir shows, it would have been perfectly easy for Julia to have money brought to her in Vienna by an open courier; Miss Hellman herself says that the Morgan Bank had been sending Julia large sums of money all over Europe. Why then the need to smuggle? And even if we grant that need, why could Julia not accept the money from Miss Hellman in Vienna rather than taking a trip north to Berlin? An underground operative on crutches, with a badly fitting false leg, is a sight easily marked. Why should Julia have involved herself so visibly in the exchange? (p. 37)

Why is Miss Hellman sent as a courier on the same train with the thin woman and the heavy woman? Either of these two could have carried the money without involving Miss Hellman. . . . And if the two women, as members of a resistance group, are subject to surveillance, why are *they* on the mission? Especially, why are two of them on the train, both exposing themselves to arrest when one would have served to nursemaid Miss Hellman? For the operation is certainly overstaffed: in addition to Julia herself, there are two people in Paris, two on the train, two waiting for Miss Hellman in Berlin, an unspecified number trailing Miss Hellman in Berlin, and the man on the train to Warsaw. Most of these could have been replaced with a single operative in Paris, bringing her the candy and the hatbox. Miss Hellman says that her instructions for the border crossing were conveyed to her in a note from Julia; this note could also have contained instructions for the Berlin rendezvous.

Other questions present themselves. Miss Hellman's uncertainty about when the train from Paris will reach the border is surprising in one who had lived for extended periods in Germany and France; could she have thought Berlin might be a suburb of Paris? If the heavier of the two women is on her way to Cologne, why does she stay on the train to Berlin, 250 miles beyond her stop? What is the significance of the box of candy, which makes repeated appearances but for no apparent reasons? When Miss Hellman is met in Berlin, why should her welcomers loudly announce that she will spend a few hours

with them and then leave immediately after telling her to go straight to Julia? Why is the money transferred in public? Why does Julia tell Miss Hellman to take the train for Moscow at Bahnhof Zoo, requiring her to double back several miles to the west and use a small station, where she would be more conspicuous than at a large one? When Julia tells Miss Hellman that her escort will be in a car to the left, how can she know not only the order in which various carriages would be cut into the long train but also whether Miss Hellman's own carriage would be positioned with the corridor on the left or right?

To all these questions, one might answer that truth is stranger than fiction. But besides these internal inconsistencies and puzzlements there are a great many more involving Miss Hellman's other published work and the world of reality.

In the account of the Paris-Moscow trip given in *An Unfinished Woman*, Miss Hellman says that she had a five-hour layover in Berlin and that the Soviets sent a young consular officer to look after her during that period. This functionary simply disappears from the tale as told in *Pentimento*. In *An Unfinished Woman*, Miss Hellman tells us that her trunk disappeared from the Berlin-Moscow train after the train left Germany. She records that the Polish conductor told her "I would receive it in Moscow, the Nazis were not barbarians, a mistake had been made, my name was German." . . .

There is an alternative version to all this in *Pentimento*. The Polish conductor's *sang-froid* is much less marked: "He was upset when he told me the German customs people had removed the trunk, that often happened, but he was sure it would be sent on to me in Moscow after a few days, nothing unusual, the German swine [non-barbarian swine, to be sure] often did it now." (p. 38)

The narrative of her trip to Moscow is one key passage in Miss Hellman's story of Julia; the other key passage recounts Julia's death in May 1938 and Miss Hellman's journey to London to claim her body.

On May 23 she receives in New York a telegram from London:

> Julia has been killed stop please advise Moore's funeral home Whitechapel Road London what disposition stop my sorrow for you for all of us.

The cable, signed John Watson, bears no address.

Miss Hellman's reaction to this is to get drunk for two days. On the third morning, she goes around to the home of Julia's grandparents, finds them out of the country, and engages the butler in an argument. That evening, Dashiell Hammett, who ordinarily does not like her to travel, persuades her to go to London to look into matters. Miss Hellman makes her way thither and proceeds to the funeral home, where Mr. Moore apologizes to her for his inability to cover the wounds on Julia's face, but remarks that the scars on the body are worse. She leaves for a brief time and when she returns the undertaker gives her a note:

> Dear Miss Hellman,
>
> We have counted on your coming but perhaps it is not possible for you, so I will send a carbon of this to your New York address. No one of us knows what disposition her family wishes to make, where they might want what should be a hero's funeral. It is your right to know that the Nazis found her in Frankfurt, in the apartment of a colleague. We got her to London in the hope of saving her. Sorry that I cannot be here to help you. It is better that I take my sorrow for this

wonderful woman into action and perhaps revenge. Yours, John Watson, who speaks here for many others. Salud.

Miss Hellman leaves the funeral home again, and when she later calls to get John Watson's address, she is told that the funeral man has never heard of Watson. He had received the body from one Dr. Chester Lowe at 30 Downshire Hill. Miss Hellman goes there and finds a large house converted to flats; Dr. Lowe's name is not on the nameplate. She then returns with the body to New York, sailing on "the old *De Grasse*."

In America, she goes to the house of Julia's grandmother, where the family shows no interest in receiving the body. She has it cremated and the ashes deposited in an unspecified location. In later years, she makes unsuccessful attempts to locate Julia's daughter, whom Julia had told her in Berlin was living with foster parents in Mulhouse, in Alsace. The family is notably uncooperative in her efforts. The tale ends years later with Miss Hellman meeting a distant cousin of Julia who denies any knowledge of the child's existence.

This account, like that of the trip to Berlin, is troubled with improbabilities. Why did Watson and his associates inform Miss Hellman rather than Julia's family? Why did he "count on" Miss Hellman's coming to London when he did not ask her to do so? Why did Julia's colleagues, once having gotten her out of Germany, bring her, gravely wounded, all the way to London rather than stopping in the Netherlands, Luxembourg, Belgium, or France? . . . Would they have taken a badly wounded, indeed, dying, woman aboard a Channel or North Sea steamer? Or, more improbably still in 1938, an airliner? And why did Miss Hellman return home on a ship that, as one can verify from a check of the records, sailed from Le Havre and called at no British port?

Diane Johnson, in a new biography of Dashiell Hammett, written with Miss Hellman's full cooperation, reports that in the spring of 1938 Hammett, while working in Hollywood, suffered a serious physical and mental breakdown. His friends put him on a plane to New York, where he was received by what Miss Johnson describes as a "terrified Lillian." On May 23, when Miss Hellman received Watson's telegram, Hammett was in Lenox Hill Hospital in serious condition, and did not leave there until the middle of June. Miss Hellman mentions none of this; but it seems on the face of it improbable that she would have left Hammett's bedside, and even more improbable that she would not have mentioned the fact in her account. (p. 39)

It is also inconceivable that Julia's death would not have come to the attention of the English authorities. . . . The undertaker would have insisted on a death certificate for the body, which no doctor would have given, for under English law, any doctor who cannot certify a natural cause for a death must notify the police, who then set an inquest in motion. And there would have been complicated legal formalities attendant on exporting the corpse. Yet two separate searches by Scotland Yard (made at my request in August and September 1983) failed to find any record of Julia's presence in London: no report to the police of her violent death, no record of the inevitable coroner's inquest. Nor are there any records of the corpse leaving the United Kingdom, in or out of Miss Hellman's company.

Finally, Miss Hellman tells us that she returned home on "the old *De Grasse*." . . . The *De Grasse* sailed from Le Havre on June 9, reaching New York on the 17th. The passenger list of the *De Grasse* for this crossing has survived, and Miss Hellman does not appear on it. Nor does she appear on the passenger lists of the *Normandie* or the *Aquitania* or any of the two dozen ships that arrived in New York from Channel and North Sea ports during the first through the third weeks of June. Was she traveling incognito? To have done so would have required a false passport, something useful in underground work but which she nowhere mentions as being among her effects.

In short, the account of the 1938 London trip is no more satisfactory than that of the 1937 Berlin one: it is improbable on its face, and its details are at sharp variance with the public record.

But the *Pentimento* account is not the end of the matter. Miss Hellman continues the tale in her 1979 commentary on **"Julia"** in *Three*. There she relates that many people had been trying to guess the true identity of Julia, but only one, a distant cousin, had succeeded. Miss Hellman tells us further that she cannot identify Julia for legal reasons: her publishers fear a lawsuit for invasion of privacy. As any author knows, publishers' lawyers do tend toward caution in these matters, but considering that the subject of this memoir had already been dead for thirty-five years when it was published, this caution seems excessive.

Still more interestingly, Miss Hellman writes that after the English edition of *Pentimento* appeared, a London physician to whom she assigns the pseudonym "Smith" contacted her claiming to have been raised in the house—30 Downshire Hill—from which the undertaker had obtained Julia's body. He objected, she says, to her having accused his father, also a doctor, of having issued a false death certificate for Julia. . . . Miss Hellman says that she knew she had changed the name of the physician from his real one to "Lowe," and that she *thought* she had changed the address as well. . . . Miss Hellman must know the real name of "Lowe" in order to know that she had changed it; if it was not the same as the real name of "Smith," then "Smith's" entire claim to knowledge of the affair is demolished. But if it is the same, Miss Hellman does not say so. . . .

There is more that Miss Hellman reports in *Three*. On her next visit to London following this first exchange, the younger Dr. Smith telephoned and proposed a rendezvous which he did not in the event attend. He then telephoned again, and there were confused background conversations with his infirm parent, who conveyed his approbation of Miss Hellman's having done "some justice" to Julia. Finally, the younger Dr. Smith told Miss Hellman that his family had always known the whereabouts and fate of Julia's daughter. The Germans, invading Alsace, had made straight for the house where she was living and had killed both her and her foster parents.

Miss Hellman, inexplicably, remarks that she was glad to hear the child was dead. She ends her 1979 commentary on **"Julia"** by justifying her reluctance to research the Smith/Lowe connection further on the grounds that no nation pays honor to its premature anti-Nazis. There is a classical fitness about this, for it is with a similar passage that she began her tale of Julia. It is no more intelligible here: the most distinguished British premature anti-Nazi was named Winston Churchill, and he and his fellows who opposed Hitler in the 1930's derived great honor thereby as long as they lived. It is preposterous to imagine that anyone in England could suffer by being recognized today as having been anti-Nazi in 1937 or 1938. All the passage does is to smear British society with the charge of pro-fascism. (p. 40)

Before leaving the topic of Julia altogether, we should notice an earlier appearance by her in Miss Hellman's *An Unfinished*

Woman. The reference comes in Miss Hellman's account of her early days as a manuscript reader for the publishing firm of Horace Liveright. One of Liveright's prize authors, Samuel Hopkins Adams, is working on a sequel to his novel, *Flaming Youth.* In order to update his knowledge of the sexual mores of the young, he interviews Miss Hellman and two of her colleagues. They cannot resist the temptation to guy him: one of them, named Alice, tells him that only her confessor has the full details of her experience, but that she can make him write them down, her father being a papal count. At this point in the narrative, Miss Hellman inserts a characteristic aside about Alice's later career: "Her father was a rich Jew from Detroit and she was already started on the road to Marxism that would lead her, as a student doctor, to be killed in the Vienna riots of 1934."

Here at last, if not long before, we must reject the long arm of coincidence. It is simply beyond believing that in addition to the undoubted existence of Muriel Gardiner, there were *two* other rich young American Marxist women at the University of Vienna medical school during the 1930's, and that both of them were personal friends of Miss Hellman. She mentions no such extraordinary coincidence in *Pentimento.* In Dr. Gardiner's *Code Name: "MARY,"* Alice no more appears than does Julia, nor does she appear—under any name—in the New York *Times* account of the February 1934 fighting.

It is, however, suggestive that having inserted Alice/Julia into the narrative of her own life, Miss Hellman kills her off—in *An Unfinished Woman* in 1934, in *Pentimento* four years later (after first mutilating her by the loss of a leg). Readers of a Freudian bent may have something to ponder here.

If the tale of Julia were the only example of untrustworthiness in Miss Hellman's memoirs, one might conclude that it represents no more than a bizarre aberration in the career of a writer otherwise deserving of the reputation for fierce integrity that she has claimed for herself and that has brought her widespread esteem. But if Martha Gellhorn is to be believed, Miss Hellman's account of her 1937 trip to Spain is as little to be trusted as her account of Julia. And other such problems in Miss Hellman's work exist as well. (pp. 40-1)

Another very large area in which Miss Hellman's latter-day memory does not square with history is her treatment of her former political opinions. Since this is one realm in which others—particularly in reviews of *Scoundrel Time*—have pointed out misstatements and inconsistencies in her account, our discussion of it here can be brief.

Miss Hellman has been hesitant to put a name to her political stand in the 1930's. She was, she says in one place, "nobody's girl"; in **"Julia,"** she suggests that she was somewhere between a Jeffersonian Democrat and a simple agrarian reformer, full of "the strong feelings the early Roosevelt period brought to many people." She does admit on two occasions that she was slow to see the faults in what she calls "Stalin Communism." But she also says, "The truth is that I never thought about Stalin at all."

This is a rather odd failing in someone who had visited Moscow during the Great Purge. Miss Hellman has an explanation for this, and she repeats it twice in the expanded version of *An Unfinished Woman*— once in the 1969 account of her 1937 trip to Moscow, and once in her 1979 reflection on her account of a later trip to Moscow. The explanation is that she did not know about the purge trials when she went to Moscow; the people at the U.S. embassy were full of dark stories about the

Soviet regime, but their malice toward it was so apparent that she did not believe them.

If she did not know about the purge trials before she went to Moscow, presumably some time in September or October 1937, she was remarkably ill-informed. By this time, the 1935 trial of Kamenev and Zinoviev, as well as their 1936 retrial (the first of the great show trials), and the 1937 show trial of the alleged Trotskyists, had all been held and fully reported in the press. Additionally, in 1937 Marshal Tukhachevsky and other members of the general staff had been tried *in camera* and their executions announced. If Miss Hellman was in fact unaware of all this, she had to be living in a cave.

That she was not living in a cave is evident from two statements published in the Communist party newspaper, the *Daily Worker.* The first, on February 9, 1937, just after the defendants in the 1937 show trial had been shot, appeals to American liberals to reject the proposal of John Dewey and Sidney Hook for a thorough investigation of the second Moscow trial; the statement defends the trial as entirely justified. One of the signatories is Lillian Hellman, "dramatist and author." The second, on April 28, 1938, states the belief of the signatories—Miss Hellman among them—that the third show trial was entirely fair, that the Soviet Union should be allowed to deal with its traitors in its own way, and that the United States is facing a fascist attempt to destroy democracy similar to that just nipped in the bud by the Soviet Union.

The fact is that the signatories had no independent evidence whatsoever as to the truth of the charges. They simply accepted, without a trace of skepticism, the monstrously false case of the prosecutor. Nor were they bothered by the oddity that defendants who had pled guilty were then tried. This alone ought to have alerted them that something other than the efficient and fair administration of criminal justice was afoot. Finally, it is inconceivable that someone who thus twice joined with others to defend Stalin's crimes "never thought about Stalin at all." (p. 42)

In 1980, Miss Hellman published a fourth memoir with the pregnant title of *Maybe.* Although *Maybe* is apposite to a study of Miss Hellman because it is about a woman who lies about her past, its substance need not concern us. Its theme should, however, for it is largely about memory, fallibility, and the need to be honest.

Miss Hellman interrupts her narrative at one point to interpose a reflection:

> It goes without saying that in their memoirs people should try to tell the truth as they see it or else what's the sense? Maybe time blurs or changes things for them. But you try, anyway. In the three memoir books I wrote, I tried very hard for the truth.

This dogged proclamation echoes two earlier passages. One appears in the preface to *Three:* "I tried in these books to tell the truth. I did not fool with facts." The other appears in **"Julia,"** and it is the most pointed of all:

> I think I have always known about my memory: I know when it is to be trusted and when some dream or fantasy entered on the life, and the dream, the need of dream, led to the distortion of what happened. And so I knew early that the rampage angers of an only child were distorted nightmares of reality. But I trust absolutely what I remember about Julia.

This is a remarkable statement: that part of her past which, when placed against the template of reality, displays the most incongruities, is just the part of her past about which Miss Hellman feels the surest.

Many of the facts misrepresented by Miss Hellman are not in themselves terribly important. Nor is her inaccurate reporting on various people she has known unique among memoirists. In time, if literary historians learn to use her cautiously, her contaminating effect on our knowledge of our times may prove minor.

The real issue posed by Miss Hellman's behavior is that she has manipulated millions of readers and moviegoers into admiring her as an ethical exemplar, and as a ruthlessly honest writer. Her eventual reputation in this regard—whatever might be the outcome of her suit against Mary McCarthy—will tell us a good deal about the health, intellectual no less than moral, of our literary establishment. (p. 43)

> Samuel McCracken, "'Julia' & Other Fictions by Lillian Hellman," in Commentary, Vol. 77, No. 6, June, 1984, pp. 35-43.

HILTON KRAMER

Of the many remarkable things to be noted about the life of Lillian Hellman . . . none was more remarkable than the quality of the sentiment that greeted its end. Even as the obligatory eulogies were delivered, they seemed to contain an unmistakable note of embarrassment—a grudging awareness that at the time of her death the reputation of Lillian Hellman was well on its way to becoming a shambles. (p. 1)

It was to be expected, of course, that she would be praised at the time of her death. The etiquette of the occasion called for panegyric, and there was no shortage of admirers to provide it in ample measure. She had a great many friends in positions of power, influence, and high reputation. She had many political allies who supported her various vendettas. And she had something else, too—the kind of money and position that enabled her to bestow (and withhold) rewards. For a good many years, moreover, it had been an established practice in the literary world for writers to lavish her work with the most extravagant encomiums; and her personal political history—notwithstanding the fact that she was the very model of the American literary Stalinist—had likewise won her a special status as, of all things, a moral heroine. The chorus of acclaim that had become an expected accompaniment to every new turn in Hellman's career had reached its fulsome climax in 1976 with the publication of *Scoundrel Time*—the third volume in the trilogy of her so-called "memoirs," and one of the most poisonous and dishonest testaments ever written by an American author.

It tells us a good deal about the temper of the times that this malicious and mendacious book, written to even old scores with her anti-Stalinist "friends," was widely hailed on its publication as a work of awesome moral probity. Reviewing it on the front page of *The New York Times Book Review*, Maureen Howard was moved to invoke the shades of Emerson and Thoreau as appropriate points of comparison, and ended her catalogue of praise with a reference to Camus—a writer whose entire career as an artist and a moralist represented a complete repudiation of everything Lillian Hellman stood for [see *CLC*, Vol. 8]. Oh, how her friends rallied round that detestable book! John Hersey spoke of Hellman as "a moral force, almost an institution of conscience" in the pages of *The New Republic*—the same *New Republic*, incidentally, whose

editor had just rejected a less favorable account of *Scoundrel Time* written by Alfred Kazin. And when Diana Trilling sought to set the record straight by answering the charges made against her and Lionel Trilling in *Scoundrel Time*, her publisher—who was also Hellman's publisher—promptly refused to publish what she had written on this subject, an act that elicited not the slightest word of protest from this "institution of conscience."

Yet it was undoubtedly with *Scoundrel Time* that Lillian Hellman, flushed with money, spite, overconfidence, and the incipient paranoia which dominated her later years, began to overplay her hand. Memories might be short and a sense of moral discrimination nonexistent in the well-heeled literary and theatrical society that had made her its heroine, but elsewhere history—and Lillian Hellman's role in it—had not been entirely forgotten. Writers who had reason to remember what the blight of Stalinism had once visited upon American political and cultural life began to speak up—not only Diana Trilling, but Murray Kempton in *The New York Review of Books*, William Phillips in *Partisan Review*, and Irving Howe in *Dissent*, among others. One focus of Hellman's attack in *Scoundrel Time* had been the anti-Communist Left and the liberals allied with it, and she specifically maligned the editors and writers of *Partisan Review* and *Commentary* for their alleged failure to come to the defense of those who were questioned about their Communist Party activities by Senator McCarthy's committee and other committees of the United States Congress in the late Forties and Fifties. She explained their alleged delinquency in the following manner:

> Perhaps that, in part, was the penalty of nineteenth-century immigration. The children of timid immigrants are often remarkable people: energetic, intelligent, hardworking; and often they make it so good that they are determined to keep it at any cost.

Her explanation, in other words, was the customary Stalinist charge of sellout, only in this case embellished with a touch of snobbery that was distinctly her own.

She had clearly gone too far and claimed too much. Writing in the aftermath of the Vietnam war and the Watergate scandal, she no doubt felt she could get away with anything—even Garry Wills's wholesale misrepresentation of the history of the Cold War that served as the introduction to *Scoundrel Time* . . . Yet favorable as the Zeitgeist was to the lies and accusations propounded in the pages of *Scoundrel Time* and its introduction, American intellectual life had not, after all, become so lost to the corruptions of revisionist history that there were not some writers left to remind us of the truth, and they now began to mount their counterattack—not only in their own defense, but in defense of veracity itself. In the critical responses of William Phillips, Diana Trilling, et al., to the fabrications and allegations of *Scoundrel Time*, we saw the first round in what was to become, by 1984, a sweeping exposé of the falsehoods that formed the very fabric of Hellman's autobiographical writings—those writings that brought her, as Robert Brustein correctly noted, "renewed fame, wealth, and the respect of the literary community, besides making her a model for independent women everywhere" [see *CLC*, Vol. 34].

It would be tedious as well as unnecessary to rehearse all the voluminous detail that is now on public record to show how often and how profoundly Lillian Hellman misrepresented, distorted, and ignored the truth in writing the autobiographical trilogy that consists of *An Unfinished Woman* (1969), *Pentimento: A Book of Portraits* (1973), and *Scoundrel Time* (1976).

The key documents in the case are Martha Gellhorn's "Guerre de Plume", Dr. Muriel Gardiner's memoirs, *Code Name: Mary* and Samuel McCracken's "'Julia' and Other Fictions" [see excerpt above]. Martha Gellhorn's piece is particularly hilarious and devastating in showing how virtually every word written by Hellman about her adventures in and on behalf of the Spanish Civil War and about her acquaintance with Ernest Hemingway—Gellhorn was married to Hemingway at the time—was sheer invention. Dr. Gardiner's *Code Name: Mary* is an account of her own work in the anti-facist underground in the Thirties—the work that Hellman not only fictionalized and embellished in her famous "memoir" of **"Julia,"** but in the story of which she falsely claimed to have played a role herself. Devastating, too, is Samuel McCracken's documentary research into the specific circumstantial detail on which the veracity of **"Julia"** must finally be judged. To say that Lillian Hellman emerges from this literature as a false and self-serving witness would be an understatement. She stands exposed as a shameless liar, and Mary McCarthy was only stating the truth when she said, in her famous charge on the Dick Cavett Show, that "Every word she writes is a lie." (pp. 3-4)

[The] question that inevitably arises is: on what basis *are* we being invited to admire either the woman or her work? Her claim to being considered an "institution of conscience" was bogus, for it was based on her political activities and these were wholly devoted to Communist causes in a period when Communism had shown itself to be a system of murder and terror. The "memoirs" that brought her wealth, fame, and honors of every sort are now shown to have been a fraud. Is it, then, on the basis of her superior contribution to the art of the drama that we are being asked to admire Lillian Hellman? Not at all. . . . For what we are being asked to admire, finally, is that fictional character which Lillian Hellman so adroitly created in her "memoirs" and which she performed so consummately in the "theater" that she had made of her life. What we are being asked to admire, in other words, is a carefully constructed illusion. (p. 5)

> *Hilton Kramer, "The Life and Death of Lillian Hellman," in* The New Criterion, *Vol. III, No. 2, October, 1984, pp. 1-6.*

MAURICE F. BROWN

Lillian Hellman's autobiographical writing is of interest because it extends the range of the form and explores significant theoretical issues. Hellman presents herself as both human being and writer in process, exposing her methods of recall, probing the multiple meanings of the past, and commenting on her problems as investigator and writer. Her focus has been on the nature of her personal involvement with herself and others, not on her career as dramatist nor on herself as a political person. Hellman's "life-record" is a full one: among her documents are the many detailed notebooks she began keeping when she was fourteen. While she turned to a fully-documented autobiographical format in *Scoundrel Time,* the body of her work presents a quest for the truth of life as experienced—for the poetic and philosophical life. Hellman confronts the tension in her motives in this passage from the Dashiell Hammett chapter of her first volume, *An Unfinished Woman:*

> Thirty years is a long time, I guess, and yet as I come now to write about them the memories skip about and make no pattern and I know only certain of them are to be trusted. I know about that first meeting and the next, and there are many other pictures and sounds,

but they are out of order and out of time, and I don't seem to want to put them into place. (I could have done a research job, I have on other people, but I didn't want to do one on Hammett, or to be a bookkeeper of my own life.)

Hellman is grappling with the issue central to any consideration of biography as a literary form. The historian's instinct and training lead him to seek pattern by arranging documents and memories chronologically and evoking meaning with the aid of the discursive reason. But memory is "out of order and out of time." Or rather, it has its own perverse order, its irrational metonymies and opaque symbolisms. The "memory work" is poetic in nature. As such, it bears relation to the dream work as Freud came to understand it. If the dream work sometimes takes the form of disguised wish fulfillment, the memory work should be viewed as a restructuring of the past to sustain and integrate a positive personality structure. Contemporary theoretical work by Erik Erikson in ego psychology suggests the complexity of the memory work, which involves self-creation through a non-rational process of rejection of "negative identity fragments." . . . [Disciplined] study of poetry, of myth and dream, of legend and folklore, and of subliminal psychological process has provided students of life-writing with insights and analytical tools by which we have gained access to the poetics of memory. We cannot accept mere "memory," even when well-documented, as valid life-history; and the truth revealed by critical probing of memory is more relevant to the structure of human personality and life than a bookkeeper's record, however adequate that might be to the historian.

For such probing in the context of literary criticism, William C. Spengemann has recently provided a promising approach. In *The Forms of Autobiography* he identifies St. Augustine's *Confessions* as a formal paradigm for Western autobiography, distinguishing three modes which are interwoven but given different emphasis in any given text. Drawing upon his paradigm, I shall consider Hellman's quest for her life and its appropriate form as a dialectical process in which life is presented as 1) history of the self (a chronological, developmental record of actions and conscious motivations); 2) philosophy (a process of discovery of the self); and 3) poetry (the presentation of self and its contexts in literary form). Spengemann's modes have a relationship to traditional classifications of autobiography: the memoir tends to take on the historical mode; confession, the philosophical; and apology, the poetic. But Spengemann's approach frees us from these casual nineteenth-century classifications to focus on literary process and style.

There are strong movements to all three of Spengemann's modes in Hellman's work. *An Unfinished Woman* (1969) opens in historical mode. The work's first half is structured chronologically in terms of life-stages identified by developmental psychology (childhood, latency, adolescence, etc.). . . . The later portion of the volume rests heavily on long sections of selected but apparently undoctored diary relating to Hellman's European trips and her involvement in anti-Fascist movements. At the end of the book, three portraits are presented—one of Dorothy Parker (her closest friend), one of Hammett (with whom she lived tumultuously for over thirty years), and one of the two black women of significance in her life. Hellman's second and third autobiographical volumes develop the two sides of her antithetical approaches to autobiography. She treats her personal life in poetic mode in *Pentimento* (1973), and her political life in a relentlessly documented historical mode in *Scoundrel Time* (1977). *Maybe* (1980) is subtitled "a story," but it is an extension of the mode of *Pentimento*. Perhaps Hellman is suggesting that life fragments that do not take palpable form can stand as contemporary fiction but not as authentic life-writing. Here autobiographical materials turn into a fascinating tone-poem, steeped in dream/alcohol/disguise states of semi-awareness with sharp, irrational leaps and turns of motive, character, and event. Hellman presents two metaphors for her autobiographical memory data: 1) memory is a hodgepodge of bundles of ribbons and rags, and 2) life is a puzzle with missing pieces. . . . At book's end we are left with six or seven characters, including Hellman, in search of an author. In brief, the sequence of volumes suggests an underlying philosophical concern which increasingly dictates autobiographical form. Hellman's life-writing turned into a quest for her "true" life—a quest which pushed both her historical and poetic commitments to their ragged outer edges.

Considered in the context of Hellman's entire body of work, much of *An Unfinished Woman* is a frustrated venture in autobiography. Long periods of Hellman's life—1931-35, 1942-44, and 1945-65—are omitted except for a casual reference here and there. Though we can perhaps excuse fragmented and bored treatment of her career, several relationships central to her personal life are practically ignored. . . . There is conscious concealment in that volume, and perhaps throughout her autobiographical writing, which represents an effort to avoid embarrassment of herself and others. And some segments of her life simply do not interest her. But more often, especially in regard to sexual relationships and political activity, Hellman seems to have been unable to arrive at a coherent sense of her actions and motives.

On the public side, mere inclusion of the European diaries in *An Unfinished Woman* suggests the conflict between her deeply personal human involvements and the vagueness of her public, political stance and its implications. The abrupt stylistic shift to direct documentation of life through diary entries seems almost desperate, with an extreme analogue, perhaps, in the later pages of Rousseau's *Confessions*. It took Hellman seven more years to come to terms with the trauma of the McCarthy witch hunt, and she was torn by her sense of the conflicting commitments and perspectives of her multiple audiences for that book. The intensity of Hellman's desire to find the truth about herself is present in the text, and even more in her later displeasure with the way she came to feel *Scoundrel Time* misrepresented her. Commenting on the book in 1979, she wrote:

> I am angrier now than I hope I will ever be again; more disturbed now than when it all took place. I tried to avoid, when I wrote this book, what is called a moral stand. I'd like to take that stand now. I never want to live again to watch people turn into liars and cowards and others into frightened, silent collaborators. And to hell with the fancy reasons they give for what they did.

The issue is larger than that of adequate expression of emotion and moral stance in a work. Much of the fascination of autobiography for the literary critic lies in the fact that the style and form of the work are as much a revelation of the "life" of the protagonist as the ostensible content. The problem of "misrepresented" life is in part a stylistic one—Hellman's quest for appropriate style is part of our data for her "life." At the age of sixty Hellman shifted from established dramatist to autobiographer. The considerable skill she had developed in dramatic projection of experience is evident in the power of her life-writing. And she was able to draw on experimentation with the short story form that went back to her twenties. The

strengths of these "apprenticeships," together with her strong sense for historical contexts of the action in her dramas, transfer to her work in autobiography. But Hellman had to learn to deal with the problem of presentation of memory in narrative and with the larger philosophical demands of a maturely conceived autobiographical form.

Hellman's early inclination and experience had prepared her to view life as a constantly shifting pattern. Childhood experiences were uprooting, complex, and confusing. Hellman learned to approach life as a mystery which offered her tantalizing clues to dimly-understood human motivations and relationships. . . . The stance to life carries over into Hellman's writing methods. Revising—"re-seeing"—became an obsessive gesture in her work in the drama. Her manuscripts for the final book for the original Bernstein-Wilbur-Hellman production of *Candide* include twelve complete and varying versions of it and twenty-five folders of individual scenes. Hellman's need was to find a stylistic correlative to her sense of life that was appropriate to writing her own life. In the effect known as "pentimento" in painting, she located a metaphor for the method appropriate to her vision. (pp. 1-5)

Hellman's stylistic solution involves identification of both past and present selves in sensory, emotional, active immediacy. Under psychoanalysis for long periods of time beginning as early as the nineteen-thirties, Hellman was familiar with eliciting otherwise unavailable life data by the use of psychoanalytic methods of recall and interpretation. In her writing conscious analysis and artistry enter the process to develop context through description and narration or, occasionally, to make a brief observation or judgment. Hellman's desire is to strip away defenses and distortions to reveal emotions, values, motivations, traits of character, and quirks of personality basic to the evoked living presence in action and event. She writes in a tradition which looks back through contemporary writers she admired, like Faulkner and Proust, to that master autobiographer, Rousseau. (p. 6)

The portrait, "Helen," in *An Unfinished Woman* signals the method and the mature autobiographical style which was to dominate *Pentimento*. "Helen" begins, "In many places I have spent many days on small boats." The generalized scene, unlocated in space or time, shifts as a camera focus might to a descriptive revery, anchored by references to beachcombing in New Orleans and Martha's Vineyard. A concrete and specific catalogue of her findings is given: "periwinkles and mussels, driftwood, shells, horseshoe crabs, gull feathers, the small fry of bass and blues, the remarkable skin of a dead sand shark, the shining life in rockweed."

Hellman's second paragraph places the reader in a time and place, and it turns her opening into the vehicle for an extended metaphor: "One night about six months ago, when I was teaching at Harvard, it occurred to me that these childish, aimless pleasures . . . might have something to do with the digging about that occasionally happens when I am asleep." And she proceeds to develop her metaphor in an extravagant metaphysical conceit: her head becomes the sandy beach from which the pole of her attention catches a card which answers "a long-forgotten problem," now solved as if arranged for her "on a night table." Mind has retrieved a set of scraps from memory "arranged" by the poetic of dream.

Opening paragraph three with "On that night . . . ," the narrative camera zooms in on a physical event which clicks in memory networks. The night is stormy. Hellman, disturbed by a noise downstairs, descends and sees a fallen, shattered light fixture at the foot of the stairs. (The mythic motif is introduced naturally and effortlessly.) Involuntary memory flows, presented in a long tumbling sentence which piles up different but now related experiences from time-sets clued by verbs in all the tenses but future and future perfect. . . . (pp. 7-8)

Something more of the brilliance and variety of Hellman's style in **"Helen"** can be suggested by brief glances at several transitional passages in the chapter. For example, she lays bare the process of her conscious metal work in a passage like this one:

> How often Helen had made me angry, but with Sophronia nothing had ever been bad . . . But the answer there is easy: Sophronia was the anchor for a little girl, the beloved of a young woman, but by the time I had met the other, years had brought acid to a nature that hadn't begun that way—or is that a lie?—and in any case . . .

Here the reader is involved in the writer's ambivalence, one keyed by verb alternation of past-perfect with present and simple past tenses, and by her alertness to possible deception in her image of herself as a child. An outburst of emotion provides a second daring and abrupt transition from Helen to Sophronia: "Oh, Sophronia, it's you I want back always. It's by you I still so often measure, guess, transmute, translate and act." The outcry moves us into two sharply realized incidents involving Sophronia and the child, Lilly, followed by a shift back to Helen gazing at a photograph of Sophronia and young Lilly and finding a protective love there that Hellman herself had not seen in all her fifty years of living with the photograph. From this base (the first half of the chapter), Hellman moves to consider other black/white relationships in her life, presented in narration and dramatic vignettes. The chapter ends with a final reconsideration of the overlap of black and white worlds in American society. At one point she crosses the invisible line between them into a guarded all-black world, and Helen roughly thrusts her back into neutral territory. Hellman intuits and evokes an unknown black world of shadows thrown by her own lighted experience, but she cannot enter or understand it, nor does she try.

I have hoped to suggest something of the complexity of an autobiographical style and form which Hellman casually refers to as "stream-of-consciousness." I do not wish to label it, but that label is surely incorrect. In **"Helen"** Lillian Hellman finds and presents many overlapping selves in a variety of places and times in relationship with two dead black women, and she enters upon a new and life-giving love and understanding of them, of herself, and of human experience. We begin to see, not merely through a glass darkly, but in a transparency of vision, placed in time but free from its distortions and tyrannies. Hellman turns flotsam and jetsam—scraps on the surface of life or partially buried by tidal ebb and flow—to present possession and wholeness. Hellman's past, with its distinctive shades and passions, comes alive in the present, illuminating present life in a new structure of understanding and emotional balance—a fresh sense of identity. Hellman would not claim transcendence of place and time for her art—her position is too rigorously existential for that. Rather, self is found—or perhaps only a small part of self—for right now in participation by Hellman and her involved readers in the on-going process of making art and thereby making life.

Hellman's work has helped move autobiography as a literary form into our time. Her autobiographical materials have shifted from dates and historical records to memory and its processes. Voice has shifted from objective, if personal, narration to presented and involved writer/protagonist, acting, creating, revising, speculating, and questioning. From a frustrated modernist style, Hellman has moved to multi-layered pentimento and to baffling tone-poem. As a quest for self and for answerable autobiographical style and form, Hellman's is a significant achievement in contemporary autobiography and a provocative probing of philosophical issues basic to the development of autobiography as a literary form. (pp. 9-11)

> *Maurice F. Brown, "Autobiography and Memory: The Case of Lillian Hellman," in* Biography, *Vol. 8, No. 1, Winter, 1985, pp. 1-11.*

ANITA SUSAN GROSSMAN

The outline of [Lillian Hellman's] long career which ended in June 1984 is now well known: the years as a successful playwright in the 1930s, beginning with *The Children's Hour* and continuing with *The Little Foxes* and *Watch on the Rhine;* her thirty-year on-again off-again relationship with Dashiell Hammett; her appearance in 1952 before the House Un-American Activities Committee, which led to years of being blacklisted for refusing to testify; her comeback on Broadway with the production of her play *Toys in the Attic;* and, beginning in 1969 in her seventh decade of life, her new success as a writer of memoirs with *An Unfinished Woman* (1969), *Pentimento* (1972), and *Scoundrel Time* (1974). The publication of the last-named account of her life during the McCarthy era raised a storm of criticism after the initial laudatory reviews, and led to questions about her veracity as an autobiographer that remain unanswered today. To many of her critics she seemed to have minimized her own Stalinist politics during the 1930s and 40s while lashing out at anti-Communist liberals among her contemporaries; more generally, she was accused of reducing a complex era in American political history to the crudest melodrama with herself as heroine. The work occasioned further unpleasantness for the author when her publisher, Little, Brown, attempted to stop publication of Diana Trilling's *We Must March My Darlings* after the author refused to delete from it a few passages mildly critical of *Scoundrel Time.* . . . Worse yet was the feud which developed with Mary McCarthy, who had called Hellman a liar on national television and was promptly slapped with a suit—still pending at the time of Hellman's death—for having caused her mental anguish (that is to say, for slander).

Since that time Hellman's reliability as a memoirist has been attacked in other quarters. In a 1981 *Paris Review* article, Martha Gellhorn, Ernest Hemingway's third wife, contested the unflattering portrait of the writer given by Hellman in *An Unfinished Woman,* offering a point-by-point rebuttal of her account of their meetings during the Spanish Civil War. For Gellhorn, as for other critics, Hellman was attempting to glorify herself by making others (in this case, Hemingway) look like knaves and fools. Along with this was yet another dispute concerning Hellman's veracity—the long-held suspicion that the **"Julia"** episode in *Pentimento,* made into a successful film in 1978, was fiction, not fact. Critics both friendly and unfriendly have raised the suggestion over the years, most recently after the 1983 publication of Muriel Gardiner's book about her real-life work in the anti-Nazi underground which parallels some of the exploits of Julia (who Hellman claimed was killed by the Nazis in 1938).

With hindsight it is easy to see that *Scoundrel Time,* as a political memoir, was bound to be controversial because of the strong passions still aroused by its subject-matter. The book reopened old wounds among writers of the Left, and revealed the extent of the split between the younger generation of revisionist historians and the older generation of anti-Communist liberals. Indeed, while reading reviews of *Scoundrel Time* and other books about the period, such as Victor S. Navasky's *Naming Names* (1982)—an account of the testimony offered by "friendly witnesses" in the entertainment industry—one is astonished to find opinion so polarized that there is not even consensus on what should be matters of sheer fact, let alone interpretation. . . . [Whether] one sees her as a heroine or not depends a good deal on how one views the period; judgment of her account seems to depend on the political persuasion of the reviewer. Some saw her as a figure of uncompromised integrity; others detected a lack of generosity towards others in her writing—a failing Hellman readily admits to and takes pride in. (When *Scoundrel Time* was republished along with the two earlier memoirs in a volume entitled *Three* in 1979, she wrote of herself in an afterword that "you do not forgive people.") (pp. 289-91)

One should note parenthetically that there is a certain irony in Gellhorn's attacking Hellman for caricaturing Hemingway after his death when he could not defend himself. Did not Hemingway do much the same to others in his posthumously published *A Movable Feast* a decade before, where he presented Scott Fitzgerald obsessed with an adolescent anxiety about the length of his penis, Pauline Pfeiffer as a predatory *femme fatale* breaking up the happy marriage of Ernest and Hadley Hemingway, and Gertrude Stein engaged in unsavory (sado-masochistic?) rituals with her longtime companion, Alice B. Toklas? In the case of Gertrude Stein, Hemingway was getting back at her for her earlier portrayal of *him* in The Autobiography of Alice B. Toklas as an immature young writer and unwilling father-to-be, unsure of everything save his wholehearted admiration for the older, successful Gertrude. (One has a certain feeling of compassion for the hapless Hemingway, skewered early and late in the memoirs of such formidable women.) All three autobiographers can be said to have engaged in self-promotion, although Stein is the most high-spirited and least censorious, her distortions of fact being more in the interests of comedy.

At any rate, Hellman's memoirs have been questioned over the years (more politely but just as insistently) on other grounds than those that Gellhorn chose to discuss. Reviewers of both *An Unfinished Woman* and *Pentimento* have occasionally suggested that the memory pieces "read like fiction" because of their dramatic vividness and clipped dialogue of conversations recalled verbatim forty years after the fact. Nowhere is this so true as in **"Julia"** with its suspenseful action and its mythic heroine, a millionaire American socialist who comes to Vienna to study medicine and joins the anti-Nazi underground. After losing a leg in the 1934 right-wing riots, she is visited in the hospital by Hellman and later gets Hellman to smuggle $50,000 across the German border during her next visit to the Continent. She dies heroically in 1938, her mutilated body lying unclaimed in London until Hellman arrives to take charge. Her illegitimate child, named Lilly, is presumably left to die in Occupied France by Julia's uncaring American relations, for when Hellman attempts to contact them about the child, they threaten legal action.

From the beginning of her career, Hellman always had a penchant for melodrama and a tendency to view people according to simple moral categories. This is especially true of **"Julia,"** with its stark opposition of good and evil. There are the heroic few, like Julia and Hellman, who struggle against fascism, and the corrupt many, who betray Julia or her memory: her former lover, the father of her child; her idle mother, living the good life at the expense of others; her snobbish grandparents, who want no part of Julia or her child; the false friend, Ann Marie, a shallow society woman; and Ann Marie's brother, who insults Hellman for her friendship with Julia, implying that they are lesbians. Even Hellman's friend Dorothy Parker, who was with her in Paris in 1937, here represents, along with her husband, a pleasure-loving frivolity that seems almost morally culpable in comparison with Hellman's dangerous mission. Those who feel that life offers more complex choices than the either/or situation presented in **"Julia"** may feel irritated by the sentimentality of its vision, and dismiss the story as hopelessly contrived.

But aside from the stereotypes and melodrama of **"Julia,"** there were other indications of fictionality. One was the strong similarity between the character Julia and a woman friend Hellman briefly mentions as "Alice" in *An Unfinished Woman* of whom she says, "Her father was a rich Jew from Detroit and she was already started on the road to Marxism that would lead her, as a student doctor, to be killed in the Vienna riots of 1934." Clearly the two figures seem to be the same woman, revived in **"Julia"** for further anti-fascist adventures under a new name. Then, too, there was the deliberate lack of surnames in a memoir that otherwise bristles with them. Hellman claimed in **"Julia"** that she did this out of fear of litigation from Julia's surviving relations and because she was not sure, even now, that Germans honored their premature anti-fascists. As John Simon has pointed out, both arguments are implausible, and what casts further doubt on the story is that no one, after the publicity generated by the 1978 film, stepped forward with information to identify Julia. Even the film's director, Fred Zinnemann, when questioned by a skeptical London *Times* interviewer, conceded, "It's difficult to understand how a wealthy American woman, presumably a woman of a well-known family, could have been so ill-used by the Nazis without some kind of outcry being raised."

When in fact someone did appear in 1981 to confirm a part of Hellman's story, it only served to cast further suspicion on Hellman's veracity. Muriel Gardiner's autobiographical account of her life in the anti-Nazi underground pre-War Austria, *Code Name "Mary,"* had many striking parallels with Julia's life . . . The parallels were enough to convince Gardiner that she was, at least in part, the model for Julia, especially in view of the fact that although she and Hellman had never met, they shared for many years a mutual friend, the late attorney Wolf Schwabacher, who related stories of the theatrical life to Gardiner and presumably had the opportunity to tell Hellman of Gardiner's exploits in Vienna. She wrote to Hellman in October 1976 asking whether Julia was a composite figure based in part on her experience, but received no reply; when questioned by the *New York Times* about the letter from Gardiner, Hellman said that she did not remember receiving it. "She may have been the model for somebody else's Julia, but she was certainly not the model for my Julia," she remarked to the *Times.*

Hellman's denial of any relationship of her account to the life of Gardiner is understandable, for she had an enormous investment in claiming that the story of Julia is real and just as she has told it. For one thing, Gardiner's story belies the tragic, bitter moral of **"Julia":** she escaped Austria to have a long and distinguished career as a psychiatrist; she found enduring love with her third husband, Joseph Budinger, leader of the Austrian Revolutionary Socialist Party, whom she met in the 1930s; her child, Connie, far from being murdered in France, is now herself the mother of six children in Aspen, Colorado. Gardiner's account of her adventures in Austria is flatter and less artfully narrated than Hellman's. Even so, for all its occasional dullness and mass of detail, it reminds us that people are far more complex than Hellman would have them. (pp. 293-95)

Hellman instead chose to write a morality play about good and evil, and as a result painted herself into a corner: "I think I have always known about my memory: I know when it is to be trusted and when some dream or fantasy entered on the life, and the dream, the need of dream, led to distortion of what happened . . . . But I trust absolutely what I remember about Julia," she writes in the story. In later interviews she remained rock-like in her insistence on the truthfulness of her memories: to a *Rolling Stone* reporter she said that writing **"Julia"** was difficult but that "nothing on God's earth could have shaken my memory about her." In fact, the evidence points strongly to Hellman's fictionalizing in **"Julia,"** using the story of Muriel Gardiner, combined perhaps with features of a real-life friend from her youth in New York, to create simultaneously the effects of mystery and veracity. The story of Julia's life gradually unfolds in the course of Hellman's elliptical narrative using flashbacks which relate the story on several levels of time, ending with a party in 1952 where she met the son of Julia's family's lawyer. In an afterword to the story, when it was reprinted in *Three* (1979), Hellman lets drop further tantalizing hints to deepen the mystery and substantiate her claims for the truthfulness of the story: only one person half-guessed the true identity of Julia, and the son of the English doctor to whose office the dying Julia was brought, calls Hellman up when she is in London years later to baffle her with his equivocations and secrecy. (She does learn from him, however, that Julia's child was definitely murdered by the Germans.) All these sequelae further the portrayal of Hellman herself as a heroine attempting to discover the truth about Julia and her child. Just as the living Julia stood for truth, Hellman, in recounting the story of her friend and seeking to locate the missing daughter, participates by extension in her noble mission. Needless to say, the entire effect of the story—its heroic portrayal of Julia and Hellman, and its air of mystery—depends on the assertion of Julia's real-life existence. Once we perceive that **"Julia"** is indeed a work of fiction, and that Hellman may well have fictionalized some of the other episodes in her memoirs, we read the pieces very differently. We may perhaps enjoy them as much, and be more appreciative of Hellman's creative powers; or we may instead simply feel disillusioned, seeing the **"Julia"** episode as a meaningless exercise in sentimental melodrama. In either case her work now belongs to a different realm of discourse. Is such fictionalizing a legitimate prerequisite of the autobiographer, or are we to agree with Martha Gellhorn that Hellman is an "apocryphiar?"

For Hellman apologists like Bernard Dick, there is no problem at all. She has fictionalized, but never mind: "Hellman was not aiming for factual accuracy in her memoirs; she was seeking the essence of events," he claims as though there were a natural antipathy between "facts" on the one hand and "the essence of events" on the other. (Do we live in a Platonic universe in which earthly life as we know it is but a dim shadow of the real?) At another point he attempts another argument: "What Gellhorn keeps forgetting is that Hellman is not writing history,

and that what might be reprehensible to a journalist might not be to a literary critic," implying that autobiographers need not be called on to tell the truth and that Gellhorn's insistence on veracity is merely the idiosyncrasy of her particular profession (we all have our narrow specialities). The same arguments have appeared of late in more general form in the work of literary critics of autobiography, who find the reader's intuitive expectations of veracity evidence of a naive and benighted literalism; for them a person who inquires as to the truth-value of an autobiography is cousin to the puritan who centuries ago scorned art for not being "true." Unlike biography, autobiography for these writers is inherently subjective and therefore must give up all claims to historicity. (pp. 296-97)

This is not to say that the autobiographer should be treated with automatic suspicion like a prisoner in the dock, his most trivial assertions requiring external verification. But just as one naturally looks for internal coherence within the text and perceives the self-portrait the writer has constructed from the totality of images he gives us, one may also need the additional perspective afforded by biography or history in order to make sense of his story—that is, to evaluate it in the proper context. Certainly in the case of a political figure like Hellman, one needs to know something of the period she is discussing, particularly in a polemical work like *Scoundrel Time,* with its accusations against her contemporaries and her dramatic presentation of her own behavior. In reading the book one cannot wholly separate the literary from the extra-literary experience: instead we are forced to take a stand on the case she presents. The passionate critics of Hellman's autobiographical writings may have been wrong-headed and biased by their own political orientation, but they paid the author the ultimate compliment of taking her ideas seriously, unlike those for whom she is merely a literary icon. Among the latter critics is Linda W. Wagner, in "Lillian Hellman: Autobiography and Truth" [see excerpt above], who sees no disharmony between the demands of art and veracity in Hellman's writing, and who blandly ignores the controversy swirling around so much of her work. At times Wagner contends that historical truth is irrelevant to Hellman's purpose, since she is attempting to capture a more subjective truth than that of historical fact, one that must be re-created by the literary imagination—a reasonable contention, as far as it goes—but in dealing with *Scoundrel Time,* a work whose claims to historical veracity would be hard to ignore, Wagner simply assumes that Hellman's account is unquestionably the last word on the subject and that it presents no problem in interpretation. (p. 303)

It is entirely understandable that, after the bitter disputes occasioned by *Scoundrel Time,* Lillian Hellman retreated into the quasifictional form and purely private content of her last autobiographical work. With *Maybe* there was no chance that anyone would come forth to contest her account because the matters narrated therein are so shadowy to begin with: Sarah Cameron, her friends and family, are seen through a blur of time and contradictory evidence, and the whole book is testimony to the impossibility of ever knowing anything real about such a mysterious, distant figure. Hellman's own inability to learn the truth about Sarah is evidently meant to have metaphysical reverberations for us, the readers, and give us a sense of the ultimate elusiveness of truth. (Hellman uses the poor vision that has afflicted her later years to symbolic effect here.) Unfortunately, the slightness of the story cannot sustain the weight of import it was intended to bear, as Hellman herself admits halfway through the book when she asks, "Why am I writing about Sarah? I really only began to think about her a few years ago, and then not often. Although I always rather liked her, she is of no importance to my life and never was. I do not know the truth about her or much of what I write here." By denying that her given subject-matter was either real or important to her, Hellman undermines the very structure she is erecting and works against her considerable gifts as a narrator. The book seems especially uncharacteristic of a writer who is best known for her uncompromising stand on issues and her passionate commitment, whether to individuals or causes. On the other hand, her last work can be seen as the logical extension of the tendency toward fiction already present in her earlier volumes: there, too, we found the famous elliptical, laconic style, the deliberate blurring of chronology, the juxtaposition of fragments of experience which lift her account out of the here and now to take on the dimensions of myth. The relative failure of *Maybe* was in the execution rather than in its conception as a literary experiment *per se*. That is, for all of her mystification about the Camerons, Hellman simply had not come up with a subject which could lay claim to significance, at least in the form she gave it. What was needed, perhaps, was more invention rather than less.

It remains to be seen whether Hellman left behind further autobiographical fragments for eventual publication which will cause us to reevaluate her collection of memoirs. Through the controversies attendant on her first three volumes, she found autobiography to be a risky business, particularly when—as in the case of "**Julia**" and *Scoundrel Time*—her need for a coherent aesthetic and moral vision went against the expectations of documentary veracity inherent in her chosen form. Perhaps such a conflict is inevitable in all memoirs by literary figures, with hers merely an extreme example of a general condition. Whatever the case, it seems likely that the issue of truth in autobiography raised by her work will continue to arouse debate among her readers for years to come. (pp. 304-05)

> Anita Susan Grossman, "Art Versus Truth in Autobiography: The Case of Lillian Hellman," in CLIO, Vol. 14, No. 3, Spring, 1985, pp. 289-308.

WILLIAM WRIGHT

On the evening of January 16, 1986, a play called *Lillian* opened at the Ethel Barrymore Theater in New York, a few blocks from the theater in which a half century earlier Lillian Hellman propelled herself into the American cultural scene with the success of her first play, *The Children's Hour*. . . . [*Lillian* is] a portrait of Lillian Hellman based on the playwright's three memoirs and a series of interviews on public television. For a writer to be the subject of such an autobiographical monologue was in itself a rare accolade and placed Hellman in an elite that included Mark Twain, Oscar Wilde and Gertrude Stein. And Hellman did not have to wait as long as the others; her Broadway canonization came eighteen months after her death.

The reaction of the newspaper critics to *Lillian* was unanimous. None quarreled with Hellman as a subject for evening-long focus; all criticized the dramatization for presenting only one side of her, the side that was tough, principled and courageous. Apparently they knew, as many in the audience knew, that there were other less praiseworthy sides to this complex woman. They also had reason to believe that the events and encounters

she described in the memoirs of her long and productive life were not necessarily true.

Had the play appeared ten years earlier, few would have questioned its validity. Two of Hellman's three memoirs had just enjoyed long runs on the best-seller lists without a murmur that they contained exaggerations, distortions or worse. The last memoir, *Scoundrel Time*, Hellman's account of her confrontation with the House Committee on Un-American Activities, provoked vociferous controversy but it always remained within the bounds of political disagreement. To be sure, she was accused of self-aggrandizement and of bending the truth to bolster her opinions, but it was not until the last five years of her life that her overall honesty came under a series of attacks. In January 1980, on national television, Mary McCarthy, a higher-ranking intellectual than Hellman but a less successful writer, accused her of being a persistent liar. (pp. 11-12)

For many, the cloud of doubt that had gathered over Hellman and because of her death was left undisturbed, only heightened curiosity about a woman with an array of claims to prominence, many of them beyond the reach of skeptics. She had written more hit plays than any other female playwright, all of them on serious themes. Only a small handful of American dramatists of her period—Eugene O'Neill, Arthur Miller and Tennessee Williams—are revived as frequently. Her three memoirs had not only broad sales, but were widely praised for their literary quality. Three of her six screenplays, written during Hollywood's *premier cru* years of the thirties and forties, are considered classics and were produced in collaboration with such film giants as William Wyler, Bette Davis and Samuel Goldwyn. She counted among her friends many of the most prominent people of her day. Her three-decade bond with that brilliant writer and enigmatic man Dashiell Hammett would, in itself, have assured her a place in the period's literary lore. (p. 12)

Interwoven through her variegated creative and personal life were passionate political convictions that placed Hellman at the center of the labor turmoil of the 1930s, the progressive movement of the 1940s and, as a victim, the radical witch hunts of the 1950s. Her sympathy for Communist Russia dominated her political vision and had such hurtful consequences, both before and after the McCarthy years, that, while the wisdom and clarity of her views could be questioned, her sincerity could not.

Hellman had a talent for placing herself at the scene of momentous events: Germany during the rise of Nazism, Russia during the purge trials, Spain during the civil war, the Russian front during World War II and Yugoslavia soon after Tito broke with Moscow. While other literary figures are forced to tint lackluster histories, Hellman was beneficiary of as colorful a background as America can offer: Southern Jewish forebears, some rich and avaricious, others poor and eccentric. As a child, she commuted between a New Orleans boardinghouse and Manhattan's Upper West Side. In her early twenties she circled the glamorous fringes of New York publishing and Hollywood filmmaking until she leaped to major prominence at the age of twenty-nine with the brilliant success of her first play. Her thirty-year career as a dramatist was punctuated with theatrical milestones and monumental feuds. . . . Indeed, her life had so much well-documented color, drama and achievement, it would seem to require no embellishment. Yet, according to her critics, embellish it she did in fashioning her memoirs with a skillful blend of fact, fiction and pure fantasy.

Hellman would hardly be the first American literary figure to indulge in touching up an unsatisfactory reality. It has gone on happily since Hawthorne inserted the "w" in his name, Whitman added six children to his family tree and Faulkner complained that his wife wasn't interested in his work. But if Hellman was not alone in truth-doctoring, she was definitely alone in the way she was publicly excoriated for it. Perhaps her rare and enviable combination of commercial and artistic success made her a tempting target. Her politics, extreme and rigid, may have brought her further enmity. Or her own combativeness may have provoked a compensatory aggression, just as her well-publicized moral displays made denigrators eager to catch her in a compromise. There was also the possibility that she had gone much further than others in manufacturing myths. Whatever the reason, the Lillian Hellman persona was tarnished by the suspicion that she was not the woman she claimed to be.

Even before her death, the life that had received such extensive and artful examination by the person who lived it seemed to need examination of a different sort, an impartial search for the truth behind the legend. That search would lead, after a thorough study of the memoirs, to lovers, friends, enemies, professional colleagues, widely scattered correspondence and manuscripts, a half century of interviews and news items. The picture that emerged was different in many significant ways from the portrait Hellman had painted of herself. The memoirs abounded in the self-aggrandizing fabrications she had been accused of, but she had also omitted episodes that did her credit and enhanced the sweep of her life. Both her frequent excursions from the rigid confines of nonfiction and her quirky omissions raised questions that defied simple answers. What was the reality behind her romance with Hammett—and what was the extent of his influence on her plays? Was she, in fact, a member of the Communist party—an allegiance she denied? Had she ever known Julia, whom she claimed as her closest friend in her memoirs' most famous chapter? And what, finally, were the reasons that compelled her to distort the circumstances of an already extraordinary life?

The real Hellman was a woman far more complex and controversial than the paragon of *Lillian*. Funny, tough, courageous—but also temperamental, obstinate, dogmatic and, at times, unscrupulous. . . . Her life as she really lived it proved to be much more intriguing than the Hellman of the memoirs, much more dramatic than that of any character in her plays. (pp. 13-14)

William Wright, in his Lillian Hellman: The Image, the Woman, *Simon and Schuster, 1986, 507 p.*

Christopher (David Tully) Hope

1944-

South African novelist, poet, short story writer, scriptwriter, nonfiction writer, critic, and author of children's books.

A citizen of South Africa who emigrated to England in 1975, Hope has earned praise for his witty observations on the social problems of his homeland. In his fiction, he draws from the techniques of such contemporary satirists as Herman Charles Bosman and Tom Sharpe, contending that humor is the only means by which individuals can cope with the contradictions and absurdities of apartheid. His protest of the South African government is softened by an ironic narrative tone that has become a standard element of his writings. Although some critics cite weaknesses in his handling of dialogue, many are impressed with Hope's poignant humor, his metaphorical language, and the pathos with which he infuses his portrayals of protagonists victimized by discrimination. Phil Goffe stated: "Hope's art lies in creating fictional characters rendered with precision and force so that the real horror of their actions is suggested, while the comic control of the writing disarms the reader and sets him up for the satiric bite which is its intention."

Hope's first novel, *A Separate Development* (1980), centers upon Harry Moto, a dark-skinned Afrikaner teenager whose quick-witted impudence and wry observations prompted Darryl Pinckney to liken him to Holden Caulfield, the protagonist of J. D. Salinger's novel *The Catcher in the Rye*. When Harry's racial ancestry becomes a topic of debate among residents of his suburban town, he moves to a black district, where he finds the lifestyle better suited to his personality. Later, after being falsely charged with rape, Harry relates his life story from a prison cell with a buoyant humor that belies the injustices for which he has suffered. Banned in South Africa upon its publication, *A Separate Development* was well received by critics for its humor, energy, and credibility. In his next work, *Kruger's Alp* (1984), a slapstick parody of John Bunyan's moralistic tale *Pilgrim's Progress,* Hope makes use of allegory, myth, and dreamlike imagery to chronicle the adventures of a former priest's search for the legendary "city of gold" that supposedly was built near Geneva by exiled Boer revolutionary leader Paul Kruger in 1900. While some critics contended that considerable knowledge of South African history is required to understand this novel, most applauded Hope's metaphorical images and farcical plot complications. Ron Loewinsohn commented: "[Mr. Hope] is an intelligent and gifted writer, with an eye for realistic detail and an incisive but fluent style that together give substance to his allegory and complement his mordant wit."

Hope's next novel, *The Hottentot Room* (1986), examines the static lives of exiled South Africans living in London. These characters spend their days drinking in a dismal pub, enduring the present by living through their memories of the past. Critics noticed revealing parallels between this novel's stagnant atmosphere and the plights of present-day expatriates. *Black Swan* (1987) is the ironic tale of Lucky, a mentally retarded black South African boy whose disability allows him to defuse the grim realities of his country's political situation. While the protagonist's guileless vision serves to represent the beliefs of the South African people, the government regards him as a subversive, and the novel ends with Lucky in prison, unaware

that he has been sentenced to death. Praising its cohesive imagery and poignancy, critics generally regarded *Black Swan* as among Hope's most moving works.

Hope's poetry and short stories share many of the concerns of his novels. *Cape Drives* (1974) includes confessional verse describing the difficulties of coping with feelings of displacement in an authoritarian society. *In the Country of the Black Pig* (1981) contains poems which explore the dilemmas of white South Africans while ridiculing the delusions postulated by proponents of apartheid. Impressed by Hope's blend of imagination and social realism, Douglas Dunn commented: "It is heartening . . . to read a poet who can balance conscience and compassion with literary good taste, distributing powerful ironies and pictures with discretion as well as concern." *Englishmen* (1985) is a long epic poem that mocks the complacency of white South Africans while attempting to trace the origins of Afrikaner nationalism. Included among the characters of this work are the ghosts of English settlers, implying that the English will always dominate South Africa. *Englishmen* was acclaimed for the warmth that Hope ironically instills in his unpleasant characters, but most critics found its apathetic tone an unwelcome change from his usual fervor. Hope's short stories collected in *Private Parts and Other Tales* (1981) satirize the self-serving attitudes of many people involved in antiapartheid movements. S. M. Mowbray stated that the stories depict "a strange, bitter world of fear, hatred and desperately illogical self-justification, of fanaticism and wilful blindness. They provide ample evidence of the author's prickly, witty, original talent."

Hope has also written several plays produced by South African television, including *Ducktails* (1976), *Bye-Bye Booysens* (1979), and *An Entirely New Concept in Packaging* (1983). In addition, he has published *White Boy Running* (1988), which combines a chronicle of his return to South Africa in 1987 to observe the country's national elections with autobiographical sketches of his childhood and adolescence. Hermione Lee observed: "Writing in the admirable, unsympathetic, formidable tradition of cold satirists like Orwell or V. S. Naipaul, Hope sees nothing but apocalypse in view."

(See also *Contemporary Authors*, Vol. 106.)

THE TIMES LITERARY SUPPLEMENT

Christopher Hope is a White South African poet who explains in the blurb to his new collection [*Cape Drives*] that his work is an attempt to come to terms with a society within which he is spiritually displaced. Not much of this, however, emerges as an immediate issue in the poems themselves; for the most part they are sinewy, sardonic, descriptive pieces, tough and faintly Lowellish in their imagery but without the complex moral depths which the blurb seems to promise:

> Fifty years he savaged the parish
> In his bull-nose Morris:
> Commanding the field behind the wheel,
> Wrestling the gears, foot on the engine's throat.
>
> He sped his Mass until its Latin changed
> To a high-pitched hum;
> Spoke it like a Roman who'd seen
> Ceremony dry like saliva after years of saying.

These poems, too, seem to bull-nose briskly through the South African scene, crammed with dynamic verbs and craggy epithets but avoiding any self-indulgent grit. Their verbal burliness is controlled by a taut emotional discipline which allows for moments of metaphorical *brio* or clinching wit, heightening without overcolouring their tenacious social realism. . . .

Mr. Hope's poems do not easily yield sympathy to their subjects, but their emotional tight-lippedness is not to be mistaken for neutrality. It seems rather the necessary stringency of a poet who needs to feel his way back into an increasingly alien world by a process of precise observation, clarifying and defining its textures so that perception itself becomes a kind of moral act.

> *"Revving Up," in* The Times Literary Supplement, *No. 3772, June 21, 1974, p. 667.*

ROGER GARFITT

Christopher Hope's first collection [*Cape Drives*] centres on his situation as an English-speaking White South African, a situation, as he puts it, of a man 'fearing displacement, not realising that he is already displaced.' Satire is his natural medium, and the natural target the Afrikaner: but it is a mark of his intelligence that he understands his opponent well enough

to get inside as well as under his skin, and uses this understanding to set up counter-currents within the poetry, creating the sense of a world as contrary as the mind of his planter, who

> since his boy's a clod
> Who wants smashing, plans a trip to France
> To trace the Huguenots who'll purge his blood's
> Distemper, got upon a Coloured maid,
> Restoring whitewash to a stained facade.
>
> (p. 119)

The problem of satire is always to contain its energy. While some of the structures here seem a little random, and some of the more *outré* images may reflect laziness rather than imagination, too ready an acceptance of association's free gifts— 'Old men's bellies,' for instance, 'show like whales', 'their eyes are oysters', so 'their laughs are snails', or there are Greeks in their corner cafés 'whose minds are mosquitoes behind dark netting'—the best and most characteristic of this work is thoroughly achieved, making an effective use of strict forms, whether in the sonnets of ["**Cape Drives**"], or in the ironic quatrains of "**An Affair of the Heart**", or in this rollicking take-off of Kipling:

> O it was dop and dam and a willing girl when we were young and green,
> But Jewish money and the easy life are the ruin of the Boerseun,
> He disappears into the ladies' bars and is never seen again
> Where women flash their thighs at you and drink beside the men,
> And sits with moffies and piepiejollers and primps his nice long hair:
> 'You'd take him for an Englishman,' said Kobus Le Grange Marais.

Christopher Hope adds to one's growing impression that some of the most assured new poetry in English is now coming from writers overseas. (pp. 119-20)

> *Roger Garfitt, "In Retreat to the Edges," in* London Magazine, *n.s. Vol. 14, No. 4, October-November, 1974, pp. 113-20.*

EDNA LONGLEY

[In *In the Country of the Black Pig* Christopher Hope accumulates] odd details until the overall impact exceeds their sum. "**At the Country Club**", one of his South African poems, throws in shocks like 'This week's tennis prize is a personalised Luger', as it builds up to a more roundly resonant climax:

> Beneath the trees which hide the security fence
> nannies doze among children who pick at their
> soft black undersides as if they were fallen fruit.

As opposed to just railing at the system, Hope explores the white paranoia and self-deception that knows 'deep down / they go on dreaming of driving us into the sea, / not caring even to notice how well we swim / or that we are all in the middle of nowhere'. This poem ends on a fine ambiguity: 'Dying will be the last thing we do for them'. Hope's strategy relies on good endings, because it risks not only a prose content but a prose rhythm. Often elongated beyond ten syllables, and more usually arranged in slabs than in stanzas, his lines can discard even the skeleton of metre: 'Everyone says beyond the town lies freedom, a new hinterland / but difficult to identify because its name is changing constantly'. Also, it is possible to overdo the flat-toned moralizing of landscape, however suitable a terrain South Africa may be.

Edna Longley, "Fencing with Forks," in New Statesman, Vol. 102, No. 2629, August 7, 1981, p. 19.

PETER BLAND

[Christopher Hope's] South African poems (emotion recollected in love and anger) have a pace and urgency of imagination rare in current English poetry. The 'realities' prior to his poems are as dangerous as those in Ulster or Brixton and they inform his best work with a similar sense of 'things falling apart.' The colonial tea-garden is going to pot, 'only rust eats at the tables.' Though he remembers a time when 'the African sun itself was taken and hung out over the trees / like a brass gong.' . . . There's a gusto and physicality to the voice. Hope writes as though he's never been hemmed in. I got the same whole-hearted enjoyment out of his new book *In the Country of the Black Pig* as I did from Hecht's *Venetian Vespers* or Jim Baxter's *Jerusalem Poems* or Ferlingetti's marvellous *The Old Italians Dying* or Allen Curnow's latest flowering in downtown Auckland. In all these instances there's a controlled generosity of response to the world about us that one can only be grateful for. Sure, Hope's less polished than some of the above, but the same feeling is there. ["**In the Country of the Black Pig**"], together with "**African Tea Ceremony**," "**Coming Round**," "**Atonal Blues**," and "**At the Country Club**," are brilliant evocations of South African racialism in crumbling retreat. . . . Closer to home Hope looks at British funerals "**On Highgate Hill**" . . . 'the black hearses slip by, pooled in gloss' . . . and nervously watches his hands rebel and run off in the surrealist poem "**Pen in the Mouth**." He's beginning to look at the English scene with increasing astringency. There *are* touches of verbal over-kill in poems like "**Sterling**" and some slackness in the "**Songs for Masters**" sequence, but the overall quality of imagination at work here is outstanding. (p. 82)

Peter Bland, "Exiles at Home," in London Magazine, n.s. Vol. 21, No. 7, October, 1981, pp. 79-82.

JAMES LASDUN

[In Christopher Hope's first novel *A Separate Development*, the] hero, a young, apparently white, South African called Harry Moto, finds himself in a predicament akin to that of Forster's Aziz and Paul Scott's Hari Kumer. A suspicion that he may have a touch of the tar brush is confirmed just as he has been caught in a highly compromising position with a girl at the school matric dance. Fearing that particularly gross manifestation of Apartheid, the Immorality Act, he lights out for the Indian territory of Koelietown, there to seek the invisibility that shrouds coloured people living on the fringes of white society.

Unlike Forster or Scott, Hope has chosen to treat his theme in an almost exclusively comic way. True, there is no shirking of the humiliation and violence suffered by non-whites in South Africa, but Harry Moto's account of his life gives the same breezy, light-hearted attention to an attempt to torture him, as it does to his first adolescent gropings or his comic antics as an assistant salesman selling skin bleach to black villagers. This may be a question of the style which, while always energetic and sometimes wonderfully vivid, seems incapable of much tonal variation. Or again, it may be that Hope is making

a subtle point, whereby the most eloquent possible damnation of a political system based on a quibble about colour, is a refusal to treat it seriously.

Either way, however, the result is much the same. *A Separate Development* is an amusing, readable book, which one enjoys as one might enjoy a mildly satirical farce by Tom Sharpe. Nothing wrong with that, but it is perhaps a trifle disappointing in a novel that has apparently been suppressed, if only temporarily, in South Africa. This one will not have them choking with shame in Pretoria. (p. 38)

James Lasdun, "Flashes of Wit," in The Spectator, Vol. 247, No. 8000, November 7, 1981, pp. 37-8.

DARRYL PINCKNEY

Holden Caulfield has turned up in an unlikely place: South Africa. He is now called Harry Moto, and he is the hero of *A Separate Development*, the first novel of the South African poet Christopher Hope. A clever, cheeky Catholic schoolboy, Harry has done what is forbidden—fled the white suburbs to live and work among the Coloureds. His is a particular and baffling form of heresy against Afrikaner society, and it is from a prison cell that Harry tells the story of his decline and fall into the back streets and alleys of racial classification.

Before Harry's fall, he has the worries of all 17-year-olds: flat feet, girls, deranged parents, boring school. Harry is also sensitive and self-conscious about two other things: his "breasts," or "fleshy hillocks," as he refers to the abnormal development of his chest, and the darkness of his skin. His classmates tease him about both.

The problem of Harry's skin, however, is crucial. "It worried my mother and father. It was never something we could discuss over the breakfast table—though it lay between us, somewhere above the salt and to the left of the marmalade, all the days of my boyhood." . . .

Harry and his friends are aware of the peculiarity of their society. "I'm not for *apartheid*, mind you, but I think you have to admit people are different," one of his chums says. Harry is struck by the invisibility of servants. The garden boys tending the pools of his richer friends, the janitor at his school—they are all called John. . . .

Harry's world is flat; teen-agers were put there to "die of boredom," boast about girls and engage in combat with their dotty dads, and anyone who attempted to escape that world would, apparently, fall off the edge. The state controls every aspect of daily life, and there are many rules. There is much paranoia among the adults Harry knows; they carry weapons, invest in costly burglar alarms, fret that their daughters will be raped, worry over possible infringements of the Immorality Act. (Paranoia, someone said, is just having the facts.)

Harry is one of the "bad eggs boys," disgusted by the mafia of saints who pray and toady at the front of the class. Years of the lunacy of Catholic education have acquainted him with the road to perdition. Harry embarks on this road in a hilarious scene: the big dance after matriculation exams. Everything that could go wrong for an adolescent does so, culminating at the moment when Harry is caught with his date, Mary, just as his trousers fall down. By the time Harry gets home, the good friar who saw him in this situation has reported his crime—hashish and drinking have been added—and his parents are on the rampage. "It didn't matter. I was out."

Being "out" means slipping into the black world of Koelietown, where "the living were packed in like the dead in the old cemetery next door." Harry becomes a runner for a clothes retailer, an Indian named Raboobie, and learns the tricks of survival and the importance of camaraderie among outlaws. Race relations are just as intricate in Koelietown as elsewhere, but Harry's ambiguous skin tone is an advantage there. His social education is also a political one. About passive resistance Harry remarks: "They'll just drive their Jags and Pontiacs slap over you. Without even noticing, could be. No hard feelings, right. Ooops! Sorry! Didn't see you lying there, ahem."

Whites force the merchants out of Koelietown, and Harry gets a job driving for a salesman of "Gloria Sunshine Skin Care Products." Wigs and skin bleaches are among the items sold. "Everything I sell adds up to one thing, Harry," the salesman tells him, "and that's a damn big bucket of whitewash. In a way I think of myself as being a bit like Saint Paul. More than a businessman, a *missionary,* that's me. Except that I'm not out for souls. I'm in the business of saving skins."

Later, circumstances force Harry to accept even more menial "kaffir work," but still the invisibility he craves is impossible. His former girlfriend, Mary, recognizes him, and eventually they are caught in *flagrante delicto* once again, not by a teacher but by the police, who have been pursuing Harry.

[*A Separate Development*] is a wildly funny novel, and Christopher Hope sustains its ironic tone even during Harry's brutal interrogation. The jaunty manner of Harry's narration is in striking contrast to the bitter experiences he relates. There is much savage ridicule of apartheid and even the national psychoses about race and sex, which find expression through the apparatus of the state. As in most restricted societies, there is little real history available, only propaganda, and Mr. Hope makes great fun of that. The message, however, is not so funny, and in a society where no one is permitted *not* to have an official, legislated identity, it is significant that the story Harry tells is called *A Separate Development* and not *A Separate Peace.* (p. 10)

> Darryl Pinckney, "Fictions of Race," in The New York Times Book Review, *December 20, 1981, pp. 10, 19.*

JUDITH CHETTLE

Exceptions do not always prove the rule, for Christopher Hope's *A Separate Development* is quite singular in its attempt to deal humorously with contemporary South Africa. South Africa's political system and troubles have long been the concern of the country's best writers, and Hope is following a very well-worn path. But he has written a book that despite the gravity of its concerns is very funny.

Though comedy in the classic sense has always been regarded as close to tragedy, writers on South Africa for understandable reasons have felt humor to be out of place. But humor not only intensifies the tragic aspects but also adds credibility to the characters—they sound more like ourselves.

The hero of Hope's book, Harry Moto, is arrested for contravening the Immorality Act. He buys time from the policeman in charge, who sees South Africa's problems in sweeping philosophical terms, by promising to write an explanation of his own separate development. The policeman is expecting another *Cry, the Beloved Country,* but in describing Moto's journey from a member of the graduating class in the white St. Bon-

aventure school to a bus boy at a drive-in restaurant, Hope neatly turns most of South Africa's shibboleths on their heads. . . .

Hope has an ear for the way people really talk, and though his characters are never idealized, his sense of humor emphasizes the absurdity of many of South Africa's laws and conventions.

> Judith Chettle, in a review of "A Separate Development," in Book World—The Washington Post, *January 3, 1982, p. 7.*

ANTHONY DELIUS

Until recently South Africa's literary protesters against apartheid have tended to be solemn if not dour. But there has also been from quite early on in the country's literature another, less morally glum, vein of comment on its social practices. It may be said to have originated with Roy Campbell's *Veld Eclogue,* though this poet's satire later became concentrated on English sexual habits. It emerged again in another form in the prose tales of Herman Charles Bosman, whose story "The Yellow Dog" is a superb brief satire on racial antagonism. But for a while humour in this field seemed to dry up. Tom Sharpe's early books showed glints of satire, but he was not a local product. Now, however, Christopher Hope, a talented South-African-born poet, has taken to prose to give us an exuberant view of the painfully funny side of apartheid.

His novel, *A Separate Development,* . . . was awarded the David Higham Memorial prize. It is the story of a young man of dubious colour, neither black nor white, not even identifiable with any certainty as a "coloured." . . . [He] finally winds up in Security Headquarters clad only in a blanket, charged with interracial rape and writing the story of his life as a "statement" for Boss in a desperate attempt to save his testicles from a further application of the electric shock machine.

One of the themes of the novel is that however inconspicuous a South African attempts to make himself, he will never escape the attentions of the Security Police. They are the all-seeing male nurses in the madhouse which South Africa is increasingly becoming. . . . In charge of all sits the Head of Security reading Trevor Huddleston's *Naught for Your Comfort* and Alan Paton's *Cry the Beloved Country* to increase his knowledge of the more subtle threats to party and country.

In his new book of short stories, *Private Parts,* Hope carries his readers further into the sunlit realms of South African dementia. The whites are shown becoming more fixed in their crazed attitudes and the blacks react more hopelessly to them. In **"Ndbele's People"**, a little black priest has gone quietly mad in an attempt to challenge the white community out of its racial prejudices by ministering to them as if the situation was absolutely normal. He finally spends his time making strange papier-mâché figures of his parishioners and populating the church garden with them. Perhaps the most foreboding preview of what the policy of apartheid is accomplishing for blacks and whites is given in **"Learning to Fly"**, where the toughest victim of police torture turns up after the revolution as the chief torturer himself.

No doubt the contemplation of apartheid and its effects still fills Hope with savage and hair-raising comic inventiveness. Yet [*Private Parts*] seems to strain even harder both to be funny and to evoke horror. The effect is to create a feeling of sinking into an underworld of calcified demons.

Anthony Delius, "Brothers in Bedlam," in The Times Literary Supplement, *No. 4153, November 5, 1982, p. 1231.*

JOHN MELLORS

Christopher Hope has shown in his novel, *A Separate Development,* how to use ridicule to deflate the pernicious pomposities of the South African establishment. In *Private Parts* he satirizes, equally successfully, the radical chic flank of the protest movement. (pp. 112-13)

Other targets for Hope's stinging wit are the Roman Catholic Church, redneck Boer farmers, racialist bigots, black power thugs, ineffectual liberals, and hypocrites in every social stratum. In ["**Private Parts**"], about a Calvinist 'Dominee', who lectures in theology even when he is not in front of a class, Hope has evident sympathy for his victim. The dominee is obsessed by the backs of his black maid's knees, revealed to be 'smooth and honey-coloured' when she stoops to put a teapot down. It is sex that leads the dominee to lie to the police—and, in the pulpit, to relish his own words as he attacks skimpily-dressed women who 'disclose the thighs, which are sexually mixed up in a man's mind with the private parts of a woman'.

Hope is too good a stylist to embroider his narratives with any unnecessary flourishes. His descriptions are sharp, exact and relevant. The reader can almost feel 'the mechanical summer sunshine that seemed to switch itself on every morning and rose to an unvarying solar whine, shrillest at noon'. You can picture, too, the 'girls in bikinis shining like buttered kippers under their suntan oil'. Not every story succeeds. There are startling images in **"Whites Only"**, but the characters do not come to life. One cannot believe in either the self-assured dwarf, who comes out of the night to ask impertinent questions, or the sexy 'Grannie', who stands naked to the waist in front of her Bantu history class, showing the black labourers her white and powdered breasts, shaped like rugby balls. However, the failures are few, and all in all *Private Parts* is a worthy successor to *A Separate Development.* (p. 113)

John Mellors, "Love and War," in London Magazine, *n.s. Vol. 22, No. 11, February, 1983, pp. 112-15.*

S. M. MOWBRAY

Private Parts (which is not pornographic, despite its catchpenny title) is a collection of sardonic and disturbing short stories, set in South Africa and shot through with the absurdities and injustices of apartheid. There is much about university life, with rich white students playing at being radicals and ... a Calvinist theology lecturer trapped ridiculously in danger and lust by a mercy trip with his innocent black housekeeper. There are allegorical fantasies, in which the whites are seen as stupid and brutish; and scenes of Catholic school life in which the white boys are far more humane in their attitude to blacks than their Christian Brother mentors. . . . Fantasy, in fact, is Christopher Hope's long suit. In an ugly story about interrogation techniques, the black hero confounds his Boer questioner by flying out of the high window from which he has been invited to jump. Readers unfamiliar with South Africa will find these stories odd, and every reader will find them frightening. They show a strange, bitter world of fear, hatred and desperately illogical self-justification, of fanaticism and wilful blindness.

They provide ample evidence of the author's prickly, witty, original talent.

S. M. Mowbray, in a review of "Private Parts and Other Tales," in British Book News, *March, 1983, p. 194.*

D. J. ENRIGHT

Myth is no longer able to give shape and significance to what Eliot, with *Ulysses* in mind, called "the immense panorama of futility and anarchy which is contemporary history". In this line of endeavour we have progressed—or regressed—to harsh fantasy. Christopher Hope's new novel [*Kruger's Alp*] is in some sense a moral history of South Africa, from the simple believing Boers to the sophisticated and opportunistic "New Men", akin to Salman Rushdie's picture of Pakistan in *Shame,* and—behind that—to the Germany of Günter Grass's *Dog Years,* where the refrain "There was once" is the equivalent of Hope's "And I saw in my dream". . . . Perhaps this kind of fantasy, an extrapolation from fact, is now the predominant mode of the novel. If so, it is good news for fiction, but bad news in respect of the reality in which we have to live. The world cannot be soberly described or usefully criticized; it can only be choked over.

The framework of *Kruger's Alp* is a pilgrim's progress through a wilderness about to be burned with fire from Heaven, or indeed (the term used is "the Total Onslaught") from all sides, to "that shining city on the hill" which, according to legend, Paul Kruger prepared for "the pure remnants of the *volk*". This house of many mansions, the story has it, was established with the help of the gold Kruger took with him when fleeing the British in 1900. The hero of Hope's first novel, *A Separate Development,* fell among philosophers: important conclusions were surely to be drawn from the case of a white boy who turned into some sort of kaffir! Here, ex-Father Blanchaille has fallen among accountants: all that matters now, behind the façade of "the sanctity of separate lavatories", is money—money working wonders, moving in strange directions, being salted away here and there. Christian duty means "get what you can and keep it"; God and Mammon are reconciled, the Dragon of Geneva and the Whore of Rome are in cahoots, and with the Russian Bear as well.

Bunyan's hobgoblins, satyrs and monsters, his Worldly Wiseman and Giant Despair, take the shape of itinerant and bemused civil servants, policemen, patriots, rugby players, priests and presidents, of Bantustans and casinostans. . . . This is a world where function is smothered in surmise, and nothing is but what is not. The fantasy, or comic nightmare, or tragic farce, is sustained with gusto, and with surprising propriety of tone. Recruited to lay out the bodies of those killed in a township "riot", Blanchaille is told by a police colonel who expects them to leap up and attack his men, "I'm in charge here and I'll decide who's dead or not." The Straf Kaffir Brigade, we hear, has released syphilis-infected white mice in the multiracial casinos newly opened in Bantu homelands. . . .

Even though he has borrowed Bunyan's allegoric licence, it may be that Hope bears down a little too heavily. The syphilitic mice crop up twice; one almost feels sorry for the temporizing bishop, Blashford, who contrives to be right—for example in "embracing the suffering Christ" of the transit camps—without being prematurely right; while the ins and outs of cabal and fiddle border on the vertiginous. Truth is often weirder (and less measured and elegant) than fiction dare be. Who would swallow the pilgrim's progress of Zola Budd, from running among the ostriches to running across Mary Decker, except for the evidence of television? But Hope's generalizations lend substance to his imaginings: "The capacity to praise today what you executed people for yesterday, and of course vice versa, always vice versa, and with complete sincerity is essential for the maintenance of power." . . .

Bunyan was privileged. He had a celestial city for his pilgrims to reach, where "there shall be no more crying, nor sorrow". All the modern author can offer Blanchaille and Kipsel, his Christian and Hopeful, at the end of the road is a shabby spa or geriatric clinic, above Montreux, so overcrowded that meals ("good, if rather heavy") have to be served in several sittings. A last refuge, a neutral place of terminal exile, where the promised crowns are fancy brooches and medallions made from gold coins, and the inmates recount their pathetic and confused stories, perhaps throughout eternity. They—and not the supposed riches—are "Kruger's millions". The final message is a negative one: the belief that a determined people of good will, ingenuity and courage can survive in South Africa is simply a delusion.

Sad it may be, but it must be. In the end secular fantasy falls back into realism, and the writer, his satire achieved, has to settle for some feasible reality. The trek and the incidental encounters and anecdotes matter, not the arrival. . . . When Kipsel protests, "More stories!", the cheroot-smoking matron of *Bad Kruger* says what we take to be the last word. "We all need stories. We owe our lives to stories", she scolds him. "Do not spit on stories, Mr. Kipsel, or stories might spit on you."

> *D. J. Enright, "The Wrath to Come," in* The Times Literary Supplement, *No. 4252, September 28, 1984, p. 1085.*

MARY HOPE

After the death in detention of Dr Neil Aggett, there was a parliamentary debate in Cape Town, during which one Nationalist MP attacked the Opposition's objections to his prolonged solitary confinement. How could they complain, he asked, when the inquest had revealed that, far from being alone, Dr Aggett had been interrogated for 15 hours a day? How to cap such random, casual, crass, callous everyday lunacies is a challenge which Christopher Hope . . . tackles with bitter allegorical sparkle [in *Kruger's Alp*].

Hope does well to follow his first, exuberantly cynical novel, *A Separate Development,* with a far more biting and dense allegory which, for full effect, demands and rewards a detailed knowledge of current South African events and personalities. Blanchaille is a priest whose mentor, Father Lynch, trains his altar boys in political realities. The Catholic Church and the regime are both after the same thing:

> . . . all power institutions could be expected to adapt in similar ways. Their trick was to forbid individual alterations to the status quo while presenting their own changes as a genuine response to popular demands and altered circumstances . . .

Lynch has also instilled into his acolytes the dream of discovering the lost gold of the exiled President Kruger, together with a haven for the keepers of the faith of the *Volk*. The novel is Blanchaille's quest, during which pilgrimage he meets every kind of self-server and all actions of the regime are seen as far

removed from the tenets they are supposed to enforce. Nothing is what it seems: policemen are dissidents in disguise, comrades are traitors, self-interest is king and morality, of any kind, is dead. It is a completely bleak view, bursting with very naughty jokes about thinly disguised contemporary South African events and figures. . . .

By using Blanchaille as a holy innocent, Hope allows explanations of the more arcane contortions of South African politics, while letting his essentially boisterous poetic imagination rip along the allegorical front. His invention never flags and his scathing intelligence forcefully points up the sheer, outrageous contradictions of the system. . . . Towards the end of his pilgrimage, Blanchaille is shown a film of young soldiers dead on the border: 'civilisations may have died of old age, or decadence, or boredom, or neglect, but what you are seeing for the first time is a nation going to the wall for its belief in the sanctity of separate lavatories . . .'. Anger honed into the bitterest satire and wielded by an acute intelligence which dances most entertainingly around the unacceptable with splendid vigour and bite; but also a plangent lament for the loss of national morality.

> *Mary Hope, "Journeys to the Heartland," in* The Spectator, *Vol. 253, No. 8152, October 6, 1984, p. 33.*

ROBERT WINDER

If any place looks likely to supplant India as the most fashionable of literary locations, then it is South Africa. Ostracised, brutal, beautiful, a barnacle stuck implacably onto the great hull of the continent, South Africa seems set fair for a period of high popularity as a fictional milieu. . . .

[Christopher Hope's *Kruger's Alp*] is a dream conjured up by his Brideshead-like revisit to the village of his youth. The dream features an inverted crusade: its hero Blanchaille is a Catholic priest in the black townships, until disillusionment defrocks him, and sends him in search of more material mysteries. The form of the novel, too, is that of a Romance. Blanchaille undertakes his quest in the manner of a medieval knight, arming himself against the "formidable enemy", mounting to the crossroads on Kruger's Alp where stands a strange figure with "teeth flashing like a sword". As his pilgrimage progresses, a pageant unfurls before his bewildered eyes, of faces and voices, each with a story to tell.

At the Airport hotel, as Blanchaille prepares to leave South Africa, he is confronted, in masque-like sequence, by four girls, each with a long story about the contrariness of life under the regime. "Now it's Happy's turn," introduces the third girl. "She'll give you a different view of things." When Happy has finished, leaving Blanchaille "punished by parable", the girls ask him for his story, which we have just read. Blanchaille's adventure, the subject of the book and potentially the root archetype for many generalisations about the South African predicament, becomes just another "story", one of five.

It's a telling trick. By persistently denying us room to elaborate incidents into schemes, Hope confronts with only the narrow banality of staying alive. . . .

By collapsing opposites—priests merge, blur, and become policemen; whores dress as nuns; prisoners insist on their captivity—Hope approaches his climactic sentence: "What do you do," he asks, "when you find that the world you imagined to be bad, decently evil and have judged this by observation and report and legend, is none of these, but is instead flat, dull, ordinary, and very much like anywhere else.'' Without an enemy, whom is one to fight?

It is ironic that Hope, though he persistently fractures the notion of an order in things, should have compiled so rigorously schematic a book. It lacks ''characters'', of course, since it rejects the idea of anything so stable; and as a result it lacks drama. But the dazzling control of image and metaphor makes it a brilliant literary disquisition on dreams and truth, as well as on South Africa.

> Robert Winder, in a review of ''Kruger's Alp,'' in Books and Bookmen, No. 353, February, 1985, p. 34.

RON LOEWINSOHN

A dream seems a pathetic weapon to turn against repression. Yet in the life of the mind and in politics it is precisely in the dream that the repressed—both emotions and individuals—return to haunt and perhaps to stir us to action.

The South African writer Christopher Hope has successfully applied precisely this aspect of dreams and dream imagery. He is outraged by his government's institutionalized repression, exploitation and murder of his black countrymen. He is outraged too at the whole formidable machinery of double-think and doublespeak that government employs to rationalize and gain support for its crimes, and he has articulated his rage in *Kruger's Alp,* a novel in the form of a dream allegory, a very literary genre that we usually associate with Chaucer, Langland and Bunyan—the exotic domain of the literary antiquarian.

But a dream allegory today? Against apartheid? In its explicit artifice, the form distances us from the events it describes, and its allegorical machinery reduces both character and scene to two dimensions. Yet against an evil as grotesque and contradictory as apartheid, the comic book surrealism of this genre seems appropriate. Mr. Hope might argue, in fact, that he has given us a thoroughly realistic, documentary slice of contemporary South African life.

Kruger's Alp begins with its unnamed narrator lying down to sleep in the garden of Father Lynch's little church just as it is being bulldozed to make room for a further expansion or metastasis of the University of National Christian Education. (Church and state, hand in glove with business, demolish the garden.) His dream is the substance of the narrative that follows, the tale of Theodore Blanchaille, a lapsed Roman Catholic priest searching for or fleeing to—not the City of God, but the City of Gold, the legendary mountain retreat or hostel or retirement home for homeless white South Africans established (legend persists) in the Swiss Alps by Paul Kruger....

While Blanchaille flees from his last provincial parish (his flock actually besieges him for preaching to them about the brutality of the ''relocation camps'' for blacks) to the City of Gold above Lake Geneva, he is educated in the interconnections of power and the disguises it wears as he meets all the relevant members of the regime (also fleeing) and every one of the former altar boys he served and studied with under Father Lynch....

The comic-book ''Who's-on-first?'' quality of a lot of the dialogue and many of the situations ... recalls Joseph Heller's *Catch-22.* When Blanchaille points out that many of the allegedly attacking (and now dead) black people in a ''pacified''

township were shot in the back, a colonel replies, ''They are a crafty lot.... For all you know some of them turned around and were running at us backwards. Have you thought of that?'' But mostly Mr. Hope's barely controlled rage recalls Swift as he relentlessly exposes the anti-logic of authoritarian power in the acid bath of his scorn....

[Mr. Hope] is an intelligent and gifted writer, with an eye for realistic detail and an incisive but fluent style that together give substance to his allegory and complement his mordant wit. If he sometimes lapses into the flatly explanatory language of a sociology text, or goes inexcusably out of his way for a groan-worthy pun, or too-mechanically halts his narrative to give us a background sketch every time he introduces a new character, these seem minor flaws, given the importance of what he has to say to us—about South Africa in particular, but also about authoritarian power everywhere.

However, this is much more than a political tract. Mr. Hope has combined his themes and metaphors—particularly the political and the sexual—so that they illuminate each other: at its bawdiest, the book joins the drive for freedom and the need for love in a protest against all forms of repression. The regime must work ceaselessly to keep them in check; eventually—in the near future, Mr. Hope suggests—it will be exhausted by the vanity of its own impotent labor. *Kruger's Alp* is a testament to that dream of a justice long deferred.

> Ron Loewinsohn, ''In Dreams Persists Apartheid,'' in The New York Times Book Review, May 5, 1985, p. 9.

SIMON RAE

Christopher Hope's satirical explorations, in both prose and poetry, of the attitudes and evasions necessary for his native South Africa's fanatical defence of apartheid and ''the hierarchy of lavatories'', culminated in his brilliant novel *Kruger's Alp.* ... His latest work, *Englishmen,* ''a poem for voices'' in fourteen parts, dips back into history to seek out the roots of the Afrikaner identity. Two representative compound ghosts, Mr Silvero (distant cousin of the minor character in [T. S. Eliot's] ''Gerontion''?), and Mrs Oribi, whose name also has an Eliotic ring to it (though in fact *oribi* is the name of a South African antelope), meet on a coach. They are ''Setting out to find all we left behind'', taking ''the ghost trail, South to North'', ''travelling'', as Mr Silvero puts it, with playful allusiveness, ''the road we did not take, / on the bus we did not miss''.

Their magical history tour takes in the Voortrekkers' migrations away from Cape Colony and British rule in the 1830s; their conflict with the Zulus on whose territory they encroached; the Battle of Blood River, where the Zulu army was massacred; the Battle of Boomplats some ten years later where the gung-ho expansionist Sir Harry Smith routed Pretorius; and the subsequent Sand River Convention which gave the Boers their land back and guaranteed their virtual independence in the Transvaal (it being less trouble for the British to ''let the Dutch fight the kaffirs for them'').

Mrs Oribi was apparently a fly on the wall when the Zulu chief Dingaan had the Kommando leader Piet Retief impaled on a stake, an event she takes a certain pleasure in reenacting with a leather purse and ''a hatpin as long as a bicycle spoke''. Mr Silvero was present at Blood River and witnessed the Boers' covenant with God to ensure victory....

As well as compressing a lot of history into relatively few pages, Hope's poem also gives potent thumb-nail sketches of the protagonists: Sir Harry Smith—"Fair-handed / Harry is shooting a prisoner here, / a deserter there. Bone like nutmeg on the wall, / his slugs lift half their heads away." [Mostyn Owen and William Hogge, the] two shadowy bureaucrats sent out to curb his excesses, are nicely differentiated. . . . It is Hogge who justifies the Sand River Convention with the thought, "Why should we worry? Whoever wins will end up / Englishmen."

That prophecy overlooks the Boers' enduring hatred ("dreaming / of frying Englishmen basted with Zulu fat"), and the eventual realization, succinctly expressed in *Kruger's Alp,* that "if you couldn't out-gun the English, you could out-vote the bastards"—that a majority of the white minority could in time dominate Southern Africa through the ballot box.

But for how long? Mr Silvero sounds tired as he contemplates the future: "Dawn or Armageddon, / it's all the same to me. A series of strategic halts / called progress, / a long road between water-holes, / A long trek into winter."

As the recent Radio 3 production of *Englishmen . . .* showed, Hope's poetry is capable of a wide range of effects, and admirably suited to the speaking voice. The poem marks a new and exciting departure for this extremely versatile writer.

Simon Rae, "Dawn or Armageddon," in The Times Literary Supplement, No. 4340, June 6, 1986, p. 616.

DAVID SEXTON

[Exile is] the subject of Christopher Hope's *The Hottentot Room.* It is a curiously lugubrious tale of a club for African expatriates in Earls Court, presided over by the ageing Frau Katie, herself an exile from Hitler's Europe. Breytenbach typifies exiles as

> drenched in self-pity; at odds with themselves and blaming invariably "the oppressors" or history; petrified in a time warp where the reference points are a rosily remembered past; victims to the corruption of suffering; up to their necks in dog-eat-dog exile politics.

These are precisely the afflictions of the members of The Hottentot Room. A South African double agent, Caleb Looper, infiltrates the club to spy on its expatriate dissidents, but finds himself infected by its atmosphere of moral paralysis. He forms a strange bond with Frau Katie which results in him taking her ashes home at last, to the Berlin she has never really left. Having made this quixotic gesture he dies there himself, recognising that he no longer has a home or a place in history. 'History simply isn't interested. It was out when we called. We provided no occasions to which it could rise.'

Hope himself was an Irish Catholic South African before he left the country, and so already had 'an oblique way of looking at things.' The indirections of *The Hottentot Room* reflect this double detachment from the homeland of exiles. The book is amiable, prolix, oddly old-fashioned, rather falling victim in formal terms to its static subject matter—the story of a story coming to a stop. (p. 30)

David Sexton, "Exiled from Home," in Books and Bookmen, No. 371, September, 1986, pp. 29-30.

HARRIETT GILBERT

[*The Hottentot Room* is] about South Africans, black and white, who find themselves exiled in contemporary London and the myths that all exiles make of their past in the desperate hope of creating some warmth to soften the ice of their present.

The 'room' of the title is a club. . . . It's run by the German Frau Katie, a Jew who didn't realise she was until her Nazi Colonel husband informed her of the fact in 1938. In it, the slush of Earls Court's winter is escaped by Looper (a South African reporter, in more senses than one), by Wyngate Hossein, philandering General Secretary of Via Afrika, by Elize from Zimbabwe and her friend Mona May, a highjumper from the Bushveld who 'trained, it was said, back at home by competing against a tame springbok named Hendrik'.

Hope's satire here, as in his previous fictions, is driven by the anger that people feel when love and belief aren't quite destroyed, when they still know why they feel angry. One running gag/running wound in the novel occurs in the letters that Looper keeps getting from his right-of-President-Botha father, who's convinced not only that his son is a commie but that he's in daily, conspiratorial contact with the evil David Owen. . . .

It should be added that the lidless eye being cast on South Africans at home and abroad is no more blinking when it comes to the British. Our own dear form of racism, the delusion that we have a democracy, our habit of parking in laybys and 'eating sandwiches at folding tables': from start to finish we're despised. Whether at home or in frustrated exile, South Africans are producing some vital and provocative fiction. (p. 29)

Harriett Gilbert, "Island Stories," in New Statesman, Vol. 112, No. 2894, September 12, 1986, pp. 28-9.

ROBERT BRAIN

Through discarded polystyrene, hamburger boxes and paper napkins, the Hottentots of Christopher Hope's new novel [*The Hottentot Room*] walk past the travel agents, late-night grocers and fast-food bars of Earls Court and enter a dilapidated house with a pointed sign over its front door showing a seventeenth-century Hottentot woman with the fabled steatopygous buttocks. Inside, under the benign green eyes of Frau Katie, keeper of The Hottentot Room, a group of expatriate southern Africans pass the time of night. . . .

Washed up and marooned on this horrible northern island, the Hottentots are determined not to grow old and cold. Their thoughts, even their gestures, are those of southern Africa. Consumed with despair, they wait with the colossal hope of a revolution which is receding majestically like a great ship. They dream of going home (like Coree the Hottentot brought to England in the seventeenth century for display purposes, whose first English words, much repeated, were "Coree home go"), unconsciously wiping sweat from their brows, smacking at imaginary mosquitoes, feeling blindly for the sun and listening for the surf.

The Hottentots move under their queen's direction, Frau Katie insisting on only two rules: one, that she is the person to choose or blackball a member, and two, that none of her Hottentots should ever—under threat of expulsion—form couples. Hottentots are libidinous, not monogamous, and are happy to be under Frau Katie's whimsical care, having lost most of their earlier African impetus. They are all heroes who have been diminished in some way. . . .

Outside The Hottentot Room the members are just about aware that the natives are at large, but mostly invisible like natives everywhere. The English are laughed at, maliciously attacked: they are a clothed race, a depressed race inhabiting a dirty, run-down country, wearing car coats, waiting to go for a long drive on cold days and have a cup of tea in a layby. They are a people putting up with an over-long peace, waiting for the day when they can all get back into uniform, a people slowly being driven mad by petty economics. The English are devoted to Mammon, with a mystical reverence for profit similar to that felt by the medieval peasant for God. England for the Hottentots is a greyish, penny-pinching island of ant-heads, and their only fear is that some of them might go native, have pink babies and spend the rest of their lives talking about the weather, mortgages, the Royal Family and the rate of sterling against the holiday currencies. The Hottentots allow no English members in their club, and Hope allows no English characters in his novel—except for the fool who walks on and says "Absolutely right" and "Oh quite" a few times and then walks out, and a couple of weird tour operators found on an aeroplane.

The Hottentots are certainly in crisis, and not only identity-wise: Caleb Looper most of all. Looper is the son of a deranged inspector of mines living in a South Africa where Africans do not exist, who is nevertheless organizing a secret *putsch* to save his country. Caleb hates his father, but is forced to protect him when the government finds polluted sap in their family tree and uses the information that the Loopers are descendants of the Strandloopers (Beachwalkers)—an old Afrikaans name for the Hottentots—to blackmail the son and send him to London and the Hottentot Room to spy on his fellow countrymen. Frau Katie loves Looper, however, recognizing him as a victim of a country which, like her own, kills people for their beliefs, imprisons them for their poetry and trains racial inspectors to sniff out the blood of subspecies. Frau Katie has always planned to elope with Looper, but her illness prevents it and in the end only her ashes accompany him out of the country, to East Berlin, where he dies beside them. Back in Earls Court, The Hottentot Room has been rapidly transformed by Katie's native-loving daughter into the Colony Bar. . . .

The Hottentot Room is an entertaining novel, elegantly written and intricately plotted. It is also more than that, since the entertainment seduces us into coming to grips with dirty politics and ruthless power games. For a reader of the book for the first time, the surprise beginnings, contrivances and contraptions seem tiresomely unnecessary. They are not, of course, since in the end they add up to a balanced structure aimed squarely at its target, the complete nature of which, however, is one no non-Hottentot may ever fully grasp.

> Robert Brain, "Camaraderie of the Marooned," in The Times Literary Supplement, No. 4355, September 19, 1986, p. 1028.

WALTER GOODMAN

The premise of Christopher Hope's new novel [*The Hottentot Room*] is so promising and the premises where it takes place are so flavorsome that it takes a while to realize that something is lacking in such basics as narrative and character. Even so, the smart writing and sharp thinking afford their own considerable pleasures.

The Hottentot Room of the title is a pub in the Earl's Court section of London, whose regulars are a "little tribe" of expatriates from South Africa, constituting many shades of color, character and commitment to the anti-apartheid cause. Running the rundown establishment is old Frau Katie, who came to England as a refugee from Nazi Germany. Parallels between South Africa now and Germany then run strongly through the book.

The story, told by a droll, dry narrator, takes place as Frau Katie lies dying. The main mourner is her devoted Caleb Looper, a journalist who was kicked out of South Africa because of his activities in behalf of the regime's opponents. Or so it seems. Hints are dropped early that Looper may be something more or less than an expatriate, and before long our suspicions are confirmed that he is in the pay of Pretoria to inform on his pals in the Hottentot Room. Yet his loyalties lie entirely with those on whom he is peaching.

Here, then, we have a Graham Greene character, a complex, conscience-troubled fellow, but every time we begin to close in on his feelings or ideas, Mr. Hope . . . draws back. He keeps circling his prey but declines to make the capture. That applies as well to the other denizens of the Hottentot Room, whom Frau Katie's English-bred and socially aspiring daughter, Rose, dismisses, pretty accurately, as "feckless, dirty, unreliable, undependable, lazy, childlike, wasteful, treacherous and utterly out of place in the new world she was planning."

They make a picturesque pack. As they are introduced, our expectations are whetted for the complications to come when they mix it up. There's a black African leader of Zulu stock, named Wyngate Hossein, who "sounds like an Indian, speaks like a white man and looks like a black", his wife, Gladys, and his mistress, the radical intellectual Biddy Hogan. . . .

Other regulars at the pub include Buffy Lestrade, a "Maoist to the left of Moscow, Germanist, Sartrean existentialist, tea drinker extraordinaire," who has turned into a food faddist; Mona May, a woman who is a champion high jumper from the Bushveld; Elize, a nursing sister from Zimbabwe, now marching with Jewish Lesbians Against Racialism; an ex-priest named Morris Morrision, and several Africans known as the Soweto Knights, who don pelts and drum rhythms from their homeland—former firebrands now "lonely, cold, homesick and getting rather plump."

Plenty of material here for fun and philosophy, if only the narrator would let us get close. He is like a security guard, keeping the reader at a safe distance from the principals. We catch tantalizing glimpses, but despite flashes of color, the figures remain dim. . . .

Mr. Hope suggests a lot, in a kind of outline. His aloof style delivers the characters' stories from afar. The conclusion, a straightforward account of Looper's last brave effort to make up to Frau Katie and to himself for their lives of dubious commitment, for what he thinks of as "the damned slippage of things," demonstrates that Mr. Hope can tell a story when he sets his pen to it. Even this adventure, however, is turned into anticlimax, as we learn its conclusion almost as an aside.

You may leave this novel, so full of intelligence and possibilities, with regret that Mr. Hope has been holding back. Yet you can hardly help taking with you the atmosphere of exile and longing that clouds the Hottentot Room.

> Walter Goodman, in a review of "The Hottentot Room," in The New York Times, June 25, 1987, p. 25.

JULIA O'FAOLAIN

Black Swan is about a retarded teenager living in a black township in the South Africa of the 1960s. It starts with a joke: "They called him 'Lucky'. It was said he had been named after the brand of cigarettes his father smoked—*Lucky Strike*. 'Strike' would have been better, it was suggested.... Some things did best when struck: drums, gongs, matches . . . and the boy, Lucky.'' The metaphor resonates with old echoes and has prophetic force, since Lucky will indeed be battered but will also, unforeseeably, earn the jokers' respect. Meanwhile, on a realistic level, the streetwise humour tethers the narrative to a time and place so bleak that Lucky shrinks from them—as readers might, too, without the therapeutic comforts of laughter.

Lucky's escape-route is mental. "Like a bird or a plane" his mind takes off regularly, and though he is considered mad it is clear that in that dead-end place even normal youths are heavily hooked on fantasy. American gangster films provide their style, and the names they give each other are "many, various, vivid: Chop-Chop Molefe and Big Boy Mantanzima, the Duke and Mr. Ice . . . all dreamed of becoming Public Enemy Number One."

Into this world of yearners comes Ilse, a young German missionary teacher who has been insufficiently briefed about South Africa. She is desperate to do good and, when her other pupils prove too disturbed to be teachable, Lucky, the last precarious survivor, becomes a challenge. He is hard to reach but Ilse has a teaching-aid: a film of *Swan Lake* which she projects for him on the classroom wall. It is "her way into the fantastical recesses of Lucky's mind".....

Unaware that her relations with him are being misinterpreted by the scandalized authorities, she ends up as a piece of flotsam in a dusty local lake.

After this the action, seen increasingly through Lucky's baffled eyes, mingles farce with fable. Recruited as a guerrilla-fighter, he is flown to East Germany for training, fails, returns and, almost by accident, achieves the old ambition of the township youths, becoming Public Enemy Number One when a bomb he has planted blows off his own leg and kills two policemen. Impressed, his former mockers attend his trial and wave a pair of ballet shoes as a token of solidarity which comes to a climax when the bemused Lucky, stumbling on wisdom like a blind seer, tells the court, "I know that a small bird can break a big egg. An ostrich can speak with the voice of a lion. And one day we will all dance." He is sentenced to hang but doesn't realize this. A victim turned visionary, he is responsible for disturbances in the township where "young men were to be seen dancing in the streets".

Airborne by the coherence of its imagery, this exhilarating fable is, and is about, a triumph of the imagination over an obdurate and intolerable status quo.

Julia O'Faolain, "Taking Flight," in The Times Literary Supplement, *No. 4395, June 26, 1987, p. 697.*

LINDA TAYLOR

Most people long to get away from home: to leave the nest, to fly. In *Black Swan,* Christopher Hope has given his main character, Lucky, the ability to 'go away' whenever he pleases: 'he left his body and entered his mind, which took off like a

bird or a plane for somewhere else . . . The place might be wild or pretty, he didn't really mind. Its great attraction was that it took him away from where he was.' Lucky lives in one of those meagre, dusty South African townships, a marginal slice of life without electricity, piped water or sewage facilities, which Hope conveys graphically and uncompromisingly.

Freedom is the book's major issue for which the retarded or mad Lucky plays a symbolic part. His mental defectiveness is his strength; Lucky is used by Hope as the only one who can have 'vision' in such circumstances, just because he doesn't make the same connections as anyone else. Ilse, Lucky's teacher and an uneasy representative of white liberalism, wants to save Lucky (and, thus, black South Africa). But Ilse cannot control the disparate 'handicaps' of her group of pupils. They resist her love, her attempts to free them; one even dies. In a last attempt to break through Lucky's barrier of exclusion, Ilse shows him a film of *Swan Lake*. Lucky instantly recognises the sense in which ballet transforms the ordinary....

Lucky's other 'tutor' (the 'General') utilises his desire for other places by sending Lucky away to train as a liberation fighter.... [Hope] specialises in ironic poignancy: he sets up frail persecuted characters as unlikely focuses of massive political issues. In his last novel, *The Hottentot Room,* he gave them an enclave in London—the 'Room' which accommodated a ragbag of perplexed defectors from issues that they barely knew they represented. So it is that Lucky becomes a hero, and, in court, numerous pairs of ballet shoes are held up by the black 'rowdy elements' in support of Lucky who has already 'gone away'.

Linda Taylor, "In Search of Liberation," in The Listener, *Vol. 118, No. 3019, July 9, 1987, p. 31.*

HERMIONE LEE

'Funny' things sound less and less like jokes in South Africa, election year, 1987. There is said to be a man with a saw in Durban who goes around the beaches cutting through all the segregation notices. In Johannesburg, advertisements for wall-top spikes read 'Angled Right To Bite Right' or 'Surprisingly Attractive'. In the farming country, immigrants from Rhodesia used to be known as the 'Whenwees' ('When we were in Rhodesia . . .'); now they are known as the 'Sowetos' ('So where to now?')....

Given 'the deep surreality" of a place 'so absurd, so incredible, so terrifyingly funny' that it seems itself to be a fiction, the 'horrifying comedy' of South Africa may be, literally, unspeakable. Christopher Hope, a white South African novelist of Irish-Catholic parentage and upbringing, who left for England in 1974, went back in election year to try to make sense of it but found, frequently, only non-sense. Over and over again his ferociously sharp-eyed, edgy, ironic quest for meanings lacerates itself with the impossibility of its task.

So *White Boy Running* is a book about language and its misuse.... The language of a government that simultaneously proffers and resists change is all camouflage. Words such as 'reform', 'international', 'group' and 'gratitude' are coded threats and warnings. Politics is supremely, in this country, 'the ability to say radically incompatible things in the same breath'.

Hope's own life story makes one version of South African history, a vivid, witty autobiography dating from the election of 1948 (when he was four). From that point, 'Calvinist, racialist, isolationist' policy took hold. But Hope's Irish grandfather, who brought him up after his father's death, in a pub in backwoods Balfour, had been tolerated enough by his Afrikaner neighbours to be elected mayor. Tolerance vanished in Pretoria, where as one of an embattled community of Catholic schoolboys in Kruger's Calvinist capital (a ludicrous anomaly, described with relish) Hope learnt 'to live on the edge of things'. Then, naval service in Cape Town (but the real war, an instructor told them, would be in their own backyard). Then, another kind of training 'in the heady delights of crusading politics' at the liberal University of Witwatersrand in the mid-1960s. Now, looking back, he sees that not one of those liberal crusades has been won.

But no single life can speak for the country where nobody is a definitive 'South African'. Hope has a passion for long views, and 'memory is the truly subversive weapon'. So we are taken to the crucial places: the scene of the treaty which ended the Boer War but determined the Afrikaner drive for supremacy; the spot in the White Chamber of Parliament where Verwoerd was assassinated. . . .

Writing in the admirable, unsympathetic, formidable tradition of cold satirists like Orwell or V. S. Naipaul, Hope sees nothing but apocalypse in view. There are no consolations: well-meaning liberals are as savagely dismissed as the men in power, and the election results—a retreat to the *laager*—confirm all his fears.

[*White Boy Running*] is sometimes repetitive and heavy-handed. As a reporter, Hope seems to hanker for the anarchic licence of his fictions, where 'funny things' can be bizarre and surreal without having to be defined as such. And some prickly questions are raised. Writers in South Africa might ask if Hope has the right, as an 'escapee', to pop back, sum up, and get out again. Black readers might find him irrelevant. (This challenge, which the book has very much in mind, is brilliantly taken up in a scene when Hope reads to a Sowetan audience.)

Still, it is a gripping and necessary book for the times. It bites into the monstrous stuff and cuts through it like the man with the saw.

> Hermione Lee, "In Botha's Madhouse," in The Observer, *February 21, 1988, p. 26.*

J. M. COETZEE

White Boy Running is the story of the [1987 South African] election as Hope saw it, interwoven with the story of his childhood in South Africa. Partly reportage and political analysis, partly autobiography, partly satire, it is in essence a diagnosis of the condition of white South Africa today. Its conclusion is pessimistic, not to say dark.

Though Hope has lived since 1975 in England, where he has established himself as a novelist and a critic, he does not call himself an Englishman. On the other hand, he does not call himself a South African, even an ex-South African. For his thesis is that "South Africa" is a fiction, that there is no such thing as a South African nation, only "a conglomerate of an-

tagonistic groups." . . . "The sense of exile we felt within our own country is something which has never left me. We were a generation that went into exile before we left home."

Hope left South Africa, but he did not cut his ties with it. He couldn't, he says, because "the place is a fever, an infection, a lingering childhood disease I simply cannot get over." Hope's fictions—his novels *A Separate Development, Kruger's Alp,* and *The Hottentot Room,* and his stories in *Private Parts*—can be read as attempts to cure himself of the disease, to exorcise the demon of South Africa. "Since the nightfall of 1948 we have not been living in a country, but in someone else's dream," he writes. To find a way out of the stifling, obsessional dream (or nightmare) imposed on him in his childhood, he has undertaken the imaginative project of *outwriting* a society that, as it lives out its fantasies, ventures deeper and deeper into a theater of cruelty, enacting a tangled, horrifying, dark comedy. . . .

[This] is, by and large, a book of "straight" criticism, rather than one of the wilder satirical counterblasts through which Hope in his fiction wages war on the big lie of South Africa. It is straight political commentary, straight reportage, though with an emphasis on the aesthetic monstrosity of the system that distinguishes Hope's account from such other recent reports as Joseph Lelyveld's *Move Your Shadow* and Vincent Crapanzano's *Waiting.* . . .

I do not wish to imply that Hope replaces a moral or political criticism of apartheid with an aesthetic criticism. Moral outrage is certainly present, beneath the surface. But, as he makes clear in his story of a childhood and youth spent in a land of dreary moral orthodoxy and rigid ethnic separation, the attainment of freedom meant to him, in the first instance, escaping from the enemy's dream, finding ways of living in the interstices of the system, staying on the run (hence the title of his book). To a man of words, it also meant fostering the magical powers of jeering, deriding, laughing (hence Hope's other books, as well as parts of this one).

As a political commentator Hope is deft and amusing, and knows his way around. But as with certain other South African writers (one thinks particularly of Breyten Breytenbach), the world of power and intrigue is not one in which he is naturally at home. Like most literary people, he tends to overvalue the symbolic. He has little to say about black life or black politics, though watching a student protest in Johannesburg, he does note the "terrifying anger" of black students: "What police and students really want . . . eagerly, horribly, is a real showdown. They want to start shooting, they are full of hatred and wish to kill each other." He visits Soweto to give a reading from his work. The audience stops him in midflight and makes him strip away, layer by layer, the ironies, nuances, ambiguities lovingly crafted into his poem. "Not the usual literary evening," he comments; but then, he reminds himself, "this is the front line." (p. 38)

> J. M. Coetzee, "The Liberal Retreat," in The New Republic, *Vol. 198, No. 24, June 13, 1988, pp. 37-9.*

(John) Robin Jenkins

1912-

Scottish novelist and short story writer.

A respected figure in contemporary Scottish literature, Jenkins is best known for novels that examine the moral, religious, and social conflicts of his homeland. In these books, Jenkins often combines realistic details with fantastical and symbolic characterizations to explore, according to Francis Russell Hart, "the fascination and the perils of innocence, the many grotesque shapes of love, the terrible imperatives of humility, [and] the eccentricities of grace." Jenkins has also earned praise for his novels set in Afghanistan and Malaysia. Although some critics consider his characterizations unconvincing and agree with the contention of a reviewer for the *Times Literary Supplement* that Jenkins fails to "dwell on his concerns long enough, brood on them and fathom them and find the reserves of intensity to rise to them," many admire his descriptive skills and his ability to convey the inherent humor and irony of the human condition.

Jenkins's early novels established him as an insightful chronicler of individual and social tensions of contemporary Scotland. In *Happy for the Child* (1953), Jenkins addresses one of his predominant concerns—the decay of innocence—by detailing conflicts that result when a boy from a Glasgow slum wins a scholarship to a prestigious academy. E. McNaught remarked that the boy's "desperate efforts to conceal the fact that his mother is a scrub-woman, and the solemn matter of obtaining the proper school clothing, are told with unaffected poignancy of one who understands childhood." In *The Cone-Gatherers* (1955), which William Boyd called "a moral tale of evil confronting innocence," a mentally retarded hunchback who collects pinecones on an expansive Highland estate is reviled and later murdered by a misanthropic gameskeeper. *The Changeling* (1958) presents the story of an impoverished Glasgow youth who accompanies his teacher's family on an island vacation. Unable to readjust to his squalid home environment after being exposed to the lifestyle of his teacher, the boy commits suicide. Jenkins's other early novels include *So Gaily Sings the Lark* (1951), *The Thistle and the Grail* (1954), *Guests of War* (1956), *The Missionaries* (1957), and *Love Is a Fervent Fire* (1959).

Several of Jenkins's later novels continue his exploration of contemporary Scottish society. *A Very Scottish Affair* (1968) is a stark portrait of a lecherous Glaswegian man who abandons his dying wife and familial obligations for the material pleasures offered by a wealthy woman. In *A Toast to the Lord* (1972), a Puritan minister kills himself after brutally murdering a seaman who was wrongfully accused of seducing his daughter. *A Would-Be Saint* (1978) details the life of a devout Presbyterian whose renunciation of modern society leads to his isolation in a remote Scottish forest. Christopher Nouryeh heralded *A Would-Be Saint* as "a rich, rewarding history told with economy of language, in the tradition of modern realism. . . . Both setting and narrative rest upon Jenkins's artistic practice—his faith in the truth of language responsibly, candidly and carefully employed." Jenkins's next work, *Fergus Lamont* (1979), chronicles the life of a young Scotsman who emerges from the Glasgow slums to become a nationally respected poet.

The Awakening of George Darroch (1985) is a historical novel in which Jenkins documents the events that precipitated the separation of the Church of Scotland in 1843.

Jenkins's novels set outside Scotland draw from his experiences as a teacher in Afghanistan and Malaysia. While critics generally consider these works less successful than those set in Scotland, Jenkins is complimented for his skill in rendering exotic and diverse regional lifestyles. *Some Kind of Grace* (1960) recounts John McLeod's efforts to locate a Scottish couple believed murdered in Afghanistan. *Dust on the Paw* (1961), which elicited comparisons to E. M. Forster's novel *A Passage to India,* addresses racial relations in Kabul by depicting an Afghan's engagement to an Englishwoman. Orville Prescott observed: "Mr. Jenkins artfully demonstrates that deep-seated prejudices and habitual habits of thought can pose fearful problems; but he also concludes on a note of hope, suggesting that with sufficient love, patience and generosity such problems can be surmounted." *The Holy Tree* (1969) focuses upon a Borneo native obsessed with Western culture, while *The Expatriates* (1971) depicts a man's efforts to locate a Malaysian girl he fathered prior to his marriage in Scotland. Other works by Jenkins detailing life in Afghanistan and Southeast Asia include the novels *The Tiger of Gold* (1962), *The Sardana Dancers* (1964), and *A Figure of Fun* (1974), as well as a collection of short fiction, *A Far Cry from Bowmore and Other Stories* (1973).

(See also *Contemporary Authors*, Vols. 1-4, rev. ed.; *Contemporary Authors New Revision Series*, Vol. 1; and *Dictionary of Literary Biography*, Vol. 14.)

E. McNAUGHT

[*Happy for the Child* is a] penetrating and sympathetic study of a young Scottish schoolboy whose brilliant winning of a scholarship is only the beginning of his troubles. From a poverty-stricken home, supported by the Homeric struggles of his mother, and from an unspeakably sordid neighborhood, John Stirling at the age of twelve is expected to hold his own in a select Academy of wealthy and alien boys. His desperate efforts to conceal the fact that his mother is a scrub-woman, and the solemn matter of obtaining the proper school clothing, are told with unaffected poignancy of one who understands childhood. (p. 164)

Robin Jenkins is a fairly new writer. His picture of some phases of Glasgow life is most depressing, but there can be no doubt as to his skill in portraying them. (p. 165)

> *E. McNaught, in a review of "Happy for the Child," in* The Canadian Forum, *Vol. XXXIII, No. 393, October, 1953, pp. 164-65.*

BURNS SINGER

Robin Jenkins was once the most promising of all living Scottish novelists. His latest work [*Some Kind of Grace*] makes me doubt if he still is. It takes us back to all the tosh and blarney about the mysterious East, the very thing that Miss Markandaya has so cleverly debunked. True, Mr. Jenkins' North-West Frontier is more up-to-date than Kipling's. It contains its quota of Russians and Americans, for example. But it still abounds in paradisal villages and disappearing English—or rather Scottish—men and maidens. With this strange flora and fauna Mr. Jenkins has certainly constructed a novel that explores a number of unusual moral dilemmas and ambiguities. The point is that they are so unusual as to be almost entirely divorced from the experience of most of us. It seems to me high time that Mr. Jenkins returned to his native country and gave us another book about the life he knows so well and in which some of the customs at least are familiar enough to his English-speaking readers for them to be able to judge the authenticity of his background. (p. 86)

> *Burns Singer, "The Face of Evil," in* Encounter, *Vol. XVI, No. 3, March, 1961, pp. 82-6.*

R. G. G. PRICE

Dust on the Paw is a good example of the Can-Europeans-and-Asians-be-Pals novel, an honourable descendant of *A Passage to India*. Wahab is an excitable, sensitive, hypocritical, idealistic, go-getting teacher in Nurania, an Afghan-type monarchy. When he was a science student in Manchester, he got engaged to a white economist, a woman grimly keen on many good causes, including inter-racial friendship. While he is waiting for her to come out to him, he is taken up by a secret society which gets him appointed Principal of his school, with glittering further prospects, and he begins to wonder whether a European wife is such a good idea. The central figure is surrounded with European and partly-European couples, some from the Embassy, some from the University, and there are many vigorously executed scenes of rather bitter farce, marital and political. One of Mr. Jenkin's strong points is that he recognises that Asian nationalism has been successful enough for Asia to take its share of criticism. There is no longer any need for English novels about the East to be written with patronising condonation of oriental weaknesses.

What is wrong in Nurania gets blasted as hard as if Mr. Jenkins were writing about the Gorbals, and quite right too.

> *R. G. G. Price, in a review of "Dust on the Paw," in* Punch, *Vol. CCXLI, No. 6308, August 9, 1961, pp. 223-24.*

ORVILLE PRESCOTT

Robin Jenkins, a Scot, has written eight other novels, none of which has been published in this country. If they are in the same class as *Dust on the Paw,* American publishers have overlooked one of the most professionally competent of contemporary British novelists.

Mr. Jenkins is a storyteller who does not think it beneath his dignity to keep his narrative moving briskly from one dramatic episode to another. He is adroit in characterization. His book swarms with neatly, sometimes acidly, portrayed people, of whom several are revealed in depth with much psychological perception and sympathy. He has a sardonic sense of humor and a sense of the irony of human affairs that fill his book not with laughter but with the glitter of a rather cold-blooded comedy.

This is a story about life in Kabul, the remote capital of Afghanistan where Mr. Jenkins himself spent two years as a teacher. . . .

There are two basic themes twisted together in *Dust on the Paw*. One might be called how to succeed in Afghanistan without really trying. The other is the inability of well-meaning people to live up to their own ideals. Mr. Jenkins arranges matters so that his most humanitarian and intellectually high-minded characters betray others and disgrace themselves. And both these themes are deeply entangled in the problem of interracial love and marriage. *Dust on the Paw* is as intricately constructed as a Chinese puzzle.

Abdul Wahab, like Dr. Aziz [of *A Passage to India*] before him, was fiercely emotional, super-sensitive, proud, bitter and suspicious; and also humble, servile and tearful. He could be brave and he could be timidly obsequious. A science teacher in Kabul never knew when some whim of the ruling clique, some treachery or conspiracy, might not rob him of his job, and of his pitiful wage. He had to walk softly. But Wahab was engaged to an English girl. He yearned for the patronage of his own Afghan rulers and for the respect and friendship of the English.

Neither could be counted on. But by a series of ironic twists of plot Wahab found himself rising in the hierarchy of Kabul without any effort of his own and also achieving some progress in his relations with the English. This last was managed only after some of the most painful and unpleasantly embarrassing scenes in modern fiction. Mr. Jenkins makes one squirm and twist with shame and that desire not to witness such goings-on that we all have experienced too often in our own lives. As for interracial marriages, Mr. Jenkins artfully demonstrates that deep-seated prejudices and habitual habits of thought can pose fearful problems; but he also concludes on a note of hope, suggesting that with sufficient love, patience and generosity such problems can be surmounted.

One of the interesting elements of **Dust on th Paw** is what Mr. Jenkins has to say about Afghanistan itself: the charm and intelligence of young people; corruption and intrigues in the government; the dirt, flies, germs and stenches; and the courage, dignity and patience with which the people endure their terrible poverty.

Orville Prescott, in a review of "Dust on the Paw,"
in The New York Times, *February 7, 1962, p. 35.*

ALASTAIR R. THOMPSON

"Gazing down at the fat, shy, simple, elderly cripple in the shabby clothes, Rutherford felt a warm cleansing affection for him. There was, of course, no way by which to show it. The cap on the grave waited not for money, but for faith and love."

This sentence, from the end of Robin Jenkins' novel, **The Thistle and the Grail,** is, I believe, a key to the most urgent thing that Jenkins has been trying to say in the ten novels he has hitherto had published. It suggests also the justification for claiming him as a novelist of consequence not only in Scottish letters of the 20th century but in the whole course of our national literature.

I pick on this passage because it states in a few words the double nature of the sharpest of human needs. We need faith and love, not material things, and there is, of course, in the world as well as in Scotland, no easy way to give or receive that love. In each of his novels, Mr. Jenkins explores and exposes with an earnest, stern, tender intensity the many shapes of love. There is love between man and man, love between man and his social group, love between man and the faceless mass of his fellow-men, love between man and woman and, perhaps most movingly, love between child and man. But if there is love, there must also be, to give completion and knowledge to the study, the failure of love. (p. 57)

In his latest book, **Dust on the Paw,** men and women work out in a series of sympathetically detailed encounters a few of the many variants of that inexhaustibly absorbing form of communication, marriage. Mr. Jenkins is too subtle an observer to arrange the pairs in any obvious order of merit. It is enough that love is a precondition of existence for the failure as much as for the successful. Finally, and perhaps most successfully, Mr. Jenkins has plotted the strange, hidden world of a child's mind. He knows the anguished need for love and the horrifying accuracy, far too mature for the surrounding adults, lost in much experience, to understand, with which a child charts the depths of the uncomprehending world which dominates him. Tom Curdie and Sam Gourlay are unforgettable portraits of disquieting accuracy.

Mr. Jenkins' theme is then, not alone the need for love and faith—any advice column in a magazine will tell us of that but the tormenting difficulties of communication that beset us, the misery of wanting to love but knowing no words to express that need, of having no universal and dependable language in which to send and receive the urgent signals for help that each human being sends out. And yet, he suggests, when we fail in our endeavour to find this medium of mutual understanding, we emphasise our very humanity and may hope to achieve, by accepting that fact, a tolerable compromise. (p. 58)

If I may borrow a word Mr. Jenkins has often used himself, "awareness" is the quality he demands of men and women. Awareness of, responsiveness to, the condition of humanity is not a gentle, effete tolerance, but an active, difficult discipline. It is akin to that other humanitarian motto of a novelist, "only connect". Like it, it demands imagination, a stretching out from the known world of self to the mysterious country of another's self, a capacity to interpret, even if not wholly accurately, the signals other personalities send out and above all, a refusal to consider any state of mind or soul alien to the human struggle.

I think I am being fair, if I say that in Mr. Jenkins' awareness there is something of the uncompromising, unrelenting moral precision of the Presbyterian tradition. No sound Presbyterian is ever guilty of intellectual or spiritual vagueness or untested benevolence. Scots Presbyterians test each anxious judgement by moral standards whatever the nature of the subject to be judged. An unwillingness to weed the garden, the urge to put off yet again answering a letter are not merely little weaknesses amiably to be laughed off. They are moral failings, symptomatic of a central weakness. There are standards, we sternly remind ourselves, and they must be upheld. That cracked pillar, the human heart, must be maintained, or the tabernacle will fall.

I feel that many of Mr. Jenkins' characters have this stern scrupulousness and have it because such a quality infuses the mind of their creator. They are perpetually involved in a rigorous, not lightly forgiving self-examination. They sense that we must not only know the enemy in our own hearts before we face the enemy in the hearts of others but we must learn to forgive ourselves before we dare to forgive others. The danger is this. When we fall short of what we know we ought to have felt or done, we are angry and do not always attack the real malefactor. We find a scapegoat. Our ideals curdle and sour. We see our nastiness in others and hate them as if conspirators with us in some dark business. When men and women approach us, asking for love, we are angry for they are asking trustfully for what we have learned is no longer fit to be trusted, our capacity for loving. Therefore, to play our part, we must first forgive ourselves.

Duror, the stern, tormented, frustrated gamekeeper in **The Cone-gatherers,** slowly tries to work out his answer to the problem of marriage to a deformed and diseased wife in the gospel of endurance. He forgives himself, however, nothing of his hatred of his useless wife, least of all his transference of that hatred to the "holy fool", Calum, the cone-gatherer, innocent of all but deformity. Duror finds that he cannot endure the corrosions of hatred and kills what he hates—the misshapen dwarf and himself.

The sombre tone of this book, the almost obsessive concern with the love of, and hatred of, goodness, the haunting symbolism of the wood and its aspiring trees, which represent a sweet naturalness which Duror can never find in humanity and the superbly unsentimental evocation of the Highland scene help us to overlook the unsatisfactory attempt to portray the too self-consciously snobbish Lady up at the Big House. The book is a noble tragedy, only faintly flawed.

Auld Gourlay, father of the delinquent Sam in **Happy for the Child** has a vision of his world as disenchanted as Duror's but less diseased. A former Socialist miner, unemployed for years, he too is corroded but into a bitter half-humour; society does not want him, his fat, disgusting she-bear of a wife despises him. Gourlay's revenge is simple; he will have no illusions; he will accept any insult. He and an angry farmer seeking compensation for damage young Gourlay has committed pass along a pavement where girls are playing peaver. Gourlay, half wistfully gesturing towards lost youth, "nudged the peaver into another square". The farmer notices "a furtive sadness in the grey weaselly face".

> 'Ye're auld for the peaver', he said.
>
> 'I used to be a champion at it when I was younger'.
>
> 'I thought it was a lassie's game. I thought a boy would be found deid rather than be seen playing peaver'.
>
> 'I was found deid hundreds of times', said Gourlay bitterly.

Universally rejected, Gourlay has, however, forgiven himself his failure and derives from that achievement a dusty peace. Sometimes he risks undoing his peace even if he knows he will suffer as when his wife reminds him of the poetry he had whispered to her in their courting days. (pp. 58-60)

Perhaps the clearest example of this pattern of reconciliation to one's own failures lies in the mind of Harold Moffat, the liberal-minded intellectual of *Dust on the Paw* who finds himself furiously opposing a mixed marriage between an English-woman and an Asiatic because it externalises his own dilemma, married to a Chinese wife. He hates the thought of children of a mixed marriage suffering and so will have none. He cannot forgive himself this cruelty to his wife, even less can forgive her the greater serenity she brings to the problem and in despair not only does all he can to spoil the coming marriage but publicly and grossly insults his wife.

There is one scene in the novel which is characteristic of Jenkins' oblique way of making one of his self-torturers examine himself. Moffat has betrayed his Asiatic friend Wahab polit-ically in the hope of making his marriage with English Laura impossible. Sitting, symbolically enough, by a part of the river associated with his wife, Moffat is obsessed with the memory of an apparently irrelevant person, a brother-officer, killed years before in Burma. Puzzled, he reviews the man's character which was unexceptional, his own relationship with him which was unremarkable and half decides that he has remembered the man merely for the photograph, bloodstained in the moment of death, that he carried, showing his wife and child. Perhaps marriage and children are the clue, he thinks, but the reader has seen that it is more than that. ". . . he had done what he had to do in that quiet, dogged, self-preserving way which among soldiers makes for anonymity . . ." The dead man had achieved an order, a calm centre in his life, where the living Moffat had created only a desert. He had not managed to come to terms with himself.

To balance these characters who fight their way into awareness, Mr. Jenkins has created a succession of people who have a natural awareness which flowers readily. There is Mrs. McShelvie, the embodiment of Scots working-class strength who, when her not very bright son, Sammy, is killed, acts with an almost ballad-like serenity. Mrs. McKerrol, patient, willing to suffer any indignity if it will protect her children, is another. Indeed, in that strange anguished novel, *Love is a Fervent Fire*, she stands out as the only character who is truly warmed by that eternal bonfire. Jeannie, the struggling, un-lovely sister of young Gourlay, is of the same courageous breed as the other women. Indeed when one glances back over these ten novels, one realises that the people who have achieved wholeness by coming to terms with themselves and what life is likely to do with them are all either women or children. The torments of an acute consciousness of one's disharmony with the environment cynically provided by God, the miseries of recognising one's inadequacies but not the way of forgiving oneself for having them, all these are reserved for men.

I suggested above that Mr. Jenkins' first claim to distinction lay in his shrewd understanding of the human condition and his diagnostician's skill in tackling it. It is foolish to berate ourselves, whether as readers or critics for the rising urge to place authors in grades and to award them the alpha-plus of greatness, the alpha-beta of "importance" or the beta-plus of "significance". Any artist who offers his work to the public is offering something of value to him and we are right to assess its value for us. What qualities do we look for? I suggest that, to be an important writer, a novelist must deal with constant and urgent issues in a responsible way, unfettered by popularity or any non-literary theory. Greatness adds to these qualities an extra quality—perhaps an extra dimension—of finality, of imaginative originality which expresses itself in the power of producing hitherto unused images and combinations of words or by using traditional ones in a new way. Maurice Richardson, in a recent review, enunciated the qualities of the great novelist thus, "Gross creative energy; powerful imagination; high in-telligence; active temperament; plenty of sensitivity". Proba-bly the first is the rarest of the ingredients. In Scottish fiction, Scott had it, Grassic Gibbon had it and, at his highest, Jenkins all but has it. There are scenes in almost all the novels when a kind of ultimate perception descends upon his imagination so blindingly keen and white-hot that for a scene or so, nothing can go wrong. At these moments, the dangerous word "poetic" comes to mind. I call it dangerous because it suggests the hushed voice, the plummy big words and the cloying sweetness of epithet. I use poetic, however, in its true sense that the scene moves with the powerful compulsion of a poem, and that it is constructed out of images in themselves striking which strike sparks of illumination from each other as they come together in the mind. (pp. 60-2)

In *The Missionaries*, a Sheriff and a posse of officials and policemen have come to evict a party of religious enthusiasts who have invaded a Hebridean island, sacred to an ancient saint. The book is a study of faith in decline and of faith discovered. It is rich in allegorical overtones and full of half-realised myths, none of which obtrudes any more than the shadow of a passing gull. Something of the light and clarity of the Hebrides seems to have got into the writing which has a crisp, dry passion about it. The Sanctuary Stone stands chal-lengingly on the wide wet beach and had not lost its reputation for miracles. The very shells on the beach, the larks above the machair and the moving clouds have an almost Wordsworthian power over these thin-blooded missionaries of faithless civili-sation. (p. 62)

It is the supple strength wherein character, story and revelation move together with a unified flow that elevates the scene to the condition of poetry and is one of the marks of greatness.

One last example must suffice. Mrs. McShelvie, that timeless figure of enduring strength and goodness, has been evacuated from wartime Glasgow. She has a rebellious fineness of per-ception her neighbours lack and in the country lifts her eyes to the hills as a symbol of her aspirations. At the end of the book, having suffered much, culminating in the loss of her son, Sammy, and beset by "inward anxieties, self-accusations, scruples and forebodings" she makes a ritual pilgrimage up Brack Fell, a hill that has hung tantalisingly over her all through the book. She fails to reach the summit. To reach that elusive peak would be, she had felt, an act of cleansing and renewal in which she would make a vow of dedication to the grim task of returning to the slums of the city "prepared to create as much light there as she could not only for herself and her family, but for her neighbours." The journey has been a failure because her physical strength has failed. Her spiritual strength wavers, but does not flicker out. The book ends on a note of quiet, unrhetorical but utterly Scottish moral passion and purity. (pp. 63-4)

It is a just measure of Mr. Jenkins' achievement that to find Mrs. McShelvie's equals, we have to look back to Jeanie Deans and Chris Guthrie, those two Scotswomen of a like strength and moral beauty. (p. 64)

> *Alastair R. Thompson, "Faith and Love: An Examination of Some Themes in the Novels of Robin Jenkins," in* New Saltire, *No. 3, Spring, 1962, pp. 57-64.*

THE TIMES LITERARY SUPPLEMENT

[Jenkins's *The Tiger of Gold*] is, like the excellent *Dust on the Paw,* set in the east, in the independent kingdom of "Nurania" and in India. Unfortunately it is unlikely to add anything at all to his reputation, and indeed is novelettish both in story and treatment. A young Scots lass of eighteen falls in love with the princely heir to an Indian state, and he with her. Immediately the inevitable—the only too inevitable—complications caused by different race and social position arise and enmesh them. But two things in particular go wrong with the handling of this story. In the first place, Mr. Jenkins has made the eighteen-year-old girl the narrator. Everything is seen through her eyes, and neither her responses, nor the language chosen to express them, are sensitive or even acute. Secondly quite a large part of the novel is taken up with a trip taken with an American family through India to Rajpur State where the Prince now rules. This . . . is strictly tourist stuff.

Miss Quested's famous remark "I'm tired of seeing picturesque figures pass before me as a frieze" has often been quoted, but nowhere is it more apt than in connexion with this novel. She continues, it may be recalled, "It was wonderful when we landed, but that superficial glamour soon goes."

> *"All That Glitters," in* The Times Literary Supplement, *No. 3143, May 25, 1962, p. 377.*

R. G. G. PRICE

The Tiger of Gold has the courage to begin as though the reader were in for a study of the barriers to marriage between a Scots girl and a Maharajah and then to shift its stance until the centre of the novel is the American hick millionaire who befriends her. It moves from the north-western state where her father is a veterinary surgeon to a tour across India, during which she slips off to the principality where her lover rules, hoping against hope that he will not marry the girl betrothed to him in childhood. The story is, as usual, very readable and packed with vivid pictures of the locale. Like Mr. Norman Lewis, whom he slightly resembles, Mr. Jenkins makes his interest in the contemporary world sharpen his narrative, not blur it, and he

also shares the Lewis eye for the particularity of place. All his ambitions for this novel have not been realised. The decision to tell the story in the first person has led to interlarding the tale with spurts of sonsie gush and there is some uncertainty about what level it is written on: sometimes a Forster or Scott Fitzgerald theme is tackled with the no-nonsense relish of Nevil Shute getting at the innards of a plane with a Parker 51. (p. 842)

> *R. G. G. Price, in a review of "The Tiger of Gold," in* Punch, *Vol. CCXLII, No. 6351, May 30, 1962, pp. 841-42.*

THE TIMES LITERARY SUPPLEMENT

Mr. Robin Jenkins has travelled a long way since, in *Happy for the Child,* he established his claim to be considered the most promising of the younger Scottish novelists. At last, with *A Love of Innocence,* he is showing signs of fulfilling that early promise. Leaving India and the rest of the world behind him, he returns to his native heath, to Scotland, a Hebridean island called Calisay and the grim conurbation of Glasgow, and he seems refreshed by this new contact with his roots. Not that he depends on local colour. He is too ambitious, as well as too honest, for that. His theme is self-knowledge and the destructive elements that lie at the heart of knowing who one is. His approach is varied. He takes a motley collection of people, children and adults, in various stages of self-ignorance and shows, through the catalysis of an ugly relevation, how their growing awareness of their own limitations and follies commits them still further to their natural vices.

The hero-villain of the piece must be among the most complex characters of modern fiction. He is called Angus McArthur, is charming, intelligent and completely unscrupulous. Of all the characters he is perhaps farthest advanced along the road to self-knowledge and he knows himself to be completely immoral and self-interested. . . .

Opposed to him, and complementing his self-awareness, is a child welfare officer called Margaret Mathieson who knows a great deal about children and some adults but is totally ignorant of her own vulnerability. She falls victim to his charms and is soon deliriously happy, only to be disillusioned as she learns more of herself and of him. Her fall from the grace of ignorance is recited with a delicate and humorous compassion.

Even more remarkable, though, than the veracity with which Mr. Jenkins treats the world of adults is the intuitive candour he shows when dealing with the more distant but no less dreadful territories of the children. The whole book rings of children and sings with their laughter. Nor does it ignore the darker side of their experience. The key incident, indeed, in the plot is the witnessing, by a six-year-old boy, of his mother's murder at the hand of his father. . . .

But these characters, though rich enough in themselves, by no means exhaust the fertility of Mr. Jenkins's imagination. He creates dozens of others, all convincing and all peculiarly Scottish. . . . And all these varied people are held together by a plot as simple and as tortuous as a Grand Master's chess game. Mr. Jenkins has, in fact, written the novel which we knew he had in him but which he has been reluctant so far to commit to paper.

> *"Know Thyself," in* The Times Literary Supplement, *No. 3195, May 24, 1963, p. 369.*

R. G. G. PRICE

A Love of Innocence is a grave, serious study of irresponsibility. Two sons of a murderer are adopted from a children's home by a couple on an island off the west coast of Scotland. Around them several other relationships are formed, some sentimental, some productive of incautious cruelty. The people are odd and intense, the places lyrically pure and calm. Credibility wavers but not interest. Mr. Jenkins is a bit like Paul Scott, with the same kind of professionalism and integrity. (p. 866)

> *R. G. G. Price, in a review of "A Love of Innocence," in* Punch, *Vol. CCXLIV, No. 6405, June 12, 1963, pp. 865-66.*

DAVID CRAIG

[Robin Jenkins] is a popular library-novelist, and he does tend to skate along the surface with a facility that sometimes disguises a failure to more than sketch the outlines of the very complex characters, especially women, that he sets out to present. Yet at his best, which means not infrequently since *The Changeling* (1958), his lightness can, as in the early E. M. Forster, serve as the attitude of an unpartisan intelligence, not too heavily invested in any one of the characters or milieux he creates and thus able to bring out the value of each. Like Forster, and like T. F. Powys, Jenkins is forever concerned with the need for tenderness and humility—that we should be ready for and open to one another, not so afraid of being thought fools by the worldly-wise that we harden ourselves off into some role of self-importance or self-righteousness that stultifies the living impulse. Jenkins is acutely aware of how people can be hurt—he evidently feels deeply the wound of the Second War and the sheer knowledge that the Glasgow slums are there. He is moved to atone by warm love, and the feelings involved are indeed hard to dramatise without sentimentality. In Jenkins this comes out sometimes as a quite swamping tendency to the arch and whimsical: the likeness to Forster and Powys is too often to their weakest work, the quasi-supernatural whimsies of Forster's short stories or Powys' poorest novel, *Kindness in a Corner*. In *The Missionaries* (1957), for example, about the eviction of a community of religious devotees from an old holy island in the west, there is little respite from the flow of heavily gnomic conversations, crankily oracular characters, and moments of "miracle" that are left much too nearly endorsed by the author himself.

Nevertheless, the startling likeness of the style at many points to Forster and Powys is something Jenkins has a right to. Many a touch in his novels shows his Powys-like ability to note in a symbolic way the smallest symptoms of cruelty or malice, e.g. this image of a bland, treacherous shopkeeper looking at the corpse of a boy, from a novel about evacuees from Glasgow, *Guests of War:* "Michaelson dabbed now at one side of his moustache and now at the other, with his knuckle: he was imitating the swing of the gravedigger's spade." The most obvious likeness to Forster is Jenkins's ability to generalise, often paradoxically, on the dramatic moments he has created, as in this passage from a novel about a Scottish girl in love with a high-born Indian—*The Tiger of Gold*:

> Remembering Chandra, with my eyes, my lips, my breasts even rather than with my intellectual memory, I was convinced he had been sincere in Isban; but even sincerity in love was not, I realised with a spontaneous gush of thankfulness, as unchangeable as those stars. If Chandra no longer wished to marry

me, it did not mean he never had; and the change was insulting to neither of us.

I think Jenkins's problem has been to find his way to subjects good not only for entertaining story-telling but also for the treatment of his deepest preoccupations at a level more deep-reaching than an easy opposition of the priggish and the warm-hearted, the self-righteous and the tolerant, and so forth. *The Changeling* shows him at his best—and strikes me as one of the finest things in British fiction since the War—because in it the meaning isn't issued to us in little wise mottoes and the drama stands up by itself. The theme is, characteristically, that of a man trying to do good and finding that good, as the world receives it, can turn painfully into its opposite. Forbes, a rather pompous good-hearted Glasgow schoolteacher, decides to take a slum lad on holiday with his own family, to "give the boy a chance." For though the lad is clever, well-behaved, and mature, he is reputed a rogue because no-one can believe anything else could come from so squalid a home and because authority is constantly being nettled by the impenetrable *suffisance* the lad has developed simply to survive. On the holiday everything goes wrong—Mrs. Forbes is on edge waiting for signs of criminal slumminess, the other children are jealous, Forbes can't help wanting *some* sign of warmth or oncomingness from the imperturbably civil lad. (pp. 166-68)

Nothing could be finer than the sure way in which the novel then moves to what we feel to be its only possible end—a tragic end, which implicitly recognises the hopeless difficulties of thinking to solve dilemmas of class and inequality by single acts of kindness. The final pages are unerring, and show how Jenkins's gift as a narrator springs from his keen, loving knowledge of how people feel and behave. This open-hearted interest in people, the humane radicalism which gives an edge to his writing whenever it deals with privilege and inequality, the marked distrust of fanaticism—these are qualities which put him with the "liberal" tradition in modern British writing. From the Scottish point of view what is so heartening is the breadth of his interest in not particularly "national" subjects (like many an English liberal, especially Joyce Cary, he is interested in children and in the backward countries). In him we have a talent that richly typifies what I meant when I said at the end of *Scottish Literature and the Scottish People* that "a freer spirit, facing up more openly to experience at large whatever its origins, might better enable the Scottish writer to cope with the problems of living in this place at this time." (p. 169)

> *David Craig, "A National Literature? Recent Scottish Writing," in* Studies in Scottish Literature, *Vol. I, No. 3, January, 1964, pp. 151-69.*

THE TIMES LITERARY SUPPLEMENT

Whether the affair is distinctively Scottish is rather doubtful, but what happens [in *A Very Scotch Affair*] is that an insurance inspector in his forties, who considers himself sensitive, can at last no longer stand the constant teasing of his fat affectionate wife, his daughter's tacit disapproval of his pretensions to culture, and the grim ugliness of the tenements where he lives. As the novel starts we see him turning to a well-off intellectual spinster whose talk is sown with cultured pearls and who understands, or at least sees through, him. It is potentially a rich subject, and with his usual fertility in imagining situations Robin Jenkins draws in a tight network of friends, relatives, enemies, acquaintances as the dilemma ramifies. He has the fund of observations necessary to give the whole the restless air of life: he can catch the feel of an ordinary place (a shabby wind-scoured bus stop on a winter night) and the bite of vernacular talk. . . .

This new novel, however, would have had to establish character more solidly for us to feel that the underside of behaviour had been revealed in proportion to the richness of the subject. Two weeks after a first reading it is too hard to recall more than a few slight instances of what Mungo Niven is supposed to be. . . . Perhaps Robin Jenkins should have presented him in a sustained way through the eyes of selected other characters. He is not embodied enough. His incessant aggrieved interior monologue invites us to sympathize with him; we get signals that we are not meant to, wholly; but he is too little of an objective presence for us to know finally what our view of him is to be.

It is a painful novel: at every point, the uglinesses, discouragements, meannesses, harshnesses, failures of life are harped on as unrelentingly as by the Graham Greene of *Brighton Rock*. This devotion to meanness would not provoke so much resentment if the novel were in sum convincing. There are striking chapters, with admirably dramatized shifts, typical of Robin Jenkins, between the painful and the gross or hearty that goes on next door to suffering. The ending, with its perspective of a dubious future, is perfect, especially for a fiction or tale of *nouvelle* length. But too many moments are passed off with a whimsical epigram or with a startling clumsiness of phrase, including even "His eyes bulged". As often before, one is left wishing that Robin Jenkins would think it worth his while to write less skimmingly, more deliberately, sinking deep into his material, and fusing together his wealth of Scottish impressions into the excellent novel that at times he seems to have in him.

> *"Disembodied," in* The Times Literary Supplement, *No. 3464, July 18, 1968, p. 745.*

GILLIAN TINDALL

The very Scottish pessimism of Robin Jenkins's [*A Very Scotch Affair*] impresses, but fails to be very moving because such care is taken to ensure that *every* character forfeits our sympathy to a large extent. Set in one of Glasgow's better tenements, it deals with the disintegration of a family when the father takes off with another woman while his wife is dying. He is a lecher, with intellectual aspirations too feeble to save him, his wife is a fat Glaswegian whose kind heart will not save her, his son is a creep, his daughter a ban-the-bomber who refuses to make moral judgments. Wandering round with a cough and hair permanently rain-sodden, she is too carefully posed and labelled once and for all to be entirely convincing—and the same is true, in diferent ways, of the others. Rather than causing events, they seem violently manipulated by the plot in order to make a general point about the human predicament. The minor parts in this morality play, a chorus exemplifying Lust, Pride, Hate, etc., are excellent.

> *Gillian Tindall, "Devious Method," in* New Statesman, *Vol. 76, No. 1949, July 19, 1968, p. 86.*

CLAIR TOMALIN

[Colonial history is implied] in Robin Jenkins's *The Holy Tree*. It starts as a Burgess-like comedy, English schoolmasters and police with their raddled womenfolk engaging in a series of misjudged dealings with the Chinese, Malay, Indian and other racial groups of 'Kalimantam.' The hero is a bright mountain boy who yearns for education; his ambition is to become a politician; en route he betrays the shibboleths of every group and offends everybody, including one of those terrifying randy schoolmistresses Robin Jenkins specializes in. The end of the book is not comic, but the observation is always sharp and humane and it is well worth reading.

> *Claire Tomalin, "The Poisoning of X," in* The Observer, *May 4, 1969, p. 30.*

THE TIMES LITERARY SUPPLEMENT

Aldridge and Forster (and Joyce Cary) are surely the standard one needs in considering what *The Holy Tree* amounts to. It is set in Borneo (not Malaya as the dust-jacket says). At the centre of what Mr. Jenkins is trying to bring to life is a young villager, Michael Eking. He is possessed by Western culture—its speech and writing, its skill with books, its prestige, all of which he conceives of and seeks to use as the one way out of the life where "at the bottom lay the padi-fields in which he would find himself up to the thighs in muddy water, clutching rice plants, like a man returned from a dream". There are some poignant details: a taciturn Chinese shopkeeper refusing even to lend the newspaper from which Michael deciphers the news in case it might be stolen: Michael walking for miles along hot tracks, limping with the sores on his legs, getting to a school or a town or a government office by the hardest of roads. But the essence of such a character, if successfully created, would surely lie in the contradictory thoughts that seethed in him as he struggled between two ways of life, and Eking's trains of thought never have the feel of a consciousness in action: they remain synopses, coming from the author, conventionally grafted on to the figure moving on the screen. There is little of the immediacy with which Joyce Cary presents his Nigerian counterparts, especially Johnson in *Mister Johnson*, excited with visions of esteem and an easy life. Cary's method is constantly to cut quickly from a scene or piece of behaviour seen objectively to what is being made of it by minds taken up by poverty and primitive fears or longings. By contrast Mr. Jenkins seems never to have thought out the special ways that would have been needed to suggest the mind of an undeveloped country.

The novel is good-hearted and well-informed enough in its dramatization of the communal pressures that work in such a country with its mixture of British, Chinese, Dusun (the indigenous people), and Tamil, and especially in its feeling for the Dusuns, stagnating in poverty, politically feeble. But it would have taken a far more studied technique, expressing a greater intensity of concern, for it to rise above a kind of B-picture treatment of its subject.

> *"Colonial Crudities," in* The Times Literary Supplement, *No. 3506, May 8, 1969, p. 481.*

THE TIMES LITERARY SUPPLEMENT

[In *The Expatriates*] a Scottish family—McDonald, who has previously worked in Malaysia, his new wife, who runs an expensive dress shop in Glasgow, and his mother, a retired matron, Agnes McDonald, O.B.E.—go back briefly to the man's old Eastern station, called Kalamantan, to try and bring back with them the little girl, now seven, whom McDonald had fathered on his former servant, a girl twelve years younger than himself. The situation swarms with possibilities. Yet a lacklustre novel has come of it. As Henry James so often affirmed, a culture or a literature "is a matter of attitude quite as much as of opportunity'', and it now looks as though Robin Jenkins will never dwell on his concerns long enough, brood on them and fathom them and find the reserves of intensity to rise to them. Ever since the clear-eyed realism of *The Changeling* and the fine perception of feelings in *Guests of War* and *Love is a Fervent Fire,* he seems to have been content to write, rather quickly, the sort of 256-page novel that suits the printer because it is the right length, the publisher because it has a bit of everything—sleeping-around, exotic colour, and so on— and the reader because it is just interesting enough to make him think yet never deep or subtle enough to leave him debating with himself which characters are meant to be egoistical or selfless, laughable or impressive. . . .

[The] thinness of this novel can be at least partly traced to the nullity of the main man. Mr. Jenkins seems almost to have forgotten to characterize McDonald. Little time is spent inside his self, as a physical presence he hardly begins to exist, the crucial experience has happened long before. Possibly this kind of thing explains the thinness as a whole. The intense life is all off-stage. We have it reported and judged and gossiped about, and sometimes the colonial Yacht Club flickers into life. . . . Yet we are given scarcely a probe into the motivation or the aftermath of this action that he takes at the time above all when he would probably have been on his best behaviour.

> *"Offstage Intensities," in* The Times Literary Supplement, *No. 3606, April 9, 1971, p. 413.*

CLAIRE TOMALIN

Robin Jenkins has a kindred theme in *The Expatriates,* which is set largely in Kalimantan (the name he has already used for Malaya in an earlier book). Jenkins is a straightforward leisurely and well-informed writer, never rising to great heights but reliably observant and intelligent. Ronald McDonald, a conventional Scotsman, now married to a countrywoman, returns with his wife and mother to claim the little daughter born to him in Kalimantan by Jenny, a Sino-Dusun girl whose beauty and docility are in marked contrast to that of the European women he knows.

The sweating and boozing European community is cruelly detailed by Jenkins, who once again devotes many pages to the portrayal of sexually predatory and unappetising middle-aged women. Gentle Jenny, to whom the prejudiced Ronald is a god she will sacrifice everything for in silence, is described by one such woman as 'the worst traitress ever to your own sex.' The author does not commit himself to a verdict on whether it is best to be crushed like a beautiful and ineffectual butterfly or survive to squawking discontent; nor does he propose solutions to the racial and sexual tangle beyond the brisk common sense tempered with kindness displayed by the Scottish mother. Even that, he knows, does not preserve the innocent from their fate.

> *Claire Tomalin, ''An Illiberal Education,'' in* The Observer, *April 11, 1971, p. 29.*

THE TIMES LITERARY SUPPLEMENT

Robin Jenkins's novels are often at odds with their own morality. *The Expatriates,* for example, taught us to be unself-conscious about race; but the characterization of the coloured mistress—all humility and perfection—was patronizing beyond words. Now in *A Toast to the Lord* race gives way to sex and religion: but there is still the same vast gap between what the novel says it is doing and what it actually does.

Agnes is the daughter of a strict Puritan preacher: she believes that everything in the small Scottish town of Ardhallow has been sent by God—including an American nuclear submarine and a sailor called Luke. With Luke she starts to experience what Mr Jenkins intends to be sexual liberation. . . . Sex in this novel is really a very nasty business: so nasty, in fact, that Agnes's joy at finding herself pregnant becomes totally incomprehensible.

But Mr Jenkins's handling of religion is even more awry. Ann, the daughter of the respectable Presbyterian minister, goes to pieces completely when some boys from Glasgow wantonly destroy her dog. But Agnes, armed with a gentle faith, can sail calmly through a night in which an orphan boy wanders out into the storm, her mother dies of cancer in hospital, her father chops Luke to pieces with a hatchet and leaps to a spectacular death from a bridge. . . . The effect of all this on the reader is to imagine that Agnes must be off her head. But the effect on the sceptical headmistress—whose remarks end the novel—is an unaccountable renewal of faith. It is almost as though Mr Jenkins is frightened by the conclusions his novel is coming to. He stops everything, closes his eyes and firmly toasts the Lord.

> *''Quite a Night,'' in* The Times Literary Supplement, *No. 3676, August 11, 1972, p. 935.*

EDWIN MORGAN

Over the last twenty years Robin Jenkins has published almost as many novels and built up a considerable reputation. He is not the sort of author who has written one book of such unquestioned artistic success that all his other books have to be measured against it, and, in fact, reviewers have often been strikingly at variance in their estimates of his merits. But it would be fairly generally agreed that his most valuable and interesting work is in *Happy for the Child, The Thistle and the Grail, The Cone-Gatherers, The Changeling, Some Kind of Grace, Dust on the Paw* and *A Love of Innocence.* Most of his best books, though not all, are set in the West of Scotland (whether Lowland or Highland), where his naturally sharp observation combines with his sense of basic and recurring Scottish themes.

In an article in the *Saltire Review* in 1955, he argued that the novelist's job in Scotland was, above all, to be honest: to use the life he saw round about him, as a novelist in any other country would do, and be confident that it could be made interesting to readers outside Scotland. 'We have been a long time in acquiring our peculiarities: in spite of ourselves, they are profound, vigorous and important; and it is the duty of the Scottish novelist to portray them.' The wry awareness of that 'in spite of ourselves' is good, and typical of Jenkins, but perhaps the operative word is 'peculiarities', since there is no doubt that Jenkins's novels, for all their emphasis on honest reporting, do sometimes present an extremely peculiar world: a world that can only be regarded as in part symbolic and fabulous, however much local detail and dialect may be employed. . . . [The] religious preoccupation is constant, and it is the mingling of this preoccupation with two other things—the flavour of ordinariness, and the sudden very marked irruptions of violence and melodrama—which gives his books their characteristically odd and often enigmatic sort of resonance. The religious preoccupation wavers between residual Northern Calvinism, observed both sympathetically and tartly, and intimations of a wider kind of grace. The ordinariness is children at school, football matches, holidays at the coast. The melodrama is a hunchback shot in a tree by a neurotic gamekeeper, a schoolboy hanging himself in a hut, a boy watching his mild father murder his faithless mother with a hatchet, an orphan boy eaten by crows, a lay preacher taking his hatchet to an American sailor who he thinks has seduced his daughter and jumping to his death from a bridge. It is into this grim wasteland of a gap between the placidity of everyday expectations of order and habit and the fearful potential of horror that Jenkins drives his questions, which not surprisingly turn out to have a metaphysical dimension. (pp. 242-43)

Jenkins concentrates, in the main, not on characters in the prime of life but on children, the middle-aged and the old. This is unusual in itself, but it helps him to present with greater immediacy and sharpness contrasts between expectancy and knowledge, innocence and guilt, obedience and freedom, as well as the tangle of frustrated or late or twisted or consuming erotic experience in the over-thirties which is another curious and at times grotesque feature of his work. Some of the books offer a wary hope, some are tragic, some are deeply ambiguous. In *The Changeling,* a Glasgow school-teacher takes one of his East End kids with him and his family when they go on holiday. The boy is a thief and a liar but intelligent, sensitive but stoically inhibited, conditioned by poverty but capable of change, yet dogged by an almost malicious bad luck so that the teacher begins to feel 'inimical non-human forces' using the boy as their instrument: he is a changeling. Although one can see that the changeling's anguish has clear social roots—he can neither leave nor (by the end) rejoin his own class, home and family— his suicide on the last page seems rather forced, rather too didactic. The teacher (an unsuccessful one) has been brutally rewarded for his do-gooding.

Children are again at the centre of *A Love of Innocence.* Two brothers from an orphanage in Glasgow are boarded out in the Western Highlands, into a God-fearing community. Must the sin of their father, who murdered their mother, be visited on them? Even to those who are sympathetic and who like the boys, 'they seemed to lie under some kind of guilt.' But those who would send them away as contaminators of Highland purity are defeated, and the novel ends in some optimism. Its title, however, is not unambiguous, since if it offers a positive on the one hand, this seems to be turned inside out on the other, considering the fact that the main adult character, a philanderer, bigamist, fraud and blarneyman, and very far from 'innocence', is presented as a likeable rogue and by no means devoid of good qualities.

Extreme vulnerability is shown as, in the end, defenceless in *The Cone-Gatherers,* the most atmospheric and mysteriously suggestive of his books, marred only by novelettish touches (great ladies and their gamekeepers are not Jenkins' forte). Here, guilt and cruelty and suffering are shown, not as social or personal, but as written into the world of nature of which man can only be a part. During a world war, two brothers are working in a Highland forest, gathering cones for seed. Both are strange, Hardyesque earth-creatures. Against malice and rumour they have poor defences. The grimness of the ending, when the hunchback brother is killed by the gamekeeper, is only relieved by the implausible catharsis of Lady Runcie-Campbell, weeping in pity on her knees among the pine-cones.

For some years Jenkins taught in Afghanistan and Borneo, and he uses these countries as background in some of his novels. It is generally thought that he works best with Scottish material, but the attempt to break out from this was certainly justified in *Dust on the Paw* and *Some Kind of Grace,* if not in *The Tiger*

of Gold or *The Holy Tree. Dust on the Paw* is a long and ambitious novel. The main theme of mixed marriage is probed with insight and humour, within the broader political context of a recently independent state trying to find its identity among the new dollar and rouble imperialists. (pp. 243-44)

In his novels since *a Love of Innocence* (1963) Jenkins has shown some uncertainty of aim, and his last book *A Toast to the Lord* was an exceedingly odd production. There are improbabilities in many of his stories, but here they are as bold as brass and as hard to swallow. It is as if James Hogg should be talking about justified sinners, go out half-way, come back disguised as Muriel Spark and start talking about miracles. (pp. 244-45)

There is much greater satisfaction to be had from his new book, *A Far Cry from Bowmore,* which is a collection of six short stories. Here, the Malaysian setting in a post-colonial era, where a large part of the inhabitants are Indian or Chinese, though many an angular expatriate Scot is also to be seen, provides a jungle of ironies which he picks his way through humorously and well. He is good at illustrating his recurring theme of the clash of moralities, not only Western v. Oriental but intra-Oriental as well, until terms like 'bribery', 'flattery' and 'veracity' are turned inside out, and nothing solid seems to remain except the ability to hold on to threads of tolerance or hope or the mere persistence of life. ["**A Far Cry from Bowmore**"] shows the loveless and prejudiced Presbyterian rectitude of a Scottish engineer being broken into at last by pagan funeral gongs and the dignity of a Malaysian woman at the death-bed of her Scottish husband, whom he had once met in Islay. But in this story the narrative is rather contrived. In the freer, more comic, novella-length "**Bonny Chung**", which is the strongest story in the collection, didacticism is kept at bay: this spectacle of a young expatriate Chinese on the make, with the unfolding of his educational and sexual adventures in a mixed-race society, is excellently done, and ends the volume on its best note of irony. (p. 245)

Edwin Morgan, "The Novels of Robin Jenkins," in his Essays, *Carcanet New Press, 1974, pp. 242-45.*

ANNE STEVENSON

In *A Would-Be Saint,* Robin Jenkins . . . attempts to create a good man who withdraws from the world on ideological— Christian—grounds. . . . [His hero, Gavin Hamilton], remains remote, holy, unsympathetic and priggish to the end. I have never read a novel whose hero I disliked—and disbelieved in— so entirely. By Gavin's repeated confession—in which, unfortunately, he is backed by a lot of Scots Presbyterian doctrine—goodness consists not of warm, positive feelings towards other human beings, but of the cold, negative virtue of never being beholden to anyone less holy than thou.

Gavin, the good, bright boy in a Lanarkshire mining community, naturally suffers all he can be made to suffer. His father is killed in the 1914-18 War. His mother, suspiciously pretty, dies not much later. Gavin is reared by a horrible Scots grandmother—the one believable character in the book—who puts an end to his education. In an effort to make Gavin seem human, Mr Jenkins turns him into a football star—a role which is, of course, the next thing to sainthood in the Scottish calendar of virtues.

Predictably, though, Gavin gives up football because it is too violent just as he gives up, or rather puts himself in a position to be given up by his rich girl-friend when he takes a prostitute into his house—but, of course, never into his bed. No drink, no sex, no violence, no political loyalties, no dependence on anyone, no taking sides in the war: such are the negative teachings of Presbyterianism as preached by this latter-day Christ. . . .

Towards the end of the book Gavin is shunted off to do forestry work with a collection of conscientious objectors near Loch Fyne. He lies awake on his first night listening to the rats scuffling behind the wall, "thinking about that *moral position, imaginable*, if not possible where a man had *cleansed himself of responsibility* for all evils of the war and so had *acquired the right to pity* not only those who had suffered from them but also those who had perpetrated them" (my italics).

Even if goodness *were* a matter of taking "moral positions" and cleansing the soul in order to acquire "the right to pity", Mr Jenkins's book would never convince us of the reality of this cold-hearted universe of moral debts and payments. The novel is full of talk by various characters, admittedly Scottish in nature, about the rights and wrongs of Gavin's behaviour. But the interior struggle of Gavin—or anyone else—never appears. We are *told* about it—much as we are told about the feelings of the characters in an Agatha Christie whodunit. Given the shallowness of the characterization and the superficial quickness of pace in this book, one half wonders in the end why Gavin didn't at least inadvertently bring about a death or two. In this, at least, he would have been a truer representative of the kind of Christianity he practises. But the irony of Gavin's position, alas, totally escapes Mr Jenkins, and Gavin isn't even allowed the dignity of martyrdom.

> Anne Stevenson, "Presbyter Writ Large," in The Times Literary Supplement, *No. 3985, August 18, 1978, p. 924.*

FRANCIS RUSSELL HART

The Scottish situation as Jenkins portrays it is desperately polarized between natural beauty and human ugliness; he dwells on the illusory temptation of pastoral retreat in the face of urban degradation. He pictures faith corrupted into football worship and into the loveless fanaticisms of orthodoxy. His imagination centers on two figures: the innocent child and the quixotic guardian. His innocents are most moving when they are both naive and corruptible; his guardians, when in their love of innocence they learn to know its limits and acquire humility. (p. 272)

Jenkins's purpose leads him into large-scale books with many characters and complex plots resting on numerous evolving relationships. It is hard to judge whether this challenge of scope and complexity stirs Jenkins to his best, or whether a limited, intense focus serves him better. Three of the largest books— *The Thistle and the Grail, Guests of War,* and *A Love of Innocence*—are among his best. But so are four of the most sharply focused: *The Cone-Gatherers, The Changeling,* and more recently *A Very Scotch Affair* and *The Holy Tree.* In the larger books a comprehensive moral interest requires a complex structure of thematic parallel and variation. In the smaller ones it requires characters of extreme symbolic weight—archetypal figures rendered psychologically in polarized settings. (p. 273)

Jenkins's novels show a remarkable continuity of motif and theme, a cluster of situations and problems alternatively worked and reworked, without marked shifts in mode or method. His feelings for Scotland fluctuate widely between anger—for what

his artist in *Sardana Dancers* calls "the cold, murk, and inspissated philistinism" that "tormented him too into vision"— and a marveling compassion for the sheer will to survive in those ground down by a life of Glasgow poverty. . . . Jenkins's concern with the degradation of modern Scotland is not that of the socioeconomic naturalist, but rather that of the theological moralist, with ways of living in the face of that degradation, and in the face of another undeniable given: a love of innocence. Innocence is always the lovely menace, the source of renewal and hope, but also the temptation to forget how far one is from Eden, how limited is one's humanity, how flawed one's love.

Lovely, ambiguous nature can provide "a morning that seemed to beguile the mind with recollections of a time of innocence before evil and unhappiness were born" (*Cone-Gatherers*), or a place which seems to the deluded romantic a "kingdom, where regret, humiliation, mercenariness, and failure, did not exist" (*Changeling*). The reminder comes often in the figure of the child; Jenkins, like the schoolmistress in *Love Is a Fervent Fire,* is never without the faculty "of being able to see in any man or woman the child betrayed and corrupted." . . . For one of the foster parents of *A Love of Innocence,* thinking of the cast-offs of lust and murder brought to her peaceful island from a city orphanage, it seemed "miraculous that out of so much human misery and sordid violence two such delightful little boys should have emerged, not only innocent in themselves, but inspiring innocence in everyone who met them." Why is it, then, asks the cone-gatherer Neil, "that the innocent have always to be sacrificed?" Why, as the town councillor's wife in *Guests of War* comes to see, should there be in her husband, "as in all humanity . . . a dark hell where she and his children suffered for his sins"? Often, Jenkins implies, it is because the guardians of innocence have not yet discovered the risks and imperfections of their love and the narrow limits of their humanity. It seems an innocent must die to impart the lesson.

Jenkins's protagonists often find themselves in the trap discovered by Moffatt in *Dust on the Paw:* "He found himself tormented by his love as by an enemy who knew him profoundly," or by Margaret Mathieson in *Love of Innocence:* "The need for love had revealed to her imperfections that only love granted could cure." Angus, her Lothario, speaks for all of the novels: "The truth was, of course, that everybody fundamentally could love only himself; selfless love was beyond the capabilities of human beings; when it appeared to exist it was really self-love in some pathetically ineffectual disguise." . . . But "love had to be accepted, in all its shapes; to sift and censor it, and leave out all that was neither respectable nor aesthetic, was to destroy it as an adventure"—so learns Andrew in *The Missionaries.* "Love by its nature is bound to be a little grotesque, but it need not be destructive." "Cherish love," comes the imperative, "especially if it's maimed or ashamed or comic" (*Sardana*), and the novels specialize in such versions of love. The result is a melancholy vision of "the vaster universal sorrow of humanity thwarted in its love by its own limitations" (*Guests of War*). The central revelation is always the same: "Maybe it's a miracle that love is able to exist here. But it does" (*Scotch Affair*).

The discovery of one's love as a coward or betrayer, the sensing of one's distance from Eden, brings with it the chance for "that maturest of virtues," humility (*Fervent Fire*). Charlie Forbes can no longer return in enchantment, a romantic Crusoe, to his glorious holiday heritage on the Firth of Clyde. He has learned that "his heart was of ordinary size, composition, and quality; only if he acted accordingly would he find peace; that it would be the peace of mediocrity could not be helped" (*Changeling*). The romantic heroine of *The Tiger of Gold* must give up her visions of her maharajah and go home, "resolved to cultivate a little humility." Bell McShelvie won't allow herself false hopes: "There was, then, Mrs. McShelvie knew, to be no complete redemption, no cleansing and healing of the wound. A little humility had been learned, and might as soon as tomorrow be forgotten" (*Guests*). (pp. 279-82)

Love without humility, Jenkins suggests, is cruelly perfectionist; and in the face of its pretensions, betrayal is inevitable. Mungo Niven, deserter of his slatternly wife, realizes too late that "if she had since degenerated, so had he; and he was not so sure now that she had contributed more to his degeneration than he had to hers. He had perhaps blamed and punished her for inadequacies neither of them could help" (*Scotch Affair*). . . . Lynedoch, the artist of *Sardana Dancers*, finds the want of humility a national trait: "I took a scunner because we're a small country that has never had the humility to admit its smallness, or even to recognize it. We stand on our own midden and try to blow our heads off crowing. Who hears? Who notices? Not even the English. In the past it was a miserably small contribution we made to the world's art. Now we make none, and never will. How can we? We've neither faith nor interest." (p. 282)

Humility is "the maturest of virtues," but without a love of innocence it turns into amoral quietism or despairing renunciation of the "world's falseness and triviality" (*Expatriates*). The challenges and commitments are not to be shunned because "we're not fit to face them." Such are the words of one of many deniers, and the deniers are always inferior in humanity to fools such as Charlie Forbes.

The deniers give up human community and long instead for the conscienceless grace of nature, a kind of innocence not to be recovered. In *Some Kind of Grace*, McLeod knows it for a moment: "Trembling, he sat and gazed at the house. His hand still hung down, as if maimed. Out of some green vines that covered part of the wall a bird flew, with a crest and a soft, cooing call. He watched it alight on a tree. For a moment he seemed to escape into life, where morality did not exist." (pp. 282-83)

We find in Jenkins several states of life that call for the term grotesque. There are the innocents who by some mystery are monstrous. . . . There are the physically battered or gross figures of middle age in whom, almost hidden, the innocent child still lingers. There are the degenerate, aging women feigning a naive sexuality in their longing for love. There is poisoned love breaking out of repression into perverse violence. All these states are tests of love and compassion, trials in humility; to those who cannot pass the tests but cling fanatically to a vision of edenic innocence and loveliness, they seem grotesque. . . . But the horror need be no more than natural pity and revulsion and amusement at what modern Glasgow makes of human beings, or what human beings make of themselves and one another. There are no clear hints from Jenkins that we need to believe in a hell or a heaven outside of the human psyche and human society.

Yet the hints, however unclear, must be recognized. For Jenkins is nothing if not a religious moralist, and some of his most potent images and key terms are theological in suggestion. There is the negative side, the bitter attack on puritanical morality and Calvinist theology, from the frightening self-righteousness of Charlie Forbes's mother-in-law, to that of spinster-virgin Margaret Ormiston in *The Expatriates;* from the "lecherous bigots" of *The Missionaries* to the holy hypocrites who feel no charity for Mungo in *A Very Scotch Affair*, reaching a peak of intensity in the ascetic fanaticism of the missionaries in *Some Kind of Grace.*

But that title is subtly elucidated. It is not just the sarcastic reference of the searcher McLeod to the way these ascetics must have made love: "There could be little doubt that before it she would have gasped out some kind of grace and after it a thanksgiving." To Jenkins, all kinds of grace, like all kinds of love, must be cherished. McLeod, whether he knows it or not, is searching for some kind of grace, the kind to be found in the filthy, suffering Afghan poor, or in the call of a bird, or in Kemp's remembered vision of Eden on a Wester Ross mountain top. The trick is in learning to recognize signs of grace. In *Love Is a Fervent Fire*, the conservator glimpses it in Carstares' wit: "Such self-condemnation, fairly seasoned with wit, was, he thought, a sign of grace." Andrew Doig learns more generous thoughts in *The Missionaries:* "They did not take into consideration the eccentricity of grace, which in human beings could assume strange shapes. God sometimes chose to honour those whom their fellow mortals would never have thought of honouring." At tea with his sluttish, dying wife, Mungo Niven says, "I suppose it's too late for grace," and she replies, "It should never be too late for that, Mungo" (*Scotch Affair*). Bell McShelvie reflects on the miracle that people somehow "by their very separate existence on the earth were granted this virtue of diminishing the accumulated evil that was in the world. Some called it, she knew, the grace of God" (*Guests*). She is no church-goer and presumably would not think to call it that.

It appears not to matter what Jenkins would call it. It remains for him a central miracle, and perhaps faith in such miracles is the faith whose loss he laments. But Andrew Rutherford, remembering his Covenanting heritage while en route over the moors to Carnick, finds football a poor substitute for faith: "Scotland was a country where faith lay rotted like neglected roses, and the secret of resurrection was lost. We are a dreich, miserable, back-biting, self-tormenting, haunted, self-pitying crew, he thought. This sunshine is as bright as any on earth, these moors are splendid: why are not the brightness and splendour in our lives" (*Thistle and Grail*). What faith, what love, could redeem such a crew? For Andrew, "If human love failed, was there not God's love to revive and strengthen it?" Another good man—Uncle Dave of *A Very Scotch Affair*—"sought always to find good in people, not because he was a Christian, for he never went to church, but because it was simply a seeking he had been born with."

Is grace, then, an accident of birth? Or faith an accident of national culture? Jenkins is too much a natural moralist to offer answers to such questions. But his narrative preoccupations and his explicit, moralistic stances as narrator repeatedly raise them. The same themes—the fascination and the perils of innocence, the many grotesque shapes of love, the terrible imperatives of humility, the eccentricities of grace—are investigated anew in each novel, in a few basic plots, with each novel growing from a germ in an earlier novel, or returning with a new view or emphasis. (pp. 284-86)

Francis Russell Hart, "Novelists of Survival: Linklater and Jenkins," in his The Scottish Novel: From

Smollett to Spark, *Cambridge, Mass.: Harvard University Press, 1978, pp. 246-86.*

JAMES PARK SLOAN

[In *Fergus Lamont*] Mr. Jenkins returns to the Glasgow slums of his childhood for a ruminative novel, into which he pours a life's reflection on art and moral choice.

Orphaned at 7 when his disreputable mother drowns herself, young Fergus Lamont is left with only the kilt he has that day buckled on and the secret conviction that he is somehow "special." He pursues that conviction down the dubious path of snobbery, seeking to recover by military valor and marriage his mythic aristocratic inheritance. While in the trenches, he begins to write poetry. In time, like such artistic cousins as Tonio Kröger, Stephen Dedalus and, especially, Gulley Jimson, he grows into the kind of brilliant, marginal man who simultaneously makes love and war with family, country and kind.

In Mr. Jenkins's scheme of things, place assumes a special importance, and his Scotland becomes a realm more exotic than Afghanistan, comparable, perhaps, to Joyce's Dublin. Poetry itself is the discovery of a radiant inner essence in what others pass over as commonplace. The poet extracts and exhibits that radiance, converting stairhead lavatories into "Stairhead Lavatories" and gathering dung into "Gathering Dung." While he is at it, Mr. Jenkins lets us know what art is not—a list that includes politics, cynicism, facile popularity, academic gentility and the fashionable avant-garde. (pp. 14-15)

James Park Sloan, "Other Times and Places," in The New York Times Book Review, *February 3, 1980, pp. 14-15.*

L. B. MITTLEMAN

Fergus Lamont, an old-fashioned, richly textured novel in which the author demonstrates . . . the older virtues of lucidity, restraint and intelligence, is a straightforward moral history of a man and of his country. To Jenkins, the Scottish people are nearly as central to the novel as is Lamont: Scots who have inherited a rigid, artificial class structure, a narrow Calvinistic religion and a still narrower moral imagination. Nevertheless, Lamont smashes the iron barriers that subdue many of his fellow Scots. He rises from the lowest class to a position of great wealth and distinction: he frees himself from the intolerance of family and caste to become a genuinely compassionate human being; and, greatest of his triumphs, he becomes a poet of the common people whom he had once despised.

Like the protagonist of Philip O'Connor's *Memoirs of a Public Baby*, Lamont is the son of a whore, a waif who manages to rise above his sordid environment to earn his manhood. Unlike O'Connor's neurotic hero, however, Lamont is strengthened by poverty, not traumatized by its abuses. Rather, it is luxury that nearly destroys him. His marriage to the wealthy, calculating Betty T. Shields, hack writer of popular romances, saps his integrity. But his love for Kirstie McDonald, the sturdy lass of the Hebrides, restores him both as a man and a poet. . . . The conclusion—ah, Betty T. Shields would have admired the romance of it all! And that is a pity. For Jenkins writes with a depth of conviction, a lyricism that deserves a more ironical treatment of his kilted hero—and perhaps also a harder look at Scotland. (p. 440)

L. B. Mittleman, in a review of "Fergus Lamont," in World Literature Today, *Vol. 54, No. 3, Summer, 1980, pp. 439-40.*

THE CRITIC, CHICAGO

Gavin Hamilton, the hero of this unusual novel [*A Would-Be Saint*], is a man with the soul of a medieval saint in a world where people are "sorry for Christ, not inspired by Him." Set in Scotland during the 30s and 40s, the story concentrates on Gavin's service in a forestry camp as a conscientious objector in World War Two. His decision to "take up his cross daily" makes him a lonely, enigmatic figure who only finds peace in the end by becoming a hermit. Robin Jenkins demonstrates his skill as a writer by refusing to take the easy way out and make Gavin a martyr. . . . Gavin suffers only a dry martyrdom in his anguish over the war. If you are tired of the current crop of novels about super-Popes and scheming bishops, you should find this book refreshing and disturbing.

A review of "A Would-Be Saint," in The Critic, *Chicago, Vol. 39, No. 6, October, 1980, p. 8.*

WILLIAM BOYD

The Cone-Gatherers (first published 1955) is a moody, heavy-hearted story of two brothers, one tall and sullen, the other hunchbacked and angelic, whose job it is to harvest pine-cones—for eventual reforestation—during the Second World War. This they do on the massive estate of one Lady Runcie-Campbell somewhere on the west coast of Scotland. The hunchback, Calum, a timorous, nature-loving simpleton with, yes, a face like a Donatello cupid, pale and ringed with soft curls, attracts the venom of the Lady Squire and of her baleful gamekeeper Duror. Lady Runcie-Campbell's distaste is based on solid bourgeois *snobisme*. Her frail son Roderick is fascinated by the cone-gatherers' arboreal expertise and it just isn't right that the little chap should be intrigued by the lower orders (Jenkins indulges in some ponderous satire on this point). Accordingly Lady Runcie-Campbell colludes with the grimmer motives of Duror, whose splenetic loathing of Calum is less easy to understand, even though the hapless cripple has made the mistake of freeing half-throttled rabbits from the game-keeper's snares.

Duror's poisonous hatred, however, provides much of the narrative impulse of the book, insofar as it compels him, again and again, to attempt to rid the estate of the cone-gatherers' presence. . . .

Drawing on Scottish ballads and minstrel songs, *The Cone-Gatherers* is evidently meant to function as a fable: a moral tale of evil confronting innocence. However it largely fails in this respect because its mood and atmosphere are so tried and tested, so much a feature of hack Scots mythology.

Indeed the only character who truly comes alive is Duror, the gamekeeper. Duror's wife is an obese wreck, a quivering bed-ridden tub of lard whispering endearments everytime he returns home. Calum is the handy objective correlative upon which Duror can vent his frustration and poignant misery. The hunch-back's exultation in the simple natural pleasures of life stands as an intolerable rebuke, a permanent reminder of an attitude to life that he, Duror, can never hope to attain. Eventually—inevitably—Duror has his way and Calum becomes the victim of the gamekeeper's violent expiation. The ending—blood and sap dripping from the cones—comes as no surprise.

It's a pity really, because in the figure of Duror, with his grotesque wife and his perfervid misanthropy, one senses an altogether different history striving to take shape: an altogether more unpleasant, malevolent, and—dare one say it?—more Scottish novel.

William Boyd, "A Walk in the Wuid," in The Times Literary Supplement, *No. 4050, November 14, 1980, p. 1294.*

PHILIP SMELT

In the foreword to his new novel [*The Awakening of George Darroch*] Robin Jenkins outlines the history of the division in the Church of Scotland between evangelicals and moderates which led to the Great Disruption of 1843 and the formation of the Free Church. . . . Jenkins says that in the ten years leading up to the rift Queen Victoria ascended the throne, Britain acquired Hong Kong and slavery was abolished, but historians have neglected the Scottish ecclesiastical row, the 'soul-shaking disruption'. Jenkins has set himself a tall order if he wants his novel to readjust historical perspectives; in this respect it fails.

For the rest, it is a successful treatment of one man's resolution of a moral and theological conflict. George Darroch is a faint-hearted evangelical minister who faces a lonely struggle to square his conscience with the practical and financial demands of his large family, weakened by the early death of his wife. The plight of the poor in his own congregation and the hypocrisy of the moderate Church leaders encourage Darroch to believe that his conscience demands his withdrawal from the established Church; but his responsibility towards his family suggests that he should seek the patronage and parish of a rich landlord. . . . His final awakening is colourful, if not convincing, and it is clear that for him, at least, the Great Disruption was indeed soul-shaking.

Philip Smelt, in a review of "The Awakening of George Darroch," in British Book News, *February, 1986, p. 110.*

Denis Johnson

1949-

West German-born American poet, novelist, and short story writer.

In his verse and fiction, Johnson often depicts anomic individuals who strive to attain spiritual fulfillment or transcendence. Frequently compared by critics to Flannery O'Connor and Robert Stone for his grotesque characters and religious concerns, Johnson brings a visionary poetic sensibility to his prose while evoking the psychological states of people who experience extreme emotional conflicts. In both genres, Johnson portrays the urban United States as spiritually decadent, but his work usually suggests the possibility of survival and redemption.

Born in Munich, West Germany, Johnson moved frequently as a child, infusing in him the belief that life and relationships are impermanent and unstable. He began his literary career as a poet; although not overtly autobiographical, Johnson's early verse includes references to his problems with drugs and alcohol, his interest in film and rock music, and his travels. Johnson's first two collections of poetry, *The Man among the Seals* (1969) and *Inner Weather* (1976), were published by small presses and received scant commentary. However, a critic for the *Virginia Quarterly Review* praised the poems in *The Man among the Seals* for their "sophistication and controlled intensity," noting that "Denis Johnson finds moments of psychological nakedness, moments when the devious corners of our minds are illuminated, and presents them in an imaginative and gracefully colloquial manner." Johnson's first volume to earn substantial recognition, *The Incognito Lounge and Other Poems* (1982), established him as a documenter of American subcultures. Employing various forms of narration and surreal, kaleidoscopic imagery, Johnson portrays with humor and compassion the attempts of alienated urban characters to establish and maintain various types of relationships. Robert Miklitsch remarked that the poems in *The Incognito Lounge* "speak to the neglected, shadow sides of our selves, [and] illuminate . . . the prosaic world in which men and women go doggedly about their dark lives of desperation." Johnson's recent volume, *The Veil* (1987), consists of stylistically diverse poems marked by vivid imagery, esoteric vocabulary, unconventional syntax, and frequent shifts from colloquial to abstract language.

Johnson has also garnered critical acclaim as a fiction writer. His first novel, *Angels* (1983), is an episodic, realistic depiction of the tragic misadventures of drifters Jamie Mays and Bill Houston in a spiritually deteriorating United States. Bill, an ex-convict, attempts a bank robbery with his brothers; he kills a guard, is convicted, and is sentenced to die. Jamie, meanwhile, is committed to a mental institution after an experience with drugs. In his review of *Angels,* Keith Abbott lauded Johnson's "remarkable job of capturing the street people life in a novel whose structure approximates their dizzying spirals of diminishing options." Johnson's second novel, *Fiskadoro* (1985), is set in Florida two generations after a nuclear disaster has destroyed most of civilization. The survivors, who live in a primitive community known as "the Quarantine" and speak in a colorful language that incorporates elements of English, Spanish, and technological jargon, have forgotten their pasts

but nonetheless experience the same feelings of loss, estrangement, and imminent ruin that afflicted their ancestors. Johnson focuses on the efforts of three characters to rebuild civilization: a teenage boy, a middle-aged man, and a one hundred-year-old woman. Eva Hoffman called *Fiskadoro* a "startlingly original book" that examines "the cataclysmic imagination, a parable of apocalypse that is always present and precedes redemption in a cycle of death and birth, forgetting and remembering." In *The Stars at Noon* (1986), a cynical, unreliable female narrator posing as a journalist travels to Nicaragua and becomes involved with an Englishman who has divulged industrial secrets to the Sandinistas. Through the activities of these characters, Johnson attempts to underscore the problematic consequences of American intervention in Central America.

(See also *Contemporary Authors,* Vols. 117, 121.)

PETER STITT

The first thing that strikes the reader of Denis Johnson's *The Incognito Lounge and Other Poems* is its neon style. The adjective is suggested not just by the title, drawn from the supposed name of a bar, but by the inspired design of the book as well. Johnson's writing crackles with electricity, as in the opening lines of the poem **"Heat"**: "Here in the electric dusk your naked lover / tips the glass high and the ice cubes fall against her teeth. / It's beautiful Susan, her hair sticky with gin, / Our Lady of Wet-Glass-Rings on the Album Cover." Of course this poem is comedic and so the poet has gone to special lengths almost to parody himself. Still, the lines are representative of a lot here, and show a further extension of the baroque style that is fast coming to dominate contemporary poetry. (p. 920)

To begin with such an example, however, is to give a false impression of what Johnson is most importantly attempting in this book. Despite the pervasiveness of the poet's sense of humor, this ultimately is far more of a heart-rending than a comic volume. The characters who people these poems are drawn from the streets, the diners, the lounges, and especially the buses of America. They possess neither money nor college diplomas, have no status and not much dignity. They are people we might be tempted to condescend to, if Johnson did not handle them so well, handle them in a way that reveals the love he feels for them. . . . Failed dreams, and the sense that somewhere inside the self that one presents with so little distinction to the world there is a person we wish it could know, wish someone would love.

There appear to be three separate forms of narration in the book. The weakest poems are the several in the second section written in a personal voice seeming to speak literally of problems in love and marriage, the resulting loneliness. Much better are the several dramatic monologues scattered throughout the volume in which Johnson gives voice to characters clearly different from himself. Between these extremes are poems in which Johnson both maintains a kind of third-person distance from his characters, presenting them from a slightly more knowledgeable position than they themselves occupy, and identifies with them as well. Although this doesn't make much sense when stated so baldly, it is something we are familiar with—it is the way Raymond Carver writes his incredible little stories, "both in and out of the game, and watching and wondering at it." We see this voice in poems like **"The Song,"** which attempts to define "The small, high wailing / that envelops us here, / distant, indistinct." At the end of the poem we learn that the sound "is actually the terrible / keening of the ones / / whose hearts have been broken / by lives spent in search / of its source, / / by our lives of failure, / spent looking everywhere / for someone to say these words." Johnson is both one of those who wail and one of those who searches, he is the one who says "these words" and the one who wants "someone to say these words." A remarkable achievement in a young poet. One reviewer has asked that Johnson write more dramatic monologues; actually, given the nature of this doubling voice, which is both the poet's and someone else's, he may already have done so. (p. 921)

Denis Johnson may well be the best of a number of unusually talented and interesting young poets who have recently begun to appear. (p. 922)

> *Peter Stitt, "A Remarkable Diversity," in* The Georgia Review, *Vol. XXXVI, No. 4, Winter, 1982, pp. 911-22.*

ROBERT MIKLITSCH

"Surrealism" is one of the catchwords of this century which, like "wit" in the seventeenth, has been used so often and in such widely differing contexts as to have retained only a vaguely pejorative meaning. Though it was first used by Apollinaire (in a subsidiary and not entirely serious manner), it is usually associated with its most polemical spokesman and publicizer, Andre Breton, and later practitioners in French poetry such as Aragon, Char, Desnos, Eluard and Peret and, in painting, Dali, Tanguy, Ernst, Delvaux, Miro and Magritte. In some sense, it is a product of a unique historical climate: in Europe after the Great War, there was still a solidified bourgeoisie to rebel against and, for Breton at least, surrealism was an instrument for social change, a revolutionary force. In the recent past, though, it has also been used—much too loosely I should emphasize—to designate a certain style of American poetry fashionable in the sixties and seventies, one that sought to undermine that Eliotic-inspired, New Critical tradition and its emphasis on rationality and self-consciousness. It can be seen at work, for instance, in Bly's aesthetic of the "deep image," a later diluted version of which became known as "barnyard surrealism," and in the New York School, whose poets (O'Hara, Ashbery and Schuyler, to name three) were widely read in and influenced by French surrealism.

Polemics aside . . . , it seems to me that, in terms of the artist—whether poet or painter—it is most useful to speak of surrealism as an attitude or sensibility: in other words, it presupposes that one has a novel, if not revolutionary, apprehension of the world. In this sense, it is something you are born with, *not* something you can learn. A surrealist work, in turn, should involve what the Russian Formalists called a "making strange" and produce an effect of "defamiliarization," an estrangement of the familiar. I rehearse all this because there are readers of American poetry who have despaired of finding a genuine surrealism in the dross that has passed for it over the years; I think I can safely say, however, that they need look no farther than Denis Johnson. When I first came across his work in a recent "anniversary" issue of *Antaeus*, I immediately thought: *this is the real stuff.* Though the issue was not short on good, and in some cases even excellent poems, **"The Incognito Lounge"** was the only one that I returned to with the obsessive regularity that I associate with the excitement of hearing a new voice, one that twists tradition in such a way as to *seem* wholly independent of it.

Now, having read and re-read *The Incognito Lounge and Other Poems,* which was chosen by Mark Strand for the National Poetry Series, I would be less than honest if I did not begin by admitting that the book is not as original or as consistently surprising as the title poem ["**The Incognito Lounge**"] led me to believe. Like every poet, especially young ones, Denis Johnson owes a debt or two to his precursors, not least to Strand himself (obvious in Johnson's recourse to "the story of our lives"). And if he cannot be accused of being a poseur in the annoying way that Breton and Dali and even, say, Ashbery can be (the last another influence on Johnson), a number of poems are unfinished, technically speaking (e.g. **"From a Berkeley Notebook"**). And yet, given these caveats (not, I might add, unusual ones for a first book), I am still struck by how *extraordinary* Johnson can on occasion be. Coleridge said that some poets make the extraordinary ordinary (he was thinking of Wordsworth), and some make the ordinary extraordinary. Johnson, like Coleridge, belongs in the second category.

Here is the first stanza or "strophe" of the title, and premiere, poem of *The Incognito Lounge:*

> The manager lady of this
> apartment dwelling has a face
> like a baseball with glasses on and pathetically
> repeats herself. The man next door

has a dog with a face that talks
of stupidity to the night, the swimming pool
has an empty, empty face.
My neighbor has his underwear on
tonight, standing among the parking spaces
advising his friend never to show
his face around here again.
I go everywhere with my eyes closed and two
eyeballs painted on my face. There is a woman
across the court with no face at all.

Clearly, this is not the kind of verse which relies for its effects on acoustics in general or metrics in particular or, for that matter, rhyme and enjambment (the rhyming, mostly internal and off, is minimal and only the breaks in line two and twelve carry any real poetic charge). What the above passage obviously does rely on is the obsessive image: in this case, one of the most intimate and seemingly familiar of images, the human face. Though surrealism has frequently been understood as the immediate juxtaposition of the quotidian and the strange, this is a static, derivative version of its true subject and *modus operandi:* metamorphosis. The latter, more profound form is evident in Johnson's metaphoric and metonymic variations on the image of the human face which, in his hands, suffers a number of sea changes. To be more precise (and mechanical), there is an initial substitution of the inanimate for the animate (''a face / like a baseball with glasses on''), a reversal of that process (''the swimming pool / has an empty, empty face''), a repetition and displacement of the initial image (''I go everywhere with my eyes closed and two / eyeballs painted on my face'') and, finally, a ''negative'' or *effacement* of it (''a woman / across the court with no face at all''). A fantastic world this, one both frightening and fascinating where nothing is what it seems because nothing stays the same, because everything is always changing into everything else.

Johnson's protean, surrealist poetics may be too painterly (i.e. merely decorative) for some—in the way that some painting is criticized for being too ''literary''—but the concluding strophe of **''The Incognito Lounge''** should dispel any doubts as to the authenticity of his vision:

Maybe you permit yourself to find
it beautiful on this bus as it wafts
like a dirigible toward suburbia
over a continent of saloons,
over the robot desert that now turns
purple and comes slowly through the dust.
This is the moment you'll seek
the words for over the imitation
and actual wood of successive
tabletops indefatigably,
when you watched a baby child
catch a bee against the tinted glass
and were married to a deep
comprehension and terror.

In the concluding lines above, the speaker experiences a moment of identification and regression that cannot be attributed to ''painterly'' contrivances or *trompe l'oeil,* coming as it does out of that ''deep comprehension and terror'' which is one of the continual sources of poetry.

I should note here that in order to suggest some of the pleasures and surprises of **''The Incognito Lounge,''** I have not done complete justice to it, having quoted only two (the beginning and end) of its nine strophes. This is not to say that its fragments form some kind of ''whole'' or totality; on the contrary, its individual parts are connected only by the speaker's compelling voice and the episodic history he presents, scene by scene, like

technicolor slides of a foreign country we have read about but never seen. Johnson's imagination, however, seems particularly suited to this kind of poem, one composed of seemingly self-contained anecdotes that, put together, produce a skewed but strangely satisfying story. (pp. 246-49)

Surrealism may be Johnson's privileged view of things and what makes his work seem so distinct in the context of contemporary American poetry, but that work would be nothing without his sympathetic imagination. The result is poems that speak to the neglected, shadow sides of our selves, that illuminate, like the neon light on the cover of the book, the prosaic world in which men and women go doggedly about their dark lives of desperation. (p. 250)

> *Robert Miklitsch, in a review of ''The Incognito Lounge and Other Poems,''* in The Iowa Review, *Vol. 13, Nos. 3 & 4, Spring, 1982, pp. 246-50.*

PETER ORESICK

[*The Incognito Lounge* is] flawed by a distracting habit, though not an unconscious one, and it eclipses much of the book's best writing. I'm referring to Denis Johnson's apparent difficulty in writing a poem without mentioning the word *light.* After several readings what I remember too well is the fluorescent light, the refrigerator light, dance hall light, cups of light, half-light, fiery light, roads of light, light like whiskey, etc. Of the thirty-one poems in the book, twenty use the word. Five of those use the word three times or more within the same poem. The result, obviously, is predictability and annoyance. The more the image reoccurs, the more it loses meaning, not accumulates meaning, because of the dramatic attention it calls to itself. I'm sure Johnson would rather call this an obsession, but after close reading I'm hard pressed to believe it. Obsessions are central to the vision of the poet. Most often the *light* bit is gratuitous, a stagey device, and the repetition creates a rhetoric, not a deep image.

What is central to Johnson's poetic vision, however, is the idea of alienation. His poems are peopled by high school truants, office workers, bag ladies, refugees and barflies, and no amount of light imagery can illuminate them. They are faceless. . . . Johnson's characters are not memorable as individuals. An achievement of his book is its success as a kind of collective biography of a mass type: alienated man. Johnson means to keep them faceless because this underclass is faceless. His strategy assumes that alienated man is an abstraction because little remains of his relations to his activity, work, or fellow human beings, and he has lost touch with human specificity. . . .

Johnson's response to his subjects is ultimately what interests me most about **The Incognito Lounge,** and that response varies—sometimes self-identification, compassion, sometimes revulsion or detachment. Yet what bothers me at times is an emotional distancing that is really nothing less than grandstanding. . . .

In the final analysis I believe in Johnson's integrity (and God will forgive him). I'll be curious to see more of his work, to see if the rich texture and scenic quality of the poems are maintained, and to see if the hocus-pocus with light is abandoned.

> *Peter Oresick, in a review of ''The Incognito Lounge,''* in The American Book Review, *Vol. 5, No. 2, January-February, 1983, p. 18.*

WILLIAM HARMON

The best poems in *The Incognito Lounge* remind me of eerily lucid lines written by other Americans born in the forties—James Tate, Louise Glück, Kathleen Norris, Albert Goldbarth, and Robert Morgan. For *The Incognito Lounge,* especially for its incandescent title-poem, "surrealism" is not quite the word, because a plain-text "real" Arizona exists in the same space as "unreal," "surreal," or "irreal" states, confederated in a Union potentiated and sponsored by the mechanisms of metaphor, enjambment, syntax, rhyme, and rhetoric. Consider these passages from **"The Incognito Lounge"** itself:

> The center of the world is closed.
> The Beehive, the 8-Ball, the Yo-Yo,
> the Granite and the Lightning and the Melody.
> Only the Incognito Lounge is open.
> My neighbor arrives.
> They have the television on.
>
> It's a show about
> my neighbor in a loneliness, a light,
> walking the hour when every bed is a mouth.
> Alleys of dark trash, exhaustion
> shaped into residences—and what are the dogs
> so sure of that they shout like citizens
> driven from their minds in a stadium?
>
> . . . . .
>
> But these shoppers of America—
> carrying their hearts toward the bluffs
> of the counters like thoughtless purchases,
> walking home under the sea,
> standing in a dark house at midnight
> before the open refrigerator, completely
> transformed in the light. . . .

The surface and pace here seem smooth and even, but they turn out to contain an efficient hive of activity. In the passage beginning "Alleys of dark trash," for example, the dramatic anacoluthon (what begins as a declaration abruptly becomes a question) calls up the same vivid rhetorical device as at the end of Yeats's "A Second Coming" and is just as horripilating. Throughout, Johnson manipulates a slight dislocation of idiom—"*a* loneliness," "walking" made into a transitive verb, "from their minds" instead of "out of their minds"—that inhibits too smug a conclusion or reaction. The use of explicit simile in "like citizens" and "like thoughtless purchases" causes other metaphors to seem less like comparisons and more like anecdotal equations: every bed is indeed a mouth. The witty ambiguity of "bluffs" (topographical and commercial) and the submarine environment, probably derived from Poe, are both given crisp definition and resolution by rhymes at the end: "sea," "midnight," "completely," "light." (pp. 461-62)

Five of Johnson's finest poems are sonnets, or nearly so: **"White, White Collars," "Heat," "Vespers," "Sway,"** and **"Passengers."** I wish I could quote all five in full, to show his virtuosity in launching a poem, as it were, in the ice and water of its own melting, where it rides to some breathtaking destination. . . . When I finished reading Johnson's book and still had the humor and depth of **"The Confession of St. Jim-Ralph: Our Patron of Falling Short, Who Became a Prayer"** haunting my memory, I happened to turn back to a piece of perfunctory front-matter: "The author is most grateful to the Book-of-the-Month Club, the National Endowment for the Arts, and the Arizona Arts Commission for gifts that made these poems possible." No way. The gift that made these poems possible is Johnson's own unique personal property. The charitable institutions ought to line up to guarantee continued financial support for Johnson's poetry, because it is terrific. (pp. 462-63)

William Harmon, "A Poetry Odyssey," in The Sewanee Review, *Vol. XCI, No. 3, Summer, 1983, pp. 457-73.*

ANATOLE BROYARD

When we first meet Jamie, the heroine shall we say, of *Angels,* she's sleeping in a bus, dreaming about men dying in a cloud of poison. We read that "she wished she could smother her baby," one of two children she seems to have conceived for the sole purpose of extending her indecisiveness. Jamie is running away from her husband because his conviction that "one moment goes to the next" strikes her as a very limiting way of looking at things.

On the bus, Jamie meets Bill, an ex-convict who is covered with pornographic tattoos. They go together to a hotel where the bedding "smells of sorrow." Jamie tries to persuade Bill to take her to Philadelphia to see the Liberty Bell because she can't think of anything else to do. Her life is narrowing down to national monuments. Every time she does her laundry, Jamie throws away some clothes, because it's less to wash, carry, or know about. She keeps throwing away bits of her life, too.

As you can see, *Angels* begins badly, but after Mr. Johnson settles down, the novel actually turns out to be pretty good. Mr. Johnson . . . has a nice way with details, which is always a promising sign. There is an interesting moment when Bill is sobbing drunk, leaning on the wall of a building, and he cries out, to himself really, "I wanna meet my *responsibilities!*"

He and Jamie go back to Phoenix, his hometown, where his mother lives on a street "where things could only fail to occur." Like so many contemporary writers, Mr. Johnson catches the terrifying *absence* of beauty in our cities, a quality far more dire than dirt or threat. Here, again, we have a heroism of ugliness, as if our writers were boasting to everybody from Baudelaire to John Berryman that we have outstripped their darkest imaginings.

"All the songs on the radio," Bill reflects, "talked about his experience." It's hard to imagine a worse fate. Because he has all the impatience of a man with nothing to live for, Bill decides to rob a bank with his two brothers and another fellow. . . .

The bank robbery is well described. Though they have rehearsed it many times, James, the middle brother, is taken aback this time by the actuality, the largeness and the seriousness of the bank. He feels that "he wanted to detain his partners, invite them to get a sense of the place." It sounds as if the bank, seen under pressure, is the first environment that ever moved him.

They are all caught, of course, and since Bill has killed a man in the bank, he receives the death penalty. Unluckily for him, the authorities are in a punitive mood just at this time. In Death Row, he is put next to the only other murderer in the prison and, because they both throw off such a strange light to each other, they tape up old newspapers on the bars between their cells.

Jamie, meanwhile, goes insane as a result of taking drugs, and Mr. Johnson reverts to his bad habits. Her insanity is like the acid trips in the novels of the 1960's, full of third-rate poetry. When we get back to Bill, though, we find that, as Samuel

Johnson said, the threat of death has wonderfully concentrated his mind. He "speaks directly to the heart of the moment," and worries about the fact that people "with motels in their eyes" will see him, or imagine him, in the chair in the gas chamber.

Before Bill leaves his cell for the gas chamber, the guard asks him to take off his pants. When Bill asks why, the guard says, "We can't have a big pile of clothes all soaked with gas." There are quite a few other good moments in the second half of *Angels,* as if Mr. Johnson needed a universal subject like death to sober him up and bring out the quality in him.

Anatole Broyard, "Throwaway Lives," in The New York Times, *September 14, 1983, p. 14.*

JOHN CLUTE

The great direction of the American soul is Westwards. No American novel of any ambition can begin in a California bus terminal and head straight towards Pittsburgh, as does Denis Johnson's *Angels,* without waving metaphysical flags that warn of dire things to come. . . .

Two main characters emerge from the squalor of this initial transit. With her two monotonous children, Jamie is trying to escape a marriage gone wrong, back in Oakland. There are relatives of some sort (we never meet them) somewhere in Pennsylvania. Middle-aged drifter Bill Houston has some money to burn, and offers to burn it with Jamie. She is easily distracted from her relatives. After four or five days the bus deposits them in Hell. . . .

In the first third of *Angels,* which is the telling and brilliant part of this very uneven first novel, Jamie and Bill undergo a Hogarthian Progress to the filthiest acre of Hell, somewhere in Chicago, where she is tortured, raped and drugged out of her mind. He rescues her.

He takes her to his criminal family in Phoenix, Arizona, but the Westward movement is a cruel pretence. Robbing a bank, he kills a guard. He is arrested. He is executed. Jamie survives a stint in the psychiatric wards. In her crazed state she sees something like angels. They tell her that she has fallen through into reality, reality being who she is and where she abides, for there is no Dream left.

Acute, muscular, and quite relentless, Johnson . . . is about to write a major novel, if *Angels* can be taken as a guide. In this book there is the metaphysical bite, the eye for terrible detail, the grasp of character. But he got his venues wrong. His Phoenix is hollow and strained; Bill Houston's God-ridden mother and brothers tip the whole horrific narrative into hyperbole, at just the point where we need to believe every word. All the same, we believe enough of *Angels* to recognize a new voice.

John Clute, "Heading Downwards," in The Times Literary Supplement, *No. 4231, May 4, 1984, p. 486.*

JOHN SUTHERLAND

Angels introduces us to its heroine, Jamie, at the Oakland Greyhound station. She is running away from a trailer-park marriage gone wrong. On the five-day journey to her sister in Hershey, Pennsylvania, she falls in with Bill Houston. 'A nice man', Bill is a loser: three times divorced, an ex-sailor and ex-con. He is going, as he says, to Pittsburgh, for a spell of 'wine, women and song'. They get loaded on his bourbon.

Jamie turns out to be the woman he's looking for, and they both end up in Pittsburgh. Having spent all his fun-money, made rather a half-hearted attempt to prostitute Jamie and knocked her little girl about, Bill moves on to Chicago. (Dylan's "Like a Rolling Stone" is a leitmotif in the narrative.) Reduced to selling her blood, Jamie takes the money her long-suffering sister has wired her and instead of going where she should, to Hershey, never arrived at in this novel, she follows Bill to Chicago. At that city's bus station (where she hopefully posts herself and simply waits for him to pass by) she is picked up, drugged and raped by another nice man. Bill reads about her ordeal in the *Tribune,* and they are reunited. For no particular reason, they move on to Phoenix, where they gather a little moss in the shape of Bill's Bible-crazy mother and his two brothers, one of whom is a drunk, the other a junky. The Houston brothers hamfistedly attempt bank robbery. Bill kills a guard, and qualifies as the first criminal to go to the gas chamber under Arizona's new capital punishment statute. The last section of the novel follows his weeks in Death Row, and Jamie's psychotic nightmares, drying out in the Mamie Eisenhower wing of the local mental institution. Wherever it starts, the journey's end, as AA solemnly informs its members, leads to the prison, the asylum or the morgue.

Summarised, it's a grim, hopeless chronicle of little, insignificant lives: tales of the transient, no-account pilgrims who travel Greyhound. As Johnson narrates it, the whole thing is consistently tender and on occasion hilarious. All the characters—even the Chicago rapist—are oddly amiable. And the whole thing is told with a wry detachment which contrives to be both wisecracking and poetic. . . . Johnson's balance is admirable; his tone is never so cool as to be heartless, nor does his affection for his hopeless bunglers descend into sentimentality. The novel flirts with higher meaning, signalled in the title (the epigraph is a sombre nugget of Catholicism from Greene's *The End of the Affair*). There is a lot of byplay about souls, immortality and the manichean. 'Everybody's religious in the Death House,' as the guard tells Bill, before he takes his last walk. But Johnson contrives to smuggle in his seriousness obliquely, using as couriers a troupe of varied religious nuts who comically garble the novel's message. Serio-comic is a hard trick to pull off, but Johnson succeeds so well as to make one eager for more fiction from him. (pp. 19-20)

John Sutherland, "Johnsons," in London Review of Books, *Vol. 6, No. 10, June 7 to June 20, 1984, pp. 19-20.*

MICHIKO KAKUTANI

Denis Johnson's *Fiskadoro* is not the easiest novel to describe. It's the sort of book that a young Herman Melville might have written had he lived today and studied such disparate works as the Bible, *The Waste Land, Fahrenheit 451* and *Dog Soldiers,* screened *Star Wars* and *Apocalypse Now* several times, dropped a lot of acid and listened to hours of Jimi Hendrix and the Rolling Stones. It's a wildly ambitious book, *Fiskadoro*—full of mythology and philosophical speculation about the nature of time and memory and the endurance of language and art. At times it's beautifully poetic, at times insanely rhetorical, but its strange, hallucinatory vision of America and modern history is never less than compelling.

Although it's set in the near future (about 80 years from now), *Fiskadoro* creates a portrait of America that mirrors the one in *Angels,* Mr. Johnson's one previous novel—a portrait of America as a cultural and spiritual wasteland, peopled by drifters, con men and disaffected poets; a hot, violent land, eager for salvation, susceptible to madness and tottering on the edge of apocalypse.

In *Fiskadoro,* that apocalypse has already occurred; World War III or some form of nuclear disaster has wiped out most of civilization, leaving the survivors of "the Quarantine" to live in a primitive, pre-machine-age world. Yet if these people seem to have lost their historical memory . . . they nonetheless suffer from the same feelings of loss, alienation and impending doom that afflicted previous generations of Americans. They, too, live in a strangely disembodied dream state, unable to distinguish between what is real, imagined and remembered; and they, too, are waiting for the time when "everything we have, all we are, will meet its end, will be overcome, taken up, washed away."

It is one of Mr. Johnson's achievements in *Fiskadoro* that he makes the brave new world of the Quarantine thoroughly palpable, through his acute ear for language—most of the people in this book speak a resonant patois of English and Spanish that lends their words a certain mythic dimension—and his gift for visually precise description. He has chosen as his setting the sullen, exotic terrain of the Florida Keys, but he has reassembled this favorite fictional landscape like so many pieces of a shattered mirror, turning it into a place at once familiar and disturbingly unreal.

Key West has been renamed Twicetown, in honor of the two dud bombs that crashed there during the war, and its motley residents now conduct provisional lives amid the wreckage of earlier cultures: automobile seats, broken Xerox machines and moldy church pews dot the landscape, lyrics to old rock-and-roll songs buzz on the radio at night, and would-be messiahs go by such names as Bob Marley, Jake Barnes and Cassius Clay Sugar Ray. There is much talk of magic abroad in the land, and people seek deliverance in talismans and charms. Pirates, trading in contaminated goods, prowl the waters close to shore, and on the beach, gangs of pinheads, "the sightless and deaf, and creatures obliged to cover up their faces" wander in search of a home.

Nearly everyone in Twicetown, in fact, suffers from some kind of incompleteness, some kind of longing for a past they can't recover. . . .

Fiskadoro, the 14-year-old hero of Mr. Johnson's epic tale, will . . . learn that the price of survival—or salvation—may well be memory and a sense of self. Certainly his name, which comes from *pescador* (meaning fisherman) and *flagador* (harpooner), invokes associations with Christ, the fisher of souls; and Fiskadoro will in fact be heralded, in Twicetown, as a sort of new man—someone who promises to redeem the wasteland, or at least usher it into another age. Before he can assume that role, however, he must undergo a series of classic initiation rites that will leave him "all cleaned out inside like a baby": he will lose his father and his mother, as well as his manhood and his power to remember; he will descend to purgatory and return "not like other men."

The ritual ordeals that Fiskadoro experiences   are described in heightened, surreal terms. Toward the end of the novel, these hallucinatory riffs become longer and longer, the prose increasingly windy. . . . The reader is inclined, at moments, to say "enough," but these moments are rare. Such is the power of the narrative that one can only finish *Fiskadoro* with ad-

miration for Mr. Johnson's ambition—and a keen appreciation of his prodigal imagination.

> *Michiko Kakutani, in a review of "Fiskadoro," in*
> The New York Times, *May 1, 1985, p. C23.*

EVA HOFFMAN

Postnuclear literature often springs from ambiguous impulses. We all understand the big fear that propels it: what is more difficult to acknowledge is the element of wish fulfillment often present in fantasies of a world that has been swept clean of everything we know, and can therefore return to a pastoral innocence. In *Fiskadoro,* which joins the growing ranks of novels set beyond the end of the world, the poet and novelist Denis Johnson attempts something much more daring and provocative. He doesn't entirely avoid the millenarian impulse. But his startlingly original book is an examination of the cataclysmic imagination, a parable of apocalypse that is always present and precedes redemption in a cycle of death and birth, forgetting and remembering.

It is a complex and finally problematic vision. To convey it, Mr. Johnson constructs a fictional cosmos that is hard to enter, but whose resonant power becomes increasingly evident. *Fiskadoro*'s physical geography is gritty, lyrical, surrealistic—a landscape so densely concrete, and so disjointed, that it affects one like a feverish dream whose symbols and images demand interpretation. It is set in a time-warp described as the Quarantine, some 60 years after the nuclear destruction. . . .

It is a disturbingly familiar world, barbaric with both age and youth, and so are the populations inhabiting it. These vaguely multi-ethnic tribes engage in basic human occupations: they fish, barter, smoke, drink, form families and indulge in escapist nights of sex and music. They also speak a language that is the book's most interesting presence and invention—a hybrid dialect that mixes elements of Spanish, English, occasional injections of technological vocabulary and a distorted, primitive syntax all its own.

Like all the reduced circumstances of *Fiskadoro,* this impoverished idiom is a way of posing certain fundamental questions. What, in a world stripped of accumulated "cultural" knowledge, are the minimal units of communication and meaning? What, in our naked helplessness, are the available modes of knowledge? And how, given the central fact of death, can we wake from the troubled sleep of denial?

Death dominates the atmosphere, and forms the heart of the allegory. It is, of course, most hugely present in the event that shattered the previous world and gave rise to this one—the event that, in the novel, functions as the model and archetype for every death, every seemingly ultimate catastrophe. Evidence of this catastrophe is all around (a harmless nuclear missile lies, like a dark totem, outside Twicetown) but the characters, suspended in a limbo of semiconsciousness, can no longer decipher it.

In one of the central scenes, a group of people gather in a library, in nervous anticipation, to listen to a newly found book that may hold the key to what happened. It is simply a factual account of the atomic bombing of Nagasaki in 1945; but as passages are read aloud, the audience becomes increasingly hysterical, questioning its truth and finally drowning out its words. But a character called Mr. Cheung, who represents a more civilized sensibility and "believed in the importance of remembering," understands that the bomb is the cause of his world's amnesia. "As the bombs fell," he thinks, "already we were forgotten."

The scene is a powerful dramatization of our desire not to know the worst, even after it has happened. And the worst, Mr. Johnson implies, has happened many times over. "The world is repeating itself," one character reflects. But if the end recurs, so does the drive for meaning that is the beginning of the world, the counterpoint to entropy and dissolution. This drive, which is as strong and primal as hunger, is manifested in the various cults, rituals and tales proliferating in *Fiskadoro*—jumbled versions of the religions and legends we know, through which the characters reinvent their world and search for talismans to protect them from chaos and death. There are voodoo cults and followers of Allah, wild Israelites who construct a boat to await the coming of Jah. A man who calls himself Cassius Clay Sugar Ray creates his own cult by retelling his Odysseus-like adventures; when a woman finds out she has breast cancer, she recruits the help of a voodoo deity, Atomic Bomber Major Colonel Overdoze.

But the more elaborate quests are conducted through *Fiskadoro*'s three major characters, each of whom represents a different search for wisdom. Perhaps the most poignant figure is Mr. Cheung, the Chinese manager of the pitiable band called the Miami Symphony Orchestra, who clings to the few bits of knowledge remaining from the preapocalyptic time as if these fragments could really shore him up against his ruin. . . .

Yet for all the sympathy with which he is treated, Mr. Cheung's search for historical memory does not bring him into contact with the underlying significance of his world, and he becomes disillusioned with his efforts. The past, Mr. Johnson seems to imply, must not be forgotten, but it doesn't save; history is a nightmare that leads most of us into sleep.

The more efficacious spiritual alternatives are represented by the adolescent boy called Fiskadoro and by Mr. Cheung's grandmother, Grandmother Wright, who at more than 100 years is the only survivor of the earlier civilization. Both she and Fiskadoro plunge near the bottom of death, and from that dive retrieve a more direct knowledge of reality. . . .

Fiskadoro comes to his epiphany through an impersonal, tribal ritual of male subincision practiced by the nocturnal swamp people who have abducted him. In their hallucinatory, nightmarish id-region, he is taken through a strange ceremony, echoing various myths of origin, that leads both to a self-wounding and a total loss of self. He is also, in his state of delirium, initiated into a powerful language that gives voice and shape to the deepest forms of experience, connecting him to knowledge and meaning.

At the end of the rite, Fiskadoro has a vision of corpses, people killed in their automobiles. After that, he forgets almost everything he has known. But he has gained a deeper knowledge; he now plays the clarinet better than Mr. Cheung, and when a floating shape appears on the horizon from Cuba—another apocalypse? a redemption into a new age?—he is the only one, we are told, who is ready.

Somehow, Fiskadoro . . . has become initiated into our collective Platonic, or Jungian, memory. Like many mythical heroes, he has gained identity by daring to lose himself entirely. It is majestic stuff, and its intensity is heightened by Mr. Johnson's ability to release language like a full-throated, many-voiced choir. And yet there is something in *Fiskadoro* that resists the reader's full submission, or suspension of disbelief.

Perhaps there are some subjects that are too overwhelming to be taken out of their historical context and serve as a pretext for allegory. Why make a nuclear Armageddon—a potential fact whose implications are all too real—the point of departure for a parable of eternal recurrence, a universal fable that favors the mythical imagination? The specific event, with its possibilities for truly final destruction, overwhelms the book's symbolic layers, and makes them seem too close to mere psycholiterary games. Not that those games aren't very serious. Mr. Johnson has fashioned an enormously ambitious and highly condensed work of fiction that nevertheless has an allusive grandeur and depth. It is an odd case of a book that succeeds in everything but its subject—or at least is marred by the shadow of its very premise.

Eva Hoffman, "Postapocalyptic Pastoral," in The New York Times Book Review, *May 26, 1985, p. 7.*

KEITH ABBOTT

The two people [in *Angels*] whose lives make up the bulk of the narrative, Jamie Mays and Bill Houston, operate in a world almost bereft of motivation. Things happen to them, they do this, they do that. They are called "street people" and their world runs on the hidden logic of the fitful abandonment of will. In street talk, they are "space cases." This novel is appropriately "spacey" in its structure, consisting of short realistic scenes with hardly any connections. So for this narration, it is quite correct to have Bill Houston, in the midst of an alcoholic blackout, walk into a bar and try to guess what town he is in by talking to the bartender. There's a bravado to this life; the pointblank refusal to use "commonsense," or to even consider one's motivation, fuels its worse excesses. In *Angels* Denis Johnson has this world down pat; this is the book's greatest strength.

However, this world also becomes the biggest problem that Johnson faces: how to make a novel of this Brownian movement. The risks of a space case narrative are major: the reader may *not* supply the necessary attention, holding the emotional impact of the scenes in mind and letting them build. Even then, the reader can still simply dismiss the book as a disconnected series of blackouts with confused violent people. This is the undercurrent that gives the novel its narrative tension, not its characters' predicaments. The characters don't create tension, simply because they do not know that what they do matters to any larger scheme of things. They don't want to know. The novelist has to assume so much control that he is left with finding a solution. . . . So the tension in the telling of the story remains: when will these lives knit up into a semblance of meaning?

The novel's narrative strategy of creating bright, spacey scenes forms a discrete series which mirrors the life of the characters in its structures. This is a modern poetic method and it comes as no surprise to read that Johnson is a poet. This also shows up in the handling of the prose. Early in the book he tries for a poetic prose which seems at odds with the characters. Jamie, who never seems a poetic character, "pushes words away" and feels "the weightlessness of fear." This poetic prose goes awry at times. . . . Luckily, as the book progresses, these lapses into poetic prose decline and the power of the scenes takes over the narrative. The cumulative effect of viewing these scenes can be quite strong, given that the reader must expect no necessary connections. It also can become, as a friend remarked of the novel, "a jeweler's tray of samples."

The story runs something like this: Jamie runs away from her husband with her two children. She meets Bill on a bus. They go to Pittsburgh and spend Bill's money in increasingly random ways. Bill goes to Chicago. Jamie borrows money, goes there too. She is raped. Bill sees her story in the newspaper, goes to her and declares his love for her in one of the few statements of purpose by a character in the entire book. To provide for her and her family, he reverts to his criminal past and returns to Arizona to his weird family and plans a bank robbery. Jamie gets hooked on pills, cracks up, and Bill kills a bank guard and goes to his death in the gas chamber.

Now, very little of this rather bald story engages our sympathies since both characters are continually drunk or stoned and only wish to have their miserable consciousnesses blotted out in some way. Jamie's rape, as horrifying and sensational as it is, creates remarkably little sympathy for her. As Bill tells her, being out on Clark St. in Chicago in her condition is to invite it. When Bill shoots the bank guard, the act doesn't seem to be fraught with tension and relief, but merely inevitable. Another fuckup in a life full of them. In this, *Angels* is close to the terminal barrenness of *The Executioner's Song,* a book I am sure influenced the writing.

The reader doesn't care what Jamie does with her children; the reader cares not what Bill does with his money or his life, but the book accumulates power despite this, simply because each phase of their rush to some final blot gives rise to the hope that the end must have some meaning, some sign that these two lives come to rest in a bigger pattern. Instead, as the law imposes its will on Bill, and the psychiatric ward its will on Jamie, both institutions are shown to be as random and vindictive as life out on the streets. Johnson tries to let a pattern emerge within this space case narrative. In Bill's case, his last wish as he dies, to pray for another human being, seems quite affecting. But because it occurs as another scene in a row of scenes, it comes *very* close to having almost no cumulative impact. Indeed, it is his last act before death and changes little about how we feel about him. It is only the previous words of the death chamber attendant which give this thought much credence. He says of Bill, before Bill dies, "I think you been healed." (pp. 15-16)

Like many long modern poems, the feeling one gets from the structure of the book is one of process; it does not close off but continues. For all that, this is a minor flaw in the novel, not a crippling one. I think Johnson has done a remarkable job of capturing the street people life in a novel whose structure approximates their dizzying spirals of diminishing options. *Angels* is a powerful book, exact in its detail and its vision. (p. 16)

> Keith Abbott, *"Denis' Angels,"* in The American Book Review, *Vol. 7, No. 4, May-June, 1985, pp. 15-16.*

SUSAN LARDNER

Fiskadoro is an ambitious book both in its method and in its subject—the end of the world. Could it be, as in Johnson's cyclical eschatology, that in a nuclear war two missiles could fall on Key West and fail to go off? Might the descendants of whatever survivors there were be found, sixty years later or so, huddled in small, primitive communities between the Gulf of Mexico and the Atlantic, speaking in pidgin dialects, living in huts and houses furnished with leftovers, thinking unclearly and remembering in loose ends? Johnson imagines the possibilities and raises the question of whether the people and the place he describes represent a renewal of life on earth (as we more or less understand it) or just a delayed extinction. Despite Johnson's formal acknowledgment of his debt to a number of stately scholars—"students and teachers of humankind"—*Fiskadoro* is not heavy with the weight of its sources (mainly psychological and anthropological treatises) or ponderous as a result of its grim suppositions. His account of an earthly afterlife, or half-life, is constructed as a tale of the past related by a spokesman for a future civilization, who apologizes for its reactionary aspect, saying, "Thinking about the past contributes nothing to the present endeavor," and "Can we help it if sometimes we like to tell stories that want, as their holiest purpose, to excite us with pictures of danger and chaos?" Once past the first few pages, in which there is reference to "the god Quetzalcoatl, the god Bob Marley, the god Jesus," the rather condescending voice of the narrator fades out, and the story is left to speak for itself. . . .

[There] are three main characters: Grandmother Wright, one hundred years old, a witness to the end of the world, now too old to tell . . . ; her grandson, known as Mr. Cheung, a middle-aged man who grows sugarcane, plays the clarinet, and struggles to hold on to what he remembers of the past, including the names of the fifty states and the words of the Declaration of Independence; and Fiskadoro, an adolescent native of a fishing village that has replaced an old military base. Identified enigmatically by the narrator as a famous figure, "the only one who was ready when we came," Fiskadoro is portrayed by Johnson as an ordinary restless teen-ager. (pp. 83-4)

Although Johnson uses the narrator to frame the story and to indicate an ending, he concentrates on the fractured mentality of his interim society, an assortment of fishermen, housewives, entrepreneurs, and bums, with a handful of scholars and musicians—racially mixed, semiliterate, superstitious, or, as Johnson more objectively describes them, entertaining a variety of religious beliefs: disciples of Voodoo, Bob Marley, and/or Allah, black Israelites, Jimi Hendrix devotees. (p. 84)

Johnson moves through the minds of his characters without judging them or their prospects—describing their lives and the places they live in as they see and understand them, attending their occupied and idle moments. . . . In this way, he breaks down the reader's defenses against uncertainty and revives the frightening sense of mystery that is blunted by reliable experience and predictable turns of phrase. With analogies and metaphors that are suggestive but not definitive—sugarcane, for example, and Grandmother's amazing escapes—he suggests questions that have no sure answers: about the destiny of his survivors (what is likely and what each imagines it will be); about the reality and the exact nature of an event like Fiskadoro's initiation ceremony, from which he emerges both like and unlike other men; about the importance of remembering the past, compared with forgetfulness, which in one case releases musical talent and the ability to read. Are there really Cubans, fellow-survivors, ninety miles away, broadcasting and biding their time? Is there really a future or only lingering death, spread by the enterprising scavengers, who may represent human curiosity turned against itself, ultimately destructive? What kind of future? The introductory voice seems to speak for a complacent theocracy—"Thanked be the compassion and mercy of Allah"—and belittles the significance of the story. But by the end the voice is forgotten—thanked be the prose and ingenuity of Denis Johnson—and the reader has landed with Cheung, Fiskadoro, and all the rest, waiting silently on the beach for something from the "place out there beyond the end of all thought" to take shape. (pp. 84-5)

Susan Lardner, "Complications," in The New Yorker, *Vol. LXI, No. 21, July 15, 1985, pp. 83-5.*

PHILLIP CORWIN

Visionary novelists are a rare breed, and seldom optimistic. Whether their pessimism is due to a personal crisis, to what they see as their immutable and involuntary membership in a doomed human race, to a feeling that the social class they represent is soon to become vestigial, or to the belief they are the abused orphans of an indifferent universe, is a matter for their critics to debate.

Denis Johnson's second novel, *Fiskadoro,* carries heavy intellectual baggage with it on the way to the literary forum, and invites this kind of philosophical debate. It is, indeed, about the doomed human race, and has grandiose pretensions. And yet, the nihilism and cerebral meanderings in this novel are almost *trompe l'oeil.* For what distinguishes *Fiskadoro,* ultimately, is an original, visceral prose style that assaults the conventional bastions of naturalism and approaches the creation of a new form in fiction.

To start with, Johnson has given us an ingenious collage of poetic, often melodramatic, happenings and situations, peopled with eccentric, semi-articulate, deranged survivors of a nuclear holocaust. There is no hope and no joy in this novel, and all of the author's considerable narrative skills have been used to emphasize the pointlessness of human survival. Yet the technique itself survives, as though, to borrow Yeats's metaphor, the dance survives the dancer. (p. 444)

The imagined events in this novel are absurdly sensational, and often savage. Yet, Johnson seems to ask, how could their fictitious brutality even begin to approach the inescapable facts of human brutality evidenced in wars, or even in peacetime? And it is that very savagery of the human species, the impulse to do evil or whatever other name may be given to mankind's murderous instincts, that is the focus of Johnson's visionary work.

Of course, this terrain has been explored before. But what makes *Fiskadoro* a literary achievement is not its intellectual framework; rather, it is Johnson's ability to enhance fantasy with fact, to juxtapose realism and surrealism, to be able to place Marianne Moore's fabled "imaginary gardens with real toads in them."

The business of this novel, finally, is art itself. (p. 445)

Phillip Corwin, "Creating a New Form in Fiction," in Commonweal, *Vol. CXII, No. 14, August 9, 1985, pp. 444-45.*

MICHIKO KAKUTANI

With the opening sentences of *The Stars at Noon,* we're deposited in a menacing but familiar world—a hot, tropical world of sleazy bars and cheap motels, third-rate spies and disaffected drifters, a world familiar to us from old Sydney Greenstreet movies, and novels by Graham Greene and Robert Stone. Sometimes the setting is Southeast Asia, sometimes it's Mexico or South America. In this case, it happens to be Nicaragua,

1984; and the protagonist is a "North American female prostitute-drifter with a press card, which has been revoked."

A poet as well as a novelist, Mr. Johnson possesses a gift for visually precise description, and in *The Stars,* he conjures up a hellish vision of Managua and the outlying country through dozens of details and heat-glazed images. . . .

Mr. Johnson is equally persuasive in describing certain emotional states—conveying to the reader the panicky sensation of traveling in a war-torn foreign country, cut off from everything familiar and subject not only to the palpable dangers of gunfire and ambush, but also the more insidious assaults of the unknown. . . .

Brilliant as Mr. Johnson's poetic reportage is, however, it can't sustain the novel's thick, histrionic plot or carry us through his extended excursions into melodrama. As he demonstrated in his last two novels, *Angels* (a disturbing look at two drifters' unraveling lives) and *Fiskadoro* (a fierce, hallucinatory portrait of America, postnuclear holocaust), he is an ambitious writer, blessed or cursed with an apocalyptic vision of America as a spiritual wasteland. And in *Stars* he seems to want to extend this vision further—by obliquely examining the consequences of American political/business intervention in Central America and by more directly looking at the consequences of one American woman's careless cynicism.

The problem is that the story never becomes more than a sort of hokey retread of *Angels,* set in the third world and garnished with a twist of betrayal: drifter-woman meets down-and-out male, the two hit the road together, become lovers, meet up with other unsavory types, get into further trouble, etc. This time, the "crime" the man has committed—giving away industrial secrets to foreign governments—is so sketchily delineated that the reader is never sure whether he's just incredibly dumb or the author, himself, is naïve.

As for the woman, she swiftly disintegrates into a carelessly packaged collection of clichés—the hard-bitten prostitute, the hard-drinking lady journalist, the world-weary war tourist—and as the narrator, she unfortunately gives the entire novel a tricked-up tone. Half the time she sounds like a parody of one of Joan Didion's disaffected heroines, trying to hide her spiritual emptiness through aimless affairs and equally aimless wandering: "But I'm saying that I was in the habit of walking the midnights after work, barefoot, dangling a high-heeled shoe from either hand, in the only hour when the temperature was bearable." The rest of the time she comes across as a second-rate female Bogart:

> "Look, . . . everybody sells everybody out down here. They can't afford not to, it's basic, that's the situation. If you hang on to even one little tiny scruple it'll be the death of you, I promise. This is Hell, it's Hell, how many times do you have to be told?"

Though such remarks supposedly belie a deeper vulnerability and pain, we grow so sick of this woman's posturing, so weary of her self-pity and tattered cynicism that we just want her story to end. We never really care whether or not she betrays her lover, and we certainly never care what eventually happens to her. Mr. Johnson's shimmering descriptions of Central America provide us with moments of relief, but in the end, his narrator's tiresome voice drags the novel down, submerging the magic of his prose.

Michiko Kakutani, "Adrift in Nicaragua," in The New York Times, *September 13, 1986, p. 14.*

CARYN JAMES

For Denis Johnson, hell is a world without meaning—or, as the flippant, philosophical narrator of **The Stars at Noon** tells us, hell is Nicaragua in 1984. She is a down-and-out American trapped in Managua and through her Mr. Johnson creates a vision bleaker than the madness and murder of his first novel, **Angels,** more desperate than the postapocalyptic world of his second, **Fiskadoro.** What better setting for such pessimism than the political and moral morass of 1980's Nicaragua? Here, as the narrator says, is "the hyper-new, all-leftist figure coming at us at the rate of rock-n-roll," where she finds no usable past or hopeful future, just a torturous present of ramshackle McDonald's and starving children.

An unreliable narrator especially short on veracity, she claims she has come to Nicaragua to discover "the exact dimensions of Hell," but seems bent on losing all trace of consciousness or conscience. We never learn her name; she is appalled by the corruption of both the Sandinistas and "the stupid CIA." And though she arrived in Central America as a Witness for Peace-style observer, she lasted two and a half days before escaping into Managua's shady underworld, where she halfheartedly masquerades as a journalist, sidelines as a prostitute and lives on her cache of black market Nicaraguan cordobas. In the Managua she has discovered, everything is debased—the currency, the minor officials who sleep with her and renege on their part of the bargain, and especially language itself.

The English businessman who starts as her john and becomes her lover is another nameless sort, a weak-jawed Brit caricature who passes industrial secrets to rival countries and calls it humanitarianism. "A humanitarian in Hell," the narrator thinks. "This guy, at some point in his earthly existence, must have been truly evil, possibly Hitlerian." It's true, he's in trouble. His company and the Costa Ricans knew of a possible oil deposit under Lake Nicaragua; in the interest of fair play, he gave the information to the Nicaraguans, who apparently told the Costa Ricans they'd been double-crossed. Now the Costa Ricans are after the Englishman, and from there the plot grows as convoluted as Mr. Johnson can make it. The narrator's assessment of things is what truly matters, though, and with her determined amorality she easily equates industrial espionage and political power plays with the Holocaust.

The hell Mr. Johnson invents for this muddled narrator is no Dantesque vision of sin and retribution, but a more ironic, sinister inferno than any she could imagine. He cruelly grants both her desires—for nihilism and meaning. "I tried to lock my attention onto the problems ahead of me and mislaid all sense of the goal," she says while driving to meet a man who might exchange her illegal cordobas for the dollars needed to buy a plane ticket out. "The fumes and smells and roaring temperature of Managua's roadways savaged all mental effort." Yet, tipped off that the Nicaraguan officials suspect her of something—related, she guesses, to "the Englishman's activities as a blabbermouth"—she instinctively tries to warn him. Suddenly, the Nicaraguans are after both of them, and as they head for the border she glides straight toward the emotional bond she so consciously avoids.

Abruptly, the novel takes on elements of an escape thriller. Will the Nicaraguans let them cross the border? Will the Costa Ricans let him live if they do? More important, will she betray him to save herself? . . .

In her careless way, [the protagonist] is relieved to have her choices narrowed by border guards and the American and the pressure of circumstances. And though she later says, "I had a revelation. Nothing fancy. . . . Either I'm Christ or I'm Judas: it's kill or be killed," her discovery is glib, despite its "nothing fancy" disclaimer. It points to the novel's most serious flaw— the narrator is a cardboard mouthpiece for the author. With her religious imagery and taste for irony, her philosophical attitudes toward everything from her own prostitution to Managua's oppressive heat, it's not plausible that she could remain so willfully dazed. Mr. Johnson's first-rate soul-searching is trapped in her second-rate mind, which frequently borrows the author's eloquence and intellectual rigor. . . .

In **The Stars at Noon,** language slides off its moorings, as style mirrors substance almost too well. Just as often as it is debased, the language is inflated by the empty abstractions of the narrator, who is "trying to make clear what can't be understood or forgiven"—whether she is tortured by free-floating original sin or by political murders she has witnessed, the author doesn't say. . . .

[This] novel is an encapsulated narrative, begging to be fleshed out. Still, it is daring, this political novel that disdains politics, this philosophical work that rejects all philosophies.

Caryn James, "Nameless Lovers Chased through Hell," in The New York Times Book Review, *September 28, 1986, p. 7.*

ANDREW KLAVAN

The Hell of Denis Johnson's fine third novel, **The Stars at Noon,** is Nicaragua. His main characters—a man and woman who are given no names—are searching for its borderlines. . . .

He is an English oil executive, a sorry and befuddled adulterer with a pasty face and Clark Kent glasses. She's an American woman who may once have been a journalist. She's now a whore. They meet in Managua in the way of business—her business. But she soon finds out the Englishman has done a very dumb thing. He has tried to be fair. He's told Nicaraguan officials the location of some oil fields on the Costa Rican border. Or as his nemesis, the American Spy, puts it, "'he's done a minor something that upsets the balance more knowledgeable people are trying to maintain from day to day down here, moment to moment even.'" In any case, just about everybody now wants his ass. The woman (like Dante before Virgil teaches him better) shows compassion for the poor condemned idiot. She phones to warn him of impending danger and, thanks to that single act, she too becomes a fugitive.

From then on, where reality ends and hell begins is a moot point. This Nicaragua is a landscape of damnation. Its government, its revolutions, even the clockwork of its love affairs—all are founded on lies. For the fugitives, the attempted journey out must be made through baffling obscurity. It's nearly impossible for them to tell what's required, whom to pay and in what currency. The threat to their lives is definite enough, but the source of the danger always lies somewhere beyond the vanishing point. The phone lines, as well as all other lines of communication, are generally down.

The American Spy is the spokesman for the place. He is dogging the fugitives across the country, tempting the woman to turn the man in. Replete with a golly-gee vocabulary of double-talk and double-dealing, he is the words of Ronald Reagan made flesh: a sweet-faced fountain of sincere, confused, and patriotic rage, looking to avenge the humiliations of Cuba and Vietnam on everybody in sight. He's Johnson's best character by far, a quiet American for the '80s. But whereas Graham Greene's Pyle poisoned Southeast Asia with innocent, if puritanical, idealism, even this remnant of the Spy's best self has been thwarted and transformed. He has become a jackanapes, so smug in his anger that at one point the woman cries out to him (as many a nation to the U.S.): "'What are you sitting at my table for?... [I]f you only knew how sick everybody gets looking at you, even knowing you exist. Don't you know what an asshole you are?'" Nope, he doesn't. If he did, he wouldn't care. To paraphrase Rambo and Ron: he's gonna win this time. It doesn't matter what he has to turn himself into to do it. If the fugitives are in hell, the American Spy is the hand they will shake when they shake hands with the Devil. He'll be waiting for them at every crossroad along the Way Out.

With the creation of the American—and in the interplay between the American and his prey—Johnson takes an important step toward making the underlying mythos of his story come to life. That life is, to my mind, what separates this novel from his two others, and what makes it worth reading, even with its flaws. *Angels,* Johnson's first novel, was a realistic tour de force heavily influenced by the writings of Robert Stone. Like *The Stars at Noon,* it concerned a man and woman on the run. *Fiskadoro,* an intelligent but schematic work, also traced a mythic journey, though it was through the mythic territory of a post-apocalyptic world. With *Stars,* Johnson seems to be striving to put it all together. If it costs him something in originality—if, that is, he reuses elements he's used before—it's because those elements matter to him, I think, and he's trying to get them right. He wants to keep the grit he showed in *Angels.* He wants to borrow some of Stone's backdrops and despair. But Johnson has had a vision, a vision he first explored in *Fiskadoro,* and he wants to see if his fiction can make it vital, can make it (as Stone might say) *apply.*

The Stars at Noon goes wrong when it tries too hard to inform us of its mythic proportions, when it becomes so full of itself it floats away. The fact that the characters have no names, for instance, or that the story takes place in 1984, or that Johnson's historico-political concerns remain vague—these things are irritating; they detach the legend from the life. On top of which, we are told Nicaragua is hell so many times that I, for one, canceled my plane reservation. But the book works, and works beautifully, when it finds its hell in reality, when it allows its myth to grow out of the story and characters rather than shape them.

The myth that has come to mean so much to Johnson is central to the works of Joseph Campbell and Norman O. Brown: the heroic descent into the abyss, the attempt to retrieve the repressed from the subconscious and unite the mind's underworld with the self....

The conclusion of the novel is inevitable, but Johnson avoids allowing it to become schematic. Like many others bent on self-destruction, his characters remain mystified by what they do to themselves; their actions appear sourceless to them, like an uncanny string of bad luck. The reader, up until the very end, is allowed to participate in their ignorance, which lends an aura of suspense to the unavoidable.

And, in fact, when it comes right down to it, the sources of the characters' actions seem less important than their effects. We are told vaguely that the woman's need to betray her own escape has something to do with her father, but it doesn't much matter what. It's enough for Johnson that the repressed comes back, arising like the cream of the crap. Once the journey out of hell has failed, the past, though not transformed into an instrument of torture, becomes eternal. We are back in Dante's Inferno, a place disturbingly like the unconscious mind. In the novel's powerful final images—of a man poised impotent above his deepest fantasy and of a woman divided from her double—eternity has become a recurring nightmare, without a life to wake to.

It's that sort of imagery—when the real and mythic merge—that makes this such a strong novel. It's a tragic vision presented with authority and evil wit. If it manages to deliver a message of hope, it's the hope implied by the act of telling an old, old story one more time, even if it is the old story of all hope abandoned.

Andrew Klavan, "Infernal Combustion," in The Village Voice, *Vol. XXXI, No. 43, October 28, 1986, p. 51.*

STEPHEN DOBYNS

Denis Johnson has a powerful ability to crank up the English language. Using rhetorical repetitions, Nerudaisms ("Disappointment lights its stupid fire in my heart") and direct, emotional statements ("Young girls accelerating through the intersection make me want to live forever"), he heightens language until it's like a man on tall stilts strapped to roller skates on the slippery dance floor of an ocean liner plowing through typhoon-ridden seas. When he has a subject equal to the language, the result can be wonderful. When he doesn't, it is hokum. In *The Veil,* his second collection of poems, there is a lot of brilliance and a lot of hokum.

Mr. Johnson can wax elegant and rhapsodic on any subject, deserving or undeserving. But in terms of structure and development and in the use of line, the poems are almost always uneven. However, Mr. Johnson has many striking sentences, compelling beginnings and strong endings. These are ragged poems of great imagination and often of great lyric beauty....

The best work here is a group of dramatic monologues that begin the book and another group about a marriage and a relationship with a stepson that end it. Scattered in between are other fine poems, but few are satisfying in their entirety and many are obscure.... Many of the poems have... impenetrable passages and the result is a gnawing irritation that I suppose would not have arisen if the poems had not had so many fine moments. But the ragged quality, the hokum, the obscurity weigh them down and irritation finally outweighs pleasure.

Stephen Dobyns, "Some Happy Moments, Some Very Tall Language," in The New York Times Book Review, *October 18, 1987, p. 46.*

Mervyn Jones

1922-

English novelist, nonfiction writer, critic, translator, editor, and short story writer.

In his fiction, Jones frequently focuses on human relationships and social and political issues. He has stated that a recurring theme in his work is "the nobility and irony of idealism." Writing in a straightforward, objective prose style, Jones meticulously develops conflicts between characters to represent opposing values or beliefs, complications of love and sexuality, historical or topical issues, and the struggles of the working class. All of his publications reflect his commitment to the cause of socialism.

Jones's socialist orientation is particularly evident in his historical novels. *Joseph* (1970), a sympathetic version of the life of Joseph Stalin, concentrates on the experiences that shaped the Soviet leader's political views and actions. *Holding On* (1973; published in the United States as *Twilight of the Day*), which was adapted for television, presents the virtues and heroic struggles of a London working-class family. *Today the Struggle* (1978) depicts characters from various social classes to explore the socialist movement in England from the 1930s to the 1970s.

Several of Jones's novels examine contemporary issues. *John and Mary* (1966), which was adapted for film, centers on the more liberal social attitudes toward sexuality that arose during the 1960s. This work dramatizes the gradual development of a meaningful and enduring relationship between a young couple who become sexually intimate soon after they meet. In *Mr. Armitage Isn't Back Yet* (1971), which explores the values of the counterculture movement of the 1960s, a middle-aged industrialist is kidnapped by a group of young idealists who eventually convert him to a more carefree and less materialistic lifestyle. *Strangers* (1974) concerns a rich young Englishwoman's confrontation with class attitudes and her reevaluation of her own political views. These conflicts are exacerbated by her relationship with an older man who lacks social status and her encounters with violence and political intrigue while traveling in Africa. *The Pursuit of Happiness* (1975), which depicts a woman's struggle to find satisfaction in her career and personal life, reflects Jones's interest in feminist issues. This topic, as well as themes relating to sexuality and the plight of an unmarried pregnant woman, is also treated in *Joanna's Luck* (1984), in which a young female is victimized by economic conditions that prevent her from pursuing her career.

Several of Jones's other novels have drawn significant critical attention. These include *A Survivor* (1968), which revolves around feelings of creative and emotional emptiness in the life of a novelist following the death of his wife; *Lord Richard's Passion* (1974), which portrays a love affair in Victorian England that is ruined by sexual repression; and *The Beautiful Words* (1979), which relates the tragic life of a mentally handicapped young man. In addition to his novels, Jones has published *Scenes from Bourgeois Life* (1976), a collection of novellas, and *Chances: An Autobiography* (1988).

(See also *CLC*, Vol. 10; *Contemporary Authors*, Vols. 45-48; *Contemporary Authors New Revision Series*, Vol. 1; and *Contemporary Authors Autobiography Series*, Vol. 5.)

THE TIMES LITERARY SUPPLEMENT

A Set of Wives is a subtle study in resilience, moral and sexual. It concerns, principally, three sisters, all members of the "liberal establishment", left-wing, intellectual. Beatrice, a lecturer in sociology, is married to a precise and successful barrister, an espouser of causes, who said, both of her large build and of her virginity, that "they were not indictable offences". Beautiful Miranda, after an unsuccessful, but on her side wholehearted, affair with a novelist, has been married for fifteen years to a rising Labour M.P. Their relationship is close, scrupulous and passionate, although Miranda came to love Eric only after marriage. . . . Jill is married, with four children and a grown-up stepson, to a television personality with whom she had a casual affair before his apparently casual divorce. They live in the inevitable colourful and cheerful chaos. The story unfolds during the mounting tension before the 1964 election.

In their private lives all three sisters have reached that stage where speculation about the possibility and nature of infidelity can be absorbing. This speculation, as Mr. Jones demonstrates excellently, runs alongside a lessening of resilience as a result of security, love and time. . . .

All three are exposed to jokes and gossip about casual infidelity and divorce. . . . It is the perfect Miranda, ''beyond reproach'', to whom, as her ex-lover remarks, ''women like that'' appear ''not merely immoral but unnatural'' who falls. . . . Her personality disintegrates; her fastidious husband shows signs of strain, perhaps because of the election. The story ends abruptly in violence and madness. As Jill tells Miranda, ''not being a flirt is part of your trouble''.

The novel is disturbing and gripping; it is excellently written with precision, intelligence and wit. Mr. Jones gives, with economy, enough background information about his characters for their thoughts and actions to seem plausible. The climax, nevertheless, however well foreshadowed by hints, seems somehow imposed by the novelist. But the true novelist's gift for seeing a character or an action from several points of view is abundantly there.

> *''The Ways of Three Wives,''* in The Times Literary
> Supplement, *No. 3321, October 21, 1965, p. 933.*

EDWIN MORGAN

[*A Set of Wives*] is a curious affair, gripping without satisfying: an odd mixture of potent observation and unexplained human motives. The 'set of wives' are three sisters, married into the upper-bracket left-wing London world of 1964. Jill and her TV-personality husband live in an amorphously large household of parties, children, au pairs, and much coming and going. Beatrice is a lecturer married to a lawyer, and their highly ordered and earnest life is presented with some nicely ironic touches. Miranda, who turns out to be the focal study of the novel, despite intermittent opposition from two political themes (an approaching general election, and the case of a Greek Cypriot about to be deported for assault), is apparently the most securely and contentedly married of the three, but her MP husband fails to realise that she is cracking up inwardly, moving from nightmares and forgetfulness to adultery with a worthless and unattractive man for whom she feels nothing, except that he becomes necessary to her. Her complete mental breakdown ends the novel, but inconclusively and tantalisingly, because there is so little analysis which would offer a clue about what Mr. Jones is up to. As Jill's husband says, 'understanding Miranda isn't the easiest thing in the world.' Yet the steps of her growing panic are admirably traced, and she is a sympathetic figure, quite apart from any use the author may intend to make of her, relative to the theme of 'helping someone before it is too late' which Jill ironically puts forward in talking about the Cypriot. Social satire and the desperation of a soul coexist uneasily.

> *Edwin Morgan, ''Mighty Wind,'' in* New Statesman,
> *Vol. LXX, No. 1813, December 10, 1965, p. 941.*

DAVID CRAIG

[*John and Mary*] condenses an understanding of human nature quite exceptionally exact and unillusioned. The form is original and simple, emerging inevitably from the life at issue. A man and a woman, alone in a flat high up in a new tower, concentrate on each other with the absorption of strong attraction growing towards love. So the chapters are made to alternate between the man's view and the woman's, sometimes with an overlap that brings out graphically how much minds and their contents can differ even when two people have touched as closely as bodies can. The precision of it all—the following out of how

the balance of feelings between the two trembles and swings—is consummate, and strikes one as rooted in a sanity free of *parti pris* or underlying emotional vested interests of any kind whatsoever. The ending is actually up-beat, although the *milieu* (with its alienation of neighbour from neighbour, short-lived affairs, and infidelity taken for granted) would have tempted many a writer into self-indulgent styles whereby the variety of life, the efforts and satisfactions, all dissolved either into a nice, foggy, atmospheric *angst* or else the cruel puppet shows of the Absurd.

When all that is said, the whole seems a bit clipped, wanting in some dynamic which is hard to define yet would be recognisable if there. The book is about coupling, essential marriage, and the two are sensual people, yet their sensuality is evoked in rather brief, curtailed (though unerring) touches and then at once placed—more placed than evoked. After a deep kiss John thinks of it as 'the X-certificate kiss'. The flip style is perfectly the character's, but since the novel is wholly first-person, it leaves the author no channel for expressing any further vision of his own. (p. 524)

> *David Craig, ''Metropolitan,'' in* New Statesman,
> *Vol. 73, No. 1856, October 7, 1966, pp. 524-26.*

THE TIMES LITERARY SUPPLEMENT

John and Mary is a love story, touching on such traditional themes as each lover's wondering how much the other cares, his doubts whether this is the right time to kiss her and her hope that he will. Its point is that it opens with John and Mary waking in bed, still strangers after a night together. . . .

They manoeuvre, seeking or evading commitment, coming to terms with partners who are sexual intimates but social and emotional strangers. This allows amusing effects of perspective, but the need for articulate monologues by characters who are not unusually eloquent leads to a good deal of contrivance on the lines of: ''The social context was indispensable to the personal relationship. I got that phrase from a man who was a deadset Marxist.'' More damagingly, the technique makes them appear more calculating than is consistent with the sympathy which Mr. Jones obviously wants. John is a somewhat withdrawn character; the technical procedure turns him into a very cold fish. At times he resembles a computer with a libido.

The real trouble is that the characters' valuations are the only ones presented and their status is uncertain. Towards the end the prose becomes lyrically elevated; it seems that we are to think that John has admitted someone else into his over-protected privacy and Mary is about to free herself from a train of six-month affairs; for the first time they use the word ''love''. But the book also admits of a totally different interpretation. Mary refers several times to ''that girl who was shut up in a tower of brass, where Zeus got at her''. When John tells her, correctly, that Danaë was in a dungeon, she is upset, for she sees herself as Danaë in the tower-block. Why does Mary have this rather implausible obsession with a Greek myth if not to suggest both that the tower is a prison and also that she is wrong in her conviction that their love affair will last? In this view, the moment in the tower has no validity outside and the somewhat inferior quality of the lyricism is an international device to show that they deceive themselves.

But this more complex interpretation, though it presents itself rather markedly in places, does not impose itself throughout enough to carry conviction. Perhaps the talk of Danaë is a flourish and the lyricism is meant to ring true. The uncertainty is radical, extending to our response to every detail of the prose, and though the novel is at first sight an unusually neat and controlled performance, at a more serious level of criticism its author is not sufficiently in control.

> *"Getting to Know You," in* The Times Literary Supplement, *No. 3372, October 13, 1966, p. 946.*

THE TIMES LITERARY SUPPLEMENT

Probably Mervyn Jones's new novel [*A Survivor*] will be of most interest to his fellow-novelists, since a principal theme in it is the relationship between an author's personal experience and his use of that experience in his fiction. . . .

The sad, successful novelist is a "survivor", escaping from a wartime air crash which resulted in his friend's death, marrying the man's mistress and acting as father of their child, and then surviving his wife—whom he had loved but not fully known. The widower survives at least four mistresses: they can read about their predecessors in his novels and feel dissatisfied. . . .

[He] has preserved his experience, however unsatisfactory to his set of mistresses, in the sense that he has set them down in an ordered pattern; their experience is in the past, but his survives.

One of the departing women tells him: "It's not too hard to keep a woman's love. And another thing: it's not too hard to write the books you have in you. All it takes is a bit of good faith." This is a hard saying. The reader knows about the experience which has been left out of the man's writings, and can well understand the reasons why. He is severely judged by the women, especially by his supposed daughter who resents his affair with her school friend, and doubts that he was "really in love" with her: "It's what people do that matters, I think—the results of what they do."

This may all sound rather cerebral, for an account of a man's sexual life; but the style and the manner seem appropriate for discussing a man whose literary faults are supposed to be over-much discretion and a lack of involvement. *A Survivor* is extremely well organized and is convincing as a story—even if some of the women seem almost too good to be true. They are easier for the reader to know and understand than is the principal character himself: for instance, his occasional political actions (over Suez, Hungary, C.N.D.) seem unrelated to any other aspect of his character. But again, the essence of the man is that he is hard to know, a writer unable to communicate all that he wants to tell.

> *"In Good Faith," in* The Times Literary Supplement, *No. 3446, March 14, 1968, p. 245.*

GILLIAN TINDALL

[In *A Survivor* Mervyn Jones] attempts to suggest the inconclusive complexity of real experience, and partly succeeds. The central figure, the 'survivor', is—perilously—a successful writer who has drawn his novels closely from his own life. He is fortyish, intensity has seeped out of his existence, his relationship with his daughter is non-existent; but this is not, we seem meant to conclude, so much because he has cannibalised his life to feed his writing, as because he can't forget his dead wife, which I found a less convincing proposition. Several absorbing and important themes are broached: the relationship between truth and invention, fiction as self-compensatory, the

'necessary selfishness' of the writer; but early signs that Mervyn Jones is planning to confront this material directly, in the manner of Julian Mitchell or Doris Lessing, are disappointed.

The impetus of the book peters out in relating a series of affairs too essentially unimportant (and unconvincing) to fill the space they occupy. Each acts as a substantial red herring, and because the narrative hops around in time with the casual agility of an avant-garde film, most of the action is described retrospectively and therefore with diminished impact. Time remembered is not, after all, the same thing as time lived—though this is one aspect of the novelist's problem which is not here stated.

Something is missing from this book which would give it both immediacy and greater depth, and I suspect that what is missing is the front level of reality: a commentary on it in Mervyn Jones's own person. (p. 489)

> *Gillian Tindall, "Versions of Girls," in* New Statesman, *Vol. 75, No. 1935, April 12, 1968, pp. 488-89.*

CLIVE JORDAN

Joseph is an attempt to explain in human terms the phenomenon of Stalin. It's a novel, not a biography, and Mervyn Jones takes some quite unMarxist liberties with history, on the whole justifiably. We are asked to shrug off the received historical facts and start again, as if seeing Stalin, his family and main victims—Trotsky, Kamenev, Zinoviev and Bukharin—for the first time. To this end, the names of all the characters are anglicised—as well as the obvious Joseph, Lenin becomes Victor, Leon Trotsky is Leonard and so on. Though this does make them more human, it must be said that it also levels them out and makes them surprisingly unRussian. I found myself sneaking frequent looks at the check-list to remind me who they were. Indeed, the whole style of the novel—quiet, down-to-earth, unadorned—seems far removed from the brutality and excitement of the 1917 Revolution. Perhaps intentionally, the great events somehow seem to happen just off-stage.

The attempt to personalise the famous is typical of Mervyn Jones's treatment. The results of Stalin's use of power are seen not so much nationally as in their progressive impact on the Alvey (really, 'Alliluyev') family of old-guard communists into which Stalin has married. Their estrangement and sufferings mirror Stalin's relationship with the Party elite and the people at large. Remote, all-powerful, godlike, he withdraws into the gloomy keeps of the Kremlin, symbol of 'fortress Russia' which gives him his finest hour in the defence of Moscow, the climax of the book.

The lengthy narrative of *Joseph* is a worthy mirror of its subject in all except cunning. Dogged, thorough, carried through doldrums by the inherent interest of the enterprise, its success is one of perseverance rather than brilliance. The insights into Stalin are on the whole historical—such as the revealing account of his early career as a political gangster—rather than human. The appalling sufferings of the victims in the Purges are brought painfully to life. But Stalin himself remains as Mervyn Jones leaves him, a monolithic figure towering over puny mortals on the stage of history: in the final instance, unknown and unknowable.

> *Clive Jordan, "Death's Emblems," in* New Statesman, *Vol. 79, No. 2042, May 1, 1970, p. 634.*

RICHARD BOSTON

[The title character of *Joseph*] is Joseph Vissarionovich Dju-gashvili, known to the Czarist secret police and to his fellow Bolsheviks as (among other names) Koba, Soso and—the name by which he became known to the world and to history—the Man of Steel, Stalin.

Of all 20th-century tyrants he is the most enigmatic. Looking at old newsreels we can laugh at the comic-opera Mussolini; through Chaplin's genius we can even laugh at the histrionics of Hitler; and by laughing at them we are able to some extent to come to terms with them. But there is nothing comic about Stalin. When we see him on film, he does not rant and scream and wave his arms about. . . .

He was infinitely patient, and he was also willfully capricious; he was ruthless, bloody and vengeful; he was relentlessly am-bitious and possessed inflexible will power; he was a monster, one of the greatest killers of this, or any other, century; though his intellect was completely undistinguished, he affected the history of not only Soviet Russia but the whole world as much as any man in this century.

Fortunately there is a considerable literature of a high standard to help us understand Stalin's sphinxlike character. To this literature, which includes the biographies by Trotsky and Isaac Deutscher, Mervyn Jones's novel is a valuable addition. *Joseph* does not provide fresh historical information or even particu-larly new interpretations; for these it sticks fairly close to Isaac Deutscher. Rather, what it has to offer is compulsive readability and a portrait of Stalin that is (most of the time, anyway) psychologically convincing. By putting his portrait into the form of a novel, Jones is able to invent the sort of intimate personal details that are obviously highly important in any person's life but are too often unknown in the case of so remote a figure as Stalin. Of these inventions we can say, as John Womack Jr. says of Elia Kazan's *Viva Zapata!*, that they are inaccurate but historically true.

An example of Jones's method is to be found in the description of Stalin's mother, one of the best things in the book. Trotsky remarks in his life of Stalin that "any Georgian matron past thirty years was regarded as almost an old woman." Jones describes how, when Joseph has been expelled from a semi-nary, he makes a journey to his mother, whom he hasn't seen for years. He is shocked by her appearance. . . . (p. 5)

In this passage Jones not only breathes life into the bare bones of Trotsky's statement, but also helps us to understand Stalin's later behavior. "After the revolution, when cruelty and injus-tice had been swept away with poverty, no one would suffer again as his mother had suffered. He could offer her no other comfort, but he could offer her that." Perhaps Stalin felt that for a whole generation of Russians like his mother, nothing could be done, and that they could therefore be sacrificed for the sake of later generations.

Jones offers Stalin's hatred of Trotsky as another motive force in his drive for power. In his biography of Stalin, Trotsky quotes a French writer who said that "in London Stalin for the first time saw Trotsky. But the latter hardly noticed him." Out of this bald statement (at least, I suppose it is the source) Jones makes one of the most telling moments of the book. After Trotsky has dazzled a London congress with his rhetorical mastery, the unknown Stalin speaks. . . . He confronts Trot-sky's oratory with hammer-blows of logic. Only at the end of the speech does he turn to look at his adversary's face. Trotsky is not there. Joseph does not know whether Trotsky left before

or during the speech; "anyway, he had been cheated—he had slammed his hammer on an empty anvil. He sat down in a state of confused anger." It is a brilliant moment, and Jones describes it (as indeed he does all the events in the book) with vividness and economy. (pp. 5, 29)

The country in which the events take place is not named. The result is presumably intended to universalize what is being described, and to remind the reader all the time that this is a novel and not history. I can see this, but I don't think it comes off. . . .

Mervyn Jones's account has not got the astonishing sharpness and wit of Solzhenitsyn's description of the Kremlin and its boss in *The First Circle*. But by any other standards the book is a considerable success. (p. 29)

Richard Boston, "On First-name Terms with Sta-lin," in The New York Times Book Review, *August 16, 1970, pp. 5, 29.*

NEAL ASCHERSON

Joseph seems, at first sight, a curiosity. Mervyn Jones has transformed the life of Stalin into a novel. But this is neither a mere "reconstruction" which decorates a chronicle with dia-logue, nor an imitation of those laborious late Upton Sinclair novels in which the insufferable Lanny Budd dashes about like a hijacker on a time machine, instructing historical personalities on their next move. Jones has taken fictionalization a step further. The names of the principal actors of the Revolution and the first Soviet decades have been changed, episodes have been invented, other events telescoped or switched about in time.

This is where opinions about *Joseph* are going to divide. For many readers, the shadow of the Georgian is too cold and close to be tampered with so confidently. Victor, Leonard, Clem, and Sandra sound more like the stalwarts of a Labour Party branch in outer London than Lenin, Trotsky, Voroshilov, and Kollontaj (and, unlike the reviewer, readers don't get a pub-licity slip telling them that Vivian is really Vyacheslav Mol-otov). Joseph goes to bed with Sandra, and his son turns out to be a homosexual. What's this?

Jones knows all these objections perfectly well, and doesn't seem to lose courage. He adds an appendix explaining what he has invented or transposed. He does not tell us why he has done so, except to say that "I have used the facts as novelists often use the facts." The explanation lies in the book itself, and it is an impressive book. Beginning with the remote birth in Georgia and ending, in effect, with the Red Army parade through Moscow in 1941, the Germans at the gates, and Joseph on the reviewing stand, Jones tries to construct a hypothesis of Stalin's nature. It is, as it should be, a respectful novel. Joseph slowly emerges from the seminary, from clandestine work and revolution, as a man totally ordinary in his tastes and perceptions, totally extraordinary in the relationship of his loneliness to his will to power. By a pun on both that ordi-nariness and the derivation of Stalin's name, Jones calls him "Joseph Smith."

The book is also about the prime and the fate of the old Bol-sheviks. Through the characters of Gregory and Leo and Ni-cholas and Richard, Mr. Jones tries to raise the ghosts of Zinoviev, Kamenev, Bukharin, and Rykov. As in his other novels, *In Famine's Shadow, John and Mary*, and *A Survivor,* he takes particular care to make his women authentic and believable.

Joseph is a moving book, but it does not entirely succeed. Lifting men and events out of the mythic Russian context in order to make them somehow more intimate and familiar was a risk. The dimensions of that episode are of an unalterably mythic scale. Clever Leonard and bald Victor do not quite fit their background, because those who helped to make those times themselves ceased, in some sense, to be "ordinary" people. If the ghosts of Stalin and Beria are to be taken for a walk, then let their closest escort be veracity. (pp. 45-6)

Neal Ascherson, "Heretics," in The New York Review of Books, *Vol. XV, No. 9, November 19, 1970, pp. 45-6.*

THE TIMES LITERARY SUPPLEMENT

Mr. Armitage isn't back yet because he has been kidnapped by a couple of hippy-type hitch-hikers and whisked off to a convenient deserted island. . . . His captors, two boys and two girls, are preternaturally vague on the political purpose of their dangerous project and on the exigencies of daily life in society. But while summer lasts they pursue their herbivorous kicks and nurture the insufferable sense of superiority that comes to those who wash their clothes in mountain streams (they came out perfectly clean, according to the author). One's time between orgasms is spent hewing wood and reading Scott Fitzgerald, and naturally Mr. Armitage, who struggles through *Karamazov* during the long hot summer and makes some effort to comply with their wishes, finds himself rather left out of things. His reward comes from the wide-eyed innocent Sue, in purple passages which make the toes curl with embarrassment. Project and summer end with Armitage redeeming himself by remembering a good deed once done. Middle age and youth part on goodish terms.

[*Mr. Armitage Isn't Back Yet*] is a bad novel, and the more irritating for being written by an intelligent man, one of the best socialist journalists we have. In attempting to address itself to a political matter, the clash of ideologies, the book gets bogged down in the mire of good intentions and subjective impressions.

"Guinea Pig," in The Times Literary Supplement, *No. 3615, June 6, 1971, p. 667.*

EDWIN MORGAN

Mr. Armitage Isn't Back Yet hovers between story and fable. The story shows how Mr. Armitage, wealthy managing director of a plastics combine, reacts to being kidnapped by four young people who are living on an island and want to study him. The fable comes with the fact of the island: the classic isolation from complexity, the re-examination of fundamentals, the return to 'nature'. It is an attractive idea, clearly and simply presented, and if there are some improbabilities, both in the story and in the dialogue, these may be regarded as necessary hostages held by the fable. Armitage comes across much more vividly than his captors, and the book conveys very well the disorientation of the executive uprooted from secretary, telephone, calendar, cigarettes, Jaguar and regular occupation. From raving and ranting, through prideful withdrawal, he comes to co-operation, and pours his life and thoughts into the tape-recorder. Basically, what he says is that while no doubt money is power, the drive is towards power itself. 'Business isn't about profits, as most people think. Business is about success.' But with this success, this power, he has lost both friends and freedom. On the island he can do what he wants with his time, and he can involve himself in personal relationships with two men and two women who are themselves freely and changingly associated. He learns, they learn. Tensions develop, the summer ends, and with it the fable. A Victorian-type afterword projects both sadness and optimism into the future lives of the five. It is a thoughtful, well-managed book.

Edwin Morgan, "President Chance," in The Listener, *Vol. 85, No. 2202, June 10, 1971, p. 760.*

CLIVE JORDAN

The labouring classes, in fiction as in fact, are always with us. A Zola can orchestrate their lives, a Gorki extol their individual energies, a Brecht allow them to break through in one final revolutionary flood. Mervyn Jones's new novel [*Holding On*] gives them a much more British role; as his title suggests, they endure. And his London East End family, the Wheelwrights, certainly have a lot to put up with: two world wars, the General Strike, the slump of the Thirties, wartime evacuation, the post-war brutalisation of their environment in the name of progress—in short, the major economic and social events of this century.

That such experiences were general rather than unique underlines the fact that Mervyn Jones clearly intends this family chronicle of four generations to be typical of working-class life. The dominant figure is partly a type also: Charlie Wheelwright, a lifelong stevedore in the Albert Dock like his father before him, is born with the century and breathes the last of his three-score years and ten in an NHS ward. He embodies, as well as energy and decency, the narrow socialist belief that virtue resides in the working class, with 'its honesty, its manifest values, its dignity', in the words of Charlie's politically-conscious wife Ann. As Charlie Wheelwright in old age is at odds with the greater complexity of post-war political realities, so the author seems to share his nostalgia for the old times and the work ethic. Sometimes the polarities seem justified: strike-breaking students in 1926 may well have been gangling public-school idiots, recent events remind us that Tory MPs have been known to take mistresses. But for all Mervyn Jones's keen sense of the minutiae of class differences, the underlying romantic assumption seems to be that the working class, like a force of nature, can do no wrong.

There's a dogged accumulation of social detail, a meticulous explanation of relationships, which sometimes recall those endless Biblical genealogies, and threaten to induce something uncomfortably like the loneliness of the long-distance reader. The narrative proceeds, more often than not, from the general to the particular, yet another sign that the abstract idea of the working class, as much as its representative Charlie Wheelwright, is the hero of the novel. The context of experience remains determinedly mainstream, even to the inner lives of the characters. The bias is towards the exploration of their sexual needs, women as well as men. The working class seem here to be depressingly devoid of visionaries or even eccentrics. Yet the sheer weight of detail makes these limited characters real and known enough for their deaths to provoke a sense of loss, and even of anguish.

The same romanticism that weakens the picture of working-class life gives rise to one of the novel's strengths: a finely realised sense of place. Charlie's home and his terraced street, as much as Charlie himself and the class he represents, can lay claim to being the heroes of the novel. The wholeness of the humble street, the ties of neighbourliness, the routine of departure and return, are evoked no less strongly than the ravages of the blitz and the contemporary barbarism of the post-war planners, which combine to make Charlie's East End a thing of the past.

Clive Jordan, "For Dear Life," in New Statesman, Vol. 85, No. 2203, June 8, 1973, p. 853.

THE TIMES LITERARY SUPPLEMENT

More than seventy years of a London dockside family's history have been neatly stowed into the continued space of this brief novel [*Holding On*]. The author is as handy as a stevedore. No overloading: there still seems room for much more information. But, if we think of the book's contents as a cargo, we soon begin to wonder what it's for, and where it's going.

Mervyn Jones records, most credibly, the lives of the ever-growing family of Jack Wheelwright, a stevedore at the Albert Docks during the Boer War. His widow marries a Tory insurance salesman; his son Charles, another stevedore, has one German-Jewish brother-in-law and another in Latin America; his grandson marries an ambassador's daughter who later elopes with a literary gent. These are a few of the more striking deviations from the way of a stevedore's world which Jack passes on to Charlie. But none of the incidents is treated very dramatically. The narratives are terse and short on dialogue. Events are recorded with the passionless serenity an archivist might bring to the history of a "great family". . . .

Holding On is a good title for this serious, quiet, simple book: encouraging but not enforcing a democratic and populist critique of twentieth-century London's history and planned future. It has a spirit of elegy, perhaps, rather than defiance, on behalf of the working-class tradition it celebrates.

"Dock Brief," in The Times Literary Supplement, No. 3721, June 29, 1973, p. 736.

RONALD BRYDEN

In principle, the territory Jones tackles [in *Holding On*] is fascinating. Starting, I'd guess, from the premise that the generation since Freud has said everything of interest about the individual psyche, the human animal's struggle to cohabit with mind, he sets out to explore the wider psychology of our life within cultures: the struggle of the animal in us with the communal patterns which provide our minds with their definitions. His chronicle of the Wheelwrights of West Ham traces the breakdown of that working-class culture which, for a century or so, united generations of East Enders within shared notions of manliness, womanliness, fatherhood, motherhood, family life and duty, virtue and criminality.

The flaw is that, trying to generalise from one family, he makes them too representative to carry conviction as individuals. Charlie Wheelwright, paragon of dockland virtue and virility, embodies too many traditional East End attitudes and decencies to ring quite true. For him, a man is a docker, a straight back and strong working hands, who keeps a roof over his family, and has many women but loves only one. His wife Ann, who resists the pressure of his certainties and recognises a wider world in which books and privacy have their use, is a more complex figure: but Charlie is meant to overshadow her, and

does. Together, they stand for the norm the East End has lost, and their unquestioning willingness to accept that norm and embody it makes them something less than individuals, something less than real. The book often shows a fine, subtle sense of how different lives grow or stop growing, and is always rich in the detail of East End landscape, history and custom. Reading it, you become enclosed in its horizons of brick, masts and Thames cranes, a world which ended at Aldgate to the west, Hackney marshes to the east. But the generalisations will creep in, Orwell-fashion—large men prefer small women, all Cockneys mistrust language—and each time they do, reality is diluted. The best part of the novel is the early section, where trams, tin baths and pub life are simply themselves, part of a living Edwardian landscape.

It's interesting, in this connection, how much more powerful a sense of cultural pull Mervyn Jones achieves by indirection in his other new book, **The Revolving Door,** which reads like a frivolous afterthought to *Holding On*. Dmitri Myslov, a handsome, divorced Russian geographer, defects on an academic visit to London and throws himself joyously into the fleshpots of Western decadence. Like a Slavic Tom Jones, he progresses from bed to aristocratic bed, indulging to the full a sensuality which has felt cabined and cribbed within the earnestness of Soviet culture. What he wants is freedom for a basically anti-cultural animal self. The life that matters to him is personal, achievable wherever girls are pretty and beddable. Yet once he's exhausted his round of London affairs, he suddenly finds his anywhere life tiresome. He needs to feel somewhere and, safe in the news that his ex-wife has defected after him, returns to Moscow, happily making passes at the Aeroflot stewardess. There's more life, I'm afraid, in this un-Russian Russian, simply because he's atypical, than in most of Mr. Jones's carefully-studied representatives of East End representativeness. And here the generalisations about the English and their classes are jokes. They work better that way: very sharply, cynically and funnily indeed. (pp. 155-56)

Ronald Bryden, "Dockland Decencies," in The Listener, Vol. 90, No. 2314, August 2, 1973, pp. 155-56.

PETER PRINCE

With Andrew Stanton, hero of his absorbing new novel [*Strangers*], Mervyn Jones attempts the difficult task of portraying a truly saintly man. Other novelists before him, of course, have successfully done the same, but in their pessimism they have taken care to equip their saints with some fatal weakness (booze, dope, secret pride), or else presented them as holy fools, Idiots, possessed of ultimate wisdom perhaps, but apparently ill-equipped to deal with the vulgar practicalities of everyday life.

In *Strangers*, Mr. Jones will have none of these get-outs. Stanton is not only uncompromisingly Good, he is also thoroughly Practical. In his time he has been a journalist, a farmer, a game warden, written a few books—now, at 52, he is a UN field officer in Uganda, imaginatively caring for a miserable and menaced band of refugees from the Sudan. His perfection extends even into competencies not normally required of earlier saints: sprawled on the dry earth of Africa, Stanton lights extravagant fires within his passionate young wife, and during their lengthy enforced separations, thousands of miles apart, is able quite effortlessly to govern her mind and (almost) her body.

It says a great deal for Mervyn Jones's calm, persistent advocacy that the reader's disbelief in this paragon is held at bay for so long. And if it does triumph in the end, one has the uncomfortable feeling that this may be due not so much to the novelist's failings as to the absolute refusal of the modern mind, perhaps foolishly, even to consider the possibility of a wholly good man. I don't know if the parallel was in Mr. Jones's mind, but Stanton is a Christ-like figure in a complete sense, not just in his goodness, but as an *effectively* good man, as a leader, organiser, persuader. And with one as with the other, whether correct or not, it is much easier to decide to admire them as the products of sublimely wishful thinking than to tangle with the consequences of their being real men.

> Peter Prince, "Paragons," in New Statesman, *Vol. 87, No. 2250, May 3, 1974, p. 633.*

THE TIMES LITERARY SUPPLEMENT

[*Strangers*] can be read as an adventure story, and there is nothing to provoke a borrower to reject it with words like "intellectual" or "high-brow". This happy result is brought about not by lack of ambition but by craft and self-restraint. *Strangers* is a serious novel, and will be felt to be serious by even its most casual readers.

The principal character is Val Stanton. . . . Val has made rather a surprising marriage to a widower of fifty who's old enough to be her father. This man, Andrew Stanton, is a South African liberal of a very well-to-do family, a pacifist whose career has been one of working for benevolent international organizations run by Quakers and United Nations agencies. . . . He is persuasively presented as a truly unselfish man, worthy of his young wife's love.

When the story begins, Andrew is in Uganda, living in a settlement of Dinka refugees from the Sudan. He has to protect them from a local tribe, the Karamajong. Val goes out to see him, and his serious problems are something of a relief to her, after her own rather dreary, petty worries in London. . . . [Val] comes to understand the frame of mind of the Dinka refugees, listless and with no sense of a future because they are in a strange country and, therefore, without their gods. Earlier in the book, thinking in bed of her friends, she had "offered what, in another language, could have been a prayer". It becomes clear that Mr. Jones is sketching the religious sensibility of a conventional agnostic starting, unwillingly, to change.

The political attitudes which inform the novel are distinctly left-of-centre by the standards of adventure-story and romance, but not in a polemical, overt, challenging way: the assumption is that left-of-centre views are quite conventional. Mr. Jones has a similar trick to play with libertarian sexual attitudes: for instance, he contrives to suggest that it is conventional for middle-class women to use Lawrence's aggressive language, quite coolly, when describing their sex-lives in polite conversation. This does not seem unrealistic, since his spokes-women are Val herself, a social worker and [an] unmarried mother (an art-school drop-out).

But what happens in London is made to seem much less important and compelling than what happens in Andrew's remote and neglected little patch of Africa. Briefly, the refugees regain their vitality through a savage and deplorable attack upon their Karamajong persecutors, the Uganda Army arrives on a punitive expedition, and Andrew effectively prevents further bloodshed with a courageous demonstration of his pacifist philos-

ophy. Then there is a sour little Brechtian twist, when it is suggested that his stand for non-violence has succeeded only because of the secret support of his capitalist brother, a South African businessman with influence over the Uganda Government. *Strangers,* for all the simplicity of its manner, is probably the most subtle of Mr. Jones's recent novels.

> *"Fair Dinka," in* The Times Literary Supplement, *No. 3774, July 5, 1974, p. 705.*

KARL MILLER

[Mervyn Jones] is a prominent left-wing journalist and, latterly, a copious novelist, one of whose recent books [*Holding On*] was a panorama of working-class life in London's East End. Now it is the turn of the West End—of the toffs, in Edwardian parlance. The English, it is said, dearly love a lord, and so, it is rumored, do the Americans. Mr. Jones [in *Lord Richard's Passion*] dearly loves Lord Richard, second son of the Duke of Berkshire, who comes of age during Britain's Imperial heyday and weathers the reckoning of the Great War. Is this a popular novel, in the line of Ouida, and about the old ruling class, but written by a melting latter-day leftist? A wild thought.

Lord Richard falls in love with Lord Farnham's daughter, a pale, austere, golden-haired, piano-playing, Pre-Raphaelite beauty called Ellie Colmore, and he loves her unhappily ever after. Ellie is very squeamish and declines to be the usual sort of debutante. She is not in any obtrusive way interesting. . . . She has a secret sorrow, which presently earns the period diagnosis of dementia praecox. As a girl, she had stumbled in the middle of the night through a bedroom door (left unlocked by novelistic license) to be astonished by the sight of a hairy major lying on top of her sister. This confirms Ellie in her horror of possession by a man. She loves Lord Richard but does not wish him to lie on top of her.

Richard had previously kept a servant girl as a mistress, but she could not hope to compete with Ellie. After Ellie has broken off their engagement, he marries a third woman, who can't hope to compete with Ellie either. He lives with the virtuous and managing Geraldine for a number of years, and has two sons. An army officer at the outset, he is now a politician, having noticed that the House of Commons was pretty much like Eton: an insight achieved by more than a few. He is promised the Foreign Secretaryship by Lord Salisbury, for which mark of favor he has groomed himself by acquiring a favorable opinion of Germany, and the belief that Britain and Germany must come to an understanding. In time, the Great War proves that he was right all along.

He divorces Geraldine after renewing his friendship with Ellie and prevailing on her to agree to marry him. But she cracks under the strain of thinking of "the thing he would do to her as her husband," and takes leave of her senses. Richard sets up house in Florence with an Englishwoman, who, once again, means far less to him than Ellie does, and he leaves her like a shot when the time comes for him to be the Duke of Berkshire and inhabit the palace of Severalls. At this point Ellie drowns herself. Neither kicking nor screaming, but distinctly perplexed, Richard enters the twentieth century, with its suffragettes and assertive women. Then comes the Great War, and the Somme: the novel treats very well the gradual realization, on the home front, of the scale and futility of the carnage. Late in life, liked and deferred-to, but put off by the politics that has emerged from the war, Richard takes to believing that he is visited by his Ophelia.

Lord Richard's Passion is agreeable to read, and the social and political bearings which it devises for its hero do not disturb. . . . [The] real worry with the book has to do with the question of how far it can be seen as a celebration of its hero. Does it come out with what socialists generally repress? There is no way of knowing. Is it a quiet way of saying, through a scrutiny of what this kind duke gets up to, how awful these ruling classes were: does its anodyne air conceal a stratagem, which may even involve some use of the fact that Severalls is the name of a psychiatric hospital? I am inclined to reject this idea too, but there were times when it gained a certain potency.

Looked at with a dispassionate eye, Richard's politics are fairly thin, and his private life is calamitous, though by no means for the reasons he supposes. His noble passion has, in fact, some of the attributes of a natural disaster. Three women at least are sacrificed to it: those women, including the mother of his children, are held to impose claims on him which it would be laughable to compare with the claim imposed by the phantasmal, almost speechless Ellie. He couldn't desert his Florence woman "without feelings of pity, of uncertainty and—it had to be faced—of guilt." The novel continues: "He could make out a solid case in his defence." The novel hardly seems to be making out a solid case here in favor of Lord Richard's passion.

Nevertheless, it can't seriously be doubted that it is chiefly his passion which is meant to make Lord Richard sympathetic. All for love, and the Foreign Office well lost. *Amor vincit* the Duke of Berkshire, amid clouds of cigar smoke and odors of dementia. . . . Mr. Jones goes to great lengths, and inspires the uncouth thought that such loves belong, as doubles do, mostly to books—to masterpieces and penny dreadfuls alike. In one respect, however, there is nothing bookish about the scenario which accompanies Lord Richard's passion. Ellie's refusal of life is not veiled is euphemism: it is revealed and explained as an illness. (pp. 26-7)

> *Karl Miller, "Gothic Guesswork," in* The New York Review of Books, *Vol. XXI, No. 12, July 18, 1974, pp. 24-7.*

THE TIMES LITERARY SUPPLEMENT

It is surprising to find Mervyn Jones writing a novel [*Lord Richard's Passion*] about a duke's younger son who allows a lifelong passion for a woman to ruin his marriage and a promising political career. The world Lord Richard inhabits continues from Trollope's—he was born in 1855. There is no strenuous period detail and there are some curious anachronisms, but Mr. Jones appears to have cast his story at this time and in this milieu to emphasize the implications of the case-history at the centre of the novel. Ellie is a beautiful young woman with a terror of sex which is confirmed by the sight of her sister in a state of trance beneath the hairy body of a major to whom she is not married. Ellie, her sister, and even Lord Richard are seen as victims of the Victorian romanticizing of women.

It is not possible to believe in his passion, so that much of what happens in the novel is lifeless and contrived. But Mr. Jones has done well to leave his characters, their views of their personalities and possibilities, to speak for themselves, rather than interpreting them, as he might have been tempted to, in terms of what Ibsen or Freud would have made of them. Ellie's torturing sense of her own perverse nature might still be made to look charming and provocative today, and it is not clear that

a well-set-up man of the world, however much in love, would necessarily be any better than Lord Richard at detecting or remedying her difficulties.

> *"Ducal Delusions," in* The Times Literary Supplement, *No. 3790, October 25, 1974, p. 1206.*

JULIAN BARNES

'He clenched his fist and the knuckles went white—I'm sorry that moments of emotion so often have to be described in clichés, but it's a fact.' Mervyn Jones's sceptical examination of the final limb of Jefferson's triad [*Pursuit of Happiness*] certainly exudes the courage of its clichés. In writing about a girl's emotional and sexual maturing, and her rocky marriage to a superhead, it's clearly a calculated risk to tell it all from her point of view and then offer as stylistic apologia her remark that 'I wasn't concerned with style, even with good English, nor with achieving any kind of effect'. Some sections are well handled, notably the girl's early sexual experiences, in which a sense of adventure does service for lust. But mostly we are left with propositions like 'To ask why women get married is like asking why a moth flies into a flame', with characters 'without an ounce of surplus fat', and with seductions which are 'a ritual surrender, like the surrender of a temple maiden to a priest'. It's difficult not to itch for a less self-effacing author.

> *Julian Barnes, "Semi-Bold," in* New Statesman, *Vol. 90, No. 2328, October 31, 1975, p. 550.*

VALENTINE CUNNINGHAM

There is little that is sprightly about Mervyn Jones's *Pursuit of Happiness:* more a plod into unhappiness in fact. A girl called Pat Bell narrates (and were she dubbed String-Along or Touch-Pacey the reader would not have to linger even the thirty-odd pages he does have to before getting whiffs of the particular fictional ozone in store). She offers the flimsiest of hoary old excuses for writing: "I'm writing for myself, with fanciful notions of being read by some daughter or granddaughter years hence . . ." (no excuses, it appears, like the old excuses—they will be discovering editable confessions in trunks soon). And ways with words never came stolider: culinarily speaking, *The Pursuit of Happiness* is a protracted feast of Spotted Dick without even the occasional covenanted mercy of currants. . . .

No doubt [the development of plot and characters] felt good at the ur-novel stage: but it has not exactly leapt happily from the drawing board. The situations and people persist in being unbelievably stereotyped, ever calqued on a colour supplement adman's dreams. Or perhaps, more calculatedly, the mixture has been rigged for a script conference with some meat-headed film executive. We need some Glossy Birds! (They are here, O Mogul.) Time for a Trendy Don! (Here he comes, Mogul.) Chuck in some Middle Class Anguish! (That is in too, sir.) Now for a Liberated Woman Bit! (That is in as well.) And never less than immoderately in: not a couple of slick chicks, but a flat-full; not a talking head, but a shouting big head; not just a posh wedding, but one attended by a vice-chancellor, the editor of *The Times*, the director-general of the BBC and the "Minister for the Arts Council". And even on the occasions when sentiments manage to be as laudable as they are credible they are dwelt on ever so lengthily. . . .

Not for a long time has the anti-Midas touch—at which everything that is not already dross turns into it before the reader's startled eyes—received such an orchestrating in a novel of allegedly serious pretensions.

Valentine Cunningham, "Unspotted Dick," in The Times Literary Supplement, *No. 3843, November 7, 1975, p. 1325.*

JULIAN BARNES

Choice, rather than circumstance, makes Mervyn Jones's style [in *Scenes from Bourgeois Life*] the unflashy thing that it is. Flat, monochrome and Maughamish, it avoids imagery, and the constant priority of sense over sound makes for the occasional aural collapse (try saying 'the cessation of the foursome left the twosomes to function as usual' without frothing). It is, however, appropriate prose for describing the flat, monochrome etc. lives of the likeable but corrupt professional middle-classes of Epping, Dorking and Wimbledon. Bourgeois life no longer operates a system of rigid laws designed to suffocate Emma Bovarys; instead, its keynote is a sort of voluntary sleepiness. Disturbance expresses itself not in social but sexual terms: some find adultery the only way of invoking authentic and powerful feelings; others merely slide into sexual inertness; while in one of these stories, an isolated quartet of siblings enforces its solidarity by incest. Summary makes Mr. Jones sound lurid; in fact, his forte is conveying the jogging half-awareness of the bourgeois mind (where equal brainspace is given to the misfortune of friends and the non-arrival of the plumber), and the passionlessness of much of the life: spouses walk out not in anger but in empty, incommunicable finality. Best of all he captures the timbre of thought, and the inherent selfishness, of his subjects: 'At the end of the day,' remarks husband comfortingly to wife about a failing marriage, 'they're other people, and we're us.'

Julian Barnes, "Any Old Irony," in New Statesman, *Vol. 92, No. 2367, July 30, 1976, p. 152.*

JOHN MELLORS

Mervyn Jones has written five longish short stories, in four of which he charts the sickness of good living in Hampstead, Epping, Dorking and Wimbledon. The fifth, an unconvincing description of a mysteriously incestuous family of half-siblings on the Lancashire moors, seems to have wandered by mistake into *Scenes from Bourgeois Life*. **"The Syndrome"**, about men who decide monogamy is tame and women who have 'a gift for coming along at the right moment', and **"Such a Lovely Girl"**, about a beautiful but cold and heartless wife, suffer from the author's lack of sympathy with his characters.

The last two stories in the book are a cut above the rest. **"Senior Citizens"** is a picture in the round of a thoroughly 'nice', unassuming woman who finds, when her husband retires, that it was a mistake to have married for stability rather than love. After more than 30 years of married life, she excites her husband's anger when she confronts him with the truth: 'We're not very successful at living together.' **"Happiness is . . ."** tells of Carol Talbot's escape from the prosperous home of her chartered accountant father, where she is astonished that people can be so indifferent to 'what shaped and enclosed their lives: the great evil, the great goodness', to a prison-cell in Russian-occupied Czechoslovakia, where she 'rested her bruised cheek against the stone wall' and 'felt truly happy'. (p. 158)

John Mellors, "Council Writers," in The Listener, *Vol. 96, No. 2469, August 5, 1976, pp. 158-59.*

JEREMY TREGLOWN

To breed or not to breed is a question that crops up . . . [in *Nobody's Fault*], about Tamsin's affairs and marriages with her two former co-editors on the university literary mag., Brian, now a failed poet, and Keith, a rich pop-music promoter. Keith wants children but turns out to be infertile. Brian, on the other hand, neither wants nor indeed can afford the infant with whom he temporarily impregnates the careless Tamsin.

It's a readable, well-observed fiction which somehow misses out because of its own self-assurance, its easy acceptance of a style of realism which makes reality itself seem like a set of literary conventions. When we're told, for example, that Tamsin's family have lunch but Keith's call the same meal dinner, the code is so instantly decoded as to forfeit any interest in the broader distinction it tries to suggest. There's a clear-eyed chapter or two about Brian and Tamsin's attempt to live in a snowbound croft in Scotland, but on the whole it's a performance difficult to feel strongly about.

Jeremy Treglown, "Kithflicks," in New Statesman, *Vol. 93, No. 2403, April 8, 1977, p. 471.*

ALAN MASSIE

> She hadn't thought yet about whether to tell Brian. If she was convinced of what she said—that what she'd done didn't mean anything, that there was no space in her life for a lover—then there was no harm in telling Brian; indeed, not telling him was creating a conspiracy with Keith. And if that was so, staying with Keith for the evening, or the night for that matter, made no difference.

It seems worth giving this quotation in full, not merely because it states clearly the theme of Mervyn Jones's highly readable novel [*Nobody's Fault*], but because it exemplifies so completely the virtues and weaknesses of his characteristic manner and method.

First, Mr. Jones is so clearly fair and concerned; concerned not only with his characters' fates and with how they behave but also, in an Orwellian sense, with decency. Second, Mr. Jones is scrupulously honest. And third, he has a driving sense of narrative, even here when he tries to disguise it beneath some not entirely satisfactory time-shifts.

Why, in the face of these virtues, does one find oneself less than wildly enthusiastic about the novel? . . . The characters, rather predictable at the start, never go on to surprise us. And this points up the central inescapable weakness in Mr. Jones's work, why one is eventually disappointed. Mr. Jones is always anxious to tell us; but he does not make us see or hear. "Dramatize", said Henry James, but Mr. Jones prefers to explain; just in case we get anything wrong.

Alan Massie, "Keeping It Decent," in The Times Literary Supplement, *No. 3936, August 19, 1977, p. 997.*

PATRICIA CRAIG

Neither style nor subtlety may be claimed for *The Beautiful Words*. It reads like one of those books for adolescents written with a social objective, in this case to inculcate an attitude of kindness to the unfortunate. Tommy—he has no surname—is a charming 17-year-old with a defective brain. He has every good quality except intelligence. His behaviour is that of a docile child, and the point of the novel is that he's in search of a parent: but the hearts of his benefactors can never be as pure as Tommy's. Circumstances place him successively in the care of a prostitute named Rita ('Some of the men Rita knew were perfectly horrid'), a dirty old tramp, a couple of squatters in a derelict house (yes, the author has gone deeply into the question of squalor in urban life) and a rich old lady with an ungenerous spirit.

It is sentimental to keep stressing the positive aspect of Tommy's disabilities: he is incorruptible as the result of a congenital deficiency, and he retains innocence only to the extent that he's incapable of elementary reasoning. His virtues are inadvertent, and there is nothing in the facile realism of the novel to suggest that he is meant to stand for more than endearing simplicity. We may be reminded of another innocent, Eric in Sylvia Townsend Warner's *The True Heart*, but Eric's thoughts and impressions were not rendered in terms of the utmost banality. That novel has a strangeness, a fairy-tale quality entirely missing from *The Beautiful Words*. Of course it's splendid, as Mervyn Jones implies, that someone has taken the trouble to teach the boy to recite Wordsworth (the beautiful words); and it's easy for the reader to relish the pleasure he gets from this unanticipated gift. The moral point appears to be that it's wrong to make assumptions about the degree of incapacity in these cases. But it isn't enough to enliven a sad and boring tale. (p. 63)

> *Patricia Craig, "Cripples," in* New Statesman, *Vol. 98, No. 2521, July 13, 1979, pp. 62-3.*

REGINALD HILL

[*The Beautiful Words*] are those of Herrick's "To Daffodils" and Wordsworth's "My Heart Leaps Up", which have been learnt with great difficulty by Tommy, the novel's mentally sub-normal hero. The Wordsworthian connection is particularly apt both because of the poem's assertion of the value of the child in man and because in Tommy we quickly recognise Johnny Foy, Wordsworth's "Idiot Boy". Those selfsame qualities of simplemindedness which caught the poet's imagination are here—the attractiveness, the capacity to inspire love, the suggestion of some almost magical healing power—but we have come a long way from the *Lyrical Ballads* and Mr. Jones can hold out no promise of a joyous reunion with a loving mother at the end of his story. Tommy is doomed from the start, to neglect, abuse, malice. He meets kindness too, but not enough to protect him. Unfortunately, or perhaps necessarily, the novel seems to hesitate between the pathetic and the tragic, and at times promises rather more than in the end it gives. But it is never less than interesting and often moves with a Wordsworthian intensity.

> *Reginald Hill, "Puzzlement," in* Books and Bookmen, *Vol. 24, No. 11, August, 1979, p. 50.*

NICHOLAS SPOLIAR

The title of Mervyn Jones's new novel [*A Short Time to Live*] echoes both the burial service and Herrick's "Daffodils", a poem often quoted by Jones in his 1979 novel, *The Beautiful Words*. The associations suggested by these references are en-tirely appropriate, for the story is dominated by a sense of loss and uncertainty: a woman has lost her husband, a man has wasted his life, someone has been killed (indirectly) by his best friend, and the most interesting character in the novel reflects that: "The only truth was this: what happened was the opposite of what you intended or expected. (Hardcastle's Law)." The structuring of developments like these is a tricky problem for the novelist, and in *A Short Time to Live* we are offered a deftly organized, craftsmanlike work, in which Jones neatly harmonizes the framework of an Old School novel with some of the conventions of a thriller.

Michael Kellett has been killed, supposedly by a snake, while on a mysterious (journalistic) mission to a Pacific Island. His funeral is the starting-point of the book and it brings together the novel's cast: his school-mates from his suburban grammar school, with some wives and parents. "It's wonderful how they've stuck together, that bunch who was together at school", his father remarks, and the comment appears a straightforward one. But during the course of the novel it acquires an ironic code of reference made up of all the other ways in which the characters have been or become stuck together: murder, adultery, the exposure of a character's activities in the House of Commons by a former school-mate. The loyalties that are established for us in the opening scene are undermined or reversed, to be only partially re-established in the novel's concluding scene, another funeral. . . .

A counterpart to this tale of loss is the account of events on Tamatavu, the scene of Kellett's death and a Pacific paradise garishly depicted, with serpent, on the book's dust-jacket. By the end of the novel Tamatavu, like the old school, is a lost Eden, violently made one with the modern world. Philip Zane comments on the island's absolute peacefulness when he was there, and for him it seems to have acquired a symbolic importance as the "world's still centre", but for another school-mate, Titus Hardcastle, it is a place "practically made of chrome", and he cannot wait to educate its inhabitants in the benefits of work and conquest. . . .

The affair is a central irony of the book, as Hardcastle has uncharacteristically remained faithful to his wife, but unfortunately the sections in which it is described do not really come to life. . . .

Mervyn Jones is not afraid of clichés, and *A Short Time to Live* has its share of them: clues on post-cards, Kellett's mysterious mission, a Welsh Mr. Chips (Mr. Evans), and some rather tired descriptions of "successful" people. . . . There are other, consciously modern clichés—first wife becomes friendly with wife husband left her for—and the central contrast between Titus Hardcastle and Philip Zane is itself somewhat obvious. But the description of the Hardcastles (Emma surely so named in irony) is genuinely touching and also extremely funny, with walk-on parts for a couple of shady chrome-prospectors and an even more dubious tropical Prime Minister. The suspense element is neatly handled and it is a nice touch to channel vital items of news through Titus's fragmenting consciousness.

> *Nicholas Spoliar, "A Private Island," in* The Times Literary Supplement, *No. 4044, October 3, 1980, p. 1087.*

PAUL ABLEMAN

Eighteen months ago, John Updike's *The Coup* was published in England. . . . I hailed the book as a modern masterpiece while Mervyn Jones was reported as thinking it overwritten and pretentious. In his strictures, I sensed a kind of puritanical distaste for what he perhaps considered mere ornamental rhetoric, even verbal decadence. Now Mervyn Jones has published his own novel about a coup [*A Short Time to Live*], almost as if to demonstrate how the theme should be handled by a serious novelist concerned with life and not an aesthete obsessed with spinning ecstatic prose. He has done a very good job and I can imagine a type of reader who would find his book more pertinent and exciting than Updike's luscious satire.

The structure of *A Short Time to Live* is really quite different from that of Updike's book. Mr. Jones's coup, although the pivot of much of the action, occurs off-stage. The author is not concerned to examine its mechanism or, in any detail, its dramatic confrontations. His scene is set in London, 10,000 miles from the site of the uprising on a Polynesian island partitioned into francophone and anglophone mini-states and which, presumably by chance, sounds remarkably like the New Hebrides where all the confusing hugger-mugger erupted recently. Mr. Jones analyses the impact of the distant event on the lives of a group of ex-school-friends. He does it expertly and without any implausible coincidence. The web of event and hazard which binds us all, and the disclosure of which is a traditional and central part of the task of fiction, is convincingly exposed.

The structure of the book is admirable. It spans a year, bracketed between two funerals, in the life of a group of loosely connected people. The book has some of the qualities of a thriller and the suspense is sustained to the end.

But Mr. Jones seems chiefly preoccupied with ambiguity, with how the best-laid schemes of merchant bankers and heads of state gang aft agley, and with how what seems least probable is often the most likely to occur. This is movingly expressed in the account of the graceless wife who, among the elegant and passionate women that surround her, seems the most unlikely candidate for a high romance but who achieves just that.

Mr. Jones has a wide range of human sympathy but he seems to me even more in tune with the subtleties of the female mind than with the more robust aspirations of the male. None of the characters in the present work dwindles into symbol or type, as they showed a tendency to do in *Today the Struggle,* the last work of Mr. Jones's that I read. A particular success is Mr. Evans; the pawky retired schoolmaster, to whom many of the male characters repair from time to time to sample his sister's teas and receive his sardonic commentary on their lives.

With one exception, the central characters in this book are worldly, sophisticated and fully involved with contemporary life. The exception is Philip Zane who, after a conventional middle-class education, rejects the world in favour of spiritual development. He thus has a heavy fictional burden to bear since he represents the huge dimension of experience that is not expressed by orthodox society. For me, he remained a rather shadowy figure and I felt that Mr. Jones never really succeeded in penetrating the mind of such a man. As if in an attempt to compensate for his lack of true substance, Zane is endowed with quasi-mystical properties. He emerges from a grove of trees with his golden beard glowing like a redeemer's and is credited with a kind of authority that is never really earned by what he says or does. This struck me as the chief flaw in a novel which, in every other respect, is a splendid achievement.

Paul Ableman, "Island Story," in The Spectator, *Vol. 245, No. 7943, October 4, 1980, p. 26.*

MIKE POOLE

Two Women and their Man might almost have been written to illustrate Orwell's definition of the traditional English murder as a crime of guilt rather than passion: illicit sexuality running up against the demands of respectability and taking the desperate way out in an irrational bid to stay within the bounds of propriety.

Mervyn Jones is an enormously prolific writer with something approaching a score of novels to his name, mostly social realist in intention and leftist in inflection. Some of them, like *Today the Struggle,* attempt to dramatise large historical movements; others are more reflective. It is typical, then, that this rather slight story of a sexual triangle—husband, wife and American divorcée—should be set in 1939 and its in-built tragedy unfolded against the wider backdrop of Munich and the descent from phoney peace into WW2. For what it describes is the most precarious of equilibriums: a wife who knows her husband is having an affair with her best friend, but doesn't let on; a husband who isn't even aware that his wife and mistress know each other; and a mistress caught in the middle, genuinely torn between the two. The inevitable happens when hubby resorts to his service pistol to prevent his wife finding out what she already knows. The man he kills is a reclusive painter who had threatened to spill the beans—news travels fast in a small Welsh village—and whose primitivist work was later to achieve a posthumous cult status, turning the case into a *cause célèbre*.

The novel presents itself from this later perspective as a sort of art history document—a reconstruction of the circumstances leading up to the murder compiled from the first person accounts of the three surviving protagonists. As their narratives intertwine it becomes clear that the painter was a peripheral figure. The real interest lies in the sexual drama he had the misfortune to stumble upon. The three conflicting points of view are deftly handled and the novel's considerable pleasures derive from the way their fractured versions of events fail to coincide. But there is a fatal lack of verisimilitude about much of what happens—two women held in Lawrentian thrall by the sexual magnetism of a man who is also a big prick in the other sense—and in the end one is left with the feeling of having participated in little more than a well-made male fantasy, albeit in a beguiling period setting. (pp. 23-4)

Mike Poole, "English Murder," in New Statesman, *Vol. 103, No. 2656, February 12, 1982, pp. 23-4.*

ANTHONY THWAITE

Mysterious resonance isn't something Mervyn Jones ever goes in for. But *Two Women and Their Man* is a reminder of other qualities and strengths available in fiction, such as the making of characters through an accumulation of 'facts' and the familiar device of giving the characters self-contained but interlocking narratives which change the reader's perspective. Mr. Jones is a commonsensical traditional craftsman, never producing a shoddy piece of goods, judiciously reinforcing his storyteller's instinct with the convincing touch of detail that is part of his journalistic experience.

It's a measure of how successfully the detail is built up and built in that a crisp analysis of the three main characters is so difficult. The man, David, is perhaps more perfunctorily done than the two women; or perhaps it's just that he is less generously seen. A prosperous Anglo-Welsh landowner and sheep-farmer, his reclusive reticence comes over as pompous priggishness.

I couldn't raise much enthusiasm for his agonised erotic enthralment by Estelle, the worldly American on whose cottage mattress he discovers that 'there was no longer a choice, but only an acceptance of the inevitable'. Much more interesting is the relationship between Estelle and David's wife, Martha. Mervyn Jones has always been good at sympathetic portraits of women; and here, seen from the inside, presenting themselves, their unexpected bonding is believable.

Anthony Thwaite, "Ghosts in the Mirror," in The Observer, February 14, 1982, p. 33.

KIERNAN RYAN

The prolific imagination of Mervyn Jones (born 1922) has produced to date some nineteen novels which between them map an impressively wide and varied fictional territory, embracing both the immensely public and the intensely private, the sweepingly historical and the vividly contemporary. Jones' first novel, *No Time To Be Young,* appeared in 1952, but it was not until the successfully filmed *John and Mary* (1966) that his fiction really began to claim the wider attention and respect which it now regularly commands.

John and Mary remains, indeed, one of the best novels Jones has written. In his customary lean and lucid, often deceptively simple prose, it narrates the superficially trite experience of a man and a woman spending the day together, sealed off from the everyday world, following a casual sexual encounter the night before; a day in which they gradually learn to know each other truly and in the end, 'under a silent pressure of unbroken time and unchanging place', fall authentically in love.

The achievement is in the penetration beneath the prosaic surface of the incident to reveal the subtle psychological dynamics and implications of this process of falling in love: all the wary tactical manoeuvrings on both sides through impulsion and restraint, overture and resistance; all the fraught subliminal conflicts of anticipation and inhibition before the final courageous breakthrough into the vulnerable commitment of full and honest mutuality. The narration proceeds in stereoscopic depth through the alternating and independent first-person accounts of each phase by John and Mary. For Jones is thus able to show how the man and the woman alike must struggle out through their socialised preconceptions of each other's character and motivation to a genuine recognition and trust beyond the confines of conventional assumptions. The novel pursues its hermeneutics of desire and relationship with spare intensity, quietly dramatising and celebrating the power of men and women to surmount the acquired illusions, fears and prejudices barring their way to mutual self-realisation.

The same strategy of creating a deliberately insulated situation, under whose special pressures an exemplary process of development can be magnified and accelerated, is deployed in *Mr. Armitage Isn't Back Yet* (1971), which concerns a much more drastic emancipative shedding of internalised constraints and presuppositions. A wealthy executive is kidnapped by four benign hippies and 'imprisoned' with them over a long period on a deserted, inaccessible island. Their aim is to study and understand the capitalist species *homo economicus* under whose domination they will have to spend the rest of their lives. The

fascination of the book lies in Armitage's account of what becomes for him an experience of radical transformation.

By the surreptitious force of circumstance and the irresistibly gentle, humane example of the two young couples, Armitage is gradually driven to overcome his initially traumatic symptoms of dislocation and withdrawal from bourgeois 'civilisation', and to question his most basic suppositions regarding property, money, work, time and sexuality; to completely revise his least-considered presumptions as to what is 'natural' and 'normal' and 'common sense', and what really constitutes happiness. In short, he is induced to dismantle the whole individualist and instrumentalist way of life hitherto deceiving and degrading him, and to edge his way towards an alternative way of living in equal community with others. To be sure, the novel fails to evolve a reciprocal interrogation of the hippies' naive and apolitical anti-authoritarianism; the objective fragility of their vision in the face of the everyday world being but hastily adumbrated at the end. And the abruptly bitten off closure and generally uneven narrative structure leave much to be desired. But, like *John and Mary,* the text does succeed in producing a genuinely illuminating collision of the social modes of containment with the human drive for release into more and better, which other Jones' novels, in spite of themselves, do not always manage to achieve.

Strangers (1974), for example, is (as the title might suggest) a comparative study in the many forms of our alienation, but one whose preoccupation with charting the negative effects of division and estrangement leaves little scope for projecting preferable versions of feeling and relationship. The novel is overcast by the sense of our living 'in the century of the refugee', in an age when 'everybody's leaving somewhere'; the liberal middle-class heroine Val learning on her pulse the bitter truth of 'how many prisoners and how few free people there [are] in the world'.

The narrative shuttles between Val in London and her pacifist husband Andrew in Uganda in charge of a precarious settlement of tribal refugees from the Sudan. In London and Africa by turns Val's liberal complacencies are put increasingly to the test, and the awareness grows that the experience of oppressive estrangement is not restricted to the wretched tribe abandoned and despised in Uganda, but is shared in different degrees and forms (social, political, sexual, racial, generational) by all the members of Val's ill-assorted London household: the lonely American draft-dodger; the pregnant girl evading her parents; the black student harassed for his relationship with a white schoolgirl; the working-class tenants in the basement flat, to whom Val feels bound by nothing but her sense of class guilt. Through Val the categories of the English and the African experiences cross-question and relativise each other, and the novel does at least begin to shape a liberating sense of the virtual common humanity existing across all these arbitrary barriers provisionally dividing people. So that, despite a closing feeling of blockage, uncertainty and dismay, what prevails overall is the recognition that 'there wasn't a battle to be won or lost; there was an endless effort, never likely to be wholly successful, yet never to be abandoned, always worth while.'

This scaled-down yet realistic and resilient appraisal of our situation and our task likewise structures Jones' much more ambitious novel *Today The Struggle* (1978), a panoramic social and political chronicle of England over the last forty years. Here Jones traces the closely intertwining fates of various families and associated characters representative of the whole class spectrum of English society during the period. Through their personal experiences he endeavours to lock in on the nation's history at three specific moments: the intensely political 1930s, with the Spanish Civil War and the growing menace of Fascism; the late 1950s and early 1960s, centring on the exuberant rise but eventual subsidence of the CND movement (of which Jones himself was a prominent member); and finally, in stark contrast with these politically rich moments of united commitment and aspiration, the apathetic 1970s, the decade in which 'what was missing . . . was the quality of idealism. The striving to make a better world—the reaching for a vision . . . they led their lives, all of them, without trying to change the world.'

Jones deliberately juxtaposes the promise generated in past struggles with the conditions and attitudes blocking the continued effort to realise that promise in the present. And although on the one hand this leads to a deadening apprehension of stagnation and impasse, it generates at the same time a correspondingly urgent insistence on the stubborn need nevertheless to defend unflaggingly the ground already won, 'to offer the whole of oneself, without calculation and even without hope: to resist'. For in the end 'always something was gained, if only the awareness of greater possibilities; but always the success was partial, the impetus melted away. What mattered was to remember. What was vital was not to lose hope.'

But the structure and the vision do not always come through as clearly and forcefully as this. In several novels Jones sets out to explore an initially arresting narrative situation, the terms of whose conflict seem bound to generate a whole spectrum of valuable recognitions. But somehow the drive to attain a full imaginative seizure of the subject flags and fades, and the embryonic, ideal parameters of the fiction dissolve in a blur of mere circumstantial anecdote, obliterating all but the vestiges of the really significant narrative the text might have become.

Lord Richard's Passion (1974) is a typical example of the Jones novel which never quite manages to grasp and articulate its own central concern, and whose interstices afford maddening glimpses of the other, unwritten novel which could not finally be lured to the surface. Set in the Victorian period, it describes how the passionate love of a young aristocrat for a beautiful woman of his own class is persistently thwarted by personal and social-historical forces which neither of them can fully understand, but which are focused in the submerged contradictions between her nascent feminist consciousness and his unconsciously domineering sexism. But because the author fails to characterise the protagonists in such a way as to invest their imputed hunger for fulfilment with a more fully human, oppositional authority capable of interrogating and indicting the social relations which defeat them, the novel never realises the representative tragic status to which it aspires but remains a merely particular, incidental case-study in sad misfortune. Unable to select and structure the kind of telling action and charged detail calculated to impart general symbolic force to the narrative, the compositional focus slithers promiscuously all over the place and the novel peters out in a stammer of structurally superfluous gossip.

Much the same critique, *mutatis mutandis,* could be made of *A Survivor* (1968) or even Jones' most recent, disappointing novels, *The Beautiful Words* (1979) and *A Short Time To Live* (1980). In all of these that nagging sense of the repressed true text, swelling insistently beneath the actual diffuse and uncentred surface novel, is inescapable. Each defaults on its implicit narrative contract to illuminate the tragic tension between what could be and what is: to expand our cognizance both of the socially produced circumstances severing people from their potential selves, and of the irrepressible latent power of humans to subdue those circumstances nevertheless to their will.

At times, moreover, there is a clear feeling that what's stifling the fully dynamic and subversive tragic vision at birth is a deep-lying, profoundly static notion of social reality, an informing world view bordering at moments on paralysed resignation and finding its aesthetic expression all too readily in the spare descriptive naturalism into which Jones' novels tendentially veer. The problem with this minimal, anecdotal style being that it hypostatises the in fact processive reality which it addresses, confirming and stabilising even where it would disrupt. In place of a conflictive drama of becoming, the evolving narration of human fates in volatile, contingent solution, such a naturalistic descriptive mode, as Lukács observes, 'transforms people into conditions, into components of still lives. . . . The result is a series of static pictures. . . . The so-called action is only a thread on which the still lives are disposed in a superficial, ineffective, fortuitous sequence of isolated, static pictures.'

The problem is manifest in one of Jones' most popular books, *Holding On* (1973). . . . This novel chronicles the working-class experience of this century through the particular history of the East End docker Charlie Wheelwright. It recounts his life and times from his birth at the turn of the century through to his bitterly lonely yet proud death as an old man at the start of the 1970s, taking in his experience of both World Wars, the General Strike and the Depression, and the dehumanising 'progress' of an increasingly callous and sordid postwar Britain. The courage, human warmth and dignity of Charlie and his class under even the most appalling conditions are rightly stressed throughout. And yet the overall picture is finally just too acceptably rosy and contented with itself altogether. For under the pressure of the naturalistic style and vision the proletarian experience of the twentieth century is implicitly depicted not as a series of socially and historically produced tragedies made and changeable by men, but as having been a 'natural', ineluctably fixed and necessary condition of being to be simply endured—the wars being conceived as deadly plagues, the Depression as a vicious winter, through which the working class stoically 'held on'. History, thus naturalised and stunned, is deprived of its conditionality and optionality, and thereby robbed of its constant inherent potential, displayed both in the past and in the present, to produce worlds other than those which have prevailed. (pp. 168-72)

Kiernan Ryan, ''Socialist Fiction and the Education of Desire: Mervyn Jones, Raymond Williams and John Berger,'' in The Socialist Novel in Britain: Towards the Recovery of a Tradition, *edited by H. Gustav Klaus, St. Martin's Press, 1982, pp. 166-85.*

STUART EVANS

Joanna's Luck is a resolutely, if at times deceptively, unsentimental account of a young woman's determination to live her life on her own terms. Without Mervyn Jones's intelligence, narrative discrimination and social acerbity, the theme and mood of the novel might well have been the substance of a story in a popular magazine or a television playlet. Joanna, far from unattractive, engaging of mind and enticing of bosom, thinks herself down on her luck. Public funds dry up to deprive her of a worthwhile job which she enjoys: so she has to work as a part-time restaurant waitress where she despises the ersatz pretentions of patrons and management alike. . . .

Joanna frets that at the age of 24 in the early 1980s she is still a virgin! After one or two forays into licence, she divests herself of the slurred state twice on the same evening, at the hands (as it were) of different partners. She is accordingly not certain who is the father of the child she ultimately decides to bring to term: it might have been a drunken semi-rapist at a New Year party, or the taxi-driver who cheered her aftermath confusion on the drive home. Unpromising as it may sound, the novel is for the most part sympathetic and its underlying premises demand consideration. Mr. Jones is, not surprisingly, angry about the waste of young and talented people in a society of fatuous values.

Stuart Evans, "A Life of Her Own," in The Times, *London, February 7, 1985, p. 11.*

MARY HOPE

Mervyn Jones is a highly professional journalist who has written novels which have been often praised and have also been turned into effective film and television scripts. He has a strong sense of the currents swirling around in society at any time; his finger is on the pulse. *Joanna's Luck* is the story of a young girl who, although well qualified, loses her job, through no fault of her own; fails, like three million others to find another one, falls pregnant—innocence rather than experience—and chooses to have and keep the baby. The twist is that, although she is the child of a swinging Sixties couple who have subsequently gone their separate ways, she is, until her fateful impregnatory encounter at a party, a virgin; not from principle or morality, but rather because she is a rather shy, self-contained, intelligent girl who has, in a quiet way, withstood the social pressures around her. She has one good male friend, the earnest well-informed Henry, who at one stage she proposes shall relieve her of her by now outdated virginity, but who finds himself unable to oblige when confronted by the demands of a real chum: the recurrent problem of the relationship of sex to friendship. This leads to a certain frostiness between them, though he does have the priggish decency to offer to marry her and adopt the baby. Sensibly and self-reliantly, she refuses, choosing rather to remain in London and earn her living doing other people's typing: virtue is in the end rewarded, and she lands a coveted job.

This is a pedestrian account of a pretty pedestrian plot; but the novel has an honest charm, a feeling for the potential waste of so many young people reduced to becoming waitresses, languishing on the dole, or worse. Mervyn Jones is no supporter of the present regime, but he refuses to make political capital in this novel, and indeed points out the virtues of self-reliance, a ratiocinative approach to life's problems and a refusal to go along with the crowd if it doesn't suit you. It is a kind of updated Victorian novel: trouble, teethgritting and then triumph. I just hope that whoever tries to film it doesn't fall into the trap of coy casting: there is just a hint of the Georgie-Girl or Tushingham trap here. (p. 26)

Mary Hope, "Decencies," in The Spectator, *Vol. 254, No. 8170, February 9, 1985, pp. 25-6.*

JOHN MELLORS

[*Coming Home* is] about first love and its revival in later life. Owen and Vera were at school together in Walthamstow. Still in their teens, they had a passionate affair. It was brought to an abrupt end when Owen, doing his National Service, was posted to Malaya. Vera refused to marry him before he went, saying that 'a piece of paper's no guarantee'. Owen had stayed in the Far East, in various enterprises, enjoying a string of mistresses for whom he felt affection but not love. Vera had married a sculptor.

Some 30 years later, on leave in England, Owen hears that Vera is divorced and living in North Wales. He finds her, courts her, sleeps with her, and marries her—but she is dying. She has been looking after young people in need: a cripple, a schizophrenic and her own blind son. After her death, Owen decides to stay and look after them rather than return to Sarawak. That could be the plot of a weepie, but Mervyn Jones tells his story in a plain, straightforward way that convinces by its evenness of tone and avoidance of histrionics. Young Owen had said, "'I'm in love with you, Vera. And nothing else matters." The words sounded flat, utterly inadequate. She deserved eloquence, and he had none. Truth would have to be enough.' Jones may lack eloquence, but his book, like Owen's declaration of love, has the ring of truth. (p. 26)

John Mellors, "Going Back to First Love," in The Listener, *Vol. 115, No. 2962, May 29, 1986, pp. 25-6.*

Ismail Kadare

1936-

Albanian novelist, short story writer, and poet.

Albania's most respected contemporary author, Kadare is a prolific writer whose works have been translated into more than thirty languages. His presentation of such universal topics as traditional values, tyranny, prejudice, and the futility of war is considered by many critics to have contributed to the international appeal of his books. Especially popular in France, Kadare's fiction is also noted for its surrealistic blend of Albanian history and folklore with elements of realism. Although some commentators fault Kadare for overreliance on detail, most laud his warm, lyrical prose that conveys love for his country and its people.

Kadare's anti-war chronicle *Gjenerali i ushtrisë së vdekur* (1963; *The General of the Dead Army*) was the first Albanian novel to be published in the United States. A harsh examination of the repercussions of war, this book tells of an Italian general who is sent to Albania to bring back the bodies of his countrymen killed in World War II. The general's search for his soldiers' remains reveals his need to discover his own identity. His subsequent descent into madness is caused by the absurdity of his mission and the guilt that stems from his participation in the war. A reviewer for *Publishers Weekly* called *The General of the Dead Army* "an impressive, sustained act of imagination."

Kadare further addresses the subject of war in *Kronikë në gur* (1971; *Chronicle in Stone*), a semiautobiographical account of his childhood in the town of Gjirokastër during World War II. This novel garnered critical acclaim in Europe and the United States for its frank depiction of an Albanian mountain village that is alternately occupied by the armies of Italy, Greece, and Germany. Kadare captures the senselessness of war through a young boy's candid observations of the townspeople and their captors. *Chronicle in Stone* prompted comparisons to the works of Colombian author Gabriel García Márquez for its combination of wonder, magic, and poignant social observation. Leonie Caldecott noted: "Although on one level the boy misunderstands the events that affect his life, the very lack of adult prejudice guarantees a clearsightedness that conveys the pain of his people more vividly than anything else could hope to do." *Le crépuscule des dieux de la steppe* (1981), another autobiographical work, recreates Kadare's experiences as a student at Moscow's Gorky Institute of World Literature during the 1950s. The most humorous of Kadare's novels, this book offers a broadly satirical view of Russia's totalitarian regime under Joseph Stalin.

Kadare has published several historical novels in which Albania's ancient traditions and superstitions conflict with its recent socialist regime. In *Dasma* (1968; *The Wedding*), Kadare addresses this friction in the story of a young peasant girl who is reluctantly awaiting the finalization of a traditional arranged marriage. When the girl is sent to work in a government railroad camp, she learns of equal rights based on socialist doctrines and subsequently breaks the engagement. In *Ura me tri harqe* (1978), a suspenseful tale of murder and exploitation of ignorance set in medieval Albania, a Catholic monk relates the

discovery of a man entombed in a bridge's arch. In Albanian folklore, immurement was a common practice believed to protect structures from evil forces; the man's killers hope that their crime will be interpreted as a superstitious ritual. *Prilli i thyer* (1982) takes place in the early twentieth century and focuses upon an ancient set of laws, collectively known as the Code of Lekë Dukagjini, which is designed to protect the family and secure individual justice. Gjorg, a young man who has avenged the murder of a relative, becomes the object of revenge by his victim's family, according to the Code. While fleeing from his tormentors, Gjorg befriends a honeymooning couple whose lives are vastly altered by their indirect involvement with the Code. Critics regarded *Prilli i thyer* as Kadare's most ironic work, for the laws that he chastises are tyrannical and barbaric but nonetheless provide emotional strength and courage. *Qui a ramené Doruntine?* (1986) is loosely based on the Albanian legend of a man who returns from the grave to honor an important commitment. Kadare turns this simple tale of integrity into a Gothic thriller with sudden deaths, empty coffins, possible incest, and numerous suspects. Robert Elsie stated: "Those who enjoyed Umberto Eco's *Name of the Rose* will not be disappointed by the atmosphere of medieval intrigue which Kadare offers [in *Qui a ramené Doruntine?*]."

Kadare has also published several short story and poetry collections. *Qyteti i jugut* (1964) resembles *Chronicle in Stone* in its presentation of autobiographical tales of socialist life in wartime Albania that are narrated by a child. The compassionate strength of the stories in *Invitation à un concert officiel et autres récits* (1985) prompted Bettina Knapp to comment that Kadare "writes with pith and point, with the verve of a Voltaire and the excitement of a Balzac." Kadare's volumes of verse include *Frymëzimet djaloshare* (1954), *Motive me diell* (1968), *Koha* (1976), and *Buzëqeshje mbi botë* (1980).

KIRKUS REVIEWS

[Ismail Kadare's *The General of the Dead Army* is a] very good novel, slightly too Kafkaesque in tone, about a general of an unnamed country (Italy) who is sent to Albania to recover the bones of his dead countrymen who were buried there some twenty years before during the war. The strange, rather savage customs of the still-hated (and hating) Albanians and the drudgery of a year-and-a-half of grave-digging in almost unremitting rain have their inevitable effect on the general, who goes slightly insane, culminating in his throwing the bones of the highest ranking dead officer, Colonel Z., former leader of the infamous "Blue Battalion," into a mountain stream in an attempt to rid himself of the evil spell that is surely the objective correlative of his unrecognized war guilt. This sparsely written [novel's] slightly surreal mood arises from the accumulation of detail and rather stylized conversations between the general and the rather distant priest who accompanies him. . . .

> *A review of "The General of the Dead Army," in* Kirkus Reviews, *Vol. XXXIX, No. 22, November 15, 1971, p. 1228.*

PUBLISHERS WEEKLY

[In *The General of the Dead Army,* a] general of a "great and civilized country" (which we have no trouble identifying as Italy), is sent on a mission to Albania to search for and to repatriate the remains of his country's soldiers killed in World War II. Opening grave after grave, in a land of blood and mourning, he soon finds his pride and his illusions fading in the perpetual rain, mud and snow of a country that is full of grief, hostile, at best indifferent. He drinks too much. He listens to the tales of partisans and prostitutes. Soon he cannot tell the difference between the tragic and the grotesque, the heroic and the depressing. . . . The general begins to feel that there is no way of leaving, or disengaging honorably; his mission appears to him to be blind, deaf, and absurd. He feels himself to be outside of time, frozen, petrified. He sees all the participants in this grim charade as "pitiful clowns of war." A stern reminder of the futility and tragedy of war, a remarkable exposition of guilt, *The General* is an impressive, sustained act of imagination.

> *A review of "The General of the Dead Army," in* Publishers Weekly, *Vol. 200, No. 22, November 29, 1971, p. 30.*

ARSHI PIPA

[*Le général de l'armée morte (The General of the Dead Army)*] is a bitter satire against the militarism and fascism which caused Albania so much harm in the recent past. The sarcasm yields

to contempt when the author, moving from the past to the present, considers the government's hypocritical policy of using the soldiers' bones to buttress the cause of bourgeois patriotism which serves the interests of those in power. The author is both an Albanian and a communist, his perspective resulting from the intersection of socialism and patriotism. His point of view seems to reflect the official doctrine of Albanian communism which is permeated by nationalism. The reflection is a refraction in fact, since the two elements are dissociated. Kadaré tells a lot about Albanian ethics and life, but almost nothing about Albanian communism, its leaders and institutions. Kadaré's unorthodoxy consists first and foremost in that he never mentions the Party in his novel. The main characteristic of Albanian communism, the celebration of work as the essence and purpose of life, is also ignored. The satire of Italian militarism is done at the expense of military heroism in general, for the novel is decidedly anti-heroic, emphasis being laid on the intrinsic value of life, life enjoyed for its own pleasure . . . , regardless of ideological strings—another heresy.

Willingly or not, the author is following the protest movement in the Eastern European countries which has Solzhenitsyn for its major representative. A great deal of the narrative occurs in Tirana, but one never sees a street of the city, let alone a park, the hotel to which foreigners are herded being the only living place offered to the reader's sight. The desolation of military cemeteries has a counterpart in the feeling of a secluded prison-like life. The depressing atmosphere thus created would be intolerable if the author did not dispel it by parenthetically inserting some lively episodes: the journal of an Italian soldier disguised, for fear of the Germans, as a field worker at the service of a peasant who shelters him; the story of a whore killed by the father of a young man who has fallen in love with her and therefore abandoned his fiancée, causing a scandal in the village; the wedding episode illustrating such national characteristics as hospitality and vendetta. With such devices the author manages to sustain the narrative until the end.

[*Le général de l'armée morte*] is not a "roman de stature mondiale," as Robert Escarpit describes it in his preface to the French translation, but it is the first Albanian novel which can stand the proof of criticism. It has been a controversial novel since its publication in 1963, and may continue to be so as long as Albanian writers repeatedly ape each other while obediently following the official line. With this novel, as well as with his poems which are equally good, Kadaré brings to adolescence a literature which for some twenty years has been an uninterrupted series of propagandistic works devoid of artistic value, coming from the same bag invariably marked "socialist realism." Such a literature exchanges reality for a sequence of ideological clichés, and consequently fails to capture the life of the Albanian people in its present condition. Kadaré instead is able to produce a picture of the real Albania, a country which has suffered a great deal from foreign invasions but has never lost its national pride. (pp. 162-63)

> *Arshi Pipa, in a review of "Le général de l'armée morte," in* Books Abroad, *Vol. 46, No. 1, Winter, 1972, pp. 162-63.*

JANET BYRON

Ismail Kadare is the only modern Albanian writer who is known widely outside his own country. Although he writes both poetry and prose fiction, he is known primarily for the latter. Thematically, Kadare's fiction contains strains of Albanian nationalist thinking and of twentieth-century socialist thought. But Kadare avoids the idolatry of nationalism and socialism by disavowing the notion that the deeds of the traditional "old man" or of the socialist "new man" are sufficient, *independently*, to secure the well-being of the nation. The strengths of socialism must redeem the weaknesses of national traditions; and conversely, the virtues of national thought must overcome the imperfections of socialist practice. In Kadare's works collectively, the old national symbol is hence resurrected, but Kadare endows the two heads of the eagle with fresh significance and the eagle itself with unfamiliar vitality.

Of his numerous works, three are rich in Kadarean conceptions: the novel *Gjenerali i ushtrisë së vdekur (The General of the Dead Army)*, the collection of short stories *Qyteti i jugut (The Southern City)* and the novel *Dasma (The Wedding)*. In *Gjenerali* a nameless Italian general is sent to Albania by his government in order to recover the bones of Italian soldiers who had died and were buried there during World War II. A priest, also nameless, accompanies the general on his mission. These two are in an uncomfortable relationship: they dislike each other; only necessity binds them together. Although characterization of the men is sympathetic, what they symbolize is unlovable. While the general is a symbol of militarism, he is also more than that: he stands for Western attitudes toward life and love, the indestructible matters of human existence. The priest epitomizes the religious support which is accorded Western views. In the general's precise and diligent search for the bones of dead men, and in the sad consequences of this search for himself—anxiety, insomnia, nightmares and alcoholism—Kadare wants us to discover a terrifying aspect of Western ways, namely, that these ways serve the forces of death, not life.

The life-promoting forces are found in Albanian character and in socialist action. As the general and his partner move from one locality to the next in their search for bones, they encounter Albanians of different ranks. . . . Albanians are portrayed as vigorous, self-controlled, altruistic and proud in contrast to Westerners, who are debilitated, sexually lawless, selfish and greedy. Whatever vice exists among Albanians is imported.

Despite so much national commendation, however, *Gjenerali* is not a piece of nationalistic propaganda promoting the tired but attractive notion that the West is corrupt while Albania is pure. Kadare weakens the allure of this notion by showing that while vice is unevenly distributed, suffering is not. The wartime intruders and their descendants do not suffer any more on account of their corruption, nor do the Albanians suffer any less because of their virtue. (p. 614)

[Regardless], Western ways remain inherently punitive, for they spell the destruction of moral character, while Albanian ways remain life-promoting, because they sustain moral character. . . . This idealistic picture of Albanian character starts to fade, however, in *Qyteti i jugut* and in *Dasma*. In these later works the foreign intruder is not so conspicuous; and in taking a more relaxed view of the character of Albanian society, Kadare uncovers indigenous, not imported, evils against which he warns his countrymen.

Katrina, the heroine of *Dasma*, is a peasant girl from the mountains. In accordance with the custom of arranged marriages, she was engaged at a young age and was expected from that time on to begin learning the skills which would prepare her to be a wife. However, the hopes of her father are disappointed

several years later when the authorities send Katrina, along with other students, to southern Albania in order to work at a railroad camp. (The location is significant, for southern Albania has been regarded as more cultivated than the mountainous north, within whose formidable fastnesses the mountaineers have been able to preserve ancient customs. Not surprisingly, the Albanian Communist movement began in the south.) The trip to the south is Katrina's first encounter with the world outside her village. . . .

In her new surroundings Katrina becomes acquainted with what she calls "paja e partisë" (the dowry of the Party), which does not involve clothes and linen, but freedom and knowledge for women. She begins to despise her background and to pity her father for his submission to a social system which relies for its survival upon conformity, violence and the oppression of women. Katrina breaks her engagement, and not long thereafter she falls in love with a young worker named Xheviti, who wishes to marry her. She consents; and through this independent course of action, she not only severs herself from her family, but also compromises her family's integrity: for since the traditional marriage is really a marriage of families, the moral failure of one individual affects many others. . . .

The wedding (*dasma*) of Katrina and Xheviti, a wedding which they have arranged themselves, is the central event of the novel. . . . The guests represent, in short, every stratum of Albanian culture. Through a series of subplots Kadare explores the character of relationships between the sexes in Albania. The novel is a condemnation of traditional marriage, its patriarchal basis and its indifference to the happiness of the young. It also attacks the matchmaking negotiations, which barter lives as though people were on a level no higher than that of sheep, donkeys and goats. Finally, the novel denounces the violence which is often used to avenge a serious breach of trust.

In Katrina's and Xheviti's case, trust has been breached, for the girl's parents had promised her to another. The tension pervading the novel arises from the unarticulated understanding of everyone that sooner or later a broken promise will be avenged. But the newlyweds are not afraid; they know that their personal rights are protected by the Party. The shades of tragedy which have clouded the marriage festivities materialize when the father and the matchmaker unexpectedly appear. In the dark woods near the wedding hall, they attack each other, then mysteriously disappear, "si dy përbindësha të plagosur" (like two wounded monsters), leaving drops of blood on the ground as evidence of their savage encounter. But the wedding joy is undiminished, and when the long celebration ends at daybreak, the sun rises on yet another couple to be married with their own consent in socialist Albania.

The message is clear: the old customs are vicious and will crumble under the weight of their own contradictions, without in the least hindering the establishment of more humane relationships between men and women. (p. 615)

Dasma's picture of the suppression of women is the antithesis of *Gjenerali*'s celebration of the purity and stability of male-female relationships. And the violent tendencies of Albanian men, deplored in *Dasma*, are either lauded in *Gjenerali* as examples of Albanian masculine pride, or else excused as excrescences alien to the true character of Albanians. The traditional Albanians in *Gjenerali* are portrayed as noble, while many of those in *Dasma* are pictured as ignoble. It is as though Kadare were describing two different peoples. But he is not. They are the same; it is the basis of evaluation which differs in the two novels. For in *Gjenerali* Albanians measure up well when they are compared against the militaristic and debilitated West, but these same Albanians are found wanting when their customs are evaluated against professed socialist ideals.

The test of an honest observer lies in his willingness to subject even his ideals to scrutiny. Kadare passes the test in *Qyteti i jugut*. *Qyteti* is a collection of short stories, many of which are set in or around the "southern city." This would be Gjirokastër, Kadare's birthplace, in southern Albania. Many of the stories are autobiographical and recount impressions (sometimes through the eyes of a small boy) of wartime and socialist Albania.

Love and marriage reappear in *Qyteti*. "Në kafe" ("In the Café") is the account of two fathers conducting matchmaking negotiations. Because these have become illegal, the fathers must negotiate stealthily. They have met in the café in order to settle the issue of the bride price. The bride-to-be is the same Katrina who appears in *Dasma*. Kadare exposes the materialistic thinking which often governs arranged marriages.... The negotiations are abruptly halted by Party officials who had been secretly observing them.

In contrast to this picture of Party diligence, **"Sezoni dimëror i Kafe Rivierës" ("Winter Season at the Café Riviera")** depicts a leadership which is apathetic in the face of arranged marriages. In this story a young idealistic waiter loses his job for speaking out against the participation of Party members and enthusiasts in arranged marriages. The criticism is open and unambiguous, but it is not a criticism of socialism. On the contrary, Kadare's point is that the leadership is not living up to the socialist ideal of freedom for women.

But *Dasma*'s notion that relationships in the new society are invariably better than those in the old is shattered in **"Historia,"** which relates a brief romantic encounter between two students. The girl is appealing, but her immodesty, frivolity and shallow urbanity distress the moral young man who is attracted to her. Through rediscovering the beauty inherent in his country's struggle to shape its history, and most of all through realizing that he is necessary to that struggle, the young man is delivered from bewilderment and from shallow attachment. **"Historia"** is therefore also a lesson on the obligation of the new man to maintain zealous commitment to socialist freedom. (pp. 615-16)

Besides narratives of socialist life, *Qyteti* also includes stories which explore several aspects of Albanian national character. Especially in the narratives which are set during World War II, we are shown a brave and proud people trying to survive against formidable odds. But these narratives also indicate that while courage and pride are adequate to form a strong nationality, they are insufficient to construct a strong *nation*. For this latter purpose Albanians must overcome ignorance, backwardness and superstitious trusts.

Kadare's major works reveal a remarkable writer who is appreciative of both his countrymen and his nation. Yet he is spared the temptation of self-congratulatory nationalism by Albanian history, which provides too many tragic warnings of the impotence of national virtue unsupported by progressive thinking. At the same time, although the author is committed to socialism, his awareness of its failures and of its ambiguous successes restrains the thoughtless exuberance that too frequently attends ideological allegiance. (p. 616)

Janet Byron, "Albanian Nationalism and Socialism in the Fiction of Ismail Kadare," in World Literature Today, *Vol. 53, No. 4, Autumn, 1979, pp. 614-16.*

EDOUARD RODITI

[Ismail Kadare's *Le Crépuscule des dieux de la steppe* (*The Twilight of the Gods of the Steppe*)], however surrealist it may appear in some of its satirical fantasies and in much of its brilliant imagery, is nevertheless an autobiographical novel that follows very faithfully the official Albanian Marxist-Leninist party line in describing with unabashed critical vigor the author's personal impressions of his life as a foreign student at Moscow's Gorky Institute. Kadaré's descriptions, for instance, of the absurdly virulent press and radio campaign to discredit Pasternak after the latter had been awarded the Nobel Prize in 1958 are extremely humorous and might well remind English or American readers of George Orwell's satires on totalitarian propagandistic ballyhoo. (pp. 149-50)

Kadaré's accounts of the drunkenness, corruption, opportunistic treachery and frustrations of Soviet "intellectual" life are truly devastating. His only "decent" fictional character is a Greek communist refugee with whom the autobiographical hero sympathizes in occasional sessions of mutual nostalgia for their distant Balkan homelands. An interesting theme that occasionally appears as a kind of undercurrent throughout the novel concerns the great pressures that appear to be exerted on the institute's many ethnic-minority students to abandon their native languages or dialects and to express themselves as writers in Russian. (p. 150)

Edouard Roditi, in a review of "Le crépuscule des dieux de la steppe," in World Literature Today, *Vol. 57, No. 1, Winter, 1983, pp. 149-50.*

JANET BYRON

The early eighties have been years of ideological and political disturbance among Albanians in Albania and among their compatriots across the border in the Albanian-speaking autonomous province of Kosova, in Yugoslavia. In 1981 Mehmet Shehu, second in command to Albania's Enver Hoxha, died—whether by suicide or homicide was disputed at the time. And across the border in Kosova, the Albanian minority rioted in Prishtina, capital of the province, over political, economic and social injustices.

The literary field did not escape agitation. At the 1982 assembly of the League of Albanian Writers and Artists..., Dritëro Agolli, president of the organization, accused Albania's leading writer, Ismail Kadare, of lately having written folkloristic and historical novels whose themes and esthetic character lent themselves to ambiguous ideological interpretation. This criticism of modern Albania's most gifted writer has ruffled the grace that Kadare had long enjoyed under the Albanian regime. But any criticisms he might endure will probably only enhance his already considerable popularity in the West, particularly in France. Two recent French translations of his novels are certain to promote this outcome.

Le pont aux trois arches, a translation of *Ura me tri harqe,* is set in feudal Albania in the late fourteenth century, on the eve of the Turkish conquest of the country. The narrative, recounted through the mouth of Gjon, a Catholic monk, concerns construction of a bridge over a river in southern Albania. The builders (a mysterious foreign enterprise) have resorted to shrewd techniques in order to secure legal rights to construction, and while the bridge is being built, a man is discovered immured at the foot of one of the arches.

Immurement is a common theme in Balkan—including Albanian—folklore. In many tales bearing the immurement motif, human sacrifice is connected with the construction of edifices: folk belief embodied in the tales holds that the spirit of the immolated victim will secure and protect the structure. . . . In *Le pont* a simple mason, one Murrash Zenebishe, was immolated in secret. Through a series of suspicions and anguished hypotheses, the monk arrives at the conclusion that Zenebishe had probably, for ulterior motives, entered into agreement with a rival enterprise to sabotage the building of the bridge. Getting caught in the act, he was killed by the original builders, who then immured him. They were confident that the crime would be interpreted as a ritualistic murder instigated by a superstitious people, who wished the bridge to be protected. The plot is complex and suspenseful. . . .

Through interweaving Albanian history and mythology, Kadare has constructed an allegory of the depredation of Albania by the sophisticated rival interests of Eastern and Western powers. He shows that with all the differences between the two camps, they shrewdly discerned on Albanian soil cultural vulnerabilities (superstition, poverty, credulousness, et cetera) that they could exploit in order to despoil a simple people. (p. 40)

At first glance, the content of the novel appears to be ideologically safe: Albanian historians have of one accord denounced the centuries-long exploitation of Albania by alien powers. But upon closer inspection, the reader becomes aware that Kadare is taking some ideological risks. First of all, the narrator is a problem. Although the clergy constituted a real, socially accepted class in feudal Albania (Kadare's narrative is therefore historically plausible), in Communist Albania, which prides itself on being the only avowed atheist state in the world, it is unfashionable to respect the religious mentality, especially in retrospect, inasmuch as that mind, with its associated superstitions, is perceived as belonging to the unliberated era of Albania's past. In recounting the events of *Le pont* from the vantage point of a good-hearted though credulous monk, Kadare seems to intimate that a certain *kind* of religion can be the compassionate ally rather than the brutal despoiler of the people. (pp. 40-1)

What is more, Kadare has implicated not only the aristocracy (symbolized by the lord in whose service Gjon is employed) and clergy, but also the common people in the ancient victimization of the nation; for through Gjon's evaluation of events, the novel clearly indicates that the ordinary people (who, incidentally, are depicted as devoid of heroic qualities) were blind to the insidiousness of exploitation. This viewpoint is also different from the official one, which, on the contrary, erects an unscalable wall between the historical victims and victimizers of the Albanian people.

Kadare moves closer to our own time in the second novel under review, *Avril brisé,* a translation of *Prilli i thyer.* This too is a historical novel, but its events unfold at the beginning of the present century in the north Albanian mountains. Before centralized government became established in Albania, northern Albania was a tribally structured area that governed itself by an ancient set of rules known collectively as the *Kanuni i Lekë Dukagjinit* (the Code of Lekë Dukagjini), as well as other traditional practices, many of which antedated Christianization of the country. These rules were designed to protect the soli-

darity of clan and family. . . . *Avril Brisé* tells of the indoctrination of Gjorg, a sensitive northern man of twenty-six, into the rules of the blood feud: according to custom, Gjorg avenges the murder of a blood relative by murdering, in his turn, the original killer. Thenceforth he becomes a hunted man. In escaping the vengeance of the victim's kin, Gjorg crosses paths with an urbane young Albanian couple, Diane and Bessian (a writer), who have been invited to spend their honeymoon in the northern highlands. The novel details the disturbance that this extraordinary encounter between urbanites and mountaineers wreaks on the seemingly harmonious relationship between wife and husband. . . .

The dominant angle from which the reader views events of the novel is the vantage point of Bessian and Diane. Bessian, who is *not* a northerner, had studied mountain customs as a researcher and was fond of descanting upon them to his young, convent-educated wife. Bessian's perception of the customs—and particularly the blood feud—is romantic: he finds transcendental value in it. . . . He perceives and appreciates as well the sturdiness that life under the austere regulations of the *Kanun* exacted from men. Even Gjorg the hunted is momentarily overcome with pride at having become an avenger; for although his lack of experience initially made him reluctant to destroy life, once the deed was accomplished, he perceived himself—despite his fears—as having entered a privileged community of feuders who were superior to people untouched by the feud. . . . (p. 41)

When Diane saw these men juxtaposed in the rugged environment of the north, she was assailed by unacceptable sentiments. Although she abhorred the feud, she nevertheless seemed to view the men of the mountains with compassion and even mild respect: even though it was true that blood and courage were needlessly sacrificed to the vendetta, nevertheless, in satisfying the demands of vengeance, mountain men continually placed their stability, peace and life in jeopardy. During the honeymoon, Diane grew distant from her husband; one suspects that in the mountains she saw him as he might really have been: a poseur, a man whose manliness was lived out on the gentle lowland of words, and in absolute safety; a man to whom the worst that could apparently happen was a bad review of one of his articles.

All this in itself would have been sufficient for a novel, but Kadare also interweaves another theme into *Avril brisé.* He depicts the mountain customs as deific, tyrannical: as the narrative proceeds, it becomes clear that one cannot dwell in the highlands for long without becoming subservient to them, without having the intellectual and spiritual capacities subverted by their traditional demands. It is here that the reader encounters another of Kadare's ironies, for it now becomes possible to view Diane's loss of respect for Bessian not as an injury she inflicted upon him, but as an injury the mountains inflicted upon the two of them.

Superficially, the themes of *Avril brisé* appear to be in keeping with the political imperative for writers to scrutinize traditional folkways, so that the destructive feudal and patriarchal ones can be the more effectively combatted through socialist and communist enlightenment. But the novel is ideologically unnerving in that amidst all its ironies, it depicts these folkways as providing at least some psychological strength and integrity which appear not to be provided by the customs and assumptions of an urbanized, excessively intellectualized existence. The setting of the narrative in a remote, presocialist period only thinly conceals the fact that the themes of the work—or at the very least, the *implications* of these themes—do not nourish socialist optimism. (pp. 41-2)

Janet Byron, "Albanian Folklore and History in the Fiction of Ismail Kadare: A Review of Two French Translations," in World Literature Today, *Vol. 58, No. 1, Winter, 1984, pp. 40-2.*

BETTINA L. KNAPP

Because few Americans have read the works of Ismail Kadare, they have been deprived of hours of delightful tale telling. Although his works are plentiful—e.g., *Le général de l'armé morte, Les tambours de la pluie, Chronique de la ville de pierre,* and many more—his name unfortunately has remained in the background. Still, Kadare . . . writes with pith and point, with the verve of a Voltaire and the excitement of a Balzac.

In [*Invitation à un concert officiel et autres récits*], a series of short stories, readers are kept enthralled by the manner in which he fuses pathos and humor, naïveté and satire. In such stories as **"La caravane des férédjés,"** for example, the hero is a traveling salesman who takes 500,000 veils destined to cover the faces of the women in countries conquered by the Ottomans. His shock and admiration at the sight of the spectacularly beautiful faces of the young girls he sees during his travels is both mirth-provoking and sad. Only by reading this story and others, such as **"La commission des fêtes"** and **"Le crime de Suzana,"** can one hope to understand the meaning of tyranny, bigotry, and religious and political fanaticism, all interwoven in mirthful, fascinating, and beguiling fabulations.

Bettina L. Knapp, in a review of "Invitation à un concert officiel et autres récits," in World Literature Today, *Vol. 60, No. 1, Winter, 1986, p. 158.*

ROBERT ELSIE

Once again Ismail Kadare plunges into Albania's legendary past, legendary in the purest sense. The story of Constantine and his sister Doruntine, alternatively known as Garentine, is one of the best-known in Albanian folklore—simple, yet, as we see, with many possibilities.

An old woman had nine sons and one daughter. Eight of the sons had already died by the time the daughter was to marry a distant suitor. Because the aging mother was apprehensive about giving her consent to the marriage and thereby losing her daughter too, perhaps forever, the only surviving son, young Constantine, made a solemn pledge (*besa* in Albanian) to his mother to bring back his sister whenever the mother should express the desire to see her. Time passed, but of the surviving members of the bereft lineage, it was Constantine who died first. The old woman, now alone, regretted her decision, longed for her daughter, and cursed the dead Constantine for having broken his *besa*. Thereupon, Constantine, faithful beyond the grave to his pledge, rose from the tomb, mounted his horse, and set off in the night to find his sister, whom he returned to the arms of their dying mother.

Such is the Balkan legend which Kadare has skillfully transformed into the period thriller [*Qui a ramené Doruntine? (Who Brought Doruntine Back?)*]. The action revolves around Captain Stres, a minor official in medieval Albania who is re-

sponsible for sorting out the facts of the case and preparing a report: the daughter's unexpected arrival from distant Bohemia on a misty October night, the sudden death of mother and daughter, persistent rumors of an incestuous relationship—a desire so strong as to overcome death itself—the gravestone ajar, devious attempts to hush up the growing scandal and preserve the interests of Church and state, and finally, a suspect. But who did bring Doruntine back? Those who enjoyed Umberto Eco's *Name of the Rose* will not be disappointed by the atmosphere of medieval intrigue which Kadare offers.

Robert Elsie, in a review of "Qui a ramené Doruntine?," in World Literature Today, *Vol. 61, No. 2, Spring, 1987, p. 331.*

SAVKAR ALTINEL

With the second of his books to appear in English published only months after the reissuing in paperback of his best-known work, *The General of the Dead Army,* . . . the Albanian novelist Ismail Kadare must now be deemed to have accomplished the doubly difficult feat of breaking through all the barriers against exporting culture from his native land (though for political reasons the translator of *Chronicle in Stone* is not identified) and gaining acceptance in the only marginally less impenetrable literary world of Great Britain.

Chronicle in Stone is a somewhat slighter creation than its predecessor. It is set during the Second World War in an unnamed Albanian mountain town of grey stone buildings which is referred to as a "city", but is small enough for a ten-day visit to Tirana by one of its inhabitants to make the local paper, and is so steeply banked that the top of one house often grazes the foundations of another, and drunks who fall down in the street roll on to roofs. The changing fortunes of this settlement, which passes back and forth between the Italians and the Greeks before finally being occupied by the Germans, and is also home throughout this period to a communist resistance movement, are narrated by a small boy who records, as well as the ravages of the war and his own growing pains, juicy scandals involving hermaphroditism, impotence, murder and black magic, and the doings of an inventor who is determined to develop an engineless aircraft powered by perpetual motion.

The blurb suggests that Kadare is "a genius of modern literature" to be mentioned in the same breath as Gabriel García Márquez and Günter Grass. In fact, there is little modernity in evidence here. The passages set in italics or beginning and ending in mid-sentence do not add much to the strictly chronological and fully accessible narrative. . . . [*Chronicle in Stone*] manages to pack a great deal of warmth and lyricism into its child's-eye view of the upheavals of Balkan life without being especially adventurous or innovative.

Savkar Altinel, "More Growing Pains," in The Times Literary Supplement, *No. 4396, July 3, 1987, p. 715.*

LEONIE CALDECOTT

At the heart of *Chronicle in Stone* is a scene in which the narrator, a young Albanian boy whose hometown is caught up in the vicissitudes of World War II, is taken by his grandmother to visit the house of a local inventor, the town's resident genius. He is said to be designing a plane powered by the principle of perpetual motion. As the inhabitants of the town have recently begun to suffer aerial bombing, the miraculous invention holds out a promise, not only of practical defense but also of honor to a people humiliated by the war machine that has been deployed against them.

All too soon, however, the boy perceives that the inventor's fragile, elegant model represents a hopeless pipe dream. This perception is based partly on realism, and partly on fantasy, which, informed by the harsh times, demands that anything powerful and effective have a suitably menacing appearance, like the Italian bombers on the newly hewn airfield below the old stone city. This encounter, in which faith in the traditional philosopher-sage is exchanged for the metallic certitude of modern technology, encapsulates all the sadness of this compelling novel. . . .

Speaking through the consciousness of a child just short of adolescence enables Mr. Kadare to blur the line between fact and fantasy without for a moment sacrificing the essential realism of the novel. The animistic manner in which the boy perceives his environment—for example, he views water as both friend and foe of the old stone city, where "it was not easy to be a child"—is essentially a poet's way of conveying the truth about his situation. Mr. Kadare's stylistic tour de force here has been well served by a skilled, though anonymous, translation from the Albanian. Although on one level the boy misunderstands the events that affect his life, the very lack of adult prejudice guarantees a clear-sightedness that conveys the pain of his people more vividly than anything else could hope to do. At the beginning of the novel, he and his best friend flee in disgust from the sight of animals being slaughtered. By the end, the bloodletting has overwhelmed the city to such an extent that hangings, shootings and throat-cuttings of friends, relatives and neighbors are described with the steady gaze of accepted inevitability. As in the scene at the inventor's house, the children's mood has passed from joy, through sadness, to indifference.

Thus Mr. Kadare has succeeded in creating a tale that breaches the boundaries of Albania's specific tragedy. The coming-of-age of his nameless narrator stands for a whole generation's initiation into the numbing effects of violence. . . .

Ismail Kadare's work—which includes poetry and eight other novels—has yet to gain the attention in the United States that it enjoys in Europe. His fiction has been compared with that of Gabriel García Márquez. Certainly he induces the same ironic double take in his readers, by means of the child's magical view of life that is larger than most adults realize. The triumph of **Chronicle in Stone**—only the second of his novels to be published here—is that it does not need to depart from the esthetically satisfying unities of time, space and action in order to achieve this beguiling conjunction of realism and fantasy.

> Leonie Caldecott, "Shrugging Off the Invaders," in The New York Times Book Review, *January 24, 1988, p. 18.*

KEN KALFUS

Despite its political and geographic isolation and its lack of foreign trade, Albania proudly offers the world market at least one product of distinctive Albanian origin. Tucked away at the bottom of its balance sheet, among the miscellaneous entries in favor of its meager hard-currency earnings, lies the nation's most remarkable export: the novels of Ismail Kadare. . . .

The 51-year-old Kadare inherited an oral literary tradition concerned with blood feuds and the supernatural. He plies these themes in a variety of settings, drawing his inspiration from recent history as well as legend. *The Three-Arched Bridge* and *Who Brought Back Doruntine?* take place in a medieval Albania, where curses are potent magic, avengers return from the dead, and all pledge allegience to the Albanian code of honor, the *Kanun,* and of vengeance, the *Besa.* In *The Twilight of the Steppe Gods* and *The Great Winter,* Kadare writes the story of his country's bitter falling-out with the Soviet Union in 1960.

First published in the Albanian capital, Tirana, in 1971, *Chronicle in Stone* adds to the international childhood-in-wartime genre. It is set in Gjirokastra, a southern city near the Greek border, the birthplace of both the founder of theAlbanian Communist state, Enver Hoxha, and the author. . . .

Precocious and peculiar observations illuminate the novel, narrated by an unnamed young boy presumably based on Kadare himself. . . . Because of the resemblance that Turkish script bears to ant trails, he believes his grandfather should be able to read both, and is disappointed to learn that he can't. The boy enjoys his myopia, disdaining an older friend's eyeglasses:

> I was used to looking at the world through a puff of steam, so that the edges of things ran together and separated freely, not according to any fixed rules. . . . But through the round glass the world looked rigid and greedy, full of rules, showing no more than what there was. It was like a house where everything— oil, flour, even water—was measured to the last drop.

Mussolini had taken Albania in 1939, ousting King Zog and establishing a puppet government in Tirana. Southern Albania became a battleground in Italy's war against Greece, which sporadically held Albanian territory. The boy's "puff of steam" romanticism shields him in part from the ugliness of the conflict, as one army after another occupies, flees, and reoccupies the city. . . . When he is told his family must take refuge in Tirana's ancient stone citadel, it is "one of the happiest evenings of my life. . . . Everything would be marvelous there, terrifying and extraordinary."

But this sentiment hardly flows from native optimism. Rather, Kadare's Albania is an enchanted nation imagined from centuries of legend, a land where "crones" and slightly younger *katenxhikas* are said to live well into their hundreds, a land where the marvelous and the terrifying are easily appositive. Even the names of its women cast a spell; Xhexho, Mane Voco, Selfixhe, Kako Pino. . . .

War provides a host of auguries. An anti-aircraft gun kills a British pilot, whose severed arm is paraded through the streets and placed in the city museum, from which it is eventually stolen. Xhexho warns, "Heaven dropped that Englishman's arm down on us, and now you'll see, German hair and Chinese beards will rain down on us next, and then nails of Jews and Arabs' noses." Mother Hanko, who is 132 years old, announces, "The world is changing blood. . . . A person changes blood every four or five years, and the world every four or five hundred years. These are the winters of blood."

Given Albania's reputation as a doctrinaire Stalinist state, the reader might expect to find in this novel the heavy-handed expression of Communist verities. But Kadare has an easy touch, occasionally evincing nostalgia for precommunist Albania. He's neither condescending nor hostile to his people's superstitions and political naïveté. Although Enver Hoxha, who ruled from 1944 until his death in 1985, towers over his country's history, the book's few references to him are modest. Told that Hoxha is leading a class war, Selfixhe remarks, "That's hard to believe. He was such a well-behaved boy." . . .

[The Albanian government] is clearly satisfied with Kadare: he gets permission to travel to foreign countries, where he's beset by reporters as curious about his politics as they are about his literary sensibility. His French interviewers dance around the difficult questions, hoping to find in his work metaphorical criticism of the current regime. Kadare dismisses the "sometimes sinister speculation of vulgar propaganda," chiding, "It is not serious for a writer to write one thing while meaning something else. . . . You must have the courage to write that something else." . . .

In an interview with *Le Monde* in 1986, Kadare reported that he had just finished a long short story touching on the current Albanian-Serbian strife in the Kosovo region of Yugoslavia, inhabited by some 1.5 million ethnic Albanians. **"The Frozen Wedding Party,"** based on legend, tells how the plans for a marriage between an Albanian boy and a Serbian girl miscarry when their people's hatred turns the groom's wedding caravan into stone. Kadare calls for an end to this millennial feud, but in the interview he adds a partisan shot that takes a typically Balkan long view of things: "It is true that the Slavs have been there [in Kòsovo] since the seventh century. But who was there before that? The Illyrians. Us."

In *Chronicle in Stone,* Albanian nationalism, like Kadare's ideology, remains muted, free of high-flown language. The old artilleryman, Avdo Babaramo, is a patriot, of course, but only after some rather prosaic reasoning:

> In Smyrna one time, a dervish asked me, 'which do you love more, your family or Albania?' Albania, of course, I told him. A family you can make overnight. You walk out of a coffee-house, run into a woman on the corner, take her to a hotel, and boom—wife and children. But you can't make Albania overnight after a quick drink in a coffee-house, can you? No, not in one night, and not in a thousand and one nights, either.

> *Ken Kalfus, "The Witches of Gjirokastra: Ismail Kadare's Albanian Chronicles," in VLS, No. 62, February, 1988, p. 17.*

JOHN UPDIKE

Albanians are known for their ferocity, isolation, and ultra-Communism, and not for their modern literature; yet Ismail Kadare . . . has a considerable European reputation, [and his] . . . *Chronicle in Stone* is no mere curiosity but a thoroughly enchanting novel—sophisticated and accomplished in its poetic prose and narrative deftness, yet drawing resonance from its roots in one of Europe's most primitive societies. Kadare has been likened to Gabriel García Márquez, and both writers tell of towns still shimmering with magic and dominated by clannishness; Kadare's nameless mountain city, no doubt based upon his own native Gjirokastër, seems less whimsical than García Márquez's Macondo, less willfully twisted into surreality. . . .

Though the narrative takes place during the Second World War, the city harbors timeless customs; brides' faces are decorated with "star-like dots, cypress branches, and signs of the zodiac, all floating in the white mystery of powder," and outbreaks of magic cause people to lock up their hair clippings and fireplace ashes. The erection of a statue in the town square had seemed to the natives an alarming novelty:

> A metal man? Was such a creation really necessary? Might it not cause trouble? At night, when everyone was sleeping as God had ordained, the statue would be out there standing erect. Day and night, summer and winter, it would stand. . . . To avoid trouble there was no unveiling ceremony. People stood and stared in wonder at the bronze warrior, hand on his pistol, who gazed severely down into the square as if asking, 'Why didn't you want me?' That night someone threw a blanket over the bronze man's shoulders. From then on, the city's heart went out to its statue. . . .

The prevalent animism is doubly intense in the sensibility of the unnamed child at the center of the novel. He anthropomorphizes the raindrops talking in the gutter, and the cistern beneath the house which they flow into: "I liked the cistern a lot and often leaned over its rim and had long talks with it. It had always been ready to answer me in its deep, cavernous voice." . . .

The voice of innocence and gusts of gossip relay the tale, though the chapters are interlarded with fragments of newspaper, proclamation, and historical chronicle. The Italians occupy the city, bringing with them nuns, a brothel, and an airfield; the British bomb the city; the Greeks momentarily occupy it; the Italians return and retreat again; Albanian partisans of various political stripes descend from the hills; and, finally, the Germans occupy the city. Most of its inhabitants flee ahead of the yellow-haired invader, and then slowly return: "Again the tender flesh of life was filling the carapace of stone." With the German occupation, the chronicle ends, as if its marvellous tone of childish fable could no longer be supported by memory. An adult voice tells us at the end,

> A very long time later I came back to the grey immortal city. My feet timidly trod the spine of its stone-paved streets. . . . Often, striding along wide lighted boulevards in foreign cities, I sometimes stumble in places where no one ever trips. Passersby turn in surprise, but I always know it's you. Rising up suddenly out of the asphalt and then sinking back in, deep down.

One would like to know where these foreign boulevards were, and how Ismail Kadare was able to produce, under the notoriously repressive and xenophobic Hoxha regime, an art so refined and so free in its feeling. Hoxha is referred to in a late chapter, as a hunted resistance leader and former, once "well-behaved" resident of the city, but without any flattery or obsequious emphasis. The waves of competing authority that move through the city are seen, like spells of weather, in terms of their local effects purely, and the Communist characters participate in the internecine brutality without rising above it. The bits of prose between the first-person chapters reduce history to a non-progressive flutter of old feuds and fresh slogans. The most ominous event is the execution, by the German occupiers, of old Kako Pino, the painter of brides' faces, who is seized by a patrol on her way to one of the weddings that have absurdly, miraculously persisted through all the bombings and invasions. Her picturesque magic is perfunctorily and, one feels, irretrievably erased from the world. (p. 112)

[Kadare's] stone city emerges as a persuasive analogue for anyone's childhood—friendly even in its mysteries, precious even in its recollected hardships and barbarities. Nostalgic reminiscence, of course, is one of the safer havens for a creative writer under a totalitarian regime. . . . Ismail Kadare, the jacket flap tells us, after first finding fame as a poet, "has mined medieval and modern historical events, legend and reality" in the writing of nine novels. It will be ineresting to see, as these novels are translated into English, if they maintain the superb balance and unforced amplitude of this one or slip, under the pressures of a watchful regime, into false naïveté and prudent stylizations. (pp. 112-13)

> *John Updike, "Chronicles and Processions," in* The New Yorker, *Vol. LXIV, No. 4, March 14, 1988, pp. 112-15.*

George Washington Lee

1894-1976

American novelist, short story writer, essayist, and editor.

A successful businessman and politician in Memphis, Tennessee, during his lifetime, Lee also wrote literature as a means of reaffirming racial pride and promoting the prosperity of black-owned businesses in the decade following the Depression. His novels and short stories also elicited attention among white readers for their realistic portrayals of Southern black milieus. While Lee's unadorned prose style and tendency to enumerate facts and figures to support his themes caused several critics to comment upon the overly didactic nature of his works, his descriptive powers and attention to detail were acknowledged as significant literary contributions.

Lee's first novel, *Beale Street: Where the Blues Began* (1934), is an informal cultural history of the Memphis avenue that profoundly influenced the lives of innumerable black Tennesseans. Lee relates the financial, artistic, and moral successes and failures of Beale Street through detailed vignettes of its residents. Although some critics maintained that Lee was openly biased toward financial accomplishments, his animated descriptions of life on Beale Street prompted Percy Hutchison to comment: "Mr. Lee's tremendously living picture, barbaric in its colors, raucous just as often as it is melodious, was the book's raison d'être and the alluring thing about it." Lee's next novel, *River George* (1937), was written to vindicate himself among black intellectuals and writers who had attributed the success of *Beale Street* to the prominence and notoriety of its subject rather than the book's literary qualities. *River George* exposes the injustices of Southern tenant farming through the adventures of the title character, a college-educated young black man first introduced in *Beale Street* who attempts to organize sharecropping families to fight for better wages and equitable treatment. Accused of a murder he did not commit, George flees his hometown, first seeking refuge with a Beale Street prostitute, and later joining the Army. Upon his return home, George is captured and lynched by an angry mob. While some critics praised Lee's authentic rendering of the tenant farming system, others echoed the reviewer for the *Brooklyn Eagle* who stated: "[There] are not enough facts to make *River George* good propaganda, and there is not enough artistry to make *River George* a good novel."

With his political career thriving during the late 1930s and early 1940s, Lee became less involved with movements of social protest and black pride, and critics contended that the pieces in his next volume, *Beale Street Sundown* (1942), were less didactic than his earlier works. Comprising nine stories previously published in the *Negro Digest*, the *World's Digest*, and the *Southern Literary Messenger*, *Beale Street Sundown* includes accounts of a former prostitute who captivates a minister, a congregation that professes hate instead of love, and a young vocalist torn between careers as a classical singer and a blues stylist. While little national attention was given to *Beale Street Sundown*, a reviewer for the *Memphis Press-Scimitar* commented: "The Boswell of Beale Street has spun the best book of his literary career." Lee also wrote a number of political and fraternal essays, many of which were published in black periodicals and newspapers during the 1950s and 1960s.

(See also *Contemporary Authors*, Vol. 125 and *Dictionary of Literary Biography*, Vol. 51.)

PERCY HUTCHISON

For many reasons such a book as [*Beale Street: Where the Blues Began*] is neither easy to describe nor to evaluate; the crosscurrents are so many that a reviewer feels as if he had launched into a more than ordinarily choppy sea. To begin with: How is he to begin? Of course, he might start grandiloquently by saying that New York has its Fifth Avenue, Paris its Rue de la Paix, but Memphis has its Beale Street; and all he would have accomplished would be to have got off on the wrong foot.

Again, if he likened Beale Street to Lenox Avenue, the boulevard both of trade and of fashion of New York's Harlem black belt, he would have done no better. Perhaps if he were to imagine Fifth Avenue as skirting the Wailing Wall of Jerusalem he would come nearer, for if Beale Street is, or has been, the dusky thoroughfare of fashion and of trade, it also has been the road of tribulation of a race. And it is such a dramatic contrast which this book by George W. Lee, himself a Memphis Negro—a book often well written, but in part ineptly written—brings out forcibly. Let it be said, however, that the good in the volume so far outweighs the bad as very much to reduce the intrusion of the latter. . . .

The reviewer believes it possible that, purely as a commercial proposition, Mr. Lee's book might have been difficult to place had he not tied it up with the history of the beginnings of syncopation, thereby making possible its subtitle of *Where the Blues Began*. But for this reviewer the chapters devoted to this bit of musical history proved the least interesting. For him, Mr. Lee's tremendously living picture, barbaric in its colors, raucous just as often as it is melodious, was the book's raison d'être and the alluring thing about it. Comedy and tragedy walk hand in hand down George Lee's *Beale Street*; high yellows, light chocolates and coal blacks work, parade the avenue, crowd the dance halls; river roustabouts, where Beale Street meets the Mississippi, heave their bales and roar their songs. And the author has caught something of the rhythm of the Mississippi. "Old Man River" seems to be intoning in his lines. . . .

W. C. Handy, who, incidentally, has written a foreword for the book, is accredited with being the originator of [the Blues] the fundamental of which is, unquestionably, nothing above simple wailing. . . .

It was the political situation of 1909 which put Handy and his new type of music on the map. Three men were running for Mayor of Memphis, of whom one was E. H. Crump. Handy, who had a band and was hired to play for Crump, composed a piece based on the "backward, over-and-over wailing" of his people, to which he had so long listened. (p. 3)

"That tune," writes Lee, "was the vehicle which carried two to victory," Crump and Handy "who rode on it from Beale Street to Broadway.". . .

Yet for all of this information, interesting as it is, we still prefer the more objective features of the book. It is an illuminating picture of a civilization within a civilization that George W. Lee has drawn. Far from being a purely dependent growth, parasitically clinging to the white man's culture, the Negro is here displayed as developing a culture of his own, caring for his own needs in medicine, in the law, in religion, education and recreation. One sees Negro life insurance companies proceeding on their useful way; Negro banks operating; burial associations performing their necessary duty. So many of the books on the Negro have dealt with the rural black that not all of us have guessed at the multiple civic life of the urban black. *Beale Street* opens one's eyes.

And because it does, we wish it had no stylistic imperfections to mar its otherwise even flow and compelling force. It is the sort of work which should be carried through objectively from start to finish, and this Mr. Lee seems to have been unable to do. Too often he lapses into mere statistics, becomes solely the recorder. (p. 13)

> *Percy Hutchison, "Beale Street, Memphis, Where the Blues Began," in* The New York Times Book Review, *July 29, 1934, pp. 3, 13.*

CLINTON SIMPSON

Beale Street, "where the blues began," is famous for other reasons than its nurture of a particular, characteristic type of popular music. According to the author, it has long been the centre of Negro culture, and represents Negro life in its various

phases at its most civilized. George W. Lee, himself a business man on Beale Street, has written a book about it [*Beale Street*] that tells its history, recounts its popular legends and describes the Street as it is now and as it was in its heyday. . . .

The book summarizes the history of the Negroes in Memphis since the Civil War, describes the changing aspects of Beale Street and recounts the careers of some of its citizens—politicians, crooks, musicians, dope peddlers, prostitutes, teachers, and many others. The color of a unique section of American life is here in plenty. Such a book can scarcely avoid being interesting, and this one is interesting—and valuable, too, since it contains material not printed elsewhere. The chief positive lack in the book is its lack of perspective, resulting in lengthy treatment of purely local matters to the exclusion of general issues—and of "blues" where we should like to hear more of other Negro music. . . .

> *Clinton Simpson, in a review of "Beale Street," in* Scribner's Magazine, *Vol. XCVI, No. 3, September, 1934, p. 14.*

MARGARET LARKIN

Where the Blues Began is a misleading subtitle for a miscellany of success stories and local legends about the Negro section of Memphis, Tennessee. It is not about music. Two of its twenty chapters deal with Negro bands and orchestras and with the rise to fame of colored entertainers. . . . Another fifteen pages are devoted to W. C. Handy, who changed the course of American popular music with his "St. Louis Blues" and made a fortune out of it because he had the financial acumen to publish it himself. George W. Lee, a business man on Beale Street, obviously is not equipped to tell Handy's story in any other terms than those of financial success. What he really has written is "Beale Street: Where the Negro Business Man Began.". . .

[*Beale Street*] opens with a eulogy of a colored banker and "realtor" who controlled most of the businesses on Beale Street in the late eighties, and ends with a eulogy of his son, a Republican boss there today. It contains biographies and anecdotes of Beale Street's gamblers, dope peddlers, and dark courtesans, whose charms were officially reserved for white men; of colored preachers, bankers, "beauticians," tailors, doctors. It recalls the long, shameful history of lynchings in Memphis and the rumors, lies, and racial slanders that set them off; gives a somewhat technical account of how a few white men were backed by the Ku Klux Klan in seizing control of the Negro insurance companies; gives full details, including speeches and newspaper accounts, of the opening of a park named after a colored philanthropist; solves murders and fixes the blame for the local bank crash. Much of the material of the book is fascinating. But many pages, even chapters, are given over to facts of the kind a census taker might collect, gathered into little biographies that serve to conceal the subjects as effectively as so many obituaries. The valuable portions of the book are drowned in undistinguished matter which obviously did not interest even the author. . . .

The one personality who emerges from the book is Robert R. Church, Tennessee's colored Republican boss. Mr. Lee's admiration for him is naively uncritical; he presents the reader with a full view of his hero's political chicaneries, paternalism, patronage system, trade-ins with the Democrats, and sell-out to the Hoover machine, which he disapproved and which betrayed him. Mr. Church helped to nominate Hoover but threatened to withdraw votes because of the presence of Klan members on the campaign committee. Slight concessions brought him into line. But Hoover did not reward him with handsome patronage as Harding had done; expected Negro appointments were canceled and lily-whites were installed in every important place. Years of careful building to make the Negro a politically important factor in Tennessee politics were swept away. . . . The next campaign saw him maneuvering to hold his power in the county convention. Futile as it had proved, position in the Republican Party was preferable to political extinction.

The bourgeois Negro is in a peculiarly tragic position in America. By raising himself above the proletarian and farmer Negro he cuts himself off from his own main stream. The whites bar him from further advancement. The correct Babbittry of the middle class is intensified by the incessant need to prove that a Negro banker, doctor, merchant, or civil servant is as good as his white prototype or even better. This is the point of view in *Beale Street.* It accounts for the pedestrian dulness with which Mr. Lee has handled the dramatic and heroic story of a Negro community struggling for economic and political power in the midst of the intolerant South.

> Margaret Larkin, "Success Stories," in The Nation,
> New York, Vol. CXXXIX, No. 3609, September 5,
> 1934, p. 279.

ELMER ANDERSON CARTER

Here is the biography of a street, a narrow, poorly lighted, dingy street that has exerted tremendous influence on the lives of countless Negroes; that has given inspiration to one of America's most famous composers; that has produced one of the nation's most astute politicians; and that has played a major role in determining the kind of government which the citizens of the city of Memphis and of the State of Tennessee enjoy or from which they suffer.

Of this street George W. Lee, himself one of its products, has written with gusto and enthusiasm. [In *Beale Street,* he] has succeeded in transferring to the printed page a great deal of the color and movement, the sounds and smells of this remarkable street, and where he has failed from the standpoint of literary excellence, his failure can in part be ascribed to the inherent difficulty of his subject. For there are many books in Beale Street . . . , and their compression in a single volume demanded exceptional power of organization which would have proven a task for a writer of much greater experience than Mr. Lee claims to be. . . .

Mr. Lee's story of Beale Street is "rotarian" in its concept and execution. He sets out to glorify Beale Street as the greatest Negro thoroughfare in America. Therefore this book is almost wholly lacking in that critical evaluation of social forces which alone could give understanding to Beale Street's influence on Negro life in Memphis. We catch glimpses of it here and there, but only glimpses. There are questions which persist in coming up in the reviewer's mind. How much, for instance, has Beale Street contributed to the dubious distinction which Memphis has attained of possessing the highest homicide rate of any city in the western hemisphere? Aye, of any city in the civilized world.

A rare organizer, as exemplified by his leadership in the field of Negro insurance and the American Legion, an able politician, perhaps it is unfair to expect from Mr. Lee in his first

work more than an interesting and intriguing narrative. And this he has given us.

> Elmer Anderson Carter, in a review of "Beale Street:
> Where the Blues Began," in Opportunity, Vol. XII,
> No. 10, October, 1934, p. 314.

E. C. BECKWITH

Mr. Lee's novel [*River George*] reflects the conditions prevalent at a large plantation in Western Tennessee, a fertile property owned by unscrupulous whites and worked by numerous black sharecroppers. These laborers, forced to buy the necessities of life on tick at the plantation store, are ruthlessly defrauded each harvest of their meager profits, and so held in thrall by fictitious debts to their masters from year to year.

The plight of his exploited people arouses to action young Aaron George, a stalwart, enlightened Negro, when he returns from three years of study at a colored college to the cabin of his parents on the plantation. His father, a docile, pious field hand, lies dying, and Aaron, after the old man's death, remains at the cabin to farm the land which then passes on to him. His keen sense of economic and social justice for his race impels Aaron to protest the cause of his fellow Negroes to the white men in control of the plantation. For so doing, Aaron is marked a trouble maker, incurs the animosity of his employers, and on the false charge of killing a worthless white is forced to flee the threat of lynching. . . .

The subsequent adventures which overtake Aaron in his endeavor to conceal his identity, remain free, and keep touch with his loved ones back home on the plantation are many, arduous and far-flung, though generally plausible. Persisting in his dream of bettering the masses of his race, he finally recognizes and accepts the hopelessness of his task. He has been bitterly frustrated in all his generous aspirations, and at the close one wishes for him some kindlier recompense than the fate to which he is subjected. The story, told from the viewpoint of the Negro, abounds in expressive character types (nearly all of them colored), illuminating incidents and sidelights, which graphically amplify the novel's scope and human interest.

> E. C. Beckwith, "Sharecroppers," in The New York
> Times Book Review, June 20, 1937, p. 16.

HUGH M. GLOSTER

Like [George Wylie Henderson's] *Ollie Miss,* George W. Lee's ***River George*** treats the lives of Negro sharecroppers in the deep South, but here the similarity ends. *Ollie Miss,* evading racial issues, presents black landowners and sharecroppers far removed from the interference of whites. Lee's work, on the other hand, provides a more realistic depiction of Negro tenant farmers in their relations with one another and with white members of the community. Deriving much of its plot from the life of a semi-legendary Mississippi River rouster discussed in Lee's earlier book, ***Beale Street: Where the Blues Began,*** ***River George*** offers as a hero a Mississippi college student who hopes that through the practice of law he may help to free his race "from a bitter bondage which did not end with the signing of the Emancipation Proclamation." George is keenly aware of the hardships of the Negro:

> It is a battle with the majority of the whites, who
> insist on holding up, as most representative of the

Negro, his worst, rather than his best. It is a battle with the majority of the Negroes themselves who crucify their own kind upon a cross of indifference or desire for personal gain through gaining favor with the whites; it is a battle with one's own self in which one is forced to accept life on a lower level and yet keep faith with his highest convictions. It is a battle against despair, life's deadliest sin.

Shunted from his professional ambitions by the death of his father, George assumes support of his mother and becomes a sharecropper on the Beaver Dam Plantation. He gives up his work, however, upon being cheated by the plantation book-keeper and upon discovering that Ada Smith, the woman he loves, is the mistress of Fred Smith, "a mean-faced, mean-souled white man." George's efforts to organize the Negro tenant farmers of the district lead directly to a fight with Smith, who is determined not to share his concubine "with any nigger." After killing his opponent George flees to Memphis, where he lives with Annie Bell, proprietress of a Beale Street brothel, until detectives learn of his whereabouts. The fugitive next joins the Army with the hope that the Negro, after fighting beside the white man to preserve democracy, will receive justice in America. After the Armistice, however, the activities of the Ku Klux Klan convince him that Annie was right when she said:

> Don't fool yourself. If you go over there to fight and get back here, so far as this man's country is concerned, you'll still be a nigger and you'll still be treated like a nigger.

Returning to America, George spends a short while in Harlem and then, with the hope of getting in touch with his mother and Ada, goes to Vicksburg, Mississippi, which he is forced to leave because of resentment for his officer's uniform. In Memphis he is captured by a Negro detective but makes a daring escape. Getting work as a Mississippi River rouster, he establishes himself as a notorious bad man by defeating Black Bill. During a southward trip on a steamboat George is recognized by three white passengers and later lynched by a Mississippi mob for the murder of Smith.

In its earlier chapters *River George* authentically portrays Negro sharecroppers who work from dawn to dusk throughout the year and derive their chief diversion from Saturday night break-downs and Sunday religious excesses. Revealing the tension between overlords and peons of the Cotton Belt, the novel shows how black workers are fleeced and oppressed. (pp. 238-40)

Almost as well developed as the sharecropping background is the Beale Street setting, where George lives as a fugitive after fleeing from Beaver Dam Plantation. In this "Blues Heben" river rats, rousters, rustics, and spruce city dandies mingle in an atmosphere reeking with corn liquor and barbecue. With George we visit the Panama, Hammett's Place, the Hole in the Wall, the Monarch, Peewee's Place, and the voodoo head-quarters of Mary the Wonder, each of which the author knew firsthand. Less intimately done is the description of Harlem, where George spends two days; and altogether neglected is the presentation of the European scene, where he gives over a year of service in the United States Army. *River George* is chiefly important, therefore, for its exposure of the abuses of the tenant farmer system. (pp. 240-41)

> *Hugh M. Gloster, "Negro Fiction of the Depression," in his* Negro Voices in American Fiction, *1948. Reprint by Russell & Russell, Inc., 1965, pp. 208-51.*

DAVID M. TUCKER

Since writing offered a medium for promoting the racial pride upon which black business thrived, George Lee took up the pen as a tool for creating profits. His first published articles called for the race to unite against the evils of poverty and discrimination, and his first book celebrated the achievements of Negro Memphians. After the great depression delivered a devastating blow to the black economy of Beale Street, turning the once prosperous street into "one of the longest bread-lines in the life of the city," George Lee felt compelled to begin work on a book that might revive his people's flagging faith in black business.

George Lee had long followed the *Crisis* symposiums on the literary portrayal of Negro characters and naturally hoped that by beating white writers to the Beale Street story he might discourage any local creation of dialect farces such as those with which Octavus Roy Cohen had caricatured Birmingham Negroes. Featuring Hop Sure Peters, a shuffling Pullman porter, who clowned on the Birmingham-to-New York line and was "considerable social pumpkins" in the 18th Street circles, Cohen's blackface caricatures had ignored the very existence of an accomplished middle class, deprived the Negro of human dignity, and exploited the race for the amusement of the whites. It would be tragic, Lee felt, if Beale Street society were rid-iculed as Birmingham's 18th Street had been, and so he sought to tell it the way it should be told. Lee wanted to draw a realistic picture which would show Memphis Negroes not as Hop Sures or Hambones but as successful businessmen who, though segregated and deprived, had shown the same potential for self-improvement as the Anglo-Saxon. Nowhere had this potential been realized more dramatically than by the elder Robert R. Church, who gained his freedom in 1862 when the Union Army came to Memphis and went on to build an estate worth more than a million dollars. Since it was Church who had made Beale Street the center of commercial life for Negroes, Lee decided to enclose his picture of the district's life within the frame of Robert Church's success story. George Lee would give his readers closeups of all the bankers, lawyers, druggists, funeral directors, and insurance men who lived on the street, and who like the beautician, Madame Gorine Morgan Young, had come up from Mississippi and "established themselves solidly in Beale Street's commercial life." (pp. 105-06)

A black Babbitt would have collected only Negro success stories and ignored the sordid and seamy side of life, but George Lee, following the trend of the Negro literary renaissance, also sought a sympathetic portrayal of the lowdown black Negroes, the gamesters who rolled the dice at the Hole in the Wall, dope peddlers such as Ten Dollar Jimmy, and courtesans who ran black and white pleasure palaces. Carl Van Vechten's *Nigger Heaven* had made it current literary fashion to view the Negro as an erotic primitive who was uninhibited by the puritanism that had stifled the spontaneity of the white middle classes. So Lee documented the existence of dissolute blacks alongside the respectable middle class of Beale Street. (pp. 106-07)

[Local] book stores refused to stock *Beale Street: Where the Blues Began* until after Clifton Fadiman had reviewed it in the July *New Yorker*. "I wish to pin a small but distinctive badge (with ribbons) upon the honest colored breast of Lieutenant George Washington Lee," Fadiman wrote. "Mr. Lee's naïve Memphis recitals have the authentic color of good crackerbox gossip." After Fadiman's review, the book began selling everywhere, and George Lee's ego swelled as he received the favorable writeups. (p. 111)

Beale Street became popular because it captured so successfully the tempo of the district's life. The street was, George Lee said, "owned largely by Jews, policed by whites, and enjoyed by Negroes." There were hog-nose sandwiches, chitterling cafes, and an underworld with every vice known to man. The author had told of the bad black roustabout, River George, whose career had carried him through Beale Street like a "bloody comet." No detail had seemed too small for Lee's tableau. The reader learned that gamblers at the Hole In The Wall were normally fined five cents for spitting on the dice, and that while the favors of the bordellos were officially reserved for a white clientele, the alley doors were always opened to the blacks after 3 A.M. This racy, graphic description of Negro Americana made fascinating reading for thousands of whites who lived quiet and routine lives. But the splendor of these descriptions of the colorful activity on Beale was dulled by the uninspired documentary on Negro middle-class achievements. Almost without exception, the critics complained of George Lee's self-imposed mission to catalogue the names and contributions of the street's businessmen, churches, schools, banks, and of course, insurance companies. "Half of it could and should have been junked," said the New York *Sun*. "The rest is pure gold." (p. 113)

Actually, Lee had no further ambitions for writing, until he learned that Negro intellectuals in the East were unimpressed with his literary effort. Bob Church brought back the news from New York that Walter White, secretary of the NAACP, and his Harlem circle of friends felt that Lee himself had no talent as a writer, but that the subject, not its literary treatment, had made **Beale Street** a success. Such reaction made it clear to George Lee that he would have to write another book to show Harlem's pseudosophisticates that the East had no monopoly on talent.

Lee decided to take his third chapter from **Beale Street,** the chapter about River George, a semimythical bad man in the community, and expand it to a full length antisharecrop novel. Ever since George Lee's escape from a Mississippi tenant farm, he had longed to strike a blow at what he called the "damnable sharecrop system"; and now, by telling his story of the half-legendary bad man of Beale Street, he would finally have his chance.

Lee tried to be fair in his work of protest fiction, however, and never denounced all the landlords categorically. His own relationship with [a former employer], Mr. Klingman of Indianola, had been such a happy one that the author put his white benefactor in the novel as Mr. King. . . . In the novel, this kindly old white man has been the owner of Beaver Dam plantation, a well-run, impressive estate of which he boasted, "I got the best niggers and the best cotton in the whole delta." The old gentleman, however, sells the plantation to the greedy, self-made Mr. Tyler, and under this new owner the potentially vicious system forces the workers into conditions as deplorable as slavery. The exorbitant prices at the plantation store and the shameless dishonesty of the plantation bookkeeper reduces the tenants to virtual peonage; for no matter how many bales of cotton a sharecropper on Beaver Dam produces, he cannot pay off his debt to the plantation.

The central character of the novel, Aaron George, returns home from Alcorn College to his family's sharecrop on Tyler's plantation. Eager to put his education to work by emancipating his people, he promises his dying father he will go to the owner and protest his criminal system. (pp. 114-15)

[Education] has liberated Aaron from his parents' peasant conservatism, and he resolves to improve the condition of the sharecroppers. At the first opportunity, he asks Sam Turner, the plantation agent, to induce Mr. Tyler to make the sharecropper's efforts a bit more profitable when the annual settlements are computed. But only the most naïve of southern Negroes can expect to receive a sympathetic audience from a white overseer. "Ain't no place on Beaver Dam for a nigger that talks like you," Turner snaps. "You better get such damn fool notions out of your head; cause if you try to start anything among these niggers, it's going to be mighty unhealthy for you." (p. 115)

The hero might have moved his mother north and escaped the hopeless Delta, but George Lee has made Aaron an extremely idealistic character, unwilling to run until he has put the system, and himself, to the test. . . .

Just as he had always done in his own life, George Lee's character, Aaron George, turns to influential white folks for help. Since Mississippi ethics forbid an outsider from intervening in disputes between a planter and his Negroes, Aaron cannot take his complaints about the unjust settlement itself to any white man; yet he can ask his father's former employer to help him find a second job in town. So Aaron goes to Mr. King who is able to place him in a cotton-oil mill in Indianola. There Aaron makes more money in a single month than he had earned in a year on the sharecrop, and other workers begin to follow his example until a score of men are riding their mules into Indianola to work in town rather than spend the short winter months on the plantation in idleness. (p. 116)

George Lee destroyed the unity of his agrarian novel by moving Aaron from the rural South when he was only halfway through the book. The subsequent chapters follow Aaron George to Beale Street, Harlem, and through the First World War before returning him somewhat unconvincingly to Beaver Dam where he is lynched upon arrival. Artistically, these later chapters detracted from the force of the book, but they gave Lee the chance to include a wider range of autobiographical material and, above all, to retaliate against his Harlem critics. "Listen, big boy," Lee has one eastern Negro say, "we aren't much interested in Harlem in doing anything for the race. The fellows who worry about that usually push their faces into trouble. And who cares? Harlem has a good time." As Lee depicts them, the dissolute Harlemites lack the staunch integrity, the racial concern, and the simple emotional depth of the southern Negro. The spiritual emancipation of the race, Aaron concludes, will never come from Harlem. (pp. 117-18)

[*River George*] was never the success that Lee's first book had been. Although it represented a distinct advance artistically, some reviewers fairly, if ruthlessly, concluded, "there are not enough facts to make **River George** good propaganda, and there is not enough artistry to make **River George** a good novel." At the same time, however, critics generally did appreciate the realistic picture of southern sharecropping with its protest against white violence and bigotry. From Louisville, Kentucky, a reviewer wrote, "Keep writing, books like yours . . . will make you more friends than all the articles on racial questions put together. Dickens helped children in old London, Black Beauty helped a lot of dumb animals. River George is helping the colored people." So George Lee's second book did draw some degree of applause, at least enough to encourage the author to go on writing. (pp. 118-19)

[George Lee] no longer looked to writing as a medium of social protest, but rather as an outlet for his creative energy. Now he wanted to paint scenes of Beale Street life which were works of art and not merely racial tracts. Lee's stories describe a church congregation filled with hate instead of love, the confidence game which fleeced Beale Streeters out to get rich quick, a Negro girl who was ''passing'' in a white whore house, and how the Blues created tensions between the brown middle-class and the common black masses. George Lee had his stories published in the *Negro Digest, The World's Digest,* and the *Southern Literary Messenger,* and later published them as **Beale Street Sundown,** a collection which, though attracting little national interest, at least won him the satisfaction of great local praise. ''The Boswell of Beale Street,'' the Memphis *Press-Scimitar* raved, ''has spun the best book of his literary career.'' (p. 119)

> *David M. Tucker, in his* Lieutenant Lee of Beale Street, *Vanderbilt University Press, 1971, 217 p.*

John (Clarke) L'Heureux

1934-

American novelist, poet, short story writer, and editor.

A former Jesuit priest, L'Heureux is best known for novels in which he portrays members of the clergy whose personal crises often arise from the tension between their spiritual and carnal impulses. While his poetry is usually whimsical and optimistic in detailing the search for personal understanding, L'Heureux reveals a darker, more bitterly ironic viewpoint in his fiction to expand the dichotomy between religious belief and sexuality and to address parallels between what Richard Eder defined as "normality and monstrosity" in personal relationships. Despite their respect for religion, L'Heureux's characters often learn that the ideal Christian existence conceals what Ralph McInerny described as "an egocentric sexuality" that is characteristic of "the hard and ugly nature of things."

L'Heureux became an ordained priest in 1965. With the publication of his first two works, the poetry collections *Quick as Dandelions* ('1964) and *Rubrics for a Revolution* (1967), he elicited critical praise for ironic wit, lyricism, and the ability to enliven devotional subject matter by playfully synthesizing religious and laic imagery. *Picnic in Babylon: A Jesuit Priest's Journal, 1963-1967* (1967) incorporates entries from L'Heureux's personal diary as well as portions of business and personal letters to chronicle his three years of theological study at Woodstock College, Maryland, prior to his ordination. While regarded by some critics as disingenuous, *Picnic in Babylon* won approval for L'Heureux's lucid, self-effacing exploration of his spiritual maturation during the mid-1960s. His next two verse collections, *One Eye and a Measuring Rod* (1968) and *No Place for Hiding* (1971), examine both secular and religious themes. Although L'Heureux garnered praise for his wry, humanistic approach, most reviewers faulted the poems in these volumes as complacent or derivative.

Upon leaving the priesthood in 1971, L'Heureux wrote two novels in which he questions the validity of a religious life. *Tight White Collar* (1972) recounts a priest's crisis of faith and subsequent search for self-knowledge following his return home for the funeral of a distant relative, and *The Clang Birds* (1972) employs scatological humor to satirically examine the relationships that develop among the "Thomasites," a group of priests and nuns who establish an experimental urban colony while protesting the Vietnam War during the 1960s. Although several critics contended that L'Heureux sacrifices the wit and intimacy of his early poetry for a cynicism that results in unattractive, stereotypical characters, others praised his acute observation of detail.

In his short story collection *Family Affairs* (1974), L'Heureux diverges from the exclusively religious subjects of his previous works. While several commentators deemed some stories in this volume unconvincing, others applauded their ability to recapture the humor of L'Heureux's poetry while retaining his stark, well-crafted narrative style. Doris Grumbach commented: "[L'Heureux] can fix a situation to the page with a few sentences and then expand it, explore it, bring it to an inevitable conclusion . . . without striking a single false note." In his next work, *Jessica Fayer* (1976), an elderly former nun

reflects on her past following a violent incident. This novel, as well as L'Heureux's second short story collection, *Desires* (1981), received mixed reviews.

In L'Heureux's suspense novel *A Woman Run Mad* (1987), a self-involved professor's dissatisfaction with his intellectual but emotionally unstable wife and his obsessive sexual relationship with a beautiful but disturbed shoplifter result in violence and madness. Although this work was faulted for melodrama and sensationalism, several reviewers commended L'Heureux's portrayal of the precarious balance between sanity and psychosis. Richard Eder compared L'Heureux to Iris Murdoch for his ability to make readers identify with the horror underlying the apparently normal lives of his characters, stating: "[Even] in their most matter-of-fact moments, we feel a horror closing in on them without knowing where it comes from."

(See also *Contemporary Authors*, Vols. 13-16, rev. ed. and *Contemporary Authors New Revision Series*, Vol. 23.)

DeWITT BELL

John L'Heureux is a lyric poet. The language [in *Quick as Dandelions*] sings for him—in his own special way. His way is rhetorical and traditional and intuitive, as shown in these lines from **"Van Gogh"**

> To have failed all and every failure sobbing
> I am Vincent, blind from laddering sunlight

The lines would be unimpressive without "laddering." The leap to this word gives the passage its penetration and individuality. In poems where he is able to make the leap from the conventional framework, L'Heureux presents us with startling insight; where he is unable, the poems are merely conventional.

The author is a Jesuit, and most of the poems are religious. This constricts him to a tradition and limits his range of subject matter. He does manage to add something of his own to that tradition, though, and infuse new life into it. For example, in **"Flowering Sudden,"** a poem about the Crucifixion, he speaks of "These hallowed hands now streaming light / like Gothic windows" an image remarkable for its compression and scope. To his often excellent metaphoric language, he adds wit, playfulness and, in poems dealing with the Virgin especially, a great gentleness. In **"The Imperfect Eye,"** he writes, "Sometimes joy is like that, coming quick as dandelions." Sometimes the book is like that.

> DeWitt Bell, "Plain and Fancy," in The New York Times, September 19, 1965, p. 50.

SISTER M. THÉRÈSE

At a time when as never before critics of poetry have been awaiting the sound of new voices, poems by a young Jesuit, John L'Heureux, began appearing in such magazines as *Atlantic, Harpers, The Beloit Journal,* and the *Kenyon* and *Yale* reviews—poems that were fresh, singularly modern in form and structure, and highly imaged, with a certain dramatic quality about them which gave them power and movement. It was *Atlantic* . . . that carried John L'Heureux's **"Death of a Man,"** one of the few *real* poems among the many. It is a delight to find it among the titles in [*Quick as Dandelions*] which contains sixty-two poems in a three group arrangement, namely, **"All Grass is Flesh," "A Solemne Musick,"** and **"Ashes and Wrath."** Opening the book at random the reader is confronted with a variety of interesting stanza patterns and forms in which the poet has engemmed a wide range of subject-matter. . . . The poems are full of delightful surprises.

But it is to those of the second division of the book, **"A Solemne Musick,"** that one must give special attention. For in this cluster of seven poems—a brilliant *tour de force* for any poet— Mr. L'Heureux has enshrined a whole theology of man and his world, from the moment of creation. . . . In a rich interplay of symbolisms ancient and modern he sings of the creation of the animals when "velvet tigers with tails / of braided hemp, puffy / lions regal and prim" parade the landscape. Then came man— "a dream worth building vision on." And on the day when "bullfrogs sang in rhymed hexameters / and all the trees clapped hands / for music" came the eternal woman: "Helen / coming home with her basket of apples. . . ." The last poem of the group one might have expected to be a *finale,* but it is nothing of the sort, as its title indicates, it is an **"Improvisation."** For it is of man, universal, particular, for whom life goes on and "value is a question / after all of meaning;" and we hear the poet's voice very distinctly: "If at the end / my heart is iron still / think no harsh truths . . . think it is because / a base of metal has been / long required as alloy / to the pain

of being / golden . . ." Mr. L'Heureux is as far from *angelism* in his poetic statement as one can hope to be for "Eden's blood / is gold / A stream ambivalent and clouded, / Alloy being found essential / For survival."

Poems of a deeply (though not obtrusively) philosophic and theological dimension are everywhere—though having their source in concrete event, as in **"One Winter Morning by the Footbridge,"** [**"A Bat in a Monastery,"** and **"Death of a Man"**] . . ., in which symbolisms of "apples, stables, bullets," which carry the weight of meaning resolve themselves into that mystery of providence wherein "God sees, allows, and loves / in ways we do not ripely understand. / Let mankind hobble home now on its knees."

Throughout the collection there is a deft control of forms, open and freely moving, though to this reviewer there are occasional lapses where lines seem to be broken in strange places, perhaps to conform to a specific pattern on the page such as "mind uncluttered by / Complexities of / Truth." But the poet must have had some sound rhythmic reason for his usage; nor are the poems much marred thereby. One wonders too about the use of capital letters at the beginning of lines in certain patternings. But *Quick as Dandelions* is a memorable first collection spiced with a keen verbal wit and gentle yet incisive irony, which is always intellectually in order.

To read John L'Heureux's poems is to have an exciting encounter with the mind of a poet of strikingly individual voice and vision. His work is fresh, daring, sprung from a rich experience of life and wonderfully alive with the movement of a free Christian spirit. A fine new poet, and a handsome book. (pp. 166-67)

> Sister M. Thérèse, in a review of "Quick as Dandelions," in Renascence, Vol. XVIII, No. 3, Spring, 1966, pp. 166-67.

JAMES TORRENS

[L'Heureux] has just come out with his second book of poems, **Rubrics for a Revolution.** The title itself of this new volume is rather subtle. There is little enough of tumultuous revolution; instead, one lone intelligence striving to point out unnoticed things, good and bad, at the core of human experience, and feel its way through disillusionment to wisdom.

Morse Allen, who reviewed his first book, **Quick as Dandelions,** was disappointed not to find more Easter joy in the earlier collection. But John L'Heureux does not like rhetoric, or faith with a contrived "oomph." His "cuckoo's voice," he says, was not made for the traditional resurrection songs (though his sequence **"A Solemne Musick"** in **Quick as Dandelions** is as fine an example in this genre as one could wish).

Many people still look for poetry to be a key to Philip Sidney's "golden world," and are disappointed not to find it so. They are unaware that the best of modern poetry has been designedly anti-romantic. So John L'Heureux (in **"The Garden House"**):

> Sun ripened on
> The fully grown
> Bewildered vine as one
> By one the clusters
> Of ripeness festered.

This is not gimmickry. It proceeds from a mind fully aware that things are not as rosy as we dream. Hence the deep distrust of rhyme that L'Heureux openly proclaimed in **Quick as Dan-**

delions. Reliance on rhyme today would be specious, too facile a solution of dissonance and complexity. (Despite this, one of the author's most striking poems, "Hollow," is set in the traditional frame.) The irregular and more subtly contrived patterns of L'Heureux's poetry strive to cope with the unlikely juncture of ape and angel that we find to be man.

The book has five divisions. **"The Concert: Oratorio for a Season of Wrath"** strikes the note of small-town New England people scrabbling for survival in a world of muted violence. The poems are lighted up by some fine ironic humor. **"Poem #5,"** extremely complex and skillful in its weaving of motifs, is among the best in the volume.

Intelligent poetry yields its secrets very slowly. This is particularly true of L'Heureux's second section, **"Eleven Poems of Exhaustion."** On first reading they will perhaps appall, certainly puzzle. . . . But this may well be the most skillful and effective group of the lot. They challenge careful thought (this, apparently, is their "rubric"), and turn out to be far less flinty than at first sight.

A third section, **"The Semantic Waltz,"** continues in a topical and personal vein. **"Valentine for Ophelia,"** which deals with the Nazi persecution of our Lady's people, the Jews, is especially unforgettable.

"Transparencies," part four, is a random group of imaginative musings, plus three fine poems on Emily Dickinson, Marilyn Monroe and our Lady (**"The Quince"**). A few are very hard going—**"Isomorphism,"** parts of **"The Swan."** One of them, **"Marginal Notes in a Theology Text,"** is a standout among artistic approaches to a Christian anthropology.

In part five, **"That Mortal Knot,"** John L'Heureux springs a dramatic sequence upon the unsuspecting reader. The result is memorable: a *journal intime,* leading from the apples and eelgrass of youth, through a particular species of the dark night, up to the point of mystery where we find Christ "risen from the night of our impatience."

Rubrics for a Revolution will repay a sympathetic and careful reader many times over, but him alone. (pp. 479-80)

> *James Torrens, in a review of "Rubrics for a Revolution," in* America, *Vol. 116, No. 12, March 25, 1967, pp. 479-80.*

JAMES DICKEY

John L'Heureux is well named. [In *Rubrics for a Revolution,* he] is not only happy, but whimsically imaginative. He is a religious poet, indeed a priest, but with a refreshing difference. His feeling for sacramental relationships has nothing of the owlish or scholastic; it is a form of worship that includes, as most religious verse does not, humor and a very wide latitude of tolerance. "Let us rejoice / that we are compassed round / by madness." Even the device of irony, very nearly an essential one in modern poetry, is here simply another form of appreciation, of connecting things in an affectionate and graceful manner. . . .

If L'Heureux infrequently strikes one as a little too accepting, there nevertheless is in most of his work a sense of the poet's going eagerly toward events and people, open-handed and open-hearted, wanting to understand and love. . . . In this, he reminds me somewhat of George Herbert, another gentle and profoundly imaginative soul, a poet not of wrath but of balm and of a wide, mild peace: not the peace that passeth under-

standing, but that which is a product of it, if understanding is seen—or felt—to include the blood and muscles, the whole being, as well as the mind. This is a good book, but better than that, it is a healing, reconciling one. (p. 10)

> *James Dickey, "Of Mind and Soul," in* The New York Times Book Review, *June 18, 1967, pp. 10, 12.*

JOHN MOFFITT

John L'Heureux's chatty and diverting journal [*Picnic in Babylon*] is a very incomplete and very human record of the three years he spent at Woodstock College, in Maryland, during his theological studies prior to ordination as a priest. . . .

The idea for this book, as is made clear by the author, came from the editor who handled the publication of his first book of poems, *Quick as Dandelions.* Charmed by his letters, she felt that, if written in such a lively style, something autobiographical about one preparing for the priesthood would be worth publishing. He himself was not without qualms. Apropos of a letter from his editor about the first hundred pages he had submitted (asking him to make them more intimate), L'Heureux says, in his entry for July 27, 1964: "The notion of a very personal journal gives me the willies. This one seems already too naked and I don't like walking around naked in a room full of clothed people." . . .

As the author reveals in a matter-of-fact preface, the first half-year's "entries" were not written as part of a journal at all. They were assembled from letters returned by friends, from carbon copies of business letters, and from random notes kept by accident. About the work as it finally appeared, he writes in his preface: "*Picnic in Babylon* is an amalgam of lies and half-truths and a larger, more important care for that truth which can be approached only tangentially."

Though there is no narrative in the strict sense, as you read you gradually become aware that a very real story underlies the whole: the story of the slow maturing of a rather special person, one whose very excesses—as they are set down here—are perhaps necessary to convey the spit and image of the original. John L'Heureux is not unaware of these excesses. . . . (p. 480)

But though it is practically impossible to trace a story, what can indeed be traced is some of the strands that make of the book such varied—and rewarding—fare. There is first of all, of course, the informing presence of the blithe spirit destined for the priesthood, who somehow manages to see himself and his calling without pretense. There is, almost as constantly, the friend who most humanly cherishes the responses of friends and honestly winces at a failure (perhaps largely his own fault) in friendship. And again, there is the literary critic, whose business is to fathom the ambiguities or expose the shallownesses of his subjects: through much of the book L'Heureux comments about his labors on an article on Edward Albee's *Who's Afraid of Virginia Woolf?,* which he rashly undertook for a scholarly journal; but he includes also intelligent comment on writers such as Muriel Spark, Flannery O'Connor, Evelyn Waugh and Virginia Woolf herself—to mention only a few. There is, as well, the amused observer, who sets down the foibles—but the greatnesses, too—of teachers and fellow novices alike; and who, I should add, does not spare himself.

Last of all, there is the conscious and conscientious poet, already receiving a measure of acclaim . . . , who still finds it worth his while to record his elation at editors' approval, his distress at their indifference, and at last, to his credit, his own unconcern.

In the course of these pages, one comes upon not a few passages of startling intensity—passages relating not only to Christ and the priesthood, but to the central position of love and to men's failure in love. There are also intimations of profound human understanding, as in the final paragraph of the entry for June 22, 1964, where he tells of a mother's pitiable discomfiture in front of one of her son's friends, who has stopped in on his way to say his first Mass. (pp. 480, 482)

There are at least three stories in this volume that are so funny you won't forget them. And flashes of the L'Heureux humor and good humor constantly light up the text. Also, on a first reading, there are a few passages you might wish had been left out. In the entry for Dec. 21, 1963, for instance, you trip on the sentence: "I love God, you know. I really do." (This is surely culled from a letter; no one would ever write this way for himself.) Again, in a rather penetrating discussion of Mary McCarthy and *The Company She Keeps,* in the entry for April 12, 1964, comes the following: "Her Catholicism is like a ripe scar on a white and pampered body. I must pray for her."

Yet this gives way immediately to the April 13 entry, where you read: "I gave the kids a Latin assignment that consisted in kneeling down next to a kitty ('If you don't have one, borrow a neighbor's') and listening to the purr. It caused all sorts of alarm among the parents, but a few students, for the first time in their lives, became aware of a life other than their own." This is perhaps the most revealing passage in the book. Yet would the whole work carry the impact it does if those other two passages had been deleted?

The most piquant element for me, as a poet, is what John L'Heureux writes about himself as a poet. In the March 24, 1964, entry occurs this estimate: "Don Hinfey says that as a poet I give a good virtuoso performance, my range of technique is fine, but there is no consuming passion, no fire. Is he right? I think he is. I had fire once but it died of a little awareness." I doubt if L'Heureux holds this opinion of himself now. Nevertheless it strikes me as very odd that so accomplished a poet writes a prose that conveys himself, as a person, far more faithfully than most of his poetry.

Two poets immediately come to mind who have succeeded in expressing their total selves as vividly and authentically in their poetry as John L'Heureux has in his prose. They are Walt Whitman and Paul Goodman. But of Whitman he says in this book: "Whitman at his best was never more than an overdeveloped ego attached to a bellows. . . ."

So what are we to make of this 301-page record? There are those who will—for one reason or another—raise fastidious eyebrows at the apparent *gaucheries,* and so miss its central honesty and goodness. No matter. The old reticences die hard. But for anyone who may care to know a real, even though perhaps difficult person, a person whose ways of thinking and feeling can help him perceive his own self more clearly, I can think of no better prescription.

What we need today—what we have always needed—is a little unvarnished truth-telling, a little nakedness, if you will, amid all the clothing. Here it is. Make the most of an opportunity you may not have again, and become bosom companion of one who surely deserves his name, "John the Happy." (p. 482)

John Moffitt, in a review of "Picnic in Babylon," in America, *Vol. 117, No. 18, October 28, 1967, pp. 480, 482.*

PETER A. STITT

John L'Heureux is a poet of lyric sensibility whose best work is to be seen in small, tight poems based on an observation or an incident. But he is also a member of the Society of Jesus, and he writes many poems, like the long **"A Solemne Musick,"** that are theological in content and symbolic in technique— poems which seem to betray his real talent. Perhaps I reveal a lack of catholic taste by condemning these poems, but I must confess that they bore me, even though they are skillfully written. In addition to the theological, there is another voice which I would object to in L'Heureux's verse [collected in **Quick as Dandelions**]—that of the morally indignant preacher who looks out at life from his gilded cage and sees nothing but filth and sinning toads ("your / sticky tongues serve only / your distended bellies"), who live in a world that is a "worn out harlot." Amen, Brother, but deal me out. (p. 359)

We can be thankful, however, that L'Heureux often transcends theological speculation and moral didacticism, for when he does he writes some very good poems indeed. One thing L'Heureux is particularly skilled at is startling the reader through the use of an unexpected and witty phrase. A good example of this is the beginning of **"The Storm":**

> After the great rain
> I came upon a hare's bone
> chilled white against black rock
> It was Edith Sitwell.

The subject of the poem is Miss Sitwell and her poetry; however, the first three lines lead us to expect, perhaps, a neo-Roethkean metaphysical allegory such as we might find in a translation by Robert Bly. A similarly shocking effect is achieved in the opening of **"A Bat in the Monastery"**—a poem which shows that L'Heureux is not unacquainted with the poems of another monk, Thomas Merton. . . . (pp. 359-60)

Two of the finest poems in the book—**"The Recluse"** and **"The Citadel"**—are concerned with the monastic life; I find them ruthlessly and startlingly honest, especially in contrast to L'Heureux's rather too confident theological poems. **"The Recluse"** is a brilliant poem. . . . It is in poems like this that John L'Heureux's real talent is revealed; he carefully mixes and modulates images and phrases in such a way that the frightening and startling final line is fully justified. In many ways, this is an amazingly good first book—already L'Heureux seems a master of his craft, and one feels that, if he will employ this craft in the lyrical rather than the didactic mode, then he will be well on his way toward becoming a major contemporary poet. (pp. 360-61)

Peter A. Stitt, "The Ancient Croaking," in The Minnesota Review, *Vol. VII, No. 4, 1967, pp. 359-62.*

GERALD BURNS

As a Bourgeois priest John L'Heureux's spirituality owes less to the coffee house than the coffee table. He is sufficiently juvenile to imagine readers will find religious clichés surprising—that, for instance, conjunctions of the divine and the human are often silly (**"Perichoresis and the Single Seminarian"**) or not quite polite (**"Three Awful Picnics"**). Maybe he's right, but **"The Last Veil"** is a mighty cheap win. *One Eye and a*

Measuring Rod has the worst Kennedy elegy yet, and too many echoes—Roethke, Stafford, Muir, Field . . . but he may go on with the poetry of flat statement (in the section called **"Facts"**), which would be interesting. . . . [**"The Municipal Park," "The Berry Stain,"** and **"Tiffany Alexander"**] show he can break his lines effectively when he wants to. Short lines no. In **"Lines to be Recited While Burning at the Stake"** the words don't do all the work yet. The trick meter does nothing for **"The Gift"**; I'm not sure if the trick rhyme in **"Brother Jordan's Fox"** kills or cures. The only verse with half the life of his cummings epigraph is **"Six Varieties of Religious Experience."** (pp. 448-49)

> *Gerald Burns, "Dark Horses, Front-Runners, a Gelding, a Unicorn," in* Southwest Review, *Vol. LIII, No. 4, Autumn, 1968, pp. 445-50.*

BEST SELLERS

There are some taut yet delicate lyrics in [*No Place for Hiding*]—pieces like **"The Reply"** that stand up in splendid control of thought and word; and there are enough of them to give the slim volume considerable distinction. John L'Heureux does, however, seem to attribute an unwarranted amount of importance to the slightest things, as though he thought they were exceptional when they are not: his drinking of Scotch, for instance. . . . Some of the forms are mannered, some of the words lack the freshness necessary to convey experience, but the best poems are very good indeed.

> *A review of "No Place for Hiding," in* Best Sellers, *Vol. 31, No. 3, May 1, 1971, p. 58.*

JOHN KOETHE

I didn't care for John L'Heureux's fourth book of poems, *No Place For Hiding.* No doubt most books don't come off in some way or other, but at least there are usually enough happy moments in them for us to be able to respect the author's aspirations if not always his achievements. The thing that irked me most about L'Heureux's book is its complacency—there is a satisfied air about it, but no authority. While he is after self-knowledge, what we get here is self-dramatization, which he tries to deflate into knowledge by means of a sort of sophisticated patter. The effect is one of smugness. . . . (p. 57)

To make matters worse, L'Heureux seems conscious of the fact that in his more controlled efforts he comes across as something of a *poseur;* his attempts to relax are downright embarrassing. . . . (p. 58)

> *John Koethe, "The Poetry Room," in* Poetry, *Vol. CXX, No. 1, April, 1972, pp. 49-58.*

MARTIN LEVIN

Delivering an unofficial eulogy at the wake of a Protestant relative, a young Jesuit priest named Ransom is thrown off-stride: "He had not taken into consideration the likelihood of genuine feeling." This oversight signifies a flaw in his vocation, which Mr. L'Heureux magnifies with cumulative power [in *Tight White Collar*]. In the day it takes for a round trip on the New Haven . . . Ransom's physical exhaustion makes him susceptible to an almost visionary insight as he continues painful self-analysis.

The author skillfully homogenizes bits and pieces of the priest's memory with the external actions that trigger their recall. In this detached interlude, Ransom begins to believe that he was driven to the priesthood by negative motives. . . . The Jesuit's uneasy truce with his doubts is finally shaped into a subtle composition of shadows and substance.

> *Martin Levin, in a review of "Tight White Collar," in* The New York Times Book Review, *April 9, 1972, p. 42.*

CORNELIA HOLBERT

There was a Jesuit named John L'Heureux who wrote several books of fine-boned poetry, who set before us *Picnic in Babylon,* a diary of the last three years before his ordination. . . . (p. 40)

When liturgical changes were in progress, L'Heureux's proposed canon was of such Franciscan quality that one can only marvel at its being ignored in favor of the four Eucharistic prayers chosen, pedestrian save for the phrase "pilgrim Church."

Tight White Collar is a diary-novel of one day in the life of a young priest, exhausted from pastoral work and writing, harassed by his mother into attending the wake of a distant relative. Ill and supersensitive to his environment in the train, in his parents' house, at the funeral home, he is dealt a mortal blow of misunderstanding by a former nun who had been his friend. When his gastric ulcer hemorrhages he is offered comfort by the one man he has openly avoided in the course of the painful day, a homosexual whose beat is the railroad station.

L'Heureux owes nothing to Bernanos, but it is no irreverence to either author to detect the pain and nausea of the country priest under the tight white collar. The rebellion an adult can still feel toward his parents he shows in anguished perfection: the almost hopeless revolt, the silent seething. One thinks of Merton's definition of original sin as the rejection of disinterested love. L'Heureux faces with damning courage his own weaknesses and his bitter dislikes; he despairs at the near impossibility of valid communication, at the damage a child can do to his parents and parents to their child—above all, at the damage each of us can, at any moment, do to all the rest.

One of the truths of life singled out in this novel is the malady Gehenno considers endemic among women and which Dr. Harry Stack Sullivan terms "alagonia": the proclivity for exchanging and relishing bad news. Could it be that this sickness affects us all, male and female, rich and poor—this sad-faced rejoicing in one another's sins and misfortunes, this spirit-killing censure (both public and private) which sets the ripples of dislike going from the venomous center infinitely outward? Could it be that in some small way we have all helped to drive a man from the priesthood or from his marriage, or a woman to her overdose of sleeping capsules—could it be? (pp. 40-1)

Love and peace to John L'Heureux, balm for his bitterness, flowering for his talents, and, in return, we watch for continuing publication by him and ultimately a great Christian novel. (p. 41)

> *Cornelia Holbert, in a review of "Tight White Collar," in* Best Sellers, *Vol. 32, No. 2, April 15, 1972, pp. 40-1.*

DORIS GRUMBACH

I have publicly and privately admired [L'Heureux] and his poetry. Now I am constrained to write a less-than-kind review of [*Tight White Collar*], which I very much *wanted* to like and resolved at the start to treat kindly.

I suspect that what goes wrong in this brief book can be traced to L'Heureux's optimistic premise that the reader will stay with a repellently self-involved, egotistical, uncharming, humorless and, what is worse, *dull* young hero-priest through five-sixths of the story in order to be present at his final epiphany about himself. Others with greater fictional skills—John Updike in *Rabbit Run* and Mary McCarthy in *The Groves of Academe*— have brought this feat off and written whole novels with unsavory heroes, but L'Heureux lacks Updike's beautiful prose rhetoric and Mary McCarthy's ironic skill. In this one long day's journey into night for the young Jesuit who goes home reluctantly to be present at the wake of a Protestant relative, the reader becomes impatient with the seeming pointlessness of the episodes and the milk-toast quality of the dialogue.

Even the realization that the flashbacks and forecastings, the talk and thoughts, are purposeful, that they are intended to demonstrate truths about Father Ransom, his friend Father Daniel, his family, his nun-correspondent, does not help the reader to bear their flat quality. For me the story itself fails in interest and in what Henry James demanded in fiction: intensity. To watch a hero vomit in a public bathroom, ironically helped in his agony by a homosexual, does not serve to persuade me of the genuineness of his new self-awareness; it is merely another episode, like the story told of the priest made mad by a night spent with a boa-constrictor. Both lack vital roots in a motivational compost which might have produced a living tale. I suppose what I am saying is that the novel has parts but no convincing whole.

This truth is, sadly, underscored by stylistic defects. I am one of those who dislike constant resort to sliding tenses in telling a story. . . . I am opposed as well to constant references to writing by a novel's hero when no part or sample of his work is given, especially since we are assured that Ransom's work ''would be widely and favorably reviewed,'' . . . and that, most improbable construct of all, the book would be called *Jesuit Letters to a Jewish Psychiatrist.* . . .

I can forgive Ransom's selfishness, his egoism, his lack of charity, his whole unsavory self in a way that John L'Heureux seemingly cannot. What I cannot forgive, the Lord and the author forgive *me,* is L'Heureux's thinking that he had here a novel, or the makings of a novel, or even a palatable subject for one. For myself, and readers like me, *Tight White Collar* is three or four sizes too small.

> Doris Grumbach, in a review of ''Tight White Collar,'' in America, Vol. 126, No. 23, June 10, 1972, p. 619.

MARTIN LEVIN

[In *The Clang Birds,* five] priests, members of an obscure order, decide to leave the seminary and set up a radical commune in a two-family house. . . . What this has to do with ''clang birds,'' what *they* are, you will have to discover from the author's whimsical epigraph. From me, you can have the disclosure that [*The Clang Birds*] is a bitterly funny once-over of relevancy and religion. After a year of protest, the score is relevancy 2, religion 3, two priests having left the church. . . .

Mr. L'Heureux's way with his characters is at once splenetic and sympathetic, if you can imagine such a parlay. He deplores hypocrisy and yet is kindly toward the hypocrites. Most of the action comes together in the trashing of a Selective Service office. In the end, the communards and a couple of liberated nuns are left wrestling with their consciences—and, occasionally, with one another—in a dazzling juxtaposition of ironies.

> Martin Levin, in a review of ''The Clang Birds,'' in The New York Times Book Review, October 8, 1972, p. 42.

RALPH McINERNY

[*Tight White Collar* is] the first of John L'Heureux's novels devoted to the religious life. . . . If the cheap shot were a literary genre, one would have to say that L'Heureux shows himself an unhappy master of it in *Tight White Collar* and his more recent *The Clang Birds.* The priests and nuns of these stories are a far cry from the characters in the saccharine novels once published by Bruce and Benziger; they are equally distant from those we meet in J. F. Powers and Edwin O'Connor or in what one is tempted to call the fiction of the Irish school; they have little in common with the priests of Mauriac, Bernanos and Greene. Bocaccio suggests a comparison, perhaps, but the world of L'Heureux is closer to that of Maria Monk and the Marquis de Sade. Whatever the surface phenomena, whatever the apparent softness and beauty of the religious vocation, L'Heureux is here to tell us that the hard and ugly nature of the lives of priests and nuns is a matter of booze and sex and selfishness, with little redeeming social value. We are asked to exchange the bodiless heroes and heroines of those Bruce and Benziger sagas for hollow soulless characters who move across a lunar landscape uttering smirking *double entendres,* their thoughts and language scatological, cloacal, lubricious, vinous. (pp. 184, 186)

Tight White Collar, rather a longish short story than a novel, gathering as it does to a murky epiphany on the part of the young Jesuit, Father Ransom, tells of a priest doing graduate work in Boston. Ransom despises his fellow man, begrudges any demands made upon him as a priest, seemingly confines his reading to *The New Yorker* and newsmagazines; he is a man wholly self-centered who should never have become a priest and by all the logic of the story should get out. He does and he doesn't. The opening passage of the novel, one extremely well-written and which promises so much more than the sequel provides, informs us that after the time of the novel Ransom does indeed leave and marry but, in the framework of the story, he decides to remain. The great difficulty of the story is that we are not provided with any vantage point from which to interpret what is going on. L'Heureux pays lip service to some ideal that Ransom does not and cannot embody but the net impression the novel leaves us with is that the ideal is illusory and unreal. Certainly none of the other characters embodies it. They are, if possible, more odious than Ransom himself. A curiosity of the narrative is that through other characters as well as the author himself, the suggestion is several times made that Ransom is a pleasant, attractive young man, eager to help others. There is no evidence whatsoever provided for such a view of him. When his epiphany comes his realization would seem to be that it is the world, and not himself, that is awry.

The Clang Birds is billed as a savage satirical novel about the bright young people in the Christian anti-war movement. It is also self-described as wicked and hilarious. At least one side of those dual descriptions of the novel is accurate. The *Tight White Collar* can be dismissed as unsuccessful and unsavory and slight. The failure of *The Clang Birds* is multi-faceted. Perhaps it was only seemingly to spare his former fellows, the Jesuits, but, by inventing the Order of St. Thomas, L'Heureux invites comparison with *Morte D'Urban,* and from this his novel can only suffer. St. Gomer, the founder of the Thomasites, is the source of the title. "The Clang Bird," he wrote, "is a rare creature that flies in ever decreasing circles at ever increasing speeds until with a terrible clang it disappears up its own ass. It is only because of the will of god that the Clang Bird is not extinct." Unfortunately, this passage effectively captures the level of wit in the novel. The choice of "clang" here, which is unintelligible, would not bother a writer of grafitti, but L'Heureux is a poet.

At the outset of [*The Clang Birds*] we are back in the Boston residence for Jesuits we encountered in *Tight White Collar.* A group of priests and scholastics, characters cut from the same cardboard as before, are given permission to set up an independent experimental residence. A sexual circus of overlapping rings with much self-dramatizing and confused self-examination is here offered as the hard and ugly underpinning of the anti-war movement. All the mandatory scenes are here: marches, meetings, the assault on the draft board office. Again, the difficulty is one of vantage point. All the mandatory scenes are here: marches, meetings, the assault on the draft board office. Again, the difficulty is one of vantage point. Are these characters found wanting with reference to a more adequate conception of the religious life? Are they found wanting by comparison with a more effective anti-war agitation? One who read *The Clang Birds* as a *roman à clef,* decoding in the direction of Berrigans and Sister Elizabeths, would be responding to a clear invitation. The book's message then is that those priests and nuns whose trials and tribulations you have been reading of are finally a group of horny lushes whose private frustrations have been transposed into a public key. But L'Heureux waffles on this and destroys the book's satirical potential.

The main reason that the book lacks a single attitude toward its characters, however unjust and however unestablished within the narrative, is that John L'Heureux himself intrudes upon the story. *Picnic in Babylon,* a book L'Heureux wrote while he was still a Jesuit, is passed around among the characters. . . . "The book eventually reached Reginald and disturbed him profoundly because he kept identifying with the author." . . . Since Reginald is the book's main character, it is difficult to avoid the realization that L'Heureux is the protagonist of this novel just as, masked as Ransom, he was of the first. Reginald, like Ransom, is *said* to be charming, . . . generous, kind, etc., but he is never *shown* to be any of these.

Tight White Collar would seem to provide the motif of both books. "It's not my fault and it's not theirs either. I was trying to do something that was too hard for me to do." The remark refers to the priesthood, but it can cover these two novels as well. . . . L'Heureux is perhaps too close to all this to effect the credible self-exculpation he is after. His novels do not suggest that the religious vocation is, while difficult, a worthy ideal of pursuit. Guilt is exorcized by portraying the priesthood, the Jesuits, the religious life, as so many masks which imperfectly conceal an egocentric sexuality, the latter being, so far as these novels are concerned, the hard and ugly nature of things. Nor is it only the priests and nuns who are distorted (and I mean distortion within the confines of fictive credibility).

L'Heureux's children are hideous grotesques, his few domestic scenes suggest unrelieved bitterness, vacuity, flaccid bestiality. Everything and everyone is as suffocatingly depressing as his world of religious graduate students. There is little point in discussing the massive lapse in taste and tact and charity these novels represent. It is enough that they fail as fiction and that is a fault that L'Heureux must shoulder as his own. (pp. 186-88)

> *Ralph McInerny, "Religious Life: Is It Really a Matter of Booze, Sex and Selfishness?" in* Commonweal, *Vol. XCVII, No. 8, November 24, 1972, pp. 184, 186-88.*

MARY ELLMANN

In *The Clang Birds,* John L'Heureux reminds me of Kingsley Amis: against one's will—because they are both so anti-liberal—one has to laugh at what they laugh at. Nobody wants particularly to reduce to mockery candidates for the Roman Catholic clergy or members of their congregation. I suppose L'Heureux is the first to exploit the new subject matter, which is the slipping grip of monastic and conventual life. His priests and nuns are heatedly against the war and hotly in pursuit of each other. When they all are not in bed, they are Protesting. Their effort, which I find more worthy than does Mr. L'Heureux, is antidraft and antiwar. If the young are preposterous, the war is more so, but Mr. L'Heureux is too jocular to admit the fact.

We follow a small group of what Mr. L'Heureux calls Thomasites, bent on a Protest Community, to 42 Oak Road, where their next door neighbors are the McReedys—the second target of the book, cruel but genuinely funny. . . . Although one wearies of the fledgling priests and their forbidden but still monotonous sex, one never tires of the McReedys. Their last action is to dynamite . . . , by inadvertence, one of the Thomasites. His exit drastically reduces the masturbation rate at 42 Oak Road.

> *Mary Ellmann, in a review of "The Clang Birds,"* in The Yale Review, *Vol. LXII, No. 3, Spring, 1973, p. 467.*

DORIS GRUMBACH

During the summer, the short stories of John L'Heureux appeared (*Family Affairs*) to precisely the kind of general nonnotice that such collections usually achieve. So I call this book to your attention, because of the unusual craft of L'Heureux's work and the uncommon amount of sensitivity, feeling, acutely accurate observation that results from his craft. When I first encountered him years ago he was a Jesuit and a poet. This new volume draws upon his religious experiences, his new (to me) achievement in narrative prose (I remember being not so impressed with his novel, *Tight White Collar* [see excerpt above]; I suspect short fiction is his metier), the material of his Boston years . . . , his departure from his Order, his often remarkable ability to make his characters agonizingly real. Whether he is writing about nuns, priests, ex-priests, an old plumber on his unhappy way to a home, . . . his qualities remain impressive. He can fix a situation to the page with a few sentences and then expand it, explore it, bring it to an inevitable conclusion—often by the use of a fine moment of epiphany—without striking a single false note. I liked most of these nine stories, and I can think of few serious readers who will not agree.

Doris Grumbach, *"Fine Print,"* in The New Republic, *Vol. 171, No. 11, September 14, 1974, p. 32.*

MICHAEL MEWSHAW

Family Affairs, a collection of stories by John L'Heureux, splits down the middle like a windfallen apple—one half bruised and unpalatable, the other ripe and relatively undamaged.

The first stories are variations on a single theme that inevitably involves fear, desperation and despair. L'Heureux has thrust his characters into a dark tunnel whose only exit is death, real or imagined. This might suggest tragic potential, but since all escape routes have been closed, the characters don't display their personalities through choice, and the action fails to move the reader to awe or understanding. Instead hopelessness appears on the first page and everything that follows reiterates this one emotion which is already attained.

In **"Something Missing"** a young pianist is tormented by his father, who berates him for lacking genius. At school the boy, who is ugly and Jewish, is tormented even more cruelly by both teachers and classmates.... Not a splinter of light intrudes. One doesn't wish for cheery brightness, only enough illumination to permit insight and a sense of chiaroscuro.

In **"A Family Affair"** a girl struggles through adolescence in a desert town.... [Her] story, told in a flat, monochromatic style, doesn't develop, doesn't deepen. It enlarges like a cancer and simply stops.

By sharp contrast, the stories in Part II are witty, vital and perspicacious. All five deal with priests, nuns and brothers who have left the church or are starting to have doubts. Since John L'Heureux was once a priest, it may be he feels on firmer ground when writing about the foibles of Catholicism. Whatever the reason, his style improves radically, gaining verve and texture, and his vision grows more acute.

In **"Swan and Fox,"** for example, an ex-seminarian's initial sexual encounter has obvious comic impact, but more importantly it achieves a neat balance between theology and biology, Jesuitical reasoning and physical imperatives, knowledge and experience, and masculine and feminine inclinations. This one story contains greater tension and irony, and leads to a profounder understanding than the grim earlier stories, which seem forced and at odds with L'Heureux's talent. (pp. 38-9)

Michael Mewshaw, in a review of "Family Affairs," in The New York Times Book Review, *September 15, 1974, pp. 38-9.*

CARMEN P. COLLIER

[L'Heureux] is a professional writer and his work has appeared in a number of magazines.

Consequently *Family Affairs* was appraised for the craftsmanship and the talent which we have come to expect of L'Heureux's work.... Each of the stories differs essentially from the others and the collection ranges from pathos to that subtle brand of humor which has been known as "Jesuit humor." The title, *Family Affairs,* follows closely that of the longest of the stories and perhaps the most tragic and the most disturbing in the collection.

John Gardner has said that L'Heureux observes real human beings and puts them on paper, pore by pore. In *Family Affairs,*

L'Heureux has done that in each counterpart of life as he depicts each being with clarity and compassion. With swift and precise control his vividly pictorial writing establishes mood and scene, with an economy of narration but with the authenticity of a documentary.

Carmen P. Collier, in a review of "Family Affairs," in Best Sellers, *Vol. 34, No. 15, November 1, 1974, p. 337.*

THE NEW YORKER

There is enough material for three or four novels in [*Jessica Fayer*], about an old woman whose life passes before her as she sits in a daze after being mugged on the streets of Boston. Unfortunately, there is far too much for one. Among the episodes in Jessica Fayer's life of which we have interesting but all too fleeting glimpses are ... [her] brief life as a nun, her unhappy marriage to a wounded war veteran, her sexual interest in a black hired hand, a long period in which she runs a boarding house for old people in Amherst, ... and, in the last few pages, another encounter, with a handsome Boston surgeon whose homosexuality she "cures." The flashbacks and flash-forwards required to keep all this going are, as may be imagined, dizzying, and though the author has a gift for quick characterizations, even his most interesting characters (like Mrs. Fayer herself) get lost in the blur of activity.

A review of "Jessica Fayer," in The New Yorker, *Vol. LII, No. 7, April 5, 1976, p. 135.*

WILLIAM B. HILL, S.J.

Weaving together the strands of life—to use a useful cliché—is the work of the novelist. [In *Jessica Fayer*], John L'Heureux starts with the year 1976, with a woman who, symmetrically, is seventy-six years old. He then floats out the strands, not chronologically but with a well-managed impressionistic technique, and ends with a clear picture of a complex history.

From the stunning dismay of a mugging attack in Boston's Louisburg Square, Mrs. Jessica Fayer goes back to Amherst, the last days of her nursing home and the decay of a brilliant namesake, and then to her days in the convent. Bit by bit, the people are made whole....

The picture is a clear one. Like others before him, however, L'Heureux has tried hard to blend the dancer and the dance. Jessica Fayer is not an overwhelming character, and much depends on the effectiveness of the technique—it is effective but how valuable is the experience it transmits? L'Heureux seems to be new to this sort of thing; wisely, he uses signboards for the years and does not attempt the masterful but not explicit time-blends of Old Master Faulkner.

The language of the novel is remarkably economical, spare without being sparse. The imagery is functional and occasionally trite. It is difficult to believe that the author did the proofreading and allowed "lays" for "lies" on page 86.

William B. Hill, S.J., in a review of "Jessica Fayer," in Best Sellers, *Vol. 36, No. 3, June, 1976, p. 71.*

JOHANNA KAPLAN

John L'Heureux's vision is eerie and unmistakably his own. . . .

[The short stories collected in *Desires*] are oblique, ironic moral fables, and they are written in a spare, elegant and witty prose. The tone is one of extreme detachment, a methodically distanced wry remove—as if all earthly passion and purpose were futile, the locutions of everyday speech necessarily hollow and any full-bodied, acknowledged emotion somehow absurd. "'What's the use,'" says the baffled academic husband in the story **"The Anatomy of Bliss."** "'What's the use of anything.'" He is not so much asking a question as offering up the despairing, flat, embittered refrain that haunts so many of the characters in this book. As Morgan Childs, the afflicted statistics professor in **"Witness,"** says: "There's no escape." For when we enter the world of Mr. L'Heureux's fiction, we are immured in a landscape of hopelessness and disillusion, a cruel and unforgiving place in which any commonplace pursuit—a professor teaching literature, a couple making love, an old woman having coffee—is a doomed and foolish hoax. It's not that these characters are staring into the abyss; but rather that the abyss has always been right there staring up at them, only they, unfortunate life-deluded fools, don't know it. They find out, though. (pp. 14-15)

Priests and ex-priests in these stories tend to fare better than anyone else, though their lives are no less anguished. But perhaps because their choice of vocation embodies a spiritual seriousness, Mr. L'Heureux endows his strange tormented priests and seminarians with complexity and compassion, giving them a resonant, compelling fictional life.

In **"Departures,"** a young man decides to become a priest because he thinks it will allow him to live in a world of "not feeling." On his first visit home after six years in the seminary, he is so repelled by the vulgarity of other people on the train that even though the sight of his waiting parents makes him think "they are a picture of order in all this chaos," he refuses to let his mother embrace him. The result of this betrayal, "the look of drowning in her eyes," will haunt him all his life, even breaking into his attempts at meditation.

The desire for transcendence is the preeminent desire in Mr. L'Heureux's fiction. Some of his characters seek it in mystical union with God. Mr. L'Heureux, in stories like **"Departures"** or **"The Priest's Wife"** (an astonishingly beautiful story, austere, shapely and imbued with a sense of wonder), achieves another kind of transcendence through his art. (p. 15)

> *Johanna Kaplan, in a review of "Desires," in* The New York Times Book Review, *April 12, 1981, pp. 14-15.*

DAVID J. LEIGH, S.J.

[In *Desires*, L'Heureux] has produced a volume of short stories that baffle those who have followed his career as poet, novelist and satirist. Of his poetry (all written in the 1960's while he was still a seminarian), James Dickey has said: "There is in most of his work a sense of the poet's going eagerly toward events and people, open-handed and open-hearted, wanting to understand and love" [see excerpt above]. This 'whimsically imaginative' strain in L'Heureux almost totally disappeared in his fiction since 1972, particularly in his novellas about priests, *Tight White Collar* and *Clang Birds*. It was replaced by a constant over-satirizing, a heavy-handed irony and caricature, two qualities that led critics and readers to dismiss these books.

Since taking up the short story, L'Heureux has achieved remarkable success. . . . In the present collection of stories from 1974-1980 [*Desires*], I find three varieties, almost exactly divided by the three sections of the book. In the first section entitled "Marriages," the stories offer clever but superficial portraits of frustrated couples, most of whose predicaments are subordinated to several innovative devices attempted by the author. The second section, "Mysteries," presents four fairly conventional stories, heavy with satire somewhat cynical in tone. . . . Despite L'Heureux' usual control and crafted sentences, the stories seem to manipulate their characters as if the author were fighting personal battles through them.

Only in the final section (plus, perhaps, **"The Priest's Wife"** from the first section) does L'Heureux recapture some of the imaginative 'happiness' found in his poetry and his journal, *Picnic in Babylon.* Amid the rather bizarre plots . . . we find complexity of character and suggestiveness of meaning missing in the earlier stories in the volume. Here L'Heureux manages to combine wit and warmth (despite continued authorial aloofness) to achieve an integration which he himself could not find in an article he wrote in the 1960's about the dilemma of the modern religious novelist. In that article he lamented the tension between his vocation as a religious to communicate compassion and his call as a modern writer to employ irony and detachment. Let us hope he can find new ways to resolve the dilemma.

> *David J. Leigh, S.J., in a review of "Desires," in* Best Sellers, *Vol. 41, No. 4, July, 1981, p. 131.*

PETER LaSALLE

John L'Heureux's 1972 novel *The Clang Birds* was a timely and entertaining satire showing the potential for excess in priests and nuns immersing themselves in the trendy social-cause scene in the 1960's.

In this new collection of 11 short stories [*Desires*], the best also are about the religious life or its lingering effects on those who chose to leave it. However, the mood here is more serious, more intriguing too. (p. 387)

In **"The Priest's Wife,"** a former nun marries a former priest, a troubled man who dislikes his job teaching at a high school. . . . He growls at her in frustration as he tries to write his own poems, and she supports him quietly and lovingly. Eventually she leaves him. She establishes a literary career for herself. . . . Years later, when each is more understanding of himself or herself, they decide to resume the marriage.

L'Heureux writes in [this story] with enough feeling, control and graceful language to remind us again what a marvelous form the short story is—how apt it is in its concision, for painting those halftones, conjuring up unexplained the important little mysteries that seem to characterize the complexity of contemporary life.

Actually, what disturbed me about reading this collection was realizing just how solid a L'Heureux story can be and then having to admit that several stories fail painfully. Sometimes the problem appears to be that L'Heureux is struggling to do what other, and very well-known, short story writers . . . already have done much better in their own special ways. Other stories do not work because the underlying premise is slick or, worse, presumptuous in trying to get at big issues with rather tawdry hipness. **"Consolations of Philosophy"** is a dull black comedy in which a stoical doctor in a nursing home engages in perfunctory sex with a stoical daughter of a patient who comes to visit her father there.

Conclusions? Well, as I said, when L'Heureux is good he can be quite good. (pp. 387-88)

Peter LaSalle, in a review of "Desires," in America, *Vol. 145, No. 19, December 12, 1981, pp. 387-88.*

DONNA KITTA

A Woman Run Mad is about educated, self-aware people whose very intensity of being—fears, visions, ambitions, fantasies—drives them into deadly circumstances. The plot is tight, suspenseful; the cast of characters superb, each offering an equally compelling perspective on the bizarre events that bring them together. Quinn, untenured professor/writer, finds inspiration and love with a glamorous shoplifter while epitomizing the selfishness inherent in the artistic temperament. Claire, his "too good" wife, is a raving success—scholar, author, professor, victorious dieter—who does, ultimately, rave. And then there's mad Sarah Slade, the shoplifter, driven insane by sexual horror. . . . Their interactions generate a mesmerizing, terrifying web of sexual struggle. Contemptuous of ambiguity, L'Heureux knows exactly what he means and how to say it. Bedtime reading this isn't.

Donna Kitta, in a review of "A Woman Run Mad," in Booklist, *Vol. 84, No. 6, November 15, 1987, p. 513.*

JOHN GROSS

John L'Heureux is an accomplished writer . . . and he knows how to keep a narrative moving. Both the action and the locales of *A Woman Run Mad* are firmly realized, in clear, economical prose: there are some telling psychological strokes; the characters' idiosyncrasies . . . are never allowed to degenerate into mechanical tricks.

But what does it all prove? At the very least, the book qualifies as a superior suspense story, but is it anything more?

The semi-philosophical conversations between Claire and Angelo represent a bid for high seriousness, I suppose; so do the classical allusions that prepare us for what is to come later in the book, the references to Dido and Medea. . . . But neither bid seems to me to get very far, and what counts in the end is simply the story itself.

It is the kind of story that might well have appealed to a writer like Patricia Highsmith, a drama of interlocking obsessions and overheated imaginations. But in Highsmith you would feel the full force of the characters' involvement with one another, by contrast, Mr. L'Heureux's neatly worked out tale reads like the blueprint for an obsession rather than the obsession itself. A fairly exciting book—but not much remains once the excitement has worn off.

John Gross, in a review of "A Woman Run Mad," in The New York Times, *January 8, 1988, p. C32.*

RICHARD EDER

If John L'Heureux had wanted an epigraph for his comic horror story, *A Woman Run Mad,* he could have used Goya's ambiguous inscription, in one of its possible translations: "The dream of reason brings forth monsters."

The book's four main characters represent in different ways the rational flower of our contemporary urbanity and the canker that eats it. They live in the gracious part of Boston, and they are more or less talented or charming or funny. The worst one is selfish and self-centered, but in a comfortably recognizable way. By the end of the book, they have fallen into madness and monstrosity.

In Sarah, a handsome and cultivated Brahmin, the madness is visible from the start, though misted by a vulnerable allure. Quinn, who taught English at Williams College and is now trying to write a novel, encounters her shoplifting a purse at the Back Bay branch of Bonwit Teller.

He is intrigued; and anyway, his writing is going badly. He follows her to her Beacon Hill apartment, only to be accosted on the doorstep by a young man [named Angelo] who makes a crude sexual overture. (p. 3)

[Sarah] some years earlier had killed and mutilated a sexually sadistic lover and had escaped jail by a judgment of temporary insanity. When, at the end of the book, we learn the details of Sarah's mistreatment and her reprisal, they are so terrible as to blur the lines between the two and arouse a kind of desolate sympathy for her.

The above may begin to tell us what L'Heureux, a moralist of untrammeled imagination, is doing. But it takes us a long way from how he is doing it.

The horror in *A Woman Run Mad* is both serious and extreme. But we get to it gradually, by way of premonitions in which we have no real trust, in the course of a book that is blithe, witty and so coolly laid back as to constantly tell us that nothing really awful can be happening. (pp. 3, 15)

The blitheness begins with Quinn and his wife, Claire. She has prevailed over handicaps—orphanhood, poverty and a tendency to get fat—to become a brilliant Latinist and win a tenured position at Williams. Quinn, on the other hand, is shallow and self-absorbed. . . .

There is an angry passion in Claire, but it is concealed—from herself among others—by a need to put aside her former ordeals and find gentleness and repose. . . . She clings to Quinn and is confident that he shares her commitment to marital coziness. For a while, we will get rather fed up with Claire.

Quinn does. Sarah's shoplifting seems exotic to him when he first spots her. So does the languorous and kinky sex she introduces him to when they finally get together. A touch of perversity is appropriate to the contemporary urbane. Even Angelo's cruising doesn't make him a monster, though it does get him savagely beaten up; he is genuinely kind to Sarah and loves to talk about ideas. . . .

Normality—as our time understands the word—and monstrosity are L'Heureux's poles, and he joins them with extraordinary dexterity. Sarah and Angelo, despite a sweetness that finally attaches us to them, are the monsters, seemingly. Quinn, despite his unlikableness, and Claire, despite her excessive striving, are the normal ones, seemingly.

The ending is not to be revealed, other than to say that it is bloody and grotesque and that normality and monstrosity become utterly indistinguishable.

But it is in his style as much as in his plot that the author manages to connect his opposites. *A Woman Run Mad* is, for much of the time, witty and almost lighthearted. L'Heureux treats his characters somewhat in the manner of Iris Murdoch; even in their most matter-of-fact moments, we feel a horror closing in on them without knowing where it comes from. Conversely, representing large and terrible things, they are chatty and crotchety and sometimes very funny indeed. . . .

L'Heureux, in a sentence, can convey enormous pain. Quinn has told Claire he will leave her. She walks out, swivels and tries to come back in; he holds the door shut against her. "They stood there, pressing wildly against one another, the heavy door between them," L'Heureux writes in a stunning reverse image.

The author is not always in full command of his odd and original novel. It bogs down in a series of internal monologues, particularly Claire's and Angelo's.

Having Claire discover a pistol in Angelo's bedside drawer early on, and introducing a peculiar little boy who spends his day sitting on the staircase and watching what is going on, may recall Chekhov's caution: Show us a pistol in the first act and we know it will go off in the last. Show us a watch bird at the start, we might add, and we know he will see something before the end.

A Woman Run Mad is quirky and unbalanced. Its excesses at the end hardly seem excessive, and that is the author's remarkable achievement. It is accomplished at the price of a large distancing.

It is hard to feel close to this talented book, which is clever most of the time and wise at least some of the time. It may be hard to love it. Perhaps it is not hard to dislike it. It is easy, in any case, to admire it and its author extravagantly. (p. 15)

> *Richard Eder, in a review of "A Woman Run Mad,"* in Los Angeles Times Book Review, *January 17, 1988, pp. 3, 15.*

LAURIE STONE

[*A Woman Run Mad*] got me going on page one and peeved me at the same time. It kept peeving me, all the while I was racing through it. . . . [L'Heureux has] written a piece of slippy pulp, but he wants it to seem fancier, so he hobbles it with lapsed Catholic maundering about God's abandonment, Kierkegaard, and Iris Murdoch. It's like running an editorial on the cancer-causing properties of beef right next to the meat-loaf recipe.

L'Heureux wants to have it both ways with the characters too: entreating us to care about them while playing up their most unlikable traits. . . . Claire is described as "witty, brilliant and acid-tongued," but the sentences she speaks don't amuse, or amaze, or bite. Quinn is described as "funny, lovable, and absurd," but his actions aren't comical, endearing, or puzzling. Sarah, who's allegedly a torch between the sheets, doesn't generate enough heat to light a match. And Angelo, the philosopher, is given to oh-wow insights. As the book chugs on, the portrayals grow even lazier. Sarah is reduced to a schizo space cadet, Angelo to a hell-bent masochist, Quinn to a rampant egotist, and Claire to a binging fat girl.

Claire's fatness is but a pimple amid the book's acne of female disgust. Men and women alike find women's bodies repellent. Although Quinn is shown to be a self-absorbed bastard, a fraudulent novelist who justifies betraying his wife as research for art, L'Heureux can't repress his affection for, his *understanding* of this man. L'Heureux lavishes more attention on Quinn's psyche than on any other. And while women get to murder men—supposedly evening the score with the beasts—the female characters still come off punished and deprived. Losing love drives them completely crazy, and they reveal they hate sex, body parts, and physical functions. . . .

But occasionally—like wild mint beside a compost heap—a bit of perspicacity crops up. Says Sarah's brother Porter, who survives a heart attack, "It's amazing how the fear of dying becomes just another fear—like losing at squash. . . ." However, the book's main pleasures—and they're seductive enough to raft you over its rocks—reside elsewhere. For one, in its *National Enquirer* cheesiness. Wacko heiress, famed for stuffing Latin playboy's severed parts in stolen purse, at it again, suitably summarizes the intrigue. The plot line, on the way to nothing . . . , nonetheless gallops. And steady pleasure bubbles from the delightfully whorey narrative voice. It invades every mind, every heart, every groin—with exactly the same glancing tone and shallow probe, but also with unflagging prurience and radar for the telling detail. . . .

This narrative voice is like having Joan Rivers inside every consciousness, including that of a grotesquely ugly, eavesdropping tot. The voice would talk from the perspective of a turtle if one figured in the story. As with overindulging in Joan herself, *A Woman Run Mad* won't make you fat or make your face break out, but it may make you hate yourself in the morning.

> *Laurie Stone, "Love You Madly," in* The Village Voice, *Vol. XXXIII, No. 8, February 23, 1988, p. 51.*

MADELEINE BLAIS

L'Heureux's characters have an engaging uniqueness [in *A Woman Run Mad*]. . . . Claire quite often speaks in Latin, and Angelo, the homosexual bodyguard, finds sex and Kierkegaard equally engaging passions.

These are nice touches that promise a less formulaic work, but ultimately *A Woman Run Mad* seems to rely on the tricks of the genre rather than transcending them. The ending is blood-soaked and not for the weak of stomach. The obligatory book-jacket blurbs invite comparison with Scott Spencer's *Endless Love*, presumably because both works share a certain compulsion to turn menstrual blood into a main character in certain pivotal scenes.

This remains a troubling book that will intrigue some and frustrate others. It has some elements of high art, some elements of pot-boiling page-turners. It seeks to marry the two, but this gene-splicing seems to have created something ugly rather than excitingly elegant.

> *Madeleine Blais, "A Quirky Novel Runs Wild," in* Chicago Tribune—Books, *March 13, 1988, p. 7.*

Ron(ald William) Loewinsohn

1937-

Philippine-born American poet, novelist, editor, fiction writer, and critic.

An author whose writings emphasize observation and fact, Loewinsohn utilizes idiomatic speech patterns and casual rhythms to celebrate objective reality and stress the commonality of human experience. Influenced by the verse of William Carlos Williams, Loewinsohn examines life's physical aspects, often exploring distinctly American landscapes, cultures, and artifacts while featuring musical analogies and structures. Employing counterpoint, repetition, and variation, Loewinsohn considers numerous topics, including love, marriage, sexuality, baseball, travel, and friendship, and probes such themes as the relationship between art and existence, the significance of imagination in daily life, and the nature of attraction and repulsion.

In his first volume of poetry, *Watermelons* (1959), which contains an introduction by Allen Ginsberg and a commendation by William Carlos Williams, Loewinsohn uses concrete visual imagery and colloquial language to interweave dissimilar elements and introduce his poetic concerns. In his subsequent works, including *The World of the Lie* (1963), *Against the Silences to Come* (1965), *L'autre* (1967), *The Step* (1968), *Meat Air: Poems, 1957-1969* (1970), and *Goat Dances: Poems and Prose* (1976), Loewinsohn extends the techniques and themes of his first book by blending poetry and prose, incorporating elements of Japanese verse, and examining, among other subjects, the nature of artistic experience, loss of innocence and youth, and the burdens of poverty.

In his first novel, *Magnetic Field(s)* (1983), Loewinsohn portrays the lives of several characters to examine the interconnections of human existence. Arranged in three sections, this novel initially centers upon a professional burglar who invades the private lives of strangers by breaking into homes, thus hoping to relieve his feelings of exclusion and loneliness. In the second section, Loewinsohn depicts events in the life of burglary victim David Lyman, a middle-aged avant-garde composer and musician. Section three reveals Lyman's discovery of his best friend's extramarital affair and concentrates on his imaginings of its details. Utilizing self-reflexive techniques, recurring phrases and motifs, and occasionally violent and disturbing imagery and descriptions, *Magnetic Field(s)* elaborates on such themes as the relevance of vicarious experience, the correlation between imagination and reality, and the significance of achievement and loss. In his second novel, *Where All the Ladders Start* (1987), Loewinsohn again focuses on David Lyman, depicting his mid-life personal and spiritual crises, his unfulfilling relationship with his family, and his affair with a twenty-year-old music student. Concerned in this work with examining the unforeseen consequences of an individual's actions, Loewinsohn offers, in Susan Braudy's words, "a passionate literary novel of one man's complex, painful and manic turning—at the sacrifice of his own safety and his family's peace of mind—toward what he comes to see as the love of his life."

(See also *Contemporary Authors*, Vols. 25-28, rev. ed.)

WILLIAM CARLOS WILLIAMS

Now I come to a great pleasure, the acknowledgement of some excellent poems, saluti! Nothing of that nature which is postponed is ever lost except due to a neglect on the part of an interested party and I do not want that.

My wife read the poems aloud to me last night. Part of one of them completely won us, **"The Stillness of the Poem."** The way you slowed down the third line and made it go over to the following line at the end did all that had to be done to me to convince me of your poetic gift. After that nothing will ever convince me that you can fail as a poet.

You have a difficult road to follow, but what poet has any different? And you alone know your fate unless you are turned from your course by events of the day which may discourage you. Technical problems that beset the modern poet, the division of the poem into lines is your own concern. So far you have shown great knowledge or sensitivity let us say for the line.

Your choice of words and images, is sensitive, accurate, fresh, you convince that you are actively searching for a particular effect and putting down only that which you have accepted, lie as it may upon the page. It's a fastidiousness which only the accomplished artist accomplishes and only at rare intervals. It is that that we in the end recognize. Civilizations which lack that, are damned, they cannot survive even when we have to take to the caves like animals to outlive them.

All your poems are not of the same character but in general their character is high. **"La Mer,"** is ambitious. It is worthy of all your study. Finish it, you will learn a lot in your art by persisting and using your wits to circumvent yourself in keeping a freshness in the attack. **"The Sea-Gull,"** is tops. The modesty and intelligence with which you refrain from touching draws you to the reader who feels that he wants to trust you. **"The Occasional Room,"** is very well done, trust your own instincts. There is lots more that might be said.

> *William Carlos Williams, in a letter to Ron Loewinsohn on April 8, 1958, in* Watermelons *by Ron Loewinsohn, Totem Press, 1959, p. 2.*

ALLEN GINSBERG

Ron Loewinsohn's first verse five years ago was vague. Then something happened: "The Daisy made recognisable / suddenly / by a flash of / magic light, the tongue / of fire, Pentecost." . . .

His verse began to sharpen into hard fact images, humane detail; his epiphanous Daisies & Seagulls recurred into poems. He fitted his prosody to what he wanted to say, began reading Williams to pick up on the half-century old tradition of American measure. It prepared a usable classical medium for him, & he saw it in time to eliminate bullshit. It's a rare thing for anyone to get anywhere, but he makes it.

He picked up on the technical competence abounding in 1956-San Francisco, and the local trust in Poetry. He's a romantic visionary, not afraid of his own senses—can transcribe his breakthroughs even if they come from his "own body in the shower." Not scared of a verbal jump—the Ox waking in the cellar "rusty and contemplative." Rusty, that's good. Eerie universal ear at moments: **"The Stillness of the Poem,"** "Portent, like / the sudden halt of great machines / Silence . . ." Exit from the **"Occasional Room"**—you can see he gets hung up on his actual experience and writes about it, wife, young job, & mystic melons. **"The Thing Made Real,"** a kid walking down the street dreaming of life, "Till it thunders into / the consciousness / in all its pure and beautiful / absurdity / like a White Rhinoceros." This is innate poetic understanding already, (age 21, almost a miracle) expressed without affectation (really a miracle.)

A great wave of Poetry is breaking over America now & Loewinsohn's early hip beauty helps wet everybody.

> *Allen Ginsberg, in an introduction to* Watermelons *by Ron Loewinsohn, Totem Press, 1959, p. 1.*

FELIX STEFANILE

[Ron Loewinsohn's work in **Watermelons**] is completely out of the mainstream of Official Culture, having by-passed the Donne-Eliot-Tate-&-Ransom steps to success for the lonely mountain path of William Carlos Williams. He indulges in all the risks of craft for the sake of love and rage, the thing said and finally said. This kind of awkward, grasping, aggressive talent doesn't stand a snowball's chances in hell of getting

"correct" publication, and if it weren't for the "small" press, he might be singing in the back-yards for all we know.

Yet he is easily better than the average doctoral candidate at the Ode Factory. Already, he has discovered a personal myth, always a valuable tension. . . . (p. 182)

[He] states

> Later
> on another road, I smelled myself
> the fetor of the living
> like locker room & loving beds

This may not be Lessing's "Ugly made Beautiful", but it is a far cry from the pretty toads, dead dogs, and old houses some of us have been raving about. In **"The Occasional Room"**, one of the strongest poems in this little pamphlet, filled with the saucy delinquence of youth meaning what it says, a touching mixture of love, poverty, imitations of Williams, and intense feeling really creates "New countries who beckon to us, / who aren't born until / we reach out & embrace them".

At his best, Loewinsohn fixes on the moment, visualizes, plays with normal speech cadences, particularizes by using modifiers, "red", "yellow", anything to catch the picture. Naturally, hero-worship goes too far, but he is not trying to reach across the centuries toward a dead language. What he is copying is not only available, but viable. If his "Spring not far enough / along to make a difference" is not original, his "God whom I resemble but am not" is as un-Miltonic as it is true. An introduction by Allen Ginsberg, a letter from Williams [see excerpts above], are interesting paraphernalia, and not necessary. Ron Loewinsohn is a poet in his own right, and I am glad for his future. (pp. 182-83)

> *Felix Stefanile, "The Angels of Discombooberation," in* Poetry, *Vol. XCVI, No. 3, June, 1960, pp. 179-85.*

DABNEY STUART

Ron Loewinsohn's visual vignettes [in **The World of the Lie**] give the effect of casualness. They are pleasant to read, but, because he is primarily interested in focusing his reader's sight, they lack the vitality of language that makes poetry. One feels he is either using the wrong medium (words) or the wrong form for the medium (poems), that he should be a motion-picture director or a story teller. Indeed, many of his pieces are about artists who create in other media, or about the media themselves: Bach, Miles Davis, Henry Moore, drawing. One would rather hear jazz, or see sculpture, than read about them. In this sense much of Loewinsohn's writing deals with artistic experience second hand. For the rest, the theory of the world of the lie he sketches in the title section of the book may be the stuff of a good novel. (p. 261)

> *Dabney Stuart, "Seven Poets and a Playwright," in* Poetry, *Vol. CIV, No. 4, July, 1964, pp. 258-64.*

JIM HARRISON

Ron Loewinsohn's **Against The Silences To Come** is a single poem of eight pages. . . . It is a strange poem and, I think, genuinely accomplished. Loewinsohn's poem reminds one of Eli Siegel's *Hot Afternoons* in the manner in which dissimilar events are woven together—in Loewinsohn's case, a parade, a murder in Reno, the sinking of a submarine, the actions taking place in a school playground across the street from the poet's window. The poem, addressed to his wife or mistress, in a deeper sense the source of the poet's music, makes the attempt to soften the intrusions, the texture of discord. The teacher in the schoolyard "raises the bullhorn to her lips as if to drink" and one shudders. The dismembered body in Reno will scream perpetually. Loewinsohn forces the events to swim through each other, becoming integral parts of the total harmony of the poem. It is an excellent, skillful piece of work. I hope it will manage to reach a larger audience than that intended by its pamphlet form. (p. 199)

> *Jim Harrison, "California Hybrid," in* Poetry, *Vol. CVIII, No. 3, June, 1966, pp. 198-201.*

WILLIAM DICKEY

Ron Loewinsohn accepts [in *L'autre*], if not entirely a poetry of accident, at least a poetry which is determined by the observed fact, rather than inventing or determining it.... Loewinsohn's exact honesty to what he sees and hears is in the tradition of William Carlos Williams; it assumes no essential difference between a colloquial voice and a poetic voice, though it allows the second to be a sometimes heightened form of the first. It also assumes, I think, an equivalency between poetic experience and general sensory experience: the poem becomes a form of our general consciousness, rather than a specialized consciousness of its own.

A good deal is gained here. Loewinsohn, with his attentiveness to spoken language, will not over-ornament, nor of course will he be tempted by the kinds of inflation that come from [some poets'].... confusion of the human and the divine.

But something is lost.... Loewinsohn's world is very alive and very clear in its *human* way—one cannot help admiring it and feeling affection for it. But Loewinsohn knows, as we all must, that sense of the other, of the transparent architectural shape and proportion which is reflected, clearly or unclearly, in the things we build. I don't yet see how he (or Robert Creeley, whom he admires) can deal with that architectonic. So far, their only effort has been by the implications of objects—the pattern of resonance of the haiku. Such a pattern may permit one to say or imply something about ideal presences, but it will not let what is said be very precise. Loewinsohn's language is over and over again true, accurate—accurate enough sometimes to be infuriating—but there is an area of ideal eloquence that is so far closed to him, yet which has a relevance to our lives. (pp. 696-97)

> *William Dickey, "Intention and Accident," in* The Hudson Review, *Vol. XX, No. 4, Winter, 1967-68, pp. 687-98.*

GERALD WILLIAM BARRAX

[*L'autre*'s] unity operates through the diversity of Ron Loewinsohn's subjects: marriage, baseball, music, travel, friends, and strangers. This diversity, modulated by the poet's daily concern for the concrete ("The abstractions fall away, / like shoes, lying there by the door / to my kitchen"), is responsible for the particular character of the book. What unifies Mr. Loewinsohn's work is that he is often saying the same thing over and over: something like *connect*. Yes, we've all heard that before; what he tells us is how simple it is—and deadly important. (The mottoes which preface the book take the form of a dialogue between Sartre and Jim St. Jim: "L'enfer, c'est les autres." "Oui, mais notre seule redemption reste entre nous

et l'autre.") In many of these poems there is a horror that screams against silence. In **"Toward"** he says, "We talk a damned lot & it goes / a long way toward saving us." But he suggests in **"Watch for Flag Man"** that we may all be saved by the absurdly simple act of noticing someone—like the old man with the red flag in the road work crew who pleads

> Take note of me, this red & yellow
> vest isn't an armor, but a visual aid,
> the better for you to see me with. Notice
> me standing here in your way, inconveniencing
> you. But notice me, see me. . . .

And the poet says "Ignorance is murder [and] suicide," remembering how a friend once turned away without returning his hello. Were it not for poems like **"Better Homes & Gardens," "Gentle Reader,"** and the almost surrealistic **"It Is Very Distinct at the Ballpark,"** I would be compelled to say that **"Against the Silences To Come,"** is Loewinsohn's most successful—a well-handled long poem that sometimes nags with the feeling that the poet didn't quite know what to leave out. (pp. 343-44)

> *Gerald William Barrax, in a review of "L'autre," in* Poetry, *Vol. CXII, No. 5, August, 1968, pp. 343-44.*

PAUL WEST

Ron Loewinsohn is an alert, sensual man fingering [in *Meat Air: Poems, 1957-1969*] the ephemeral configurations that each day brings: configurations of ball players, lovers, barbers, teachers, eaters, drivers, old women who water flowers. It's not euphony, syllable count, or symmetry that matters to him; it's the meticulous palping of givens, with the words not only referring to them but also pacing the eye during its tour:

> The cloverleaf isn't isolate but operates
> to serve the surrounding towns;
> 75 feet across US 101, a concrete subtle
> arch supported in the center by
> 3 square pillars set down single file
> in the dividing island of the roadway.

So "operates" in the first line has an intransitive phase; "subtle" in the third has briefly almost a noun's force; the arch in the fourth looks temporarily unsupported, and the three pillars seem for a little while unfounded. More obviously there is this:

> . . . boxes filled with
> wadded newspaper,
> each breakable thing wrapped in a husk of paper,
> blooming as we peeled it:
> a glass,   a vase,   an ugly,
> "gift,"   a pottery monkey,
> a red sandstone woman,
> a favorite cup.

Here the words enact the things' "blooming," and the eye has chance to linger, has an improved sense of the physical space they're in. Best of all, though, in this mode of decombination or disassembly, is **"Semicolon; for Philip Whalen,"** which begins:

> Semicolon ; like the head & forearm of a
> man swimming, the arm in foreshortened per-
> spective, his head looking away ;

Observant and ingenious Loewinsohn certainly is. As well as being an uncoyly appetitive erotic poet he makes room in his poems for what is measurable in its shoddiness (a girl picked up who has to be gotten rid of, maybe gently) or miraculous in its novelty (a urine dump done at sunset by astronauts freezes into tiny orbiting crystals that create a golden nimbus). Reverentially puzzling away at specifics, he writes poems that swell the mind, exercise the eye, and fill the palm.

> *Paul West, in a review of "Meat Air: Poems, 1957-1969," in* Book World—The Washington Post, *May 31, 1970, p. 6.*

WILLIAM H. PRITCHARD

There is nothing so high-minded as a sex snob: when Ron Loewinsohn tells us [in a poem from *Meat Air*] how it was with "the weight of your ass in both my hands, / your head thrown back & thrashing & your lips / forced open . . ." it's clear no joking around is to be permitted, for we are in the realm of Meat Air, sensations too deep for tears or laughter. But Loewinsohn also moves in less meatier realms, as when he sings to a famous man's wife: "Of course he'll love you Mrs. McCovey— / but will the swing of your hips / replace the swing of his bat?" or takes the time to render a moment with some care:

> The weather clear, late June afternoon,
>   the evening seeming to hold back
> for us, coming out of the Adirondacks
>   in that failing light we saw
> down in the valley a lake, in a lake's
>   shape, so still grey water in what
> light there was, down there among the trees. . . .
>
> ("**Lots of Lakes**")

The sentence is beautifully laid into the stanza, and you can see the point of all W. C. Williams' talk about how the line must change, the necessity matriculate. Williams, the presiding spirit behind this book, has perhaps helped Loewinsohn to see beyond the quirks of his own spirit. Which is in effect what Robert Creeley praises him for on the jacket, but he seems to me less pretentious than Creeley and does not stutter too much about The Language or The Poem, subjects on which too many shags have talked too much piss recently. (pp. 566-67)

> *William H. Pritchard, in a review of "Meat Air," in* The Hudson Review, *Vol. XXIII, No. 3, Autumn, 1970, pp. 566-67.*

JAMES ATLAS

Ron Loewinsohn's book, *Meat Air,* dedicated to William Carlos Williams, from whom he seems to have learned a great deal about poetics, is a compendium of four small-press editions published over several years, subtitled *Poems 1957-1969.* Loewinsohn is highly stylized in his work—even consciously archaic, as in the "**Book of Ayres**", a chapter of love poems. Complex and circumspect, or cautious, he takes in his hands various reports about life in our time, and transforms them, assigns them meaning. . . . His prose poems ("**The World of the Lie,**" *L'Autre,* "**Hope Springs,**" and "**The Sipapu**") are as self-conscious as his lyrics, and as precise; nothing seems random or diffuse. Allusions to Rimbaud ("If the season is hell"), to Blake (the "dark satanic mills of enterprise"), to Frost (a poem called "**The Silken Tent**"), are interspersed with constant reference to what surrounds us in America; "a parade, a murder in Reno, / a sub lost in the Atlantic". Rather than simply ignoring our inheritance, Loewinsohn revives its uses, and claims them as his own. (p. 49)

> *James Atlas, "What Is to Be Done?" in* Poetry, *Vol. CXIX, No. 1, October, 1971, pp. 45-51.*

LISEL MUELLER

There are prose pieces and poems in Ron Loewinsohn's book [*The Step*]. He writes good prose, energetic and witty. The trouble is that many of the ostensible poems are really prose too, the rhythms prosy and the language and treatment literal. On the other hand, Mr. Loewinsohn tries his hand at various styles, and he can come up with a luminous, flowing poem ("**Royal Blue**") and a poem of pure grace ("**The Distractions; the Music**"). I also thought "**Backyard Dramas, with Mamas;**" "**The Sea, Around Us;**" "**Lying Together . . . ;**" and "**Another State**" successful. These poems don't really contain any more imagery than the rest, but they succeed by the way they *move.* (Movement—not meter, but in a larger structural sense involving pace and gravity—seems to me to be the most important, yet least analyzed, element in poetry; perhaps it is the least analyzable.)

Altogether this is a likable book, breezy, friendly, often playful, some of it pastiche and collage, its plethora of sources cheerfully and scrupulously acknowledged. There is lots of fun and games, including the dedication to no less than thirty-five people, including Aristotle and Philip Whalen. (p. 298)

> *Lisel Mueller, "Five," in* Poetry, *Vol. CXXII, No. 5, August, 1973, pp. 293-98.*

CONNIE FLETCHER

While Loewinsohn frequently bewails the "poverty of language," his range and style are among the most expressive in contemporary verse. *Goat Dances* alternates between sensuality and higher self (intellect) which he finds equally baffling. Loewinsohn's philosophical excursions can sparkle over some fine point of intellect, while erotic poems have the ease and softness of the best Japanese poetry. Many readers will find this "inside-out" perspective fascinating.

> *Connie Fletcher, in a review of "Goat Dances," in* Booklist, *Vol. 73, No. 12, February 15, 1977, p. 876.*

ANATOLE BROYARD

Only a first novelist, one with five published volumes of poetry behind him, would be brash enough to tackle the kind of theme Ron Loewinsohn has taken on in *Magnetic Field(s).* His male characters are all investigating, in their separate ways, the texture of their lives, the structure of the things we call happiness, or belonging.

Of course, this is what all novels are about in a sense, but Mr. Loewinsohn is explicit about it. He interrogates being as if he were playing ontology on a piano.

He begins *Magnetic Field(s)* with Albert, a thief who uses stealing only as "a public reason" for entering other people's houses and feeling there the thrill of their being. Albert becomes more and more involved in the houses themselves, less and less in the stealing. He lights a cigarette and looks at television, uses the bathroom, pokes around searching for the occupants' secrets.

After Albert is arrested, Mr. Loewinsohn moves on to David, a composer who takes down Albert's license number as he is driving away from an aborted burglary of David's place. David is a composer who includes the environment in his "music": "The imperfect fifth" of a house "cracking its joints" as it settles, or the noises of the woods behind his property. Through art and technology, David rediscovers his environment, or the texture of his life. He rediscovers it on a conscious plane, appreciates it in a more complex, theoretical way, rather like Andy Warhol with his paintings of soup cans.

Magnetic Field(s) is full of the sorts of correspondences, parallels or universals that are dear to poets. The various characters in the book repeat one another's gestures under slightly different circumstances, as if the author were trying to get at the human constants we all live by. When Daniel, a close friend of David's, begins having an affair with Connie, a former student, he invents an entire new life of squash games, night classes and fishing trips to explain his time with Connie to Annie, his wife. And this invented time gradually drains the reality out of his real time with Annie so that he can leave her. His cover stories make him feel like a criminal, like Albert, and this gives his affair with Connie an additional dimension of forbiddenness.

Daniel achieves what the philosopher Arthur C. Danto calls "the transfiguration of the commonplace." But David wonders what it costs Daniel to do this. Where does he really "have his being?" David wonders. And we wonder too: Is Daniel just talking to himself in his affair with Connie, making love like a character in a novel he has "written"? How can we tell what is real and what is art? David asks himself. And perhaps the answer is that we cannot, that life and art are inextricably tangled, and that most of us suffer from an overdose of one or the other.

Mr. Loewinsohn knows how to conjure, how to surprise the reader, which may be the best, or at least the rarest, of the novelist's talents. But he's still too much of a poet, too fond of modulations and musical structures. His book is too tense with too many meanings. As Wallace Stevens, another poet, put it, he is "too conscious of too many things at once." The same is true of his characters: They think too much and do too little. They seem to have almost no ordinary existence.

Yet these are lovely flaws, excesses of the author's imagination, an overeagerness to give us something, everything. Reading *Magnetic Field(s)*, one is reminded of a line from Paul Valdry's *Mister Head*, whose protagonist says, "I know my heart by heart." Though there is both pride and sadness in the line, Mr. Loewinsohn need not be sad. If his book is not altogether a success, it is only because he is too much in love with knowing, with consciousness, which is exactly as it should be in a first novel.

Anatole Broyard, in a review of "Magnetic Field(s)," in The New York Times, *June 22, 1983, p. C24.*

TOM LeCLAIR

Ron Loewinsohn brings us into his remarkably poised first novel [*Magnetic Field(s)*] with the traditional attractions of crime and suspense. We enter the book with a burglar entering a house. But once inside, we cannot remain voyeurs. Rather we are compelled to circulate among the book's parts to recognize and even help produce the power, intricacy and mystery that the novel generates. (p. 1)

Mr. Loewinsohn, the author of five books of poetry, has some high-tech predecessors in fiction. Though not nearly so exhaustive in his science as Thomas Pynchon in *Gravity's Rainbow* and not as devious with the reader as John Barth and Robert Coover, Mr. Loewinsohn synthesizes their experimental energies. *Magnetic Field(s)* is a second-generation model, a compact system designed for home use, deeply attentive to daily American particulars as well as to the structures that contain and energize them.

Magnetic Field(s) has three sections, a form rather than a plot. In the first, we are in the mind of Albert Boone, a 25-year-old skilled burglar who enters San Francisco homes and then attempts to enter the owners' lives by pocketing personal objects and leaving some sinister trace of himself behind. (pp. 1, 23)

Through the details of Boone's professionalism and the acute observations of the lives in which Boone can intervene but not participate, Mr. Loewinsohn creates in fewer than 50 pages a frightening and sympathetic figure of urban life. Boone wins our sympathy as well as our fear, because the magnet that draws him into his victims' homes is not money or drugs but the hope of shelter, relief from what he calls his "exclusion," his loneliness. . . .

Part Two begins with David Lyman returning home to find Boone coming out of his San Francisco house. It then quickly shifts to the 40-year-old Lyman's life with his wife and adolescent son in a rented summer house in New York's Hudson Valley. Now Lyman becomes a kind of prowler and thief, discovering the house's secret rooms and hidden life. He steals ideas for his avant-garde music from the noises of the house and reconstructs out of odd-lot materials—old correspondence, gossip, physical objects—the relation between the house's owner, Charles Mortimer, and Mortimer's prodigy son, who was killed in a freak accident at the age of 12.

The affecting story of Mortimer and his beloved son, framed by Lyman's more distanced relation to his own son, is about the desperate spaces—playrooms, tree houses, secret studios—parents make to preserve, perhaps seal off, intimacy with their children. It's also about the killing rage one feels against intruders upon this intimacy. In reconstructing Mortimer's story, Lyman discovers that Mortimer killed *his* intruder, Anthony Blaquere, the truck driver who ran over his son and who, in one of the novel's many coincidences, has the same initials as Lyman's own threat, Albert Boone. "How many lives could he stand in the middle of at once?" Lyman wonders, without realizing that the middle of his own life is even more complex than he suspects.

Along with the analogies between Lyman and Boone and between Lyman and Mortimer, the reader finds, in this middle section, not only objects but phrases and whole sentences repeated from Part One. Roland Barthes said that avant-garde literature resists consumption by refusing to answer the question "Who speaks?" Mr. Loewinsohn plants the question and ultimately shows its uselessness, for an answer would take the reader outside the novel for some single cause or authority or explanation. Inside the novel, inside the magnetic field, it's the ever-changing, reciprocal and multiple relationships that matter, leaving the reader to measure the lines of force among the characters, to trace the circular patterns of their invention of each other and consider the mystery of their attraction and repulsion.

This description may make the novel seem dauntingly abstract or difficult, but it's no molecular paper chase. Mr. Loewinsohn's metaphor and method are absolutely right for his realistic, almost commonplace themes: How imaginative participation in others' lives can be both sympathetic understanding and egotistical domination, how projection of our secret desires and primal fears onto others is a way of rehearsing desire and evading fear, how our spaces are conduits and enclosures, windows and mirrors. Loss is the emotional center of *Magnetic Field(s)*—loss of privacy, of a child, of a friend, of self. Mr. Loewinsohn imagines the imagination trying to fill the empty spaces that those losses leave in our lives. He wants us inside the novel to see to it that we try too.

Immediately accessible and yet coiled with secret connections, *Magnetic Field(s)* occasionally gets caught between these intentions. In the third section of the book, which circles back to the San Francisco settings of the first section, Lyman discovers that his best friend has been having an extramarital affair. . . .

Lyman then imagines the details of his friend's affair, but while this invention is readily believable, it doesn't have the alien precision of Lyman's earlier imaginative appropriation of the spaces and objects and emotions that defined Mortimer's life.

Mr. Loewinsohn's arrangements are intricate—"the rose in the steel dust," says a character, referring to the pattern a magnet makes of iron filings—but the novel's language, perhaps too carefully obeying large structures, lacks the shading of the live flower. And the book's self-reference, its artists on art and in art, sometimes explains too much. But these are only flaws. *Magnetic Field(s)* is humanely imagined and mathematically constructed. It should be entered. (p. 23)

> *Tom LeClair, in a review of "Magnetic Field(s),"*
> *in* The New York Times Book Review, *July 31,*
> *1983, pp. 1, 23.*

IRVING MALIN

Magnetic Field(s) is, on the surface, a study of attraction and repulsion, a perverse exploration of "entries" or, to use the common term, "break-ins." The novel is divided into three sections: in each one we have the sense that privacy is being invaded, that souls (and properties) are attractive because they offer spiritual—and, of course, monetary—consolation to the criminal.

Loewinsohn, however, turns things upside-down. His criminals and victims are "married"—hence the novel's title—and need some kind of communication, some *environment* in which they can share "poles". They are caught in action-fields. Thus Albert, the common criminal and Daniel, the middle-class citizen, are subtly united as the novel, moves slowly, surely, circuitously from one to the other. They—and their creator—apparently reflect similar thoughts; they are echoes.

Loewinsohn goes one step beyond. By writing Albert, Daniel, and indeed, all the other characters in the novel, he creates a total environment, a field in which language itself is borrowed. One character echoes another; all echo the author. Reading the novel I become part of the field, another invader of consciousness.

> *Irving Malin, in a review of "Magnetic Field(s),"*
> *in* The Hollins Critic, *Vol. XX, No. 5, December,*
> *1983, p. 15.*

MARK ROYDEN WINCHELL

Magnetic Field(s) reads like what it is—the first novel of a talented poet. It possesses the concision and suggestiveness that we associate with the best modern poetry. (Indeed the paltriness of Loewinsohn's narrative line makes his book less a novel than an extended prose poem.) Although we gain various degrees of access to the consciousness of several characters, Loewinsohn's third-person narrative voice provides the novel with a consistent tone. As a result what his characters see (or imagine) becomes part of a seamless tapestry woven by self-effacing—if not entirely anonymous—hands. Yet the narrative reality of any scene in that tapestry is, at best, provisional.

Loewinsohn has elaborated upon a common motif in modern fiction—the subjunctive imagination. From Conrad onward novelists have bestowed a projective omniscience upon their narrators. A perceiving consciousness will imagine the thoughts of other characters and fabulate scenes that it has not witnessed. Thus the objective events of the story become less important than the narrator's own subjectivity. By giving us two centers of consciousness and very little enveloping action, Loewinsohn makes the act of fabulation itself the focus of his novel. (pp. xliii-xliv)

Consequently *Magnetic Field(s)* is a self-regarding artifact that is its own excuse for being. Its central image is a model-train set surrounded by a village that contains a house like the one in which the train is found. Open up the house and you see a representation of a train set surrounded by a village that contains a house . . . (p. xliv)

> *Mark Royden Winchell, "Other Voices, Other Runes,"*
> *in* The Sewanee Review, *Vol. XCII, No. 2, Spring,*
> *1984, pp. xliii-xlv.*

LINDA W. WAGNER

Magnetic Field(s) orchestrates the intersection of several characters' lives, trying on its own terms, as the novel says, to bring readers inside those fields ("If you stand outside it, all you can see is the *effects* of its being there, the designs of the iron filings . . ."). The attempt is all the more interesting because it ties together several fields, and thereby shows the inveterate relatedness of all human motivation. . . .

The taut novel is connected not only by this ostensible action, but, more effectively, by fragments of vision (a woman draped over the arm of a chair, about to be invaded; a toy seal made from some tinny kind of metal); by repeated descriptions; even by repeated names and characters (the dedicatee appears too as a character in the text, much as Norman Mailer appears in the movie *Ragtime*). Self-reflexive fiction seldom works as well as this: Loewinsohn's patterns are surprising; they further the action, and call attention to his presence as author with humor rather than with self-consciousness. Yet the reader is eventually conscious of the written work as performance (as Daniel, the most aware of the characters, notes toward the end of the text: "Daniel regretted only that all this acting, this performance, was going unacknowledged. . . . A job of acting presumed an audience aware that the actor is playing a role"). And Loewinsohn succeeds too in drawing characters that are able to exist independent of judgments—the burglar is shown to be much like the stable composer; whereas the composer's best friend, who leads a double life with mistress and wife, echoes the base behavior of the truck driver who runs over a child and never admits it. Social, moral categories prove unreliable, established and then destroyed by the moving fabric of Loewinsohn's seemingly straight-forward narrative.

From the sheer excitement of the house-robbing narrative (complete with deaths of both human beings and animals), to the introverted life story of the child genius and his history-professor father, to the mirroring coupled and coupling fables of the third segment, *Magnetic Field(s)* assumes a vision of the world that appeals because of its honesty. People *can* perform to their best or to their worst qualities, and often their "success" or "failure" does depend on influences as intangible as their place, their surroundings. For Loewinsohn's novel is aptly named: all his characters derive strength, or madness, from what is around them—woods, walls, secret rooms, yards—and from the sounds of those surroundings. It is no accident that several of the main characters are composers, creating works as individual as their psyches, as impermanent as their sojourns on earth. And just as they attempt to find a way of recording their sense of life, so does the novelist. As Loewinsohn has Boone think, mulling over his attraction for the house *per se* that he robs, "what was so exciting about being in the other houses where people were living was just the fact of standing in the middle of someone else's life." The reason we all read, to capture someone else's life, is admirably achieved—in every section—in this novel. . . .

In this novel, . . . Loewinsohn pays tribute to, but goes well beyond, [William Carlos] Williams' "no ideas but in things," as he creates the essence of place, home, character (or of placelessness, homelessness, characterlessness) through the very things of our tepid existence. But in *Magnetic Field(s)* the objects shift, they appear and disappear, they show themselves as mutable as personhood. Loewinsohn reaches dimensions Williams and our other great modernists would never have attempted. For his aim seems to be to re-create the enormity as well as the immensity of human consciousness. The amazing point to be made is that this novel succeeds in that aim, and that we are left with the fragments of a civilization that coalesce to give us moments of audacious brutality, set consistently in a narrative that assures us of affirmation. The last character of the novel, finally, does *not* injure the animals. It is a small achievement, but it is a rare, and an exceedingly human, accomplishment.

> *Linda W. Wagner, "Orchestrated Lives," in* The American Book Review, *Vol. 7, No. 4, May-June, 1985, p. 15.*

LAURA D. KUHN

It is perhaps unfair to judge one book by another, but given that Ron Loewinsohn's second novel, *Where All the Ladders Start,* is a quasi-sequel to his first, *Magnetic Field(s),* one can't help but look back comparatively—and with a bit of longing.

For unlike *Magnetic Field(s),* which was violent and disturbing drama, *Where All the Ladders Start* is a relatively uneventful story of a not entirely successful composer/conductor, David Lyman, who, in the throes of mid-life crisis and assisted by a young composer/musician lover, struggles to piece together a psyche alarmingly fragmented by long-term marriage with a preoccupied nuclear freeze groupie and a son possessed by punk rock. The weakness is not in the time-worn tale, but in the central figure, who is simply not interesting in Loewinsohn's treatment. After reading *Magnetic Field(s),* from which Lyman emerged, one may also question the choice of protag-

onists here—any number of other characters, left beautifully suspended, could have provided stronger substantive material. Loewinsohn's second novel does share a propensity for music with his first, but while *Magnetic Field(s) is* music—with rich, tonal subjects masterfully intertwined into a fugue-like structure—*Where All the Ladders Start* is simply *about* music, the objectification of which falls surprisingly flat.

> *Laura D. Kuhn, in a review of "Where All the Ladders Start," in* Los Angeles Times Book Review, *June 14, 1987, p. 4.*

MICHIKO KAKUTANI

Ron Loewinsohn's intricately patterned—and highly praised—first novel *Magnetic Field(s)* (1983) introduced us to several male characters whose intersecting lives provided variations on the themes of vicarious living and loss. . . .

A sequel of sorts to that earlier novel, *Where All the Ladders Start* is less concerned with the pressures that other peoples' lives exert on our actions, than with the unforeseen consequences that our actions have on those we love. Like *Magnetic Field(s),* it relates ordinary, domestic events in a coolly formalistic style; and like *Magnetic Field(s),* it uses musical devices—refrains, counterpoint and cross-rhythms—to invest its characters' actions with added resonance. It catches up with David Lyman as he's preparing to embark upon an affair—much like his friend Daniel's.

Though he's reviled Daniel's actions as the silly self-indulgences of a confused middle-aged man (and consequently terminated their 20-year friendship), David also realizes that he's envious of Daniel's decision to start over. He realizes that his own life has slid into a boring, unfulfilling rut: his wife, Jane, has become so absorbed in her antinuclear protest work that she has little time or energy left over for him; his son, Danny, is drifting out of reach, caught up in the urgencies and secrets of adolescence, and his own work as a composer has started to reflect his spiritual malaise—it's been years now since he's written anything truly daring or new. . . .

How does David cope with this realization? Fairly predictably, it turns out. He develops severe headaches, spends more and more time alone in his studio and he begins fantasizing about a new member of his music group—a pretty college student by the name of Ginny. He and Ginny begin talking after rehearsals. They meet for tea. They find they like one another. Time passes. Ginny inspires David with new ideas for his work. He helps her win an award. More time passes. They sleep together. Their surreptitious meetings grow more elaborate. David figures it's a nice, safe, manageable affair—it can't get out of hand since he's married and she has a boyfriend out of town. Then he discovers that he's fallen in love.

As Mr. Loewinsohn recounts these events, we notice that his characters are constantly repeating themselves, and as their conversations and actions loop back and forth in time, a sort of echo chamber is created that leaves us with a constant sense of déjà vu. This applies not only to the overall shape of the narrative (David's unwitting duplication of his friend Daniel's choices), but also to small bits of observation and phrasing. David's sad meditations about some discarded clothing found in a church basement are echoed some 40 pages later by Ginny's celebration of vintage fashion, just as one of his early come-on lines ("Isn't what's real always better?") is later echoed by a sobering self-assessment: "He had not felt real himself before he'd fallen in love with Ginny, and now that she was gone, there was no one for whom his own reality, his own experience of the world, had an inside.''

Just in case we fail to notice such patterning on our own, Mr. Loewinsohn inserts various statements about technique in his characters' mouths. Referring to a certain piece of music, David talks about how ''the incremental repetitions created a pattern that dissolved time, in which it was always *now*.'' And Ginny later tells him that she likes the part of his composition ''where you've got the same theme in all the different time signatures all going at the same time.''

In a richer, more detailed story, such self-conscious references might just seem like extra icing on the cake—clever, if superfluous jokes, shared by author and reader. In *Ladders,* however, there's little else to sustain our attention. The language in this volume is less poetic than in *Magnetic Field(s)*—for the most part, it's plain, flat-footed prose, garbled here and there by sentimental excess (''The water of life,' he said, handing her the whiskey bottle, feeling his whole body smiling.'') Further, the experimental innovations of the earlier book have grown attenuated, leaving us with the bland, generic characters of high-tech fiction, unsupported by the full complement of narrative pyrotechnics they need to really function.

What then does the reader think of *Ladders* in the end? Frankly, one's inclined to echo the assessment of Ginny's composition offered by one of the characters in the novel. ''David, the piece is pleasant,'' he says, ''but it doesn't go anyplace, it doesn't develop any of its material. It just seems to go around and around.''

> *Michiko Kakutani, in a review of ''Where All the Ladders Start,'' in* The New York Times, *June 24, 1987, p. C25.*

SUSAN BRAUDY

In *Where All the Ladders Start,* his persuasive second novel, the poet Ron Loewinsohn spills all the details of a passionate love story. Mr. Loewinsohn is so brilliant at describing dangerous new romantic feelings that I suspect he (like his cerebral and married third-person narrator) has just waked up to feel his heart beat.

In his first, acclaimed novel, *Magnetic Field(s)* Mr. Loewinsohn told part of the story through the eyes of a demonic burglar and then switched third-person narrators to the husband upon whose family the burglar intrudes. (That husband, David Lyman, and his family are pretty much the same bunch portrayed in this new lyric novel.)

But this time Mr. Loewinsohn really probes the innards of David, a self-absorbed, middle-aged head-of-family who falls in love in every way you can possibly imagine with his adoring student. The difference between the 20-year-old composer and flute player Ginny Johnson and nearly everybody else in the world is that she isn't making any deals—she is simply willing to give David everything she has.

Before he discovered his student David was bleak because nobody paid attention to his composing. He woke up at the side of his wife, Jane, every morning with a depressed ''goddamn'' on his lips. (To Mr. Loewinsohn's credit, I like Jane, an overworking woman whose sour reserve vanishes at antinuke rallies.)

The book opens in the late-night solitary moment when David realizes that after a year of linking up at the soul and the brain, he and Ginny Johnson will have a physical affair. David vows to control his passion; it will not destroy—that is, change—his life.

It was while rehearsing his small chamber orchestra in the dismal church basement full of cartons of discarded clothing that David observed his new flute player. Respecting her musical intuitions, David found himself studying the way her tongue licked her flute mouthpiece. But the girl with Southern twangy music in her voice, nice little breasts and green eyes didn't strike him until she said how much she loved and imitated his music. (No wonder he respects her intuition—it's based on his own.) In fact, Ginny thanks him, confessing that she is the anonymous composing student for whom he fought to award an important prize.

Now, a year later, David finds Ginny at her birthday party kneeling to dig ice cubes out of a cooler. Suddenly she ''was holding his head and kissing his face, her close-cropped hair tousled and her eyes wide with a kind of excitement she couldn't have controlled even if it had ever occurred to her to want to try.''

David's mind skids. Then he exults. ''Had he ever made anyone this happy simply by being there? It was like asking for an apple and getting the whole orchard.''

Unreal? Right? Wrong? What will happen to David's new high energy when they first (Heaven forbid) disagree?

Don't worry for now. Just enjoy the book. The sex scenes, for instance, take lusty poetic license. They are first-rate as are all of David's ruminations (except alas for the few paragraphs of musical description).

A more objective novelist might force David to worry that his marital decay is his fault. To put it mildly, our David doesn't share easily. Wrapped up in his reveries, David just keeps asking his sullen wife to stop her chores to listen to music. But before I lapse into egalitarian bickers, let me add that Mr. Loewinsohn's verbal skills forced me to accept his premises.

Throughout the book, David affirms his love for nearly all sounds except those punk music noises his son makes. But finally, purged of resentment and high as a kite on his new feelings, David weeps with his wife at their son's punk concert: She shouts into his ear over the music, '''We *made* that!' He could not stop crying. He could not speak. He nodded. Oh, damn.'' However, true to form, David accepts the punk music by congratulating himself that it is he who taught the boy to rebel musically.

It is very much to Ron Loewinsohn's credit that he has written such a passionate literary novel of one man's complex, painful and manic turning—at the sacrifice of his own safety and his family's peace of mind—toward what he comes to see as the love of his life.

> *Susan Braudy, ''Heating Up at the Cooler,'' in* The New York Times Book Review, *July 19, 1987, p. 14.*

JACK SULLIVAN

Loewinsohn's [*Where All the Ladders Start*] is an allusion to Yeats' ''The Circus Animals' Desertion,'' which identifies the ''foul rag-and-bone shop of the heart'' as the source of all that is important in life and art. When 43-old David Lyman, a San Francisco composer and conductor, begins having an affair with Ginny, a 20-year-old flute player, he assumes it will be brief and that no one will get hurt. But gradually he falls in love, a process so sweetly intense that it obliterates the tenuous happiness he enjoys with his wife "like one melody drowning out another."

As this simile indicates, Loewinsohn is fond of musical analogies and scenarios, some of which are ingeniously embedded in the structure of the story. Something of his method is suggested in David's obsession with the Bartók Third String Quartet, which he listens to in his car as he drives to Ginny's apartment and which features "two versions of the same theme playing catch with each other in a fugue . . . Both versions move toward the same point of resolution; they would get there at the same moment, although by different routes."

Indeed, very often in the novel different versions of the same experience play catch on the page, usually in the form of brief images or memories. This is not to say that *Where All the Ladders Start* is a cold, technical book. The tone is seductively romantic and many of the musical analogies are intensely sexual, with the similarities between these two pleasures drawn tautly and dramatically.

Unfortunately the novel's ending lacks the kind of satisfying cadence we might expect from such a richly musical work. David is also the protagonist in Loewinsohn's celebrated first novel, *Magnetic Field(s),* where, ironically, he watched in dismay as a good friend ditched his wife for a sweet young thing. Loewinsohn may well have plans for another sequel, for after a crescendo of back-and-forth interior monologues about what to do with his crisis, David simply affirms his abstract resolve to change, and the novel grinds to a halt. The final muddle here is not only David's, but the reader's.

Jack Sullivan, in a review of "Where All the Ladders Start," in Book World—The Washington Post, *August 2, 1987, p. 8.*

Najīb Mahfūz

1912-

(Also transliterated as Naguib Mahfouz) Egyptian novelist, short story writer, dramatist, and scriptwriter.

The recipient of the 1988 Nobel Prize in literature, Mahfūz is generally regarded as modern Egypt's leading literary figure. He is best known for his novels, in which he creates psychological portraits of characters whose personal struggles mirror the social, political, and cultural concerns confronting his homeland. Mahfūz first won respect during the mid-1940s for a series of novels set among the impoverished districts of Cairo that depict the futility and tragedy of lower-class characters who contend with social injustice and the ineluctability of fate. He secured his reputation during the mid-1950s with a trilogy of novels that chronicles significant experiences in the lives of a middle-class Cairo family while detailing Egypt's changing social and political milieu from 1917 to 1944. In his later work, Mahfūz makes extensive use of literary devices and experimental techniques to explore political issues, social and cultural malaise, spiritual crises, and decadence in contemporary Egypt.

Mahfūz's first three novels, *'Abath al aqdār* (1939), *Rādūbīs* (1943), and *Kifāh Tiba* (1944), are historical narratives set in ancient Egypt that contain allusions to modern society. Most critics agree that Mahfūz's talent matured with *Khān al-Khalīlī* (1945), his first novel set in contemporary Cairo. M. M. Badawi commented: "[*Khan al-Khalīlī*] began a series of eight novels in which [Mahfūz] emerged as the master *par excellence* of the Egyptian realistic novel, the chronicler of twentieth-century Egypt, and its most vocal social and political conscience. . . . [Mahfūz's Cairo] is a recognizable physical presence; its powerful impact upon the lives of characters is as memorable as that of Dickens's London, Dostoevsky's St. Petersburg or Zola's Paris." Evoking life in the Cairo slums during World War II, *Khan al-Khalīlī* and two other acclaimed works from this period, *Zuqāq al-Midaqq* (1947; *Midaq Alley*) and *Bidāya wa-nihāya* (1951; *The Beginning and the End*), depict the various ways in which individuals attempt to overcome oppressive circumstances and also examine the prospects for political and economic reform.

Mahfūz's trilogy of novels, *Bayn al-Qasrayn* (1956), *Qasr al-Shawq* (1957), and *al-Sukkariyya* (1957), is considered a masterpiece of Middle Eastern literature. Fusing colorful evocations of ordinary events in the lives of several generations of a middle-class Cairo family with detailed descriptions of the transforming patterns of Egyptian society, these works encompass such topics as the Egyptian Revolution of 1919, the effects of modernization on cultural and religious values, and changing attitudes towards women, education, and science. Sasson Somekh stated: "No future student of Egyptian politics, society or folklore will be able to overlook the material embodied in Mahfūz's Trilogy."

In his later work, Mahfūz shifts from his characteristic style of objective realism to make more extensive use of symbolism and various unconventional narrative techniques. For example, *Awlād Hāratinā* (1959; *The Children of Gebelawi*) is an allegory in which Egypt's present-day social concerns are linked with those of the past. Mahfūz explores broad themes, includ-

ing the nature of evil and the meaning of life, by modeling his characters on such figures as Adam, Satan, Moses, Jesus Christ, and Mohammed, and he ambivalently personifies science and technology as the modern prophets of humanity. In *al-Liss wa-al-kilāb* (1961; *The Thief and the Dogs*), Mahfūz employs a stream-of-consciousness narrative to create a psychological portrait of a wrongly imprisoned man who wreaks revenge on his betrayers upon his release. *al-Summān wa-al-kharif* (1962; *Autumn Quail*) concerns a corrupt bureaucrat who loses his pension following the revolution of 1952, when Egypt's wealthy King Faruk was forced to abdicate. Refusing to work under the new regime, the man gradually sinks into decadence and despair. *Tharthara fawq al-Nīl* (1966) documents the cynicism and superficial lifestyles of young professionals in Egypt. Most of the scenes in this novel take place on a houseboat, where a group of bureaucrats and artists congregate to share drugs and sex. *Mīrāmār* (1967), one of Mahfūz's most acclaimed works, juxtaposes the observations of several narrators to examine the actions of five male residents of an Alexandrian hotel when a beautiful and naive young woman is hired as a maid. *Hob taht al-Matar* (1973) and *al-Karnak* (1974) contrast the repressive actions of authorities during the regime of Gamal Abdel Nasser with the idealism of young people hoping for political and social reform. Reflecting the content of much of Mahfūz's later work, these novels also examine the disillusionment and malaise that affected Egyptian society following the country's military defeat in the Six-Day War of 1967.

THE TIMES LITERARY SUPPLEMENT

A new book by Nagib Mahfuz is a great occasion, at any rate throughout the Arab world, whose leading writer of fiction he is. This one [*Hikāya bilā Bidāya walā Nihāya*] is something of a disappointment, taken as a whole, but it nevertheless contains a good deal that is of interest to his admirers.

The book consists of five short stories, almost entirely in dialogue. The first two, the eponymous **"A Tale without Beginning or End"** and **"The Lovers' Quarter"**, hark back to the second and most acclaimed period of Mahfuz's work, when he established himself as the chronicler of twentieth-century Cairo. They deal in realistic fashion with minor crises in the life of the metropolis. . . .

"The Scrap Merchant" is in a different class, and has clearly been inspired by such members of the Egyptian literary avant-garde as Muhammad Hafiz Ragab and Magid Tubiya. Imbued by the spirit of the absurd, and full of suspense, it charts the decline of a rich jeweller through a mysterious marriage and unmotivated beatings-up to the final degradation—the seat of honour in the wheelbarrow of a sinister junk dealer. . . .

The atmosphere [in **"The Man Who Lost His Memory Twice"**] is gripping and the occurrence of one ghastly calamity after another is moving, but the story shows a fatal lack of direction. . . .

[**"Anbarlulu"**] is the most complete work in the book, and is a fine example of Mahfuz's post-Revolutionary style. It recounts the simplest of episodes: a girl and a middle-aged man, discussing their problems in a Cairo park, are interrupted first by gunfire and then by the youth who did the shooting, from the top of the Cairo Tower, as an individual protest against Israel; they persuade him to give himself up to the police; and finally, their inhibitions scattered by the spontaneity of his actions, they give voice to their repressed thoughts and reveal that each feels the solution of their difficulties is to make their lives together. The contrast between a quietly developing love affair and the violence of current political events gives **"Anbarlulu"** its effectiveness; it has a unity which only **"The Scrap Merchant"**, in this collection, also attains.

> *"Chronicles of Cairo," in* The Times Literary Supplement, *No. 3621, July 23, 1971, p. 850.*

SASSON SOMEKH

Mahfūz's début in the field of the novel can hardly be regarded as a great literary event in itself. His first novels ['*Abath al aqdār, Rādūbīs,* and *Kifāh Tība*], the Pharaonic ones, though important in the context of contemporary Egyptian fiction, are amongst the author's least original. They lack both the accurate hand of a craftsman and the touch of a genuine artist. Admittedly, one would not demand virtuosity or artistic perfection from a beginner. Nevertheless in the case of a great number of artists, their early works impressed their readers as "an event" from the outset, or at least foreshadowed a fresh literary style and "vision". Mahfūz's first novels do not strike us as such.

Mahfūz was, for one thing, ill-equipped to write historical novels. His knowledge of ancient Egypt was fragmentary and his acquaintance with the western historical novel was slight. Thus one is not surprised to discover that the outcome is nothing but a romantic reflection of the national past, full of marvellous occurrences and stock characters. . . .

Furthermore these novels betray a meagre individual style and tone. True, many of the themes and ideas which are to become essential components of Mahfūz's mature art are discernible in these early works (e.g., Fate, Death, social injustice, patriotic passion), but at this stage they are handled with little originality. (p. 60)

It would not be fair, however, to deny these novels some merit. They form an ambitious effort to give a panoramic view of ancient Egypt with clear reference to the contemporary scene, adhering as far as possible to the cold historical facts, yet furnishing an imaginative framework. The allusions to the continuity of the Egyptian character and aspirations are neatly interwoven into the fabric of the narrative. The patriotic theme is introduced in an intelligent and calm way.

As opposed to these "thematic" novels, *Rādūbīs* is less straightforward, dealing with individual human beings rather than a period or an idea. It reveals a richer grasp of human emotions, and an ability to penetrate beyond superficial human appearances. Furthermore, this novel represents a mood and key more akin to that of the real Mahfūz as he is to emerge: not heroic-flamboyant, but tragic-elegaic. The language is less rhetorical and assertive. True, both the themes of Fate and Patriotism are present in *Rādūbīs* as well, but they no longer occupy a central position. They are, rather, two of many components of which *love* is the most prominent. (p. 61)

In the next group of novels, those published between 1945-1951, Mahfūz's bent becomes clear. Life as embodied in these works is rather different from that of the historical novels. What distinguishes these five books [*Khān al-Khalīlī, al-Qāhira al-jadīda, Zuqāq al-Midaqq, al-Sarāb,* and *Bidāya wa-nihāya*] is not merely the fact that they are all set in contemporary Cairo, and that they are populated, except for one case, with poor and simple people, not members of noble dynasties; it is above all their mood and underlying philosophy that gives the novels their distinct quality. Here we encounter, more than before, the pessimistic, often fatalistic, outlook. Four of the stories end in death—two of them in double death. There is a depressing atmosphere which is not mitigated even by the occasional humorous situation or utterance. A tragic air, that of an impending catastrophe, is ever dominant. Hope only produces a mirage. "Death is more pitiful than hope", says Husayn, one of the characters in *Bidāya wa-nihāya*, "and this does not seem strange to me, for while death is a creation of God, hope is the offspring of our stupidity."

It has often been professed that the gloomy vision has its roots in the stifling conditions prevalent in Egypt at the time, the very conditions that Mahfūz wishes to portray. But such a contention does not hold water. Many an author concerned with a depressing social scene has evinced a more sanguine state of mind. In Egypt itself, authors can be found whose view is not as pessimistic, even when they tackle the same scene. (p. 65)

All four novels depict the lives of the poor or lower middle-classes, mostly those living in the old squalid alleys of Cairo. They are oppressed and helpless. A host of overwhelming forces—poverty being only one—seem to coalesce to perpetuate the misery of these men and women, and to inflict yet greater tragedies. Everything works to trample them down, to starve and humiliate them. (p. 66)

The social theme then is dominant in these novels. They can truly be said to belong to the literature of social protest. The characters themselves are often aware that they are oppressed by an unjust social and political order. Ḥusayn, the pious son in *Bidāya wa-nihāya,* sums up this awareness. "As a matter of fact," he says to his brother, "we go too far in making God responsible for our numerous hardships. Can't you see that even if He is responsible for our father's death, He is by no means to blame for the meagreness of his pension?"

Moreover, there are also representatives of a revolutionary solution, such as 'Alī Ṭāhā in *Al-Qahira al-jadīda* and Aḥmad Rāshid in *Khan al-Khalīlī,* who have a clear vision of the sources of social evil; and although such characters are never central in these novels, they constitute foci of dissatisfaction with the present, stressing the need for a new social order.

The tone of these novels is restrained and neutral. Ostensibly the author does not take sides. Yet his very interest in the poor and oppressed shows where his sympathy lies. Mahfūz, to be sure, shows a special relish in portraying exotic characters and scenes. . . . Furthermore, the people are very often portrayed from within; and seeing them in this manner we more often than not have our sympathies on their side. In fact, the neutral stance is only a disguise under which the author is able to elicit sympathy for his people in a more subtle way. There is no doubt whatever that his heart is with them, although he is occasionally cruel to them. . . . On the other hand, whenever representatives of the wealthier classes make an appearance, . . . they are ignoble.

It is this attitude to his unfortunate protagonists that distinguishes Mahfūz's art from that of the Naturalists, who regard their characters as specimens and their plots as cold studies, or even "case studies" to illustrate their so-called scientific theories. There are a few qualities, however, which link these novels to the practices of the Naturalists, rendering it untrue to say that they are *solely* concerned with social criticism. There is a certain emphasis on the role of inherited qualities. This trend is to become more prominent in the Trilogy, but is discernible here as well. The environment too, plays a certain role; sexual impulses are important in the make-up and subsequently in the fates of a great many characters. But while these elements appear only in the background of the novels discussed, there is one theme which is ever present and which comes out nearly as strongly as that of the social theme. This can be called fate, accident or chance. The theme of the "Mockery of Fate," which in the novel bearing that name (*'Abath al-aqdār*) was treated in a rather naïve and didactic manner, is now introduced stealthily but forcibly. It is ever-present, omnipotent, and devastating. (pp. 67-9)

· · · · ·

No sooner did Mahfūz publish the first volume of his Trilogy in 1956 (*Bayn al-Qaṣrayn*), than it became clear to many readers that this was the beginning of a great literary event. With the appearance in 1957 of the second and third volumes (*Qaṣr al-Shawq* and *al-Sukkariyya*), these expectations proved to be fully justified. The author was now unanimously acclaimed as the foremost novelist of modern Egypt.

The work, an enormous personal testimony, portrays the political scene of Egypt, and the daily life of the middle-class Cairene through a period of twenty-seven years (1917-1944). No future student of Egyptian politics, society or folklore will be able to overlook the material embodied in Mahfūz's Trilogy.

The portrait of the 1919 Egyptian revolution is, for one thing, more accurate, and at the same time more lively than that of any previous attempt in the field of literature (not excluding that of Tawfīq al-Hakīm).

The change of social patterns is not less admirably recorded; the rapid rejection of time-honoured social norms, the slow emancipation of woman from medieval shackles, the spread of education and scientific thinking, the increasing influence of western culture, the decline of religious adherence among the urban middle-class.

But while the process of change is at the forefront of this work, the world of yesterday, that which is rapidly losing ground, receives no less meticulous a treatment. It is delineated with great competence and love (sometimes even with a tinge of nostalgia). Throughout the pages of the Trilogy, and especially its first part, this world is recalled in its minutest details. The people of Cairo in the early twenties come alive before us, as do their habits, entertainments, songs, prejudices, dress and furniture.

Yet it cannot be stressed too strongly that this is not a sociological or historical study. Neither is it a body of social or political criticism in the guise of narrative. Mahfūz's Trilogy, is, above all, a *novel* and a very enjoyable one at that.

The many, ever-widening circles which constitute the material of this work are at all times under control, and one has to look very hard if one is to discover discrepancies or inconsistencies. Similarly the reader finds no difficulty whatever in following the comings and goings of the numerous protagonists. The tension is nearly always kept at a high pitch and there are very few dull passages in the whole of the 1500 pages comprising the Trilogy.

The Trilogy admittedly draws on autobiographical material, yet it is by no means an autobiographical novel. Neither the social background nor the personages are fully identifiable with those of Mahfūz's own life. The main character, Kamāl, resembles the author in more than one detail, but the two differ in many others. Certain fragments of the author's own story are delegated to other characters. The general tone is detached and balanced, so different in fact from that of many confessional novels.

In more than one way the Trilogy can be compared to Thomas Mann's first major novel *Buddenbrooks* (1901). Both novels deal with the history of a family through several generations. Both are characterized by patient accumulation of detail, and combine autobiographical and imaginary material; above all, both describe, albeit the difference in background, the decline of the merchant and the appearance of the intellectual.

None of the stories embodied in the Trilogy are simple and there are no happy endings. Life is a complicated web where tragedy lies in every corner. On reading the Trilogy one is continually shocked by the most cruel manifestations of life and human relations. In this way it is saved from being one of those middle-brow family chronicles. (pp. 106-08)

The function of Mahfūz's Trilogy is precisely "to fundamentally shake." . . .

The structure and technique are . . . in harmony with the intrinsic qualities of the characters. The [rhythm of the Trilogy] is dictated by the changing pace of life in Cairo. (p. 108)

Above all it can be noticed that there is much less determinism here than in Maḥfūẓ's other novels. In fact the stress is not on the perennial, the static, the immutable. On the contrary: the main theme of the Trilogy is precisely the *change*. It is in fact a study of a rapidly changing human community, a change which finds expression in every aspect of the lives and values of these people.

The change, it must be added, is not confined to superficial aspects of life. In this respect one should not make the mistake of seeing the Trilogy as a political novel as indeed a few critics have done.

True, the interest in politics is here, as in practically all of Maḥfūẓ's works, a central issue. . . . The major political events are at all times recorded with great accuracy. Many of the important upheavals in politics have parallels in the life of al-Sayyid's family. (p. 110)

Yet a closer look at the work—again as one entity—will reveal that politics is only one of many facets. A great number of protagonists of al-Sayyid's family, and to a certain degree Kamāl himself, are only marginally politically minded. Furthermore, although a certain bias towards the Left is discernible in the third volume, the novel is far removed from what is known as socialist-realism. It has no "positive hero" (Fahmī, the only one who comes near to that description, disappears as early as the first volume). It has no easy way out to offer and does not end in either resounding triumph or defeat. Politics, in a word, is brought into the novel only to the extent that it constitutes an integral part of the life-fabric of the urban Arab (and the Arab intelligentsia in particular). (p. 111)

Politics, then, is only one of many manifestations of life which Maḥfūẓ tackles in his Trilogy. The question might now be asked: Is there one central point around which the whole work pivots? Is it a philosophical "inquiry" into the effect on human beings of time, death, and fate? In a way it is. These issues are ever-present and no reader can fail to notice them. But as has already been pointed out, the author, while greatly interested in all matters philosophical or metaphysical, is always aware of the basic demands of the art of story-telling. His main concern is to tell the *story* of his own world, past and present, mundane and spiritual. Having lived in an age of dramatic change, of seething revolution, he is fascinated above all by the process of that change. He dwells upon the fate of his nation, groping for a quick way out of the medieval world and, at the same time, fighting to rid itself of foreign domination. He is fascinated by the *rapidly changing rhythm of life*. It is this changing rhythm . . . that determines the structure and style of the whole work. (p. 112)

A wide gulf separates the Trilogy and its predecessors from *Awlād Ḥaratinā*, 1959. The early works were realistic novels *par excellence*, although a rudimentary symbolism crops up here and there. *Awlād Ḥaratinā* on the other hand is an allegory. The early Cairene novels of Maḥfūẓ are concerned with the lives of contemporary people. *Awlād Ḥaratinā* is concerned with anything but individual characters of our day.

Neither is *Awlād Ḥaratinā* a historical novel in any sense of the word. Historical novels aim at reconstructing the intimate lives of people of whom we know little, and, above all, representing them as living human beings, often relating events of the past to those of the present. *Awlād Ḥaratinā*, however, depicts its historical (or legendary) personalities more or less following the outlines of the sacred books, the interpretations of their deeds being sometimes different. Moreover, people of the past are not represented in their own historical settings or even under their original names. They are transplanted into that world which Maḥfūẓ knows best, namely that part of Cairo in which most of his "social" novels are set.

Furthermore, both the literary style and method of characterization in *Awlād Ḥaratinā* are totally different from those we have encountered earlier. (p. 137)

Awlād Ḥaratinā then is a philosophical tale in its purest form. Yet there are no cut and dried conclusions which it is out to prove. The converse is true. The gist of the book is an enquiry, a search for an answer. As is the case in all the author's other works, no definitive answer emerges. As the work ends, the struggle is still as fierce as ever, the questions as disturbing.

Nevertheless there are certain points of departure in the work which can be summed up as follows:

1. The majority of the human race have always lived in destitution, because their rulers have taken for themselves the wealth of the earth, a wealth which was meant to be shared equally by all God's children. Tyranny and poverty have since the dawn of history been two sides of the same coin. Consequently the world has become impure, full of evil, lust, hatred and wars.

2. The three great prophets came, in reality, to save us from these evils. The first prophet (Jabal = Moses) delivered his people and obtained justice for them. The second (Rifāʿa = Jesus) was not concerned with power or property. His sole object was to purge the soul of the people from evil. He preached love and gave his life for it. The third (Qāsim = Muhammad) was also a prophet of mercy and love, but he saw that it can be achieved only by violent means. His mission was confined, not only to his own people but to peoples of all races and colours.

However, the successes of these prophets are short-lived. Their goodwill and victories are squandered. No sooner did they disappear from the scene than their teachings were distorted and the old pattern of tyranny-cum-destitution was resumed.

3. Science (the magician ʿArafa = scientist) is capable of bringing about the downfall of evil. Science is able to produce weapons which can potentially be used to destroy unjust political and social orders, and can provide a better and richer life for all. Unfortunately it is used not for the benefit of humanity, but to serve the ends of tyranny. Further, it secures a monopoly of power. The super-power, aided by science-made weapons, suppresses the whole of the human race. Thus, instead of bettering the lot of man, science has changed nightmares into realities.

4. Religion, it is true, has throughout the ages been at the service of wicked rulers, but man needs a belief. He does not live by bread alone. Science, which unwittingly brought about the death of God, again served humanity ill. Indeed the killing of God was possibly to the benefit of the tyrants of the earth because faith often gave simple people hope and courage.

5. Science, despite its setbacks, is the hope of our race. Possibly an elusive hope but the last remaining one. If he is ever to succeed, the scientist has to be both humanist and militant, and to lead his people as did the prophets. The risks are great,

but so are the hopes. If science and justice ever win the battle and the energies of man are liberated, we shall all become scientists endeavouring to discover the secrets of nature and possibly, to put an end to death. The existential question might be solved. Belief itself might one day be revived.

So much for the abstractions of *Awlād Ḥāratinā*. By what means did the author contrive to make them concrete? And has his story any literary value as such?

The ideas are brought to life through the characters of "modern" Cairo. The story begins when Jabalāwī, the Master of the Big House, expels two of his sons (Adham = Adam; Idrīs = Satan), for different reasons. Their seed multiplies and their houses form the *Ḥāra* ('living quarters'). The *Ḥāra* is divided into alleys (*aḥyā'*, sing, *ḥayy*), each inhabited by one branch of Jabalāwī's descendants and dominated by a *futuwwa* (pl. *futuwwāt* 'strong-arm man'). Jabal, Rifā'a and Qāsim arise in these alleys in separate generations. The period of time separating each message is not specified, but it is not longer than one or two generations in each case.

The events throughout the work are intended to be plausible. There are no supernatural incidents. The protagonists, including the three who were entrusted with messages by Jabalāwī, are ordinary men who rise to help their fellows. There is nothing miraculous about their encounters with Jabalāwī or with his messengers, encounters which set them off on their separate ways. The battles they win or lose are also plausible in the context of the *Ḥāra*. Jabalāwī himself is simply one of the domineering patriarchs of old Cairo, in some ways resembling the Master in *Bayn al-Qaṣrayn*. (pp. 139-41)

The question now arises as to how far the ideas embodied in the work benefited from its allegorical or semi-allegorical form. In other words, what extra dimension is added when the historic-philosophical concept is conveyed through character and action. The author himself believes that this method offers a profounder understanding of the subject. On one occasion he draws a comparison between his work and *Gulliver's Travels*. He suggests that *Awlād Ḥāratinā* is "the converse of what Swift has done in his well-known journey. He criticized reality by means of a legend [sic], while I am criticizing the legend through reality."

The legends, indeed, are retold in terms of a reality much close to the modern Arabic reader than that of the sacred books. The special flavour of Cairo with the typically *baladī* names of places, people, and things; their specific problems, entertainments, jokes—all these are part of a reality which Mahfūẓ knows very well.

But is such a realistic coating in itself sufficient to make *Awlād Ḥāratinā* a novel as are his earlier works? For if Maḥfūẓ was to succeed in criticizing the legend by transferring it into a familiar realistic setting, he would have had to make the characters individual and convincing, so that the thoughts and actions of the underlying prototypes would be better comprehended. Is there any human depth to the characters of *Awlād Ḥāratinā*?

The answer tends to be negative. The great majority of the characters are black-and-white. The *nāẓirs* and *futuwwāt* are, without exception, absolute monsters, lacking any trace of human feeling. The masses of the *Ḥāra* are faceless, mostly passive and cowardly. Above all, the main protagonists of the five different sections are only portrayed in quick-moving sketches. The main bulk of each section is occupied by endless

events, battles, and adventures. The love stories (one in each section) are conventional and the women often unnatural. (p. 142)

• • • • •

> The days passed and brought with them many illnesses from which I was able, without too much trouble, and at a cost I could afford, to find a cure; until I became afflicted with that illness for which no one possesses a remedy. Every way out was closed and I was encircled by despair.

These words from a short story published by Maḥfūẓ in 1961 adequately provide us with the dominant mood, and at the same time they point to the focal themes, of the five short novels which the author published between 1961-1966.

The feeling of despair, doom and siege is at all times at the forefront of these works. Admittedly none of Maḥfūẓ's works, as we have seen, is free from pessimism. But whereas in the early Cairene novels the catastrophe comes towards the end of the story and as the culmination of the plot, in these short novels despair is the *starting point*. Furthermore, while in the early novels the root of the tragedy lies in social conditions, the works of the sixties give prominence to tragedy of a different kind—spiritual or existential. The malady is much more insidious, more consuming than the social one. The roads are closed and there is no remedy to be found. (p. 156)

The first two of these novels, *al-Liṣṣ wal-kilāb*, 1961, and *al-Summān al-kharīf*, 1962, are clearly set in the social and political realities of present day Egypt. In the former, the protagonist, Sa'īd, is a thief just released from prison. Having been betrayed by the people closest to him, he is intent on punishing the traitors. He comes to believe that his mission of revenge is symbolic, and it is in fact aimed at all traitors and bullies. His struggle, however, ends in his destruction.

'Īsā, the protagonist of *al-Summān al-kharīf*, his promising career in ruins following the 1952 revolution, refuses to compromise with the new realities. He cuts himself off from the mainstream of society, thereby destroying himself as a person.

Both of these novels, then, provide a down-to-earth setting and motivation. Yet the interest in the external circumstances is reduced to a minimum, while the more intimate aspects of the crisis are given prominence. Furthermore, both of these stories, especially the first one, have a strong air of mysticism about them. Reference is repeatedly made to the search for certainty and the craving for an otherworldly repose.

The next novel, *al-Ṭarīq*, 1964, does not start with a spiritual crisis. Ṣābir, its hero, sets out to look for his lost father because his mother has urged him to do so on her deathbed, and also because he hoped that his father might save him from impending poverty. In the course of his search he becomes entangled with two women, one of whom goads him to kill her aged husband. Eventually he kills both husband and wife, and it is only after he is sentenced to death for these crimes that he finds a clue to the identity of his lost father.

The outline of *al-Tarīq* might not strike one as esoteric, but the novel has many indications of being a double-layered story; in other words, the lost father who is sought by Ṣābir is more than a flesh-and-blood one. He is, to all appearances, another version of that great ancestor who, in *Awlād Ḥāratinā*, was also unreachable by his children. Hence the events which start Ṣābir on his quest for his father can be interpreted as having a deeper meaning. His crisis, then, is no less a spiritual one.

In the two novels that follow *al-Shaḥḥādh,* 1965, and *Tharthara fawq al-Nīl,* 1966, there is no attempt to disguise the spiritual ordeal. They are straightforward portrayals of people searching for the secrets of life or attempting to explore the ultimate riddle.

al-Shaḥḥādh is, in fact, a direct study of the process of rejection of the realities of life and society, and the drift into the mystical labyrinth. 'Umar, its hero, is a successful lawyer and a happy father who for no conceivable reason (conceivable, that is, to other people) loses interest in everything surrounding him and sets out to elicit the "secret of secrets of life" first through sex, and then through mystical literature. Finally, he deserts his home to seek a life of mystical hallucinations in seclusion.

Anīs, the chief character in *Tharthara fawq al-Nīl,* is similarly immersed in his visions, albeit by means of hashish. He has long since detached himself from society to live in a boathouse, never to be separated from his fantasies, even during office hours. A great part of *Tharthara fawq al-Nīl* portrays his moods and hallucinations. Apart from the few quick-moving incidents occurring at the end of the book, there is no action except for the daily hashish sessions of Anīs and his friends.

The drift away from stark realities towards mysticism is, then, the most prominent feature of this group of novels. There is a great change in the thematical stress as compared to the author's earlier works. The change, moreover, is not only in subject matter, but also in the structure, style and treatment of the characters. . . . [It] would be useful to dwell upon certain features which are common to this group and the rest of Maḥfūz's works.

The social theme, for one thing, is not altogether absent. This is especially true of *al-Liṣṣ wal-kilāb* where the hero's poverty in his youth is recalled tersely but clearly, especially that scene in which his ailing mother was taken, bleeding, to a private hospital, but was turned away on account of her poverty. It is this poverty that first made him steal. Moreover, he comes to see his "profession" as one of social protest, directed against the rich. In the same novel we encounter the prostitute Nūr, another victim of an unjust social order.

In the other four novels most of the characters are less bedevilled by need. Yet in each of these works, the theme of social protest makes an occasional appearance. In *al-Tariq* Ṣābir remarks to his lawyer, when the latter informs him that his lost father is a millionaire, "More important, the law of the land has no power over him." To this the lawyer replies, "At any rate you were aware [when committing the murders] that you are poor and subject to the laws of the land."

The subject of current politics, at times closely related to the latter, is often raised. As in the early novels and in the Trilogy, there is a sharp awareness of the political scene, domestic and international. References of that nature are especially frequent in *al-Shaḥḥādh* and *Tharthara fawq al-Nīl.* Furthermore, one novel, *al-Summān al-Kharīf,* has as its main character a career politician (rather, ex-politician), and that book comes as close as any to being a straightforward political novel.

Another theme which is present in many of these novels is the old preoccupation with the validity of science and knowledge. The search often starts after the character has despaired of scientific or rational solutions. The first chapter of *al-Shaḥḥādh* takes place in the doctor's clinic. 'Umar has come to consult him about his depressive mood. He explains that he has come to find out whether this mood of his has an organic cause. To this the doctor remarks, "Wouldn't it be wonderful if our great problems could be solved by a pill-after-meal or a spoonful-before-bed!"

The question of the limits of science; the claims of science on the one hand, and philosophy, art and death on the other hand—occupy, in fact, a great part of the conversations between 'Umar and other characters of that novel. The same kind of question is touched upon in other novels as well, at times in a straightforward manner and at others esoterically. In *al-Tariq,* for instance, Ṣābir, on arriving in Cairo to look for his father, starts with a doctor—this time a heart specialist—bearing the same name as his father. He too, like 'Umar, is disappointed: the man has never heard of his father.

Fate is as cruel in these stories as ever; the Mockery of Fate as shattering. In *al-Liṣṣ wal-kilāb,* Sa'īd, whose bullets in the past never missed their targets, now manages to hit only innocent people. Ṣābir in *al-Tariq* receives Ilhām's selfless offer of help only after he has committed his murder and has thus become irredeemably entangled with Karīma. Later he discovers the identity of his father only after having been sentenced to death. 'Īsā, in *al-Summān al-Kharīf,* plans to marry Salwā in August, but the *coup d'état* which occurs on the twenty-third of July shatters his life.

Finally, the scene of action is the self-same Cairo; and the houseboat of *Tharthara fawq al-Nīl* is also nothing new. Also present are the Ṣūfī, the beggar, the harlot, and similar characters.

Yet these and other elements in the short novels, reminiscent as they are of Maḥfūz's earlier works, have to be seen in their right perspective. Their function, arrangement, interplay and order of prominence, in other words, their aesthetic treatment, is unmistakably different from anything we have seen earlier. (pp. 157-60)

> *Sasson Somekh, in his* The Changing Rhythm: A Study of Najīb Maḥfūz's Novels, *E. J. Brill, 1973, 241 p.*

[S. EL KHADEM]

In short (4 pp.) and very short (2 pp.) dramatic scenes, Najib Mahfuz depicts [in *Hob taht al-Matar*] a very bleak picture of Egypt after the military defeat of 1967 and the philosophical bankruptcy of its "glorious" revolution. The main characters of his story are young university graduates striving for a better life. Because of the political deadlock and the military stalemate they are confused and troubled. They are completely lost amidst unfeasible materialistic goals, an unworkable social structure and irrelevant moral codes. In their search for a way out of their dilemma, they try love, marriage, and even prostitution. They resist, revolt, and surrender. No matter what they venture, they always end up bitter and disenchanted. The representatives of the older generation, handicapped by their physical debility and moral deficiencies, indulge themselves in old lies, secondhand dreams, and exhausted memories. They are, therefore, unable to give the younger generation any support or guidance. With the explosive military situation and the despondent political condition in the background, the story moves rapidly from one gloomy scene to another till it comes to a halt without reaching any end.

The skill and artistry of Najib Mahfuz, who is undoubtedly the greatest narrative writer in the history of Arabic literature, is due to the fact that, although he deals with many social problems and tackles earnest moral issues, he is always aware of his function as an amusing storyteller and beguiling fabulist. Never does he sacrifice the development of plot in favor of philosophical question or a political argument. His style, which is always plain, lucid, and unaffected, is another reason for his extreme popularity.

> *[S. El Khadem], in a review of "Hob Taht al-Matar (Love in the Rain)," in* The International Fiction Review, *Vol. 1, No. 1, January, 1974, p. 68.*

S. EL KHADEM

In his novel *Hob taht al-Matar,* Najib Mahfouz has dealt narratively with the dilemma of young intellectuals in Egypt after the military defeat of 1967; in *al-Karnak,* he returns to the same subject matter, to the situation before and after this defeat, shedding more light on the political and moral bankruptcy of Egypt's "glorious revolution." Once again his heroes are the "true children of the revolution".

The narrator, an uncommitted and objective middle-aged man, spends most of his time in "al Karnak" (a café in downtown Cairo), watching the customers and the owner of the café, a retired belly dancer. He is mainly interested in a group of university students who come to the café, from time to time, to chat and discuss the political and social problems of their country. For no apparent reason, the vicious secret police incarcerate and chastise them; Zainab, the only girl among them, is raped in prison in front of the chief of police. Nevertheless, these patriotic young people do not lose faith in the cause of the revolution, simply because they believe, like most people, that the "suffering of the masses is the price of great revolutions". But when Egypt is defeated and humiliated during the six-day war, they, like the rest of the people, find no justification for what they have endured.

In spite of the many similarities between this novel and *Hob taht al-Matar,* it is obvious that Najib Mahfouz is now preoccupied with many ideological aspects of his society in a way that makes him neglect the development of a coherent plot and the creation of engaging and radiant characters. These two qualities, incidentally, established his reputation as an accomplished novelist and a beguiling storyteller. For instance, the love affair between Qronfola, the owner of the café, and one of the students, and the relationship between Zainab and Ismail—her playmate, colleague, and lover—are kept far in the background, so that the writer can devote himself both to the impact of certain political incidents on the younger generation and to the way in which this generation is driven to disenchantment, alienation, and moral corruption. Due to this uneven blending of enlightening and entertaining elements, readers who usually appreciate coherent plots and exciting incidents will be disappointed by this heavy political novel.

> *S. El Khadem, in a review of "al-Karnak," in* The International Fiction Review, *Vol. 2, No. 1, January, 1975, p. 81.*

SAAD EL-GABALAWY

Many of the pieces in the collection *Khamāret al-Qitt al-Asward (The Tavern of the Black Cat)* indicate that [Mahfouz] has an exquisite taste for uncommon and mysterious events. In his code of thought, the story must be exceptional enough to provide its *raison d'être.* Therefore, he introduces extraordinary incidents freely into his stories, regardless of the objective representation of reality which approaches the scientific method. In order to assimilate the irrational and mysterious elements, the reader should attempt to suspend disbelief, for he is witnessing another world bound by its own logic and necessities.

Perhaps the best example in this regard is the first story in the collection, **"A Vague Word,"** where a gangster has a strange dream of the enemy he had murdered many years before, echoing his last words before death: "I shall kill you from my grave." This evokes recollections of the day the man was buried and his wife raised her baby over the grave, making a solemn oath that the infant would one day take revenge on his father's murderer. Nurtured upon local tradition and superstition, the gangster's mind is totally preoccupied with interpretations of the dream. Most of the old women, who claim to be knowledgeable in the art of dream-reading, agree that the ghost of the father might urge his son to seek revenge.

With intolerable premonitions dominating his mind and heart, the gangster starts the agonizing search for the son to destroy him, or rather to destroy his own fear. Guided by rumors about the place of the young man, all the tough members of the gang follow their leader to a remote area in the desert. . . .

The journey follows a labyrinthine pattern of striving towards a goal across a difficult and dangerous terrain. Mahfouz vividly represents the imminent doom through the strangeness, the adventurousness, and the sinuous forward movement of this fatal pilgrimage. (p. 7)

In terms of modern psychology, the dream may be regarded as an expression of suppressed fears, but this does not explain the mysterious end of a man rushing irrevocably to his destiny. The pivotal character in attempting to avoid his fate, acts in such a way as to seal it inexorably. Mahfouz seems to believe in the existence of an actively malign power in the universe. The forces of fate in some of his stories appear to be hostile, vicious, and whimsical. The essence of man's tragic plight lies in the notion that he is lifted up only to be dashed down. His self-made threads of aspiration finally serve to entangle him in the recognition of his helplessness. He sees himself doomed to be perpetually cheated of his aims and mocked by a superior power which takes no heed of his hopes and fears.

The theme of fate in Mahfouz's work is closely related to the limits of vision in man. There is an important aspect in the actual page-by-page experience of reading the stories: the uneasiness or confusion of the reader, his sense of being afloat on a troubled conceptual and ethical sea. Much of the reader's bewilderment is due to the pervasive and obvious shortsightedness of most characters. In fact, these myopic characters are very similar to us, with our limited vision and incomplete knowledge of the truth. Many of the stories present the spectacle of several limited and inadequate points of view at indecisive war with each other. The writer addresses himself less to vision than to blindness: to man's refusal to overlook his prejudices, and his inability to discern what lies beyond his limitations. In different ways, Mahfouz seems to insist upon the relativity and shortcomings of his characters' perceptions and of their codes of judgement which often cancel each other.

"A Miracle" accentuates poignantly the wide gap between illusions and reality. At the beginning of the story, the central character is sitting alone in a tavern and, out of boredom, thinks of a strange game to while away the time. He fabricates a very uncommon name of a fictitious man and asks the waiter if that person is one of his customers. As might be expected, the waiter has never heard the name before. To the utter surprise of the protagonist, a few minutes later he hears the manager of the tavern shouting the same name to answer a telephone call. This, for him, could not be mere coincidence, since the man has no real existence except in his own fancy; he is the creator of the name. The experience gradually leads him to a vague feeling that he possesses some innate power of super-human vision, of extra sensory perception. Baffled by the "miracle," he decides to test his newly-discovered gift by repeating the experiment. When he coins another very strange name and asks the waiter about it, there is a similar telephone call. (p. 8)

The experience gradually isolated him from his family and friends, when he became obsessed by this inner light which might change his barren life and transform him into a transparent being with a miraculous power. The fixed idea caused him to delve deeper and deeper into studies of occult and mystical phenomena of spiritual illumination. After months of reading and meditation, he decided to test his power again. Moving from one café to another, he played the same game, but to no end. Eventually he went to the tavern where he had the first revelation of this "extra sensory perception." There, he was approached by a boisterous drunken man who gave him the most unexpected interpretation of the "miracle." He told him how in that first night, a group of drunks were sitting next to his table and heard him asking the waiter about the strange names. As a practical joke, they sent one of them twice to the nearest shop in order to make the telephone calls. While listening to this cheap and mundane explanation of his mysterious power, the protagonist felt his soul disintegrating with grief and despair. His infantile harmony was cruelly shattered by the discovery. In the tempestuous fury of disillusionment, he stabbed the drunk's neck with the fork on his table, then collapsed completely.

In symbolic terms, the drunk represents the ugliness of reality, reversing all the protagonist's expectations. The latter's fantasy world is a mental phenomenon which reveals the irrationality and absurdity of man's attempts to create his own version of reality, to change the facts of life and defeat suffering. Mahfouz repeatedly suggests that human vision is illusory, fragmented, and negative. The mind tends to accept what it expects, which is often conditioned by needs and desires, hopes and fears, weaknesses and follies, preconceptions and prejudices. The writer is not perplexing his characters out of mere whimsy, or playing a hoax on his reader. In my view, he renders the reader less rather than more ready to speculate about the true nature of situations or to anticipate the frustration of the fanciful by the actual. Instead of providing him with a back door, so to speak, he presents him with a veritable labyrinth of alternatives which lie beyond human visibility. The reader sees too much blindness and confusion in all, including himself, to trust the views of anyone. (p. 9)

The essence of the truth is again hidden by misleading appearances in **"The Defendant,"** where a man finds himself unjustly accused of a crime, without any hope of proving his innocence. A young villager is hit by a truck on the highway, but the driver runs away to escape from responsibility. Another driver, who has witnessed the accident, stops out of compassion to help the dying youth. At that moment, the fellaheen rush from their fields and, judging by appearances, jump to the conclusion that he is the guilty one. The class conflict is poignantly depicted in the confrontation, charged with hatred and hostility, between the barefooted peasants and the owner of the car. The reader becomes keenly aware of the plight of the man, trapped by circumstances beyond his control, so that he suddenly and inevitably declines from happiness to misery. . . . Although the plot lacks originality and complexity, the story is redeemed by the subtle moment of illumination at the end, where the peasants and the investigating officer derive a morbid pleasure from the victim's death, since it serves to confirm the man's guilt. Out of sheer perversity and prejudice, they refuse to transcend the limitations of vision and never try to explore the truth.

The problem of the limited vision assumes a different form in the story entitled **"The Tavern of the Black Cat,"** where the writer adopts the allegorical mode to set his symbols in motion. The tavern is full of riotous drunkards when a stranger arrives and starts to intimidate them. . . . In spite of their attempt to resume merrymaking, they become gradually convinced that there is no point in staying any longer. The stranger, however, prevents [them] forcibly from leaving the tavern and insists they must know his story. "The minutes ticked away in the strained atmosphere. Their low spirits sobered them after the intoxicating effect of the wine". To escape from the stranger's oppression, they ignore him completely, drinking and singing, unrestrained and uninhibited. . . . Finally, the stranger, sadly and tearfully, walks away, leaving the drunkards with a deep sense of wonder: "When and where have [we] seen that man?"

In sustaining the literal dimension of his narrative, Mahfouz gives the story the hard convincing texture of authenticated fact. Through its dramatic movement, it has the potentialities of an actual experience. Through close attention to vivid and minute details, the writer creates an air of verisimilitude. This is not only the effect of the sober tone; it springs also from the sensitive and subtle movement. But the literal surface is not transparent enough for the reader to establish immediately a definite relationship between the two levels of meaning. The tavern, with its oppressive darkness and iron-barred window, seems to signify the world as a prison of the soul. The stranger can be regarded as a personification of the truth from which the customers of the tavern try to escape for fear of pain. Although they are momentarily shocked into awareness and sobriety, these men prefer the lethargy of oblivion.

It is also possible to assume that the stranger typifies death, coming suddenly and stealthily to shock human beings who indulge in earthly pleasures and ignore the ultimate moment of truth. Perhaps the greatest strength of the story lies in its ambiguity. The more we explore its dynamic images, the more they expand in the mind. Simultaneously, we become increasingly aware of our failure to grasp the full significance of the personified abstractions which stand for a system of ideas. Presumably, the writer is deliberately attempting to accentuate the lack of meaning, which is the great dilemma of man.

Many of Mahfouz's characters are exiles, suffering from alienation and psychic homelessness. They are often outcasts who have failed to find their spiritual home in society: drunkards, drug addicts, gangsters, prostitutes, and the like. Man is isolated from man by unsurmountable barriers of religion, illusion, apathy, prejudice, preconception, irrational hostility, and spiritual blindness. Again and again, the writer reveals the failure of communion and the almost complete absence of compassion.

Significantly, the genuine feeling of human brotherhood can be perceived in Mahfouz's **"Paradise of Children,"** which is cast in the form of a dialogue between a young girl and her father. The child wonders why she and her closest friend go to different classes in religious lessons; this artificial separation does not make any sense to her. The father tries in vain to explain the difference between Islam and Christianity, and fails pathetically to give adequate answers to the girl's questions about the nature of God and eternity, or about the duality of heaven and hell, good and evil, life and death. Mahfouz communicates in the simplest terms the child's magnificent vision of the universal man, uncorrupted and unrestrained by the complications of formal religion. There are no obstacles of preconceptions to mar her spirit of real sympathy and communion. The reader clearly hears the voices of innocence and experience, the spontaneous intuition of the child versus the sophisticated mind of the adult. Apparently, the more we grow up, the more we progress backwards in terms of vision. The father is totally conditioned by years of indoctrination, which inevitably create barriers of fanaticism and intolerance. Until challenged by his daughter's questions, he has not given any serious thought to abstract issues of doctrine and faith, blindly accepting the fact of isolation.

Generally speaking, this collection of short stories clearly reflects the writer's basic pessimism and tragic view of life. He is more inclined to protest against the inadequacy of human existence than to extol its fulness. Instead of a balanced and benign order in man and society, Mahfouz finds maladjustment, disillusionment, cruelty, perversity, and frustration. Love is absent from his world. Men approach each other to destroy and to be destroyed, never to attain plenitude of being. For the author, the earth is not paradise, life is not a theme for rapture. The tragic nature of his characters stems mainly from their inability to alter their condition. The universe he sees as a place of blind necessity and inexorable law, ruled by a capricious power which takes no account of human aims. (pp. 9-11)

> *Saad El-Gabalawy, "The Tragic Vision in Najib Mahfouz's 'The Tavern of the Black Cat'," in* The International Fiction Review, *Vol. 3, No. 1, January, 1976, pp. 7-11.*

P. J. VATIKIOTIS

Naguib Mahfouz, the leading Egyptian and Arab novelist today, has produced the most professional novels of all about Cairo, its people and life. He portrays the changes that have occurred in the lives of the petit bourgeois Cairenes, highlighting the difference between one generation and another as these are influenced by new forces, ideas and events. With the publication of his famous trilogy in 1956-57 he established the Egyptian novel as a highly artistic literary form. His early novels were on specifically Egyptian historical themes, both as symbols of national aspirations and mirrors of his country's actual political condition. Immediately after the war he exploded into print with three major novels depicting the life, trials and tribulations of the poorer classes in the native quarters of Cairo.

Midaq Alley (1947) belongs to this period. It is on one level the story of one alley in the city and its inhabitants. On another level it portrays the tragic attraction of modernity for those who seek a means of escaping the oppressive destitution of life in the alley. Its structure really consists of a series of plots but with a central character, the alley's belle Hamida, who dreams of modern Cairo and better prospects only to end up in extreme degradation as a prostitute. In her desperate defiance of her traditional social milieu, Hamida is unconsciously willing to be trapped, because that for her represents adventure away from the filth and poverty symbolized in her lousy hair.

The dialogue is vital and spontaneous, using transposition from Cairene dialect or idiom to literary Arabic, which perhaps makes it in the end somewhat formalistic and unrealistic, forcing the writer on occasion to speak for his characters. But the tension is constant, the precise detail and meticulous description of foods, smells and the like absolutely superb. The pull of modernity does not relieve Hamida and the other characters of the alley from the tragedy of life and the conundrums of existence, familiar themes in Mahfouz's novels. But the very dilemma stresses the oppressiveness of an unjust order and the dissatisfaction with the present. It is interesting to note that the leading Arabic novelist today is least attentive to the Arab and Islamic past. Instead, he is thoroughly secular and Egyptian in his thinking, art and concerns, influenced mainly as he is by twentieth-century European fiction and his university education in philosophy and psychology.

> *P. J. Vatikiotis, "The Way of the Storyteller," in* The Times Literary Supplement, *No. 3868, April 30, 1976, p. 523.*

MICHAEL BEARD

The title [of *Miramar*] is not an Arabic word but a composite of those disembodied Romance stems from which the names of hotels are put together. The Miramar is a seaside *pension* in Alexandria, the home of five single men and the maid Zohra, a peasant girl escaping from an arranged engagement. Everyone is interested in Zohra—romantically, exploitatively or protectively—and consequently the *pension* becomes a microcosm of the Egyptian political situation of the time (the original was published in 1967).

The bare minimum of events takes place, but according to some mysterious dialectic, Mahfouz's writing becomes more interesting when less is happening. The story is narrated by four of the boarders, who recount with slight variations the same simple events (a dinner conversation, an evening listening to Umm Kulthum on the radio). Zohra defends her honor, one of the boarders commits suicide; but what intrigues us is the kind of endless variation and witty restatement which keeps us interested in village gossip once we are attuned to its rhythms. This sense of benign serenity (which outweighs its effect as social satire) makes *Miramar,* with last year's *Mirrors* (with its tone of leisurely recollection . . .), the most appealing Mahfouz yet translated. (pp. 739-40)

> *Michael Beard, in a review of "Miramar," in* World Literature Today, *Vol. 53, No. 4, Autumn, 1979, pp. 739-40.*

M. M. BADAWI

Mahfouz began his career as a novelist with historical fiction, publishing three novels in the genre between 1939 and 1944. In these works, the imaginative reconstruction of the ancient Egyptian past is less important than Mahfouz's use of the distant Pharaonic setting as a vehicle for commentary on the political and social situation of contemporary Egypt. In this he succeeded to some extent: there is implied criticism of the tyranny of King Farouk in *Radubis* and a pronounced feeling of nationalist resentment against the foreign (and hence British) occupation of Egypt in [*Kifāh Tība, Thebes' Struggle*]. However, Mahfouz soon abandoned Pharaonic times for the contemporary Egyptian and specifically Cairene setting. This was a wise decision, not least because he was ill-suited to the historical novel. His next work, *Khan al-Khalili* (1945), began a series of eight novels in which he emerged as the master *par excellence* of the Egyptian realistic novel, the chronicler of twentieth-century Egypt, and its most vocal social and political conscience. With titles taken from the names of streets of old Cairo, the novels offer a panoramic vista of the Egyptian lower and lower-middle classes, with the minute details of their daily lives vividly and lovingly portrayed. Unlike Lawrence Durrell's Alexandria, Mahfouz's Cairo has more than mere romantic imaginative validity: it is a recognizable physical presence; its powerful impact upon the lives of characters is as memorable as that of Dickens's London, Dostoevsky's St Petersburg or Zola's Paris.

Mahfouz's realistic art reaches its pinnacle in his trilogy, published in 1956-57, but clearly written before the 1952 Revolution. The earlier novels, *Khan al-Khalili* (1945), [*al-Qāhira al-jadīda, New Cairo*] (1946), *Midaq Alley* (1947) (available in English translation), and [*Bidāya wa-nihāya, A Beginning and an End*] (1951) deal in the main with the pressures and drama of life in Egypt during the Second World War. The trilogy, on the other hand, *Bayn al-Qasrayn, Qasr al-Shawq* and *al-Sukkariyya,* traces the fortunes of a Cairene family over three generations, beginning in the second decade of the twentieth century, roughly coinciding with the growth of the nationalist movement that culminated in the 1919 revolution, and ending with the Second World War. The destinies of the individual characters are the microcosm, but the macrocosm is the destiny of modern Egypt. The tragedies, the sufferings, the conflicts of the men and women who people these novels reflect the larger social, intellectual and political changes in one significant part of the modern Arab world. The struggle of the younger generation to attain their domestic freedom, to shape their own lives, mirrors the nation's struggle to achieve political independence and to free itself from the shackles of outworn and debilitating, almost medieval conventions in a gigantic endeavour to become part of the modern world. The slow unfolding of events, the meticulous enumeration of detail, the heavy sociological documentation, the constant authorial presence, the anxious concern to produce a tightly knit plot, the scrupulous care to maintain an objective stance, give these novels, despite their unmistakable Egyptian character, the air of nineteenth-century European fiction. To the criticism that they took no account of modernist techniques, Mahfouz replied that, although he was not unaware of Modernism, he felt that technique was determined by the writer's material and vision of life, and was not something to be imposed arbitrarily from without. Herein lies Mahfouz's strength: unlike lesser writers he has never been dazzled by the latest literary fashion.

Between the completion of the trilogy and the appearance of *The Children of Gebelawi* in 1959 . . . , Mahfouz wrote nothing for more than five years, a silence all the more baffling in view of the prolific output of earlier and later years. His own recorded explanation is that with the coming of the Nasser Revolution he felt he had nothing further to say, since it was pointless to continue to criticize the *ancien régime*. But clearly the novelist must have experienced something of a spiritual crisis, partly responsible for the change in emphasis, form and theme which occurred in his work when it was later resumed. *The Children of Gebelawi* (in Arabic: *Awlad Haratina*) is one of the few allegorical novels in Arabic. The events, true enough, still take place in Cairo, but unlike the earlier novels, which are set in a particular place and at a particular juncture in modern Egyptian history, *The Children of Gebelawi* evokes the *general* atmosphere of Old Cairo, in an almost timeless period,

although it is clearly before the late nineteenth century. The timelessness is perhaps appropriate, since the theme is, in fact, the whole of human history and man's quest for religion from Adam and Eve, Cain and Abel, Moses, Jesus, Muhammad, right down to the last of the prophets, the modern man of science, the man indirectly responsible for the death of their ancestor, Gebelawi, the Mountain Man, who clearly stands for God. These figures are given thinly disguised Arabic names which, together with a brief outline of the main events in their lives, immediately reveal their true identity. They are portrayed as the heroes of an imaginary alley who from time to time rise up in rebellion against the violent tyranny of the *status quo*. Structurally it is an interesting work: instead of the slow tempo of the earlier novels we have in effect a number of very fast-moving short *nouvelles*, held together by means of certain parallelisms and continuities and, of course, one unifying concept. Significantly, the novel is divided into 114 chapters, the same number as that of the chapters or *suras* of the Koran, a feature which in this context cannot be dismissed as mere coincidence: Mahfouz here is giving modern man's view of the stories of prophecy narrated in the Koran.

Yet although *The Children of Gebelawi* deals primarily with metaphysical questions such as the nature of evil and the meaning of life, the moments of spiritual illumination or religious ecstasy are few and far between. The driving force behind all the prophets is not so much the sense of man's essential need for God's comfort in a frighteningly insecure universe, as a keen awareness of social injustice and the evil perpetrated by man against man. In this respect *The Children of Gebelawi* forms a link with the rest of Mahfouz's work. On the other hand, even in his sociological novels Mahfouz's philosophical preoccupations, no doubt the product of his early intellectual formation, are never entirely absent. The conflict between science and religion, and the influence of Auguste Comte's logical positivism are clearly marked in his early writings, particularly in the character of Kamal Abd al-Jawwad in the trilogy. And it is this interpenetration of the philosophical/religious and the social, political and psychological that gives Mahfouz's novels, particularly his later works, their peculiar resonance and richness of texture, their many layers of meaning.

For Mahfouz went on to write more, and much greater, novels after *The Children of Gebelawi,* which constitutes an impressive, though imperfect, landmark in the development of his art as a novelist (in fact, more than twenty volumes of short stories and novels have appeared since 1959). As a novel *The Children of Gebelawi* suffers from serious defects: it is too repetitive, too full of fighting, too fast-moving; too thickly populated to allow for convincing characterization and, for a work on man's religious quest, it is too explicitly prosaic and lacking in the poetic spirit. Its interest lies chiefly on the level of themes and ideas, although its message is not exactly redolent of hope. Yet its spiritual preoccupations, its existentialist terror of death, point forward to future works. The next novel Mahfouz published was [*al-Līss wal-kilāb, The Thief and the Dogs* (1961)], which marked the beginning of a new phase of shorter novels concentrating on one protagonist, more dramatic in nature, more lyrical in style, more subtly symbolical in mode, employing stream-of-consciousness techniques as well as other modernistic devices in keeping with the nature of their subject. In them we have the poetry of realism, an indissoluble mixture of the political, the psychological, the metaphysical and the mystical. In several, notably in [*al-Shahhādh, The Beggar* (1965)] and [*Tharthara fawq al-Nīl, Chit-Chat on the Nile* (1966)], the obsessive spiritual quest leads to disturbing states of consciousness in which the borderline between illusion and reality is blurred and the distinction between past and present obliterated. Yet, despite their metaphysical dimension, they provide an eloquent and sensitive index to the mood and temper of Egypt since Nasser's revolution.

> *M. M. Badawi, "Microcosms of Old Cairo," in* The Times Literary Supplement, *No. 4095, September 25, 1981, p. 1104.*

ISSA PETERS

In the fall of 1959 one of the novels of Egypt's foremost writer of modern times, Naguib Mahfouz, called *Awlād Hāratinā*, was serialized in Cairo's major newspaper *Al-Ahrām*. Customarily, the serialized version would later be published in book form. Indeed, the novel was advertised on the back of Mahfouz's other works as being under publication and would presumably come out shortly thereafter. But this did not come to pass. It was not until 1967 and in Beirut that *Awlād* was to be published. The religious authorities in Egypt had opposed its publication there apparently because it subjects a religious topic to secular use, the novel being a transparent allegory of the three monotheistic religions. The names of the characters and the action in the novel thinly disguise those of the Old Testament and the Koran. For instance, Gebelawi, "Man of the Mountain," stands for God. Adham stands for "Adam" and Idrīs for "Iblis," Arabic for Satan.

Following biblical and Koranic accounts, the novel identifies the present-day problems of a Cairo neighborhood with the religious ones of the past, thus turning the religious figures into social reformers rather than prophets impelled by an apocalyptic vision of the divine. The analogy of the allegory culminates in a modern-day prophet, Arafa, who stands for science. It is not only the prophets of old who have failed in alleviating the social misery of the Cairene neighborhood, but also modern science, since Arafa's magic, instead of helping the district, is now at the disposal of the tyrannical trustee. What had been hoped to be a weapon of social justice turns out to be a tool of tyranny. The novel therefore strikes a gloomy note, except near the very end where the tone of gloom is transformed into one of ambivalence, since Arafa's disciple Hanash is portrayed as someone who may someday continue the struggle for human deliverance.

The novel marks a significant point of transition in Mahfouz's career. Except for his first three historical romances which appeared in the late 1930s and early 1940s, all his novels prior to the one under review were in the "realistic" and relatively "optimistic" vein. *Awlād*, however, reflects a transition toward an introspective phase characterized by an increasing sense of personal futility and political disillusionment. *Awlād* is Mahfouz's first major expression of the danger of the new scientific technology which his earlier heroes had welcomed.

The importance of this novel lies in its dramatic power to portray a vision of social reality as well as in its place in the philosophical and artistic development of the greatest Arab novelist of modern times.

> *Issa Peters, in a review of "Children of Gebelawi,"*
> *in* World Literature Today, *Vol. 56, No. 2, Spring, 1982, p. 398.*

ROGER ALLEN

Those critics who have considered the group of novels which Najīb Maḥfūẓ published during the 1960s have generally tended to regard the first of the group, *al-Liṣṣ wa-al-kilāb* (*The thief and the dogs,* 1961) as the best. Indeed, there is little doubt that this study of oppression and betrayal provides a most convincing fusion of symbol and reality in order to make some telling comments about socialist values. The fact that this work ends on such a negative note and that Maḥfūẓ's next novel, *al-Summān wa-al-kharīf* (*Quail and autumn,* 1962), has such an optimistic conclusion may even suggest that there was some official concern about Maḥfūẓ's views as expressed in the first novel. In any case, I have always regarded *Tharthara fawq al-Nīl* (*Chatter on the Nile,* 1966) as a work of equal distinction; in fact, in view of the extremely difficult task which Mahfūẓ sets himself in this later work, I find the results, if anything, even more impressive. In the first place, the spatial dimension in this novel is extremely restricted: the setting is an *'awwāma*, a houseboat on the Nile in Cairo. Within such an environment the action is, needless to say, confined, and one of the major features of the novel is an almost total lack of movement or change of scene. The narrative opens with a sarcastic description of the ministry office in which the novel's pivotal character, Anīs Zakī, works as a civil servant. He has finished a report and submitted it to his superior. He is summoned into the latter's office to explain how it is that the last pages of the report are completely blank; Anīs Zakī's pen has run dry in the process of writing the report and he has not even noticed. Apart from this introduction to one of the situations in Anīs Zakī's life, the only other occasion on which the scene shifts from the houseboat is when the characters of the novel pile into a car and go on a crazy ride down the Pyramids Road to Sakkāra, knock down and kill a peasant on the road, and do not stop to face the consequences.

The opening of the novel does more than depict the tedious environment of life in the civil service. In fact, that goal may be considered as ancillary to another literary task of some difficulty which Maḥfūẓ set himself in this work, namely of portraying Anīs Zakī in an almost permanently-drugged stupor, taciturn and inward-looking, hardly ever contributing to the "chatter" but responding to the comments of his superior in the ministry or his evening companions on the houseboat with streams of consciousness which resurrect episodes from past history and illustrate his own griefs and failures. The picture of Anīs Zakī's life and the activities on the houseboat which Maḥfūẓ gives is obviously important in that Anīs Zakī is, to quote one of the other characters, "in charge of our houseboat", a phrase which has more than a merely surface import within the atmosphere which Maḥfūẓ creates in this novel. Further details and descriptions are provided at different stages of the work by other characters; Maḥfūẓ in this work is using a limited multi-narrator technique which he exploits to a fuller extent in his next work, *Mīrāmār*. (pp. 101-02)

This then is not a novel of action; it is indeed concerned with "chatter on the Nile". The houseboat itself can, of course, be regarded as a means of detachment. It is moored to the land which in this case may be considered as the haven of a brutal reality, but the symbol of water allows for a lulling feeling of removal from such unpleasant facts of life which Anīs Zakī has to face in his office every day. It is from this environment that he escapes to his houseboat wafted by the cool evening breezes and to the circle of companions who join him in the evening for encounters with drugs and sex. The symbolism implicit in this escape from land and reality is further underlined by the presence on the boat of 'Amm 'Abduh, the houseboat's general factotum, a huge man who, in addition to arranging all the necessary equipment for the evening's gathering and procuring girls for Anīs Zakī and the company when asked, also serves as Imām for a local group of Muslims. . . . 'Amm 'Abduh then is the guardian of the houseboat and the provider of all the needs and comforts for the group of individuals who come to share in the atmosphere of detached irreality which Anīs Zakī has created for himself.

The group who come to the houseboat are from a variety of professions: there is Muṣṭafā Rāshid, the lawyer; Khālid 'Azūz the writer of short stories; Laylā Zaydān, a graduate of the American University in Cairo who has espoused feminist causes; Aḥmad Naṣr, a civil servant and book-keeper who is devoted to his wife and is described as "in sum a completely ordinary person"; 'Alī al-Sayyid, an art critic and companion to Saniyya Kāmil, who, "at times of marital trouble comes back to her old friends, a woman of experience who learned all about womanhood while still a virgin, a wife and mother, who is a veritable treasure-house of experience for the young girls who come to our houseboat". Much of the above description about these characters is given to the reader by Rajab al-Qāḍī, a celebrated film actor, who brings a new girl friend, Sanā' al-Rashīdī, to the group for the first time and introduces them to her one by one at the beginning of the fourth chapter. She is amazed at the blatant way in which the company indulges in illegalities, and this affords the characters—and, no doubt, the author—the opportunity to supply just one of a series of political comments which are scattered throughout the novel:

> "Aren't you afraid of the police?" she asked.
>
> "We're afraid of the police", 'Alī al-Sayyid responded, "the army, the English, the Americans, the overt and the covert. It's reached the stage now that we're not afraid of anything."
>
> "But the door is wide open!"
>
> "'Amm 'Abduh is outside. He can keep out any intruders."
>
> "Don't worry, gorgeous," Rajab said with a smile, "the government's so busy building things, it hasn't got time to bother us."
>
> "Why don't you try this type of fortitude?" asked Muṣṭafā Rāshid, offering her the hashish pipe.

The cynicism of the group, the reliance on 'Amm 'Abduh, and the desire to run away from reality and to persuade others to do so, all these features are evident in this short extract. Into this situation comes the figure of Sammāra Bahjat. We first hear of her at the beginning of the fifth chapter when 'Alī al-Sayyid announces that his journalistic colleague wants to visit them, since her curiosity has been aroused both by his conversations to her about the group and also by the publications in a variety of media of the artists who frequent the group. It is this same Sammāra Bahjat who provides another level of insight into the characters on the houseboat when, in the tenth chapter, Anīs Zakī reads from her diary the outline of a play which she has written, one in which all the personae are taken from the group on the houseboat. She has provided a cameo sketch of each of the "characters" in her play which reflects her own opinion of the person concerned. She has, in fact, told them earlier of her extreme interest in the theatre as something which "has focus and where every word has to have its own particular meaning". She ignores Muṣṭafā Rāshid's retort to this comment, to the effect that the theatre is thus totally opposite to what goes on on the houseboat, and instead asks the stupefied Anīs Zakī why he is not saying anything. This sends Anīs off on one of his journeys into history and his own consciousness, and yet typically he makes no response.

As Sammāra begins to attend the group regularly, they begin to worry about the fact that she is too serious; she poses a threat to their escapism. (pp. 102-05)

After Anīs Zakī has read Sammāra's diary which, unknown to the group, contains her impressions based on these conversations, an amusing chapter follows in which he argues with the group about their priorities in life, quoting throughout from Sammāra's diary. Even though he does not reveal the source of his comments and the group seems only moderately disturbed by his unusual loquaciousness, Sammāra herself feels most uneasy and eventually succeeds in getting the diary back after refusing to sleep with him. The fact that Anīs Zakī serves as a mouthpiece for the views of Sammāra about the group may perhaps be seen as a premonition of what is to come. When the grossly-overcrowded car in which they are speeding along the Pyramid Road kills the peasant, Sammāra insists that they stop, true to her role within the group and confirming their fears about her. Anīs Zakī is unable to sleep and only succeeds in doing so at his desk the next day, whereupon he is arrested after assaulting the Director General who has reprimanded him for his conduct. When the group meets that night, the atmosphere is tense. Sammāra insists that they go to the police, whereas everyone else is afraid of being exposed. Their efforts to point out to her that her own reputation will also be soiled are of no avail. Rajab al-Qāḍī, the driver of the car and would-be lover of Sammāra, becomes increasingly furious at Anīs Zakī's comments, and a terrible fight ensues, during which the figure of 'Amm 'Abduh appears, only to be sent away again by Aḥmad Naṣr. However, the group is not ready for the consequence of this fracas; for, when Anīs Zakī recovers, it is to tell his colleagues that murder is one thing which cannot be taken lightly, and he makes it clear that he is referring to the death of the peasant on the road. He says unequivocally that he is fully cognisant of what he is saying and that he will go to the police himself. Rajab tries to attack again, but the group take him away. 'Amm 'Abduh now reappears with a cup of coffee which, he hints, will make him feel better. Anīs Zakī is now left with Sammāra, and she only has time for a short conversation about the implications of their position before the laced coffee sends Anīs Zakī off into a final reverie concerning the tragedy of man's evolution "from the paradise of apes in trees to the ground in the forest".

From this brief, yet somewhat complex description, it will, I hope, be clear that we are dealing with one of Maḥfūẓ's richest essays in the use of symbolism. We have already made several suggestions on this topic, but the store is by no means exhausted. It should, for example, be pointed out that all the members of the group which meets on the houseboat belong to the intellectual class and more specifically to those in the sphere of culture. That Maḥfūẓ should have addressed himself to the issues evoked by the problems, life style and expectations of this group during the period of the early 1960s is in itself of extreme significance. For, as many people have since shown and as Maḥfūẓ himself has recorded in more recent fictional works such as *al-Marāyā* (**"Mirrors"**, 1972) and *al-Karnak* (the name of a café, 1974), these years may have witnessed some of the most oppressive political constraints on the artist during the entire revolutionary period. (pp. 105-06)

Roger Allen, ''Eight Arabic Novels,'' in his The Arabic Novel: An Historical and Critical Introduction,
Syracuse University Press, 1982, pp. 99-162.

SAAD EL-GABALAWY

The dilemma of the tormented self is . . . a thematic motif in
Najīb Mahfūz's *Al-Karnak* (1974), a relentlessly political novel,
representing in a conventional form the trend of committed
social realism. The author, one of Egypt's leading literary
figures, focuses on the trauma of totalitarianism in Nasser's
days, which inevitably created an atmosphere of prevalent fear
and suspicion, of moral disintegration and intellectual prostitution. The so-called ''Revolution'' is exposed as a corrupting
process, thriving on torture and treachery, violence and oppression, humiliation and degradation. It is not unreasonable in
this respect to suggest that Mahfūz, while depicting the Egyptian milieu accurately, may have taken as his primary model
Isherwood's Germany, Solzhenitsyn's Moscow or even Orwell's Oceania.

The totalitarian nightmare unfolds through the human tragedy
of the central characters, Ismail El-Sheikh and Zeinab Diab,
who are supposedly ''children of the Revolution.'' These young
lovers have known each other since childhood and planned to
get married after graduation from the university. It is likely
that the novelist intends them to incarnate the spirit of ''purity
and innocence'' before the fall. Ismail and Zeinab regard the
advent of the Revolution as the new dawn of freedom, equality
and justice. There is strong emphasis in the first part of the
book on their revolutionary idealism, based on blind faith in
Nasser as the savior of the nation from poverty and bondage.
In their eyes, Egypt is, so to speak, the phoenix that will rise
from its ashes in the freshness of youth.

But the Revolution starts to prey upon its children, particularly
the intellectuals who may pose a menace to the new regime.
Ismail and Zeinab are among the early victims, dragged barefoot and blindfolded by the secret police from their beds in the
middle of the night and thrown in dark prison cells, where they
are stripped of all dignity. (p. 87)

Thus the young idealists suddenly find a serpent in the cradle
of the revolutionary paradise. In the novel, the brutal chief of
the secret police, Khaled Safwan, seems to embody the spirit
of evil, leading to the fall of ''innocence and purity.'' Such
symbolism is strongly suggested by Mahfûz's description of
Safwan's encounters with Ismail and Zeinab, where his actions
are pathologically sadistic and venomous. With the young man,
he uses emotional blackmail to extract a confession that he is
a Communist: ''Can't you visualize what may happen to this
innocent girl if you insist on silence?'' Despite the fact that he
has never joined the Communists and has always asserted his
allegiance to the Revolution, Ismail desperately signs the
confession in order to protect Zeinab from torture. There is
striking irony when Safwan starts to reiterate mechanically the
hollow slogans of the Revolution: ''We are protecting the state
which has liberated you from all kinds of slavery''.

His sadism culminates in a scene of sheer horror when he
''decided to watch a thrilling, delightful, and most unusual
spectacle!'' Zeinab is raped by one of Safwan's thugs in front
of his eyes, in order to crush her pride and dignity, reducing
her to nothing. Her sense of innocence and harmony is suddenly
shattered by new awareness of evil. She is stunned by the
incredible outrage, by the blight of intolerable pollution, by
the deep feeling of contamination and irrevocable loss. Mahfūz

displays effectively the plight of the victim facing unpredictable
and uncontrollable circumstances. It is a diabolical trap which
leaves the victim alive but in torment and without hope of
release or even relief. For Zeinab, it is a dilemma with no
possible resolution in satisfactory human terms; its only sur-
cease lies in the merciful coup de grace of death.

Though considering for a moment the notion of suicide, she
is resilient enough to defeat the death wish and accept her stain.
No only that. Both Zeinab and Ismail, overwhelmed by grief
and despair, are forced to work as informers, suffering constantly the pangs of betrayal. . . . In the face of such degeneration, the reader becomes intensely conscious of the annihilation of values caused by ruthless dictatorship. The young
lovers, step by painful step, drift apart as a result of the agonies
of shame and guilt, of humiliation and degradation. Perhaps
the most terrifying aspect of Zeinab's life after the fall is her
bizarre form of atonement. Crucified by guilt, she starts to sell
her body: ''I kept repeating persistently, I'm a whore and a
spy! . . . I refused to make a false pretence of honor and decided
to live as a woman without dignity''.

This is not only atonement but a perverse and cruel punishment
which she inflicts upon herself out of self-hate. In this regard,
Zeinab adopts a strange kind of logic: ''I'm a child of the
Revolution and, in spite of everything, haven't lost faith in its
essence. I'm therefore responsible for it, and must carry the
full burden of this responsibility. Implicitly, I'm to blame for
what happened to me''. The novelist reveals here a deep insight
into the psychology of revolutionary idealism, which calls to
mind a similar perception in Arthur Koestler's *Darkness at
Noon* (1941), where the old Bolshevik Rubashov confesses to
crimes he had not committed and willingly accepts the guilty
verdict and execution as a last service to the party to which he
had dedicated his whole life.

The young idealists are, however, shocked into awareness by
the military defeat of 1967. For them, disillusionment is enlightenment, so that they acquire a clear vision of the devastating effects of tyranny. (pp. 87-8)

Mahfūz thus reveals how the political atmosphere, with its
ominous ramifications, can separate friends and lovers, undermining human relationships. *Al-Karnak* involves a process
of reduction and annihilation, with hardly any hope of renewal.
(pp. 88-9)

Saad El-Gabalawy, ''Tormented Selves in Three
Contemporary Egyptian Novels,'' in The International Fiction Review, Vol. 12, No. 2, Summer, 1985,
pp. 84-91.

ISSA PETERS

Al-Liṣṣ wa-al-Kilāb, here translated as *The Thief and the Dogs,*
is a study of the passion for revenge on the part of an intellectual
who had been convicted of theft and was later betrayed by his
wife and his former ideological mentors, who have become
turncoats. He faces his inevitable destiny with a quasi-exis-
tential courage and without indulging in romanticizing or self-
pity. The author lays bare the feelings of this bitter man while
exposing his tenderness toward people who are kind to him.
On a social level, however, the disillusionment of the protagonist may refer to the failure of Egyptian society to achieve
the hopes of the 1952 revolution and to the betrayal of the
Egyptian intellectuals and their ideals of social justice and equal
distribution of wealth.

The novel, which appeared in 1961, marks a significant change in the career of Naguib Mahfouz. . . . The concern with external reality, which characterizes the early novels, gives way to an analysis of the individual's inner life. Whenever there is a tragedy in the early novels, the root cause lies in the social conditions. *The Thief and the Dogs,* however, reflects a tragedy of a different kind—that of a psychological nature. The protagonist here seems bent on confrontation and ultimate self-destruction.

Moreover, the novel reveals two technical innovations in the development of Mahfouz's literary career. The first is an economy of expression, whereby the author's earlier propensity to indulge in prolific description of external reality is gone; now every word counts. Second, new points of view are employed to reflect the new domain of interest such as the stream of consciousness; this technique is employed in order to dramatize the protagonist's internal crises as well as to provide information on his background and to explain his feelings and motivations.

The novel under review therefore represents a turning point in the philosophic and artistic development of the greatest Arab novelist of modern times.

> Issa Peters, in a review of "The Thief and the Dogs,"
> in World Literature Today, *Vol. 60, No. 4, Autumn,*
> *1986, p. 684.*

ROGER ALLEN

The story [in *Wedding Song*] is one of sordid intrigue and hatred within the ersatz world of the theatre in Egypt. The title, itself a bitter pun on traditional wedding rites, refers in fact to a play written by Abbas Karam Younis, one of the four narrators of the tale. Like one of the novel's predecessors, *Miramar,* the work represents the telling of the same story by four different characters and reveals their differing points of view toward the events which take place. I must add immediately that *Wedding Song* is no equal of the earlier novel, either in the subtlety of its presentation of the situation and the characters who are involved, or in its brilliant use of style to convey the differing attitudes of the participants in the action. I am, of course, aware that many critics have spoken in terms of a further "phase" in Mahfouz's novelistic output, and certainly there is no letup in the author's determination to reflect current attitudes and concerns in his works. There is much reference to overflowing sewers, rising prices, and transportation problems, all of them distressingly frequent facets of current life in the huge metropolis which Cairo has now become. All this allows Mahfouz to engage in some of his famous "one-liners": "We're living in times when sex has become a national pursuit," for example, and "I'm liberated. I belong to the good old days, before religion and moral behavior became all the rage." It all makes for enjoyable and profitable reading, but I can hardly say that it serves as a further enhancement of Mahfouz's reputation as a novelist. . . .

In summary, *Wedding Song* is an interesting example of the recent output by the Arab world's most illustrious writer of fiction and, as a reflection of his views on current life in Egypt, a useful addition to the list of works translated from modern Arabic fiction.

> Roger Allen, in a review of "Wedding Song," in
> World Literature Today, *Vol. 61, No. 1, Winter,*
> *1987, p. 149.*

IVAN HILL

[*Miramar* is set] in an Alexandrian boarding house. A young girl comes to work there from the country, where she has refused an arranged marriage. She wishes to be independent, to study, and so to become a "modern" woman. Unfortunately, the other residents regard opportunity as justification. Incited by her beauty, they quarrel and fight over her. In the end there is a death. . . . [The] narrative is passed from one character to another. . . . [The] result is magnificent. There is no authorial intervention at all; the characters, using very different idioms, address the reader in turn, revealing their memories and thoughts. A complex counterpoint is built up, and, because of the different ages, backgrounds and experience of the characters, we are presented with a microcosm of Egypt.

Mahfouz is considered by many to be the most significant writer of the Arab novel. Certainly, in his long and prolific career, he has experimented with a form not organic in Arabic literature. In some ways the different stages of his work parallel the development of the novel in the West. Early works such as *Midaq Alley* and *The Beginning and the End* . . . have a strong feel of the nineteenth century about them. The alley is a character in its own right, in a poor quarter of Cairo, used rather like Egdon Heath or Bleak House. A rich collection of characters is built up with Dickensian detail. (It is curious to note that Mahfouz has not read Dickens, although he has read extensively in Balzac and Dostoevsky.) In the centre is Hamida, beautiful and haughty, with aspirations above the squalor and social limitations of her environment. She becomes engaged to the barber, who goes away to earn money by working for the British forces. During his absence, Hamida is attracted by a sophisticated stranger, who turns out to be a pimp and presses her into service for up-market clients. This elegant prostitution suits her. The returning fiancé, inflamed by passion and drink, sees her surrounded by soldiers in a Cairo bar, attacks her, and is killed in the ensuing fight. As with *The Beginning and the End,* the tragic saga of a family, the story is sequential and in the social realist tradition.

The Thief and the Dogs is from an entirely different genre. Written in 1961, it makes extensive use of "stream of consciousness". It is a fast-moving psychological study of a man, freed after wrongful imprisonment, seeking revenge on his wife and her lover. He kills the wrong people and is hunted by the police, who finally surround him in a cemetery. Mahfouz, despite his new form, does not lose his social concerns. The quest for justice is symbolic:

> "Whoever kills me will be killing the millions. I am
> the hope and the dream, the redemption of cowards;
> I am good principles, consolation. . . . The decla-
> ration that I'm mad must encompass all who are
> loving." . . .

The plot of *Autumn Quail* (1962) . . . [is also] clearly intended to have a wider significance. Isa al Dabagh was a senior civil servant before the revolution. He was pensioned off because of his fondness for bribes, but refuses to seek employment under the new régime. Married to a barren divorcee, he strikes up, rather unwillingly, a relationship with a prostitute, but abandons her when she becomes pregnant. Later, he pines for his child, but the mother refuses to recognize his paternity. Disillusioned and depressed, he encounters a man whom he had previously sent to jail unjustly. Their exchange leads him to new hope, as he follows the young man out of the shadows. This, set against a historical background, is easy to understand, the old order embracing the new dawn with renewed optimism.

But the exact significance of individual elements is harder to pin down. One could say that the barren wife was the old system, under which those capable of creation had to prostitute themselves. His abandonment of the child could be refusal to accept social responsibility. But what of the child? Is this the new régime which he was unable to embrace? We should not look too hard for rigid structures here, for the general drift is clear. What is not so clear is why Mahfouz should have written such an optimistic book so soon after *The Thief and the Dogs,* with its strongly critical tone. There have been suggestions of political pressure or expediency. *Wedding Song* (1981) is a return to a bleaker outlook (the compromises that every character makes lead to dishonesty, treachery, corruption and death), but employs a similar form to *Miramar.*

> *Ivan Hill, "Adapting the Alien," in* The Times Literary Supplement, *No. 4422, January 1-7, 1988, p. 15.*

MICHAEL BEARD

Naguib Mahfouz's international reputation makes him the generic Egyptian writer, an institution, one of those seemingly inexhaustible factories of narrative we like to compare with Balzac or Zola. Consequently he suffers the fate of national authors, being read abroad for local color, for his crowded canvases and the closely observed social detail. It may be that a slim book like *Respected Sir* (published in Arabic in 1975), which is sparing in detail and less anchored in social specifics than most of his other novels, can help attune us to Mr. Mahfouz's subtleties as a writer. . . .

Respected Sir follows [the entire career of bureaucrat Othman Bayyumi], from the day when he is introduced at the Director-General's office as one of a group of neophyte clerks. The historical background is colonial Egypt, sometime between the 1920's and the revolution of 1952, but the period is unspecified and unfocused. Beyond the fact of Othman's humble origins, Mr. Mahfouz takes no particular interest in showing us what motivates him. . . .

Mr. Mahfouz's dexterity in shunting us along the corridors of Othman's career is so subtle that we may want to see *Respected Sir* as a simple cautionary tale—a latter-day *Bleak House* in Arabic, with Othman Bayyumi as an overreacher whose ambition costs him his soul. Othman is on a misguided quest, unmistakably, but Mr. Mahfouz also makes it clear that his protagonist is talented, sensitive and not without charm. Othman does become the admirable bureaucrat he sets out to be, and when he compromises himself morally (in his stinginess, in his refusal of socially disadvantageous marriage offers) we see his remorse. When he catches himself momentarily wishing the death of a sick superior, "the thought made him feel ashamed, as his thought often did, and he prayed to God for forgiveness." . . .

Naguib Mahfouz doesn't allow us any clear-cut moral judgments; our attention flows back not to a list of sins but to the space Othman has crossed, and the novel's revelation is one of scale. So this is how long it takes to get from one side of the bureaucracy to the other: an entire life. It is a complex, delicate effect, and with it *Respected Sir* urges us to take a closer look at this author's other novels to see what we might have missed.

> *Michael Beard, "Othman Makes It," in* The New York Times Book Review, *January 31, 1988, p. 29.*

Harry Mathews

1930-

American novelist, poet, short story writer, and translator.

In his writing, Mathews affirms the ability of language to reveal unexpected meanings. A proponent of the experimental techniques formulated among the group of European writers, philosophers, and mathematicians who constitute Oulipo—Ouvroir de littérature potentielle, or Workshop of Potential Literature—Mathews employs arbitrary, constrictive rules to explore new possibilities in fiction and poetry. According to Mathews, rigid adherence to these self-imposed rules forces the author to write material he would not have otherwise conceived. Influenced by the work of experimental French writer Raymond Roussel, Mathews's fiction is characterized by artifice, bizarre imagery, subtle humor, language games, contingent plots, fantastical situations, and complex searches for solutions to riddles. Mathews believes that language, rather than experience or reality, generates literature and that literary art is not a product but part of the process of writing and reading. Joseph McElroy observed: ''Like Italo Calvino, [Mathews] has practiced an agile faith in the imagination's autonomy. Like Raymond Roussel earlier in the century, Mathews has conjured the unforeseeable out of the seemingly random.''

After graduating from Harvard University in 1952, Mathews moved to France, where he has since lived most of his life. He began his literary career as a poet but turned to fiction after reading Roussel's novels and plays, which convinced Mathews that prose could be as inventive as verse and that fiction need not be representational. Each of Mathews's first three novels—*The Conversions* (1962), *Tlooth* (1966), and *The Sinking of the Odradek Stadium* (1975)—details a convoluted search for an obscure goal. In *The Conversions*, an anonymous narrator must solve three apparently incongruous and cryptic riddles engraved on a cutting tool in order to claim a fortune left by an eccentric millionaire. This quest encompasses several misleading clues and seemingly pointless tales framed within other mysteries. The narrator ultimately discovers that he has been the victim of a practical joke. Thomas R. Edwards compared *The Conversions* to Thomas Pynchon's *V.*, noting that the two novels share an interest ''in the messages that may be concealed in history, the necessity and absurdity of trying to make sense of a senseless world.'' *Tlooth* is a picaresque story about an androgynous violinist-turned-dentist who seeks revenge against the person who unnecessarily amputated two fingers from her left hand. The protagonist deciphers coded texts and documents and travels great distances while attempting to attain her goal. In *The Sinking of the Odradek Stadium*, a husband and wife exchange letters in hopes of finding lost gold. The wife eventually locates the treasure on a ship called the Odradek Stadium, but, as the title of the book suggests, the gold will not reach its destination. Brian Stonehill described Mathews's first three novels as ''intricate allegories of the reader or listener caught in the act of interpretation.''

Mathews's fourth novel, *Cigarettes* (1987), is regarded as his most conventionally plotted work. Each of the chapters in this book centers on two major characters within a series of interrelated stories focusing on such themes as business ethics, personal and familial relationships, the nature of friendship,

and the social connotations of wealth and power. Tom Clark commented: ''[Mathews] has made himself surprisingly comprehensible in order to illuminate humanity's general state of mutual incomprehension; he has written a novel that's like a message-in-a-bottle proposing that *all* messages—even art's—are lost from the moment they are composed, because each is inscribed in the self's subjective language.''

Mathews's verse and short fiction also make use of techniques devised in Oulipo. In *Le savoir des rois: Poèmes à perverbes* (1976) and the texts collected in *Selected Declarations of Dependence* (1977), Mathews displays his penchant for linguistic playfulness by juxtaposing the first parts of well-known proverbs with the second parts of others to create unforeseen new meanings, which Mathews calls ''perverbs.'' *Trial Impressions* (1977) comprises thirty permutations of a lyric by seventeenth-century poet John Dowland on the theme of permanence and change. In *Country Cooking and Other Stories* (1980), Mathews parodies writings from such fields as musicology, anthropology, historiography, and the history of science, as well as cookbook recipes. *Plaisirs singuliers* (1983; *Singular Pleasures*) explores the social and political implications of onanism. *Armenian Papers: Poems, 1954-1984* (1987) collects all of Mathews's poetry and features ''The Armenian Papers,'' a series of prose poems about the genocide of Armenians in Turkey. With poets John Ashbery, Kenneth Koch, and James

Schuyler, Mathews also founded and edited the literary journal *Locus Solus*.

(See also *CLC*, Vol. 6; *Contemporary Authors*, Vols. 21-24, rev. ed.; *Contemporary Authors New Revision Series*, Vol. 18; and *Contemporary Authors Autobiography Series*, Vol. 6.)

SHAUN O'CONNELL

Strange to the point of incommunicability, *The Sinking of the Odradek Stadium and Other Novels,* by Harry Mathews, offers three fictional designs (?) which give shape to little beyond themselves. In *The Conversions* the narrator meets the strange Mr. Wayl, who will award a fortune to the first who can decode a cryptic message on his ritual adze; Mr. Wayl has "Midas fingers," a beam which touches all with gold: "one by one, all the guests were subjected to the illusory transformation." So too all Mathews' characters. In Pynchon fashion, they seek to decipher riddles (*Tlooth*) and uncover clues to buried treasure (*Sinking*); of course, the more they pursue, the farther the prize (the tlooth-truth) recedes; all goes batty. Mathews has a following which ranges from *Paris Review* to *NY Times Book Review,* but his novels constitute painful reads, *ad hoc* journeys into the *outre*. In Modern fiction no truth is more universally and predictably acknowledged than that no truth can be acknowledged. (p. 169)

> Shaun O'Connell, "American Fiction, 1975: Celebration in Wonderland," in The Massachusetts Review, *Vol. XVII, No. 1, Spring, 1976, pp. 165-94.*

DAVID LEHMAN

Mathews is one of our great experimentalists, and *Selected Declarations of Dependence* is a magnificent feat of verbal gamesmanship, providing conclusive evidence of his ability to create a proliferation of texts from the least promising of origins, to harness the generative power of language through the agency of applied mathematical principles. The book's *donnée* is a set of well-worn proverbs, forty-six of them, that supply the "theme" for an apparently inexhaustible number of variations. Capitalizing on typos is one way of renewing a dead metaphor, as Mathews shows in such "Snips of the Tongue" as "The road to help is paved with good intentions." A more reliable method involves the equivoque, an arcane form in which the first half of any given line couples with the second half of the following line. Mathews calls the results he comes up with "perverbs." And here is where the fun begins: the main body of the work consists of ingenious paraphrases of some of the permutated proverbs. The example Mathews proffers as a kind of reader's guide goes as follows:

> "The sky was clear except for the fog rising to the east—fermentation from the oak bog" is a *paraphrase* of the *proverb* "Every cloud from little acorns grows."

A voice may be expected to raise objections at roughly this point: that Mathews' "rules" tend to value the bizarre as an intrinsic good and, further, that all individuality is forfeited during the task—the writer has "merely" to apply the rules "and let the sounds take care of themselves." The paraphrases themselves rebut these charges more effectively than the abstract arguments to which they give weight—the age-old ar-

guments in favor of constrictive forms, not as evasions of individual authority, but as elaborate tests of the writer's skill, challenges to his imagination. That such arguments are "age-old" suggests that the experimental ideal to which Mathews is committed represents a more complex attitude toward tradition than one might expect. If, as Richard Howard has said, originality implies a return to origins, then Mathews is certainly an original in both senses of the word. (pp. 147-48)

Reminiscent of the strategems for composition introduced by Raymond Roussel, *Selected Declarations of Dependence* is as useful a book as any I know for serious students in poetry writing seminars; it affords a long loving look at the process by which airy nothings are given a local habitation and a choice of names. (p. 149)

> *David Lehman, "In the Cool Element of Prose," in* Parnassus: Poetry in Review, *Vol. 8, No. 2, 1980, pp. 137-51.*

WELCH D. EVERMAN

The fiction of Harry Mathews is fiction that poses as something else (mythology, linguistics, history, etc.) posing as fiction. This dialectical process is intricate and confusing, for it is always a process without a product: a lecture on linguistics that refers to no real language; a history that circles back to its own present; instructions for the preparation of a meal which the chef will lose all desire to eat. These fictions consume themselves. Once read, there is no remainder. For Mathews, each text is the process of having written. For the reader, each is the process of having read.

The title story of [*Country Cooking and Other Stories*] presents cook book instructions for the making of "farce double" ("literally, double stuffing"), the specialty of a mountain village in the Auvergne. The directions are deceptively complete and straightforward, though the ingredients would be impossible to obtain and the dish impossible to prepare. The meal itself is only half of the "farce double"; the other half is the ceremony which accompanies the serving of the dish, a celebration based on a long and involved song about a young man's first travels into the world. Mathews presents both the culinary and the anthropological "facts" in such detail that one is tempted to believe everything one reads. And yet [**"Country Cooking"**] cancels itself; the meal is merely the excuse for the ceremony and the ceremony merely the excuse for the meal. Mathews' "realistic" details are betrayed by his obvious fictions (e.g., his instruction to the reader to see page 888 of this 88 page book). The farce poses as a factive treatise which seems to betray its own fictivity. In the end, the text has not produced an account of a process (the preparation of "farce double"); it is the process itself. Neither the dish nor the ceremony can exist beyond the signifiers that present them. These signifiers are facts; what they signify is fiction.

Are there only the words?

How is this possible? How is it done? . . .

Mathews' fictions seem to be written in a language that demands translation. That language is English. The reader's translation produces a text that is identical to the original, word for word. If there was a meaning hidden in the original text, it is hidden in the translation as well.

There are only the words.

But, in fact, the meaning is not hidden at all; it is there in the act of translating. . . .

Like the texts of Raymond Roussel, Mathews' texts are motivated by their own language, and that language does not point beyond itself. As *Impressions of Africa* is not the travelogue it pretends to be (because there is no Rousselian Africa beyond the text), so Mathews' **"The Dialect of the Tribe"** is not a treatise on primitive language, and **"Tradition and the Individual Talent"** is not an exercise in the history of music. Both Roussel and Mathews often make use of "real" names (Africa or Boris Christoff), but these names do not factualize the fictions, for they are neither more nor less "real" than any of the other (uncapitalized) words in the texts. Instead, Africa and Christoff become fictions, i.e. mere words.

For Mathews, it is the shape of the sign, the material signifier, that matters, and each signifier points to and/or cancels the next (see the recurring moreovers and howevers of **"The Network"**), just as the two halves of *Impressions of Africa* account for and erase each other.

What is left?

There only are the words. . . .

Like many of Italo Calvino's invisible cities, Harry Mathews' imaginary histories are often so probable that that they ought to be true, at least as true as any historian's history. Calvino's "real" characters, Kublai Khan and Marco Polo, have their counterparts in Mathews' Dietrich Fischer-Dieskau and Nathan Milstein, and Mathews' musical/genealogical history of the Bratislava Spiccato in **"Tradition and the Individual Talent"** seems as likely as any other historical treatise (except, of course, for the fact that it appears in a collection of short fiction).

Only an expert in European music history could tell fact from fiction here (and Mathews holds a degree in music from Harvard). The story could be disproved or verified, of course, but in order to do so, one would have to rewrite Mathews' piece, as Pierre Menard did for Cervantes or as Mathews himself has done for John Dowland in his collection of poems, *Trial Impressions*.

Such a rewriting could have two possible results:

(1) The new text would be identical to Mathews'.

(2) The new text would be different from Mathews'.

In either case, one would have another text which, in its turn, could be disproved or verified, altered or left to stand. Mathews shows us why this is so. History is not fact. Fact is fact. History is invented after the fact. And what comes after the fact is fiction.

There only the words are.

Therefore, a rewriting is not necessary. A simple (?) reading of the text is enough.

Mathews is an innovative fiction writer precisely because he does not seem to be one. In fact, he does not seem to be a fiction writer at all. Perhaps he is not. Or perhaps all writers are fiction writers. (p. 7)

Calvino has written: "Literature is a combinatorial game which plays on the possibilities intrinsic to its own material." The game as Mathews plays it is one of mathematical precision. Each element balances and is balanced by another. The equation is always perfect (see **"The Ledge"**), i.e. always a tautology which leaves no remainder, which teaches nothing.

Only the words are there. (pp. 7-8)

Harry Mathews writes words. On the surface, these words seem to be about history, linguistics, anthropology, cooking, etc. And yet it is this "about" that Mathews betrays through the words themselves. On the surface, the words appear to be about something else, something that is not language, i.e. facts. In fact, they are about themselves. On the surface, the words offer a sense of depth and seem capable of explaining, accounting for, transforming the world beyond words. Paradoxically, a deeper reading shows that the words remain on the surface.

For Mathews, words do not transform the world beyond words, and there is every reason to believe that the words of Jacob Burkhardt, Ferdinand de Saussure, Claude Levi-Strauss, and Betty Crocker are as fictitious as those of *Country Cooking*. No doubt the yearning to transform the world with/into language is real, but the effort can only fail.

Are only the words there?

What remains is not fact or science or knowledge. It is fiction. It is the linguistic act, "that supremely human gift."

What more could you want? (p. 8)

Welch D. Everman, in a review of "Country Cooking and Other Stories," in The American Book Review, *Vol. 3, No. 3, March-April, 1981, pp. 7-8.*

GEORGES PEREC

[The essay excerpted below was originally published in French in the publication Le monde, *April 3, 1981.]*

It is undeniable that the first impression given by Mathews's books is that of a narrative world determined by rules from another planet, rules that with agreeable liveliness undermine the conventions surrounding our concepts of fiction in general and the novel in particular. No doubt the continuity of these tales resembles that of an ordinary adventure story, so that at the start one finds oneself concerned, in a perfectly traditional manner, with solving the riddle on which the fortune of a rich eccentric depends, with the fulfillment of a terrible vengeance, or with the search for clues to a fabulous treasure. But within the framework of these simple plots, at first sight hardly likely to present an author with significant difficulties, characters apparently behave according to an imaginative system at once whimsical and bewildering, one that obliges them to play baseball in a Soviet labor camp or weave linen in the sewers of Miami. At every moment the vicissitudes of their existence transport us a thousand leagues from the place we expected to find them.

In these utterly unpredictable, utterly precise works of fiction, anything can happen. And anything does happen: we encounter a Russian lieutenant defending himself for a night and a day from Kirghiz bandits behind a wall of rusk sacks; three Americans who meet at the Copenhagen airport and discover a common fondness for pickled onions and old German music before facing death and devastation on the floes of the Arctic; a modern Perseus rescuing his Andromeda by subduing a dragon with his Swiss army knife. Without batting an eyelash, the author shifts us from an outbreak of plague in Bengal to a surefire method of fixing horse races by training horses to constipate themselves. (p. 82)

It was through an excerpt from *The Conversions* published in 1970 in *Les Lettres nouvelles* that I first entered this improbable world where nothing happens according to the customs of to-day's fiction. From the outset I was fascinated by the prolif-eration of meticulous and obsessive images that turns every situation into a pretext for unimaginable twists of the plot; where space and time become no more than inconsequential variables, through which the author and his protagonists move as though unaware of them; where a character's fate is abruptly revealed, because of the working of some unknown code, to hang on the momentary inattention of a cook in Brittany; and where prodigious verbal apparatuses are assembled in a few pages or a few lines only to vanish like mirages, leaving behind them no more than the slightly misty sight of twelve sarru-sophones, or of an uprooted graveyard floating intact on the waters of the flooded Kabul.

For the first time since Raymond Roussel, Harry Mathews has provided us with a novelistic configuration whose imperious requirements, contiguous with the written text itself, secrete symbols, allegories, points of contact and discontinuity, true and false scientific discoveries, lexical, verbal, and syntactic deformations, myths and obscurities, none of them having, ultimately, reference to anything beyond themselves. Every-thing that happens in these books—the least details of their vicissitudes, their erudite digressions, their *langoureux ver-tiges*—are nothing more than the ghostly, frail delineations of the legendary wrestling match in which from the beginning of time we have been engaged with the world of words, signs, meanings, and dreams, and which we call fiction. (p. 83)

> *Georges Perec, "Avez-vous lu Harry Mathews?" in* The Review of Contemporary Fiction, *Vol. VII, No. 3, Fall, 1987, pp. 82-3.*

BRIAN STONEHILL

Harry Mathews takes semiotics out of the seminar and makes it live as fiction. Language is anything but transparent for him. He is not a self-centered performer, or a member of the Look Ma, I'm Writing! school. Nor does he make us uncomfortably aware of ourselves as readers. But (although he ridicules McLuhan) Mathews does treat his medium as his message; language, in all of its many-meaninged, ambiguous, tragicomic potential, is itself his subject matter. His first three novels are in fact intricate allegories of the reader or listener caught in the act of interpretation.

The distinctive appeal of Mathews's novels lies in their ex-traordinarily rich and playful linguistic texture, rather than in the plot structures that are relatively straightforward and easy to recount. *The Conversions* (1962) begins when its anonymous narrator is given a golden ceremonial adze by a wealthy ec-centric named Grent Wayl. The adze is engraved with a series of seven mysterious scenes which the narrator attempts, ten-tatively, to explain. When Wayl dies, a provision in his will turns the narrator's mild curiosity into exegetical zeal, by con-ferring immense wealth on the person who can answer three riddles:

1) When was a stone not a king?

2) What was *La Messe de Sire Fadevant?*

3) Who shaved the Old Man's Beard?

The riddles all have to do with the engravings on the adze, and all seem to depend upon puns. Along with the narrator, we gradually learn of a secret society that has persisted through the centuries despite repeated persecution, a society that, in a ceremony involving the golden adze, crowns its leader King

and calls him Sylvius. An imposter named Johnstone once claimed falsely to be Sylvius—hence the "stone" that was "not a king". *La Messe de Sire Fadevant* devolves upon mu-sical and translingual puns: *Sire* denotes not a noble title but two musical notes, while *Fadevant* places a third note in front: *fa-si-re*. Tracking down a Mass that begins with these notes, the narrator finds that its words shed further light upon the followers of Sylvius. The third riddle stumps him, however, and he abandons the quest, seemingly inconclusively, at nov-el's end.

Mathews's second novel, *Tlooth* (1966), achieved some re-nown when Martin Gardner described it glowingly in his col-umn in *Scientific American*. Its narrator and protagonist (whose name and even gender are concealed from us until close to the end) spends the novel pursuing a fellow ex-convict, for reasons that are tucked away as an aside to a footnote on the novel's first page. (It appears that the object of pursuit, a criminally perverse surgeon, unnecessarily amputated two fingers from the left hand of the narrator, who until then had been a vio-linist.)

"Texts True and False" (one of *Tlooth*'s chapter titles) litter the trail of vengeance, as do documents in a dozen lingos, clashing symbols, and uncracked codes. "Tlooth" itself, the sound uttered by a bizarre oracle, is, when properly construed, a prophecy that comes true: the narrator, now turned dentist, succeeds in strapping the object of her pursuit into her own dentist's chair. Mercifully for both reader and quarry, no pain-ful drilling takes place, for reasons I will not divulge.

In 1975, Harper & Row published Mathews's epistolary novel *The Sinking of the Odradek Stadium* in a handy omnibus volume that includes the two previous works. *The Sinking . . .* consists of the letters of two correspondents, Zachary McCaltex, an American treasure-hunter writing from Miami, and Twang, his obscurely Asian wife, answering in comically bad but melior-ative English from various spots in Italy. The two of them are pursuing, by diverse machinations, a fortune in gold hidden in a chest and then lost by the Medici family. Again much of the action consists of the perusal, translation, interpretation, and verification of a host of documents, maps, clues, and false leads. In the very last letter of the book we learn that Twang has actually got her hands on the gold, and is about to ship it to Zachary via the freighter *Odradek Stadium*. Only the novel's title hints at what happens next.

Clearly, depth psychology counts for little in these three novels. Their plots, while seemingly serpentine, studded with endo-narratives, framed tales, and convoluted digressions, are es-sentially linear in structure, and derive all their motivation from the pattern of the Quest. In *The Conversions* and *The Sink-ing . . .* the narrator-protagonists are driven by a desire for money: an inheritance and hidden treasure, respectively. Hun-ger for revenge gives *Tlooth* its bite. The same narrative struc-ture, though, animates all three novels, the same one, in fact, that underlies the action of *Pilgrim's Progress* and *Moby Dick*. (Grent Wayl, the millionaire who starts the narrator of *The Conversions* on his quest, is probably named in punning al-lusion to both the Whale and the Grail, conflating secular and religious Quests in much the same way that similar references converge in the novel's title.) The Quest motif, it is worth noting, similarly dominates the novels of Mathews's near-con-temporary Thomas Pynchon. Stencil pursues V. in *V.*, a con-geries of characters chases the V-2 in *Gravity's Rainbow*, and, especially close to the secret followers of Sylvius in *The Con-*

versions, there are the conspirators who await silent Trystero's empire in *The Crying of Lot 49.*

Oedipa Maas, the heroine of *The Crying of Lot 49,* may even be seen as a near relation of the narrator-protagonist of *The Conversions.* Just as Oedipa comes to feel that the entire Trystero system has been invented so as to lure her into attempting to decode it, so the narrator of *The Conversions* winds up suspecting that the whole Sylvius conspiracy was contrived as "an elaborate trick on me." Furthermore, there is ambiguous but potent evidence concealed throughout Mathews's novel suggesting that the narrator, who is of obscure parentage, is himself the present rightful Sylvius—that this is what Grent Wayl wished him to discover—but that, at novel's end, he remains ignorant of his own identity. If this is true, then the novel's central character is linked not only to Pynchon's Oedipa but to the Sophoclean Oedipus Rex: the Sphinx poses riddles, which the hero can only partially answer while remaining blind to his own identity. In Mathews's crafty updating of the myth, the close exegetical reading which the novel teaches us to perform grants us knowledge that is denied to the narrator himself.

In Pynchon's work, too, the plots are made of metaphors for the act of interpretation. This is most explicit in *Gravity's Rainbow,* where Pynchon finds an analogy for the characters' pursuit of scraps of Rocket information in the study by Talmudic scholars of some all-important Text. Paranoia strikes deep in both these writers, for just as Slothrop starts "finding in every bone and cabbage leaf paraphrases of himself," so, in *The Sinking . . . ,* Zachary writes to Twang, "I have become convinced that in my dealings with the Knights everything that happens is symbolic; even if I don't know of what, that doesn't matter, what counts is that I am being guided along a spiritual itinerary."

I'm not suggesting, of course, that Mathews has cribbed from Pynchon; these are filiations, not derivations, and besides, Mathews's first two novels *precede The Crying of Lot 49.* Yet another curious link between these two writers, however, lies in the similar degree to which their characters, as metaphoric "readers" of ambiguous "texts", are faced with the obligation of sorting out signs and signals that mean something from arbitrary occurrences signifying nothing. They, the characters, and we, the readers, are together launched on the same quest to distinguish signal from noise, to find a message in the mess. Is it a map, or is it the terrain? Live or Memorex? Mathews and Pynchon both dramatize this essentially semiotic challenge of inferring the intention behind a sign by mingling elements of obvious randomness with those of undeniable conspiracy. Mathews loves to give long, manically detailed descriptions of intricate, often impossible machines, stressing the connections of part to part and to the function of the whole in a way that glorifies the bonds of cause-and-effect. At the same time, much of his action is generated by games of chance: races of all sorts (the narrator of *The Conversions* wins his golden adze by gambling on a worm-race), card games, variations on spin-the-bottle. We become hopers and doubters like the characters themselves; any word might conceal a hidden meaning, or a half-dozen hidden meanings, or it might mean nothing at all. Or both, or all three. Language congeals, opacifies, deliquesces, and clarifies before our very eyes, while the story rolls on. This is not easily done.

As for the human quality of the stories, their emotional texture, I find *The Conversions* and *Tlooth* delightfully engaging and intriguing as intellectual puzzles, marvelously playful in their linguistic vitality, but somewhat arid or harsh in their unconcern with a reader's natural sympathies for this character or that. (To each his or her own criteria, obviously.) The range and richness of Mathews's invention are truly phenomenal and not to be gainsaid. But it is not until *The Sinking of the Odradek Stadium* that I find myself *touched* by his work; and here, strangely enough, it is because the novel is as much about feelings of love as about ideas of language.

The Sinking of the Odradek Stadium is, in my opinion, a superior novel because the letters that pass between Twang and Zachary McCaltex are motivated not only by their greed for the Medici gold but also by a burning urge to throw down their pens and reading glasses, cross the ocean that separates them, and leap into each other's arms. Part of every letter is given over to expressions of longing, loneliness, or lust, and these passages provide an emotional depth and resonance that the other two novels lack. (pp. 107-09)

If *The Conversions* is Harry Mathews's most Pynchonesque novel, *The Sinking of the Odradek Stadium* is his most Nabokovian. There is some unacknowledged play on the epigraph to *Pale Fire,* a sentence that Boswell heard Johnson say about his cat: "Hodge shall not be shot." In *The Sinking . . .* a character named Dexter Hodge apparently receives a bullet in the chest and bleeds profusely, but it turns out to have been all theater. More significantly, perhaps, *The Sinking . . . ,* again like *Pale Fire* but unlike any other novel I know of, comes equipped with a meticulous but tantalizingly incomplete index. In addition to burying wealths of meaning in their own wordplay, both fictions also concern actual buried treasure. As John Barth reminds us in a more recent epistolary novel, "language is always also but seldom simply about itself." (p. 110)

Brian Stonehill, *"On Harry Mathews,"* in Chicago Review, *Vol. 33, No. 2, Autumn, 1982, pp. 107-11.*

IRVING MALIN

Although Mathews uses the exchange of letters [in *The Sinking of the Odradek Stadium*]—the entire novel is, in effect, an attempt to relive (or rewrite or "re-rite") the past—he refuses to accept easy historical conventions; the letter-novel, for example, is deliberately destroyed. We have communications in various forms, languages, and pictures so that we are never sure *where* we are. There are puns, parodies, and obscure references. The juxtapositions of language are subtly offered to sink stadia, structures, "reality."

The novel—written as a series of letters (love) between Zachary and Twang— is a complex interlocking of culture, romance, "scholarship," but we quickly discover—as do the absurdly named characters—that such dense texture is rent with holes.

The novel is a hunt for treasure. Unfortunately, Zachary and Twang discover that treasure of any sort—materialistic or spiritual—is fool's gold. They find that the quest produces more forests than chapels. There is, if you will, dark comedy here. History is a cheat; love is a cheat; language is, perhaps, less of a cheat than the others.

It is impossible to summarize the various turns, schemes, coincidences of the novel. We are, therefore, initiated—as are Zachary and Twang in various ways—into the "religion" of Wittgenstein (Mathews mentions the name several times). We discover that, no matter how we move, we cannot free ourselves from the perplexities of language. Although we are tempted—the novel is filled with references to various kinds of temptation—to assign *meaning* to words, we sadly, heroically learn that they are, in effect, merely marks on a page. They cannot point the way; they cannot *map* sunken treasure.

Let us look at one brief, typical example of the entire book. (Mathews, of course, would dismiss this search for clues because he maintains that there are *no clues to ultimate meanings*.) The first words of the novel are "confidence in words, Twang." The last words of the novel are: "Alone I cannot carry this burden of joy and doubt." The novel is a loop— "doubt" leads us back to "confidence in words." Thus, on the one hand we can find a circular pattern; but the pattern warns us not to be confident, not to assume that we have decoded the system, found an overarching structure. Continuity *and* discontinuity—all words, including the ones which make up this novel—give *and* take away meaning. Yet words are the only things we can accept (according to Mathews) for our momentary salvation. (pp. 186-87)

Mathews refuses to rest in one world. He accepts the "absurdity" of real life, but he underlines this absurdity by his elaborate, erudite game playing. He implies that he and we are alone in a world of his own discourse. He winks knowingly, hoping that perhaps we can share *some* of his world. (p. 187)

Irving Malin, in a review of "The Sinking of the Odradek Stadium," in The Review of Contemporary Fiction, *Vol. V, No. 3, Fall, 1985, pp. 186-87.*

EDMUND WHITE

The most obvious precedent for Harry Mathews's *Cigarettes* is [Jane Austen's] prose. Austen's involving circumstantiality and her elaborate structuring of plot are both here in Mathews's work, as is a ready appreciation of the social consequences of wealth and power. Mathews, following Austen's example, scarcely describes even the main characters or principal settings. Like her, he alternates between scenes of direct dialogue and narratives covering longer periods and employing indirect discourse—that most novelistic of all tones, the "flying narrative" ("They were happy for two years until . . ."). More importantly, Austen's peculiar tone of grave seriousness towards morals and satirical benevolence towards manners finds an echo in Mathews's approach.

Of course the differences are as marked as the similarities. Unlike the race of recent or contemporary English women novelists, from Barbara Pym to Anita Brookner, who are routinely compared to Austen, Mathews is more psychological than sociological, more fascinated by the genteel rich than the genteel poor, by artists or would-be artists than by retired civil servants or teachers, and he is far more bizarre and violent than Austen or any of her progeny would ever dare to be.

More concretely, Mathews is not afraid to exchange Austen's "inch of ivory" for a whole tusk. He roams over several decades and many locales, manipulates a large cast and assimilates the point of view of many characters, old and young, male and female. This range and flexibility relates his sophisticated fictional world to our own largest sense of experience; we are never able to smile at the charming foibles and self-deceptions of his people, as we might smilingly condescend towards Austen's.

But Mathews's expansive ambitions, of course, threaten his design. Social comedy cannot sustain a lack of rigor and compression; *Le jeu de l'amour et du hasard* does not properly admit of too much *hasard*. Austen's narrow preoccupation with

finding suitable husbands for her eligible and not-so-eligible girls Mathews has replaced with a quite broad interest in such subjects as: sexual conquest; the fostering of reputation; the love and hate between mother and son, father and daughter, brother and sister; the links (and abysses) between affection and imagination; the parallels between homosexuality and heterosexuality; and the nature of the amorous friendships linking quite old people.

No one would deny the intrinsic fascination inherent in Mathews's topoi nor the wisdom and compassion he brings to his human situations, but he has not been content merely to catalog them. He's sought to impose on them a necessary form, one that would lend his book the concision Austen achieves through unities of place, cast and problem.

Mathews's formal rigor is precisely what makes him modern. His structures are not imposed on preexistent contents; rather the exigencies of form generate incidents and even descriptions. The analogy is with poetry (verses suggested by rhymes) and music (variations hatched out of themes, themes out of motives). Future studies will reveal the almost maniacal regularity of his form, an aspect I will not dwell on lest it overshadow the even more marked sense of lived life, of spontaneous event in this *breathing* text. Suffice it to say that *Cigarettes,* which at first (and last) glance seems his most realistic book, is also the one most manipulated by combinatorial devices, such as those Mathews has described in an essay in Oulipo's *Atlas de littérature potentielle.* After all, Mathews has long been a member—along with such writers as Italo Calvino, Raymond Queneau and Georges Perec . . . —of this Parisian literary group, so fancifully serious, devoted to fictional research. In *Cigarettes* the "time signature" varies in every chapter as does the "key" (i.e., "Louisa and Lewis: 1938-1963" or "Priscilla and Walter: Summer 1962-Winter 1963"). Moreover, certain themes (the portrait of Elizabeth, shady business deals, the problems of inheritance, horses) repeat and evolve in "free" (i.e., undetermined) fashion. In short, several elements follow a program, whereas others are introduced ad libitum.

Another thoroughly contemporary aspect of the text is its language. The syntax is intricate but nimble, the sentences short but never falsely naive or monotonous, the mode nominative rather than adjectival, verbal rather than adverbial. The comic tone depends on shifting neatly from one register to a quite different one. . . . (pp. 77-8)

The quirkiness of Mathews's style enables its humor, just as the leanness makes for efficiency in getting tales told. Throughout his career, in his four major novels, Mathews has always loved telling stories; indeed adventure and mystery have been his preferred genres, just as religion and science have been his preoccupations. . . .

In *Cigarettes* Mathews has forged his most expressive style, although never does he allow the language to exhort or persuade—he's always a bit cool. As in the earlier books, suspense is ubiquitous (will Maud find out that Allan is cheating on her? will the true nature of Phoebe's illness be diagnosed in time to save her? are Irene and Morris plotting against Walter?). Science in the form of probability theories of betting and medical definitions of Phoebe's illness is invoked, as is religion in the form of art and love.

But the book is mainly funny, though the humor no longer depends on freaks such as Zachary and Twang. Now it is enacted by well-heeled exurbanites as glamorous as Fitzgerald's characters and as silkily hedonistic as Henry Green's.

The omniscient narrator (who, at the last minute, we discover is one of the characters—though we should have suspected it sooner) shows us Louisa from the point of view of her son Lewis, then after we're convinced she's a meddling neurotic, plunges us into her thoughts only to reveal her loving solicitude for her difficult children. In the same way we see Maud from Pauline's viewpoint and Pauline from Maud's. (p. 79)

The plot of *Cigarettes* is as dense and sensationalistic as that of any good melodrama. Maud and Pauline are sisters, though Maud inherits and Pauline doesn't. Pauline pretends she's rich and tricks Oliver into marrying her, though the marriage of course is unhappy. Maud marries Allan, who's a successful insurance man but who feels so outclassed by his wife's wealth that he indulges in shady business deals. Their daughter Priscilla becomes the mistress of the painter Walter Thrale and the friend and business partner of Morris. Morris's sister Irene is Walter's dealer. Morris's lover is Lewis, brother of Phoebe, Walter's studio assistant. Phoebe's parents are Louisa and Owen Lewison; Owen decides to investigate Allan's shady deals with the help of Pauline, who's always been eager to sleep with Allan, partly to get revenge on her sister Maud, who "cheated" her out of her inheritance. Allan is gratified by Pauline's apparent interest in him, since he has just lost his last girlfriend Elizabeth to his wife Maud.

Elizabeth was the subject of an early portrait by Walter Thrale, his "breakthrough" painting. The portrait has been scrupulously copied by Phoebe. The painting (or the copy) is sold, destroyed, stolen. One of the dealers involved, Morris, dies of a heart attack while Lewis, his masochistic lover, immobilized inside a plaster cast, watches helplessly.

This résumé, no matter how cursory, should suggest opera buffa twists and turns. (p. 80)

The soap-opera plot also turns up implausible occasions, which Mathews knows how to write with exquisite veracity. . . .

There are two things that make this book remarkable. First, it is as involving as a nineteenth-century saga and as original as any modernist invention—a rare combination of readability and ingenuity. Second, it shows compassion towards characters usually slighted or ridiculed in contemporary fiction—the middle-aged and old, the successful, mothers, homosexuals, even sadists. Nor does it treat these characters with a governessy solicitude; rather it judges them on the basis of the good they do and the happiness they feel and give. (p. 81)

> Edmund White, "Their Masks, Their Lives—Harry Mathews's 'Cigarettes'," in The Review of Contemporary Fiction, Vol. VII, No. 3, Fall, 1987, pp. 77-81.

KEITH COHEN

Once when I told Kenneth Koch that I had just finished reading a new story by Harry Mathews, he responded, "Have you figured out the secret formula it's based on?" This seemed at the time an innocent remark, perhaps a kind of indirect compliment to Mathews's artistry. But since then, it has become clear to me that Koch's question held a precious insight about the seemingly hermetic writings of one of our most critically neglected authors. Harry Mathews's work is always based on a hidden pattern, sometimes as obvious as a cooking recipe, other times as obscure as a Latin rebus.

After looking more closely at Mathews's short stories, I realized that the procedures used in these pieces are more con-

densed (and more accessible) versions of those used in the novels. In this essay I will suggest a few of the patterns I have found in Mathews's short fiction, which, I will argue, may serve as a model for analyzing his longer works. What all these patterns have in common is their bearing on a story about one or more characters engaged in a certain labor of deciphering some mysteriously encoded string of signifiers. These labors of the signifier are precisely the task then assigned to the reader who, in discovering the secret formula underlying the fiction, begins to see the relation, often ironic, between the story and the pattern.

One of the most obvious devices Mathews uses to organize his baffling plots is that of attribution. Parodying a wide range of literature, from the Homeric catalogs and epithets to the family tree, he foregrounds the simple habit of supplying a bit of genealogical information each time a new character is introduced. This practice is common in Racine's theater: one is constantly reminded, for example, of Phèdre's lineage, in the famous line, "Fille de Minos et de Pasiphae." The function of the line in the play is to compress the past and future into the present. . . . (p. 173)

Mathews's use of the device is not aimed, however, at compressing time, nor even at focusing the destiny of a single character. On the contrary, the irony of the way he uses it in a story like **"Tradition and the Individual Talent: The 'Bratislava Spiccato'"** is that "tradition" ends up trivializing "individual talent." Parodying musical biographies, which often insist on the renown of the individual's lineage by citing famous relatives and teachers, Mathews supplies every conceivable connection by blood or marriage between his characters and other musical celebrities. (pp. 173-74)

[The] history of the Bratislava spiccato, which could have been rendered in two or three sentences, plods on over seven pages by taking us on a tour of the minor dignitaries in the musical world of Eastern Europe. The effect is, of course, one of parody, as the text foregrounds the irrelevance of blood relations in musical history (at least in this one) and skimps on what appear to be fascinating details about the musical maneuver itself. . . .

"The Novel as History" makes a similarly ironic comment on the relation between the novel and history. It begins as a parody of a Conrad novel, with Robinson, the narrator, seated before a fire, speaking to unnamed auditors. The reference to Conrad is significant, since in his novels more than any others the aura of "history" is belied by the subjectivity of the narrator. . . . Like **"Tradition and the Individual Talent,"** this tale is impeded by irrelevant details about the characters' relations. One of the initial characters, Borgmann, for example, is traveling at one point with Jeremiah Keats, "who is best remembered as having been confidential secretary to Kuromato, the original Japanese ambassador to St. Petersburg." Other such details abound. . . . (p. 174)

The main effect of the digressions here is to make clear that "history" has little or nothing to do with the "novel" that is being fleshed out. Historical references to Philip of Burgundy or to Betsy Ross have no bearing whatsoever on the fictional content of the story. Instead, they appear to be mere filler. In light of what we know about Mathews's art, the point of **"The Novel as History"** serves as justification for his own novels, which rarely bear on historical events. As the French structuralists have pointed out on numerous occasions, History is a discourse that becomes just as fictional as the novel. There is no "true" history of anything. In this light, Mathews's title suggests its opposite, history as a novel.

The other pervasive technique I have found in Mathews's stories is what I shall call the "set piece." Working from models of discursive prose which, once detected, reveal themselves in their entirety, Mathews can at once use the quirks of the set piece and parody it at the same time. One of the most hilarious examples is **"Country Cooking from Central France: Roast Boned Rolled Stuffed Shoulder of Lamb (Farce Double),"** which is, in this case very obviously, a cooking recipe. The "farce" of the title, of course, is at once the complex stuffing used in the recipe and the increasingly incredible feats of cuisine and acrobatics required to complete the dish. The projected task, which the recipe-speaker claims, contrary to local skeptics, can be accomplished even by someone not from the Auvergne region, becomes a literary farce through exaggeration and incongruity.

The type of recipe Mathews parodies here is the chatty one that addresses the cook in familiar terms and does not hesitate to digress with an apt story. The most preposterous example of this is the song related to us as characteristic of those sung in Auvergne during the five-hour roasting of the lamb. It is relevant, the speaker tells us, in that it "provides valuable insight into the character of the Auvergnat community." Such a pretext might be comprehensible if the text were anthropological and not culinary; it is hard to see what possible help can come from knowledge of Auvergnat mores. In any case, it is a story of a blacksmith's son who undertakes to find his long-lost mother and, in so doing, encounters a series of women who "do for him what mother never did for her son." This quest tale begins inauspiciously enough, but reaches a very moving climax when the blacksmith's son meets a shepherdess who "has loved him for many years." It is she who, in the middle of the night, reveals to the young man that his mother is actually dead and can be seen among the souls of the dead who "have gathered into one blazing light" in the night sky. The shepherdess then proclaims to him that she will become his "mother" "—even if now, and tomorrow, and all the days of my life, I do for you what mother never did for her son." These words produce in the blacksmith's son a feeling of ecstasy, for "he has discovered his desire."

We recognize in the premises of this tale a retelling of the basic Oedipal story, whereby the son searches for a mother-substitute. This aspect of the tale is, in fact, overdetermined by the repetition of women who "do for him what mother never did for her son." It is as though the son must sleep with every woman he encounters in an effort to accomplish his disavowed desire to sleep with his mother. The prohibition against incest is, moreover, built into the phrase "what mother never did for her son." And the unconscious dread of what fulfilling his desire might mean is figured in the three evil women who, after doing for him what the other women have done, try to kill him. Rather than simply saving himself, the blacksmith's son instead turns on each woman and slays her. In this way, the story seems to suggest not simply the accomplishment of sublimation but also the ridding of the desires of the mother, which the son presumably experiences as guilt. In this sense, it is a troubling tale in which the mother figure must be slaughtered before true desire can be fulfilled.

The real or symbolic connection between this interpolated tale and the lamb recipe presents the major challenge in analyzing the text. The speaker ingenuously suggests that the connection lies "in an analogy between the stars" (which the son beholds as the shepherdess explains to him that they "are chinks in the night through which the fateful light of the dead and the unborn is revealed to the world") and "the holes in the lid of the roasting pit." The most striking feature of this relation, it seems to me, is not between the stars and the holes in the lid, nor in the shepherdess's connection with lambs, but rather in the discrepancy between the triviality of the recipe and the gravity of the tale. In a manner that recalls the work of Lévi-Strauss, a common ritual pertaining to cuisine is combined with a unique story that tells of a rite de passage. Like the feathers from the hunt worn in an apron over the genitals in the initiation rites of certain primitive tribes, the recipe, structurally, dangles around the story of initiation and maturation. What is thus suggested is that the elaborate cooking of the lamb is an ancient cultural pretext for the telling of the tale, which, like myth according to Lévi-Strauss, functions to mediate a basic contradiction of the society, that of a son's devotion to his mother which, though tinged with feelings of sexual attraction, can never be manifested in an erotic way.

This conclusion is interesting in that it suggests that the ultimate purpose of some elaborate cultural discourses lies not in their apparent proclaimed object but rather in the digressions or tangents that they spawn. (pp. 174-77)

A very different kind of set piece, the academic lecture, is used in **"Remarks of the Scholar Graduate."** Like **"Country Cooking,"** this text is addressed to a group of listeners but who, in this case, are presumably present as the "scholar" presents the results of his research on early Bactrian writing. The specific branch of knowledge that is here parodied is linguistics. In a gesture that recalls [the] pseudoscientific texts of Borges, the speaker proposes to interpret a system of writing whose basic sign is the horizontal line. Phonetic values are then attributed to series of parallel lines that may fall, in any combination, on several different levels. The result is not merely the deciphering of an esoteric language but, as it turns out, the discovery of the origin of the Indo-European alphabet. (pp. 177-78)

There is, in this most preposterous account of the origin of our writing system, a quality of wonder. Mathews strikes the chords of verisimilitude just often enough that his false attribution begins to seem very attractive as a theory. This is part of the point. Theory is sometimes believable to the extent that it is beautiful. (This is the problem with the philosophy of origins, as Montaigne pointed out long ago, since many great authors, "when they write about causes, adduce not only those they think are true but also those they do not believe in, provided they have some originality and beauty.") This fictional account of the origin of writing is just as believable or unbelievable as some of the etymological accounts we read in the works of learned linguists.

"Remarks of the Scholar Graduate" provides a glimpse of what might be considered Mathews's fundamental procedure, that of providing a false attribution to a common phenomenon. Just as **"Tradition and the Individual Talent"** uses attribution to obscure the origin of the Bratislava spiccato, just as **"Novel as History"** uses attribution to show the *a*historical nature of the novel, Mathews here uses attribution (or perhaps, more properly, derivation), to have the scholar convince his audience of the authenticity of his findings. As in the works of Borges, false attribution becomes here an end in itself: writing a fiction that tells of the origin of writing.

A set piece closely related to the academic lecture is the festschrift, used as the basis for **"The Dialect of the Tribe."** Actually, the text is not the festschrift itself, but rather a letter responding to an invitation to contribute. Like **"Remarks of the Scholar Graduate,"** this piece is a parody of linguistics. But whereas the former treated the origin of writing, this one treats the origin of a mythical language, Pagolak, and the mysteries of translation that this language unravels. The writer here seems to be the same person as the one who addressed us in **"Remarks,"** since he is continuing his "research on the Bactrian controversy." But by accident he gets sidetracked by a book offered him by a diligent librarian, Ms. Maxine Moon, devoted to an examination of the language of "a small hill tribe in northern New Guinea." The book explains, in particular, the unique method of translating out of Pagolak: while the method "produced translations that foreign listeners could understand and accept, it also concealed from them the original meaning of every statement made."

The writer is attracted to this book because he has always had a high regard for translation. Indeed, he believes it to be "the paradigm, the exemplar of all writing." As he learns Pagolak, he begins to understand its meanings. However, when he attempts to repeat what he has read "in other terms," he finds himself utterly incapable. The passage in question is where the *abanika,* or "chief word-chief," talks about translation. As the scholar ponders it, he realizes that the declaration "*was* the very process of transforming language that I expected it to be *about*. It was not an account of the process, it was the process itself."

A language capable of being translated without revealing the meaning of the original suggests something like "pure" language, in the way the Symbolists aspired toward "pure poetry." The title, in fact, **"The Dialect of the Tribe,"** recalls Mallarmé's line from "Le Tombeau d'Edgar Poe": "Donner un sens plus pur aux mots de la tribu" ("To give a purer meaning to the words of the tribe"). Pagolak takes on the attributes of music, suggesting ultimately that translation, far from the paradigm of all writing, is a hopelessly deluded activity, since one can never truly convey the original except by repeating the original itself. Furthermore, the idea of purifying language reaches its apogee with Pagolak. If the meaning of this curious language can never be seized through translation, then the language must have been purged of all referentiality (the dream of Mallarmé, as well as that of Gertrude Stein). The translation that is created must be considered a sort of arabesque, a degraded distillation of the original which can never hope to convey anything but a meaningless string of signifiers.

In sharing his joy of discovery with the person he is writing to, the recipient of his eventual festschrift, the scholar goes into the details of certain key phrases, which refer to initiation rites and higher states of existence. Parodying here oriental systems of belief that include forces like Karma and states like Nirvana, Mathews has his speaker explain the complexities of *namele* and *namalan,* two aspects of the highly sacred act of translating. The changes one undergoes in attaining these states are called *kalo gap.* While *kalo gap* is embodied in the speaking of Pagolak (note that the term is a palindrome for the name of the language), awareness of it must be learned. Initiation rites, practiced to train young males to acquire this awareness, culminate in their emergence from *ajanu,* or boyhood, "like seabirds from chicken eggs." Thus, Pagolak is not merely a language that has developed a unique method of translation; it includes in the very speaking of it a constant awareness of the magical properties of this translating process.

The comic conclusion one must draw from **"The Dialect of the Tribe"** is, first of all, that translation can never succeed except by sabotaging the original, and, secondly, that the notion of "pure language" would mean the disappearance of meaning as such (i.e., the necessary absence of a nugget of translatable stuff subtending written or spoken words).

Mathews's fondness for a secret formula is carried over in experiments he has done using set texts and proverbs in what the French call *exercises de style*. The technique, made famous by Raymond Queneau but also practiced by other writers such as William Carlos Williams and Kenneth Koch, takes as its point of departure a text written by another author or else so well known as to require no quoting. The imitator then composes a number of variations of the original according to slight modifications in style, tone, or register.

In *Trial Impressions,* for example, Mathews takes a poem by John Dowland, "Deare, if you change, Ile never chuse againe," and submits it to various stylistic modifications, as indicated by a brief notice following each version, such as "Up to Date" and "Male Chauvinist." Particularly inspiring in Dowland's original is the final couplet of each of the two stanzas, which summarizes the terms of the poet's declaration of love:

> Dear, sweete, fayre, wise, change, shrinke nor be not weake,
> And on my faith, my faith shall never breake.

> Earth, heaven, fire, ayre, the world transformed shall view,
> E're I prove false to faith, or strange to you.

This is transformed in the first stanza of the "Male Chauvinist" variation to:

> Pain, kvetch, potato nose, dope, keep acting this way
> And as sure as there's sand in spinach I'll keep kicking your ass.

(pp. 178-80)

A different type of *exercise de style* is used in *Selected Declarations of Dependence*. Here Mathews takes as his point of departure a series of common proverbs and, by changing a key word each time one is repeated, deconstructs the meaning of the original. The new creations, which Mathews calls "perverbs," are often astonishing in their positing of a strange homily, hinting, like a typo, at the original, yet suggesting a new perception that is far from bromidic. The most successful are formed by fusing the chopped off beginning of one proverb with the truncated ending of another. For example, "Every cloud from little acorns grows." An expanded version of this procedure makes up a little poem:

> When in Rome,
>   Few are chosen,
> Six of one
>   Are another man's poison.

Or again:

> Leave no stone
>   Before you leap,
> Six of one
>   The twain shall meet.

Perhaps the pithiest, and most suggestive, of this type is "Rome is another man's poison," since it suggests some profound thought about the fall of Rome or about the vicissitudes of conformity.

When such a sudden revelation of possible profundity occurs, the result is hilarious, since one realizes that the perverb has been created entirely haphazardly. The aura of eternal verity hangs onto each segment, through a kind of proverb intertextuality, even though the words themselves are fairly ordinary. (p. 182)

As I suggested at the beginning of this essay, one value of identifying the secret formula procedure in Mathews's short fiction is that it provides a means of better understanding the composition of the longer works. Let us now consider one example, typical of what I perceive to be a major technical trait of Mathews's novels, from *Tlooth*. In the chapter "Spires and Squares," Robin Marr recounts an experience she had during her last year in college. The metadiegesis, which takes up most of the chapter, concerns a copy of Frost's *Lives of Eminent Christians*, into which someone had slipped a piece of paper on which is written, at the top of the page, the letters

r

e

s

and below, three incomplete sentences:

> The Mother cannot ＿＿＿ her Son.
>
> The Son ＿＿＿ his Father.
>
> The Mother ＿＿＿ their Spirit.

A clue that this episode may have certain compositional similarities to the shorter (and, in this case, later) fiction is the penultimate sentence: "Robin stirred the dying fire." It is like the final sentence of **"The Novel as History"**: "Irritably, Robinson poked the lowering coals." This frame device is, like other elements in this short text, reminiscent of the way Conrad treats Marlowe as intradiegetic narrator. It suggests a conscious staging, and hence the set piece.

In attempting to find a clue about the missing words in the three sentences, Robin hits on the idea that *res*, which she had taken as the Latin word for matter, might be an anagram or a fragment of them. She discovers that, indeed, the three words each begin and end with the letters r, e, s: resire(s), restores, and respires. Furthermore, when written one on top of the other, the non-res words form the phrase "I to pi." All these elements, she concluded, had to do with the three-part God of Christianity and the nature of Christ's divinity. The three sentences, accordingly, address the question of how Christ could be both God and man at once. "I to pi" is explained by connecting God embodied as a man with "I" and discovering in "pi" not simply an expression of the ratio between the radius and circumference of a circle, but a symbol of the Holy Spirit. "I to pi," then, comes to mean "the man becoming Spirit, and so remaining God."

What might be taken as an excess of exegetical zeal on Robin Marr's part turns out to be a passion shared by at least one other person. Three years after finding the piece of paper, Robin receives a letter from an Englishman who, familiar with the article in which she summarizes her conclusions, claims he has found in Edward Davies's *Celtic Researches* a reference to the sixteenth-century Latin translation of the *Bazaar of Heraclides*. A typographical ornament on the translation includes what might be taken as an allusion to one of the three sentences Robin had found:

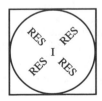

The Englishman furthers Robin's own analysis of the mysterious words by observing that the square around the circle suggests another "res" word, "resquares," which, when taken apart spells the Latin phrase "res qua res," or "the thing in itself." He goes one more step by pointing out that the German phrase on the bottom of the page which Robin had ignored till now, "Zwei Herzen in Dreivierteltakt," refers again to the tripartite God: "The 'two hearts' were the two natures of God, human and divine. They were 'in three-quarter time' because they were joined in the consubstantial union of the Trinity, which formed a single perfect measure."

This episode is typical of Mathews's novels in the way it presents an unlikely concatenation of events and signifiers, apparently devoid of connection or signification, and then proceeds to discover a rich underlying meaning to them all. Mathews's novels are all informed by this sort of epistemological quest through a forest of signifiers, but, whereas in the medieval allegories composed around such quests the signifiers endowed with special meaning are obvious (the rose, the path, the abyss), Mathews takes the most esoteric or unsuspecting of signifiers to endow with a secret message. One thinks of the teeth composed, in Raymond Roussel's *Locus Solus*, by an airhammer into a portrait of a Polish military officer, and indeed the texture of *The Conversions*, for example, is very reminiscent of Roussel's work. Both Roussel and Mathews seem to base their plots on key words whose meanings are not known at the beginning, or central objects whose true function is revealed after arduous mental labor.

This labor becomes all the more significant when it is lifted out of the story and grafted onto the reading process. In *The Sinking of the Odradek Stadium* we encounter a preeminent instance of this procedure. The work is an epistolary novel composed of letters written between an American man and a Vietnamese woman. The woman's English, at the beginning of the novel, is so fragmentary and confused that the reader is forced to decipher nearly every sentence with particular care. These labors of the signifier are brought into sharp relief near the end of the novel when the man, Mr. McCaltex, wishes to place a long-distance call to the woman, Trotsi Panattapam, who is in Italy. In order to make himself understood, Mr. McCaltex must spell each letter of his name and that of Ms. Panattapam. The result is a hilarious confusion on the part of the Italian operator, suggesting the impossibility not only of translation but of transcription from the speaker of one phonic system to that of another. The episode ends ironically with Mr. McCaltex about to spell his message, "Arrive tomorrow," to the hotel clerk, beginning with the Italian word *addio* for A, when the clerk interrupts him to say, "I understand perfect: 'Arrive tomorrow.'"

This last example forms the flip side of the example from *Tlooth*. While the impossibility of communicating the English and Vietnamese names through an Italian phonological frame suggests the lack of reliable meaning in the most humdrum of verbal interactions, Robin Marr's deciphering of the "res" riddle suggests the opposite, that any verbal signifier, no matter how outlandish or esoteric, may contain some hidden significance. Between these two poles, that of impossible signification and that of pansignification, Harry Mathews's fiction swings continually, setting the time for a new music, rarely heard in the Anglo-American literary world. (pp. 184-86)

Keith Cohen, "The Labors of the Signifier," in The Review of Contemporary Fiction, *Vol. VII, No. 3, Fall, 1987, pp. 173-86.*

TOM CLARK

Cigarettes is Harry Mathews' fourth novel, his first in 12 years. It follows *The Conversions* (1962) . . . , *Tlooth* (1966) . . . , [and] *The Sinking of the Odradek Stadium* (1975). That early trio of books can now be seen as a unit, and probably a closed chapter in the novelist's career.

Certainly their shared characteristics make them unique in American fiction. A blend of wild intellectual comedy and bizarre fantasy, arcane data and flamboyant verbal gamesmanship, they are disarming and delightful works with few precedents in the language. If *Tristram Shandy, Finnegans Wake* and Lewis Carroll's *Alice* books perhaps broke some ground for the early Mathews, one must search beyond the bounds of English for closer analogies. Borges and Calvino, to whom Mathews has been compared, were never this weird; and Raymond Roussel, the turn-of-the-century herald of French surrealism (*Impressions of Africa, Locus Solus*) from whom Mathews did indeed borrow the anti-referential, language-playing elements of his early style, was never quite this funny. (p. 3)

The self-enclosed verbal performance of *The Conversions* and *Tlooth* strains linguistic reference to its limit, creating a subjective universe in which the mind's ceaseless inventiveness runs up against an opaque barrier of "facts" and "words." Mathews' heroes are detectives of the absurd who don't realize they're trapped in this baffling puzzle-universe; the task the novelist has assigned them is to discover and investigate a world that gradually reveals itself to be a compound delusion. In *Cigarettes,* this tragic joke turns unexpectedly into something that for all its elegance, sophistication and irony looks suspiciously like real tragedy.

For *Cigarettes* is about nothing less than the built-in impossibility of human relationships. Our addictive drive to know and understand each other not only consumes us, Mathews seems to be saying in his new novel, but does so with as little real meaning as the consumption, one by one, of cigarettes from a pack: flaring glow, some smoke, and then gone. The only truth perceptible by the light of this brief flame is that subjectively titled "deformed truth" defined so well by Freud as the product of wishful thinking; trapped inside the mirror-filled halls of their wishful illusions, Mathews' characters struggle valiantly but unsuccessfully to relate, each speaking a language of Self that may sound clear but ultimately proves as unintelligible to the surrounding selves as Esperanto to a Martian.

At first glance, the new novel appears as conventional as its predecessors are exotic: Gone are the maps, charts, diagrams, musical scores, acrostics, puzzles and word games that make the early books resemble brain-teaser kits for occupying child prodigies on prolonged car trips. This time around Mathews' fantasy and *bizarrerie* give way to a surface realism not too different from what you might encounter in a *New Yorker* short story. Even as I use the words *Mathews* and *realism* in the same sentence, though, I race to qualify. The *Cigarettes* characters dwell in a super-Elysium of money and class that may not actually exist on this Earth, even in the extremely well-heeled slice of it that Mathews commands as his setting: a thin strip extending from Manhattan's downtown financial district and artists' enclaves through its uptown galleries and watering holes to the "horse-and-dog-world" of the upper reaches of the Hudson. All along this circuit, the blood and the chips run a deep patrician blue. (pp. 3, 9)

Mathews dedicates *Cigarettes* to the late French novelist Georges Perec. Like Perec's 1978 masterpiece *La Vie Mode D'Emploi*, this novel gradually unfolds through a series of interlocking tales, revealing its essence only in progressive skin-of-the-onion stages. Each of its 14 short-story-like chapters pairs off two of its 13 main characters, and chapter by chapter these characters rotate positions, forming an increasingly incestuous ring of relationships whose shape keeps changing before our eyes. The focus of Mathews' relentless ingenuity, source of so many dazzling comic moments in the earlier books, is here transferred from the verbal surface to the plot architecture. He weaves into each of his several story-threads more unexpected twists than you'll find in the average multivolume Victorian novel.

Cigarettes is a brilliant and unsettling book that turns on a typically Mathewsian paradox. Here this erstwhile master of High Nonsense has made himself surprisingly comprehensible in order to illuminate humanity's general state of mutual incomprehension; he has written a novel that's like a message-in-a-bottle proposing that *all* messages—even art's—are lost from the moment they are composed, because each is inscribed in the self's special subjective language.

If there is a God in Harry Mathews' universe, it is the joker-deity of *comedie noir*, continually winding people up to embark on the impossible—whether it be finding a golden adze or relating without deception to each other. After each predictable failure, he chuckles behind his hand and then winds them up to start again. The beauty of these novels is that we get to share the joke even while realizing it's on us. (p. 9)

> Tom Clark, "Out, Out, Brief Cigarette," in Los Angeles Times Book Review, *October 11, 1987, pp. 3, 9.*

ALBERT MOBILIO

Harry Mathews, Jacques Roubaud, and the late Georges Perec are all members of a Paris-based group of experimental writers dedicated to the high art of game. Founded in 1960 by mathematician François Le Lionnais and novelist Raymond Queneau, Oulipo (*Ouvroir de Littérature Potentielle,* or Workshop of Potential Literature) produces literary puzzles whose spirit and shape derive from mathematical formulae and linguistic high jinks. Inspired by Lewis Carroll, Stein, Joyce, and Raymond Roussel, Oulipians craft puzzle-palace poems and novels for which solutions are not nearly as crucial as the process of solving. Some typical bits of Oulipo business include palindromes like Perec's "Straw? No, too stupid a fad. I put soot on warts," snowball sentences adding one letter to each successive word, or Queneau's *Cent Mille Milliard de Poèmes* (*A Hundred Thousand Billion Poems*), a book of 10 sonnets, sliced into 14 strips, so that flipping a line creates a new poem—10^{14} of them. Less analytic ploys can be found in Mathews's *Selected Declarations of Dependence,* in which proverbs mix and match—"When in Rome / Few are chosen, / Six of one / Are another man's poison"—acquiring surreal vigor. These games are not as flat as they sound. The N-7 algorithm takes a familiar passage and replaces each noun with the seventh noun that follows in the dictionary. Try it. Any domesticated phrase— Our fathom who art in hebetude hallowed be thy nanny-berry— yields laughs and a glimpse of sound and sense at work.

Unabashedly arbitrary in conception, Oulipian constructions nonetheless adhere to an internal logic. Formal constraints spur the imagination to thrive within strict limits similar to those of sonnets and sestinas. Of course, language presents its own brick wall of rules: grammar and available vocabulary. Self-contained and ingeniously coherent, Oulipian sub-systems derange the grid and impose a fresh, idiosyncratic order that mirrors language's own arbitrary nature. (p. 11)

After traveling around the world, Raymond Roussel, Oulipo's spiritual godfather, proudly declared that none of the experience had entered his writing. Imagination, he said, accounted for everything in his work. Harry Mathews, former editor of a magazine named after Roussel's pun-twisting novel *Locus Solus,* maintains similar faith in pure invention. . . . Whether indulging in linguistic arcana or the Swiftian bizarre, Mathews always seems to be using a *chromaturge,* an imaginary device from his first novel, ***The Conversions,*** which systematically distorts color to produce fantastical paintings. It is fiction built around lexical sports and fueled by an energetic abuse of reality.

At first glance, his new book appears to mark a radical departure. Very much a social novel in a 19th century sense, ***Cigarettes*** charts the backstabbings, infidelities, and sexual traumas of an upper-class New York clique in the early '60s. A jaded, inbred set obsessed with horse racing, trust funds, and art, they have smothered their inadequacies in petty triumphs over one another. Mathews pries open these lives with Jamesian precision to trace their circuitous fears and power plays to the source, an abiding conviction of loss.

The plot is a soap opera's Möbius strip of intimacies, of characters doubling back upon themselves. Allan runs insurance scams to feel better about himself and cheats on his wife, Maud, with Elizabeth. Owen is blackmailing Allan for Elizabeth's portrait; he once discovered his own daughter, Phoebe, posing nude for the painter, Walter. Walter's lover, Priscilla, is Allan and Maud's daughter. Walter wins recognition in the art world because of an essay by Morris, whose sister Irene may possess a forgery done by Phoebe of Elizabeth's portrait. And Phoebe's brother, Lewis, is involved in a sadomasochistic relationship with Morris. That's just one way of putting it. The combinatorial gymnastics—the 13 characters are paired and re-paired in 14 relationships—permit mutual perceptions to reflect and be reflected. As a result, the reader is caught in the same trap of subjectivity as the characters; each binary relationship produces a sum of conflicting impressions.

Mathews's dexterous shifts in perspective uncover the resentment and heartache binding Owen and his daughter, Phoebe. Feeling "swindled" by her decision to leave school and paint in the Village, Owen withholds her trust fund. But Phoebe finds a niche in the downtown art crowd and wins back his affection. He delights in sharing her boho lifestyle on visits to the city until she reasserts her independence. Owen wakes up in her studio to discover she's "slept elsewhere" and begins to brood. . . . He becomes convinced Phoebe has lured him into enjoying a world that could only be hers as revenge for his initial opposition. The "noticeable thrill" Owen experiences from the prospect of this betrayal suggests that possessiveness has blossomed into paranoia. But when the narration takes Phoebe's point of view we learn that Owen is quite correct. Phoebe believes her father faked interest in her painting, that he shrewdly "pretended to encourage her freedom only to attack it better." Each misperceives the other, their flawed readings sharpening the hurt and poisoning their love.

While this depth of psychological exchange makes ***Cigarettes*** Mathews's most realistic work, the novel retains the themes and formal rigor found in his explicitly Oulipian texts. Betting strategies and N-7 wordgames crop up occasionally, but much more significant is the daisy-chain recombination of cast and plot. Like Roubaud and Perec, Mathews engineers a funhouse labyrinth in which guise disfigures guise and the logic that reigns is that of representation. Skillfully planned to disrupt perceptions (especially the reader's), the mirrored lattice reveals the human genius for misapprehension; solving the jigsaw of other lives seems to lie beyond the narrow vantage of the self. (p. 12)

Albert Mobilio, "Perpetual Notion Machines," in VLS, *No. 60, November, 1987, pp. 11-12.*

LISA ZEIDNER

Harry Mathews's haunting fourth novel [*Cigarettes*] provides enough plot for a season of mini-series. Three wealthy couples from upstate New York, along with their friends and relations, pair and re-pair in a chain of dangerous liaisons. We have the requisite infidelities, rivalries and shady business. But this is no stock melodrama. In Mr. Mathews's most subtly experimental novel, the plot is used as bait to lure us into confronting love's darker side.

Cigarettes traces the connections among 13 characters, between 1936 and 1963, in Saratoga Springs and Greenwich Village: artists, critics, gallery owners, patrons and society hangers-on. . . .

Because of the novel's ingenious structure, you don't need a flow chart, or hired help, to keep track of the plot. Each chapter examines one relationship—between husband and wife, parent and child, between friends or siblings. A partial view thus expands and reverberates as the chapters unfurl. But the chapters aren't chronological, with consecutive clues revealed until, at the end, we have a completed jigsaw. Instead, Mr. Mathews often strands us in one character's perceptions, or presents the puzzling effect before the cause. As Lewis, the novel's young modernist writer, must learn, "creation begins by annihilating typical forms and procedures, especially the illusory 'naturalness' of sequence and coherence."

That strategy is particularly effective in the chapters on Phoebe and Lewis. Phoebe suffers from a misdiagnosed thyroid condition that causes severe depression. Awash in hallucinations, she locks herself into battle with her father. . . .

Her brother, Lewis, suffers from his own "ecstatic pain" when he begins to practice homosexual sadomasochism. . . . The point of view in these scenes forces the reader to be voyeuristic, complicit—like Lewis's mother. A chapter on the mother and son's conspiracy against the father is a harrowing case study in the tactics of shame and guilt

While such relationships may be extreme, Mr. Mathews implies that all relationships are treacherous. All of the novel's partners volley for "the right to control," or accept roles of dangerous dependency. Walter, with his swagger of heterosexual virility, mirrors Lewis: "Some males claim to dislike women, others to like them, but all share an original, undying fear. . . . Woman, having created him, can destroy him as well."

Much of the stylistic invention that has distinguished Mr. Mathews's earlier novels and poetry can be found here as well. There's humor in his incestuous naming of characters (Morris-Lewis-Louisa) and in the taunting, Jamesian formality of his diction. There's some fun with Zen paradox ("You don't have any money problems—you don't even have any money"). But the powerful characterizations dominate, and keep the inventiveness from seeming like mere trickery.

Beneath the mechanism of the plot lurks a complex vision of parents and children, of how disappointments and dependencies are bequeathed from generation to degeneration. Mr. Mathews has the good sense to choose enigma over dogma. Like the novel's mysterious title (a Sphinxy riddle from one of Phoebe's hallucinations), much is left dangling.

> Lisa Zeidner, *"From Generation to Degeneration,"* in The New York Times Book Review, *November 29, 1987, p. 23.*

LEWIS WARSH

As a title, *Cigarettes* is an antimetaphor; it works on so many different levels, each one cancels the other out. It's an impenetrable image, embodying both pleasure and death, yet if you try to think about what the title "means" (assuming it means any one thing) you'll come up with an empty pack. The sense of contrariness embedded in the word "cigarettes" carries over to the book, which consists of fifteen chapters, each dealing with a relationship between two people; the titles of the chapters are the names of the characters—Owen and Phoebe, Lewis and Morris, etc.—and the book chronicles their overlapping histories between 1936 and 1963. Even the similarity between these two dates is significant: Mathews, in his earlier novels, was obsessed with deciphering codes, raising the quest for the combination of words and numbers to an epic scale worthy of Poe or the Kabbalists. In these books . . . , the characters are functions of the language, as if the author were making love to words, not the people these words are describing.

The Conversions (1962), *Tlooth* (1966), and *The Sinking of the Odradek Stadium* (1975) are exuberant language games where the possibilities of what a novel can be are shattered like an expensive vase and put back together so that the vase resembles the Chinese drawing engraved on its side and the flowers in the vase and the vase itself become one. *Tlooth,* my favorite of the three, chronicles the adventures of a dentist who escapes from a camp for political/religious heretics and travels through Europe and Africa. Part of his quest is to discover the mysterious disease fomenting below the stumps of his fingers (he has only three fingers on his left hand), but the quest is less important than what happens to him along the way. Mathews is like an anthropologist who invents the tribes he studies, and *Tlooth* is a series of case histories and descriptions, all tangential to the void which is at the illusory center of most novels. In *Cigarettes,* however, he gives up the attempt to locate pleasure within an imaginary frame; instead of the manic wit and the feeling of timelessness of the earlier books we have the suffering and abuse of real people in real time, and this return to earth, as it were (implying that the world we live in is as scary and insane as anything he could invent), results in his most beautiful and most hair-raising work.

Mathews keeps the crystallization of plots and subplots (enough, really, to fill another trilogy of novels) purposely vague, as if to say that beneath even the most transparent and obviously realistic surface there's a code of enigma which is the function of merely being alive. . . .

In a lecture he gave at Queens College a few years ago, Mathews talked about the reader's participation in the act of writing as if it were the reader's task to fill in the "absences, negations, voids," the "nothings" as he called them, much the same way he or she might go about finding the solution to a puzzle or code. *Cigarettes,* contradicting the author's own prescription for novel-writing, is less a collaboration between reader and writer than an act of generosity, filled with as much subdued anguish as his earlier novels were with bravado, and aspires towards some notion of what the truth of being alive might be.

> Lewis Warsh, *"Full Pack,"* in The American Book Review, *Vol. 10, No. 2, May-June, 1988, p. 16.*

Gloria Naylor

1950-

American novelist, short story writer, and critic.

In her fiction, Naylor illuminates representative black American experiences from various perspectives within contemporary society. She is best known as the author of *The Women of Brewster Place* (1982), for which she received the American Book Award for best first novel. In this work, Naylor chronicles the aspirations and disappointments of seven female residents of Brewster Place, a dilapidated ghetto housing project located in an unidentified northern city. Naylor devotes individual chapters to the lives of her characters, detailing the circumstances that brought the women to the neighborhood, their relationships with each other, and the devastating events that heighten the difficulty of leaving Brewster Place. As the women cope with living in a racially polarized and sexist society, they also encounter abuse and indifference from their husbands, lovers, and children. To alleviate these conditions, Naylor advocates female solidarity and nurturing, an ideal that prompted comparisons to the concept of female bonding that Alice Walker propounds in her novel *The Color Purple*. While *The Women of Brewster Place*, like much traditional Afro-American literature, portrays impoverished blacks trapped in urban squalor, many critics noted that Naylor's work avoids stereotypes and didacticism. Judith V. Branzburg commented: "Without being overtly critical of the racism of America, Naylor manages to make the reader understand how the economic and social situation of black lives becomes one with personal lives, with the relationships between men and women, women and women, and parents and children, without diminishing the humanity of the individuals involved."

In her second novel, *Linden Hills* (1984), Naylor abandons the gritty realism of *The Women of Brewster Place* for an allegorical commentary on the fallacies of upward mobility and material success. Linden Hills, an exclusive suburb located near Brewster Place, is headed by the satanic Luther Nedeed. A real estate tycoon and mortician, Nedeed is a descendant of the man who founded the community during the 1830s by selling his wife and six children into slavery. While his ancestors developed Linden Hills into an affluent suburb, intending to showcase the economic and educational achievements of blacks, Luther has turned his family's mission into a perverse legacy in which prospective residents must forfeit their heritage and sell their humanity to obtain a home. *Linden Hills* revolves around two young men, Willie and Lester, who encounter several residents while working odd jobs over the Christmas holidays. As Willie and Lester proffer their services throughout the neighborhood, they witness Nedeed's malevolent control over the community and expose the idleness, hypocrisy, and bigotry of the townspeople. Critics cited similarities between *Linden Hills* and Dante's *Inferno*. For example, Dante's hell consists of nine circles, with each descending layer populated by more repugnant sinners; in Naylor's novel, Linden Hills is composed of nine circular streets on a hill at the bottom of which reside the wealthiest and most decadent citizens. Michiko Kakutani observed: "Although the notion of using Dante's *Inferno* to illuminate the co-opting of black aspirations in contemporary America may strike the prospective reader as pre-

tentious, one is quickly beguiled by the actual novel—so gracefully does Miss Naylor fuse together the epic and the naturalistic, the magical and the real."

Mama Day (1987), Naylor's recent work, is set in an all-black rural community named Willow Springs, where citizens have successfully eluded commercialization for nearly two hundred years. An island located off the coasts of South Carolina and Georgia yet legally independent from both states, Willow Springs was founded by Sapphira Wade, an African slave and sorceress who married and later murdered her owner after forcing him to bequeath his land to his slaves and their offspring. The novel centers on two of Sapphira's descendants—Mama Day, the elderly leader of Willow Springs, who possesses mystical healing powers, and Cocoa, Mama Day's strong-willed grandniece, who lives in New York City but returns to Willow Springs every summer. The book's chapters alternate between a summation by Cocoa and her husband George of their stormy courtship and marriage and the narration of an unnamed island resident who relates the story of Willow Springs and its two legendary matriarchs. Critics praised Naylor's accurate rendering of southern idioms and use of folklore to advance her story. A reviewer for *Publishers Weekly* asserted: "The rhythmic alternation of voices and locales [in *Mama Day*] has a narcotic effect that inspires trust and belief in both Mama Day and Naylor herself, who illustrates with convincing simplicity and clear-sighted intelligence the magical interconnectedness of people with nature, with God and with each other.''

(See also *CLC*, Vol. 28 and *Contemporary Authors*, Vol. 107.)

JUDITH V. BRANZBURG

Black writers often feel compelled to ask themselves in what ways and to what extent their art should serve the political-social needs of their race. The answer is not easy to find. Failure to write with a crusading mentality has often brought on accusations of betrayal of the race, while polemical writing had been criticized as dull and lacking in artistry or subtlety. For Afro-American women writers the perils of politics and art are more numerous than for the men. Not only must the women remain true to their race, they must also support racial unity by not being too hard on black men.

A number of contemporary women novelists, including Toni Morrison and Toni Cade Bambara, have succeeded in being faithful to art and their race while writing honestly about relationships between black men and women. Their writing has the power to move both through the situations of the characters and the beauty of the prose. Their novels also have a ring of truth because the women write with a black sensibility, with black rhythms, and in a black vernacular, exhibiting a type of imagination which takes its substance from the experience of being black, not non-white, in the United States.

This is the tradition in which Gloria Naylor has placed herself with *The Women of Brewster Place*. The success of her novel is in her rendering, in rich, sensuous, rhythmic language, a sense of the reality of Afro-American women's lives while including serious examination of racial and sexual politics. Without being overtly critical of the racism of America, Naylor manages to make the reader understand how the economic and social situation of black lives becomes one with personal lives, with the relationships between men and women, women and women, and parents and children, without diminishing the humanity of the individuals involved. She makes it clear that the socio-economic reality of black lives creates black men's tendency to leave their lovers and children. She knows that black children need special training to survive in a society which holds blacks in disdain. But Naylor is also certain that black men are capable of taking more responsibility than they do, and that mothers of any color will try to do their best for their children. (p. 116)

Brewster Place is separated from the rest of the city by a brick wall erected to control traffic in the major part of the town. Disconnected from the business of the city by a wall, Brewster Place has become a dead end, literally and figuratively, for the black people who finally come to inhabit it. By setting Brewster Place off, Naylor is able to write of Afro-Americans untouched by whites in their daily, domestic lives.

The novel is organized around the lives of seven women, all of whom live on Brewster Place. Each chapter, or story, is devoted to detailing the circumstances of one of the women's lives. Naylor's intent is not to present all the different possible types or situations of Afro-American women, but to present a range that illustrates the difference in detail but the sameness in effect. Mattie Michael, the emotional center of the novel, is a middle aged women who comes to Brewster Place from the South. Her story is the only one that does not take place entirely on Brewster Place. Before her coming, she has dedicated her life to raising her son, only to have him fail her. Etta Mae Johnson, an old friend of Mattie's southern childhood, comes to Brewster Place and Mattie to make a final attempt at finding a man who will stay with and support her. She is fearful that the charms which have stood her in good stead, allowing her to seduce men when she needed them, will now fail her. Kiswana Browne, a young political activist whose vision of her people was born in the Black Power movement, comes from the good side of the tracks, Linden Hills, to live and work with ''the people'' on Brewster Place. Another young woman, Lucielia Louise Turner, a kind of stepchild to Mattie, learns the pain of loving a man, Eugene, who cannot give her any kind of support, emotional or economic, and the anguish of the death of a child. Cora Lee, the welfare mother, seems a child herself. But she spends her life having babies, fascinated by them yet unable to deal with them once they are no longer infants. Finally, ''The Two,'' is the story of the lesbians Lorraine and Theresa. They live isolated from the others on the street, separated because of their sexual love for each other. They become symbols both of women's pain and women's unity by the end of the novel.

Except in the ''Kiswana'' chapter, which is the least fully realized portrait, and ''The Two'' up until the point of Lorraine's rape, patterns of attraction to and abandonment by men, too much caring for children, and the realization of the solace, comfort and love that black women can give one another are repeated throughout the novel. But each retelling of the black women's tale is not simply a repetition. It is a building on the previous telling, gaining force and culminating in Lorraine's rape and its aftermath, Mattie's final vision. Both of these beautifully rendered last scenes address the question from Langston Hughes' poem, ''What happens to a dream deferred?'' which is posed on the prefatory pages of the novel. The rape is a male response, the tearing down the wall of Mattie's dream a female one. (pp. 117-18)

In each case, the women accept responsibility for their parts in their relationships with men, and can then continue their lives. By taking responsibility for mistakes, pain, and love, and in choosing each other, the women accept that they can, at least to some extent, control their lives. Such an acceptance means ceasing to be victims of others' wills or circumstances. . . . The men are finally incidental, good for pain and not much more. They come, do their dirty work, and go. The children fail too, for they are not strong enough to carry their parents' dreams. The women stay and support each other.

Naylor is as successful as she is at presenting the complexity of black lives without reducing the people to types simply because she is an accomplished writer. She is especially good at describing the sensuous and at evoking the sounds, smells, and feelings of any given situation. Her talent for creating rich, emotional characters makes her failings particularly disappointing. Kiswana, the Black Power activist and the two lesbians are flat characters, especially Kiswana. The only time Kiswana seems to come alive is in the few lines when she is thinking of her lover Abshu. The lesbians also fail because Naylor does not invest them with the sensuousness and fullness of feeling that characterizes the other women. The ''Kiswana'' chapter is also the only one in which Naylor fails to show the seamless intermingling of the political and the personal and resorts to a lecture from Kiswana's middle class and bourgeois, yet very proud mother. Naylor seems to have difficulty portraying women whose life choices or circumstances have separated them from the pain of financial struggle and heterosexual relations that mark all of Naylor's other women. But, taken as part of the whole, these are minor complaints. Naylor's ability to present the pain and love of her characters' lives carries her through.

So, although at the end of the novel the people leave a dying Brewster Place with their dreams still deferred, there is a sense of hope. The women have, at the very least, gained respect, the readers' and their own. (pp. 118-19)

> *Judith V. Branzburg, "Seven Women and a Wall,"*
> in Callaloo, *Vol. 7, No. 2, Spring-Summer, 1984,*
> *pp. 116-19.*

MICHIKO KAKUTANI

In *The Women of Brewster Place,* her award-winning first novel, Gloria Naylor conjured up an entire fictional world by sifting through the lives of eight black women, trapped in an urban housing development, at "the end of the line." . . . [In *Linden Hills*], she is again concerned with the foundering of black dreams within a particular community, but she has moved up the social ladder, to an upper-middle class neighborhood of mock-Tudor homes and Georgian mansions known as Linden Hills.

By letting her mythic imagination spring free from the constraints of old-fashioned realism, Miss Naylor has produced an ambitious novel that aspires to be nothing less than a contemporary reading of Dante's *Inferno*. Not only are the residents of Linden Hills lost souls, condemned to a "city of woe" for their embracing of material pleasures, but they also live on a series of circular drives that correspond, geographically, to Dante's nine circles of hell. At the bottom of the hill, there's a frozen lake—just like the one in which Lucifer was immersed—and on the lake lives Miss Naylor's own version of Satan, a short, frog-eyed real estate tycoon, named Luther Nedeed, who maintains his hold over Linden Hills by appealing to its citizens' baser ambitions. . . .

Although the notion of using Dante's *Inferno* to illuminate the co-opting of black aspirations in contemporary America may strike the prospective reader as pretentious, one is quickly beguiled by the actual novel—so gracefully does Miss Naylor fuse together the epic and the naturalistic, the magical and the real. If the narrative relies rather too much on baroque symbols and withheld secrets—What terrible rites take place in the mortuary at the bottom of the hill? Whatever happened to Luther Nedeed's wife and baby son?—it is redeemed by the author's confident way with a story; her sassy, street-wise humor; her ability to empathize with her characters' dilemmas.

As written by Miss Naylor, those characters represent a spectrum black opinions. One member of Linden Hills denounces his ancestors for their passivity and their faith: "These people, his people, were always out of step, a step behind or a step ahead, still griping and crying about slavery, hanging up portraits of Abraham Lincoln in those lousy shacks. They couldn't do nothing because they were slaves or because they *will* be in heaven."

Another mocks his wealthy family and their neighbors as yuppified Uncle Toms: They're the "saddest niggers you'll ever wanna meet."

And a third sympathizes with these same people for wanting a better life: "My mom got beat up every night after payday by a man who couldn't bear the thought of bringing home a paycheck only large enough for three people and making it stretch over eight people, so he drank up half of it." . . .

There is a certain sociological impulse at work here, as though Miss Naylor wanted to play Studs Terkel—wanted to make sure to include every representative viewpoint. And yet for all their symbolic value, her characters never become caricatures, outlined by a condescending observer. Roxanne, the bright, spoiled princess who wants to grow up to be a combination of Eleanor Roosevelt and Diana Ross; Xavier, her ambitious boyfriend who's afraid to declare his love; Michael, the Harvard track star who becomes a minister, only to lose his faith—these people emerge, bit by bit, as conflicted individuals whose dilemmas are as much products of personal chemistry, as abstract, environmental forces.

We get to know these residents of Linden Hills through the eyes of Lester and Willie, two characters out of an Eddie Murphy movie and two of the most charming heroes to talk their way through a recent novel. These two hip dudes are doing odd jobs in Linden Hills to earn some extra Christmas money, and in narrating their adventures there, Miss Naylor captures, perfectly, the flavor of youthful male friendship— that peculiar combination of boasting and joke-telling that belies deeper bonds of shared insecurities and fears.

Both young men happen to be poets, blessed with sensitivity and a way with words, but as our guides through the inferno of Linden Hills they remind us less of Virgil and Dante, than of another pair of friends—Tom Sawyer and Huckleberry Finn.

> *Michiko Kakutani, "Dante in Suburbia," in* The New
> York Times, *February 9, 1985, p. 14.*

MEL WATKINS

Gloria Naylor's first novel, *The Women of Brewster Place,* which won an American Book Award in 1983, chronicled the plight of eight black women living in an urban lower-class cul-de-sac. With few exceptions—most notably the portrayal of a ghastly gang rape, which took on mythic proportions—that book realistically portrayed the characters' efforts to overcome the poverty and anguish of their lives. *Linden Hills,* Miss Naylor's second novel, also uses a confined geographic setting to construct a tale about the interconnected lives of a group of black characters. It is, however, a much more ambitious work in which realism is subordinated to allegory. Although flawed, it tackles a controversial subject with boldness and originality.

Like Amiri Baraka in *The Systems of Dante's Hell* (1965), Miss Naylor has adapted Dante's *Inferno* to her own fictional purposes—in this instance a tale of lost black souls trapped in the American dream. The setting is Linden Hills, an upper-middle-class black community built on a huge plot of land owned by the mysterious Nedeed family (the locale is not specified). Purchased by Luther Nedeed in 1820—after he had sold his octoroon wife and six children into slavery and moved from Tupelo, Miss., we are told—the land has remained under the proprietorship of the Nedeeds for more than 150 years. Luther (read Lucifer), as all the males in the Nedeed family are named, opened a funeral parlor, then developed the land and leased sections to black families. His sons and grandsons, all of whom are physical copies of the original landowner, furthered his plan—to establish a showcase black community.

That community, as the original Luther says, would not only be an "ebony jewel" representing black achievement, but also "a beautiful, black wad of spit right in the white eye of America."

When Miss Naylor picks up the story in the present, Luther's vision has been realized. Linden Hills is a thriving community of successful black professionals. But Luther's domain is not all it seems. We discover why when introduced to the residents of Linden Hills by Willie and Lester (read Dante and Virgil), two young poets who take odd jobs with the Hills inhabitants to earn money for Christmas. As they work their way down the circular drives—a structural hierarchy wherein the wealthier and more successful families live closer to the Nedeed home, which is surrounded by a frozen lake at the bottom of the hill—Miss Naylor strips away the facade of material success to reveal a nether-world of chaos and despair. . . .

Simply stated, Miss Naylor's version of the *Inferno* suggests that blacks who aspire to the white world and material success are pawns of the Devil and will experience the torments of hell. It is an intriguing allegory, and for the most part Miss Naylor presents it with wit and insight into the tensions and anxieties that plague assimilated blacks. (There is even a sense of tongue-in-cheek humor here—why else would the author's Dante and Virgil bear the names of a well-known ventriloquist-and-dummy team?) The problem is that, perhaps because of the rigid allegorical structure, the narrative lists toward the didactic. Moreover, intimations of some bizarre rituals are never made quite clear. Why does one of the Nedeed wives order snakeroot, powdered dove's heart and castor oil for her kitchen? And what exactly are the strange ministrations Luther performs on the corpses in his mortuary?

Although Miss Naylor has not been completely successful in adapting the *Inferno* to the world of the black middle class, in *Linden Hills* she has shown a willingness to expand her fictional realm and to take risks. Its flaws notwithstanding, the novel's ominous atmosphere and inspired set pieces—such as the minister's drunken fundamentalist sermon before an incredulous Hills congregation—make it a fascinating departure for Miss Naylor, as well as a provocative, iconoclastic novel about a seldom-addressed subject.

> Mel Watkins, "The Circular Driveways of Hell," in
> The New York Times Book Review, *March 3, 1985,*
> *p. 11.*

ROBERT JONES

For the women who live on Brewster Place, Linden Hills rises above their dead-end street as a dream to be achieved. Linden Hills may be indistinguishable from any colorless, American suburb, but it flaunts everything that has been denied to those exiled from the standard baggage and measure of middle-class success. Gloria Naylor has not given the name of a place to her two novels accidentally. She understands the ways in which geography infiltrates the mind and how our identification with a particular landscape determines our understanding of ourselves and our connection to a history.

Few histories have been as psychically linked to the land as ours. To a large degree, our spirit of omnipotence and invincibility as a culture cannot be separated from the belief that the land will never run out. There will always be room to breathe and an opportunity for limitless growth. . . . Even places that have failed, like the ghost towns of California and Nevada,

are predicated on this belief in expansion. These jinxed, desert towns stay in our memory as monuments to an eternal faith in the possibility of renewal, the belief that when the water runs dry or the gold disappears, we can begin again somewhere else. Geographical memory feeds our most potent legends and self-understanding and makes the country, even at its most desolate outposts, perpetually seem to be the isolate land of promise.

But these myths of origin and development are always the property of the sovereign culture. Gloria Naylor writes of ghost towns of another variety, for when she looks to the past, it is to a history of exclusion rather than promise. The urban grave-yards of Brewster Place have not been deserted by settlers, but abandoned by hope. Brewster Place lies at the end of a city; its inhabitants live on the outskirts of history. When Naylor's characters speak of the past, it is always in terms of family, never in terms of a larger, cultural tradition. The family is what they remember and the history of which they are part. It is not the memory of a historical past shared by the culture encircling them.

In *Black Boy,* Richard Wright said, "when I thought of the essential bleakness of black life in America, I knew that Negroes had never been allowed to catch the full spirit of western civilization, that somehow they lived in it but not of it." Naylor is a generation forty years subsequent to Wright's. Her vision is of the aftershocks of assimilation and the double-loss it entails: the forfeiture by black Americans of a tenuous sense of a distinct past for the doubts and failings inherent in the world to which they so long dreamed of belonging.

Both of Naylor's novels concern the death of remembrance. In "A Sketch of the Past," Virginia Woolf defined memory as the base upon which all of experience rests, the tie that binds all impressions and ideas, all life, to a context. It is this memorial event which allows meaning to unfold and enables us to imagine a future as we attempt to make sense of the past. Understanding is remembrance, and the greatest novels of this century, Proust's *La Recherche du Temps Perdu,* Andrey Biely's *St. Petersburg,* Woolf's *The Waves,* all reconstruct a past as the present recedes into diffusion and meaninglessness. Self-knowledge is made possible only by memory. This idea is integral to Dante and, before him, to Augustine, for only in memory can we glimpse the possibility of eternity. Memory sets you free.

In *Linden Hills,* Naylor recreates Dante's city of Dis in *The Inferno* in an American suburb. Her meaning is founded on the same sense of damnation that overwhelmed Dante's journey into hell. Dis is Lucifer's city, the place of souls turned against themselves, those damned for ill-will, corruption of the spirit, and the perversion of social good for self-dreaming and glory. At the end of *The Women of Brewster Place,* Naylor says that a street dies when it becomes lost to memory. Her characters are bereft of any link to a past or to a place that allows them to imagine an end to their exile, so they suffer oblivion. . . . In *Linden Hills,* Naylor brings us into the world to which the residents of Brewster Place aspired, and shows us that it too is a place of dead roads.

As Lester Tilson and Willie Mason stroll down the crescent drives of Linden Hills to the home of its ancestral founder, Luther Nedeed, we experience an unnerving sense of a culture gone out of control. It is the province of Lacan's *ça parle:* the voice of a culture that jabbers noisily at its people as they search in vain for meaning. *It speaks:* language simply goes on; the meanings embedded in the encompassing world generate their own life and we find ourselves in society after-the-fact. Naylor's vision is uniquely modern in its depiction of culture as something independent to the lives struggling to adjust to its advancement.

For Naylor, damnation begins with the loss of memory of origins. *Linden Hills* is about the fallacy of independence and the seduction of will-lessness and forgetfulness. The loss of memory engenders the loss of will, and both precurse the slide into oblivion. As Lester and Willie make their descent, Luther's wife, Willa, lies locked in a basement as punishment for her husband's paranoia. Willa gradually unearths relics of past Nedeed women driven mad as she is now. . . . Luwana Packerville, Evelyn Creton Nedeed. There is an elegiac quality in these passages that is unrivaled in contemporary fiction. In the litany of the dead's secrets, Naylor bears witness to the possibility that we can disappear without a trace and be trampled unnoticed by a culture we have set in motion and are powerless to stop.

Tales of the American dream gone sour have become a truism in cultural criticism and a genre-unto-itself in twentieth-century fiction. . . . Almost as soon as America created itself, its literature cast a stern eye toward its progress and predicted its decline. Especially in the present age, no ''serious'' writer earns his or her credentials without lamenting our lost innocence and our fall from grace. We have become so accustomed to hearing of our lemming-like plunge into futility, that despair has lost its affect. Naylor understands the contagion of an imaginative lack and our susceptibility to hopelessness. But her work diverges from fashionable, nihilistic novels in its evocation of the cruelty culture inflicts on all of its missing persons and the damnation awaiting those of us who automatically follow its course.

In John Ciardi's translation of *The Inferno*, Dante hears the anguish of hell's dead spirits and asks:

> Master, what shades are these who lie
> buried in these chests and fill the air
> with such a painful and unending cry?

Willa Nedeed's cries haunt Lester's and Willie's walk through Linden Hills. In Willa, Naylor echoes the bewilderment of those who unwittingly lost their way and find themselves deceived by a life they never imagined having. And who, at their moment of starkest reflection, cannot remember how any of it began or how they have come so far. (pp. 283-85)

> Robert Jones, ''A Place in the Suburbs,'' in Commonweal, *Vol. CXII, No. 9, May 3, 1985, pp. 283-85.*

JEWELLE GOMEZ

It's hard for me to be overly critical of a young, black woman writer who has achieved national success, something so rarely offered to women of color in this country. It is doubly difficult when the work of that writer, Gloria Naylor, shows seriousness and intelligence, and, next to Toni Morrison, creates the most complex black women characters in modern literature. Still, Gloria Naylor's first novel, *The Women of Brewster Place* and now her second, *Linden Hills,* leave me unsatisfied, somewhat like I've felt after my grandmother's *Reader's Digest* condensations. I sense something important was happening but the abridgement left a bare skeleton, not a full experience. (p. 7)

Perhaps it is the sweeping scope of her story which makes Naylor believe she must wave characters and situations before us quickly rather than let us interact with them in an intimate way. But given her flair for lyrical narrative and pungent dialog there is no reason not to expect more from her. Too often, [*Linden Hills*] reads like a screenplay. Naylor gives us a visual effect or the rhythm of an event but we get no clear sense of either the impact on the characters or the emotional subtext. If there is no subtext, if this is merely the unfolding of a tapestry of diverse characters whose paths cross at random, then it is even more crucial for Naylor to attach her characters more firmly to the framework.

The Inferno motif shapes the narrative—which is fine, as the lives of black people are more than suitable for epic legends—but it often feels like a literary exercise rather than a ground-breaking adaptation. But having chosen a classical European tale to emulate, Naylor then does nothing to utilize the endless and rich African mythology to embellish the story and give it a more timeless significance. The first disappointment comes early and is woven throughout the book. Skin color has been a source of contention for Afro-Americans since we were forced onto these shores. Our color marked us as slaves and as inferior. We, as well as Europeans, have been taught that the fairer our skin the closer we are to human. Naylor uses that symbology liberally: the endless Nedeed men are coal black, squat, ugly and evil but Ruth, Willie's dream girl, has a face like ''smokey caramel.'' All of the Nedeed wives have been fair-skinned and nearly invisible presences in the household. The current Mrs. Nedeed, somewhat darker, ironically delivers the first fair-skinned son; both are doomed from the beginning of the book. Given the complex and oppressive part that skin color has played in the economic, social and psychological lives of Afro-Americans I expected a more meaningful treatment of it. If ''black'' only symbolizes evil here, just as it does in most western literature, then why does neither the author nor her characters comment on that, either directly or obliquely? Perhaps Naylor feels she has done so by giving Willie the nickname ''White,'' awarded to him because of his dark skin. But the reiteration of the symbolism here feels like simple acceptance of it.

Another weakness in the novel is the preponderance of mad people. This is, perhaps, where clinging to Dante has been most disadvantageous. On their descent Willie and Lester encounter their old friend Norman, a man who appears healthy most of the time until he is attacked by ''the pinks.'' Then he claws madly at his skin, gouging and scraping to rid himself of imagined pink ooze which threatens to envelope him. His wife has reduced their household to the most harmless furnishings (paper plates, plastic flatware, only two chairs) in order to protect him when he is possessed. Laurel, the beautiful, ''coffee-colored'' heir to a house in Linden Hills, retreats into silence, classical music and endless swims in her backyard pool. She leaves her devoted grandmother bewildered and her ''sketch'' of a husband impatient. Laurel finally does a high dive into her empty pool on a snowy Christmas eve to escape the demons that haunt her—demons which, like ''the pinks,'' are rather fantastic and ill-defined.

The Nedeed patriarchs pursue riches and power through their mortuary business and the conversion of Linden Hills into a desirable property. They shape the competition which drives others to scheme and connive to win a place in Linden Hills. The last Luther Nedeed loses control when his dark-skinned wife gives birth to a light-skinned son: he locks them both in the basement of their home. (And as if that were not enough, he has already been seen doing unsettling things with the corpses at the mortuary.) Then there are the Nedeed wives, most of whom have been chosen for their obsequiousness and malleability. The current Mrs. Nedeed (whose name, Willa, we learn only at the end of the book) seems to be in atypically good control of her faculties until her son dies in the basement and Luther refuses to let her out. Leafing through journals and photograph albums during her imprisonment, Willa sees a pattern of overbearance and abuse that has left the Nedeed women less than whole. And in one particularly chilling section she flips through a picture album that begins with the wedding of a vibrant girl named Priscilla to an antecedent Luther. As the pictures progress the shadow of Priscilla's son, yet another Luther, grows ominously until it covers her completely. Soon all traces of her once lively face appear to have been deliberately burned away from the photos. In another journal Willa watches the normal check list of groceries and recipes metamorphose into a grotesque catalogue of binging and purging.

Willa's explorations of the past prove to be the most engaging parts of the book, although so many people (good and evil) are crippled with neuroses it is hard to find one to hold on to. Perhaps that is part of the relentless descent into hell; but after a while I longed for one ordinary somebody who just goes home and watches television. Naylor sets a tone of relentless gothic horror but her bedlam is out of hand. . . . There are no innocents here except for Willie and Lester, and they are her weakest characters. Perhaps in light of the insanity around them their mundane concerns (where to find a job, what to do about being in love with a friend's wife) can only seem insignificant. Naylor does not give these concerns nearly as much attention as the more histrionic ones. A paragraph here and there touches on one boy's unease at the real intimacy he feels with his pal, or the other's bitterness toward his mother, but these are only passing moments on the way to the snake pit. Willie and Lester should be our link but they have neither wisdom or naiveté. They are young boys who have opted out of the system for no particular reason; they are not significantly oppressed by poverty nor inspired by genius; they have no driving vision of their own and so cannot compete dramatically with the really extraordinary characters.

I would have loved to see this trip through the eyes of Ruth, who does battle against her husband's ''pinks'' with a fierceness and love unmatched by any other character in the novel (a battle dropped half way through the book!). Or through the testimony of the alcoholic Reverend Hollis who is the only active adversary of Luther Nedeed. The telescope of Dr. Braithwaite, the town historian, would certainly have been revealing: he has killed the roots of the willow trees surrounding his home to provide an unobscured perspective from which to observe the life of most residents, including Luther, while he writes the definitive history of Linden Hills.

Time is another problem. As in *The Women of Brewster Place,* I am never secure in my sense of time. The history of Linden Hills is laid out from before the Civil War to the recent present but all events are set curiously adrift on the social and political sea that buffets Afro-Americans in this country. I don't need to know exactly where Willie and Lester are in relation to Brown vs. Board of Education, but even Dante worked within a specific sociopolitical milieu which shaped his vision. In Linden Hills some people behave like it is still the turn of the century while others talk about ''disc cameras.'' For many of the issues Naylor touches upon, a clear sense of historical time is pivotal. For example, one character disavows a liaison with his male lover in order to marry the appropriate woman and inherit the coveted Linden Hills home, all at the direction of Luther Nedeed. This feudal machination is certainly not completely outdated (and never will be as long as there is greed), but who is the young man beset by this trauma? We receive so little personal information about him that his motivations are obscure. For a middle-class, educated gay man to be blind to alternative lifestyles in 1985 is not inconceivable but it's still hard to accept the melodrama of his arranged marriage without screaming ''dump the girl and buy a ticket to Grand Rapids!'' Naylor's earlier novel presented a similar limitation. While she admirably attempts to portray black gays as integral to the fabric of black life she seems incapable of imagining black gays functioning as healthy, average people. In her fiction, although they are not at fault, gays must still be made to pay. This makes her books sound like a return to the forties, not a chronicle of the eighties. (pp. 7-8)

All of that said, the reason I have such high expectations is that Naylor is talented. Her writing can be lyrical and powerful, so I demand more than emulation. . . .

I want Gloria Naylor to engage me, to intrigue, horrify and move me. She is eminently capable of that and more. But her writing jumps around from character to event as if it's not important how we feel about them. Naylor's work is important and intelligent. She takes black people and black women in particular more seriously than most writers do today. I want her craft to be equal to her vision. We know that we can master European forms. That's easy. I'm still looking for the evenly shaped work that I know will be crafted from Naylor's raw talent. A work that stands on its own in world literature. (p. 8)

Jewelle Gomez, ''Naylor's Inferno,'' in The Women's Review of Books, *Vol. II, No. 11, August, 1985, pp. 7-8.*

PUBLISHERS WEEKLY

The beauty of Naylor's prose is its plainness, and the secret power of her third novel [*Mama Day*] is that she does not simply tell a story but brings you face to face with human beings living through the complexity, pain and mystery of real life. But *Mama Day* is a black story in particular which is, paradoxically, why it is such a satisfying and all-encompassing experience. A young black couple meet in New York and fall in love. Ophelia (''Cocoa'') is from Willow Island, off the coast of South Carolina and Georgia but part of neither state, and George is an orphan who was born and raised in New York. Every August, Cocoa visits her grandmother Abigail and great-aunt Miranda (''Mama Day'') back home. The lure of New York and the magic of home and Mama Day's folk medicines and mystical powers pull at the couple and bring about unforeseen, yet utterly believable, changes in them and their relationship. Naylor interweaves three simple narratives—Cocoa and George alternately tell about their relationship, while a third-person narrative relates the story of Mama Day and Willow Island. . . . Naylor's (*The Women of Brewster Place, Linden Hills*) skills as a teller of tales are equal to her philosophical and moral aims. The rhythmic alternation of voices and locales here has a narcotic effect that inspires trust and belief in both Mama Day and Naylor herself, who illustrates with convincing simplicity and clear-sighted intelligence the magical interconnectedness of people with nature, with God and with each other. (pp. 54-5)

A review of ''Mama Day,'' in Publishers Weekly, *Vol. 232, No. 25, December 18, 1987, pp. 54-5.*

MICHIKO KAKUTANI

In her previous novel, *Linden Hills,* Gloria Naylor created an intimate portrait of a "perverted Eden," in which upper-middle-class blacks discover that they've achieved wealth and success at the expense of their own history and identity, that they've sold their souls and are now living in a kind of spiritual hell. *Mama Day,* her latest novel, similarly describes a hermetic black community, but this time, it's a pastoral world named Willow Springs—a small, paradisal island, situated off the southeast coast of the United States, somewhere off South Carolina and Georgia, but utterly sovereign in its history and traditions.

Legend has it that the island initially belonged to a Norwegian landowner named Bascombe Wade, and that one of his slaves—"a true conjure woman" by the name of Sapphira, who "could walk through a lightning storm without being touched"—married him, persuaded him to leave all his holdings to his slaves, then "poisoned him for his trouble." Before killing him, she bore him seven sons. The youngest of that generation also had seven sons, and the last of them fathered Miranda, or Mama Day. The great-nieces of Mama Day are Willa Prescott Nedeed, who readers of *Linden Hills* will recall came to an ugly and untimely end; and Ophelia, the heroine of this novel, who is likewise threatened with early and disfiguring death. . . .

To set up the fast-paced events that conclude *Mama Day,* Ms. Naylor spends much of the first portion of the book giving us menacing hints and planting time bombs set to detonate later. We're told that Ophelia's the namesake of another Day, an unhappy woman who never recovered from one of the misfortunes that befell the family, and that her own hot temper is liable to get her into trouble. We're told that George suffers from a bad heart and that he shouldn't over-exert himself. We're told that Miss Ruby, a neighbor in Willow Springs, plans to use her magical powers against any woman who comes near her husband, and that her husband happens to be attracted to Ophelia. We're also told that Mama Day herself possesses potent conjuring powers, which she will use to defend her family.

One of the problems with this information is that it's force-fed into the story line, at the expense of character development and narrative flow. The plot is made to pivot around melodramatically withheld secrets (concerning the history of Willow Springs, the nature of Mama Day's second sight, the mysterious "hoodoo" rites practiced on the island); and we are constantly being reminded of the novel's themes by trite observations that are meant to pass as folk wisdom: "Home. You can move away from it, but you never leave it"; "they say every blessing hides a curse, and every curse a blessing" or "nothing would be real until the end."

To make matters worse, the island's residents, who are given to uttering such lines, come across as pasteboard figures, devoid of the carefully observed individuality that distinguished their counterparts in *Linden Hills.* Mama Day is just the sort of matriarchal figure that her name indicates—strong, wise and resolute; her neighbor, a "hoodoo" man known as Dr. Buzzard, is a folksy con man, who plays a crooked game of poker and makes moonshine on the side, and Ruby is the manipulative devil woman, absurdly possessive of her man. As for the visitors to Willow Springs, they're initially just as two-dimensional: Ophelia is a bigoted, demanding woman, who seems lucky to have found a husband at all, given her large mouth and even larger ego, while George appears to be a conscientious yuppie, neatly dividing his time between work, his wife and his passion for football.

Fortunately, as *Mama Day* progresses, Ms. Naylor's considerable storytelling powers begin to take over, and her central characters slowly take on the heat of felt emotion. The bantering exchanges between George and Ophelia demonstrate their affection, as well as their knowledge of each other's weaknesses, and George's gradual immersion in the world of Willow Springs serves to reveal much about both him and his wife.

Still, for all the narrative energy of the novel's second half, there's something contrived and forced about the story. Whereas Toni Morrison's recent novel *Beloved,* which dealt with many of the same themes of familial love and guilt, had a beautiful organic quality to it, weaving together the ordinary and the mythic in a frightening tapestry of fate, *Mama Day* remains a readable, but lumpy, amalgam of styles and allusions. The reader eventually becomes absorbed in George and Ophelia's story, but is never persuaded that the events, which overtake them, are plausible, much less inevitable or real.

> *Michiko Kakutani, in a review of "Mama Day," in*
> The New York Times, *February 10, 1988, p. C25.*

BHARATI MUKHERJEE

On a note card above my writing desk hang the words of the late American original, Liberace: "Too much of a good thing is simply wonderful."

Excess—of plots and subplots, of major characters and walk-ons, of political issues and literary allusions—is what Gloria Naylor's *Mama Day,* her third and most ambitious book, is blessed with. "There are just too many sides to the whole story," Cocoa, Mama Day's grandniece, explains at the end of this longish novel, and the story obviously feels urgent enough to both Cocoa and to Ms. Naylor that they present it to us whole.

If novels are viewed as having the power to save, then novelists are obliged, first, to relive the history of the errors of earlier chroniclers and filling in the missing parts. Recent novels like *Mama Day,* Toni Morrison's *Beloved* and Louise Erdrich's *Love Medicine* resonate with the genuine excitement of authors discovering ways, for the first time it seems, to write down what had only been intuited or heard. These are novelists with an old-fashioned "calling" (to bear witness, to affirm public virtues) in a post-modernist world; their books are scaled down for today's microwavable taste, but still linked to the great public voice of 19th-century storytelling.

Mama Day has its roots in *The Tempest.* The theme is reconciliation, the title character is Miranda (also the name of Prospero's daughter), and Willow Springs is an isolated island where, as on Prospero's isle, magical and mysterious events come to pass. As in *The Tempest,* one story line concerns the magician Miranda Day, nicknamed Mama Day, and her acquisition, exercise and relinquishment of magical powers. The other story line concerns a pair of "star-crossed" (Ms. Naylor's phrase, too) lovers: Ophelia Day, nicknamed Cocoa, and George Andrews.

Willow Springs is a wondrous island, wonderfully rendered. We learn its secrets only if we let ourselves listen to inaudible voices in boarded-up houses and hard-to-reach graveyards. We find out the way the locals do, "sitting on our porches and shelling June peas, quieting the midnight cough of a baby, taking apart the engine of a car—you done heard it without a single living soul really saying a word."

On this wondrous island, slavery and race relations, lovers' quarrels, family scandals, professional jealousies all become the "stuff as dreams are made on." The island itself sits just out of the legal reaches of Georgia and South Carolina. "And the way we saw it," ghosts whisper, "America ain't entered the question at all when it come to our land. . . . We wasn't even Americans when we got it—[we] was slaves. And the laws about slaves not owning nothing in Georgia and South Carolina don't apply, 'cause the land wasn't then—and isn't now—in either of them places."

America, with all its greed and chicanery, exists beyond a bridge. The island was "settled" (if that word is ever appropriate in American history) in the first quarter of the 19th century by an Africa-born slave, a spirited woman named Sapphira who, according to legend, bore her master, a Norwegian immigrant named Bascombe Wade, and maybe person or persons unknown, a total of seven sons. She then persuaded Bascombe to deed the children every square inch of Willow Springs, after which she either poisoned or stabbed the poor man in bed and vanished ahead of a posse. We find out the conditions of Sapphira's bondage only at the end of the novel: love, and not a bill of sale, had kept Bascombe and Sapphira together. Bascombe had given up his land to her sons willingly. This disclosure may make for "incorrect" politics, but it is in keeping with the *Tempest*-like atmosphere of benevolence, light and harmony that Ms. Naylor wishes to have prevail on Willow Springs.

Mama Day, who made a brief appearance in Ms. Naylor's earlier novel, *Linden Hills,* as the toothless, illiterate aunt, the wearer of ugly, comfortable shoes, the hauler of cheap cardboard suitcases and leaky jars of homemade preserves, the caster of hoodoo spells, comes into her own in this novel. . . .

Mama Day—over 100 years old if we are to believe what folks in Willow Springs say, unmarried, stern, wise, crotchety, comforting—is the true heir of Sapphira Wade. Sapphira and Bascombe's love nest, a yellow house set deep in the woods, yields secrets about the future as well as the past to the witch-prophet-matriarch Mama Day. She is the ur-Daughter to Sapphira's ur-Mother and, in turn, through a Leda-and-the-Swan kind of mysterious dead-of-night visitations, she peoples the land herself. . . .

As long as the narrative confines itself to Mama Day and daily life on the bizarre island full of rogues, frauds, crazies, martyrs and clairvoyants, the novel moves quickly. Curiously, the slow sections are about the love story of 27-year-old Cocoa, who has relocated from Willow Springs to New York, and George Andrews, who is meant to be emblematic of the good-hearted, hard-driving but culturally orphaned Northern black man. The courtship occurs all over Manhattan—in greasy diners, in three-star restaurants, in midtown offices, on subways—giving Ms. Naylor a chance to accommodate several set pieces. But she is less proficient in making the familiar wondrous than she is in making the wondrous familiar. Discussions of black bigotry (Cocoa uses kumquats, tacos and bagels as race-related shorthand and has to be scolded into greater tolerance) or of the alienating effects of Barnard College on black women ("those too bright, too jaded colored girls" is George's put-down) seem like arbitrary asides.

The love story suffers from a more serious flaw. Ms. Naylor, through strident parallels, wants us to compare Cocoa and George to Romeo and Juliet, and their courtship process to the taming of Katharina, the "shrew." The literary plan calls for George to sacrifice his life so that Cocoa might be saved, but the lovers never quite fill out their assigned mythic proportions. Cocoa just seems shallow and self-centered; and George is a priggish young man who wears dry-cleaned blue jeans for roughing it on weekends. For their love story to overwhelm us, with "all passion spent," the lovers' intensity should make whole paragraphs resonate. This, unfortunately, Ms. Naylor does not do. It seems the unchallenged domain of the 19th-century novel to link personal passion with the broader politics of an age. Cocoa is not Madame Bovary, Anna Karenina, Jane Eyre, Dorothea Brooke.

But I'd rather dwell on *Mama Day*'s strengths. Gloria Naylor has written a big, strong, dense, admirable novel; spacious, sometimes a little drafty like all public monuments, designed to last and intended for many levels of use.

> *Bharati Mukherjee, "There Are Four Sides to Everything," in* The New York Times Book Review, *February 21, 1988, p. 7.*

DAVID NICHOLSON

In *Mama Day,* her third novel, Gloria Naylor manages a considerable feat: She bends black folk and spiritual lore to her uses, all the while scrupulously respecting the integrity of that lore. At the same time, she tells the moving modern-day story of love between two people who have every reason not to expect or get the happiness they eventually earn. It is a neat, and long overdue trick, for too much contemporary black writing retreats into games of language or form (the novels of Clarence Major or John Wideman) or into an imaginary, idealized past (Wideman, again, or Sherley Anne Williams). I do not mean to deny the obvious talents of these writers I have cited, but simply to say that black writing in the '80s seems to have failed to address many of the realities of black life in the '80s.

Here, Naylor manages to avoid both traps. While there are three narrators—the two lovers, George and Cocoa, tell their own stories and a third-person narrator relates the happenings on Willow Springs, a small sea island somewhere off the southeast coast—the effect is only a little confusing, and only at first. Eventually, we see that Naylor has told the story the way the story demanded to be told. Her writing, clear, precise and apt, is always a delight to read; it is often poetic, and yet the narrative thrust of the story is never made subordinate to the poetry. . . .

It is refreshing to read a book by a black woman in which black men are not objects of ridicule or instruments of torture. While Naylor gives us characters who are fools—vain, egocentric, given to making wrong choices or simply with too high an opinion of themselves and their abilities—these characters are always human, and their number equally divided between male and female.

George and Cocoa's story is in the foreground, but those parts that feature Mama Day, matriarch, healer and Willow Springs' vessel of wisdom, are not of lesser importance. In the chapters that alternate with George and Cocoa's story, we see Mama Day aiding a woman unable to bear children, quilting with her sister, Abigail, chiding the bootlegger and would-be conjure man, Dr. Buzzard. She is a woman of power, and it is on

Willow Springs, where George accompanies Cocoa on her annual August return home for the first time in their four-year marriage, that her knowledge receives its ultimate test when Cocoa's life is threatened.

To tell more would be to spoil the novel for the reader. Naylor has made **Mama Day** suspenseful, but the suspense is of the best kind—the reader continues to read, not because something is being withheld, but because something is always being revealed. And what is revealed is not simply who is threatening Cocoa and why, but something infinitely more valuable: insights into the complex nature of people and matters of the heart such as the difficulty of accepting love. . . .

[**Mama Day**] is a wonderful novel, full of spirit and sass and wisdom and completely realized.

> *David Nicholson, ''Gloria Naylor's Island of Magic and Romance,'' in* Book World—The Washington Post, *February 28, 1988, p. 5.*

Joyce Carol Oates

1938-

(Has also written under pseudonym of Rosamond Smith) American novelist, short story writer, poet, dramatist, essayist, critic, and editor.

One of the United States's most prolific and versatile contemporary writers, Oates has published nearly twenty novels, sixteen volumes of short stories, nine collections of verse, several plays, and numerous nonfiction works since her first book appeared in 1963. In her fiction, Oates focuses upon the spiritual, sexual, and intellectual decline of modern American society. Employing a dense, elliptical prose style, she depicts such cruel and macabre actions as rape, incest, murder, mutilation, child abuse, and suicide to delineate the forces of evil with which individuals must contend. Oates's protagonists often suffer at the hands of others as a result of emotional deficiencies or socioeconomic conditions. Greg Johnson commented: ''[Oates's] particular genius is her ability to convey psychological states with unerring fidelity, and to relate the intense private experiences of her characters to the larger realities of American life.''

Much of Oates's work takes place in the small towns that make up Eden County, a fictional region based on her birthplace of Erie County, New York. Her first novel, *With Shuddering Fall* (1964), foreshadows her preoccupation with evil and violence in the story of a destructive romance between a teenage girl and a thirty-year-old stock car driver that ends with his death in an accident. Oates's best-known and critically acclaimed early novels form a trilogy exploring three distinct segments of American society. Critics attribute the naturalistic ambience of these works to the influence of such twentieth-century authors as William Faulkner, Theodore Dreiser, and James T. Farrell. Oates's first installment, *A Garden of Earthly Delights* (1967), is set in rural Eden County and chronicles the life of the daughter of a migrant worker who marries a wealthy farmer in order to provide for her illegitimate son. The woman's idyllic existence is destroyed, however, when the boy murders his stepfather and kills himself. In *Expensive People* (1967), the second work in the series, Oates exposes the superficial world of suburbanites whose preoccupation with material comforts reveals their spiritual poverty. The final volume in the trilogy, *them* (1969), which won the National Book Award for fiction, depicts the violence and degradation endured by three generations of an inner-city Detroit family. Critics acknowledge that Oates's experiences as a teacher in Detroit during the early 1960s contributed to her accurate rendering of the city and its social problems. Betty DeRamus stated: ''Her days in Detroit did more for Joyce Carol Oates than bring her together with new people—it gave her a tradition to write from, the so-called American Gothic tradition of exaggerated horror and gloom and mysterious and violent incidents.''

Oates's novels of the 1970s explore characters involved with various American professional and cultural institutions while interweaving elements of human malevolence and tragedy. *Wonderland* (1971), for example, depicts a brilliant surgeon who is unable to build a satisfying home life, resulting in estrangement from his wife, children, and society. *Do with Me What You Will* (1973) focuses upon a young attorney who is

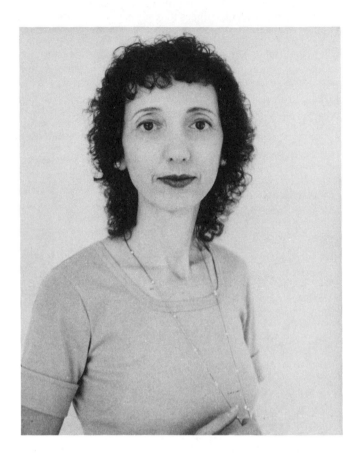

lauded by his peers for his devotion to liberal causes. *The Assassins: A Book of Hours* (1975) is a psychological tale which dramatizes the effects of the murder of a conservative politician on his wife and two brothers. *Son of the Morning* (1978) documents the rise and fall from grace of Nathan Vickery, an evangelist whose spirituality is alternately challenged and affirmed by various events in his life. *Unholy Loves* (1979) revolves around the lives of several faculty members of a small New York college. Considered the least emotionally disturbing of Oates's novels, *Unholy Loves* was praised for its indirect humor and gentle satire.

During the early 1980s, Oates published several novels that parody works by such nineteenth-century authors as Louisa May Alcott, Charles Dickens, Edgar Allan Poe, and Charlotte and Emily Brontë. *Bellefleur* (1980) follows the prescribed formula for a Gothic multigenerational saga, utilizing supernatural occurrences while tracing the lineage of an exploitative American family. Oates includes explicit violence in this work; for example, a man deliberately crashes his plane into the Bellefleur mansion, killing himself and his family. *A Bloodsmoor Romance* (1982) displays such elements of Gothic romance as mysterious kidnappings and psychic phenomena in the story of five maiden sisters living in rural Pennsylvania in the late 1800s. In *Mysteries of Winterthurn* (1984), Oates borrows heavily from the works of Poe as she explores the conventions of the nineteenth-century mystery novel. The protagonist of this work is a brilliant young detective who models his career after the exploits of Sir Arthur Conan Doyle's fictional sleuth, Sherlock Holmes. While some critics viewed these works as whimsical, Anne Collins maintained that they are significant literary achievements: "Joyce Carol Oates resurrects an old form so that she can unabashedly resurrect [the word 'evil'] and apply it to the destructive mysteries of the human psyche."

Oates's recent novels explore the nature and ramifications of obsession. *Solstice* (1985) revolves around a relationship between a young divorcée and an older woman that evolves into an emotional power struggle. In *Marya: A Life* (1986), a successful writer and academician attempts to locate her alcoholic mother, who had abused and later abandoned her as a child. *Lives of the Twins* (1987), which Oates wrote under the pseudonym of Rosamond Smith, presents a tale of love and erotic infatuation involving a woman, her lover, and her lover's twin brother. With *You Must Remember This* (1987), Oates returns to a naturalistic portrait of families under emotional and moral distress. Suicide attempts, violent beatings, disfiguring accidents, and incest take place in this novel, which centers on an intense love affair between a former boxer and his adolescent niece. Set in Eden County and containing references to such historical events as McCarthyism, the Rosenberg executions, and the Korean War, *You Must Remember This* earned high praise for its evocation of American life during the early 1950s. John Updike stated that this work "rallies all [of Oates's] strengths and is exceedingly fine—a storm of experience whose reality we cannot doubt, a fusion of fact and feeling, vision and circumstance which holds together, and holds us to it, through our terror and dismay."

Oates's works in other genres also address darker aspects of the human condition. Most critics contend that Oates's short fiction, for which she has twice received the O. Henry Special Award for Continuing Achievement, is best suited for evoking the urgency and emotional power of her principal themes. Such collections as *By the North Gate* (1963), *Where Are You Going, Where Have You Been?: Stories of Young America* (1974), *The Lamb of Abyssalia* (1980), and *Raven's Wing* (1986) contain pieces that focus upon violent and abusive relationships between the sexes. One widely anthologized story, "Where Are You Going, Where Have You Been?," a tale of female adolescence and sexual awakening, is considered a classic of modern short fiction and was adapted for film. Oates has also composed several dramas that were produced off-Broadway in New York and has published numerous volumes of poetry. In addition, she is a respected essayist and literary critic whose nonfiction works are praised for the logic and sensibility with which she examines a variety of subjects.

(See also *CLC*, Vols. 1, 2, 3, 6, 9, 11, 15, 19, 33; *Contemporary Authors*, Vols. 5-8, rev. ed.; *Contemporary Authors New Revision Series*, Vol. 25; *Dictionary of Literary Biography*, Vols. 2, 5; and *Dictionary of Literary Biography Yearbook: 1981*.)

MARY GORDON

We punish Joyce Carol Oates for the crime of her productivity. A book a year, in some years two—we respond as if she did it just to make us look bad, the A student who hands in for a geography assignment not only a weather map of the Hawaiian Islands, but a papier-mâché model of a volcano as well. Our sense of her work as a mass ready at any moment to engulf us makes us reluctant to read, as they come toward us, the individual works and to differentiate among them. Partly, we assume that if there are that many none can be any good, as if literature were a finite resource like, say, a soup meant to serve 10 which had been cynically thinned to fill the bowls of 36.

This is, of course, nonsense. There is no formula for the correct amount of time it takes to write a good book. There are the Flauberts; there are also, the Trollopes, and the Ford Madox Fords. We are uncritically in love with the notion that the writer's vocation is like the sculptor's, forgetting that words, being immaterial, shift shape. Sometimes they are obdurate and sometimes biddable good children ready to fall into line. And if we as readers allow ourselves to see Joyce Carol Oates as an industry or a phenomenon rather than the serious writer she is, we do her and ourselves an injustice. It should not be forgotten that she has rendered better than anyone else the texture of the daily life of a particular kind of American: the lower-middle- or working-class woman whose limited possibilities can quickly move from simple frustration to nightmare.

For myself, I am glad to see Miss Oates back in K Mart territory, the territory of *them* and her powerful Detroit stories; I find *Marya* her strongest book in years. uglier, grittier, less literary than *Solstice* or the Gothic *Mysteries of Winterthurn* or *A Bloodsmoor Romance*, *Marya* is the story of the life of a deprived child mysteriously transformed not into a princess but a scholarship girl. The transformation is no less the stuff of fairy tale, the reward not the palace but the library, the tenured university seat, the place, God help us, at the international conference where the princess knows her worth because her face is recognizable from pictures on the dust jackets of her books.

The beginning of *Marya* is searing in its rendering of the treatment of young children by a drunken slattern of a mother, and the children's garbled understanding of their father's murder. We see before us the brutality of deficient parents who impose upon their children—usually, but not exclusively, their daughter—premature responsibility. . . .

Vera Sanjek Knauer, Marya's mother, is a terrible and wonderful creation. She is the kind of mother a child can never feel safe with. Any word spoken, any act performed can be a danger, can lead to punishment: you never know where you are.

Marya's mother insists upon bringing Marya with her to see the ruined body of Marya's father laid out on a metal table in the sheriff's office: "She goes with me . . . she's the same as me—she knows everything I know." Soon after this, Vera abandons Marya, age 8, and her two brothers, leaving them in the care of their reluctantly and only partially nurturing aunt and uncle. Marya must live in the same house as her cousin Lee, four years older, who regularly but inefficiently—he really doesn't know what goes where—assaults Marya sexually from the age of 8 onward in his father's junk car lot. Marya excels in high school and wins a scholarship to the State University of New York at Port Oriskany—the landscape of western New York state is rendered with a damning precision. I cannot think of reading anywhere before such an intensely and compassionately observed account of the lives of dirt-poor but intellectually passionate young women "uneasily preoccupied with studies, grades, parttime employment, finances of a minute and degrading nature . . . grimly energetic, easily distracted . . . susceptible to tears at odd unprovoked moments, to eating binges, to outbursts of temper . . . capable of keeping their doors closed for days on end and speaking to no one when they did appear." For these young women, learning is a miracle, a liberation and a gift. . . .

Marya's brilliant undergraduate career buys her a place in graduate school at a wealthy Ivy League university; there, her achievements earn her the attentions of a famous medievalist who takes her as his lover. She then gets a job at a small New England liberal arts college, which she puzzlingly gives up to become a political journalist specializing in reporting atrocities around the world, but particularly in Latin America.

When Marya's life materially improves, the novel grows weaker. This is because its strength emanates from the brilliance of Miss Oates's descriptions of objects and place. Her instinct for the telling physical detail is unerring: the hair caught in the zipper, the fake brick siding on the family house, the junk car lot, the overturned container of potato salad and the smashed watermelon at the lakeside picnic site, the befouled toilet and used sanitary napkin that the college janitor leaves behind to torment Marya—these exist for the reader with a solidity that shimmers and condemns. But when Marya prospers, Miss Oates grows abstract.

Her moving away from the strongly observed physical detail occurs, I believe, for two reasons. The first is that the objects of middle-class and academic life don't *tell* the way the objects of the working class do, and are therefore of less use to a writer. They are things, merely, and not portents. Marya's professor-lover's Hieronymous Bosch tells us less about him than the rubber band around Marya's aunt's ponytail tells us about her. Or perhaps it is that all readers of serious novels are, by the very fact of their reading, middle class. . . .

But the second reason for Miss Oates's shift of vision is more serious in its consequences for the novel. Marya's life is marked by the presence in it of three rescuing men, all of whom die while she is involved with them. The first is a cancer-ridden priest who engages the teen-age Marya as his amanuensis. The second is her graduate adviser, a German prone to odd visitations from demon figures whose death forces Marya to change her field to 19th century America. The third, who is killed on the thruway driving back from Albany, is the editor of a politically courageous little magazine under whose influence, one imagines, Marya gave up her tenured job. I am reminded of certain gangsters' molls known as "Kiss of Death Girls." It was never clear to anyone whether hooking up with these women caused the gangsters' deaths, or whether the women smelled closeness to death in their men and took it for an aphrodisiac. In all other contexts cynical, resentful, punitive and closed, Marya blossoms inexplicably in the presence of mentors, and Miss Oates's prose falters. (p. 7)

Women with Marya's history of being sexually abused do not fall happily into the arms of treasuring, appreciative lovers, and as if Miss Oates knows that, she races through the sections of the novel having to do with the men, unbalancing her structure. This is particularly true in the section that has to do with Marya's life as a journalist after her lover's death. We experience another lurch when Marya suddenly decides to find her mother. This decision is a wise one on Miss Oates's part, but she should have prepared her ground more carefully. The book's

ending, however, is a marvelous, elliptical return to her hometown, Innisfail, transformed now by shopping-mall chic. When Marya's aunt tells her the truth about her mother, they are in a local coffee shop eating croissants.

The final scene of *Marya,* suggestive, understated, returns it to the sure ground on which it began. Tantalizingly and rightly, we are left with the mere glimpse of a photograph of her mother, Vera, tucked in the letter she has just written to Marya. We see a woman who "wore a dark dress with white trim, her shoulders . . . sloping and her bust rather heavy, her head defiant, erect. The print was just perceptibly blurred as if whoever had taken the picture had moved the camera at precisely the wrong moment." We last see Marya trying to get a better look at her mother's unfocused face. And this is just right. For the real romance of the novel has nothing to do with men. It is the romance of the daughter abandoned by her witch mother, who leaves, whispering over her shoulder the worst curse of all: "She's the same as me." (p. 9)

Mary Gordon, "The Life and Hard Times of Cinderella," in The New York Times Book Review, *March 2, 1986, pp. 7, 9.*

DOROTHY ALLISON

Joyce Carol Oates has just published [*Marya: A Life*] her 17th novel, an event that can be roughly compared to the return of spring. We knew it was going to happen. We were even looking forward to it, but we hadn't expected it would come this soon or be this disappointing. (p. 56)

Marya is a less than satisfying psychological portrait of a successful author and teacher who dwells in that poverty-stricken landscape of violence and repression Oates evoked so well in her early novels. In fact, the first chapter of *Marya* reads like one of her more extraordinary short stories. Unfortunately, Marya's tragedy is encapsulated in the moment when her mother pulls her into the morgue to see her father's corpse; nothing that follows is as powerful.

"If you start crying, you'll never be able to stop," Marya is told, so she never starts. Not when her father is murdered, not when her mother abandons her, not when her adopted brother rapes her at age eight; not when she is beaten by boys from her high school for getting a scholarship to college; not when she is treated with contempt by her professor-lover; and not when the man she loves dies without getting around to leaving his wife for her. The final blow comes when she discovers that her mother is still alive and living the peaceable suburban life that will never be Marya's. Theoretically, this should be a wrenching event, but it is instead frustratingly obscure. Marya responds to this discovery the way she responds to everything else—she doesn't.

Marya is the quintessential third person, the perpetual observer, scrutinizing herself as well as everything around her. Seeing a young girl on a street corner, Marya wonders if it's someone she knows. Her heart pounds. We think something is going to happen, but Marya simply looks the other way, telling herself she knows no one in town. Eventually the reader becomes as impatient with Marya as everyone around her is. Though a gifted intellectual, emotionally the woman is unfathomable, so impassive she's brittle. We keep expecting her to shatter with all the violence and suffering she's suppressed, but she doesn't. She simply pushes it down further inside her. It makes for a detailed character study but very dry prose. Never mind: novel number 18 should be published sometime soon, and if we're lucky it will be back up to Oates's own high standards. . . . (pp. 56-7)

Dorothy Allison, "Tame Oates," in The Village Voice, *Vol. XXXI, No. 20, May 20, 1986, pp. 56-7.*

DEAN FLOWER

Joyce Carol Oates has been turning out a lot of costume fiction over the last five years: the family saga (*Bellefleur*), the allegorical romance *(Angel of Light),* and the gothic *(A Bloodsmoor Romance; Mysteries of Winterthurn).* She has long had a fatal facility for these ready-made forms, as the titles alone suggest. If only they were parodies! But her latest novel [*Marya: A Life*], happily enough, is genuinely novel: a portrait of the artist, or say rather of someone whose background and talents closely parallel Oates's own. Marya Knauer grows up poor and parentless in rural upstate New York, not far—metaphorically speaking—from where her creator began. Each of the novel's chapters forms a short story, a slice of Marya's life: the story of her father's violent death and the family's disintegration when she was seven; the story of her uncle's family, with her diffident "mother" Wilma (whom she is drawn to) and of her mindless cousin Lee (who abuses her sexually). Subsequent chapters focus on each particular person who defined Marya's life for a time: Emmet Schroeder, who wanted her to marry him after high school; Mr. Schwilk, her screwball English teacher who inspired her; Father Shearing, the dying priest whom she served and would have died for; Imogene Skillman, her college friend who uses and betrays her; Maximilian Fein, the arrogant professor who takes her as mistress and graduate student; and so on.

The strategy works well, providing the economy and concentration of the short story (which has always served Oates well as a constraint on her impulse toward lavish rhetoric) and also aptly expressing Marya's central problem: she is defined by others. There is nothing unnatural or surprising about this when Marya is young—what is childhood, after all, but a time when all the choices are made for you? But as she matures her passive, adaptive, chameleonic nature becomes clear: all her images of herself come from others or from books. She surrenders herself to them—usually they are confident, willful males—and subsumes her identity in theirs. The high school glamor boy whom every girl covets, the theologian-priest, the world-famous literary scholar, the idealistic intellectual who edits an important journal: all these succeed—for a time—in providing Marya with a self, "a life."

But she is too intelligent, and too willful herself, to be wholly taken in by others. Marya has the capacity to throw herself into work, especially reading and writing, with an escapist's suicidal zeal. In college she goes on late-night binges of imaginative writing—setting down stories "she seemed to be hearing in a kind of trance," full of "wild, disturbing, unanticipated" subjects that threatened to "push her over the brink—into despair, into madness, into sheer extinction." Here I think we have the paradoxical and prolific Joyce Carol Oates in essence: a writer struggling violently (if it is not too melodramatic to say so) to escape and create herself in words. Her narrative voices are indeed heard in a kind of trance, and it has never been certain what her own authentic voice was. Perhaps there were too many of them, or else as in *Bloodsmoor* and *Bellefleur* the voices were merely derivative. In any case, *Marya: A Life* constitutes the author's coming to grips with her

problem and so transcending it. The epigraph from William James gives a hint of this liberation: "My first act of freedom will be to believe in freedom." Her second act of freedom was to go back to her origins and find her own voice. At the end of the novel we see Marya looking at the blurred outlines of her long-lost mother: that won't solve her identity problems, but she is at last looking in the right direction. (pp. 309-10)

Dean Flower, "Fables of Identity," in The Hudson Review, *Vol. XXXIX, No. 2, Summer, 1986, pp. 309-21.*

JACK MATTHEWS

Sometimes fictional characters reveal with startling directness one of the secrets of the artist who made them. In Joyce Carol Oates's latest collection, *Raven's Wing,* such significations occur often. The story **"Harrow Street at Linden"** begins ominously with a college student named Katherine Stickney—aware that she has been married exactly 108 days—surprising her husband with his ear to the wall as he listens to the couple in the next apartment. She is perplexed, concerned, intrigued—what, exactly, is happening? Later, near the end of the story, she takes notes during a lecture: *"It is the improvised nature of human life that accounts for the prevalence of unhappiness."*

This "improvised nature" accounts for anxiety too, along with suspense and the hunger for self-knowledge—materials of which stories are made. Katherine's unhappiness is characteristic of most of the troubled and limited people in this collection. Her insecurity is the obverse of her fascination with the possibilities of life, a fascination shared and reflected by her husband. They become obsessed with the sounds made by the couple next door and from these fragments of evidence try to re-create some sense of what their neighbors must be. Why do they need to know? Why should they care? Because we are always mirrored by others—a truth that is celebrated throughout the stories in *Raven's Wing.*

The reflections are literal, as well. One story begins with a woman gazing into a three-way mirror; in another, a character's face is reflected in a knife blade; a woman teaching at a Jesuit college looks in a mirror to see what it is about her that a priest colleague hates; in still another, a man, half-drunk, sees his image in the mirror in a lavatory and thinks, "Who the hell's *that*, I don't want nothin' to do with *that*." But there are also those more mysterious projections: cats are treated as babies and, in ["**Raven's Wing**"], the horse Raven's Wing reflects all that is distant and mythic for a young couple, becoming an image of some Other Lover.

Characters are thus haunted by the treachery of appearances and the threat of desolation. . . . And yet, sealed off in themselves, they are so filled with sensation that they verge constantly upon dissociation and hysteria—they fail to recognize their own spouses when they come upon them unexpectedly in public; and women, especially, are prone to seizures of trembling, lightheadedness and actual fainting.

Similarly, these characters inhabit the perilous edge of the present—an effect that is uniquely communicated by Ms. Oates's style, in which the reader feels the relentless power of invention as the narrative moves forward. The "improvised nature of human life" is constantly at work in the accumulation of those details that make up realities. In **"Nairobi"** a young woman throws away the shoes she's wearing after buying a new pair, saying "the hell with them"—an act "she might regret afterward: but it was the right thing to say at that particular moment.''

''The right thing . . . at that particular moment'' is impulsive, intimate; and sometimes, according to a related artistic principle, Ms. Oates's narratives seem to yaw dangerously, blown by whim and notion. The stories are literally monotonous—even the first-person narrative voices sound alike—but they are never boring. And they are humorless, in spite of the rich variety of grotesque physical and psychological attributes that might be comic if the tone were less earnest.

But fashionable ironies are not part of Ms. Oates's testimony in this book. The conveyance of her fictional truths merges with those truths themselves, creating an effect of higher seriousness that seems to me unique in today's fiction. Many of the characters are of the uneducated working class; they are physically unattractive and psychologically flawed (references to pimples, greasy hair, sweat-stained clothes, filth and drunkenness abound); more important, they seethe with the pent-up wrath of those who are inarticulate and self-deluded. And yet, in spite of their human defects, they are created with an urgency that signifies that they *matter*; and because of this urgency, they matter to the reader as well.

> Jack Matthews, ''108 Days of Marriage, and Counting,'' in The New York Times Book Review, October 5, 1986, p. 9.

STEPHEN GOODWIN

A friend once charged up to me in a state of high excitement, brandishing a literary magazine which, he claimed, was a rare collector's item. Why? Because it did not contain a story by Joyce Carol Oates.

Like the many other jokes about her . . . , that one expressed envy and a certain grudging admiration for her prodigious energy. Now in mid-career, Oates is still going strong, and her talent is still protean. In *Raven's Wing,* her 13th collection of short fiction, she not only explores new territory but raids two traditionally male sanctuaries, the race track and the gym.

[''**Raven's Wing**''], about a small-time handicapper, crackles with rage. The man's huge anger is directed—where else?—mostly at the woman who is carrying his child, but the story turns on his visit to an injured race horse. For once in his life the man comes face-to-face with a force that awes him:

> The size, and the silky sheen of the coat, the jet-black coat, that skittish air, head bobbing, teeth bared, Billy could feel his warm breath, Billy sucked in the strong *smell* . . . Jesus did he look good, Jesus this was the real thing, wasn't it?—Billy's heart beat fast as if he'd been popping pills, he wished to hell Linda was here, yeah, the bitch should see *this*.

That same charged-up, visceral excitement is present in ''**Golden Gloves**,'' a story about a young boxer. Has a woman ever written a boxing story? Oates has. She gets inside the skin and muscle of the boxer, born with deformed feet, and conveys all the pride and glamour of sheer physical prowess. There is an odd, touching purity in this young man's pride, and the blow that ends his career is a blow the reader will literally feel.

A number of the 18 stories in *Raven's Wing* deal with characters in their late teens. It is an age that has always intrigued Oates; she gives to the confused passions of late adolescence an unusual respect and dignity. She seems drawn to the turmoil, which enables her to place her stories right on the edge of

violence. Perhaps her greatest gift—and it seems also to be the spark of her energy—is to catch a cresting emotion and ride it; she's not a tame writer, nor is she fussy. Sometimes, in fact, she seems downright careless. The end of ''**Golden Gloves**'' reads like an afterthought, as if she'd lost interest in the story, but why not? The explosive, volatile moment is what she wanted to get, and did. (p. 3)

> Stephen Goodwin, ''Short Stories: The Art of the Matter,'' in Book World—The Washington Post, November 30, 1986, pp. 3-4.

ANITA BROOKNER

In her now novel [*Marya: A Life*] Joyce Carol Oates has dealt herself a superficially attractive proposition: to tell the story of her heroine in disjunctive episodes until landing her, at some point in her late thirties, with evidence of her earliest beginnings. The attraction is superficial because the story is a bitter one, and one which leaves the reader with a feeling of dismay that accumulates with each successive chapter and reaches its apogee as the narrative breaks off, abruptly, on the last page. Just why this feeling should arise is quite puzzling. Certainly the story is a bleak one, but one which should be familiar by now through the comparatively recent outpouring of women's fiction, the sort of fiction that is disguised feminine autobiography: wrongs explained but not righted, bafflement deepening, anger growing through the sedulously impassive narrative voice. If women have suffered so greatly in the 20th century, one is almost bound to ask, how on earth did they manage in the 19th? The answer, unpalatable as it may seem, would appear to be that they are now attempting more than they have ever attempted before, becoming doctors, judges, engineers, often from beginnings which did nothing to prepare them for such freedom or such loneliness. 'My first act of freedom will be to believe in freedom' is the epigraph (from William James) that Joyce Carol Oates chooses to introduce her difficult story. But freedom, to those brought up in servitude of any kind is not so easily attained. (p. 26)

The growing unease which the reader may feel is not entirely attached to the powerful story which Joyce Carol Oates has to tell. It proceeds, rather, from something unresolved, not only in Marya's life, which could be called a success, but in the manner in which it is achieved, or overachieved. These lonely exaltations, unmatched by physical strength (as in the nightmarish episode of an ambitious bicycle ride) are not a sign of success or even of normal growing and aging. I am not sure how much of this Joyce Carol Oates intends. Something wilfully absent in the narrative indicates personal involvement of a high order. Marya is still a young woman as the story ends but my guess is that her future will be as a writer of fiction. (p. 27)

> Anita Brookner, ''An Uncomfortable Voice,'' in The Spectator, Vol. 258, No. 8270, January 10, 1987, pp. 26-7.

ANATOLE BROYARD

While many people will be surprised to learn that Joyce Carol Oates has written a book on boxing, there's no reason they should be. Women are no less familiar than men with desire, pride, anger, aggression, selfishness and greed. Nor are they strangers to deception and cruelty. Women too can appreciate the melancholy of the fact that when two persons are passionately joined together, one must win and the other lose.

Like boxing, Ms. Oates's stories are about people struggling with one another, trying to wrest temporary victories from the recalcitrance of love and fate. They are about the triumph and the failure of the will, and about disappointment, which waits for us all, like age and death.

The thing to watch out for in writing about boxing is sentimentality. Whitney Balliett said that jazz, the least sentimental kind of music, always seems to inspire sentimental writing—and the same is true of boxing. While Ms. Oates is too intelligent to be sentimental, she is romantic, which is one of the indulgences of the intelligence. To see something romantically is to assume that it deserves all its implications, its analogies, its symbolism, its metaphysics.

In spite of its romanticism, *On Boxing* is a very good book. And in fact it would hardly be worth writing about boxing in any other way, unless of course you were a newspaperman. Ms. Oates tells us that her father was a fan who took her to fights, and we have to try to imagine how this might have influenced her view of boxing and tinged it with nostalgia and other classical emotions. . . .

"All is style," according to Ms. Oates, but can the word "style" be applied to Rocky Marciano or Mike Tyson? The referee, she says, frees the boxer's conscience. "The boxing ring is an altar of sorts, one of those legendary spaces where the laws of a nation are suspended. . . ." This is an appealing formulation—yet it seems to me that a boxer is far from free. He can't hit below the belt, in the kidneys or on the back of the neck. He can't hold and hit, or butt. He's not even allowed to hit backhand. . . .

Ms. Oates is so interesting on boxing that I wish she had gone further, had not written such a shapely book, but allowed herself to speculate and free-associate ad libitum. While she's wonderful on the great fights, what escapes her—or at least what she has not written about—is the recent vulgarization of boxing, in which the boxer has been knocked not out of Time, but too much into our own time, has become too much a part of time's erosion. For example, the brutality of boxing today lies as much in the fighter's ego as in his fists. When boxers talk on television, there is no referee.

Though Ms. Oates does not comment on this, one of the remarkable things about boxing today is the *lack* of aggression in so many boxers. Manic in interviews, they're depressive in the ring. . . . All of the aggression seems to be in [a contestant's] corner as his handlers scream at him to do something. . . .

As Ms. Oates points out, boxers do not always try to injure one another: "subdue" is a more accurate word. And I hope she would agree with me that it's not an altogether unwelcome spectacle to see male aggression subdued. Boxing usefully reminds us of the conception of fairness, the fair fight between near equals. The motions of boxing used to be part of the choreography of a boy's life, but now, if no knives, guns or baseball bats are used, young American men import their aggressive tactics from Japan.

Ms. Oates takes the violence of boxing in her stride, for she knows as well as anyone that many of us do violence to other people—in love, in business, in friendship and in print, and that each of these is more painful than punches.

On Boxing is better than its subject. Ms. Oates is truer to the sport than most boxers are. She is game, as they say in the vernacular. If it is too coarse a verdict to call *On Boxing* a knockout, Ms. Oates has certainly scored a stunning TKO, or technical victory.

            Anatole Broyard, "The Romance of a Left Hook,"
            in The New York Times Book Review, *March 15,*
            1987, p. 8.

ALLEN BARRA

I'm sure she didn't set out to do it, but it's a measure of her success in *On Boxing* that Joyce Carol Oates has pissed off so many old fart sportswriters. My two favorite comments so far: "Just what we need: 'Oh let us now examine these quaint brutes'" and "How does she rate a book on boxing? Where did she pay her dues?" Translation of comment one: "This chick can *write*." Translation of comment two: "How many left hooks has her rib cage stopped?"

I looked up Joyce Carol Oates in the latest *Ring Record Book* and found out her credentials are as good as those of any writer currently doing a boxing beat—though, among novelists, she takes a backseat to Norman Mailer, who went three rounds with José Torres on *The Dick Cavett Show* in 1969. On paper, at least, Oates could probably hold Mailer to a draw; *On Boxing* is the best work on the subject since Mailer's 1971 essay about the first Ali-Frazier fight, *King of the Hill.*

Like Mailer, Oates is resented by the sportswriting establishment because she's a novelist, an *outsider*. And Mailer is probably the only other boxing writer who would agree with her conclusion that "boxing has become America's tragic theatre" (though modern boxing, dominated by head cases like Don King and Gerry Cooney, might have more in common with theater of the absurd). Mailer and Oates are hip, in a way beat writers almost never are, to how a fighter's fans impose pressures on him more severe than any he faces in the ring. . . .

Where Oates parts company with Mailer (and almost every other writer on boxing) is in not wanting to be Sugar Ray Robinson or Muhammad Ali; there isn't the slightest trace of jockstrap envy. . . . Being shut off from so much of the boxing world doesn't alienate her, it intrigues her: "Men fighting men to determine worh (i.e., masculinity) excludes women as completely as the female experience of childbirth excludes men. And is there, perhaps, some connection?"

Oates knows a truth about boxing that Martin Scorsese and many admirers of *Raging Bull* do not. In perhaps the book's best passage—and, I think, one of the shrewdest observtions on boxing ever made—she writes:

> There is an instinct in our species to fight but is there an instinct to *kill?* And would a "born" killer have the discipline, let alone the moral integrity, to subordinate himself to boxing's rigors in order to exercise it? Surely there are easier ways: we read about them in the daily newspaper.

This is light years from the jokey attitude of A. J. Liebling, who countered arguments of boxing's brutality with, "If a boxer, for example, ever went as batty as Nijinsky, all the wowsers in the world would be screaming 'Punch-drunk.' Well, who hit Nijinsky?" It's not surprising then, to find that Oates isn't a Liebling fan: "The problem for Liebling and for *The New Yorker* must have been how to sell a blood sport like boxing to a genteel, affluent readership. . . . It is a problem that, for all his verbal cleverness, Liebling never entirely solves.''

A lot of what Oates says about Liebling is true—at his worst, he could sound like a road-show Damon Runyon. What disturbs me about *On Boxing* is the way she exempts herself from the problem she attributes to Liebling. Does she think the crowd at O'Reilly's is going to read this book? Isn't Joyce Carol Oates about the last writer you'd expect to forget that all readerships are primarily genteel and affluent?

''I don't 'enjoy' boxing in the usual sense of the word,'' she says. What is the ''usual'' sense of the word when applied to boxing? Liebling's, I fear, and probably mine. Not that I can't identify with Oates's insight into the affinity between writers and fighters, which I think is her greatest contribution to boxing lit. She prizes ''the sport's systematic cultivation of pain in the interests of a project, a life-goal. . . . It is an act of consummate self-determination—the constant reestablishment of the parameters of one's being.''

        Allen Barra, "A Ring Cycle," in The Village Voice, *Vol. XXXII, No. 15, April 14, 1987, p. 56.*

JEFFREY BERNARD

[*On Boxing*] is an idle romance. It is a celebration of a violence as remote to her as is childbirth to me. I have seen a baby being born and I have been flattened in the ring and you will be delighted to hear that my reminiscences of childbirth are not going to be submitted to the Bloomsbury Press. Mind you, Miss Oates is a damn sight cleverer than I am but there is a world of difference between a punch on the nose as viewed from a ringside seat and one as received in the souped-up, hyped-up ring itself.

What draws Miss Oates to the fight business is that it is American National Theatre at its best. Nightly heroics and tragedies performed from coast to coast to an audience of thousands. But is it as theatrical to the protagonists as it is to the author? For most of the fighters I have known over the years it is about as untheatrical as was Noël Coward's advice to a young actor, 'Remember your lines and don't bump into the furniture.' It isn't all cake. There's a lot of bread and butter to be got through first and before you get to be a champion you have to finish up all your greens. (pp. 35-6)

And it was even less theatrical then when most fighters had daytime jobs—Cooper was a greengrocer who took time off to train. Jack Dempsey to Miss Oates was a John Barrymore and the greatest of them all, Ali, is now touring in a production of *Pagliacci*, poor sod. And it must be an exceedingly glamorous kind of relief to sit in an expensive ringside seat to watch a physical game of chess between two men 'who have to think standing up' after a long day at Princeton trying to explain Jane Austen to a load of numbskulls.

As a book on the psychology of boxing it is unnecessarily illustrated. Badly too. . . . But it has to be said—and the Bloomsbury Press are welcome to quote me out of context—that speaking as a sports freak it is a book I wouldn't do without. Not that I *need* it. . . . Miss Oates is what they call in racing 'a rider on the stand'. That is a spectator who thinks he knows better than a Lester P.

I also think that Miss Oates is a trifle confused about the so-called killer instinct. That fascinates her. I've never met any fighters who wanted to kill anyone; they just wanted to win because the idea of losing is frightening. People like Roberto Duran who fought like a psychopath are really not a lot more than dogs straining on the leash when they go walkies. You may as well berate a cobra for having a killer instinct as it tries to bite you. No, they are not killers, these great fighters, but perfect fear driveth out all love. There are moments when a boxer's back suddenly feels the hemp ropes and he knows in a moment that he is on the slide. That is the moment when 'killing' his opponent becomes his first priority. He doesn't need a psychological explanation or a prompt from Miss Oates. Another great psychologist, Jack Dempsey, put most of it into one nutshell, 'When you're fighting you're fighting for one thing: money.' And there is a black equivalent of that uttered by Larry Holmes. 'It's hard being black. You ever been black? I was black once—when I was poor.' (p. 36)

        Jeffrey Bernard, "A Rider on the Stand," in The Spectator, *Vol. 259, No. 8296, July 11, 1987, pp. 35-6.*

MICHIKO KAKUTANI

The title of Joyce Carol Oates's 18th novel, *You Must Remember This,* comes, of course, from the song ''As Time Goes By,'' but there are no love songs and little moonlight in this book; only lots of passion, jealousy and hate. Love, for the characters in this novel, is not about romance or redemption; rather it's a kind of obsession, a ''blood-heavy extinction of their minds,'' which undermines their already precarious hold on reality and draws them closer and closer to madness and death.

As in much of Ms. Oates's previous fiction, acts of emotional and physical violence proliferate throughout the text. Grandfather Stevick walks out on his wife and children to take up with a showgirl, then blows his brains out in a hospital bed. His illegitimate son, Felix, will think about running head on into an abutment on the expressway; his other son, Lyle, will contemplate hanging himself, and in the opening pages of the novel, Lyle's daughter Enid Maria will try to kill herself by taking an overdose of aspirin. In addition to these suicide attempts, there are several beatings, an abortion, an incestuous rape, a terrible boxing mishap and a couple of car accidents.

Though the sheer accumulation of these events has a certain numbing effect on the reader, there is nothing gratuitous or contrived about them. As expertly dramatized by Ms. Oates, they not only underline the characters' fears about the randomness of life, but they also project a fierce vision of America during the 1950's—an America still reeling from the revelations of the deathcamps of World War II, an America rocked by the Rosenberg case, the McCarthy hearings and new anxieties about the Bomb. In fact, as the novel progresses, the characters' private bewilderment becomes a mirror of a larger, public sense of dislocation; their sense of being overwhelmed a reflection of our inability to fully comprehend modern history.

In this respect, certainly, *You Must Remember This* recalls Ms. Oates's highly acclaimed novel *Them* (1969), in which the disorders in her characters' lives converge with the Detroit riots of 1967; and like that earlier novel, *Remember* is similarly grounded in a rich, Balzacklan matrix of social detail. Indeed with *Remember* and her last novel *Marya: A Life,* Ms. Oates seems to have returned to the storytelling impulses that animated her first books; and in the wake of her uneven experiments with genre fiction . . . , the result is a most felicitous one. Whereas such earlier novels as **With Shuddering Fall, Them** and **Wonderland** held the author's penchants for the naturalistic and the Gothic in an uneasy balance. **Remember** welds them together to create a portrait of family life in the 50's that is both recognizable and horrifying, mundane and disturbing.

While it cuts back and forth in time to show us three generations of the Stevick family, **You Must Remember This** is principally concerned with the youngest daughter, Enid Maria. Enid is a strange, watchful child, at once the model student and obedient daughter—and a cynical, sexually precocious brat. Perched on the brink of adolescence, she is initiated into the confusions and cruelties of the adult world by her uncle Felix, a former boxer, who's taken his brash arrogance from the ring and turned it on the world at large. Felix seduces Enid when she is 14, and as she grows increasingly obsessed with him, it becomes apparent that she is another one of those Oatesian victims whose passivity acts as a magnet for destruction. Though Felix is cold, manipulative and cruel, Enid is totally dependent on him and soon cannot conceive of life without him. . . .

Writing in powerful, meticulous prose, Ms. Oates conjures up for the reader the physical passion shared by Felix and Enid with the same brutalizing immediacy that she lavishes on the scenes of Felix boxing in the ring. We are made to see the dark, chaotic currents of guilt, anger and eroticism that run beneath the seemingly placid surface of the Stevicks' lower-middle-class existence, and in doing so, we are also given a glimpse of the enormous gap between appearance and reality that exists in their lives: both the bourgeois hypocrisy that colors their acts . . . , and their futile efforts to reconcile their dreams of safety and their intimations of disaster.

Enid, whom we've seen engaged in the simple rites of girlhood (having her ears pierced, putting Noxema on a sunburn, copying hairdos out of Screen World), will trade her youthful fantasies of romance for an ugly abortion and a weary cynicism. Her father will realize that all his efforts to protect his family, from dispensing advice to building a bomb shelter in the backyard, can't prevent his loved ones from drifting away. Unable to cope with what has happened to them, these characters adopt the policy that "the wisest procedure is simply to forget"—something that the reader, mesmerized by Ms. Oates's masterly storytelling, cannot easily do.

> *Michiko Kakutani, in a review of "You Must Remember This," in* The New York Times, *August 10, 1987, p. C20.*

PUBLISHERS WEEKLY

Sparely told, in contrast to Oates's usual prolix style, this intriguing tale of psychological suspense [*Lives of the Twins,* written under the pseudonym of Rosamond Smith] holds the reader in a tight vise. Having been a dabbler and a dilettante (and something of a liar) all her life, Molly Marks is surprised to find heady love when she drifts into the office of therapist Jonathan McElwain. Instead of answers, he offers Molly a safe, though stolid, berth to anchor her quicksilver personality. But Jonathan has a secret—an identical twin he refuses to speak about—and the less he says, the more Molly is consumed by curiosity. She tracks down James McElwain, also a therapist, but finds herself in deep water when his abusive, feral attraction becomes a magnet for her, and she tumbles into position as a pawn in the brothers' lifelong war for domination. This brief story of obsession gradually builds in emotional and erotic tension as Molly's by now helpless fascination strips away a

thin patina of civilization to expose her own need to be brutally dominated and abused. . . . Oates is exploring here the undercurrents of animal savagery that lie just beneath the surface of some psychopathic personalities. Though a shade too glib to stand up to scrutiny, this horror story will undoubtedly be a talked about book. (pp. 51-2)

> *A review of "Lives of the Twins," in* Publishers Weekly, *Vol. 232, No. 18, October 30, 1987, pp. 51-2.*

ROBERT PHILLIPS

Twenty pages from the end of her magisterial new novel [*You Must Remember This*], Joyce Carol Oates summarizes the book's central theme, through a letter written by Warren Stevick, a pacifist, to his sister, Enid Maria, its heroine: "Strange isn't it—how 'love' seems to carry with it no knowledge. The people I have loved most in my lifetime (including you) I haven't known at all. Nor have they known me. . . ." Familial love, romantic love and lust provide the plotlines for this novel, together with subplots about love of power, love of music and love of boxing. The latter is a subject about which Oates knows a great deal, as was demonstrated in her recent nonfiction study, **On Boxing,** and is further displayed here.

It should be said at the outset that [*You Must Remember This*] is Oates's most blatantly sexual book. Some of the scenes would make John Updike appear a prude, and the number of couplings—in cars, showers, hotels, motels and occasionally at home in bed (and once, in a bombshelter!)—is astonishing. She catalogues these acts in more detail than is to be found anywhere else in her work. I hope this is not the reason for the popular success the novel is having, because sex here is not in the least gratuitous. It is central to the book's theme. To have been less graphic would be to have been less honest. In the act of sex her characters literally lose themselves. And only when they are away from family and lovers, where people do not know them or have not known them for very long, do they find themselves. The novel, in one sense, is a toccata and fugue on the mysterious and unfathomable nature of sexual desire. . . . The novel's concluding scene is an act of love between an aging and overweight married couple who have not coupled in nearly 18 years. It is a moving tableau. (p. 360)

Oates unfolds the chronicle of the Stevick family against a backdrop of the late 1940's and 1950's. The McCarthy hearings, the Rosenberg trial, Jack Benny, Adlai Stevenson, the Korean "conflict," Ted Mack's Original Amateur Hour, Marilyn Monroe—all here, adding authenticity and scope to what ultimately becomes an epic.

You Must Remember This is filled with set pieces—long passages that could and should be studied and admired for the writing alone. These include the description of two minutes into the eighth round of a disastrous prizefight of Felix ("The Cat") with an opponent named Corvino. The sounds, the sights, the smells, the pains, even the tastes of the event are all here. It is as if Oates herself had taken the blows and fallen insensible. Other remarkable sequences describe Enid's abortion, her brother Warren's war experiences and their father's intellectual despair. . . .

The two lovers, 15-year-old Enid Maria and her older uncle, prizefighter Felix, are complex characters who give in to their incestuous desire with disastrous results for both. In this sense, the novel is a very old-fashioned moral tale—not unlike Dreiser's *An American Tragedy*, which it superficially resembles with its class distinctions, its naturalism, its unwanted unborn love-child who must be contended with and accounted for. Because of Enid Maria's extreme youth and Felix's relationship with her family, plus the depictions of American motel life, the book even more superficially resembles Nabokov's *Lolita*, though Oates displays none of Nabokov's puckish humor here. A more logical comparison would be to more erotic works of D. H. Lawrence.

But ultimately, this work is no one's but Joyce Carol Oates's. It is the book she has been moving toward, novel after novel, if readers would notice. Her most recent novels—*Solstice* and *Marya: A Life*—seem more personal, more psychologically penetrating, than her earlier, more violent novels. . . . Now Oates applies her penetration and technique to produce her best novel. Critics complain that she writes too much, and committees have not showered her with prizes; a National Book Award for *them* back in 1970 is the only major recognition she has received. For its sweeping depiction of American life and thought, this book deserves the Pulitzer Prize. (pp. 360, 362)

> *Robert Phillips, in a review of "You Must Remember This," in* America, *Vol. 157, No. 14, November 14, 1987, pp. 360, 362.*

JOHN UPDIKE

Joyce Carol Oates, born in 1938, was perhaps born a hundred years too late; she needs a lustier audience, a race of Victorian word-eaters, to be worthy of her astounding productivity, her tireless gift of self-enthrallment. Not since Faulkner has an American writer seemed so mesmerized by a field of imaginary material, and so headstrong in the cultivation of that field. She has, I fear, rather overwhelmed the puny, parsimonious critical establishment of this country; after the first wave of stories and novels (most notably, *A Garden of Earthly Delights* and *them*) crashed in and swept away a debris of praise and prizes, protective seawalls were built, and a sullen reaction set in. Many of the critics began to treat Miss Oates as one of her many scholar heroines, Marya Knauer, is treated by her eighth-grade instructor Mr. Schwilk:

> Finally, Schwilk said airily, "You have a most *feverish* imagination," and handed the story back; and that was that.
>
> (p. 119)

Miss Oates has continued to devote her energy to literature in almost all its forms. Her short stories seem to be everywhere, from fledgling quarterlies to annual "best" anthologies. Her one-act plays have been produced Off Broadway. Her poems are being readied for a collected edition. Her criticism is generous and wide-ranging. With her husband, Raymond Smith, she edits the elegant *Ontario Review* and its line of books. Single-mindedness and efficiency rather than haste underlie her prolificacy; if the phrase "woman of letters" existed, she would be, foremost in this country, entitled to it.

As a reader and critic, I have been as overwhelmed as the next, and cannot offer to lay out for dissection the hydra-headed monster of Miss Oates' œuvre. But I can, and do, report that her latest novel, *You Must Remember This*, rallies all her strengths and is exceedingly fine—a storm of experience whose reality we cannot doubt, a fusion of fact and feeling, vision and circumstance which holds together, and holds us to it, through our terror and dismay. While some of her fiction appears to be built almost entirely out of projected anxieties, this book

has a sentimental substance; its title (from, of course, the lyrics of "As Time Goes By," of *Casablanca* fame) might be addressed by the author to herself. It is a historical novel of sorts, centered on the mid-fifties, with traces of research in its passing references to Adlai Stevenson, Senator McCarthy, the Korean War, the Rosenberg execution, bomb shelters, the popular songs and prizefights and automobiles of the time. Some of the glimpsed headlines seem a touch opportune, and some of the historical themes (such as that of bomb shelters) feel rubbed into the plot with a bit too much determination, but the background events of the period are by and large feelingly translated into subjective experience, by an author who was there. (pp. 119-20)

The stale little Stevick household—father and mother and three daughters, Geraldine and Lizzie and Enid Maria, and one son, Warren—is the core of *You Must Remember This,* and its central action is the affair between Enid Maria and her half uncle, Felix, a former prizefighter who is sixteen years older than she. The setting is one that has figured in Miss Oates' fiction from the start—a tough small upstate [New York] city, here called Port Oriskany and situated, like her native Lockport, on a canal. Her authority within this city, her ability to move through its schools and streets and stores and bars, evoking a gritty social grid on which individual lives and dreams and passions bloom and quickly wilt, is grimly absolute. (p. 120)

Miss Oates knows her protoplasm. She sees our dark softness churn like flame. The novel begins with one of her ominous prologues, all in italics . . . a string of one-sentence paragraphs describing fifteen-year-old Enid Maria Stevick happily attempting suicide by ingesting forty-seven aspirin tablets. In these days of not uncommon but still shocking teen-age suicide, this fictional example, dated June 7, 1953, enlightens us; we are admitted to the seethe of passion, delusion, and calculation that rages behind the façade of a bright middle-class girl, and are shown how thin the membrane is between her erotic and her self-destructive compulsions. When she masturbates, it is felt as a flirtation with death. . . . She flirts, too, on the trampoline at school, bouncing "high and higher still, risking her neck," so that the gym teacher rebukes her; and in the swimming pool, "a place where Death was possible," diving and swimming underwater to exhaustion, so that afterward "nothing could startle or hurt, for hours;" and by shoplifting downtown; and by losing herself in contemplation of her room's intricately patterned wallpaper, "feeling her soul slip thinly from her into the wallpaper where there was no harm, never any danger;" and by being drawn to the steep-sided canal that flows through Port Oriskany, and the narrow footbridge that crosses below the railroad trestle. . . .

Her affair with her uncle, too, is a flirtation with nothingness, beginning with a clumsy assault in a deserted Adirondacks hotel. . . . She accepts the obliteration, writing him, "*Anything you do to me—it's what I want.*" Her attempted suicide, insofar as it is a romantic stratagem, demonstrates to him her toughness and places them on a plane of equality as death-defiers, as familiars of violence. (p. 121)

Violence is not just the projection of inward tumult and fear; it *exists*—"there it *was*." Joyce Carol Oates, both the writer and the person, is drawn to boxing as a curiously intimate, visible, regulated, caged yet living specimen of the nightmare that surrounds our fragile shelters and delusively peaceful lives. Like Hemingway and Mailer, she suggests that violence is uniquely authentic. But Mailer's writing on boxing is sports journalism compared with the fight descriptions in *You Must Remember This*—especially the terrific pages that show the destruction of young Jo-Jo Pearl by an older fighter, Byron McCord.... We learn that a boxer goes for the other's eyes, with the thumbs and laces of his gloves; we learn that a hazard of ringside seats is having your camel-hair coat spattered with blood; we experience a young boxer's child-like daze as he sinks toward death of "subarachnoid hemorrhaging." As far as this reader is concerned, the sport could be outlawed on the strength of this single horrendous, yet briskly factual, fight scene.

Sex, too, in Miss Oates's telling, is a nightmare come true.... Unblinkingly the processes are detailed whereby an adolescent girl is loosened up by red wine and vodka and enjoyed in a succession of motels, and initiated into the full range of sensual possibility, and so habituated to lying that she comes to like it, and kidnapped from her high-school lunch hour by her jealous older lover in his cream-colored Cadillac Eldorado, and impregnated in their erotic fury, and then subjected to an abortion. The abortion is as harrowing, and as calmly detailed, as Jo-Jo's fight. All earthly experience, it comes to seem, except for Enid's homework and her piano lessons, is founded on some basic desecration. Not only chemical smells haunt Port Oriskany but Roman Catholicism, a creed shunned by most of the characters yet present in whiffs, as when Enid thinks, "Whatever happened she deserved. She knew she deserved it because it happened." This echoes a saying of Nietzsche's that appears in Miss Oates' *Marya,* a recent book of linked short stories that presents, as it were, the academic, intellectually achieving aspect of Enid:"Marya noted a chilling aphorism of Nietzsche's. *Terrible experiences give one cause to speculate whether the one who experiences them may not be something terrible.*" Victim and criminal, death and love, dream and reality can fuse when subjectivity, instead of being regarded as a mere epiphenomenon within objective reality, is granted a power of its own. Miss Oates, her earlier jacket flaps told us, majored in English at Syracuse University and minored in philosophy; quotes from Heraclitus, Spinoza, William James, and others offer to orient us in her seething fiction. Something Neoplatonic, of Berkeley's *esse est percipi,* licenses her visionary outpouring. Her fictional worlds exist to be consumed by her characters' passions and perceptions; the universe has no meaning beyond its uses by the feverish human spirit, and does not receive, therefore, the kind of artistic homage that imitates its enduring structure. Her plots suggest not architecture but cloud formation, beginning and ending in air; there is rarely a sentence that arrests a moment for its own cherishable sake, in a crystallization of language. All is flowing, shifting context. Her worlds refuse to enclose, to be pleasant. Prayers arise from them, but no praise.

You Must Remember This, away from its consummate portraits of two violent wills, is relatively thin, but solid enough to frame those portraits. Lyle Stevick's tatty secondhand-furniture store and his jumbled timorous mind convince us; his obsession with a back-yard bomb shelter seems somewhat allegorical. His three daughters neatly enact, as in a fairy tale, three possibilities open to girls in the fifties: Geraldine marries into a local life of chronic pregnancy and domestic drudgery; Lizzie becomes a singer, an entertainer, and possibly a hooker in New York City; and Enid goes off to college. Their brother, Warren, a Korean vet and early antinuclear protester, is complex and almost interesting enough to deserve a novel of his own. In this novel, Miss Oates does a daring amount of male stream of consciousness; she lets us know how men feel battering at each other in a prize ring, lusting after hat-check girls, watching each other financially sink or swim, speeding along in their fancy cars, and struggling against their wandering thoughts to maintain an erection during lovemaking. A very full model of Port Oriskany (O, any risk!) is clairvoyantly, affectionately constructed, so we can watch it burn. (pp. 122-23)

John Updike, "What You Deserve Is What You Get," in The New Yorker, *Vol. LXIII, No. 45, December 28, 1987, pp. 119-23.*

GREG JOHNSON

In the 1980s Oates remains a major force in contemporary American writing. Aside from her fiction and her teaching, she is a prolific poet, critic, and book reviewer; several of her plays have been produced in New York; and she is an extremely popular, engaging speaker on college campuses across the country. She also serves as coeditor of *The Ontario Review,* a literary magazine which she and her husband inaugurated in 1974 in Windsor, and continue to operate from their home in Princeton. Her achievement is all the more extraordinary when one considers that she is still in her forties and may now be viewed as entering the middle stage of her illustrious career.

Joyce Carol Oates's versatility as a fiction writer relates directly to her overwhelming fascination with the phenomenon of contemporary America: its colliding social and economic forces, its philosophical contradictions, its wayward, often violent energies. Taken as a whole, Oates's fiction portrays America as a seething, vibrant "wonderland" in which individual lives are frequently subject to disorder, dislocation, and extreme psychological turmoil. Her protagonists range from inner-city dwellers and migrant workers to intellectuals and affluent suburbanites; but all her characters, regardless of background, suffer intensely the conflicts and contradictions at the heart of our culture—a suffering Oates conveys with both scrupulous accuracy and great compassion.

Her particular genius is her ability to convey psychological states with unerring fidelity, and to relate the intense private experiences of her characters to the larger realities of American life. "I think I have a vulnerability to a vibrating field of other people's experiences," she told an interviewer in 1972. "I lived through the '60s in the United States, I was aware of hatreds and powerful feelings all around me." Her frequently remarked tendency to focus upon psychological terror and imbalance thus relates directly to her vision of America, what Alfred Kazin has called "her sweetly brutal sense of what American experience is really like" [see *CLC,* Vol. 2]. Though she has been accused of using gratuitous or obsessive violence in her work, Oates has insisted that her violent materials accurately mirror the psychological and social convulsions of our time. In an acerbic essay titled **"Why Is Your Writing So Violent?,"** she points out that "serious writers, as distinct from entertainers or propagandists, take for their natural subjects the complexity of the world, its evils as well as its goods.... The serious writer, after all, bears witness."

In responding to the "vibrating field of other people's experiences," Oates's imagination has created hundreds and possibly thousands of fictional characters: people coping with the phantasmagoric wonderland of American life and suffering various degrees of psychological and spiritual isolation. Her typical protagonist is tragically blinded to the possibility of the "communal consciousness" that Oates sees as a likely salvation for our culture.... Positing the hopeful idea that the violent conflicts in American culture represent not an "apocalyptic close" but a "transformation of being," Oates suggests that we are experiencing "a simple evolution into a higher humanism, perhaps a kind of intelligent pantheism, in which all substance in the universe (including the substance fortunate enough to perceive it) is there by equal right."

Because this epoch of cultural transcendence has not yet arrived, Oates has conceived her primary role as an artist who must dramatize the nightmarish conditions of the present, with all its anxiety, paranoia, dislocation, and explosive conflict. Her fiction has often focused particularly on the moment when a combined psychological and cultural malaise erupts into violence; and despite the notable variety of her character portrayals, there are several representative "types" that recur frequently and present distinctive facets of the turbulent American experience.

There are the confused adolescents, for instance, like Connie in **"Where Are You Going, Where Have You Been?"** and Jules in *them,* essentially innocent, romantic souls whose fantasies and ideals collide with the environment and with the imperatives of their own maturity. There are the young women seeking fulfillment in adulterous love, like the heroines of **"Unmailed, Unwritten Letters"** and **"The Lady with the Pet Dog,"** and like Elena of *Do With Me What You Will,* all of whom seek redemption outside marriages originally based upon the expectations of others. There are the tough, earthy women like Clara in *A Garden of Earthly Delights,* Loretta in *them,* and Arlene in *Childwold,* each rising from an impoverished childhood, developing considerable resilience and cunning, and dealing shrewdly with a male-dominated society. There are the brilliant but emotionally needy intellectuals like Hugh in *The Assassins* (1975), Kasch in *Childwold,* Brigit in *Unholy Loves* (1979), and Marya in *Marya: A Life,* whose lives dramatize Oates's ironic view of a culture that values "masculine" intellect at the expense of "feminine" intuitive knowledge and that inhibits, on the individual level, a healthy integration of reason and emotion. There are the middle-aged men who control society, like the businessman Curt Revere in *A Garden of Earthly Delights,* the megalomaniac Dr. Pedersen in *Wonderland,* and the lawyer Marvin Howe in *Do With Me What You Will.* And there are the doomed, literally "mad" characters, like Allen Weinstein in **"In the Region of Ice,"** Richard Everett in *Expensive People,* and T. W. Monk in *Wonderland,* young people whose inner conflicts drive them to the point of madness or suicide.

This bare-bones summary of the most frequently recurring character types in Oates's fiction scarcely does justice to the subtlety of individual characterization she lavishes on each, but it does suggest Oates's major fictional concerns and the distinct ways in which her work focuses upon the intense conflict between the individual and his social environment. While some aspects of her work—especially the increasingly hopeful resolutions of her more recent novels—may hint at "transcendence," she remains notable as an industrious chronicler of America's personal and collective nightmares.

Understanding the violent and frequently ironic terms of the American experience, Oates has employed a notable variety of aesthetic approaches in her attempt to convey such an immense, kaleidoscopic, and frequently grotesque reality. In a much-quoted remark Philip Roth has said that "the American writer in the middle of the 20th century has his hands full in trying to describe, and then to make credible, much of the American reality. It stupefies, it sickens, it infuriates, and finally it is even a kind of embarrassment to one's own meager imagination. The actuality is continually outdoing our talents."

Yet Joyce Carol Oates has met this challenge with increasingly bold and resourceful experiments in fiction, sharing not the postmodernist concerns of John Barth or William Gass solely with language and its aesthetic possibilities, but rather the Victorian faith of Dickens or George Eliot in the efficacy of the novel in dealing with profound social and philosophical themes. Oates has thus adhered throughout her career to the novel of ideas and to the mode of psychological realism, while at the same time producing highly experimental works of fiction that both complement her more traditional work and allow her to present the daunting American reality in terms of myth, antirealism, and other forms of literary intrigue. As John Barth noted in a seminal essay dealing with the traditional versus the experimental in fiction, "Joyce Carol Oates writes all over the aesthetical map." (pp. 7-13)

Some of Oates's best-known short stories published during this same period showed similar concerns, dealing with such "representative" characters as the adolescent girl from an affluent home who has a compulsion to shoplift and eventually serves as the sardonic narrator for **"How I Contemplated the World from the Detroit House of Correction and Began My Life Over Again"**; the reserved Catholic nun of **"In the Region of Ice,"** suffering a crisis of faith and conscience in her dealings with an unstable Jewish student; the well-to-do businessman in **"Stray Children,"** drawn unwillingly into a relationship with a dependent, drug-saturated girl who claims to be his daughter; and the married woman conducting a doomed love affair in **"The Lady with the Pet Dog,"** Oates's "re-imagining" of the famous Chekhov story. These stories along with dozens of others published in *The Wheel of Love, Marriages and Infidelities* and other collections have in common both a riveting psychological intensity and an authoritative, all-inclusive vision of "what American experience is really like" for people who suffer various kinds of emotional turmoil and who, like the title characters in *them,* become emblematic of America as a whole.

Oates's attempts to dramatize this turmoil, and often to convey psychological states at the very border of sanity, have often led her into the fictional mode loosely described as "gothicism." Her work combines such traditionally gothic elements as extreme personal isolation, violent physical and psychological conflict, settings and symbolic action used to convey painfully heightened psychological states, and a prose style of passionate, often melodramatic intensity. The combination of rural settings and psychological malaise in her earlier fiction, for instance, prompted some reviewers to align Oates with the gothic tradition of Southern literature, suggesting that she had been influenced by William Faulkner, Flannery O'Connor, and Carson McCullers. Certainly her bewildered, inarticulate characters, fighting their losing battles against a backdrop of brooding fatalism, do bear a spiritual kinship to the Southern isolates of Faulkner and McCullers in particular. Oates has often stated her admiration for Southern fiction, but the dynamic, hallucinatory power of her best work recalls not only Southern gothicism but also the psychological explorations of Dostoevsky, the nightmare visions of Franz Kafka, and even the fantastic world of Lewis Carroll. . . . (pp. 15-17)

To describe much of Oates's fiction as gothic in nature is not to resort to a convenient label or to suggest any limitations of theme or subject matter. The tenor of Oates's prose, however—her distinctive "voice"—often conveys the kind of extreme psychological intensity, and occasionally the outright horror, traditionally associated with gothic fiction. As Oates commented in 1980, "gothic with a small-letter 'g'" suggests "a work in which extremes of emotion are unleashed''—a description which could be applied to virtually all her novels. Whether rich or poor, cultured or uneducated, the majority of her characters live within a psychological pressure-cooker, responding to intense personal and societal conflicts which lead almost inevitably to violence. The critic G. F. Waller has discussed at length this ''obsessive vision'' at the heart of Oates's rendering of the American reality [see *CLC,* Vol. 19]. As Oates herself has observed, ''Gothicism, whatever it is, is not a literary tradition so much as a fairly realistic assessment of modern life.''

Oates has also used the gothic tradition explicitly in short stories dealing with the paranormal, collected in *Night-Side* (1979), and in her cycle of genre novels begun in 1980, novels appropriately described by Oates as Gothic ''with a capital-letter G.'' In *Bellefleur* (1980), *A Bloodsmoor Romance* (1982) and *Mysteries of Winterthurn* (1984), Oates combines her usual psychological realism with a free-wheeling, explicit use of fantasy, fairy tales, horror stories, and other Gothic elements; the central settings of all three novels, for instance, include a huge, forbidding mansion and such assorted horrors as a female vampire (*Bellefleur*) and a painting which comes to life and murders a couple on their honeymoon (*Mysteries of Winterthurn*). . . . [Of *Bellefleur,* Oates said] ''I set out originally to create an elaborate, baroque, barbarous metaphor for the unfathomable mysteries of the human imagination, but soon became involved in very literal events.''

Her handling of these ''literal events'' shows a characteristic inclusiveness in her desire to present a sweeping social and philosophical vision of American history. Oates has described her specific attraction to the Gothic mode in these novels:

> To 'see' the world in terms of heredity and family destiny and the vicissitudes of Time (for all five novels are secretly fables of the American family); to explore historically authentic crimes against women, children, and the poor; to create, and to identify with, heroes and heroines whose existence would be problematic in the clinical, unkind, and one might almost say, fluorescent-lit atmosphere of present-day fiction—these factors proved irresistible.

(pp. 17-20)

It should be clear that despite the sheer abundance and inclusiveness of Oates's fiction, her work does not represent an aesthetic surrender to the chaos of ''real life'' or the failure of a driven, highly productive artist to organize her materials; yet such well-known critics as Alfred Kazin and Walter Sullivan, accustomed to the more typical modern writer who might manage a single book every five or even ten years, leveled exactly these charges against her work in the 1970s and helped create the impression of Oates as a careless, haphazard writer, working in a trancelike state and continually pouring forth novels and stories without adequate concern for their literary integrity or coherence. (pp. 20-1)

Critics in the 1980s occasionally repeat these charges, but one suspects that they cannot have read Oates's work very extensively or thoughtfully. As the late John Gardner remarked in an appreciative review of *Bellefleur,* ''for pseudo-intellectuals there are always too many books'' [see *CLC,* Vol 19], and over the years Oates has patiently responded to the charges of excessive productivity. (pp. 21-2)

Late twentieth-century criticism, nourished on modernist and postmodernist works, has frequently devalued or simply lost sight of the artist as a committed, energetic craftsman, pro-

ducing the kinds of ambitious, socially relevant novels that had virtually defined the genre in the Victorian era. Such esteemed nineteenth-century writers as Dickens, Balzac, Trollope and Henry James all wrote steadily, daily, and produced many volumes, unharassed by critical suggestions that they slow down or stop altogether. The modernist conception of the creative process as infinitely slow and tortuous, resulting in a single exquisite work after long years of painstaking labor, combined with the particularly American view of the writer as a hero of experience, like Ernest Hemingway or F. Scott Fitzgerald, someone who must travel the world, live as colorfully as possible, and preferably drink to excess, has perhaps influenced critical attacks on Oates, who not only writes voluminously but leads a quiet, disciplined life that she once called ''a study in conventionality.'' And much of the criticism clearly stems, as Oates herself has noted, from simple envy.

Any reader making his way through such a skillfully paced family chronicle as *them,* or the complicated series of interlocking tales that comprise *Bellefleur,* or an intricately constructed political novel like *Angel of Light* (1981), can have little doubt that Oates is an extremely careful and deliberate craftsman. . . . Occasionally her patience in the face of critical attacks has worn thin. In 1979 she emphasized her dedication to craftsmanship, reacting angrily to one critic's speculation that she wrote in a trancelike state, ''a fever of possession'': ''I revise extensively. I am passionate about the craftsmanship of writing. I am perfectly conscious when I write, and at other selected times. . . . Will I never escape such literary-journalism drivel? Year after year, the same old cliches.''

Oates will probably never escape the ''drivel'' of those critics who prefer attacking her to considering thoughtfully her voluminous, carefully written works. What matters to Oates is the work itself, not its critical reception or her own notoriety. Despite her occasional remarks hinting at exhaustion, her passionate engagement with her craft continues. . . . Despite the occasional criticism, her reputation continues to grow not only in the United States but worldwide: she is a member of the American Academy and Institute of Arts and Letters, and has been nominated several times for the Nobel Prize for literature. Although it is pointless to speculate about which of her works future generations will consider her masterpiece—quite possibly, she has not yet written the book that will be viewed as representing the full range of her talents—it is clear that Joyce Carol Oates has already earned her place alongside the major American writers of the twentieth century. (pp. 22-5)

Greg Johnson, in his Understanding Joyce Carol Oates, *University of South Carolina Press, 1987, 224 p.*

SUSAN FROMBERG SCHAEFFER

''Nothing will happen to you that isn't an expression of your own deepest desire. I promise.'' This is both the promise and the threat of *Lives of the Twins*. It explains the odd sequence of events forming the novel and points to the riddle at its center: what exactly *are* the deepest desires of human beings? Are they ever known? In Rosamond Smith's novel, human beings, no matter how aware, mistake their deepest desires or fail to know them, wear their personalities like masks, unaware of what lies beneath, and act out roles they believe suit them (Antigone, Ophelia, Hedda Gabler) until, often tragically, the role becomes the reality. What they cannot do is confront their deepest desires, the face beneath the mask. *Lives of the Twins* is a masterly exploration of what happens when the mask drops, when the real desire manifests itself, when the person stops playing roles and, standing on the knife's edge, acts on his own impulses. It is a truly rare book.

Reading Rosamond Smith (she is Joyce Carol Oates, writing under a pseudonym, as has been previously reported) reminded me of reading Vladimir Nabokov. Precisely because the actual plot so little reflects the novel's real concerns (as in the best of Nabokov), preoccupation with events or surface leads nowhere. The real concerns of *Lives of the Twins* lie beneath the plot. "Human beings," says one of the characters, "impose a more or less arbitrary narrative framework upon their more or less formless lives in order to tell their lives to themselves and others, presenting their actions in the best possible light— usually as heroes but sometimes, surprisingly, as victims. 'Innocent' victims." According to this theory, "Truth is not irrelevant, but it isn't an issue." Life is like a dream. Whether events in the dream are or aren't real is irrelevant. The dreamer's interpretation is everything.

Seen as a dreamscape, *Lives of the Twins* becomes completely satisfying, even logical. As a realistic novel, portraying a young modern woman seeking a lover and a man to father the children she wants to have before 30, it is likely to appear contrived, even preposterous. Molly Marks, from whose point of view we see the world, meets and falls in love with a psychotherapist, Jonathan McEwan, who stops seeing her as a client and becomes her lover. Their idyllic love affair is disrupted by Jonathan's revelation that he has an identical twin, also a psychotherapist, by whom he has been injured and from whom he is estranged. For reasons that she does not understand, Molly makes an appointment with James McEwan, her lover's twin, beginning both therapy and an affair with him also. At the same time, she becomes obsessed by the twins' secret—what is the injury Jonathan believes James to have done him?—and ruthlessly, thoughtlessly, she proceeds to solve the mystery. . . .

Lives of the Twins abounds in doubles—is, in fact, obsessed by them—and in paradox. What one needs and wants most is also what is most poisonous and hateful. As a child, Molly had a fantasy twin who later metamorphosed into a ghost vision of her mother who stood by sadly, watching her. As an adult, she owns a tortoise-shell cat whose double she finds in James

McEwan's apartment. The cat is, in himself, twins, because, as Ms. Smith tells us, all tortoise-shell cats begin in the womb as identical twins; the dominant twin then absorbs the chromosomes of the weaker twin, becoming two cats in one. Jonathan McEwan keeps turtles as pets, so much the same they cannot be told apart. Molly Marks overhears a woman in a restaurant discussing a tumor found in another woman's body, all that remains of *her* identical (and previously unsuspected) twin. Molly tries unsuccessfully to make a twin of herself when, taking the pseudonym Holly Hawkes, she goes to see James McEwan. There are "twin" gifts, twin lunches, twin deceptions, even a baby "fathered" by twins.

Twins are first seen as enormously seductive, enviable in every way. They "duplicate" themselves in the world, and consequently feel more secure, less fragile—but their very doubleness becomes the source of their torment. The McEwan twins are like the very rich, constantly asking if they are loved for themselves, or only because they are twins and hence curiosities, objects fascinating to others. Are they loved because one has been mistaken for the other? If people around them believe they are incomplete halves of a whole, can they ever be loved for themselves? Can they distinguish themselves from each other any more than other people can distinguish between them?

And how important is the face in this quest for personal significance or salvation? Is it the sign of achieved uniqueness? Or is it most frequently worn as a mask, covering what lies beneath?. . .

Lives of the Twins is a marvelous metaphysical novel; the fact that Joyce Carol Oates published it under the pseudonym Rosamond Smith, a feminization of *Raymond Smith*, her husband's name, inevitably extends the resonances of this novel about identity (or the illusion of identity), freedom (or the illusion of freedom), outward into everyone's blood-real daily life. The use of a pseudonym oddly clarifies the novel's concerns—the pressing need both for a double (or soul-mate) and for a unique viewing, a new look at a face we think we already know.

Susan Fromberg Schaeffer, "The Lover Had a Brother," in The New York Times Book Review, *January 3, 1988, p. 5.*

James (Amos) Purdy

1923-

American novelist, short story writer, dramatist, and poet.

In his fiction, Purdy presents a bleak vision of human nature through a blend of realism, fantasy, and black humor. Central to Purdy's pessimistic view is his belief that contemporary materialistic values are destructive to the individual and have contributed to the disintegration of familial relationships. In Purdy's novels and stories, this breakdown of communication results in the inability to love. All of his characters are emotionally crippled and removed from mainstream society, prompting many critics to compare Purdy's writings to those of such authors as Carson McCullers, Flannery O'Connor, and Tennessee Williams. Miranda Seymour remarked: "All that emerges clearly and consistently from Purdy's works is a despairing sense of a grotesque world in which our beliefs and expectations are distorted and horribly magnified, and in which happiness becomes the most dangerous of illusions."

Purdy's early short fiction collections establish his focus on the exploitation of children by adults and the inability of families to give and receive love. Such volumes as the novella *63: Dream Palace* (1956), *Don't Call Me By My Right Name and Other Stories* (1956), and *Children Is All* (1962) often feature adolescent males searching for love who are victimized by physically or emotionally absent fathers and narcissistic or sadistic mothers. The troubled, loveless marriages that abound in Purdy's stories produce alienated, spiritually empty children who are unable to discover their individual identities.

Purdy's first novel, *Malcolm* (1959), is a grotesquely humorous subversion of the picaresque genre that continues the thematic focus of his short fiction. While searching for the father who abandoned him, fifteen-year-old Malcolm is manipulated by the people from whom he expects help. Unlike most traditional heroes, he learns nothing about human nature, and ultimately he is coerced into a self-destructive marriage. In *The Nephew* (1960), the title character's aunt tries to decipher her nephew's life by writing a memorial for him when informed that he is missing in action in Korea. The woman discovers, however, that she knows virtually nothing about her relative. *The Nephew* illustrates the failure of art to reveal the significance of human experience, a theme that also pervades Purdy's next novel, *Cabot Wright Begins* (1964), which depicts the difficulties of producing a biography about a businessman who rapes to relieve his boredom. This book indicts the American literary establishment and modern culture as being corrupted by the ethics of commerce and advertising. *Eustace Chisholm and the Works* (1967), set during the Depression, revolves around the tragic consequences that result among homosexual characters who cannot acknowledge their love.

Jeremy's Version (1970) and *The House of the Solitary Maggot* (1974) are the first two volumes in a planned series of interconnected novels entitled *Sleepers in Moon-Crowned Valleys*. Based on anecdotes that Purdy heard from his relatives, these works examine the repressiveness of family life in deteriorating rural communities and represent his most comprehensive use of the memoirist narrative. *I Am Elijah Thrush* (1972) focuses on the effects of extreme love among millionaire Millicent de

Frayne, artist Elijah Thrush, and his mute great-grandson, called the Bird of Heaven. *In a Shallow Grave* (1976), which is regarded by some critics as Purdy's most affirmative novel, concerns a disfigured soldier who is nursed back to physical and spiritual health by two men. *Narrow Rooms* (1978) is a study of a group of men whose lives have been ruined by their thwarted passions for each other. Paul Bresnick observed: "*Narrow Rooms* is the most thorough, honest, *human* treatment of homosexual love by a writer of serious fiction in America."

Purdy's works of the 1980s explore many of his characteristic themes. In *Mourners Below* (1981), teenaged Duane Bledsoe is haunted by the ghosts of his two half-brothers, who were killed in an unidentified war. Sensing that he is fulfilling the wishes of his late half-brother Justin, Duane endures violent sexual rites of passage and eventually fathers a child with Justin's ex-lover. Julia M. Klein noted: "*Mourners Below* recapitulates many of Purdy's concerns—with small-town families in crisis, the explosiveness of contained emotion, the marriage between the dead and the living. Purdy sees to the heart of relations between the sexes, mourning the dreadful chasm between them." *On Glory's Course* (1984) underscores problems that ensue from emotional and sexual repression. In this novel, a search by a millionaire's mistress for the illegitimate son that was taken from her at birth provides the impetus for a narrative reminiscent of the works of Sherwood Anderson and Edgar Lee Masters. *In the Hollow of His Hand* (1986) portrays the dilemma of a young half-breed whose biological father, an enigmatic Indian, and legal father, a reputable white man, vie for his love and attention. Lee Smith called *In the Hollow of His Hand* a "grimly antic antipicaresque" that typifies Purdy's work "in its vision of a violent, meaningless world in which only bizarre, obsessive love is possible." *The Candles of Your Eyes and Thirteen Other Stories* (1987) collects Purdy's short fiction spanning a twenty-year period. Purdy has also written several volumes of poetry, including *The Running Sun* (1971) and *The Brooklyn Branding Parlors* (1985), and such plays as *Cracks* (1963) and *Proud Flesh* (1981).

(See also *CLC*, Vols. 2, 4, 10, 28; *Comtemporary Authors*, Vols. 33-36, rev. ed.; *Contemporary Authors New Revision Series*, Vol. 19; *Contemporary Authors Autobiography Series*, Vol. 1; and *Dictionary of Literary Biography*, Vol. 2.)

WARREN FRENCH

Both [*Jeremy's Version* and *The House of the Solitary Maggot*] are in the form of memoir-confessions of the "waste land" school, authorized by T. S. Eliot's epigraph to "The Love Song of J. Alfred Prufrock," drawn from Dante's *Inferno* and promising the revelation of terrible secrets only on the supposition that they will never be published to the world.

One might well wish to conceal the history of family irresponsibility unraveled in *Jeremy's Version*, although any diligent enough researcher could have found most of it in the public record, since it all came out in the divorce proceedings that climax the novel. Fergus Wilders descends from a family that was involved in the Battle of Culloden at which the British defeated the Scots highlanders in 1746, an event that has been the source of much mischief in American letters. Fergus had insisted on marrying Elvira Summerlad over his family's objections. Then after swindling his wife's family out of all its money, he decamps, leaving her to bring up three sons by running a boarding house and rendering other services to her customers. About a decade later, broke after his get-rich-quick schemes have failed, he returns at the time of the Depression to the decaying county seat of Boutflour to appropriate and then gamble away the small inheritance that would have freed his eldest son to escape to New York and become an actor.

After trembling on the brink of decision for years, Elvira is now determined to divorce Fergus; but she is opposed by his madly imperious sister, who has become as intent on keeping them married as she once was on preventing their marrying. Finally, when the sons appeal to the judge in Elvira's behalf, the decree is granted; but during a celebratory picnic, the second son (who has recorded most of this sordid history in his private notebook) tries to kill her. The reasons behind this erratic behavior are brought out in a speech that the eldest son, Rick, with the kind of flagrant disregard for courtroom procedures that usually characterizes Purdy's creations, addresses to his father during the trial—an extraordinary oration that sums up what most of Purdy's betrayed children feel about their parents and guardians. It reaches its climax with these sentiments:

> "For if you are my father, Wilders, and I'm not some bastard got by a traveler who spent the night under our unprotected roof, why did you leave and desert me in the first place to the complete power and endless claims of Elvira Summerlad, allowing her to do with me anything her wishes dictated. If you can answer that, Wilders, the court can adjourn, and the case can come to rest . . . Give me, in other words, Wilders, the reason for my existence, since you were never here before to teach it to me, and I had only Elvira to crush out manhood with her lessons!" (ellipsis in text)

Even *Jeremy's Version,* however, provides no preparation for what is to come in *The House of the Solitary Maggot,* in which three handsome and talented sons are destroyed because of their parents' inability to control their passionately selfish drives and accept responsibility for their offspring. "In our family," the eldest son explains, "we always do the wrong thing." The father's remark to the mother late in the book, "You are making a terrible mistake of judgment here" might appropriately appear on almost every page of the chronicle, addressed to any one of the principals. (pp. 85-6)

Purdy is principally concerned to employ his relentless imaginative power to decry the failure of the *clan* to rally to the aid of its inheritors—a point that William Faulkner stresses also when he traces the history of a family's degeneration in *The Sound and the Fury* to the Battle of Culloden . . . , which marked the destruction of the power of the Scottish clans in their native highlands and the transfer of their traditions—especially of the blood feud—to our Southern mountains and Ohio River Valley.

It may be unfortunate here to have to evoke the word *clansman,* since it has fallen into disrepute in this country ever since, early in this century, the notorious Reverend Thomas Dixon used it as the title of the racist novel that provided the basis for D. W. Griffith's epic film, *The Birth of a Nation* (1915). If, however, we can extricate the term from Dixon's particular racist context, we perceive that the impetus of the *clan* mentality has always been to protect one's blood relations from the encroachments of all outsiders. . . . Inevitably such an obsession with family leads to bigotry, because it places private obligation above any public good. But Purdy's obsessive concern with the failure of clan commitment is motivated, I believe, less by any sense of the superiority of a particular group than by his conviction that if there is no family solidarity, there can be no larger community (a point made again, though from an entirely new viewpoint, in the recent novel *Mourners Below*). If we cannot count on our kin, what can we expect from the impersonal state?

This conflict of loyalties and expectations goes as far back in our literature as the prehistoric crisis dramatized in Sophocles' *Antigone.* The work of what now seems distinguishable as James Purdy's first period (1956-1974) endures as a tragic reminder that after millenia, the question of the individual's primary loyalty to clan or larger community remains one of the most troublesome confronting us; and certainly nothing that has happened in our time gives us confidence that the dilemma can be resolved by making the individual a creature of the state. We can accept society only ambivalently, weighing our gains against our losses in any submission to it; yet Purdy's narratives also suggest that clan solidarity is threatened basically not by pressures from larger systems so much as by lack of individual self-discipline. Civilization can flourish only if individuals can effect a compromise. (pp. 87-8)

Although Purdy's tone is often cynical, bitter, hysterical, it remains the same kind of affirmation of a life force that we find in Dylan Thomas's "Do Not Go Gentle into That Good Night"—"Rage, rage, against the dying of the light," another oracle of a Celtic clansman. Eneas Rex Harmond in *The House of the Solitary Maggot,* withdrawing behind his "Do not disturb" plaque, is no more a spokesman for Purdy than is Mrs. Curt Bickle [in *Cabot Wright Begins*].

Yet so overpowering are Purdy's portrayals of self-destructive forces that, before a change in direction suggested by the novel *Mourners Below* that appeared only as I was revising this essay, it would have been difficult to discern a murmuring stream of affirmation running beneath the chorus of shrill denunciations if we could not have obtained a perspective on the polemical works of this writer by viewing them in juxtaposition with the calmer meditations of stoic observer like Will Moses, whose work flows steadily between the wildly oscillating wave of Purdy's despair and hope. (pp. 90-1)

I must cite Will Moses a final time on a matter where the differences that I have been urging between the sensibilities that inform his work and James Purdy's do converge in assessing the cause of much of mankind's grief. In a poem more ostentatiously titled than most of his, "American History," Moses comments on the pioneers' conquest of the wilderness, but observes at last, "It is hidden that they were the easy enemy." "An older, harder war is still at its start," he concludes.

The physical conquest of "the blue-grey devils of nature" was ultimately "the easy diversion" in comparison with the struggle to follow. While he is not specific about "those other devils," clearly he feels that the taming of the wilderness by isolated men is easier than people's learning to live communally in peace. His Manichean use of the term "devils" to describe the tough opposition suggests a battle with no end. Wearied of this, we might prefer to remain fixed under a cedar tree while ghosts smile in waiting rooms.

Even agreed about the source of human problems, however, these writers part company in their reactions. Purdy rancorously insists that stasis is the death that has overtaken the characters from his earliest writings like *63: Dream Palace* to *Narrow Rooms.* Even though the passionate dead litter the field, the Battle of Culloden continues. (In *Mourners Below,* however, Purdy envisions the emergence of a restored sense of family responsibility out of our disastrous national involvement in Viet Nam.)

What we may be able to learn from the joint contemplation of these two writers as we end our projections in the dark with two images of peaceful resignation achieved by the very different means of submission to the wilderness, on one hand, and, on the other, the struggle even to death to sustain the clan is not what choice we should make, but that there are choices, however difficult, and that the function of *creative* writing is not to make the choices for us, but to show us that alternatives exist. (p. 91)

Warren French, "James Purdy, Will Moses: Against the Wilderness," in Kansas Quarterly, *Vol. 14, No. 2, Spring, 1982, pp. 81-92.*

DONALD PEASE

Perhaps more than any other recent American novelist, James Purdy highlights in his work the difficult problem of narrative beginnings. Through the seemingly exhaustive interplay of enveloped and enveloping contexts held together by the compelling concerns of developing plot lines, novelists have traditionally finessed the problem of what remains unnarrated. Having begun with a narrative plot organized around the rhythmic alternation of exposure and concealment, deception and recognition, most novelists simply render moot the question of whether another story line, finally unassimilable to the one told, is possible. But since James Purdy characteristically begins his novels with a character who cannot be drawn into the narrated plot on its own terms, his novels expose an arbitrary, seemingly contingent quality in the world of his fiction; or, to use a distinction introduced by Edward Said, Purdy's narrative beginnings appear intransitive rather than transitive.

As Said explains, a transitive beginning authorizes a continuous narrative line. Given such a beginning, Said compares "the house of fiction" with a dynastic line fathered by a concerned patriarch. "It is the institution of a humanized abode, populated with beings and maintained by an authority that conserves itself." In contrast to the author as legitimate patriarch, James Purdy peoples his novels with orphans, abandoned children, foundlings and outcasts, who share a common inability to be salvaged by the world that pre-exists them. And instead of founding their own world, these "starters" only emphasize the distance between themselves and a world that cannot "adopt" them. In wavering between some unnarrated, mute past and the present world of the novel, these characters introduce an irreconcilable gap between these worlds. Through persistent anticipation of beginnings they fail to initiate, Purdy's characters at once call into question a world that will not permit them an authentic beginning and recall a silent world that haunts the narrated one with intimations of an irreversible priority. Consequently, in Purdy's novels the metaphor of a house of fiction must be stripped of all genealogical pretensions until only an abandoned frame, cluttered with the signs and traces of departure and decay, remains as the haunting central image.

Purdy's "starters" do not fail because of overriding ambition to be initiated into the world. If anything, their desires are simple, even typical enough to be immediately gratified by even the most commonplace of worlds. (pp. 335-36)

When [Purdy's] haunted characters turn to writing, it is not surprising that they produce the literary equivalent of a haunted house. Not only Alma's memoirs [in *The Nephew*], but those of Matt Lacey (*Jeremy's Version*), Parkhearst Cratty (*63: Dream Palace*), Zoe Bickle (*Cabot Wright Begins*), Madame Girard, Millicent de Frayne (*I Am Elijah Thrush*), Lady Nora Bythewaite (*The House of the Solitary Maggot*), and Eustace Chisholm are allegories, which, as Walter Benjamin has observed, "are in the realm of thoughts what ruins are in the realm of things." Allegories presuppose the deaths of persons described, for in this genre persons possess all the lost significance of stuffed owls, exotic plants, and trinkets; but, whereas these "memorabilia" decorate the spacious interiors of Purdy's haunted houses, characters once allegorized decorate the spacious interiors of haunted memoirs.

Emptied of the possibility for any meaning but that projected onto him, an allegorical character really exists only as the allegorist's compulsive wish to reconcile projection with character. Unlike the symbol, which utterly unites subject and significance, an allegory presupposes their separation; and this separation only exposes allegory as a form of *wishful thinking*, a longing to join together what must always be recognized as a breach in the order of things. A modern allegorist, in any case, must always be aware at least peripherally of the morbidity of his task. Possessed as he is of a disembodied intention, whether it be a moral, a psychologism, or just an insight, he can only invest a corpse with this intelligence, for only a vessel completely devoid of its own significance will admit the "truth" of the allegorist. But even when the operation is complete, it is difficult to determine whether the allegorical significance is really a psychological justification for the allegorist's compulsive need to deny the death he always must presuppose.

Of course, allegories were not always such wounded symbols. In the Middle Ages, allegories possessed ontological sanction as the revelation of eternal truths—not dead letters but invitations to participate in the illumination of the same spirit which had gone into the act of creation. Allegories then provided a progressive journey into the mind of the Eternal Father, a journey bound to reveal to the allegorist his place in the family of man.

But Purdy sets his novels in a world in which such divine sanction, along with the paternal principle in general, has obviously disappeared and the allegorical intention has been reduced to a wish not to deny the separation of object from spirit but to perfect it. As in the case of Aunt Alma's memoir, the allegorist first loses sight of the supposed subject and then memorializes this loss. Ironically, however, these allegorical memoirs assume enough priority over the persons commemorated to appropriate some of their powers. Most eerily, in this world devoid of any generative principle, the memoirs rather than the persons become procreative. Just as social roles and grand gestures replaced human actions in *Malcolm*, so memoirs replace human reproduction in *The Nephew*, and not merely in the sense that persons exist in order to be turned into memoirs. In Purdy's novels, characters cannot generate children but only memoirs, but memoirs can produce more and more memoirs in the form of different versions and revisions of the same subject.

Instead of producing a continuous line of descent from a father or mother, Purdy's memoirists reflect on their sense of disconnection from all the characters who surround them until only this sense of estrangement remains alive enough to record or be recorded. And in a world in which everyone has already been converted into a memory vague enough to need to be recorded (in order, we might add, to be forgotten), authority itself is only another vague illusion. But while Purdy's characters possess only the illusion of authority, none of them is reluctant to assert the authority of this illusion in a world in which—as is implicit in Madame Girard's authoritative assertion, "Texture is all, substance nothing"—keeping up appearances is the only reality.

In a world wherein the father principle has been converted into the illusion of an authority figure who can hold sway only by imposing the authority of his illusion, sado-masochism turns out to be the inevitable if not the natural expression of human relationships. In practically all of Purdy's novels, the actual father has either been killed, divorced, abandoned, exiled, or otherwise lost, while in his absence the other characters play his part. Uncannily, they play this part not in order to usurp the father's authority but to expose this authority as an illusion—the illusion necessary before one character can impose his will upon another. In the novel *Eustace Chisholm and the Works*, we can clearly see the activity of paternal substitution at work in almost all of Amos Radcliffe's activities. His decision to go to bed with his mother after he has stabbed his estranged father is oedipal enough in the traditional sense to require only its citation, but his later sexual episode with his homosexual patron, Reuben Masterson, is complex enough to

require elucidation. Whereas in his incestuous relationship with his mother, Amos was an actual son playing the role of his father, in his affair with Reuben, Amos plays the role of a son with a man who plays the role of his father. Thus in both sexual episodes the roleplaying of the father remains constant. But since this roleplaying denies the actual presence of the father, the role of the father begins to accrue power through the force of this denial. In the figure of Captain Stadger, it is the force of the *denied father* who assumes human shape and wreaks furious revenge on Daniel Haws, the figure of the son who has denied him.

If Captain Stadger seems sadistic, he only refines the role that Daniel, in his office as father figure, earlier played with Amos, Eustace with Carla, and, in other novels, Alma with Boyd, Girard Girard with Madame Girard. Only after Beaufort Vance aborts Maureen O'Dell's unborn child, however, can we begin to see how sado-masochism also refines Purdy's allegorical emblem of the abandoned house. This act of destruction directed against the generative principle immediately transforms Maureen O'Dell's body, formerly the "humanized abode" for another living being, into the equivalent of a haunted house.

Maureen's abortion also clarifies a rather obvious point. In a world without fathers it would also follow that there would be no actual mothers, but only memories of mothers, as it were, at one remove—grandmothers, half-sisters, great-aunts, great ladies, and patrons. In Purdy's novels, patrons complicate sado-masochism and then apply this complex to the arts. Here patrons are neither father figures nor mother figures, but characters who are in actuality mother figures yet play the roles of the father. These patrons do not wish to see or hear anything artistic, but only their own memoirs, dictated to memoirists who do not understand what they are commanded to write. Such patrons never grow old for like Millicent de Frayne they never actually enter life but instead live on the memory of the "impossibility" of a past event:

> Millicent de Frayne had not actually grown any older since 1913 because in that year having fallen in love with Elijah Thrush . . . each day succeeding their backstage meeting she had done nothing but think of the impossibility of their love.

Yet at least Millicent lives on the memory of the impossible love of a man who still lives. Such other great ladies as Grainger in *63: Dream Palace*, living as they do on the memory of their dead husbands, search for young men like Fenton Riddleway, dress them up in their deceased husband's clothes, and then engage to marry them. But these ladies do not actually consummate the marriage ceremony, but rather only await the news of their newly discovered fiancé's death so that through these substitutes they can relive the deaths of their first husbands.

Although Millicent never actually marries her "dream lover," Elijah Thrush, her memoirs of their relationship, recorded by the paid memoirist, Albert Peggs, do effectively transform this young man into the equivalent of their child, so that at the end of the novel, after, that is, Millicent has ceremonially castrated the authentic Elijah, Peggs announces, much as would an orphan who has discovered his real father, "I am Elijah Thrush."

The accuracy of even this pronouncement gets eerily qualified by a revelation Elijah made to Albert earlier in the novel, "The thing that now really afflicts me . . . is simply this: do I require her everlasting obsession with me, and the cruelty toward me for the sake of feeling I exist. . . . Am I, do you attend me, am I, Albert, really her?"

We may want to bring a curtain down on the narrated action in Purdy's novels by considering Albert's assertion in the light of Elijah's question. If Albert asserts his identity to be the same as that of Elijah, who in turn fears he may have lost his identity to a woman who lives only in the memory of his unrequited love, neither Millicent nor Elijah nor Albert (nor for that matter any of Purdy's "initiated" characters) possesses any existence apart from the haunting memory of an estranged relationship. The feeling of estrangement inhabits all of these characters, converting them into haunting replicas if not of each other then of that image of the abandoned house we have isolated at the heart of Purdy's imagination.

But this description provokes a question that has perhaps been shadowing this discussion from the outset. If the father figure has been abrogated from this quite literally *de*-generating world, where does James Purdy as author, the putative father figure of this world, come to abide in his fiction? Like Albert Peggs, who at one point complains, "More than anything else . . . it was the language spoken which was more becoming mine that made me go out of my head," has he been absorbed into the world he transcribes? If not, how does Purdy's language differ from his characters? Has Purdy inadvertently condemned himself to the fate of the satirist or parodist whose existence has been reduced to the impersonation of the characters he caricatures? Put succinctly, is there a fundamental difference between the unreal dreams of his solitary characters and the vision of James Purdy?

To answer these questions we need to return to the problem which served as the point of departure for this entire discussion; that is, the status of the "beginners" in Purdy's fiction—Malcolm, Jethro, Fergus, Cabot Wright, Claire Riddleway, Eustace Chisholm, and Owen—who never do finally "begin," but remain marginal figures whose detachment places them both in and out of the world that surrounds and absorbs the other characters.

Though these characters never are exactly disillusioned (for them to be so would imply their movement *through* and out of the world of the fiction), their ever-renewed beginning relationship to this world constitutes the disillusioning force pervading Purdy's fiction. If these novels describe the separation of man from his generative role, himself, and his intentions, these beginners constitute the very essence of these repeated separations. As ciphers, rather than developed characters, they are the generative force envisioned as a pure anteriority, a pure origin which discloses the strength of its negation by its failure to be narrated.

Unlike a satirist, who must finally invoke pre-existent ethical systems as the justification for the venom in his satire, Purdy finds all morals and all customs caught up in the same deluded ceremony of authority at play among the social circles within his fictions. So to extract a humanistic virtue as a coda for Purdy's work would only return it to the status of an authoritative gesture which is, at least in Purdy's fiction, a mere illusion of authority. A more fruitful, though admittedly more stark direction to take would be to see how Purdy's beginners disclose the presence of a selfhood so radically innocent of all "social" character that is has more in common with the "anonymity of a pure negation," than with any recognizable character from fiction. Indeed, these characters are closer to the process of disillusionment every character in a traditional fiction undergoes when he recognizes the distinction between his own expectations and what the world will offer. But Purdy's beginners are disillusioned with the world before they begin:

they have no expectations because there is nothing this world can offer them capable of disturbing the powerful negation in their being.

It is their detachment from the world that enables them to return the rigidly delineated social world back to the status of indistinguishable sounds of silence and colors of darkness, "So that it came to me that everything that had ever happened from the beginning of the world was going on now and at the same time, and there were no dead and no living but all were together in steady, if often flickering band of light." Since these characters emanate from a place of radical priority, their "intransitive beginnings" threaten the existence of the other characters who, as we have seen, exist in and for memories. These beginners exist prior to memory, and what exists before memory can, as it does in this reflection of Joe Bickle's in *Cabot Wright Begins*, obliterate a character's life by revealing it to be a memory in origin:

> First we are here she said to herself, being this sort of person and then so little later we have lost all track of that time and who we were then until some trifle brings us back to that period for a brief lightning-illumined second, then back again to the now.

But it is not merely these "beginners" who achieve this marginal status. Purdy, or at least the narrative voice he adopts, speaks from the point of view of one of these beginners, which is to say, from the point of view of a character so detached from the surrounding world that he can mouth its language while remaining utterly free of any commitment to it. This is not a rebellious point of view for that would commit Purdy to this world enough to want to overthrow it. And his is clearly not, as we have seen, a satirical point of view. Purdy's perspective is much more akin to that of an allegorist, but a disillusioned allegorist aware of the hollowness at the core of every idea he would project into the corpse he himself has, as we have seen, willed into existence.

Unlike the traditional allegorist who would deny the death that haunts his labors by projecting an insight profound enough to shroud the presence of the corpse, Purdy affirms the universal presence of death and takes possession of it in characterizing scenes and language revealing nothing else. Purdy's writing always works at the level of the cliché, the language of the corpse. The cliché is an expression which has always already been said, yet because it has already been said it eludes meaning. It is not spoken so much as it is mouthed and it is not heard so much as it is forgotten before it reaches one's ears. As such it is the hollow voice of silence itself. No real person speaks in clichés; a person speaking in clichés is a non-person impersonating a person. Purdy's language invariably listens for the moment when words are about to turn into clichés; then he coaxes them in their turn to resound the hollow rumblings of what remains unsaid, yet speaks through every other expression, as if this were what they were all struggling to recall into Being, the voice of a pure origin—a voice calling out from a home so utterly original that it makes all the world of personified clichés seem utterly homeless in comparison. (pp. 342-48)

> Donald Pease, *"False Starts and Wounded Allegories in the Abandoned House of Fiction of James Purdy," in* Twentieth Century Literature, *Vol. 28, No. 3, Fall, 1982, pp. 335-49.*

ROBERT J. SEIDMAN

[*On Glory's Course*] is ostensibly about the 1930's. In it, Mr. Purdy dramatizes at length the long past "fall" of Adele Bevington, the beautiful, aristocratic 50-year-old damned *belle dame* of Fonthill, a tiny Midwestern town of suffocating insularity. Roughly 30 years earlier Adele had been persuaded by both her lover, the wealthy George Etheredge, and her father to give up her illegitimate son. Since then, it seems, Adele has spent most waking hours staring out of the windows of her hilltop mansion, hoping to catch a glimpse of her own flesh and blood coming out of the local movie theater. She hasn't seen the boy since infancy, yet somehow she believes he is alive and well and still in town.

In recompense for her suffering, her lover literally covered Adele in diamonds, which, years after his death, she breaks out on memorable (usually erotic) occasions. Adele is still beautiful and, like the other significant middle-aged woman in the novel, miraculously "free of lines." . . .

Adele Bevington's alter ego and rival, the Mrs. Goody Two-shoes of Fonthill, is the beautiful, also unlined Elaine Cottrell, "widowed mother of two strong-willed boys, Ned and Alec, aged 15 and nearly 20 respectively." Elaine mounts a doomed, tedious campaign to keep her sons roped to her heavily floured apron strings; to Elaine, beef stews, dumplings and glazed carrots are the chains that bind.

The two women's self-sacrifice is opposed to the unfeeling youthful male struggle to grow up and leave home. In Adele's son's case, of course, unfeeling is accompanied by unknowing. This well-documented conflict is not exactly a breaking story, though it could have worked novelistically if Purdy had invented more compelling characters. To be sure, there are some affecting moments in the war between these representative mothers and sons. Adele, the embattled town rebel, has courage and wit, even stature, although the thought of a three-decade-old sin arousing such concern, even in this Depression-era Peyton Place, strains credulity.

Mr. Purdy does mount a few hilariously comic scenes, as when the dotty Widow Hughes, parodying Leporello's list of Don Giovanni's conquests, gives us Judge Hitchmough's amorous biography. . . . But these moments are all too sparsely scattered. For the first 150 pages I was afraid that the novel would be limited to Alex's rage at his younger brother Ned for having "outstripped him sexually." . . .

In attempting to catch the verbal rhythms of the 30's, Mr. Purdy has employed an idiom so ponderous that, with the single exception of the rough-hewn Val Dougherty, all of his characters have trouble speaking their lines. It's hard to believe that anybody, even during Prohibition, called brandy "the illicit distillation of the grape" and liquor "a corrosive draft." The generation buffeted by World War I and the seemingly unending deprivations of the Great Depression wanted language to supply what their experience denied—something solid, permanent, normal. The failure of the novel's style makes *On Glory's Course* seem long-winded and self-conscious. Mr. Purdy has written—and probably will write—better novels.

Robert J. Seidman, "War between Mothers and Sons," in The New York Times Book Review, *February 26, 1984, p. 25.*

T. O. TREADWELL

Contempt for American cultural values is a persistent theme in Purdy's fiction, while a sense of himself as an outsider and a defiant acceptance of his position as an unpopular writer seems to have freed him from any fear of the experimental or difficult. *Mourners Below* . . . continues his quest for unusual ways of rendering his vision of American life.

The terrible emptiness and sterility of this life is, as always, his theme. *Mourners Below* is set during the Second World War in an anonymous locality in the Middle West which the narrator refers to only as "our town", suggesting (besides a swipe at Thornton Wilder folksiness) an identification of the place with American society in general. The central character is Duane Bledsoe, the adolescent son of Eugene Bledsoe, one of the town's leading citizens. The novel opens on the day the Bledsoes receive notice that Duane's two older half-brothers have been killed in battle, their bodies destroyed so completely that only the identity tags and a few scraps of uniform remain.

The elder Bledsoe responds to this catastrophe by refusing to speak of it, or even to allow mention of his dead sons' names, a reaction which Duane finds baffling and intensely painful. As the novel progresses, it becomes clear that the father's iron repression of his grief is an aspect of his emotional deadness, a terrified rejection of human feelings and the natural rhythms of life. . . .

In direct contrast to this is the coarse animal vitality with which Duane's dead half-brothers had been endowed. One of them is so lightly sketched that his presence in the novel is itself mysterious, but the other, Justin, had been a brawling, sweating, rutting giant to whom Duane had looked up with adoration and a marked sense of his own inferiority. Duane's desolation at the loss of all this energy and at his father's cold refusal to mourn for it turns to baffled anguish when the ghosts of his older brothers literally return to haunt him, seemingly to no purpose other than to remind him of his loss.

The third major character is Estelle Dumont, a rich and attractive young widow of equivocal reputation who has been Justin's mistress. In the novel's central episode she organizes a masquerade ball as a memorial to the dead Bledsoes, at which Duane is guest of honour. In the course of the masquerade she seduces him and subsequently announces her pregnancy, at which point she insists on marrying, not Duane, but his tutor, Duke LaRoche, who has long been hopelessly in love with her; the child, however, is to be given to Duane. A boy is born, Duane takes it from the delivery room, names it Justin Bledsoe II, and devotes himself to it entirely, so much so that in the novel's closing words his father wonders "if there had ever been a boy before in all recorded history who was so destined to do nothing but raise a son".

The dead, the story tell us, are more alive than the living; Duane's own identity is submerged in Justin's, and even in the act of creating life in Estelle Dumont's bed he is, as he comes to see, doing his brother's will. His only purpose is to bring Justin back to life in the form of the child. The masquerade ball, presided over by the Circe-like Estelle (who is identified allusively with America itself), is the novel's master-image. . . .

The masquerade marks Duane's initiation into an adult masculine potency, but on emerging into the real world the next day he is stripped of his expensive costume, beaten and sexually humiliated.

The meaning of *Mourners Below* lies on the symbolic, even allegorical level—where spiritual desolation is suggested by houses with too many rooms, and sweat and saliva become the waters of life. The problem with it is nearer the surface. Duane Bledsoe is so charmlessly priggish that his ingenuousness is irritating rather than affecting, and the voice which narrates the melodramatic events of his story is a listless monotone of circumlocution and faded cliché. This may be an appropriately tedious medium for a story about deadness; and it is tempting to see in his technique Purdy facing his role as an unpopular writer in the most direct way. He is, of course, quite entitled to demand that his readers work to get below the arid surface of the novel, but the rewards for making the effort are meagre.

> *T. O. Treadwell, "The Dead More Alive than the Living," in* The Times Literary Supplement, *No. 4248, August 31, 1984, p. 977.*

PATRICK PARRINDER

[*On Glory's Course*] is set in Fonthill, an oil town somewhere in the Midwestern hinterland at the beginning of the Great Depression, and at first the small town's peace and quiet is disrupted by nothing more unusual than an aging beauty heckling the preacher in the middle of his sermon. The novel proceeds in brief, dramatised scenes, and before long the tempo of bizarre revelations becomes so heady that it seems likely to overwhelm the deadpan narrative. And on and on it goes, in an immensely skilful stylised melodrama, a tornado of small-town gossip.

Adele Bevington, descendant of one of the founding families of Fonthill, is the deserted mistress of a millionaire who took away her illegitimate son at birth and plied her, instead, with jewellery from a safe distance. Mouldering away in solitude in her ancestral home (now opposite Fonthill's 'photoplay house'), Adele sees herself, and is viewed by others, as an abandoned movie queen. Her lifelong search for her lost son provides the formal structure of the narrative. Does she find him, or doesn't she? Are all the young men of Fonthill, in a sense, her sons? And does it matter anyway? What can be said is that the novel is almost entirely populated by corrupt male authority figures, sex-starved widows who in more stringent times might have been burned as witches, ruined boys of whom one, Alec Cottrell, escapes from the suffocating town, and young and not-so-young women who are all, in one or other of the senses of a capacious word, whores. The men of Fonthill, according to crazy old Widow Hughes, 'burn even in the grave . . . the fire that is in them may indeed be behind the makeup of our entire universe. . . .'

[Purdy] once seemed tailor-made as a prototype of the self-conscious American novelist, playing with themes of writing and identity, and questioning reality and character-consistency. In *On Glory's Course* the playful and self-conscious touches have declined to the status of mechanical mannerisms. (p. 22)

Purdy, like many other American novelists, is noted for being haunted by a sense of entropic collapse. The sentiments released by his latest book are indeed those of loss, loss of sexual and emotional fulfilment, and the loss of youth and vigour. Brooding over Fonthill are the mutilated veterans of the Great War such as Keith Gresham (who lost his manhood in a battle in which he killed 27 Germans), and the shell-shocked physical and mental cases of the local Soldiers' Home. Yet, thanks to a wealth of period detail, props and costumes, the reader is kept well-cushioned against these intimations of mortality. . . .

This hothouse atmosphere is, intentionally, pure Hollywood. Seeing the same movies again and again is probably the nearest that Purdy's characters get to ordinary life. Only one of these movies is actually described, a film about a rancher dispossessed by thugs in the pay of a mining company, which bores Purdy's protagonists to tears. Fonthill does not like social realism in the cinema, preferring instead the revelations found in other people's secret diaries. These diaries, we are told, are like 'expensive confections, jellies and jams hidden high on the pantry shelf'. And that is the trouble with *On Glory's Course.* Superb confectionery, but there's a lot of it, and in the end you've had a surfeit of jellies and jams. (p. 23)

> *Patrick Parrinder, "Father, Son and Sewing-Machine," in* London Review of Books, *Vol. 7, No. 3, February 21, 1985, pp. 22-3.*

VERNON BOGDANOR

The House of the Solitary Maggot revolves around a contest for the fortune of the late Mr. Skegg, the magnate, or maggot as he is called by the villagers of Prince's Crossing. The contestants are three rather implausible illegitimate sons, the product of Skegg's liaison with Lady Bythewaite whose character could not be better described than it is in the blurb: 'a woman with a past whose passions can never be satisfied and who bends everyone to her will'. *The House of the Solitary Maggot* is a Gothic tale of Oedipal conflicts and shameful desires, resembling nothing so much as a pseud's version of *Peyton Place,* overladen as it is with heady symbolism and the promise of momentous consequences. Its language is too heavy for its limited emotional substance, and its final effect one of empty rhetoric.

> *Vernon Bogdanor, "Atoms Not Actors," in* The Listener, *Vol. 115, No. 2948, February 20, 1986, p. 28.*

VINCE ALETTI

Purdy's novels are both mundane and fantastic, rooted not only in the suffocating insularity of smalltown America but in the "'nature,' sweat, pain, sickness, madness, heavy breathing and tears, sorrow, and death—all the things that had to do with blood." . . . Even at their most uneventful, Purdy's midwestern melodramas are played at fever pitch, full of awkwardly operatic passions, unrestrained crying, impulsive couplings; "just short of hysteria" is a typical Purdy condition. Hysteria pales beside the truly berserk moments: the barn-door crucifixion that climaxes *Narrow Rooms,* the disembowelment at the end of *Eustace Chisholm and the Works,* Duane's humiliating rape in *Mourners Below,* Vickie's violent deflowering in *Jeremy's Version.* Yet Purdy always combines the appalling with the absurd, and many of his most outrageous scenes—particularly the sexual encounters—are as hilarious as they are horrifying: Terry Southern meets Nathanael West and Tennessee Williams for a circle jerk.

Although even Purdy's urban settings—notably in *Malcolm* and *Cabot Wright Begins,* his most sophisticated comic novels— are compressed to gossipy, back-stabbing coteries as narrow and crushing as any small town's, his recent work is steeped in rural American Gothic, a grotesque and glorious territory all his own. Going back to memories of the Ohio country towns he grew up in during the 1920s, Purdy strews a mythic landscape with grandiose, 25-room mansions, vaguely scandalous boarding houses, cornfields, fairgrounds, courthouses, and sweetshops. Though he insists he's a realist, Purdy has the savage, satirical eye of a primitive painter, and his scale is oddly askew; his huge homes loom like beached liners, improbably luxurious souvenirs from another era. But if the towns seem fanciful—Fonthill, Boutflour, Prince's Crossing, and Paulding Meadows often have the quality of dreamscapes—perhaps it's because their inhabitants, behind quite ordinary facades, are such a volatile, extraordinary crew.

With the extreme exceptions of the hideously disfigured war vet of *In a Shallow Grave* and the sadistic, driven teenagers in *Narrow Rooms,* Purdy's sprawling towns are typically peopled with broken, one-parent families, tortured young men, assorted busybodies, and mysterious, often fabulously (or formerly) rich older women who play unlikely sirens for the restless teen protagonists. These women—Estelle Dumont in *Mourners Below,* Adele Bevington in *On Glory's Course,* and, to a different degree, Elvira Summerlad in *Jeremy's Version*—are compulsive seductresses, but they're also manipulative sex-Moms, voraciously maternal, relentlessly demanding. Next to them, Purdy's men seem strangely ineffectual—insensitive, swaggering, frequently absent fathers; oversensitive, confused aesthetes; and big brother types. At the center of this tight-knit but utterly unhinged universe there's usually a curious, sharp-eyed young boy who's both caught up in and estranged from his family, already haunted by the past (Duane in *Mourners Below* is visited by his brother's ghost), desperate with apprehension for his future, but reckless enough to follow an impulse of the moment.

Like Malcolm, the eponymous waif in his first novel, these kids make Purdy's plots run. Citing Mark Twain and Herman Melville, Purdy points out that questing, "lost boys" are "one of the big American themes," but there's an obsessiveness in Purdy's work that goes beyond literary motifs. Does it help to know that, after his parents were divorced when he was ill, Purdy was shunted from father to mother to grandmother in various Ohio villages? That he ran away to Chicago at 16 and had an adventurous, "nightmare" time . . . until he joined the army? Maybe that's why there are no true innocents in Purdy's work—certainly not among the children, who are wise beyond their years and fiercely observant. Even when they are pawns in an adult world, they have more power—and frequently more daring—than the selfish, deluded grown-ups that surround them.

Nowhere is this clearer than in Purdy's knockout new novel, *In the Hollow of His Hand,* whose 14-year-old hero, Chad Coultas, is a Main Street Malcolm cut loose from family ties and set adrift in an American fantasyland as outlandishly marvelous as Kafka's Oklahoma. The first half of *In the Hollow of His Hand* is set during the 1920s . . . in an overwrought Purdyville, Yellow Brook, where Chad, the son of a prominent, once-wealthy family, is being taken for long, silent car rides by "the town Indian," Decatur. . . . Decatur, who has been away for 14 years, is convinced he's Chad's real father, though he barely remembers having stumbled into Eva Coultas's bedroom one afternoon while she was zonked on laudanum.

After a few intense rides in the Indian's company . . . , Chad begins to wonder about his own dark skin and black hair, his one blue eye and one black eye, and his . . . webbed feet. This last, uniquely Purdyesque detail leads to a bizarre scene of mutual desocking in Decatur's front seat (the Indian's feet are webbed, too), and Chad's slashing of his own feet to destroy the evidence and sever the connection. But even as the blood flows, Chad knows that the truth of his paternity can't be denied, so when Decatur decides to kidnap him, he goes willingly. And when the pair are quickly found and captured, Chad testifies in Decatur's defense. "I had never been claimed before by anybody, never had a father before," he tells the sheriff and his legal father, Lewis Coultas. "I knew even if I came

back to Yellow Brook I would only be coming back to it now as a stranger because I had become his son."

Once Decatur is jailed, Lewis Coultas, in a frantic effort to assert his role as a father and "begin all over again," takes Chad from bed one night and runs off with him on a train to Chicago. In the metropolis, Coultas acts more like a big shot with a client than a father with his son, dazzling Chad with luxuries and introducing him to a pair of bimbos named Cora and Minnie. That night, when the boy discovers his father naked and asleep between the women, he flees in shock and decides to walk all the way home.

As if leaving Yellow Brook has cut his ties to reality, Chad is suddenly spun free to begin a series of ever more incredible adventures, many of them with eccentric older men who say they want nothing more than to be his father, but who usually have other motives for giving him a ride. Pursued by Coultas, Minnie and Cora, and a loony private detective named Wilbur Harkey, Chad plunges from one encounter to the next with the hallucinatory logic of an acid trip (liberal doses of his mother's "elixir" keep him "fortified" and spaced out). He escapes a run-in with Decatur's crazed grandfather, who wants to cut out his blue eye, by flaying the old man savagely with a bullwhip. Taken up as a prophet by a religious cult, he addresses the startled congregation with a babbled "sermon" about his two fathers, then flees the riot that ensues. Like Lewis Coultas, he sleeps with two women in one night, but Chad leaves them to search for an Indian named Chief Silver Fox. Instead, he finds a party of white men playing at being wild Indians who attack him with burning branches when they find out he's the real thing. Finally, he meets an Indian "desperado" named Shelldrake who spirits him away from the approaching search party, tells Chad, "I need a son more than I need air to breathe," but is killed by a rain of police bullets before they get very far. (pp. 18-19)

Chad wakes up (was it all a dream?) in a train back to Yellow Brook with Wilbur Harkey, who informs him that Lewis Coultas has fled the country after being exposed as a swindler. Harkey hands Chad a mirror so he can see for himself that both his eyes are now the same color: black. The chaotic reception in Yellow Brook, with a torchlight parade through a snowstorm and a welcoming ceremony at the old Opera House, is one of the book's most surreal spectacles. It begins to seem that Chad will never again find his reality, his roots. But as the storm reaches a thunderous peak, Decatur appears, Chad throws himself at the man's feet, and father and son walk off arm in arm "while above them the sky flashed with a kind of cerise fire." After so many false daddies, Chad is united with his real father in an elemental extravaganza of biblical proportions. And Decatur, who early in the book asked, "Without a son, what is a man?" is complete, back in touch with his natural self. As Eva Coultas declares in an otherwise delicate, stiflingly civilized final scene, Chad was never really hers. She bows to Decatur's love for the boy: "not a human love . . . maybe it is divine, I don't know—but it is immoderate like the lake in a storm, and the forest when riven by lightning. It comes out of the sky and the thunder. I can't vie with that." . . .

Purdy's work has a freakish, compulsive quality uncontrolled by logic or grammar. Astounding events, unpredictable turns of phrase keep the reader in a state of alarm and incomprehension. You're constantly amazed by incidents that Purdy shrugs off matter-of-factly in a few sentences. . . . Some passages are so extravagant that they seem unmediated by any editorial hand. . . .

Oddly, you get accustomed to Purdy's unlikely plot twists sooner than his provocative prose. Teetering between elevated, old-fashioned elocution and common, frequently uneducated speech, Purdy's writing seems undigested, full of raw spots and whole paragraphs that feel impulsive, blurted out.... He creates a jolting, dizzying, loopy language, at once prim and profane, that's perfectly suited to his astonishing stories. Purdy's voice is as insinuating and unsettling as his tales; he lulls you with stilted refinement, then kicks you in the ass. "I show what people really do and never tell," he says. Purdy, the devil, always tells. (p. 19)

> Vince Aletti, *"American Gothic: James Purdy's Divine Madness,"* in VLS, *No. 48, September, 1986, pp. 18-19.*

LEE SMITH

It's as if Cormac McCarthy with his dark genius and Edward Bulwer-Lytton with his overblown prose style had joined hands to rewrite *Joseph Andrews,* sending their young protagonist forth across a landscape provided by Louis L'Amour. In this grimly antic antipicaresque [*In the Hollow of His Hand*], the passive young half-Indian Chad—instead of setting out on a traditional quest to find his own father—is kidnapped repeatedly by potential fathers eager to adopt *him.* And yet, many of the conventions of the picaresque are observed: the importance of coincidence; the totally episodic nature of the journey itself; its consequent lack of cause and effect; the stock characters who never develop; the bawdy encounters; the use of talismans.

For three decades James Purdy has been spinning his tales of foundlings lost in a grotesque and absurd world. *In the Hollow of His Hand* is a good introduction to his work for anyone unfamiliar with this author's considerable output.... Mr. Purdy's latest novel is typical of the whole in its vision of a violent, meaningless world in which only bizarre, obsessive love is possible; where the emblematic characters behave in nonrational ways; where the author's black humor often fails to alleviate the final bleakness of his world view. Mr. Purdy writes again and again about the search for—and the impossibility of finding—an identity.

But *In the Hollow of His Hand* is in some ways a departure for him. Not quite so far, finally, the book's ending offers a resolution; not quite so violent, this novel's plot lacks the gratuitous bloodletting sometimes seen in the earlier novels. And the absence of a writer-character (a Purdy trademark) makes this book more real, less self-consciously a fiction....

The mysterious Indian Decatur starts showing up at school to give Chad Coultas—who has one blue and one black eye—a ride home. Then Chad drops an "object" labeled "Bear Grease" on Miss Lytle's classroom floor: " 'Who gave this to you?' she thundered. He glared at her.... 'You'll stay after school, Chad Coultas,' she fulminated."

The conscious use of melodramatic clichés parallels the one-dimensional characters. Despised by his laudanum-loving wife, Eva, adored by Eva's mother, Pauline, whose fortune he has lost, Lewis Coultas is a "rugged white American male." He is enraged when Decatur, inevitably, kidnaps Chad, claiming to be his father. Decatur's motivation is clear. He says, "Without a son, what is a man?" Chad resists him initially..., yet when the police bring him home he unaccountably asserts that Decatur *is* his father, after all. Lewis Coultas is so angered by

this defection that he kidnaps Chad next, treating him to a "palatial" hotel. Chad, awake early the following morning, sees Coultas sprawled out naked with two "somewhat young women," the infamous Cora and Minnie, and so decides to "walk home" to Yellow Brook.

Here the picaresque begins in earnest. Chad is taken up by "the silk-hatted Mr. Elmo Lejeune and his bus filled with life-size wax dolls," then has a bloody encounter with Decatur's maniacal grandfather, finds himself deified by a weird religious cult, spends a wild night with the innkeeper Viola Franey's two daughters. Meanwhile, he is pursued by two unlikely parties: Lewis Coultas, Eva and Minnie; and the ancient detective Wilbur Harkey, his young wife, Emma Lou, and their libidinous chauffeur, Hibbard Grady.

Entering a nightmarish land . . . , Chad conceives of his journey as a kind of quest, perhaps to meet the legendary Chief Silver Fox. But the Indian desperado Shelldrake tells the boy that "in this life, there are no guides. There are no chiefs waiting to tell us something," and he involves Chad in a violent shoot-out that ends in a rapturous bloody union. Finally Chad is on his way home, ready for a mystical encounter with Decatur, who—after a welcome-home parade and ceremony—"led him from the Opera House into the street now piled in snowdrifts above their heads, while above them the sky flashed with a kind of cerise fire."

The reader has been vastly entertained, enraged and baffled—just as Mr. Purdy, no doubt, intends.

> Lee Smith, *"Kidnapped by Everyone,"* in The New York Times Book Review, *October 19, 1986, p. 15.*

DAVID R. SLAVITT

James Purdy is a marvel. His new collection of stories [*The Candles of Your Eyes*] confirms the wacky elegance that has been Purdy's stock in the writing trade during a distinguished career that goes back to the middle '50s. What other writer would dare sentences like these?

"Tim made a grimace with his lips that looked like the smile on a man I once saw lying dead of gunshot wounds on the street."

Or, "Jess shot once, then twice, the bowl of morning cereal was covered with red like a dish of fresh-gathered berries."

The near-hysterical heartlessness, the preposterous precision—not just berries, but fresh-gathered ones—is no mere embellishment but comes from the core of Purdy's basilisk vision. These are, after all, love stories one way or another. And love is, for Purdy, as much a sickness as anything else.

The kinds of love hardly matter, and the mixes of ages and sexual proclivities seem all but random—as perhaps they should....

Purdy's usual strategy is to set up a grotesque and bizarre exaggeration or a distortion of some kind, let it run a little, and then reel it back with a long, strong, all-but-invisible filament of his sympathy and humane understanding. But that thread of humanity that keeps him honest also allows us to share with an untroubled conscience the demoniac glee he takes in the unpredictable contortions of the human heart when it finds itself engaged or afflicted.

It would be an intolerably bleak vision of human experience, if it were not redeemed by Purdy's quirky compassion and illuminated by the virtuoso linguistic turns with which he bedecks and mollifies these acid etchings.

Inevitably, some of the stories are better than others. But the general level in this collection is very high—Himalayan in fact.

David R. Slavitt, *"James Purdy's Wacky but Elegant Love Stories,"* in Chicago Tribune—Books, *July 5, 1987, p. 5.*

ERIKA MUNK

James Purdy has always been celebrated for his ''voice''—the unpredictable but unmistakable sentences, at once plain-spoken and eccentric, that spin from his narrators no matter who they are or what kind of tales they're telling. Listening to Mr. Purdy's autodidacts, semiliterates, social climbers and outcasts, the reader, however charmed, always knows a bit more than they do and is kept at a bit of a distance. Mr. Purdy's stories have the self-conscious attractions of a ventriloquist's show.

This is not necessarily a good thing, of course. *The Candles of Your Eyes* includes 14 pieces, many of them extremely short, covering almost 20 years of Mr. Purdy's writing; it's his third collection and, no surprise, wildly uneven. The near-magical delights of a thrown voice neatly caught in midflight are too often overtaken by the clacking of dummy figures crudely manipulated to give us a scare or a giggle, and the writer's compassion for his characters' naïveté can turn into a complicitous wink at the audience.

"Some of These Days," the opening story, is eloquent. A young ex-convict painstakingly sets down an account of his final months: while looking for his former landlord, who had been his lover, helper and victim, the young man has grown deathly ill of ''a sickness'' . . . for which unfortunately there is today no cure.'' He searches in porno cinemas; running low on money, he buys tickets rather than food; he has sex with the moviegoers, hoping they'll help him find his landlord. Clearly—but not too oppressively—the quest is mystic and the illness spiritual, for he calls the landlord ''my lord,'' and the story was written in 1975, before one could read into the disease the terrible reality it now has. The young man's innocence is neither patronized nor romanticized, and every sentence is precise and surprising. Unfortunately, **"Some of These Days"** sets up expectations that are then pretty thoroughly dashed.

The voice in Mr. Purdy's stories can grow sticky and arch or old-hat hammy . . . or forced. . . .

Many of these narratives combine semi-ironic nostalgia for some unspecified rural past—those pillars—with a racism and misogyny so bizarre they're almost funny, with the joke on Mr. Purdy for his unawareness. Thus **"On the Rebound"** is about a white woman novelist who decides to regain her social position by making love to a chic black novelist, who vengefully tars and feathers her. Servant-master attachments generally loom large, and the only good thing a woman can do, as mother or lover, is collaborate in men's affections for each other.

The last three stories, including the title one [**"The Candles of Your Eyes"**], are the most recent, and quite different from the rest. Their substance is unhedgingly gay; the malice is gone; they take place in a recognizable present. Most of the mannerisms have fallen away, replaced for better or worse by a sentimental realism. Yet even in his newly romantic mode,

Mr. Purdy can set himself to the side and ventriloquize: ''And strange to say I felt almost refreshed at shedding so many bitter tears,'' says an otherwise flip and prosaic young 1980s actor, creating for a moment the author's old, sly voice.

Erika Munk, *"Scares and Giggles,"* in The New York Times Book Review, *September 6, 1987, p. 23.*

LOXLEY F. NICHOLS

Made up of work written over the last twenty years, Purdy's third collection of stories [*The Candles of Your Eyes*] is basically more of what has come before. Although somewhat milder in tone than *Color of Darkness* and *Children Is All,* this new collection is nevertheless full of foreboding, ennui, and despair. Relationships are tenuous and adversarial; families are partial entities, usually with one parent missing and the other inoperative. Identities are hard to tack down, and deception may be accidental or intentional, significant or trivial, but it is always present.

In Purdy's fiction the sentimental and the macabre are common bedfellows. Tears and blood flow easily onstage, while bruises and blackened nails give evidence of violence offstage. Although it bears no resemblance in plot to the Alban Berg opera, **"Sleep Tight"** has a pervasive red hue and atonal *Wozzeck*-like resonance. In this story a dead man's blood becomes the medium of a child's ''watercolor'' paintings, and children's screams echo to the tune of a popular song.

Impulses, too, are deceptively interchangeable, and appetites, when they exist at all, are insatiable. In **"Lily's Party"** two men and a woman engage in an orgy of compulsive eating and grotesque fornicating that measures the extremity of their emotional and spiritual deprivation. (pp. 50-1)

Talk is important in these stories. Six are written in the first person and many are conveyed as gossip. When the narrator is effaced, a story may adhere to an oral tradition, such as the ballad-like **"Ruthanna Elder"** or the fable **"Mud Toe the Cannibal."** Dialogue, however, is usually full of non-sequiturs. Operating in a spiritual vacuum, Purdy's characters feel invisible, expressing the sentiments of the naïve protagonist of *Malcolm,* who admits, ''I hardly feel I exist.'' Thus the act of telling becomes more an attempt at clarification, justification, or validation of *self* than communication with another.

About half the stories in this collection are successful—the first four, plus **"Sleep Tight," "Short Papa,"** and **"The Candles of Your Eyes."** Purdy's quirky, angular prose style can turn wooden and trite, and he has a tiresome preoccupation with homosexuality. Frequently his stories are so reductive they read like synopses.

Yet the titles of this collection and [*In the Hollow of His Hand*] illustrate the author's lyrical bent. Set in the Midwest after World War I, *In the Hollow of His Hand* is an initiation story that marks a new dimension in Purdy's exploration of the relationship between fathers and sons and the search for self. Instead of being abandoned and fatherless, young Chad Coultas suddenly finds himself with two fathers and must choose between his natural one, the outcast Indian Decatur, and his legal one, the upstanding (and unscrupulous) Lewis Coultas. (pp. 51-2)

The writing, especially in the first 105 pages, is luxuriant and masterly, and the characters are compelling not only to the reader, but to one another as well. . . . What begins in a tide of rhapsodic splendor, however, later becomes stymied in an allegorical bog. After a while we lost interest in Chad's wild adventures, which become too numerous and random to keep track of.

This arbitrary and seemingly artless quality of Purdy's writing has been viewed differently. "The cool inconsequence of the narrative [in *Malcolm*]—the inconsequence of real life with the impression of fantasy and the suggestion of vast but always escaping meanings—" was for David Daiches "proof of [Purdy's] supreme control." For Flannery O'Connor, who was also a Purdy admirer of sorts, this quality was a sign of sloppy writing: "the stories seem to me merely thrown together." Whether intentional or accidental, such abstruseness finally becomes monotonous, oppressive, and just plain unsatisfying. Reading James Purdy is rather like eating kumquats: colorful and exotic experimentation but hardly substantial enough for a meal. (p. 52)

> *Loxley F. Nichols, "Kumquats for Supper," in* National Review, *New York, Vol. XL, No. 4, March 4, 1988, pp. 50-2.*

Erika Ritter

1948?-

Canadian dramatist, essayist, and scriptwriter.

In her plays, Ritter explores the plight of independent contemporary women who attempt to assert their individuality and principles while maintaining careers and romances. Paul Milliken commented: "[The] individual expression, through work, and the sexual expression, through relationships, combine to form the core of Ritter's plays. . . . The central characters are young women who, by acting out their expressions of work and sex, struggle to define themselves to those around them." Ritter is often praised for her dialogue, particularly the sardonic remarks uttered by her protagonists that poignantly reflect the ambiguities in their lives.

Ritter first gained critical recognition with *The Splits* (1978). This play depicts a female protagonist who has written a novel that the Canadian Broadcasting Corporation wishes to adapt into a situation comedy series for television. Resisting the financial advantages of working for television and leaving behind unfulfilling relationships with her husband and her lover, the heroine sets off at the play's conclusion to begin a new life and to continue writing serious fiction. *Winter 1671* (1979) concerns a group of women shipped from France to Quebec as wives for Canadian settlers. Ritter suggests parallels between this seventeenth-century practice and the status of women in contemporary society. *Automatic Pilot* (1980), Ritter's first work to draw significant critical and popular attention, contrasts the onstage poise and control of a stand-up comedienne with the disorder of her personal life. Troubled relationships are also examined in *The Passing Scene* (1982), in which the problems between a pair of married journalists are reflected in their failure to converse about anything except work-related matters. *Murder at McQueen* (1986) focuses on four women who meet regularly at an exclusive health club to discuss their careers and love interests. Featuring Ritter's characteristic blending of poignant dialogue with a satire of modern urban lifestyles, this play explores what Martin Knelman identified as "the dilemma of the modern woman whose twentieth-century political programmes and mastery of power dressing keep bumping against her nineteenth-century psyche."

In addition to her work as a playwright, Ritter has served as hostess of several radio programs on contemporary lifestyles. Many of her commentaries on urban trends and preoccupations are collected in *Urban Scrawl* (1985) and *Ritter in Residence* (1987).

MARTIN KNELMAN

Megan [the main character in *The Splits*] is a 1970s Toronto version of the wisecracking heroines who used to be played in 1930s Hollywood comedies by Carole Lombard or Rosalind Russell. She lives in a decaying downtown apartment, keeps mice as pets, and refuses to eat meat. She's a sassy fighter who has not only taken honours English at university but has

also learned how to talk dirty—and funny dirty—with the boys. At first the play seems to be about the men in her life: she's caught between her ex-husband, a charming drunk whose prodigious talent is divided between writing and screwing . . . , and an insufferably well-organized lover (married) who works as a travel agent for executives. There's also a weak-kneed CBC story editor who gets into the act. But as things turn out, the play is really about Megan's career—and especially about the degradation involved when she's tempted to sell her novel to the CBC for a series. The last straw comes when Megan discovers the worst—that the CBC has been plotting to turn her material into a situation comedy. As it hurtles toward Megan's decision to throw all the demanding, disruptive people out of her life so she can devote herself to her writing, *The Splits* resembles a feminist version of Martin Kinch's play *Me?* But Megan goes the hero of *Me?* one better; she throws out everything, including her CBC scripts, walks out even on her dumpy apartment, and hits the street. At the end, the main question the audience is left with is: but who's going to feed the mice?

It's a shame that Ritter has such contempt for situation comedy, because she has the talent to be a wonderful comedy writer. The play is most alive when Megan is jousting with Joe, her impossibly free-wheeling ex-husband. With his macho bull about sexual conquests, Joe is a walking definition of what women are trying to get liberated from. It's implicit in Ritter's way of seeing things that in order to be free, a woman has to live without sexual excitement. The way she has stacked the deck, the more enlightened a man is in his conduct toward women, the more boring and limp he's likely to be, too. When Joe is off stage, Megan has no one worth struggling with, and the play falls apart. In order to prove her integrity, Megan/Ritter seems willing to give up not only sex but also drama. . . . Megan hangs onto her artistic integrity the way Doris Day used to hang onto her virginity, and the little nuggets of consolation wisdom—such as, It's time somebody fought back—are so blatantly self-serving they're excruciating. The audience is invited to cheer Megan for throwing her sit-com series in the trash can and hitting the street so she can be free to write her great Canadian novel. But I wanted to tell Erika Ritter to do just the opposite—to toss her how-I-became-a-serious-writer ideas in the garbage and go with what she's got—an ear for witty drama that could be a blessing if she got it out from under the clutter of Significant Ideas. (pp. 60, 62)

> *Martin Knelman, "The Playwright as Star of the Play," in* Saturday Night, *Vol. 93, No. 3, April, 1978, pp. 59-60, 62.*

MARK CZARNECKI

Automatic Pilot [a play about a stand-up comedienne named Charlie] shoots down the pretensions of "those half-assed '70s people who always have to keep their options open," but Ritter should have followed her own moral—too many melodramatic options spoil the froth, starting with a pitfall-laden plot about Charlie's marriage breakdown, apparently precipitated by her husband, Alan, turning gay. However, the author is unabashed about keeping her sabre-sharp wit as sheathed as possible: "For me comedy is only an incidental payoff—life is full of one-liners." High seriousness has escaped her, though, its place usurped by excessive bitterness and makeshift sentiment derived from set-up situations.

In her stand-up routines Charlie tries to objectify and transcend the pain she suffers in her aimless relationships with men. But although Charlie is an immediately recognizable, overly trusting and dipsomaniacal child of the '70s, the self-gouging comedienne persona arising from her soft, confused "real" self appears more schizophrenic than therapeutic. Neither the script nor the performance conceals Charlie's convoluted masochism sufficiently in the first half of the play to make her final flight from love dramatically forceful—there's no point in ultimately unveiling the truth when it's been parading around naked for two hours. . . .

Ritter's comic gifts are considerable—not just a hodge-podge of one-liners, *Pilot* is actually a highly intelligent satiric vision of urban alienation. Prodigal with her talent, the playwright also demonstrates in the brief seduction and parting scenes between Charlie and Nick's kid brother, Gene, the sensitivity to the intricacies of relationships she prizes even more than her caustic insights. That the two visions can't be happily united here is the result of high comedy at war with realism, a conflict in which the audience inevitably dies laughing.

> *Mark Czarnecki, "Bound for Glory of the Commercial Kind," in* Maclean's Magazine, *Vol. 93, No. 28, July 14, 1980, p. 54.*

RICHARD PLANT

"Erika Ritter's dazzling play [*Automatic Pilot*] . . . just keeps going on and on," Bruce Blackadar wrote in the Toronto *Star*. . . . But why? Certainly it is funny, in the same way a stand-up comedian's patter of one-liners is funny. In addition, the idea of a comedienne whose comedy routines come out of her own personal anguish, although not new, offers rich potential for drama. The lightly veiled comments on the exploitation of women, achieved through the metaphor of women as stand-up comediennes, offer some substance to the piece. But in the end what we get is a love story involving Charlie, the comedienne, and the younger brother of her short-term lover who, in turn, had replaced her former husband when she (and he) discovered he was a homosexual. As tangled and potentially informative as these problems of sexual identity are, thoughtful audiences surely want more than the superficial insights this play gives us. Like David French, Erika Ritter has demonstrated a quick ear for dialogue and an apt dramatic sense. One hopes she will put these tools to use in creating plays of more substance than this one. (p. 11)

> *Richard Plant, "Future Schlock," in* Books in Canada, *Vol. 10, No. 4, April, 1981, pp. 10-13.*

RONALD HUEBERT

With her fourth play, *Automatic Pilot*, Erika Ritter won the Chalmers Award for 1980. In a sense this . . . is a one-woman show, though the cast includes three supporting male actors; and this play . . . is based on the author's personal experience, this time 'as a stand-up comic.'

The one woman is named, with a touch of ambiguity, Charlie. A touch did I say? No, Charlie's name is virtually an announcement that this is a play about sexual roles. Turned out in her Annie Hall costume and grasping the mike at her local nightclub (The Canada Goose), Charlie is every inch a professional. She is funny, and she is in control. But in her private world, unprotected by clothing or custom, she becomes slavishly vulnerable to her need for men. And she chooses her men with a flawless instinct for frustration. Now thirty years old, she is separated from her husband, Alan. Alan Merritt the actor, that is, pathologically dishonest, chronically out of work, socially devious, and gay. She is seduced, bedazzled, and betrayed by Nick Bolton, the ambitious motion-picture executive who sleeps with all the girls but gives himself to none. And at last she is passed on to Nick's younger brother, Gene, age 23, law-school dropout, Hudson's Bay salesclerk, and aspiring novelist.

This trio of male stereotypes allows Ritter to dish out an amusing meal of feminist revenge. Nick is by far the stupidest and most cruel of the three men, so nobody minds when Charlie deflates him. . . . Charlie's 'late husband,' Alan, is just as roundly punished; he is the butt of a series of anti-homosexual jokes that no male writer today could dream of putting into print. And poor Gene is just a babe in arms compared with his jaded patrona. He falls in love with her, moves into her apartment, wears her aprons, cooks her soufflés, tolerates her infidelities, and leaves when she no longer needs him.

If the hollowness of her male manikins is Ritter's gravest artistic fault, her biggest technical error is the starring role she gives to Bell Canada. Imagine all the wonderful things an alienated single woman in apartment city can accomplish through the impersonal medium of the telephone. She can place a long-distance call to her estranged homosexual husband in Stratford. She can unplug the jack when she's depressed and wants to get drunk by herself. She can forget to plug it back in when she's still depressed but wants her lover to call. She can overhear her estranged husband making a rendezvous with his gay boyfriend. And there are further combinations, limited only by the number of extensions which the theatre can supply. Still, a playwright who relies so heavily on the telephone for conducting the social life and revealing the emotional self of her protagonist must be suffering from poverty of theatrical inventiveness.

Somehow, I should emphatically add, the character of Charlie surmounts her environment. Hers is a magnificently actable part: witty, tender, flamboyant, defensive, always the centre of attention, yet always alone. . . . None the less, I think Ritter is at her best, not when she's providing Charlie with polished one-liners (as she frequently does), but when she has Gene sit down at his desk to write his novel. Gene composes by reading into a tape recorder:

> It came as a surprise to him that this was what being in love felt like. He'd imagined the feeling many times, of course, and it had been different. Better circumstances, more exotic locations, a different kind of woman. For he wasn't so caught up in emotion that he couldn't admit that to himself. He'd simply never expected to fall, when he fell, for a woman like her. She was taller than what he'd had in mind, she smoked too much, and she was absolutely nothing like Jane Fonda. And she was older than he was. Most of all, she was older. . . .

(pp. 57-8)

This passage is enough to convince me that Erika Ritter is already a very fine writer. Furthermore, there is evidence here of a deeply dramatic imagination at work: the kind of imagination which can see the world through *someone else's* eyes, and find the words which allow that otherness to express itself. I am not saying that Ritter should abandon the theatre to complete Eugene Bolton's novel for him. But I am saying that she is a better writer with a richer imagination than one might guess from her achievements as a playwright thus far. (p. 58)

> *Ronald Huebert, in a review of "Automatic Pilot,"* *in* University of Toronto Quarterly, *Vol. L, No. 4, Summer, 1981, pp. 57-8.*

MARK CZARNECKI

When the dirty linen of public affairs becomes too offensive for private eyes, disengaged members of society firmly believe journalists will do the wash for them. This belief was revealed as a delusion in the aftermath of Watergate, when the scandal that could have transformed a society was instead transformed into a movie celebrating two reporters. The worship of false idols continues. . . .

Erika Ritter's new play, *The Passing Scene,* explores this phenomenon with a "moral compass" held by two journalists whose private ethical codes fluctuate according to the events they cover. Their courtship and marriage span the Watergate years (1971 to 1976); Dan is patterned after Carl Bernstein of *The Washington Post,* but Kitty has no obvious public counterpart. The title of her book of essays, *Urbane Guerrillas,* says it all: she scorns ideology—only the inner life is sacred. Yet, at their first meeting, Dan, the obtuse investigative reporter, digs up a confession of emotional betrayal from her

past. They fall in love, part, bitch, act silly and finally marry. Dan breaks the big story but, rather than toppling the government, he pulls his punches and films the tale. Meanwhile, Kitty wins notoriety writing a lifestyle column for a soft porn magazine. The end mirrors the beginning. Under her pointed questions, Dan—now a full-fledged media whore fallen victim to the tabloids—confesses to an affair while protesting his love for Kitty. She tersely forgives: the moral compass is dropped, and their exploration of a life together continues, blindly.

Playwright Ritter is her own worst enemy. She has not yet found a voice that will blend her magical, biting wit—also amply displayed in her previous hit, *Automatic Pilot*—with her more profound issues and characters. Instead of pushing further into the promising land of her initial premise, Ritter misplaces her faith in easy laughs and shallow satire ("I see our hotel rooms have the same decorator—Fisher-Price"). . . . Formally structured into three acts, the play moves like a sonata from New York to Hollywood and back, inviting a restrained, almost classical playing style as a counterpoint to the dominant mode of crude realism. . . .

Happily, [the final confrontation between Dan and Kitty] is gripping and bittersweet, a tantalizing glimmer of the fires Ritter might have lit had she pursued *The Passing Scene* with greater tenacity and less wit.

> *Mark Czarnecki, "Caught between the Lines," in* Maclean's Magazine, *Vol. 95, No. 3, January 18, 1982, p. 62.*

PAUL MILLIKEN

[Individual] expression, through work, and the sexual expression, through relationships, combine to form the core of Ritter's plays. In terms of style, the plays fit into the mainstream of Canadian drama—what she calls "TV-style realistic theatre." But her subject matter and thematic approach set them apart. Unlike much of our realistic drama, which lays all of its eggs in the family basket, Ritter's work isolates the individual in a situation where she must cope on her own. The central characters are young women who, by acting out their expressions of work and sex, struggle to define themselves to those around them. They are apartment people who inhabit a world of bosses, boyfriends, and landlords; and any links they may have to a traditional home are only tentatively maintained by long distance telephone. (p. 33)

The plays have no specific axe to grind, and Ritter isn't lashing out at society as an ultimate villain. (pp. 33, 36)

As a chronicler of contemporary relationships, Ritter brings to her work a well-informed view of what's happening in the world, and a realistic sense of how the individual sinks or swims in the modern current. She has a keen ear for dialogue. . . .

Her least-known play, *Winter 1671,* takes a more Brechtian approach to the expression of character. The play deals with *les filles du Roi,* who were shipped from France to Quebec as wives for the colony. The society they arrive in in *Winter 1671* is a very uncertain place—part military garrison, part clerical outpost, part trading terminal. The expectations that each aspect of the society has for these women make their expression of self almost impossible. But Ritter arms each of them with a past. As the play progresses, the audience comes to know more about who each woman has been, and thereby come to an awareness of who they might like to be. The women appear trapped between a sense of their past and a desire for the future; our understanding of their dramatic present is defined by the various discrepancies. . . . As a statement of male domination in Canada and of our view of woman-as-object, it's one of the more important plays created here to date. (p. 36)

The sense of integrity that [Ritter's] characters try to gain for themselves is the kind of attitude that our theatre has been trying to create. If we are going to have theatre in this country, there must be room in it for writers whose outspokenness and truthfulness will expose the unfair ways in which we respond to one another. Relationships—the way we use and abuse each other for the sake of pairing—have been Erika Ritter's domain. (p. 37)

> *Paul Milliken, "Erika Ritter's Search for Integrity on the Stage," in* Performing Arts in Canada, *Vol. XIX, No. 2, Summer, 1982, pp. 33, 36-7.*

RACHEL WYATT

I was eager to read Erika Ritter's **Urban Scrawl** to find out whether much has changed since I used to write and broadcast essays, vignettes, and comment for the CBC 20 years ago. . . .

Almost everything . . . is different, including the language, but the use of "us" and "we" remains the same. In Ritter's book, much use is made of the plural pronoun, as though to embrace all the world. Yet it tends to have a special and local application.

Twenty years ago "we" were leading a dark-age life. "We" lived in Don Mills on the outskirts of Toronto. At age 33.3 all of "us" had 1.75 children, with a promise of making it four or five in that fertile breeding ground. We worried a lot about hot and cold wars and having no future, and on weekends we drank whisky and barbecued red, raw flesh. . . .

So what has become of "us"? We have moved into the city, into high-rise buildings or shared houses in Toronto's Beaches district. We cycle about looking for love or listening attentively to the beeps of our friends' answering machines. We are a rootless lot, we pre-middle-aged, middling folk. We lie there in society wedged between the powerful rich and the interesting poor like a jurassic layer in the rocks of time. We lack connection. (p. 20)

The picture that Erika Ritter paints is clear and detailed if not totally desirable. We can run for cover and shout that "we" are not like that. But the book is shot through with moments of recognition.

Writing for the unsighted, capturing the listening ear fast, is an art that Ritter understands well. . . . It is those tricks of beginning in the middle, of creating an instant picture, of employing a relaxed, chatting-to-friends style, of moving on quickly and occasionally startling people out of their socks that mark the real radio writer and modern essayist. Nobody will sit still long enough nowadays to listen to reams of pith on matters of moment. That demanding audience out there wants instant gratification. And that is what, in **Urban Scrawl,** it gets.

The shorter pieces are the best. **"Bicycles"** and **"The Invasion of the Airline Stewardesses"** are good examples of the cockeyed look at this tiny segment of the world that we are promised on the book jacket. In some of the longer essays the humour and the ideas are stretched thin, and occasionally there are touches of the whimsical and the cute. But readers will argue

about this book, each making a case for his or her favourite piece.

I will stand up for **"Club Dread."** I think I've been there. I was a little worried when it changed course in midstream and took on heavy, almost Conradian overtones. Then I began to recognize those put-upon holiday-makers, playing their awful games to win approval, eternally seeking love. On the other hand, I couldn't make myself care what happened to Holden Caulfield in **"Catcher in the rye-and-water."** The essay called **"Guilt"** has much that is pertinent to say about our my-guilt-is-heavier-than-yours society, with its background cries of *mea culpa*. (pp. 20-1)

I didn't hear much music in this book, or poetry, or love of any kind. What I could hear was the plaintive voice of the time asking, "What have we done to deserve this?" And the answer is there on those pages. . . .

I hope that Erika Ritter will continue to cast her beady eye over the world she lives in, and tell us what she sees. (p. 21)

> *Rachel Wyatt, "Pith and Vinegar," in* Books in Canada, *Vol. 13, No. 9, November, 1984, pp. 20-1.*

SHERIE POSESORSKI

Urban Scrawl is a collection of 24 comic essays by Erika Ritter who is best known for her play **Automatic Pilot**. The majority of the pieces were first aired on Ritter's adult-phenomenon segment on CBC's "Stereo Morning." . . .

Her speculative essays are comic anthropological queries of urban trends. She aims her helium-filled shots at the urban species and inflates their preoccupations until they burst with absurdity. In **"Bicycles,"** she wonders why adults are postponing their adolescence to senility by playing with bats and bikes. In **"Guilt,"** she meditates on guilt in Canada after receiving a guilt-inducing notice from her credit-card company informing her that she has to pay a surcharge because clients have the nerve to pay their bills on time. . . . Her comic fantasies include a Ph.D. dissertation on phone messages and a nightmare where all women start talking like airline stewardesses.

A true wit combines superior mental powers with self-deprecating humour. These qualities abound in Ritter's work.

> *Sherie Posesorski, in a review of "Urban Scrawl," in* Quill and Quire, *Vol. 50, No. 11, November, 1984, p. 37.*

W. H. NEW

If there isn't already a generic term "urban irony," there needs to be one for [**Urban Scrawl**]. It's a controlled-caustic glimpse of city mores, in two dozen essays on such subjects as women's attitudes to their purses, the faddishness of riding bicycles as an adult, Grey Cup football, drinks, cats, and language: mostly language. . . . What makes the humour contagious here is not the topics themselves; it's the fact that Ritter cares enough about people to find a way to deal with Mass Woman, Mass Man, and the plastic aesthetics of Mass Design. The wry wit is a cocky human answer to the doomsayers, a gasp of breath in an airtight room.

> *W. H. New, in a review of "Urban Scrawl," in* Canadian Literature, *No. 104, Spring, 1985, p. 183.*

LAWRENCE CHANIN

In this collection of humour pieces [*Urban Scrawl*], the majority selected from her CBC radio shows, Ritter roams across the passing social scene from bicycles and exotic vacations to fashions and bumper stickers. With abundant insouciance and an excellent ear for funny dialogue, Ritter treats the reader to her cock-eyed conceptions of urban professional life.

Urban Scrawl is social commentary of sweetness and light, totally unconcerned with urban blight.

In only a few pieces is the humour stretched thin, for example, an easy entitled, **"Guilt,"** Ritter's one ambitious attempt to tickle a serious subject.

Like a good comedienne, Ritter leaves her audience laughing with her best sketch, **"Great Expectations."**

Urban Scrawl is a collection of high quality scribbles that provide quick shots of gratification for the consumer society.

> *Lawrence Chanin, in a review of "Urban Scrawl,"*
> *in* Canadian Author & Bookman, *Vol. 61, No. 2,*
> *Winter, 1986, p. 24.*

JOHN BEMROSE

[*Murder at McQueen*] is set in the exclusive, all-female McQueen Club, where the characters meet regularly. Success and independence have taken their toll on relationships with the opposite sex, and much of their acerbic talk is devoted to the eternal problem of men. The fact that two of the women unwittingly share the same lover, talk-show host Rex Hahn, adds a melodramatic twist to their friendship and points to the central meaning of the play's title. *Murder at McQueen* is about the small murders that people commit when trust is betrayed.

The best moments of the play sparkle with Ritter's sardonic, slightly melancholy wit.... But [these] lines, while entertaining, have little new to say about the problems of contemporary women. Of the characters, only Norah Tratt, a corporate lawyer and rock-hard feminist, shows any complexity. The men in the drama—Hahn and private detective Jesse Butler—are victims of arrested development. Their lines are either woefully wooden or burdened with Ritter's facile tendency to be cute instead of psychologically accurate. *Murder at McQueen* is a pleasantly tart diversion, but not much more.

> *John Bemrose, in a review of "Murder at Mc-*
> *Queen," in* Maclean's Magazine, *Vol. 99, No. 47,*
> *November 24, 1986, p. 66.*

MARTIN KNELMAN

In Erika Ritter's new comedy, *Murder at McQueen,* four smart city women track that elusive creature, the perfect post-liberation man, and joke bitterly among themselves about the odds against the quest. They know their expectations are absurd, but they can't stop hoping. Meanwhile they sift through the wreckage of failed relationships.

"If old lovers were dead, you'd never have to worry about running into them on the street," says Mitzi, who runs a trendy women's club. "You've done fine without anyone," she's told by Norah, a militantly aggressive young lawyer who likes to call phone-in radio shows to complain about the male conspiracy. And Mitzi replies: "I've done without anyone. It's not quite the same thing."

When Blythe and Hilary, two eager writers in the group, question Norah about her definition of the ideal man, she replies with a flippancy traditionally associated with coarse males: "My ideal man flies in for the weekend, doesn't snore or watch sports on TV, fucks like a dream—and then flies out again."

"Bullshit," retorts Mitzi, who sees through Norah's veneer of invulnerability. "You want what everyone wants."

The exchange sums up the subject-matter of *Murder at McQueen*—the contradictions and ambiguities at the heart of the feminist movement. There is probably no-one better qualified to write a knowing play about this than Erika Ritter, who has been chronicling the plight of the beleaguered urban woman—the kind sometimes accused of being too smart for her own good—for a decade. Ritter has worked as a journalist, fiction writer, and radio commentator: in her latest incarnation she's on the air five afternoons a week, two hours a day, as host of CBC Radio's "Dayshift"—a programme devoted to those subjects usually grouped together under the umbrella term "life style." (p. 61)

[The plot of *Murder at McQueen*] has a deliciously gossipy edge. The fictitious McQueen Club was clearly inspired by a real club—originally called Twenty-One McGill, now The McGill Club—which began as the symbolic capital of 1970s-Toronto-style feminism. And the play's most dramatic event—a great fire—recalls a real incident with mythic reverberations. (pp. 61-2)

In the case of Erika Ritter as well as the case of The McGill Club, what seemed radical or daring or beyond the fringe a decade ago has now been absorbed into the mainstream and become almost too respectable. Can a satirist find happiness doing radio interviews about dental floss and premature babies? "Dayshift" ... is a classic example of CBC Radio's controversial attempt to increase its ratings by going after a wider audience. Actually, Ritter handles the assignment with grace. Yet listening to "Dayshift" I sometimes feel I can almost catch Ritter stifling the impulse to deliver a sarcastic remark, and making an effort to be, well, *nice to people*. Which raises the question of why anyone should want to make an exotic tiger into a plain old pussycat.

But in a play Ritter's voice and her way of seeing come through without a filter; she doesn't have to serve somebody else's point of view, and she doesn't have to make nice. Ritter and the stage are perfect, if reluctant, mates. She's free to talk dirty and inject feminist rage into shock words formerly appropriated by men. And she's freer to explore her favourite subject—the dilemma of the modern woman whose twentieth-century political programmes and mastery of power dressing keep bumping against her nineteenth-century psyche. To newsmagazines and academic demographers the growing futility of the successful single woman's mate-seeking is the current hot topic: serious, worrying stuff. To Ritter, who's been alert to it all along, it's also comic. The theatre liberates the side of Erika Ritter that is entertainingly Not Nice.

Most of the six Ritter plays produced so far feature a wise-cracking heroine who finds it almost impossible to sustain a decent relationship with a man. One of the characters in her new play works for a magazine called *Urban Lady* ..., and that's not a bad description of her target. (Mercifully, Ritter is not one of those writers trying to get back to the land or discover the Canadian identity in a simple rural setting.) Her protagonists are updated Toronto versions of the smart working girls played in 1930s Hollywood comedies by Carole Lombard, Barbara Stanwyck, Rosalind Russell, or Eve Arden.

In *The Splits* (1978), the heroine, named Megan, is a sassy writer caught between a charming drunk of a husband and an insufferably well-organized lover, and coping at the same time with the treachery of CBC story editors who want to turn her serious work into sitcom. In *The Passing Scene* (1982), the heroine, Kitty Frank, is a journalist/author messily involved with a Washington political journalist who bears more than a passing resemblance to Carl Bernstein. The more intelligent and discriminating a woman is, these plays seem to suggest, the less chance that she's going to have a fulfilling love life.

In Ritter's most polished and successful play, *Automatic Pilot* (1980), expanded from a short story published the year before in *Saturday Night,* the heroine, Charlie, is a performer at a comedy club named The Canada Goose. She's involved with two brothers—the older a retrograde Don Juan, the younger a would-be writer who works at The Bay—and she also has an ex-husband who is a bisexual Stratford actor.

According to Charlie—described by one of the characters as the sort of girl who puts "sleep around" on her list of things to do—single straight men are hard to find. The problem, as Charlie sees it, is that men don't come on to big, capable girls like her—"girls who speak English as if it was their native language." Still, for Charlie, being a loser in the game of love has its fringe benefits. Seeing the faults of the men around her with a merciless eye, she fails to find happiness with any of them. But she gets a lot of zippy jokes out of her misery, and gives the distinct impression of thriving on it. Charlie's punch lines are like a string of multiple orgasms.

Probably Ritter's most complicated and ambitious play, *Murder at McQueen* goes further than her earlier work by showing the audience a group of discontented women rather than a single beset heroine. With its ultrachic setting, its hive of queen bees, and its buzz of bitchy banter, it's like an update of Clare Boothe Luce's 1936 opus *The Women.*

There's Mitzi, the club owner with a tragic past; Hilary, the eager private-school girl who writes reports for *Urban Lady* from the life-style front lines; Blythe, the aspiring writer who gives seminars on detective fiction; and Norah, the brilliant young lawyer who vents rage through anonymous calls to a phone-in show.

By their sheer numbers, they demonstrate the point that everyone is now noticing but that hardly any contemporary playwright has written about: that so many interesting, unattached women are stranded without men in prospect if they happen to be over twenty-five. Not counting a bewildering cop who's half fantasy, half reality, the only eligible man in sight is Rex, the rumpled, chain-smoking host of a morning radio show. Rex is not only an arrogant chauvinist, he's also a heartbreaker.

Ritter plays the club fire for both comedy and melodrama, and she turns the question of who lit the match into a parlour mystery game. Naturally the sacking of the McQueen is viewed as a male attack on feminists; naturally the incident has to be dissected on Rex's show.

Murder at McQueen is a far from perfect play. It raises expectations it can't fulfil, strays into whimsy, and ends with an upbeat message—a woman shouldn't settle for a less-than-great relationship just because she hasn't figured out who or what she wants—that sounds like something from the sort of self-improvement guide Ritter might be expected to savage. (Maybe "Dayshift" is getting to her.) Yet for all its shortcomings, *Murder at McQueen* puts a zing into the theatre season by giving the audience a shock of comic recognition. If Ritter has chronic trouble with endings, maybe that's because she takes the risk of charting unknown territory. She appears to be that rarity, a feminist writer with a sense of humour. Her knack for funny, lively dialogue may lead reviewers to dismiss her as a frivolous practitioner of one-liners. But she's not just cracking jokes; she's covering the biggest life-style story of our time from her own gleefully subversive point of view. (pp. 62-3)

> Martin Knelman, "Urban Lady," in Saturday Night, Vol. 101, No. 12, December, 1986, pp. 61-3.

CAROL BOLT

To some, Erika Ritter's *Murder at McQueen* does not seem to make a feminist statement at all. It is about women, of course, but it's about women who are shown living through and for their men. The characters have problems like "Will my best friend find out I'm sleeping with her ex-husband?" when "What am I doing with this guy?" might seem a more enlightened question. When one of the characters discovers that her dream-lover-come-to-life is actually a married man, the announcement at one performance was greeted with hisses. For some in the audience, this reaction was prompted not so much by the news of the dream lover's perfidy, but because the female character seemed so devastated by this somewhat less than earthshaking revelation. . . .

[These women] are fondly created characters, drawn with Ritter's characteristic warmth and wit and accurately drawn as well. Of course women often live through and for men. These characters remind us of an enduring and rather endearing feminist dilemma, instantly recognizable to most women in the audience. Hilary, Mitzi, Norah, and Blythe do not need consciousness raising and sending them all off to take night-school classes to improve themselves will not improve the play. Perhaps our focus on the story needs adjustment before we can really enjoy the irony of these thoroughly modern women with thoroughly old-fashioned love affairs.

The play received mixed reviews and Ritter is rewriting it. I hope the new *Murder at McQueen* will include passages like Hilary's thoughtful and chilling reflections on an abortion: "I came to with this enormous sense of accomplishment, dying to find out what a brave and clever thing I'd done. You know for a moment I couldn't remember at all. And then I remembered." (p. 40)

> Carol Bolt, "Female Leads: Search for Feminism in the Theatre," in The Canadian Forum, Vol. LXVII, No. 770, June-July, 1987, pp. 37-40.

James Salter

1925-

American novelist, short story writer, dramatist, and script-writer.

In his fiction, Salter combines personal experience and imagination to explore the nature of desire while illuminating the dynamics of human relationships. Utilizing elements of literary impressionism, a technique derived from painting in which atmosphere and mood are evoked through subjective observation, Salter depicts tensions within his characters' psyches, focusing particularly on obsession, sexuality, ambition, and failure. In his prose, which has been compared to that of Ernest Hemingway for its staccato rhythms and direct tone, Salter employs such devices as repetition, imagery, and episodic narration to construct adventurous plots that probe aspects of human perception and motivation. Margaret Winchell Miller observed: "James Salter's novels celebrate passion in its loveliest and most insufferable moments. He is one who realizes the balance in which most of us live, between the holy and the imperfect; the gravity of desire that draws us naturally towards that which we perceive as good; the error in our judgement which leads us into temptation; the graceful fate that retrieves us from danger, redeems us in death. His books . . . give a glimpse, through the secret hexagons of the heart, 'deep into the life we all agree is so greatly to be desired.'"

Salter's first two novels, *The Hunters* (1957) and *The Arm of Flesh* (1961), reflect his experiences in the United States Air Force. Set in Korea and Germany, respectively, these works are noted for their technical proficiency and their lyrical treatments of life and death during wartime. *A Sport and a Pastime* (1967), which was described by Webster Schott as "a tour de force in erotic realism, a romantic cliff-hanger, an opaline vision of Americans in France," is generally considered Salter's first major work. Ostensibly an explicit account of a twenty-four-year-old college dropout's romantic involvement with a young woman while on an extended vacation in France, this novel is actually a fantasy invented by the narrator to compensate for inadequacies in his social and sexual experience. A study of desire and its inability to transform human existence, *A Sport and a Pastime* documents the narrator's failure to reconcile his imagination with reality.

In his next novel, *Light Years* (1975), Salter chronicles the dissolution of a twenty-year marriage of a moderately successful New York City architect and his culturally ostentatious wife. Related in a loosely connected series of impressionistic scenes, this work examines commitment, habit, and change while offering extensive digressions on highbrow culture and cuisine. *Solo Faces* (1979), which relates the story of a man's passion for mountain climbing, examines such typical Salter concerns as personal obsession and self-discovery. Salter's recent book, *Dusk and Other Stories* (1988), collects previously published and unpublished fiction from throughout his career. Displaying various styles, settings, and subjects, these pieces focus on many themes explored in his novels, including sexuality, desire, failure, exile, and death, while featuring shifting points of view and evocative imagery.

(See also *CLC*, Vol. 7 and *Contemporary Authors*, Vols. 73-76.)

THE VIRGINIA QUARTERLY REVIEW

[*The Arm of Flesh* is a] straightforward yarn about two fighter pilots lost from their Rhineland base in a thick fog with a fast dwindling fuel supply [that] . . . receives unusual treatment by the author who elects to tell his exciting tale in roundabout and piecemeal fashion through a dozen or so narrators, each of whom advances the action almost imperceptibly as meanwhile he discloses a sometimes pertinent fact about himself. If the intention were to heighten suspense, the device assumes an added invalidity, if only because the delay becomes not intolerable, but interminable. Each narrator speaks with the voice of his predecessor; none has a character or a personality of his own. One may indeed detect the insistent tones of the author himself, cozening his readers with his display of technique instead of getting on with the story. His lyrical attitude toward dying does result in a certain eloquence, but he rides a good many thousand feet below the late Antoine de Saint-Exupéry. (pp. lxxxiv-lxxxv)

A review of "The Arm of Flesh," in The Virginia Quarterly Review, *Vol. 37, No. 3, Summer, 1961, pp. lxxxiv-lxxxv.*

RONALD BRYDEN

The Arm of Flesh describes that private civilisation, scattered from airfield to airfield across the Continent, of young men from Alabama, Ohio, Minnesota, who guard a Europe we have never seen: a huge sky whose provinces are weather-systems, drifting up from Africa to the Arctic. . . . Mr. Salter achieves lyricism in his evocation of their life: scrambling from dark hangars to scale cold dawns, sprawling on barrack beds in farm-boy card games, reading little but comics, combing the Munich bars for girls; men with no skills but outracing birds and sound, who will be senile and twitching at thirty-five. If they survive: in a radio-play pattern of monologues, one voice taking the narrative from another, Mr. Salter tells the story of Cassada, the young Puerto Rican pilot who doesn't quite fit, is never quite accepted, and crashes trying to prove himself to the others. The scene of the crash, in grey, drizzling dusk over the airfield, has anguished suspense, but you know from the start Cassada must die. In such strong, closed societies, the primitive superstitions work: there is a doom upon the hero and outsider. Mr. Salter, who survived twelve years as a pilot, shows himself not only an insider but a kind of poet of his dizzy new element. (p. 48)

> Ronald Bryden, "Men at Arms," in The Spectator, Vol. 208, No. 6968, January 12, 1962, pp. 48-9.

WEBSTER SCHOTT

James Salter's *A Sport and a Pastime* slowly explodes. Arching gracefully, like a glorious 4th of July rocket, it illuminates the dark sky of sex. It's a tour de force in erotic realism, a romantic cliff-hanger, an opaline vision of Americans in France. Fiction survives through minor novels like this one. They assert its power to make us suffer shock, compassion, regret. They bring the private news history never records.

A West Pointer and former fighter pilot, Mr. Salter published two previous novels, *The Hunters* (1956) and *The Arm of Flesh* (1961). He wrote of air war in Korea and supersonic military society in Germany as if he were a pressure-suited poet of tissued metal and death. *A Sport and a Pastime* lyricizes the flesh and France with the same ardent intensity. With a jagged, faintly Hemingwayesque style, he wanders into the murk of reality and appearance. He goes beyond the animalistic use of human beings. He lifts the chains of conscience and finds personality locked against change by the past.

Salter's narrator is a voyeur of the imagination. A 24-year-old American, he lives in Autun, a village near Dijon, in the house of friends who lay siege to Paris, drinking the city dry. In retreat to the provinces, he lusts after a divorcée, breathes in bourgeois France and agonizes over the raptures of a chance acquaintance. A Yale drop-out, son of a famous critic and a suicide mother, traveling on borrowed money and driving a demonic automobile, Philip Dean drops by Autun for a few days and stays months. Dean, a born operator, immediately steals a 19-year-old French girl from a Negro G.I. The rest of the novel is a continuous journey of the soul via the flesh. . . .

This is a direct novel, not a grimy one. Salter celebrates the rites of erotic innovation and understands their literary uses. He creates a small, flaming world of sensualism inhabited by Dean and Anne-Marie, and invaded by the imagination of the narrator. We enter it. We feel it. It has the force of a hundred repressed fantasies. And it carries purpose: Salter details lust

in search of its passage into love. Sometimes it makes it. Here it can't.

Slowly eroticism fails. The reality of total human need intrudes into the golden bedrooms of the lovers' weekends. Anne-Marie may be Aphrodite; she's also a dumbbell with bad breath. She dreams babies and an American refrigerator. Dean is on a voyage to total sensations, death. His desire to give is feeble counterweight to his drive to take and consume. Devoid of hope—Karl Menninger's "dim awareness of wishes which, like dreams, tend to come true"—their relationship crumbles.

Like Joyce's artist paring his fingernails, Salter's narrator watches and imagines in cold isolation. As unable as the lover to break into fullness, he risks nothing and gains nothing. Against the background of sunlight, rains, the ancient vitality of France, he makes a ticking sound. He is a feeling gauge, flawed as a person and instantly forgettable as a character. He plays a functional role, picking up Salter's instructions in reality. Sex is beautiful. To live without it, is to be less than alive—in this case a throbbing, unoiled mechanical man. And to live for sex alone is to be less than human. *A Sport and a Pastime* succeeds as art must. It tells us about ourselves.

> Webster Schott, "Toujours L'Amour," in The New York Times Book Review, April 2, 1967, p. 47.

TIME, NEW YORK

Salter sets [*A Sport and a Pastime*] in France. His subject is the love affair between Anne-Marie Costallat, an 18-year-old who looks like a child but eats like a dock hand, and young Phillip Dean, a Yale dropout who has been wandering through Europe with "that touch of indolence and occasional luxury that comes only from having real resources."

The affair is viewed, or rather voyeured, by an unnamed narrator. In the hazy New-Novel fashion, the exact locale is uncertain: it may be Autun, or it may be Auxerre. And the events described may have happened or they may have been invented. As the narrator puts it: "I see myself as an *agent provocateur* or a double agent, first on one side—that of truth—and then on the other." He is also a shadowless personality, inept in his love life. Thus, to compensate for his own inadequacies, he exaggerates Dean's qualities almost to the point of inventing a new character; he fears his creation as he must fear "all men who are successful in love."

This curiously distilled method of storytelling proves effective and makes something lyrical of a rather commonplace romance. Dream-walking, the reader follows the narrator and his lovers through a lightly perfumed garden of erotic nuances. The encounters of Dean and Anne-Marie seem to reqire not reading but sensing, as if the touch of the eye were almost too much for reality. And when at last the dream breaks, it is not with a shatter but a silent splintering of crystal fragments. (pp. 120, 122)

> "Ways of Love," in Time, New York, Vol. 89, No. 15, April 14, 1967, pp. 120, 122.

ANATOLE BROYARD

In his last novel, *A Sport and a Pastime,* James Salter described a provocatively mismatched love affair so hauntingly that I couldn't for the life of me see how these people could possibly get along either with or without each other. Neither, apparently, could the author, for he unforgivably killed off his hero in a meaningless car crash. The thrilling question of the novel shriveled and died with him

Light Years is worse in several ways. The characters and their alleged incompatibility are both less interesting and less convincing. Once separated, they are even more boring than they were together. The woman dies, in her 40's, of a mysterious disease, and the man settles down to the most predictable sort of resignation. They are not only unredeemed: in retrospect, they are seen as insulting to our patience and our expectations. I feel like asking the author: "Didn't you have something more in mind? Do you really feel that you have fulfilled your obligations?"

The prose style of *A Sport and a Pastime* was brilliant. Much of the action occurred in Autun, a medieval French town, and Mr. Salter can describe rain falling in a square, seen from the window of the lovers' hotel, better than anyone I know. It is almost unbelievable what he can do with a few pigeons—just pigeons—rising or settling to the ground. He writes short sentences that are like caresses. He looks at a landscape or a corner of a town the way a lover looks at his mistress's body. After finishing *A Sport and a Pastime,* I forgave the awkwardness of the unnecessary narrator, the wasteful death of the hero, everything.

Light Years, though, is something else again. The prose is still rich and ambitious, but it seems exiled in the house on the Hudson where the characters live. I got the impression that the author was always trying to force mystery into American people and places. Everyone has a Lawrence Durrell sort of name: Viri, Nedra, Franca, Jivan, Daya, Nile, Arnaud. Even the dog is named Hadji.

Nedra, Viri's wife, reminds me of Mona in Henry Miller's *Tropic of Cancer.* I remember Mr. Miller wincing when his beloved Mona says, "There is no central hall in this house." Nedra says things like that " 'You're right,' she said abruptly. 'Celine was an absolute bastard.' " How the hell would she know? And "absolutely"? Like Mr. Durrell again, Mr. Salter condemns his people to speculative conversations, abortive attempts at aphorisms about large issues. One character, a man, actually says, "I adore biography." . . .

"Real goodness was different, it was irresistible, murderous, it had victims like any other aggression; in short, it conquered. We must be vague, we must be gentle, we are killing people otherwise, whatever our intentions, we are crushing them beneath a vision of light." "The inward curve of the bidet's edge, the smoothness of it gave him for a moment a sensation of deepest longing." These are fair samples of the degeneration of Mr. Salter's prose style between *A Sport and a Pastime* and *Light Years.* The fact that the character concerned had never seen a woman on a bidet makes the image that much more affected. And "light," by the way, appears on almost every other page in this book. The author glues the novel together with it, using it as a structural constant or point of reference in the aimless movement of the characters. When Nedra feels lonely in her German hotel, after leaving Viri in America, she thinks, "swallows were screaming over the stained roofs of Rome." Why Rome? Because it's baroque, dummy!

Yes, of course, *Light Years* is about the crisis of marriage. Is there any other kind of novel? It is not enough to be content, even happy; there's a whole world out there waiting to be experienced. We must cut every tie, turn every stone, open up every blade of the self like a Swedish army knife and slash, saw, snip, file, screw, pick, scale and punch away for all we are worth. As Wallace Stevens said:

> These days of disinheritance, we feast
> On human heads.

Anatole Broyard, "Ending in the Middle," in The New York Times, *June 25, 1975, p. 41.*

RODERICK NORDELL

James Salter's fourth novel [*Light Years*] fondly, ruefully preserves the essence of a certain comfortable and complacent stratum of New York living that will become history if the age of austerity arrives and that even now tends to be a subject of satire rather than romanticization. For unfamed architect Viri and wife Nedra, it's a house in the country and work, pleasure, shopping in the city: "They had certain places for everything, discovered in the days when they were first married. . . ." Their friends and possessions are interesting. They nurture warm family rituals, entertain with seasoned style, go to parties that sometimes include celebrities, mean no harm to anyone.

Mr. Salter draws them to appear the way another couple looks to Viri: "He tried to see the blemishes in their contentment, but the surface blinded him." . . .

But there are blemishes in their contentment, as in the book itself, whose dubious plotting and outlook finally outweigh its impressionistic successes. Viri and Nedra have affairs, as a daughter later does, and Mr. Salter's prose becomes almost ludicrously awestruck in describing their sexual feelings. They are so essentially self-centered that they seem compartmentalized from the tragedies of others. In a sense they are insufferable. After all of Nedra's self-pleasing efforts to reject "ordinary life" she is asking for the daughterly teen-age outburst she gets: "I want to be like everyone else!"

Sometimes Mr. Salter's writing seems as effortfully unordinary as Nedra. But it is a measure of his skill that he presents her in a way to explain other characters' conflicting estimates of her as "very generous" and "the most selfish woman on earth." And the ironical and the typical touchingly mingle in such moments as when, after we have begun to see beneath the surfaces of these lives, a grown-up neighbor girl pays a visit and is "drenched with love for these people who, though they had lived nearby all through her childhood, it seemed she was suddenly seeing for the first time, who were treating her as someone she longed at that moment to be: one of themselves."

Roderick Nordell, "Comfortable New Yorkers Portrayed in Skillful Impressionistic Novel," in The Christian Science Monitor, *July 30, 1975, p. 23.*

MICHAEL IRWIN

Light Years is made up of glimpses, half-scenes, reveries, snatches of talk. It describes impressionistically the dissolution, over two decades, of a once happy marriage. The husband, Viri Berland, is an architect, sufficiently prosperous and not untalented, but never able to fulfil his higher professional ambitions. Nedra, his wife, is beautiful, "interesting", a woman of taste. For some years they create together a secure life for themselves and their two daughters, a life of pets, excursions, stories, games, endless summer holidays. But temperamentally they are too dissimilar: they begin to drift apart. Each takes a lover. Viri is essentially a mild man, eager to keep the marriage together for the sake of the children, or even for its own sake, for wholeness. Nedra feels obliged to seek freedom, to explore her own individuality. Eventually they divorce and go their different ways: Viri to a doubtful second marriage, Nedra to a succession of experiments and affairs. As they enter middle age the question is how far the memories and experiences of the happier years can sustain them in the face of loneliness, illness or even death.

Odd transitions, unexpected emphases and omissions, and especially the cumulative effect of many passages of rapt description convey a dream-like sense of the passing of time, the shift of relationships, the growing-up of children. James Salter creates a languorous atmosphere in which motives, aims and needs seem uncertain, and the patterns of living establish themselves unperceived. By the standards it sets itself, however, *Light Years* is less than fully successful. The author works too hard to sustain the dominant mood. Too many of the descriptive passages are a little overwritten, a little too self-conscious. The short sentences can seem mannered, the similes obtrusive. Hyperbole comes too easily: repeatedly characters are "overwhelmed" or "stunned".

The very scheme of the book involves a calculated risk. So much is to be left out:

> Life is weather. Life is meals. Lunches on a blue checked cloth on which salt has spilled. The smell of tobacco. Brie, yellow apples, wood-handled knives.

Life is these things, of course, but it is a great many other things besides, most of them less obviously picturesque. The pattern of the novel demands that the characters are almost invariably seen in an aesthetically interesting context. As a result they and their doings come to seem insubstantial. Work and the workaday are inconspicuous and a conventional notion of Good Living bulks far too large. Viri and Nedra spend too much of their time sipping Margaux or St. Raphael or retsina or ouzo or Rémy Martin and talking lightly of Mahler or Céline or Europe or Nureyev or India. It is not easy to take their agonies or their ecstasies as seriously as the author invites us to. *Light Years* is a graceful novel but neither in style nor material is it sufficiently vital to lend power to the author's larger comments on life and death.

> *Michael Irwin, "Built on Sand," in* The Times Literary Supplement, *No. 3877, July 2, 1976, p. 815.*

VANCE BOURJAILY

Although it uses a technical device that may not please every reader, James Salter's *Solo Faces* is on the whole a beautifully fashioned and satisfying novel. The story it tells is not so much about mountain climbing as of a man obsessed with the sport.

Before we know that he is a climber, we meet Vernon Rand while he is working with a younger man, a student named Gary, on the roof of a church in California. Gary connects Rand with "a breed of aimless wanderers . . . working as mason's helpers, carpenters, parking cars. They somehow keep a certain dignity, they are surprisingly unashamed.". . . The young man both scorns and envies these "men whose friend he would like to be, stories he would like to know."

Gary doesn't stay on in the book to learn Rand's story, but before their encounter is over Rand has saved Gary's life, a deft piece of foreshadowing, for later, in the Alps, Rand will save others.

Before this can happen, Rand must shed his aimlessness. It happens on a brief climb, at the end of which he meets an old friend named Cabot, "the kind of man who mapped out continents." Rand himself "had had a brilliant start and then defected. Something had weakened in him. That was long ago. He was like an animal that has wintered somewhere, in the shadow of a hedgerow or barn, and one morning mudstained and dazed, shakes itself and comes to life."

The images and the rhythm of these descriptions are suggestive of Mr. Salter's rhetorical control.

As a hero, and he is one, Vernon Rand is laconic, a realist, a loner, and bad news for the women who find him attractive. There are several such women, as well as some minor male characters in this short novel, and Mr. Salter has developed a resourcefully elliptical way of describing them. Here, for example, enters Susan,

> a girl he first saw outside American Express. She was blonde, clean-faced and an heiress. . . . In spite of her life, she had a healthy appearance. She was tanned from being in Sicily. Her arms had a golden down. She was scrubbed, alert, casual.
>
> "Where are you staying?" she asked. He was her friend, she'd made up her mind. "Can I trust you?" She had gone to good schools, a brilliant student in fact. She'd been married to a man in Kenya. "He was fabulous but he was a drunk. . . . You want to go in here?" she asked.

Along with the elision of Rand's replies, and the compression of time, Mr. Salter has moved us temporarily into Susan's point of view. It is an arbitrary shift in point of view, a questionable technical device that some excellent writers use freely— Robert Stone, for example, in *Dog Soldiers.*

This technique is exactly the opposite of dramatic irony. When dramatic irony is used, the author shares a more complete understanding with the reader than with the point-of-view character. In its reverse, the reader is somewhat excluded from what the author and the character know because the point of view has been switched.

Sometimes this can be effective. For example, Rand is leading a rescue party up a difficult and dangerous body called the Dru to reach a pair of stranded Italian climbers, one of them injured. We see some of it through the eyes of Dennis, a less experienced man: "All that allowed him to go on, all that preserved him from panic, was a kind of numbness, an absolute concentration on every hold and a faith complete, unthinking, in the tall figure above." And later: "Dennis had outclimbed his fear. An exhilaration that was almost dizzying came over him. He was one of them, he was holding his own." Good enough. Since we have been up the Dru with Rand before, it is refreshing to make the second ascent with someone quite different.

But in the violent, climactic sequence on which the main action ends, the technique becomes risky. Out of the mountains and back in California, Rand is doing some hair-raising stuff with a gun; but now the point of view has switched to that of Rand's friend Cabot, who is crippled. Since Cabot doesn't know what Rand is up to, neither do we. Whether it is wise to deny the reader full knowledge of what is happening at a crucial point is something each storyteller has to decide for himself. But there is this risk in the denial: that the reader will have to come to a stop sometime, during or after the scene, and turn back to discover what has been missed. Whatever advantages the method may have, it is not a good servant of narrative drive.

Perhaps I have made too much of this. Like the sport it celebrates, *Solo Faces* is an adventurous and exciting book.

Vance Bourjaily, "*Different Points of View,*" in The New York Times Book Review, *August 5, 1979, p. 11.*

VERNON SCANNELL

Solo Faces carries on the back of its dust-wrapper encomia from Norman Mailer, Al Alvarez, Irwin Shaw, and a more restrained commendation from Graham Greene. It is a readable piece of work but not, I think, a novel of any real importance. The principal characters are two Americans, Rand and Cabot, both dedicated mountaineers, whom we first meet in California where Rand has been working as a building labourer and shacking up with a divorced lady who has a twelve-year-old son. A chance reunion occurs: Cabot says that he has recently been climbing in France; Rand, inspired by his friend's stories of the vertiginous challenges to be found in Europe, leaves his mistress and goes to Chamonix where, after surviving a hard winter of privation and loneliness, he is joined by Cabot. Together they climb the Dru, a mountain in the French Alps which for decades has been regarded by the cognoscenti as unscalable. Cabot is injured on the climb and his companion has virtually to carry him to the summit.

As a consequence of their achievement in mastering the formidable Dru they become locally and nationally famous, and Rand is impartially corrupted by adulation and relatively soft living. When he later attempts another hazardous and solitary climb he finds that he has lost that obsessive, even suicidal, determination to succeed that must be part of a mountaineer's psychological equipment.

Rand has a number of sexual encounters, one with a woman he lives with for a time in Chamonix who becomes pregnant. We are told that he loves her but little of his behaviour would appear to confirm this and he tells her that he does not want her to have the child. Realizing that he is committed to the conquest of barren mountain-faces she leaves him and returns to a former lover. . . .

The men and women in *Solo Faces* are neat bundles of attributes rather than complex, contradictory, human beings. Rand is presented as the Noble Savage, physically beautiful, brave, strong and brainless. Cabot, the author suggests, has a few ideas to rummage around in, but from the little we see of them they don't amount to a row of beans.

One shouldn't, however, be over-critical. Though *Solo Faces* loses momentum once the climbing has to stop, the prose, deriving from Hemingway, with a few tints from glossier influences, is always adequate and, in the descriptions of Rand's responses to his first visit to Paris, succeeds admirably in conveying the excitement, sexuality, the sense of suppressed violence, the watchful greed and cynicism beneath the lyric surface. The account of the two climbers' ordeal on the Dru is also very well handled and, on the whole, Salter manages to avoid the sentimentality that so often and fatally softens the fiction of those writers, usually American, who would extol the hairy, masculine virtues of physical strength, resolution and comradeship.

Vernon Scannell, "*Rock Steady,*" in The Times Literary Supplement, *No. 4012, February 15, 1980, p. 171.*

FRANCIS KING

I can think of no novel that comes closer to explaining the nature of [mountain climbing's] mystique than James Salter's *Solo Faces.* The force that drives his hero, Vernon Rand, and Rand's colleague and rival, Jack Cabot, to make their always uncomfortable, often painful and sometimes dangerous ascents of rock faces in California or glaciers in the Alps, is akin to the force that, in the West, drives a man or woman to abandon family, friends and personal possessions and enter a closed order, and, in the East, to squat under pelting rain or scorching sun beside a begging-bowl. 'This thing is bigger than myself' is the explanation, spoken or unspoken, of such people; and because it is bigger than themselves, it leads them to perform actions that, to people incapable of seeing the 'bigness' of the 'thing', often seem ruthlessly self-centered.

At the beginning of the novel, Rand, who is working as a builder in Los Angeles, is shacked up with a husbandless woman, whose adolescent son he takes climbing with him. It is almost without a qualm that he abandons the two of them and sets off for France, where he plans to climb in the Alps. In Chamonix he takes up with another woman, a half-English shop-assistant, and eventually gets her with child; but her too he deserts, fearing that domesticity will get in the way of his 'vocation'.

Most of Rand's climbing feats are performed alone; and when there are others with him, there is little of the comradeship that shared danger usually produces. He is instrumental in saving first his arch-rival, Cabot, and then two Italians marooned by accident and a storm on the Dru; but the intensity of these shared experiences fades as soon as the men have descended from thin air and the glitter of snowy peaks to the mundane life of bars, lodging-houses, restaurants and tourist shops.

Rand lives shamelessly on the women whom his spreading fame attracts to him. No less shamelessly, he swaps one woman for another, out of caprice, boredom or the fear of being trapped. His mountaineering gift is akin to a gift for music or mathematics—it is independent of any distinction in any other sphere of life. When he climbs, he becomes, like a great musician or a great mathematician, 'inspired', and he himself acknowledges this: 'Supreme climbs need more than courage, they need inspiration.'

Climbing also yields an intense aesthetic satisfaction. 'There are routes the boldness and logic of which are overwhelming. The purely vertical is, of course, the ideal. If one could follow, or nearly, the path that a pebble takes falling from the top and climb scarcely deviating to right or left . . . one would leave behind something inextirpable, a line that led past a mere summit.'

Eventually Jack Cabot is destroyed by a combination of hubris and loss of nerve; and Rand forsakes climbing, having detected in himself the onset of similar defects. Rand has had a vision of 'an immortal image of himself high up among the ridges'; but now, he has realised, this image is only too mortal.

The actual climbs, even to someone like myself who does not know the difference between a piton and a crampon and would have no idea what to do if commanded 'Off belay!', are wonderfully exciting; and Mr. Salter has a rare gift for evoking landscape and weather—now the aridity of California and now the lusciousness of France. He resembles Hemingway in the economy of means with which he communicates the most complex of emotions.

As one reads his novel, one realises that though, ostensibly, its theme is 'What is a man profited, if he shall gain every summit and lose his own soul?'—and though, on that level, it makes a gripping yarn—yet the singlemindedness with which Rand sets out on his lonely conquests is a potent metaphor of the artistic vocation. Climbing and the highest artistic achievements demand a similar ruthlessness both with self and with others; and in each the aspirant may suffer an inexplicable loss of nerve or of inspiration, so that in a moment he plunges from the airiest heights to the darkest depths. So too, just as 'the mountains make you do it' (Rand's words), great literature, art or music imposes the same kind of imperative in its creation.

This is a strange, haunting book, the climax of which—in which Rand uses the threat of a gun to make his crippled former buddy get out of a wheel-chair and walk—baffles me. But it has illuminated the whole mystique of climbing for me, as some inspired preacher might illuminate some hermetic religion.

Francis King, "Climbers," in The Spectator, *Vol. 244, No. 7910, February 16, 1980, p. 22.*

MARGARET WINCHELL MILLER

Admittedly, Salter's first two novels, **The Hunters** and **The Arm of Flesh** (1961), are not especially noteworthy at first glance; they manifest ordinary episodes, characters and details which reflect his twelve-year Air Force career (1945-1957). And they resemble a dozen other first novels whose central attraction is high adventure and a neatly expedited plot. As structurally linear as these two novels are, however, they could not escape critics' watchful eyes for a perception and a voice unusually poetic. "A distinctly experimental . . . deliberately oblique technique . . . a clean, luminous quality," wrote *Kirkus* of **The Arm of Flesh**. Salter was heralded by *Spec* as "a kind of poet of his dizzy new element" [see excerpt above by Ronald Bryden]. And it is the best of this poetry which trademarks the last three of his five novels—**A Sport and a Pastime, Light Years,** and **Solo Faces. A Sport and a Pastime** (1967) marks what Salter himself deems the real beginning of his career as a writer. It reveals his two most compelling gifts: a poet's ear for lyricism, and an obsession—like the novel's young Phillip Dean—with the power of desire. Under its influence Dean is drawn to France in an ingenuous pursuit of happiness which becomes the bloodline of Salter's subsequent works:

> 'Life is composed of certain basic elements,' [Dean] says. 'Of course, there are a lot of impurities, that's what's misleading . . . What I'm saying may sound mystical, but in everybody, in all of us, there's the desire to find those elements somehow, to discover them, you know . . . When you enter certain rooms, when you look at certain faces, suddenly you realize you're in the presence of them. Do you know what I mean?'
>
> 'Of course I do,' she says. 'If you could achieve that, you'd have everything.'
>
> 'And without it you have . . .' he shrugs 'a life.'

It is this exaltation of life's pleasures, this search to discover the basic elements that perfect it, which illuminates Salter's last three novels. They are rare and deliberative chronicles of passion that have for some reason existed only on the outskirts of commercial success. Not that popularity is the writer's ticket to a glorious life. But fortunately, in the past year Salter's last three novels have been re-released in paperback. And as *Time*

magazine wrote of **A Sport and a Pastime,** "There are best-selling novelists who could learn from this cool and quiet book" [see excerpt above]. Perhaps, in an age in which there is a marked absence of passion, and a host of "bestsellers" which reflect that somber reality, Salter's day of atonement has come.

Life's imperfections, or "impurities," are rarely illuminated in Salter's fiction. Instead he elects to reconcile a world and its relationships in terms of what is graceful and splendid, unblemished, perfect. The result is a tension which exists *within* his characters rather than *between* them as each faces a disheartening acknowledgement of what is, after all, a flawed, malignant world. Phillip Dean, a 24-year-old self-seeking nomad; Viri and Nedra Berland in their rich yet paradoxically empty lives; and Vernon Rand, whose single ambition it is to scale the most dangerous mountains in France, have a dream in common. They seek life's purest elements; they desire, in Dean's words, Everything. (pp. 2-3)

The settings of Salter's novels are evidential. Paris; Chamonix; Autun, France; even the Victorian house belonging to Viri and Nedra Berland, although they're clearly New Yorkers, is furnished in the European style—its wines, its arts. They are straight out of Salter's own history, reflecting his early years in New York, his extensive travels, his seclusion in Magagnose, a small village in northern France. And they are the first and most obvious clues toward his own perception of where life's purest elements lie.

If place is a distinguishing feature of Salter's paradise, then voice is the qualifying factor. It is usually inappropriate to definitively categorize a novelist's voice and probably, in the end, inaccurate. But it is a result of his language that Salter has been called, by various critics, a "sensuous, suggestive, ethereal, atmospheric, pointillist, impressionistic" writer. The comparative reference to impressionism is even more apropos, perhaps, than critic Duncan Fallowell of *The Spectator* (1976) intended [see *CLC*, Vol. 7]. Very likely he perceived the same "eye" in Salter's fiction that Jules Laforgue, the French poet, admired in the painter Monet: "The Impressionist eye is the most advanced eye in human evolution," wrote Laforgue, "that which up to now has seized upon and rendered the most complicated nuances known." Salter's "eye" is a kind of combined organ synthesizing rhythm and tone, a complex sense which memorizes sounds and repeats them in periodic cadence so that the nuances of every paragraph sing. . . . Descriptions are studded with exaggerated perceptions of movement, like film on an oversized screen, the images rolling slowly forward:

> Four in the afternoon. The blue sky of France *flooding* with clouds. Snow is *streaming* into the headlights, *pouring* against us, *exploding* on the glass . . . Across the road a river of snow is *flowing, spilling* sideways, *shifting, rushing* away.

One reviewer called this "relentlessly poetic prose . . . strained, unearned lyricism." Perhaps it is a matter of taste. . . . Clearly neither the poetry nor its precept is incidental in Salter's fiction. It is part of a deliberate effort to recreate, just as Monet did in his day, a vision of this world in a more hallowed and flawless light. **A Sport and a Pastime, Light Years** and **Solo Faces,** despite their differences, are variations on this theme of elusive perfection. They reveal a curious movement in Salter's work, a pursuit which circles inward, centering finally—in **Solo Faces**—at a point designated *self.* It is an indication that Salter remains faithful to the credo expressed by Dean—and, like Dean, pursues a desire to discover those several basic "elements" of perfect life and to place himself, and all of us, in their presence.

A Sport and a Pastime is ostensibly the story of Phillip Dean, a 24-year-old Yale dropout on holiday in France who, like Fitzgerald's young Jay Gatz, attempts to spring from his Platonic conception of himself. Salter has created an Adam whose Eden lies abroad. Episodic soirees with Anne-Marie Costallat, an 18-year-old shop girl, soon reveal his second desire—naturally, to lay claim to his Eve. Both of Dean's dreams are realized through a baptism of sorts, in the night he spends with her; the affair consummates, at once, partner and place: "The sum of small acts begins to unite them, the pure calculus of love . . . Dean lies beside her. The real France, he is thinking. The real France. He is lost in it, in the smell of the very sheets. The next morning they do it again." These bedroom scenes fill the book. Described in meticulous detail, they serve to initiate and fervently recommit Dean to his new mainland. The *New York Times Book Review* [see excerpt above by Webster Schott]—and many other reviewers—hailed Salter for "celebrating the rites of erotic innovation" while other more prudent critics—*Library Journal*—took offense at what they called "vigorous 'love' scenes (which) occur with the regularity of TV commercials in language suitable for telling it to marines." But the incredible frequency of this act, the insatiable lust and self-indulgence with which it is carried out, is the core of Dean's existence. Northrop Frye notes in his *Anatomy of Criticism* that "every crucial periodicity of experience: dawn, sunset, the phases of the moon, seed-time and harvest, the equinoxes and the solstices, birth, initiation, marriage and death, get rituals attached to them." For Dean, sex is all of these things, a ritual linking him not only to Anne-Marie but to his promised land. This consuming passion moves him, just months after his arrival, to seek his return plane ticket as a means to afford prolonging the dream existence. Dean's only chance at wealth—the wealth he left behind him—lies in the sale of his American identity; in a single redeeming gesture, like a grasp of the apple, he inherits the new and beloved place and a handful of its currency—his ticket, for a time, to survival: "He has money, everything is changed. . . . He can speak the language suddenly with (it) in his possession. . . . They are important, these inexhaustible ten-franc notes. They are the essence of invention. They are the warrants of his life."

It is only the most genuine believer who can earn a place in Paradise. Clearly—sadly—Dean's new loyalty can last only as long as the expendable "warrants of his life" hold out. Foolishly he lavishes them on Anne-Marie in his deep confusion of a love affair with person and place. And in the same way Dean is convinced by Anne-Marie's purity to join her, he is soon enlightened to her imperfections. And this, too, changes his life. Immediately after selling his ticket, his pockets bulging with new franc notes, Dean splurges on an enormous dinner which Anne-Marie promises she is hungry enough to finish. Afterwards, as they walk home, she without warning "vomits up the whole meal at her feet, frogs' legs and oysters splashing onto the stone." At that moment Dean is certain he will not marry her. In fact, he is so "depressed by her imperfections" that he will last only a few months longer in France. It is when his sister visits him in Paris that his realization of "Life's basic elements" strikes and only pages later that he begs her for the $350.00 which will take him home, buy back an identity that he had attempted to barter, like a soul, for the heart of the thing he loved.

The end is quick in coming; in the chapter immediately following Dean's flight home (we are not told how much later it happens) Anne-Marie announces his death—a car accident of which he was an innocent victim. And realistically there is no other way the novel could end. Dean had vowed to send for her, a lie which no one, including the reader who has come to know his conscience, can believe. Where is the tragedy in this conclusion, then? The sympathy evoked is not for either of the lovers. Dean's sudden death is more a confirmation of his exodus than it is a heartbreak. We do not care for him enough to mourn his loss; nor have we grown to love Anne-Marie, who has served primarily to trigger, reflect and magnify his dreams. Without our knowing it, Salter has disguised the tragic figure as the narrator of this novel who all along has related their doomed affair.

Although this purports to be the story of Phillip Dean, his desires are made known through the consciousness of an anonymous "somnambulist" historian who tells his story. But with Dean's death the several lives which once so intimately converged through him immediately unravel. The man we knew as Dean is now no more than a legend; Anne-Marie vanishes into the arms of France. And shutting the book we realize that we have just been witness to a queer yet convincing trick. The narrator is a magician; the story he has related is not a real story at all, but a product of his self-conscious imagination. Details of the love affair—and he had repeatedly made this clear—have been invented, fabricated, created in the best of his own image. Dean is, as Virginia Woolf said all characters must be, merely a view; personality has been avoided at all costs. *A Sport and a Pastime,* rather than being a tale of two lovers, is instead an intimate glimpse of one man's vision of paradise, of paradise lost. Reading it is rather like spying on the mind of a self-proclaimed God who has created and is responsible for all that we see. (pp. 3-6)

This is narrative in its purest form, *narrative* being derived from the Latin root *gnoscere, to know*. The tale, born in the mind of the one who tells it, entitles its narrative Creator to all the liberties of invention. Such duplicity is difficult to take seriously in a novel which has fooled us into thinking of Dean as its hero, of Autun and Anne-Marie as its story. "We are all at his mercy," Salter warns of Dean. "We are subject to his friendship, his love. It is the principles of his world to which we respond, which we seek to find in ourselves." If this is so, what remains when Dean is gone is not the ghost of what he was but the ghost of what he dreamed. His principles must be traced back to the narrator who has created him— inevitably, to Salter's own perceptions of a flawed, inadequate world blurred, changed and imagined to perfection.

Salter gives evidence—as though each possession were a component of the crime—of what it is to be "rich" in Dean's eyes, in the sense of having Everything. He relates riches to knowledge, knowledge to power: as Dean enters Anne-Marie "he discovers the world. He knows the source of numbers, the path of stars"; her breasts "hang sweetly . . . like handfuls of money"; the new francs allow him to speak her language; his eye is drawn to "the chaste gold of cufflinks, a gold watchband, the mesh dense as grain, a gold lighter from Cartier. . ." It is interesting, if not crushing, to also recall Fitzgerald's paradigm of wealth which culminates in Gatsby's demise—the expensive car, the beautiful shirts, ebullient meals, stunning women draped over the divan. All of this results in an equally tragic finale: death to the visionary, the woman's collapse into the nearest embrace, and a narrator who can do nothing more than observe as the curtain falls, which Nick does:

> They were careless people, Tom and Daisy—they
> smashed up things and creatures and then retreated

back into their money or their vast carelessness, or whatever it was that kept them together. . . .

And as Salter finally must—"They visit friends," he says of Anne-Marie and the man she has married, "talk, go home in the evening, deep in the life we all agree is so greatly to be desired." Desire is the password concluding this novel, and it is the *mot d'ordre* which opens all doors to Salter's work. Here he admits and names the particular gravity that keeps us moving. It is the impetus behind his creation of Dean, behind Dean's infatuation with Anne-Marie, and finally behind the credo which leads Dean home. Roethke defines this force in his poem "The Manifestation": "What does what it should do needs nothing more. / The body moves, though slowly, toward desire. / We come to something without knowing why." And it is, with the same assurance, voiced later in Salter's *Light Years:* "If you do what you really should do, you will have what you want." In his desire, the narrator/dreamer, like Salter, is perpetually drawn to the source of his discontent, the real, imperfect world. His creation of Dean and the affair is actually a *recreation* as he alters his perceptions of reality and magnifies life's certain perfect elements to compensate for its countless impurities.

If desire is the essential element, what appears to be the least "pure" in Salter's fiction, and the greatest source of man's discontent, is the object of his desire, women. Or perhaps it would be more fair to say that his *relationships* are his undoing. As Jorge Borges wrote, "Man is the imperfect librarian in a universe which can only be the work of a god." (*Ficciones,* "The Library of Babel") Salter illustrates relationships as man's only means of cataloguing his inborn desires. Clearly it is our nature to attempt to satisfy those desires with which we were born. But our imperfections are most manifest in our passionate, often misdirected, affections. Thus, the "pursuit of happiness" is very often fruitless or, at best, moves us only a few steps closer to the *something* Roethke says we seek rather than bringing us to its gates. Salter hesitates to name this "something." Dean calls it "life's basic elements." Borges calls it God:

> In some shelf of some hexagon, there must exist a book which is the cipher and a perfect compendium *of all the rest:* some librarian has perused it, and it is analogous to a god . . . Many pilgrimages have sought Him out. How to locate the secret hexagon which harbored it? Someone proposed a regressive approach: in order to locate book A, first consult book B which will indicate the location of A; in order to locate book B, first consult C and so on ad infinitum. . ."
>
> *Ficciones,* "The Library of Babel"

It is the search for this source of perfection (life's elements, God, if you will) with which Salter through his characters is obsessed. Viri Berland, in fact, at one point in *Light Years,* confirms Borges' allegory: "The best education comes from knowing only one book," he tells Nedra. "Purity comes from that, and proportion, and the comfort of always having an example close at hand." In *A Sport and a Pastime* Salter merely hints at the desolation brought on by the process of seeking perfection. Dean is able to come only a single step closer to it before his death. In *Light Years* (1975), however, Salter conducts a slow tour, via the lives of Viri and Nedra Berland, through several "hexagons" towards the supernal volume A.

While this novel is not a sequel to *A Sport and a Pastime,* the life assumed by the Berlands in their house on the Hudson is reminiscent of Dean's prediction about the future he would spend with Anne-Marie: "Yes, Dean thinks, America. They will live in a studio downtown with a small garden, a terrace perhaps, and a few good friends." Viri and Nedra are Phillip Dean and Anne-Marie twenty years later in a marriage wearing away at its seams. And New York or not, their subsistence is filled with Dean's "elements"—the same criminal components that won his heart: French knives, Brie cheese, LU's imported biscuits which Viri's daughters (*Papa,* they call him) adore. Extensive conversations of and over elaborate repasts: Grand marnier, Pernod, *pâté maison,* cassis, *fromages,* Cinzano, *rosti, paella,* ouzo, Margaux, *bollito misto,* brandy, *tagliatelle* and more. So much more that a few reviewers reduced *Light Years* to "foolishness . . . a book about food and drink." But these are drastic simplifications of Salter's intent. It is admittedly puzzling at first to see Nedra move about with such facility in this highborn, Mediterranean life. The Berlands are middle class, we are told, Viri an architect of minor talent, and Nedra has never travelled anywhere, not even to Canada. But the *paella* and Pernod are not an arbitrary *mise en scène.* They imply a double life, a second set of values which pertain only to a dream reality. Again it is this duplicity, as in *A Sport and a Pastime,* which compels Viri and Nedra to move—though slowly—toward their individual desires, eventually bringing a separation of lives.

It is probably the eroticism that saved *A Sport and a Pastime* from the several somewhat caustic sorts of reviews that *Light Years* received. The *New York Times Book Review* called Dean's story "a tour de force in erotic realism" [see excerpt above by Webster Schott]. "Dream-walking," wrote *Time* magazine, "the reader follows the narrator and his lovers through a lightly perfumed garden of erotic nuances" [see excerpt above]. Because it is a longer and seemingly more complex novel, *Light Years* tricked some readers—reviewers, anyway—into expecting a more commercially "readable" or linear work. But this is impressionism, not realism; Salter's fiction must be read keeping in mind the "complicated nuances rendered." *Light Years* is a Bible to its own religion, supporting the theology that "there are really two kinds of life. There is, as Viri says, the one people believe you are living, and there is the other. It is this other which causes the trouble, this other we long to see." Salter illustrates the prayers and proverbs of lone disciples, the pilgrimage of two people whose lives are devoted to discovering this "other" life, the hidden and mysterious perfection they desire, the "cipher and compendium of all the rest."

At its simplest level, *Light Years* is a memoir—the record of a marriage which in time, like worn rope, unbraids of itself, its twin strands drifting in opposite directions. That both Nedra and Viri become involved in extramarital affairs implies an injurious regression, a moving away from the union which was meant to be their source of strength. But regression, if you recall, is Boges' proposal. The difference in the Berlands' search is their method. Unfortunately, whether possessed more by greed or by insecurity, the imperfect librarian is curiously unwilling to give up whatever truth it is that he holds—be it library book or lover—and equally unwilling to resist any temptation which promises something more. And it is in this double grasp, the opening of book B before closing book C, that the Berlands' complex *ménages à trois* are formed. Salter portrays love as a comparative practice, a measurement of one emotion against another like hypotheses of truth. But whatever the method, there remains an impetus to progress towards the object of desire. Thus the pilgrimage—the library tour—is begun.

Viri and Nedra's several affairs prompt the periodic introspection involved in any quest of the spirit. Prayer, in the traditional sense, serves this purpose as a reverent petition— a thanksgiving, an adoration, a confession, a call for guidance and direction—to the god one worships and wishes to reach. The "prayers" voiced by Viri and Nedra, or those moments when each cries out to what he desires and moves slowly towards it, measure their individual progress. Desire, again, is the vehicle by which they are moved, but the objects of their desire differ greatly and therein lies the rub.

Of the pair it is Viri's steps which are most easily traced. It is 1958; Nedra has been Viri's wife for seven years—the seven fat years, perhaps. What has gone before we cannot know, but in the course of one afternoon whatever loyalty he has practiced in their marriage is broken. Viri's attraction to his secretary culminates in an impulsive affair very much like the night Dean spends with Anne-Marie: "[Viri] touched his forehead to her like a servant, like a believer in God. He could not speak. He embraced her knees." Afterwards they walk to a museum to see the Egyptian jewelry. "Do you know who Isis is?" "A goddess," says Kaya. "Yes," Viri answers. "Another one." There is a brief stroke of guilt resulting from this disobedient devotion when Viri must face Nedra. Beguiled by temptation, he did eat, and is ashamed. But more importantly, he has discovered the secret and carnal pleasures of passion revealed to him by this other woman:

> In some way he was suddenly equal to [Nedra] his love did not depend on her alone, it was more vast, a love for women, largely ungratified, an unattainable love focused for him in this one wilful, mysterious creature, but not only this one. He had divided his agony; it was cleaved at last.

This theme—women for women's sake—is reminiscent of Dean who adored everything innately female about Anne-Marie (His lips formed *reverent* phrases, his hands touched her *carefully*) but none of the qualities that characterized the particular woman that she was. It was those particulars, in fact—the fever blister on her chin, her "cheap shoes," her bad English, the poverty of which she was a product—that he considered imperfections. It was her simple sexuality that he instinctively desired, as Adam desired Eve. So Viri has discovered a second Eve, as Dean undoubtedly would have, had he lived to see the day. He wants "to speak to her, to fall on his knees before her" in a primitive and passionate idolatry. The helplessness of his devotion is clarified when one afternoon he visits Kaya's apartment to find her with another lover: "His existence vanished: 'I need you,' he said. 'I can't do anything without you.'" Viri's realization destroys him. But it is one which will come to him again, even more urgently, later when Nedra leaves him. Though Viri worships not god but a pagan goddess, Salter uses him to confirm in a peculiar way a theme inherent in the Christian pursuit of holiness: that it is not only possible but necessary for one to lose his life in order to eventually find it. While this is Viri's only real "affair," and while it is quite short-lived, Kaya remains fixed in his consciousness as the idol he has allowed her to become. In fact, she takes on all the traits of an omnipresent God. Viri envisions her in place of the young woman behind the pastry counter; in his dreams she steps out of an elevator, a man on either arm; at a restaurant when he is with Nedra, Kaya appears and sits just tables away. And when she leaves, Viri—in the humble posture of a seraphim—hides his face.

In our vanity, we are accustomed to claiming what we love. Those of us who are willing and wise somehow find the courage, albeit in the last moments of our lives, to let go. "The others," Rilke writes in his *Book of Hours,* "will not learn / that in the beggary of their wandering / they cannot claim a bond with any thing, / but, driven from possessions they have prized, / not by their own belongings recognized, / they can own wives no more than they own flowers, whose life is alien and apart from ours." Viri is one of these others. His "cleaved agony," though it taps an otherwise unknown vast love for women, separates him from Nedra, the single source of affection and stability he had come to trust. And he is devastated when she drives away just days after their divorce has become final: "He was suddenly parted from his life . . . the simple greed that makes one cling to a woman left him suddenly desperate, stunned." Salter is persistent in emphasizing the ineffectualness of Viri as husband, breadwinner, lover. After Dean, the theme of man's weakness seems to be pervasive. Each can sense his own life only in terms of relationship; left alone, godless, they are like children, every facet of their existence subject to doubt. They are pious men, but it is a false deity which fills them. Once Kaya has left Viri and Nedra is gone, he rediscovers his idol in Lia, the woman he marries in Italy. Or, more specifically, he falls in love with her femininity. She is the holy *la belle dame; "en un mot, elle est femme"*:

> It was as if he had never seen a woman before; the sight of her nakedness, the darkness of its core overwhelmed him, his mind mumbled devotions. . . . He saw Rome like one of God's angels, from above, from afar, its lights, its poorest rooms. He blessed it, he fell into its heart. He became its apostle, he believed in its grace.

This is the familiar *cri de coeur* of Salter's archetypal lover, and it is not surprising that Viri grows no stronger, no wiser with each devotion, still perceiving himself as disciple. The act of love, the embrace, the voice and shape of a woman, which are her purest elements—these things compel him and compose what have come to be the sanctuary of his theology, his clean, well-lighted place. Safely imbedded in it, he is in heaven. Apart from it—as a believer separated from God—he is not merely crippled but paralyzed in a solitude which may as well be called hell.

Critics have lamented many of Salter's women as feeble characters without substance or desire, passion, ambition or humor. This is necessarily true of Anne-Marie, Dean's prop in *A Sport and a Pastime.* Even in *Solo Faces* (1979) the many women— Nicole Vix, Colette Roberts, Catherin, Carol, Paula—are featureless, merely decorating the lives of the men they love. At one point, Rand's lover Louise resembles Viri in her simplistic passion: "She felt a shameful urge to reach out, put her arms around him, fall to her knees." Salter has created, instead of multi-dimensional women, a collection of hollow-headed dolls: the "women who once were models" that attend parties given by Viri's friends: both Madame Roberts in *Solo Faces* and the ornamental Anne-Marie who once worked as mannequins, who live their lives in a fixed pose, beauty their only virtue. This is what prompts Vernon Rand to remark, "One woman is like another. Two are like another two. Once you begin there is no end." But in *Light Years* Salter allows at least one of his women to flower. She is stunning, gifted, thoughtful, witty, passionate, strong. She is all of the things that every other woman Salter has brought to life are not—and many things that his men, by virtue of their sex, can never be.

Nedra's desires are, for a time, equally as complex and triangular as Viri's. But in the end her life is far more gratifying. She is habitually reflective of her lovers' qualities rather than reverent: Jivan, the one who "seemed to be the man Viri was hiding, the negative image that had somehow escaped;" Brom, the actor, "the self she envied but had never been able to create." This allows her to leave them in a way that Viri, in his awe, finds impossible. As Goethe wrote, you must be the blade or be the block. Nedra is finally the blade which severs their hopeless marriage. She possesses the capabilities which whole women prize, the intuition and wisdom that perpetuate strength. She is strongest and most confident not in the presence of her lovers, as Dean, Viri and—in a sense—Rand are, but when she is apart from them—at the beach house with her daughters, reading Alma Mahler, and alone, finally, as she contemplates her death. Her "pilgrimage" is an altogether different, more loyal one for this reason. "Life is movement," Nedra at one point explains, like Stevenson who wrote that "the great affair is to move." Nedra's great affair leads her nearer to the secret hexagon of Borges' library. It is for this peace that, much earlier, she leaves Viri—and it is clear that in losing her life with him, she is able to find it. "It was as if her eyes had been finally opened; she saw everything, she was filled with a great unhurried strength." Gradually she relinquishes the possessions of their rich life; yoga becomes a practice, the meditation whose very name means *yoke*, or union, with God. These steps compose the required regression, and only in the end—just months before her death—are her hands finally emptied of all they once held, as though the riches contained, like Dean's warrants, her life: "Gone from her completely was the knowledge she once was sure she would keep forever: the taste, the exaltation of days made luminous by love—with it one had everything. 'That's an illusion,' she said." A grand and grievous illusion.

Viri, in the end, returning to the yard of their abandoned house on the Hudson, finds himself still at the point at which he began searching years ago. He has walked a circular path, having been misled by a series of weak, impulsive desires. Yet his is not a journey without discovery. As he reviews his past, the house and garden like a remnant, what is true and valid becomes clear:

> It happens in an instant. It is all one long day, one endless afternoon, friends leave, we stand on the shore. Yes, he thought, I am ready, I have always been ready, I am ready at last.

Ready for what? Death, perhaps—perhaps he jumps off of the bank into the rolling river below. Or perhaps he is ready, finally, to live—life and death being, after all, the only things for which any of us must finally prepare. These are Viri's last words, and with them the novel ends. Salter very carefully draws it to a close without ever finishing his story. What we are witness to is the first and perhaps only significant discovery of Viri's life. He is, as Thomas Wolfe said, "forever a stranger and alone;" and he has finally, as the apostle Paul said all men must, put away childish things. And this is the truth which sets him free. The regressive path, obviously, leads not outward, into the embrace of others, but inward—into the self, the powerhouse of passion and devotion, the fountain from which our purest desires flow. The process takes a lifetime, as Dean, Nedra and Viri prove. Until the end they can know but in part; only then is the whole revealed.

In *Solo Faces,* Salter's most recent novel (1979), the world is reduced to a range of perilous mountains, the best of the human race summed up in a single man, Vernon Rand. In Salter's illustration of the individual through courtship, marriage, divorce, and finally a career of individual pursuit, it is reasonable that this novel should follow *Light Years*. Although Rand is an American, the nature of his desires draws him, once again, to France where the Dru, his greatest challenge, lies. Like Dean, Rand arrives abroad a college dropout pursuing dreams. Like Nadine's pursuer in **"The Destruction of Goetheanum"** *(O. Henry Prize Stories,* 1972) he is convinced that "there is always one moment, it never comes again." *Solo Faces* is a parable of that single moment, the single mountain to be climbed, the one man who must do it. In the same way that Viri and Nedra's lives were projections of Dean and Anne-Marie's, Vernon Rand undergoes the personal challenge for which Viri, in *Light years*' final chapter, has only prepared.

This novel was reasonably successful commercially—perhaps because of its skeleton which resembles that of an adventure story. But as Vance Bourjaily of the *New York Times* points out [see excerpt above], this is not really a story about mountain climbing any more than *Light Years* is a story of marriage. Rather, it is a book based on the theme of individual pursuit pervasive in Salter's many works and first expressed in *A Sport and a Pastime:* "Life is a game of solitaire," theorizes the narrator, "and every once in a while there is a move." Certainly this is true for Dean, in whose game Anne-Marie is trump. In **"The Destruction of the Goetheanum"** Nadine's disillusioned suitor plays solitaire in his room reflecting sadly that "the person he had been had somehow vanished, it was impossible to create another." In *Solo Faces* Rand's lover Colette plays solitaire on their bed, naming the kings and queens. But, as the title suggests, the real sport and pastime in this novel is Rand's solo mountain climbing, the most dangerous and self-indulgent form of solitaire possible. There is, necessarily, the "lack of any real action" cited in one review, the "women in the book (who) exist merely to provide sex for their climber lovers and then to be dropped" noted in another. Rand has passed through that hexagon, so to speak—"passing the love of women," as the Bible says, for the love of something yet more desirable. Solitaire imposes an absence of partner; women can serve as nothing more than cards which periodically may be drawn to the hand or played. The real "action" takes place in the mind of the gambler who holds the deck and plays to the tables of fate. Salter, rather than illuminating love's relationships once again, focuses on Rand alone and his peculiar fears and precautions which, paired with one another, carry him through the final descent.

Rand is drawn to Chamonix as Dean is to Autun. What each seeks is not example but exemplar. "A great mountain," Rand says, "must be difficult and also beautiful, it must lie in the memory like the image of an unforgettable woman. *It must be unsoiled.*" Only in this way can Rand—and Dean—be certain of the purity of that thing to which each is prepared to give his life. Throughout his fiction, Salter repeatedly designs and describes his characters as athletes of a sort—runners. In *Light Years* it is not Viri but Nedra's lover Brom who is built like a competitor: "Strong, like rope. . . . He had a chest like a runner's flat as boards, extraordinary." Malcolm, the insouciant artist in **"Am Strande Von Tanger"** *(O. Henry Prize Stories,* 1970) possesses "a runner's body, *a body without flaws.*" Dean is, before making love, "like a runner before a race"; asleep, "like a dead musician, like a spent runner." But Vernon Rand is a sportsman in the way that these men, whose pleasure it is to court, can only pretend to be. Rand, Salter's only real athlete, is physically put to the test not only on his solo climbs, but in his rescue of two Italians trapped on the West face of the Dru. Afterwards he is a savior, a hero, "the envoy of a breed one had forgotten," Salter writes, "generous, unafraid, with a saintly smile *and the vascular system of a marathon runner.''*

Not surprisingly, there is a laurel in each of these ''marathons,'' that thing which is priceless and must be won in order to be possessed. For Dean the prize is the gilded Anne-Marie, the heart of France, whose impurities and imperfections eventually surface and depress him so that he must give her up rather than remain with her and endure them. Brom, for his strength, attracts Nedra. She knows that Viri is no runner. He moves in place, so to speak, in the small circle that is practice. He is deceived by weak women into perceiving himself as strong. And eventually even they, more mannequin than goddess after all, betray and desert him until he must finally calculate and hold to what, amid all of life's sham, is the truth.

The ''prize'' that Vernon Rand covets is more complex and less attainable than any other. He arrives in France ''ready'' for something in the way that Viri was ready. And although he never makes it to the peak of the Walker to learn what prize—what Law—lies thereon, there is, as the proverb promises, profit in all labor. The desire which leads Rand is of as much significance as the unclaimed laurel. Of Salter's three novels in which desire is the moving force, *Solo Faces* illustrates it most graphically as Rand, like Moses, ascends.

We shall all be changed, the apostle Paul assures the Corinthians, in a moment—in the twinkling of an eye. The gravity which drew Dean and Viri to Europe also draws Rand from Los Angeles to France where the great and various challenges lie. For Dean the months in Autun are ''like the wilderness. 'It's changed my life,' he says. 'It's changing my life.' '' And Rand, at first sight of Mont Blanc (Byron called it *the monarch of mountains),* is a convert, a disciple: ''That first immense image,'' Salter writes, ''changed his life.'' Conversion is the reason Rand has come. He is reverent of the mountains, as Viri is of his goddesses, and pursues them devotedly. His life change, like Dean's, is permanent in as much as all experiences inspire irrevocable transformations. And Rand—like Viri, like Dean—is eventually enlightened to the reality of the thing that has changed him and, in the end, also turns away. But the difference lies in the nature of their separate recognitions. Dean and Viri realize the imperfections of the women they worshipped. Rand is awakened to the imperfection within himself. Encouraged by the completion of a dangerous climb up the Dru which has made him a savior and a hero, he attempts to scale the monarch Walker. But soon, having come only part way up, slowed by the perilous, icy conditions, Rand realizes that he is not stronger than the elements, that ''he could be killed, that he was only a speck.'' His will to persevere vanishes. He faces inevitable defeat.

In adventure each notch on the belt can be counted. Heroism is measured not by one blow but by the number of times a man can stand up again after a fall. But Salter has composed in *Solo Faces* an allegory rather than an adventure. He treats every blow as a death, a step. It takes only one mountain to send Rand home, just as it took only Anne-Marie to open Dean's eyes to the darker side of the France he adored. He returns to California with a single experience, like a lifetime, behind him. ''The acts themselves are surpassed,'' Salter writes, ''But the singular figure lives on.'' Rand is a composite of all he has seen and done—the initial sight of the mountains, the climb, the triumph, the defeat. He is resolved in the end—rather like Nedra—and in the same way emptied, filled—humbled and calm, having come closer to the source than ever before. Who can say? Perhaps as close as any of us is meant to come before

we finally stand alone, face to face with something toward which our desires have moved us, though slowly, all the long days of our lives. (pp. 6-13)

James Salter's novels celebrate passion in its loveliest and most insufferable moments. He is one who realizes the balance in which most of us live, between the holy and the imperfect; the gravity of desire that draws us naturally towards that which we perceive as good; the error in our judgement which leads us into temptation; the graceful fate that retrieves us from danger, redeems us in death. His books paint the life that, as Nedra said, is movement. They give a glimpse, through the secret hexagons of the heart, ''deep into the life we all agree is so greatly to be desired.'' (p. 13)

Margaret Winchell Miller, ''Glimpses of a Secular Holy Land: The Novels of James Salter,'' *in* The Hollins Critic, *Vol. XIX, No. 1, February, 1982, pp. 1-13.*

A. R. GURNEY

What is impressive, first of all, in [*Dusk and Other Stories*] . . . is the range of setting and subject. During the course of the book, we move from a beach near Barcelona to a bar in the Southwest, from Italy to Colorado, from a reunion at West Point to the dissolution of a film company in Rome. We see things through the eyes of young men, older women, children, artists and artisans. Most of the important characters are Americans, and many of these are well educated and well off, but none of them lives a settled domestic life.

James Salter is a long underestimated American writer. He has written several novels; the best known is probably *A Sport and a Pastime,* about Americans in Paris, published in 1967. In these new stories, he is again writing primarily about exiles, at home as well as abroad, people who seem cut off from their roots, their pasts and their cultural traditions.

The stories are for the most part eventful and filled with odd surprises and sudden reversals. There is a restlessness, a constant shifting of position or perspective in the characters and in the prose. People wander through cities, drift across Europe, strike out impulsively for new terrain without real purpose or conviction. They are usually held to a particular course by a temporary sexual fascination or else by a need to escape it. Occasionally, as in a story entitled **''Via Negativa,''** a man is driven to obsessive action, in this case by artistic jealousy and spite. But as the title suggests, this is the negative way. The problem, for most of Mr. Salter's characters, is that they have few positives to act on.

Several stories stand out with particular brilliance: **''Twenty Minutes,''** for example, describes the death, and through it the life, of a woman in Carbondale, Colo., as she lies injured from a riding accident. The story recalls Hemingway's ''Snows of Kilimanjaro'' yet moves beyond it in some ways, by avoiding the occasional misogyny and self-pity. **''American Express''** follows the peregrinations through the Upper East Side and northern Italy of two young lawyers who are suddenly rich. Their cavalier attitude toward the people they meet reminds one of Fitzgerald, though in Mr. Salter there is little of Fitzgerald's dewey-eyed awe for the rich. **''Foreign Shores''** deals with a young divorced mother in the Hamptons and her Dutch *au pair* and explores the erotic tension between them and the mother's young son. Lest it seem that Mr. Salter confines himself only to the concerns of the privileged, it should be added that the final story, **"Dirt,"** is about a relationship which is cemented through common manual labor, and evokes in some ways the world of Robert Frost.

The fact that *Dusk* brings to mind other American writers who have explored the same thematic veins should in no way diminish Mr. Salter's originality or contemporaneity. He is an ultimately modern writer, or a post-modern one. His prose style is simultaneously terse and elegant, with alternately hectic and hypnotic rhythms. The images he uses are complicated and sometimes oblique. The point of view can shift suddenly and surprisingly, and we may find ourselves temporarily viewing a scene from an entirely different perspective or drifting into an excursion which only retrospectively relates to the main theme.

But time and again, what could become mannered is redeemed by the precision of a writer who observes accurately and intensely. (pp. 9, 11)

Within the disarming virtuosity of this style and the wide diversity of these settings, there seems to be one issue around which all these stories turn. *Dusk* is no idle title. It is a central image and an underlying concept. Dusk, of course, is that time of day when the light changes, when we suddenly see things differently, when we are made aware of the inevitable approach of chaos and dark night. Mr. Salter writes about the "dusk" that suddenly arrives in a relationship, in a life, and—most grimly—in a culture or civilization. To use a word which never crops up in his laconic style, these are crepuscular stories, obsessed with twilight, constantly aware of the precariously thin net of trust which supports what we call civilization and of the darkness which lies underneath. . . .

This is fine writing, these are first-rate stories, and James Salter is an author worth more attention than he has received so far. (p. 11)

> *A. R. Gurney, "Those Going Up and Those Coming Down," in* The New York Times Book Review, *February 21, 1988, pp. 9, 11.*

NED ROREM

Although still something of a cult figure, James Salter, because of his short fiction, inhabits the same rarefied heights as such establishment idols as Flannery O'Connor, Paul Bowles, Tennessee Williams (whose stories are much superior to his plays) and John Cheever. Like that of the first three, his style is opulent and his content excruciating; like Cheever's, his characters are mostly well-off, youngish, suburban American WASPs who spend time in Europe. Beyond this, I'm at a loss for literary comparisons.

I have always avoided linking the arts. Despite Pater's "architecture is frozen music," the arts are not interchangeable; if they were, we'd need only one. Yet at times, confronted by James Salter's unique verbal world, I find myself involuntarily turning to music and movies for my metaphors. His prose is true prose—cliff-hanging prose—not poetry, but its spell stems less from a gift to spin yarns than from rhythm and echo, from color in the guise of "dark" vowels and clipped consonants, and from tune-like phrases with their repetition and variation— aural attributes ringing through the pages with a sensuality as continual, and as impossible to depict in words, as the continual sensuality in, say, Debussy. His prose is also visual, decep-

tively unplotted, elliptical, with "silent" spots where we can nonetheless "hear" what's going on for long periods without dialogue, as in an Antonioni film. Indeed, as with Antonioni, décor *chez* Salter, if not actually a hero, is at least a catalyst; with a few deft strokes the sun and shadow of Barcelona, Rome, Long Island, West Point, southern France or central Germany are evoked as tellingly as any of the unsettled humans that dwell in his paragraphs.

At other times his pen seems dipped in what some liberationists used to call—without defining it—gay sensibility (he focuses on expensive soap or women's clothes with an unapologetically delicate relish that would be shunned by a Mailer or a Wolfe, lest we get funny ideas), except that Salter is not gay. Definitions are elusive, and shift with the times.

Rather, his sensibility is French. That is, his perceptions are superficial in the best sense—crucially "impressionistic" like a Monet lily caught in a fugitive second and imprinted on our brain forever. This French sensibility, rare in America, falls like dew into Salter's sentences, emitting a specialized flavor without, thank heaven, being "experimental" or even quirky.

Dusk, an assemblage of 11 stories . . . , represents more of a continuation than an evolution in Salter's relatively spare catalogue. He does not improve (do even the greatest, after a point, really improve?) but merely recasts his always perfect notions into alternative shapes. Like composer Maurice Ravel, Salter sprouted full-blown from the muse's head. His ideas, ebbing and swelling with messages of sex and death, never much change with the passing tides. Each of the first five stories, by design or not, portrays male-female intercourse with a carnal urgency that throbs on the page. The remaining six contain nothing sexually explicit, although they're "about" sex, or the pangs thereof.

Salter's early novel, *A Sport and a Pastime,* published 23 years ago, is, in skill of diction and in erotic intent, identical with the first story here, **"Am Strande von Tanger,"** recounted all in the present tense. It displays the delusion of the creator spirit in an expatriate American, "an artist in the truly modern sense which is to say without accomplishment but with the conviction of genius."

Similarly, the last story, **"The Destruction of Goetheanum,"** concerns an obscure writer ("If he was not great, he was following the path of greatness which is the same as disaster"), a woman ("She moved with a kind of negligent grace, like a dancer whose career has ended"), his work ("Nothing is heavier than paper"), and the collapse of an ideal. Musical names— Scriabin, *Wozzeck, The Magic Flute*—are dropped like scented bath crystals that permeate a Germany as unique to Salter's imagination (but as real a locus for the reader) as *Amerika* was to Kafka's. Past and present interweave with diary-like non sequiturs that ultimately cohere in a sensible, melancholy fabric.

Many of these stories are wistful, melancholy. **"Twenty Minutes"** is the period of grace between sudden fatal trauma and the moment when pain begins, granted in this case to a woman, thrown from a horse, who sees her life pass before her, juxtaposing hopeless horror with fleshly frivolity. (pp. 1-2)

A Roman tale called **"The Cinema,"** a cynical backstage glimpse at moviemaking and a romance twixt the stars, provides an odd contrast, in theme if not in texture, to a tale called **"Lost Sons"** about a military academy graduate at the reunion of

1960 (''a class on which Vietnam had fallen as stars fell on 1915 and 1931'') who turns out to be *sensitive*—an artist. ''Of course he did not really think of himself as weird, it was only in their eyes.''

Polish is the keynote of a Salter melody—the polish of an exquisitely necessary trope, which in a measure or two can set the tone, desperate or wistful, of a whole little work gleaming with the economy of a good song; indeed, this garland of stories, at its best, resembles an elegant cycle of songs which could hardly be changed for the better. If, however, there were to be a 12th or 13th offering, one could ask for something giddy; for Salter, long on wit, is short on humor.

What lingers? This:

If James Salter steps sideways rather than forward, he's on the path of many great artists. His writing, as it's being read, feels abstract (but music is always abstract) until in quick retrospect it settles into a stream of pure narrative. The narrative is generally of failure, a writer's failure, and one guesses the writer to be *our* writer.

Now in reality Salter is a success, in the only way that any artist need be: he is appreciated by people he does not know. Still, no serious artist, no matter how appreciated, thinks of himself as a success; he knows wherein he has *not* succeeded and that knowledge obsesses him. The writers about whom Salter writes, write of the senselessness of writing, and yet, in the face of all odds, and whether or not they are ''any good,'' they persist. This paradox—writing about the writing about that which may not be worth writing about—is in the final analysis elating and hopeful. Hope is what lingers. (p. 2)

Ned Rorem, ''The Artistry of James Salter,'' in Book World—The Washington Post, *March 6, 1988, pp. 1-2.*

Jean-Paul (Charles Aymard) Sartre

1905-1980

French philosopher, dramatist, novelist, essayist, biographer, short story writer, journalist, editor, scriptwriter, and autobiographer.

Sartre is regarded as among the most influential contributors to world literature in the twentieth century and, along with Martin Heidegger and Albert Camus, one of the leading proponents of the philosophical concept of existentialism. Sartre's interpretation of existentialism emphasizes that existence precedes essence and that human beings are alone in a godless, meaningless universe. He believed that individuals are thus absolutely free but also morally responsible for their actions. Sartre acknowledged the inherent absurdity of life and the despair that results from this realization but maintained that such malaise could be transcended through social and political commitment. In his prolific and diverse literary output, Sartre examined virtually every aspect of human endeavor from the position of a search for total freedom. Arthur C. Danto commented: "Sartre totalized the [twentieth] century . . . in the sense that he was responsive with theories to each of the great events he lived through." In 1964, Sartre was awarded, but refused to accept, the Nobel Prize in literature.

Sartre's earliest influence was his grandfather, Charles Schweitzer, with whom he and his mother lived after his father's early death. As Sartre recalls in his childhood memoir, *Les mots* (1964; *The Words*), Schweitzer, a professor of German, instilled in him a passion for literature. An only child who was doted on by the adults in the Schweitzer home, Sartre perceived hypocrisy in his middle-class environment as manifested in his family's penchant for self-indulgence and role-playing. As a result, Sartre held anti-bourgeois sentiments throughout his life. While attending the École Normale Supérieure, Sartre met fellow philosophy student Simone de Beauvoir, with whom he maintained a lifelong personal and intellectual relationship. Sartre spent much of the 1930s teaching philosophy and studying the works of German philosophers Edmund Husserl and Martin Heidegger. Sartre's early philosophical volumes—*L'imagination* (1936; *Imagination: A Psychological Critique*), *Esquisse d'une théorie des émotions* (1939; *The Emotions: Outline of a Theory*, published in Great Britain as *Sketch for a Theory of the Emotions*), and *L'imaginaire: Psychologie phénoménologique de l'imagination* (1940; *The Psychology of Imagination*)—reflect the influence of Husserl's phenomenology and focus on the workings and structure of consciousness.

While serving with the French Army during World War II, Sartre was taken prisoner by the Germans and held captive for nine months. His experiences among fellow inmates affected Sartre strongly, and his subsequent literary work demonstrated an increased awareness of history and politics. In 1945, Sartre quit teaching and co-founded the leftist review *Les temps modernes*. Throughout the 1950s and 1960s, Sartre devoted much attention to world affairs, participating in political demonstrations and espousing Marxist solutions to social problems in articles later collected, along with philosophical and literary essays, in the ten-volume *Situations* (1947-1976). In *Critique de la raison dialectique, Volume I: Théorie des ensembles*

pratiques (1960; *Critique of Dialectical Reason: Theory of Practical Ensembles*), Sartre attempts to fuse Marxism and existentialism to provide a new approach to historical analysis. Condemning capitalism and Western democratic institutions, Sartre calls for a synthesis of personal freedom and moral duty within a neo-Marxian context in order to create the foundation for social revolution.

Several of Sartre's philosophical themes are adapted from the works of Heidegger. Among Heidegger's most significant theories in the development of Sartre's ideas are the importance of history as a requisite for philosophical analysis, the belief that individuals are continuously inventing their identities, and the contention that inquiry into the human condition should derive from an examination of the results of social change throughout history. Sartre and Camus, who were among the leading French intellectuals during the World War II era, also shared many similar ideas. Both writers were interested in exploring the significance of human endeavor in the twentieth century, and each recognized the need to acknowledge and overcome the absurdity of the world through commitment and action. Their fundamental philosophical differences lay in their interpretations of "the absurd"; Camus saw absurdity as the disparity between an individual's rational expectations and the irrationality of the universe, whereas Sartre viewed absurdity in terms of contingency, or the superfluous nature of existence.

The relationship between Sartre and Camus soured following the publication of an essay by Camus in 1952 that attacked communism.

L'être et le néant: Essai d'ontologie phénoménologique (1943; *Being and Nothingness: An Essay on Phenomenological Ontology*) is considered by many scholars to be Sartre's masterpiece. Combining technical philosophical terminology with specific, fictionalized scenarios, Sartre systematically examines what he terms "being-in-itself," or the world of things, and "being-for-itself," or the world of human consciousness. Sartre also explores such issues as how individuals view reality, how they perceive themselves and others, and how they interact, stressing humanity's complete freedom and resultant responsibility to overcome the role prescribed by society. Failure to act on this responsibility, Sartre contends, results in "bad faith" and represents an inauthentic existence. Lionel Abel remarked: "*Being and Nothingness* is probably the most complete effort that has been made in modern times to deal in a philosophically precise manner with questions which by their very nature had seemed to condemn the theorist to inexactitude."

Sartre made use of existential psychoanalysis in his biographies of authors Charles Baudelaire, Jean Genet, and Gustave Flaubert. These books—*Baudelaire* (1947), *Saint Genet, comédien et martyr* (1952; *Saint Genet, Actor and Martyr*), and *L'idiot de la famille: Gustave Flaubert de 1821 à 1857* (1971-1972; *The Family Idiot: Gustave Flaubert, 1821-1857*)—examine their subjects through the social conditions under which they wrote and the changes they underwent as a result of historical events. This method is delineated in part in the essay "Qu'est-ce que la litterature?" (1948; "What Is Literature?"). In this work, Sartre denies the necessity of critical analysis of a writer's style, which he believes is important only as a means for stating a theme. Instead, he promotes "engaged" writing, that which raises social consciousness.

Sartre's plays are generally recognized as successful elaborations of his philosophical themes. His first drama, *Les mouches* (1943; *The Flies*), produced during the German occupation of France, subtly denounces nazism through a reenactment of the Electra and Orestes legend. Sartre's next play, *Huis clos* (1945; *No Exit*), presents three characters who have been condemned to hell. This existence is symbolized by a small room from which there is no escape—the result of having lived in bad faith. The protagonists eventually realize that "hell is other people" and that the ultimate torture is to ponder one's faults for eternity through the eyes of others. *Morts sans sépulture* (1946; *The Victors*, published in Great Britain as *Men without Shadows*) centers on a crisis of consciousness among French Resistance fighters who have been captured and tortured by the Vichy militia. *Les mains sales* (1948; *Dirty Hands*, published in Great Britain as *Crime passionnel*) focuses on the struggle of Hugo, a bourgeois idealist, to prove his worth to his comrades in the Communist party. Ordered to assassinate Hoederer, a Communist leader whom he admires for his political views, Hugo wavers but finally kills him for reasons unrelated to politics. When given a chance to renounce his action after Hoederer is declared a hero, Hugo refuses, thereby affirming his good faith. *Le diable et le bon dieu* (1951; *The Devil and the Good Lord*, published in Great Britain as *Lucifer and the Lord*), set in Reformation Germany, revolves around a man who first pursues absolute evil and then absolute good, only to discover the falseness of both paths. This play is generally viewed as Sartre's strongest affirmation of atheism. In

Les séquestrés d'Altona (1960; *The Condemned of Altona*, published in Great Britain as *Loser Wins*), a German boy goes insane after contemplating his father's role in the Nazi Holocaust. The boy locks himself in a room in an attempt to expiate guilt and sustain his delusion that Germany won World War II. This play also indirectly addresses the French Army's crimes during the Algerian war.

Sartre's first novel, *La nausée* (1938; *Nausea*, published in Great Britain as *The Diary of Antoine Roquentin*), is widely considered a classic of existentialist literature and the precursor of the *nouveau roman*, or New Novel. Taking the form of a journal kept by Antoine Roquentin, a historian working on a biography, *Nausea* relates the protagonist's growing realization of the gratuitousness and senselessness of physical objects and of his own existence, which manifests itself as a feeling of nausea and a resolve to invest meaning in his life by writing a novel that would alert the bourgeoisie to the absurdity of their existence. Sartre implies in *Nausea* that the only authentic mode of being is the aesthetic.

During World War II, Sartre developed the idea for a tetralogy of novels entitled *Les chemins de la liberté* (*The Roads of Freedom*). In this series, which he never completed, Sartre intended to dramatize the conflict between individual liberty and social obligation among French intellectuals and artists in crisis situations. The first novel of *The Roads of Freedom*, *L'age de raison* (1945; *The Age of Reason*), centers on philosophy student Mathieu Delarue's uncertainty over whether to devote himself to his pregnant mistress or to his political party. The second volume, *Le sursis* (1945; *The Reprieve*), which employs simultaneous narratives influenced by the novels of John Dos Passos, explores the ramifications of the appeasement pact that Great Britain and France signed with Nazi Germany in 1938. In the third book, *La mort dans l'âme* (1949; *Troubled Sleep*, published in Great Britain as *Iron in the Soul*), Delarue ends his indecisiveness by attempting to defend a village under attack from the Germans. Although he is killed, Delarue expresses his ultimate freedom through his bravery.

In addition to his novels, dramas, and philosophical writings, Sartre published the short story collection *Le mur* (1939; *The Wall and Other Stories*, published in Great Britain as *Intimacy and Other Stories*), which contains pieces that depict instances of characters acting in bad faith. Sartre also wrote several screenplays, including *Le jeux sont faits* (1947; *The Chips Are Down*) and the various works edited and posthumously published as *Le scénario Freud* (1984; *The Freud Scenario*).

(See also *CLC*, Vols. 1, 4, 7, 9, 13, 18, 24, 44; *Contemporary Authors*, Vols. 9-12, rev. ed., Vols. 97-100 [obituary]; *Contemporary Authors New Revision Series*, Vol. 21; and *Dictionary of Literary Biography*, Vol. 72.)

WILLIAM GASS

Sartre on Theater is a beautifully edited collection of all the bits and pieces of opinion which Sartre has left behind in this place or that while he's had his show on the road: a sanatorium at Bouffémont or the main hall of the Sorbonne, a reel of tape here, another there, as though he had forgotten his coat in Tokyo or lost his left shoe in New York—feuilletons, fusillades, conversations, interviews, debates, book blurb, a bit of letter, record liner, squib, a casual talk, a few formal lectures—now raked together the way Isis gathered the body of her brother, and restored not to Sartre exactly but to us; for we might not have recognized the first time that these aperçus and appraisals were gifts, we might have naïvely thought they were merely left shoes.

The earliest piece dates from 1940, but except for the most recent which consists of a few short selections on "the paradox of the actor" from Sartre's study of Flaubert, *L'Idiot de la famille,* these are responses to specific questions or occasions, directed toward particular audiences, the shots of an author zigzagging under fire more than the reflections of a philosopher calmly waiting to be dunked, and in that way they partake of the theater in terms of form, occasion, and delivery, as well as subject.

So these are the notes of an old campaigner: they focus on present issues as if the present were more than of passing importance; theories are regarded as programs for action; positions are presented with three-line simplicity; slogans are flashed; there is much easy assessment and plenty of name-calling; and it is thought very important that the masses think alike and rightly.

The distance between Sartre's serious work as a philosopher (in *Being and Nothingness,* say, or the *Critique of Dialectical Reason*) and the mainly momentary verbal encounters recorded here is more than customarily enormous. Sartre's changes of mind are legendary, and he now confesses to being shocked by some of his earlier opinions. (p. 16)

Sartre will doubtless find some of his current opinions equally extreme, since he likes to look over the edge of an idea like a tourist at a canyon; and his mind has always been both centrifugal and parochially sensitive to the present; so when he uses the word "universal," it most often means, "generally obtaining at the time." That's why the Greeks grow out of date. And why the conflict between clan and city can no longer interest us. That's why the recurrent word in these interviews and statements on the theater is "now," though in this volume "now" lasts thirty years; why it made sense to devote a half of *What Is Literature?* to "The Situation of the Writer in 1947," and why, in reply to criticisms, Sartre can calmly say: "I wrote *L'Etre et Le Néant* after the defeat of France, after all . . ." or respond to the suggestion that *The Flies* is perhaps not the best play to perform before Germans because it "bestows a gigantic pardon," by admitting that the issue turns "on the question how far a play which may have been good in 1943, which was valid at the time, still has the same validity and, in particular, validity in 1948. The play must be accounted for by the circumstances of the time."

So throughout these pieces he serenely repeats the collective "we don't think that way now" when he means that although most of us are always out of step, we ought to keep up, perceive the immediate situation, just as, when existentialism became *passé,* Sartre nonetheless kept *au courant* (in 1943 anxiety was a universal sickness of the spirit, but mankind had so recovered by 1947 that the disease was confined to the bourgeoisie), and who can predict what character will follow the letter Mao?

It is this recurrent certainty, this calm acceptance of the nonce, this franchising of fads, which has made his readers morally uneasy. There is in the reduction of ideas to praxis, in a too noisily vibrating intelligence, a not very carefully concealed determinism of circumstances like the song of the wind-harp; just as one might praise or excuse Plato by saying that after

all, the *Republic* was written after the disgrace of Greek democracy, the fall of Athens, and the death of Socrates—facts which no one will dispute, and facts which remain philosophically irrelevant. To suggest that a work is principally a reply to local conditions is to suggest that it is unimportant. Ideas have their sordid grounds and conditions, their secret social motives, a private itch they are a public scratch to, but what is exactly central to philosophy is the effort to propose and argue views whose validity will transcend their occasions, and not to manufacture notions which, when squeezed, will simply squirt out causes like a sponge. If that effort cannot succeed (as we know in many cases it does not), then philosophy becomes a form of conceptual fiction, and new determinants of quality, equally harsh and public, must be employed. (pp. 16-17)

Aristotle had argued that virtue ought to be a habit; that honesty was second nature to the honest man (who thus has, after all, a created essence), but Sartre prefers the Christian position: that virtue consists of a continuous self-conscious triumph over temptation; and it would appear that in order to prove that the temptation is there, it is periodically necessary to succumb to it. How will *les autres* know I'm free, if my behavior is consistent?

There is no such thing as an isolated freedom—any circumstance will contain the intersection of my projects with others—and the new religious theater of the folk which Sartre speaks about will give us *agons*—conflicts of right in the form of reenacted clashes of passion; because only by means of passion can we portray the whole man. In 1944 Sartre was saying that "anyone performing an act is convinced that he has a right to perform it." In 1960 he is making this claim about the passions: "passion is a way of finding oneself in the right, of referring to a whole social world of claims and values to justify the fact that one wishes to keep, take, destroy, or construct something." I happen to agree with Sartre that feelings are cognitions (though frequently faulty) and that values are fundamental ingredients of them, but Sartre draws a thick line between feelings and passions and rolls with characteristic unconcern over an entire series of faulty implications like a train over a bad track.

> For what is passion? Does a jealous man, for instance, emptying a revolver into his rival, kill for passion? No, he kills because he believes he has a right to kill. . . . jealousy implies a right; if you have no right over the person with you, you may be very unhappy because she does not like you any more, because she is deceiving you; but there will be no passion. ["**Epic Theatre and Dramatic Theatre**"]
>
> (p. 19)

Observe not the speaker or the speech then, but the techniques. Sartre first locates something that may sometimes be true of some feelings (and perhaps *ought* to be true of them all). This is universalized. Then objectified. We may begin with a claim, but we end with an implication. The ontological proof got along on less. Finally, if someone produces a case where there is a feeling but clearly no right, let alone a claim of one, as in the case of the mother who beats her chid, he points out that he was not speaking of mere feelings, but of passions (which always do claim a right). In short, he turns his statement into a definition and begs the question.

The point I am belaboring is essential to Sartre's theory of the theater: it is an arena in which we perceive ultimate projects in collision, these represented to us through the display of passions which claim a right to the acts which express them.

These actions, furthermore, are irreversible and must be ridden like a bobsled to the end, becoming more and more radical, picking up speed. Language must be seen as a kind of action, too. Its function is not to describe conditions or reveal character, but in effect to do battle.

We are once again confronted by an emotional definition like still another snake on the trail. "A real action is irreversible," he says. Then the following are not real actions: (1) I write "phooey" in the margin of a book and then decide the word is too adolescent so I erase it; (2) I buy a TV but return it to the store when I find that it's defective; (3) I sign your death warrant but countermand the order before the soldiers reach your cell; (4) I swallow rather too many sleeping pills but help is at hand and they pump out my stomach in time. Of course there is a trivial sense in which nothing done can be wholly undone, and there are always varying degrees of doing and undoing, but that is not what Sartre has in mind.

I think we can detect in Sartre's attitude here, as elsewhere, the need to push a thought toward an extreme formulation, and to hurtle every obstacle, logical or otherwise, which may lie in the path of that push. The free act may be irreversible, but the theatrical act must be irrevocable; the free man can always stop, abandon his project, change direction, for actions do not stay up to party after their agents have gone to bed, but Sartre is perfectly aware that an aborted tragic action will not look well on the stage; that we cannot have Macbeth decide he's had enough of the usurpation business and refuse to murder Banquo, who, after all, is a fine brave fellow. The theatrical act, as he says, "wipes out the characters who were there at the beginning" in its demand to express itself. Yet this dramatic necessity gives us a Macbeth who is overpowered by his passions, who is weaker than his wife, who is increasingly constrained by circumstances, who is ridden by the actions he once rode.

Antigone and Creon represent opposing terms of a fundamental political contradiction which rent but also animated Greek society. According to Sartre, the contemporary theater places such conflicts inside the protagonist, and the action of the play arises from and reflects these contradictions. However Sartre immediately slips from the stage into psychology. "A man," he says, "only acts insofar as internal contradictions are the driving force of his action." By his action he severs himself from these contradictions (how this happens isn't clear), escaping them to achieve an end, but the act itself must continue to embody contradictions (whether the same ones or others isn't clear).

Freud provides us with many examples of such acts, the inappropriate gift, for instance. You can't drive, hate every shade of red, all ostentation, and own a house with a dinky garage, so I give you a pink Cadillac. This gift beautifully blends my generosity and my meanness, my knowledge of your likes and my disdain for them, my sense of indebtedness to you and my dislike of that situation. But Sartre's principal case (Brecht's Galileo, who both pioneers a new science and abjures it) reveals the contradiction by successive actions, and furthermore the conflict is not truly an *inner* one. Left to himself, Galileo would have continued to advance science. Left to himself, he would not have abjured his doctrines.

The bourgeois theater tries to persuade people (for its own foul purposes) that all acts are failures, and so the People's Theater, which Sartre supports, must show that this simply isn't so. The tragic action achieves success in the radicalization of itself, but

it is hard to imagine what the success of inherently contradictory acts would be, for the various aims are likely to inhibit one another, making it impossible for any one to fully express itself—neither my meanness nor my generosity. They are crippled by the conflict which gave rise to them, and of which they are an expression. We may understand what this flummery-mummery on the stage is all about, but what is it for? It is for the good of the Folk, and the reformation of the Bourgeoisie? O dear.

There are two kinds of theater which are satisfactory to Sartre: dramatic theater and epic theater. The difference lies mainly in the relation established between those on the boards and those in the seats. It is characteristic of epic theater to put the audience at an aesthetic distance from the action, as Brecht famously does; to insist that what is being seen is a performance; and to inhibit participation and identification. In dramatic theater the audience is presented with an image of itself which it recognizes and joins, but bourgeois theater also does this, and Sartre begins by rejecting the idea of participation because the bourgeois use it so effectively as a weapon. (pp. 20-1)

As Sartre sees it, the advantage of dramatic theater is its greater emotional effect. It fashions an image of my situation. It plays my song. I sing along. Dickens can effectively expose the Victorian exploitation of children, for example; but he can also encourage me to be sentimental about poverty and find the poor in some ways privileged. It is difficult, furthermore, to limit identification. A bourgeois can worm his way into the soul of a militant radical who dies for his cause, because "while he rejects the *substance* of the play, he will be attracted by the formal design of heroism." In any case, when I am singing my song, I do not quite hear it, and epic theater forces me to listen as if I were hearing my voice on tape. It is a pedagogically superior technique. *That's* how I sound? My god.

Another reason why Sartre waffles on this issue is that he really wants a religious theater. He longs for the interpenetration of values characteristic of the Greek arena. Sartre certainly approves of Brecht's effort to educate his audiences concerning the social determinations of individual action, but Sartre wants to involve his audience in myth, to touch them at their deepest emotional level, while showing them their common situation (and, in later Sartre, the contradictions which comprise it). He wants to enlist the people's participation in breaking the chains which the system has fastened around them and which the play has shown are there. Brecht's theater is not sufficiently kinetic. It informs, it does not energize, its audience. It does not create a true community.

Common interests don't necessarily unify. (p. 21)

So the drama cannot rest with revealing a mutual plight, nor is any play able to appeal to human universals of whatever sort (sin and salvation, for example, happiness or entelechy), because for Sartre there aren't any; therefore the appeal must be to a concept of collective action: the need to hold property in common or to unionize, to seize the utilities or run the railroads. The formula for successful plays of this kind consists first in revelation: this is your situation and here is the enemy mainly responsible for it (early Sartre might have bravely blamed the masses for their own enslavement); second, the individual's only hope lies in collective action; third, there is value in collective action which transcends utility: cooperation becomes brotherhood. This last part is vital, because in establishing a common cause through a common enemy, one must be careful that the joint venture isn't nevertheless still held together by self-interest, in which case the collective will dissolve like a team at the end of the season, or incorporate itself and become a business. . . .

The qualities which make great plays, especially great tragedies, require (exactly contrary to Sartre's formula) that justice be done every opposition, all aspects, each element. When a pie is cut there is pie on both sides of the knife. Brecht regularly wrote plays which were too artful, too original, too *just*, to be acceptable to the narrowly political mind which invariably expects the poet to condemn other wars than his, other lies than his, other necessary disciplinary actions, expediencies, confinements, interrogations, tortures, murders, than his—and never wars, lies, secrecy, or tyranny in general.

In play after play, even the most dogmatic and didactic (*The Mother* or *The Measures Taken,* for example, *The Trial of Lucullus*), the text undermines its intended message, and the party growls its displeasure, admonishes and threatens. One part of Brecht wanted to sell out to discipline, order, and utility, to replace religion with politics, to take a belief like a Teddy bear to bed; another part wanted to compose great plays and have them properly performed. And while that first half tried to submerge us all in the collective, the other continued rather shrewdly to define the special divided self that was Brecht.

Sartre is himself a sufferer from this saving split of feeling and value. His own play, **Dirty Hands,** was "misunderstood" because the characters for once escaped the program they were tied to and became problems. Sartre, at his deepest point, is anarchistic, playful, ironic, proud, lonely, detached, superior, unique. It is a painful position and it is not surprising that the surface flow of his life and his thinking should run so strongly in the direction of humorless moralizing and the obliteration of the self. . . .

The key concept again, as in all of Sartre, is freedom; but there are as many freedoms as there are threatening pairs—like frying pan and fire. Do we avoid essence only to fall victim to accidents? And in our escape from sufficient reason will we wind up in the arms of chance? Is our freedom going to be metaphysical, physical, psychological, economic, or political? Sartre has bounced the same word off each of them like a yodel from a mountain. These echoes don't sing harmony. (p. 22)

Sartre's examples inform us that it is the determinism of the family and the state that troubles him most: character and government—the clash of classes—the constraints on man placed there by man himself, not selfish cells or designs depicted in the stars; yet he has made his objection to social and political coercion into a freedom from human *physis* as mythological as the *Moirai* themselves. Against *Ananke* not even the gods fight, Simonides says, and it makes desperate good sense to distinguish between physical necessities and social constraints, and to kick against the pricks and not against the laws which enable us, as Aristotle says, to be an ensouled body rather than an unarticulated boneless ham or silent pitted stone.

Freedom is a wonderful dream, but Sartre's defense of human freedom has been too strongly asserted, too badly stated, too weakly reasoned, too plainly *caused,* and by now the freedom he speaks of has been reduced to a blind Lucretian swerve within a steady rain of atoms.

> This is the limit I would today accord to freedom: the small movement which makes of a totally conditioned social being someone who does not render back completely what his conditioning has given him.

Which makes Genet a poet when he had been rigorously conditioned to be a thief.

Yet Genet could become a poet because he possessed his enormous talent from the beginning. The fact is that social and political categories of this kind (God and His Dominions and His Powers) don't adapt well to the rarefications of metaphysics . . . unless Denmark's a prison, of course, and the world's one.

Sartre explains that Beckett's plays are admired by the bourgeois because the bourgeois enjoy being told that man is a depraved lost vicious lonely bored but frightened meaningless creature. Such a view will justify the severe social order they favor: the cage man is to be safely kept in. Yet the bourgeois do not like Beckett. The vast mass of the middle class like *The Sound of Music.* Those few self-selected members of the class who respond to *Waiting for Godot* are hardly characteristic of the whole. They are, furthermore, the same intelligentsia who provide Sartre with his audience and readers. It was a collection of *clercs* who nearly made existentialism commercial.

It is the word "bourgeois" which Sartre brings down like a club on most of his traditional opposition. Wouldn't we all like to have such a weapon? (p. 23)

Sartre insists that "you always have a right to speak evil of the bourgeois as man, but not as bourgeois," but I should have thought that no one spoke well of the bourgeois . . . not under that rubric. Of course everyone has his own bourgeois (Sartre his, I mine, you yours), but to prefer content to form—what could be more bourgeois? to think of art in terms of social utility—what could be more bourgeois? to be an intellectual good Samaritan—what could be more bourgeois? to dislike plays that are too gloomy and pessimistic—what could be more bourgeois? to believe that the artist holds some sort of mirror up to nature, or like Taine that a successful work must be in harmony with its era—what could be more bourgeois? and then to feel that plays ought to do you good, that the aim of theater should be "telling the truth"—what could be more bourgeois? to hector, to teach, to drag morality into everything like the worst Victorian Pa—what could be more bourgeois? above all to put on plays which will be eaten like ice creams at intermissions (and for new times there will be new plays, new plans, new truths, and new demands)—what could be more bourgeois, or more in keeping with our consumer society where long novels burn like cigarettes, poems don't outlast their speaking, paintings fade into the walls they hang on as though the sun were their only patron, and sculpture is made to look as if it had already been thrown away? to use up the whole of the present and dispose of it in history like trash thrown in a can—what could be more bourgeois, more vulgarly commercial, more nightschool, more USA.

Sartre admits that a revolutionary movement needs a reactionary aesthetic, and it is perfectly true that if Sartre entered stage left, he is leaving stage right, for he has managed to forsake every aesthetic norm in favor of a praxis about as effective (though no doubt immensely satisfying) as spit on a wall. The editors inform us in their introduction [to **Sartre on Theater**] that Sartre has given up writing plays because "the time for individual creation is over and . . . the dramatist's new role is to share in a theatrical company's collective work." One can readily imagine the excitement of working in the company of gifted and committed people toward a cause which confusion allows everyone to believe is common. Once perhaps men were more like ants and toiled at cathedrals as if they were hills, though I don't believe it. In any case, the individual, in-formed, isolated, and sometimes lonely consciousness which wrote Sartre's books and (like Rilke) wrote the rest, is the supreme achievement of our tradition in the West, and if (which again I do not believe) the creative consciousness has become too expensive and in any case rather useless to the struggle of mankind for general animal ease, then general animal ease is too expensive and in any case rather useless to accomplishment, which is the task at hand. Groups feel with a shallow though terrifying strength like a wind over an inland lake; they *cause*, but they neither think nor create, nor did the Greeks suppose their many gods together jerrybuilt the world. (p. 24)

William Gass, *"Theatrical Sartre,"* in The New York Review of Books, *Vol. XXIII, No. 16, October 14, 1976, pp. 16-24.*

THOMAS R. WHITAKER

Why insist on playing hell? Critics and playwrights often attribute our obsession to the anguished clarity of a modern disillusionment. A truly modern mind, they say, can accept no ontological ground for any predications of truth or value. It must understand the non-self to be a blind energy, an absurd chaos, or a meaningless flux; and the self to be a will to power, a set of determined responses, or a mere nothingness; and its own language to be an essentially misleading convention, a subtle means of coercion, or a tangle of ambiguous games. Such a mind, they assure us, can seriously imagine its own existence as occurring nowhere but in some fiction of a hell in which it can not believe. (p. 168)

Sartre's *No Exit,* Beckett's *Play,* Genet's *Screens,* and Pinter's *No Man's Land* do not just set before us images of existential inauthenticity, self-consciously theatrical isolation, lyrical nihilism, and ambiguously frozen violence. They invite us to play such images, and to discover in our playing their necessary conditions and complements. And they lead us to experience in quite various ways the meaning of that remarkable moment near the end of the *Inferno* when Virgil, bearing Dante downward along the icy flanks of the ruler of despair, turns downside up and begins to grapple as one who mounts.

Of these four circles beyond apparent hope, *No Exit* most obviously gives us a self-contradictory negation of the authentic life it must assume. Not that it merely illustrates certain arguments in *Being and Nothingness.* Our playing of what Sartre had called 'a dead life' requires participation in the mode of dialogue that the characters persistently corrupt and that Sartre himself was never able or willing to describe. But what we most easily see, of course, is the predicament in that closed room.

'It has happened *already*, do you understand?' taunts Inez at the play's end. 'Once and for all. So here we are, forever.' As Estelle and Garcin echo her sardonic laughter, and as all three then collapse on their sofas in hysterical recognition, they seem extreme images of the 'triumph of the Other' that Sartre had declared to be the meaning of death. Each has grudgingly relinquished the realm of earthly life. Inez has heard the whispering of lovers on what was once her bed, and then has failed to hear even that. Estelle, before a similar fading of all earthly sounds, has heard Peter and Olga enliven their dance with gossip about 'Poor Estelle'. Garcin, whose reputation is longer in dying, has heard himself denounced by Gomez as a coward. But each is also an image of a subtler triumph of others that had begun long before the time of physical death. Estelle, a narcissist who complains that she has no sense of existing

unless provided with some visible self-reflection, depends on the mirroring gaze of others to make her seem a valued object. Inez, a self-declared sadist, needs the suffering of others in order to maintain that of herself. Though some critics have said that she entered hell with 'self-knowledge' or 'represents Sartre's point of view', she clearly exhibits what Sartre had called sincerity in bad faith, the self-deceptive attempt to identify oneself with the content of previous acts. And Garcin, who is narcissist and sadist by turns, a confused idealist with a self-deceiving will to self-sufficiency, finally sees that one who identifies consciousness with any role or ideal must submit to the unpredictable validating judgement of others. 'Hell is—other people!' So it is for those who depend in principle on an alienating and objectifying look. At every moment they will have *already* lived.

No doubt the torture in this room (where Garcin needs Inez, who needs Estelle, who needs Garcin) is increased by the fact that no one or two can withdraw or establish some gratifying relation without being interrupted by another who has been left out. But could earthly life release them from such ironic blockage into anything more than self-stultification or *folie à deux?* Did it ever do so? As the play closes, its entire form threatens to become an image of the human condition as nothing but a 'dead life' of which 'the Other makes itself the guardian'. For theatrical 'realism' here discloses itself to be an instrument of our inauthentic self-objectification. What is the box-stage? A claustral space posited in a void and supplied with props in derivative bourgeois styles: Second Empire furniture, a bronze by Barbedienne. Within that setting, recognized by Garcin as appropriately bogus, three melodramatic characters fill up their quasi-eternal stage time by going through the motions of a sexual power struggle as they gradually expose their past lives (shades of Strindberg and Ibsen?). But they can be 'characters' for us only because they are frozen in their own grotesquely self-contradictory effort to freeze themselves as characters (shades of Pirandello?). And their useless self-recognition, punctuated by an attempt to murder the dead that recalls the climax of *Six Characters in Search of an Author,* has been decreed by a script that seems itself the 'design' of the omnipotent 'they' of whom Inez repeatedly speaks, a 'they' whose many 'eyes' Garcin finally feels are devouring him. But those eyes belong to us. Who are we, in fact, but the spectator-gods of this hell to which we have condemned the images of our actual lives? Have we not become the 'look' of the 'Other'? In engineering this exposure of the self-alienation that pervades our lives in and out of the theatre, Sartre has covered much of the distance from Ibsen to Beckett.

'Authenticity' here seems as unlikely as the 'radical conversion' and the 'ethics of deliverance and salvation' that Sartre had notoriously relegated to a footnote in *Being and Nothingness.* But the self-contradictions in this performed action are patent. A dead life is a living death, which can be nothing but life that continually negates itself. When critics say that *No Exit* lacks what is ordinarily called action, that its 'acts' are 'in the past', that its characters 'had surrendered' their 'freedom' before death, or that its 'existence after death lacks the essential condition which time possesses for Sartre', they simply forget what Sartre knew quite well: that the theatre can represent nothing but action. No more than *Rosmersholm* or *Six Characters in Search of an Author* is this play merely retrospective. Its irreversible action manifests itself in every taut exchange of speeches, for, as Sartre also knew, in the theatre 'language is action'. Each character is here trying to become a self-conscious object. Each therefore wants and fears to be defined by others. And as the characters interact, they move towards the mutual blockage that will ironically heighten both the want and the fear. The import of their shared action, which proceeds through unique choices in a realistic time that is simply out of phase with the accelerated time they glimpse on the off-stage earth, becomes explicit when the door of the room flies open and all nevertheless insist on remaining inside. In that moment of truth . . . Sartre challenges the characters with the opportunity to abandon the known and enter the void of the uncreated. All bluffs are called. Who can say what would happen if someone walked out of that open door?

No doubt we sympathize with their refusal to risk that exit from the hell of attempted self-objectification. But just such an 'exit' would begin to appear even within this room if Garcin relaxed his grip on his claimed moral identity, or Inez let her painful self-image lapse toward oblivion, or Estelle contented herself with being nothing. Such tranformations are unimaginable only because they seem formally precluded by the self-contradictory field of this 'design,' which is both free and determined, planned in advance but also generated before our eyes by the shared efforts of self-isolating wills that are ostensibly past the point of willing. Through our own predictable but quite un-Sartrean desire to fix those three as intelligible 'characters' who would not violate their given 'motives', we have collaborated in that design. But we must nevertheless admit that precisely when Garcin says, 'Well, well, let's get on with it', the curtains must close upon this hell. For 'getting on with it' is also unimaginable. The characters' action of mutual discovery and entanglement could hardly be repeated, and any continuation of this blockage would now be for us a formless and meaningless bore. In reaching its moment of endless closure, the play has actually completed its illuminating trajectory. Sartre himself later said, 'there is no art which is not a "qualitative unit" of contradictions'. The world of authenticity would have to be a very different world.

Or would it? *No Exit* seems to have cast its witnesses in the role of bodiless subjects who observe as object the doomed attempt of subjectivity to turn itself into an object. But that self-contradictory model of the performed action is itself a negation of our action of performance, which requires that the actors be *with* each other, their roles, and their witnesses in the imperfect mutual inclusion that always characterizes the reality between human beings. Here we must firmly set aside a number of Sartre's own pronouncements. A character, he could say, 'is always definitely someone else, someone who is not me and into whose skin I cannot slide'. But that half-truth would make acting impossible and would reduce witnessing (our mediated participation in the actor's discovery of the role in himself and himself in the role) to the merely external vision that Sartre's philosophy requires. In the theatre, he could say, 'I no longer exist except as pure sight'. Hence 'the real meaning of theater is to put the world of men at an absolute distance'. That half-truth would indeed turn us into the spectator-gods of *No Exit* and deny our ability to perform the play. We must here trust the performance and not the philosopher, whose Cartesian assumptions have always prevented him from explicitly recognizing the inter-human dimension of his own plays and their dependence on the expressive reciprocity of our bodily existence.

What happens if we trust the performance? Moment by moment, we attend to the contradictions between 'staying dead', the self-isolating action never to be understood by Estelle, Inez, Garcin, or any Medusa-eyed spectator-gods, and 'playing dead',

the analogous but antithetical action that we share in the theatre as we move towards understanding. As actors speak with witnesses through the expressive forms that mediate for us those 'dead lives', we live each character's attempt to be an unchanging reality, and also live the implications of exploring our undefined selves by lending them to that self-deceptive attempt. We live each character's insensitive use of others as mirror, victim, or judge, and also our sensitive collaboration in the heuristic miming of such use. As we render the self-defeating insistence that each subject must become an object, our intersubjective play is for us a non-objectifiable and participatory act, not some Sartrean project for a fleeting 'We-subject' that might dream itself 'master of the earth' but the unfolding of a reciprocity that is prior to every individual 'I'. And as we play the script's apparent reduction of the world to a Cartesian dualism of subject and object trapped in an instant of lucidity that ironically closes on itself, we inhabit a moving field of mutual disclosure where our shared action emerges prior to any such dualistic lucidities, and where the play's style can therefore declare itself to be the symbolic form of the blockage it portrays.

Finally, of course, *No Exit* invites us to exit through the open door of the theatre in which we have played it. And Sartre himself readily asserted that this hell need not be for 'me' unless 'I' choose it. But the play's meaning does not consist of an externally imposed and merely conceptual contradiction between the inauthenticity of its characters and the hypothetical authenticity of some arbitrary and agonizing choice to be made by the inherently solitary consciousness that is posited by the verbal dialectic of *Being and Nothingness*. The play's meaning lives in the enacted and witnessed contradictions of our performance, as we commit ourselves in dialogue to realizing the values implicit in a script that seems to deny the possibility of such commitment. Because authenticity, like art, inhabits a world of paradox, it requires a lived dialectic with the images of the inauthentic. We approach it here by playing hell. (pp. 170-74)

> *Thomas R. Whitaker, "Playing Hell," in* The Yearbook of English Studies, *Vol. 9, 1979, pp. 167-87.*

ARTHUR C. DANTO

"If you were a phenomenologist," Raymond Aron once said, over drinks, to Jean-Paul Sartre, "you could talk about this cocktail glass and make philosophy out of it." Simone de Beauvoir, who recorded this now-famous conversation, recalls that Sartre turned pale with emotion: "Here was just the thing he had been longing to achieve for years—to describe objects just as he saw and touched them, and extract philosophy from the process." These journals [*The War Diaries of Jean-Paul Sartre: November 1939-March 1940*]—of the 14 notebooks, 5 have survived—which Sartre assiduously kept during a portion of his service as a meteorologist stationed in Alsace during the *drôle de guerre*—the "phony war" of 1939-40 before the Germans invaded France—display the results of phenomenology as Aron explained it: the extraction of philosophy from the episodes and objects of Sartre's dislocated life. But for just this reason, they are not what Sartre meant them to be: "The notebook of a witness. . . . the testimony of a 1939 bourgeois draftee on the war he's being made to fight." Sartre's mind was that of a philosophical oyster, for whom the perturbations of life were so many stimulants to the secretion of theory.

Much of what he writes is giddily abstract, with the thick nacre of philosophical interpretation interposed between the text and whatever actually happened to have occasioned an entry. It is scarcely testimony at all, by comparison with the vivid diaries Simone de Beauvoir kept at the time in which the cold sour taste of a world settling into war is still pungent. Sartre's notebooks, instead, are a philosophical distillery in which the spare materials of soldierly existence are alchemized into reflection. . . .

In the first few months, the diarist makes an effort to comply with the imperatives of being a witness. Sartre dutifully reports the plight of the Alsatians who had been evacuated to the rear because of their uncertain national loyalties. He draws portraits of his comrades and sets down the conversations through which they emerge as personalities for one another. He notes the weather and transcribes items from the newspaper in the spirit of someone stocking a time capsule. But irresistibly, observation yields to speculation: "War, when all's said and done, is a concrete idea that contains within itself its own destruction and that accomplishes this by an equally concrete dialectic." And by the end of the last notebook, Sartre perceives that the labors of the witness are not for someone who stands at such an alienating distance from the realities in which everyone else is immersed—as though the weather balloons that were sent aloft each day, which seems to have been his only task, were a metaphor for his own condition.

"I'm not at ease except in Nothingness—I'm a true nothingness," he writes in a late entry. "I'm a *lack* and I precisely lack *the world*." Perhaps the diary served its purpose in bringing this fact home to him, but it is characteristic that he should generalize a self-discovery into a metaphysics of consciousness. He is feeling his way, in such passages, toward the grand declarations of *Being and Nothingness,* one of the philosophical masterpieces of the century. The diaries enable us to see the personal circumstances from which he extracted a philosophy and gave it an abrupt universality. It is this that gives the notebooks their value and their poignancy. . . .

Sartre's own personality is of an astonishing lightness and, curiously in view of his brilliance and his age—he was 35— of an almost extreme adolescence. Like a young girl trying on her mother's clothes, Sartre stumbles about in a philosophical costume as yet too large for him and almost comically trips over the hem. The most ordinary episodes are given philosophical portent. He distills a philosophy of freedom from his efforts to lose weight. He does not describe his leave in Paris, but agonizes over whether he is "authentic" enough to *take* the leave that is being given him. "I'm a bit afraid of finding, in the very midst of those ten days, the copious, lymphatic foam of my time here. . . . leave is *difficult*." Afterward, he laments that "the rare quality I was hoping for failed to materialize." Throughout, he struggles with the issue of his authenticity. From reflections on his ugliness he derives a theory of being-with-others. He finds a metaphysical axiom to deduce his taste for beautiful women.

The 14th notebook breaks off well before the phony war ended with France's invasion. I have the sense that Sartre had wearied of being a witness. . . . In any case, he got a lot out of the enterprise. He learned something about himself, framed a deep philosophical theory, went on to become an engaged consciousness and to lead one of the exemplary lives, perhaps even to achieve authenticity.

Arthur C. Danto, "Thoughts of a Bourgeois Draftee," in The New York Times Book Review, *March 31, 1985, p. 12.*

RICHARD RORTY

The images that will always be associated with Sartre are tactile contrasts: solid and fluid, firm and squishy, impervious and absorbent, metallic and fleshy. He is forever describing a hard and impregnable core beneath a soft fleshy exterior, or conversely, imagining a squishy center concealed within an apparently solid object. *Being and Nothingness* hits its stride when he begins to say things like "Nothingness lies coiled in the heart of being—like a worm." Mathieu's homosexual friend Daniel feels "hard and resolute, with an underside of strange sickliness, reminiscent of raw meat." Roquentin, the protagonist of *Nausea,* feels as if he were "filled with lymph or with tepid milk." In [*The War Diaries of Jean-Paul Sartre: November 1939-March 1940*], criticizing Flaubert's attempt at a marmoreal style, Sartre diagnoses "the secret flabbiness of that marble." He sees things as concealing "wizardly malevolence beneath a show of corpse-like stiffness." . . .

Many of the best ideas of *Being and Nothingness* are already to be found in these diaries, in particular those that were to appear under the heading "Quality as Revelation of Being." The qualities Sartre dwells on are stickiness, sliminess, slipperiness, slickness. What made Sartre's fascination with such textures more than an obsession was his use of them to transform our understanding of all the old philosophical dichotomies: fixed inner essence as against undulating outward appearance, the crystalline intellect deep inside us and the impressionable senses on our outer surface, the hard sciences and the soft arts, rigid morality versus flexible prudence, firm logic and slippery rhetoric. After Sartrean "existential psychoanalysis" all these distinctions begin to look like symptoms rather than platitudes. To invoke them seems a sign of emotional tension rather than of intellectual clarity. (p. 32)

By the time the war ended, Sartre had produced a fabulous variety of books, each reflecting and enhancing every other. No other philosopher has had such success in using stories, plays, novels, critical essays, and philosophical treatises to complement and reinforce each other. His "ontological" treatment of mouths, wombs, and anuses—of cavities and holes generally—as incursions of Nothingness into Being parallels, for example, Mathieu's reaction to the news that his mistress is pregnant: "a child: a consciousness, a little centerpoint of light that would flutter round and round, dashing against the walls, and never be able to escape." All of his works during World War II argue this "existentialist" thesis that human life is "a useless passion": the attempt to be both capable of objective moral knowledge and radically free, to be subject to an unyielding code while fully aware that it is only one of many, equally plausible, codes.

Sartre thought of this passion as the inevitable and doomd effort to be simultaneously hard and soft, completely committed and completely open to alternative possibilities, simultaneously slick and porous. He saw philosophy as the paradigmatic expression of this self-deceptive attempt to have everything both ways: the attempt to pull one's decisions up by their bootstraps, so that they might be absolutely obligatory (expressing "the will of God," or "human nature," or "the moral law") and also be the products of perfect, rational freedom.

Sartre was never again able to focus his energies as tightly as in the years when he was working out the ideas sketched in these diaries. After he had become successful, he had to become political. It went with the job of being Top French Intellectual; and he was eager to take on the assignment. But he was not as good at politics as he had been at existential psychoanalysis. The antifascist who had written in his diary that one is "either an accomplice or a martyr" became first an accomplice of Stalinism, and later, after the Hungarian invasion, a geyser of moral indignation, aware of many evils but of no good. He presages his postwar political dilemmas in these diaries when he says of a fellow-soldier, "With that great, coarse, brutal man—to whom belching and farting come as naturally as breathing—I act the whore because he's a worker."

The desperate honesty of this self-description is typical. Sartre knew that his need for a hard-muscled unselfconscious proletarian to serve as moral exemplar—an antithesis to the self-involved bourgeois bookworm whom he saw reflected in this proletarian's eye—was self-deceptive. He was (almost) able to make fun of it, as when he yearns to be like a fantasized "worker or hobo in the Eastern USA" who "resembles Gary Cooper"—one who can "boil with great, obscure rages; faint from great, motiveless outpourings of tenderness." Sartre knew that such fantasies, as well as Marxist doctrines about "the march of history," were just further attempts to synthesize necessity and freedom, to be both perfectly hard and perfectly soft. But he was no more immune from this useless passion than are any of the rest of us.

In the end he stopped resisting. By 1960 he had announced that existentialism was only "an enclave within Marxism." Remembering his own earlier analysis of the nature of cavities, it is difficult not to think of this enclave as a soft-walled rumpus room in which the bourgeois intellectual endlessly reauthenticates himself by dissolving and remolding himself. (pp. 32-3)

I suspect that it will be the earlier Sartre—the Sartre whom we see in these diaries—who will be remembered. Despite Quintin Hoare's claim in the introduction, the diaries are not "a marvelously successful work." They are not a work, but a mixture of striking self-analyses, everyday trivia, and (sometimes acute, sometimes tiresome) comments on the books Sartre was reading. Nor was the loss of most of the notebooks that contained them "one of the great intellectual losses of the kind in our century." But we are, in fact, lucky that a few notebooks survived to be published. It is always useful to know something more about the decisive years in the life of a great writer. The surviving diaries show Sartre busy creating himself—not yet ravaged by the question of whether self-creation is a sufficient justification for a human life, and so not yet split between the private and the public, political man. (pp. 33-4)

Richard Rorty, "Feeling His Way," in The New Republic, *Vol. 192, No. 15, April 15, 1985, pp. 32-4.*

TOM BISHOP

Sartre's *War Diaries* is no afterthought to an illustrious career; it is one of his most brilliant books, essential for anyone even vaguely interested in the chief exponent of postwar existentialism. It ranks with *The Words* for its insight into this complex personality—the leading intellectual figure of his era. It is a dazzling work, humorous and philosophic, introspective yet ready to embrace the world, concerned both with daily life a few miles from the front lines and with complex speculations on existence. Written when he was 34, the war diaries provide the most human portrait of Sartre the man, while prefiguring almost all his later works.

With all that, the diaries represent only a fragment of what Sartre wrote each day from September 1939 to March 1940. Of the fourteen notebooks he filled during that period, only the five that make up the current volume have been found. The loss of the remaining nine is staggering considering the treasures available here.

This was the *drôle de guerre,* the "phony war," that strange period of waiting after the declaration of war when German and French troops stared at each other from behind their fortifications, the Siegfried and Maginot lines. (p. 470)

By the time Hitler invaded Poland, Sartre had acquired an important reputation in Parisian intellectual circles. He had taught philosophy and had published a landmark novel, *Nausea,* and a striking collection of stories, *The Wall,* as well as philosophic treatises and literary criticism. The cognoscenti already conceded that he was the most brilliant mind of his generation. The war was to divide his life in two. Before it, he engaged in relatively unstructured philosophic inquiry, aligned principally with Husserl, and was essentially aloof from the public concerns of his time; afterward, he developed the basic tenets of his existentialist theories, which were Heideggerian in spirit, and became passionately committed to the political and social issues of the postwar world. It is in *The War Diaries* that we can see Sartre become the Sartre who left his indelible mark on this century.

Sartre decided to keep a diary for a number of reasons. He said he wanted to preserve the testimony of an average soldier, but beyond that the diaries allowed him to explore his own identity and authenticity, to free himself from past influences and to prepare himself for future work, to be alone in the claustrophobia of communal living, "to accentuate the isolation I was in, and the rupture between my past and present lives." Prior to his mobilization, Sartre had gone "fifteen years without looking at myself living"; he was now to observe himself closely and record with humor and sensitivity what was happening within him. He wrote his notebooks with the clear conviction that they would one day be published, and they show it.

Many of Sartre's subsequent philosophic concerns surface here. The pages on the problem of nothingness, more readily comprehensible than *Being and Nothingness,* obviously prepared the way for that treatise. Philosophic speculations on such topics as the "other," authenticity and bad faith are more compelling than elsewhere because they are accompanied by references to his own behavior. (pp. 470-71)

In the diaries, too, are the first traces of the brilliant autobiography, *The Words,* of his later studies of Genet and Flaubert, of the future novels and plays and of his struggles with the difficulty of formulating a moral philosophy. The analyses of time and history (and especially his readings of Emil Ludwig's biography of William II), the exploration of his links to his own characters and his dismay at not being a poet make equally engrossing reading. Sartre's literary judgments reveal much about his taste and his mentors. He repeatedly mentions Gide with admiration; with Malraux, he respects the many insights in *Man's Fate* but denies their influence on him. "I could have written that," he notes apropos a line from Malraux's novel, and he admits to a "brotherly" resemblance between Malraux's literary techniques" and his own. For Flaubert, to whom he was to devote more than three thousand pages of biography, Sartre has only contempt and irritation, deeming his style clumsy, disagreeable and pretentious. He clearly prefers Stendhal. . . . (p. 471)

Even more captivating than these dense, stimulating and often stunning pages on philosophy and literature are the many passages in which Sartre talks about himself. Taken together with the broader perspective offered by Simone de Beauvoir's autobiographical writings and *Lettres au Castor* they compose the most revealing portrait available of the man. The reader is struck first by Sartre's astounding clarity about himself, his perpetual need for self-analysis. If ever there was a prototype of the intellectual's mania for watching himself doing, it lies in the diaries. A soldier among soldiers, he is caught up in the dull military routines of the waiting war; he eats, works, drinks and talks with his colleagues. But he is equally absorbed by reflections about his past, present and future. Sartre knows himself to be cut off from people and things: ''I feel no solidarity with anything, not even with myself: I don't need anybody or anything.'' . . .

Sartre's concern with fame and honors in *The War Diaries*, comes as something of a surprise in a man who refused to be lionized and who turned down everything from the Legion of Honor to the Nobel Prize. . . .

Finally, *The War Diaries*, provides a particularly perceptive account of the phony war. Although he is not happy to be in the army, Sartre is not eager to see the war end, undoubtedly because those strange uneventful months were a sort of vacation for him, an interruption which afforded him time to think and write. Finding the war not so terrible during this stagnant period, he predicts, with a singular lack of foresight, that it ''has a modest little future of destruction and death.'' It is this failure to see what was still to come that enabled him to write, ''it's much easier to live decently and authentically in wartime than in peacetime.'' Nowhere does one find any hatred or even dislike for the Germans; there are signs of a theoretical distaste for Nazis, but Hitler is mentioned rarely and with no special emphasis. Sartre is more rigorous with respect to his own country; he wonders how the future will judge prewar France but rejects the notion that the period has been a decadent one.

Sartre betrays several astonishing notions in the diaries. He dismisses scientists, doctors and engineers as inauthentic and self-impressed and their work as boring. Several times he refers to Jews as members of a special classification. There is never any hostility, nor could anyone suggest that the author of *Anti-Semite and Jew* was remotely anti-Semitic. Yet it is odd to find Sartre referring to Jews as if they were, to use his philosophic terminology, ''a category in itself.'' (p. 472)

''How can a man be grasped in his entirety?'' asks Sartre in the diaries. This posthumous publication represents his clearest, most compelling self-portrait, and earns a place among his best writings. (p. 473)

> Tom Bishop, ''Becoming Sartre,'' in The Nation, New York, Vol. 240, No. 15, April 20, 1985, pp. 470-73.

DOUGLAS KIRSNER

Sartre was always interested in the relation between an individual and his or her time. The early Sartre seemed to focus on the manner in which we deny the freedom which constitutes us, while the later Sartre emphasises the limits to this freedom, which result from our familial and social contexts. In fact,

Sartre devoted more pages to understanding the individual in context than to any other matter. How much can we know about a person who is free and yet situated? Sartre's study of Genet [*Saint Genet*] shows what Genet made of what was made of him. His study of Flaubert [*The Family Idiot*] asks both what Flaubert can tell us about his time and what the time can tell us about Flaubert:

> For a man is never an individual; it would be more fitting to call him a *universal singular*. Summed up and for this reason universalized by his epoch, he in turn resumes it by reproducing himself in it as a singularity. Universal by the singular universality of human history, singular by the universalizing singularity in his projects, he requires simultaneous examination from both ends.

In this article I want to look at Sartre in the same way in which Sartre treated Genet and Flaubert. Sartre himself wanted to be ''as transparent to posterity . . . as Flaubert is to [him].'' I want to investigate empathically Sartre's ''lived experience,'' as the way his culture lived him as well as the way he lived his culture, in order to achieve the same end as Sartre achieved with Flaubert. How did Sartre live our contemporary culture? How did he reflect and express central problems of our time as a ''universal singular''? Sartre's own view of our age is depicted in *The Critique of Dialectical Reason.* It is a pessimistic work which focusses on our radical alienation from ourselves and our world. The groups into which we are born terrorize us and dominate the very categories with which we think. Our Western world of late capitalism is ruled by a counterfinality in which loser wins. Advanced technological rationality may be seen to enshrine the final outcome of the fetishism of commodities— human beings are constituted as objects of administration. We blindly produce a world that controls us. Where technology has become the prevailing ideology, human relations often become relations between things. Freedom and choice are fundamentally illusions for there is no ground on which freedom and choice can become realized. In *Search for a Method* Sartre shows how we can use a method of cross-reference to explain the relation of the individual to society and, in *The Family Idiot,* Sartre goes further in developing a way of characterizing our time. He understands Flaubert's neurosis as

> a neurosis *required* by what I call the objective spirit . . . In the first two volumes I seem to be showing Flaubert as inventing the idea of art for art's sake because of his personal conflicts in reality, he invented it because the history of the objective spirit led someone who wanted to write in the period 1835 to 1840 to take the neurotic position of post-romanticism, that is to say, the position of art for art's sake

The ''objective neurosis'' of Flaubert's time then provided the setting and the impetus for Flaubert's subjectively conditioned creativity. Sartre's work is specific—he understands Flaubert through documents and texts and also as reflecting and expressing his own time. Sartre uses the method of empathy, which he could not use in writing about himself, in understanding the writer's lived experience.

How are we to define the ''objective spirit'' of our age in an effort to understand Sartre in his time and ours? I will attempt to cross-reference Sartre's own statements and writings with a view of our time in which the psychological is firmly rooted in the sociological. Sartre has often criticized psychoanalysis for its stereotyped use of categories as labels, as though psychoanalytic categories were final explanations. Sartre's work is antipsychological insofar as psychology is seen as stripping responsibility from us and placing it somewhere else in the past, i.e. insofar as it is reductionist. Yet Sartre himself uses psychological categories in a nonreductionist way in his works on Genet and Flaubert: it is difficult to discuss the singularity of an individual which includes experience of childhood without it. Sartre's ambivalence about psychoanalysis does not prevent his using a similar approach in his later works, although it is neither stereotyped nor reductionist. I will approach Sartre himself as a universal singular of our time in terms of the relationship between the objective or collective neurosis and the subjective neurosis that Sartre discusses in Flaubert. (pp. 206-08)

According to Harry Guntrip, a leading analytic thinker of the British school of object-relations, many people today suffer from schizoid problems which concern identity, "people who have deep-seated doubts about the reality and validity of their very 'Self,' who are ultimately found to be suffering various degrees of depersonalisation, unreality, the dread feeling of 'not belonging,' of being fundamentally isolated and out of touch with their world." They do not feel other people at all as being capable of being related to as they are trapped inside their own fantasy world. These people "feel cut off, apart, different, unable to become involved with real relationships."

> The schizoid sense of futility, disillusionment and underlying anxiety (is apparent) in existentialism. These thinkers, from Kierkegaard to Heidegger and Sartre, find human existence to be rooted in anxiety and insecurity, a fundamental dread that ultimately we have no certainties and the only thing we can affirm is "nothingness," "unreality," a final sense of triviality and meaninglessness. This surely is schizoid despair and loss of contact with the verities of emotional reality, rationalised into a philosophy. Yet existentialist thinkers, unlike the logical positivists, are calling us to face and deal with these real problems of the human situation. It is a sign of our age.

I want to argue that Sartre's problematic fits this view. The most important issues in Sartre's life and work express and reflect these issues and tell us much about Sartre and our age. Often the creative writer distills much of the mood of an era, and is especially sensitive about the flavor and problems of human relations. This is not to say that Sartre's views are to be dismissed as "metaphysical pathology" (as Garaudy once called *Being and Nothingness*.) On the contrary we must read them as enlightening us about ourselves and our experience today. For the world Sartre describes is no alien one and his work has been very popular and influential. As many theories in the history of ideas express an age and are thus historically situated, so Sartre's ideas need to be historicized. This does not detract from the very real insights he made but rather tells us about the way he lived out history.

Herbert Marcuse has argued that Sartre's ontological categories are in fact the historical categories of late capitalism. While this may be true, it does not go far enough. As Sartre says, we are not lumps of clay; and what is important is not what people make of us, "but what we ourselves make of what they have made of us." We are obviously conditioned by our historical context but are also "transhistorical" beings, that is, the fact that we are born small and dependent in need of suckling is true of all cultures and of all times. We live our historical conditioning in individual ways which emanate from our own childhood relations, as Sartre reminds us in *Search for a Method*. . . . If Sartre's life and work are taken as a whole, a thread emerges which also links his world with our time— Sartre's schizoid and narcissistic world can be viewed as an instance of our neurosis. Let us look at this world in more detail. Sartre's worldview is essentially pessimistic. The world is an unfriendly viscosity bereft of meaning. Confronted with a godless world, human beings who are themselves defined as absence have an abiding sense of futility. We are not defined by what we are and will, but by what we do. There is no inner core of being. Our actions are not even within our control— loser so often wins.

Sartre's world is radically split. The "for-itself" will never be united with the "in-itself". We are "the desire to be God" but in this we are a "useless passion." Human relations are intrinsically "locked in conflict" and sadomasochistic pleasures are poor substitutes for love and friendship—all relationships are between exploiters and exploited. As the individual is an empty nonentity, life becomes a grim and constant struggle to preserve a minimal personal integrity against hostile others or else a self-deceiving loss of identity in another person, ideology or organization. We long to escape the freedom to which we are condemned. But in this we are doomed to frustration and despair.

In the world Sartre describes there is a fundamental failure of basic trust in both self and environment to provide the basis or the development of what Laing terms "primary ontological security." We are abandoned by a God who does not care and life becomes a losing battle with despair. Condemned to a freedom we do not want, we are basically deprived of the fullness of being. The good Lord does not exist but acts as a silent partner in Sartrean ontology. In fact the dialogue with the silent bespeaks a manichaeism without God—deprived of God, the world is evil and liberation is not possible.

Except perhaps in the battle of Sisyphus. For joy consists in our consciousness of not being overwhelmed and controlled by the circumstances to which we are condemned. The ability to say "no" which constituted a final refusal was, for Sartre, the ultimate foundation of choice. There was never the Promethean vision of an open future. The ability to turn the tables on one's torturers means an *incontrovertible conviction of meaning*. But even here as in *The Wall* we cannot be certain of the consequences of our not giving in to the demands of our masters. Sartre's optimism is that we "do not suffer from nothing" and Sisyphean freedom is a last-ditch stand against an otherwise invasive world. Certainly it is the freedom in chains that Sartre proclaims and sometimes rails against, but defiance can be seen as appropriate for a world where this is the only real freedom left; the very emphasis on our ontological freedom is an index of how far social freedom has ceased to exist.

Even where there are dreams of freedom, there is no exit anywhere. The theme of sequestration provides a vital underlying theme in Sartre's work. Many scenes in Sartre's literary works are set in rooms almost hermetically sealed off from the outer world. The room of the madman Pierre in *La Chambre,* the second empire drawing room of *Huis Clos,* the room in *Morts sans sépulture* where the resistance fighters await torture and death, Hoederer's room in *Les Mains sales* and that of Franz in *Les Séquestrés d'Altona,* provide some examples.

These symbolize the human situation as one of imprisonment. We are enveloped by forces beyond our control and condemned to possessing a freedom we cannot use authentically. Our inner void which demands fulfillment can never be filled. Our relations with others are intrinsically frustrating and, as if this were not enough, death destroys all the significance we thought we could attain. For Sartre, "Life does not only take place in a prison, it is itself a prison."

Sartre's interest in sequestration finds its origin in his own childhood experience of being an only child without peers who was shut up in a house where his only friends were his grandfather's books. Sartre's mother was treated as a child in the household which was ruled by Sartre's domineering grandfather. Sartre had no respect for her and came to regard her as an older sister in need of his protection. He was treated as a doll, a cute exhibition piece, an object—even a little prince. But never was he treated as a worthwhile person in his own right with real and valued feelings of his own. The young Sartre's internal reality was systematically invalidated: his being became his being-for-others. Sartre felt himself to be in the hands of adults. Feeling empty, he was an impostor playing the part he understood was expected of him by adults. The world of reason, books and ideas was substituted for the emotionally real, meaningful and confirming experience he lacked. As he experienced only his false self, he felt as malleable as clay, like a jelly fish inside, and was disgusted with what he saw as the "trivial unreality" as the world. Sartre sees childhood as a "solitary" reality in which what and how the child internalizes is beyond his control. It is scarcely surprising that his work denigrates the reality of feeling in favor of an intellectual rationality which sees the human being as a void, a lack, a nothingness.

Sartre always saw himself as marginal—as never really being in anything. He missed the games with other children in early childhood, and later only watched others' games. The proletariat was only on his horizon at the Ecole Normale and it was really only the war that brought him a sense of solidarity and membership in society. But even then, Sartre felt envious of those who did the actual fighting; as a writer he was still on the sidelines. After the war he continued to feel marginal, since he wasn't a worker but a "useless mouth" so far as the communist party was concerned. Sartre's portrait of the party man Brunet [in *The Roads of Freedom*], certainly depicts a man deceiving himself, yet the opposite position, that of Mathieu, is also untenable. Sartre says in the interviews following *La Cérémonie des adieux:* "Mathieu, Antoinne Roquentin had lives other than mine, but neighbouring lives, expressing what, in my own eyes, was most profound in my own life."

Brunet's solidity was given by his identification with the party. Mathieu, the indecisive, intellectualized, evasive, bourgeois, impotent, self-searching philosophy teacher is counterposed to the solid, powerful, resolute, real proletarian man of action, Brunet. Duped by nature we are, like Mathieu, nothing at all, or else we impersonate what we are, like Brunet. Brunet, who seems like a whole man, is really a caricature, for his raison d'être is based on self-deception, on the delusional identification of being a soldier of the Party. Thus, Mathieu is ambivalent towards Brunet. He would love nothing more than to be able to make the leap of bad faith to become like Brunet. Yet he cannot act without sufficient reason—conviction must follow reason and not vice versa.

For Mathieu there is a complete split between reason and feeling. A life based on reason alone is as much a lie as one based exclusively on feeling. Demanding absolute certainty in his actions, Mathieu sees himself as an embodied refusal whose identity would be at stake in a world in which he would have to say "Yes." He defines himself *against*—like Sisyphus he

knows what he is by what he is not. His nothingness forms the boundary between himself and others and prevents his merging with them. Brunet, on the other hand, does not experience his nothingness as he has merged with the Party. But Brunet's strength and identity are based on a collusively accepted myth.

Mathieu can either renounce his freedom by joining the Party or he can maintain his precarious identity by keeping his distance from the menacing world that threatens to engulf him. Mathieu has a constant grip on himself; feelings will never rule him. He will not let himself go for fear of losing himself. Feeling that there is nothing inside him is preferable to losing his boundaries altogether. To keep away from his feelings he represses them. His attachment to reason is rationalization. Mathieu and Brunet can be seen as two parts of the same person, a split personality that can never come together. The vitality is in Brunet, yet Mathieu can never reason himself into embracing it. Intellect and emotion are radically split.

Feeling himself to be a shell, Mathieu never explores any core feelings, only his defenses against them. His lack of commitment is not a happy one since there is nothing he desires more, yet at the same time fears more. He can do neither with nor without relationships. If he forgets himself for a moment, flies and cockroaches appear. If he commits himself to an action, he loses control of its consequences. Yet by not doing anything, he is pushed around by personal or impersonal forces.

Mathieu has only a pseudoindependence, invoking the outer world to give his life meaning. This characterizes the schizoid dilemma in which the self feels so empty that it relies suicidally on relationships with precisely those others who might swallow it up. Mathieu reaches a schizoid compromise in which he is "half-in and half-out" of relationship. He is sympathetic to the Party but will not join, has a lover but will not commit himself, attacks bourgeois living but remains bourgeois. His compromise means diminished desires but also diminished rewards. Feeling is erased in his general state of continuous withdrawnness. He is never really unhappy, but his life is full of chronic frustration. He is cut adrift in his own futile world, floating aimlessly, ruminating, waiting. In the aloofness and fastidiousness he so enjoys, Mathieu can remain cold, detached, even icy. Mathieu has committed a form of psychic suicide; devoid of feeling, how can he feel any point to life? Living becomes an intellectual exercise. In a life full only of missed opportunities Mathieu waits for the lightning flash which could fuse reason and emotion in a self-certain conviction; this is precisely what his radically split ego cannot achieve. Mathieu sees himself as a rotter, a washout who needs to be thoroughly cleansed. Purification comes only in his putative suicide in which he takes revenge on his past failures through firing on the approaching Germans. Mathieu knows this absurd and futile act will put the German timetable back only fifteen minutes and has warned a comrade against doing just that. Killing his first German is his first definite action—it is his own German. Commitment is for Mathieu linked with self-destruction. But Mathieu's first definite live action means that he has not only projected his bad parts on to the Germans, but also that he has put his vitality into them. This is suicidal as there is nothing left in him emotionally after his act. This demonstrates the final loss of self on the one hand subjectively and on the other a magical feeling of omnipotence which in fact is the likelihood of actual self-annihilation. Commitment for Mathieu is life and death at the same time. Doing what he most wants means self-annihilation. Moreover, Mathieu projectively identified parts of himself with the Germans as he had with the Party. The other often serves as a repository for menacing projections in the Sartrean world.

For Sartre action means losing oneself in it. There is no autonomous self behind an action or role. The waiter sees himself and is seen primarily as a Waiter. His role defines him—he cannot be in *his* actions without being his actions. The self as shell remains by not being engulfed, for neither symbiosis nor aloneness is a viable alternative. Symbiosis means a total dependence on a constricting and frustrating mother who will contract to supply all needs only at the price of the child's soul. It involves the ultimate in projective identification—everything is in the other with whom one is psychologically merged. Aloneness is being cast out helpless without relationship into the unfriendly and untrustworthy menacing wilderness. This represents the paranoid position described by the psychoanalyst Melanie Klein in which all the badness is outside and normal introjections have failed. Real relationships as opposed simply to projections of oneself on to others, are not possible. Sartre presents an ego in a primitive stage of infantile dependence, in a state of projective identification with the parent.

Sartre's analysis of "being-for-others" in *Being and Nothingness* confirms this. All human relationships are of a mutually devouring kind—one's being is swallowed up by or absorbed by another and vice versa. (pp. 211-17)

All relationships involve either sadism or masochism; one attempts to "appropriate" the "freedom" of the Other or surrenders one's own to him. But "the Other is on principle inapprehensible; he flees me when I seek him and possesses me when I flee him." Thus a satisfying sado-masochistic equilibrium is impossible; relationships are doomed to frustration. One wishes to "absorb" and "assimilate" the Other to achieve recognition, one is in perpetual danger and has no security. Again we find the paranoid position described by Melanie Klein where relationship is equivalent to persecution.

Apart from indifference—which is no relationship at all or withdrawal from relationship—hate is the only alternative relation to love. For Sartre hate involes my wishing the Other dead so that I will not be an object for him. (pp. 217-18)

According to Sartre the self, as a nothingness, is so empty, so inherently deprived of satisfactory fulfilment that he feels he needs to be certain of the Other—which he cannot be by the nature of the Other's separateness and subjectivity. This leads to a sadistic drive to incorporate or absorb the Other with the concomitant fear of destroying the very person he desires. One wants to have the Other as subject or person, not as an object or instrument. But one cannot have one's cake and eat it. One seeks to control and secure the freedom of the Other, but it is precisely the unconstrained freedom of the Other, upon which the self cannot depend, that is required for secure recognition.

Sartre's conceptions of being-for-others in the outer world are generated by the emotions of the inner world. The relationships that Sartre describes reflect the internal bad objects of a barely developed inner world. The Other upon whom the self cannot rely is the breast that may be snatched away at any time. As Guntrip remarks, "The schizoid is very sensitive and quickly feels unwanted, because he is always feeling deserted in his inner world." (p. 218)

Huis Clos is a dramatization of Sartre's analysis of being-for-others in *Being and Nothingness*. The three occupants constantly thwart and frustrate each other in the hermetically closed "*Second Empire*" drawing-room which is their Hell. Garcin concludes that "Hell is other people" since each person acts as torturer of the other two. However at one stage the door to their prison opens to Garcin's insistent knocking, but no one, including Garcin, leaves. They are "*inséparables.*" Garcin claims that his reason for not leaving and for his not pushing Inez, who hates him, out of the room is his need for her "confirmation." However, if Hell really is other people, why does no one leave?

Huis Clos may be regarded as an image of the inner bad object world which is a "closed system" that is a "static internal situation." This closed system is what Sartre's concern with sequestration, with imprisonment, is basically about. This inner world of bad objects revealed by Melanie Klein is understood by Fairbairn to constitute "the most formidable resistance in psychoanalytical treatment." This inner world is often dreamed of as a torture house, a prison, or a concentration camp in which the self is a prisoner. This system is "run on hate," and the self is the victim of a large amount of persecution. Of course the prison in which the person finds himself has been erected by himself. But it is a prison which is very difficult to breach, and this indicates just how strongly the person holds on to his persecutory system of internal object-relations. Many people do not want to leave their prisons—it is felt to be far more dangerous outside.

The persecutory internal object-relationship is that of the internalized bad parents whom it is impossible to do without, since the person would then be all alone without any relationship at all. It is better to be hated than ignored—far better to be something than nothing. The closed system is part of a struggle to keep going, to have some degree of independence. Further, the internal closed system of persecution "confers a sense of power, if only over the self." Identification with powerful objects, even where these are self-destructive, gives some security. Guntrip writes:

> The entire world of internal bad objects is a colossal defence against loss of the ego by depersonalisation. The one issue that is much worse than the choice between good and bad objects is the choice between any sort of objects and no objects at all. Persecution is preferable to depersonalisation.

This is why the inmates in *Huis Clos* dare not leave their prison. Garcin, for example, has a hate relationship with Inez, which is preferable to being alone in absolute isolation. Further, since Estelle is of no account to Garcin, it is imperative that Inez stay to provide a meaningful, if hostile, relationship. The worst ultimate terror is to be a "psyche in a vacuum." The irresolvable relationships of *Huis Clos* are staunch defenses against personal annihilation. Hell is not other people—it is being utterly alone. (pp. 219-20)

Sartre wanted to rescue subjectivity in a dehumanized world, and to find the possibility of good reciprocal relationships in a better society, yet the deeper he probed the less real these possibilities seemed. The early Sartrean self can at least refuse to be controlled, yet we find a still bleaker view developing as Sartre senses the increasing power of the social world to control even the perception of the alternatives available to us. For Sartre the world is a vast prison in which the prisoners wittingly or unwittingly collaborate in the perpetuation of their servitude.

In his personal and philosophical refusal of surrender, Sartre wants consciously directed activity to dominate the body and nature. Sartre is echoing the view of the body and the world that has enshrined the project of Western civilisation for many centuries. This is the logic of domination which views the world as there to be subdued and controlled and uses an instrumental, managerial form of rationality that regards oneself, others and the environment as objects to be quantified and manipulated. Near nuclear catastrophe and ecological disaster are part of the runaway madness of a system that uses a logic whose "paradoxical" consequence is thoughtless technologization and "development." Why should we accuse Sartrean philosophy of being schizoid when the logic of the world at large pushes us so far in that direction?

Sartre is truly a "universal singular" of our time in that he describes in his work, and represents in his approaches and perspectives, some of the foremost problems of our era. Sartre's refusal of surrender to the body, the Other, and nature is itself an instance of the logic which has led to our collective insanity today. It represents the total abandonment of basic trust in ourselves and our world to provide for our vital needs. Yet has Sartre gone too far?

The world Sartre portrays is one in which our worst fears are seen to be finally true, but this situation need not be understood as ontologically inherent in history. Whatever else he has contributed, Sartre has expressed the vagaries and paradoxes of life in the modern world. (pp. 224-25)

> *Douglas Kirsner, "Sartre and the Collective Neurosis of Our Time," in* Yale French Studies, *No. 68, 1985, pp. 206-25.*

ARTHUR C. DANTO

The terms "totality" and "totalization" occur with increasing frequency in the late philosophical writings of Sartre, and though the concepts to which they correspond were present at the beginning, they refer, in his earlier thought, primarily to the structure of the single life, whereas in the later writings they refer to social and political structures, as well as to the way or ways the individual life and the enveloping structures relate to one another. In those last, swollen, difficult works, desperately in need of editorial modulation, the problem with which Sartre struggled as a thinker almost perfectly coincided with his struggle as a person, to reconcile both his extreme independence with the social commitments in which he increasingly believed, and the unqualified metaphysical freedom of the person with his visions of societies in which the individual was fully and fulfillingly integrated. Ideologically speaking, the effort was to reconcile Existentialism, which he never forsook, with Marxism, which he could not resist. Perhaps no more revealing approach to either his life or his philosophy could be found than in tracing the adventures of totalization as the leading idea in both. In terms of one of his most audacious theses, one might say that totalization was his original project, with his life and his philosophy parallel examples of what it meant.

In *L'Être et le néant* he had written (my translation):

> Man is a totality and not a collection. Consequently he expresses himself as a whole in even his most insignificant and most superficial behaviour. In other words there is not a taste, a mannerism, or a human act that is not revealing.

It would be inevitable—it would be a matter of totalistic necessity—that Sartre would be concerned with biography in a philosophical way: that biography would be an enfleshment of his metaphysics. In *L'Être et le néant* he announces two biographies—one of Flaubert and one of Dostoevsky—but biographical preoccupations possessed him already in his philosophical novel, *La Nausée,* whose hero, after all, is the biographer Roquentin. The difficulties Roquentin encounters in getting at the life of his subject moved Sartre, in his philosophical writings, to elaborate them as matters of ontology, and, in the other direction, moved the hero of the novel to undertake a novel which, just because a work of art, must exemplify the totalistic structure he fails to find in life. *La Nausée* itself has the form of a diary, a series of notations and memoranda—a collection—which, when read as a narrative, is fused into a totality. Since in any case "everything is revealing", since "there are no accidents in life", the concern with totalization must itself be totalized as an expression of the totality that is Sartre. Whatever else he may do, he expresses the full totality of his being, and his biographies—of Baudelaire, of Genet, and of course of Flaubert—have often been perceived as disguised essays in autobiography. It is not surprising—it is no accident, as totalizing thinkers like to say—that his one absolute masterpiece is his autobiography, in which he could confront directly, and with narcissistic enthusiasm, the personage he knew himself to be. But even in the most remote and abstract of his texts, we are never very far from autobiography. And the texts come most forcefully to life when we recognize that it is his own life he is describing.

Sartre characterizes a totality as follows in the first volume of the *Critique de la raison dialectique:* . . .

> A being which, radically distinct from the sum of its parts, is to be found, under one form or another, in each of those parts, and which enters into a relationship with itself, either with respect to one or several of its parts, or with respect to [*par rapport à*] relations which all or several of its parts sustain among themselves. . . .

Sartre uses works of art as his best examples of totalities, and insists that a totality is something made, or constructed, and hence has the status of what he terms *l'imaginaire*—the product of an act of imagination. Thus, by reading in a certain way, we confer totality on what is but a set of jottings, as in *La Nausée.* But totalization is a synthesizing activity found throughout the sphere of human practice, and dialectical reason itself is "nothing other than the movement of totalization as such". Totalization consists in an ensemble, or set, "making itself manifest to itself through the mediation of its parts". Imagination and the imaginary were among the first of Sartre's philosophical concerns. They reappear, under the rubric of totalization and totality, twenty-five years later, in the *Critique,* and seeing them together is itself an act of totalization if Sartre's evolving system is a totality.

La raison dialectique is sharply counterposed to *la raison analytique,* and Sartre over and over again throughout the *Critique* is at pains to point to things revealed to dialectical reason to which analytical reason is blind. Indeed, analytical reason is misapplied to human reality since its primary field is the *En-soi*—the world as mere object as opposed to practice (Heidegger's distinction between *Vorhandene* and *Zuhandene* peers out from behind Sartre's terms) or the world as mere body as opposed to consciousness or the *Pour-soi.* The *En-soi* is inert and "rongée par une infinie divisibilité". Dialectical reason, or totalization, exemplifies human reality construed as practice. Infinite divisibility was tendered by Descartes in the Synopsis to the *Meditations* as the criterion of the bodily, with indivisibility as the correlative distinguishing property of the soul or mind. Totalization is then meant, in Sartre's system, to express the kind of unity the mind has. It is a constructed or imagined unity, as with a work of art. It is not that a life need be a work of art, as in Goethe's famous imperative, but only that lives on the one hand and works of art on the other are examples of (forgive me) totalizing totalities.

Critique de la raison dialectique is addressed to social and historical unities—the second, posthumously published volume is specifically concerned with the totalization of conflict—but it is also concerned with the structure of thought or reason appropriate to these matters, so that the book moves on two levels at once. One must be reminded of the way in which Descartes, in the *Second Meditation*, demonstrates that whatever we may have learned about physical bodies, in thinking out the criteria of identity and change for the celebrated piece of wax, we have learned even more about ourselves, in reflecting on the way we have just been thinking. We are always led back to the self. It is this that perhaps vindicates the bold use of "critique" in the title—one does not lightly invite comparison with Kant—since the *Critique of Pure Reason* reflects back on to the act of reading it, almost as though the text serves as a *repoussoir* for what the mind goes through in coming to terms with it, and we learn about ourselves not just as its subject but as its readers. Sartre's *Critique* is intended, then, to exemplify what it also addresses, and we are to catch dialectical reason in the act, as we read about it. Admittedly, this is to give Sartre a certain credit not altogether licensed by the text, sprawling and arid but punctuated with brilliancies, as one might expect of a mind like his, prodded and sustained by the desperate administration of amphetamines during its composition (if that is the word). It is easier, in a way, to totalize it into the larger enterprise of Sartre's philosophy than to totalize it as such. Thus the central idea of totality and of totalization connects with the early notions of original choice and of existential psychoanalysis, both of which refer us to the single life . . . and thence to the topic of philosophical biography.

In *Les Mots,* Sartre addressed the question of what could have accounted for his having become precisely the individual he was. This, in its most general form, was the animating question of his philosophy, and certainly of the *Critique.* In "Questions de méthode"—which prefaces the *Critique* exactly as the *Discours de la méthode* (that paradigm of *la raison analytique*) prefaced Descartes's treatises on geometry, optics and meteors—Sartre lays out the problem that Existentialism raises for Marxism:

> Valéry was a petit-bourgeois intellectual. Of that there is no doubt. But not every petit-bourgeois intellectual is Valéry. The heuristic insufficiency of contemporary Marxism is contained in these two sentences. Existentialism . . . means, without being unfaithful to the principles of Marxism [*aux thèses marxistes*], to find the mediations which permit the concrete singular to be engendered—the life, the real and dated conflict, the person—from the general contradictions of productive forces and the relations to production.

It was thus that the immense study of Flaubert was meant to be a philosophical demonstration, an existentialist-marxist biography, and the crowning achievement of his life, seen as a whole. *L'Être et le néant* is about *individual consciousness,* the *Pour-soi* being almost a metaphor for the *légèreté* Sartre rued in his own personality. The *Critique* is about consciousness as social, the individual as penetrated by the social whole of which he is a part. The three-volume life of Flaubert [*L'Idiot de la famille*], with the projected study of *Madame Bovary,* was to bring all this together in a *Gesamtwerk*: the social made concrete in the individual artist, the artist totalizing the structures that made him thinkable. Philosophy and biography at once, it was to be a triumph of the progressive-regressive method bravely announced in the *Critique*. (p. 753)

Sartre totalized the century, I suppose, in the sense that he was responsive with theories to each of the great events he lived through. And for a few years he did more—he represented history, he *was* history during the *années sartre,* just after 1945, when the world saw the meaning of the war, of occupation, of a Europe liberated, of a night lifted, in his work and his life. This utter identification may have spelled the *has-been-ness* to come, when the theories seemed to grate against the consciousness of the French, to be arbitrary and out of contact with reality to the point that his countrymen seemed glad to walk him to his grave and forget him. (p. 754)

> Arthur C. Danto, "A Prodigious Dream of Totality," in The Times Literary Supplement, No. 4345, July 11, 1986, pp. 753-54.

JOHN STURROCK

The Freud Scenario is extraordinarily good to read. . . . The volume, edited by J.-B. Pontalis, contains the full text of Sartre's first version and extracts from the rather more melodramatic second version. The scenario is in three acts, of numerous short scenes, each of which tends mercilessly to one end, the self-creation of the therapist. And this being Freud's world, the drama isn't all on the surface; Sartre plants subtle cues all over the place as a come-on to fellow psychopathologists who already know that every small banality masks some big psychical trouble. Sartre's Freud, above all, is not the simply compassionate, scientific medical man but someone disturbed by an unacknowledged hostility toward his father, as well as by the prevalent anti-Semitism of Austria. This Freud is harsh, even at times a little Stalinist in Sartrean terms, prepared to defend the most ruthless practices in the consulting room by the benign prospect of an eventual cure. He is also taking his revenge on the stiff-necked hypocrites of middle-class Vienna by bringing to light their foul secrets, which is another sign that Sartre the hater of the French bourgeoisie is in charge here.

Most of this of course would have passed the cinema customers by, so it is a good thing that Sartre's noble scenario has survived among his papers as a text when it might have been mangled, cheapened and ruined as a feasible movie. . . . Love it or deride it, Freud's therapeutic method has never been dramatized so theatrically or so intelligently as here by Sartre; this scenario should not be wasted.

> John Sturrock, "M. Sartre Goes to Hollywood," in The New York Times Book Review, October 12, 1986, p. 15.

MICHAEL WOOD

The Family Idiot runs to some 2,800 pages in French. It isn't finished, indeed seems to be only just getting going as it fades out, promising the critical reading of *Madame Bovary* everyone was waiting for. (p. 55)

The book that one might pick up as a good deed (as I did) turns out to be an extraordinary adventure, some sort of rambling masterpiece, taking in more of the late modern landscape than any of us thought we would see in one work. It is garrulous and repetitive . . . but it is also relaxed and witty, full of elegant throwaways (the aim of Mallarmé's art, for example, is "quietly to ruin sumptuous words"). The book requires our concentration and our patience, but it tolerates, even welcomes, our skepticism. And it is exactly the reverse of "Cyclopean," as Vargas Llosa calls it. It incorporates Lacan, Derrida, and Barthes as if they were just part of the air we breathe; and it is more lucid and less mannered than any of them.

What we have now in English . . . are two books (they match the first French volume) that take the young Flaubert through the process of "constitution" (the action upon you of your world and especially your family, everything that makes you what you are) and into the beginning of "personalization" (your own response to what your world makes you, your way of turning these pressures and conditions into a life).

The great theme of the book is how one becomes a writer, how what Sartre nicely calls "the child without qualities" became "the author of *Madame Bovary*." Or, how the family idiot turned out to be a genius. It is unlikely that anyone ever called the child Flaubert the family idiot. Sartre is more convincing when he suggests only that Flaubert's family made him *feel* like the family idiot, like a misfit and a failure. He was a distinguished doctor's son who couldn't become either a doctor or a lawyer. He was not the daughter his mother was hoping for. He was a perennial second son, daunted by the "Trinity" of the Father, the Mother, and the Older Brother.

His father teased him, kept him at a distance. His mother offered him "love without tenderness," the reflection of a feelingless devotion to the idea of the family. The family is everything in this reading. It is, in turn, determined by the larger structures of history; and Sartre has many astute things to say about the social and cultural contradictions of the time. But for Flaubert, and for almost all of the early parts of this book, the family is the only horizon. The great hermit, the solitary figure of the legend, never became an individualist, as the sociable Stendhal did, because the "terrible family"— the respectable, self-important Flaubert clan, pride of the province—haunted him to the end. (pp. 55-6)

Is Sartre's reading of Flaubert's life and times true? "This is a fabrication, I confess. I have no proof that it was so. . . . Never mind . . . the *real* explanation, I can imagine without the least vexation, may be precisely the contrary of what I invent, but *in any case* it will have to follow the paths I have indicated." No. Other explanations could follow other paths, but they could not, I suggest, be "precisely the contrary" of Sartre's, because he, with his tact and creative imagination, has picked up so much of what any explanation would have to contain. Neither truth nor fiction in any simple sense, Sartre's book admirably answers his own large question, the one he asked in *Search for a Method* and which led him to Flaubert: "What, at this point in time, can we know about a man?" The answer is: not much and a tremendous amount. We know as much as we are willing to work for, as much as we can sympathetically imagine. What we know is the sense we make of the evidence we have. But we shall always have to *make* the sense, and this is what we watch Sartre doing, all his cards on the table.

How do we know Flaubert's family made him feel he was an idiot? Sartre's work begins with a brilliant analysis of a reminiscence by Flaubert's niece, his sister's child:

> My grandmother had taught her elder son to read. She wanted to do as much for the second and set to work. Little Caroline at Gustave's side learned rapidly; he could not keep up, and after straining to understand these signs that meant nothing to him, he would begin to sob, He was, however, avid for knowledge. . . .

Sartre comments that "this poor relationship with words" was to be decisive. Language is a "poor conductor," in the electrical sense; the child suffers from a "poor insertion into the universe of language." "He will read, he will write, but language will always remain in his eyes a double, suspect creature that talks to itself all alone inside him. . . ." For the adult Flaubert, language is "an interminable commonplace," a sort of deadwood that only others (the real idiots) can actually believe in. All this is very interesting. It suggests that a great writer might have something like the reverse of a gift: a deprivation, or a despair. . . .

Sartre mocks Flaubert, gets angry with him, suffers with him, is sorry for him, gets angry on his behalf—all as befits a writer who knows his man. This may not be our Flaubert—it can't be, it's Sartre's—but it is as close as we shall get to the person who hid in the legend and vanished in the books. Flaubert described what most tempted him as a writer as "comedy taken to extremes, comedy that doesn't make you laugh." Sartre allows us to see the pain and the pathos in such an idea, and its centrality to Flaubert's life and art. (p. 56)

Michael Wood, "The Human Pen," in The New Republic, *Vol. 196, No. 23, June 8, 1987, pp. 54-6.*

NAOMI BLIVEN

At his death, in 1980, Jean-Paul Sartre left unfinished *The Family Idiot: Gustave Flaubert, 1821-1857,* in which he set out to uncover all the reasons that Flaubert became the man who wrote *Madame Bovary.* . . . In its scale and ambition, Sartre's investigation of a man who is the model of a writer dedicated to art, and who thus embodies a challenge to Sartre's own choice of political engagement, is almost absurd. It is also grand, inventive, compelling, and in some sense true: Sartre's readings give us both a Flaubert who never was and a Flaubert who surely was. Sartre's last major work is an epitome of its gifted, complex, opinionated, and original author, and, like him, it is sometimes exasperating but never insignificant.

Sartre tells us that he undertook this work to answer his own question: "What, at this point in time, can we know about a man?" (He assumes that we know the biographical facts concerning Flaubert—that he was born in 1821, published *Madame Bovary* in 1857, and so on—and that we have read Flaubert's fiction.) Readers trained in the skeptical, English tradition of philosophy might reply that, since we cannot logically prove even the existence of another person, strictly speaking we can *know* nothing—we only infer or invent. Sartre's philosophical traditions—his tools in this study—are existentialism, Marxism, and psychoanalysis. However, as he frequently admits, he has nonetheless found it necessary to infer and invent. I doubt whether all his inventions are true—or true of Flaubert—but they are true as artistic creations. This biography reads like an anthology of novels, stories, and dramatic scenes slipped into the hypothetical narrative of a psyche.

In its claustrophobic closeness, which fostered both dependence and ambivalence, Sartre's Flaubert family is reminiscent of another nineteenth-century bourgeois family, the Buddenbrooks. Sartre argues that the Flauberts, parents and children (Gustave had an older brother and a younger sister), unconsciously conspired to make Flaubert a passive, neurotic personality—the family idiot. He insists that Flaubert's seizure in 1844, which his father and his brother, both doctors, thought was epileptoid, was really a "refusal to become an adult": a neurotic or hysterical tactic to keep him from retaking the law examinations he had already failed and to allow him to retire into family-supported invalidism, so that he could write. Even as a boy, however, Gustave fell into trances or absences, and Sartre's refusal to accept the evidence of organic illness seems intellectually wayward.

Sartre's thesis—a fairy tale about the mistreated child who becomes a neurotic and a great man—requires a witch, and he gives us one. He makes the infant Flaubert the victim of a destructive mother. He fancies that Mme. Flaubert, having produced one son, wanted a girl instead of Gustave. (In his autobiography, **The Words,** Sartre supposed that his own mother would rather have had a daughter than him.) Besides the three children who lived, Mme. Flaubert bore three boys who died in infancy, and Sartre says, melodramatically, "The death of those three young males has always seemed suspect to me." His Mme. Flaubert is less brutal than unloving; she tends her baby Gustave with mechanical, glacial conscientiousness. The Mme. Flaubert of this volume is strikingly old-fashioned, a personage probably formed by masculine fears—the icy monster of a mother whose coldness destroys her children. I think it more likely, though less dramatic, that Mme. Flaubert and the rest of the family were baffled by a child with undiagnosed neurological problems; Flaubert's difficulty in learning to read suggests dyslexia, which was unrecognized in the eighteen-twenties. (p. 94)

Flaubert's generation inherited the intellectual debris of three demolished systems—the ancien régime, the First Republic, and the Napoleonic Empire—but while Sartre is as harsh as Flaubert himself in appraising the mental furniture of the provincial bourgeoisie of nineteenth-century France, he never lacks empathy for individuals. He is generous in his approach to Gustave's brother Achille, for example. The older boy was the perfect son, a brilliant medical student who followed the lines traced for him by his father and inherited his father's position at the hospital. Achille became at the same time a success and a nullity; his attainments were always his father's, not his own.

Sartre remarks that as an adolescent Flaubert could not think through or reflect upon his misery as the family idiot; instead, he wrote stories. He calls that procedure "reflection through imagining." Sartre's own method is the reverse: he seems to need reflection—abstract thought—to spur his imagination. He occasionally takes his abstractions too concretely, but several of his theoretical disquisitions are fascinating, among them his discussion of the relation of acting and writing to reality. In any case, Sartre's theories do not infect his characters; the Flauberts and their world do not read as if they had been constructed out of doctrines.

In his second volume Sartre has included two entirely credible novellas about dominance between friends. The characters in the first are Gustave and Alfred Le Poittevin, a friend of his youth, and in the second they are Gustave and Edmond Laporte, a friend of his later years. Most biographers think that Flaubert felt betrayed by Le Poittevin's marriage and that he quarrelled with Laporte about money. Sartre uses the same research but elicits the theme of rivalry hidden beneath amity. Since no one, and no friendship, is all of a piece, the tacit struggle for supremacy he sees may have coexisted with the sentiments that other biographers descry. Whatever the historical reality, in Sartre's minute tracking of the shifts in feeling between friends analysis becomes narrative: he has created a story about the pleasure of a disciple (Gustave) who feels he has surpassed his master (Alfred), and a story about the fury of a celebrity (Gustave) when a subordinate (Edmond) asserts independent judgment.

There are areas in which, I think, Sartre has unmistakably caught the bedrock Flaubert. One is the pervasiveness or inclusiveness of Flaubert's anger. Sartre notes that in Flaubert's juvenile writings—tales that work off the lad's rage at his kinfolk—everybody loses, every character is punished. There is no winner, no endearing little hero who represents the unappreciated self, the dreamer and author. Sartre's emphasis on Flaubert's rejection even of himself points to a source of the strength of *Madame Bovary*. The desolation in that work is painful, total, and bracing. As in King Lear, we face the worst. . . . And the dissatisfaction in Madame Bovary is a force that denies any evasion. Thoreau, who was, like Flaubert, a middle-class dropout from the nineteenth century, and more dependent than he admitted on the society he rejected, found nature an antidote to a life of quiet desperation. Flaubert's letters express his pleasure in nature, but he would not let the fact that grass grows in Normandy console Emma or the reader. His rage becomes the extremism that makes art: it takes us to, or beyond, the limit.

A second area in which Sartre seems exact is his emphasis on Flaubert the actor, who never ceases dramatizing himself. Sartre rightly notes that in his letters Flaubert writes "to produce a resonance in the ears of his correspondents." He writes letters not only to inform or to keep in touch but to plead his case, to sway his reader. Sartre thinks that the plays Flaubert wrote and acted in as a child were a struggle for acceptance: "*On stage* Gustave . . . receives a guarantee that his conduct is justified. 'Off stage' he is always criticized." (p. 95)

One wonders how the future will assess the multiplicity of roles Sartre chose to play: which of his philosophical issues will preoccupy future generations, and how they will judge his compulsive activism. I suspect that scholars seeking Sartre in *The Family Idiot* will find, in his encounter with a man who would be nothing but an artist, the very artist that Sartre was not content to be. The older man dominates: you might say that Sartre's Flaubert became Flaubert's Sartre. (p. 96)

Naomi Bliven, "Inventing Flaubert," in The New Yorker, *Vol. LXIII, No. 18, June 22, 1987, pp. 94-6.*

JAY PARINI

This inventive, highly speculative novel [*Nausea*] is, I think, the best thing Sartre ever did. It sounds like cruel and unusual criticism to say that a writer's first book was his best, but it seems true. *Nausea,* as Iris Murdoch points out in her terse but brilliant study of Sartre's career as a writer and philosopher, "contains all his main interests except the political ones." In it, Sartre meditates on the nature of memory and of thought itself. Its hero, Antoine Roquentin, "discovers" that life is contingent, that we relate to the world not intuitively but discursively. I doubt that it's an either-or situation, but Sartre doesn't. His hero, in the process of learning how to read the world and his relation to it, becomes the embodiment of philosophical man, though Roquentin is hardly a man: he is a vehicle for Sartre's speculation. As such, he is fascinating.

The novel is not a novel, per se; it is a prose-poem. Like Virginia Woolf or Joyce, Sartre often conjures moments of pure aesthetic reflection. The book is noticeably apolitical, though Roquentin's disgust with bourgeois society amounts to something like the beginning of a political position. What's good about *Nausea* is the way Sartre has reduced the human condition to its essentials, revealing a bare, abstract pattern that produces, as the title suggests, a kind of nausea.

For a man who would later become hyper-political, Sartre began with the usual Modernist detachment from overt politics, a carryover from the aestheticism of the Belle Epoque. He took no interest in the Spanish Civil War, for instance. His personal life, relations with women, his writing and teaching, absorbed him utterly. Even World War II seems to have had little effect on him. Though he formed a discussion group called "Socialism and Freedom" during the Occupation, they did little but meet periodically for a chat. Sartre never wrote an explicit word about Nazi atrocities, nor did he contribute much to the Resistance.

He began, nonetheless, to think that philosophy and literature should impinge on life. What he did was to mix his own blend of phenomenology from the previous work of Husserl and Heidegger, adding his own concern for "freedom" as it relates to individual action. He called this mixture a "philosophy of existence," and when the media labeled the new thinking "Existentialism," Sartre gladly accepted the term, realizing it was catchy. And why not? The central concerns of the new philosophy are contained in his massive text of 1943, *Being and Nothingness.* That somewhat impenetrable tome takes up and develops the themes presented in *Nausea,* the main one being the nature of consciousness.

Here, Sartre is a philosopher in the tradition of Descartes. His concern with "freedom" is inextricably involved with his concern for picturing consciousness. He insists, like Descartes, on the supremacy of the *cogito,* but his interests (unlike most other serious philosophers of consciousness) are psychological rather than linguistic. For him (as for Roquentin), consciousness becomes the flux between moments of perception, of being, wherein objects exist "in-them-selves" against a background of negation, of nothingness, the empty spaces between the stars. To perceive the "thinginess" of things is the beginning of Sartrean wisdom. But what about the Self? Here value comes into play (*la valeur*): that mystical entity which is non-contingent but real nonetheless. "The supreme value towards which consciousness, by its very nature, is constantly transcending itself is the absolute being of the self, with its qualities of identity, purity, permanence," writes Sartre.

Humankind seems endlessly shifting between Being and Nothing, between value and non-value, between Being-in-Itself (*être-en-soi*) and Being-for-Itself (*être-pour-soi*). This latter contrast, the in-itself versus the for-itself, has become famous. We seek, according to Sartre, the former, the (valued) thinginess of reality, the in-itself. The for-itself is an "outside" state, the sense of consciousness playing over the world of things, a state of pure consciousness. Only God, says Sartre, ever attains both senses of reality, the condition of being *en-soi-pour-soi*; the human condition denies it. This is ultimately a depressing philosophy, wherein human nature defines itself as a lack of completeness. Sartrean man is, as he notes toward the end of *Being and Nothingness,* a reverse Christ, aspiring to lose his humanness, to become God. But since God doesn't exist (because His existence defies logic), man is perpetually foiled: *"L'homme est une passion inutile."*

What's interesting, and noble, is that Sartre refuses to sink into a self-satisfied, rational despair. He declares an end to "the reign of value" in the old sense. The discovery that all human activity is a vain attempt to transmogrify man into God is the pre-condition of freedom. In *Being and Nothingness,* Sartre does not develop the implications of this newfound freedom, though, as Denis Hollier notes, in this work Sartre "encountered the imperative of an ethics." That ethics will unfold in **"Existentialism Is a Humanism,"** the great essay of 1946, where the Existentialist creed is codified (if not ossified). It becomes an underlying theme in the four novels gathered under the title, *The Roads of Freedom*—all written during the war and shortly after.

Oddly enough, the war years were amazingly conducive to productivity for Sartre, who wrote much of his best creative work then, excluding *Nausea.* The novels have been mentioned: not one of them has the centripetal energy of *Nausea,* but the sum of the four is considerable. As in *Nausea,* all human communication seems difficult, even impossible. The superabundance of *things* produces nausea in *Nausea;* in *Roads of Freedom* it is the horror of the flesh that produces loathing. Murdoch says: "The flesh symbolises the absolute loss of freedom, and references to its inertness, flabbiness, stickiness, heaviness form a continual accompaniment to the narrative."

It was also during the war years that Sartre wrote his two finest plays, *The Flies* (1943) and *No Exit* (1944), the former a Sartrean riff on the Electra-Orestes theme, the latter an "existential" portrait of hell, defined here as "other people." These are remarkable works, very much in accord with the Modernist theater in France. Jean Giraudoux, Cocteau, and Jean Anouilh had all refashioned Greek myths for the contemporary theater, so Sartre's *The Flies* was, if anything, *á la mode.* In his version of the myth, Orestes returns to Argos and finds it wallowing in regret, choked; the citizens "held their tongues . . . said nothing," as Jupiter says, trying to convey the cowardice of the town in the face of its king's death. The men of Argos, in a moment of recognition, plead: "Forgive us for living while you are dead." The parallel with the Occupation is implicit, with Sartre arguing that free men should assume responsibility for their actions, no matter what the consequences. (pp. 364-66)

Sartre became increasingly political—fanatically so— in the post-war years, supporting a wide range of left-wing causes and revolutionary committees. He played cat-and-mouse with the Communist Party, writing an anti-Communist play (*Dirty Hands*) in 1948 that, later, he would renounce. Wanting desperately to believe that the Soviets had, in fact, managed to create a genuine Marxist society, Sartre bent over backwards in the early fifties to support them; but this became impossible after the invasion of Hungary in 1956, and he withdrew his endorsement. In his later years, he supported a group of student Maoists called the Proletarian Left, becoming their figurehead for a while as "editor" of their crudely printed handouts. In fact, Sartre was in the late sixties a kind of hero to the student left throughout the world.

The need to rationalize his commitment to political activity led to his last major philosophical effort, *The Critique of Dialectical Reason* (1960), a projected two-volume effort of which only the first was ever published. The work was written—thirty to forty pages a day—in what Cohen-Solal describes as "a wild rush of words and juxtaposed ideas, pouring forth during crises of hyperexcitement, under the effect of contradictory drugs. . . . Everything in excess." The work meditates on the meeting between Marxism and Existentialism: an attempt to get Marxists to recognize, as Murdoch says, that "the *aventure singuliére* of human existence must be returned to the centre of the picture." Sartre was looking for ways in which individuals relate to their historical surroundings via a continuous mediation between the general and the particular; he was trying to understand the nature and place of free choice in this overall scheme.

Methods of "mediation" were sought in the human sciences—psychology, anthropology, and sociology—though Sartre keeps returning to his philosophical base, which is always the phenomenology of consciousness. Sartre came to see history as driven, as he says, "not by scientific laws or by an abstract inhuman super-purpose, but by human willed purposes, so that its explanation and being lie in a study of conscious human activity." Historical inevitability, the baseline of Orthodox Marxism, went out the window. In general, Sartre was trying to connect Marxism with the old Hegelian subject-object phenomenology of mind, and to reinstate the theme of human purpose in history. He was also trying to formulate a critique of Western culture in the guise of philosophy, though he never really accomplished this goal. Instead of making a sustained analysis of existing institutions with concrete proposals for change, he indulged in random indictments, his rhetoric swelling at times to something approaching the apocalyptic.

The failure of coherence which mars *The Critique* is even more troublesome in his last great work, ***The Family Idiot,*** a biographical study of Flaubert. This work obsessed Sartre in his later years, and it was finally published (in French) in 1971 (volumes I and II) and 1972 (volume III). Like his previous "biographies" of Baudelaire (1946) and Genet (1956), Sartre takes huge liberties with the genre, mixing in autobiography, philosophical rumination, and criticism. He pays scant allegiance to the facts, using them as a launching pad for speculation. The unique *mythos* of each life provides instances galore of existential choices, though one suspects that Sartre distorts the lives to fit them to his philosophical schema. He should have followed the example of his earliest hero, Roquentin, who abandons his biography of de Rollebon when he sees that no amount of factual knowledge can make another person's life any more "real." In *Nausea,* this is all part of Roquentin's mounting awareness that one cannot form an absolute notion of one's past. It is also part of Sartre's typically Modernist lack of faith in epistemological certainty. One wonders what drove him to attempt in his last major work what he had previously decided was impossible. (pp. 368-69)

Jay Parini, "Sartre's Life of Writing," in The Hudson Review, *Vol. XLI, No. 2, Summer, 1988, pp. 363-69.*

Larry Shue

1946-1985

American dramatist and actor.

Shue garnered recognition in Great Britain and the United States for his comic farces *The Nerd* (1981) and *The Foreigner* (1982). In *The Nerd,* a social misfit who had saved the life of a soldier during the Vietnam War unexpectedly decides to accept the man's longstanding offer of hospitality and moves in with him. The soldier, now an aspiring architect, soon loses patience with his obnoxious visitor and attempts to oust him from his home. Although *The Nerd* became one of the longest-running American productions in Great Britain and was also a popular success in the United States, many critics deemed inappropriate the play's similarities to television situation comedies. Most reviewers agreed with Clive Barnes's assessment: ''[*The Nerd*] is not—by any means—a good play. . . . It made me want to scream with agony—although, in fairness, many of the preview audience sharing this experience were, to all appearances, screaming with laughter.''

In Shue's next comedy, *The Foreigner,* an excessively shy Englishman on a three-day visit to the United States takes a room at a Georgia fishing lodge. Pretending that he understands no English in order to avoid contact with other guests, the man soon overhears discussion of several conspiracies, including one by the Ku Klux Klan to establish a post at the lodge. Although some reviewers faulted the play's characters for lack of motivation and considered the plot unbelievable, Edith Oliver admitted that she ''laughed start to finish at one comic surprise after another,'' and John Beaufort contended that ''the theatrical high jinks create their own kind of loony fun.'' Shue's last drama, *Wenceslas Square* (1984), is a serious examination of the effect of governmental oppression upon artistic expression. Deriving from Shue's personal experiences, this play details the attempts of a young man and his former college professor to complete a book on reactions to the presence of Russian communism in Czechoslovakia as reflected in Czech theatrical productions of the 1960s.

(See also *Contemporary Authors,* Vol. 117 [obituary].)

DOUGLAS WATT

[In *The Foreigner*] Larry Shue has contrived to rout the forces of social injustice by farcical means. But I'm afraid in doing so all he has produced is an unpalatable hash.

For reasons never made very clear, the title character, a young Englishman named Charlie Baker, accompanies a pal, an older chap named Froggy LeSueur, on a mission to a lake resort in Georgia. A demolition expert, LeSueur is supposedly hired by the U. S. military periodically to demonstrate his expertise in blowing up a mountain or two, as if we hadn't long since graduated from such kid stuff.

Froggy regularly lodges with Betty Meeks, whose humble rooming house is about to be condemned through trickery in

order to make way for Ku Klux Klan headquarters with the lofty goal of promoting white Christianity throughout the land.

But enough of the old-homestead plot, in which a sizeable inheritance also figures, and on to that title character. Being a shy man and a reluctant companion of Froggy's to begin with, Charlie declares his unwillingness to talk to anybody right from the start. So Froggy introduces him as a foreigner and a complete stranger to the English language. This allows the author to set up scenes of nonsense talk, ones in which a young minister and his pregnant bride-to-be discuss intimate matters in Charlie's presence, and gradually ones in which Charlie learns of the plot being concocted by the local Klan head Owen Musser, a villain popped right out of 19th-century melodrama minus only black hat and mustache, and (horrors!) the young minister himself.

Naturally, Charlie, who has gradually been picking up bits of Georgia patois, foils the racists at the last moment, and all ends happily, and sappily, with the promise of a new life for Charlie . . . and the disgraced minister's former intended, though what they'll name the child is anybody's guess.

Though his story is ridiculous, Shue does get off a few funny lines. . . .

Douglas Watt, '' 'Foreigner' Sounds Like a Lot of Nonsense Talk,'' in Daily News, *New York, November 2, 1984.*

FRANK RICH

The Foreigner desperately wants to provide some silly fun. As the author's incredible premise has it, Charlie has traveled from England to a fishing lodge in rural Georgia for a weekend of relaxation. So fearful is the man of having to engage in conversation with strangers, however, that he masquerades as a non-English-speaking "foreigner" of indeterminate national origin. The gullible local yokels fall for the ruse, and soon they are blithely spilling their darkest secrets in the presence of their seemingly mute and uncomprehending visitor.

This preposterous plot requires a full act to set up—with much of the exposition delivered by the playwright himself, appearing in the role of an English soldier who unaccountably deposits Charlie in Georgia. Yet, when *The Foreigner* finally gets going, its convoluted shenanigans hardly seem worth the effort. The other occupants of the lodge are all stereotypical rubes; their tedious crises, which the eavesdropping Charlie must ultimately straighten out, include a dispute over an inheritance, an ill-advised shotgun marriage and a clandestine Ku Klux Klan conspiracy to establish the headquarters for "a new Christian white nation."

Perhaps a master of buffoonery, such as Michael Frayn or Larry Gelbart, could cook up something from this inane recipe. With Mr. Shue, we usually spot both the story twists and punchlines well before they actually arrive. We also guess the play's supposedly heartwarming payoff well in advance: Once the nebbishy Charlie is forced to come to the rescue of the evening's victims, he is destined to acquire both the self-confidence and devoted romantic partner that have always eluded him back in England.

> *Frank Rich, "Anthony Heald in 'Foreigner'," in* The New York Times, *November 2, 1984, p. 3.*

JOHN SIMON

James Agee classified certain movies as "intelligent trash," a category that he neither respected nor contemned, but recognized as having its uses.... In the theater, too, there is room for some slumming, which, I imagine, is what Larry Shue's *The Foreigner* means to provide. After seeing this farce by the actor-playwright, I suspect that he is quite capable of writing intelligent trash for well-bred pigs to wallow in, as the play does, at times, rise to this level. Mostly, however, it is content to be unintelligent trash.

The Foreigner brings an unlikely pair of Englishmen—"Froggy" LeSueur, a boisterous corporal and demolition expert, and Charlie Baker, a timid, boring reserve officer, ... to Betty Meeker's Fishing Lodge Resort in Tilghman County, the heart of Georgia darkness. Here the smooth Reverend David Marshall Lee and his rough pal, Owen Musser, are planning to take over, with the help of the Klan, today the lodge, tomorrow America. David is about to marry the pretty but somewhat benighted ex-debutante and heiress Catherine Simms, who has a semi-idiot brother, Ellard, and a fortune with which David and Owen plan to finance the takeover of what they propose to turn into White America. Because of his extreme shyness, which makes talking to strangers agonizing, Charlie is passed off as a foreigner having no English while Froggy goes off on some demolition job. Betty, the aging proprietress, the exploited and dimly suspicious postdeb, and the rather speculative half-wit are enormously taken with the cute "foreigner," who, in turn, takes to being fussed over as any lamb would to being lionized.

Now, what prevents this farce—in which, typically, bumbling good overcomes cunning but fallible evil—from being intelligent trash is its utter implausibility. What makes good farce a valid art form is its keeping a firm grip on reality no matter how much its feet may slip on banana peels. In *The Foreigner,* however, people are stupid and inept beyond any relation to reality, except when they become, equally unbelievably, improbably clever or wise. And the author cannot even make his premise seem credible enough to support the airiest of fantasies. Furthermore, his wit, despite occasional flashes, goes into lengthy eclipses during which we seem to be viewing the proceedings through smoky glass. Take this line of Catherine's to her brother: "You couldn't catch a chipmunk if all his legs were broken and if he were glued to the palm of your hand." This kind of line is trying too hard. Not feeling confident that it has scored with the broken legs, it huffs on to that sticky hand in the hope of clinching a laugh, and doesn't get it in either place. Ellard replies, "I wouldn't want him then," which in its pseudologic is mildly amusing; but because the big yocks have failed to come, the answer makes us conjure up in all seriousness a broken-legged beastie, and the fun turns sour.

One main source of humor in the play is the language of the nonexistent country from which Charlie claims to hail. In this double-talk, he improvises everything from badinage to lengthy anecdotes, and Froggy must fall in with it, however clumsily. The word for "yes," Charlie tells us, is "*gok*," and the word for "no" is "*blint*"; otherwise, the lingo sounds mostly like pig Russian, and less funny than it could be. Rather more amusing is the rapid progress Charlie makes in English—as are also his recidivisms whenever it pays to act dumb—and the status of genius this confers upon him. (p. 135)

> *John Simon, "If the Shue Doesn't Fit," in* New York Mazagine, *Vol. 17, No. 45, November 12, 1984, pp. 135-36.*

EDITH OLIVER

[*The Foreigner*] is a silly, funny farce, for Shue has a truly humorous and jokey mind and the knack of turning a phrase. A British Army officer, a demolitions expert, comes to an inn in Georgia on some assignment or other, bringing with him a friend called Charlie.... Charlie, a shy man, is overcome by panic at the thought of having to make conversation with strangers, so, to protect him, the officer tells the proprietress of the inn that Charlie is a foreigner unable to understand English, much less speak it. That is the premise (and basic joke) of the play, and what you do is place it on the tip of your tongue and gulp it down. Just when Charlie, alone, has decided to confess to the hoax, a sinister, two-faced minister enters, and down the stairs rushes his pretty fiancée to announce that she is pregnant. Loud, intimate conversation follows, and suddenly she notices Charlie, head in hands, and raises hell. Proprietress reassures her that Charlie can understand nothing. In the course of the action, Charlie overhears quite a lot—there is villainy and skulduggery afoot, but the villains take no notice of him whatever. Since surprise is the essence of farce, you'll get no more from me.... (pp. 187-88)

I have no critical comment to make, unless expressing enjoyment can be considered criticism. I laughed start to finish at one comic surprise after another. (p. 188)

> *Edith Oliver, "Not Much to Celebrate," in* The New Yorker, *Vol. LX, No. 40, November 19, 1984, pp. 184, 187-88.*

HOWARD KISSEL

[Like *The Foreigner, The Nerd*] relies on an air of high school hijinx.

The play is about a group of friends (unaccountably named Willum, Tansy and Axel) who are visited by a man Willum has never met, but who saved his life in Vietnam. He at least has a reasonable name: Rick. . . .

Rick is indeed moronic enough to deserve the title "nerd," though it apparently never occurs to anyone (not even Axel, who must be extremely shrewd and perceptive since he is a drama critic) to question how someone so idiotic could have been capable of great bravery.

The Vietnam episode, in fact, is never even discussed, which is odd given the fact this is the two men's first meeting.

I won't reveal the reason for this or other unaccountable turns of plot, because it would spoil the play's "surprise"—though any script with such consistent lack of plausibility ill-deserves such consideration. The silly twists here recall that most contrived of '50s sitcoms, *The Stu Erwin Show*.

Shue's sense of humor reminded me of jokes in the high school cafeteria. Sample: "You're a hard man, Axel." "Am I good to find?" . . .

Occasionally there are amusing non sequiturs, but on the whole Shue's appeal seems to be his childlike belief that if you are a clever actor you can fool the world into being a better place.

Howard Kissel, " 'The Nerd': Well-Acted Junk," in Daily News, *New York, March 23, 1987.*

ALLAN WALLACH

Larry Shue's *The Nerd* is flimsy and preposterous, with enough gaping holes in its negligible plot to sink an aircraft carrier. So why was I laughing?

More comic strip than comedy, *The Nerd* builds its jokes on exaggerated character traits, just as Shue's *The Foreigner* did. The biggest exaggeration is the outrageous, obtuse and overwhelming hayseed dumbness of its title character. And this guy, this *nerd*, completely disrupts the lives of people we'd expect to toss him out on his ear.

Silly? Sure. But funny. . . .

I didn't crack a smile when Shue turned painful shyness into a one-joke comedy in *The Foreigner*, but *The Nerd* is harder to resist. It softened me up with the wisecracks of a stock character, an acerbic theater critic. And when bumptious bumpkin Rick Steadman showed up, swiftly reducing a birthday party to a shambles, I waved the white flag. . . .

[Shue's] excuse for making Rick his live-in tormentor is one of those playwright's devices you just have to accept: Rick saved Willum's life in Vietnam, and though he'd never even seen his savior, Willum promised to do anything for him. Now Rick has moved in with him, maybe for good.

As it turns out, it's for bad.

The comedy sags once Rick starts destroying Willum's life, but the letdown is sandwiched between two mirthful scenes. The first is the wrecked party, which lets us savor reactions to Rick that include the slow burn of a hotel owner, the repressed rage of his wife, and the terror of their obnoxious son.

The second comic setpiece is a frantic attempt to get rid of Rick—an exorcism that aims for terror and approaches hysteria.

Allan Wallach, " 'Nerd': A Comic-Strip Throwback," in Newsday, *March 23, 1987.*

CLIVE BARNES

To portray boredom and not be boring is one of the classic conundrums of art. By the same token, to write about a nerd and not be nerdish, or even nerdlike, was the task undertaken by Larry Shue in his play, uncompromisingly called *The Nerd*. . . .

[*The Nerd*] is not—by any means—a good play. It is nerdlike, or even nerdish. It made me want to scream with agony—although, in fairness, many of the preview audience sharing this experience were, to all appearances, screaming with laughter.

A case, perhaps of different screams for different strokes for different folks.

It takes place in Terre Haute, Ind., a town where they doubtless know a nerd when they see one. Willum Cubbert is a youngish architect who has everything going for him except that reliant common sense that the playwright terms gumption. . . .

Willum has two friends—his girl Tansy . . . , [and Axel], a sour-mouthed, smart-assed, alcoholic drama critic.

Some years ago, when Willum was serving in Vietnam, his life was saved by a stranger, Rich Steadman, who, although wounded himself, dragged Willum's body back to camp.

Willum had woken up in base hospital in Tokyo, wondering what had hit him. He never met his savior, but they corresponded, and Willum assured Rick that if there was ever anything he could do for him—anything at all—he only had to ask.

So now it is Willum's 34th birthday. He is feeling the first intimations of male menopause, . . . and his hotelier client is bullying Willum to betray his architectural ideals and turn his hotel design into something looking like something between a box and an air-conditioner.

Willum thinks he has troubles; but then Rick unexpectedly arrives. To take up Willum's offer. To stay. To live with Willum. To share his life. Seemingly forever. And Willum thought he had troubles before!

Rick is unbearable. Crass, stupid, boring—he is a walking lexicon of adjectives you don't want to stay with for more than two minutes. He is also oblivious to insult, impenetrable to reason, impervious to rejection. . . .

That is the story—it does have a sort of outcome I will not reveal—that is the situation, that is the character. It is one joke embellished with semi-slick one-liners, mostly one-lined by semi-slick Axel. Rick, with his party games and tambourine, his high-pitched voice and low-pitched mind, is intolerable.

He is not the sort of person you want to spend a play with. And as the play itself is nothing much more than an averagely written TV sit-com with the canned laugh track omitted, I personally wondered what I was doing in the theater at all.

Hearing that Axel took his own duties as a drama critic so lightly that he never stayed to the end of a play awakened a fierce feel of wanderlust in the soul of my boots. . . .

I left *The Nerd* with some relief but conscious of two things. One was that I didn't like it, and the other was a certainty that quite a lot of people will.

> Clive Barnes, *"The Nerd? Absurd,"* in New York Post, *March 23, 1987.*

FRANK RICH

Connoisseurs of nerdiness—a group that includes anyone who ever passed through an American high school—will recognize all the symptoms in [the title character of *The Nerd*]. . . .

[Rick is] a fellow who could drive a person crazy. . . . Act I of *The Nerd* recounts what happens when . . . [he] travels to the Terre Haute home of an old Vietnam war buddy, an architect named Willum, and settles in for an extended stay. Act II describes the farcical pranks by which Willum and his pals try to evict Rick once their hospitality and patience run out.

As readers of the *National Lampoon* and *Mad* magazine know best, nerds are eternally ripe for comic ridicule. Mr. Shue . . . provides pockets of ace material in his first act. . . . Rick insists that everyone play an exasperating parlor game featuring incomprehensible rules, paper-bag masks, eye poking and the mutilation of footwear.

Along the way, Mr. Shue provides some bright one-liners as well, on such eclectic topics as Marjorie Main, Saturday-morning television animation, the fifth act of *Hamlet* and the least likely flavor for ice cream. But its plot similarities notwithstanding, *The Nerd* does not prove to be *The Nerd Who Came to Dinner*. Mr. Shue aspires instead to the formulas of the old-time television sitcom. When Willum's best-laid plans for playing host to his pompous boss are upended by Rick's accidental sowings of chaos, we're back in the cartoon world of Lucille Ball and Gale Gordon.

Fair enough, but network sitcoms run a half-hour, and *The Nerd* is five times that length, including intermission. It takes the playwright nearly 30 minutes to bring on Rick in Act I. Much of that warm-up is devoted to laborious, ultimately inessential exposition about Willum's architectural and romantic interests—far too much of it delivered by telephone answering machine. The prolonged, intentionally "infantile" slapstick shenanigans of Act II turn out to be more exhausting than hysterical. . . .

> Frank Rich, *"Robert Joy in 'The Nerd',"* in The New York Times, *March 23, 1987, p. 16.*

JACK CURRY

Buried within *The Nerd* . . . is a single insight that keeps this often exasperating play from ever becoming pointless:

It is the nerd's capacity for turning everyone around him into nerds that makes him truly dangerous. As ably demonstrated here, when normal people react to the gonzo antics of the titular geek, their own worst sides come out.

Willum, his life saved by an unknown soldier while serving in Vietnam, has set up his architecture business in Terre Haute, Ind. . . .

Out of the blue—or out of a factory in Wisconsin, more exactly—comes Rick, Willum's battlefield savior. Within minutes, the visitor's loser behavior . . . presents Willum with the

play's central problem: What do you do when you owe your life to a jerk?

Quickly, [Willum's, Tansy's, and Axel's] cool melts down as they find themselves resorting to dork-level maneuvers to rid themselves of the nerd. But while this who-can-out-nerd-who set-up creates some enormously funny moments, the joke becomes monotonous by final curtain. . . .

The Nerd certainly isn't Broadway's first geek comedy—although it may be the first one to put its most likely audience in the title.

> Jack Curry, *"Too Many Nerds Spoil the Froth,"* in USA Today, *March 23, 1987.*

JOHN BEAUFORT

Farcical absurdities, daffy gags, and loony conceits run riot in *The Nerd*. . . . Larry Shue sets up a situation made for hokey-jokey maneuvering and then proceeds to maneuver. While results in the present case are variable, farce nevertheless befits Mr. Shue.

The Nerd stresses the unforeseen perils that may attend the effort to pay a debt of gratitude. Terre Haute architect Willum Cubbert has waited for years to demonstrate with hospitality the thanks he owes Rick Steadman for having saved Willum's life in Vietnam. (The men were separated immediately following the brave deed.) Then one November day in 1981, Rick shows up. It soon becomes clear that, notwithstanding his moment of heroic glory, Rick must have been the nerdiest nerd in Uncle Sam's army.

Shue's comic props, devices, and general silliness start with the green monster getup in which Rick first appears, mistakenly thinking he has been invited to a costume party. Among other things, the over-extended proceedings involve a totally weird parlor game, a chatter-box phone answering machine, and specimens of Terre Haute cuisine undreamed of back home in Indiana. . . .

According to the [play's program], *"The Nerd* became the highest-grossing play of the West End season when it was staged at London's Aldwych Theatre in 1984." While Broadway playgoers may prove harder to please, it can be reported that a preview audience found the Shue shenanigans irresistibly funny.

> John Beaufort, *" 'The Nerd': Hokey-Jokey Farce on Stage,"* in The Christian Science Monitor, *March 25, 1987, p. 23.*

VARIETY

The naivete of Americans encountering totalitarian political repression is poignantly and gently dramatized in the late Larry Shue's *Wenceslas Square*. . . .

The evidently autobiographical play recounts a 1974 return visit to Prague by a midwestern theater academic who's wrapping up a book on the flowering of artistic free expression that preceded the Soviet clampdown. Play has a flashback structure, narrated by a scenic designer who, then a rube student, accompanied the prof.

Less farcical and more thoughtful than Shue's *The Foreigner* and *The Nerd,* the play reaps a sizable laugh harvest through the encounters of the impressionable Yanks with an assortment of Czech theater people and literati, all of whom are played by two actors.

It's this multiple-character feature and the opportunities for virtuoso versatility that give the play its theatrical energy. . . .

Shue let the returning academic take far too long to get the obvious point, that the Prague Spring which so impressed him has turned to Soviet winter, and the character of the tagalong student isn't properly developed or assimilated into the action. . . .

It's a play in *sotto voce,* but none the less pleasing for that. . . .

Shue's sad death in a 1985 plane crash deprived the theater of a fast-growing talent. . . .

> *Humm., in a review of "Wenceslas Square," in* Variety, *March 9, 1988, p. 69.*

EDITH OLIVER

[*Wenceslas Square*], for all the enjoyment it offers, seems to evaporate before our eyes. It is about the memories of a scenic designer named Dooley, who in 1974 paid a short visit to Czechoslovakia with a professor of his named Vince. Vince had been there in 1968, during that interlude of freedom called the Prague Spring, and he has written an as yet unpublished book about it, which he brings with him as he looks up old acquaintances. . . . The play opens some years later with Dooley as narrator, now grown older . . . , and immediately shifts to 1974, with a younger actor . . . in the role. The action itself consists of an assortment of brief encounters with an assortment of people, making do or not under Soviet repression. Although the atmosphere is often sombre, even menacing, no opportunity for comedy has been overlooked by Mr. Shue. . . .

As we move from person to person, from place to place, and back and forth in time, the effect is kaleidoscopic. . . . (p. 80)

At this point in his tragically short career . . . , Mr. Shue was striking out into new territory; he was still as adept as ever when trying to be funny, somewhat insubstantial when trying to be serious. But who knows what could have been? (pp. 80-1)

> *Edith Oliver, "Colloquy," in* The New Yorker, *Vol. LXIV, No. 4, March 14, 1988, pp. 80-1.*

Emma Tennant

1937-

(Has also written under pseudonym of Catherine Aydy) English novelist, editor, critic, short story writer, and author of children's books.

Tennant's novels examine themes relating to human relationships and individual identity. Employing an ornate prose style replete with elaborate imagery and symbolism, Tennant blurs distinctions between fantasy and reality and frequently evokes an ominous Gothic atmosphere. She utilizes elements of satire, allegory, and parody to comment on contemporary social conditions and the idiosyncrasies of the British upper class while exploring the psychological motivations of her characters. Tennant's works often center on vulnerable and bewildered female protagonists whose attempts to develop a stronger sense of personal understanding are challenged by strange people and events.

Tennant's first novel, *The Colour of Rain* (1964), which she published under the pseudonym of Catherine Aydy, is a conventional study of London's upper-class milieu. Nominated by its publisher for a European fiction prize, the novel was condemned as "an example of British decadence" by Alberto Moravia, a renowned Italian literary figure who served as one of the judges for the award. Discouraged by this assessment, Tennant continued writing fiction but refused to submit her work to publishers for nearly a decade. Her next three novels satirize contemporary English society. In *The Time of the Crack* (1973), an earthquake creates a wide fissure that separates London into halves, one of which is nearly destroyed, while the other remains secure and prosperous. Concentrating on the struggles of characters in the ruined half of the city to reach the other side, Tennant creates an allegory of modern society. *The Last of the Country House Murders* (1974), which parodies English murder mysteries, depicts near-future England as a totalitarian state with an economy dependent upon tourism. The leaders of this nation plan to murder the country's only remaining aristocrat and use his estate as a tourist attraction. *Hotel de Dream* (1976), which explores the nature of illusion and reality, revolves around hotel inhabitants whose dreams begin to control their lives. Further complications arise as residents become intertwined in each others' fantasies and two characters created by a writer gradually develop into actual human beings.

Tennant has stated that her next few novels concern "the female Gothic—particularly the theme of the double and the myths and fairy tales that go to make up the female psyche." The structure and subject matter of *The Bad Sister* (1978) parallel and parody James Hogg's 1824 novel *The Private Memoirs and Confessions of a Justified Sinner,* in which a young man, possibly possessed by demons, murders his mother and brother. Tennant changes the sexes of the principal characters and sets the story in contemporary times to examine themes related to female identity. *The Bad Sister* is written in the form of a journal compiled by the protagonist that simultaneously reveals her quest for identity and the disintegration of her personality. *Wild Nights* (1979), which is set in a Scottish manor and features several eccentric characters, is narrated by an adolescent girl who becomes enchanted by a witchlike aunt. In *Alice Fell*

(1980), a reworking of the Greek myth of Persephone, a young woman living in the seedy underworld of London returns to the large estate where she was raised and reverses the decline of her family. This novel also examines English social and political issues from the 1950s and 1960s. In *Queen of Stones* (1982), Tennant recreates from a feminine perspective the scenario and themes of William Golding's novel *Lord of the Flies,* focusing on a group of young girls who find themselves lost and alone in an unfamiliar area. Separated from the adult world, the girls take on various roles and identities in their struggle for survival. Adam Mars-Jones commented: "The greater part of the book is brilliantly suspended between . . . two styles, the mythical and the intuitive, and flirts boldly with a succession of genres (case-history, fairy story, dream diary, Gothic, thriller) without tying itself down."

In her later work, Tennant continues to examine the eccentricities of wealthy characters as well as relationships among people from different social classes. The narrator of *Woman Beware Woman* (1983; published in the United States as *The Half-Mother*) returns after a ten-year absence to the home of a famous novelist following his mysterious murder. Utilizing such elements of Gothic fiction as revenge, sexual obsession, and a haunting landscape that contributes an aura of mystery and decadence, this novel blends present events and the narrator's memories to depict the strained relationships among several women associated with the victim. *Black Marina* (1985), set on a Caribbean island, includes elements of international intrigue and such characteristic devices of Tennant's work as an unreliable narrator, violent deaths, and sudden plot twists. In *The Adventures of Robina, by Herself* (1985), Tennant parodies Daniel Defoe's novels *Roxana* and *Moll Flanders* to detail the misadventures of a 1950s debutante. *The House of Hospitalities* (1987) is the first in a projected series of novels following the relationships of four schoolgirls from various social classes. The narrator of this novel reminisces about the decadence and luxury she observed while a guest at the home of one of the other girls. According to Sara Maitland, Tennant's lush prose and poignant observations of upper-class English life allow "the dream world and the real world—the fantasy of class privilege, with its beauty and generosity, and the snobbish, petty, pompous and frightening practice—to flow in and out of each other in a very rich and courageous way."

In addition to her fiction, Tennant founded *Bananas*, a literary magazine that concentrated on publishing the work of young writers between 1975 and 1978. Tennant has also edited several anthologies of fiction, and she is the author of a book for young adults, *The Search for Treasure Island* (1981), based on the novel by Robert Louis Stevenson.

(See also *CLC*, Vol. 13; *Contemporary Authors*, Vols. 65-68; *Contemporary Authors New Revision Series*, Vol. 10; and *Dictionary of Literary Biography*, Vol. 14.)

TONY PALMER

[In *The Time of the Crack*], Emma Tennant has written a (mercifully short) satirical parable about the day the world came to an end when a crack appeared in it right down the middle of the Thames and swallowed up all that was nearest and dearest in our civilisation including, presumably, the sewage which had polluted the river. All that remains is the Playboy Club, although that too eventually crumbles. Clearly, a very symbolical tale. (p. 753)

[Tennant] relies for the energy of her piece (a short story rather than a novel) upon the curiosity of the story and the mock seriousness of its incidents. Not that her book lacks the picturesque phrase. For example, she describes the tottering towers of Cheyne Walk following the earthquake as being like "exhausted guests at the end of a fancy dress party". There are also numerous genuflections toward fashionable causes—intellectualised Women's Lib being the most odious—although Miss Tennant's disgust at these sociological warts is too genteel to be effective. But then, she *is* genteel. Nothing wrong with that, except it does tend to precondition one to expect. To expect to be admired, to expect to be wanted, and to expect to write easily. Which is exactly what Miss Tennant does, but not *about* anything. Her central idea, that a physical earthquake which disrupts accepted social harmony will not necessarily be replaced by a better scheme, lies plonk on the page. It should have been grappled with until the last drop of significance however absurd had been wrested from it. But it has not. (p. 754)

Tony Palmer, "Enjoyable But . . . ," in The Spectator, Vol. 230, No. 7564, June 16, 1973, pp. 753-54.

JOHN SPURLING

Emma Tennant's first novel *The Time of the Crack* is a short, staccato account of how a great crack opens in the bed of the Thames reducing London to rubble and its inhabitants to corpses or hysterics. The book threatens at times to turn into one of those high-minded attempts, like Penelope Gilliatt's *One by One,* to show us all what worms we are, how shallow and mean our civilisation is, when submitted to the test of a great natural disaster. Fortunately Miss Tennant is content with what she can extract from the situation moment by moment in the way of jokes, surrealist cadenzas and passages of bizarre description that occasionally remind one of Mervyn Peake—a concourse of bald heads seen far below through a crack in the dome of the British Museum Reading Room, lead gargoyles dripping in the heat of the sun, and 'by the armless Peter Pan statue, a pile of grey-flannelled nannies lying on the ground'. It is an odd book, not so much a novel, more a series of slightly macabre cartoons.

John Spurling, "Losing Caste," in New Statesman, Vol. 86, No. 2207, July 6, 1973, p. 26.

STEPHEN CLARK

Between one revolution and the next the people of the British Isles are starving in their shacks throughout the countryside, the once-rich play out games of bridge and banter at a perpetual party too tawdry to be called theatrical, there is a nameless government with tired officers, and there are a few recalcitrants, such as Jules Tanner. The last caged inmate of the last country house, Tanner has beguiled the last years permitted to him by wrecking the artistic and historic heritage the government has planned to unveil, on his death, to the world's tourists. The time has finally come: Tanner is to be the victim of a dramatic murder—his murderer selected, and then revealed, by a government spy dressed up as Lord Peter Wimsey. . . .

Everything goes wrong. Jules finds death a little premature, and tries to bribe the ersatz Wimsey. Bessy, a woman wronged because Jules could not wrong her, pursues a death-or-marriage policy. Enter left the saviour, Cedric, actor supreme. . . .

[This] farrago offers few insights into England as it is or as it might become. We may yet be doomed to mass starvation, idiot bureaucracy, the final retreat of imagination, but when it comes it will not be like this. Nor do I suppose Ms Tennant thinks it will be. The work's point, and merit, lies elsewhere. In the superfluous invention: Jules's metallic birds mechanically tip-tap down the gravel paths—every week he starts them off again. In Cedric's impeccable mime of Bogart, Fagin and—his greatest part—"Mein Fuehrer". Revolutions are made in drab landscapes by the evocation of past phantoms.

The state spy, "a sort of Pooter", is the government's best copy of Cedric: both are without personal characteristics, both move in permanent and changing disguise, both stand in at some point in the tale for Jules. But whereas Cedric is supremely competent at anything he tries—too competent indeed—the poor detective, bridling his nostalgia for fear his face betray his feelings, torn between the old revolution and the new, can produce only a murder as prosaically unconvincing as Ms Tennant's own ending is grotesquely perfect.

What the moral of this very moral tale is, I cannot tell. The only surviving named character is Jules, aesthete and pederast: are love and artistry, however twisted from their proper end, our only, feeble hope till the Great Ones come from their retreat? The other stars are gone, there is no world but this. To shatter the dead past, to make a new covenant with our creative powers: there, perhaps, an insight lies. The second revolution, in a burst of running feet, may promise better than poor Jules can see. These, at any rate, are the formulations of what is spoken so trippingly in this minor, but elegant and sometimes moving satire.

> *Stephen Clark, "Minimum Revolutions," in* The Times Literary Supplement, *No. 3804, January 31, 1975, p. 102.*

JAMES BROCKWAY

[*The Last of the Country House Murders*] is a delightful extravaganza told with verve and set in the future, when the faceless bureaucrats have got us all firmly in their grip. They order a murder to be staged as a tourist attraction and sop to the masses, whom years of television and radio conditioning have rendered perfectly passive and mindless. The event is to be combined with a spot-the-murderer quiz, via closed-circuit television, and will turn Woodiscombe Manor, the scene of the crime, into a Grade One Tourist Attraction. . . .

Attractive though the idea is, the main attractions are the writing, always sprightly, and Miss Tennant's clever mind and assured technique. She reminds me of Brigid Brophy and her fables, though she skates around on the surface more lightly. She knows exactly how to employ improbability and skip all the pedestrian business of logic and verisimilitude, leaping from scene to scene and character to character with great agility and vivacity—and the right touch of arbitrariness. A glance at the physical structure of the book—152 pages divided up into twenty-five brisk chapters—tells a lot. . . .

This novel is not merely an extravaganza though. Its futuristic picture of a public stultified and stupefied by electronics and an utterly pliable quantity in the hands of the Powers That Be is not *all that* futuristic. The emphasis the book lays on the part played in this by technology, by radio and television, as a tool of power, as a means of manipulating the masses, is highly relevant to our society today and a deeply serious issue. To defeat those who would use—are using—technology as such we need sharp minds and talents like Emma Tennant. A highly entertaining and necessary book.

> *James Brockway, in a review of "The Last of the Country House Murders," in* Books and Bookmen, *Vol. 20, No. 12, September, 1975, p. 64.*

EDWIN MORGAN

It does not require any detective work to realize that *The Bad Sister* is a variant of James Hogg's *The Private Memoirs and Confessions of a Justified Sinner* (1824). Hogg is mentioned towards the end of the novel, and the parallels are close and fairly pervasive. There is the same construction, a confessional journal sandwiched between two sections of editorial narrative and comment; the satanic figure of Gil-Martin appears in both books . . . ; and both books raise the same questions about certain murders—whether the murderer was psychologically disturbed or demonically possessed. The two main differences are sexual and political. The central character in Hogg's novel is a young man who is responsible for the deaths of his mother and brother, and in Ms Tennant's it is a young woman who (apparently) kills her father and sister; in addition to this, Ms Tennant makes the nature and role of women in society a central theme. The political aspect is dangled somewhat desultorily across her book, with the suggestion that the murders might have been politically motivated. . . . The period is the late 1970s (the "editor" writes from the near future, in 1986) and at times a slight suggestion of Patty Hearst or Ulrike Meinhof steals over the reader's mind, but on the whole not very much is made of these possibilities, and the concerns of the book seem to be more psychological than political.

Jane, illegitimate daughter of Michael Dalzell, has an immediate and consuming jealousy of his legitimate daughter Ishbel, whom she fights as a child, haunts, and (it is suggested) kills, just as Robert fights, haunts, and kills his brother George in Hogg's *Confessions*. But jealousy, and the other possible motivation of money, are only a part of it. There are strong intimations of demonic control, both from Jane's sculptor friend Gala who "needs the spirit world for her work" and more especially from the witchlike Meg who leads the women's community and who is urging Jane (according to Jane's account) to break free into the spirit world. Meg is "reversing science, translating the known into the unknown"; she offers new powers, but at a classically high cost: Jane's body is found with a stake through its heart. What Jane is searching for is described as a new wholeness, an end to the "double female self" if she can kill her sister, and a gaining of the necessary "male principle" if she can find Gil-martin, which she imagines herself doing at the close of her journal. She is really searching for a power that women are surmised to have had in pre-scientific times, lost, and now begun in various ways to set about retrieving. A house for battered wives and a lesbian club are features of the scene where much of the action takes place, and the male characters are for the most part uninteresting, ineffectual, or marked for death.

As Jane's identity crisis becomes more acute—and a psychiatric report included by the editor labels her as "a schizophrenic with paranoid delusions"—she sees herself as shadowing or being shadowed by other female figures who are sometimes quite clearly projections of herself. The nightmarish ambiguities of these later scenes, with their vivid evocations of mingled real and unreal environments, and their acrid infusion of suspense, really grip the reader. Overall, Ms Tennant's novel does not have the relentless drive of Hogg's because it lacks the foundation of hard and defined theological doctrine out of which Hogg nurtured his nightmare; on the other hand, *The Bad Sister* has a jagged, shifting, cinematic quality which is of its time. To some, its concerns—feminism, witchcraft, "wholeness"—will seem modish. If this is a criticism, it is a criticism which has to be placed against the informing perspective of Hogg's original *Confessions*.

> *Edwin Morgan, "Devil's Work," in* The Times Literary Supplement, *No. 3981, July 21, 1978, p. 817.*

SONIA JAFFE ROBBINS

[*The Bad Sister*] hits on so many elements of the '70s, both profound and banal—feminism, political murder, occultism—that reading the dust jacket ("a brilliant anatomy of today's woman, trapped in society and torn by its conflict") may tempt you to put it aside as a potboiler. Resist the temptation. This is a powerful novel, small in focus yet intense in effect.

The fulcrum of the story is the murders in 1976 of a Scottish landowner [Michael Dalzell] and his 24-year-old legitimate daughter. Ten years later, a rather stuffy, elderly reporter investigating the still-unsolved crimes comes across new "evidence'' in the form of a journal, which leads him to suspect that its writer, the landowner's illegitimate daughter Jane, is the murderer. The journal makes up the bulk of the novel and is as different in tone from the reporter's prologue and epilogue as possible.

The reporter is dry, rational, straightforward. He gives us the facts. . . .

Jane's journal is a masterful emotional document, plunging us directly into her mind as she is driven mad by the fragmentation women often feel in trying to discover who they are. Jane literally cannot live in her own skin, and her journal cascades through fantasies and dreams as she tries to escape from herself. She is battered by the traditional rivalries between women, and seems unable to face directly the primal rivalry between herself and her mother. (p. 132)

Ultimately, the puzzles—was Jane the victim of a feminist ideology that saw Dalzell as "the symbol of the father of all women," or was she possessed by demons using her to extend their power, or was she suffering a psychotic breakdown?—are less important than Jane's progress through femaleness as madness. (p. 134)

Sonia Jaffe Robbins, in a review of "The Bad Sister," in The Village Voice, Vol. XXIII, No. 41, October 16, 1978, pp. 132, 134.

HERMIONE LEE

There's nothing simple or modest about Emma Tennant's weird, ambitious phantasmagoria [*Wild Nights*], which looks like a cross between Mervyn Peake and Angela Carter. She has used fantasy before, in *Hotel de Dream* and *The Time of the Crack*, but *Wild Nights* is much wilder than its predecessors. No distinctions are now drawn between the real and the bizarre; the reader is at the mercy of a clotted, glittering accumulation of unlikely details.

In a mock-Gothic castle, the imposition of mid-nineteenth century capitalism on a remote Scottish valley, the remnants of a family—disconsolate parents, reclusive Uncle Ralph, forever working on a machine to make the house revolve or 'in some cupboard hanging like a great bat upside down in the darkness, proving a new biological clock'—await the coming of winter and Aunt Zita's visitation. To the child-narrator it seems that Aunt Zita can raise the dead, turn herself into animals, summon ghostly attendants and ride on the north wind. But her exotic powers are thwarted by the pious influence of the mother's family, and by the sinister hostilities of the half-civilized villagers. After Aunt Zita is destroyed ('she burned as quickly as paper'), the family flees south for the painful onset of spring, leaving the house to its ghosts.

Lurking beneath this black masque is a surplusage of themes: the battle against the past, in history, families, and the seasons; the ancient conflict of Christian and pagan forces; the decline of a Victorian industrialist's family, sapped by sexual repression and by two wars. And the whole novel might be read as the over-intense pubescent fantasy life of the watching child. These possibilities are contained within a narrative which enacts the main idea of metamorphosis by a display of ostentatious similes. . . . This novel will be an irritant to those who dislike the self-validating sensationalism of fantasy. Even so, its sustained imaginative audacity must be admired.

Hermione Lee, "Enter a Stranger," in The Observer, September 16, 1979, p. 37.

CAROLE ANGIER

Wild Nights is more a poem than a novel. It is wild, lyrical and—to me—utterly obscure. The narrator seems to be the only child of the Big House which dominates, and owns, a bleak northern valley. Mother and father hang on to shreds of ordinariness, but the rest of the family are very queer. . . . Strangest of all is Aunt Zita, who comes to visit for three weeks every year. Pale, magenta-lipped and spewing fire, she is, at least to the narrator, magical. . . . Aunt Zita, however, seems to be vanquished by the next visitor, pious Aunt Thelma; Zita is burnt by the villagers, and the family go south. They stay with Uncle Rainbow, who lives somewhere swampy and wet and near the sea. Here they are washed over by the spring—only to return to the north, where spring has hardly reached, and to start the annual cycle of aunts and uncles all over again.

Emma Tennant must be telling us something about the cycle of the seasons, about growth and sex, and about the past and the nature of time. But *what* is not at all clear. Perhaps just that the past is always there, either buried below the surface of our minds—as the old village is buried beneath the new in *Wild Nights*—or, as it is to Zita and the child, always present and visible. But that could be said less confusingly and more interestingly than it is here. Occasionally the language is beautiful; but more often it is, to my ear, overdone, vague and obscure. Towards the end of the book Emma Tennant writes: 'From the stone mouths of the sea came riddles, impossible to understand, and spewings of foam'. It is probably my own fault, but that is just how I feel about *Wild Nights*. (pp. 121-22)

Carole Angier, in a review of "Wild Nights," in British Book News, February, 1980, pp. 121-22.

CAROL RUMENS

Large, faded country houses and hotels form an important part of the imaginative terrain of Emma Tennant. They seem to provide a metaphor both for the individual human consciousness and for historical change, particularly as it is played out between the generations. [*Alice fell*] revolves around just such a house, set vaguely among "the Downs" and occupied by its owner, the Old Man, and by the Paxton family and their child Alice.

The fictional method, familiar to readers of Tennant, is not entirely allegorical, though allegory plays a major part and the "real" world is presented at a remove, stylized and symbol-strewn. As *Alice fell* unwinds in its chapterless sections it suggests a medieval tapestry, or perhaps a more ancient frieze depicting godlike characters, larger and simpler than life. The difficulty is that by stylizing the Paxton household and treating the members as agents of myth (Alice herself is, of course, Persephone) Ms Tennant sacrifices the novelist's most effective means of holding the reader's attention—the sense of chance exercising itself within a life. As archetypes her characters have a limited choice of actions. With the exception of Alice, they scarcely develop over the twenty or so years of the narrative. . . .

Within their allegorical limits, however, the characters and the family structure are credible. . . .

At times, a delicate comic sense takes over, as when Mrs Paxton devotes herself to abolishing the ghostly presences of Great Men: "Freud's pinstripe trousers were quickly dismissed, no more than a wasp shadow lying by the door to the third room off the landing. Picasso was more difficult, leaving as he did a mass of angles for Mrs Paxton to walk through". Elsewhere, there are some vivid surreal touches: "The cries of the child were a distant cutting: trees fell, giving out flakes of red dust as the chain of high sound bit the bark". But when the outside world is more realistically introduced it seems as oddly intrusive in the text as in the lives of the Paxtons themselves: "Water boiled. Mr. Paxton went over to the wireless in the corner and twiddled a knob to hear news from Sir Anthony Eden". . . .

The symbolism can seem over-obvious and rather simplistic. George's Analytic Engine, supposedly introduced to represent the rising dominance of dry rationalism, is one example. Alice's obsession with equal sizes as she divides chocolate amounts almost to a parody of the democratic concerns of the 1960s. But on the whole *Alice fell* is stronger, less whimsical stuff than the predecessor it most resembles, *Wild Nights.* Against the imperfectly realized sense of historical development, Emma Tennant sets the more compelling counterpoint of cyclical change, as represented by the turning seasons in the countryside around the house. Despite its short length, the novel achieves an impressive feeling of spaciousness. The prose itself is beautifully measured and graceful, and though perhaps one wouldn't turn the page on account of the story's narrative impetus, one certainly does so for the pure pleasure of the style.

> Carol Rumens, *"Agents of Myth,"* in The Times Literary Supplement, *No. 4049, November 7, 1980, p. 1250.*

JUDY COOKE

Emma Tennant's brand of Gothicism may be less disturbing [than Robert Nye's] but it proves to be equally demanding. *Alice Fell* is an extraordinary book, poetic and bizarre, with the wild logic of a surrealist painting or a dream. Alice falls into a wonderland of past civilisations and certainties and promptly destroys them; she is like a comet, blazing the way to a new age. Delivered by Mrs Grogan and born to Mrs Paxton, her childhood home is gradually revealed as the great house, beautiful but decaying, in which her mother works as a servant to the Old Man. The writing is superb taken line by line, at its best when it deals in symbols, at its weakest in the characterisation. Who is Alice? What is her growing awareness to do with the real events interpolated in the text, the Suez crisis, Porton Down? The novel is flawed, being obscure; exhilarating, impossible to classify. (p. 23)

> Judy Cooke, *"Black Mass,"* in New Statesman, *Vol. 100, No. 2592, November 21, 1980, pp. 22-3.*

ADAM MARS-JONES

Queen of Stones ends with a Short Bibliography; and though the booklist is compiled by the narrator rather than the author, it gives a fair idea of the novel's concerns. There are books on psychology (Freud, Ferenczi) and on children's imaginative worlds (Bruno Bettelheim, the Opies). . . .

The book's opening also makes appeal to the authority of print; it purports to reproduce an item from the *Bridport Advertiser* of October 19, 1981, with the headline "Missing Girls—Fears Grow". There follows an "Author's Note" which offers sketches of the main characters, based on photographs given to the press by their parents.

The eldest, Bess, is thirteen, bright, beautiful and apparently stable; the youngest girls, at six, are much more suggestible. But even Bess is profoundly affected when a dense fog, the worst ever recorded on the west coast of Dorset, separates her party from the adult who is leading their sponsored walk.

The impressively circumstantial opening represents one pole of the novel's style, and is taken up by subsequent reports from psychiatrists and social workers. The other pole is a free fantasy, lucid but discontinuous, which turns the girls' experiences into a vivid series of threats and epiphanies. The greater part of the book is brilliantly suspended between these two styles, the mythical and the intuitive, and flirts boldly with a succession of genres (case-history, fairy story, dream diary, Gothic, thriller) without tying itself down. . . .

The book moves with great excitement towards the violent death promised by the Author's Note. Who will be struck down? And who will strike? Bess? Melanie? Mary and Mathilda, the sinister twins? Fey, withdrawn Nat Minges?

It is at this point that the excitement so cleverly generated begins to disperse. The book abandons its games with genre and settles down to become a thriller. It loses much by doing so; the manipulative pleasures of a thriller are achieved at the expense of the consistent focus demanded by a case-history.

The novel remains Freudian in its ideas about human behaviour; though the character of the retired analyst Dr Ross is mildly ridiculed, his conclusions are upheld. But as the story proceeds, the girls seem less and less plausible a group, and the whole project runs into difficulties. Freud's innovation, after all, was not the suggestion that people in extreme situations behave irrationally, but that there is an element of extremity in all behaviour, and a lurid logic to mental events. . . . Emma Tennant's procedure in this book is essentially the opposite; she dramatizes what is already dramatic, and ends up creating mysteries instead of revealing them.

The book's climactic atrocity is also a compromise between exegesis and mystification. The motives are properly symbolic, as befits a case-history; but there must be a twist in the tail, if a thriller is to thrill to the end, and so neither the murderer nor the victim are the expected candidates for their roles.

The result is an abrupt and disastrous relaxation of tension. The book moves into high rhetorical gear, but disengages the reader; and the subtle workings of the unconscious mind (so remarkably conveyed by the book for much of its length) are finally abandoned in favour of the coarser substitutions and displacements of thriller technique.

> Adam Mars-Jones, *"Fog with Thrills,"* in The Times Literary Supplement, *No. 4155, November 19, 1982, p. 1268.*

LORNA SAGE

Twice-told tales and stories made out of stones are at once sophisticated and primitive devices. A writer adding a new layer of speculation to familiar motifs is more often than not obeying an atavistic urge to revisit childhood haunts, no matter how conscious and literary the technique seems. William Golding's *Lord of the Flies* was a book of this kind—a cento of earlier island fantasies, located on the threshold between the adult's and the child's consciousness. And now *Queen of Stones* by Emma Tennant repeats the trick by re-writing *Lord of the*

Flies itself, once again in search of a route back to childhood's kingdom by the sea.

Or rather, queendom, since this time the cast of lost children is all-female . . . , a bevy of schoolgirls cut off on a promontory of the Dorset coast by a sudden and semi-mythic mist, acting out the changeling roles they remember from fairy tales and games and dreams. Their characters are distinct. . . .

As the hours of fog-bound wandering draw out, however, the girls' half-formed personalities splinter and recombine in increasingly ominous patterns. Like Gulliver, or Alice, the older ones find themselves alarmingly large (and realistic, and adult) one moment, frighteningly small and fantasy-bound the next. Soon, though, after a false start or two, they learn to synchronise their new selves, and agree on a deadly game to play.

The ending (we've been here before) is never in doubt. We know what will happen—if not, until the last, who it will happen to. And in a sense, though the suspense is real enough, the identity of the scapegoat is almost irrelevant, since the murder is a rite of passage. Ms Tennant's characters are killing off their childhoods in one final festival of role playing, before they settle into the skins of the women they'll be as adults, and forget the impossible love-affairs (you be good Queen Bess, I'll be Mary Queen of Scots) that official history says can't happen. What the violent climax does establish is that, in contrast with Golding's book, *Queen of Stones* is finally sceptical about the efficacy of its rites. Ms Tennant, deconstructing her oft-told tale, seems to be wondering, off-stage, whether the archetypes themselves aren't somehow unsatisfying, whatever games you play with them. As a result the novel misses out on the compulsive quality of real regression, and stays, after all, reluctantly grown-up.

> Lorna Sage, "Dark Doings in Old Wessex," *in* The Observer, *November 21, 1982, p. 34.*

JOHN WALSH

A party of Dorset schoolgirls on a sponsored walk are lost in fog, separated from their Women's Legion supervisor. A search party takes days to find them, . . . days in which their young minds are assailed by terrors of assault and loss, until their strange journey leads to madness and ritual execution. . . .

Emma Tennant is an experienced hand at extracting the last drop of Gothic suggestion from everyday circumstance. Her highly-charged prose [in *Queen of Stones*] wreathes the stranded infants in a miasma of bizarre fantasies—The Wind Man, who steals babies and substitutes changelings; the Posy Tree with its connotations of plague; the court of Elizabeth I with its retinue of swans and ruffled waves. And in addition, to lend an air of analytical rigour to what is apparently a true life story, she intersperses the poetic narrative with formal psychiatric reports on the central characters, diagnosing Electra complexes, personality transference and sexual jealousy.

It's a strange, unsettling novel with a chequered parentage: by *Lord of the Flies,* out of *Picnic at Hanging Rock,* with some genetic strains of *White Hotel* pop-psychology, the whole dressed up in Fay Weldonish detached paragraphs. It's not, unfortunately, quite enough: though the dénouement startles, it is affecting only in a disconnected, thrillerish way. The elements of sub-conscious obsession and desire simply fail to cohere. but it's nonetheless an absorbing study of pre-pubescent dreams of power and majesty.

> John Walsh, in a review of "Queen of Stones," in Books and Bookmen, *No. 327, December, 1982, p. 36.*

STEPHEN BANN

In order to envisage the curious achievement of Emma Tennant's *Queen of Stones,* you must first imagine that Virginia Woolf has rewritten *Lord of the Flies.* Interior monologues and painfully acute perceptions of a seaside landscape combine to colour in what is essentially a tale of a group of girls wrecked on a desert island. The fact that the desert island is just off the coast of Dorset, and has been isolated by an exceptionally heavy fog, is quite immaterial. It is the isolation from the adult world that counts—and of course the fateful pattern of relationships that emerges from that isolation. But having imagined Mrs Woolf at this recuperative task, you must then take into account the likelihood that she has been nosing through the Hogarth Press edition of the works of Freud. Intercalated with the story of rivalries and affiliations among the hapless castaways is a series of reports by 'Dr Ross, Freudian Psychoanalyst, aged 76'. Despite his great age, Dr Ross has a shrewd diagnosis to make about Bess Plantain, the adolescent girl who initiates the collective violence.

Emma Tennant's novel thus proceeds through a kind of lurching counterpoint. One moment we are under the blanket of fog, observing the fact that twins stick together and mysterious foreign girls have an odd effect on the homogeneity of the group. The next moment, we are back in the consulting-room. Dr. Ross is painstakingly reviewing the symptoms of Bess's earlier life, and moving towards an interpretation which seems unashamedly parasitic on Freud's case-history of Dora. The psychoanalytic commentary is not the only adult vantage-point in this dialogue between event and interpretation. Bess Plantain comes from a wealthy background, and can therefore be offered the luxury of a Freudian psychoanalysis. But Melanie Ayres, a companion on the sponsored walk which led to the fog-bound isolation, is not so fortunately placed. The commentary on her deprived and eventful life is provided by 'Social Worker Ms S. B. Potts' (no age given).

It is not all that difficult to grasp Emma Tennant's strategy at this point. *Lord of the Flies* is a novel about boys. *Queen of Stones* is a novel about girls. *Lord of the Flies* is a story which makes use of the exotic props of the desert island location, and accepts the inheritance of Defoe and Stevenson. *Queen of Stones* keeps closer to home, making the psychological as well as the socio-economic backgrounds of the children impinge upon the exceptional series of actions which takes place on the Dorset coast. It would be possible to proceed from here to the suggestion that *Lord of the Flies* is a mythologising book, which deliberately exploits the sacred and mysterious aspects of collective violence, while *Queen of Stones* is a demythologising book, which places the instruments for analysing the violence in the reader's hands. That is certainly the implication of the 'Short Bibliography' at the close of the novel, which adds Bettelheim's *The Uses of Enchantment,* the Opies' *Lore and Language of Schoolchildren* and Zweig's *Mary, Queen of Scots* to the psychoanalytic resources of Freud, Ferenczi and Winnicott. If *Queen of Stones* is not quite convincing enough to persuade us to accept it on its own terms, that is not for want of clarity and definition. At least we are provoked to think carefully about the different varieties of myth-making, and their relationship both to the stories we tell and the lives we lead. (p. 10)

Stephen Bann, "Mythic Elements," in London Review of Books, *Vol. 4, December 30, 1982 to January 19, 1983, pp. 10-11.*

FRANCIS KING

As its title [*Woman Beware Woman*], echoing that of a tragedy by Middleton, would suggest, this short, allusive, packed novel is primarily about the terrible damage that women can inflict on each other. At its start, its heroine, Minnie, who is also its narrator, resolves, after a lapse of ten dreary years, once more to make the journey, even more arduous emotionally than physically, from her home with her mother in North Kensington to the house on the southern coast of Ireland in which she passed some of the most exciting times of her life with a family not her own. What precipitates this decision is the news that the head of the family, a famous writer called Hugo, has been found dead in some woods, in circumstances that suggest that he may have been murdered.

Though we learn a lot about Hugo—his death becomes the pivot on which the whole story swings back and forth between past and present—it is significant that, of all the characters, he alone remains implausible. . . .

In contrast to Hugo himself, his women are all brilliantly realised. There is, first and foremost, his wife Moura, a painter believed to be the possessor of the evil eye. There is his American daughter-in-law Fran, an insensitive reporter, who guesses that in the mysterious circumstances of his death, perhaps at the hands of the IRA, there may be a story for her. There is the working-class woman, persecuted by her husband, whom Hugo wished to help and so brought on himself the enmity of her in-laws. There is the family retainer, Lily, presiding over the house like an elderly nanny over a fractious nursery. Last, there is Minnie.

In novel-writing I know of no task technically more difficult than to make a narrator inadvertently reveal about himself things which he either has never acknowledged or wishes to suppress. This task Emma Tennant brings off impeccably in her handling of Minnie. With her mysterious atacks of what one assumes to be epilepsy, her drab existence as a tutor in London, and her abiding obsession with the man who never married her, she at first excites only sympathy for her lovelessness and loneliness. But then, as we listen to her plaintively insistent voice telling the story of how someone—Hugo, Moura, her own mother?—cheated her out of the marriage on which she had set her heart, a far more formidable, less likeable figure emerges.

Equally masterly is Emma Tennant's evocation of the house, Cliff Hold, perched on an eyrie of rock high above the sea, and of the wild countryside around it. She paints in her landscape in pale, flat washes of colour, so that the narrow lanes, the huddle of cottages that make up the remote, tiny village, Moura's sub-tropical garden and the ever-present sea all seem to be viewed through a soft, clinging mist.

This story of treachery, sexual obsession, murder and Moura's revenge subsumed in another even more implacable, is told in so devious a manner, with constant time-shifts, that it demands of the reader an intense concentration; but that concentration is amply repaid by the satisfaction of a dénouement that, in a book part whodunnit, part why-dunnit and part psychological study of misdirected love, it would be unfair to reveal. The narrative stretches before the reader like some dank, menacing tunnel, at the distant end of which the view constantly changes, a succession of hallucinations. The reader must be left to explore it for himself, certain of a journey full of unexpected pleasures and shocks.

Francis King, "Gazing In," in The Spectator, *Vol. 251, No. 8107, November 26, 1983, p. 27.*

GRAHAM HOUGH

On the archetypal theme of lost children, [*Queen of Stones*] combines the factual and circumstantial with vision and nightmare—a newspaper cutting, a social worker's report, a psychiatrist's case-history with the terrors and confusions of a band of children lost in a sea-fog, and the disturbed fantasies of those of them who are nearing adolescence. And there is a shocking ending, the explanation of which remains obscure. No one knows what happened and no one can find out. The strength and imaginative intensity are inescapable. Some doubts set in, on reflection. The sheer physical implausibility of some parts of the children's three-day ordeal, including the grisly finale. But that it ends in an unsolved mystery is not a failing, it is integral to the conception, which revolves round the impenetrable obscurity of the children's minds.

Woman Beware Woman is quite evidently by the same hand. There is no similarity in the theme or setting, but the air of obscure foreboding, the fog-wreathed uncertainty, is the same. The quasi-Elizabethan title suggests a drama of revenge, which this is. The scene is Ireland. Minnie, the narrator, is summoned from a dreary life in London to go back after ten years' absence to the house on the West coast where she has spent much of her childhood. It is the residence of Hugo Pierce, the celebrated novelist. But Hugo has just been found dead in the neighbouring woods, and Minnie is needed to stand by and help Moura his widow. There are two sons, Gareth and Philip, both gone to America. Years ago Minnie was engaged, or thought she was engaged, to Philip: but it came to nothing and her life has been empty ever since. So Minnie comes to a house dense with painful memories. Dense, too, with mysteries. It seems likely that Hugo has not as was thought died of a heart attack, but has been murdered; and this provides the surface plot. Who killed him and why? But a host of other ambiguities springs up.

Emma Tennant is extremely skilful at packing into a very short compass long perspectives into the background of her characters and dark surmises for their future. 'Everybody loved Hugo'—but it seems on further examination that he was a posturing humbug with a charm as bogus as his Irish accent. A few pungent scenes give a blood-chilling impression of modern Irish society: the big houses taken over by Germans and rich Americans, a populace ever ready to gang up in support of a murderer. And it soon begins to appear that Moura the widow has her own suspicions and her own obscure scheme of retribution. I cannot pretend to outline the intricacies of the plot, for two reasons. The first is the extraordinary compression. There is enough complex human material here for a long novel, besides much glowingly vivid scene-painting. The second reason is that I really don't know what happens. A powerful sense of menace and of the obscurity of human motives is conveyed, but in the end I do not know who went where, and when, and what was in which mackintosh pocket. And since much stress is laid on these circumstances one is clearly meant to know. The difficulty is compounded because there are many hints throughout that Minnie is an unreliable narrator, and finally, perhaps, that she has been deceived and deluded throughout. This sets out to be more than a mystery story of the whodunnit variety, but for all the power and authority of the writing it runs the risk of ending up as rather less. Or perhaps I am being stupid. All the same I feel that Emma Tennant has such a masterful hand with mystery that she enjoys it a little too much.

Graham Hough, "Auld Lang Syne," in London Review of Books, *Vol. 5, Nos. 22-3, December 1 to December 21, 1983, p. 14.*

GRACE INGOLDBY

Memory is a vital part of *Woman Beware Woman* . . .: a novel about loyalty and betrayal among women, family and friends, on a level with the Last Supper. Minnie, the narrator, returns to Cliff Hold in Ireland after an absence of ten years to a house and a family she has long and unquestionably considered to be a home from home. Hugo, the father of the man to whom she was once engaged, has died; his widow, Maura, will surely need her now? Everything is as it always was—or is it?—for Minnie's memory is, of course, selective, shaped by need, perilously blurred by nostalgia. In the following scenes—who dun it, why, and how to react?—Ms Tennant manoeuvres with surgical skill, sympathy flares and flickers for the deluded Minnie, rising to points of outstanding chill and cold surprise.

Tennant's cat and mouse game and subtle suggestion are the strengths of a novel otherwise flawed by the implausibility of many of its characters. The Irish belong to Donleavy if not Somerville and Ross, and Fran, the Fonda-type, feminist American film-maker, who goes for skeletons in cupboards with the fury of a terrier unleashed, whose pursuit of international terrorists has blunted any shadow of sensitivity, would be happier in *Dallas*. The novel slips inexorably over the cliff—so brilliantly constructed in its opening passages—and into a sea of lyrical incredibility. But as an exposure of self-delusion and the nightmare of misplaced loyalty and affection, it has moments of ice-cold come-uppance for reader and narrator alike.

Grace Ingoldby, "Past Imperfect," in New Statesman, *Vol. 106, Nos. 2752 & 2753, December 16 & December 23, 1983, p. 44.*

RACHEL BILLINGTON

[*The Half-Mother*] is Emma Tennant's eighth novel and, although short, it is complex and ambitious. She uses the first person to tell her story of strange passions. But that often most limiting technique is here moved so boldly through time and memory and the reader's changing perceptions that the effect is many-layered. In this way, *The Half-Mother* is immediately reminiscent of Ford Madox Ford's masterpiece, *The Good Soldier,* in which the final picture is only perceived at the very end.

Like *The Good Soldier*, *The Half-Mother* starts with an evocation of beauty and apparent peace. Minnie, our narrator, is returning from London to southwestern Ireland, scene of the happiest days of her childhood. . . .

[In] the woods above the house, Hugo, its owner and a Nobel Prize-winning writer, has just been found dead, apparently from natural causes. And in the house, Moura, his beautiful painter wife and Minnie's substitute mother, seems to be curiously unmoved. Hugo's death brings back Minnie to her child-hood and brings Hugo and Moura's children back from around the world. . . .

[Minnie's] story, its currents ever darkening, unwinds in parallel narrative with the present day of a village Ireland, of wife-battering and petty thievery beneath the shadow of political violence. . . .

Gradually a book that begins with emphasis on character and description, giving it a fairly static feel, sharpens and moves into the narrative flow of a thriller. "Who killed Hugo?" turns out to be only the first of many questions. Minnie, who presents herself at first as an insignificant spectator, grows in power until she turns out to be the novel's protagonist.

Even as her mind begins to fragment and distort our view, Minnie is an exciting central figure. . . .

Miss Tennant is most successful in the detail and subtlety of her scenes between the women in her novel. . . . Moura seems perhaps an even subtler creation than Minnie, as we watch her turn from the warm earth-mother into the "Half-Mother" of the title. Lily, the old family retainer, a thankless role in constant danger of cliché, seems to smell of the old kitchen like a much-washed pot. Miss Tennant is determined not to lose that essential grip on reality that Lily represents.

Yet there is a period just before the climax when the delicate fabric of the book with its evocative language and imagery is not strong enough to take the rapid buildup of passionate events, involving by now a large number of characters. The author's plan suddenly emerges uncomfortably into view. Miss Tennant is not quite such a good thriller writer as she is a novelist. That aside, *The Half-Mother* is a most accomplished and compelling tale, distinguished by the coherence and subtle detail of its visual imagery.

Rachel Billington, "Ireland, with Corpse," in The New York Times Book Review, *May 12, 1985, p. 14.*

PETER KEMP

Bar-tenders should love Emma Tennant's new novel [*Black Marina*]. Spilling over with instructions on how to prepare cocktails, it frequently reads like a manual for them. . . .

In keeping with this concern with exotic concoctions, *Black Marina* is something of a cocktail itself. Pouring out a tale of rum doings in the Caribbean, it mixes into this a variety of ingredients Tennant also shook together in her last book, *Woman Beware Woman*. There, an untrustworthy narrator, travelling to Ireland, misleadingly recounted a story of violent death and mistaken identity. Here, things are strikingly similar. Once again, the narrator is deceptive; the setting is a politically troubled island; violent death and mistaken identity lie at the heart of it all. As in the earlier book, too, Tennant tops off this latest blend with her favourite garnish: a sour concluding twist.

Set on the Caribbean island of St James, only four miles from Grenada, *Black Marina* brims with references to political chicanery—from Marxist machinations to CIA infiltration. Drawn from second-hand sources—parallels with the 1983 invasion of Grenada are very copiously tapped—all this seems weak and stale, though. The strongest and freshest parts—sometimes pleasantly tangy—of *Black Marina*, in fact, are those which aren't concerned with the Caribbean in the 1980s at all, but with bitter-sweet memories of London in the 1960s. Holly

Baker, the book's narrator, is a product of that era. In her element in swinging London, she has ill-advisedly left it to bar-hop her feckless way across the United States, and ended up managing a ramshackle store on the tiny island of St James. Here, still got up in hippie garb—thonged sandals, tinkling bangles, a faded caftan—she has torpidly become a kind of local landmark.

Around her, though, sprawls a world about to be blasted out of its calypso-and-coconut drowsiness into violent upheaval. Opening with the pastiche of a travel-brochure advertisement—all talk of tranquil lagoons, white beaches and "fabled spices"—the novel closes with a newspaper report of its brutal take-over by American marines. In between—confining her story to one Christmas Eve, throughout the afternoon, evening and night of which events escalate towards crisis—Tennant attempts to show how super-power intrigue and cynical ideologies have worked to undermine the island's picture-postcard calm.

The most authentic-seeming sections in the novel's account of happenings on St James are those which sardonically survey its vulgar tourist world.... Nice incongruities are caught in Tennant's pictures of the Caribbean Christmas with its hibiscus and mistletoe, tinsel and sun-tan oil, plastic reindeers and swooping fruit bats. Attempting to penetrate deeper into the hinterland of the island than this flimsy overlay of hotels and marinas, though, the book merely blunders into a Gothic milieu of lush rottenness: Creole in-breeding, madness, incest, strawberry birthmarks, voodoo women and albino Negroes. Always easily lured into the melodramatic, Tennant plunges into it wholesale with her novel's concluding scenes, where too much comes to light too abruptly and in too unprepared-for a way. Her lurid disclosures about the decadent doings of the island's last feudal grandee and her panting intimations of international skulduggery are alike garishly stagey. Strained parallels with Shakespeare's late plays—for example, what is intended to be a shocking parody of the motif of reunion with a long-lost daughter—add to the unreal atmosphere. Increasingly highly coloured, *Black Marina* is infused with what Emma Tennant clearly hopes is strong stuff. But—unlike a novel such as Margaret Atwood's *Bodily Harm*, with which it has some very marked similarities—it never convincingly captures the rank flavour of Caribbean political ferment.

> Peter Kemp, "A White Dry-Snow-Cauldron Christmas," in The Times Literary Supplement, *No. 4290, June 21, 1985, p. 689.*

LORNA SAGE

Emma Tennant's *Black Marina* belongs in a [strange] ... 'bubble of time,' a Caribbean island setting suddenly invaded by international tourism and international political intrigue. British-but-independent St James becomes the focus for exploring our brave new world, which is seen as made up of islands—of isolated, separate, divided interests that compete and clash invisibly, until they finally, briefly make the headlines. Obviously Ms Tennant's story takes off from the invasion of Grenada, but it's about the psycho-history of such visible events, which it traces back to 'roots, roots, roots'—roots that go back to Robinson Crusoe, and so aren't roots at all, or at best lost ones (Africa) or discarded ones (England).

The narrative is oblique, at once sinisterly swift and inert, as if to mimic tropical torpor. Holly Baker, an English Sixties drifter becalmed for 15 years on the island, tells most of it in a patchy, surreal style, savagely shorthand.... Only gradually

do you realise that Holly herself is part of the action, making things happen, in obscure revenge for her own private paradise lost.

As with other of Emma Tennant's novels ... the writing is dense and allusive, resembling a kind of bloody-minded poetry. This makes the mere plot hard to follow, as if what she wants is to arrange its elements around the reader simultaneously, like the black magic with plants and chicken-feathers her islanders go in for. It's worth the struggle, though, because it does in the end convey exactly the eerie feeling she's after, of a world grown at once enormous and tiny, imploding into violence.

> Lorna Sage, "How We Live Now," in The Observer, *June 23, 1985, p. 22.*

NICHOLAS SPICE

Black Marina is a parable, oblique and elusive in its message, working more by allusion and the suggestion of a correspondence in the underlying forms of things, than by unambiguous and open statement. It succeeds less in the portrayal of particular places and people than in the evocation of a mood and the intimation of certain general truths about the way our world works these days. The mood is one of apprehension and unease, the truths, broadly speaking, that the forces which govern events are far more complex and sinister than they seem, and that evil walks along paths which even the vigilant may overlook. The malignity at work in Tennant's imagined world is not, however, motiveless, and the baddies are clearly identifiable: big business, big politics, big news. Their theatre of operation is the Grenadines, those 'sad thickly green islands in the blue' to the west of Trinidad and the north of Venezuela.

On 27 October 1983, two months before the events described in *Black Marina,* the Americans invaded Grenada, displacing the extreme leftist regime of Hudson Austin and Bernard Coard, leaders of the coup which only eight days previously had ousted the populist government of Maurice Bishop. Now there is a rumour that Austin and Coard's party is planning to infiltrate St James (a tiny island, four miles to the south of Grenada), intending to use it as a base for their subversive activities in the region. It's thought that a landing has been planned for Christmas Eve and the action of *Black Marina* is taken up with this possibility.

The story is divided into three parts—'Afternoon', 'Evening' and 'Night'. It is told, for the most part, by Holly Baker, an English woman in her mid-thirties, who came to St James in the Sixties and ended up staying 16 years, working as the island store-keeper. Holly's narrative is suspended between two violent events, the shooting of a man and the occurrence of something unspecified but dreadful which took place late on Christmas Eve. Although she is only an incidental player in the drama which unfolds, her position as trusted bystander gives Holly an insight which no one else possesses into the links between events. Her narrative is an attempt to join these links into a coherent and consequential chain. Like all acts of remembering where the recollection involves a complex history going back many years, Holly's story proceeds associatively. Her mind moves back and forth across the hours which led to the nameless tragedy, sometimes casting the story in the past tense, sometimes in the present—as one might retell a long and complicated dream. Gradually, the various pieces begin to fall into place....

A picture of international intrigue emerges, of powerful and sinister forces pitted against one another for the possession of the island, of callous manoeuvring and cynical manipulations. . . . At the centre of all this, drawing the threads together, is Holly, a sort of gentle Cassandra, on the edge of the action, aware of the magnitude of what is developing but unable to do anything effective against it. . . .

The sophistication of Emma Tennant's narrative technique in **Black Marina** is considerable. At times it seems to borrow from the minimalist procedures of the Nouveau Roman, elongating over fifty pages or more a sequence of actions that lasts only a few minutes. In the sky a helicopter buzzes, a girl's head bobs on the surface of the sea as she swims towards the shore, a man walks down the beach, the girl approaches Holly's store, she asks a question. Each shot in this slow-motion sequence is the starting-point for a digression or train of association. By such means, Tennant succeeds in creating a disorientating uncertainty in the reader's mind. The constant references and allusions forwards and backwards to mysterious acts of violence and imminent disasters produce a generalised anxiety and undefined menace which is the book's main expressive achievement. Reading **Black Marina,** I felt exposed and vulnerable, as if threatened by a blow but unsure of the direction it would come from. At times, however, I found the portentousness of the style, its heavy load of dark hints, veiled allusions and questions left hanging in the air, monotonous and tiresome. And the dénouement, held back until the last few pages of the novel, is too cryptic to be altogether satisfactory. (p. 11)

> *Nicholas Spice, "Costa del Pym," in* London Review of Books, *Vol. 7, No. 12, July 4, 1985, pp. 10-11.*

HOWARD JACOBSON

[In *The Adventures of Robina, by Herself*] Emma Tennant, although she cites Defoe and Smollett as exemplars, and would even remind us, by verbal echo, of the remorseless tragedy of *Roxana,* takes her obligatory turn with the archaisms and plays them primarily for laughs, offering what amounts almost to a pastiche of the pastiche. Robina's weighty sentences relate, literally from anti-climax to anti-climax, nothing less (that's to say nothing more) than the making of a modern debutante: one destined to curtsey before Queen Elizabeth II, to do 'Obeisance to a Cake'; and one who is therefore otherwise at the mercy of fate, since she possesses no other preparation for life. 'I hadn't even, remember, Shorthand Typing.'

Even when the device falters, as the mock-heroic always must, there can be no doubting that Robina knows whereof she speaks. To a mere Commoner, whose ears prick at the mention of certain Royal Dukes and Noble Princes, or of Earls who mistakenly murder their wives' nannies when they mean to murder their wives, a teasing sense of exclusion prevails, as if this were a *roman* to which the *clef* is denied him, by blood. By the absence of blood, that is.

Nonetheless, the most gleefully farcical sections are those which do the dirt, as it were from the inside, on life down in the mortgaged rural retreats of the English Upper Classes. During her stay at the Estate of L—in the County of W-Shire, . . . Robina comes upon the old Marchioness standing upon a stone hearth, talking to friends: 'and if it is said that there is nothing unusual in that, I can only add that the Dignified Old Lady was Peeing as she Stood there . . . which none of her friends affected to Notice or Care About.' Breeding, you see.

Who can say what makes for authenticity in a fiction? The more fantastic the behaviour of Robina's noble connections, the more believable they are. So that if we complain, at last, that the Dukes and Earls are all, to a man, too interested in finding a way up Robina's skirts and too incapacitated by drink or congenital defect to do much once they get there, it is not because the idea of an aristocracy saved from depravity only by its own enfeeblement is more than we can take. The very opposite is the case.

Having hit upon a powerful vehicle for savage satire, Emma Tennant disappoints only by not being savage enough. The picaresque relies upon an absolute assumption of wickedness. Robina might be surprised by the Cupidity and Concupiscence of the Nobility, but we who aren't innocent know all that already. The reliance on scenes of passing venery—not tumultuous, not tragic, but merely venereal—makes us think of Cleland before Defoe or Smollett. Robina's Adventures might have been devastating. As it is, they're good fun.

> *Howard Jacobson, "Period Postures," in* The Observer, *January 19, 1986, p. 48.*

CHLOE CHARD

[The eccentricities of *The Adventures of Robina, by Herself*] are the product of a return to the slightly haphazard form of narration employed by Defoe in *Moll Flanders* and *Roxana;* Tennant mentions the influence of this latter novel, in fact, in a prefatory 'Editor's Note' (which itself echoes the 'Author's Preface' in *Moll Flanders,* in insisting that the story is a true one, told by a 'real' heroine and merely written down by the author).

One of the disconcerting features of Defoe's novels which is imitated in **Robina** is the way in which the heroine—a young debutante of the late 1950s, describing her education at 'Establishments for Young Ladies' in Oxford and Paris, and her 'Coming Out' in London—constantly interrupts her tale with allusions to future developments, often hinting at the 'dire consequences' which are to result from her own follies and from the lust, avarice, parsimony, malice and stupidity of the various representatives of the gentry and aristocracy who surround her. The novel also mimics Defoe in its alternation between the voice of Robina identifying with her younger, cheerfully wayward self and the voice of the older, repentant Robina, commenting gloomily on her past 'crimes'.

The bouts of heavy moralising in which the older Robina indulges often seem uneasily at odds with her younger levity, despite the fact that the puritanism of her Scottish education is implicitly put forward as an explanation for her sharp sense of sin. Tennant attempts to resolve this difficulty by showing her heroine to be utterly confused—and, at the same time, enduringly delinquent. Unlike *Moll Flanders* and *Roxana,* the novel contains a strong element of irony; the words of the heroine are constantly used to expose her own amiable inanity, in the manner of Anita Loos' *Gentlemen Prefer Blondes.* (pp. 34-5)

Robina's conviction that a continuation of her extremely desultory studies in French History of Art might have offered her a means of making 'my Own Way in the World', moreover, is ingeniously used to construct a link between her upper-class silliness and the mercantile outlook which she shares with Defoe's heroines: she declares earnestly, at one point, that more extensive instruction in this area of knowledge would have left her 'Qualified for Serious Work . . . rather than a Prey both to Men's Emotions and my Own, and continually searching for Love. . . .'

Despite uncertainties of tone, and the fact that the novel's satirisation of the upper classes is of too well-established a kind to acquire much sharpness, *Robina* is sufficiently energetic, brief and witty to provide constant amusement. The echoes of 18th century language which are incorporated in the heroine's narration are often cleverly fused with her own artless speech patterns. (p. 35)

> Chloe Chard, "Playing Around," in Books and Bookmen, *No. 364, February, 1986, pp. 34-5.*

SARA MAITLAND

I have an enduring affection for Emma Tennant's wonderful prose. . . . At its best, Tennant's writing can sustain narrative, without losing its poetic quality, to a level that I had not thought possible before.

To my considerable sorrow I have enjoyed her more recent novels less, so I am particularly delighted that *The House of Hospitalities* is lovely—with all that old lush extravagance of writing and fantasy, a dream quality concentrating on the beautiful and the artificial, and now, as well, a more specific focus on the social question of class: its reality, its influence, its danger.

At first sight it might seem that Tennant is one of the authors around least suited to such political-analytical novel writing. First because she is actually one of the best prose lyricists I know of, with deep, succulent sentences and an extraordinary skill at evoking the beauty of buildings, gardens, clothes, food, moods in groups, in rooms. And such writing is practically an impossible vehicle for satire—the usual literary way to examine and condemn the foibles of the British upper classes. Second, the very material that draws out her richest prose is the particular possession of the class that she wants to criticise here. And how to condemn that which you love, that which has, in some way, informed your own sensibility so deeply?

Tennant, however, has found a clever novelistic solution to the problem. The story is narrated by an adult remembering herself as a child, with all the striving upward mobility and willingness to be impressed by riches and class and social clout that almost all 14-year-olds have. Jenny has been invited, despite her socialist aunt's objections, to stay with a school friend, the daughter of an 'emminent' family in their 'famous' country house, in 1953. Beyond the walls of Lovegrove everyone knows that everything is changed since the war, but, within its sacred precincts, the assumptions of privilege are untouched. . . . The emerging sexual energies of the schoolgirls—Jenny, Amy the daughter of the house, two other highly drawn but still recognisable teenagers—can be contained, even channelled, in the 'real world', but here in this hidden, elaborate paradise, where even licentiousness has become a game and a fraud, the girls are not only damaged themselves but also become destructive. The grown-ups who are damaging them expel them back into the mundane world to protect their own unreality. Expulsion from Eden is a necessary consequence of sexual knowledge, the old story tells us, but Tennant asks quite subtly and sadly whether this shallow paradise is really all it's cracked up to be.

I am making it all sound rather earnest. It is lightened both by the writing (see above) and by the author's love for what she is standing in judgment over—much as God must have felt, I suspect. It is this latter which allows Tennant some extremely funny *coup-de-théâtre* scenes. . . . More importantly it allows the dream world and the real world—the fantasy of class privilege, with its beauty and generosity, and the snobbish, petty, pompous and frightening practice—to flow in and out of each other in a very rich and courageous way. (pp. 28-9)

> Sara Maitland, "Lovegrove Revisited," in New Statesman, *Vol. 114, No. 2947, September 18, 1987, pp. 28-9.*

ANNE HAVERTY

Novelists tend to stake out a milieu, a perspective on life, a style, and stick to it throughout their careers. You can generally identify a novel by Iris Murdoch, Margaret Drabble or Graham Greene from the first page or two. But it is more difficult to tell one by Emma Tennant because she takes such gleeful pleasure in her versatility. Last year, in *The Adventures of Robina,* she abandoned the school of magic realism for a *jeu d'esprit* about the rollicking, degenerate aristocracy of the 1950s in the style of Defoe's *Roxana.* Now, in *The House of Hospitalities,* she stays with the stately homes of England of that period but writes in a dense, mannered style very akin to that of Anthony Powell.

The fascination of the noble houses of England for the middle classes has been a fruitful subject for novels since those houses began to seem anachronistic. Emma Tennant uses the bewilderment of a middle-class schoolgirl who penetrates the walls of the great pile of Lovegrove to suggest that, while life within the walls is not very well, it goes on and will go on through its instinct for survival and exclusiveness.

Amy, the daughter of Lovegrove, is adored by everyone, pupils and teachers alike, at the middle-class day-school in West London which she (rather improbably) attends. This may not be entirely due to snobbery. Amy is beautiful; fair-haired, pale, long-legged like a thoroughbred; while the other girls, notably Candida Tarn who adores Amy to the point of obsession, are dumpy by comparison and inclined to go different shades of red in bourgeois discomfiture. Jenny lives in the grimy Portobello Road with her homely Labour Party aunt, and it is she, the narrator, not Candida, who goes to stay at Lovegrove when Candida contracts chicken-pox. Jenny, avidly observant and erudite, but otherwise colourless, witnesses the goings-on at Lovegrove. Readers of Powell and Evelyn Waugh will not find these particularly strange.

There is the usual weekend assembly of people of uncertain marital status, disreputable in-laws, a painter or two, a retainer called Boltie. . . . Who is having relations with whom becomes increasingly obscure and inconsequential; until with the denouement on the last page, Emma Tennant very skilfully succeeds in shocking our jaded sense of *déja vu* to almost the same degree as the baffled and involved Jenny is shocked.

Tennant's style in *The House of Hospitalities* is irritatingly convoluted, but it is always amusing. The most memorable scene is set not at Lovegrove, but at the house of Candida's parents, the Tarns, on an evening when the boisterous Carmen arrives to suggest that the girls gate-crash the ball at the Lovescombes' London house. The Tarns are German academics who speak bad English and Mrs Tarn serves up a gruesome supper of hard-boiled eggs, sausage and sauerkraut before Candida, usually so dutiful, goes off to the ball, her school hat moving "with lunar serenity" through the streets. The evocation of the puddingy Tarns in their dim, linoleum-covered rooms is well done, but it is tinged with racism—just as the people without the walls, once inside Lovegrove, seem a motley set in comparison with the flawed but "different" people who live in it.

Dinner at Lovegrove, too, is gruesome, with soup-plates tilting into *décolletages* and pheasants falling off platters, but it is an eccentric gruesomeness, sanctified not by the grandness but by the autonomy and separateness of the Lovescombes. What seems shocking is not their coldness or their sexual peccadilloes, but that of which these are a symptom: their self-image as the most powerful, the autonomous, a contrivedly in-bred race who will own Lovegrove and England for ever.

Anne Haverty, "Still Standing," in The Times Literary Supplement, *No. 4407, September 18-24, 1987, p. 1025.*

ELAINE FEINSTEIN

In this warm and witty novel [*The House of Hospitalities*], Emma Tennant looks at the deadly glamour that has always dominated the English imagination: the excitements and corruptions of privilege. . . .

It is crucial to the plot that the narrator should come from a modest, middle-class background, bewildered by the customs of the people she meets. Unlike Waugh, however, who is unequivocally in love with the society he longs to enter, Miss Tennant uses the innocence of an outsider to mock an exclusivity too confident of its power to be particularly put out by lechery in the gardens, drunks in the drawing-room, or even the discovery of Lady Lovescombe bathing nude in a shallow pool with a guest.

That the narrator should be a child is equally important. It is the device that Miss Tennant has employed before, in *Wild Nights* and *Alice Fell,* to focus on the language as the vision of a child learns to focus on the world. In this elegant novel, which could only have been written by Tennant, we are taken into the very heartland of those who believe that England belongs to them.

Elaine Feinstein, "Comic Corruptions of High Life," in The Times, *London, October 8, 1987, p. 21.*

ANITA BROOKNER

[*The House of Hospitalities*] is something defiantly unfashionable and supremely well carried out, a novel that is the first of a series which will deal with the lives of four friends over a period stretching from 1953 to the present day. The four friends are four women who meet as schoolgirls, but for once the formula is sunk in the matrix of another formula, that of a great house and its bizarre inhabitants. The nightmarish weekend spent at Lovegrove by Jenny Carter, the narrator, forms a very successful separate novel, and the considerable unease experienced by Jenny is foisted effortlessly onto the reader, who may have expected something like *Le Grand Meaulnes* but who ends up panting for release and the safety of the Portobello Road. 'Period' details merely intensify the strangeness of the narrative. Gravely, and almost classically, in long winding sentences, Emma Tennant conveys one definitively away from everything that can be thought of as home, and a sense of displacement, intensified by the bewildering topography of the great house and its proliferating gardens, is underlined by the inordinate behaviour of its owners, all of whom confound the expectations of the unprepared guest, herself only too willing to experience the glamour that surrounds the daughter of the house, Amy Rudd.

'The daughter of the house' is an old-fashioned phrase that perfectly describes Amy, who is several cuts above the other girls who vie for her friendship at St Peter's School. None of these other girls could be described in such a manner. Jenny lives with Aunt Babs who has an antiques stall in the Portobello Road. Candida's parents are German refugees, while no one knows where Carmen comes from, and she is such a liar anyway that anything and nothing about her might be true. . . . Although it was Candida who hoped for the invitation to Lovegrove, Amy's house, it was Jenny Carter on whom the honour finally fell, and the honour turned out to be a dubious one. Between her arrival, and her fleeting sense of recognition of Lovegrove as the sort of ideal home she has never had herself, and her appalled induction into certain matters which are perhaps the secret of great houses and noble families, the narrative takes one deeper into the semi-farcical but altogether frightening imbroglios that constitute—again, perhaps—life in such places. The total lack of innocence encountered by the innocent narrator is never explained, merely stated as fact. A hard grasp of the realities of money is the only matter of substance that would be recognised by the outside world. Everything else is a mystery. . . .

[Normal] amenities are not observed: meals are interrupted by unwelcome arrivals, drunken guests, and accidents such as slipping platters and hands accidentally plunged into containers of bread sauce. The absence of nourishment and the forced marches to different parts of the estate increase the discomfort of the child guest, who writes not as a child but as a particularly grave adult, looking back on this ordeal from a vantage point outside the time span of the novel. Indeed, the unusually stately prose adds another dimension to the feeling of alienation that steals over the reader, forced into this weekend which promises to be all that the narrator wants it to be and discovering with her that some invitations are better left unrealised. The shock at the end is a powerful *coup de théâtre.* . . .

Recollected in the tranquillity that comes from the measured sentences, the mysterious affairs that take place in the house of hospitalities—the least hospitable house imaginable—remain disconcerting. It is to Emma Tennant's credit that she invests none of this with the clichés of adolescent awakening, although the weekend embodies a classic rite of passage from childhood into the future. What the future holds will be revealed in the forthcoming volumes. *The House of Hospitalities* constitutes a more than satisfying beginning.

Anita Brookner, "Mysterious Affairs in Style," in The Spectator, *Vol. 259, No. 8308, October 10, 1987, p. 38.*

ELIZABETH BAINES

Emma Tennant's point [in *The Adventures of Robina, By Herself*], that 'the ways and manners of a certain section of the society in which we live are virtually unchanged since the early eighteenth century', is something of a truism. Yet, paradoxically, her device of telling the tale in the style of Defoe's *Roxana* does not for me entirely succeed in proving that point: so faithfully (and wittily) has she replicated the early-eighteenth-century form and flavour, that any sense of a post-war twentieth-century world is almost entirely lacking in the book. With so little evidence then of the modern world to which, according to Tennant's implication, the British aristocracy is impervious, or oblivious, or which, in the traditional manner, it is using for its own ends (it is consequently hard to know precisely what she *is* implying), the reader is required to extrapolate. In this way, and seeming in her 'Editor's Note' to make no distinction between the aristocracy of the 1950s and that of the present day, Tennant lays herself open to objections that the social changes of the past thirty years have necessitated some adjustments on the part of the upper classes—to begin with, the Season (the focus of this book) as we had known it (or known of it), was due at the time in which the book is set to come to an end. The question of whether the aristocracy carries on the same regardless, whatever the outward signs, is one I find extremely interesting, but Emma Tennant's assertion that it does is not convincingly carried by the form she has chosen.

Only now and again does she bridge the gap, showing the most up-to-date twentieth-century upper-class slang to be based on the most ancient colonial and regressive patterns of thought and behaviour. . . . For the most part, however, so potent is the ethos conjured up by the diction, syntax and narrative form of the book, that, reading for instance the episode where our heroine escapes yet another trauma in a country castle and hears wheels on the road behind her, I imagined carriage-wheels before I remembered that, of course, they must be car-wheels; indeed, since wheels are mentioned, rather than an engine, one wonders whether here the twentieth century has been entirely displaced from the consciousness of the author herself. It is hard at times to keep in mind that it is the upper classes of the 1950s that Tennant is aiming to ridicule and expose, and she is in danger of veiling them, in fact, in the gutsy but quaint historicism which has always been the aristocracy's own excuse; the whole book is so outrageously amusing that, should we accept it as a true picture of our present-day aristocracy, one conclusion we might be inclined to draw is that it's just a jolly good laugh that they're such a load of rogues.

What Tennant appears to have attempted is to apply language and literary form cosmetically as simply symbols of a predetermined social fact, but the sheer dynamism with which language operates has swept the question aside, imposing a forceful and unassailable world of its own. It is an interesting experiment, conducted with panache, but for me the novel reveals far more about the associative power of language than it ever does convincingly about twentieth-century High Society.

Still, as Lord C—M— would say, in the Unlikely Event of his Tearing his Mind off Ladies and Money: It's a Damned Good Read.

Elizabeth Baines, "Plus ça Change," in PN Review 58, *Vol. 14, No. 2, 1987, p. 68.*

Tomas (Gösta) Tranströmer

1931-

Swedish poet, translator, and critic.

Recognized as one of Sweden's outstanding contemporary poets, Tranströmer juxtaposes dissimilar images in order to transform conventional interpretations of reality. Employing an unadorned style and laconic tone, Tranströmer often links artifacts from modern industrial society with natural phenomena to evoke civilization's relationship with nature. His verse frequently incorporates his experiences as a psychologist and world traveler while examining such concerns as the influence of environment on individuals, the functions within society of history and mythology, and the nature of conscious and unconscious existence. Although faulted by several of Sweden's Marxist-influenced critics for refusing to commit his art to political ends, Tranströmer has been praised for displaying technical accomplishment, vast thematic scope, and creative insight. Joanna Bankier stated: "[Tranströmer's] work provides, in its formal perfection and attention to the weight and resonance of words, an imaginative realm where words have not lost their sensuous reality and where the self can be affirmed and recreated."

In his initial collection, *17 dikter* (1954), Tranströmer employs predominantly classical verse forms to present impressionistic portraits of Swedish landscapes, focusing particularly on the atmosphere of Runmäro, a small island in the Stockholm skerries. *Hemligheter på vägen* (1958) adopts an international scope, as Tranströmer draws upon his travels to the Balkans, Turkey, Italy, and Spain. This volume also includes poems directly inspired by works of art, including paintings by Francisco Goya and Vincent Van Gogh. The objective viewpoint prominent in Tranströmer's early volumes becomes increasingly personal in his subsequent collections, moving from a detached serenity toward a darker vision fraught with insecurity and pain. In these later books, he demonstrates an acute awareness of the brutality and indifference of the natural world and the precariousness of existence. In addition to these themes, *Den halvfärdiga himlen* (1962) continues Tranströmer's travel impressions of Italy, Greece, and Egypt and includes romantic lyrics which affirm the musicality of his verse. In *Klanger och spår* (1966), Tranströmer places less emphasis on form and highlights autobiographical elements, while in *Mörkerseende* (1970; *Night Vision*), he relates personal encounters with death, disease, and other crises.

Östersjöar (1974; *Baltics*) is commonly considered Tranströmer's most ambitious and expansive work. Replete with nature imagery and authentic evocations of past eras, this volume reflects upon family traditions and legacies by interweaving history, locale, memory, and social history through loose structures and rhythms. *Sanningsbarriären* (1978; *Truth Barriers*) comprises four sections of poems written mainly in free verse and prose in which Tranströmer considers various topics, including the music of Franz Schubert, art, memory, hallucination, and dreams. *Windows and Stones* (1972) contains translated verse from Tranströmer's first four volumes, while *Selected Poems* (1980) includes all of *Baltics* and *Truth Barriers*, and *Selected Poems, 1954-1986* (1987) features previously unpublished works. Tranströmer has also published *Stigar* (1973), which incorporates several of his own pieces with his trans-

lations into Swedish of the works of Robert Bly and Hungarian poet János Pilinszky.

(See also *Contemporary Authors*, Vol. 117.)

SVEN CHRISTER SWAHN

Tomas Tranströmer belongs to the young generation of writers around thirty who, since almost a decade, have been occupied in all possible ways with refuting the generation that is around forty now. World War II and, maybe still more, the feeling of guilt to which a neutral state is subjected had made the poetic style disturbed and had made hard feelings during the Forties. At the time of Tranströmer's debut in 1954 with *17 dikter* (*17 Poems*)—a matter-of-fact title that also says something about Dylan Thomas's position in the lyrics of the Fifties—his contemporaries in age were beginning to occupy themselves with a Romantic land clearing or with a cult of form in the spirit of Empson.

But, what can be said about all lyrical poets worthy of interest is true of Tranströmer: that it is quite possible to find connecting threads with their contemporaries but that they continually shift the point of gravity to a certain degree, weighing what is elemental in their time in a characteristic manner.

Tranströmer, too, can feel the painful breaking up of a lost summer and, in a sensitive way, see traces of a wrecked human idyll in nature. He, too, has turned aside from the Forties; however, he did not become either academic or romantic in gliding away. With a great deal of caution, he put up a fence around his poetical resources and is on his guard against anything that glitters but is not gold. His scanty production—*17 dikter, Hemligheter på vägen* (*Secrets on the Way,* 1958) and now, in the fall, *Den halvfärdiga himlen* (*The Half Finished Sky*)—speaks of a writer who selects and ponders more than is usual in our hurried times and, likewise, of the author's self-confidence, his feeling that haste is unnecessary. There is nothing he needs to catch up with, and his position has been clear from his first collection. He needs and also takes his time for an increased concentration. From the reader, he demands a similar concentration and, maybe, also a kind of sensibility similar to his own. (p. 402)

His lyrical poetry has two tendencies as far as themes are concerned. In part, he sketches an almost novelistic course of events in an unheard of abbreviation: two people, a trip, a walk. In part, he gives us poetry on nature, often in relation to a moral problem or from a point of view that admits a suddenly extended field; people's life in common; a man face to face with nature. This is not new; it becomes new.

The language of his poetry is the one of concentration, of acts of remembrance, of the short-cut; it is a system of metaphors with modern components but with a baroque appetite to strike and astonish.

These leaps, sometimes violent, from object to object—in order to put a paradoxical stress, by means of the fast and tremendous movement, on the isolated experiences to be illuminated—have no parallel in the arrangement of the poem, in its strophic form. He has been able to use Sapphic verse or to come, rhythmically, close to the part of Swedish poetry of the Thirties that was academically pruned in the means of expression. He has no contact with the fluid form of the Forties; however, in his naturally illogical way of dealing with a series of images, the heritage of the nearest preceding generation is, of course, evident.

Like most poets, he is sometimes a word creator. The new experience which a poet implies requires, naturally, new words. But an experiment with words, strophes, images is not—it should be repeated—essential to him. The experiment takes place on another level. He wants to fire impressions at man and to see how fast, how painfully they may change; and then let the whole of the poem, its weight and motion, give a mute answer to questions about poetry and life, a poem's motion toward the reader, the man's motion—under changeable stars—toward death.

Yes, in such a sense, one trait of an experimenter can be found in Tranströmer. He examines, again and again, how fiercely a remembrance can bite, how wide a compass a moral position can have.... The visual moment in his system of metaphors is quite obvious. And through him one more incommunicable vision has become common property. However, it hardly will become an everyday product, even if he has many energetic followers in young Sweden. (pp. 402-03)

> Sven Christer Swahn, "Tomas Tranströmer," in
> Books Abroad, *Vol. 37, No. 4, Autumn, 1963, pp. 402-03.*

ERIC SELLIN

Tranströmer has been a major figure on the Swedish literary scene ever since his debut, and an indication of his impact is his pole position in Karl Erik Lagerlöf's anthology *Ny svensk lyrik från Tranströmer till Bengt Emil Johnson,* published in 1966 when Tranströmer was thirty-five. Since then one can say that he has acceded to the next stratum and joined the likes of Martinson, Lundkvist, Lindegren, and Setterlind. Tomas Tranströmer has made his living as a psychologist, first for many years at Roxtuna youth prison and then in the Stockholm area as an occupational psychologist, dealing especially with the handicapped. Although his poems are on one plane very unreal, they are, on another plane, extremely autobiographical. If one knows Tranströmer well, he will recognize in the poems many references to Tranströmer's surroundings and experiences at Roxtuna (e.g. **"Vinterns formler"**), in the islands of the Stockholm *skärgård* (**"Andrum juli"**), and his travels to Egypt (**"I Nildeltat"**), Greece (**"Syros"**), Black Africa (**"Ur en afrikansk dagbok"**), the United States (**"Oklahoma"**), and elsewhere. Some of the references are very personal, but are not so readily recognizable. For example, the very curious and uncharacteristic long poem **"Balakirevs dröm"** in *Hemligheter på vägen* seems more consistent with the poet's vision when we realize that the poem is based on a real dream which Tranströmer himself had, a fact he himself has attested to.

During a career spanning almost twenty years, Tomas has relentlessly pursued his personal idiom and in that idiom the most radical changes have been, at best, subtle. Whereas many modern poets are nervously fretting from poem to poem and from book to book in search of some divine insight, some shamanistic role bestowed by any available spiritual being, force, or chemical, Tomas Tranströmer has developed the context of his imagery and never forsaken it for the surrealistic mode of free-association or trance writing. The synapses are not bared but made of nothingness. In explicating the poems we find ourselves dwelling on the unsaid, on what is blank between contexts, but it is the clever manipulation of the contiguities which guides our explication. Thus, even while forfeiting the author's traditional right to specify his reader's thought through what is said (cf *Alice in Wonderland*), Tranströmer makes our manifold interpretation of an image retain some sense of boundary, some sense of direction. (pp. 44-5)

One might well say that to pursue a personal sense of miracle in modern times is to behave as a mandarin, an obsolete man of letters or cultural patrician—in a word, to behave irrelevantly. The Swedish New Left press has not remained neutral, often berating Tranströmer for not committing his art to politics. He even gets piqued by these barbs, and self-justification has crept into his work, although I feel that his steadfast adherence to the tenets of poiesis rather than politics is justification enough. (p. 46)

Within Tranströmer's poems, the mechanism of truth and enlightenment has unstintingly remained the poetic image, and the freshness of this poet's idiom was clear right from the first lines of his first book, *17 dikter:* "Uppvaknandet är ett fallskärmshopp från drömmen. / Fri från den kvävande virveln sjunker / resenären mot morgonens gröna zon." (The awakening is a parachute jump from the dream. / Freed from the suffocating vortex the traveler / sinks toward the morning's green zone.) Tranströmer's brilliance at seizing upon the unexpected but perfectly apt image has become his trademark, so much so that one tends to overlook the metrical intricacies to which he has restricted himself in certain poems, notably the classical **"Strof och motstrof"** and **"Fem strofer till Thoreau"** in *17 dikter*. Indeed, the principal evolution of Tranströmer's idiom has been to move slowly away from the metric rationale either toward a "field" rationale—that is, letting words somehow stake out their own claims on the page on the basis of shape, respiration, and the general terms of each poem's needs and laws, not unlike iron fillings responding to a magnetic field—or, as in **"Upprätt,"** toward the elimination of such concerns and the adoption of straight prose. The one common denominator in all the works is the well-tooled image, such as that ending **"Lamento"** in *Den halvfärdiga himlen:* "Det blir långsamt natt. / Malarna sätter sig på rutan: / små bleka telegram från världen." (It slowly becomes night. / Moths sit upon the windowpane: / small pale telegrams from the world.)

At the core of Tranströmer's imagery is a meticulous attention to the oft-overlooked wonders of nature, and this devotion makes him a deeply "religious" poet in the best sense of the word. His images are miraculous interventions, moments of communion which surpass understanding: participation is a prerequisite but the essential process is one of overwhelming. If one lies under an August night sky in New England, the stars will seem to generate in space and rain down as the eye grows accustomed to the night. The process is in the eye of the beholder, but the miracle surely lies in the stars. A good reader will be thus affected by Tomas' images which contain a dynamics linking the banal and the infinite. (pp. 46-7)

> *Eric Sellin, "Tomas Transtömer, Trafficker in Miracles," in* Books Abroad, *Vol. 46, No. 1, Winter, 1972, pp. 44-7.*

LEIF SJÖBERG

Tomas Transtömer (born in Stockholm in 1931) created a bit of sensation with a slim volume entitled *17 dikter* (*17 Poems*, 1954). Its perfect employment of classical metrics, its startling new discoveries in Swedish landscapes and seascapes, its amazing density of acute images (written in a mild modernism which is more suggestive of Éluard and Dylan Thomas than of Lindegren and Ekelöf) soon made Tomas Transtömer the most imitated poet in Sweden. As one critic remarked not long ago, it would seem that for some years "everybody heard and saw the same as Tomas Transtömer."

The point of departure for his nature impressions was most often Rummarö, a small island in the Stockholm skerries, where the poet has spent his summer since childhood. (p. 37)

While his *17 dikter* (*17 Poems*) was quite Swedish in themes, his next book, *Hemligheter på vägen* (*Secrets on the Way*, 1958) was more international and also more dependent on "crutches." This dependency can be seen in his employment of themes from travels, i.e. the Balkans, Turkey, Italy, and Spain. The title of the poem **"Caprichos"** is Spanish for "whims" or "fancies," but it also alludes to one of Goya's series of etchings. Among poems directly inspired by art works there should be mentioned **"A Man from Benin,"** which can be seen at the Museum für Völkerkunde in Vienna, and **"After an Attack,"** which refers to a Van Gogh painting.

Den halvfärdiga himlen (*The Half-finished Heaven,* or *The Half-ready Sky*), his third book, 1962, continues with further travel impressions from Italy, Greece, and Egypt. It also contains a few love poems. Music, which has been an important source of inspiration to Tomas Transtömer, is quite prevalent in this collection. Besides poems with obvious musical titles such as

"Nocturne," **"Allegro,"** and **"C Major,"** there are other poems which owe a debt to music. The volume also reveals the poet's feeling of being threatened by something dark which occasionally leads to depressions and unproductivity. (p. 38)

In his fourth book, *Klanger och spår* (*Echoes and Traces*, 1966), *form* is less emphasized than before. Instead of nature impromptus there are larger statements and greater cohesiveness. The startling juxtapositions with a mystical isolation of phenomena, reminiscent of dream flight, are less frequent than in the earlier collections. The poet appears less anonymous. In the poem **"Loneliness"** he describes in an almost documentary way an authentic experience, a traffic accident threatening his life! This volume also contains poems on Lisbon, Oklahoma, and Central Africa (**"From the African Diary,"** 1963). Furthermore there are two notable portraits. One of them portrays a friend about whose father we are told that he "earned money like dew. / But no one nonetheless was completely safe at home—." The other is concerned with the great Norwegian composer Edvard Grieg, who urges himself to "simplify!"

Transtömer's fifth and last collection to date, *Mörkerseende* (*Dark Adaptation*, 1970) reveals a great deal of simplification in regard to *form*. The biographical element in these eleven poems is more pronounced than earlier. The poems are entirely documentary, almost confessional. Although many earlier poems by Transtömer also are documentary, in one sense or another, they never revealed the poet's private experiences as directly as now. In a friend's copy of the book, he has even jotted down the names of places and the circumstances under which the experiences occurred. (pp. 38-9)

Mörkerseende, which Robert Bly translated as *Night Vision,* and the Scottish poet Robin Fulton called "Seeing in the dark," (*Lines Review,* 35), reflects a serious crisis or perhaps a series of crises. It speaks of great and shattering changes in his personal life, such as death and disease among his kin, a feeling of lost identity, worries about the war between technology and nature, etc. A poem like **"The Bookcase"** opens with the line, "It was brought from the dead woman's apartment." The poet who has been particularly close to his mother (in the absence of a father ever since childhood, when the parents were divorced) has been faced with her death. In **"Preludes"** he has emptied his mother's apartment, which he, too, has inhabited for the better part of his life. Hope has vanished. "The anchor has let go—but despite the mournful air it's still the lightest apartment in the city." How come? One can guess that the poet can cherish his memories undisturbed, that he is more on his own, and that he possesses some new, deeper insight: "Truth needs no furniture. I've gone one round on life's circle and come back to the starting point: a bare room." His childhood experiences fade in the strong light, and give way to concentration on the present, the "here and now." His vision is widened—but also markedly darkened, as the very title, *Dark Adaptation,* reminds us—"the windows have enlarged." "The empty apartment is a big telescope pointed at the sky."

A similar development in the poet is discernible in **"Preludes,"** where efforts to escape from the truth of the self are called futile. A confrontation with one's self is unavoidable. Whether it results in inward or outward activity, you will finally have to face yourself, at the moment of truth. In a most recent poem, **"Guard Duty,"** the idea of the present is reinforced. . . . The philistine's concept of a poet as an impractical, impulsive, irresponsible individual with a generally weak human organization could not easily be applied to Tomas Transtömer. He is a psychologist by profession and as such has served as counselor to juvenile delinquents at the modern Roxtuna institution, 1960-66, sometimes being in charge of the whole institution. He then moved with his family, wife and two daughters, to the city of Västerås where he took up a half-time job in order to give readings, do translations, etc. He still devotes much of his energy to problem cases in occupational psychology and aptitude tests for handicapped people. The criminal element is a smaller portion of his present clientele.

While no criminals appear in his poems, Tranströmer has naturally incorporated his experiences from his work as psychologist, usually in an unobtrusive, indirect way, in such poems as **"Under Pressure,"** and in **"Winter's Formulae."**. . . . As a psychologist Tranströmer is interested in sleep, especially the dream intervals, and awakening. In this respect he is like Pierre Reverdy. Many of the poems deal with awakening. In his wakeful hours Tranströmer is a frequent participant in conferences of social psychologists and social workers, and he has led study groups for probation officers on how to treat prisoners. Being afraid of the proliferation of superimposed patterns of any kind, be they social or political, he has never worked as a journalist who expresses and creates opinions. He maintains that a poet can be *engagé* without writing manifestos. Like most of his Swedish compatriots he reacted *early* against the Vietnam war. (pp. 39-40)

He considers his chief task as a poet to be independent of any groups or coteries, so that he best can illuminate reality and perceive it as if for the first time. Ideally Tranströmer's reader should respond to his own inner stirrings, not to "dictates" or pressure from the outside, such as commercial or political indoctrination, not even from the *poet's* modest directives. . . .

How did the forceful turn to the left among his contemporaries effect Tranströmer? "Politics, world events, society, the power struggle, are all inevitable," said Tranströmer in an interview (1968) upon which I will draw here, and continued, "All of them are also to be found in my later books. But in youthful audiences there are always a few who take me to task for allegedly being 'turned away from the world.' They want me to write in a political way, use political language. Actually they would allow me to write about anything, flowers and bees, as long as I did it in a 'political' way," he said. "But the language of poetry, at least the language of my poetry, gets its meaning when it engages itself in a political reality without being politicized." A politicized language he defines as one which serves as a means to exert pressure and through which false alternatives are presented, such as 'If you don't choose A, you have actually chosen B.' "Political consciousness includes ability to see through these language patterns, not to subordinate oneself to them," maintained Tranströmer.

What does he then expect from poetry? He wants to see the poetic language as some kind of catalyst, something that liberates man instead of restricting him. As a new communication between experience. Above all, poetry should set man's inspiration free, give him a chance to know himself and to discover dimensions in himself whose existence he had not been aware of before, dimensions which the commercial society does not consider useful, since they cannot readily be manipulated. Poetry differs from other types of language in regard to density. Poetry is, among other things, the densest form of information. Senses, memories, intuition, position-takings to questions—everything is in poetry. Poetry is the contrary of what many people believe, says Tranströmer, i.e. those who think that it is a way of embellishing, confusing, or inflating reality. Farthest away from poetry, at the very end of the scale, are those

language exercises with the smallest density, such as those great talk bubbles which spread themselves when one gives a speech. (p. 41)

Although Tranströmer is no longer imitated in Sweden, where more aggressive and goal-directed poetry is presently flourishing, it should be noted that Tranströmer together with Ekelöf is the most translated poet, at least into English, and that he is indeed one of the outstanding poets of our day. (p. 42)

Leif Sjöberg, "The Poetry of Tomas Tranströmer," in The American-Scandinavian Review, *Vol. LX, No. 1, March, 1972, pp. 37-42.*

JOHN HAINES

A consequence of modern history is that the world has become increasingly an object, to be viewed from a distance. We are less and less a part of nature, or at least it can be said that we function at considerable inner, as well as outer, distance from it. The old presences of nature are no longer there, at least not in the old forms. Or if they return, they are apt to do so as social and political aberrations with a malevolent character. The world is dominated by machines and products of manufacture, things which looked at objectively are incapable of self-sustaining life, and of passion. In any valid sense the world most modern people live in is dead.

But the inner man is not satisfied with this. He feels a great emptiness in and around him; his deep ear and his spirit are still tuned to the sounds of the forest, to the snap of twigs, the cry of animals and birds, and the murmur of moving water. He looks back to a time when even rocks might speak to men. Yet he cannot live in a dead world. And to satisfy his imagination he begins to endow machines and factory-made objects with life and thought. . . .

It is part of the struggle of poetry with history to find its liberation in understanding, in image and metaphor. (p. 6)

In Tranströmer's poems we find abundant evidence of this struggle. Again and again industrial objects collide with or are combined with, act against or in concert with, the old shapes of nature. We learn of cicadas "strong as electric razors," of trees that instead of producing blossoms, threaten to put forth clusters of iron gloves; pollen is "determined to live in asphalt." A house seen from a distance reminds him in its redness of a bouillon cube; another house, struck by the evening light, has shot itself in the forehead. A train comes by and collects faces and portfolios. The poet's wristwatch gleams "with Time's imprisoned insect." The historical and political content is seldom absent; swept by more than the wind of April, even the grass whispers, "Amnesty."

We may have reduced the world to mechanism, to dead object; the earth will be divided into lots and sold to the next high bid. But the poet cannot live with that state of things. He must set the world in motion again, put things on their feet and have them speak. And in doing this he renews an old and needed function of poetry: the reconciliation of warring and unlike things, that we may live in a comprehensible world. Thus, contemporary events become entangled with prehistory; shapes from the past erect themselves in the present-day soil. Reading Tranströmer's poems is like being introduced to a new stone age, in which the tools and conveniences of modern society are becoming artifacts and fossils. Another wilderness springs up around his images, where the concrete piping "laps at the light with cold tongues,'' as the industrial age slowly goes back to rust and earth. . . . (p. 7)

Laconic, careful in what he says, in the space he allows for his images, Tranströmer restores to us some of the lost mystery and surprise of life. Much of the exposure and confession we have grown used to in recent years ends in dullness. Instead of mystery we have information; nothing, or almost nothing, is withheld. Yet poetry lies as much in concealment as in revelation, more often in what is not said or shown. We should remember the hiddenness of so much early art, in caves, places where it would not be seen easily and stripped of its meaning. There were places once that one did not go, mountains no one thought to walk on, for the sake of the spirit living there. Our compulsion now is to climb every peak, to pry into every corner of life, to expose every secret. In the end we find the world empty, the mystery vanished, retreated stubbornly to a place we will never find by looking for it.

Yet the mystery is alive; at the irreducible source of things, a fire, a smoke. As Tranströmer demonstrates in his poems, only a small amount of quiet and space are necessary for it to reappear ''among good-sized stones with peaceful backs.''. . . (pp. 7-8)

Let me conclude by saying that I find Tranströmer's poems contemporary in the best and truest sense. They display to an amazing degree that ability to combine and synthesize and renew which has always been one of the strengths of the poetic intelligence. Behind his images we sense the ever-encroaching menace of our time; a thing sinister, nearly invisible, impossible to name exactly. And the human life feeling its way forward under this menace, surviving somehow, as in the near-crash of **"Solitude"**; or as he tells us in **"The Name,"** of awakening suddenly in the backseat of his car in a brief panic and confusion, to understand that his existence and identity are in question. . . . (pp. 8-9)

He is contemporary in the uncertainty with which he faces the world: the predicament of the modern individual who must question and name and personify everything, to have it speak to him, unsure otherwise who he is and where he is. We feel in him the nervousness of the contemporary man afraid that he is not at home in the world, that things are not as true as they once were, neither nature nor history, nor the emotions these things once guaranteed us. Aware possibly also that what he sees and understands may have no meaning at all in the general life. And yet convinced, as good poets tend to be everywhere, that the writing of a poem is a social act in which the poet finds himself in dialogue with his time, to be called to account for what he says. . . . (p. 9)

I respect the brevity and concentration of [Tranströmer's] poems. In a time of noise, of abuse of speech and of writing, the volume of talk may require as its adequate response the closest thing we can have to silence, the briefest, most concentrated thing we can make. More words do not make the truth. The wave of print we are witnessing may conceal on its far side a gulf, an absence.

It is hardly a contradiction to add that Tranströmer seems to understand, on the evidence of his poems, that poetry, the rare good writing whatever form it takes, may be one of the few ways we have of continuing ourselves in some truth, of escaping from the arrogance and tyranny of official history and its half-willing spokesman, the *news*.

Night vision? Or, seeing in the dark? There may be nothing obscure or mystical about this, but rather a means of finding one's way in a time that will be known by its corrosive light, itself a kind of darkness. (pp. 9-10)

> *John Haines, ''On Our Way to the Address,'' in* Ironwood, *Vol. 7, No. 13, 1979, pp. 5-10.*

JOANNA BANKIER

When Tranströmer made his début in 1954 with *17 Poems*, he received immediate recognition. There was a poise and a maturity in his first work that was compelling. After the publication of the two subsequent volumes *Secrets on the Way* (1958) and *The Half-finished Heaven* (1962), his position as the major poet of his generation was well established. Here were guidelines for a new poetry. Here was a poet who articulated what was as yet only vaguely perceived by others. As one critic remarks,

> he articulates changes in style which we have barely felt the scent of. He gives shape to things that in others are only lights and shades, hazy shifts in ways of perceiving and writing.

In the late 50's, modernism, which was the predominant style by then and had produced such outstanding poetry as that of Gunnar Ekelöf, was degenerating in the lesser poets into a cliché-ridden, vaporous kind of writing, from which anything not ''poetic'' was excluded. In this context, Tranströmer's dry matter-of-factness must have been felt as refreshing. When Urban Torhamn, in a brilliant essay entitled ''Tranströmer's Poetic Method,'' spoke of the ''poetically factual'' quality of his work, he formulated what for many readers, to this day, appears as the dominant feature of Tranströmer's style. ''The almost pedantic accuracy makes even the wildest flights of fancy seem real and accessible even to the conventional imagination. If we are informed when something unbelievable or timeless is happening we somehow know where we stand.''. . . Torhamn is obviously and understandably delighted with the precision in Tranströmer's poetry, yet I am uneasy about the reasons he advances for liking it. I am not sure Tranströmer is concerned with staying within the confines of the conventional imagination. There is not, on the one hand, dream and vision, and on the other, realistic factual information that somehow combined make the whole more palatable to the conventional imagination, but a visual imagination that is astoundingly factual and precise. Furthermore, the precise indications of time and place add a sense of further estrangement; unreality becomes real and the commonplace acquires a stranger coloring. As to the sense of lived reality that emanates from the poetic vision, it originates in its authenticity, not in the factual information it happens to contain.

Nevertheless, Torhamn is quick to recognize the poet's originality in this unusual combination of vision and factual accuracy. Torhamn is also quite perceptive of Tranströmer's unique handling of metaphors. These are no longer comparisons or near-comparisons with a tenor and a corresponding vehicle. ''They are charged abstract or abstract-sensual visions, explosions that aim at a metamorphosis of experience.'' Here, I would have liked Torhamn to make the connection with Surrealist practice and theory. Although he does mention Surrealist aesthetic influence on Tranströmer, he seems unaware of the deep affinity of purpose they share: ''metamorphosis of experience'' was precisely what the Surrealists tried to achieve; herein lies the radical subversive element of their art. Tranströmer is not only a Surrealist in the technical sense, but also in the way his poetry works on the mind, freeing it from set, habitual ways of ordering experience, and making the reified objective reality we are living in suddenly seem unreal. Shifts of perspective from what we actually see to what we could see if our lives spanned millions of years, have a way of pulling the rug from under our established notions (pp. 29-30)

But this kind of specific probing of his moral-political values and serious concern with Tranströmer's relation to Surrealist theory are alien to Torhamn's reading. The whole question of values is dealt with under the blanket notion of the maturity of the artist and his development as a human being. Torhamn is ready to admit that, if there was in the first volume a certain *noli-me-tangere* attitude, a distance between the poet and the motif, a danger of reduction to the merely decorative, it has disappeared in the following books. Tranströmer has now abandoned his position as the objective observer. The poems have become more personal, the I is involved in the "transformations to which he subjects his material" (Torhamn). Brita Wigfors and Agneta Pleijel follow Torhamn in praising the development in Tranströmer's work from an aesthetic, objectifying stance with its easy serenity towards a darker vision, fraught with insecurity and pain. Lasse Söderberg, in a poem dedicated to Tranströmer, once likened his perspective to that of a buzzard. Now the poet must struggle to form his material, or as he says himself, abandoning his distances, "travel at the same time mole and eagle."

Torhamn concludes with the hope that Tranströmer will move toward increasing depth and range in his exploration of human experience and advises readers to follow his development closely, because the dominant position that Tranströmer holds in Swedish poetry makes the direction he takes crucial to future generations of poets.

Five years later things had changed. "I am today as estranged from Tranströmer's poetry as I admire it." Critical response to Tranströmer in Sweden from the mid 60's on has found its most adequate expression in this polished little paradox, which appeared in [*Bonniers Litterära Magasin*] in 1966, in Leif Nylén's critical review of *Resonance and Tracks*. For ten years after his début, Tranströmer had remained the leading poet of his generation, the one on whom the style and sensibility of the decade was patterned. In the mid 60's, however, the literary canon shifted to the left and Swedish writers and critics, or "culture workers" as they like to call themselves, became increasingly concerned with social realities at home and in the Third World. Marxism, often in combination with Structuralism on the French model (Lévi-Strauss, Foucault) had a profound effect. Here, the world is seen as far less stable and given. Most of what we are accustomed to regard as real, as an integral part of the human condition, is seen as the product of the ideology of the ruling class. Thus, human nature is an illusion, nurtured by conservative forces and the notion of the individual fictitious, a nexus of learned cultural patterns of behavior. If the world has become more shifting and uncertain, by the same token it is also more susceptible to change; it will respond to our efforts at manipulation. Words being the obvious tools for the restructuring of reality, for creating a new consciousness, it is generally felt that the poet has acquired new powers and new responsibilities. He is expected to develop a social conscience and to attempt in his writing to affect the course of history in the direction of a more equal distribution of wealth and opportunities. He must cease his preoccupation with self and turn his attention to the economic and social

realities. A strong and vociferous majority has imposed silence on recalcitrant old-timers and succeeded in making concern with aesthetic form, inwardness, resignation, not to mention despair, tantamount to shirking one's duty. Since Björn Håkansson's seminal essay in *Rondo* (1962), it has become customary to label Tranströmer a religious poet, who seeks refuge in the healing perspectives of eternity. He is alternately branded a romantic and an idealist. His pessimism is resented and his lack of involvement with current social problems in a positive, dynamic way is considered a "lack" (Nylén). . . . The world Nylén speaks of is that of a political praxis, of the material base, in which the question of domination is crucial. Tranströmer's mythical, historical consciousness is infinitely vaster in scope and includes the awareness of the limited place occupied by modern industrialized society and even of the history of mankind in the millennial development of natural life. He attempts to incorporate into his sensibility the concept of an infinite universe, with all the concomitant notions of brutality and indifference. As Brita Wigfors observes: "The storm that is heard at the horizon comes from the evil side of existence. It is the eruption of primeval brutality and power mounted by emptiness. . ." It is the result of this cosmic awareness that we encounter in the poetry taking the form of an acute sense of the fragility and precariousness of existence. In *The Baltics* (1974), silence and desolation are the basic conditions. All human activity is a great effort, a Sisyphean work, a barrage against nothingness. Existence is a hushed murmur against the background of the pandemonium of natural forces. Now here, now there, governed by hazard, life appears on our shores and is blown out by the wind of war, of quiet death, of disasters.

However, the moment the poet reckons with the frightening perspectives of infinity, he also restores a sense of connectedness with the universe he inhabits, with forces larger than himself and the present moment. Thus the link between man and the world is restored; alienation, whose roots Tranströmer sees in the reduction of the value of human beings to that bestowed on them in the market place, can be bridged. . . . The shift of perspective has a freeing power, without rhetorical strain it creates a natural link with the world, which the ugly artificiality and commercial shallowness of our civilization ordinarily obscures. We are made to experience the whole modern industrialized society as a passing phenomenon. . . . The apparently perennial factories are made to seem transitory, as exposed to forces of disintegration as are the life and memory of individuals. Political events, that seem crucial and tend to make us feel their crushing weight, are shown to be timebound, ephemeral. An abandoned newspaper is already on the way to becoming a plant, a cabbage head . . . If Nylén here perceives a metaphysical dimension, he is quite justified in doing so. But surely he must be aware of the difference. Tranströmer's metaphysics includes a revolt against present social conditions and goes beyond Marxism in questioning the lingering aspects of 19th century materialism and belief in progress, which makes Marxism, in its pure ideological form, so dated and unfit to tackle the problems we are facing in the late 20th century.

Moreover, what Nylén and his colleagues are blind to in their ideological rigor is that the homogeneity and integrity of Transtömer's world is not easily come by. They tend to view the poetry as the direct expression of the poet's personality: serenity in the poem equals serenity in the poet; forgetting that art is also creation, i.e. will, intention, and project. Good poetry, like that of Transtömer, is not unmediated self-expression, a replica of the artist's soul. In asserting its aesthetic autonomy from the contingencies of personality and social class, it provides a forum for the finer shades of feeling that remain unarticulated in everyday existence; it reflects the deep-seated inner longings and needs of the individual. In its formal perfection, it offers a mimesis, an imitation of an ideal human order, all the more necessary as its absence is keenly felt in a fragmented existence uncertain of its values. It could be compared to the rain dances performed by the ancients when rainfall was imitated in order to make the rain come by imitation, by sympathetic magic. (pp. 30-4)

Not every Swedish writer toes the orthodox Marxist line. There are voices that break out of the chorus, like that of Lars Gustafson, a significant writer in his own right. Gustafson, in a collection of essays published in 1974, advances an opinion similar to the one I am defending. He brushes aside the accusation of elitism, disposing at the same time of the notion of development in the poet's work. "Tranströmer is remarkable," he writes, "if you read his poems carefully, you'll notice that he has changed very little since the 50's. He attempts to do one single thing with a tremendous intensity." There is in his work a single-minded, obstinate search back to a pristine sensibility that actually belongs in childhood. A state of mind where perceptions were more intense and one felt alive, a lost state of happiness. There is nothing unique or elitist about this; on the contrary, it is the most common experience in our culture. What could be more widespread than alienation under the present working and living conditions? "Life has to be lived outside life if at all. Tomas Tranströmer speaks of the narrow slit in between the walls in a life occupied by foreign powers. He does not dwell on our lack of freedom, hope, and action but expresses the emptiness negatively in our flight away from it." Gustafson admits to the charges of escapism, but shows it is a symptom, not a goal in itself. Besides, he says, if the Marxists see escapism here as the goal and most important aspect, it only means they have not understood the meaning of dialectical philosophy. The important element in Tranströmer's poetry is that it transcends its social determination and emancipates itself from the given universe of behavior and discourse, showing us what we eminently need.

Paradoxically enough, it is Tranströmer's poetry—elitist, escapist, and individualistic—that offers the greatest hope for change and the promise of a less reified society. Against structuralist atomistic notions and Marxist ideas of man as the sum of social conditioning, he affirms that individual man exists, or at least that he will have to be recreated in our actions and our poems. He does not deny the pressures of social conditioning, language, behavior patterns, and ideology, but he strongly affirms the need to oppose them, mustering whatever we have of imaginative and visionary powers. It might well be that Sweden's most elitist poet is also the most radical, and this in spite of the fact that the accusations of pessimism and resignation are quite accurate. For his work provides, in its formal perfection and attention to the weight and resonance of words, an imaginative realm where words have not lost their sensuous reality and where the self can be affirmed and recreated. As it must be if the disintegrating powers of social conditioning are to be opposed at all. It seems obvious that an art that does not assert its aesthetic autonomy is bound to perpetuate the conditions of oppression and carry them into the heart of the work. (pp. 35-6)

Joanna Bankier, "Critical Response to Tranströmer in Sweden," in Ironwood, *Vol. 7, No. 13, 1979, pp. 29-37.*

ROBIN FULTON

[The] title of Tranströmer's eighth collection, **The Truth Barrier,** meets us full in the eye before we even open the book. Since the late sixties Tranströmer's poetry has shown an increasing concern for a certain kind of "truth-telling," which in shorthand could perhaps best be described as a faithfulness to his own verifiable experience, or a refusal to invent simply for the sake of poetry. This has not resulted in a "plain" poetry—on the contrary, his startling metaphors and his exhilarating charges of focus gain in intensity through this sense they carry of resulting from personal testimony. In practice this means, among many other things, that when in the long poem **"The Gallery"** he imagines (?) faces "forcing through the white wall of oblivion / to breathe, to ask about something," describes in miniature what seem to be individual histories or fates and then tells us that the faces are not "imagined" but "real," we should take him at his word.

A barrier can of course be an obstacle, a wall between the dead and the living, between memory and oblivion, between ourselves and others, between our everyday selves and our deeper selves. An idea that often occurs in Tranströmer's poetry is that beyond this wall there is considerable activity, even if we cannot see or hear or understand it: things we forget may remember us, the forgotten fragments may reassemble into the mosaic. But a truth barrier, like a sound barrier, is clearly something we can break through now and then, though hardly in as clear-cut and measurable a manner.

The collection is in four parts: a sequence on Schubert (music being one means of breaking the barrier) and **"The Gallery"** are framed by two sets of shorter pieces, about half of which are in prose. The more destructive and sterile kinds of truth are carefully placed in the total pattern to serve the moments of gratitude and affirmation. We can start to consider this wider pattern simply by looking at the first poem, an enigmatic nightmare, and the last one, which celebrates a personal relationship and ends in a group of six glowing paradoxes. (pp. 306-07)

Robin Fulton, in a review of "Sanningsbarriären," in World Literature Today, *Vol. 53, No. 2, Spring, 1979, pp. 306-07.*

LEONARD NATHAN

Baltics is divided into six loosely connected sections, the first taking us back "before the time of radio masts." Here we are introduced to the poet's pilot grandfather, who is also a metaphorical pilot for a voyage into an era when man's occupation could still be almost fully human. We are given a sample of his grandfather's nearly surreal shorthand log—names, sizes, and ports—all that's left of the modest heroism and subtle art that guided long-forgotten vessels through fog and reefs. There was a profound piety in their task, and in that life where "lands and reefs" were "memorized like hymn verses" and men still had the power to humanize, even domesticate, their tools: "The compound engine, as long lived as a human heart, worked / with great soft recoiling movements, steel acrobatics, and / the smells rising from it as from a kitchen." Nothing is concluded from this, no generalizations drawn, only a sense of those routinely mysterious ventures into the fog.

The second section begins in seeming contrast to the first. We are in a pine forest, thinking the thoughts of a woman (the poet's grandmother, it seems) dead thirty years, but the sea is still present in the wind sighing through the branches, feared and hated, but more than that; for it bears a message, the feeling of a shared fate, of the "broad current that blows some flames into life and blows / others out. Conditions." The feeling is almost overwhelming, but out of it comes something like a vision: "where everything becomes boundaries. An open square sunk in / darkness. People streaming out of the dimly lit buildings / around it. A murmuring." That is, the whole numinous complex of lives that have gone into the poet's own. Then he turns outward to "other shores," to the modern world, a far off, vast landscape of conflict and oppression where the kinlike and personal are compromised by "something dark." He brings us to what is immediate and powerfully human, an encounter with a mine, its defusing and transformation into a harmless object of local interest. But we are not left with this comfortable domestication of evil and danger. The section circles back to the wind which passes over the cemetery where pilots are buried; it recalls the lost art of his grandfather, and in the gale's "dry sighing," the boundaries of shared fate: "large gates opening and large gates closing."

The third, fourth and fifth sections display the echoes and circlings—and add interesting and moving material—by which the poet gathers his poem into a unity. The leaps in space and time are all surface; below there is a strong cohesive tide.

The last section is a memorial to the grandmother, linked with the poet by their shared sense of common fate, and here revealed as at least as brave and daring as his pilot grandfather. An orphan who refused to be cowed into servitude, she passes her spirit like a message on to her grandson. The message: "She never looked back. / But because of this she could see The New / and seize it. / Break out of the bonds." That is, break out of those boundaries of fate that keep reappearing in the poem. The last line is at once a description of what she *could* do, and an imperative for what the poet *must* do. And we may wonder why the heir to so forward-looking a spirit looks back for so much of the poem, and who, in fact, concludes *Baltics* by taking us to the oldest house on the island (Gotland). This fisherman's hut reminds him "of an old bull / that refuses to get up" weary, yes, but still stubbornly potent. The roof tiles suggest an old Jewish cemetery in Prague: "So much encircled love! The tiles with the lichen's letters in an unknown language / are the stones in the archipelago people's ghetto cemetery, the stones erected and fallen down." This complex metaphor—this work of "style"—serves as the "truth" about the poet's own past, as the final lines of the poem make clear: "The ramshackle hut shines / with the light of all the people carried by a certain wave, a certain wind, / out here to their fates."

So Tranströmer has been looking back, not in violation of his grandmother's spirit or out of nostalgia, but to trace back, honor, and understand the source of that light which it is his duty as poet (and perhaps pilot) to record and interpret.

It would be folly to translate all this into a glib summary, but perhaps this much can be said without abusing the necessary aphasia before the truth: What we experience in reading *Baltics* is an organic composite of a particular life which speaks for all life only out of its own richly witnessed details. The life given us in *Baltics* is circumscribed by mystery, but a mystery less baffling than the response the poem received in its Englished version. My hope is that a few readers may go out and find why the poem has been so admired by those who have had the good fortune to know it in the original or [translated] . . . version. (pp. 95-6)

Leonard Nathan, in a review of "Baltics," in The Chowder Review, *Nos. 16 & 17, Spring-Winter, 1981, pp. 95-6.*

ROLF FJELDE

Of his spare and incisive work produced over nearly 30 years, the Swedish poet Tomas Tranströmer has written, "My poems are meeting places." The metaphor is singularly apt for his divided career, his dominant concerns, his wide-ranging subject matter and, not least, for his claim on a growing audience of American readers—a claim well served, in different ways, by these two collections of translations [*Selected Poems* and *Truth Barriers*].

Mr. Tranströmer has published eight volumes of verse, beginning with *17 Poems* (1954), but the first two have the cribbed, cabined and confined preciosity of a poet who has not yet found his sea legs. With *The Half-finished Heaven* (1962), however, the always exhilarating voyage of a major talent was clearly underway, marked by an authority of arresting image, a resonance with outer and inner depths of nature and the self, and as much self-assurance as could be expected from any poet vulnerable to the shocks of our world. In a poem called **"Night Duty"** he conceives himself in the figure of a ballast stone in the deepest hold of a ship: "I am one of those silent weights / which prevent the vessel overturning!". . . [*Selected Poems*] is particularly useful in charting the course of Mr. Tranströmer's development since it includes substantial samples from all eight books, three of them translated intact. (p. 24)

Mr. Tranströmer has traveled extensively, and much of the pleasure of his art is in the wit and accuracy of his imagination as it expands our awareness and renews the familiar. In a smoky hut in Madeira, two fish are frying with "tiny garlic explosions." New York City seen at night from a distant prospect is like "a spiral galaxy seen from the side," the dozing bodies in its subway cars becoming catacombs in motion." Sometimes these deft formulations go beyond pungent perception to express an esthetic credo, a moral stance, as in a prose-poem titled **"Upright,"** which captures the condition of living "free but wary" in the memory of a visit to the Sara tribe in Africa. It recalls being welcomed there aboard a canoe that represents "A balancing act. If the heart lies on the left side you must incline your head a little to the right, nothing in the pockets, no large gestures, all rhetoric must be left behind. Just this: rhetoric is impossible here. The canoe glides out of the water."

The exotic provenance of these images is balanced in Mr. Tranströmer's work by the stones, forests, villages and cities of his native Sweden, the chief metaphors of his meditations on existence. For a poet to be judged important and to reach toward greatness requires more than a gift for isolated insights, however penetrating—the random jewels need the ordered background setting of a world-view. There is evidence of such in one obsessively recurring image-complex: the car, the driver, the mass migration of traffic. The motif of driving somewhere, anywhere, becomes an effective symbol for contemporary man, encased in his technology, separated from the earth, prone to sudden accident, moving in the blind flow of traffic like "a sluggish dragon" over asphalt where "seeds try to grow."

Meanwhile, around, beneath, above the insulated figure in the car and his starved, diminished capacity for response, a universe of natural revelation offers itself and bides its time. . . .

Even man's artifacts enjoy a sentience ignored by the imperceptive: "the house feels its own constellation of nails / holding the walls together." The ominous result of abandoning the meeting places where awarenesses mingle in their full complexity is a falling away from poetry, which is a communication of being most completely alive, to the public prose of jackbooted, manipulative efficiency....

In Mr. Tranströmer's work one senses that the novelist who refuses to sell experience short (one of the finest prose-poems is called **"Start of a Late Autumn Novel"**), the dramatist unable to cheapen life for a lucrative effect, the poet who lives like his squat pinetree in the swamp, of whom "what you see is nothing / compared to the roots, the widespread, secretly / creeping, immortal or half-mortal / root system"—are all partisans in a common resistance movement that will not collaborate with literal, or figurative, death-dealers.

Truth Barriers (1978), Mr. Tranströmer's most recent volume, is an exploration of a diversity of boundaries that both close in and shut out, and the truths of larger consciousness—art, memory, hallucination, dream—that undermine those walls of the psyche. Robert Bly has written a sympathetically informed introduction, and out of his own temperamental affinity contributes translations as consonant with the Swedish as one could hope. The Swedish originals are provided for comparison in an appendix. The poems of Tomas Tranströmer are points of entry "upward into / the depths" of an imagination, a spirit that is regeneratively inventive, capacious, unillusioned, undaunted, admirable. (p. 26)

> Rolf Fjelde, "Poems as Meeting Places," in The New York Times Book Review, April 26, 1981, pp. 24, 26.

MICHAEL SCHMIDT

[*Selected Poems*] is disappointing, and the quality of the translations uneven. In some poems what appears to be a literal approach has stanched the rhythm altogether. But the main problem is with the poems themselves. In an interview appended to this book, the poet discusses his 1968 poem **"Night Duty"**. It grew directly out of six years' work with young offenders (by profession Tranströmer is a psychologist). The year is important: the tension for change was great, and for Tranströmer the recurrent imagery of pulse, footsteps, and clocks in his early work looked to be at an end. "The language marches in step with the executioners. Therefore we must get a new language." There are various difficulties here. The "we" addressed would hardly understand the hermetic metaphors of the poem which are obscure in a *fin de siècle* way. The poem has lost its occasion in them. More important, this poem and its successors fail to "get a new language". They hardly even seem to try. The line was only a gesture, without consequence in or for the verse.

Tranströmer in his more recent work writes on the move, when he gets away on journeys from the fortunate constraints of home and family. He remains conscious of audience in his poems, even when he is most confiding. The good "dishonest line" will be admitted for effect. There is a lack of repose, a sense that he is always busy about his poems. This is congenial and implicates us—up to a point. We remain a collective audience. He is deliberate and cosmopolitan in what has become a conventional way. The poet "with roots" looks hopelessly provincial from the airport bus; but then the tourist poet may be travelling light. It's no wonder that *Baltics* (1974), in which

Tranströmer invests his own history, is the most compelling and original work in this book....

> Michael Schmidt, "Open to Otherness," in The Times Literary Supplement, No. 4092, September 4, 1981, p. 1019.

SVEN BIRKERTS

Tomas Tranströmer has been publishing his sharp, disquieting poems in Sweden since 1954. English-language translators . . . only began to catch up with him in the late 1960s. And we have had to wait until 1981 for a compendium. The publication [of *Selected Poems*] gives us our first full overview of this singular poet. Here we have generous selections from the first six books, and complete texts of *Baltics* and *The Truth Barrier,* Tranströmer's two most recent books. (An interview by Gunnar Harding is included as an appendix.) (p. 202)

Tranströmer, like [Gunnar] Ekelöf, is a poet preoccupied with the Unknown, with all that is excluded by the bright efficiency of an aggressively modern country. Time, identity, the bottomless psyche, and death—these are the boundary stones of his terrain. Where Ekelöf has the mystic's drive to get past the phenomenal, however, Tranströmer does not. He roots himself in it. In his work, the perceived world—stones, trees, cars, electric razors—reverberates with phenomenality. Instead of stripping away the perception of the here and now, Tranströmer uses it. His images tirelessly animate the object world: fluttering laundry is a butterfly, bicycles are beasts with horns, rubber stamps are the hooves of horses.... Nothing escapes his Ovidian eye. The result of this thorough re-processing of the world is, for the reader, a sharp sense of displacement. For there is no point of rest, no place at which things hug their usual forms or conform to our expectations. This obsessive animation is the expression of a dissolving ego. In Tranströmer's poems the "I" is not a coherent entity; it is almost entirely porous to the surrounding world. Each poem is a vibrant, uncentered perceptual field, a mystery. But Tranströmer is not a mystic. The mystery is there for itself. The poet will not put a higher interpretation upon it. The suggestion is now and again made that there are hidden windows and doors and that they will lead somewhere. Nothing, however, comes of it. And where all is provisional, including the self of the narrator, the ethical dimension is necessarily absent.

In Tranströmer's poems the image is dominant, prevailing over the line, and the individual poem progresses by way of stacked perceptual units. This is where Tranströmer reveals his mastery: he is an engineer of uncanny effects. Synaesthesia, telescoped metaphor, unpredicated transitions and leaps, sudden shifts in scale all combine to form tight linguistic circuits working at maximum load-capacity.... Underlying this image world is a great metaphysical unease, the absence of a higher claim. The surface of the work is varied and rich, but beneath it we find a man in deadlock. The images conjure great mystery and strike the complacent senses with all kinds of startling connections. The reader is plucked from the network of the familiar and hooked into something self-contained and ominous. But while intimations gather and build pressure, they ultimately lead nowhere because there is, in the vision of the self dissolved, no place to get to.... (pp. 202-04)

Tranströmer is intent upon the provisionality of all structures, whether internal (structures generated by the psyche), conceptual (social orders and worldviews), or even literal (objects and the edifices of material civilization). He is suspicious of the very *idea* of order. And thus, his eye is always looking for the anomaly, the slip, the contradiction, whatever will buttress his case: that we live blindly in the midst of the unknown, that we have evolved our personalities and social orders to defend us from this, that they are never quite adequate.... The poems set out to subvert this "normal everyday reason" and to open the reader to that "greater context." But what this greater context involves is never made clear. The reference to the "religious character" of the mystery is not very helpful, for there is no sense in which the work bears this out. At best we might say that there are moments of discontinuity in the psyche—when we go into sleep, or wake from sleep, or suffer sudden shock—that are avenues to higher apprehension. But "higher" only in that they are truer. These brief displacements are the only time that we come face to face with unstructured reality. They are glimpses of the noumenal through unexpected chinks in the phenomenal. We perceive that our "normal" order is a phantom architecture. Tranströmer re-creates in his poems the "feel" of a psyche suddenly jarred from its track.

If we look closely at the dynamic of these displacements, we see that they are, in fact, instances of collapsing ego. The "normal everyday reason," Plato's "charioteer," is nothing more or less than the conscious "I." As Ekelöf wrote:

> In reality you are no one.
> Reality is so without I, naked and shapeless!

But what for Ekelöf were superior forces permeating the universe are, in Tranströmer's poetry, the forces of the unconscious. (Tranströmer, it should be noted, is a trained psychologist.) In both poets there is a sense of the porous "I," an "I" that may at any time lose its contours. The difference is that for Ekelöf this effacement is a spiritual process, a surrender to a higher law; for Tranströmer there are overtones of psychosis: it is never clear whether the unconscious is a hoard of higher meaning or merely an undifferentiated mass of material, some of it useful, most of it anarchic and dangerous.

Tranströmer repeatedly searches out the line where the "I" stops and the unconscious begins. Once he has found the frontier, he will work from both sides.... (pp. 204-05)

To call Tranströmer's poetry a series of onslaughts upon the ego would be too reductive. For one thing, Tranströmer does not confine himself to the psychologist's standard map of the psyche. As a maker of images he requires greater latitude. And if some of his premises have empirical sanction, the effects he achieves from them place him well outside the academy. Psychologists do affirm, for instance, that the unconscious does not differentiate time, that it is, in effect, atemporal. Tranströmer gets much poetic use out of this absence of tenses. When he writes:

> the stains pushing through the wallpaper
> It was the living dead
> who wanted their portraits painted.
>   (from **"From the Winter of 1947"**)

he is being neither metaphoric nor surreal. These unnervingly straightforward lines express the conviction that in the realm of the unconscious the dead are very much alive. What's more, the unconscious, throughout Tranströmer's work, is shown to have as great if not a greater claim upon the real than the ego. Thus, we keep encountering these unclassifiable presences. They are not exactly ghosts, or hallucinations, or memories—they are not even metaphors. It is as if we are looking at time through the undiscriminating eye of the id. Past, present, and future want to merge into a state of pure duration. Only the structural limitation of the "I" prevents it.... (p. 207)

That inner frontier line between conscious and unconscious has a spatial counterpart in Tranströmer's poetry in the ever-shifting boundary between the natural world and the structures of civilization. In a sense they are the same line, for nature and the unconscious are vitally linked, and technology is very much a conscious manifestation. This is, of course, a simplistic mapping—as simplistic as correlating individual and collective unconscious—but it may give us some access to Tranströmer's conceptions.

Tranströmer has been, from the earliest poetry on, attentive to landscape and geography. As he notes in the interview: "... my poems always have a definite geographical starting point." But he is less interested in description or detailing *per se* than in finding the various points of contact between the man-made and the natural order. Just as he is fascinated by situations in which the balance of the psyche teeters, so he wants to uncover terrestrial tension points. We find in the poems a natural world penetrated by telephone cables and dotted with industrial debris, suburbs where man and nature are in pitched battle, and city-scapes that are subtly imprinted with other signs.... (pp. 207-08)

Nature, like the unconscious, is seen as an ultimately mysterious entity, a code that will never be cracked. The tools of reason cannot hope to penetrate their own original source—that would be a tautology. Still, indifferent and dangerous, dangerous in its indifference, nature may yet be where the saving powers are concealed. And though there seems to be an undeclared war between nature and "civilization," reconciliation is not impossible. Perhaps it will be effected by some unknown principle within nature ... or else by some access of vision in man.... (pp. 208-09)

The six books leading up to the long poem *Baltics* (1974) bring us repeatedly to these inner and outer border zones, startle us with uncanny imagery, force us to a recognition of peril, instability, and indeterminacy. The landscapes are depopulated and ominous, the voice always solitary. This consistency of effects would be a liability—or more of a liability—if Tranströmer were not so inventive with his surfaces: the poems are like mobiles, where the pendants and disposition of weights change, but where the principle remains the same.

But with the publication of *Baltics* (1974), Tranströmer finally strikes out from his norm. His longest and most ambitious work (and a long poem is no small accomplishment for a poet accustomed to working with compacted image units), *Baltics* plaits history and locale, personal and communal memory, and generates an affecting texture of tenuously interconnected lives. The commerce between interior and exterior worlds is a great deal freer than what we have seen in the previous work. And, no less importantly, Tranströmer takes the liberty of a looser and freer line. There are fewer signs of compaction and construction, more bursts of lyricism. The imagery is now in the service of evocation, less calculated to startle.... (p. 209)

We sense that a new conception has thrown up its challenge. The poem moves with energy and assurance. Tranströmer has not changed his fundamental perception. He is still hovering among border zones, between day vision and night vision, always directing us to the *mysterium rerum*. But now the setting, an archipelago of islands in the Baltic, supplies structural freedom. The sea, all surrounding, is his mediating element. He has less need to set up transitions: the steady movement of water is itself perpetual transition. The narrative voice is free to shift among tenses, pronouns, and places. Not surprisingly, *Baltics* contains some of Tranströmer's freshest writing. . . . Formerly Tranströmer avoided the human presence. One sensed a considered epistemological position: other lives could not be known. His willingness, in *Baltics,* to evoke other lives indicates a major transition.

The Truth Barrier, the most recent collection, is a paradox in this light. It is, on the one hand, a consolidation of many of the gains made in *Baltics*. The poems are looser, with longer lines. Indeed, six of the fifteen are prose poems—further evidence that tight patterns have become stifling. . . . (p. 210)

The problem is that the promise of transformation given in *Baltics* has not been realized. The humane discursiveness of **"Schubertiana"** is an exception. Too many of the other poems simply reenact the familiar Tranströmer procedures. A poem like **"Homewards"** is little more than self-pastiche. . . . A big step forward has been followed by a little step back.

I remarked earlier that there is an impasse at the core of Tranströmer's poetry, that for all of their brilliance his images are non-directional. Stylistic shifts and the annexation of new material suggest that Tranströmer is aware of this and is looking for ways to change. But it is a deeply rooted problem. For twenty years now Tranströmer has been atomizing the ego. He has made its insubstantiality his central preoccupation. And out of this has come a distinctive poetic voice, a voice that does not depend upon authority so much as upon the undermining of authority. In the process, however, he has painted himself into a corner. For once the ego has been dismantled and the unconscious brought forward, there are few options left. The poet can either advance into surrealism and exploit the material, or else he can remain in his corner and try to vary his effects as much as possible—and for a time it looked as if this was Tranströmer's plan.

But there may be a third option: that of reclaiming and reconstructing the "I." The process would require a reversal, the repudiation of a unique project. In other ways, though, it would be a forward motion, a return from the underworld. Tranströmer's problem right now is that of the nihilist: the vaporized self cannot establish connection to any sort of moral order. And great poetry still depends upon this order. What Tranströmer will do remains to be seen. (pp. 211-12)

Sven Birkerts, "A Cull of Trance-Roamers," in Parnassus: Poetry in Review, *Vol. 11, No. 2, Fall-Winter, 1983 & Spring-Summer, 1984, pp. 192-212.*

ROBERT LINDSEY

[*Selected Poems, 1954-1986*] includes material from Tranströmer's first collection of poems, published when he was only twenty-three, as well as his very latest. And though poets don't necessarily develop chronologically, one does get a sense that Tranströmer has come a long way from his earliest, chiefly descriptive pieces in *Seventeen Poems* to the sweeping, controlled vision of a work such as *Baltics* (1975).

In many of Tranströmer's poems, meaning derives from the juxtaposition and accumulation of packed images. This is particularly true of earlier pieces like **"Autumn in Skeries."** . . . The images are stored in curt, hard lines that release, one after the other, dense associations with striking force. These are interspersed with longer-lined observations in which the poet generalizes from concrete data. . . .

Though the work presented here is drawn from nine separate volumes and one clutch of new pieces, Tranströmer's material coheres below the surface through recurring images that crop up in the earliest poems as well as the latest—dreams, sleep, water, nautical hardware, ships, winter. The poet who described Sweden as a "hauled-up, unrigged ship" in 1954 also described it as "drag[ging] over the floor of the world like a grappling hook" in 1983. There is also a consistent perspective that juxtaposes the world of official business and responsibility and the filtration process of individual experience, which explains, in part, recurring allusions to dreams and sleep. . . .

More important is Tranströmer's quiet but pervasive sense of spiritual possibilities underlying the objects and movements of commonplace experience. Regardless of where he turns his attention, whether to a sleeping Swedish town or a deserted forest, the compass needle invariably points in this direction. It is, in fact, one of the most striking things about Tranströmer's work precisely because it is so effectively and painstakingly understated. An examined painting "begins to stretch and open behind the boy who is sick / and sunk in himself. It throws sparks and makes noise." A plane passing overhead throws a cross-shaped shadow. . . .

The religious context is assured and incorporated within a natural order, and, partly for this reason, Tranströmer's world abounds with potentialities—for dreams, transformations, music from unexpected corners, sudden changes of light, momentary engagements with the spiritual, life itself, which is "the poem which is completely possible." The spiritual element works within Tranströmer's chiseled detail.

Unlike many other contemporary poets, Tranströmer does not settle for concrete reportage. The world he evokes serves, through the vocabulary of its imagery, like the higher functions of ritual. He asserts and orders human dignity within "the mass of the endless text."

Robert Lindsey, "The Poem Which Is Completely Possible," in The Bloomsbury Review, *Vol. 7, No. 5, September-October, 1987, p. 27.*

George W. S. Trow

1943-

American short story writer, novelist, and essayist.

Trow is best known for his humorous short stories that highlight absurdities of human behavior and various American popular culture trends. His first collection, *Bullies* (1980), which is composed of pieces originally published in the *New Yorker*, is notable for Trow's accurate reproduction of slang, jargon, and cliché and his keen eye for detail. In his review of *Bullies*, Jeffrey Burke remarked: "Because he is such a careful writer and yet so stylistically adventurous, Trow is easily one of the best humorists around." Trow's second volume, *Within the Context of No Context* (1981), contains two long essays which also first appeared in the *New Yorker*. In the first piece, "Within the Context of No Context," he presents an unflattering portrait of American popular culture, which he finds morally hollow. The second essay, "Within That Context, One Style: Eclectic, Reminiscent, Amused, Fickle, Perverse (Ahmet Ertegun)," is a profile of pop music entrepreneur Ahmet Ertegun, who, Trow believes, embodies the contemporary sensibility explicated in the first essay.

Trow's first novel, *The City in the Mist* (1984), examines moral decline among upper-class Americans by chronicling more than a century in the lives of two New York families. Edward Pitoniak commented: "[Trow's vision in *The City in the Mist*] is honestly commanding, fixing without fatuity on cardinal issues: honor, manners, social authority."

EVE BABITZ

Quentin Crisp once wrote something like this: "When you say things are better than they are, they call you a romanticist. When you say things are worse than they are, they call you a cynicist. But when you say things are exactly as they are, they call you a satirist." George W. S. Trow's wonderful volume of stories [*Bullies*] is a victory for things exactly as they are.

Terrible images conjured up in these stories seem bound to linger for a lifetime in one's brain. . . .

Part of the time, Mr. Trow writes in a terminal travel-brochure style, as when his prose attempts to transcend by cheeriness an intractable resort hotel called the Hotel Reine-American, which is located on a strip of lost-cause ocean-front property called Alani Beach. . . .

Other times, George W. S. Trow writes in an innocent style you usually see in the Talk of the Town section of *The New Yorker*. Only this time the bright and genial prose is out to make bearable not reptile exhibits or a certain special cheese importer—this time Mr. Trow's friendly words are out to describe Mrs. Armand Reef (who "Likes to Entertain"). Mrs. Armand Reef, a divorcée who lives on the Upper East Side and endorses products like "Body Dew" and "Ultra Vodka," discusses who is asked to her "little dinner parties": "To be asked to one of my little dinner parties you must have great

intelligence. And wit. I value wit. I love the clever thing—the thing that just *glances off* the truth and circles back to something topical." She then goes on to say, "I find that high-powered dynamic men like to humiliate easy women and that makes a party *go*. . . ."

There is a story called **"At Lunch With the Rock Critic Establishment,"** which to me—having spent my youth in the jaws of rock'n'roll, designing album covers and spending so much time with people like those he describes that I *know* he's saying things are exactly as they are—is worth the price of the whole book. The sort of rock critics Mr. Trow describes are the ones who write three-page essays on the first four notes of the Eagles' "Take It Easy," showing these notes as proof that the Eagles are corrupt and Too L.A. and that nobody could possibly take them seriously but teen-agers. . . .

What happens when you read Mr. Trow's stories is that you begin to see everything quite clearly. Suddenly, a fabulous place that boasts of "hotels with perfect security" becomes transparent.

And Mr. Trow, who is himself a master of style when he writes, seems to be using it to show that style, taste, those little refinements used in everyday life to separate the elegant and delightful from the rest of us, are nothing more than "specifics." So that having the specifically right shoes, the right shirts, the right old furniture and new friends is nothing but a collection of specific details imposed by those in fashion. And those in fashion are nothing more than bullies. Yet those who are bullied seem so eager to soak up the specifics and details of what is in style and what isn't, that unless they read Mr. Trow's book, they may go on and on without ever stopping to think what fashion really means.

But once you've read these stories, it will seem that in fashion, bullies are all there are. Or ever will be.

Eve Babitz, "The Tyranny of Fashion," in The New York Times Book Review, *April 20, 1980, p. 14.*

ANATOLE BROYARD

[George Trow] says that "the stories in *Bullies* take place in a landscape rather like history with the tide out." The remark is attractive but flawed. Landscapes, in the strictest sense, have no tide. The tide of history is not an altogether fresh metaphor. And that "with" is awkward.

But we know what he means. He is looking for a landscape where he will be the first historian, where there will be only his footprints in the sand after the tide has gone out, a landscape that was not conventional, yet one where neither Barthelme, Beckett, nor Kafka has planted his flag. Perhaps every writer is an explorer manqué, an adventurer with bad feet or an intolerance for flies. It might be wise if Mr. Trow wore "the new serious leggings" preferred by some of his characters.

The 16 overlapping stories in *Bullies* all appeared in *The New Yorker,* which seems to be like writing with the tide out. In a story about rock music, there are death-rock clubs and a feminist rock-and-roll quarterly called *Mother Rock,* whose editor believes that "women have an innate urge toward percussion which has been thwarted by men." Dominica Davenport, Havana Davenport's sister, hates textiles of any kind and wears aluminum party pants. A rising musician named Calvin is accused of having once "done back-up for Donovan." A rock group called the Traitors is cashing in on the popular "disloyalty thing."

In Mr. Trow's landscape, "two-story commercial entities support the low sky." In this neighborhood, "a certain shrill shout has become almost common." "Rooming" is one of the new "great songs of work and effort." We learn that "the tension between intersection and juxtaposition is the generational force" that produces the songs.

Outside the hotel, which is one of Mr. Trow's archetypal images, a girl "waits through the dawn, with a piece of velvet." In the town a woman has been arrested for " 'lawning'—driving her powerful Chevrolet station wagon deep into the newly planted lawns of 20 or 30 suburban homes." Another woman, "because of the long, empty quality of her walking down the hall," reminds us of something in a foreign film. . . .

Some of Mr. Trow's devices wear thin over the long haul. His short, flat sentences, his stylized repetitions that establish irrelevant rhythms, his tunings of jargon, his reliance on damp— these become self-conscious in the longer pieces. The psychological picaresque lacks incident.

Mr. Trow has a good ear and it serves him well. The trouble with *Bullies,* though, is that it is stitched together out of symptoms. It's like listening to the story of someone's operation. Even though the operation is a literary one, it still has a chemical smell.

Anatole Broyard, "Psychological Picaresque," in The New York Times, *April 26, 1980, p. 25.*

JEFFREY BURKE

Parody and satire and a touch of madness are the distinguishing features of *Bullies,* a collection of pieces short and long by George W. S. Trow. . . . His lighter satire deals with fads, fashions, and human foibles, like the relationship, born of the self-help Seventies, between a divorced man and his rug in the opening story, **"I Expand My Horizons":**

> Like my ex-wife, my rug wants to exist in a non-judgmental atmosphere. "I am not here to meet your expectations"—that's what my rug says to me.

Though an undertone of quiet desperation may creep through even those lighter pieces, Trow continually amuses with his absurd or effectively silly details. . . . In the longer pieces, most of which describe a crumbling resort called Alani Beach, the satire is darker, and Trow signals a shift from familiar contexts to surreal ones by suggesting malevolence in what elsewhere were innocently absurd details. . . . Because he is such a careful writer and yet so stylistically adventurous, Trow is easily one of the best humorists around, as well as one of the few whose literary merit permits him to be taken seriously. (p. 91)

Jeffrey Burke, "Fielder's Choice: The Softball School of Literary Criticism," in Harper's, *Vol. 260, No. 1560, May, 1980, pp. 90-2.*

EVA HOFFMAN

White middle-class Americans growing up during the postwar decades were strangely dissatisfied. Vietnam didn't quite account for all of it, nor did other political disaffections. What was wrong? The youthful malcontents talked about how things didn't seem quite "real," and how people didn't express their true feelings. It all seemed quite banal, jejune and annoyingly self-indulgent. And yet—and yet, the talk, for all its awkwardness, wasn't about nothing. They were bothered by *something,* these well-educated and apparently pampered young, even if that something was very tenuous and very difficult to name.

It is George Trow's most interesting achievement in the first, and more important, of [*Within the Context of No Context*'s] two companion essays ["**Within the Context of No Context**"] that he has found a mode for describing this elusive middle-class malaise without being reductively analytical or vapidly sentimental. His method could be called lyrical sociology, and his diagnosis of his generation's complaint is that they have suffered from reality anemia.

In fact, the form Mr. Trow . . . has invented for this essay is so original and unabashedly idiosyncratic that on entering it one experiences a kind of reading vertigo. The immediate subject of the piece is contemporary media culture and the sensibility it fosters; but this is hardly a sociological tract or a mundane history of the period as seen through the mindless eye of the tube. Mr. Trow makes his observations on the "context of no context"—a thin cultural landscape with television much too prominently at its center—through a collage of aphorisms, personal meditations and a species of structuralist dissection. Nowhere in the essay are there diatribes on the dullness of suburbia, case histories of fed-up TV watchers turned rebels,

Marxist analyses of advertising economics or thematic critiques of specific programs. Instead, there are short riffs on such subjects as the decline of adulthood ("In the New History, the preferences of a child carried as much weight as the preferences of an adult."), the shift from history to demographics ("Groups of more than one were now united not by a common history but by common characteristics."), the supplanting of authority by experts, the ascendancy of the "problem" as a form of discourse, the scale of experience created by television ("The trivial is raised up to power in it. The powerful is lowered toward the trivial."), the distortions of psychic distance created by too many people ("The middle distance fell away. . . . Two grids remained. The grid of two hundred million and the grid of intimacy."), the special reality status of celebrities ("Celebrities have an intimate life and a life in the grid of two hundred million. . . . Of all Americans, only they are complete."), and the meretricious, make-believe power of Robert Moses's World's Fair.

What sort of way is this to slice up a subject? Where do these categories come from and what do they add up to? In some cases, their choice seems entirely subjective. Mr. Trow feels free to swoop down on whatever bits of his own experience strike him as revealing, to pick out snippets of information just because they have made a vivid impression, and in doing so he sometimes risks glibness. But eventually his selection of terms begins to take on an internal logic. For all the occasional cuteness, the deadpan naïveté, Mr. Trow is after fundamental matters. What he wants to catch, through his abstractions and his cerebral metaphors, are the underlying messages, meanings, energies behind pervasive cultural phenomena; his observations on people in masses, on the psychic distance between individuals and the crowd, and on our relationship to advertisements and products are an attempt to grasp basic conditions of the modern American environment and describe the way they affect our consciousness and organize our experience.

The most basic condition, in his view, is a kind of experiential and moral bloodlessness. Within the heart of the heart of the country, he perceives a gap, an absence, a deprivation. For some reason, in his parents' generation, he suggests, the sense of authority, of self-confidence, of adulthood felt by middle-class Americans diffused itself and evaporated. The amount of personal power inhering within any one individual diminished as it got distributed into aggregates of people—demographic units. This left his own generation—"the babies"—without frames of reference, models of certainty, a context. It left them also without comfort, without "a sense of home." (pp. 7, 24)

Television is the force that has come to fill the empty, cold spaces; but the substitutes if offers for personal experience are themselves a chilling con. (p. 24)

Television offers family hours and intimate glimpses of celebrities to give a simulacrum of warmth, discussions of problems and shells of identities (lawyer, cop, lawyer who is a cop) to give the momentary illusion of context; it even treats viewers to game shows based on the participants' discomfort to get at what feels like reality. But it cannot mask the fact that it is not real, and the pretense creates an unease of its own.

It is this weakening of experience, this failure of individual power, Mr. Trow suggests, that caused his generational cohorts their embarrassments in the face of false authority, provoked their ironies toward their own middle-class identities, even their rebellions. Speaking of the fedora hat that his father, hoping to initiate him into "the traditional manners of the high bourgeoisie," expected him to wear, he writes,

> It turns out that while I am at home in many strange places, I am not free even to visit the territory I was expected to inhabit effortlessly. To wear a fedora, I must first torture it out of shape so that it can be cleaned of the embarrassment in it.

The diagnosis seems to me penetrating. It's diametrically opposed to the myth—which continues to have some potency—of America the raw, America the energetic. But then, from Alexis de Tocqueville to Paul Goodman, there have always been observers of America who, beneath the currents of collective, mass energies, have noticed a strange lack of individual self-assurance, a languid, demoralizing anxiety. In any case, if **"Within the Context of No Context"** is convincing, it's not by virtue of a systematic analysis, but in the thrust of Mr. Trow's vision, the angle of his attack.

Aphorism is the mode of concentrated insight. Mr. Trow's aphorisms work because his relationship to the culture is intense. Unlike Marshal McLuhan, to whose later writings this essay could, in some respects, be compared, Mr. Trow does not offer a philosophy of popular culture; but his antennae are alert to its thickness and weight, the way its contents feel on the skin and mind. We live perpetually suspended between subjectivity and data; Mr. Trow locates that intersection with oblique, subjective precision. For all the urbane understatement of his tone, this is hardly a detached exercise in cultural criticism. Reality anemia—the dissociations it causes, even the ironies it requires—upsets him, and the distress makes his writing passionate as well as cool.

In his second essay, titled **"Within That Context, One Style,"** it's mostly cool. Like the first essay, this piece—a profile of Ahmet Ertegun, president of Atlantic Records and probably rock music's most prominent entrepreneur—was initially published in *The New Yorker*. Putting them together is strained. There are some thematic links. The later stages of rock, over whose development and marketing Ahmet Ertegun to some extent presided, take place against the background of no rules matter and therefore no violations are possible. There's the same attention, although on a more trivial scale, to the messages conveyed by style, to essential energies—in this case of rock—and to the twists of ironic commentary on those energies. But for the purposes of personifying his version of contemporary sensibility, Mr. Trow did not choose the most illustrative figure. . . . For a portrait of somebody firmly embedded "within the context of no context," Mr. Trow might have done better with one of those baby moguls who have risen in various media industries with meteoric speed and apparently no managerial method, or with a contemporary rock star whose music reflects the sense that it's all up for grabs in its very rhythms.

Mr. Trow is too acute an observer, though, not to give us engaging moments. (pp. 24-5)

But the subject, in this second essay, is simply too ephemeral to carry the weight of larger analysis, and Mr. Trow's tone, with its relentless low-key irony, becomes quickly annoying. As a piece of catching-the-moment, on-the-scene journalism, the profile has enough perceptive nuggets to make good reading; but its life should not have been prolonged beyond its occasion. Its companion piece was startling to come upon the first time; the surprise is how well, in spite of its stylish simplicities, it sustains itself between the covers of a book. (p. 25)

Eva Hoffman, "Reality Anemia," in The New York Times Book Review, *October 11, 1981, pp. 7, 24-5.*

BARRY GEWEN

Trow's *Within the Context of No Context* consists of two pieces, somewhat uncomfortably linked, that originally appeared as long articles in the *New Yorker*. The first, ["**Within the Context of No Context**"], is an ambitious and impressionistic survey of the cultural detritus strewn across the American landscape in the form of TV, movies, magazines and fashion. The second, **"Within That Context, One Style: Eclectic, Reminiscent, Amused, Fickle, Perverse (Ahmet Ertegun),"** narrows in on a single pop music entrepreneur who is taken as representative of our current sorry state.

The "no context" of the opening essay is the U.S. setting, where Trow finds nothing solid or substantial, only a mass market operating on the empty principles of a con game. Earlier critics of American popular culture like Dwight Macdonald will discern many familiar strains here: the tyranny of the Philistine majority, the vacuity of television, the decline of authentic values, the importance of fame, the submersion of the individual into the mob. With the deftness of a good jazz musician, Trow discovers new ways to present these old ideas, playing clever variations on standard themes. He has a hard, sinuous, absurdist, sensibility. Frequently, his comments are striking, his way of putting things exquisite; and he can be savagely funny. But irony by itself, no matter how well expressed, is ultimately unsatisfying fare, and often a reader is left feeling, as with the dissection of *People* magazine, why bother?

The second essay is the more intriguing of the two. Ostensibly expanding on the ideas of the first, it follows the activities of Ahmet Ertegun, millionaire founder of Atlantic Records. Ertegun "lacked the inflexible center," says Trow. "At the heart of his achievement there was no answer stated or question posed but, rather, only this: the rhythms of infatuation smartly expressed." Trow reports on Ertegun's business lunches, business trips and business deals, and the piece ends in a splash of jet-set parties, attended by assorted Warhols, Halstons, Vreelands, and Jaggers.

If this were all there was to Ertegun, he would be worth about a paragraph's attention but, it turns out, this son of a Turkish ambassador possesses an aristocrat's grace unique in the hustle-bustle world he inhabits. More important, as a producer during the late '40s and early '50s, he made a lasting contribution, sensitively analyzed by Trow, to American music. To his credit, Trow does not conceal his admiration for Ertegun ("I thought Ahmet was a great man in spite of himself"), yet since reverence has a way of undercutting irony, the essay has a distinct wobble. Trow's stance is out of sync with his subject.

As *Within the Context of No Context* amply demonstrates, Trow is undeniably a writer. He is intelligent and subtle, with an eye for the power relationships underlying social conventions. Nor does he lack the bitchiness that seems a prerequisite for the close observation of manners and style. But he has not, so far, succeeded in establishing a perspective that brings his taste and values fully to bear on his material. (p. 15)

Barry Gewen, "America in Three Contexts," in The New Leader, *Vol. LXIV, No. 20, November 2, 1981, pp. 14-15.*

JOHN LEGGETT

For so short a novel, *The City in the Mist* has a spacious framework. It is an account of two rich New York families over a century and a half of their spawning. First come the Coonlons, sprung from an order of waterfront criminals. Michael, the patriarch, is a brewery plug-ugly whose ambition was sparked in childhood by his father's pointing out the other family's founder, Johannes Aspair, as the richest man in America.

Come to think of it, the plan for *The City in the Mist* is like one of those genealogical charts that starts from a single marriage and fans back across 10 generations of forebears, but in reverse so that we are introduced to the founders of the Coonlon and Aspair dynasties in the middle of the last century and then brought down to the present on a spreading trellis of names.

As the marriages and the births multiply so do the odd names and random facts. . . .

The focal figure is Edward Coonlon Jones, Michael's grandson and a man who is now a 60-year-old bachelor. His mother's intensive tutoring in material possessions has contributed to his simplemindedness. He is without an occupation, and he lives in an apartment on 73d Street, where he polishes his shoes, chats on the telephone with his cousins, reads zealously about violent crime and human misfortune and looks after his legacy, which is, in part, his grandfather's wardrobe and those Adam-Sheraton chairs of his mother's.

There is an accretion of the details in Eddy's life—a whole page of the addresses of family-held real estate and objets d'art, for example—that puts the reader in mind of those portraits of Depression sharecroppers listing the contents of their bureau drawers.

Some episodes are told with a delightfully surreal dizziness. Eddy visits the Greene Club in order to play bridge and during the course of the game, the club becomes a ship at sea, and the passengers become society figures with whose scandals he is familiar. After a dramatic shipwreck, Eddy is questioned by a Congressional committee. He describes the great disaster vividly before wandering back to society gossip and the details of the bridge game to which he attaches a greater importance.

But for all its flights and dives of fancy, *The City in the Mist* is rarely fun. Mr. Trow is too much in earnest for that. Nor, given this feckless cast of characters, is there a redeeming or even convincing revelation in the idea that so materialistic a society as ours grows ever more feeble and purposeless.

There is bemusement here, a faintly contemptuous smile for such labyrinthine futility, but otherwise I found no feeling, neither love nor loathing, on the part of the author for the narrator, nor on the part of the narrator for the characters, nor on the part of the characters for each other. That's a shame too because it leaves this intriguing city socked in.

John Leggett, "Without Love or Loathing," in The New York Times Book Review, *February 5, 1984, p. 12.*

RICHARD EDER

The City in the Mist is a brief, dense fable that at its best moments soars into a witty and powerful vision of our contemporary disarray. Like Mark Helprin's *Winter's Tale*, it devises a golden and magical legend for New York's rackety energy and confusion; and seeks in that legend the means to restore to us our sense of who we might really be.

City begins by establishing two of the legend's founders. One is Michael Coonlon, a brawling Irish member of the Pearl Button Gang in the 1870s, who was reformed by marriage to the girlfriend of his best friend, Tom Guin. Under her influence, he became a wealthy brewer, moved to Albany and, by the time he died, had constructed a political and real estate empire.

The other city father is Johannes Aspair who, like Commodore Vanderbilt, made a much greater fortune much earlier, establishing one of the city's social dynasties. Coonlon was an incandescent, large-spirited man; Aspair was heavy and stuck to his account books, but both in their different ways were patriarchs and builders.

Their descendants lived in a very different world. Trow, who gives Coonlon a vivid if legendary corporeal existence, while treating Aspair more laconically and with greater mystery, makes this world as foggy, trackless and dragon-filled as Beowulf's backyard.

It is an evil place. If New York once belonged to the builders, it now, in the words of one of the descendants—an inquiring young man named William Guin—belongs to the "priers."

The speculators, redevelopers, fashion designers, trend setters have built nothing, Guin reflects. "With violent tools they pried apart some existing connection (roof to walls, floor to joists) so they could squeeze themselves or other persons into position. This done, they turned backward and paid no attention to new thoughts."

The image presents a society turned inwards, one that uses its energy to immure its talents and spirits instead of opening new ground; a society of mergers, of fugitive bottom lines, of skyscrapers built above churches, of celebrity instantly created and destroyed, of constant manipulation in belief and tastes. . . .

Trow insinuates his characters into this febrile and pathless world. They wander aimlessly. All are shadows as they come on, one by one; and this shadowiness in the book's mid-portion is a problem. Trow is arming them to go off. By the end, they all take their places in his morality tale; some as participants in the evil of the times, some as victims, some as rescuers. But for quite a while an elaborate haziness tries the reader's patience and understanding.

They include numerous Aspair descendants, among them Sophie, whose glittering parties gather all the powerful of the day; and Virginia, dreamy and dwindling, and about to be snapped up by one of the day's sharks. There is a new-style rootless gossip columnist, and an old-style columnist with roots and no purpose. There are zombie journalists and schemers and men of power who are too important to be public figures.

And there is Eddie, Coonlon's aged bachelor grandson, who becomes the channel of grace through which the ghosts of the old city return and do battle. It is a splendid battle, absurd and moving. An old friend, a talented, obscure architect, is about to be cast off by the woman who keeps him, instigated by her ambitious niece. Eddie rouses himself from contemplation and jousts to a series of comical and stirring encounters in a posh restaurant, an exclusive bridge club and a dinner party. The party, where the niece is socially routed, is a scene as richly layered as one of Proust's and as unsparing as one of Pope's. The hostess is Eddie's childhood love, a dying aristocrat. She

and Eddie preserve the old faith that power and wealth are intended to uphold style and open up the world.

Eddie moves, part-dreaming and part-possessed. He is a marvelous creation; innocent, devious and bolstered by Pearly Button ghosts who lead him through the streets and tip him off to the location of honors in his neighbor's bridge hand.

Once Eddie makes his appearance, Trow's book goes into an inspiring overdrive, powered by fancifulness, humor and a black and piercing look at the self-consuming mechanisms of our time. He uses an older notion of aristocracy to fight what now passes for one; his anger is Tory, and uplifting.

> *Richard Eder, in a review of "The City in the Mist,"*
> in Los Angeles Times Book Review, *February 12,*
> *1984, p. 1.*

RHODA KOENIG

[George W. S. Trow's ***The City in the Mist***] covers a century in the lives of two wealthy families and their hangers-on—a gangster, a socialite, a gossip columnist, a gigolo. . . . *City* is written in a bizarre, owlish style that teeters somewhere between Diana Vreeland and Gertrude Stein. What, for instance, is anyone not supplied with controlled substances supposed to make of passages like this one (italics Trow's)?: "She continued to watch him. He *touched* things. He picked things up and put them down again, moving, moving. *They will think he is stealing,* Victoria thought. But no one noticed him, because a change had come over the room. It had *parted*. A man entered who represented *the work of the moment*." The characters have as little to do with one another as the chapters, which read like self-contained profiles or particularly ineffable "Talk of the Town" pieces (Trow is a longtime *New Yorker* writer). Two chapters rise above the general murk. In one the society-and-violent-crime reporter of an unattractive newspaper not unlike the *New York Post* takes a girl with a shaven head into the ladies' room to interview her about rabbit killers; this has some nicely funky and sinister atmosphere. In the other, two people at a dinner party conspire to turn a grand dame against her niece. . . ; here some action that has a consequence is taking place. But for the most part *City in the Mist* is inhabited by hothouse plants—fragile flowers that communicate by waving their pale tendrils at one another. (p. 119)

> *Rhoda Koenig, "City of the Wimps," in* The Atlantic
> Monthly, *Vol. 253, No. 6, June, 1984, pp. 117-21.*

EDWARD PITONIAK

George Trow is indignant. His indignation is dry and oblique, but it is not slight. He is obsessed, in a highly poised manner, with the moral degeneration of our nation's upper class. His most ardent displeasure is with New York society (by which he always means high society). The domain of privilege, he wants us to know, has been overrun by the brazen and willful. To be a gentleman, distinguished by wit and bearing, is to haunt the outskirts. And it's on the patrician outskirts that you'll find George Trow, the atavist.

The City in the Mist is billed as Trow's first novel, but it makes spare effort to be a narrative. *Mist*, instead, is a series of episodes populated by figures owning, for the most part, little or no dramatic connection to each other. In one episode, for example, we follow a "Miss Quality" on her rounds—she writes a newspaper column on criminals of commanding style—

and after a brief taste of her bleak state we part ways, to meet again only briefly. But one can't fault such forays as lacunae. How can there be digression when there's no plot? Theme, not drama, is what unites Trow's tale and the theme derives from the author's recondite obsession with social authority. Therefore Miss Quality, a contestant for social credence, has a rightful place. She, among others, helps to make *City in the Mist* a very gnomic work.

The book essentially concerns itself with two families: the Coonlons and the Aspairs. Its opening sections, in which we meet the Coonlons, are marked by a pure, modest, almost antique prose. Michael Coonlon, Irish Catholic and a strongman for a New York brewery in the 1870s, is the patriarch of his line. . . . (p. 33)

Accompanied by a light-hearted wife, Michael moves to Albany and makes his fortune. His daughter, though, suffers from the family's social isolation and looks to an expatriate aunt for salvation. But—in a subverted echo of *Portrait of a Lady*'s Albany scene—Sarah Coonlon is made to see the lonely slapstick of an American falling for the Old World and its seemingly inherent grace. Redirected but still yearning for a circle to move in, Sarah marries into a notable WASP family. She finds them petrified. Chastened, Sarah bears a son—Edward Coonlon Jones—and she educates him to the complexities of living in a republic, "opening up the definition of fineness so that there was room in it for the roughness of his grandfather."

The Coonlon family history is important because in its telling Trow brings his own ideals to light. In his earlier work—*Bullies,* short stories, and *Within the Context of No Context,* essays—Trow wrote as a (wittily) censorious moralist, damning other sorts for their tawdry codes, yet never seeming to reveal his own morality. In his chronicling of the Coonlons he at last balances his indignity with an illustration of the good that has been violated. Edward Coonlon Jones, in this respect, serves as Trow's paragon, an image of an American gentleman. Blessed with a wise love of his history, Edward will not betray his rough origins even as he lives a refined life. His knowledge of society will be rich in irony and when he encounters the Aspairs late in life he will know what underlies them.

The Aspairs, the second family in *Mist,* recall the Astors, right down to an heir dying on the Titanic. Johannes Aspair begins the family's fortune in the mid-1800s simply by owning much of New York. His fortune is great, but not unruly. Johannes is still a man of the republic who *knows* what he owns and carefully husbands his properties in a ledger book.

In later generations, however, the Aspair fortune becomes immodest. Heirs wish to live princely lives. By 1980, the "last Mrs. Aspair," Sophie, will know little of honor. She pays no true respect to history, and in her character *The City in the Mist* reaches its main issue: the degeneration of society. As Trow sees it, society remains the apotheosis of our culture, the only zone in which private urges can find a public reality. Publicity is the vital element. A stunning head of hair, the deft dousing of an old flame—in society such attainments aren't ephemeral, doomed to private oblivion. They're well-noted, remembered, quoted, immortalized. Publicity is a privilege, nearly divine in its power: it certifies and commemorates.

But society people haven't borne their privilege wisely, as we see in the book's most developed episode, a Sophie Aspair dinner party. By this point Trow's prose has lost the fond tone of legend; it is now quite sinister, at once mannered and clinical. (pp. 33-4)

Bent on prominence, a single-minded American, Sophie dreads irony. To evade its unsettling power she darts about her rooms, terribly occupied, convinced "that her dinners should have about them the energy of *the crisis*," so that she can feel the gravity of "*crisis management.*" At Sophie's table we find no dignity: "What was said? It was hard to remember. Each guest spoke from his own past. He reached back to the last opinion he had held successfully and shouted that. Each one thought: When was I not embarrassed? Some people had to go back quite far."

If this elegant depiction and satire were Trow's only achievement, *Mist* wouldn't be much of a book. What ultimately makes it a valuable and even rare work is Trow's historicism. His ambition is to deepen our sense of living in time, and this ambition, we ultimately see, lends an almost sacerdotal dignity to his obsession with our society's upper reaches. He seeks a faith in which the legacy of the hallowed dead can ennoble the living. His vision is archaeological: the wise person pursues his traces back to their pure states. This vision of a life in history reaches its fulfillment in Edward Coonlon Jones, in the very way he walks the streets of his city. . . .

This idea of history as redemption is *Mist*'s most compelling undercurrent, and bears us through all the dinner parties and all the forays down menacingly up-to-date boulevards. Through his knowledge of the old pathways, Edward Jones dwells among the ancients, in a society nearer grace. This is the privileged society George Trow envisions most artfully, even fondly, though, alas, this fondness isn't offered for the reader's sake. *City in the Mist* remains a cool and impervious book. Its spirit is highly distilled, its flat landscape populated by archetypes, all serving Trow's vision, not the reader's wish for another world to live in. But this vision, which is Trow's alone—he's not asking for allies—is honestly commanding, fixing without fatuity on cardinal issues: honor, manners, social authority. Too abbreviated at times, too suave in its intelligence, *The City in the Mist* nonetheless yields an urbane satisfaction. (p. 34)

Edward Pitoniak, in a review of "The City in the Mist," in Boston Review, *Vol. IX, No. 3, June, 1984, pp. 33-4.*

James Welch

1940-

American novelist and poet.

A Native American of mixed Blackfoot and Gros-Ventre heritage, Welch is praised for universalizing the clash between the American Indian's uncertain contemporary existence and his secure, traditional way of life prior to white expansionism. He avoids sentimentality while making use of biting humor and absurdism to explore the fates of protagonists who seek to overcome alienation from both their Indian pasts and the inaccessible, white-dominated present. David M. Craig asserted: "In James Welch's fiction, the issue is not assimilation but survival. For his Indian heroes, as for Emily Dickinson in her room or for Huck Finn fleeing west, one can only find a homeland apart from the constrictions of American society. . . . [The] territory they discover, however, lies inside the self."

Welch's first book, the poetry collection *Riding the Earthboy 40*, was largely unnoticed by critics upon its publication in 1971. After it was revised and reissued in 1975, however, *Riding the Earthboy 40* elicited widespread admiration for Welch's examinations of such aspects of reservation life as social and economic exclusion and traditional matters of family and religion. This volume prompted John R. Milton to praise Welch as "the best American Indian poet in terms of techniques, production, attitudes, and what must be called competence." Welch's first novel, *Winter in the Blood* (1974), received nearly unanimous praise for imparting modernist concerns from a Native American perspective and for its avoidance of romantic myths and other stereotypes common to historical and literary treatments of the American Indian. This story concerns an unnamed Indian narrator who endures a bleak, desensitized existence in the bars and towns surrounding his reservation near Harlem, Montana. Isolated from a sense of family and identity, he is finally able to overcome his alienation by discovering the names and history of his grandparents, thus reclaiming his ancestral past. Charles R. Larson lauded *Winter in the Blood* as "a work of perfect unity and finish," while Reynolds Price maintained: "Welch's new version of the central scene in all narrative literature (the finding of lost kin) can stand proudly with its most moving predecessors in epic, drama and fiction."

Welch's second novel, *The Death of Jim Loney* (1979), features a protagonist of mixed Indian and white descent. Abandoned at a young age by an alcoholic father and a licentious mother, Loney is obsessed both by a symbolic biblical passage and by the image of a dark bird, neither of which he can comprehend because of his estrangement from both white and Indian societies. A man with no past and no future, Loney is capable of attaining a sense of self only in death; at the novel's end, he accidentally shoots a childhood friend during a hunting expedition and forces a reservation police officer to track him down. According to Helen Carr, *The Death of Jim Loney* is "on one level an enactment of Indian loss, and a plea for the continuity of Indian life; politically it appeals for acceptance of change but against assimilation. . . . [That] plea is essentially one for the continuity of family and place, for the value of affection, and for the dignity of the individual."

In *Fools Crow* (1986), Welch departs from contemporary subject matter to chronicle the maturation of a young Blackfoot warrior during critical years in High Plains Indian culture following the American Civil War. As Fools Crow attains manhood and leadership of the Blackfeet, he is forced to watch his tribe's traditional way of life destroyed by internal divisiveness, disease, and the United States Army. Robert L. Berner called the publication of *Fools Crow* "perhaps the most significant event in the recent development of Native American literature. . . . [For] in telling the story of one Blackfoot warrior Welch has evoked the total culture of a tribe, an act of historical imagination unprecedented in our literature."

(See also *CLC*, Vols. 6, 14 and *Contemporary Authors*, Vols. 85-88.)

CHOICE

[To label Welch] an "Indian writer" may be to do him a disservice, since [*Riding the Earthboy 40*] demonstrates that he is one of the best poets now writing in this country. Although many of the poems deal with the so-called "Indian problem," they do so in a way that reveals the universal truths that are the concern of all good poetry. The poems are sometimes bitter, as when they describe the man from Washington who comes to speak abut "a world of money, promise, and disease," but they are also often full of beauty, like this description of a Navaho girl: "The land / astounded by a sweeping rain / becomes her skin. Clouds / begin to mend my broken eyes."

A review of "Riding the Earthboy 40," in Choice, *Vol. 13, No. 2, April, 1976, p. 228.*

WILLIAM STAFFORD

[In his poems collected in *Riding the Earthboy 40,* Welch] reaches out in two directions. He lives in differences and connections. And his poems enable a mutual knowing. He rides his horse, "Centaur," which is "part cayuse." That mixture speaks for a whole area of bringing together: how does it feel to be on the reservation at Christmas time? How does it feel, the elation and the depression that fill the world when you are a group that meets enough exclusion to bring about in-group solidarity?

These poems are from inside a culture but enable a realization of its edge; the view here extends both ways. And not only does the reader gain a bi-focal view, but the language also reaches for a two-way gain. The language has excitement, an air of the unusual. If you go into a priest's study, you smell both incense and bourbon. The poems convey a vertigo of realization. But to attain full reading you need the sound of the voice that says the mixture of direct feelings and ironies. Any little scene may stretch out into large implications. Sometimes the lines are descriptions that then merge on, just go spacing on. . . . But here is the text of a poem called **"There Is a Right Way"**; it demonstrates the combined simplicity and complexity of view and language:

> The justice of the prairie hawk
> moved me; his wings tipped
> the wind just right and the mouse
> was any mouse. I came away,
> broken from my standing spit,
> dizzy with the sense of a world
> trying to be right, and the mouse
> a part of a wind that stirs the plains

This book has verbal events; it creates. No list of its topics can convey its effect, for those topics, such as weather, boredom, discouragement are enlivened by insight. What the seasons do, how a house feels, the perceiving of ways to live that are not yours but touch yours—on the way to subjects like these many strange things happen. (p. 107)

It's not a tame country, this book. Even its history is strange— [*Riding the Earthboy 40*] was first printed in 1971 but was through a change in company plans not then distributed. Now available in augmented form, following Welch's novel *Winter in the Blood* (a phrase from one of the poems here), this collection belongs on the good shelf, clear in its views, lively in its language. (p. 108)

William Stafford, in a review of "Riding the Earthboy 40," in The Journal of Ethnic Studies, *Vol. 4, No. 3, Fall, 1976, pp. 107-08.*

ROBERT KIELY

Between the song of noble Hiawatha and popular legends of the ferocity of Geronimo, the American Indian has been trapped in mythologies that have either ignored or justified his fate. Whether shown to be gentle and trustworthy or savage and treacherous, the Indian of stories, poems and films has continued to serve his victor's will; good or bad, the mythical redman is supposed to be entertaining. . . .

Historians have long argued against the falseness of these images and their cruel inapplicability to the Indians who have survived into the 20th century. But it has been fairly recently that the myths have been challenged on their own ground, that imaginative writers have tried to dismantle the fakery. James Welch . . . writes in *The Death of Jim Loney* about a 35-year-old halfbreed who lives in Montana. As fiction, it is almost unbearably spare. The "far" west is not a vivid terrain for this Indian; it is neither hostile nor nurturing, but rather a bleak, vast, nondescript space with a few cheap houses and bars thrown together and mountains rising on the horizon like a distant wall.

Abandoned by his parents—an alcoholic father and promiscuous mother—Loney feels no connection either with the white or Indian communities. He is not particularly rebellious, because there is no visible institution or authority at hand that seems to have been directly responsible for his lot. . . . Everything about his circumstances and surroundings is drab and unpromising except for the love of his sister and a young schoolteacher from Texas. They both see a goodness and intelligence in him that he himself cannot untangle from his inertia and his obsessive dreams of a beautiful bird.

Mr. Welch's economy of style and feeling prevents the story from becoming sentimental. His achievement is to have shown a modern American Indian, out of warpaint and costume, with no tribe and no real home in nature or in the plastic substitutes available to him. It is a very sad picture.

Robert Kiely, in a review of "The Death of Jim Loney," in The New York Times Book Review, *November 4, 1979, p. 14.*

ANATOLE BROYARD

James Welch may have the makings of a good novelist, but it's hard to tell, because he has shrouded himself in the clichés of a certain kind of contemporary writing. The protagonist of *The Death of Jim Loney* is offered to us as a hero of hopelessness. He is a half-breed, of white and Indian parents, who has been abandoned by both. His answer to his abandonment is to turn his life into one long shrug, between pulls at a wine bottle.

Jim Loney hardly talks, and when he does, it is only to describe his emotional disaffection. . . .

The reader feels that he has been here before. . . . It's time for another turn of the screw, as Henry James put it, time to move beyond disconnection and see what else is possible. Jim Loney is as static as the old wooden Indian in front of the cigar store.

While neurosis is a personal tragedy, it is not necessarily a literary one. Nor is being a member of a minority. On the dust jacket of *The Death of Jim Loney,* we read of Jim's "noble self destruction." We are asked to see him as bravely refusing the terms of the contract. Unless we give him back his mother and father, unless we connect him to society, he won't play.

Jim's lover, Rhea, is not much better. She is a rich girl who left her parents' house in Dallas to end up, improbably enough, in the small Montana town where Jim lives. . . .

[Rhea] tries to teach Jim, giving him a course in life appreciation, like those art- or music-appreciation courses we all had in school. She is strong on picnics and drives into the country. She offers Jim her own disconnection in the common belief that two disconnections, like two negatives, equal a positive. One can almost imagine her saying to Jim after their lovemaking, "You feel, therefore you are."

Jim has an older sister, Kate, who went to Washington to become something important in education. Kate has so hardened herself against the risks of life that all she can accept of it is work. Her exchanges with her brother, whom she supposedly loves, are condemned by Mr. Welch to the kind of spare, or bare, lines love is allowed in current fiction. "I don't understand you," Kate says. "I know," Jim answers. "I don't understand myself."

Just how interesting, ultimately, is all this lack of understanding? One is tempted to say that ignorance is no excuse in the eyes of the law. When Jim reflects that "in the past several years he had become something of a non-person," we agree with him.

Rhea says to Kate about Jim, "We've both come to the conclusion that he is a human being." When Kate replies by describing him as "a human being with potential," Mr. Welch himself sounds as if he is growing bored with his character.

We may have had enough of potential, for the time being. Our fiction may need an infusion of the actual. Robert Frost said that poetry seizes life by the throat, but Jim Loney talks only about trying for "some sort of controlled oblivion."

It might be a good idea, as well, to declare a moratorium on fictional drunks, to turn them all over to Alcoholics Anonymous. While in actual life, there are people who are more interesting after a couple of stiff drinks, the bottle in fiction is almost invariably filled with depression and self-pity. It contributes nothing but "the hopelessness of the early morning hangover."

Rhea proposes to save Jim by taking him to Seattle. He refuses: his integrity demands that he keep his depression indigenous. . . .

And then, too, Jim has to stay behind to shoot his friend Pretty Weasel. Why? Because Pretty Weasel is an Indian, and the only good Indian, Jim seems to feel, is a depressed one. Pretty Weasel is happy and successful in life, a traitor to his tragic destiny.

"After tomorrow," Jim says to himself, "I will have no future." Is that a lament or a boast? Is he threatening us with his unhappiness? Why do so many of our serious novels have to read like unpaid bills?

> *Anatole Broyard, in a review of "The Death of Jim Loney," in* The New York Times, *November 28, 1979, p. C25.*

ALAN R. VELIE

While some of Welch's poetry is perfectly clear, even to an unsophisticated reader, much of it is difficult to understand. The reason is that like many other American poets today—James Dickey, Kenneth Koch, John Ashbery, Robert Bly and James Wright, to name just a few—he has been influenced by surrealism. The most important direct influences have been the poetry of his friend James Wright and the works of Peruvian poet Cesar Vallejo.

Surrealism has its roots in earlier European movements like Dada and Symbolism, but as a self-conscious movement it began with Andre Breton's 1924 *Manifeste du Surrealisme*. The object of the surrealists was to free art from the logical, realistic way of viewing and depicting things. Surrealists wanted to create a new order of reality, a new way of seeing which merged dreams with waking perceptions, the real with the imaginary, the conscious with the unconscious. Wild association of ideas, linking seemingly disparate objects in striking images, became the distinguishing mark of their poems. (pp. 19-20)

There is often a playfulness and lighthearted absurdity to the writings of the first generation of [French] surrealists, Breton and his confreres. In the Spanish and South American surrealists who followed them there is a grimmer use of the same techniques. . . .

The South American who influenced Welch the most was Cesar Vallejo, a Peruvian poet (1892-1938) who spent most of his adult life in Paris, save for a brief exile in Spain when the French deported him for his Marxist activities.

Vallejo was a *cholo*—a man of white and Indian origin—and he incorporates his ethnic heritage into his poetry. (p. 21)

Vallejo published two volumes of poems before Breton's *Manifeste* appeared, highly imaginative symbolic poems, and he found surrealistic techniques congenial. In the thirties surrealistic poets came to the position that dreams were not poetry, and so rather than recording dreams they wrote dreamlike poems, poems which reproduce the atmosphere or ambiance of dreams, but which were composed by the same creative processes as traditional poetry. In these poems, as in dreams, objects change and undergo strange transformations, and normal everyday causality is suspended, but the works are carefully composed products of the conscious imagination. (p. 22)

What we have in Vallejo is a deep pessimism and sense of absurdity. He couples a passionate intensity towards life with a fatalism that human effort is wasted, human life is hopeless. Although he often writes about God, he is essentially an existentialist: God is not dead, but he is in very poor health. "Well," he writes, "on the day I was born, God was sick." (pp. 22-3)

Welch came to Vallejo through James Wright. He read Vallejo chiefly in the translation made by Wright, Robert Bly and John Knoepfle. . . .

Like Vallejo's poems, Wright's exude a defeated existentialism. God is not dead, or even sick, but he is extremely remote, unfeeling and unconcerned with man. (p. 23)

The most striking religious figure in Wright's works is Judas. . . . Judas is the hopeless sinner and loser who appears in other guises in Wright's poems—drunk, murderer, prostitute—who does a final act of kindness, but not out of hope of reward, for that is gone, but simply out of the goodness of his heart—"for nothing." God is not dead as far as these losers are concerned, but he has ceased caring about them. (p. 24)

In tone Wright's poems resemble the Spanish surrealists rather than the French. The passionate feeling, the bitter cynicism, the weary sense of defeat, and the feeling of anomie in an absurd universe that occurs in Lorca, Vallejo and Pablo Neruda is what comes through in Wright's verse.

Translated into an Indian context, Welch shares the existentialism and surrealism of Vallejo and Wright. Welch's existentialism is largely the product of the disillusionments of reservation life, and a tribal and personal habit of laughing at the absurdity of existence. Welch acknowledges his interest in Vallejo and Wright, and as their outlook was congenial to his, he borrows their surrealistic techniques.

"**Magic Fox**" is a good example of Welch's surrealism:

> They shook the green leaves down,
> those men that rattled
> in their sleep. Truth became
> a nightmare to their fox.
> He turned their horses into fish,
> or was it horses strung
> like fish, or fish like fish
> hung naked in the wind?
>
> Stars fell upon their catch,
> A girl, not yet twenty-four
> but blonde as morning birds, began
> a dance that drew the men in
> green around her skirts.
> In dust her music jangled memories
> of dawn, till fox and grief
> turned nightmare in their sleep.

> (pp. 24-5)

Explicating surrealistic poems is always a dubious business, and so I hesitate to say very much about "**Magic Fox.**" T. S. Eliot once said that "Genuine poetry can communicate before it is understood," and so the poem may transmit something to the reader even if he doesn't know what it is about. However, there is also no doubt that one gets more out of a poem that he understands intellectually as well as intuitively, and so it is worthwhile to try to see what Welch is doing in "**Magic Fox.**"

"**Magic Fox**" is about dreaming: it is a dreamlike description of dreamers. The rules that govern the poem are those of the world of dreams. The dreamers, "those men that rattled in their sleep," dream of horses, fish, stars, and a beautiful girl. The dreams are controlled by a magic fox, a sort of trickster figure, a being with power to transform things (not unlike a poet, in fact). The fox transforms the dreamers' horses into fish—or does he—the dreamers aren't sure, because the world of dreams is always uncertain, and images shift constantly.

The surrealist poem speaks through its images, and these must be apprehended by intuition rather than ratiocination. For instance, a girl "as blonde as morning birds" makes no sense logically, but is perfectly clear to anyone who is familiar with blondes or songbirds. The image evokes the girl's freshness, her outdoors, dewy beauty—the girl draws the men in "green around her skirts." Welch is not using green in any denotative sense, but the term makes sense poetically in that green is the color of blooming nature, and fits with the image of morning birds. The men swirling green around her skirts remind the reader of the green leaves in the first line. There is a connection between the leaves, men, fish and stars which fall and swirl throughout the poem.

Although Welch is not recording a dream the way the first surrealists did, his poem of an imagined dream imitates the processes of dreaming. His description is hazy, indefinite, a pastiche of fragments, full of familiar yet strange occurrences and transformations. In short, what Welch is doing is depicting a dream in language as vivid, indefinite and troubling as dreams often are.

In the first edition of *Riding the Earthboy 40,* "**Magic Fox**" was well back in the book, the first poem of the third section, "**Knives.**" The first poem in the book was "**Day after Chasing Porcupines,**" a straightforward, nonsurrealistic description of a scene from a Montana reservation farm. In the new Harper and Row edition, published in 1975, Welch has changed the order of the poems, moving "**Knives**" to the front, and "**Magic Fox**" is now the first poem in the book. Most of the poems in "**Knives**" are surrealistic, and by moving them up front where they are the first poems the reader encounters, Welch has indicated that surrealism has become the dominant mode in his poetic voice and vision.

Dreaming is a motif which runs through many of Welch's surrealistic poems. "**Dreaming Winter,**" also from the "**Knives**" section, reads in part:

> Wobble me back to a tiger's dream,
> a dream of Knives and bones too common
> to be exposed. . . .
>
> Have mercy on me, Lord. Really. If I should die
> before I wake, take me to that place I just heard
> banging in my ears. Don't ask me. Let me join
> the other kings, the ones who trade their knives
> for a sack of keys. Let me open any door,
> stand winter still and drown in a common dream.

Meaning is elusive in a poem of this sort, but it appears that Welch is contrasting the old Indian way of life, hunting and warfare, with the new uncertain world that the Indian faces. The tiger is a predator who symbolically stands for the Indian as hunter and fighter, and the dream of knives is the memory of the old life. But this life is over, for better or for worse, and so the hunter must trade his knife for the keys to the new world. Welch's attitude towards this new world is ambiguous. The "Really" in the last stanza indicates that the prayer may be ironic rather than fervent. Whatever the tone, the door Welch mentions leads to life in the white world, and drowning in a common dream means participating dubiously in American mainstream culture. "Winter" refers not only to that fierce season which savages Montana, but also to the winter in the blood that is the subject of his novel [*Winter in the Blood*]. (pp. 25-7)

Although surrealism is French in origin, and Welch gets it from South America by way of a white American poet, there is an Indian connection—a reason why surrealism would be a congenial mode of expression to a Blackfeet poet—the importance of visions to plains Indian culture.

The vision quest was a widespread phenomenon among American Indians, but figures most importantly in the culture of the plains tribes. Generally a youth approaching manhood would go to a remote place on the prairie and by fasting and often self torture would seek to have a vision which would serve as the basis of the youth's spiritual life for as long as he lived.

Among the Blackfeet it was more common for mature men rather than young boys to attempt the quest, and many failed in the attempt to have the vision. The Blackfeet warrior was to abstain from food or drink for four days and nights, and was obliged to seek a place that involved some danger, either from terrain or predatory animals. The vision, if it came, was usually in the form of some animal, which advised the man on the course his life should take, and gave him power.

There is an obvious relationship between Blackfeet visions and dreams the way surrealists perceived them. Both are visual experiences outside (and above) waking reality, which give meaning to everyday life. In fact, the surrealists were aware of this themselves, and in the thirties some studied Indian cultures in North and South America which had rituals like the vision quest.

Welch is familiar with Blackfeet vision traditions, as he reveals in **"Getting Things Straight."**

> Is the sun the same drab gold?
> The hawk—is he still rising, circling,
> falling above the field? And the rolling day,
> it will never stop? It means nothing?
> Will it end the way history ended when
> the last giant climbed Heart Butte, had his vision,
> came back to town and drank himself
> sick? The hawk has spotted a mouse. . . .
> Who offers him a friendly meal?
> Am I strangling in his grip?
> Is he my vision?

The poem is an existential statement about Welch's search for meaning in the events and phenomena of his life. He wonders if the hawk he sees might be his vision. But the fact that the poem ends with a question rather than an answer indicates that he hasn't found any meaning—that the hawk has nothing to tell him. The part about the giant's vision quest indicates why.

The giant who undertook his vision quest on Heart Butte symbolizes the last Indian who was able to find meaning in the old culture. He was a giant while on his quest, but much reduced in stature when he returned to the white bar in town and drank himself sick. In Welch's Montana Indians drift in and out of white towns and bars, estranged from their traditional culture and the security and meaning it afforded them. Welch is saying that history ended for the Indians when their traditional way of life ended, and the days, which were once filled with meaning for them, are now meaningless. History is over, and the gods are dead; events continue to happen, but there is no pattern to existence, only dreams of the past. (pp. 28-9)

Welch's poems obviously lack the playful humor of French surrealist verse, but a close look reveals a good deal of bitter, mordant wit and humor. Perhaps this humor should not surprise us, since Welch's novel, *Winter in the Blood,* is a comic novel. But the tone of Welch's poems is less genial than that of the novel; the humor is fiercer, and the laughter it calls forth is a very uneasy sort. Welch uses humor as a weapon against white bigots in poems like **"My First Hard Springtime"** and **"Harlem Montana: Just off the Reservation,"** but he also directs it against Indians because he seems to find men, red as well as white, ludicrous much of the time, and he believes that the only honest response is to lampoon them. . . . In essence, Welch's view of life is existential, and although he doesn't have as much of an absurdist perspective as Beckett or Ionesco, his heroes are anti-heroes too, floundering about in a meaningless universe. There is something of the fool or clown in many of Welch's characters, not only those in *Winter in the Blood,* Lame Bull, the Airplane Man, or even the protagonist, but also in the figures in the poems, Earthboy, Bear Child, Speakthunder, Grandma's Man, and most importantly, the persona of the poet himself in **"Arizona Highways," "Plea to Those Who Matter,"** and **"Never Give a Bum an Even Break."**

Acquaintance with Blackfeet religion may shed light on why Welch so often depicts men as fools. Napi, or Old Man, the chief deity and culture hero of the Blackfeet, is also often depicted as a fool. Like most Indian culture heroes Napi is a trickster, a complex figure who is alternately creator and destroyer, savior and menace, prankster and buffoon. Although

he is often creator of the world and all its inhabitants, he is also a saturnalian figure who breaks all the rules and mores of the tribe with impunity, to the delight of the audience. (pp. 29-30)

Every Blackfeet Welch's age would naturally grow up with a steady diet of Napi stories, and the shape of the peripatetic god who is both a fool and philanderer lurks in the background of many of Welch's characters, like the figures in his poems, and the hero of *Winter in the Blood.*

To start with Welch's portrayal of himself, let us consider **"Arizona Highways,"** a poem in which he explores his reaction to a young Navajo girl he meets while touring Arizona giving poetry readings.

> I see her seventeen,
> a lady dark, turquoise
> on her wrists. The land
> astounded by a sweeping rain
> becomes her skin. Clouds
> begin to mend my broken eyes.
>
> I see her singing by a broken shack,
> eyes so black it must be dawn.
> I hum along, act sober,
> tell her I could love her
> if she dressed better, if her father
> got a job and beat her more.
> Eulynda. There's a name
> I could live with. I could
> thrash away the nuns, tell them
> I adopt this girl, dark,
> seventeen, silver on her fingers,
> in the name of the father, son,
> and me, the holy ghost.
> Why not? Mormons do less
> with less. Didn't her ancestors
> live in cliffs, no plumbing,
> just a lot of love and corn?
> Me, that's corn, pollen
> in her hair. East, south, west, north—
> now I see my role—religious. . .
>   Fathers, forgive me.
> She knows me in her Tchindii dream,
> always a little pale, too much
> bourbon in my nose, my shoes
> too clean, belly soft as hers.
>
> I'll move on. My schedule
> says Many Farms tomorrow, then
> on to Window Rock, and finally home,
> that weathered nude, distant
> as the cloud I came in on.

The title of the poem is an ironic reference to the slick paper picture magazine of the same name—the sort of chamber of commerce publication put out to encourage tourists to visit the colorful Grand Canyon State. Welch's sardonic outlook is the antithesis of the perpetually upbeat magazine. (pp. 30-1)

The setting of **"Arizona Highways"** is a bar. Eulynda is talking to an Indian politician. She is darkskinned, with black eyes. She is poorly dressed, but wears turquoise bracelets and silver rings. She seems thoroughly at home not only in the bar, but in her cultural milieu. Moreover the imagery of the poem links her to the land.

> The land
> astounded by a sweeping rain
> becomes her skin. . .

In one sense this means that her skin is red-brown like the earth, but in a deeper sense this suggests that the girl is still a part of the Indian culture which has its roots in the earth, and so to Welch she is of the earth, earthy in a way that he no longer is. Of course it must be realized that Indian culture in the 1970's consists as much of Levis, Coors and jukeboxes as it does in hogans and horses, and Eulynda is no more Indian genetically or by virtue of her upbringing than Welch, a full-blood born and raised on a reservation. But Eulynda is Indian culturally because she lives the way Arizona Indians live now, and Welch has been cut off from his ethnic identity by his college education and his profession as poet.

Welch feels out of place in the Indian bar, and an unfit companion for Eulynda. . . . In short, he feels that he is too civilized—not man enough for a woman like Eulynda. Since he would not do as her lover, he ironically suggests alternative relationships: paternal (he would adopt her): spiritual (he would be Holy Ghost to her Virgin Mary, or medicine man putting pollen in her hair). But there is something very wrong between them. He is like a Tchindii to her. Tchindii are Navajo ghosts, the spirits of the dead, a malevolent and vengeful pack who often bedevil the living. Welch is afraid that he seems alien, frightening, wraithlike, insubstantial, malevolent to Eulynda. In short, the persona that Welch depicts is a caricature—pale, pudgy, spectral, and overdressed. He realizes that there is no relationship that he can establish with Eulynda, and so decides to move on, down the highway.

In **"Plea to Those Who Matter,"** Welch's caricature becomes a clown. Here Welch examines the question of ethnic identity from a very different standpoint. Whereas in **"Arizona Highways"** Welch wasn't Indian enough, here he is too Indian.

> You don't know I pretend my dumb.
> My songs often wise, my bells could chase
> the snow across these whistle-black plains.
> Celebrate. The days are grim. Call your winds
> to blast these bundled streets and patronize
> my past of poverty and 4-day feasts. . . .
>
> I have plans to burn my drum, move out
> and civilize this hair. See my nose? I smash it
> straight for you. These teeth? I scrub my teeth
> away with stones. I know you help me now I matter.
> And I—I come to you, head down, bleeding from my smile,
> happy for the snow clean hands of you, my friends.

The poem is difficult to understand until Welch explains the situation behind it. Before they were married, his wife, who is white, and teaches in the English Department at the University of Montana, was invited to a department party. Welch, who at that time was also in the department, was not invited. In the poem, Welch indicates that he feels that his Indianness has caused his exclusion. He feels his Indian past of "poverty and 4-day feasts" makes him inferior in the eyes of the white professors, and he pleads for a chance to change himself—to burn his drum, the symbol of Indianness, civilize his unruly hair, and straighten his nose, so that he will be welcome at their snow white hands.

The poem, like **"Arizona Highways,"** is about identity, which appears to be a matter of context: who you are depends on where you are and whom you are with. Welch sees himself as a paleface with Eulynda, but a savage to the Montana English Department. The experience is obviously painful, and Welch treats it with a mordant irony. The tone is fiercer than that of **"Arizona Highways"**; Welch again plays the buffoon in mock self-abasement, but the hyperbolic fantasies he depicts—"I scrub my teeth away with stones"—are savage in their intensity. This clown is battered—nose smashed, "bleeding from his smile." Although the pose is one of self-abasement, the poem is an attack on his fellow professors, the comedy a weapon.

This clownish persona appears again in the last poem in *Riding the Earthboy 40,* **"Never Give a Bum an Even Break."** Welch speaks of leaving home with a friend, and then concludes:

> Any day we will crawl out to settle
> old scores or create new roles, our masks
> glittering in a comic rain.

Persona is the Latin word for *mask*. Here Welch's persona speaks of donning a mask to face the comic (i.e., absurd) world, or put it another way, donning a comic mask as a way of coping with the world. (pp. 32-4)

In conclusion, James Welch is a poet with a comic way of viewing the world and a fondness for surrealism. Strange as it may appear to white readers, both of these traits can be traced to his Blackfeet heritage. The Blackfeet were able to take at times a comic view of their chief god, so they certainly were prone to see the foolish side of men as well. And, with the importance of the vision to their culture, it is not surprising that a Blackfeet poet would respond to the surrealist fascination with the world of dreams. (p. 38)

> *Alan R. Velie, "James Welch's Poetry," in* American Indian Culture and Research Journal, *Vol. 3, No. 1, 1979, pp. 19-38.*

HELEN CARR

In his earlier novel, *Winter in the Blood,* as in some of his poetry, James Welch comically exploits the distance between the romanticized Indian and the incongruous clash of new and old worlds in which he now lives. The central character and narrator of that novel describes his Cree girlfriend, shortly to run off with his gun and razor, engrossed by movie magazines and imagining herself as Raquel Welch; she sits opposite his grandmother, who, toothless, almost blind, once third wife of a Blackfoot chief, plans to murder this tribal enemy with her paring knife. That novel about a reservation Indian was concerned with continuities and renewals. In *The Death of Jim Loney,* the story of a half-breed, half-alcoholic drop-out, the struggle to find such continuities is much harder, though Loney longs "to create a past, a background, an ancestry—something to tell him who he was". . . .

James Welch writes sparely and evocatively; the structure of the novel is that of Loney's "crisis of spirit", as his lover Rhea calls it; though Harlem's bleakness and harsh winter echo his malaise, he is drifting away from awareness of the present, physical world. Gradually he repossesses the memories of his past; among others, those of his Indian mother, now crazy, and of his surrogate mother, Sandra, his father's deserted lover, now dead. Deep-seated memories of losses and betrayals have eaten away at his substance until "somewhere along the line he had started questioning his life and he had lost forever the secret of survival". He can't survive; but as he follows those questions back he comes to a kind of peace with himself. He's drawn back to his Indian past, and chooses to die on Indian land, shot down . . . by a fellow Indian, the reservation policeman.

The language of *The Death of Jim Loney* is simple and direct; it isn't possible here to do justice to the intricate and subtle unfolding of relationships or the interweaving of them. N. Scott Momaday, probably the best known Indian novelist, said once that "none but an Indian, I think, knows so much what it is like to have existence in two worlds and security in neither''. Welch suggests that Loney's position is but the extreme of that experienced by all Indians, all half-breeds now. A mythic novel as well as a psychological one, it is on one level an enactment of Indian loss, and a plea for the continuity of Indian life; politically it appeals for acceptance of change but against assimilation. As in Welch's earlier novel, however, that plea is essentially one for the continuity of family and place, for the value of affection, and for the dignity of the individual.

Helen Carr, "Up and Away in Montana," in The Times Literary Supplement, *No. 4023, May 2, 1980, p. 500.*

CHARLES WOODARD

[*The Death of Jim Loney*] is about a man's failure to establish a meaningful history or a reason for being. It is a book about death.

Welch's Jim Loney is a contrast to the hopeful narrator of *Winter in the Blood.* Loney, like Melville's Bartleby, seems ''incurably forlorn.'' He is a half-blood, unable to function effectively in either the white or the Indian world, but his situation seems strangely inadequate to explain his despair. He is comforted neither by his sister, who is materially successful in the white world, or by his lover, who seems sensitive to his sufferings. Both want to take him away from his bleak small-town environment to begin again elsewhere; but Loney mysteriously refuses to consider their offers seriously, and his death wish intensifies as the narrative moves toward realizing the book's title. His occasional attempts to find meaning are pathetically ineffectual, and the conclusion, while vaguely troublesome because of its mysterious inevitability, is poetically reminiscent of the ending of Steinbeck's ''Flight.''

Welch the poet is again evident in this book, although the language of *Winter in the Blood* seems more consistently original. He again movingly communicates the bittersweet bar-to-bar existences of purposeless people and vividly imagines the cold and lonely Midwestern distances, but at times the dialogue, especially the exchanges involving his female characters, seems somewhat artificial. Additionally, the black humor which was so integral a part of *Winter in the Blood* seems only peripherally connected to the main action in this novel and therefore not as dramatically effective as it was in the first book. Still, *The Death of Jim Loney* is a skillfully crafted and highly readable book with a variety of realizable human experiences in it, and as such it is additional evidence of James Welch's enormous potential as a creative writer. (pp. 473-74)

Charles Woodard, in a review of "The Death of Jim Loney," in World Literature Today, *Vol. 54, No. 3, Summer, 1980, pp. 473-74.*

PAUL N. PAVICH

Contemporary Native American literature spans a full range of philosophies and moods from renewal and affirmation to alienation and negation. James Welch's novel *The Death of Jim Loney* is close to the end of the negative pole. Basically it is a story of a middle-aged man of mixed Indian and white parentage. He is confused by his life and spends most of his time drunkenly trying to figure things out. Into his life comes a young white teacher who tries to make him leave Montana with her. However, their attempts at communication become clouded and he draws away from her. Loney kills one of his friends,

perhaps by accident, and flees into the hills where he awaits a ritualistic death at the hands of the reservation police.

Along with the fairly simple plot goes a spare, often ironic style. In one passage the teacher reflects on the reality of life in Montana in contrast to her romantic ideal: ''But instead of summer theaters and mountains and Glacier Park, she found herself in country that was all sky and flat land. She was in Big Sky country. With a vengeance.'' (pp. 219-20)

Beneath the uncomplex plot and the lean, concise style is a powerful, thought-provoking theme. Welch has brought to this story of a few weeks in the life of a half-breed in a small Montana town the full import of the problems of America in the twentieth century. Loney is like the anti-heroes of many contemporary novels: he cannot find a purpose to his existence; his life is a disordered array of meaningless events. . . .

Loney's consciousness is flooded by ideas and signs but he cannot impose any pattern on them. Throughout the novel he is haunted by the image of a dark bird. In traditional Indian society this may have been an omen of warning or a guiding spirit. However, he is separated from his Indian roots and hence he can never decipher the bird's meaning. He only has an uneasy feeling that it might mean something. Likewise he is repeatedly troubled by a line from the Bible, ''Turn away from man in whose nostrils is breath, for of what account is he?'' Since he is also alienated from his white upbringing he is puzzled by the implications of the Biblical injunction. Loney wants to be a part of some community, some tradition, but he is a foreigner to all. His death at the end seems to be a type of suicide because he can no longer comprehend or adapt to life.

The novel is not a very happy or a very hopeful one. However, Welch's depth of feeling and literary skill make *The Death of Jim Loney* an unforgettable statement about the destruction of the human spirit. (p. 220)

Paul N. Pavich, in a review of "The Death of Jim Loney," in Western American Literature, *Vol. XV, No. 3, November, 1980, pp. 219-20.*

KENNETH LINCOLN

A rootless, lonely dispossession troubles Indian and White alike in [*The Death of Jim Loney,* a] novel about a deadened ''breed.'' slipping a few years and scattered places on from the anonymous narrator of *Winter in the Blood,* the novelist this time names his protagonist Jim Loney, a tease on Welch's Christian name, a play with nicknaming him ''The Lone Ranger'' in a bar, a pun (loon, lunar, lonely) on a ''funny name,'' his girlfriend [Rhea] muses, watching her sleepless bedmate doze like ''a dark hummingbird at rest.''. . . The narrative keeps the reader guessing and mildly alert to small things that seem to count and that people count on, like the years. (pp. 179-80)

Jim Loney cries in his sleep, ''I'm small.'' By day he's wolfish, a ''mongrel, hungry and unpredictable, yet funny-looking,'' thinks Myron Pretty Weasel, an ex-basketball teammate. . . . Indians, too, are caught up in Indian myths. Out of the ''breed'' stereotype, Loney comes half wild animal from the reservation . . . and half poor white trash from Harlem (his ''scrawny'' father [Ike], now a 62-year old bar fly who lives on pasteurized American cheese, reminds one of Huck Finn's scurrilous Pap, ''the worst type of dirt,'' his son knows). Genders cut between bitches and bastards. Mothers and daughters run away like wild creatures; fathers and sons hang around, to no good. Transient women, sister and lover, want to rescue and hide Loney away in opposite coastal cities, Washington, D.C., and Seattle, Washington, mirroring capitals named for great White and Red "fathers.''. . . But Loney can't go anywhere, since he has no place to leave, and exiled from his past, he has no future. . . . *Nothing* matters in this novel of small revelations. Everything, in detail, remains local, down-played, and real to ordinary life. . . . The two-engine Frontier puddle-jumpers skip in and out of dusty northwest towns, mostly off-schedule; the local cop from California wants a "safe, warm life,'' makes model airplanes and housewives, drinks beer with the football coach, arrests drunks, and eats TV dinners; the bartender drops mothball jokes. A North Dakotan carries a turd in his wallet for ID, Kenny Hart quips, in a state that claims the housefly as its regional bird. . . . With all this, Loney makes the best of a "plain'' life in a kitchen smelling "the faint sourness of a man who lives alone'': the day-to-day reliefs of a sometime girlfriend, a glass of bourbon, fall rain, a losing Friday night game, the first snow on Saturday. It is a season when washing hangs frozen on the clothesline. "Loney hated the cold the way some people who had to live on it hated deer meat, hopelessly and without emotion.'' These events anticipate worse things to come. . . . At the fall end of greening seasons, the traditional color of regeneration darkens blue toward death: the promise of distance in Rhea's eyes "the color of turquoise,'' Jim thinks, "and he wondered at their coldness, but in that morning light they were the warm green of alfalfa.''. . . Loney ends his life plugging from "a green bottle'' of Rhea's Scotch, hunted like a deer in a land where mad red women run wild.

These "mean'' characters average small-town American life in a tawdry common denominator. Happiness for Kenny Hart is "a bar full of good people having themselves a real good time.'' Neither low enough to reach tragic depth, nor high enough to reveal insight, the monotony of common events picks away at these people's lives. . . . Like the cheap painting that hangs over her bed, Rhea slides through life a mildly passionless woman "waiting for something to happen,'' a Dallas Blonde with a literary M.A. from Southern Methodist. . . . (pp. 180-82)

This novel is almost too real. Little ironies intersperse a poetry of inarticulations: "Their bodies touched on the narrow bed, yet they did not touch each other.''. . . "She was a mother who was no longer a mother.'' Such a language of dying labels could fall flat if pushed for effect, but Welch unpretentiously states things as the half-living half-know them, or *don't* know: "`. . . I realized I didn't know anything,'' Loney says to his deaf dog. "Not one damn thing that was worth knowing.'' Still, the truth about commercializing Christmas and eating white bread along empty Thanksgiving streets seems too easily known, a cliché to our common understandings. "Christmas makes for strange barfellows,'' Loney muses. . . . Naturalism finds its limits here; to speak too little of the common malaise isn't quite enough. The bar jokes aren't as bizarrely funny in a novel whose plot and style seem left-over from the first. It takes two North Dakotans to eat a rabbit: "One to watch for cars.'' Street terms like tit, crotch, nuts, turd, poopface, and shithouse truncate the everyday data of small lives in small places, where Zane Grey and Mickey Spillane provide the male reading matter of bars, barbershops, and bathrooms (pp. 182-83)

Though persistently and powerfully James Welch, *The Death of Jim Loney* seems more self-consciously interior, less gutsy in detail than *Winter in the Blood*. The second novel's focus is less sharp, with less sense of place, ear for dialogue, and particularizing narrative voice. We are told that Jim Loney is half-Indian, but in voice and consciousness he could as well be a Mayflower descendent in up-state New York. The novel comes across more as ideas than execution, a sociological interior monologue neither as edged nor bitterly engaging as *Winter in the Blood*. In uneasy mix with pulp fiction, Joyce's Stephen Dedalus influences the plot at times. . . , as though this novel were Welch's portrait of the drunken artist as a not-so-young Indian. Thunderbird wine induces Jim's rotgut visions, Mogen David for holidays. The novel opens with an epigraph from *Under the Volcano* about galloping away to someone you love "into the heart of all the simplicity and peace in the world''—the tragically sentimental dream of Malcolm Lowry, the novelist of drunks, the slow suicide.

Like a surreal play, much of the action and passage of time take place off-stage, in gaps between chapters, and the corny bartender at Kennedy's serves as a low-comic stage manager. The novel tightens and quickens by mid-point, the plot congealing, prose toughening, but the overall sting is less penetrant than Welch's first fiction. The novelist goes inside Loney's mind to the extent of muffling his story, blurring his prose, imitating a boozy reality too closely. . . . (pp. 183-84)

[Toward the novel's end, Loney] confronts his father with questions about a phantom mother. "What do I know that you'd want?'' Ike challenges his son. "I'm an old man. I was born to buck and broke to ride. It's all over.'' With grainy pathos Jim toasts his "sonofabitch'' father, "to the way we are.'' The tautological solution is to commit and exorcize one's own crime, not the sins of the fathers. . . . On a "pheasant'' hunt for deer, the "wolfish'' Loney mistakes Pretty Weasel for a bear—a sad totemic confusion for a warrior—and shoots him. Blasting the window of Ike's green trailer and some of his father's face with a shotgun old as Jim himself, the Oedipal-bred Loney makes love to Rhea one last time and goes south to Mission Canyon on the reservation. . . . (pp. 184-85)

Loney can't say he loves Rhea because "there was no place to take it.'' "I have to leave, he thought, but he held her as though to prevent her from slipping away.'' A dispossessed man who must run, but can't leave someplace not there, he fears others leaving him as he drives them off, so he clutches at a displaced self trying to run away. . . . The tragedy is a loss of place, simply said, "home''—the heritage of land, family, clan, tribe, spirit world turned alcoholic nightmare. And the doubly tragic solution is ritual death, betrayed by "an old bastard'' father—cathartic for a reader who suffers with Jim Loney, potentially self-destructive for one who identifies too personally.

With his father's "perfect bird gun'' and Rhea's Scotch in below zero weather, Jim prepares his own murder at the hands of a tribal cop, Quinton Doore, a sadistic "thug'' who edged into reservation police work. . . . To die, definitively, is to end a mean existence. "This is what you wanted,'' Loney thinks at last. "And he fell, and as he was falling he felt a harsh wind where there was none and the last thing he saw were the beating wings of a dark bird as it climbed to a distant place.'' The myth of an Adamic falling Icarus informs this Hemingway out, a *denouement* to end it all, with a touch of Cooper's *The Last of the Mohicans*: "`. . . it was like everything was beginning again without a past. No lost sons, no mothers searching.'' It is an old American myth, too often reality, repeatedly fictionalized: a violent end to a life of troubles, death a "place'' to go "home'' to a lost mother. (p. 185)

And still one questions why. A suicidal culture hero, drawn from an American frontier fascination with "rich regenerative violence" (William Carlos Williams, *In the American Grain*), can perpetrate despair's self-destructive truth along with stereotypes of the blood-thirsty savage, noble redskin, cigar-store stoic, and vanishing American in the wilderness of Harlems of Native America. A reader must consciously work away from these images toward the end of civil war on reservations, the control of alcoholism, the reversal of a sense of dispossession. To be sure: to see and give voice to the truth of suffering takes the first moral step of an historical fiction whose muse is truth. . . . In internecine competition, rather than tribal reciprocity, old basketball teammates end up shooting one another after twenty years of mainstream acculturation: "he used to be the best friend I ever had. . ." Pretty Weasel jibes Loney, who replies, "Times have changed." Loney accidentally, at least without conscious motive, kills "Super Chief," the Uncle Tomahawk who went to the University of Wyoming on scholarship and quit to work a modernized ranch with his father. Myron's acculturated "success" deep-ends Loney's "breed" estrangement. And Doore, the mean second-stringer "standing right behind" Loney in the state championship photo, assassinates the lone wolf with a telescopic deer-hunting rifle. This half-breed finds his thanksgiving in death. (pp. 185-86)

> *Kenneth Lincoln, in a review of "The Death of Jim Loney," in* American Indian Culture and Research Journal, *Vol. 4, Nos. 1 & 2, 1980, pp. 179-86.*

DAVID M. CRAIG

In creating his Indian heroes of his novels *Winter in the Blood* and *The Death of Jim Loney,* Welch describes backgrounds strikingly similar to his own. His heroes grow up in northern Montana, going to school on the Fort Belknap Indian reservation, as did Welch. . . . While one cannot assume Welch's novels are autobiographical, the correspondences between Welch and his heroes serve to underscore his stance as Indian writing about Indian experience. (p. 182)

[Welch's opening passage in *Winter in the Blood* identifies his major concern: the] hero's estrangement from everything, even himself, and a homecoming which occasions a search for self and for a personal and ancestral past. In the terms of the opening passage, Welch writes about returning to the reservation, to the "Earthboy place," a phrase which recalls the name of Welch's first book, a volume of poetry, *Riding the Earthboy 40.* This "homecoming" sets Welch apart from his white readers, for to them the reservation can never be native ground. It also turns the novel inward, into the self—"the distance I felt came not from the country or people; it came from within me." And it is this exploration of the territory of the self that is Welch's primary concern. As the novels *Winter in the Blood* and *The Death of Jim Loney* make clear, Welch believes this exploration takes place for Indians in different terms than it does for whites.

Juxtaposing the events of the narrator's present with those of his past, alternating between his "homecomings" and the drunken sprees in nearby towns, the narrative structure of *Winter in the Blood* defines Welch's sense of the quest for identity. The events of the past—the narrator's father First Raise freezing to death in a borrow pit and his brother Mose's being struck and killed by a car while herding cattle—are numbing reminders that all that he has loved has died. The events of the present underscore the barren quotidian of his daily life—the

narrator's search for his girlfriend of three weeks through a succession of Indian bars in white men's towns and his mother's marriage to Lame Bull, the aspiring capitalist who prizes the land that he is gaining as much as he does the woman. Finally both plot strands unite in the death and burial of the narrator's grandmother. Through these events, the narrator learns his grandmother's story and discovers the richness of his ancestral past. These discoveries become the catalyst for the series of moments of self-discovery with which the novel ends.

The Death of Jim Loney tells a similar story but with a different narrative texture and feel. Jim Loney, a "half-breed," has no place in the white man's world, nor in the Indian's; an orphan, he has no sense of his past, nor hopes for the future. Two women try to supply these deficiencies, his sister Kate, who has translated her Indian heritage into a job in Washington, D.C., and his girlfriend Rhea, who has cut herself off from wealthy Texas parents in order to teach in a rural Montana high school. Kate offers Loney a place with her, while Rhea wants to take him to Seattle—a 1970 version of "go West young man." But like the narrator of *Winter in the Blood,* Loney turns toward the past searching for his lost father and inward searching for an identity which he can never find. Loney's inward journey is toward death, for as the passage from Isaiah that Loney remembers tells us: "Turn away from the man in whose nostrils is breath, for of what account is he?" On the reservation in Mission Canyon, the place of his happiest memories, Loney dies shot by an Indian policeman.

These skeletal outlines of *Winter in the Blood* and *The Death of Jim Loney* suggest that there is a characteristic shape to Welch's fiction—a three-part story of estrangement, of search for self, and of return to the Indian world. Each hero, the nameless narrator of *Winter in the Blood* and Jim Loney of *The Death of Jim Loney,* is cut off from everything except the pain of his consciousness. In his pain, each looks inward seeking to define his identity. The inward turn prompts a return to the reservation and a search for one's personal and ancestral past. For Welch, the hero's identity can never be defined in isolation; it stands in relation to his identity as Indian. . . . I want to explore this three-part story in greater detail, for tracing the story will both introduce Welch's fiction and isolate his essential theme: that the Indian dilemma is not assimilation but survival.

Estrangement is the defining characteristic of the Welch hero. . . . The isolation begins in childhood, for Welch's characters come from fragmented families and grow up emotional orphans. . . . Without a family, the Welch hero matures knowing only his aloneness. His emotions stunted, he yearns for connections with these lost relatives or for a healing liaison with a woman— as if physical union could make the hero forget past distances.

Isolation and distance also characterize the hero's present. The remaining relatives—the narrator's mother or Jim Loney's sister—cannot reach the hero, and their attempts to communicate with him only heighten his sense of estrangement. But the hero's isolation is not primarily familial. In the terms of *Winter in the Blood:* "the country had created a distance as deep as it was empty, and the people accepted and treated each other with distance." This is the geography of aloneness, of prairies burnished a lifeless gold in July and frozen a sepulchral white in January. The land is sterile, a natural wasteland where even the fish used to restock the rivers mysteriously disappear. The people's lives are equally distant. In Welch novels scene after scene takes place in bars, places where physical contiguity emphasizes emotional distance. (pp. 182-84)

The primary isolation comes not from outside the self but from inside.... Consciousness and action are disjunctive to the Welch hero; he watches his life unfold as if it were a film. Partially, this sense of disassociation comes from drink.... But it also results from a quality of mind which makes the self distinct from what it experiences. Unable to connect his sensations to what he is, unable to live in the present, the Welch hero either lives through his memories as the narrator of *Winter in the Blood* does or in waking dreams as Jim Loney does. The most prominent example of consciousness isolated from self comes in Loney's bird vision which recurs at central moments in [*The Death of Jim Loney*]—making love with Rhea, his girlfriend, talking with his sister about the father who denies him, and dying alone in Mission Canyon: "... I see a bird—I don't know what kind of bird it is—but I see it every night. Sometimes it flies slowly enough so that I can almost study it, but even then ... it is a bird I've never seen in real life." Attending the bird, Loney cannot experience his present and always feels disassociated from it. Thus only Loney's body makes love to Rhea; his mind watches the dark bird. (p. 185)

In the second stage of the Welch story, the hero seeks to define the self by linking his memory with his consciousness of the present. The present can never be confronted directly. The bar scenes tell us why: they are fragmented and chaotic. Rather the present becomes the catalyst for memory, as sensations stimulate past recollections.... These memories, in turn, inform the present, forcing the narrator to account for the pain that homecoming arouses.... It is through pain that the shape of the self becomes discernible.

Much of the action of a Welch novel comes as extended meditations. As memories are called to consciousness, they gain particularity—they are studied, examined, and reflected upon. (pp. 185-86)

For Welch, though, memories do not simply recall; they also create.... For Welch, memories are like wishes that create the world of our hopes and desires. They supply what the present cannot, a sense of self. The narrator of *Winter in the Blood* ... uses memory as invention when he tries to recall the aftermath of his father's death. Having "no memory of detail until we dug his grave," he can nevertheless imagine memories of his father's shoe sticking up above the snow, also a hand, and "the endless skittering whiteness." This imaginative reconstruction of the details of his father's death fills in the landscape of the experience and makes his father's frozen body materialize against the formless backdrop of snow-whitened plains. This imagined vision might remind readers of Quentin and Shreve reconstructing the events of Sutpen's life at the end of Faulkner's *Absalom, Absalom!* In each case the imagined memories are more real than experience; in each case the imagined memories bring the self into existence together with the fancied visions.

The central sections of *Winter in the Blood* provide an extended example of memory as search for self when the narrative alternates between the narrator's drunken odyssey and its aftermath and his memories of his brother's death. The world of the present provides no help in the identification process. The concluding passages of the two parts dramatize two efforts at self-definition.

> I traced the hump of my nose with a fingernail. It was very tender, and swollen, so that it was almost a straight plane from the bridge to the cheekbones. I walked down the street, out past the car lots, the

slaughterhouse, away from Havre. There were no mirrors anywhere.

> "What use," I whispered ... as though the words would rid it of the final burden of guilt, and I found myself a child again, the years shed as a snake sheds its skin, and I was standing over the awkward tangle of clothes and limbs.... And the tears in the hot sun, in the wine, the dusk, the chilly wind of dusk, the sleet that began to fall as I knelt beside the body, the first sharp pain of my smashed knee, the sleet on my neck, the blood which dribbled from his nostrils, his mouth....

By tracing the outline of his face, the narrator tries to connect his sensations with himself. He does not succeed, for neither the physical forms nor mirrors reveal the shape of the self. The second passage, however, unfolds a moment of self-discovery as the narrator returns to the moment of his brother's death. Memory relived heals. The passage records the rebirth of sensation as the narrator momentarily becomes a child again, and in doing so overcomes his sense of separation from the world outside himself. As past and present sensations intermingle—"the sleet on my neck" from the past with aftertaste of wine of the present—the narrator finds his self and experiences who he is. The emptiness occasioned by his brother's death is now filled by the self which suffered and now recalls the sense of loss.

In the final stage of the Welch story, the novels enact rituals of return. The essential movement in both *Winter in the Blood* and *The Death of Jim Loney* is toward the reservation, toward the Indian world of nature, fragmented relationships, and the Indian past. It is also a return to the roots of the self. Both novels are about homecomings, but as the opening chapters of *Winter in the Blood* tell us, such homecomings are never easy.... [Pain] has its value, however, for Welch might revise Descartes to assert: "I hurt, therefore I am."

The meaning of the narrator's homecoming in *Winter in the Blood* is symbolized in two very different events: in his discovery that the old Indian Yellow Calf is his grandfather and in the physical act of saving the cow from sinking in a mud hole. The discovery of his grandfather supplies a personal as well as ancestral past. In learning that Yellow Calf is his grandfather, the narrator can share, albeit vicariously, his grandfather's closeness to nature.... It is a world undefiled by the white man. Welch, however, does not sentimentalize the Indian past. For example, when the narrator determines his ancestry, he also learns that his grandmother has been ostracized by the Gros Ventres because she was a Blackfoot, an outsider. Nevertheless, learning about his grandfather supplies a rich heritage, for his grandfather had saved his grandmother's life by feeding her when the tribe left her to starve. The act of saving the cow has symbolic resonance as well, for it rouses the narrator to action. In saving the cow, the narrator decides to live himself, to free himself of the "winter in the blood" that has separated him from everything, even his own feelings. But even this act has its darker side for the narrator's aged and treasured horse dies in the rescue effort. Homecomings are never easy.

The Death of Jim Loney tells of a return, but of a much bleaker sort, for Jim Loney returns to the reservation in order to die. Loney leads the lawmen to the reservation where he knows that they will kill him. His actions, however, like those of Meursault in Camus's *The Stranger*, affirm the grounds of his life, affirm a self, for only by dying does Loney gain control of his life. He does so first by choosing the place of his death, Mission Canyon, where he experienced the few moments of happiness with his minister foster parents and where his most intimate lovemaking with Rhea, his girlfriend, occurred. But in death he is seeking more than a connection with these memories; he also seeks "a place where all those [his fragments of memory] pasts merged into one and everything was all right and it was like everything was beginning again without a past. No lost sons, no mothers searching." For Loney only death can provide this place; only death can provide the unity of experience for which he yearns; only death can provide a sense of self. (pp. 186-88)

In James Welch's fiction, the issue is not assimilation but survival. For his Indian heroes, as for Emily Dickinson in her room or for Huck Finn fleeing west, one can only find a homeland apart from the constrictions of American society. The present is empty—the dying, isolated towns, the stark absence of the plains, and the people united only in loneliness. Thus Welch heroes return to the reservation, but not to seek the Indian present, for that is as barren as the white man's. Rather they want to participate in the Indian past. The Indian past, as the narrator of *Winter in the Blood* discovers, makes the experience of the self intelligible. For Welch to reflect upon the past is simultaneously to experience the natural rhythms of his ancestral past and to escape the ghost-haunted memories—the "winter in the blood" that numbs the hero's sensibilities and estranges him from others. Out of the same necessity that compels Huck Finn to light out for the territory, Welch heroes return to the reservation; the territory they discover, however, lies inside the self. (p. 189)

> David M. Craig, "Beyond Assimilation: James Welch and the Indian Dilemma," in North Dakota Quarterly, Vol. 53, No. 2, Spring, 1985, pp. 182-90.

PETER WILD

Winter comes with a surreal hardness to Montana. . . . Even today, travelers keep an eye on the vast reality of the sky, a daily reminder of a whimsical power beyond human control. As did James Welch's two earlier novels, *Fools Crow* evokes this landscape where man's fate is not in his own hands.

In this case, that man is not the drunken present-day Indian stumbling through the alien smugness of small-town Montana in *Winter in the Blood* and *The Death of Jim Loney*. He is Fools Crow, the son of a Blackfoot chief in the Montana Territory in the 1870's. This marks a radical shift for Mr. Welch. Unlike his predecessor, who, in a chaos of alcoholism and cultural loss, spread pain to those around him, Fools Crow has only one flaw, if we can call it that—his youth. His task, the usual challenge to young men in traditional tribes, is to show himself an able hunter and warrior and thus prove himself a worthy member of his community. Through stealing horses, joining war parties and taking a wife, he succeeds.

On the most immediate level, Mr. Welch, himself part Blackfoot, details the intricacies of coming of age in a time and society that are long gone. To a rather loose and, some might argue, episodic plot involving Fools Crow's comings and goings on buffalo hunts and so forth, Mr. Welch fastens more compelling aspects of the culture—the prayers, ghosts, dreams and waking visions that make up a warrior's spiritual life. In their fascination with exotic religions, outsiders tend to separate them from everyday life. As Mr. Welch shows to the contrary, Native Americans didn't hike up to mountaintops on empty bellies simply to have the pleasure of chromatic hallucinations.

Indians applied revelations from the world beyond to the workings of this one, for they believed that by tapping into the spiritual they could gain power over everyday occurrences—a psychological necessity, one might suggest, a cushion against sometimes unbearable harshness. Behind the physical events of the novel, then, lie Fools Crow's visions, which tell him how to act. In this richer sense, the book becomes a series of dreams acted out, a chronicle of the Indians' visions as applied to daily life. . . .

On this score, the novel might easily drift off into an oneiric never-never land, but Mr. Welch doesn't let this happen. To say that he keeps dreams and events working nicely in tandem would be a misstatement of what finally is an unpredictable series of natural and supernatural interactions; yet the relationship always is there, the real world blending into the unreal until neither we nor the characters themselves can tell the difference. This is the book's major accomplishment. To recall again Mr. Welch's earlier work, the whim-whams of the modern-day alcoholic here give way to a spirit realm held valid by an attuned people. The former was entertaining, if painfully so; the latter is instructive. . . .

Despite a penchant for the cruelty, boastfulness and betrayal common to people everywhere, through their beliefs the Blackfeet manage to maintain an admirable, if at times brutal, stance toward the world. At the best of times, the stars are in their places at night and the mythical Above Ones give a lasting illusion of permanence, whatever the day's trials. As the novel progresses, however, there come increasing hints of a new culture approaching, a devastating power beyond the control of the Indians who are soon to be overwhelmed and even the whites who wield it.

> Peter Wild, "Visions of a Blackfoot," in The New York Times Book Review, November 2, 1986, p. 14.

LOUIS D. OWENS

When James Welch published his first novel, *Winter in the Blood,* in 1974, he joined N. Scott Momaday as only the second American Indian novelist at that time to have produced a truly outstanding work of fiction. . . . Although novels by American Indian writers have been appearing in a steady, though slim, stream since Simon Pokagon's *Queen of the Woods* in 1899, only since 1969 has the Indian novel begun to come of age. Welch's third novel, *Fools Crow,* marks an important step in that movement toward a maturation of body style and vision. . . .

Drawing upon his Blackfoot heritage, and, more critically, upon his own sense of what it means to be "Indian" in late 20th-Century America, in *Fools Crow,* Welch has written an extraordinary novel.

Fools Crow is set in the final crisis years of the American Indian High Plains culture—around 1870, when the buffalo herds are falling before the marvelous efficiency of repeating rifles and the Indians are being decimated by the less efficient but still deadly assault of smallpox and the U.S. military. Although the narrative point of view shifts at times to create a finely layered complexity, the novel focuses primarily upon the consciousness of a member of an isolated band of Blackfeet, a young man called White Man's Dog, who, in the course of the novel, grows into the hunter, warrior and healer named Fools Crow. Fools Crow's coming of age parallels the final brief period of traditional life for the Blackfeet, once the most powerful tribe on their part of the continent. As the power of Fools Crow grows, that of his people declines. It becomes the responsibility of Fools Crow to foresee and bear witness to the extermination of the traditional way of life for his people. (p. 1)

Both of Welch's first two novels [*Winter in the Blood* and *The Death of Jim Loney*] were experiments, impressively successful attempts to merge American Indian history and mythology with absurdism, surrealism, and black humor in a torturous quest for the protagonists' identity as Indians in contemporary America. In interesting ways, however, *Fools Crow* is a more dangerous book for Welch than these first two and, perhaps, his most radical experiment yet. In this work, Welch has taken the risk of writing in high seriousness, abandoning the black humor, absurdism and structural high jinks of his earlier fiction. The result is a novel that plunges the reader with startling abruptness wholly into an Indian world, a world in which reality is idyllic and bitter, hard-edged and magical.

In this novel, Welch is remembering the world of his ancestors, putting that world together again in a way that will tell both author and reader what has been lost and what saved. . . . [When] Fools Crow, in a dream-vision, is summoned three days' ride northward to meet with a figure from Blackfoot mythology and to be shown a stark outline of his people's future, the reader must accept the spiritual encounter on Indian terms. Welch's Blackfeet in *Fools Crow*, like many Indian people today, live in a world that acknowledges no separation between man and the natural or supernatural worlds.

Fools Crow is a painful, stunning act of recovery, the completion of an identity quest that began for Welch in his first poems and novels. In this novel, Welch takes a major gamble, for at times, the carefully articulated speech of the author's Blackfeet is inevitably reminiscent of the stilted Oxfordian verbiage found in romantic treatments of Indians from James Fenimore Cooper to the Hollywood Western. Rescuing this novel from such guilt by association, however, is a hardness and precision of language lacking in nearly every other fictional attempt to render Indian speech in English, an absolute certainty of voice. More important, perhaps, is the fact that no appropriation of Indian culture is going on here; the author writes from within this imagined world rather than from without. In *Fools Crow*, the non-Indian is the outsider who must recognize a new world and adapt.

The fundamentally mimetic realism of *Fools Crow* may well meet with its detractors. Even more surely, it will provide critics with another opportunity to write nostalgically about what American Indian culture was like. What Welch has accomplished, however, has been to remind us, as well as himself, of what is still there. Perhaps the most profound implication of this novel is that the culture, the world-view brought so completely to life in *Fools Crow*, is alive and accessible in the self-imagining of contemporary Blackfeet and other American Indians. In recovering the world found in this novel, Welch serves as storyteller, bearer of oral tradition and definer of what it means to be Indian today. (p. 6)

> *Louis D. Owens, in a review of "Fools Crow," in* Los Angeles Times Book Review, *December 14, 1986, pp. 1, 6.*

CHARLES R. LARSON

[When Welch published *Winter in the Blood* and *The Death of Jim Loney*], critics likened him to Ernest Hemingway and John Steinbeck. His characters were Indians because Welch happened to be an Indian. . . . Yet his characters were hardly heroes—more like drifters than anything else—lonely, displaced and guilt-ridden; human beings, suffering from pain, similar to the characters in all great literature: by-products of historical patterns that can never be rewritten.

With *Fools Crow,* his third novel, Welch has taken a major step—backwards, as it were, into the past. The heroes are there (at least a few), though time has already become a terrible burden from which there is no escape. Fools Crow, the main character, earns his name from a successful skirmish against the enemy Crow. For a time, it appears as if he will become a great leader of his people, the Lone Eaters, a band of the Pikuni (Blackfeet) living in northern Montana.

Yet it's already too late, just as it was too late once the first Europeans arrived in the New World. . . . Welch makes it clear that it is not a matter of bows and arrows against superior armaments. Rather, it's a matter of unity, and that cohesiveness within tribal units may have fallen apart because of a fatal flaw within the organizations themselves. Rampaging groups of young Pikuni males (outcasts themselves) become just as much a threat to tribal leadership as the invading traders and settlers. And against the white man's diseases, the Indian doesn't have a chance at all.

Welch focuses his story upon the human dimension, upon the break-up of family units within the tribal framework. The conflict is treated with great emotional depth and, although the story is ultimately tragic, the rendering of it is through a poet's vision. The result is an awesome beauty, unlike anything I have previously encountered. Dreams, visions, hallucinations: the Pikuni world view (a hundred years ago) is recorded in a language both poetic and mimetic.

Fools Crow is a startling encounter with a tribal viewpoint shattered by cracks from within and without. James Welch is that rare artist who writes out of his own tradition and into another; it's impossible to tell where the first one ends and the second begins.

> *Charles R. Larson, "Native American Heroes: Doomed Warriors," in* Chicago Tribune—Books, *December 21, 1986, p. 6.*

JAROLD RAMSEY

One of the most exciting features of what has been justly called "the American Indian literary renaissance" of the last twenty years or so is the way Indian poets and writers are persistently incorporating in their work the oral traditions of their peoples—myths, oral history, songs, and so on. What critics and general readers have begun to recognize as one of the newest and most interesting branches of American literature is thus in fact richly continuous with this country's first and oldest literary traditions. (p. 108)

[In] *Fools Crow,* the Blackfoot writer James Welch has . . . implicated mythic and fictive elements with one another, and the result is magnificent—a historic novel of northern Plains Indian life just after the Civil War, whose utter authenticity of detail and narrative design are given, throughout, the resonance of myth. In this respect, *Fools Crow* is very much a new departure for Welch. His first two novels, *Winter in the Blood* and *The Death of Jim Loney,* both set in modern-day Montana, are notably austere both in style and in vision; the heroes of both books are for the most part as alienated from their Indian heritage as they are from their contemporaries. . . . So for Welch to open his imagination and skills to both history and myth in writing *Fools Crow* must have been a stern undertaking, and it is good to be able to praise the well-made and compelling work that such a radical turn brought into being. (pp. 108, 110)

Fools Crow is set in . . . Blackfoot country in north-central Montana; it centers on one band of Pikuni Blackfeet, the "Lone Eaters," and its protagonist is a young Lone Eater named White Man's Dog, and later, Fools Crow. Welch vividly catches his people at the onset of rapid and terrible change. The Civil War is over, and Anglo soldiers and citizens are flocking westward, encroaching on Indian lands; smallpox, always one of destiny's shock troops in the American West, begins to devastate the Pikunis and their neighbors; and, in response to such external shocks, the traditional Pikuni way itself begins to fall apart. The customary medicine rituals seem to be losing their credibility and force; the younger generation grows increasingly at odds with their tribal elders over how to deal with the encroachment of the whites, or "Napikwans," and many of the best of the young men leave their communities to become renegades.

One such rebel is Fools Crow's boyhood friend Fast Horse, whose wasted and increasingly violent life as an outlaw exists in counterpoint to Fools Crow's own painful, conflicted career as a responsible member—son, husband, father, leader of the younger men—of the Lone Eaters band. It is Fools Crow's fate to come of age . . . just in time to take on, together with his father, the band's chief, and its medicine man, the burdens of holding the Lone Eaters together and keeping them out of harm's way with respect to the Napikwans.

Welch's use of Blackfoot mythology is not continuous and programmatic in his narrative; . . . he adduces myth *realistically*, casually, letting it appear when and how it would in the lives of his characters, especially Fools Crow. These are people for whom the old tribal stories are at once familiar possessions and full of vital power and mystery. . . . Fools Crow's spiritual mentor, Mak'api, for example, bears the name of a great Blackfoot mythic hero; and at crucial moments in his career, Fools Crow is visited and guided by the Blackfoot trickster, Raven.

Elsewhere, plausibly, the formal recitations of myths are given as episodes in the story—the origin of the sacred Beaver Medicine bundle, for example, and the creation of the Blackfeet and their world by Napi, Old Man, and Old Woman. And most sacred of all, the myth of So-at-sa-ki (Feather Woman, the wife of Morning Star): Feather Woman was banished from the Sky World for breaking a taboo and died of grief, earthbound; but her son, Scarface, returned to the Sky to be blessed by his father and his grandfather, Sun Chief, and to be given the sacred Sun Dance by them to help mankind. (pp. 110-11)

Such myths figure in Welch's novel as they must have in Blackfoot culture, as sacred charters of belief and value—with the ironic fictive significance, of course, that the narrative in which these timeless myths figure seems to be pointing to the eventual extinction of the Pikuni culture. When Old Man and Old Woman, both gamblers, contend about whether human life should be unending or mortal. Old Woman wins out for death, claiming that, because all people-to-come will die, they will "feel sorry for each other"—the mortal basis, that is, of human compassion and interdependence. The myth thus "anchors" a novel rich in instances of kindness and interdependence among the Lone Eaters as they face the possible end of their Way: Fools Crow "adopts" the family of his crippled father-in-law,

for example, and attempts, because Fast Horse's grieving father asks him to, to bring his renegade friend back to his people; when smallpox breaks out amongst the Pikunis and quarantine is suggested, it fails tragically, because the people indeed "feel sorry for each other" and take in infected survivors from other communities, with calamitous results.

Welch's most powerful use of Blackfoot mythology comes near the end of the novel when Fools Crow, desperate over his people's prospects, goes off on one last mission, an eerie, dreamlike trek to a secluded meadow where he meets Feather Woman, eternally mourning—as in her myth—the fact that she has been banished from heaven, but still hoping to be reconciled to her husband, Morning Star, and her son, Scarface. Feather Woman's predicament—cast out from a happy and unchanging world into a world of unhappiness and change, *suspended*, in fact, between those worlds—powerfully symbolizes what is happening in the novel (and in history, kept on happening!) to Fools Crow's people; and it gives their ordeals, as real as they are, the continuity and dignity of myth. (pp. 111-12)

I have engaged *Fools Crow* here as a "Native American novel," and so it is, one of the best yet written—but the real measure of Welch's achievement, I think, is that by composing the particulars of the story of Fools Crow and the Lone Eaters so beautifully, he has universalized that story. Reading this book, I think of other accounts in the world's grim and not-ended history of cultural encroachment and domination, like Chinua Achebe's harrowing narrative of the coming of the British to the Ibos of Nigeria, *Things Fall Apart*. Achebe's novel was the first of a brilliant trilogy of novels: with *Fools Crow* in hand, we can hope that James Welch has a similar design. (p. 112)

> *Jarold Ramsey, in a review of "Fools Crow," in* Parabola, *Vol. XII, No. 1, February, 1987, pp. 108, 110-12.*

ROBERT L. BERNER

The publication of [*Fools Crow*] is perhaps the most significant event in the recent development of Native American literature. Indeed, future students of the subject may well regard it as the beginning of a new stage in that development, for in telling the story of one Blackfoot warrior Welch has evoked the total culture of a tribe, an act of historical imagination unprecedented in our literature.

Fools Crow is set in the years following the American Civil War, and its subject is the "Pikunis" (Piegan) branch of the Blackfoot alliance. Welch's story is of this tribe's catastrophic encounter with white civilization, its difficulty in maintaining unity under the pressure of historical events, and its struggle to preserve its traditions and culture. It is more than a social history, however. It is also the story of an uncertain boy who almost accidentally becomes a hero of his people, receives a hero's name—Fools Crow—and then makes every effort to live up to the esteem in which his people now hold him. . . .

In telling his story Welch is able to make the tribal vision of the Pikunis believable, an extraordinary achievement considering that our own culture derives from premises so wildly different. In placing the greatest value upon physical courage and duty to the tribe, even if that duty required the warrior's death, the warrior ideal of the Plains Indians resembles that of the medieval knight or the Japanese samurai more than anything in our own history. Still, the warrior also was distinguished by a wisdom that enabled him to receive lessons from the natural world.

Fools Crow gives us an absolutely convincing sense of this vision. It is the finest presentation of a tribal culture that we have had in fiction, and as a fully rounded evocation of the physical, mental, and spiritual life of a tribe, the only work which can bear comparison to it is the autobiography of Black Elk.

> *Robert L. Berner, in a review of "Fools Crow," in* World Literature Today, *Vol. 61, No. 2, Spring, 1987, p. 333.*

LOUIS OWENS

[Any novel by Welch] is destined to receive substantial critical attention. *Fools Crow* merits the attention. Set in the late 1870s, during the final years of Blackfeet power, *Fools Crow* tells the story of a young man's coming of age. As the young man known as White Man's Dog grows into the hunter, healer, and warrior who will be called Fools Crow, the power of the Blackfeet is broken. Repeating rifles determine the end of the buffalo herds and smallpox and the U.S. Army together decimate the tribes. It falls to Welch's protagonist to witness this decline and, in visions, to foresee his people's future.

Written securely within the world-view of the traditional Blackfeet, *Fools Crow* makes unusual demands of a reader. . . . Welch's novel is purely Indian, offering no apologies or explanations for a magical interweaving of natural and supernatural.

Conflict is immediate in *Fools Crow*. The reader experiences intimately the tragedy of cultural genocide as obstacles to American expansion—the native inhabitants—are destroyed. And within this story of a people's destruction Welch has managed superbly the task of recreating that lost world of the traditional Blackfeet. For the Blackfeet-Gros Ventre author of *Winter in the Blood* and *The Death of Jim Loney*, both novels about the contemporary Indian's search for an identity—whether full- or mixed-blood—*Fools Crow* represents a distinct act of recovery, of self-discovery. (p. 56)

> *Louis Owens, "Acts of Recovery: The American Indian Novel in the '80s," in* Western American Literature, *Vol. XXII, No. 1, May, 1987, pp. 53-7.*

Acknowledgments

The following is a listing of the copyright holders who have granted us permission to reprint material in this volume of *CLC*. Every effort has been made to trace copyright, but if omissions have been made, please let us know.

THE COPYRIGHTED EXCERPTS IN CLC, VOLUME 52, WERE REPRINTED FROM THE FOLLOWING PERIODICALS:

America, v. 145, December 12, 1981 for a review of "Desires" by Peter LaSalle; v. 150, March 17, 1984 for "More than History: Flanagan's 'Year of the French'" by Gerard Reedy; v. 157, November 14, 1987 for a review of "You Must Remember This" by Robert Phillips; © 1981, 1984, 1987. All rights reserved. All reprinted with permission of the respective authors./ v. 116, March 25, 1967; v. 117, October 28, 1967; v. 126, June 10, 1972. © 1967, 1972. All rights reserved. All reprinted with permission of America Press, Inc., 106 West 56th Street, New York, NY 10019.

The American Book Review, v. 3, March-April, 1981; v. 5, January-February, 1983; v. 7, May-June, 1985; v. 9, January- February, 1988; v. 10, May-June, 1988. © 1981, 1983, 1985, 1988 by *The American Book Review.* All reprinted by permission of the publisher.

American Indian Culture and Research Journal, v. 3, 1970; v. 4, 1980. Copyright © 1979, 1980 The Regents of the University of California. Both reprinted by permission of the publisher.

The American-Scandinavian Review, v. LX, March, 1972. Copyright 1972 by The American-Scandinavian Foundation. Reprinted by permission of *Scandinavian Review.*

The American Spectator, v. 17, March, 1984. Copyright © *The American Spectator* 1984. Reprinted by permission of the publisher.

Analog Science Fiction/Science Fact, v. XCVIII, January, 1978 for a review of "In the Ocean of Night" by Lester del Rey; v. XCVIII, June, 1978 for a review of "In the Ocean of Night" by Spider Robinson. Copyright © 1977, 1978 by the Condé Nast Publications, Inc. Both reprinted by permission of the respective authors./ v. C, October, 1980 for a review of "Timescape" by Tom Easton; v. C, November, 1980 for a review of "Shiva Descending" by Tom Easton; v. CIII, September, 1983 for a review of "Against Infinity" by Tom Easton; v. CIV, September, 1984 for a review of "Across the Sea of Suns" by Tom Easton; v. CVI, July, 1986 for a review of "Heart of the Comet" by Tom Easton; v. CVIII, March, 1988 for a review of "Great Sky River" by Tom Easton. © 1980, 1983, 1984, 1986, 1988 by Davis Publications, Inc. All reprinted by permission of the respective authors.

Arizona Quarterly, v. 5, Spring, 1949 for "The World of William Faulkner" by Charles I. Glicksberg. Copyright 1949, renewed 1976 by *Arizona Quarterly.* Reprinted by permission of the publisher and the author.

The Atlantic Monthly, v. 253, June, 1984 for "City of the Wimps" by Rhoda Koenig. Copyright 1984 by The Atlantic Monthly Company, Boston, MA. Reprinted by permission of the author./ v. 192, December, 1953 for "Conrad Aiken: The Poet" by R. P. Blackmur. Copyright 1953, renewed 1981 by The Atlantic Monthly Company, Boston, MA. Reprinted by permission of the author.

Best Sellers, v. 31, May 1, 1971; v. 32, April 15, 1972; v. 34, November 1, 1974. Copyright 1971, 1972, 1974, by the University of Scranton. All reprinted by permission of the publisher./ v. 36, June, 1976; v. 41, July, 1981. Copyright © 1976, 1981 Helen Dwight Reid Educational Foundation. Both reprinted by permission of the publisher.

Biography, v. 8, Winter, 1985. © 1985 by the Biographical Research Center. All rights reserved. Reprinted by permission of the publisher.

The Bloomsbury Review, v. 7, September-October, 1987 for a review of "Weaveworld" by Phil Normand; v. 7, September-October, 1987 for "The Poem Which Is Completely Possible" by Robert Lindsey. Copyright © by Owaissa Communications Company, Inc. 1987. Both reprinted by permission of the respective authors.

Booklist, v. 73, February 15, 1977; v. 75, October 1, 1978; v. 84, November 15, 1987. Copyright © 1977, 1978, 1987 by the American Library Association. All reprinted by permission of the publisher.

Book World—Chicago Tribune, October 17, 1971. © 1971 Postrib Corp. Reprinted by courtesy of the *Chicago Tribune* and *The Washington Post.*

Book World—The Washington Post, May 31, 1970. © 1970 Postrib Corp. Reprinted by courtesy of the *Chicago Tribune* and *The Washington Post.*/ September 21, 1980; February 22, 1981; January 3, 1982; May 29, 1983; February 26, 1984; August 5, 1984; October 27, 1985; March 23, 1986; August 24, 1986; November 30, 1986; June 28, 1987; August 2, 1987; February 28, 1988; March 6, 1988. © 1980, 1981; 1982; 1983; 1984; 1985; 1986; 1987; 1988, *The Washington Post.* All reprinted by permission of the publisher.

Books Abroad, v. 37, Autumn, 1963; v. 46, Winter, 1972. Copyright 1963, 1972 by the University of Oklahoma Press. All reprinted by permission of the publisher.

Books and Bookmen, n. 353, February, 1985 for a review of "Kruger's Alp" by Robert Winder; n. 364, February, 1986 for "Playing Around" by Chloe Chard; n. 371, September, 1986 for "Exiled from Home" by David Sexton. © copyright the respective authors 1985, 1986./ v. 20, September, 1975 for a review of "The Last of the Country House Murders" by James Brockway; v. 24, August, 1979 for "Puzzlement" by Reginald Hill; n. 327, December, 1982 for a review of "Queen of Stone" by John Walsh. © copyright the respective authors 1975, 1979, 1982. All reprinted by permission of the respective authors.

Books in Canada, v. 10, April, 1981 for "Future Shlock" by Richard Plant; v. 13, November, 1984 for "Pith and Vinegar" by Rachel Wyatt. Both reprinted by permission of the respective authors.

Boston Review, v. IX, February, 1984 for a review of "Dance Script with Electric Ballerina" by Matthew Gilbert; v. IX, June, 1984 for a review of "The City in the Mist" by Edward Pitoniak; v. XI, December, 1986 for a review of "Palladium" by Sven Birkerts. Copyright © 1984, 1986 by the Boston Critic, Inc. All reprinted by permission of the respective authors.

British Book News, February, 1980; March, 1983; December, 1985; February, 1986. © *British Book News,* 1980, 1983, 1985, 1986. All courtesy of *British Book News.*

Callaloo, v. 7, Spring-Summer, 1984 for "Seven Women and a Wall" by Judith V. Branzburg. Copyright © 1984 by Charles H. Rowell. All rights reserved. Reprinted by permission of the author.

Canadian Author & Bookman, v. 61, Winter, 1986 for a review of "Urban Scrawl" by Lawrence Chanin. © 1986 by the author. Reprinted by permission of Candian Authors Assoc.

The Canadian Forum, v. LXVII, June-July, 1987. Reprinted by permission of the publisher.

Canadian Literature, n. 104, Spring, 1985 for a review of "Urban Scrawl" by W. H. New. Reprinted by permission of the author.

Carolina Quarterly, v. XXXVI, Spring, 1984. © copyright 1984 *Carolina Quarterly.* Reprinted by permission of the publisher.

Chicago Review, v. 33, Autumn, 1982. Copyright © 1982 by *Chicago Review.* Reprinted by permission of the publisher.

Chicago Tribune—Books, December 21, 1986; July 5, 1987; March 13, 1988. © copyrighted 1986, 1987, 1988, Chicago Tribune Company. All rights reserved. All used with permission.

Choice, v. 13, April, 1976. Copyright © 1976 by American Library Association. Reprinted by permission of the publisher.

The Chowder Review, n. 16 & 17, Spring-Winter, 1981. Copyright 1981. Reprinted by permission of the publisher.

The Christian Science Monitor, July 30, 1975; January 10, 1977; March 25, 1987. © 1975, 1977, 1987 The Christian Science Publishing Society. All rights reserved. All reprinted by permission from *The Christian Science Monitor.*

CLIO, v. 14, Spring, 1985. © 1985 by Robert H. Canary and Henry Kozicki. Reprinted by permission of the publisher.

Commentary, v. 77, June, 1984 for " 'Julia' & Other Fictions by Lillian Hellman" by Samuel McCracken. Copyright © 1984 by the American Jewish Committee. All rights reserved. Reprinted by permission of the publisher and the author.

Commonweal, v. XCVII, November 24, 1972; v. CVII, November 7, 1980. Copyright © 1972, 1980 Commonweal Publishing Co., Inc. Both reprinted by permission of Commonweal Foundation./ v. CXII, May 3, 1985; v. CXII, August 9, 1985. Copyright © 1985 Commonweal Foundation. Both reprinted by permission of Commonweal Foundation.

Comparative Drama, v. 14, Winter, 1980-81. © copyright 1981, by the Editors of *Comparative Drama.* Reprinted by permission of the publisher.

The Critic, Chicago, v. 39, October, 1980. © *The Critic* 1980. Reprinted with the permission of the Thomas More Association, Chicago, IL.

Critical Quarterly, v. 23, Winter, 1981. © Manchester University Press 1981. Reprinted by permission of Manchester University Press.

Daily News, New York, November 2, 1984; March 23, 1987. © 1984, 1987 New York News Inc. Both reprinted with permission.

Drama, London, n. 108, Spring, 1973; n. 147, Spring, 1983. Both reprinted by permission of the British Theatre Association.

Encounter, v. XVI, March, 1961; v. LXXI, June, 1988. © 1961, 1988 by Encounter Ltd. Both reprinted by permission of the publisher.

L'Esprit Créateur, v. XVII, Summer, 1977. Copyright © 1977 by *L'Esprit Créateur.* Reprinted by permission of the publisher.

Essays in Arts and Sciences, v. III, May, 1974 for "Conrad Aiken's Preludes and the Modern Consciousness" by Douglas Robillard. Copyright © 1974 by the University of New Haven. Reprinted by permission of the publisher and the author.

Fantasy Review, v. 8, April, 1985 for "Gregory Benford's Introductory Survey of American Literature" by Gary K. Wolfe; v. 8, April, 1985 for "Some Comments from the Minority Culture" by Gregory Benford; v. 8, June, 1985 for "Blood without End" by Michael A. Morrison; v. 8, September, 1985 for "Brilliant First Novel" by Chris Morgan; v. 8, September, 1985 for "Benford's Latest Cast in 'Thriller' Format" by Gary K. Wolfe; v. 9, February, 1986 for "Off on a Comet" by Gary K. Wolfe; v. 9, October, 1986 for "Visions of the Joyous Apocalypse" by Michael A. Morrison; v. 10, April, 1987 for "Sure Thing" by Stefan R. Dziemianowicz. Copyright © 1985,1986, 1987 by the respective authors. All reprinted by permission of the respective authors./ v. 9, July-August, 1986 for "In Human Minds" by Pascal J. Thomas. Copyright © 1986 by the author. Reprinted by permission of the publisher.

Foundation, n. 14, September, 1978 for "From Aliens to Alienation: Gregory Benford's Variations on a Theme" by David N. Samuelson. Copyright © 1978 by the Science Fiction Foundation. Reprinted by permission of the author.

The French Review, v. LX, May, 1987. Copyright 1987 by the American Association of Teachers of French. Reprinted by permission of the publisher.

The Georgia Review, v. XIV, Summer, 1960; v. XXVII, Winter, 1973; v. XXXII, Fall, 1978; v. XXXVI, Winter, 1982; v. XLI, Winter, 1987. Copyright, 1960, 1973, 1978, 1982, 1987, by the University of Georgia. All reprinted by permission of the publisher.

The Guardian, October 17, 1986. © Guardian and Manchester Evening News Ltd., 1986. Reprinted by permission of Los Angeles Times—Washington Post News Service.

Harper's, v. 260, May, 1980. Copyright © 1980 by *Harper's Magazine.* All rights reserved. Reprinted by special permission.

The Hollins Critic, v. XVIII, October, 1981; v. XIX, February, 1982; v. XX, December, 1983. Copyright 1981, 1982, 1983 by Hollins College. All reprinted by permission of the publisher.

The Hudson Review, v. XX, Winter, 1967-68; v. XXIII, Autumn, 1970-71; v. XXXIX, Summer, 1986; v. XL, Summer, 1987; v. XLI, Summer, 1988. Copyright © 1967, 1970, 1986, 1987, 1988 by The Hudson Review, Inc. All reprinted by permission of the publisher.

The International Fiction Review, v. 1, January, 1974; v. 2, January, 1975; v. 3, January, 1976. All reprinted by permission of the publisher./ v. 12, Summer, 1985. © copyright 1985 International Fiction Association. Reprinted by permission of the publisher.

The Iowa Review, v. 13, Spring, 1982 for a review of "The Incognito Lounge and Other Poems" by Robert Miklitsch. Copyright © 1982 by The University of Iowa. Reprinted by permission of the publisher and the author.

Ironwood, v. 7, 1979. Copyright © 1979 by Ironwood Press. Both reprinted by permission of the publisher.

The Journal of Ethnic Studies, v. 4, Fall, 1976. Copyright © 1976 by The Journal of Ethnic Studies. Reprinted by permission of the publisher.

Kansas Quarterly, v. 14, Spring, 1982 for "James Purdy, Will Moses: Against the Wilderness" by Warren French. © copyright 1982 by the *Kansas Quarterly.* Reprinted by permission of the publisher and the author.

Kirkus Reviews, v. XXXIX, November 15, 1971; v. LIII, June 1, 1985; v. LV, August 1, 1987. Copyright © 1971, 1985, 1987 The Kirkus Service, Inc. All rights reserved. All reprinted by permission of the publisher.

The Listener, v. 85, June 10, 1971 for "President Chance" by Edwin Morgan; v. 90, August 2, 1973 for "Dockland Decencies" by Ronald Bryden; v. 94, December 11, 1975 for "Public and Private Medicine" by Brian Winston; v. 96, July 22, 1976 for "Haggard Odysseus" by Christopher Price; v. 96, August 5, 1976 for "Council Writers" by John Mellors; v. 115, February 20, 1986 for "Atoms Not Actors" by Vernon Bogdanor; v. 115, May 29, 1986 for "Going Back to First Love" by John Mellors; v. 118, July 9, 1987 for "In Search of Liberation" by Linda

Taylor; v. 118, September 10, 1987 for "Borrowers Amok" by Rupert Christiansen. © British Broadcasting Corp. 1971, 1973, 1975, 1976, 1986, 1987. All reprinted by permission of the respective authors.

London Magazine, n.s. v. 14, October-November, 1974; n.s. v. 21, October, 1981; n.s. v. 22, February, 1983. © *London Magazine* 1974, 1981, 1983. All reprinted by permission of the publisher.

London Review of Books, v. 4, March 4 to March 17, 1982 for "Generations" by John Sutherland; v. 4, December 30, 1982 to January 19, 1983 for "Mythic Elements" by Stephen Bann; v. 5, December 1 to December 21, 1983 for "Auld Lang Syne" by Graham Hough; v. 6, June 7 to June 20, 1984 for "Johnsons" by John Sutherland; v. 7, February 21, 1985 for "Father, Son and Sewing- Machine" by Patrick Parrinder; v. 7, July 4, 1985 for "Costa del Pym" by Nicholas Spice; v. 7, October 3, 1985 for "Street Wise" by Pat Rogers; v. 9, September 3, 1987 for "Poor Toms" by Karl Miller. All appear here by permission of the *London Review of Books* and the author.

London Theatre Record, v. VI, October 8-21, 1986 for a review of "The Secret Life of Cartoons" by Nick St. George. Reprinted by permission of the author.

Los Angeles Times Book Review, February 12, 1984; December 14, 1986; June 14, 1987; October 11, 1987; December 27, 1987; January 17, 1988. Copyright, 1984, 1986, 1987, 1988, *Los Angeles Times.* All reprinted by permission of the publisher.

Maclean's Magazine, v. 93, July 14, 1980; v. 95, January 18, 1982; v. 99, November 24, 1986. © 1980, 1982, 1986 by *Maclean's Magazine.* All reprinted by permission of the publisher.

The Magazine of Fantasy and Science Fiction, v. 55, July, 1978 for a review of "In the Ocean of Night" by Algis Budrys; v. 59, December, 1980 for a review of "Shiva Descending" by John Clute; v. 60, February, 1981 for a review of "Timescape" by Thomas M. Disch; v. 65, July, 1983 for a review of "Against Infinity" by Algis Budrys. © 1978, 1980, 1981, 1983 by Mercury Press Inc. All reprinted by permission of *The Magazine of Fantasy and Science Fiction* and the respective authors.

The Massachusetts Review, v. XVII, Spring, 1976. © 1976. Reprinted from *The Massachusetts Review,* The Massachusetts Review, Inc. by permission.

Midstream, v. XXV, June-July, 1979 for "Woody Allen's Jewish American Gothic" by David M. Friend. Copyright © 1979 by The Theodor Herzl Foundation, Inc. Reprinted by permission of the publisher and the author.

The Minnesota Review, v. VII, 1967 for "The Ancient Croaking" by Peter A. Stitt. Copyright 1967 by the Bolingbroke Society, Inc. Reprinted by permission of the author.

The Mississippi Quarterly, v. XX, Winter, 1966-67. Copyright 1967 Mississippi State University. Reprinted by permission of the publisher.

The Missouri Review, v. VII, 1984 for "Acts of Will" by Mark Jarman. Copyright © 1984 by The Curators of the University of Missouri. Reprinted by permission of the author.

Modern Age, v. 23, Spring, 1979. Copyright © 1979 by the Intercollegiate Studies Institute, Inc. Reprinted by permission of the publisher.

Modernist Studies: Literature & Culture 1920-1940, v. 1, 1974-75. © 1975. Reprinted by permission of the publisher.

The Nation, New York, v. 240, April 20, 1985. Copyright 1985 *The Nation* magazine/The Nation Company, Inc. Reprinted by permission of the publisher.

National Review, New York, v. XL, March 4, 1988. © 1988 by National Review, Inc., 150 East 35th Street, New York, NY 10016. Reprinted with permission of the publisher.

The New Criterion, v. III, October, 1984 for "The Life and Death of Lillian Hellman" by Hilton Kramer. Copyright © 1984 by The Foundation for Cultural Review. Reprinted by permission of the author.

The New Leader, v. LVIII, May 26, 1975; v. LXIV, November 2, 1981. © 1975, 1981 by The American Labor Conference on International Affairs, Inc. Both reprinted by permission of the publisher.

The New Republic, v. 184, May 23, 1981 for "The Limits of Realism" by Robert Brustein. © 1981 The New Republic, Inc. Reprinted by permission of the author./ v. 171, September 14, 1974; v. 192, April 15, 1985; v. 196, June 8, 1987; v.198, June 13, 1988. © 1974, 1985, 1987, 1988 The New Republic, Inc. All reprinted by permission of *The New Republic.*

New Saltire, n. 3, Spring, 1962.

New Statesman, v. LXX, December 10, 1965; v. 73, October 7, 1966; v. 75, April 12, 1968; v. 76, July 19, 1968; v. 79, May 1, 1970; v. 82, October 29, 1971; v. 85, June 8, 1973; v. 86, July 6, 1973; v. 87, January 4, 1974; v. 87, February 8, 1974; v. 87, May 3, 1974; v. 90, October 31, 1975; v. 90, December 12, 1975; v. 92, July 30, 1976; v. 93, April 8, 1977; v. 98, July 13, 1979; v. 100, November 21, 1980; v. 102, August 7, 1981; v. 102, October 30, 1981; v. 103, February 12, 1982; v. 106, December 16 & December 23, 1983; v. 111, May 23, 1986; v. 112, July 18, 1986; v. 112, September 12, 1986; v. 114, September 18, 1987. © 1965, 1966, 1968, 1970, 1971, 1973, 1974, 1975, 1976, 1977, 1979, 1980, 1981, 1982, 1983, 1986, 1987 The Statesman & Nation Publishing Co. Ltd. All reprinted by permission of the publisher.

New York Magazine, v. 17, November 12, 1984 for "If the Shue Doesn't Fit" by John Simon. Copyright © 1988 by John Simon. All rights reserved. Reprinted with the permission of *New York* Magazine and the Wallace Literary Agency, Inc./ v. 21, January 18, 1988 for "Irish Bull" by Rhoda Koenig. Copyright © 1988 by News America Publishing, Inc. All rights reserved. Reprinted with permission of *New York* Magazine and the author.

New York Post, November 29, 1976; March 23, 1987. © 1976, 1987, *New York Post.* Both reprinted by permission of the publisher.

The New York Review of Books, v. XV, November 19, 1970; v. XXI, July 18, 1974; v. XXIII, October 14, 1976; v. XXV, June 29, 1978; v. XXXV, April 14, 1988. Copyright © 1970, 1974, 1976, 1978, 1988 Nyrev, Inc. All reprinted with permission from *The New York Review of Books.*

The New York Times, February 7, 1962; September 19, 1965; June 25, 1975; July 9, 1975; November 29, 1976; November 4, 1979; November 28, 1979; April 26, 1980; September 19, 1980; June 22, 1983; September 14, 1983; November 2, 1984; February 9, 1985; May 1, 1985; September 13, 1986; March 23, 1987; June 24, 1987; June 25, 1987; August 10, 1987; January 8, 1988; February 10, 1988. Copyright © 1962, 1965, 1975, 1976, 1979, 1980, 1983, 1984, 1985, 1986, 1987, 1988 by The New York Times Company. All reprinted by permission of the publisher.

The New York Times Book Review, July 29, 1934; November 1, 1936; June 20, 1937; March 10, 1940; September 29, 1940; March 9, 1941; October 5, 1941; July 26, 1942; January 24, 1943; June 27, 1943; January 9, 1944; July 16, 1944; March 10, 1946; October 27, 1946; September 14, 1947; September 18, 1949; June 4, 1950; March 11, 1951. Copyright 1934, 1936, 1937, 1940, 1941, 1942, 1943, 1944, 1946, 1947, 1949, 1950, 1951 by The New York Times Company. All reprinted by permission of the publisher./ April 2, 1967; June 18, 1967; August 16, 1970; April 9, 1972; October 8, 1972; September 15, 1974; March 27, 1977; June 12, 1977; July 31, 1977; May 14, 1978; August 5, 1979; February 3, 1980; April 20, 1980; October 26, 1980; April 12, 1981; April 26, 1981; October 11, 1981; December 20, 1981; July 31, 1983; February 5, 1984; February 26, 1984; October 14, 1984; March 3, 1985; March 31, 1985; May 5, 1985; May 12, 1985; May 26, 1985; July 7, 1985; August 4, 1985; January 19, 1986; March 2, 1986; September 21, 1986; September 28, 1986; October 5, 1986; October 12, 1986; October 19, 1986; November 2, 1986; February 15, 1987; March 15, 1987; May 31, 1987; June 21, 1987; July 19, 1987; September 6, 1987; October 18, 1987; November 22, 1987; November 29, 1987; January 3, 1988; January 17, 1988; January 24, 1988; January 31, 1988; February 21, 1988. Copyright © 1967, 1970, 1972, 1974, 1977, 1978, 1979, 1980, 1981, 1983, 1984, 1985, 1986, 1987, 1988 by The New York Times Company. All reprinted by permission of the publisher.

The New Yorker, v. LX, November 19, 1984 for "Not Much to Celebrate" by Edith Oliver; v. LXI, July 15, 1985 for "Complications" by Susan Lardner; v. LXIII, June 22, 1987 for "Inventing Flaubert" by Naomi Bliven; v. LXIII, December 28, 1987 for "What You Deserve Is What You Get" by John Updike; v. LXIV, March 14, 1988 for "Chronicles and Processions" by John Updike; v. LXIV, March 14, 1988 for "Colloquy" by Edith Oliver. © 1984, 1985, 1987, 1988 by the respective authors. All reprinted by permission of the publisher./ v. XII, October 31, 1936 for "Faulkner, Extra-Special, Double-Distilled" by Clifton Fadiman. Copyright 1936, renewed 1963 by The New Yorker Magazine, Inc. Reprinted by permission of the author./ v. LII, April 5, 1976. © 1976 by The New Yorker Magazine, Inc. Reprinted by permission of the publisher./ v. XXV, September 17, 1949; v. XXVI, May 20, 1950. Copyright 1949, renewed 1976; copyright 1950, renewed 1977 by The New Yorker Magazine, Inc. Both reprinted by permission of the publisher.

Newsday, March 23, 1987. © Newsday, Inc. 1987. Reprinted by permission.

Newsweek, v. LXXXV, June 23, 1975; v. LXXXVIII, December 13, 1976; v. LXXXIX, May 9, 1977; v. XCVII, May 11, 1981. Copyright 1975, 1976, 1977, 1981, by Newsweek, Inc. All rights reserved. All reprinted by permission of the publisher.

The North American Review, v. 266, March, 1981. Copyright © 1981 by the University of Northern Iowa. Reprinted by permission from *The North American Review.*

North Dakota Quarterly, v. 53, Spring, 1985. Copyright 1985 by The University of North Dakota. Reprinted by permission of the publisher.

The Observer, May 4, 1969; April 11, 1971; January 27, 1974; September 16, 1979; February 14, 1982; November 21, 1982; June 23, 1985; September 22, 1985; January 19, 1986; March 22, 1987; December 27, 1987; February 21, 1988. All reprinted by permission of The Observer Limited, London.

Parabola, v. XXI, February, 1987 for "Fools Crow" by Jarold Ramsey. Copyright © 1987 by the Society for the Study of Myth and Tradition. Reprinted by permission of the author.

Parnassus: Poetry in Review, v. 8, 1980 for "In the Cool Element of Prose" by David Lehman. Copyright © 1980 by the author. Reprinted by permission of the author./ v. 11, Fall-Winter, 1983 & Spring-Summer, 1984. Copyright © 1984 Poetry in Review Foundation, NY. Reprinted by permission of the publisher.

Performing Art In Canada, v. XIX, Summer, 1982. © 1982 by Performing Arts. Reprinted by permission of the publisher.

Plays & Players, n. 394, July, 1986; n. 404, May, 1987. (c) 1986, 1987 Brevet Limited. Both reprinted with permission of the publisher.

PN Review 58, v. 14, 1987 for "Plus ça Change" by Elizabeth Baines. © *PN Review* 1987. Reprinted by permission of the author.

Poetry, v. XCVI, June, 1960 for "The Angels of Discombooberation" by Felix Stefanile; v. CIV, July, 1964 for "Seven Poets and a Playwright" by Dabney Stuart; v. CVIII, June, 1966 for "California Hybrid" by Jim Harrison; v. CXII, August, 1968 for a review of "L'Autre" by Gerald William Barrax; v CXIX, October, 1971 for "What Is to Be Done?" by James Atlas; v. CXX, April, 1972 for "The Poetry Room" by John Koethe; v. CXXII, August, 1973 for "Five" by Lisel Mueller; v. CXLV, November, 1984 for a review of "Dance Script with Electric Ballerina" by William Logan; v. CXLIX, October, 1986 for "Mortal Listeners" by J. D. McClatchy. © 1960, 1964, 1966, 1968, 1971, 1972, 1973, 1984, 1986 by the Modern Poetry Association. All reprinted by permission of the Editor of *Poetry* and the respective authors.

Prairie Schooner, v. 60, Summer, 1985. © 1985 by University of Nebraska Press. Reprinted from *Prairie Schooner* by permission of the **University of Nebraska Press.**

Publishers Weekly, v. 200, November 29, 1971; v. 213, June 26, 1978. Copyright © 1971, 1978 by Xerox Corporation. Both reprinted from *Publishers Weekly,* published by R. R. Bowker Company, a Xerox company, by permission./ v. 231, February 6, 1987; v. 232, October 30, 1987; v. 232, December 18, 1987. Coyright 1987 by Reed Publishing USA. All reprinted from *Publishers Weekly,* published by the Bowker Magazine Group of Cahners Publishing Co., a division of Reed Publishing USA.

Punch, v. 282, February 3, 1982 for "The Hulk's Gal" by Melvyn Bragg. © 1982 by Punch Publications Ltd. All rights reserved. Reprinted by permission of Georges Borchardt, Inc. for the author./ v. CCXLI, August 9, 1961; v. CCXLII, May 30, 1962; v. CCXLIV, June 12, 1963; v. 282, April 27, 1983. © 1961, 1962, 1963, 1983 by Punch Publications Ltd. All rights reserved. All may not be reprinted without permission.

Quarterly West, n. 23, 1986. © 1986 by *Quarterly West.* Reprinted by permission of the publisher.

Quill and Quire, v. 50, November, 1984 for a review of "Urban Scrawl" by Sherie Posesorski. Reprinted by permission of *Quill and Quire* and the author.

Renascence, v. XVIII, Spring, 1966. © copyright, 1966, Marquette University Press. Reprinted by permission of the publisher.

The Review of Contemporary Fiction, v. V, Fall, 1985; v. VII, Fall, 1987. Copyright, 1985, 1987, by John O'Brien. All reprinted by permission of the publisher.

Saturday Night, v. 93, April, 1978 for "The Playwright as Star of the Play" by Martin Knelman; v. 101, December, 1986 for "Urban Lady" by Martin Knelman. Copyright © 1978, 1986 by *Saturday Night.* Both reprinted by permission of the author.

The Saturday Review of Literature, v. XV, October 31, 1936; v. XXIV, October 18, 1941. Copyright 1936, renewed 1963; copyright 1941, renewed 1968 *Saturday Review* magazine.

Science Fiction Chronicle, v. 7, October, 1985; v. 9, November, 1987. Copyright © 1985, 1987 by *Science Fiction Chronicle.* All rights reserved. Both reprinted by permission of the publisher.

Science Fiction Review, v. 6, May, 1977 for a review of "If the Stars Are Gods" by Richard E. Geis; v. 9, August, 1980 for a review of "Timescape" by David N. Samuelson; v. 9, November, 1980 for a review of "Find the Changeling" by Richard E. Geis; v. 12, August, 1983 for a review of "Against Infinity" by Gene DeWeese; v. 14, November, 1985 for a review of "Artifact" by Gene DeWeese; v. 15, May, 1986 for a review of "In Alien Flesh" by Elton T. Elliott; v. 15, May, 1986 for a review of "Heart of the Comet" by Keith Soltys. Copyright © 1977, 1980, 1983, 1985, 1986 by the respective authors. All reprinted by permission of the respective authors.

Scribner's Magazine, v. XCVI, September, 1934. Copyright, 1934, renewed 1961, by Charles Scribner's Sons. Reprinted with permission of Charles Scribner's Sons.

The Sewanee Review, v. LIII, Summer, 1945 for "William Faulkner's Legend of the South" by Malcolm Cowley. Copyright 1945, renewed 1973 by The University of the South. Reprinted by permission of the author./ v. XCI, Summer, 1983; v. XCII, Spring, 1984; v. XCVI, Winter, 1988. © 1983, 1984, 1988 by The University of the South. All reprinted by permission of the editor of *The Sewanee Review.*

SF & Fantasy Review, v. 7, March, 1984 for "Cosmic, Exciting, Depressing, Tantalizing" by Jerry L. Parsons. Reprinted by permission of the author.

The South Carolina Review, v. 11, November, 1978; v. 13, Fall, 1981; v. 17, Fall, 1984; v. 19, Fall, 1986. Copyright © 1978, 1981, 1984, 1986 by Clemson University. All reprinted by permission of the publisher.

The Southern Review, Louisiana State University, v. 19, Spring, 1983 for "Lillian Hellman: Autobiography and Truth" by Linda W. Wagner. Copyright, 1983, by the author. Reprinted by permission of the author.

Southwest Review, v. LIII, Autumn, 1968 for "Dark Horses, Front-Runners, a Gelding, a Unicorn" by Gerald Burns. © 1968 by the author. Reprinted by permission of the publisher.

The Spectator, v. 258, January 10, 1987 for "An Uncomfortable Voice" by Anita Brookner; v. 259, October 10, 1987 for "Mysterious Affairs in Style" by Anita Brookner. © 1987 by *The Spectator.* Both reprinted by permission of the author./ v. 203, January 12, 1962; v. 230, June 16, 1973; v. 232, January 5, 1974; v. 244, February 16, 1980; v. 245, October 4, 1980; v. 247, November 7, 1981; v. 248, January 30, 1982; v. 251, November 26, 1983; v. 253, October 6, 1984; v. 254, February 9, 1985; v. 255, September 28, 1985; v. 259, July 11, 1987. © 1962, 1973, 1974, 1980, 1981, 1982, 1983, 1984, 1985, 1987 by *The Spectator.* All reprinted by permission of *The Spectator.*

Studies in Scottish Literature, v. I, January, 1964. Copyright © G. Ross Roy 1964. Reprinted by permission of the editor.

The Texas Quarterly, v. I, Winter, 1958 for "Pilgrim's Progress: Conrad Aiken's Poetry" by Rufus A. Blanshard. © 1958 by The University of Texas at Austin. Reprinted by permission of the publisher and the author.

Time, New York, v. 89, April 14, 1967; v. 124, August 13, 1984; v. 131, January 11, 1988. Copyright 1967, 1984, 1988 Time Inc. All rights reserved. All reprinted by permission from *Time.*

The Times Literary Supplement, n. 3143, May 25. 1962; n. 3195, May 24, 1963; n. 3321, October 21, 1965; n. 3372, October 13, 1966; n. 3446, March 14, 1968; n. 3464, July 18, 1968; n. 3506, May 8, 1969; n. 3606, April 9, 1971; n. 3615, June 6, 1971; n. 3621, July 23, 1971; n. 3676, August 11, 1972; n. 3765, May 3, 1973; n. 3721, June 29, 1973; n. 3772, June 21, 1974; n. 3774, July 5, 1974; n. 3790, October 25, 1974; n. 3804, January 31, 1975; n. 3843, November 7, 1975; n. 3868, April 30, 1976; n. 3877, July 2, 1976; n. 3936, August 19, 1977; n. 3963, March 10, 1978; n. 3981, July 21, 1978; n. 3985, August 18, 1978; n. 4012, February 15, 1980; n. 4023, May 2, 1980; n. 4044, October 3, 1980; n. 4049, November 7, 1980; n.

4050, November 14, 1980; n. 4053, December 5, 1980; n. 4092, September 4, 1981; n. 4095, September 25, 1981; n. 4100, October 30, 1981; n. 4113, January 29, 1982; n. 4153, November 5, 1982; n. 4155, November 19, 1982; n. 4176, April 15, 1983; n. 4231, May 4, 1984; n. 4248, August 31, 1984; n. 4252, September 28, 1984; n. 4290, June 21, 1985; n. 4304, September 27, 1985; n. 4340, June 6, 1986; n. 4345, July 11, 1986; n. 4355, September 19, 1986; n. 4395, June 26, 1987; n. 4396, July 3, 1987; n. 4406, September 11-17, 1987; n. 4407, September 18-24, 1987; n. 4422, January 1-7, 1988; n. 4428, February 12-18, 1988. © Times Newspapers Ltd. (London) 1962, 1963, 1965, 1966, 1968, 1969, 1971, 1972, 1973, 1974, 1975, 1976, 1977, 1978, 1980, 1981, 1982, 1983, 1984, 1985, 1986, 1987, 1988. All reproduced from *The Times Literary Supplement* by permission.

The Times, London, February 7, 1985; October 8, 1987. © Times Newspapers Limited 1985, 1987. Both reproduced from *The Times,* London by permission.

University of Toronto Quarterly, v. L, Summer, 1981. © University of Toronto Press 1981. Reprinted by permission of University Toronto Press.

Twentieth Century Literature, v. 28, Fall, 1982. Copyright 1982, Hofstra University Press. Reprinted by permission of the publisher.

USA Today, March 23, 1987. Copyright 1987, *USA Today.* Excerpted with permission of the publisher.

Variety, March 9, 1988. Copyright 1988, by Variety, Inc. Reprinted by permission of the publisher.

The Village Voice, v. XXIII, October 16, 1978 for a review of "The Bad Sister" by Sonia Jaffe Robbins. Copyright © The Village Voice, Inc., 1978. Reprinted by permission of *The Village Voice* and the author./ v. XXXI, January 18, 1986 for "Home Is Where the Head Is" by Ellen Lesser; v. XXXI, May 20, 1986 for "Tame Oates" by Dorothy Allison; v. XXXI, October 28, 1986 for "Infernal Combustion" by Andrew Klavan; v. XXXI, December 2, 1986 for "Barker's Bite" by Richard Gehr; v. XXXII, April 14, 1987 for "A Ring Cycle" by Allen Barra; v. XXXIII, February 23, 1988 for "Love You Madly" by Laurie Stone. Copyright © News Group Publications, Inc., 1986, 1987, 1988. All reprinted by permission of *The Village Voice* and the respective authors.

The Virginia Quarterly Review, v. 37, Summer, 1961. Copyright, 1961, by *The Virginia Quarterly Review,* The University of Virginia. Reprinted by permission of the publisher.

VLS, n. 7, May, 1982 for a review of "Hombre de Paso: Just Passing Through" by Julio Marzán; n. 12, November, 1982 for a review of "Heremakhonon" by Carole Bovoso; n. 48, September, 1986 for "American Gothic: James Purdy's Divine Madness" by Vince Aletti; n. 60, November, 1987 for "Perpetual Notion Machines" by Albert Mobilio; n. 62, February, 1988 for "The Witches of Gjirokastra: Ismail Kadare's Albanian Chronicles" by Ken Kalfus. Copyright © 1982, 1986, 1987, 1988 News Group Publication, Inc. All reprinted by permission of *The Village Voice* and the respective authors.

Western American Literature, v. XV, November, 1980; v. XXII, May, 1987. Copyright, 1980, 1987, by the Western Literature Association. Both reprinted by permission of the publisher.

The Women's Review of Books, v. II, August, 1985 for "Naylor's Inferno" by Jewelle Gomez. Copyright © 1985. All rights reserved. Reprinted by permission of the author.

World Literature Today, v. 51, Summer, 1977; v. 53, Spring, 1979; v. 53, Autumn, 1979; v. 54, Summer, 1980; v. 56, Spring, 1982; v. 57, Winter, 1983; v. 58, Winter, 1984; v. 59, Winter, 1985; v. 59, Spring, 1985; v. 60, Winter, 1986; v. 60. Summer, 1986; v. 60, Autumn, 1986; v. 61, Winter, 1987; v. 61, Spring, 1987. Copyright 1977, 1979, 1980, 1982, 1983, 1984, 1985, 1986, 1987 by the University of Oklahoma Press. All reprinted by permission of the publisher.

The Writer, v. 61, June, 1948. Copyright 1948, renewed 1975 by The Writer, Inc. All rights reserved. Reprinted by permission of the publisher.

Yale French Studies, n. 68, 1985. Copyright © *Yale French Studies* 1985. Reprinted by permission of the publisher.

The Yale Review, v. LXII, Spring, 1973. Copyright 1973, by Yale University. Reprinted by permission of the editors.

The Yearbook of English Studies, v. 9, 1979. © Modern Humanities Research Association 1979. All rights reserved. Reprinted by permission of the Editor and the Modern Humanities Research Association.

THE COPYRIGHTED EXCERPTS IN CLC, VOLUME 52, WERE REPRINTED FROM THE FOLLOWING BOOKS:

Allen, Roger. From *The Arabic Novel: An Historical and Critical Introduction*. Syracuse University Press, 1982. Copyright © Roger Allen 1982. Reprinted by permission of the publisher.

Ansorge, Peter. From *Disrupting the Spectacle: Five Years of Experimental and Fringe Theatre in Britain*. Pitman Publishing, 1975. © Peter Ansorge 1975. All rights reserved. Reprinted by permission of A. & C. Black (Publishers) Ltd.

Braun, Edward. From "Trevor Griffiths," in *British Television Drama*. Edited by George W. Brandt. Cambridge University Press, 1981. © Cambridge University Press 1981. Reprinted with the permission of the publisher and the author.

Cargill, Oscar. From *Intellectual America: Ideas on the March*. The Macmillan Company, 1941. Copyright 1941 by the Macmillan Publishing Company. Renewed 1968 by Oscar Cargill. All rights reserved. Reprinted with permission of Macmillan Publishing Company.

Dick, Bernard F. From *Hellman in Hollywood*. Fairleigh Dickinson University Press, 1982. © 1982 by Associated University Presses, Inc. Reprinted by permission of the publisher.

Geismar, Maxwell. From *Writers in Crises: The American Novel Between Two Wars*. Houghton Mifflin, 1942. Copyright, 1942, renewed 1969 by Maxwell Geismar. All rights reserved. Reprinted by permission of Houghton Mifflin Company.

Gloster, Hugh M. From *Negro Voices in American Fiction*. University of North Carolina Press, 1948. Copyright, 1948, by The University of North Carolina Press. Renewed 1975 by Hugh M. Gloster. Reprinted by permission of the publisher and the author.

Grant, Steve. From "Voicing the Protest: The New Writers," in *Dreams and Deconstructions: Alternative Theatre in Britain*. Edited by Sandy Craig. Amber Lane Press, 1980. Copyright © Amber Lane Press Limited, 1980. All rights reserved. Reprinted by permission of the author.

Hart, Francis Russell. From *The Scottish Novel: From Smollett to Spark*. Cambridge, Mass.: Harvard University Press, 1978. Copyright © 1978 by Francis Russell Hart. All rights reserved. Excerpted by permission of the publishers.

Hayman, Ronald. From *British Theatre Since 1955: A Reassessment*. Oxford University Press, Oxford, 1979. © Ronald Hayman, 1979. All rights reserved. Reprinted by permission of A. D. Peters & Co. Ltd.

Howe, Irving. From *William Faulkner: A Critical Study*. Third edition. University of Chicago Press, 1975. © 1951, 1952, 1975 by Irving Howe. All rights reserved. Reprinted by permission of The University of Chicago Press and the author.

Johnson, Greg. From *Understanding Joyce Carol Oates*. University of South Carolina Press, 1987. Copyright © University of South Carolina 1987. Reprinted by permission of the publisher.

Lahr, John. From *Automatic Vaudeville: Essays on Star Turns*. Knopf, 1984. Copyright © 1975, 1978, 1979, 1981, 1982, 1984 by John Lahr. All rights reserved. Reprinted by permission of Alfred A. Knopf, Inc.

Millgate, Michael. From *William Faulkner*. Revised edition. Oliver and Boyd, 1966. © 1961 Michael Millgate. Reprinted by permission of the author.

Morgan, Edwin. From *Essays*. Carcanet New Press, 1974. Copyright © Edwin Morgan 1974. All rights reserved. Reprinted by permission Carcanet Press Ltd.

Powers, Lyall H. From *Faulkner's Yoknapatawpha Comedy*. The University of Michigan Press, 1980. Copyright © by The University of Michigan 1980. All rights reserved. Reprinted by permission of publisher.

Ryan, Kiernan. From "Socialist Fiction and the Education of Desire: Mervyn Jones, Raymond Williams and John Berger," in *The Socialist Novel in Britain: Towards the Recovery of a Tradition*. Edited by H. Gustav Klaus. St. Martin's Press, 1982. © The Harvester Press 1982. All rights reserved. Used with permission of St. Martin's Press, Inc.

Shechner, Mark. From "Woody Allen: The Failure of the Therapeutic," in *From Hester Street to Hollywood: The Jewish-American Stage and Screen*. Edited by Sarah Blacher Cohen. Indiana University Press, 1983. Copyright © 1983 by Indiana University Press. All rights reserved. Reprinted by permission of the publisher.

Snodgrass, W. D. From an introduction to *Dance Script with Electric Ballerina*. By Alice Fulton. University of Pennsylvania Press, 1983. Copyright © 1983 by the University of Pennsylvania Press. All rights reserved. Reprinted by permission of the publisher.

Somekh, Sasson. From *The Changing Rhythm: A Study of Najīb Maḥfūz's Novels*. Brill, 1973. Copyright 1973 by E. J. Brill, Leiden, Netherlands. All rights reserved. Reprinted by permission of the publisher.

Thompson, Lawrance. From *William Faulkner: An Introduction and Interpretation*. Barnes & Noble, 1963. © Copyright, 1963 by Barnes & Noble, Inc. All rights reserved. Reprinted by permission of the publisher.

Tittler, Jonathan. From *Narrative Irony in the Contemporary Spanish-American Novel*. Cornell University Press, 1984. Copyright © 1984 by Cornell University Press. All rights reserved. Used by permission of the publisher, Cornell University Press.

Tucker, David M. From *Lieutenant Lee of Beale Street*. Vanderbilt University Press, 1971. Copyright © 1971 Vanderbilt University Press. Reprinted by permission of the publisher.

Waggoner, Hyatt H. From *William Faulkner: From Jefferson to the World*. University of Kentucky Press, 1959. Copyright © 1959 by The University Press of Kentucky. Renewed 1987 by Hyatt H. Waggoner. Reprinted by permission of the publisher.

Wright, William. From *Lillian Hellman: The Image, the Woman*. Simon and Schuster, 1986. Copyright © 1986 by William C. Wright. All rights reserved. Reprinted by permission of Simon & Schuster, Inc.

Acknowledgments

PERMISSION TO REPRINT PHOTOGRAPHS APPEARING IN CLC, VOLUME 52, WAS RECEIVED FROM THE FOLLOWING SOURCES:

Photograph by Mark Gerson: p. 1

© Rollie McKenna: p. 17

© 1988 Fred W. McDarrah: p. 34

© Terry Smith: p. 51

Photograph by Jay Kay Klein: p. 58

© Jerry Bauer: pp. 78, 148, 207, 231, 328

© Meredith Waddell, courtesy of Stephen Dixon: p. 93

The Granger Collection, New York: p. 104

© Hank De Leo 1989: p. 157

Photograph by Layle Silbert: p. 163. © 1988 Layle Silbert: p. 408

Photograph by Gill Cliff, courtesy of Trevor Griffiths: p. 170

Courtesy of the *Glasgow Herald:* p. 218

Courtesy of Mervyn Jones: p. 242

Courtesy of New Amsterdam Books: p. 256

Photograph by Charles Nicholas, reproduced by permission of Vanderbilt University Press: p. 265

Photograph by Chuck Painter, courtesy of John L'Heureux: p. 271

Photograph by Howard Smagula, courtesy of Ron Loewinsohn: p. 282

Thomas Hartwell/*Time* Magazine: p. 291

© John Foley: p. 306

Photograph by Jennifer Waddell: p. 319

Courtesy of James Purdy: p. 341

Photograph by Judy B. McClard, courtesy of Erika Ritter: p. 352

Photograph by Robert Emmett Ginna, Jr., courtesy of James Salter: p. 358

© Lutfi Özkök: p. 371

Courtesy of the Milwaukee Repertory Theater: p. 390

© Tara Heinemann: p. 395

Photograph by Tom McCormack: p. 419

© 1986 Marc A. Hefty, courtesy of Viking Penguin, Inc.: p. 425

□ Contemporary
Literary Criticism
Indexes

Literary Criticism Series
    Cumulative Author Index
Cumulative Nationality Index
Title Index, Volume 52

This Index Includes References to Entries in These Gale Series

Contemporary Literary Criticism

Presents excerpts of criticism on the works of novelists, poets, dramatists, short story writers, scriptwriters, and other creative writers who are now living or who have died since 1960. Cumulative indexes to authors and nationalities are included, as well as an index to titles discussed in the individual volume. Volumes 1-52 are in print.

Twentieth-Century Literary Criticism

Contains critical excerpts by the most significant commentators on poets, novelists, short story writers, dramatists, and philosophers who died between 1900 and 1960. Cumulative indexes to authors, nationalities, and titles discussed are included in each new volume. Volumes 1-31 are in print.

Nineteenth-Century Literature Criticism

Offers significant passages from criticism on authors who died between 1800 and 1899. Cumulative indexes to authors, nationalities, and titles discussed are included in each new volume. Volumes 1-20 are in print.

Literature Criticism from 1400 to 1800

Compiles significant passages from the most noteworthy criticism on authors of the fifteenth through eighteenth centuries. Cumulative indexes to authors, nationalities, and titles discussed are included in each new volume. Volumes 1-9 are in print.

Classical and Medieval Literature Criticism

Offers excerpts of criticism on the works of world authors from classical antiquity through the fourteenth century. Cumulative indexes to authors, titles, and critics are included in each volume. Volumes 1-2 are in print.

Short Story Criticism

Compiles excerpts of criticism on short fiction by writers of all eras and nationalities. Cumulative indexes to authors, nationalities, and titles discussed are included in each new volume. Volumes 1-2 are in print.

Children's Literature Review

Includes excerpts from reviews, criticism, and commentary on works of authors and illustrators who create books for children. Cumulative indexes to authors, nationalities, and titles discussed are included in each new volume. Volumes 1-16 are in print

Contemporary Authors Series

Encompasses five related series. *Contemporary Authors* provides biographical and bibliographical information on more than 90,000 writers of fiction, nonfiction, poetry, journalism, drama, motion pictures, and other fields. Each new volume contains sketches on authors not previously covered in the series. Volumes 1-124 are in print. *Contemporary Authors New Revision Series* provides completely updated information on active authors covered in previously published volumes of *CA*. Only entries requiring significant change are revised for *CA New Revision Series*. Volumes 1-24 are in print. *Contemporary Authors Permanent Series* consists of updated listings for deceased and inactive authors removed from the original volumes 9-36 when these volumes were revised. Volumes 1-2 are in print. *Contemporary Authors Autobiography Series* presents specially commissioned autobiographies by leading contemporary writers. Volumes 1-7 are in print. *Contemporary Authors Bibliographical Series* contains primary and secondary bibliographies as well as analytical bibliographical essays by authorities on major modern authors. Volumes 1-2 are in print.

Dictionary of Literary Biography

Encompasses three related series. *Dictionary of Literary Biography* furnishes illustrated overviews of authors' lives and works and places them in the larger perspective of literary history. Volumes 1-72 are in print. *Dictionary of Literary Biography Documentary Series* illuminates the careers of major figures through a selection of literary documents, including letters, notebook and diary entries, interviews, book reviews, and photographs. Volumes 1-6 are in print. *Dictionary of Literary Biography Yearbook* summarizes the past year's literary activity with articles on genres, major prizes, conferences, and other timely subjects and includes updated and new entries on individual authors. Yearbooks for 1980-1987 are in print. A cumulative index to authors and articles is included in each new volume.

Concise Dictionary of American Literary Biography

A six-volume series that collects revised and updated sketches on major American authors that were originally presented in *Dictionary of Literary Biography*. Volumes 1-3 are in print.

Something about the Author Series

Encompasses two related series. *Something about the Author* contains heavily illustrated biographical sketches on juvenile and young adult authors and illustrators from all eras. Volumes 1-53 are in print. *Something about the Author Autobiography Series* presents specially commissioned autobiographies by prominent authors and illustrators of books for children and young adults. Volumes 1-6 are in print.

Yesterday's Authors of Books for Children

Contains heavily illustrated entries on children's writers who died before 1961. Complete in two volumes. Volumes 1-2 are in print.

Literary Criticism Series
Cumulative Author Index

This index lists all author entries in the Gale Literary Criticism Series and includes cross-references to other Gale sources. For the convenience of the reader, references to the *Yearbook* in the *Contemporary Literary Criticism* series include the page number (in parentheses) after the volume number. References in the index are identified as follows:

Author Index

Author Index

Author Index

Author Index

Author Index

Author Index

Author Index

Author Index

Munro, Alice (Laidlaw)
1931-......... CLC 6, 10, 19, 50 (207)
See also CA 33-36R
See also SATA 29
See also DLB 53
See also AITN 2

Munro, H(ector) H(ugh) 1870-1916
See Saki
See also CA 104
See also DLB 34

Murasaki, Lady c. tenth
century ....CMLC 1

Murdoch, (Jean) Iris
1919-......CLC 1, 2, 3, 4, 6, 8, 11, 15,
22, 31, 51
See also CANR 8
See also CA 13-16R
See also DLB 14

Murphy, Richard 1927-..........CLC 41
See also CA 29-32R
See also DLB 40

Murphy, Sylvia 19??-........ CLC 34 (91)

Murphy, Thomas (Bernard)
1935-......................CLC 51
See also CA 101

Murray, Les(lie) A(llan) 1938-......CLC 40
See also CANR 11
See also CA 21-24R

Murry, John Middleton
1889-1957.................TCLC 16
See also CA 118

Musgrave, Susan 1951-...........CLC 13
See also CA 69-72

Musil, Robert (Edler von)
1880-1942..................TCLC 12
See also CA 109

Musset, (Louis Charles) Alfred de
1810-1857 .... NCLC 7

Myers, Walter Dean 1937-.........CLC 35
See also CLR 4, 16
See also CANR 20
See also CA 33-36R
See also SAAS 2
See also SATA 27, 41
See also DLB 33

Nabokov, Vladimir (Vladimirovich)
1899-1977....... CLC 1, 2, 3, 6, 8, 11,
15, 23, 44 (463), 46
See also CANR 20
See also CA 5-8R
See also obituary CA 69-72
See also DLB 2
See also DLB-Y 80
See also DLB-DS 3
See also CDALB 1941-1968

Nagy, László 1925-1978 ....CLC 7
See also obituary CA 112

Naipaul, Shiva(dhar Srinivasa)
1945-1985........... CLC 32, 39 (355)
See also CA 110, 112
See also obituary CA 116
See also DLB-Y 85

Naipaul, V(idiadhar) S(urajprasad)
1932-.......... CLC 4, 7, 9, 13, 18, 37
See also CANR 1
See also CA 1-4R
See also DLB-Y 85

Nakos, Ioulia 1899?-
See Nakos, Lilika

Nakos, Lilika 1899?-..............CLC 29

Nakou, Lilika 1899?-
See Nakos, Lilika

Narayan, R(asipuram) K(rishnaswami)
1906-...............CLC 7, 28, 47
See also CA 81-84

Nash, (Frediric) Ogden
1902-1971..................CLC 23
See also CAP 1
See also CA 13-14
See also obituary CA 29-32R
See also SATA 2, 46
See also DLB 11

Nathan, George Jean
1882-1958.................TCLC 18
See also CA 114

Natsume, Kinnosuke 1867-1916
See Natsume, Sōseki
See also CA 104

Natsume, Sōseki
1867-1916...............TCLC 2, 10
See also Natsume, Kinnosuke

Natti, (Mary) Lee 1919-
See Kingman, (Mary) Lee
See also CANR 2
See also CA 7-8R

Naylor, Gloria 1950-.......... CLC 28, 52
See also CA 107

Neihardt, John G(neisenau)
1881-1973...................CLC 32
See also CAP 1
See also CA 13-14
See also DLB 9

Nekrasov, Nikolai Alekseevich
1821-1878.................. NCLC 11

Nelligan, Émile 1879-1941 ...... TCLC 14
See also CA 114

Nelson, Willie 1933- ....CLC 17
See also CA 107

Nemerov, Howard
1920-.................CLC 2, 6, 9, 36
See also CANR 1
See also CA 1-4R
See also CABS 2
See also DLB 5, 6
See also DLB-Y 83

Neruda, Pablo
1904-1973........ CLC 1, 2, 5, 7, 9, 28
See also CAP 2
See also CA 19-20
See also obituary CA 45-48

Nerval, Gérard de 1808-1855 ..... NCLC 1

Nervo, (José) Amado (Ruiz de)
1870-1919.................. TCLC 11
See also CA 109

Neufeld, John (Arthur) 1938- ......CLC 17
See also CANR 11
See also CA 25-28R
See also SAAS 3
See also SATA 6

Neville, Emily Cheney 1919- ....CLC 12
See also CANR 3
See also CA 5-8R
See also SAAS 2
See also SATA 1

Newbound, Bernard Slade 1930-
See Slade, Bernard
See also CA 81-84

Newby, P(ercy) H(oward)
1918-..................... CLC 2, 13
See also CA 5-8R
See also DLB 15

Newlove, Donald 1928-.............CLC 6
See also CANR 25
See also CA 29-32R

Newlove, John (Herbert) 1938-.....CLC 14
See also CANR 9, 25
See also CA 21-24R

Newman, Charles 1938-......... CLC 2, 8
See also CA 21-24R

Newman, Edwin (Harold)
1919-......................CLC 14
See also CANR 5
See also CA 69-72
See also AITN 1

Newton, Suzanne 1936-...........CLC 35
See also CANR 14
See also CA 41-44R
See also SATA 5

Ngugi, James (Thiong'o)
1938-................CLC 3, 7, 13, 36
See also Ngugi wa Thiong'o
See also Wa Thiong'o, Ngugi
See also CA 81-84

Ngugi wa Thiong'o
1938-................CLC 3, 7, 13, 36
See also Ngugi, James (Thiong'o)
See also Wa Thiong'o, Ngugi

Nichol, B(arrie) P(hillip) 1944- .....CLC 18
See also CA 53-56
See also DLB 53

Nichols, John (Treadwell)
1940-......................CLC 38
See also CAAS 2
See also CANR 6
See also CA 9-12R
See also DLB-Y 82

Nichols, Peter (Richard)
1927-.................... CLC 5, 36
See also CA 104
See also DLB 13

Nicolas, F.R.E. 1927-
See Freeling, Nicolas

Niedecker, Lorine
1903-1970............... CLC 10, 42
See also CAP 2
See also CA 25-28
See also DLB 48

Nietzsche, Friedrich (Wilhelm)
1844-1900...............TCLC 10, 18
See also CA 107

Nightingale, Anne Redmon 1943-
See Redmon (Nightingale), Anne
See also CA 103

Nin, Anaïs
1903-1977........ CLC 1, 4, 8, 11, 14
See also CANR 22
See also CA 13-16R
See also obituary CA 69-72
See also DLB 2, 4
See also AITN 2

Author Index

Author Index

CLC Cumulative Nationality Index

Nationality Index

Nationality Index

CLC-52 Title Index